The Cambridge H
Spanish Literature

M000286696

This first comprehensive history of Spanish literature to be published in English since the 1970s brings together experts from the USA, the United Kingdom, and Spain. Together, the essays cover the full range of Spanish poetry, prose, and theatre from the early Middle Ages to the present day. The classics of the canon of eleven centuries of Spanish literature are covered, from Berceo, Cervantes and Calderón to García Lorca and Martín Gaite, but attention is also paid to lesser-known writers and works. The chapters chart a wide range of literary periods and movements. The volume concludes with a consideration of the influences of film and new media on modern Spanish literature. This invaluable book contains an introduction, more than fifty substantial chapters, a chronology (covering key events in history, literature, and art), a bibliography, and a comprehensive index for easy reference.

The Cambridge History of
Spanish Literature

Edited by

DAVID T. GIES

CAMBRIDGE
UNIVERSITY PRESS

CAMBRIDGE
UNIVERSITY PRESS

University Printing House, Cambridge CB2 8BS, United Kingdom

Published in the United States of America by Cambridge University Press, New York

Cambridge University Press is part of the University of Cambridge.

It furthers the University's mission by disseminating knowledge in the pursuit of education, learning and research at the highest international levels of excellence.

www.cambridge.org
Information on this title: www.cambridge.org/9780521738699

First published 2004
Paperback edition (corrected) 2009

A catalogue record for this publication is available from the British Library

Library of Congress Cataloguing in Publication data
The Cambridge history of Spanish literature / edited by David T. Gies.
p.   cm.
Includes bibliographical references and index.
ISBN 0 521 80618 6 (hardback)
1. Spanish literature – History and criticism.   I. Gies, David Thatcher.
PQ6033.C36   2004
860.9 – dc22   2004045601

ISBN 978-0-521-80618-3 Hardback
ISBN 978-0-521-73869-9 Paperback

Cambridge University Press has no responsibility for the persistence or accuracy of URLs for external or third-party internet websites referred to in this publication, and does not guarantee that any content on such websites is, or will remain, accurate or appropriate.

Contents

Notes on contributors

Joaquín Álvarez Barrientos is a member of Spain's National Scientific Research Council (CSIC), and former head of its Department of Spanish Literature (Madrid). He has taught in several European and North American universities, and serves on the editorial board of numerous journals and societies dealing with Spanish eighteenth- and nineteenth-century literature. Among his many publications are *La novela del siglo XVIII* (1991), *La República de las letras en la España del siglo XVIII* (1995), *Ilustración y Neoclasicismo en las letras españolas* (2004), and *El hombre de letras en el siglo XVIII español* (2004).

Andrew A. Anderson is Professor of Spanish at the University of Virginia. His publications include *Lorca's Late Poetry: A Critical Study* (1990), *García Lorca: "La zapatera prodigiosa"* (1991), *América en un poeta. Los viajes de Federico García Lorca al Nuevo Mundo* (ed., 1999), *García Lorca: "Yerma"* (2003), six editions of García Lorca's poetry, theatre, prose, and correspondence (including *Epistolario completo* [1997], coedited with Christopher Maurer), as well as more than fifty articles on a variety of topics in modern Spanish literature. He has also compiled the bi-annual bibliography for the *Boletín de la Fundación Federico García Lorca* since 1987.

Andrew M. Beresford is Lecturer in Hispanic Language and Literature at the University of Durham, UK, where he specializes in hagiography, gender studies, and popular traditions. His publications include studies of Gonzalo de Berceo, the legend of Saint Mary of Egypt, *Celestina*, *cancionero* poetry, and the body-and-soul debate. He is one of the senior editors of Papers of the Medieval Hispanic Research Seminar and has served as a member of several other editorial boards. He is currently in the process of completing projects on the Castilian reworking of the *Legenda aurea* and the sonnets of the Marqués de Santillana.

Enric Bou is Professor of Hispanic Studies at Brown University, where he specializes in Spanish and Catalan contemporary literature. His publications include *Papers privats. Assaig sobre les formes literàries* *autobiogràfiques* (1993), *Pintura en el aire. Arte y literatura en la modernidad hispánica* (2001), and two editions of letters by Pedro Salinas, *Cartas de viaje* (1996) and *Cartas a Katherine Whitmore (1932–1947)* (2002). He is the editor of the *Nou Diccionari 62 de la Literatura Catalana* (2000) and has recently published a general anthology of visual poetry, *La crisis de la palabra. La Poesía Visual: un discurso poético alternativo* (2003).

James Burke is Professor of Spanish at the University of Toronto. He has written four books, the most recent of which are *Desire Against the Law* (1998) and *Vision, the Gaze and the Function of the Senses in "Celestina"* (2000), and in addition has published some fifty scholarly articles. He has held a number of administrative posts at Toronto, Department Chair 1983–1993, and has served on several editorial boards. He has been a frequent referee for scholarly journals, and is an Honorary Associate of the Hispanic Society of America.

Juan Cano Ballesta is Commonwealth Professor of Spanish (Emeritus) at the University of Virginia. As a literary scholar and historian he has published numerous articles and book reviews in journals in the USA and Europe. His books include *La poesía de Miguel Hernández* (1978), *La poesía española entre pureza y revolución* (1994), *Literatura y tecnología: Las letras españolas ante la revolución industrial 1900–1933* (1999), *Las estrategias de la imaginación. Utopías literarias y retórica política bajo el franquismo* (1994), *Poesía española reciente (1980–2000)* (2001), plus critical editions of Larra and Miguel Hernández. In 2003 he published *La mentira de las letras: Crítica cinematográfica de Juan Gil-Albert en la revista Romance.*

Richard A. Cardwell is Professor of Modern Spanish Literatures, Emeritus, at the University of Nottingham, UK. He has written over one hundred articles and some twenty books and editions on writers of the period 1800–1936. A number of his studies have questioned the viability of the concept of two opposed finisecular generations – *modernismo* versus *noventayocho* – arguments which will appear in definitive form in his forthcoming study of the Symbolist-Decadence in Spain. He was elected to the Real Academia de Buenas Letras de Sevilla in 1986 and serves on the editorial board of a number of journals. He presently teaches part-time in Nottingham.

Guillermo Carnero is Professor of Spanish Literature at the University of Alicante, Spain. As a poet and scholar he has received the Spanish National Prize for Criticism, the National Prize for Literature, and the Fastenrath

Prize of the Spanish Royal Academy. An expert on Spanish and comparative literature of the modern period (eighteenth through twentieth centuries), he has published editions of the works of García Malo, Jovellanos, Luzán, Martínez Colomer, Montengón, Zavala y Zamora, Espronceda, and others. He coordinated volumes 6, 7, and 8 of the *Historia de la literatura española* (1995–1996).

Lou Charnon-Deutsch is Professor of Spanish and Women's Studies at Stony Brook University. Her recent books include *Narratives of Desire: Nineteenth-Century Spanish Fiction by Women* (1994), *Culture and Gender in Nineteenth-Century Spain* (co-edited with Jo Labanyi, 1995), *Fictions of the Feminine in Nineteenth-Century Spanish Press* (2000), and *The Spanish Gypsy, History of a European Obsession* (2004). She serves on the editorial board of *Revista de Estudios Hispánicos* and *Letras Femeninas* and is American Editor of the *Journal of Hispanic Research*.

Jorge Checa is Professor of Spanish at the University of California, Santa Barbara. A Golden Age specialist also interested in medieval and contemporary literature, his publications include *Gracián y la imaginación arquitectónica* (1986), the anthology *Barroco esencial* (1992), and *Experiencia y representación en el Siglo de Oro* (1998). He has written a number of articles about Gracián, Cervantes, Lope de Vega, Calderón de la Barca, Sor Juana Inés de la Cruz, and Francisco Delicado (among other authors), in which he explores issues related to ideology, culture, and textual representation in the Hispanic world during the early modern period.

Anthony J. Close is Reader in Spanish at the University of Cambridge, UK. He is the author of *The Romantic Approach to "Don Quixote"* (1978), *Don Quixote* (1990), and *Cervantes and the Comic Mind of his Age* (2000), and some forty articles on Cervantes, Spanish Golden Age literature, the history of Cervantine criticism, and literary theory. He is a member of three editorial boards and of the Junta Directiva of the Asociación Internacional del Siglo de Oro.

John Dagenais is Professor of Spanish at the University of California, Los Angeles. His publications include *The Ethics of Reading in Manuscript Culture: Glossing the "Libro de buen amor"* (1994) and a special issue of the *Journal of Medieval and Renaissance Studies*, co-edited with Margaret Greer: "Decolonizing the Middle Ages" (2000). He has published articles, translations, and reviews on medieval Catalan, Castilian, Galician-Portuguese, and Occitan literature. Current projects include a translation of the fifteenth-century *Spill* by Jame Roig and a VR reconstruction of the

Romanesque cathedral of Santiago de Compostela. He has served on the editorial board of *Viator* since 1999.

Philip Deacon is Professor in Hispanic Studies at the University of Sheffield, UK. His published research centers on the intellectual and cultural history of eighteenth-century Spain, principally in the fields of drama, the erotic, ideological conflict, and the essay-press. Recent publications have focused on the aesthetic beliefs, social significance, and reception of the writers Nicolás and Leandro Fernández de Moratín, including a study and edition of Leandro Moratín's *El sí de las niñas*, republished in 2001.

Nigel Dennis is Professor of Spanish at the University of St Andrews, UK. His publications include *José Bergamín: A Critical Introduction 1920–1936* (1986), *Studies on Ramón Gómez de la Serna* (ed., 1988), and editions of work by Ernesto Giménez Caballero (*Visitas literarias de España*, 1995) and Ramón Gaya (*Obra completa IV*, 2000). He has published extensively on twentieth-century writers and prepared special issues of journals such as *Revista de Occidente* (1995) and *Romance Quarterly* (1999). He has been Director of the *Revista Canadiense de Estudios Hispánicos* (1992–1996) and has served as President of the Canadian Association of Hispanists (1990–1992).

Victor F. Dixon is Fellow Emeritus of Trinity College, Dublin, whose Chair of Spanish he held from 1974 to 1999. His publications include critical editions of three plays by Lope de Vega: *El sufrimiento premiado* (1967), *El perro del hortelano* (1981), and *Fuente Ovejuna* (1989), plus verse translations of the last two. He has written many reviews and over fifty journal articles on Spanish theatre; of these, apart from nine on Antonio Buero Vallejo, the vast majority relate to Lope. He has also directed and acted in some twenty Spanish plays.

Marvin D'Lugo is Professor of Spanish and Adjunct Professor of Screen Studies at Clark University, Worcester, Massachusetts, where he teaches courses on Spanish and Latin American cinemas. His publications include *The Films of Carlos Saura. The Practice of Seeing* (1991), *Guide to the Cinema of Spain* (1997), and a special issue of the journal *Post-Script: Essays in Film and the Humanities* on "Recent Spanish Cinema in Global Contexts" (2002), in addition to more than one hundred essays and reviews. He has served as a member of several editorial boards for journals, most recently *Secuencias: Revista de Historia del Cine*.

Dru Dougherty is Professor of Spanish Literature at the University of California, Berkeley. He co-directs a research project that is unearthing the stage history of Madrid's theatre from 1918 to 1936. Two volumes have appeared: *La escena madrileña entre 1918 y 1926: Análisis y documentación* (1990) and *La escena madrileña entre 1926 y 1931: Un lustro de transición* (1997), both co-authored with María Francisca Vilches. Dougherty's other major research project involves the works of Ramón del Valle-Inclán. His four books on this author include *Guía para caminantes en Santa Fe de Tierra Firme: Estudio sistémico de "Tirano Banderas"* (1999) and *Palimpsestos al cubo: Prácticas discursivas de Valle-Inclán* (2003).

Brad Epps is Professor of Romance Languages and Literatures and of the Committee on Degrees in Women's, Gender, and Sexuality Studies at Harvard University. He has published over fifty articles on literature, film, and art from Spain, Latin America, Catalonia, and France. He is the author of *Significant Violence: Oppression and Resistance in the Narratives of Juan Goytisolo* (1996) and co-editor of two forthcoming collections of essays: *Spain Beyond Spain: Modernity, Literary History, and National Identity* and *Passing Lines: Immigration and (Homo)sexuality*. He is also working on two book-length projects: *Daring to Write* and *Barcelona and Beyond*.

Sharon G. Feldman is Associate Professor of Spanish at the University of Richmond, Virginia. She is the author of *Allegories of Dissent* (1998; Spain, 2002), thirty articles and essays on Spanish and Catalan theatre and performance, as well as several play translations. She has held visiting appointments at the Universidade de Santiago de Compostela and the Institut del Teatre de la Diputació de Barcelona (including a Fulbright Senior Lectureship), and is a member of the executive board of the North American Catalan Society. Her forthcoming book on the contemporary Barcelona stage is entitled *In the Eye of the Storm*.

Derek Flitter is Head of the Department of Hispanic Studies at the University of Birmingham, UK. His publications include *Spanish Romantic Literary Theory and Criticism* (1992), *Teoría y crítica del romanticismo español* (1995), and the jointly authored *Don Alvaro et le drame romantique espagnol* (2003). His latest study, *Spanish Romanticism and the Uses of History: Ideology and the Historical Imagination*, is to appear in 2004. He is a contributor to the forthcoming Blackwell *Companion to European Romanticism* and to Continuum's *Byron in Europe* volume, and is currently completing the volume on Romanticism for Palgrave's European Culture and Society series.

Mary Malcom Gaylord is Sosland Family Professor of Romance Languages and Literatures at Harvard University. She is author of *The Historical Prose of Fernando de Herrera* and editor of "Frames for Reading:

Cervantes Studies in Honor of Peter N. Dunn," a special issue of the *Bulletin of the Cervantes Society of America*. She has published numerous essays on poetry and poetics, including studies of San Juan de la Cruz, Cervantes, Lope de Vega, Góngora, and the traditional lyric. Her current work focuses on New World resonances in sixteenth- and seventeenth-century representations of the poetic voice.

E. Michael Gerli is Commonwealth Professor of Spanish at the University of Virginia. He is a medievalist and early Modernist whose publications include eleven authored or edited books, including *Refiguring Authority: Reading, Writing, and Rewriting in Cervantes* (1995), *Medieval Iberia: An Encyclopedia* (2003), and over 150 articles and book reviews. He is a member of the editorial boards of several leading journals and presses of the profession, including the *Hispanic Review*, and the University of North Carolina Studies in Romance Languages and Literatures. Professor Gerli has held grants and fellowships for research from the National Endowment for the Humanities, the American Council of Learned Societies, and other agencies and foundations.

David T. Gies is Commonwealth Professor of Spanish at the University of Virginia. He has published twelve books and critical editions, including *The Cambridge Companion to Modern Spanish Culture* (1999), *Theatre and Politics in Nineteenth-Century Spain* (1988), *The Theatre in Nineteenth-Century Spain* (1994), *Nicolás Fernández de Moratín* (1979), and *Agustín Durán* (1975). Author of more than eighty articles and one hundred book reviews, he also edits *DIECIOCHO* and has been awarded numerous grants from agencies such as the Guggenheim Foundation, the National Endowment for the Humanities, the American Philosophical Society, and the Spanish Ministry of Culture. He serves on the Editorial Board of the *Bulletin of Spanish Studies*, *Hecho Teatral*, *Cuadernos Dieciochistas*, and *Rilce*.

Margaret R. Greer is Professor of Spanish and Chair of the Department of Romance Studies, Duke University. Her publications include: *María de Zayas Tells Baroque Tales of Love and the Cruelty of Men* (2000), *The Play of Power: Mythological Court Dramas of Pedro Calderón de la Barca* (1991), editions of Calderón de la Barca's plays *Basta callar* (2000) and *La estatua de Prometeo* (1986), and *Decolonizing the Middle Ages* (2000), edited with John Dagenais. Current book projects include *Approaches to Teaching Spanish Golden Age Drama* (with Laura Bass) and a book on early modern Spanish tragedy.

Martha Halsey is Professor of Spanish, Emerita, at Pennsylvania State University, where she has organized several international theatre symposia. In 1983 she was named Visiting Olive B. O'Connor Professor of Literature at Colgate University. Her publications include editions of plays by Buero Vallejo, Martín Recuerda, and Rodríguez Méndez, and (with P. Zatlin) *The Contemporary Spanish Theater: A Collection of Critical Essays* (1988) and *Entre Actos: Diálogos sobre teatro español entre siglos* (1999). She is the author of *From Dictatorship to Democracy: The Recent Plays of Buero Vallejo* (1994). From 1992 to 1998 she edited the journal, *Estreno*. She is an Honorary Fellow of The Hispanic Society of America.

Michael Iarocci is Assistant Professor of Spanish at the University of California – Berkeley. He is the author of *Enrique Gil y la genealogía de la lírica moderna* (1999), and he has published scholarly articles on numerous modern Spanish writers (José Cadalso, Mariano José de Larra, Gustavo Adolfo Bécquer, Benito Pérez Galdós, José María de Pereda, Federico García Lorca). He has served on the editorial board of Bucknell University Press, and he is on the advisory board of *Scripta Humanistica*. He is currently finishing a book-length study of Romantic writing in Spain and its relationship to the idea of the modern.

Susan Kirkpatrick is Professor of Spanish Literature at the University of California, San Diego. She is the author of *Larra: El inextricable laberinto de un liberal romántico* (1979), *Las Románticas: Women Writers and Subjectivity in Spain, 1835–1850* (1989), *Mujer, modernismo y vanguardia en Espana (1898–1931)* (2003), and editor of *Antología poética de escritoras del diecinueve* (1992). She has also published over fifty articles in scholarly journals and has served on the Executive Council of the MLA (1993–1996).

C. A. Longhurst is Professor Emeritus of the University of Leeds, UK; previously he was Professor of Spanish at the University of Exeter. He has held visiting appointments at the universities of Salamanca, Virginia, and Glasgow, and is currently Visiting Professor at King's College London. He is General Editor of the *Bulletin of Spanish Studies*. He is the author of *Las novelas históricas de Pío Baroja* (1974), as well as editions and critical studies of Baroja's *El mundo es ansí* (1977), Unamuno's *San Manuel Bueno, mártir / La novela de don Sandalio* (1984), *La tía Tula* (1987), and *Abel Sánchez* (1995), and Miró's *Nuestro Padre San Daniel / El obispo leproso* (1994).

José-Carlos Mainer is Professor of Spanish Literature at the University of Zaragoza, Spain. His published books include the anthology *Falange y literatura* (1971) and critical editions of works by Valera, Galdós, Baroja,

Basterra, and Martín-Santos. He is the author of *La Edad de Plata (1902–1939)* (1975, 1982), *La doma de la Quimera. Ensayos sobre nacionalismo y cultura en España* (1988), *La corona hecha trizas (1930–1960)* (1989), *De posguerra* (1995), and *La filología en el purgatorio. Los estudios literarios en 1950* (2003), in addition to dozens of articles and book reviews.

Gregorio C. Martín is Professor of Hispanic Studies at Duquesne University and Editor of *Crítica Hispánica*. His publications include *Hacia una revisión crítica de la biografía de Larra* (1975), *Lope de Vega's Las hazañas del Segundo David* (co-edited with Juan Bautista Avalle-Arce, 1985), and articles on the work of Larra, Jesús Fernández Santos, Rafael Sánchez Ferlosio, and Carlos Rojas.

Susan Martin-Márquez specializes in modern Peninsular literary narrative, film, and cultural studies. Her book *Feminist Discourse and Spanish Cinema: Sight Unseen* was published in 1999 by Oxford University Press, and she is currently working on an international collaborative oral history of cinema-going in 1940s and 1950s Spain, which analyzes the mechanisms of memory and the "performance" and practice of everyday life under Francoism. She is also completing a book, *Disorientations: Spanish Colonialism in Africa and the Cultural Mapping of Identity*, which scrutinizes the role played by Africa in the reconsolidation of Spanish national identities in the nineteenth and twentieth centuries.

Maria Rosa Menocal is the R. Selden Rose Professor of Spanish and Portuguese at Yale University where she is also Director of Special Programs in the Humanities and of the Whitney Humanities Center. Her books include *The Arabic Role in Medieval Literary History: A Forgotten Heritage*; *Writing in Dante's Cult of Truth: From Borges to Boccacio*; *Shards of Love: Exile and the Origins of the Lyric*; *The Literature of Al-Andalus* in The Cambridge History of Arabic Literature series (co-edited); and, most recently, *The Ornament of the World: How Muslims, Christians and Jews Created a Culture of Tolerance in Medieval Spain*. She is currently working on a project for Yale University Press entitled *Mosques, Churches, and Synagogues: Images of the Shared Cultures of Medieval Spain*.

Stephen Miller is Professor of Hispanic Studies at Texas A&M University. He has written *El mundo de Galdós* (1983), and edited (with Janet Pérez) *Critical Studies on Gonzalo Torrente Ballester* (1989) and (with Brian Dendle) *Critical Studies on Armando Palacio Valdés* (1993). In 2001 he published *Galdós gráfico (1861–1907): orígenes, técnicas y límites del* *socio-mimetismo*, as well as edited and introduced in facsimile volumes the five known Galdosian sketch books: *Gran teatro de la pescadería, Las Canarias, Atlas zoológico, Album arquitectónico,* and *Album marítimo.* He is currently developing a theory of composition and reading for nineteenth-century illustrated narrative.

José María Naharro-Calderón is Associate Professor of Spanish at the University of Maryland and Profesor Asociado at the Universidad de Alcalá. His publications include *Juan Ramón Jiménez* (1987), *El exilio de las Españas de 1939 en las Américas: ¿Adónde fue la canción?* (1991), *Entre el exilio y el interior: El "entresiglo" y Juan Ramón Jiménez* (1994), *Los exilios de las Españas de 1939: Por sendas de la memoria* (1999), *Manuscrit corbeau* (1998) and *Manuscrito cuervo* (1999) and editions of Max Aub's. He has recently completed *Sangrías españolas y terapias de Vichy: De los campos de concentración a las vueltas de exilio* and critical editions of Aub's *El Rapto de Europa* and *Campo francés.*

María Ángeles Naval is Professor of Spanish Literature at the University of Zaragoza, Spain. A specialist in the poetry of nineteenth-century Spain, she has written *El sentimiento apócrifo, Luis Ram de Viu (1864–1906): Vida y obra de un poeta de la Restauración* (1995) and *La novela de Vértice. La novela del Sábado* (2001). She edited *Flores de muerto* by Ram de Viu and *Recuerdos del tiempo viejo* by José Zorrilla. Coordinator of the collective volume *Cultura burguesa y letras provincianas* (1993), she has also written on José Cadalso, Bécquer, Valle-Inclán, and R. J. Sender, and has published the letters of Luis Cernuda to Gerardo Diego. She is Editor of the contemporary poetry magazine, *Poesía en el Campus.*

Nelson R. Orringer is Professor Emeritus of Spanish and Comparative Literature at the University of Connecticut (Storrs). Among his seven book-length critical studies are *Ortega y sus fuentes germánicas* (1979) and *Unamuno y los protestantes liberales* (1985). He has edited a special issue of the journal *Bulletin of Spanish Studies* (2002) on Hispanic Modernism; published the annotated English translation of Zubiri's *Estructura dinámica de la realidad* (2003); annotated critical editions of Francisco Ayala's two Caribbean novels; and authored 135 articles. He has served on six editorial boards and the Board of Directors of the Xavier Zubiri Foundation of North America.

Janet Perez is Paul Whitfield Horn Professor of Romance Languages and Qualia Chair of Spanish at Texas Tech University. She has authored books on José Ortega y Gasset, Ana María Matute, Miguel Delibes, Gonzalo Torrente Ballester, Camilo José Cela, contemporary Spanish women narrators, contemporary Spanish women poets, and edited or co-edited several essay collections and reference works. She has published more than 225 studies on contemporary Spanish poetry, drama, essays and novels, and more than 300 contributions to reference works. With past or present service on dozens of editorial boards, she is presently Editor of *Hispania*.

Joan Ramon Resina is Professor of Romance Studies and Comparative Literature at Cornell University. He is the author of *La búsqueda del Grial* (1988), *Un sueño de piedra: Ensayos sobre la literatura del modernismo europeo* (1990), *Los usos del clásico* (1991), and *El cadáver en la cocina. La novela policiaca en la cultura del desencanto* (1997). He has edited *Mythopoesis: Literatura, totalidad, ideología* (1992), *El aeroplano y la estrella: el movimiento vanguardista en los Países Catalanes (1904–1936)* (1997), *Disremembering the Dictatorship: The Politics of Memory since the Spanish Transition to Democracy* (2000), *Iberian Cities* (2001), and *After-Images of the City* (2003). He has published nearly one hundred essays and has won the Fullbright Fellowship and the Alexander von Humboldt Fellowship. He is the Editor of *Diacritics*.

Wadda C. Ríos-Font is Associate Professor of Spanish at Brown University. She is the author of two books, *Rewriting Melodrama: The Hidden Paradigm in Modern Spanish Theater* (1997) and *The Canon and the Archive: Configuring Literature in Modern Spain* (2004). She has also published and lectured extensively on nineteenth- and twentieth-century Spanish novels, theatre, and literary historiography, as well as on issues of gender, canonicity, and cultural history. Her current research concentrates on the relationships between the literary/intellectual and the juridical, legislative, and journalistic fields in modern Spain.

Jeremy Robbins is Forbes Professor of Spanish and Head of Hispanic Studies at the University of Edinburgh. He has published *Love Poetry of the Literary Academies in the Reigns of Philip IV and Charles II* and *The Challenges of Uncertainty: An Introduction to Seventeenth-Century Spanish Literature*, as well as numerous articles on the literature, art, and thought of Golden Age Spain. He has recently completed a study of the impact of skepticism on early modern Spain, entitled *Arts of Perception: The Epistemological Mentality of the Spanish Baroque 1580–1720*. He is currently working on a study of Golden Age prose fiction.

Evangelina Rodríguez Cuadros is Professor of Spanish Literature at the University of Valencia, Spain. She is the author of more than one hundred studies of Spanish Golden Age literature, among them *Calderón y la obra corta dramática del siglo XVII* (1983), and critical editions of Calderón's

plays *Los cabellos de Absalón* (1989) and *La vida es sueño* (1997), as
well as his *Entremeses, jácaras y mojigangas* (1983). Her study *La técnica
del actor en el Barroco: Hipótesis y documentos* (1998) won the Estudios
Teatrales "Leandro Fernández de Moratín" Prize in 1999. In 2001 she
published the monograph, *Calderón*.

Nil Santiáñez teaches Spanish and Literary Theory at Saint Louis Univer-
sity. His publications include *Ángel Ganivet, escritor modernista. Teoría
y novela en el fin de siglo español* (1994), *De la luna a Mecanópolis.
Antología de la ciencia ficción española (1832–1913)* (1995), *Ángel
Ganivet: Una bibliografía anotada* (1996), and *Investigaciones literarias.
Modernidad, historia de la literatura y modernismos* (2002), as well
as numerous articles on nineteenth- and twentieth-century Spanish and
European literature. He has also edited works by Gonzalo Torrente
Ballester, Ángel Ganivet, Rosalía de Castro, and Enrique Gaspar.

Charlotte D. Stern is Charles A. Dana Professor, Emerita, at Randolph-
Macon Woman's College. Her publications include *The Medieval Theater
in Castile* (1996) and more than one hundred articles and reviews on
medieval and sixteenth- and seventeenth-century Spanish literature with
emphasis on the theatre. She served on the Editorial Board of the *Journal
of Hispanic Philology* (1979–1992) and was Book Review Editor of the
Bulletin of the Comediantes (1977–1998).

Harriet S. Turner is Professor of Hispanic Studies and Director of International Affairs at the University of Nebraska-Lincoln. Her publications
include *Niebla* (co-edited with R. Gullón, 1965), *Galdós: "Fortunata y
Jacinta"* (1992), *Textos y contextos de Galdós* (co-edited with J. Kronik,
1994), a special issue of the journal *Letras Peninsulares* on the poetics of
Realism (2000), and the recent *Cambridge Companion to The Spanish
Novel* (2003), co-edited with A. López de Martínez, in addition to more
than fifty articles and reviews. She has served as President of the International Association of Galdós Scholars (1985–1988), as a member of
several editorial boards, including the Nebraska Press, and as director of
several international symposia and conferences.

Michael Ugarte is Professor of Spanish Literature at the University of
Missouri-Columbia. He has published three books in the field of Penin-
sular Spanish literature and culture: *Trilogy of Treason: An Intertextual
Study of Juan Goytisolo* (1982), *Shifting Ground: Spanish Civil War Exile
Literature* (1989) completed with the help of a Guggenheim Fellowship,
and *Madrid 1900* (1996).

Alison P. Weber is Associate Professor of Spanish at the University of Virginia. Her publications include a special issue on feminist topics for the *Journal of Hispanic Philology* (1989); *Teresa of Avila and the Rhetoric of Femininity* (1990); *For the Hour of Recreation* by María de San José (2002); a forthcoming edition of *Approaches to Teaching the Spanish Mystics*; and numerous articles on religious culture and the literature of early modern Spain. She serves on the advisory board of the Women's Studies in Religion Program at Harvard Divinity School and is a member of the editorial board for the journal *Cervantes*.

Julian Weiss is Reader in Medieval and Early Modern Spanish in the Department of Spanish and Spanish American Studies, King's College London, UK. His research interests span the Middle Ages and Renaissance, and his publications include numerous studies on early poetic theory and the lyric, such as *The Poet's Art: Literary Theory in Castile c. 1400–60* (1990) and *Poetry at Court in Trastamaran Spain* (co-edited with E. Michael Gerli, 1998). He is currently co-editing (with Antonio Cortijo) the commentary on Juan de Mena by the Renaissance humanist Hernán Nuñez.

Acknowledgments

It has become a cliché in publishing to thank one's colleagues and students for their ideas, support, and advice during the long gestation period that precedes the publication of a book. Clichés are always based in some truth, however, and, in my own case, that truth includes dozens of extraordinary colleagues and students who have made this book possible. The creation of any book is in many ways a collaborative process; the creation of a literary history is by definition collaborative, for it draws on the expertise of some of the best scholars currently writing on a broad range of topics across generations. It is therefore appropriate and with sincere gratitude that I recognize the work of all of the contributors to this book, and thank them for their dedication, knowledge, and willingness to have their words questioned, edited, shortened, expanded, eliminated, rearranged, or otherwise challenged. This book is theirs.

I would be remiss were I to fail to thank my friends and colleagues in the Department of Spanish, Italian, and Portuguese at the University of Virginia who answered queries, listened patiently to my ideas and concerns, and offered helpful correctives when needed. They are an exceptionally supportive and wise group of people, and I am grateful for their contributions and input.

Several colleagues and students pitched in to translate chapters of this book which were originally written in Spanish; in particular I am grateful to Philip Deacon, Alvin Sherman, Jr., Matthieu Raillard, Matthew J. Marr, Arantxa Ascunce, Edward Gurski and Celeste Delgado-Librera. Matthieu Raillard worked quickly and with exceptional skill to build the Chronology. The paperback edition of this book has been greatly improved by the wise observations and helpful suggestions made by Anthony H. Clarke, for which I am grateful.

I have had the great good fortune to work with Linda Bree, my editor at Cambridge University Press, on several projects. Her patient coaxing, inspired questions, and subtle reading of this book have been extremely helpful, and as the editor/author relationship deepened gradually into genuine friendship, I have come to realize that I am blessed to be able to work with one of the great editors of our time. In addition, my deepest gratitude to Leigh Mueller, whose copy-editing expertise saved us from incoherence more times than I would like to admit.

Finally, I wish to thank Janna, who is learning more about Spanish literature and culture than perhaps she ever thought she wanted to, but whose charm, cheerfulness, support, and love make even the darkest moments of scholarly activity manageable and even, in weird and wonderful ways, fun.

Note on cover illustration

Joaquín Sorolla's extraordinary painting *Cosiendo la vela* ("Sewing the Sail") was painted in Valencia in 1896 and exhibited shortly thereafter in Paris, Munich, Vienna, and Madrid. It is now housed in Venice. The play of light and shade, color and texture, depth and shimmering surfaces might be taken as a metaphor for the creation of literary history, an art form which demands that various individuals stitch together seemingly unrelated pieces of fabric in order to produce a coherent, useful, and multi-faceted cloth. We contemplate the painting awed by the artist's skill, his ability to draw us in with perspective, shape, the suggestion of movement, and the calm of eternity (what Unamuno might have said to be "history" and "intrahistory" combined). I thought this painting was particularly appropriate to grace the cover of this book, and I am grateful to the curators of the Museo d'Arte Moderna-Ca Pesaro for permission to use it.

DTG

Chronology

P: Painting F: Film M: Music S: Sculpture

	Political events		Literature		Other culture
2000 BC	Iberians inhabit Spain				
1100 BC	Phoenicians found Cádiz				
800 BC	Celts settle in Spain				
230 BC	Carthaginians found Barcelona			c. 300 BC	The Lady of Elche bust
218 BC	Roman occupation of Iberia				
133 BC	Siege of Numancia			c. 100	Aqueduct at Segovia
409	Germanic tribes invade Spain; Toledo becomes capital				
586	Recaredo is first Catholic king	c. 600	San Isidoro, *Orígenes o Etimologías*	c. 550	Basilica of Segóbriga
711	Rodrigo defeated by Moors				
718	Pelayo begins Christian reconquest; Battle of Covadonga				
1037	Fernando I becomes king of Castile and León				
1085	Alfonso VI takes Toledo			1075	Construction of Santiago de Compostela cathedral begins
1087	Almorávides conquer Spain				
1094	The Cid takes Valencia				
1146	Almohades conquer the Almorávides	c. 1105–1178	*Cantar de mio Cid*		
1212	Alfonso VIII defeats the Almohades; end of Moorish reign	c. 1150	*Auto de los reyes magos*		

1215	Alfonso IX founds University at Salamanca	c. 1252	Gonzalo de Berceo, *Milagros de Nuestra Señora*	1226	Construction of Toledo cathedral begins
1236	Fernando III conquers Córdoba and Seville	c. 1300–1310	Ferrand Martines, *Libro del caballero Zifar*	1250	Construction begins at the Alhambra
1252	Fernando III dies, Alfonso X el Sabio begins reign	c. 1330	The Archpriest of Hita, *El libro de buen amor*		
1330	Alfonso XI invades Granada	1335	Juan Manuel, *Conde Lucanor*	c. 1364	Construction of the alcazar of Seville begins
1469	Fernando de Aragón marries Isabel de Castilla	c. 1476	Jorge Manrique, *Coplas por la muerte de su padre*	c. 1434	*Retablo mayor* of the León cathedral
1480	Birth of the Inquisition			c. 1474	First printing press appears in Valencia
1492	Granada is conquered; Columbus discovers America; Jews expelled from Spain	1492	Diego de San Pedro, *Cárcel de amor*	1492	Antonio de Nebrija, *Gramática de la lengua castellana*
1499	Cisneros baptizes more than 70,000 in a day	1499	Fernando de Rojas, *Celestina*	c. 1499	Pedro Sánchez, *Entombment of Christ* (P)
1504	Conquest of Sicily and Naples	1508	*Amadís de Gaula*	c. 1509	Juan de Flandes, *Sts. Michael & Francis* (P)
1516	Carlos I of Spain (Charles V of the Holy Roman Empire) becomes king	1513	Alonso de Cardona, *Qüestión de amor*	c. 1513	Construction of Salamanca cathedral begins
1519	Conquest of Mexico	1527	Francisco de Osuna; *Abecedarios espirituales*	1530	Juan del Encina dies
1531	Conquest of Chile, Peru	1539	Antonio de Guevara, *Menosprecio de corte y alabanza de aldea*	1541	El Greco is born

(cont.)

Date	Political events	Date	Literature	Date	Other culture
1556	Carlos V abdicates; Felipe II becomes king	1554	*Lazarillo de Tormes*	c. 1548	Tomás Luis de Victoria is born
1557	Spain declares war on France (1557–1559)	1559?	Jorge de Montemayor, *Los siete libros de la Diana*	1560	Luis de Morales, *Man of Sorrows* (P)
1571	Battle of Lepanto	1582–1585	Juan de la Cruz, *Noche oscura*	1571	Cervantes injured in Battle of Lepanto
1580	Occupation of Portugal	1585	Miguel de Cervantes, *La Galatea*	1588	El Greco, *Entierro del conde de Orgaz* (P)
1588	Defeat of the Spanish Armada	1599	Mateo Alemán, *Guzmán de Alfarache*	1597	El Greco, *Vista de Toledo* (P)
1598	Felipe III becomes king	1605	Miguel de Cervantes, *Don Quijote* (Part I)	1605	Tomás Luis de Victoria, *Officium Defunctorum* (M)
1609	Felipe III expels Moors	1609	Lope de Vega, *El arte nuevo de hacer comedias*	c. 1612	El Greco, *The Marriage of the Virgin* (P)
1621	Felipe IV becomes king	1613	Miguel de Cervantes, *Novelas ejemplares*	1616	Death of Cervantes
c. 1620			Lope de Vega, *El caballero de Olmedo*	1623	Diego Velázquez, *El aguador de Sevilla* (P)
1623		1623	Pedro Calderón de la Barca, *Amor, honor y poder*	1624	Jusepe de Ribera, *St. John the Baptist* (P)
1625	Spain imposes river blockade in northern Europe	1626	Francisco de Quevedo, *El buscón*; Tirso de Molina, *El burlador de Sevilla*		

1633	Francisco de Zurbarán, *The Young Virgin* (P)	1631	Lope de Vega, *El castigo sin venganza*	1640	Uprisings in Catalonia
1635	Death of Lope de Vega	1635	Pedro Calderón de la Barca, *La vida es sueño*	1659	Treaty of the Pyrenees ends war with France
1638	Francisco de Zurbarán, *The Savior Blessing*(P)	1636	Pedro Calderón de la Barca, *El alcalde de Zalamea*	1665	Carlos II becomes king
1656	Diego Velázquez, *Las meninas* (P)	1651	Baltasar Gracián, *El Criticón*	1688	Spain declares war on France (1688–1697)
1681	Death of Pedro Calderón de la Barca			1700	Carlos II dies; end of Habsburg rule in Spain
				1701	Felipe V becomes first Bourbon king of Spain; War of Succession begins (1701–1714)
1712	Biblioteca Nacional founded			1709	Rupture with Roman Catholic Church
1714	Real Academia founded	1722	Dr. Martín Martínez, *Medicina escéptica*	1713	Treaty of Utrecht
		1726	Benito Jerónimo Feijoo, *Teatro crítico universal*		
1738	Real Academia de la Historia founded	1737	Ignacio de Luzán, *La Poética*	1737	Accord with Roman Catholic Church
				1739	Spain declares war on Great Britain
1746	Birth of Francisco de Goya	1742	Benito Jerónimo Feijoo, *Cartas eruditas y curiosas*	1746	Death of Felipe V. Fernando VI becomes king.
		1758	José Francisco de Isla, *Fray Gerundio de Campazas* (Part I)	1759	Death of Fernando VI. Carlos III becomes king

(cont.)

Political events	Literature	Other culture
1763 Real Orden of 1763 establishes first Spanish copyright	1762 Nicolás Fernández de Moratín, *La petimetra*	1762 Newspaper *El pensador* is founded by José Clavijo y Fajardo
1767 Expulsion of the Jesuits from Spain	1773 José Cadalso, *Ocios de mi juventud*	1772 Luis Paret y Alcazár, *La tienda del anticuario* (P)
1778 Liberalization of South American trade	1778 Vicente García de la Huerta, *Raquel*	1782 Death of José Cadalso
	1785 Juan Meléndez Valdés, *Poesías*	
	1786 Pedro Montengón, *Eusebio*	
1788 Death of Carlos III. Carlos IV becomes king	1788 Gaspar Melchor de Jovellanos, *Elogio de Carlos III*	1789 French Revolution
	1789 José de Cadalso, *Cartas marruecas*	
	1790 Melchor Gaspar de Jovellanos, *Policía de los espectáculos*	
1793 War with France (1793–1795)	1792 Leandro Fernández de Moratín, *La comedia nueva o el café*	c. 1795 Goya, *El marqués de Sofraga* (P)
1796 Alliance of Spain and France against Great Britain	1798 José Mor de Fuentes, *La Serafina*	
1805 Defeat of Spanish fleet by Great Britain at Trafalgar	1805 Leandro Fernández de Moratín, *El sí de las niñas*	
1808 French invasion of Spain; Carlos IV abdicates, Joseph Bonaparte declared king of Spain	1808 Manuel José Quintana, *España después de la revolución de Marzo*	1810 Goya, *Desastres de la Guerra* (P)

Date		Date		Date	
1814	Goya, *El tres de Mayo de 1808* (P)	1812	Francisco Martínez de la Rosa, *La viuda de Padilla*	1812	First Spanish constitution ratified in Cadiz
1820	Goya, *Self Portrait with Dr. Arrieta* (P)	1818	José Gorostiza, *Indulgencia para todos*	1814	Fernando VII returned as king; Constitution of 1812 abolished
1827	Goya, *La lechera de Burdeos* (P)	1824	Manuel Bretón de los Herreros, *A la vejez, viruelas*	1820	Insurgence of liberals; "trienio liberal" of 1820–1823 sees the Constitution of 1812 restored
1828	Death of Goya	1828	Agustín Durán, *Discurso*	1823	French invasion of Spain; Fernando VII restored as king. Ominous Decade begins.
1831	The Madrid Stock Market opens	1829	Juan de Grimaldi, *La pata de cabra*	1830	Birth of Isabel II
1835	Newspaper *El artista* founded	1831	Manuel Bretón de los Herreros, *Marcela, o ¿a cuál de los tres?*	1833	Death of Fernando VII; regency of Queen María Cristina begins
1837	Mariano José de Larra commits suicide	1834	Martínez de la Rosa, *La conjuración de Venecia*; Mariano José de Larra, *Macías*	1834	First Carlist War (1834–1839)
1845	Centralization of public schooling	1835	Duque de Rivas, *Don Álvaro o la fuerza del sino*	1835	María Cristina restores Constitution of 1812
		1836	Antonio García Gutiérrez, *El trovador*	1837	Liberal Constitution of 1837
		1840	José de Espronceda, *El estudiante de Salamanca*	1839	Carlist War ends with "embrace of Vergara"
		1841	Gertrúdis Gómez de Avellaneda, *Sab*	1843	Isabel II declared of age
		1844	José Zorrilla, *Don Juan Tenorio*; Enrique Gil y Carrasco, *El señor de Bembibre*	1844	The Guardia Civil is created

(cont.)

	Political events		Literature		Other culture
1848	First Spanish railway	1849	Fernán Caballero, *La gaviota*		
1854	Espartero returns to power, "bienio liberal"	1858	Gertrudis Gómez de Avellaneda, *Baltasar*	1859	The *Jocs Floral* poetry contest founded
1859	Spain enters war with Morocco			1864	Miguel de Unamuno is born
1865	War with Peru and Chile	1863	Francisco Giner de los Ríos, *Estudios*		
1868	Revolution; Isabel II is exiled	1869	Ramón de Campoamor, *El drama universal*	1870	Gustavo Adolfo Bécquer dies
1870	Amadeo of Savoy becomes king of Spain	1870	Manuel Tamayo y Baus, *Los hombres de bien*		
1871	Assassination of General Prim	1871	Gustavo Adolfo Bécquer, *Rimas*		
1872	Second Carlist War (1872–1876)	1874	Juan Valera, *Pepita Jiménez*		
1873	Amadeo abdicates; birth of First Spanish Republic	1876	Benito Pérez Galdós, *Doña Perfecta*	1873	Manuel Bretón de los Herreros dies
1875	Alfonso XII becomes king; Bourbon Restoration begins	1884	Rosalía de Castro, *A las orillas del Sar*	1882	Joaquín Sorolla, *Puerto de Valencia* (P)
1885	Alfonso XII dies	1885	Leopolda Alas / Clarín, *La regenta*		
1886	Alfonso XIII begins ruling under regency of his mother	1886	Benito Pérez Galdós, *Fortunata y Jacinta*; Emilia Pardo Bazán, *Los pazos de Ulloa*	1887	Joaquín Sorolla, *La virgen María* (P)
1888	Barcelona hosts Universal Exposition	1895	Miguel de Unamuno, *En torno al casticismo*	1898	Antoni Gaudí, Parc Güell

Year	Culture	Year	Literary works	Year	Historical events
1899	Rubén Darío visits Madrid	1898	Angel Ganivet, *Los trabajos del infatigable creador Pío Cid*	1898	Spanish American war
1901	Leopoldo Alas dies	1902	Azorín, *La voluntad*; Pío Baroja, *Camino de perfección*	1902	Alfonso XIII becomes king
1904	José Echegaray wins Nobel Prize in Literature	1904	Ramón del Valle-Inclán, *Sonata de primavera*	1906	Creation of Solidaridat Catalana
1906	Santiago Ramón y Cajal wins Nobel Prize in Medicine	1906	Antonio Machado, *Soledades, galerías y otros poemas*	1907	The "Long Government" of Antonio Maura
1908	Isaac Albéniz, *Iberia* (M)	1909	Jacinto Benavente, *Los intereses creados*	1909	Spain enters war with Morocco; fall of Maura
1909	Pablo Picasso, *Arlequín* (P)	1912	Pío Baroja, *El árbol de la ciencia*	1914	First World War begins, Spain neutral
1914	Pablo Picasso, *El jugador de cartas* (P)	1914	Miguel de Unamuno, *Niebla*	1917	General Strike in Asturias
1916	Joaquín Sorolla, *Niños en la playa* (P)	1916	Juan Ramón Jiménez, *Diario de un poeta recién casado*	1920	Spanish communist party formed
1920	Benito Pérez Galdós dies	1920	Ramón del Valle-Inclán, *Luces de bohemia*	1921	Spanish army defeated at Anual, Morocco
1922	Jacinto Benavente wins Nobel Prize in Literature	1921	Gabriel Miró, *Nuestro Padre San Daniel*	1923	Primo de Rivera begins dictatorship
1923	*Revista de Occidente* founded by José Ortega y Gasset	1924	Ramón Gómez de la Serna, *El novelista*	1925	Army lands at Alhucemas in Morocco
1926	Ramón Menéndez Pidal, *Orígenes del español*	1925	José Ortega y Gasset, *La deshumanización del arte*	1926	National Consultative Assembly established
1928	Pablo Picasso, *Baigneuse* (P)	1928	Federico García Lorca, *Romancero Gitano*; Jorge Guillén, *Cántico*		

(cont.)

	Political events		Literature		Other culture
1929	Barcelona hosts Universal Exposition	1929	Rafael Alberti, *Cal y canto* and *Sobre los ángeles*	1929	Luis Buñuel, *Un chien andalou* (F)
1930	Fall of Primo de Rivera	1930	Federico García Lorca, *Poeta en Nueva York*	1930	Salvador Dalí, *El hombre invisible* (P)
1931	Alfonso XIII exiled; Second Spanish Republic	1931	Miguel de Unamuno, *San Manuel Bueno, mártir*; Federico García Lorca, *Poema del cante jondo*	1932	Federico García Lorca creates theatre group La Barraca
1933	National Elections; center-right gains control	1933	Pedro Salinas, *La voz a ti debida*	1933	Luis Buñuel, *Las Hurdes* (F)
1936	Spanish Civil War begins	1936	Miguel Hernández, *El rayo que no cesa*	1936	Federico García Lorca assassinated; Miguel de Unamuno dies
1938	Ley de Prensa passed			1937	Pablo Picasso, *Guernica* (P)
1939	Spanish Civil War ends; fall of Second Spanish Republic; Franco rises to power; Second World War begins	1940	Dionisio Ridruejo, *Poesía en armas*	1939	Joan Miró, *Black and Red Series* (P); Joaquín Rodrigo, *Concierto de Aranjuez* (M)
1941	Death of Alfonso XIII in exile in Rome	1941	Gerardo Diego, *Alondra de verdad*	1941	Enrique del Campo, *El Crucero Baleares* (F)
1942	Spain asserts neutrality in Second World War	1942	Camilo José Cela, *La familia de Pascual Duarte*	1942	Miguel Hernández dies
1945	Second World War ends; Spain rejected by UN	1944	Carmen Laforet, *Nada*		
1947	Referendum defines Spain as Kingdom	1947	Luis Cernuda, *Como quien espera el alba*	1947	Bullfighter Manolete dies in Jaen
1949	UN lifts sanctions against Spain	1949	Antonio Buero Vallejo, *Historia de una escalera*	1948	Eduardo Chillida, *Torso* (S)
1951	Public transportation strike in Barcelona	1951	Camilo José Cela, *La colmena*	1951	Salvador Dalí, *Christ of St. John of the Cross* (P); Pedro Salinas dies

Year	Political events	Year	Literary works	Year	Cultural events
1955	Spain joins UN	1953	Ramón Sender, *Requiem por un campesino español*	1955	José Ortega y Gasset dies
1956	Student revolts	1956	Rafael Sánchez Ferlosio, *El Jarama*	1956	Juan Ramón Jiménez wins Nobel Prize in literature
1959	Cabinet composed of technocrats and Opus Dei ministers; ETA founded	1959	Ana María Matute, *Primera memoria*	1958	Juan Ramón Jiménez dies
1962	Strike in Asturian mines	1961	Luis Martín-Santos, *Tiempo de silencio*	1961	Luis Buñuel, *Viridiana* (F)
1963	Film censorship norms established	1962	Lauro Olmo, *La camisa*	1963	Mario Camus, *Los farsantes* (F)
1966	Referendum of Organic Law of the state	1966	Juan Goytisolo, *Señas de identidad*; Miguel Delibes, *Cinco horas con Mario*	1965	Alfonso Sastre, *Anatomía del realismo*
1968	First victim of ETA is killed; Prince Felipe is born	1967	Juan Benet, *Volverás a Región*	1967	Luis Buñuel, *Belle de jour* (F)
1973	Admiral Carrero Blanco killed by ETA	1970	Juan Goytisolo, *Revindicación del Conde don Julian*	1970	Carlos Saura, *El jardín de las delicias* (F)
1975	Death of Franco; Juan Carlos I becomes King	1973	Juan Marsé, *Si te dicen que caí*	1972	Luis Buñuel, *Le Charme discret de la bourgeoisie* (F)
1977	First democratic elections; attempted military coup	1975	Eduardo Mendoza, *La verdad sobre el caso Savolta*	1976	Carlos Saura, *Cría cuervos* (F); newspaper *El País* begins publication
1978	Approval of democratic Constitution	1978	Carmen Martín-Gaite, *El cuarto de atrás*	1977	Vicente Aleixandre wins Nobel Prize in Literature
1982	Socialist party PSOE wins majority; Andalusia becomes autonomous	1982	Martín Recuerda, *El engañao*	1982	Spain hosts soccer world cup

(cont.)

Political events		Literature		Other culture	
1986	Spain joins EU	1986	Antonio Muñoz Molina, *Beatus ille*	1987	Pedro Almodóvar, *Mujeres al borde de un ataque de nervios* (F); Andrés Segovia dies
1987	ETA kills twenty-one in supermarket bomb in Barcelona	1987	José Sanchis Sinisterra, *¡Ay, Carmela!*; Antonio Muñoz Molina, *El invierno en Lisboa*	1989	Camilo José Cela wins Nobel Prize in Literature; Dalí dies
		1988	Arturo Pérez Reverte, *El maestro de esgrima*	1992	Fernando Trueba, *Belle Epoque* (F)
1992	Universal Exposition in Seville; Barcelona hosts Olympic games	1994	Almudena Grandes, *Malena es un nombre de tango*	1996	Francisco Amenábar, *Tesis* (F)
1996	Socialist party defeated after thirteen-year run; Aznar forms minority government	1997	Juan Manuel de Prada, *La tempestad; Las máscaras del héroe*	1998	Ghery-designed Guggenheim Museum opens in Bilbao; Julio Medem, *Los amantes del círculo polar* (F)
1998	ETA announces truce	1998	Rafael Torres, *Ese cadáver*	2000	Carmen Martín Gaite dies
1999	Spain adopts Euro	2000	José Luis Sampedro, *El amante lesbiano*	2001	Julio Medem, *Lucía y el sexo* (F)
2000	Partido Popular gains majority in elections	2001	Javier Cercas, *Soldados de Salamina*		

Part I

Introduction

DAVID T. GIES

The Funes effect: making literary history

DAVID T. GIES

One fears that Pierre Menard might have had it right when he proclaimed, "There is no intellectual exercise which is not ultimately useless."[1] Certainly, the thorny problem of writing literary history might fit into Menard's category and he might have despaired at, if not the ultimate uselessness of the task, at least its seeming impossibility. Moreover, if Menard despaired, then his colleague (and presumed soulmate) Funes, whose implacable memory prohibited him from making connections (indeed, from thinking), merely went crazy in his attempt to sort out his own reality and reduce it to comprehensible units. As the narrator of his story reveals, "I suspect, nevertheless, that he was not very capable of thought. To think is to forget a difference, to generalize, to abstract. In the overly replete world of Funes there were nothing but details, almost contiguous details."[2] If Menard was not up to the challenge of reliving every crucial moment in the life of the author of *Don Quijote* in order to replicate not only the end product, but the experiences which informed that text, and Funes could forget nothing, and hence, not think, what, then, is to become of the modern literary historian, who faces similar challenges? How is the historian of literature to "think" when crushed by an avalanche of details (dates, categories, names, works, "-isms," movements, languages, boundaries, nationalities)? To write literary history – to rewrite literary history – must we relive literary history? Is this what Mario Valdés has in mind when he states, "every writing of literary history is inadequate to the task of reenactment, but nevertheless is a necessity for the cultural identity of the society that produces the writing"?[3] "Inadequate . . . necessity" – do the terms cancel each other out? Like Funes, are we doomed if we do, doomed if we don't?

Literary history is indeed an accumulation of contiguous details and an act of forgetting. Homi Bhabha articulated this latter belief in *The*

---

[1] Jorge Luis Borges, *Ficciones*. Ed. and trans. Anthony Kerrigan (New York: Grove Press, 1962), p. 53.
[2] Borges, *Ficciones*, p. 115.
[3] Mario J. Valdés, "Rethinking the History of Literary History." In *Rethinking Literary History*. Ed. Linda Hutcheon and Mario J. Valdés (Oxford: Oxford University Press, 2002), p. 80.

Location of Culture (but with no reference to Funes, of course).[4] The
issue is, naturally, how many details are to be included, which details
they might be, how they might be structured, and, in the end, how much
forgetting is acceptable. How does one decide what to "forget"? Does
one "forget" for ideological reasons? For aesthetic reasons? For reasons
of structure or space or power or mere convenience? If the accumulated
memory of individuals, groups, or nations informs the act of making literary history, then, whose memory is it? Is it a national memory, a repository
of canonical "greatest hits?" Is it a gendered memory? A racial memory?
Or is it a web of opinion – "opinion with dates," as Valdés calls literary
history,[5] a personalized selection based on – what? – taste, availability,
popularity, influence, aesthetic impact, ideological content, thematic concerns, or chance encounters? Louise Bernikow puts this succinctly: "What
is commonly called literary history is actually a record of choices. Which
writers have survived their times and which have not depends on who
noticed them and chose to record their notice."[6]

    If literary history consists of choices, then who chooses? And can
choice produce any semblance of objectivity? Furthermore, is objectivity possible? Is objectivity even desirable? As David Perkins, one of the
most articulate defenders of the enterprise called literary history, notes,
"The only complete literary history would be the past itself, but this would
not be a history, because it would not be interpretive and explanatory."[7]
This is what Funes finally realized, and, as we know, his inability to forget
was the road to madness.

    Literary History is, or can include, a series of dates, names, works,
titles, concepts, genres, movements, regions, schools, influences, traditions, languages, and ethnic groups. *Is Literary History Possible?*, the title
of Perkins' provocative book, captures the dilemma of the writer of literary history in the modern world, less naive than his/her forebears, who
were more confident of the necessity and possibility of the categorization,
evaluation, and selection of literature than we are today.

    As early as 1790 in Spain, Cándido María Trigueros seemed to have
had a sense of what the writing of literary history might encompass. Yet
what provided the bedrock for his interpretation of literary history is
precisely what provokes anxiety among modern literary historians. In his
Discurso sobre el estudio metódico de la Historia literaria ("Discourse on
the Methodical Study of Literary History") he wrote:

---

[4] Homi Bhabha, *The Location of Culture* (London: Routledge, 1994).
[5] Valdés, "Literary History," p. 74.
[6] Louise Bernikow, *The World Split Open: Four Centuries of Women Poets in England and
America, 1552–1950* (New York: Vintage, 1974), p. 3.
[7] David Perkins, *Is Literary History Possible?* (Baltimore: Johns Hopkins University Press,
1992), p. 13.

El mérito de los libros de cada materia respectiva, y de las ediciones de cada libro, cuyo conocimiento guía como por la mano a discernir y escoger los mejores en todas, excusando metódicamente la pérdida de tiempo y de caudal; es a lo que se dirige el estudio de la Historia Literaria; agregándose a esto el examen de los progresos del ententimiento humano, que para ser verdaderamente útil debe descubrirnos no solamente las mutaciones, adelantamientos, y atrasos de todas las Naciones en los respectivos ramos de la literatura y en el por mayor de los estudios y de las artes; pero es necesario también que averigüe las causas, o civiles, o morales o físicas, que produxeron aquellos efectos: en una palabra, para que sea loable la Historia Literaria que se estudie, debe ser *filosófica, completa, breve, imparcial* y *verdadera.*

(The value of books in each respective subject, and of editions of each book, the knowledge of which guides us toward understanding and selecting the best among them, thereby helping us to avoid wasting our time or resources: this is what Literary History tries to do. To this is added the examination of the progress of human understanding, which in order to be truly useful should reveal to us not only the changes, advances, and slips of all nations in the respective areas of literature and in the great majority of sciences and arts, but it is also necessary to discern the causes, whether civic or moral or physical, that produced those effects. In a word, for Literary History to be worthy of study, it must be *philosophical, complete, short, impartial,* and *true.*)[8]

Most of Triguero's basic assumptions are questioned today (we understand that literary history is not, nor can it be, "complete," "impartial," or even "true," and his idea of national "progress" has likewise been dismantled since the 1970s by thoughtful historians and cultural critics), but still we recognize the inherent validity of selection, aesthetic choice, and contextualization in the creation of literary history: "There must be similarities between works to justify grouping them together (in genres, periods, traditions, movements, discursive practices, and so on), for without classification and generalization, the field cannot be grasped mentally. A great many, perfectly heterogeneous objects cannot be understood."[9] Yet classification in itself has become a contested area as scholars redefine the borders between "periods" such as Medieval, Renaissance, Baroque, Modern, Contemporary, etc. We now work with more supple concepts such as Early Modern Spain, the Long Eighteenth Century, Post-Franco Literature, and even attempt to eschew or redefine "old" categories such as Generations (the Generation of 1898 is a perfect example). Mario Valdés invites us to consider such period groupings as "ideational cultural systems" rather than narrow temporal categories,[10] and we would do well to heed this advice.

---

[8] Cándido María Trigueros, *Discurso sobre el estudio metódico de la Historia literaria* (Madrid: Benito Cano, 1790), pp. 27–28.
[9] Perkins, *Literary History*, p. 126.   [10] Valdés, "Literary History," p. 69.

It may be that we have lost our innocence, and our confidence, as literary historians. Literary histories written by individuals have largely been supplanted by collective efforts. For Valdés, "The choices we make as historians are not individual – they are collective or one's own understanding of the collective sense of axial moments."[11] Or, to use Marshall Brown's terms, literary history today is more "assembled" than "written."[12] The hubris of individual protagonism has given way to the comfort of collectivity. If once upon a time we could welcome a single-authored literary history (we think of the early efforts of George Ticknor, Hippolyte Taine, Carl Van Doren, or James Fitzmaurice-Kelly), the modern world demands more reticence, and thus we get the admirable and useful *Literary History of Spain*, edited by R. O. Jones; Víctor García de la Concha's as yet unfinished *Historia de la literatura española*; or Roberto González Echevarría, Enrique Pupo-Walker, and David Haberly's *Cambridge History of Latin American Literature*, all collectively authored and in multiple volumes. I write "the modern world," since it goes without saying that Postmodern critics reject the single-authored volume out of hand, seeing in it (correctly) yet another attempt to create an untenable Master Narrative. "Useful" is a key concept here, however, for as David Perkins believes, "the function of literary history is to produce useful fictions about the past."[13]

The forces of history and historical change do not develop as a linear story or as a coherent narrative. They are *made* narrative *ex post facto*; the story is created through a process of research, selection, sequencing, and the imposition of order on often contradictory and disparate elements. Hans Kellner warns, "[W]e cannot forget that our ways of making sense of history must emphasize the *making*."[14] This is literary history, too, although the tension between the "literary" and the "history" have led to accusations of failure on both sides.[15] Linda Hutcheon reveals that literary history is "a storytelling project,"[16] while Marshall Brown insists, "We want some history in our literary history."[17] We seem to be compelled to make sense of ourselves, of our history, of our literary history, and so,

---

[11] Valdés, "Literary History," p. 70.

[12] Marshall Brown, ed., *The Uses of Literary History* (Durham: Duke University Press), p. 100.

[13] Perkins, *Literary History*, p. 182.

[14] Hans Kellner, "Language and Historical Representation." In *The Postmodern History Reader*. Ed. Keith Jenkins (London: Routledge, 1997), p. 128.

[15] Lawrence Lipking, "A Trout in the Milk." *Modern Language Quarterly* 54.1 (1993), p. 7.

[16] Linda Hutcheon, "Preface. Theorizing Literary History in Dialogue." In *Rethinking Literary History*. Ed. Linda Hutcheon and Mario J. Valdés (Oxford: Oxford University Press, 2002), p. xi.

[17] M. Brown, *Uses of Literary History*, p. 118.

like Don Quijote, armed with a smattering of knowledge and a handful
of texts, we venture into uncharted territory.

Well, not entirely uncharted. As Perkins reminds us, literary history,
from its antiquarian roots in the eighteenth century, has become a staple
of the profession of literature and has been written, contested, rejected,
criticized, and rewritten for more than 200 years. If the eighteenth century
witnessed its invention, it was the nineteenth century which expanded the
range of literary history and connected it to the nationalistic enterprises
which the twentieth century has come to reject with such force. We are
well past asking literary history to find or define the "soul" of a nation.
This "Volkgeist" was a construction of the German Romantics (of Johann
Gottfried von Herder, in particular), brought to Spain by the Romantic
theorists Johann Nikolas Böhl von Faber and Agustín Durán in the first
years of the nineteenth century, but it lost its ability to structure literary
history and fell into disuse. Indeed, by the second half of the twentieth
century, critics not only rejected such reductionist history, but were actually proclaiming the demise, fall, or obliteration of Literary History. As
René Wellek wrote in a famous paper, "something has happened to literary historiography which can be described as decline and even as fall.
Particularly in the interval between the two world wars widespread dissatisfaction with literary history was voiced in almost every country."[18]
The journal *New Literary History* even dedicated a special issue to the
question, "Is Literary History Obsolete?" in 1970.

In the present volume, Wadda Ríos-Font traces the origins of literary
history in Spain and addresses the ideological biases that inevitably inform
the enterprise. We know the impossibility of completeness, of objectivity,
of coverage, of inclusiveness, and yet we struggle on, convinced that even
an inadequate and reductive overview of a nation's literary achievements
can provide at least some guidance through the past and some keys to
interpreting the present. All decisions made by the literary historian are
necessarily arbitrary, although they are made within the boundaries of a
series of accepted codes and assumptions, codes secreted over the years
like stalagmites on the floor of a dark and unknowable cave.

What do we do when we attempt to write Literary History? Perkins
problematizes the issue well:

The question is whether the discipline can be intellectually respectable.
Hundreds of books and articles testify every year that literary history can be
written. [The aim of literary history is] to recall the literature of the past,
including much that is now seldom read; to organize the past by selecting which
authors and texts are to be discussed and by arranging them into interconnected

---

[18] René Wellek, "The Fall of Literary History." In *The Attack on Literature and Other
Essays* (Chapel Hill: University of North Carolina Press, 1982), p. 65.

groups and narrative sequences; to interpret literary works and account for their character and development by relating them to their historical contexts; to describe the styles and *Weltanschauungen* of texts, authors, ages, and so on; to express the contents of works and quote passages from them, since many readers will have no other experience of these works; to bring, through selection, interpretation, and evaluation, the literary past to bear on the present, with consequences for both the literature and the society of the future.[19]

The writing of literary history is further complicated by any attempt at a national project. The very word "nation" provokes another series of questions. What constitutes a "nation"? Whose nation? If we have learned anything from Benedict Anderson's book, *Imagined Communities*, it is that nations are constructs, formed for disparate and complex reasons. If the idea of "nation" is a contested one, then the idea of "national litera-ture" becomes even more so. Does something called "national literature" exist? When does a nation come into being? How would a "nation" pro-duce a "literature"? Such questions cannot be answered by literary his-tory, but they cannot be avoided either, since they inform the decisions, categories, and choices one must necessarily make while attempting to write a narrative of literary history. Vicente García de la Huertas' interest in creating his *Theatro Hespañol* ("Spanish Theatre," 1785) was in part (in large part) motivated by nationalistic concerns. Indignant, as were many others, at Nicholas Masson de Morviller's famously offensive article in the *Encyclopédie méthodique* ("Methodical Encyclopedia," 1782) – in which the Frenchman wondered what Spain had ever contributed to civilization in two, four, or even ten centuries of existence – García de la Huerta presented a series of texts and authors which in his view demon-strated the superiority of – at least – Spanish theatre. Ideological bias and nationalistic rhetoric informed the very roots of literary history in Spain. John Dagenais addresses this thorny issue nicely in the present volume (he writes, "The idea of 'national' literary canons and literary traditions in a national language which founds collective volumes like the present one belongs to a rapidly changing, if not already outmoded idea of the ways in which peoples, languages, and literatures exist"). "Spanish liter-ature" has been confused and conflated with "literature in Spanish," but they are not the same thing. Still, lurking beneath the narratives in all of the chapters in this volume is the inevitable issue of "Spain," "Spanish," and "Spanishness." Linda Hutcheon points out correctly that the literary past has been recounted most frequently through the categories of nation and language: "In our twentyfirst-century globalized, multinational, and diasporic world, how can we explain the continuing appeal, not only, of the single-nation/single-ethnicity focus of literary histories, but also, of

---

[19] Perkins, *Literary History*, pp. 12–13.

its familiar teleological model, deployed even by those writing the new literary histories based on race, gender, sexual choice, or any number of other identitarian categories?"[20] Perhaps we cannot explain it. Yet, can it be otherwise?

What determines what is "Spanish" about "Spanish" literature? Is it the place of birth of the author? Is it his/her native language, the language in which he/she writes, or the language in which he/she is known? Is language the main determinant for nationality? If nation and language are not organizing categories for Literary History (and many today reject such categories as reductive and/or imperialistic), what groupings can be made which avoid the reality or appearance of teleology? Certainly, any literary history organized by gender, race, theme, ideology, or even (perhaps) temporal sequences, runs the risk of falling into similar traps. If traps they are. As Brad Epps asks in his chapter on the contemporary novel, do we consider Spanish literature that which is written in Spain, in Spanish, by native-born Spaniards, or is it something else? If it is not "something else," what does one do with literature written in the Iberian Peninsula, in the country today called "Spain," but written in languages such as Basque, Catalán, or Gallego? Can there be, as Maria Rosa Menocal and Charlotte Stern ask, a "Spanish" literature before there was a concept of a country called "Spain"? Theorists today rightly question the need for, or validity of, national models of literary history.

If what we commonly believe to be a nation emerges from a shared heritage of "linguistic, cultural, political, and social values to which we must assent,"[21] then Spain is a nation, an entity which holds on to a generally shared heritage. It is, however, a hotly contested heritage, as we know from those in (particularly) the País Vasco or Catalonia who do not fully share that heritage. They elbow in and assert their own "national" identity politics, often with results that are informative, useful, and enriching. Yet where does the border begin to form between a shared national heritage and a localized, individualized heritage? How much of the latter rewrites the former? To what degree can these contested areas co-exist? Are hegemony and, concurrently, cultural imperialism the inevitable end products of a shared heritage? There is clearly no percentage, no mathematical formula which can be accessed to resolve this tension. Quotas are hardly the answer (75% Castilian? 15% Catalán? 5% Basque? 3% Gallego? 2% Other?); such renderings are obviously absurd and unhelpful.

Perhaps an even more important question would be: why are we so afraid of nationalism today? Clearly, evidence abounds in its rawest form

---

[20] Hutcheon, "Rethinking the National Model." In Hutcheon and Valdés (eds.), *Rethinking Literary History*, p. 3.
[21] Hutcheon, "Rethinking," p. 9.

that aggressive nationalism leads to exclusion, oppression, pain, and war. It can also lead to bad literary history, as exemplified in *La literatura española en el siglo XIX* ("Spanish Literature in the Nineteenth Century," 1881–1894), the aggressively nationalistic three-volume work of Father Francisco Blanco García, whose ideology frequently blurred his critical faculties. Yet is all nationalism evil? Is all nationalism hegemonic, jingoistic, chauvinistic, and bloody? Might nationalism be considered one of Perkins' "useful fictions," something which binds together disparate elements, like eggs, flour, and spices in a recipe, in order to create a palatable, even tasty, result? Are we able to think of cultural nationalism in its best sense – as an organizational category, one which allows disparate elements to coexist in a totality, one element informing the other, one drawing strength and ideas and inspiration from the other? Cervantes drew from multiple sources, literature written in Catalán, French, and Italian, and allowed his knight to absorb the noblest impulses from the literatures of the past before sending him out to save the world. It was a foolish endeavor, of course, and one doomed to failure, but don Quijote's failure has provided inspiration and laughter to millions of readers whose paths he has subsequently crossed.

This also provokes, in turn, the much broader question that Sartre first posed in 1948: what is literature? How is the category "literature" assigned? In the case of the present volume, what constitutes the corpus of texts that will be studied under the rubric "Spanish," categorized, ordered, sequenced, and placed into a narrative? Does one include "great" literature only? What constitutes "great," and, again, who decides? Trigueros? García de la Huerta? García de la Concha? Does one include literature reflective of what is normally called high culture, or low culture, or both? The eighteenth-century idea that literature was a multiplicity of texts written in many disciplines gave way in the Romantic nineteenth and early twentieth centuries to a more reductive idea of literature as something personal, more "aesthetic," and more refined. Today's multidisciplinarity, interest in cultural studies, and attention to popular literature has brought with it a broader definition of "literature" and "text" which now includes film, comics, romance novels, rap songs, and oral work of many sorts. Where does one draw the line? Is a city park a "text"? Is a T-shirt a "text"? Is a piece of pottery a "text"? The case could be made in the affirmative for each example – certainly so, if Foucault's belief, laid out in *The Archeology of Knowledge*, that all texts are equal has any validity – but when we further press the question to "is it a 'literary text'?", the category becomes inescapably more contained. Jerome McGann, looking toward Matthew Arnold, asks whether there is "something to be called 'the best that has been known and thought'? . . . Antitraditionalists have counterargued that the received Canon is also an airless structure of 'great works' organized to maintain the good order of inherited prejudice."[22] One would hope that today we see the Canon as something more subtle, something that falls somewhere between insubstantial yeastiness and choking airlessness.

So, what are we to do? Do we write only those histories that are comparative across national and linguistic boundaries, or diachronic through time and theme? Do all literary histories become multidisciplinary and "global"? Do we accept Stephen Greenblatt's view that literary history is intellectually and ideologically bankrupt, and just give up on it? Do we accept Pierre Menard's conclusion that such activity is, anyway, useless? Perkins knows that literary history is impossible to write, yet equally impossible not to read.[23] This is the dilemma, of course, and to act one way or the other is to take an ideological stance, or, perhaps in a meeker and more cowardly manner, to act merely motivated by commercial reasons. That is, literary historians might not want to write such histories (they might not be capable of doing so, even collectively), but since the histories want to be read – someone wants to read them – publishers create opportunities to revisit the enterprise and produce an object that will, indeed, be read (and, they hope, bought). Do publishers and the producers of cultural objects direct our intellectual output? How much does or should utilitarianism guide the project of writing literary history? Are we to believe José María Pozuelo Yvancos and Rosa María Aradra Sánchez when they claim, "La historia de la literatura resulta, pues, de gran utilidad porque selecciona de forma crítica a los buenos autores y les ahorra a los futuros lectores tiempo, dinero y trabajo, al informarles previamente sobre su mérito" ("The history of literature turns out to be very useful because it selects, using critical methods, the good authors and it saves future readers time, money, and effort by informing those readers of their merits")?[24] Sounds right, but sounds awfully like Trigueros too.

Linda Hutcheon equates national literary history with sectarian violence, and consequently advocates "the need to rethink the dominance of the national model of literary history, a model that has always been premised on ethnic and often linguistic singularity, not to say purity."[25] The readers of this *Cambridge History of Spanish Literature*, however, will find no attempt to discover a primordial purity anywhere in the literatures of the Iberian Peninsula. "Limpieza de sangre" (clean bloodlines), a concept that worried early modern theologians and politicians,

---

[22] Jerome McGann, "Canonade. The Academic War Over the Literary Canon." *New Literary History* 25.3 (1994), pp. 488–489.
[23] Perkins, *Literary History*, p. 17.
[24] José María Pozuelo Yvancos and Rosa María Aradra Sánchez, *Teoría del canon y literatura española* (Madrid: Cátedra, 2000), p. 155.
[25] Hutcheon, "Rethinking," p. 3.

does not concern literary or cultural historians from the early twenty-first century. This history attempts to describe what Greenblatt calls "multiple voices across vast expanses of time and space."[26] Yet its very structure, its definition and layout, carry with it unintended (or perhaps inevitable) consequences. No attempt has been made – can be made – to "forge a useable past,"[27] and we encourage readers to find value not in some artificial cohesion but in its very lack of cohesion, that is, its intentional porous and self-reflective nature. While Spanish and the political entity "Spain" naturally become the pivotal force of our history, we have tried to be sensitive to other voices that claim, rightly, a place in the Canon and in literary history. This volume makes no claim to study the whole of Spanish culture, nor the cultural production of Spanish citizens. Absent, by choice, are voices in Spanish from Latin America, from the Philippines, and from other geographical and linguistic areas not directly related to the Iberian peninsula. Rather, this book attempts to weave together strands of various colors and shapes – literature written in the Spanish language, of course, but also the literature written in Latin, Catalán, Gallego, or Basque that played a role in the creation of the country that came to be known as Spain, and can be included in the broad category called "Spanish Literature."

Many voices will be silenced; many will be forgotten. We view this volume as a collaborative effort, a dialogue between authors and critics, readers and listeners, living and dead across time. Indeed, if we are to work with "useful fictions," we must be willing to accept the discomfort of exclusion. Literary history is in essence family history, and family members will view it differently, stress different genealogical branches, and honor different things. What Lawrence Lipking wrote at the end of the twentieth century has never echoed more sonorously than now at the opening of the twenty-first century: "Literary history used to be impossible to write; lately it has become much harder."[28]

Funes, if he were capable of thinking about all of this, would surely understand.

---

[26] Stephen Greenblatt, "Rethinking Memory and Literary History." In Hutcheon and Valdés (eds.), *Rethinking Literary History*, p. 59.
[27] Greenblatt, "Rethinking Memory," p. 57.　　　[28] Lipking, "Trout," p. 7.

Part II

History and Canonicity

WADDA C. RÍOS-FONT

Literary history and canon formation

WADDA C. RÍOS-FONT

From their earliest instances, literary canons have been linked to the concept of nation and to nation-building practices. In ancient societies, they were in themselves signs of the power of sovereigns, and their contents scripts for the performance of collective identities organized around these sovereigns.[1] While Michel Foucault, in *The History of Sexuality*, has postulated premodern social orders as governed by vertical power relations characterized by the threat of force – the "power of death"[2] – the qualification can be made that, even then, such relations were enabled by the existence of shared codes generating loyalty and preventing rebellion. Among these, literature was preeminent, and, as Itamar Even-Zohar has suggested, it remained so in the making of modern nations according to "the European model."[3] This type of nation-building, of which Spain is one of the earliest and most successful examples, depends on creating "socio-cultural cohesion,"[4] vitally through the production of a standardized language that will be recognized as common by a collection of relatively heterogeneous peoples, and the ensuing production of texts in that language. These become a common patrimony for all individuals in that community, and in turn are taken to express the original and differentiating factors of their nationality.

While the grounds for the establishment of such a modern national literary system go back to King Alfonso X's (1221–1284) designation of Castilian as the shared language of culture, it is the eighteenth century that sees the outset of a veritable historical consciousness with regard to Spanish literature. Intellectuals of this century gradually implement a separation between classical or universal and Spanish literature. Already in 1727 Gregorio Mayans y Siscar lays the foundation for a historical assessment of Spanish literature in his "Oración en que se exhorta a seguir la

---

[1] Itamar Even-Zohar, "The Role of Literature in the Making of the Nations of Europe." www.tau.ac.il/~itamarez/papers/rol_lit.html. Also published in *Applied Semiotics / Sémiotique appliquée* 1 (1996), p. 21. (The latter is a refereed periodical on the Web, www.chass.utoronto.ca/french/as-sa/index.html.)
[2] Michel Foucault, *The History of Sexuality* (New York: Vintage, 1990), vol. I, p. 135.
[3] Evan-Zohar, "The Role of Literature," p. 29.
[4] Evan-Zohar, "The Role of Literature," p. 21.

verdadera idea de la eloquencia española" ("Speech Exhorting to Follow
the True Idea of Spanish Eloquence"). In his rejection of the immediate
baroque literary past, Mayans argues for the preservation and imitation
of the works of a Spanish Golden Age, and this attitude characterizes the
wave of research and compilation that will follow throughout the next
decades. Anthologies of different sorts collectively assemble a corpus of
texts that work as rhetorical, poetical, and grammatical exemplars within
a national tradition. From the *Diario de los Literatos de España* ("Diary of
Spanish Authors") founded in 1737 to Nicolás Antonio's *Bibliotheca Hispanica Vetus* and *Bibliotheca Hispanica Nova* ("Old Hispanic Library"
and "New Hispanic Library," 1788), eighteenth-century research produces – *invents*, in José Carlos Mainer's words[5] – a new object of knowledge named "Spanish literature."

Within this context, the birth of literary history signals a specific type
of impulse that moves beyond finding and collecting, and toward evaluating and encoding. Literary history, as the ambiguity in the Spanish word
historia shows, is above all a story; it participates in the assembly of a
canon, but it also shapes it into a narrative. As David Perkins explains, in
its genesis literary history is "developmental" and "narrative."[6] Like any
narrative, it constructs a plot around its protagonist, and establishes a
setting, a characterization, and a continuous line of causality. The protagonist of this narrative, whose development is chronicled, is the imagined
nation – in the case of Spain, the nation-state in particular, seen against
the background of peninsular or colonial identities not associated with
that political entity. This nation appears from the outset as engaged in
a competitive struggle with others, and literary history as an instrument
at the service of this contest. As Mayans puts it, "¿qué falta, pues, sino
superar a los extraños, o a lo menos igualarlos en el saber y uso? . . . Está
España infamada de poco elocuente. Vindicad su honra, españoles" (what
remains, then, but to surpass foreigners, or at least become equal to them
in knowledge and practice? . . . Spain is defamed as scarcely eloquent.
Avenge her honor, Spaniards).[7]

The impulses described above are evident in the first attempt at
a comprehensive Spanish literary history, that of Fathers Rafael and
Pedro Rodríguez Mohedano. Their *Historia literaria de España, desde su
primera población hasta nuestros días* ("Literary History of Spain, From

[5] José-Carlos Mainer, "La invención de la literatura española." In *Literaturas regionales en
España*. Ed. José-Carlos Mainer and José María Enguita (Zaragoza: Institución Fernando
el Católico, 1994), pp. 23–45.
[6] David Perkins, *Is Literary History Possible?* (Baltimore: Johns Hopkins University Press,
1992), p. 2.
[7] Gregorio Mayans y Siscar, "Oración en que se exhorta a seguir la verdadera idea de la
elocuencia española." In *Escritos literarios*. Ed. Jesús Pérez Magallón (Madrid: Taurus,
1994), pp. 149–151.

Its First Population to Our Day"), published in ten volumes between 1769 and 1791, establishes itself as a novelty, differentiating between a preexistent "método Bibliotecario" (librarian method) and its new "método histórico" (historical method),[8] the former "method" being something akin to mere cataloguing, while the latter attempted to insert authors and texts into a temporal and nationalistic narrative. The statements of purpose interspersed throughout the text announce a new take on the creation and preservation of a Spanish canon: the project arises out of competition with other nations, which already have literary histories; the aim, as stated in the subtitle itself, is to record the origins, progress, decadence, and restoration of Spanish letters; the procedure integrates the act of listing with its contextualization and critique; the style is a narrative concatenation that must enlighten and entertain. As they themselves write, the necessary aims of a national literary history are to give

una noticia compendiosa y exacta de lo que contienen sus Obras: informar del merito de ellas, comparadas con otras de su siglo, de los anteriores y siguientes, y aun de los Paises estraños; separar lo comun de lo particular; dar á conocer qué inventaron sus Autores, qué añadieron, ó con quantas ventajas ilustran y perfeccionan los puntos que tratan; mostrar sus adelantamientos respecto del estado en que entonces se hallaban las ciencias, qué juicio han hecho de ellos otros Sabios . . . Demas de esto, pintar el caracter y genio diferente de los Autores, formando retratos que los representen y no los desfiguren, sin que en todo esto tenga la menor parte la precipitacion de juicio, la emulacion ó la lisonja. Se necesita en fin hacer una relacion exacta de la vida de estos Heroes, y del influxo que tuvieron en los progresos y revoluciones de las Ciencias: una relacion, decimos, que sea historia, y no invectiva ni panegyrico, con enlace y coordinacion de sucesos, narracion de causas, amenidad de noticias, y dulzura de estilo.

(brief and exact notice of what their Works contain: inform of their merit, compared to that of others of the same century, of the previous and following ones, and even of foreign Countries; separate the common from the particular; make known what their Authors invented, what they added, or with what advantage they illustrate and perfect the points they treat; show their advances with respect to the state of sciences at the time, what judgment other Sages have made of them . . . In addition to this, to paint the individual character and genius of Authors, sketching portraits that represent but do not disfigure them, without rashness in judgment, emulation, or flattery having the least part in any of this. It is necessary finally to make an exact account of the lives of these Heroes, and of the influence they had on the progress and revolutions of the Sciences: an account, we say, that is a history, and not an invective or panegyric,

---

[8] Rafael Rodríguez Mohedano and Pedro Rodríguez Mohedano, *Apología del tomo V de la Historia literaria de España, con dos cartas sobre el mismo asunto* . . . (Madrid, 1779), p. 65.

with connection and coordination of events, narration of causes, amenity in contents, and softness in style.)[9]

The above statement is extremely suggestive, for it already contains much of what will become essential to literary history, even in its contradictions. It ordains, for example, the simultaneous missions of evaluation and objectivity. It seeks to separate the wheat from the chaff, and to teach its readers the subtleties of literary taste, while at the same time seeming loyal to a modern, proto-positivistic ideal that leaves the matter of the evaluator's personal taste and circumstances out of the historiographical operation. In addition, the goal of providing a compendium of Spanish literature coexists with that of shaping, and therefore editing, it into a causal and *compelling* narrative account.

The contours of such an account are guided by one ideal: the glory of Spain, and its placement among the leading nations of the Western world. For the Rodríguez Mohedanos, a literary history is a feature of advanced nations that Spain must also have – it thus belongs to what Even-Zohar has named the *indispensabilia* of power or nationhood. As they write, "concurrió también como un poderoso estímulo para poner nuestro proyecto por obra, la reflexion de que muchas Naciones cultas han dado á luz sus Historias Literarias" (a powerful stimulus to carry our work out was also the reflection that many cultured Nations have brought to light their Literary Histories).[10] The undertaking stems from a need to have Spain figure internationally at the same level as other countries. For this endeavor, comprehensive literary histories are as necessary as the histories of battles and conquests, since they are the basis for the legitimation of particular repertoires for organizing life – concerned as they are with "la conducta general de los hombres, sus costumbres, sus leyes, su establecimiento, sus intereses, alianzas y tratados, su modo de gobierno, su cultura en Artes y Ciencias" (the general conduct of men, their customs, their laws, their establishment, their interests, alliances and treaties, their form of government, their culture in arts and sciences).[11] These function internally as engines for unity, and externally as factors that consolidate a nation's position as much as war or commerce. Such consolidation is essential to Spain's structure at the time; it is unity of culture that will make the empire "natural" and legitimate it before competing powers. The Rodríguez Mohedanos virtually repeat Mayans y Siscar's formulation when they state that a central cause of the need for a literary history

---

[9] Rafael Rodríguez Mohedano and Pedro Rodríguez Mohedano, *Historia literaria de España, desde su primera población hasta nuestros días* . . . (Madrid: Antonio Pérez de Soto, 1769–1791), vol. I, p. 63.

[10] Rodríguez Mohedano and Rodríguez Mohedano, *Historia*, vol. I, p. 9.

[11] Rodríguez Mohedano and Rodríguez Mohedano, *Historia*, vol. I, p. 76.

of the nation is "la necesidad de vindicarla" (the necessity of vindicating it).[12]

The actual history written by the Rodríguez Mohedanos does not put their aims into practice, fundamentally because it remains incomplete. The last published volume is still dealing with Roman times – with writing that precedes any notion of a Spanish nation-state – and they themselves find it necessary to write an apology of their history addressing the obvious criticisms: "¿Quándo se acabará esta (Obra), en quántos siglos, y en quántos tomos? A este paso, dice (el Crítico), sin exageracion no se acabará en doce siglos, y contendrá de siete á ocho mil volúmenes" (When will this [Work] end, in how many centuries, and how many volumes? At this pace, says [the Critic], without exaggeration, it will not conclude in twelve centuries, and will contain seven to eight thousand volumes).[13] Despite their insistence on the novelty of their historical method, their work remains more an inventory than a narrative. Accordingly, it only partially serves to answer basic questions about the organization of a national literary history, and about how it constitutes its object. How is the nation related to the state? Who may be included among its peoples? What kinds of product constitute its literary endowment? How are its history and spirit expressed in the canon? Some indication of the direction in which they were moving to answer these questions nevertheless emerges.

Their basic organizational criterion is chronological, and they propose to divide the history into two parts corresponding to the ancient and modern stages of Spanish letters – the former ranging from the earliest literary activities in the peninsula to the reign of the Catholic Monarchs, and the latter to everything since then. This plan also presupposes a geographical foundation: they trace the descent of Spanish letters back to the activities of the first inhabitants of a specific territory, which will remain the gravitational center of the history. Nevertheless, at a certain point the parameters turn to a concept of common culture, as is evident in a passage that bears analysis:

Aunque pudieramos sin violencia ampliar el asunto estendiendo nuestra Historia Literaria á todos los Paises que han sido en algun tiempo de dominacion española . . . no queremos dar extension demasiada á un asunto vasto por su naturaleza . . . Asi en la Europa nos reduciremos casi á nuestra Peninsula, en la qual encontrarémos suficiente espacio y materia abundante para una Obra bien dilatada y aun dentro de ella no intentamos incluir de proposito al Reyno de Portugal . . . Por lo que toca a la America, desde luego la incluimos en el plan de nuestra Historia Literaria, en atencion á que no obstante su distancia, no podemos mirar como estraños . . . los progresos de la Literatura con los que nos

[12] Rodríguez Mohedano and Rodríguez Mohedano, *Apología*, p. 80.
[13] Rodríguez Mohedano and Rodríguez Mohedano, *Apología*, p. 273.

ha enriquecido una Region no menos fecunda en ingenios, que en minas. Asi no omitiremos trabajo, ni diligencia para hacer mas recomendable nuestra Historia con un adorno tan precioso, y un ramo tan considerable de Literatura, que echó las primeras raices en nuestro terreno, y fructificó abundantemente trasplantado allá y cultivado por manos Españolas.

(Although we could, without violence, expand the subject extending our Literary History to all the Countries that have at one point or another been under Spanish domination . . . we do not wish to prolong an inherently vast topic . . . In this way, in Europe we will almost limit ourselves to our Peninsula, where we will find enough space and plentiful matter for quite an extensive Work, and even within it we do not propose to include the Kingdom of Portugal . . . As for America, of course we include it in the plan of our Literary History, given that despite its distance, we cannot regard as foreign . . . the advances of Literature with which a Region no less fertile in wits than in mines has enriched us. So we will not omit work or diligence to make our History more praiseworthy with such a precious ornament, and such a considerable branch of Literature, which first took root on our earth, and, transplanted there and cultivated by Spanish hands, bore abundant fruit.)[14]

The character of literature as "goods" or "valuable assets"[15] is already apparent, as is the distribution of the nation into margin and center. The relationship between both is established through a metaphor that will often reappear in Spanish histories: the trunk and branches are separate and unequal parts of one central essence, and the sap that joins Spain and Spanish America (but not necessarily Portugal or other one-time Spanish dominions) is both religious (Catholic) and *linguistic*. Just as Castilian united the multicultural reign of Alfonso X, it is also the constituent element expected to give symbolic cohesion to the territories of the empire. The importance of the language factor will be increasingly palpable in many histories of the nineteenth and twentieth centuries – including the works of Marcelino Menéndez y Pelayo and Ramón Menéndez Pidal – and will dictate the different treatment given to, for example, Spanish America, and to peninsular cultures such as Catalan or Galician.

The Rodríguez Mohedanos believed that Spanish literary history should be developed domestically, since "no son los Estrangeros instrumentos proporcionados para que pase á la posteridad la fama de nuestras glorias" (Foreigners are not appropriate instruments for the fame of our glories to pass into posterity).[16] Nevertheless, no Spaniard takes up their lead until well into the nineteenth century. This circumstance is partially explained

---

[14] Rodríguez Mohedano and Rodríguez Mohedano, *Historia*, vol. I, p. 73.
[15] Itamar Even-Zohar, "Literature as Goods, Literature as Tools." www.tau.ac.il/~ itamarez/papers/lit-g-t.htm, p. 2. Also forthcoming in *Neohelicon*, a special issue in Memory of György Mihaly Vajda.
[16] Rodríguez Mohedano and Rodríguez Mohedano, *Historia*, vol. I, p. 10.

by the accidents of Spanish political history. The Napoleonic invasion of 1808 sets in motion destabilizing events on both the foreign and domestic fronts. On the one hand, the wave of successful independence movements taking place in America between 1808 and 1826 determines the crisis of the empire. On the other hand, the last domestic victories against French occupation in 1814 do not accompany a comparable triumph on the cultural plane, and throughout the century Spain, like much of Europe, will grudgingly look to France as the paradigmatic culture. A debilitated Spain must reconfigure itself as a modern nation, but this process will be further hindered by internal strife. With the death of Fernando VII in 1833, and his succession by his daughter Isabel rather than his brother Carlos, begins a period of civil war that brings to the fore the many ideological divisions in Spaniards' repertoires for understanding the nation-state. The Revolution of 1868, the First Republic of 1873, the Restoration of 1875, and the crisis of 1898 are but continuations of the previous struggles. Throughout the nineteenth century, Spain can be seen as a protean nation faced with the task of finding an image of itself to function as an element of unity inside its borders, and assure it a creditable place among Western nations. Especially in the early nineteenth century, the precarious conditions of sovereignty and government, followed by the restrictions of an absolutist monarchy, doubtless preclude concerted historiographical efforts aimed at consolidating a real or imagined national model.

In this context, the inability of Spaniards to concentrate on the development of literary history leaves the field open to precisely the foreigners the Rodríguez Mohedanos rejected. What are generally considered the first proper histories of Spanish literature are written by foreigners, as Thomas Hart has pointed out in "A History of Spanish Literary History."[17] Friedrich Bouterwek's *Geschichte der spanischen Poesie und Bereksamkeit* ("History of Spanish Literature and Eloquence") appears in Göttingen in 1804 – the third of twelve volumes in his general history of literature. It is translated into French by 1812; an English version appears in London in 1823; and the Spanish version in Madrid, in 1829. The French-Swiss author of the second history of Spanish literature, J. C. L. Simonde de Sismondi, publishes his *De la littérature du midi de l'Europe* ("Historical View of the Literature of the South of Europe") in Paris in 1813, with one volume dedicated to Spain. The English translation appears in London also in 1823; the Spanish one in Seville in 1841. The third history – the first dedicated exclusively to Spain – is George Ticknor's three-volume *History of Spanish Literature*, originally published in New York in 1849, with the Spanish translation, made even as he was working

---

[17] Thomas Hart, "A History of Spanish Literary History, 1800–1850." Ph.D. Diss. Yale University, 1952.

on the original, following in Madrid in 1851. The first foundational myths
of Spanish literary history are thus those imagined by foreigners during
a period of internal instability. Predictably, all of them point to fragmentation and unfeasibility as main features of a precarious, and decidedly
un-modern, Spanish nation.

Bouterwek was never in Spain, nor is it certain that he actually knew
Spanish. He did write a novel set in Spain, and Hart observes that "Spain
could hardly have been more to him . . . than a suitable setting for an
adventure-story."[18] Bouterwek's literary history itself reads like a novel
of adventure and chivalry. His introduction is a tale of intrigue set in a
mythical moment of origin, a story of war between Christians and Moors,
against which Spanish history is foregrounded as romance. Spaniards are
valiant and chivalrous; their gallantry is, of course, European, but it is
also *not* European. It comes, on the one hand, from the leveling influence of a specific climate, and, on the other, from miscegenation between
knights and ladies of different extraction. In this myth of origin, war
with the "infidels" is the backdrop for a sensual amalgamation, in love
adventures that the author imagines *could not be* of rare occurrence.
The conjectural language, common throughout the text, seems odd in a
literary history. In this intellectual work, intermixed with the results of
painstaking research, we find the fanciful recreation of the long-ago of
fairytales; the resulting scenarios imply through their very style that the
past they refer to is inaccessible, outside the bounds of reality. To Bouterwek, Spanish, that is, Castilian, is a powerful tongue that prevails against
other peninsular languages, like Catalan, in a proto-Darwinian struggle
for survival: "Castilian became, in the strictest sense of the word, the
reigning language of the whole Spanish monarchy."[19] Nevertheless, this
authoritative language and its literature are also doomed. At the end of
his history, Bouterwek deplores the present state of Spanish literature and
concludes that "the polite literature of the Spaniards may again rise to its
former glory, if favoured by the ancient national spirit, to the genial influence of which it owes its existence."[20] However, that spirit comes from
"the orientalism of their ancient national literature,"[21] and is therefore
not to be found in the contemporary neoclassical ambience. In the end,
Spanish literature has only a glorious past, and the very last paragraph
of the history, dedicated to mystical poetry, is a lament for what it never
achieved: "What might not this poetry have become, had reason extended
her influence over it in a more powerful degree, not, indeed, to reduce it

---

[18] Hart, "Spanish Literary History," pp. 10–11.
[19] Friedrich Bouterwek, *History of Spanish and Portuguese Literature* (London: Boosey and
Sonse, 1823), vol. I, p. 8.
[20] Bouterwek, *Spanish and Portuguese*, vol. I, p. 605.
[21] Bouterwek, *Spanish and Portuguese*, vol. I, p. 606.

to the level of prose, but to divest it of the mask of caricature, while soaring in the lofty regions of mystic invention!"[22] Spanish literature is, in summary, "decidedly national,"[23] or, in other words, exotic, essentially different from that of the rest of Europe. In attempting to be like other European literatures, it betrays its own specificity; in going back to its roots, it writes itself out of the narrative of modernity. It cannot survive the present – just as the Catalan poetry of the troubadours was too weak to compete with Castilian, so what became Spanish is ultimately too weak to stand among living literatures. The only glory it can achieve is its former glory, and only by turning to a past that goes back to even before the constitution of Spain as a nation.

In the second history of Spanish literature alluded to, Simonde de Sismondi warns that his task will be difficult, because he is not "so familiarly acquainted [with the Spanish] as with the Italian."[24] He admits that his work is somewhat derivative, and relies on the previous studies of German scholars such as Bouterwek, Dieze, and Schlegel.[25] Accordingly, from the beginning he adopts Bouterwek's characterization of Spanish literature: "The literature of the nations upon which we have hitherto been employed . . . was European: the literature of Spain, on the contrary, is decidedly oriental."[26] Nevertheless, although Sismondi, like Bouterwek, sees the Spanish character as unchanging, he confers much more importance on the influence of external developments, and thus follows the changes caused by the political history of the peninsula. For him, the tension between centralization and expansion is the principal determinant of Spanish culture. Accordingly, Sismondi's view of the relationship between peninsular nationalities differs from Bouterwek's endorsement of Castile. While he too acknowledges the power of the center, he repeatedly finds the strength of other nationalities as undercurrents within the dominant centripetal force.

For Sismondi, it is through these revolutions, produced by interaction between Castilian tradition and innovation coming from within (from centrifugal tendencies within the peninsula) or from without (for example, from Italian influences), that Spanish literature achieves what he calls its "sudden and fitful lights."[27] Rather than being simply vanquished in a struggle for survival, languages and nationalities within the peninsula energize its cultural production. Consequently, the move first toward

---

[22] Bouterwek, *Spanish and Portuguese*, vol. I, p. 609.
[23] Bouterwek, *Spanish and Portuguese*, vol. I, p. 606.
[24] J. C. L. Simone de Sismondi, *Historical View of the Literature of the South of Europe* (London: H. Colburn and Co., 1823), vol. II, p. 102.
[25] Sismondi, *Historical View*, vol. II, p. 103.
[26] Sismondi, *Historical View*, vol. II, p. 103.
[27] Sismondi, *Historical View*, vol. II, p. 104.

centralization, and then toward empire, functions as a restraint on literary greatness.

According to Sismondi, while the invigoration stemming from cultural contact contributes to the enrichment of Spanish literature, the continued absorption of cultural Others ultimately debilitates it. Spain is progressively corrupted by its constant expansion, to the detriment of liberties within the peninsula itself, and consequently of national cultural production, according to a very specifically theorized pattern: "it requires the lapse of half a century before the spirit of literature declines, or becomes extinct."[28] Thus the high period of Spanish empire may be accompanied by a brilliant literature, but it nevertheless already carries the seed of decadence. Indeed, it is decadence at which Sismondi, like Bouterwek, arrives, closing his history with the categorical remark that, after the poem of the Cid, "nothing that has since appeared can justly demand our unqualified admiration."[29] Imperial power entails the degradation of national essence and literary expression. The only saving grace Sismondi finds in Spanish literature is that it represents a bridge between West and East: "if we regard the literature of Spain as revealing to us, in some degree, the literature of the East, and as familiarizing us with a genius and taste differing so widely from our own, it will possess in our eyes a new interest."[30] Again, we are left with a national literature with no place in modern Europe. Neither Sismondi nor Bouterwek find in the Spanish state a desirable or workable national model, or envision their literary histories as legitimizing foundational myths.

In fact, Sismondi expropriates Spanish literature, turning it into a canon that constitutes neither a model to follow nor a national cultural capital. Its function is not to be the patrimony of a country, but rather a controlled channel of communication between East and West, and, even further, a source for other, presumably stronger, literatures. The work already acknowledged as the cornerstone of Spanish literature is described as "animated, witty, and pleasant" *entertainment*, thus rendering inactive the pattern set out by the Rodríguez Mohedanos, according to which Spanish literature reveals the heroic, powerful nature of national character. Here Spanish literature is not a common good symbolizing the nationhood of a particular collection of people, nor does it provide them with a repertoire of options for organizing life; rather, it is placed at the service of other cultures, and particularly of the homogenizing force of France.

Bouterwek and Sismondi prepare the ground for George Ticknor, who in 1816, while living in Göttingen, receives an invitation from Harvard

---

[28] Sismondi, *Historical View*, vol. II, p. 258.
[29] Sismondi, *Historical View*, vol. II, pp. 243–244.
[30] Sismondi, *Historical View*, vol. II, p. 248.

University to occupy a newly created professorship of French, Spanish, and Italian. He spends six months in Spain in 1818 – his only trip to this country – and, back in Boston, has elaborated by 1823 a syllabus of Spanish literature based on his lectures. The *History*, begun in the 1830s, closely follows its outline. This work is based on a much more comprehensive collection of primary works than Bouterwek's or Sismondi's histories – Ticknor made a considerable effort to be constantly provided with new texts by his Spanish translators and friends. Nevertheless, its opening premises are very close to those of the earlier histories: "Here, at the outset, we are struck with a remarkable circumstance, which announces something at least of the genius of the coming literature, the circumstance of its appearance in times of great confusion and violence."[31] As he writes, the first "wild, national poetry" of the Spaniards is a war cry. For Ticknor, as for Bouterwek, Spanish literature on the one hand absorbs the Moorish character; on the other hand, its "vigorous spirit"[32] inevitably vanquishes the Provençal, Limousin, or Catalan. Curiously, however, in cutting off "[that] delicate plant, whose flower was not permitted to expand"[33] – Catalan literature – Spanish or Castilian cuts its ties to Europe, where the troubadours of Eastern Spain ultimately had their roots. As a result, Spain continues its own literary development, separate from transpyrenean currents, and mirrored in institutions like the Inquisition, which Ticknor finds reflective of the basic intolerance of the Spanish character.

As he moves on to modern times, Ticknor too portrays Spanish literature as essentially a thing of the past. He sees the return of Fernando VII to Spain as an ominous event that brings Spanish letters in a circle back to their beginnings. The future that remains after the king's death looks eminently uncertain:

The Spanish people – that old Castilian race . . . – have, I trust, a future before them not unworthy of their ancient fortunes and fame; a future full of materials for a generous history, and a poetry still more generous; – happy if they have been taught, by the experience of the past, that, while reverence for whatever is noble and worthy is of the essence of poetical inspiration, and, while religious faith and feeling constitute its true and sure foundations, there is yet a loyalty to mere rank and place, which degrades alike its possessor and him it would honor, and a blind submission to priestly authority, which narrows and debases the nobler faculties of the soul more than any other, because it sends its poison deeper. But, if they have failed to learn this solemn lesson . . . then is their honorable history, both in civilization and letters, closed for ever.[34]

---

[31] George Ticknor, *History of Spanish Literature* (New York: Harper and Brothers, 1849), vol. I, p. 6.
[32] Ticknor, *History*, vol. I, p. 310.   [33] Ticknor, *History*, vol. I, p. 322.
[34] Ticknor, *History*, vol. III, p. 351.

The suggested possibility of a future clashes narratively with the forceful closure of this ending. Through the performative last sentence, Ticknor's text, itself the honorable history he refers to, is closed forever, in possession of finality and authority. Yet so is the crumbling institution of Spanish literature. Regeneration would, after all, depend on the Spanish letting go of their vices (religious intolerance and submission to absolutism), but these vices are simply a negative formulation of the virtues that Ticknor has elsewhere considered the basis of their literature's uniqueness (the religious and monarchical spirit). As in the histories of Bouterwek and Sismondi, there is no possible space for Spanish literature to preserve both its character and its viability. Ticknor makes this opinion even clearer in a note penciled onto one of his Spanish lectures: "an unfinished literature – a broken column – a ruin before the building was completed."[35]

The nation that emerges as the protagonist of these literary histories is a very curious creature. Metaphorically, there is that Castilian warrior, somewhere between El Cid and don Quijote, whose military conquest of the Eastern Other only masks his own penetration by that Other. Or Sismondi's now female monster of the great bosom, who feeds on the vanquished peoples from inside and outside the peninsula, destined ultimately to consume its own anthropophagic womb. There is also that site of crumbling ruin – ruins of nothing that ever truly existed. These pseudo-epics represent the history of Spain and its literature as the loss of self and loss of center of a failed nation built from, and condemned to, heterogeneity and shapelessness – features exactly opposed to the ideals of nation-building. The foreign histories of Spanish literature seize the power of naming and describing, yet do so according to models that impose an extraneous shape on the object of knowledge. Such images become the inevitable referent of native literary history when it begins, and have the counterproductive effect of further stimulating it to produce a different epic with a different hero: the strong, unified nation with a future among the modern world powers.

The lack of a native historiography during the period when the foreign texts appear does not stem from lack of awareness of its importance for national consolidation and socio-cultural cohesion. In fact, this awareness firmly develops as political events begin to make it possible. In his 1828 induction speech to the Real Academia de la Historia, Alberto Lista praises the work of Schlegel, Bouterwek, and Lord Holland, while also lamenting that Spain seems to be relying on foreigners to write its literary history: "¿Debemos esperar nosotros que vengan los extranjeros a revolver el polvo de nuestros archivos y bibliotecas y a desenterrar tesoros que, aún

---

[35] Quoted in Hart, "Spanish Literary History," p. 121.

después de encontrados, no pueden valorar en su justo precio?" (Shall we wait for foreigners to come stir up the dust in our archives and libraries, and unearth treasures that, even after finding them, they cannot accurately value?).[36] In reviewing the different epochs of Spanish letters, Lista dwells on their merit in comparison with other European literatures, insisting on their greater antiquity and superior quality; by the same token, he also deplores Spaniards' failure to establish their right to be appreciated according to what they have given Europe.

Like previous apologists of Spanish literary historiography, Lista observes that France and England already have their histories, while Spaniards lack this required cultural item. That deficiency must be remedied in order to serve the two purposes he assigns literary history. First, it is imperative to place Spanish letters and the Spanish nation in their rightful place with regard to other countries; second, it is crucial to discover, catalogue, compare, evaluate, and, above all, transmit, or *dar a conocer*, the authors, books, and ideas that signal Spanishness both within and without the peninsula.

The year 1836, three after the death of Fernando VII, is a visible turning point for Spanish literary historiography. It is marked by the transformation of what had been the Royal Library into the National Library. The government creates official task forces in charge of selecting works for deposit in the new library, from among those expropriated from the Church by Mendizábal's disentailment. The collection thus acquires 70,000 volumes, and although obviously these were not limited to the field of literature as we know it – it should be remembered that in the early nineteenth century the concept of literature still referred to a wide notion of *belles lettres* – their acquisition shows a deliberate attempt to provide the nation with a patrimony, as well as with the institutions to reproduce it. The year 1836 is also the date of a Royal Decree ordering the creation of the university discipline of Spanish Literature and the furnishing of the corresponding professorships. One of their first occupants, Antonio Gil y Zárate, authors the first real attempt at a native literary history, the 1844 *Manual de literatura* ("Handbook of Literature"), which Aradra considers a milestone in that it separates for the first time Rhetoric and Poetics from the historical subject of Spanish literature. It remains, however, a textbook, and even in a later version Gil y Zárate insists that the work of Spanish literary historiography is still to be done: "Yo me daré el parabién, si vivo lo bastante para ver publicada una *Historia* completa de nuestra literatura: y ya que un extranjero se nos ha adelantado en esto, enmendemos semejante falta con otra obra mas perfecta y digna de la

---

[36] Alberto Lista, "Discurso sobre la importancia de nuestra historia literaria." In *Vida, obra y pensamiento de Alberto Lista*. Ed. Hans Juretschke (Madrid: CSIC, 1951), pp. 476–477.

nacion española" (I will congratulate myself if I live long enough to see the
publication of a complete *History* of our literature: and, since a foreigner
has gotten ahead of us in this, let us amend this fault with another work,
more perfect and worthy of the Spanish nation).[37] Although Mainer considers Gil y Zárate "fidelísimo seguidor de Bouterwek" (a most faithful
follower of Bouterwek)[38] – which may very well be true in some respects –
the author himself explicitly positions his work against foreign historiography.

In 1861, José Amador de los Ríos publishes the first volume of what is
widely regarded as the first comprehensive (though also unfinished) native
history of Spanish literature, the *Historia crítica de la literatura española*
("Critical History of Spanish Literature"). The volume's dedication to
Queen Isabel II already characterizes the project:

Señora: El libro que hoy tengo la honra de ofrecer a V. M., no es la narración de
los hechos sangrientos, ni de las afrentosas aberraciones, ni de las aterradoras
catástrofes que anublan á la continua las brillantes páginas de la historia. Tráigo
á los pies del trono constitucional de la Reina de España la Historia critica de la
literatura española, donde si se revelan vivamente los conflictos de la patria,
templan y endulzan sus dolores las pacíficas glorias de sus preclaros hijos . . .
No olvide V. M. sin embargo que si no corresponde el fruto de mis vigilias á la
grandeza del asunto, tiene al menos la Historia . . . el mérito de ser la primera
escrita por un español en lengua castellana.

(Milady: The book I have the honor of offering you today is not the narration of
the bloody events, or the offensive aberrations, or the terrifying catastrophes
that continously cloud the brilliant pages of history. I bring before the
constitutional throne of the Queen of Spain the Critical History of Spanish
Literature, where, if one can vividly see the fatherland's conflicts, its pains are
tempered and sweetened by the peaceful glories of its illustrious sons . . . Your
Majesty should not forget, however, that if the product of my labors does not
befit the greatness of the subject, this History at least has . . . the merit of being
the first one written by a Spaniard in the Castilian tongue.)[39]

In a few sentences, Amador de los Ríos contextualizes Spanish literary
historiography before the highest representative of the field of power. The
text measures itself against political histories, and immediately defines the
nation in terms that, as the liberal revolution of 1868 would attest to, do
not yet correspond exactly to reality: as a modern constitutional monarchy. In other words, he connects directly with the Rodríguez Mohedanos'

---

[37] Antonio Gil y Zárate, *Manual de literatura: Principios generales de poética y retórica
   y resuman histórico de la literatura española* (10th edn. Paris: Garnier, 1889 [1844]),
   p. vii.
[38] Mainer, "La invención," p. 34.
[39] José Amador de los Ríos, *Historia crítica de la literatura española* (Madrid: Imprenta de
   José Rodríguez, 1861–1865), vol. I, n. p.

endeavor to employ literary history as a tool for the endorsement of a national model, thus removing it from the purely academic sphere and inserting it into the political field. Faced with this mission, the history's greatest merit is that of being "al menos" what it is, native and written in Castilian. The deceptive "at least" conceals the import of the terms "castellana" and "español." Again, literary history points to language and national unity as the key elements fundamental to the making of the modern state.

Amador de los Ríos is one in a long line of historians of Spanish literature who view Spain as a unit at once ancient *and* modern – its literature guided, from the times of Roman Iberia, by what he calls a single "idea luminosa" (luminous idea).[40] This idea is Catholicism, grounded in the medieval period, and crystallized in the Castilian language. Spain, Catholic and Castilian, destined to be One even before the onset of the unified state – this is the image imposed over the protean nation. Amador de los Ríos opposes this view to that of the foreign historians, whom he accuses of not having understood the guiding principle of Spanish literature. For example, the work of "Mr. Jorge Ticknor" lacks "un pensamiento fecundo y trascendental que le sirva de norte" (a fertile and transcendental thought that can serve as its guide), and in this "nada ha adelantado . . . respecto de los escritores que le precedieron" (he has not advanced at all over the writers that preceded him).[41] The new history substantially repeats the foreign writers' formulation of a canon (although the seventh and last volume appearing before the author's death, published in 1865, has reached only the reign of the Catholic Monarchs [Fernando de Aragón, 1452–1516, and Isabel de Castilla, 1451–1504]), but nevertheless corrects their *judgments* about it. It recasts their view of the Catholic ideology of the unified Spanish state – as incomplete (permeated by Islam), or pernicious (eliminating fine products of other extractions) – now presenting it as natural, almost divinely ordained, vital, and full of promise. According to Amador de los Ríos, it is what makes Spanish literature occupy "first place" among all the literatures that appeared since the Fall of the Roman Empire.

The centrality of political and linguistic unity to the national project determines, as it already had in the Rodríguez Mohedanos' project, the choice of what will be regarded as belonging to the culture. Already in the introduction to the first volume, for example, Amador de los Ríos spells out where Spanish-American literature should be in Spanish literary history. For the author, American writers share in a communal identity that goes beyond the nation-state. Although he only gets to the matter of

---

[40] Amador de los Ríos, *Historia crítica*, p. xcv.
[41] Amador de los Ríos, *Historia crítica*, pp. lxxxviii, lxxxix.

Spanish America in the very last paragraph of the introduction, he treats its inclusion in the history as an issue of kinship:

> Derramados al par en la Europa y en el Nuevo Mundo los cultivadores de nuestra lengua y literatura, mientras hemos procurado tejer á la exposición histórico-crítica de los ingenios que florecen en nuestro suelo la historia de la infeliz raza hebráica . . . , hemos consagrado la mayor solicitud á los ingenios que nacen de nuestra propia sangre en las vastas regiones de América, hablando nuestro idioma y cultivando el arte de . . . Lope y de Cervantes. Falta imperdonable seria en nosotros el olvidar á los poetas americanos que desde el siglo XVI logran señalado asiento en el parnaso español.

> (The cultivators of our language and literature being scattered through both Europe and the New World, while we have [on the one hand] tried to weave the history of the wretched Hebraic race into the historical-critical account of the wits that bloom in our soil, [on the other hand] we have devoted the greatest attention to the wits born of our own blood in the vast regions of America, who speak our language and cultivate the art of . . . Lope and Cervantes. It would be an unforgivable blunder on our part to forget the American poets who, from the sixteenth century, have attained a distinguished place in the Spanish parnassus.)[42]

It is interesting to observe the contrast established here between Jewish authors as "wits that bloom in our soil" and Spanish-American authors as wits born elsewhere *of Spanish blood*. While the first are to be woven into the fabric of Spanish literary history (which the author does in another work entitled *Historia social, política y religiosa de los judíos de España* ["Social, Political, and Religious History of the Jews of Spain"]), the second must figure in this work as branches of the Spanish cultural family. Here geography and even birth take second place to a transnational identity understood chiefly in terms of language, religion, and (presumed) political ideology.

The claim of sameness for Spanish-American authors is continuous with as well as different from the discourse of the Rodríguez Mohedanos. In the earlier history, there is a sense of ownership of literary goods, as part of the booty of conquest. Now there is an increased insistence on common identity, ironic since, during the period separating both works, Spanish Americans began to engage in their own nation-building practices. Despite Amador de los Ríos' description of Spain as a constitutional monarchy, his history plainly seeks to prolong the image of Spain as a legitimate empire; this not only works symbolically to validate "the glory of the nation," but has the material effect of justifying Spanish claims on the remaining American colonies, Cuba and Puerto Rico. At the same time, the insistence on familial ties with Spanish America in

---

[42] Amador de los Ríos, *Historia crítica*, pp. cv–cvi.

essence divorces the concept of nationality from that of the state. What distinguishes Spaniards and their cultural production exceeds the limits of specific places and regimes. This further substantiates the last political interests in Spanish America, implicitly labeling independence a mistake. Literary history may function as a symbolic record of the past, but it is also very conscious of its instrumentality in the game of tangible power.

Within the peninsula, Spanish literary history is also guided by "political centralism."[43] In order to serve its nationalistic purpose, the historical project needs to insist on factors of unity. Consequently, along with the imagined annexation of colonial territories even in the postcolonial period, one can observe the alienation of peninsular identities, assessed in ways ranging from taken-over competitors to completely parallel systems, never intersecting the cultural line of "Spain." As is especially evident in the treatment of Catalonia (for reasons having to do with the threat posed by its cultural renaissance movement), the national identity forms itself through the isolation of what does not fit into its legitimizing model, and its relegation to the category of "regional." Like his predecessors, Amador de los Ríos is not only reflecting, but rather creating the Spanish national identity – a project that necessitates the minimization of any sense of political crisis or cultural fragmentation, and the maximization of the sense of patriotic community. Thus, his history will depend fundamentally on the repeated cry of "Dios y la patria" ("God and country").[44]

Despite the negative future implications of this insistence on the Catholic, Castilian model, it remains important to note that, for pragmatic reasons, even Catalan intellectuals made an investment in the national undertaking. A case in point is that of Manuel Milá y Fontanals, a distinguished scholar and historian of Catalan culture, who can nevertheless make, in his *Principios de literatura general y española* ("Principles of General and Spanish Literature," 1877), the equivocal assertion that "la literatura castellana es, entre las modernas, la que presenta mayor carácter nacional" (the Castilian is, among modern literatures, the one showing the greatest national character).[45] It can be argued that it served no purpose for the Catalan nationalistic project to demand the recognition of its contribution to Spanish culture, and that separateness most strengthened its self-identification and socio-cultural cohesion. In fact, Milá's *Principios* seems to grant only common origins, devoting little attention to Catalan letters beyond the medieval period. He is caught within the allegiance to

[43] Joan Ramon Resina, "Hispanism and its Discontents." *Siglo XX / 20th Century* (1996), p. 106.
[44] Amador de los Ríos, *Historia crítica*, p. xi.
[45] Manuel Milá y Fontanals, *Principios de literatura general y española* (Barcelona: Imprenta Barcelonesa, 1877), p. 297.

a nation-state and the avowal of a nationality that does not conform to that state. As Joan Ramon Resina notes, the resulting aesthetic attitude "corresponds . . . to the historical compromise between the regulations of a centralizing despotism and the autonomy of social functions, which in Milá, as in most middle-class intellectuals of his time, is hindered by profound concessions to the religious spirit."[46] However one judges this perspective, the fact remains that Spanish nationalism and literary history impose an ideological superstructure upon other peninsular cultures; nevertheless, for their own part, these cultures negotiate this imposition in clearly utilitarian ways.

The fact that Spanish literary history is an overtly nationalistic endeavor makes its relationship with competing nationalisms reasonably evident. Perhaps more obscure is the way in which this nation-building discourse is immediately and powerfully gendered. Both in its construction of an image for Spain and in its inclusion, exclusion, and description of "los libros" (the books) and "los Autores" (the authors),[47] literary historiography institutes a radically masculine cultural space. Despite the grammatical gender of the word *España*, the emblem of the Castilian warrior prevails from the beginning over that of the nurturing motherland (*la madre patria*). Menéndez y Pelayo embodies the trend in the *Antología de poetas líricos castellanos* ("Anthology of Castilian Lyric Poets," 1890–1906), where he describes the symbolic weight of the figure of the Cid: "la figura del héroe . . . es para nosotros símbolo de nacionalidad, y fuera de España se confunde con el nombre mismo de nuestra patria" (the figure of the hero . . . is for us a symbol of nationality, and outside of Spain merges with the very name of our fatherland).[48] Literary history is in great measure a product of the century that sees the rise of the bourgeoisie and its cultural division of the world into strongly codified masculine and feminine, public and private, active and passive realms. In that context, it is interesting to observe how the adjectives used in literary histories to describe the nation and its literature are most often aligned with the first term in each of those pairs. The explicit classification carries of course an implicit valuation, where the masculine is associated with vigor and power, and the feminine signals weakness or even decadence.

It is thus the writing of men which most clearly "represents" the nation, and consequently few women enter the pages of literary histories. In the case of early modern literature, this does not even need the recourse to gender as an explanation – women producers were simply too few and too removed from the literary field to figure prominently.

[46] Milá y Fontanals, *Principios*, p. 103.
[47] Rodríguez Mohedano and Rodríguez Mohedano, *Historia*, p. 63.
[48] Marcelino Menéndez y Pelayo, *Antología de poetas líricos castellanos* (Madrid: CSIC, 1944–1945, 1890–1906), vol. VI, pp. 274–275.

A more overt consciousness of exclusion nevertheless appears when one looks at nineteenth-century histories which do get to contemporary times, since the 1800s witness the explosion of a women's literary market. The great proportion of forgotten female writers recently revisited by criticism reveals their gaping absence in the discourse of literary history. Among those who did figure in it, the case of Cuban-born Gertrudis Gómez de Avellaneda stands out for the remarkable way in which it throws into relief the relationship between gender and nationality. In his 1915 *Historia de la lengua y literatura española* ("History of Spanish Language and Literature"), José Rogerio Sánchez writes about Avellaneda that "se muestra quizá más poeta que nunca en sus composiciones *devotas*; en ellas *se apodera* del estilo de los bíblicos cantores, de . . . los salmos, y acierta á pintar en nuestra hermosa y *robusta* lengua la *terrible majestad y fortaleza omnipotente del Dios de los ejércitos*" (she perhaps most proves herself an authentic poet in her *devout* compositions; in them she *seizes* the style of the biblical singers of . . . Psalms, and succeeds in painting in our beautiful and *robust* language the *terrible majesty and omnipotent strength of the God of Armies*).[49] She is worthy of inclusion in Spanish literary history insofar as she is neither feminine nor Cuban (where both traits are, as we will see, further associated), but rather masculine, Catholic, Castilian.

Of course, not all accounts are quite as laudatory as Sánchez's, and when they are not, the criticism is explicitly the reverse of the above. In his 1891–1894 *La literatura española en el siglo XIX* ("Spanish Literature in the Nineteenth Century"), Father Francisco Blanco García decries Avellaneda's novels in the following terms: "Se notan, sin embargo, . . . un desbordamiento de pasiones y una exaltación ardiente y continua, debidos en parte á . . . las condiciones del sexo y quizá también a las del país en que vino al mundo y pasó los años de su infancia" (One nevertheless notices . . . an overflow of passions and an ardent and continuous overexcitement, owing in part to . . . the conditions of her sex, and perhaps also to those of the country where she was born and spent the years of her childhood).[50] The terms in which Blanco García describes Avellaneda's novel ("*over*flow," "*over*excitement") furthermore point to the most basic nineteenth-century associations between femininity and illness: this is clearly the discourse of hysteria. These features mark her writing as *inferior* and *foreign* – specifically, Cuban, in wording that closely replicates the contemporary discourse of Menéndez y Pelayo: "En Cuba todo el mundo hace versos . . . La ardiente fantasía de los naturales

---

[49] José Rogerio Sánchez, *Historia de la lengua y literatura española* (Madrid: Renacimiento, 1915), pp. 349–350. Emphasis added.

[50] Francisco Blanco García, *La literatura española en el siglo XIX* (Madrid: Aguado, 1891–1894), vol. I, p. 374.

de aquel suelo privilegiado en todo; lo vehemente, férvido y extremoso de sus afectos . . . son cualidades y condiciones que . . . impiden que se desarrolle con bastante pujanza el genis individual . . ." (In Cuba everyone writes verses . . . The ardent fantasy of the natives of that soil privileged in everything . . . are qualities and conditions that . . . prevent the individual genius from developing . . .).[51] In its femininity and decadence, Gómez de Avellaneda's writing is contrary to the spirit of austerity and might that normatively characterizes national literature.

Altogether, the "story" told by Spanish literary history is quite consistent and definitely consolidated by the late nineteenth century: Spanish literature expresses the glory of Spain, based on the strength of its language, its religion, and its brave character. It is a curious fact that, unlike in Spanish America, in Spain the discipline is essentially conservative. As Beatriz González Stephan has shown, Spanish-American literary history appears in the context of a liberal national project. This is obviously not to say that in the New World the nation-building impulse behind literary history skews the interests of dominant elites, but rather that its role was not to look to the past to fix a fleeting image of the nation, but to "operar sobre las condiciones materiales para hacer efectivo el progreso social, y . . . [representar] el lenguaje institucionalizado . . . de estas clases que se atribuirán la formación de los estados nacionales" (operate on material conditions to effect social progress, and . . . [represent] the institutional language . . . of those classes that will take upon themselves the formation of the nation-states).[52] In contrast, early literary history in Spain often seems designed to halt forward movement, since it understands the apex of national grandeur as anchored in the past. Tradition necessarily plays a different role in Spain than in Spanish America, and the writing of literary history works to configure it in relation to a centralizing hegemony. The legitimizing language of Menéndez y Pelayo and, later, Menéndez Pidal is plainly the crystallization of directions already present in the earliest Spanish literary history.

These directions could not be maintained throughout the twentieth century. Although a study of its trajectory through the present exceeds the bounds of my possibilities here, it is obvious that the many national crises brought about by the Second Republic, the Civil War, the Franco Regime, the transition to democracy, and the entrance into the European Union could only prove forceful challenges to the discourse of literary history. Besides political developments, intellectual developments have also contributed to radical reformulations of the discipline – postmodernism

---

[51] Marcelino Menéndez y Pelayo, *Historia de las ideas estéticas en España* (Madrid: CSIC, 1940), vol. I, pp. 279–80.
[52] Beatriz González Stephan, *La historiografía literaria del liberalismo hispano-americano del siglo XIX* (Havana: Casa de las Américas, 1987), p. 19.

questioned the possibility of any totalizing discourse, cultural studies and the sociology of culture have made it impossible to isolate literature in the way traditional literary history did. Literary history has slowly found a different place alongside other forms of philology, criticism, and theory, and evolved toward forms that do not require it to be a coherent story at all – as exemplified most recently and famously by Francisco Rico's *Historia y crítica de la literatura española* ("History and Criticism of Spanish Literature"), separated from Amador de los Ríos' *Historia crítica* not just by a century, but by an extremely meaningful conjunction. The present volume aims to revisit the issue of Spanish literary history not by substituting it for another discourse – such as the criticism excerpts that make up the bulk of Rico's useful resource – but by problematizing the notions of its authorship, national context, and ideological determination. While no form of historiography can avoid being grounded in a given conceptual or political position, hopefully this format is a definitive step forward in the balancing act between information and knowledge on one side, and the production of useful, revealing, and liberating fictions about the past on the other.

Part III

The Medieval Period

JOHN DAGENAIS, MARIA ROSA MENOCAL,
ANDREW M. BERESFORD, JAMES BURKE,
CHARLOTTE D. STERN

2

Medieval Spanish literature in the twenty-first century

JOHN DAGENAIS

Medieval Spanish literature is changing rapidly. The end of the Franco regime and Spain's membership in the European Union have transformed the Spanish nation, giving new life to cultural diversity within Spain at the same time that economic and even political differences among the nation-states of Western Europe have been renegotiated in view of common European goals. Transnational corporations and global movements of large populations have changed the way we think of centers of power and the ethnic composition of "peoples." The old European order of monolingual and monocultural nation-states has been rocked to its foundations and, to a significant extent, those foundations rested upon a particular way of conceiving the European Middle Ages. The Middle Ages provided the early evidence of the language, literature and the "soul" of the people who would create the modern nation-state. This evidence then served, in a rather circular way, to confirm the naturalness of the nation-state as the inevitable outcome of historical forces in place for centuries if not millennia. The Middle Ages legitimized the modern nation-state. Such a view is obviously reductive, not to mention teleological. It must focus on those aspects of the Middle Ages which can be made to predict the cultural, political, ethnic, and linguistic unity which constitute the founding myth of modern European nations.[1]

In this era of pan-European union and regional autonomous governments within Spain, however, the destiny of the order of nation-states seems much less manifest than it was thirty years ago. If this destiny has changed then it is also time for us to re-examine with a critical eye the foundational narratives of that destiny, including the stories we tell about the history of something we have called "medieval Spanish literature." The idea of "national" literary canons and literary traditions in a national language which founds collective volumes like the present one belongs to a rapidly changing, if not already outmoded idea of the ways in

---

[1] For a spectrum of views on "nation" and the stories we tell about it, see Benedict Anderson, *Imagined Communities: Reflections on the Origin and Spread of Nationalism* (Rev. edn. London and New York: Verso, 1991); Homi K. Bhabha, ed., *Nation and Narration* (London: Routledge, 1990); and Patrick J. Geary, *The Myth of Nations: The Medieval Origins of Europe* (Princeton: Princeton University Press, 2002).

which peoples, languages, and literatures exist. The stories such volumes tell about the Middle Ages no longer ring true. It is time to begin to think about the shape of the new stories we will tell about the medieval past of that place we now call "Spain."

"Spain" did not exist as a political unit in the Middle Ages. "Medieval Spain" (and, by extension, "medieval Spanish literature") is a back-formation, extending the idea of a unified and uniform "Spanish" political, linguistic, and cultural entity back into a period in which such an idea was very far from the minds of most inhabitants of the Iberian peninsula. For much of the period we call the Middle Ages, the idea of Hispanic unity was most often invoked by Iberians in the face of outside threats, whether from the Moorish south or the trans-Pyrenean north. Among the Christian realms of the Peninsula, however, identities were more often defined in opposition to those of other Christian kingdoms. The Catalan chronicler Ramon Muntaner provides a useful, if idealized, view of the nuances of both division and unity in the Hispania of the thirteenth century: "If those four kings of *Espanya* [that is, Castile, Aragon, Majorca and Portugal], who are one flesh and blood, hold together, they need fear little any other power in the world." Muntaner glimpses the potential strength of an alliance among these rulers, even as he recognizes how unlikely such an alliance was. As often as one hears ideals of geographical, cultural, or military unity expressed, one hears assertions of the superiority of one Crown over the other: "Pero de toda España Castilla es major, / porque fue de los otros el comienço major, / . . . , quiso acreçentar la ansí nuestro Criador" ("of all *Spanna* Castile is the best; the Creator chose to advance her because she was greater in the beginning than the other [regions]," lines 157a, b, and d) said the *Poema de Fernán González* (c. 1250, a narrative poem about the founding hero of Castile, Fernán González).[2] A Catalan admiral complains to the Aragonese King Jaume II about the difficulties of working with his temporary Castilian allies in the siege of Algeciras in 1309: "You know the people I have to deal with, for, Lord, I never knew what pains, anxiety, and care were until now."[3]

Both of these assessments will sound remarkably familiar to anyone who has spoken to modern-day Castilians or Catalans. Since the death of Franco in 1975, a variety of Peninsular cultures which trace their roots back to the Middle Ages and beyond have reasserted themselves with increasing effectiveness. The cultural and political hegemony of Castile on which Franco sought to base his rule has faded in importance as democratic government has taken firm hold in Spain. Within their own

[2] John Lihani, ed., *Poema de Fernán González* (East Lancing, MI: Colleagues Press, 1991), p. 24.

[3] J. N. Hillgarth, *The Spanish Kingdoms: 1250–1516*. 2 vols. (Oxford: Clarendon, 1976–1978), vol. I, pp. 5–10. Translations in this paragraph are Hillgarth's.

autonomous regions, Catalan, Valencian, Basque, and Galician are co-official with Castilian, the language known in most of the world as Spanish. Literature in these languages is given equal time with Castilian in secondary education. Indeed, many Spaniards educated in these regions since the late 1980s, not to mention many Spaniards in other regions of the country, might find the idea of a discussion of "medieval Spanish literature" which deals exclusively with Castilian literature to be simply the relic of another time, a time which most would prefer not to commemorate.

The goal of the present chapter is to explore the forms that a literary history of "medieval Spain" might take in the twenty-first century. How will changing ideas of what constitutes the Spanish "nation" (or "nations"), and indeed the concept of "nation" itself in a someday, perhaps, federated Europe, affect the way we tell the story of "medieval Spanish literature"? What, in fact, do we mean by "a literature"? The idea that multiple literatures exist and can be presented in volumes like this one rests ultimately not only on ideas of authorship and on aesthetic and textual categories worked out after the medieval period, but also on the now rapidly changing view that the world is composed of multiple and mutually exclusive nations. For that matter, what do we mean by "a language" when our topic is the medieval period? Like literature, this term is deeply implicated in post-medieval concepts of nationhood, especially the idea that one nation possesses one and only one language. How might we begin to achieve a balanced approach to the distinct modalities of both diversity and unity in medieval Iberia? Can we avoid egregious anachronisms of our own and resist the temptation to solve the problem by exoticizing the "difference" of the Middle Ages? In the face of a world ever more preoccupied with "presentist" concerns, what place will there be for something we might call "medieval literature," when its chief props – especially nation, ethnicity, and history – are shifting so rapidly in cultural value?

There are, of course, two ways in which we can understand the "Spanish" in "medieval Spanish literature." One is to see it as referring to the language now almost universally called "Spanish," a language which derives from the varieties of Ibero-Romance spoken in the medieval Crown of Castile. This language is spoken in two dozen countries around the world today, including Spain. Understood this way, "Spanish" refers to the language of Peninsular hegemony and world empire. This language emerged as a result of standardizing influences emanating from the Castilian court, which was ever more dominant in the Peninsula through the Middle Ages. This language went on to achieve global importance in the period immediately thereafter. Our history of "medieval Spanish literature," then, would be the literary history of a group of initially

undifferentiated dialects that would go on to become the language of
conquerors. There may well be good reasons to undertake such a history. The rise of "Spanish" is of clear historical interest for the development of world literatures in the past 500 years and for many of the
400 million people worldwide who are speakers of this language today.
Nor should we ignore the fact that in the great majority of institutions
of higher learning outside of Spain, if "medieval Spanish literature" is in
the curriculum at all it is there as an adjunct to instruction in the Spanish language in its projection as world language. Reasons exist, then, for
writing a literary history which focuses exclusively on medieval Castilian literature, the literature written in some early forms closely related
to that language which is the official language of the entire present-day
Spanish state and which is known throughout the world as "Spanish."
We cannot dismiss an exclusive focus on Castilian literature out of hand,
but we must be aware of the historically contingent reasons for choosing
such a focus.

The other meaning of "Spanish" would have it refer, not to a language but to the nation of Spain. As "Spain" did not exist as a political
entity in the Middle Ages, we will have to understand the term "medieval
Spanish literature" to be merely a useful shorthand for something like
"the literature written in the medieval period in that geographical area
corresponding, roughly, to the borders of the present-day Spanish state
(plus a few areas which were under the control of Peninsular powers in
the Middle Ages but no longer are)." Obviously the content of such a
chronologically and geographically organized study will be very different
from that of a study which is organized around the official language of
the present-day Spanish state.[4]

What would such a history include? The presence of a dynamic multi-
cultural center in al-Andalus in some key centuries of the medieval period
is discussed in the chapter by Maria Rosa Menocal. The complexities
are not limited to al-Andalus, however. The Iberian peninsula was the
crossroads of a number of languages and literary traditions we identify
today with names like Latin, Occitan, Catalan, Galician-Portuguese, and
Aragonese, in addition to the Arabic, Hebrew, and Castilian. These must
be taken into account in any history that seeks to address literary production in the geographical area of the Iberian peninsula in the medieval
period, rather than literary production in the language that became the
language of empire and nation (essentially in that sequence). If we ignore
the presence of literature written in languages or dialects other than Castilian in the Middle Ages, our resulting image of literary activity in medieval
Iberia will be deficient and fatally skewed. We cannot afford to ignore,

---

[4] Valerian Bertolucci adopts this approach to some extent. See Bertolucci *et al.*, *L'area
iberica. Storia delle letterature medievali romanze* (Rome: Laterza, 1999).

for example, the key role of the Catalan-speaking regions as receptors for the rest of Iberia, not just for the Arabic culture of the Iberian Levant and North Africa, but also, early on, of the culture of Occitania, today southern France. Later, this area will be the first to register the impact of Italian humanistic ideas, many of these arriving via the Aragonese possessions in Sicily and Naples. To understand fully literary developments in Castile in the fifteenth and early sixteenth century we will have to know what was going on in the fourteenth and fifteenth centuries in the Crown of Aragon, and, in particular, in Valencia.

The case of Galician-Portuguese literature is in some ways even more telling in this regard. Before the late fourteenth century this is the language used exclusively by many poets from Castilian-speaking areas of the Peninsula when they turn to writing lyric poetry. To put it another way: there are very few examples of lyric poetry in Castilian until the late fourteenth century. Juan Ruiz (fl. second quarter of the fourteenth century) is one notable exception, for he has given us some religious lyrics and some beggars' and student songs in Castilian. Even in the case of religious lyric, however, Galician-Portuguese dominates through the famous *Cantigas de Santa Maria* ("Songs of Saint Mary," *c.* 1250–1280), in its final form a collection of more than 400 songs in Galician-Portuguese, with music, lyrics, and illustrations, compiled under the close supervision of the Castilian king, Alfonso X, the Wise. So, once again, even if our focus were to remain on Castilian, our understanding of that literary tradition in the core centuries of its development would remain impoverished indeed if we were to ignore the presence of Galician-Portuguese lyric written by people with names like Pero Garcia Burgalês (Pedro García from Burgos, in the heart of Old Castile).

It is not the goal of this chapter to present these "other" literatures. In fact, the concept of "other literatures" can be as dangerous as that of "national literatures," as the infelicitous title of Díez Borque's otherwise excellent and important *Historia de las literaturas hispánicas no castellanas* ("History of the Non-Castilian Hispanic Literatures," 1980) illustrates. Nor do we seek to imply that the considerations here regarding the medieval period are necessarily applicable to later periods of Peninsular literary history. We merely hope to suggest that the story of "medieval Spanish literature" is far broader, far deeper, and, above all, much more complicated and more interesting than a history which focuses on the literature in a single Peninsular language can hope to portray, even if that language goes on to become one of the most important languages in the world.

As has just been suggested, it would be a fundamental mistake to believe that the way to rectify perceived imbalances in our approach to medieval Spanish literature lies in an assertion of "other" literatures – call them "national literatures," if you wish – "against" Castilian. That is, it would be an error to try to "right" the situation by allowing some sort of "equal time" to, say, a Catalan literary tradition or a Navarrese one. It is the very idea of "nation" (and its similarly anachronistic corollary "national literature") which is the impediment to our understanding of the realities of literary life in the medieval Peninsula. "Medieval Leonese literature" or "medieval Aragonese literature," in the context of the Middle Ages, are precisely the same sort of back-formations which give us "medieval Spanish literature." They have been evolved in the service of modern nationalistic goals, including resistance to Castilian hegemonic nationalism, and, as the role and function of nations changes, they will lead, increasingly, to the same intellectual dead end.

A much more productive approach for future literary histories must grow from an understanding that it is the idea of "a literature" itself which is at issue when we look at the early period. It is an outgrowth of the same search for or assertion of national identity. The idea has been that, through the centuries, certain writers and landmark texts serve to establish a corpus or canon of literature in a particular language which constitutes a repository of a national literary culture and testifies to the genius and soul of a particular culture or ethnic group. When we examine the realities of literary activity in the Iberian peninsula during the medieval period, we quickly find that this activity was at once more local and more "international" than the framework of national literature suggests. This is one of the most fundamental reasons for which "national" approaches to literature are problematic for the Middle Ages. Many works which we now view as key steps in the formation of Spanish literature never made it to "Spain."

To take the example of Gonzalo de Berceo (1196?–1264?), the first poet of the "Spanish" language whose name we know, there is evidence of just two medieval manuscript copies containing his *Vida de San Millán* ("Life of St. Emilian"): Q (around 1260, now lost) and F (around 1325), both probably based on an earlier manuscript of which no other notice has survived. As late as the 1740s, both manuscripts were still in the monastery in which Berceo presumably composed the work in the mid thirteenth century. In his edition of the work, Brian Dutton has revealed the particular admixture of local devotion and economic motivations which were behind the creation of this work: Berceo is trying to persuade some recalcitrant towns in an area roughly corresponding to La Rioja and Old Castile to resume paying to the monastery the "Voto de San Millán" ("Offering to St. Emilian" in gratitude for the saint's past aid in driving the Moors from the territory).[5] In reference to Berceo's *Milagros de Nuestra Señora*

---

[5] Gonzalo de Berceo, *Obras completas*. Ed. Brian Dutton (2nd edn. London: Támesis, 1984), vol. I, pp. 177–203.

("Miracles of Our Lady"), Dutton argues: "las obras marianas de Berceo se relacionan con un culto especial del monasterio de San Millán de Yuso, y no son puramente 'universales'" ("the Marian works of Berceo are related to a specific cult [of the Virgin] in the monastery of San Millán de Yuso and are not purely 'universal'"). At the same time, he goes on to remind us, the *Milagros* seem also to have been destined for the "entertainment and instruction" of that traveling society of pan-European pilgrims along the nearby Road to Santiago de Compostela.[6] The *Milagros* occupy two niches at once, then. One is quite local; the other pertains to the uniquely fluid society of pilgrims from all over Europe. Neither of these niches corresponds to the national Spanish niche in which modern literary histories attempt to place this work and its author.

A very different case is that of Ramon Llull (1232/3–1316), a near-contemporary of Berceo. He is considered to be the creator of *Catalan* literary language. While Berceo's life seems to have been largely circumscribed by the area between his native town and the monastery of San Millán, a few kilometers away, the Majorcan Llull traveled throughout the European and Mediterranean world of his day, from Santiago de Compostela in the west to, perhaps, as far as Cyprus in the east. In an attempt to promote, as well as to live, his dream of universal conversion to Christianity through the mechanisms of his "Art of Finding Truth," he visited North Africa and Paris, lived, studied, and taught in Montpellier, Genoa, Naples, and the Papal *curia*. He wrote more than 230 works in Catalan, Latin, and, he claims, Arabic. These works survive in well over 2,000 manuscript copies, some made as late as the eighteenth century. There are also numerous early printed editions as well as medieval or Renaissance translations into Occitan, French, Italian, Castilian, Scots, and English, including a work printed by William Caxton in London, probably in 1484.[7]

The point of this is not to assert the superiority of one artistic life or production over the other. It is merely to show that an approach to literary history which seeks to co-opt either writer to some sort of "national" literary tradition will miss the point of what either writer was striving to achieve and, more significantly, the way in which they viewed their work and their world. We would oppose the reductive view of these writers' works as mere milestones to be ticked off in the manifest destiny of an ethnic or national group to a view which gives priority to the political and economic goals of the writers themselves, that is, to the cultural context, both broad and narrow, which produced them and their works. And it seems evident that neither writer intended to found a national literary canon.

[6] Berceo, *Obras completas*, vol. II, p. 12.
[7] Ramon Llull, *Selected Works of Ramon Llull (1232–1316)*. Ed and trans. Anthony Bonner (Princeton: Princeton University Press, 1985), vol. II, pp. 1257–1304.

The foregoing should already have suggested that the same issues affect that *sine qua non* of both nation and literature: language. The idea of what constitutes "a language," in particular a medieval Iberian language, has been under serious revision of late. And with this revision comes the question of just what we mean when we say that a work of literature is written "in" a language. Until recently "dialect" (in the non-pejorative sense used by linguists) studies have been of prime importance in the presentation of medieval Iberian languages, especially in attempts to date the supposed origins of national literatures. For literary histories organized around the principle of nation, it was naturally vital to find the first written evidence of a language identifiable with the modern Castilian tongue. Indeed, for scholars interested either in demonstrating the importance of competing national languages or in showing the importance of regional traditions in the formation of such languages it was similarly important to find the first evidence of linguistic traits which show kinship with recognizable modern forms. Thus, the language of the *Razón de amor* ("Speech about Love"), a lyric poem of the early thirteenth century, has been variously characterized as Galician, Aragonese with Castilian traits, or Castilian with Aragonese traits.[8] The arguments in favor of one or the other of these often seem to have more to do with the region of origin of the scholar who makes them than with observed facts. The earliest surviving work of theatre from central Iberia, the so-called *Auto de los reyes magos* ("Play about the Three Magi," mid twelfth century), has received an even more varied set of linguistic labels through speculations that the author may have been a "Gascon," a "Mozarab" (a Christian living under Muslim rule), a "Riojan," or a "Catalan." For scholars like Carlos Alvar, the "problem" is in determining if the *Auto* represents an "autochthonous Castilian text" or is an "adaptation of a foreign model."[9] If the work turns out not to be by a "Spaniard," then its value to the enterprise of establishing a canon of works which trace the development of Spanish literature is much diminished (and this is especially unfortunate if, as is the case here, a work is the only example in its genre for the next 250 years). An emphasis on telling the story of national literature forces us into such concerns. It creates a system of authorial or linguistic *limpieza de sangre* ("purity of blood"). It obscures the significance of the simple fact that this play was almost certainly copied into this manuscript in Toledo for use in that cathedral in the very heart of Iberia, whatever the geographic or ethnic origins of its composers.

[8] Enzo Franchini, *El manuscrito, la lengua y el ser literario de la "Razón de amor"* (Madrid: CSIC, 1993), pp. 187–241.
[9] Carlos Alvar, "La letteratura castigliana medievale." In Bertolucci *et al.*, *L'area iberica*, p. 151.

More recently scholars have begun to challenge the linguistic identity of those most cherished of documents in Spanish literary and language history: the "glosses of San Millán and Silos" (second half of the eleventh century). These glosses have transformed the lovely valley in which they were found into what has been called "the cradle of the Spanish language," for they contain paraphrases of Latin texts in what has seemed to be a local Romance vernacular. The glosses, however, belong to "Spanish" only by projecting back onto them a linguistic unity which began to form, linguistically and politically, much later (recent scholarship has suggested that whatever their original language, the San Millán glosses may well have been copied in Aragon rather than La Rioja). Far from being translations from Latin into some form of vernacular, these glosses may well represent a quasi-phonetic transcription of Latin texts for oral presentation in the "accent" of the local audience. Once again, the preoccupation with appropriating these glosses for some story of linguistic development has obscured or relegated to second rank the nature of the glosses as designed to serve a very specific function in a specific local context. It seems clear to many scholars today that well into the thirteenth century, the geographical, even proto-national labels, given to these glosses and to other early "Romance" texts are anachronistic. At most we can speak of a general "Ibero-Romance" in which, outside any attempts to overdetermine specific regional traits, the Iberian Romance speech exists in an "ample elastic gamut" of shared linguistic forms and lexicon.[10]

The foregoing suggests a crazy quilt of local linguistic variety, ethnicities, political, theological, and religious motives, local and international perspectives and goals. The only element conspicuously absent is the idea that these texts, their language, and their authors belong to something we can call "Spanish." A much more powerful model for the future would be one which recognizes the sporadic nature of medieval literary traditions and the shifting and often undifferentiated identities of "language" itself in order to focus on the myriad points of intersection among traditions we might today recognize as separate literarily and linguistically. This has the additional advantage of minimizing the sort of tropes which assert one "national" tradition against another. When we take away the rigid boundaries and bloodlines enforced by the ideas of national or linguistic canons, we find, and it is probably no surprise, that these intersections are, in fact, the most fertile and productive part of Peninsular literary culture. Menocal has discussed the remarkable cross-fertilizations of al-Andalus, but this dynamic interactiveness was characteristic among literary traditions in

---

[10] See Roger Wright, *A Sociophilological Study of Late Latin* (Utrecht: Brepols, 2002), Chapter 16.

Christian areas of Iberia as well. In fact, as we examine the record of medieval Iberia and adjacent areas we find that literary activity *across* linguistic, cultural, and geographic boundaries (as we view them today) was far more prevalent than some narrow nationalistic and monolingual process of canon formation.

Until the fifteenth century Catalan poets continued to write their lyric poetry using the Occitan poetic *koiné* of what is today southern France. Among the earliest collections of Romance poetry in the Peninsula is MS V, a collection of Occitan troubadour verse copied in Catalonia in 1268. Occitan-language troubadours born in the area of Catalonia – two dozen poets in total, according to Martí de Riquer[11] – participate in the broader literary culture associated with the diffusion of troubadour lyric along that fertile West Mediterranean crescent from the Iberian Levant to Tuscany and beyond. Their works are anthologized in manuscripts compiled not just in Occitania and Catalonia, but in Italy as well. Occitan-language troubadours and minstrels from this larger European cultural world outside Iberia, in turn, refer to the Iberian kingdoms beyond the Pyrenees with remarkable frequency and more than two dozen of them visit the courts of rulers from Catalonia–Aragon to Portugal.[12] A knowledge of the Old Occitan *canso* (courtly song, generally on love) is believed to have played a key role in the development of the Galician-Portuguese *cantiga de amor* ("song about love"). Raimon Vidal from Besalú in Catalonia (fl. 1190–1220), who himself visits the court of Alfonso VIII of Castile, writes the *Razos de trobar* ("Rules for Writing Occitan Poetry"), an early attempt to make the Occitan *koiné* more accessible to would-be poets whose native language was not Occitan.[13] This treatise represents clear evidence that Iberian people were substantially interested in functioning *across* linguistic boundaries.

Poets born in Castile and adjacent areas, as we have seen, write most of their lyric verse in Galician-Portuguese, not in Castilian, until the end of the fourteenth century. The courts of Fernando III of Castile and his son Alfonso the Wise are centers of poetic activity in Galician-Portuguese and in the court of Dom Dinís, king of Portugal (ruled 1279–1325), it is the king himself who is the center of a circle of active poets. Alfonso also plays host to numerous Occitan poets, including Giraut Riquier (fl. 1254–1292), who sets a delightful *pastourelle* (poem in which a traveler, often a knight, jousts verbally with a shepherdess he encounters along his way) on the pilgrimage road to Santiago de Compostela.

[11] Martí de Riquer, *Història de la literatura catalana; Part Antiga* (Barcelona: Ariel, 1982), vol. I, p. 39.
[12] Carlos Alvar, *La poesía trovadoresca en España y Portugal* (Barcelona: Planera, 1977), p. 287.
[13] Riquer, *Història*, vol. I, pp. 111–122.

The king himself engages with Riquier – how directly is still a matter of dispute – in a poetic debate in that language. Indeed, in and around the court of Alfonso, as Aviva Doron has argued, Jewish poets such as Todros Ha-Levi Abulafia (1247–1298?) begin to produce Hebrew poetry which reveals traces of hitherto exclusively Christian literary motifs.[14]

The case of the earliest known written copy of a *romance* (ballad), a popular poetic form most often identified with Castilian, shows what we gain and lose when our first impulse is to discount works of literature which reveal linguistic and ethnic miscegenation. The poem survives because it was written into a personal copybook by Jaume d'Olesa, a Majorcan student in Bologna (*c.* 1421). Unfortunately for nationalist literary history, Olesa writes down this ballad in what has been called a "Castilian riddled with Catalanisms."[15] The preoccupation with "firsts" obliges historians of Castilian literature to mention this distressingly impure copy as proof of the early existence of the Castilian ballad form. What is missed, however, by historians of both Castilian and Catalan literature (Riquer uses the more neutral "great number of Catalan forms"[16]) is that this is a genuine piece of Iberian literary language, used by a genuine Iberian to write down a piece of Iberian "oral literature" he obviously thought was worth recording in the very Iberian context of the law school of Bologna where students from Iberia had their own college. The linguistic *limpieza de sangre* which literary histories of the national era must impose on their object of study has hitherto prevented us from appreciating this dynamic interaction – really, intermingling – of Iberian languages (and, perhaps, even to ignore the obvious appreciation of Castilian folk song which motivates it) by an Iberian student abroad.

The "impure" or "foreign" origins of the *Auto* on the Magi suggest another area in which the waning of older forms of nationalism may help us to gain new appreciation of medieval literary life: the large corpus of adaptation and translation which makes up such a large part of vernacular literature in the Peninsula. If our goal is to discover the true and authentic genius of a particular language and ethnic group (and the nation which claims inheritance from it), then translation and adaptation must necessarily be considered lesser forms: they are "borrowed" from "others," they bear a false genealogy and offer only a hybrid genius at best. For medieval writers, however, productive transformation, that is, adaptation not just to new languages but to new settings and times as well, rather than autochthonous originality, was a primary goal. Ideas of

---

[14] Aviva Doron, "La poesía de Todros Ha-Levi Abulafia como reflejo del encuentro de las culturas: la hebrea y la española en la Toledo de Alfonso X El Sabio." In *Actas del X Congreso de la Asociación de Hispanistas.* 4 vols. Ed. Antonio Vilanova *et al.* (Barcelona: PPU, 1992), vol. I, pp. 171–178.

[15] Alvar, "La letteratura," p. 287.   [16] Riquer, *Història*, vol. III, p. 379.

literary property and of a "canon" of original work possessed by a nation are far in the future. In the medieval context, we must avoid tropes like "mere translation." Berceo's *Milagros* are a translation of a preexisting Latin miracle collection, which Berceo adapts to the particular cult of the Virgin in the Monastery of San Millán de Yuso, as we have seen. The *General Estoria* ("General History"), compiled in part under Alfonso the Wise, incorporates wholesale adaptations from Ovid's *Heroides* among many other sources, Classical, biblical, and medieval. Don Juan Manuel (1282–1348) re-uses the frame of Ramon Llull's *Libre de l'orde de cavalleria* ("Book of the Order of Knighthood," 1279–1283?) in his own *Libro del cavallero et del escudero* ("Book of the Knight and the Squire," before 1330), and Joanot Martorell (*c.* 1413–1468) will use the frame yet again in the fifteenth century, although he seemed unaware of the Llullian paternity, in his *Tirant lo Blanc* (first edited 1490). A century later, translated into Castilian, *Tirant* became, in the mouth of Cervantes' priest, "por su estilo . . . el mejor libro del mundo" ("for its style . . . the best book in the world," *Don Quixote*, pt. 1, ch. 6). A lengthy section of Juan Ruiz's *Libro de buen amor* ("Book of Good Love," second quarter of the fourteenth century) is a translation of the medieval Latin comedy *Pamphilus*. Andreu Febrer (*c.* 1375 – bef. 1444) manages a Catalan translation of the *Divine Comedy* in the original *terza* rhyme scheme and meter. "Breton" *lais* are translated and adapted into Galician-Portuguese, and French Arthurian prose romances make their way into that language as well. Diego de San Pedro's *Cárcel de amor* ("Prison of Love") is translated into "valenciana prosa" (see below) by Bernadí Vallmanya in 1493, a year after its original publication.

Nor should we forget that literary multilingualism continues throughout the medieval period, whether it was Latin–vernacular, Romance–Semitic, among Romance literary languages, or in varying combinations of all of these. Enrique de Villena (1384–1434), who has ancestors in both the Castilian and the Aragonese royal families, frequents the organized poetic contests of Barcelona. He writes the *Dotze treballs d'Hercules* ("The Twelve Labors of Hercules," 1417) in Catalan, translates his own work into Castilian, and writes most of the rest of his works in Castilian. Pere Toroella (fl. 1436?–1486?) writes an extensive body of work in both Catalan and Castilian. Traditional literary histories have transformed the works these men wrote outside their "appropriate" native language into footnotes of literary history. Both should rather be seen as significant *Iberian* figures. We might wish to consider that it is these works, in fact, which are central from the historical point of view. It is multilingualism, not monolingualism, which is most characteristic of literate Iberians throughout the Middle Ages.

The focus of scholars on "texts," by "authors," and especially on texts in the proto-national vernaculars has meant that we simply have not even looked at the great bulk of the evidence for medieval written culture already easily available to us. Tens of thousands of Latin manuscripts exist, for the most part ignored, which could teach us much about the interests and level of culture in those very monasteries where, say, Berceo's work was being read. Reader's glosses abound in these manuscripts, which could teach us how medieval people who could read (and write) approached their texts. For example, a manuscript from San Millán, now in Madrid, is filled with marginal glosses of a literary nature: on the six types of allegory, on *anticipatio* (foreshadowing) and *recapitulatio* (brief review or summary) in narrative, on metaphor, irony, hyperbole, and even *geminatio* (repetition of a word or phrase in close proximity). Every once in a while we can even glimpse in medieval Latin manuscripts a comment such as "pulchra comparatio" ("a beautiful simile") which may reveal an immediate aesthetic reaction to a text (or, perhaps just as interesting, a teacher's comment to students that such and such a comparison is "pulchra"). Glosses to Latin (and vernacular) texts, whether in Latin or the vernacular, provide a wealth of information on medieval approaches to literature, whether ethical, formal, or aesthetic, which is essential to any history of medieval Iberian literature, even if our only goal is to understand the categories by which authors themselves understood the objects they sought to create.

Manuscripts and their margins provide still more to those interested in the culture of literate people in the Middle Ages, once we leave our preoccupation with texts behind. For the general public, illuminations are perhaps the most familiar non-textual feature of medieval manuscripts. As one digs deeper into manuscripts one finds everything from snippets of song to elaborate genealogical charts of Christ's lineage to doodles of faces and animals to an inscribed circle showing just how large your tonsure should be. We have a long way to go in understanding the medieval visual language of doodles and squiggles, found in the millions in medieval manuscripts. Even in the realm of textual material we can often find glimpses into the lives of those who wielded pens in the Middle Ages: someone complains in the upper margin of a manuscript "tres vezes fui azotado por Fray Juan de Campos" ("I was flogged three times by/for Friar Juan de Campos"). Two folios later we find "quatro vezes fui azotado" ("I was flogged four times"). Do the assonances of "azotado" and "Campos" suggest a snippet of song or song in creation, or is this a glimpse into the lived experience of a medieval reader who records that experience in time with the pace of his reading? Perhaps it is both. In a manuscript of Burgo de Osma, we find traces of a reader in the midst of a text from the famous passage on the origins of the Navarrese people drawn from the twelfth-century *Pilgrim's Guide* to the Road to Santiago de Compostela: "Unde Navarrus interpretatur non verus, id est non progenie aut legitima prosapia generatus" ("'Navarrese' should be glossed as *non verus* [not true], that is to say, *not* generated from a true lineage *nor* from a legitimate stock").[17] This reader, almost certainly a Navarrese, though of what period we cannot know for sure, has scratched away the "not" and the "nor" from the text, thereby restoring the legitimacy of the Navarrese with the scrape of a knife.

Taken alone, such details seem inconsequential, however charming we may find them. They offer none of the familiar gratification we may derive from editing the manuscript works of a medieval author into a "book" we can place on our shelves next to other authors in a national tradition. To date we have largely neglected the vast bulk of our evidence for literary activities in medieval Iberia, simply because it does not fit our categories of what literature is or of what literary scholars should do. Only by patiently collecting thousands of such seemingly trivial details and coming to understand their patterns and meanings will we be able, over time, to come to know that literary world completely. Unfortunately, we are far from even beginning such investigations. In fact, we have not really established which of the tens of thousands of medieval manuscripts currently held in libraries in the Iberian peninsula and other European libraries were actually *in* Iberia in the Middle Ages and could serve as a basis for such an inventory.

We have deliberately postponed discussion of Latin literature in the medieval Iberian peninsula until now. More than thirty years ago Keith Whinnom stressed the fundamental importance of Latin letters to Iberian literatures of the Middle Ages, describing the relation of vernacular letters to the Latin as that of an archipelago of islands peeking up out of a vast ocean of Latin letters.[18] This remains almost literally true, as the earliest works of vernacular literature in the central Peninsula seem to have been copied down in spaces left between Latin texts: the opening portions of the *Auto* occupy a blank space on one page at the end of a glossed biblical text; the *Razón de amor* and the Iberian texts which accompanied it are sandwiched between two Latin sermon collections, perhaps on a gathering left blank when the first of these collections was left incomplete. Another fragmentary early Ibero-Romance work, the *Debate del alma y del cuerpo* ("Debate between the Soul and the Body," *c.* 1200) is found on the

---

[17] C. Meredith-Jones, ed., *Historia Karoli Magni et Rotholandi ou Chronique du Pseudo-Turpin* (Geneva: Slatkine Reprints, 1972 [1936]), p. 257.
[18] Keith Whinnom, *Spanish Literary Historiography: Three Forms of Distortion* (Exeter: University of Exeter Press, 1967).

verso of a Latin legal document from Oña confirming the donation of a monastery. It is Latin literature which, in a very physical way, defines the shape of early vernacular literature in its interlinear spaces, margins, and blank folios.

Perhaps it is inevitable that Latin literature of the Iberian peninsula, too, clings to the margins of Latin texts. The so-called "Carmina Rivipullensia" (poems from the monastery of Ripoll) are twenty Latin poems – the core of them love poems – by an "Anonymous Lover." Despite their affinity with the Goliardic world, perhaps most familiar through the slightly later *Carmina Burana*, these poems have so far been found only in this Iberian source. The poems seem to have been copied in the late twelfth century onto some folios left blank after a tenth-century copying of a *Liber glossarum* ("Book of Glosses"). Latin will come into its own again as Humanist ideas began to enter the Peninsula in the late fourteenth century. Writers in Eastern Iberia like Bernat Metge (1340/6–1413), as well as the writers of the Aragonese royal chancellery, begin to appreciate anew the culture of Roman Antiquity and to attempt to imitate it in their works. Antoni Canals (1352–1414) translates works of Valerius Maximus and Seneca as well as Petrarch into "our beloved maternal Valencian tongue." These translations, in turn, will be re-translated into Castilian over the course of the fifteenth century. The influence of Classical Latin culture is seen most strikingly, perhaps, in the "valenciana prosa" (Valencian-style prose) of writers like Joan Roís de Corella (1433/43–1497), who used Latinate syntax (including hyperbaton, that is, unusual syntactic order) and lexicon to create an elevated and sometimes elegant rhetorical prose. Similar stylistic experiments are carried out in Castilian by writers like Juan de Mena (1411–1456) and Enrique de Villena, and in Castilian sentimental romances like Diego de San Pedro's *Cárcel de amor*.

Iberian writings in Latin and the impact of Classical, medieval, and Renaissance Latin on both Ibero-Latin and vernacular writing remain, then, one other area which we may be better able to explore once this language which belonged, in the Middle Ages, to no nation and to every nation is freed from nationalistic needs to promote the vernacular as the major index of cultural soul. Medieval Latin is doubly orphaned under the order of nation-states for its internationalism does not lend itself easily to nationalist goals, nor has its unique culture, so different from that of Antiquity, been fully appreciated by Classicists. Despite the labors of Manuel Díaz y Díaz to bring the large corpus of "Hispano-Latin" works under bibliographic control and to begin to explore its riches, significant works like the *Planeta* ("Planet," 1218) of Diego García de Campos (fl. 1138–1218?), remarkable for its exegetical and verbal pyrotechnics, remain the delight of a few specialists.[19] A reading of the *Planeta*, together with works by Rodrigo Jiménez de Rada (1170–1247), or even the fascinating work of the glossator who signs his name "S." and who may have worked in Jiménez' circle, gives an entirely different picture of culture in medieval Castile than that we can glean from the few surviving vernacular works of the time. It is time for their story to be told as an integral part of the story of medieval Iberian literary life.

The shape of that story will be subject to our understanding, not only of national destinies, but also of the function of that period with the odd name: Middle Ages. For nationalist histories the Middle Ages occupy an odd dual role as at once the grandparent of national culture and its childhood. The Middle Ages are what the culture was before it grew up to be us. This allows us both to revere the Middle Ages and to characterize the period as an age of innocence or ignorance, or both. In either case, much of what has been important for our understanding of the Middle Ages lies in our ability to measure the distance we have come from it. There is much at stake for literary historians, then, in putting an end to the Middle Ages (Iberia offers the especially convenient year of 1492 for this end), in allowing new and more sophisticated versions of national cultures to emerge. Once we are able to separate the Middle Ages from some story we would tell of national cultural maturation, however, we come to see that the Middle Ages do not go away quite so easily. Elements of what we call medieval culture continue well past any artificial periodizations we might establish. The *Spill* ("Mirror") or *Book of Women* (*c.* 1460) by the fifteenth-century Valencian medical doctor Jaume Roig (1400/10–1478) has been reprinted or translated at least once in every century since its composition. The works of Llull, as we have seen, continue to be printed, translated, and even laboriously copied in manuscript form down to the present day and the influence of his ideas was felt by Gottfried Wilhelm von Leibniz (1646–1716). The impact of medieval modes of thought and culture in the colonies established by both Castile and Portugal is part of the Iberian peninsula's legacy to the New World.[20]

Any full appreciation of medieval Iberia must also take into account the survival and continued evolution of medieval Iberian Jewish culture outside the Peninsula following the expulsion of 1492. Sephardic culture already escapes any national claims which might be made on it by Peninsular powers and offers many ironies to those who would equate language and nation. Flory Jagoda, a well-known singer of songs in Ladino (one name for the variety of Spanish spoken by Sephardic Jews), recounts in

[19] Manuel C. Díaz y Díaz, *Index scriptorum Latinorum Medii Aevi Hispanorum*. 2 vols. ([Salamanca]: Universidad de Salamanca, 1958–1959).
[20] See Luis Weckmann, *The Medieval Heritage of Mexico*. Trans. Frances M. López-Morillas (New York: Fordham University Press, 1992).

her concert appearances that, as she was growing up in Bosnia, the fact that one spoke "Spanish" was an unambiguous marker of Jewishness: anyone who spoke that language was by definition a Jew. It was not until she was eight years old that she learned the remarkable fact that there were other people in the world who spoke a variety of her language and that the great majority of them were not Jews. The remarkable flourishing of Sephardic culture, including numerous publications in Ladino, often using the Hebrew alphabet, in the centuries following the expulsion, as well as the survival today of hundreds of ballads whose origins can be traced back to late medieval Spain among the Jewish communities of North Africa, the eastern Mediterranean, the Near East, and the New World,[21] give a shape to "medieval" Iberian literature which defies not only the national and ethnic boundaries but also the temporal ones we might place upon it. It requires a rethinking, especially, of what such temporal boundaries mean.

This chapter has focused chiefly on the Latin and Romance cultures which arose in Christian-dominated Spain. Christians, Muslims, and Jews lived together in most areas of the Peninsula throughout the Middle Ages. Not surprisingly, many Iberian individuals' own lives involve a crossing of borders. As we emphasize connections among Peninsular literatures and cultures, figures such as Moisés Sefardí, baptized as Petrus Alfonsi in Huesca in 1106, or Pablo de Santa María (formerly the important Rabbi Shelomó ha-Levi), named Bishop of Burgos in 1415, become key Iberian figures, not merely signs of cultural triumphalism or betrayal. Anselm Turmeda (c. 1355 – c. 1430), a Franciscan friar from Majorca and student in Paris and Bologna, travels to Tunis and converts to Islam, changing his name to "Abdallah." From there the good friar writes, in Arabic, the anti-Christian "Tuḥfat al-ᶜarīb fi-l-radd ᶜala ahl al-ṣalib" ("Present of the Believer to the Followers of the Cross"), along with other less overtly polemical works in Catalan.

Such characters and the complex cultural currents which produced them inevitably seem exotic to those raised on the idea that the Middle Ages were the age of monolithic Christian faith. This is one danger to those who would study the Iberian Middle Ages: it is all too easy to emphasize difference, to exoticize the peculiar situation of medieval Iberia as a land of three religions. It is all too easy, too, to emphasize the attractive ideas of intercultural coexistence and cooperation, especially in present times when such ideals seem so unattainable. Positive intercultural exchange was certainly present at many points throughout the Iberian Middle Ages and this exchange constitutes a significant moment in European history.

---

[21] See Samuel G. Armistead *et al.*, *Judeo-Spanish Ballads from Oral Tradition*. 2 vols. to date (Berkeley: University of California Press, 1986).

But along with remarkable tolerance came remarkable intolerance. The challenge in reappreciating the Iberian Middle Ages is to understand the peculiar nuances of tolerance and intolerance throughout this period (David Nirenberg provides an excellent beginning in *Communities of Violence*[22]). It is easy, too, to make monoliths of each of the "Three Religions" and the political apparatus which served at least two of them. At times "Islamic Spain" was divided into as many as two dozen "Party kingdoms." We have emphasized the variety of Christian cultures in Iberia in this chapter, but such variety was also present, both geographically and across time, in medieval Iberian Islam and among the Jews. Heresies, sects, and religious controversies arose within all of the "Three Religions."

To return to the present, the European Union has, thus far, paid lip-service, at least, to the existence of "minority languages." Recently, the Educational Council of the European Union affirmed, rather tepidly, that "all European languages are equal in value and dignity from the cultural point of view and form an integral part of European culture and civilization" (14 February 2002). The European Bureau for Lesser Used Languages exists to look after the status of European languages which meet the definition of "lesser used." One thing we must hope that Europeans also keep in mind, however, is the enduring existence, in hundreds of thousands of documents tucked away in national libraries – those warehouses of the old order – of the ultimate European minority languages: those no longer spoken by anyone at all. In this respect, medieval Castilian is just as "minor" as medieval Catalan or medieval Galician. Today there is a real danger that in future generations only an increasingly diminishing minority will ever have the chance to know in the original language Pleberio's powerful lament on the death of his daughter which closes *Celestina* by Fernando de Rojas (*c.* 1475–1541); or the tormented, yet somehow affirming tones of the *Cants de mort* ("Songs of Death") by Ausiàs March (1397–1459); the crystalline beauty of the mystical prose poems "in the style of the Sufis" by Llull in his *Libre d'amic e amat* ("Book of the Lover and the Beloved"); or the deceptively simple repetitions of the Galician *cantigas de amigo* ("boyfriend songs"), written by male poets, perhaps in the style of women's folk songs. In these and hundreds of other works of medieval Iberian literature there are bits of vocabulary, turns of phrase, proverbs and similes, rhymes and meters, which must be known in the original medieval language if they are to be known at all. It would be a great shame to let go this vast treasury of human experience expressed in words. As the ideas of nation and national language shift in meaning and importance, one clear negative result is that

---

[22] David Nirenberg, *Communities of Violence: Persecution of Minorities in the Middle Ages* (Princeton: Princeton University Press, 1996).

medieval languages no longer have the cultural and political apparatus of the nation-state to defend them. Those who would wish to keep these silent languages and their texts as a part of the discourses of the present will have to find new structures – social, political, intellectual, economic – which will allow them to serve the needs of the present or they will be lost.

3

Beginnings

MARIA ROSA MENOCAL

Genesis and chronicles

At the beginnings of literary histories lie the most alluring questions. We want to know all about what we call the origins of the tradition whose story is about to be told. Few start with "once upon a time" and yet nearly all are tempted down that road marked "sources" or "birth" or "genesis," even when we know that it is a path that, nearly by definition, can have nothing like an unambiguous endpoint or resolution. Why do we persist in our scholarly tradition's most quixotic quest, the search for that grail, that moment of birth, that earliest text or, as it is often called, "monument"? Why do we persist, even when we know (for we ourselves teach this) that what does survive from the earliest sources, in relatively remote times, may be largely a trick of history, and may bear only an accidental relationship to what there really was? Why do we not begin, more simply and cleanly, in some indisputable *medias res* and from there go bravely forward into the future, rather than backwards to where the question of the source of that particular river may lie? Why are we most insistent of all, when writing about those periods often charmingly called by poetic names (such as the "springtime" of our literature), on the need to clarify what we call "influences" – and what can that mean other than the poetic company that poets kept? Why are the histories of medieval literatures (whether free-standing or, as here, as the origins stories of later literatures) so consistently our versions of the story of Adam and Eve, sometimes down to and including quasi-biblical titles such as "the creation of literature in Spanish"? Also down to and including the interpolated different accounts? Why do we lapse into our own versions of fundamentalism, even when these stories are transparently mythical, when we ourselves are at times the priests who explain the iconic – rather than historic – importance of these "where do we come from" stories?

At play is that compelling human need to establish beginnings – which means in part to establish causes and meanings – and it is why most individuals, as well as traditions, struggle mightily with competing origins stories (so that even within the Book of Genesis two story traditions about the Creation have survived alongside each other). Yet we never seriously think about abandoning the quest for the most satisfactory account of our beginnings. "A beginning: this is the source of the fascination medieval literature exercises on the mind . . . A beginning that is not really a beginning: this is the source of the complexity and originality of medieval literature," is how the senior historian of the Middle Ages in France puts it in the introduction to his own history of French medieval literature.[1] Implicit in Zink's provocative résumé of the particular interest of medieval literature is the recognition that most beginnings do not spring from any true void but rather from the destruction of something that went before. In Genesis itself the beginning of mankind, as we know it, is predicated on the destruction of that first period of innocence in the Garden of Eden.

In the beginning was . . . well, just what was there at the beginning? Was it the word, the text, the manuscript, the story, the song? What was its language? What languages did it replace? Who were the singers of those songs and the tellers of those tales? Saying just what we believe constitutes the beginning of a literary tradition – its new languages and its half-new forms – is what the philologist was created to do, and his task is really working out the etymology of a whole culture. Because both language and literature are what we take to be the vivid external markers of the most intimate qualities of communities, the stories of where they come from are of more than passing or academic interest and likely, instead, to be widely perceived as revealing the soul of a people. First there is, indeed, the word; and from the words come the songs sung with them, delighting in them; and then those stories, and then the stories about the stories, and so on. These are always difficult puzzles to piece together and often the literary historian is working from a series of fragments, and attempting to create a picture – to write a genesis story – that sheds light on much later literary phenomena. Difficult as any of this might be, however, it is still easy enough to argue that no creation story among those of the modern nations of Europe is more vexed than the one this book attempts to retell, that of Spain.

Spain's history stands out conspicuously in the annals of Western Europe and its culture, because of the singular fact that, beginning in the eighth century, it was incorporated into the expansive Islamic Empire whose center was, in that initial period, in Damascus. The far western province of a civilization that on its eastern frontier reached nearly to China, al-Andalus (as it was called in Arabic, the *lingua franca* of the Empire), was not, however, destined to remain a primitive outpost or a poor cousin of the brilliant Islamic world. In 750 a bloody coup

[1] Michel Zink, *Medieval French Literature: An Introduction*. Trans. Jeff Rider (Binghamton, NY: Medieval and Renaissance Texts and Studies, 1995), pp. 1–2.

overturned everything: while staying at their family estate at Rusafa, some 250 miles to the northeast of Damascus, the Caliph and most of his family were executed. In one bloody moment were thus eliminated the Umayyads, who had ruled the *Dar al-Islam*, the "House of Islam," since 661, and had presided over the staggering expansions of that century. The Abbasids, their rivals who engineered the dramatic rupture in the leadership, both religious and civil, of the vast Islamic polity, moved their capital to Baghdad, and there and then began a new chapter in Islamic history. This was not only an end but also the dramatic beginning of a distinctive new western history of Islam and Arabic-based culture. In this story that begins in the Near East lies the striking new foundation for medieval Spain: it turned out that one of the Umayyads had miraculously escaped the slaughter of his family. The young and intrepid Abd al-Rahman spent five years making his way to the far western provinces because that was the land of his Berber mother, and he correctly assumed he would find loyal men there. By 756 the last of the Damascus Umayyads had established himself in the colonial capital of Cordoba (and even built a new Rusafa on the outskirts of the city) and, as the first of the Andalusian Umayyads, he began the project of material transformation that would make this permanent exile of his a place worthy to eventually declare itself, as it would in the middle of the tenth century, the true caliphate.[2]

This, then, is the genesis of a transformed world order, and from this point forward the languages and cultures of Spain are markedly different from those of the rest of Europe, which is overwhelmingly Latin and Christian – and by and large still in that state of cultural dimness that had been the rule in Visigothic Spain as well. The contrast will mean that for the next four centuries or so Spain (the new Spain that is so dramatically transformed, even down to its topography and botany, with dozens of plants from the Old World soon thriving in the New) will be markedly the more civilized place, and the source of both material and intellectual innovations for the rest of Europe. Latin and its regional spoken variants survived, as did Christianity, but in virtually every respect – including the forms of Latin spoken and of Christianity practiced in the peninsula – the universe was changed.[3] The question of how to write the history of this transformation, and its many complex consequences over the next seven centuries (at least), is the toughest of historiographic problems. Many, perhaps most, of the accounts of the history of Spain after this dramatic break directly or indirectly portray the consequences as a Spain thereafter divided between, on the one hand, the true "Spaniards"

---

[2] See D. F. Ruggles, *Gardens, Landscape, and Vision in the Palaces of Islamic Spain* (State Park, PA: Pennsylvania State University Press, 2000), on the transformation of the Iberian landscape under Umayyad rule.

[3] See Maria Rosa Menocal, *The Ornament of the World* (New York: Little, Brown, 2002).

(the descendants of the Latin-speaking Christians from before the invasion of 711) and, on the other hand, the Muslim invaders who, along with the Jews (a community that in fact flourished under the Umayyads and for centuries thereafter), were a foreign and "oriental" culture. The political and demographic facts, however, as well as the cultural landscape as it evolved over some seven centuries (it is worth stating explicitly that this is as long a period as that covered by the entire literary history of the years *after* 1492: from 1492 until our own times), suggest that this simple dichotomy does little justice to the complexity of the situation and its dozens of variations over such a vast expanse of time and space.

While this is not the place to attempt any detailed retelling of that history that spans some seven centuries and at least as many languages (three classical written languages, Latin, Arabic, and Hebrew, as well as a number of distinct vernaculars, one based on Arabic and the others on Latin), it is crucial, at this beginning at least, to dismiss the most conspicuous distortions of the vision that posits that we can simply put aside, as somehow foreign to the true Spain and true Spaniards, the languages and cultures and literatures that first arrive with the Umayyads and that undergo a dozen different adaptations and flowerings and declines over those many centuries and under many different kinds of cultural circumstances. The broadest vision of what Spain was – and was not – in the Middle Ages deserves better than to remain the implausible caricature all too often accepted by those working on the literature of later periods, who are likely to see the medieval past as little more than the primitive stages of what will eventually become the real thing.

Crucially, it must be established that Arabic was from the outset, and for several centuries thereafter, the language of a book-loving and poetry-rich culture that was not remotely restricted to Muslims, but ultimately shared by most cultured Spaniards, including Jews and Christians. By the eleventh century, medieval Spain was also the place where Arabophone Jews re-invented poetry in Hebrew, and, beyond that, this was an easily multilingual society, a civilization whose aesthetic hallmarks were in creative intermarriages and adaptations and translations of all sorts. The untidy truth is that medieval Spain was home to a greater variety of interrelated religions and cultures, as well as more languages and literatures, than seem plausible or convenient to attribute, as origins, to the literature of a single modern national literature. If unified nations and single national languages are the benchmarks for the divisions of literatures established in the modern period, then the medieval universe which precedes it cannot be fit into those same parameters and divisions, without distorting the past to make it seem as if its only lasting value was in laying the groundwork for a distant and ultimately unimaginable future.

What is Spanish, before there is Spanish?

What was Spain, in the beginning? Or, more appropriately, what is the beginning of the Spain whose literary history this is? The grave difficulty for the medieval period is determining just what it is that we can legitimately call "Spanish" before any language of the peninsula is remotely understood as the unifying language of a modern nation, a time during which a remarkable range of both vernaculars and classical languages were in use and, tellingly, during which there thrived in the peninsula the most vigorous culture of translation in European history. A time and place, in other words, about as far as possible from the monolingual (and monoreligious) national culture of "Spanish" whose pre-history we presume this is. It has long been understood, in fact, that *español* was originally a trans-Pyrenean word, and that well into the Middle Ages the inhabitants of the peninsula identified themselves by their religion, or by the cities or regions they inhabited – Leon or Navarra, Toledo or Seville. Moreover, linguists understand clearly that even to conflate *castellano* with *español* – i.e. leaving aside the problem of the non-Romance languages – is a problematic procedure.

Even if we do not conflate these terms, and instead limit our canon *geographically*, to what was written in that place that is occupied by the modern nation of Spain (which comes into viable existence in the configuration we know not in the Middle Ages but, instead, in 1492), then how do we deal with the many literatures in the many languages that populate the peninsula before *that* relatively clear beginning, a beginning based in some measure on the destruction of that same long past that had included both Jews and Muslims, and their languages and literatures? If it is the language that determines filiation, then the lack of "Spanish" in the medieval period – and in fact the abundance of other languages, and the supreme literary and belletristic importance of languages that are linguistically unrelated to Spanish – presents a logical problem; and if it is the place that determines whether the literature belongs to the larger history then why do we, indeed, not count the vigorous and culturally central literatures in those other languages?

These are the toughest questions, then: what can we plausibly deem "Spanish" and "Spain" to be in the medieval period, and thus what is properly the literary tradition that lies behind that watershed year of 1492, that decisive year when both the modern state and its language were consolidated and codified? Self-evidently these are not questions that exist in isolation. Quite the contrary: they are subsections and offshoots of the largest historical questions about Spanish history and about Spanish "identity." In these most iconic realms, language and literature, these questions and especially their answers carry special weight. The matter of how we deal with these multilingual and multi-religious complexities that bear so little relationship to what follows – that one could argue is what the modern nation-state was built to deny and to destroy – is extraordinarily thorny. Perhaps the only reasonable answer is one that no modern literary history is likely to propose: to declare that what lies before that moment when Spain so dramatically turns its back on its own past and sets about disavowing it and destroying its icons (the pyres of burning Arabic books in Granada are an apt symbol of a far more widespread and deeply destructive phenomenon) is so different in its essentials, and so complex in its differences, that it no more belongs in the same literary history as what follows it than does the Latin literature written by Roman citizens born in the province of Hispania, during the "silver" years of the Roman Empire.

Of course, not including the Romans of Hispania is also a judgment call, and a matter of the cultural visions and customs of the moment at which the history is being written. The long-canonical work of José Amador de los Ríos, for example, *Historia crítica de la literatura española* ("Critical History of Spanish Literature"), fearlessly begins with the Romans from the earliest moments of their recorded writings in the peninsula, continues with the Christians of the Roman world, and after the Fall of Rome includes the Visigoths. This trajectory leads to Isidore and from there to the popular Latin poetry of the last years before the Islamic conquest. The first volume of Amador de los Ríos in fact ends with the legendary materials concerning Rodrigo and the last of the Visigoths and, without skipping a beat, or ignoring the overwhelming shift in power and social structures and religions that follow, continues with the "escritores cristianos del Califato" ("Christian writers of the Caliphate"). One might quarrel with the ideology that underpins this trajectory, which establishes that the Spaniards are defined first by geography and secondarily by conversion to Christianity, and then, ultimately, by remaining Christian in the aftermath of the Islamic invasion and colonization (which in fact led to wholesale conversions to Islam). It has, however, the merit of defining the complex terms forcefully – it is not simply geography nor a single language, but a clear identity unembarrassedly defined – and then drawing a line of descent and development consistent with those terms.

At the outset of the twenty-first century Amador de los Ríos' nineteenth-century vision, when laid out so explicitly, might seem quaint and unsustainable in a number of ways, and yet it is little different in practice from the default position developed over the course of the twentieth century, and nearly universally accepted. Our more recent versions, however, are less straightforward, since some scholars might, indeed, be embarrassed to admit that they would define medieval Spaniards as really Spaniards – or not – according to their religion. The less direct rationalization for the continuation of the same divisions used by Amador de los Ríos (if it is Castilian – or a linguistically related dialect – it counts) is that this is the linguistic first step in what will develop into the national language. This position sets the standard for inclusion within the orbit of "Spanish literature" *avant la lettre* (i.e. before 1492 and throughout the medieval period) by saying that it is the linguistic relationship to the language that will eventually become the language of the nation that makes it count or not. This now-canonical vision of the literary history of Spain subsumes a number of dubious principles: that literary history is developmental, so earlier stages are those that lead to later stages; that the literary history of a people in a given period can legitimately be defined by the extent to which their literature is composed in the linguistic harbinger of what will become, some 400 years later, the language of the nation that will succeed and replace those people and their cultures; and that the literatures in other languages, even though they may have been vibrant and indeed central in the earlier period, may be ignored altogether or, at best, studied insofar as they may have constituted "influences" on what is then understood to be the "real thing," i.e. what would one day become important. One need only begin to imagine applying these principles to other historical circumstances – or, perhaps, to imagine what its application might mean 400 years from now when scholars will be writing the literary history of our own times, based on whatever might by then have become the literature of the dominant culture of North America – to begin to understand the gross distortions of cultural history this creates and then reinforces. Beginnings, in this vision, matter only if they lead to certain ends, and this is a treacherous path indeed for the literary historian to follow.

The very widely used literary history of Juan Luis Alborg may be taken as exemplary although it is in fact superior to many (and in that comparable to Amador de los Ríos) in its direct exploration of the prickliest questions.[4] Alborg begins by raising the question of whether it is a matter of the language itself that can determine which of the premodern literatures of the peninsula belongs in a literary history of modern Spain. He does eventually answer that it is, indeed, a linguistic choice, and that *literatura española* is *literatura castellana*, and that the only historical conundrum is the question of the true first instances of Castilian literature. He does not do this, however, until he has conceded that there were a whole series of other languages that might be considered as players in that same literary history: Latin (both classical and medieval, and the versions of these used by the Visigoths and their putative descendants the Mozarabs) as well as *judia* (sic) and *árabe*. For Alborg, though, the decisive factor is ultimately, as a result of that same anachronism of working from

---

[4] Juan Luis Alborg, *Historia de la literatura española* (2nd edn. Madrid: Editorial Gredos, 1970).

back to front, what he describes as being "su repercusión en el *posterior* proceso cultural español" ("its repercussion in the *later* Spanish cultural process";[5] emphasis added), and yet even this formula suggests greater cultural or historical nuance than is really the case here. Alborg and, with him, and after him, an overwhelming majority of scholars (not to speak of the curricula of the majority of Spanish programs) simply rest the case with a direct equation of "castellano" with "español." The two other Romance dialects that were major players in the medieval cultural scene, Catalan and Galician, are, nowadays, allowed secondary roles, in part as a reaction to the rise of the regionalisms in Spain. Yet Arabic and Hebrew, and their extensive literatures, are disqualified, because those languages did not "become" Spanish – and, presumably, because their speakers and writers, and their descendants, did not become Spaniards.

By working backwards (as if the past had serving the present as its principal function) and furthermore by using linguistic criteria without cultural context (or to disguise rather simple cultural–religious prejudices), the commonplace vision of the origins of the literature of Spain has as its own beginning the dismissal of hundreds of years and many libraries' worth of writing by Spaniards, that is, Spaniards who were not Christians – in an era in which Christianity was not at all a passport to citizenship – and who wrote in languages other than Castilian – in a very long era in which Castilian was, at best, one of many legitimate languages, at worst non-existent in the world of culture and literature. Through much of the period Castilian had little or no literature and it was eventually established in great measure through a massive project of translation from Arabic. It may continue to appeal to some to tell the origins story of modern Spain focusing on the tale of how the Castilians worked their way up the literary ladder of medieval Spain, and it serves certain purposes central to the project of creating the modern (i.e. post-1492) Spanish identity. Nevertheless, it egregiously misrepresents the culture of the medieval period, which (much like our own) imagined that its importance was within its own time, and on its own terms.

What is medieval?

The truth is that a new approach to the medieval literary history of Spain – which may or may not then be regarded as the true origins of the rest of Spanish literary history – already exists. A viable model and starting point was created in the mid twentieth century: the conspicuous and exceptionally useful exception to that general practice of excluding all but

[5] Alborg, *Historia*, p. 12.

what looks like what will become Castilian is the multi-volume *Historia general de las literaturas hispánicas* ("General History of Hispanic Literatures"), published in 1949 under the general editorship of Guillermo Díaz-Plaja. The adjective "Hispanic" has been adopted (and adapted) to include *both* of those historical possibilities that make the Spanish case so different, and so much richer, than any other among the modern European national languages: the full range of literatures written by communities living in the peninsula before there was Spanish *and* literatures written in Spanish, regardless of location. That Latin-American literature is thus included as part of this history is hardly revolutionary, although perhaps in the middle of the twentieth century it would have seemed far more audacious than it does today. Still, the first of the six volumes, which has the expected and formulaic "In the beginning" title ("Desde los orígenes hasta 1400" ["From the Origins to 1400"]), is in fact anything but the expected. Instead, it is a radically unconventional depiction of those origins, and the parameters of the study are defined quite directly by Díaz-Plaja in his preface when he says that this book is "una obra en que se intenta captar cuantos valores estéticos ha producido el genio literario albergado en los confines históricos y geográficos que se conocen o que se han conocido alguna vez bajo el nombre de España" ("a work in which we try to capture whatever aesthetic values have been produced by literary genius located in the historical and geographical confines that are known, or that have at some point been known, as Spain").[6]

The first of the essays in Díaz-Plaja's volume (following a long general preface by Ramón Menéndez Pidal) takes us back to the seemingly arcane and even eccentric posture of Amador de los Ríos, beginning at the absolute beginnings of any knowable literature from the Iberian peninsula, i.e. with the literature written in Latin during the Roman period. (This literature formed a substantial part of the canon of the "Silver Age" of Latin–Roman letters, including as it does the younger Seneca, Lucan, Martial, and Quintillian.) The second of the chapters also suggests it will follow that much earlier pattern, focused as it is on the "literatura latinocristiana" ("Latin-Christian literature"), a chapter that includes the writers (not many, to be sure) of Visigothic Spain and culminates in the great Isidore of Seville, whose lifetime dovetails almost uncannily with that of the prophet Muhammad. During the sixty or so years they lived (the prophet's years are known more precisely, 570–632, and Isidore's years are generally given as *c.* 560–634), their universes were as different from each other – and as unimaginable and unknowable to each other – as can be conceived. Within a century of their deaths these starkly different

---

[6] Guillermo Díaz-Plaja, *Historia general de las literaturas hispánicas* (Barcelona: Editorial Borna, 1949), p. ix.

planets would in fact collide, that new order created by the prophet from the Arabian desert replacing and remaking the struggling old order that Isidore had valiantly attempted to keep alive. Therein lies the great challenge to writing a history of the literature of the peninsula: how do we deal with the radical transformations of the old Hispania of Isidore and his ancestors? What follows from that revolution that today would no doubt be cast as a "clash of civilizations"?

Díaz-Plaja's mid twentieth-century functional answers to these and a host of comparably difficult questions are exceptional. The structure of this first volume of the larger history recognizes the pivotal position of Isidore and the complexity and legitimacy of the heterogeneous heritage he represents, and to this the first sections are devoted. Isidore's ancestors were those who, first, shared his language, Latin, and later, and in only a partial continuum with the "HispanoRoman" ancestors (which was a linguistic kinship but a cultural and religious divide), those who shared his religion and its culture, Christianity, but who, unlike the citizens of Rome, had only the most rudimentary appreciation of anything like literature. In that sense, and in others as well, this is not only the first stage but indeed one of the crucial foundations of the medieval chapter – and the classical Latin heritage that stands behind that was important even as a shadow, as a lost standard that made men like Isidore nearly despair of their own times and cultural conditions (and that may have contributed to the attraction of the book-crazed Arabophone world, to which so many Christians would convert). Díaz-Plaja understood that this early medieval Christian culture would encompass the advent of Islam in the peninsula, as well as the flourishing of the Jewish communities and the spectacular renaissance in Hebrew letters that is one of the results of Muslim rule and universal access to Arabic letters. This history openly rejects the widespread conceit that the "Spanish" culture that Isidore represents – and the Latin foundation that lies as a haunting shadow behind that culture – went into isolation until it could re-emerge, fundamentally unscathed, centuries later. It openly maintains that the legitimate trajectory of the literary cultures of Spain must include those that developed in the peninsula that were not Christian and not Castilian or proto-Castilian – those that perhaps did not "lead" to Spanish in the reductive ways we are given to understand the concept of "leading to."

So it is that in this history the complexity of the mid eighth-century transformations get something like their due credit. The bearers of the new faith – which as it happened was radically logocentric and already had a distinctive and revered poetic tradition – were in the very first instance a band of conquering foreigners, a handful of Syrian Arabs and the majority rank-and-file Berbers from just across the Straits of Gibraltar. Within a generation, and in a steeply increasing curve thereafter, and for several centuries after that, the Muslims of this newly named place, al-Andalus, were overwhelmingly converts from all of the older ethnic and religious groups of Isidore's time, and they intermarried with the newer arrivals. "Así pues no se puede dar con propiedad el nombre de 'árabes' a los españoles, sino el de 'españoles musulmanes'" ("So we cannot with any propriety call the Spaniards 'Arabs,' but rather 'Muslim Spaniards'") is the pithy and refreshingly lucid statement on the subject by Elías Terés, author of the central chapter of this section, on "La literatura arábigoespañola" ("Arabic-Spanish Literature").[7] This means, among many other things, that the fantasy elaborated in the fifteenth and sixteenth centuries, that Christians were of a different race from Muslims (and Jews, of course), and thus always of a different language and culture along with their different blood, is delusional in various ways.

In the first instance, as Terés points out (and as most historians have known for some time), most of those Muslims participating in the extensive and rich Arabic literary culture that was the hallmark of Andalusian culture for many centuries were the descendants of converts and of intermarriages. Even beyond that, what we also know is that, with the exception of a radicalized minority, even those who remained Christians became, like the Jews, members of the multilingual community of medieval Spain, which means that even if we were explicitly to restrict the original "Spanishness" as an identity admitting to only one religion, Arabic literary culture would, even then, need to play a central role in the medieval Spanish canon. The famous lament of Paul Alvarus of Cordoba, the outspoken mid ninth-century opponent of the Arabization of the Christians, paints a vivid enough picture of the integration of Christians into the Arabophone community, which included both Muslims and Jews:

The Christians love to read the poems and romances of the Arabs; they study the Arab theologians and philosophers, not to refute them but to form a correct and elegant Arabic. Where is the layman who now reads the Latin commentaries on the Holy Scriptures, or who studies the Gospels, prophets or apostles? Alas! All talented young Christians read and study with enthusiasm the Arab books; they gather immense libraries at great expense; they despise the Christian literature as unworthy of attention. They have forgotten their own language. For every one who can write a letter in Latin to a friend, there are a thousand who can express themselves in Arabic with elegance, and write better poems in this language than the Arabs themselves.[8]

---

[7] Elías Terés, "La literatura arábigoespañola." In *Historia general de las literaturas hispánicas*. Ed. Guillermo Díaz-Plaja (Barcelona: Editorial Vergara, 1949–1968), vol. I, p. 219.
[8] Jerrilyn Dodds, *Architecture and Ideology in Early Medieval Spain* (State Park: Pennsylvania University Press, 1990), p. 67.

Like Amador de los Ríos, Díaz-Plaja includes a chapter on the culture of these Arabized Christians but the context could not be more different, following as it does both a chapter on "Literatura hebraicoespañola" (written by the then-dean of that field, Millás Vallicrosa) and, centrally, the comprehensive piece on the nearly seven centuries of literature in "arábigoespañol" by Elías Terés.

This vision of Spain in the Middle Ages, both implicit and occasionally explicit in this volume, thus provides a rather different point of departure than the one most literary histories offer, where a rough-and-tumble frontier people in the eleventh century begin the long process of creating a new literature from scratch, singing about their warrior heroes in a language that knows no written form, and which can only lay the essentially primitive (even if sometimes moving) groundwork for what will one day achieve true poetic status, roughly around the time that Castilian is well on the way to being the only form of Spanish literary culture. Here, instead, it begins with a community for which, already in the eighth century, Arabic had long been the language first and foremost of immensely sophisticated poetry (as well as of all the other belletristic forms, including philosophy and the sciences). As Terés puts it: "Siendo objeto de universal cultivo por parte de los árabes, la poesía irrumpió en España en el momento mismo de la invasión. Según una noticia – *que parece falsa pero aún en su falsedad es simbólica* – ya Táriq el conquistador cantó en verso su paso del Estrecho" ("Being the object of general cultivation by the Arabs, poetry burst into Spain at the same time as the invasion. According to one report – *which seems to be false, although in its falseness it is still symbolic* – the conquerer Tariq already sang in verse his ride over the Straits [of Gibraltar]").[9]

Even if this attribution to the conqueror of a first poem for this new beginning in Spain is apocryphal (and thus all the more telling, as Terés perceptively notes), there is a historically better documented first poem from later in that same eighth century. This different beginning for the brand-new Andalusian culture is one written by the man who, a generation later than the conqueror, is readily identifiable as its truer founding father, Abd al-Rahman. He was a first-generation immigrant in exile in what was, when he arrived, the outer province of al-Andalus. At the same time he can legitimately be understood as the first poet of the brave new world he himself would craft, transforming that outland into a new center, a homeland for the not-quite-exterminated Umayyads, and for their expansive cultural vision of Islam. Abd al-Rahman himself is a symbol of the productive fusions of that civilization, himself the child of an ethnically mixed marriage, as well as the scion of a dynasty that had promiscuously

---

[9] Terés, "La literatura arábigoespañola," p. 233. Emphasis added.

taken and reshaped so much from the cultures it had encountered during its previous century of vast expansion. In a literary history of Spain creative or audacious enough to define the radical reconfigurations of the eighth century as the legitimate beginnings of a crucial chapter in that history, Abd al-Rahman's famous ode to a palm tree could stand as an iconic first monument of Spanish literature:

> A palm tree stands in the middle of Rusafa,
> Born in the West, far from the land of palms.
> I said to it: How like me you are, far away and in exile,
> In long separation from family and friends.
> You have sprung from soil in which you are a stranger;
> And I, like you, am far from home.[10]

This linguistically, religiously, and culturally complex picture of pre-fifteenth-century Spain is eventually continued with a chapter by Menéndez Pidal on the so-called "School of Translators" and then, and only then, moves on to a section on "España romance, siglos XII–XIV" ("Ballad in Spain, 12th–14th centuries"), which now self-evidently follows in a variety of complex ways – accepting or rejecting, as often as not some of both – from everything that has preceded it. The architecture of Díaz-Plaja's volume, and the ideology that lies behind it, suggest a number of principles about Spanish literature *avant la lettre* that may seem, today, self-evident and valuable, and yet very few of them have shaped literary histories in the more than half-century since that ambitious work was published. This is a picture of a Spain which, before the establishment of Castilian as the national language (and with it Christianity as the unique national religion, and presumably with a correspondingly orthodox literary culture), was not really that later Spain at all, but rather one radically different from it, at least as different as the long-vanished Roman past, which is rarely adduced as the "origins" of Spanish literature. What does not happen here is that all-too-typical retrospective imposition of the later development on the earlier stages.

The answer to what is medieval here is simple but unusual, and it ought to be our own: it is not merely what develops into the modern, it is in fact a great deal more than what would survive (or be allowed to survive) into the properly Spanish era. Here, then, there is far more than the usual passing mention (if that) of the Jews having a reinvention of poetry in their Golden Age in Spain (which in fact occurs during the same century in which the nascent Romance vernaculars are creating new poetries). Here, instead, the Jews (to take only this example, for the moment) are as much (or as little) Spaniards as anyone else inside the volume – from Seneca to

---

[10] Cited in Ruggles, *Gardens*, p. 42.

Alfonso el Sabio – and their literature the subject of an extensive central chapter. This reflects the reality in the historical moment in which their culture flourished in Spain; their literature is in Hebrew, but that too is part of a Spanish tradition defined now as being multifaceted and encompassing languages that would later be rejected and exiled, and is thus named *literatura hebraicoespañola* ("Hebrew-Spanish literature"). One notes that here it is not even "hispánico" but "español" that is married to "hebraico" – as it is in "arábigoespañol."

What is lost?

The greatest challenge for literary histories that would want to follow this as a model is the *de facto* segregation it allows, since what these separate (if theoretically equal) chapters cannot really do is give a sense of how these different religious communities mostly also lived inside the shared cultural community that was the very essence of medieval Spain. What is lost, in the universe in which one community of scholars (and literary histories and courses and reading lists, the whole canonical apparatus that passes knowledge on, from one generation to the next) is devoted to one of the several languages of Toledo in the eleventh and twelfth and even thirteenth centuries (to take an easy example), while a completely different scholarly community, mostly incommunicado from the first, takes care of another of those languages, and the same for a third, and so forth? Clearly, we are never able to recover much of a sense of the extent to which the originality and achievements of medieval Spanish culture lay precisely in the lavish interplay of these languages – and their people, and their literature – and in all of the arts, in fact, since these productive inter-marriages are everywhere, strikingly visible in architecture, for example, and understood clearly in music. Even when there were intact and separate religious communities, with their separate religious languages and beliefs, there was at the same time a degree of cultural intermingling and interchange whose first recorded – and lamented! – instance is perhaps that complaint by Paul Alvarus, about how well all those young Christian men knew their Arabic poetry. It does not occur to most literary historians of our own time that when they exclude that Arabic literature of which those Christians were so enamored (and much of which had in fact been written by Spaniards, Muslims whose ancestry in Spain by the mid ninth century went back more years than most Americans can claim for theirs in the United States), they are following the ideological program of religious and linguistic separation that Alvarus and others like him (eventually including the whole of the Inquisitorial tradition in the fifteenth and sixteenth centuries) wanted the Spaniards of their day and age to follow. This separation has been more successful, ironically enough, among twentieth-century Hispanists, who seem to believe, by and large, that the long and venerable Arabic poetic tradition of Spain – the one so adored by even mid ninth-century Christians, who learned Arabic to read it and write it – is, after all, to be left to the Arabists.

What we should understand is that throughout the Middle Ages that segregationist and monolingual principle simply did not exist, or utterly failed when attempts were made to enforce it, and that, clearly, is what Alvarus' lament reveals: it is the depths of cultural assimilation and give-and-take that we glimpse there – and not its opposite, not what it is normally taken to mean, that the Christian community successfully resisted the cultural intermingling. Indeed, most of the other evidence surrounding the case of the famous Mozarab martyrs whom Paul Alvarus wrote about suggests that the Christian hierarchy of Cordoba was opposed to and appalled by their acts of gross and suicidal provocation of the Islamic state, into which most Christians (and churchmen) were fully integrated and within which they were protected (short of the sort of public blasphemy in which the martyrs indulged, knowing it would get them executed). Indeed, the old Visigothic liturgy in Latin was eventually translated into Arabic and it was in that language that it survived, intact and in its original form, for hundreds of years – only to be replaced eventually by the reformed Roman rite brought by the French Benedictine monks from Cluny toward the end of the eleventh century, a change bitterly contested by Spanish Christians for hundreds of years, since for them it was the Mozarabic rite, in Arabic (and not the newfangled version the northerners brought with them), that was the symbol of authentic Spanish Christianity, and its rite the remaining traditional one in Christendom. Medieval Spaniards of many different stripes appreciated that there was a radical difference between a religion, on the one hand, and a literary and philosophical culture, on the other.

It is difficult, when there are separate accounts of each of the religious–language communities, to convey how central a role both social and literary integration played in defining the character of medieval Spanish literature. One relatively straightforward example can stand for much else here: the Jews of the eleventh-century Golden Age were also, easily and simultaneously, readers and writers of the Arabic literary traditions, and in fact it was their expertise in Arabic letters that frequently won them high-ranking positions in Muslim dominions and, eventually, in Christian Spain, where their role as translators is well known. It was that intimate knowledge and love of Arabic poetry that made possible their creation of a quasi-vernacular literary Hebrew, the basis of the extraordinary reinvention of secular poetry in that long-fossilized liturgical language. At the same time, the Jews would also have been speakers of whatever the vernacular was wherever they lived, certainly the Arabic vernacular during the years of the caliphate, but also one or more of the Romance vernaculars as well, beginning with the Romance spoken by the Mozarabs, those Christians who were so thoroughly assimilated into the Arabophone world, and ending, well, ending with the fifteenth-century Castilian they called *Ladino* (from "Latino," to distinguish it from Arabic and Hebrew) and took with them into exile after 1492, and continued to speak in exile until the twentieth century. To return for just one more moment to that eleventh century: when the Andalusian Jews were dramatically rewriting the history of Hebrew poetry it just so happens that other poetries were being dramatically reinvented as well. This is the pivotal moment in the history of the nascent Romance languages when the vernaculars were boldly emerging as the poetic languages that would throw out the old (Latin) and "make it new," as Ezra Pound, a devoted student of the earliest Romance lyrics, would famously say in his 1934 Modernist manifesto.

Medieval Europe in general (and Spain exceptionally so) is infinitely more variegated than the later periods can imagine, following as they do the establishment of single and defining national languages. The powerful culture of translation – a far more ubiquitous and disorganized and defining cultural phenomenon than what might be understood if we focus only on the phenomenon of the official "School of Translators" – was the Latin-Christian reaction to its direct exposure to the riches of the vast Arabic libraries, and this too began in the same eleventh century in which the new poetries in Hebrew and Romance were the poetic avant-gardes. In 1948, when we must assume the first volume of the *Historia general de las literaturas hispánicas* was in press, a Hebraist named Samuel Stern published an article that would reveal that there were, after all, surviving texts attesting to a literature that directly reflected those very interactions among languages and traditions and peoples that are nearly impossible to account for in a scholarly universe demarcated by national (and even religious) boundaries that were anything but divisions in the Middle Ages. What Stern exposed (and deciphered) was a body of poems written in either classical Hebrew or Arabic with a refrain – which in fact sets the versification and rhyme scheme for the whole of the poem – in a vernacular, most notably in the Romance vernacular that was the other language (besides Arabic) of the Christians known as Mozarabs. These poems were, and are, self-evidently the product of that complex and energetic universe of the Spanish eleventh century, and the news of their existence provoked scholarly excitement, although principally, and very ironically, on something like "nationalistic" grounds, since it was hailed as an earlier springtime for Romance verse than anyone had imagined. The Romance part of the poems – the refrains, and only the refrains in Mozarabic, for that matter – are divorced from the rest of their poems, from the Hebrew and Arabic strophes which the Romance verses punctuate. As isolated snippets they become, in Spanish literary history, that elusive "first monument" of Spanish literature. Perhaps nothing speaks more clearly to the folly and the distortions of this backwards approach to the Spanish Middle Ages than this, the dismemberment of a bilingual poem, a poem whose bilingualism is not casual but rather foundational, and where the vernacular is not carelessly tacked on at the end, but rather, as with the society that produced it, the various languages, sometimes tied to religions and sometimes not, are intimately interlaced throughout.

What is lost in medieval Spanish literature is, in the first instance, the texts that did not survive the ravages of history: first, the commonplace conservation problems, those that wreak havoc with manuscripts, and that no doubt destroyed textual evidence of earlier versions of the story told in the famous *Poema de mío Cid* ("Poem of the Cid," written in the mid twelfth century, first copied down in 1207), to take but this one famous example; and second, the particular Spanish problems that led to the wholesale and purposeful destruction of books in Arabic and Hebrew in (especially) the sixteenth century. This latter practice was slyly satirized by Miguel de Cervantes with his "Inquisition of the Books" in Part I (chapter 5) of *Don Quijote* (1605) and then even more poignantly reflected in that most self-referential moment, in chapter 9, when the narrator discovers the manuscript that contains the story he is telling: an Arabic manuscript, about to be turned into pulp, in the old Jewish quarter of Toledo. Far more is lost than what has vanished materially, and perhaps the limits of our understanding of the literary history of medieval Spain are best symbolized by what happened to these bilingual poems after they were discovered, a fate of dismemberment worthy of Cervantine satire: we segregate the rich and interwoven traditions of the peninsula in ways that do extreme violence to the original literary cloth, that tear into rag-like pieces what was originally crafted as a luxurious fabric.[11]

If the medieval is going to constitute the "beginnings" of the Spanish tradition then it can only do that after the medieval literary scene is understood on its own terms, and in its own languages.

---

[11] Two recent books which attempt to provide a grounding in the literatures and cultures of Islamic Spain are the encyclopedic tome edited by Salma Khaddra Jayyusi (*The Legacy of Muslim* Spain [Leiden: Brill, 1992]); and *The Cambridge History of Arabic Literature: Al-Andalus.* Ed. Maria Rosa Menocal, Raymond Scheindlin, and Michael Sells (Cambridge: Cambridge University Press, 2000).

4

The poetry of medieval Spain

ANDREW M. BERESFORD

In common with other European societies, the earliest vernacular narrative poetry in Spain originated in the form of the heroic epic, a type of poem that has often been defined as dealing with the pursuit of honor through risk. Narrative poetry of this type generally developed later than its lyric equivalent, and this can be attributed to the fact that its content requires the existence of a degree of social, political, and cultural sophistication on the part of the audience for whom it was intended. This sophistication, however, does not imply that vernacular poets and their audiences were yet fully literate, because the earliest epics were likely to have been orally composed and diffused by *juglares* ("minstrels"), whose works were seldom committed to writing; of those that were, it is thought that many were obtained as a result of dictation, and none has survived in its original form. The essence of this type of poetry lies in its communal spirit and in the telling of great deeds undertaken by larger-than-life heroes whose actions embody the values of the community and celebrate the existence of a bygone, heroic age. Its effect is threefold: it informs and entertains while also inspiring the audience to emulate the heroism of their forebears.

The earliest heroic epics in Spanish dealt with the Counts of Castile and the events that were believed to have transpired under their rule. If other types of epic were composed, no record of them has survived, and so these texts represent the first steps in the establishment of an autonomous Castilian identity. The earliest poem, the *Siete infantes de Lara* ("Seven Princes of Lara"), has long since been lost, but as it was reworked into chronicles by scribes who plundered it for information, its contents can be partially reconstructed on the basis of assonance (or vowel rhyme) patterns that became fossilized within their prose. Some 550 or so lines have so far been reconstructed, and although not all critics remain convinced of their authenticity, they nonetheless tell an interesting story. What is most noticeable is that the *Siete infantes* is founded on a metrical system that consists of irregular assonanced lines of between fourteen and sixteen syllables gathered into *tiradas* ("narrative sections") of uneven length. Formulaic phrases and epithets are common, and there are many other hallmarks of an oral style; but the nature of the reconstruction makes it difficult to determine whether the arrangement is necessarily a product of oral, erudite, or mixed composition.

The text of the *Siete infantes* reveals a good deal about the nature of society at the close of the millennium: the power of bonds of kinship and of feudal loyalty, the savagery of blood feuds and of military confrontation, and the fragile nature of life itself. Nowhere are these elements more touchingly expressed than in the lament of Gonzalo Gústios over the heads of his seven sons. Yet, the poem's most important attribute lies in its religious, ethnic, and political consciousness, and in the depiction of a series of noble values challenged not by Muslim Spain, but by the enemy within. This factor underlines the vulnerability of Castilian independence in this period, and it is by no means coincidental that similar sentiments are displayed in three related texts: the *Condesa traidora* ("Treacherous Countess") and the *Romanz del infant García* ("Poem of Prince García"), which have survived only as prose, and the *Poema de Fernán González* ("Poem of Fernán González"), a mid thirteenth-century clerical reworking. These texts describe the fortunes of the Counts of Castile from the time of Fernán González through to the reign of his great-grandson, García Sánchez, and although some evidence suggests that they were composed in the form of an epic cycle, it is more likely that they appeared in isolation from one another.

The emergence of Castile as a dominant force in the peninsula is also attested by a later branch of epic dealing with the exploits of the Cid, Rodrigo (or Ruy) Díaz de Vivar. Born around 1043, the Cid served as a knight under Fernando I until the king's death in 1065; his allegiance then passed to Sancho II, king of Castile, until he was murdered as he laid siege to his brother and sister (Alfonso and Urraca) at Zamora in 1072. (These events are depicted in a lost epic known as the *Cantar de Sancho II* ["Poem of Sancho II"]). Thereafter, the Cid maintained an uneasy relationship with the new king, Alfonso, and was twice exiled from his kingdom. The second exile provides the starting point for the *Poema* or *Cantar de mío Cid* ("Poem of the Cid"), a heroic epic of some 3,700 lines, the date of which remains uncertain (critics place its composition between 1105 and 1178). The *Cantar* is a masterpiece of early Spanish literature that exists in a unique manuscript, copied in 1207. Theories concerning the composition of the text are many, but most would now agree that it is the product of a learned poet with legal training, and with ecclesiastical connections in the Burgos area, most probably with the monastery of San Pedro de Cardeña.

The *Cantar* is a subtle blend of fact and fiction that characterizes the Cid as the embodiment of a series of noble, Castilian virtues. These include the conventional characteristics of *fortitudo* ("strength") and *sapientia* ("knowledge") as well as *mesura*, a quality that embraces prudence, forbearing, and moderation. The *Cantar* itself is composed in a style akin to that of the *Siete infantes*, and this allows the poet flexibility in the way that he shapes materials. Structurally, the poem is divided into three sections, although the essence of the plot is binary: the first part dealing with the Cid's banishment, and the second, the Infantes de Carrión. These sections are unified by the Cid's loss of honor and by Alfonso's role in restoring it, and this has led critics to focus on the national sentiments of the work, and how Alfonso, a Leonese king, is educated by his Castilian vassal. This dimension is introduced at an early stage with the exclamation "¡Dios, qué buen vassallo, si oviesse buen señor!" ("God what a good vassal, if only he had a good lord!" line 20), and reaches its climax when the poet finally characterizes Alfonso as a good Castilian king. To describe the *Cantar* as a purely political text, however, would be to overlook the power of its human perspective: the concern of a man for the wellbeing of his wife and daughters. This aspect of the poem is finely blended with its wider national sentiments and produces some of the most remarkable poetry.

By the close of the twelfth century, the social and political instabilities that had coincided with the age of heroic epic had largely passed, and so literary attention turned instead toward a type of poetry that dealt with more universal, rather than strictly national, themes. These poems, composed in octosyllabic couplets, share the metrical irregularity of the epic and were probably designed for oral performance rather than private reading. Two of them, the *Disputa del alma y del cuerpo* ("Debate between the Soul and the Body") and the *Vida de Santa María Egipciaca* ("Life of Saint Mary of Egypt"), are based on near-contemporary French models, and this may reflect the expansion of Cluniac power in the peninsula and the popularization of the tomb cult of Saint James in the form of the Pilgrim Route to Santiago de Compostela. A third text, the *Libre dels tres reys d'Orient* ("Book of the Three Kings of the East"), is derived from the Apocrypha, while the source of a fourth, *Razón de amor con los denuestos del agua y del vino* ("Poem of Love with the Debate between Water and Wine") has defied attempts at identification; its second part, however, assumes the form of a debate, and this has often been taken as a hallmark of Goliardic influence. As a recognizable grouping, these poems marked a sea change in literary tastes, for in contrast to the acutely introspective nature of epic, they each deal with foreign subjects. The *Vida* and the *Libre* take place in the eastern Mediterranean, the *Disputa* describes the fate of an anonymous knight (although there is some local color), while the narrator of the *Razón* declares that he has lived in Germany, France, and Lombardy; the extent to which this can be interpreted as an indication of textual provenance, however, remains debatable, particularly in the light of a rather oblique, subsequent reference to Spain.

The most significant common denominator of these works, apart from their pan-European focus, is that they generate much of their meaning through contrasts between antithetical states of being. To some extent this could be regarded as a continuation of the partisan ethos of epic, but the themes that are considered are more wide-ranging: body versus soul, sin versus sanctity, faith versus doubt, and water versus wine. In two of the four this type of construction is a natural consequence of the narration of debates between rival parties; in the *Vida* and the *Libre*, on the other hand, the contrasts are internal: the former describes the chiasmic evolution of a libidinous sinner into a model of saintly perfection (as Mary grows spiritually, her once beautiful exterior withers and dies as her inner corruption is drawn to the surface), while the latter draws a spectacular threefold distinction between groups of virtuous and ignorant characters. In view of the binary flavor of these works, it is hardly surprising that critics have searched for similar contrasts in *Razón de amor* – the solution most commonly proposed being the distinction between chaste and sexual love. Scholarship, however, has not yet arrived at a satisfactory conclusion, or, indeed, demonstrated how the encounter between the narrator and his lady in the first part is unified with the subsequent debate between water and wine. Some have even postulated that the *Razón* consists of two poems rather than one, although there is little agreement on how they might have been joined.

The extent to which these works can be regarded as products of a school of writing is debatable, but it is noticeable that the similarities that exist between them outweigh the number of differences, chiefly in the selection of a rhyming (as opposed to assonanced) verse form, the adoption of a popular tone suited to oral delivery, and the relative universality of their content and focus. These elements are made more noticeable by the emergence in the early thirteenth century of a poetic school known as the *mester de clerecía*. These poets, whose works grew out of the monasteries of northern Spain, developed a verse form known as *cuaderna vía*: quatrains of monorhymed Alexandrines (or fourteen-syllable lines), divided by a central caesura. This type of verse lends itself both to private reading and to recitation among small groups; little is known about performance, but it is assumed that some would have been read to groups of pilgrims and monks, while secular compositions would have been read elsewhere. The earliest poem of this type, the *Libro de Alexandre* ("Book of Alexander"), offers a comment on the emergence of this style, affirming that the metrically correct poetry of the *clerecía* stands in opposition to the sinful works of the *juglaría* ("minstrels"). Although the nature of this distinction is exaggerated (the *clerecía* poets borrowed various minstrel techniques, and its most famous exponent even referred to himself as a *juglar*), the advent of this type of poetry marked the death knell of the early, popular style.

The earliest poems of the *mester de clerecía* are outward-looking, and deal not with Spain, but with the rich and exotic world of the eastern Mediterranean. The *Libro de Alexandre*, based on a subtle combination of Latin and vernacular sources, paints a vivid picture of the life and campaigns of Alexander the Great, a figure of constant fascination in the Middle Ages. The structure of the text has often been criticized, particularly the digression on the Trojan War, which seems long and cumbersome; yet, in recent years, critics have commented on its relationship to the main narrative and how it carefully underlines Alexander's flaws, chiefly his pride and his insatiable craving for yet greater glories. Similar in focus is the *Libro de Apolonio* ("Book of Apolonius"), a work that deals with an intellectual protagonist whose youthful, academic vanity leads him into a series of misadventures that are resolved only in the twilight of his life by an act of divine intervention. In many ways Apolonius and Alexander resemble each other: their lives take place in distant, bygone ages, they assemble great empires (whether by desire or default), and they suffer as a result of their imperfections. Yet, while Alexander inspires respect and awe, Apolonius elicits pity and compassion; this is partly the result of the interpolation of moralizing digressions by the *Apolonio* poet, but it can also be seen in their respective fates: Apolonius repents and spends many years in a state of strict asceticism, refusing even to cut his hair or fingernails; Alexander, in contrast, remains unrepentant and there is no clear evidence to suggest that he is saved.

Although the poems of the *mester de clerecía* differ from those of the minstrels, there is, nonetheless, a good deal of common ground. An example of this can be seen in the *Libro de Apolonio*, for, despite its status as a romance, its content is by no means dissimilar to that of hagiographic texts such as the *Vida de Santa María Egipciaca* and the *Libre dels tres reys d'Orient*. All three poems describe journeys through the lands of classical antiquity, and in each there is an evolution from youthful transgression to a mature resolution with the divine; critics have even noticed elements of hagiography in the character of Apolonius himself. In view of these similarities it hardly seems coincidental that the only surviving copies of the poems can be found in a single, unique manuscript. This type of overlap, however, is relatively common, for the development of early Spanish poetry cannot be classified according to a series of watertight categories. The *Vida de Santa María Egipciaca* and *Razón de amor* borrow much from the early lyric tradition; hagiographic elements, on the other hand, have been traced in the lives of epic heroes such as the Cid; even more noticeable is that the only early poetic treatment of the first Count of Castile (the *Poema de Fernán González*) exists not as an epic, but in a *mester de clerecía* form. The result is a fascinating hybrid: a heroic poem, composed in a clerical style (around 1250), that makes good use of history and folklore as well as the Bible and Christian tradition.

The *Poema* itself is a retrospective piece that, in common with the poems on Alexander and Apolonius, narrates the achievements of a heroic figure of the past in order to encourage the audience to imitate his actions in the present. Yet, unlike its counterparts, the national and local flavor of the piece is unmistakable: Fernán González is not a distant figure, whose deeds are of theoretical or abstract significance, but a Castilian, the sweat of whose brow was spent in ensuring the liberation of Castile from Leonese hegemony. In many ways, however, the poem is more local than that, for, just as the *Cantar de mío Cid* is related to the monastery of San Pedro de Cardeña, Fernán González maintains an equally palpable relationship with the monastery of San Pedro de Arlanza. Once again, a degree of cross-fertilization is at work: religious centers, eager to exploit the potency of the relics or reputations of secular heroes, accorded them a degree of respect that was otherwise granted only to the saints; in this way they could increase their prominence, and, as a result, attract much-needed revenues.

In the work of the Riojan poet, Gonzalo de Berceo, monastic interest in literary production reached its zenith. As far we can be certain, Berceo, the first named poet to write in the vernacular, was born in 1196 and educated at the Benedictine monastery of San Millán de la Cogolla. Following his investiture as a deacon, he may have attended classes at the University of Palencia, and then served not as a monk, but as notary to the abbot. Despite the demands of this position, Berceo dedicated much of his time to literary production, and the various poems that have survived (several others are lost) make him the most the prolific poet of the thirteenth century. Berceo's earliest works were probably written after the *Alexandre* but before the *Apolonio* and the *Fernán González*. Although many aspects of the chronology of the *mester de clerecía* remain uncertain, critics agree that his writing continued unabated until the 1260s. His poetry, therefore, straddles a period of nearly forty years, and, on this basis, critics have sometimes been tempted to overstate his involvement in the *clerecía* style: his alleged authorship of the *Alexandre* is based on stylistic similarities and the inclusion of a corrupt stanza bearing his name in one of the extant manuscripts, while his supposed association with the *Fernán González* poet in Palencia is probably no more than a geographical coincidence.

Berceo's poetic output falls into four overlapping phases. His first and most enduring love was hagiography and the cults of the saints associated with the monastery. His earliest works, the *Vida de San Millán de la Cogolla* ("Life of Saint Æmilian") and the *Vida de Santo Domingo de Silos*

("Life of Saint Dominic"), date from the 1230s and deal with saints who dedicate themselves to a variety of roles before embarking on monastic vocations. Both poems are divided into three books: the first narrating the saints' lives; the second, their miracles; and the third, their posthumous interventions in the lives of the devout. This structure produces similarities, particularly at the level of character, and this underlines an important theological principle: that the suffering of the saint is a reenactment of that of Christ, and thus, by definition, of the fact that all saints are one. Yet, in other respects, the poems are different. *San Millán*, for instance, contains a propagandistic section in which Saints Æmilian and James appear in the sky above a battle fought by Fernán González. This part of the poem exudes the spirit of heroic epic and attempts to legitimize the status of a forged decree that Castile should pay tribute to the monastery. Although *Santo Domingo* is equally propagandistic in its attempt to attract pilgrims (the most conspicuous evidence being the narrator's negative view of lengthy pilgrimages, presumably to Santiago), it includes a vivid allegorical dream and a confrontation between Church and State in which the saint comes close to suffering martyrdom. A further distinction lies in the treatment of banishment, for, like the Cid, Dominic is forced from his homelands, only to return after establishing a formidable reputation in exile. This aspect of the text represents a Christianization of the mythic hero pattern.

In the years following these poems Berceo moved away from hagiography in order to explore other subjects. Two of his works are doctrinal: *Del sacrificio de la Misa* ("On the Sacrifice of the Mass") offers a detailed analysis of the symbolism and ritual of the Mass while *Los signos del Juicio Final* ("The Signs of the Last Judgment") presents an apocalyptic vision of the end of the world. A more significant phase in Berceo's development is his treatment of the cult of the Virgin in three poems thought to have been composed between 1236 and 1252. The earliest of these, *El duelo de la Virgen* ("The Virgin's Lament") and the *Loores de Nuestra Señora* ("A Eulogy on Our Lady") deal with Mary's position as the mother of Christ and with her role in the Crucifixion and Resurrection. The poet's most accessible Marian work, however, is the *Milagros de Nuestra Señora* ("Miracles of Our Lady"). This text, arguably Berceo's most accomplished, is based on a Latin prose collection of twenty-eight miracles, the majority of which existed in various versions throughout Europe. Of these, Berceo discarded four, and, in their place, interpolated an allegorical prologue and an introductory miracle dealing with Saint Ildefonsus.

In common with the miracles in his early hagiographic texts, the quality of the *Milagros* is mixed: some are weakly constructed (notably Miracles I and X), while others contain some of the most skillful poetry to have been composed in medieval Spain. An excellent example is "El clérigo ignorante" ("The Ignorant Cleric," Miracle IX), a short, bipartite poem dealing with a cleric whose intellectual shortcomings are redeemed by his devotion to the Virgin. This text represents Berceo at his best, blending coarse vulgarity with complex theological problems relating to the development of the medieval Church. Yet, despite the nature of the collection, readers are offered few details about the identity of the Virgin herself. In *La boda y la Virgen* ("The Wedding and the Virgin," Miracle XV) she is presented as a jilted bride, angered at the marriage of a young cleric, while in *La abadesa preñada* ("The Pregnant Abbess," Miracle XXI) she becomes a female confidante, able to understand and to forgive the sexual transgression of an abbess; this text, one of the longest of the collection, offers a unique insight into ecclesiastical and lay attitudes toward women and their sexual and hierarchical status.

In the twilight of his life Berceo returned to hagiography, and composed poems in honor of two other saints associated with the monastery. The earliest of these, the *Vida de Santa Oria* ("Life of Saint Oria"), is a unique composition that focuses on the life and visions of a humble Benedictine anchoress, while the *Martirio de San Lorenzo* ("Martyrdom of Saint Lawrence") deals with the Hispano-Roman martyr. These poems underline the extent to which Berceo's interests developed, for, in contrast to his early hagiography, the tripartite structure is abandoned, and in its place we are offered a more flexible exploration of individual suffering: the inexorable physical atrophy of an anchoress in her cell and the death of a martyr roasted slowly on a grid-iron. Yet both poems are problematic: *Lorenzo* ends prematurely, while the extant manuscripts of *Oria* contain several lacunae and a sequence of stanzas that is obviously corrupt. Reasons for these problems have been considered by various critics, but there is little agreement on how they might be resolved. This is largely due to the fact that while *Lorenzo* departs significantly from its source, *Oria* is a more original composition based on local traditions and hagiographic borrowings.

With the death of Berceo the *clerecía* style fell abruptly out of fashion and was replaced by a period of innovation that soon declined into a literary crisis characterized by stagnation and decay. This was partly the result of social upheaval: the final years of the reign of Alfonso X were marked by bitter conflicts, and the succession of the child kings, Fernando IV (1295) and Alfonso XI (1312), only served to exacerbate existing tensions. The pace of the Reconquest – the campaign to recapture the peninsula from the Moors, who had successfully invaded in the year 711 – had decreased, and depopulation and economic decline had thwarted attempts at commercial development. Intellectual resources, on the other hand, remained weak, and despite a number of minor chronological overlaps, it appears that Spain could not yet sustain more than one poetic tradition at a time. The result of this crisis, while not in itself catastrophic, was nonetheless undesirable: a series of predictable and mediocre works punctuated by the occasional mature and sophisticated composition. The advances made in the early and central portions of the thirteenth century were thus neglected, and it was not until the mid fourteenth century that Spanish poetry began to reassert itself with confidence.

The latter years of the thirteenth century had in fact promised a great deal. A small but interesting group of works, many with a surprising degree of structural and metrical inventiveness, had departed from earlier traditions in order to explore more imaginative styles of poetic cohesion. One of these, a short lyrical piece known as *¡Ay Jerusalem!* ("Oh Jerusalem!"), partially fills a lacuna in the literary history of Spain, for, in contrast to the flourishing traditions of other nations, it is the only extant poem to deal with the Crusades. The absence of parallel compositions is understandable: Spain's internal struggles (against Muslim and Christian alike) prevented it from taking an interest in the eastern Mediterranean. Yet *¡Ay Jerusalem!* is by no means a simple curiosity, for it contains a series of unique features, including a polymetric verse form with long and short lines, a flexible refrain, and an acrostic derived from the first letter of each stanza. The poem is accompanied in a unique manuscript by a version of the Ten Commandments composed in rhyming couplets, and a contemplation of the Fall (*El Dio alto que los cielos sostiene* ["The God on High who Maintains the Heavens"]; this piece, composed in *cuaderna vía*, contains traces of Judaic involvement, principally in the use of *Dio* (as opposed to *Dios*). The most remarkable aspect of the manuscript, however, is the blend of poetic forms: *cuaderna vía*, rhyming couplets, and the more elaborate *¡Ay Jerusalem!* This multifaceted quality ranks it alongside the *Apolonio – Santa María – Tres reys* manuscript in terms of broad poetic diversity.

In the *Historia troyana polimétrica* ("Polymetric History of Troy") the process of innovation that characterized literary production at the close of the century is taken to an unparalleled extreme in a cycle of eleven poems that are most notable for their sophisticated fusion of form and content. The *Historia* recounts the events of the Trojan War, and, in many ways, its fascination with the lands and lessons of antiquity makes it akin to works composed more than half a century earlier. The scope of the texts, however, is more wide-ranging, with epic descriptions of battle (IV), hypnotic prophesies (II), and a particularly fine series of compositions dealing with Troilus and Cressida (V–VII). These poems, dominated by the rhetoric of courtly love, medievalize the events of antiquity by recontextualizing classical characters according to contemporary norms. A less sentimental representation of love is present in *Elena y María* ("Helen and Mary"), an incomplete debate thought to have been composed around 1280. This poem, in common with earlier French models, presents a dialogue between the mistresses of a knight and a clerk, with the two speakers making a series of absorbing, if outlandish, claims to supremacy. The courtly ethos is unmistakable, with palaces, hawks, and falcons much in evidence, but this is tempered by moments of rugged earthiness. The poem, however, is perhaps best understood as a satire of the three estates: an effete and indolent aristocracy versus a voracious and sexually corrupt clergy; the existence of the peasantry, irrelevant to the other estates, is not even recorded.

Despite the advances made by *¡Ay Jerusalem!* and the *Historia troyana*, by the turn of the century the atmosphere of poetic inventiveness had waned as writers began to look more to the past than to the future. To some extent this can be seen in the resurrection of earlier traditions: *Roncesvalles*, for instance, is a fragment of a heroic epic dealing with Charlemagne and the death of Roland. The majority of works in this period, however, are religious compositions that adopt the *cuaderna vía* stanza of the earlier *clerecía* poets. The *Vida de San Ildefonso* ("Life of Saint Ildefonsus"), composed by a "Beneficiado de Úbeda," for example, is a hagiographic narrative dealing with the celebrated Archbishop of Toledo. This poem bears an uncanny resemblance to Berceo's early hagiographic narratives, but it generally lacks his inventiveness. Similar accusations can be levelled against the *Libro de miseria de omne* ("Book of the Misery of Man"), a short hagiographic piece known as the *Oración a Santa María Magdalena* ("Prayer to Saint Mary Magdalene"), and a number of minor Marian and doctrinal works. These include the *Oficio de la Pasión* ("Office of the Passion"), a poem dealing with the Crucifixion and its relationship to the canonical hours, and two incomplete works on the Virgin: the *Oración a Santa María* ("Prayer to Saint Mary") and the *Gozos de la Virgen* ("Joys of the Virgin"). These poems, although appealing, are by no means as technically accomplished as their thirteenth-century antecedents; and it is perhaps significant that the majority of devotional and hagiographic works composed in the fourteenth century were cast as prose rather than verse. A similar type of evolution can be detected in the didactic and sapiential (dealing with wisdom) tradition with the *Proberbios de Salamón* ("Solomon's Proverbs"), a short poem on the *De contemptu mundi* theme, and two minor pieces on the philosophy of Cato.

In contrast to the majority of early fourteenth-century compositions, the *Libro de buen amor* ("Book of Good Love") displays a degree of sophistication that makes it one of the most important works to have been composed in Spanish in the Middle Ages. The *Libro* itself is cast as *cuaderna vía*, but a prose sermon at the beginning and a variety of metrical systems within it combine to make it considerably more inventive than other poems, and, to a large extent, impossible to classify. Thematically, the *Libro* is elusive: its central theme of *buen amor* ("good love") is identified by its author as being the key to the work. Yet, the nature of this love is constantly shifting, and while at some points it refers to divine love, at others the focus switches to sexual conduct and the art of seduction. Although many aspects of the *Libro* are hotly debated, the ambiguity of its focus appears to be deliberate, encouraging the reader to appreciate the subtleties of contrasting and conflicting points of view. This is partly the result of the eclectic combination of sources on which the *Libro* is based (learned and popular sermons, *exemplum* collections, the catechism, *fabliaux*, Goliardic poetry, Ovid, Latin drama, and religious and popular lyric), but it can also be attributed to a sense of mischievousness on the part of its author, Juan Ruiz, the Archpriest of Hita (d. 1351–1352). At times it seems as if Ruiz's intention is simply to undermine the reader's desire to understand the information being offered, a factor most acutely apparent in the introductory tale of the Greeks and the Romans, where the interpretations of wise and foolish readers are considered equally right and equally wrong.

The *Libro* derives much of its meaning from autobiography, and the early sections of the book describe how the protagonist falls in love and dispatches a go-between in order to woo his lady. The go-between is twice rebuffed and in each instance an *exemplum* is offered as a means with which to interpret the rejection. The delicate balance between autobiographical and didactic materials sets the tone for much of what follows, and although at times the link between the two is rather tenuous, the emphasis on generic interplay provides the *Libro* with a degree of variety that is absent in earlier compositions. In the central and latter portions of the poem the blending of such seemingly disparate materials continues unabated: we are offered descriptions of several further romantic infatuations, a number of *serrana* poems dealing with terrifying mountain women, and a series of bawdy and religious lyrics. In view of its diversity, critics have often assumed that the various sections of the *Libro* were composed over a wide chronological period, coming together only when the Archpriest decided to present them in the form of a single, unified book. The nature of this arrangement makes it suitable for private reading rather than oral performance; and yet a number of individual sections are believed to have circulated orally.

Although the *Libro de buen amor* influenced a number of eminent writers, including Chaucer, its impact on the development of contemporary poetic styles was limited. This can be attributed in part to the uniquely multifaceted genius of its author, Juan Ruiz, but an equally telling factor is the rapidly changing nature of life itself in early and mid fourteenth-century Spain. The most noticeable testament to this instability is that, in contrast to the relatively homogeneous nature of mid thirteenth-century poetry, the majority of works composed in the corresponding portion of the fourteenth century bear little relation to one another. The *Libro*, as we have seen, is a bafflingly complex analysis of varieties of love, but of the many works composed in this period, it is the only one to deal at length with such a theme. Santob de Carrión's *Proverbios morales* ("Moral Proverbs"), for instance, deals with contemporary ethical and spiritual values, while Rodrigo Yáñez's *Poema de Alfonso XI* ("Poem of Alfonso XI") and the *Mocedades de Rodrigo* ("The Youth of El Cid") have a noticeably epic and political flavor: the latter dealing with the youthful exploits of Ruy Díaz de Vivar, and the former, the life of Alfonso XI until the capture of Algeciras from the Moors in 1344.

The earliest of these works, the *Proverbios morales*, composed by Rabbi Šem Ṭob ibn Arṭudiel ben Isaac (Santob de Carrión), is thought to be the first vernacular poem to have been composed by a Jewish writer in medieval Spain. Although various other texts bear hallmarks of Jewish involvement, the *Proverbios*, completed in 1345, represent the highpoint of *convivencia* ("coexistence"), a situation that, with the pogroms of 1391, would soon decline into one of religious intolerance, culminating in 1492 with the expulsion of the entire Jewish community. In this respect the *Proverbios* stand out as a fine example of the benefits of a pluralistic cultural perspective, a feat that is achieved as the poet identifies himself with peninsular culture while reserving the right to express his own essential otherness. The result is a captivating and noticeably individualistic composition, characterized by a penetrating approach toward questions of everyday reality as well as spiritual reservation and doubt. At times, the gnomic flavor of the work produces melancholy, if not pessimism, and this can, perhaps, be taken as a reflection of the social upheaval that marked the early years of the reign of Pedro I. The poem, however, is equally important in terms of its relationship to *cuaderna vía*: some critics, for instance, see it as a work composed in rhyming Alexandrines with full internal rhyme (a modification of the *cuaderna vía* form), while others arrange it as a series of 686 heptasyllabic quatrains, rhyming ABAB.

Similar problems can be seen in Rodrigo Yáñez's fragmentary *Poema de Alfonso XI* (1348), a work that can be arranged either as sixteen-syllable couplets with full internal rhyme, or as a series of octosyllabic lines, rhyming ABAB. Unlike the text of the *Proverbios*, the majority of recent editors have preferred to print the *Poema* in octosyllabic form, thereby detaching it from *cuaderna vía* poetry, and, most conspicuously, from the *Libro de miseria de omne*, a work composed in sixteen- rather than fourteen-syllable lines. Thematically, however, the *Poema* is different: its treatment of Alfonso XI is generally optimistic, and the use of epic materials, such as descriptions of battle (many of which are embellished with images of hunting), makes it more akin to the *Mocedades de Rodrigo*, a late heroic epic, notable for its decadence and exaggeration. Although both poems are lacking in literary quality, the *Mocedades* has received a substantially greater degree of critical attention. This is partly due to the fact that it promotes a relationship between the Cid and the diocese of Palencia (recalling the propagandistic context of a number of *clerecía* compositions), and partly the result of its tendency toward chronic over-statement: its latter stages, for instance, depict the Cid at the gates of Paris in an attempt to thwart an alliance between the king of France, the Pope, and the Holy Roman Emperor.

Although epic tales continued to prove popular in the fifteenth century and thereafter, they were progressively displaced by the rise of the popular ballad, an octosyllabic form unified by assonance rather than rhyme. The origin of the ballad is far from clear and a good deal of controversy surrounds its presumed relationship to the epic. It may well be that, in certain instances, ballads were derived from epics, but a number of dissimilarities, including narratorial technique, have produced critical disagreements. The earliest ballads exist only in fifteenth-century manuscripts, but linguistic and thematic evidence suggests that they had circulated orally for many years before being collected. Some have proposed that they might first have emerged in the 1320s, but it seems safer to assign them to the final third of the fourteenth century, as they undoubtedly flourished at this time. Reasons for the success of the ballad are legion, but the most telling factors are the gradual decay of other forms of popular poetry, the social upheaval created by the Trastámaran wars, and the waning of the power of the monasteries. These factors created an explosive cocktail that effected a number of irrevocable changes in the development of early Spanish poetry.

The subject matter of ballads is varied. Some deal with epic heroes and can be read in conjunction with works such as the *Mocedades* as products of a collective yearning for the relative stability of the past. Other ballads, in contrast, focus on the bitter legacy of contemporary events such as the Trastámaran wars, often in an attempt to vilify one side or the other. A related branch of balladry deals with the events of frontier life, presenting a surprisingly ambiguous attitude toward questions of war and conflict. The most striking examples are *Álora* and *Moraima*, where Moorish protagonists can be seen either as treacherous liars or as pitiful victims of Christian aggression. The most accessible ballads, however, are those that deal with timeless problems such as love and romance. Although a good number of epic, historical, and frontier ballads deal with these themes, the so-called "novelesque ballads" explore them in greater detail, more often than not making an emotional rather than moral appeal to the reader's sensitivities. Many ballads of this type, for instance, condone behavior that, in the age of monastic literature, would have been treated with contempt. A fine example is *Blancaniña* ("The White Lady"), where it becomes difficult not to sympathize with the sexual frustration of an adulterous female protagonist (it is here, perhaps, that the role of women in transmitting and modifying ballads in the oral tradition becomes most apparent). Other ballads deal with sexual themes in a more magical and mysterious environment: *Rico Franco* is based on an unlucky hunt motif while *La dama y el pastor* ("The Lady and the Shepherd") depicts an encounter between a young country lad and a *serrana* who attempts to devour him.

Although the popularity of the ballads can be explained in many ways, it is difficult to believe that the artificial and abstract world around which so many of them are based is not in itself a form of escapism from a society consumed by civil war, urban and agricultural deprivation, and, perhaps most importantly, the Black Death, which ravaged Europe in the mid fourteenth century. In other poems of the period these problems are explored in a particularly dark and brutal manner as escapism is replaced by a macabre contemplation of the inevitability of death. The earliest of these poems, the *Disputa del cuerpo e del ánima* ("Debate between the Body and the Soul"), is a sophisticated piece that makes use of a symbolic geographical landscape in order to frame a dialogue between a human soul and a rotting body covered with worms. In contrast to the earlier body-and-soul debate, the *Disputa* is an unrelentingly desolate work that replaces feudal imagery with a shockingly realistic assessment of the nature of death and damnation. Equally ferocious in tone is the *Danza general de la Muerte* ("Dance of Death"), a more aesthetically accomplished poem, based on a simple but effective structure in which members of the ecclesiastical and secular hierarchies are summoned by Death to their fates. The success of both poems is attested by the fact that they were adapted by later poets: the *Disputa* in the form of the *Revelación de un hermitaño* ("The Hermit's Vision"), and the *Danza general* in an expanded version published in Seville in 1520.

The changing social circumstances that were a characteristic of late fourteenth-century literary production can also be seen in the emergence of *cancionero* poetry. Just as the work of the minstrels had eventually given way to other types of popular literature, the gradual decline of the power of the monasteries had produced a void in erudite poetry that was filled in this period by a group of writers who composed both *canciones* (octosyllabic pieces, generally but not exclusively concerned with love) and *decires* (longer narrative, panegyric, and satirical poems based on a twelve-syllable amphibrachic line known as *arte mayor*). This development did not happen by accident: lyric poetry, which had been composed in Galician-Portuguese until the death of King Dinis of Portugal

(1279–1325), its last great patron, had gradually yielded ground to Castilian until the latter had been adopted as a literary norm. The work of these poets is generally known through *cancioneros* ("songbooks") rather than individually, and, until recently, the complex web of relations that exists between the various *cancioneros* was little understood. A breakthrough in scholarly awareness was achieved by Brian Dutton, who catalogued the sources (and, in the majority of instances, transcribed the texts) of more than 8,000 poems composed between 1360 and 1520. As a result of his endeavor, a generation of scholars has been allowed access to a previously impenetrable area of literary inquiry.[1]

The earliest *cancionero*, compiled by Juan Alfonso de Baena, was presented to King Juan II in 1445. The anthology includes more than 600 poems by more than fifty poets, many of whom were active in the final decades of the fourteenth century at the court of Juan I. Although the *Cancionero de Baena* is not an all-encompassing collection (a prominent omission is Pablo de Santa María's *Edades del mundo* ["Ages of the World"]), it provides a wealth of information with which to counterpoint the explosion of poetic activity at around the turn of the century. Among the most noteworthy poets are Pero Ferrús, perhaps the oldest of the earliest *Baena* generation, and Macías, who, according to popular legend, became a martyr to love. The most technically accomplished writers, on the other hand, are Alfonso Álvarez de Villasandino (d. 1425) and Pero López de Ayala (d. 1407). Álvarez de Villasandino's work is most significant in view of its gradual evolution from the language and rhetoric of Galician-Portuguese to an exclusively Castilian register. Pero López de Ayala, in contrast, is acknowledged as much for his *cancionero* poetry as for his *Rimado de palacio* ("Palace Poem"), a moral and political composition of more than 2,000 stanzas. The *Rimado*, like the *Libro de buen amor*, was compiled over a wide chronological period, and its various sections deal with an impressive number of issues; these include the Great Schism and its effect on ecclesiastical unity, as well as the theme of social displacement. Yet the poem lacks the coherence of the *Libro*, and the combination of *cuaderna vía* and *arte mayor* characterizes the poet as a type of Janus, a figure conscious of the emergence of fresh poetic forms, yet unwilling to relinquish the legacy of earlier traditions.

Although the charm of the earlier *Baena* poets is undeniable, their works are generally not as proficient as those of subsequent generations. Many of the later poets were of continental or *converso* ("converts from Judaism") origin: Francisco Imperial, for instance, was the son of Genoese parents who had settled in Seville, while Mohamed el Xartose de Guadalajara

---

[1] See Brian Dutton, with Jineen Krogstad, ed. *El cancionero del siglo XV* (Salamanca: Biblioteca Española del Siglo XV / Universidad de Salamanca, 1990–1991).

was of Moorish origin; *converso* writers, on the other hand, included Ferrán Manuel de Lando, Ferrán Sánchez Calavera, and possibly Diego de Valencia and Juan Alfonso de Baena himself. The rich cultural diversity of this second generation brought an additional dimension to their work. Imperial's *Dezir a las siete virtudes* ("Poem on the Seven Virtues"), for example, reveals an easy familiarity with Dante, while Sánchez Calavera's uncomfortable attitude toward Christian ethics can be detected in much of his work. One of his poems, a *pregunta* ("question"), in fact served as a catalyst for a poetic exchange on the issue of predestination; another dealt with the Trinity. The various *respuestas* ("answers") that he received were among the earliest examples of an intellectual poetic debate, an exercise that became increasingly popular as the century developed.

A more comfortable attitude toward religious matters can be seen in the poetry of Fernán Pérez de Guzmán (d. 1460?), who composed a number of lengthy pieces, of which his *Coplas de vicios y virtudes* ("Poem on Vices and Virtues"), *Confesión rimada* ("Poetic Confession"), and *Loores de santos* ("Eulogy of the Saints") are the most significant. The most accessible of these is the latter, a partially framed series of hagiographic works containing panegyrics in honor of a number of saints. Also worthy of note are Gonzalo Martínez de Medina and Ruy Páez de Ribera, who composed a number of moral and divine works. The youngest generation of *Baena* poets, however, wrote predominantly about love, often parodying the language and rhetoric of religion in order to express their ideas. The rich and powerful Álvaro de Luna (*c.* 1388–1453), known as much for his political ambition as his poetry, is a notable example. In one of his compositions, the speaker boldly affirms: "Si Dios, Nuestro Salvador, / oviera de tomar amiga, / fuera mi competidor" ("If God, Our Saviour, took a lover, he would be my rival," lines 1–3). Luna's audaciousness is matched by that of Suero de Ribera, whose *Misa de amores* ("Mass of Love") reworks the structure and rhetoric of the Mass in order to create one of the finest examples of religious parody to have been composed in medieval Spain. The earliest works of the Galician poet, Juan Rodríguez del Padrón (d. 1450?), also belong to this period, and among the most interesting are *Los diez mandamientos de amor* ("Ten Commandments of Love") and the *Siete gozos de amor* ("Seven Joys of Love"), in which the speaker presents himself, along with Macías, as a martyr to love.

The success of *Baena* was matched in subsequent years by a plethora of new *cancioneros*. Among the most impressive are the *Cancionero de Palacio* (compiled in the 1460s), the *Cancionero de Estúñiga* (comprising the work of the court poets of Alfonso V of Aragón), and the *Cancionero general* of 1511. These compilations embrace the work of many poets whose works circulated throughout the fifteenth century. The most poetically accomplished writers, however, emerged in the latter years of the reign of Juan II; and two figures, in particular, tower above the majority of their contemporaries. The earliest of these, Íñigo López de Mendoza, Marqués de Santillana (d. 1458), spent his formative years in Aragón and was influenced by poets such as Francisco Imperial and Enrique de Villena. The poet's early works are among his most entertaining, and these include *canciones* and *decires* as well as *serranillas*, which may have been influenced by those of the *Libro de buen amor*. His best poetry, however, belongs to a period in which he dedicated himself to an ambitious series of allegorical and narrative creations, based on earlier Italian and classical models. The *Triumphete de amor* ("Triumph of Love"), for instance, is derived from Petrarch's *Trionfo d'amore*, while his *Sueño* ("Dream"), borrows material from Boccaccio's *Fiammetta* (1334) as well as Lucan's *Pharsalia* (*c.* AD 61–65). Both works deal with love from an allegorical perspective, and they are matched in quality by the *Infierno de los enamorados* ("Lovers' Hell") and the *Comedieta de Ponza* ("Comedy of Ponza"). In later years Santillana composed a series of moral and philosophical poems of which his *Bías contra Fortuna* ("Bias against Fortune") is the most distinguished example. He also composed a series of forty-two sonnets on a range of subjects; these include a contemplation of the fall of Constantinople (XXXI) and a number of hagiographic pieces, of which Sonnets XXXIV and XXXVIII (on Saint Clare of Assisi and Saint Christopher) are fine examples.

The quality and diversity of Santillana's canon is matched by that of Juan de Mena (d. 1456), the other great poet of the court of Juan II. Both men were pioneers, particularly in the adoption of continental ideas and the construction of innovative styles of poetic cohesion, but despite the extent of their similarity, they are more commonly regarded as antitheses: Mena, as a supporter of Álvaro de Luna, and Santillana, as one of his detractors. Mena's early poetry embraces a number of dimensions and includes amatory *canciones* as well as anti-clerical satires and burlesque parodies of themes such as the *malmaridada* ("unhappily married woman"). His first major poem, the *Coronación* ("Coronation"), is an octosyllabic composition that denounces the evils of contemporary society. His greatest work, however, is the *Laberinto de Fortuna* ("Labyrinth of Fortune"), a text that endorses Luna's cause, often veiling references to contemporary figures and events through the sophisticated manipulation of language and syntax. The poem itself is a complex, tripartite piece, structured through the use of allegory: the narrator, guided by Providence, is transported to a palace of Fortune where he notices three great wheels representing past, present, and future; each wheel contains seven magical spheres (representing the planets), and it is through these that he is able to catch a glimpse of the future. When in 1453, however, Luna fell from power, the effect on Mena was devastating: his last poem, the *Debate de la Razón contra la Voluntad* ("Debate between Reason and Will") exudes feelings of disillusion and personal disappointment; his *Razonamiento con la Muerte* ("Dialogue with Death") may also date from this period.

Although Mena's interest in the literary debate represents an important aspect of his work, it is significant that, in common with other debates, the *Debate* and the *Razonamiento* have seldom been appraised in terms of genre. The paucity of research in this area can be seen most acutely in relation to medieval drama, where a remarkably small number of works have received a good deal of critical attention. The corpus of literary debates, in contrast, is much larger and covers a broader range of subjects, and yet, despite the richness of the tradition, the majority of works have been virtually ignored. Poems such as the *Debate de alegría e del triste amante* ("Debate between Happiness and the Sad Lover"), Estamariu's *Debat duna senyora et de su voluntat* ("Debate between a Lady and her Will"), and Furtado's *Debate con su capa* ("Debate with his Cape") are relatively minor pieces, but it is difficult to ignore the refined elegance of Rodrigo Cota's *Diálogo entre el amor y un viejo* ("Debate between Love and an Old Man") or its anonymous reworking, the *Diálogo entre el Amor, el viejo y la Hermosa* ("The Debate Between Love, the Old Man, and the Beautiful Woman"). These works, characterized by an imaginative use of imagery, depict the fate of an ageing protagonist, who, after initially rejecting Love, eventually falls into its trap. An equally significant debate is Antonio López de Meta's *Tractado del cuerpo e del ánima* ("Debate between the Body and Soul"), an intriguing treatment of the body-and-soul theme. Although little is known about the *Tractado* and its author, critics have focused on the way in which it departs from the earlier tradition by concluding with the written sentence of an angel. Also of interest are Castillejo's (d. 1550) *Diálogo con su pluma* ("Dialogue with his Quill") and a series of poems composed by Pedro de Cartagena (d. 1486); these include debates between the Tongue and the Heart, the Heart and the Eyes, and the Lover and the God of Love.

By the time of the deaths of Santillana and Mena in the 1450s the various *cancionero* styles had long since been the dominant mode of poetic composition in the peninsula. Although this, in itself, was an improvement on *cuaderna vía* (which had outlived its usefulness by the time of its demise), in the hands of the more derivative and unimaginative poets of the period, it produced even greater complacency. Many were content to base their compositions on obscure puns and cliquish references that make their work virtually unreadable when taken out of context. Yet, other poets were more successful, and a particularly sophisticated group is that of the court of Alfonso V, the Magnanimous. These included Juan de Andújar, Carvajal (or Carvajales), Juan de Dueñas (d. 1460?), Pedro de Santa Fe (d. 1450?), Juan de Tapia, and Lope de Estúñiga (d. 1477?). In contrast to the continental influences of other groupings, these poets, who were based, paradoxically, in Naples, adhered more closely to traditional Spanish forms, particularly in their treatment of courtly love, where the speaker, devoid of the hope of attaining his lady, stoically accepts suffering as a natural consequence of his infatuation. Perhaps the most entertaining poems to emerge from this group are a series of seven *serranillas* composed by Carvajal. Although these are not as technically accomplished as those of Santillana, the poet's decision to vary the identity of his female protagonists leads to a greater degree of diversity, and, in certain instances, to an idealization of the pastoral setting.

The poets of Alfonso's court were matched in quality by those who were active in Castile during the latter stages of the reign of Juan II (1404–1454) and the early years of the turbulent rule of Enrique IV (1454–1474). A good number of these devoted themselves anonymously to satirical composition, and among the most interesting creations are the *Coplas de ¡Ay panadera!* ("Poem on the Battle of Olmedo"), the *Coplas del Provincial* ("Provincial Poem"), and the *Coplas de Mingo Revulgo* ("Poem on Mingo Revulgo"). Religious poetry, on the other hand, is perhaps best exemplified by Íñigo de Mendoza, whose *Coplas de Vita Christi* ("Poem on the Life of Christ") is composed of nearly 4,000 octosyllabic lines. Equally worthy of note is Juan de Padilla, El Cartujano (d. 1468?), the author of the *Retablo de la vida de Cristo* ("Altarpiece on the Life of Christ") and *Los doze triumphos* ("The Twelve Triumphs"), a substantial panegyric on the Apostles. Padilla's achievement in the *Retablo* is matched by that of Diego de San Pedro (d. 1500?) in his *Pasión trobada* ("Poetic Passion") and by Comendador Román in his *Trovas de la gloriosa Pasión* ("Poem on the Glorious Passion"). An equally interesting, but all too infrequently studied poet, is Juan de Luzón, whose works are known only in his *cancionero* of 1508. The most prolific religious poet of the period, however, is Fray Ambrosio Montesino (d. 1514), whose corpus includes a number of hagiographic and biblical works, many of which are cast in the style of popular lyrics and ballads. Among his most interesting compositions are poems on Saint John the Baptist and Saint John the Evangelist.

The rich vein of religious and satirical writing that emerged in mid to late fifteenth-century Castile was matched by the work of a number of more secular poets; these included Suero de Quiñones (d. 1458) and Pero Guillén de Sevilla (d. 1480?) as well as the *converso*, Antón de Montoro (d. 1477); the earliest works of Juan del Encina (d. 1529), Garci Sánchez de Badajoz (d. 1526), Juan Álvarez Gato (d. 1510?), and Florencia Pinar (the earliest significant female poet to compose in Castilian) also date from this period. Yet, the most eminent literary figures are those of the Manrique family. Gómez Manrique (d. 1490), Santillana's nephew, was a prolific poet whose work embraced a considerable degree of thematic diversity;

among his best creations are the allegorical *Planto de las virtudes e poesía* ("Lament on Virtue and Poetry") and the elegiac *Coplas para el señor Diego Arias de Ávila* ("Poem on Diego Arias de Ávila"). Jorge Manrique (d. 1479), on the other hand, is known almost as much for amatory and satirical works as for his *Coplas por la muerte de su padre* ("Poem on the Death of his Father"), arguably the most sublimely accomplished lyric ever to have been composed in Spanish. The *Coplas* deal with the death of the poet's father, but the inclusion of a number of theological and doctrinal commonplaces broadens the scope of the composition, allowing the speaker to transcend his grief and to contemplate the fundamental values of human existence. The combination of personal and universal produces an emotional intensity that is reinforced by a sophisticated fusion of form and language: a brutally direct register welded perfectly into the *pie quebrado* form (octosyllables interspersed with half lines in full rhyme). In Manrique's hands the *pie quebrado* attains an unrelentingly haunting quality, nowhere more so than in the early sections, where his precision in reworking familiar metaphors produces some remarkable poetry: "Nuestras vidas son los ríos / que van a dar en la mar, / qu'es el morir" ("Our lives are the rivers that flow into the sea, which is death," lines 25–27).

With the marriage of Isabel of Castilla and Fernando V of Aragón in 1469, the dynastic instability that had dominated the Middle Ages gave way to a mood of cautious optimism; and with the fall of Granada, the discovery of the New World, and the expulsion of the Jews in 1492, it became possible to speak of a unified Spain: a major political and military power, equipped for the first time since the early eighth century with an inkling of its own destiny. The curtain was not immediately drawn on the Middle Ages, but change was in the air. The publication of the *Cancionero general* in 1511 collated the works of a final generation of medieval poets, and in subsequent revisions various other compositions were added. Yet, the benefit of hindsight shows that the days of the poets of the *cancioneros* were already numbered, for their achievements would soon be eclipsed by those of a younger generation, whose familiarity with Italianate forms and meters would, before long, revolutionize the future trajectory of poetry composed in Spanish.

5

Medieval Spanish prose

JAMES BURKE

The foundations of the study of medieval literatures in the modern era were, of course, essentially philological. The preparation of a readable text from existing manuscripts (if more than one was available), the provenance of the manuscript(s) and the work(s) inscribed thereupon, and finally the ability to read and understand the medieval language(s) transmitted by these texts were the principal aims of an earlier generation of scholars and students. Some students of these works also understood that it was necessary to understand the modes of procedure of the scribal culture in which these literary artifacts originated. Later some scholars and critics began to apply a "new critical" approach in their analysis. Why were these pieces in and of themselves worthy of attention as literary objects?

New ways of viewing the so-called "literary text" began to emerge as the scholarly community came to appreciate and elaborate upon various approaches (linguistic, psychological, structural) which produced a notable effect upon the manner in which medieval works were read and interpreted. In recent years the "new historicists" have begun to question the validity of many of these approaches. Their views, which to some degree must have evolved from and along with those of the French historical writers concerned with "mentalités," understand the medieval text as an artifact best analyzed in context, that is, in relation to the cultural codes which prevailed when the work was composed.

For many years, analysis utilizing these new approaches has not received much attention among medievalists working in Spanish. In the latter part of the 1990s, however, several studies were either completed or initiated which incorporated recent trends, most notably those dealing with sexual identity or based upon new evaluations of the role of women in the development of literature and culture.

Prose writings in the vernacular first begin to emerge in the thirteenth century, but a tradition of writing in Latin had existed in the peninsula since Roman times. Our understanding of the relation of such compositions to those produced there in the various Romance derivatives has been complicated by Roger Wright's 1982 study, *Late Latin and Early Romance in Spain and Carolingian France*, which demonstrated that before the early thirteenth century a kind of vernacular writing system often existed camouflaged beneath a veneer of what seemed to be Latin.[1] The sudden emergence of an unhesitant written prose Castilian in the treaty of Cabreros in 1206 and in verse in the *Poema de Mío Cid* ("The Poem of the Cid") in 1207 might be the result of the prior development of this system disguised as Latin. Thus what Peter Damian-Grint has referred to as "inventing vernacular authority" among the historians of the twelfth-century Renaissance in France may have had a parallel in Hispania in historical-literary writings in Latin such as the *Historia Najerense* ("History of Nájera," *c.* 1174).[2]

Another generic type in Latin is represented by the *Disciplina clericalis*, a collection of *exempla* (short, exemplary stories) by the Jewish convert Pedro Alfonso. This work dates from the second half of the eleventh century. *Exempla* of the variety included here, particularly ones translated from the Arabic, will figure as very important in the vernacular tradition a few years later.

In the mid twelfth century a large number of translations from Arabic were undertaken, largely by Hispanic Jewish scholars and by foreigners in the old imperial city of Toledo. The so-called "School of Translators" – there seems to have had little if any formal organization – would continue its work well into the next century. In 1256 in Toledo, Hermann the German produced a translation into Latin of Averroes' commentary in Arabic on the *Poetics* of Aristotle. The terms utilized and the explanations given, however, appear to bear little resemblance to the theories of Aristotle although scholars for years attempted to resolve seeming contradictions. Judson Allen, in *The Ethical Poetic of the Later Middle Ages: A Decorum of Convenient Distinction*, was able to clarify Hermann's explanations.[3] According to Hermann's adaptation, the purpose of poetry (and we might assume prose also) is to teach ethics by means of a rhetoric involving praise and blame. Hermann must have substituted medieval concepts for many of those used by Aristotle and it would seem logical to apply his ideas to those works from the Middle Ages which we deem to be literary. John Dagenais has given direct application of Hermann's theories to the *Libro de buen amor* ("Book of Good Love"),[4] and other scholars

[1] Roger Wright, *Late Latin and Early Romance in Spain and Carolingian France* (Liverpool: Francis Cairns, 1982), pp. 240–241.

[2] Peter Damian-Grint, *The New Historians of the Twelfth-Century Renaissance. Inventing Vernacular Authority* (Woodbridge, England: Boyell, 1999).

[3] Judson Allen, *The Ethical Poetic of the Later Middle Ages: A Decorum of Convenient Distinction* (Toronto: University of Toronto Press, 1982).

[4] John Dagenais, *The Ethics of Reading in Manuscript Culture: Glossing the "Libro de buen amor"* (Princeton: Princeton University Press, 1994).

have understood the importance of the rhetoric of praise and blame for prose writings in the medieval period.

Hermann translates Aristotelian "mimesis" with the word *assimilatio* ("assimilation"). Mimesis implies a process in which an independent agent produces a copy of another free-standing entity. In the literary process the imitator is usually assumed to be attempting to produce an image which is in some manner superior to the original. The explanations of Allen make it clear that the term *assimilatio* implies some variety of connectivity between two entities and that it is not imperative to view the two in terms of original and copy. If Hermann's understanding of *assimilatio* can be taken as typical for the thirteenth century and later, it would mean that critics would necessarily have to interpret those works from the period which we deem "literary" in a way different from that which is customary in modern explanations.

The concept of *assimilatio* can also be understood as relevant in regard to another approach which is growing in importance among scholars and critics who study other medieval vernacular traditions. Very often a work which has assumed an important place in the medieval canon is based on a manuscript which contains pieces from other genres and even ones in a different language, particularly Latin. The sense of connectivity associated with the process of *assimilatio* implies that the entire physical context of a manuscript, even rubrics, illustrations, and illuminations, must be considered when attempting to understand a particular piece.

A great flowering of prose writings took place during the reign of Alfonso X (called "the Wise") who ascended to the throne of Castile-Leon in 1252. Prior to the time of Alfonso two works of some importance appeared in the vernacular. The first of them was the *Fazienda de Ultra Mar* ("Deeds Done in Other Lands"), a translation of selections probably culled from a Latin version of a Hebrew Bible. Gómez Redondo believes that one principal purpose of the work was to imply a connection between those biblical places and events described and the situation of the contemporary courtly classes.[5] The *Semejança del mundo* ("Image of the World," shortly after 1222), based in part on the *Imago mundi*, attributed to Honorius Augustodunensis (1075? – c. 1156), is an encyclopedic work which attempts to describe, probably for students in some variety of classroom circumstance, how the world is organized.

The Alphonsine opus establishes Castilian as a literary language and fixes it to such a degree that a reader acquainted with the language of the twentieth century can read works from the period fairly easily. Henceforth, official documents are to be composed in the vernacular and no longer in Latin.

5 Fernando Gómez Redondo, *Historia de la prosa medieval castellana* (Madrid: Cátedra, 1998–), vol. i, p. 119.

Alfonso's father Fernando III (1199–1252) had begun a treatise of a moral and theological nature which could serve as a guide for the principled ruler. It was called the *Setenario* ("Treatise Based Upon Seven") because of a tendency frequent in the Middle Ages to understand the divine dispensation in terms of the number seven. The son was to bring this work to completion. The number seven also figures as important in Alfonso's great jurisprudencial compilation the *Siete partidas* ("Seven Sections Pertaining to Law," 1256–1265), a comprehensive legal code which attempted to rationalize preexisting systems relating to the administration of the law. The importance of the *Siete partidas* in regard to the development of legal practice in Spain has been considerable.

Alfonso and his collaborators also realized the completion of a great project of a historical nature. The *General estoria* ("General History") was planned as a universal history stretching from the beginning of time down to the present. This lengthy work, divided into six major parts, never reached beyond the time of the birth of Christ. Episodes from the Bible are juxtaposed with stories from the classical secular tradition and other material to produce a great compendium.

The *Estoria de Espanna* ("History of Spain") consists of two parts, the first extending from the moment of Creation down to the Muslim conquest, the second ending at the death of Fernando III. The compilers of this history utilized preexisting histories, chronicles, and annals, but, as in the case of the *General estoria*, they also drew upon material which the modern historian or historiographer would by no means accept as true and useful for the purposes of research. Various pagan and Christian sources, hagiographical traditions, and legendary tales are intermingled with what appears to be documentary evidence. There seems to be no interest in making sure that what is related in reality occurred (something which would have been extremely difficult for writers in the Middle Ages to establish in any event). Reinaldo Ayerbe-Chaux has pointed out that Alfonso and his group conceived of these works as exemplary; in effect, they illustrate Hermann the German's maxim that all writing should bear ethical purpose.[6] The reader can see that true history, and what one might term "the imaginary" deriving from human writerly efforts, reveal a series of models which are worthy of either praise or blame – *laudatio* or *vituperatio*. Ayerbe-Chaux also understood that these writings were structured to bear an important political message concerning the place which Hispania should occupy in the divinely inspired scheme of historical development. The Roman Empire, divided between Rome and Constantinople, would be reunited and its center would be located in the court of Alfonso.

---

[6] Reinaldo Ayerbe-Chaux, "El uso de *exemplum* en la *Estoria de España* de Alfonso X." *La Corónica* 7 (1978–1979), pp. 28–33.

Alfonso and his collaborators adapted Ovidian tales in order to utilize them in the construction of both the *General estoria* and the *Estoria de Espanna*. Erotic elements were often discarded or downplayed so that the force of moralizations could be more effective. The heroines of the *Heroides* in Alfonso's adaptations become objective examples of the positive feminine, the virtuous woman worthy to reside and function within the imperial realm which the king hoped to establish once he finally secured the imperial crown. Marina Brownlee argues that, in the medieval exposition, allegory has replaced the mimesis of the Roman model so that "the metadiscursive breakthrough achieved by the Ovidian original" was obscured.[7] In producing these monumental histories Alfonso and his collaborators utilized a wide variety of narratological strategies in order to make their message more appealing and convincing.

Two other major groups of writings were also produced under Alfonso's aegis: the so-called "scientific" works are for the most part astronomical and astrological treatises which hope to explain the interaction between the heavenly bodies and the sublunary sphere. It is important to remember that this is a very different conception of science from that which prevails in the twenty-first century. These works are for the most part translations from Arabic sources which had built upon foundations of Greek knowledge. The *Tablas alfonsíes* ("Alphonsine Tables") described the movements of the planets and continued to be a source consulted throughout Europe almost until the Enlightenment. Other astronomical–astrological books are the *Libros del saber de astronomía* ("Books Containing Knowledge about Astronomy") and the *Libro conplido en los judizios de las estrellas* ("Book Containing Complete Knowledge about Judgement Based upon the Stars"). The *Lapidario* (a treatise discussing stones) attempts to explain the interaction of the heavenly bodies and spheres upon stones, while the very fragmentary *Picatrix* was probably in its complete version a text written to demonstrate how celestial forces might be captured and utilized in talismans.

Another important group of writings produced in and around the Alfonsine era is *exempla* or wisdom literature – treatises which Fernando Gómez Redondo describes as helping to create a courtly culture, one in which correct, mannerly, or courteous behavior is expected. One obvious and very important use of such manuals was to serve the needs of preachers who needed practical examples for their often unlearned listeners. Many of the works, such as *Calila e Digna* ("Calila and Digna") and the *Libro de los engaños e los asayamientos de las mugeres* ("Book of the Wiles and Plots of Women") are translations from Arabic. In the

---

[7] Marina Brownlee, *The Severed Word: Ovid's "Heroides" and the "Novela Sentimental"* (Princeton: Princeton University Press, 1990), p. 10.

first, a practical knowledge, that of everyday living and the marketplace, is transmitted to the reader under the guise of animal tales. The second warns against over-involvement in romantic situations with women. The authenticity of the feminine voice is a vexed question in medieval Spanish as is evidenced by the *Historia de la donzella Teodor* ("Story of the Maiden Teodor"), an adaptation of a tale from *The Thousand and One Nights* in which an extraordinarily knowledgeable young slave woman saves both herself and her master because of her formidable wisdom. Is such a tale a demonstration of the positive aspects of the feminine or a manipulation by the masculine voice to present women in yet another subservient role?

Treatises of this sort also are derived from the Latin tradition. There may have been a translation into Spanish of the *Disciplina clericalis*, while the much later *Libro de los gatos* ("Book of the Cats") (with its enigmatic title) is largely a translation of the *Fabulae* of Odo of Cheriton. The *Libro del consejo* ("Book of Advice"), which probably dates from the early fourteenth century, derives from the *Liber consolationis et consilii* ("Book of Consolation and Advice") writtten by Albertano de Brescia in 1246.

Another kind of prose realized for purposes of edification are hagiographical writings, the presentation of the lives of saints who could serve as objects of devotion and as models for imitation for the faithful. The enormous compilation in Latin, the *Legenda aurea* ("Golden Legend"), gathered together by Jacobus a Voragine around 1264, functioned as a paradigm and reference work for writers in the peninsula who would incorporate local saints' legends into the framework provided – often replacing ones in the original.

Scholars have traditionally understood these *vitae* ("lives") as didactic treatises which were used to instruct the faithful in the modes of life proper for the pious Christian. Recently it has become clear that these works must be perceived not only as directly instructive in nature but also in terms associated with the phenomenon of *assimilatio*. The recitation of the life of a saint in the presence of a listener or the presentation in iconic form of some important event from such a life serves as a catalyst to draw this person into a process in which he or she becomes a kind of co-participant in the original trajectory of events. The conditions of the individual are, thus, attracted to, assimilated into, and modified by those circumstances described in the sacred prototype. The Christian becomes a member of a group which is both real and metaphysical, a hierarchy in which the original saint occupies a much superior position.

Manuscript h-i-13 (late thirteenth- early fourteenth-century) in the library at El Escorial serves as a prime literary example of the manner in which this process was understood to function. It is a mixture of saints' lives and romances doubtless designed to demonstrate the ephemeral nature of earthly existence and the difficulties which the individual Christian might encounter on the way to salvation. The juxtaposition of the adventures of the knight-hero with the life of a saint, however, implies that it was possible for the former to participate in the kind of sanctified life experience which the vocation of the holy person implied. The *Libro del caballero Zifar* ("Book of the Knight Zifar"), composed roughly during the same period, demonstrates how it was possible for the medieval composer–compiler to assimilate the themes, ideas, and images from the two traditions into one work.

The use of materials from Ovid to prepare historical works illustrates the fact that medievals did not distinguish between what we moderns would consider imaginative works and ones which might have attempted to achieve historical veracity. Thus when the Alfonsine collaborators developed an outline for the composition of a great Crusade epic, *La gran conquista de Ultramar* ("The Great Conquest of Lands Beyond the Seas"), they took an Old French version of William of Tyre's chronicle *Historia rerum in partibus transmarinis gestarum* ("History of Things Done in Lands Beyond the Seas") and mixed in elements from the Old French Carolingian epic tradition, in particular the story of the Swan Knight. The reason for planning the book was doubtless to further Alfonso's imperial ambitions by demonstrating the prowess of some of his ancestors who had taken part in the Crusades. When *La gran conquista* was finally finished at the court of Alfonso's son Sancho IV (1284–1295), it was no doubt intended to inspire greater efforts in the king's struggles with the Moors. This long, rather amorphous work brings new modes of expression into being and serves as a kind of prototype for what will be writings of enormous importance in the Hispanic literary tradition, the novel or romance of chivalry.

Themes from the Arthurian corpus in Old French were known probably as early as the late twelfth century, circulated by roving Provençal singers. The great French Arthurian romances in verse had little direct impact in the peninsula but selections from the prose Post-Vulgate materials were adapted and translated and even mixed with elements from the so-called Vulgate cycle. Arthurian stories continued to be composed in the various peninsular vernaculars up until the sixteenth century. These works, the Hispanic versions of the Tristán legend, and a variety of other adaptations, examples of which are *Baladro del sabio Merlín* ("Tale of Wise Merlin"), *La estoria del rey Guillelme* ("Story of King William"), and the *Noble cuento del emperador Carlos Maynes* ("Noble Tale of the Emperor Charlemagne"), introduced many important themes, motifs, and ideas to the Iberian consciousness. The courtly and religious ethos conveyed in these materials had enormous impact upon the emerging ideological framework of aristocratic society. It is also clear that themes and ideas from the Arthurian context influenced the development of Hispanic novels or romances of chivalry such as the *Libro del caballero Zifar* and the *Amadís de Gaula* ("Amadís of Gaul").

It has become clear that much of the writings in the vernacular in the Middle Ages originated in the school exercises which young pupils produced as they learned the techniques of the trivium.[8] The vernacular tradition produced another great moment of literary achievement in the first part of the fourteenth century in the works of King Alfonso's nephew Juan Manuel (1282–1348). The Fourth Lateran Council in 1215 had affirmed the importance of the instruction of the faithful and the necessity of confession. Such emphasis on the centrality of personal responsibility may have been decisive in the development of a concept of the individual[9] and thus have given rise to a need for the kind of treatises produced by Juan Manuel. In essence his work can be understood as an attempt to justify in writing his political and courtly career and can thus be taken as a "mirror" in the medieval acceptance of the term but also as a move toward the autobiographical in the modern sense. This was a man of action who understood perfectly the necessity of arms in the maintenance of a political equilibrium, but who also realized the importance of written rationalizations and explanations of the knightly and courtly ethos. As well as being a man of his time, he was deeply religious, devoted to the ideals and precepts of the Dominican Order on whose behalf he founded the monastery of Peñafiel.

Although Juan Manuel, like his uncle, looked upon history as a mirror which could provide guidance for contemporary life and behavior, he, with one exception – the *Crónica abreviada* ("Brief Chronicle") which is a summary of the *Estoria de Espanna* – does not develop the kind of great overall strategies apparent in the *General estoria* and the *Estoria de Espanna*. He viewed human existence in terms of two great *carreras*, two modes, one having to do with behavior resulting in success in real human life, and the other with conduct and belief which would guarantee a positive outcome in the afterlife.

Juan Manuel was a prolific writer but unfortunately much of his work has been lost. Among those prose writings which are missing are the *Reglas de trovar* ("Guidebook for Composing") which might have given us the earliest vernacular treatise on the composition of poetry in Castilian. Minor works which have come down to us include the *Libro*

---

[8] Studies which would take into account these clerical practices could be very illuminating in regard to the later evolution of Arthurian as well as other prose works in the peninsular languages. See Douglas Kelly, *The Conspiracy of Allusion: Description, Rewriting, and Authorship from Macrobius to Medieval Romance* (Leiden: Brill, 1999).

[9] See Jerry Root, *"Space to Speke": The Confessional Subject in Medieval Literature* (New York: Peter Lang, 1997).

del cavallero et del escudero ("Book of the Knight and the Squire") which describes, through a process of questions and answers, the instruction given by an old knight to a young squire, and the *Libro de la caza* ("Book Describing Hunting") which emphasizes the author's role as magnificent and princely hunter.

The two of Juan Manuel's works which have received the most critical attention are his *Libro de los estados* ("Book Describing the Medieval Concept of Hierarchy") and the *Conde Lucanor*. The former is a retelling of the tale of Barlaam and Josaphat adapted to the circumstances of the author's situation. Juan Manuel was undergoing great political difficulties in his life and the only way that he could present a well-functioning political organization and achieve absolute resolution and even victory of one variety or another was through a narrativization of experience.

In this work an old and wise counselor gives advice to a young heir apparent who must learn to govern and to achieve success in this life, and, more importantly, salvation in the one that follows. Such success might be accomplished by fulfilling those duties and obligations which pertain to personal status in the medieval sense of the term. The Castilian word *estado* utilized in the common title of the work emphasizes this point. There are constant dangers involved in the choices which have to be made by the person in a position of superior authority, and this work, as well as the *Conde Lucanor*, is designed to help a leader circumvent and deal with such dangers. In the medieval perspective regarding human existence, earthly phenomena and processes were understood still largely in a neo-platonic sense, that is, as a reflection of a true reality which existed above in heaven and which was mediated to the sublunary realm by the stars and planetary spheres. Of course, there was also another unhappy locale for those who had not been able to achieve salvation and, although there is little medieval commentary on the fact, this place too must necessarily have had its reverberations in everyday life.

In addition to accepting that the things of this world existed as a mirroring of that which was more permanent, medieval men and women also believed that all that which occurred within it was caught up in a great play of reflections and refractions. Earthly existence was conceived in terms of a series of counter-images and counter-happenings which replicated other phenomena. Juan Manuel understood this perspective extremely well and thus both the *Libro de los estados* and the *Conde Lucanor* are constructed in terms of self-reference. The writer has injected his own being, his own persona, into most, if not all, of the characters which populate his works. He is both student and teacher, apprentice and master. His role can be that of an old knight giving instruction to a young squire or the servant–philosopher Patronio who provides advice to Count

Lucanor – a personage of course, replicating to a great degree Juan Manuel's own position in life.

The human, as the highest member of animate creation, has been endowed with something not given to lower beings: understanding and free will. Both these functions are linked to the immortal soul and are that which associate the soul with those faculties – common sense, retentive imagination, inventive imagination, estimation, and memory – which are located in the head of the individual. The examples or *semejanzas* (images and perhaps even mirror images) presented throughout the works of Juan Manuel are reflections in writing which replicate in artful and economic format the very involved and confusing happenings of real life. They are designed to aid the reader or listener to understand the "real" situation which might occur in "real" life. The individual would process the *semejanzas* through the mental faculties and develop modes of understanding and behavior which would allow him or her to deal more effectively with the world.

The *Conde Lucanor* contains three parts: the first, much longer than the others – the *Libro de los exemplos* ("Book of Examples") – consists of fifty tales plus an epilogue. Each is presented with a framing device in which the noble Count Lucanor questions his servant–advisor Patronio concerning a particular problem. Patronio responds with a story which he hopes will clarify the situation for his lord. Juan Manuel took the material for his tales from a wide variety of sources, including Spanish historical legends, oriental tales from Aesop, and ecclesiastical writings. The second part, the *Libro de los proverbios* ("Book of Proverbs or Enigmas"), is itself subdivided into a brief prologue plus three collections of proverbial sayings and a final epilogue which contains doctrinal explications. The proverbs become more and more difficult to understand as the reader progresses through the sections. The author's explanation for this is that he has spoken "plainly" in the first part of the work and now he will present more difficult, obscure exercises to challenge to a greater degree the intelligence of the reader. Whether these riddles really are to be solved or whether they present yet further illustration of the difficulties in the sign systems of this world is doubtless a matter which scholars will continue to debate. In the final section or epilogue the author presents the doctrinal affirmations of the Church. This part may be there to stand in contrast to the other two divisions and to provide a sense of closure, functioning as a nonnarrative, nonexemplary presentation of moral authority. It would serve as a summation of that which in the medieval view could only be taken as true, comprehensible, and decipherable discourse.

The very early fourteenth century is also the moment at which an important new literary prose genre comes into existence. Such writings are referred to as "novels of chivalry" but the designation "prose romance"

is doubtless more correct. The *Libro del cavallero Zifar*, probably composed between 1300 and 1310, combines themes, ideas, and techniques
from Arthurian materials with elements taken from preexisting hagiographic stories in prose. In addition, motifs adapted from the modes of
historical writings, chronicles, annals, and the great Alphonsine opus were
included. Elements from the epic tradition also are incorporated as well
as themes and ideas relating to education which were derived from the
"mirrors of princes."[10]

The *Zifar* is divided into three major sections, the first of which treats
the experiences of the knight Zifar (the name is probably based upon an
Arabic verb meaning "to travel") and his family who are forced to abandon their home and undergo a series of adventures until Zifar eventually
becomes the ruler of the kingdom of Mentón. The reason that the family
is forced to leave home, the fact that all the knight's mounts die after a
period of ten days, introduces the motif of supernatural occurrence, one
that will be of continuing prominence throughout the story. The second
major section of the book, the *Castigos del rey de Mentón* ("The Teachings of the King of Mentón"), is one in which Zifar, now king, instructs
his two sons, Garfín and Roboán, in the art of proper kingship and is thus
basically a *de regimine principum* (an instructional manual for rulers). In
the third section Roboán sets out on his own quest which will eventually
result in his becoming a great ruler. The work thus has the structure of a
diptych with the *Castigos* section serving as hinge between the two.

The succession to Alfonso X was hotly disputed. His son Sancho IV
eventually succeeded to the throne but his reign as mature sovereign was
brief and he was followed by Fernando IV (reigned 1295–1312). Before
Fernando reached maturity, royal control was exercised by Sancho's wife
(Fernando's mother), María de Molina, who acted as queen regent. Gómez
Redondo and other critics are convinced that the *Zifar* is both a reflection
of and an attempt to deal with the troubled political and social realities of
the period in which it was composed. The work would be the product of
a group effort centered around a school located at the cathedral of Toledo
under the tutelage and perhaps even direction of the queen mother herself.
Its purpose would be to demonstrate what a positive and righteous ruler
can achieve when he or she masters the art of correct behavior and proper
governance.

Most if not all the members of this group who composed the *Zifar*
would have been clerics, many even belonging to the higher orders, and
certainly they could have been aware of historical–ecclesiastical writings
which viewed the trajectory of earthly history in terms of a mirroring

---

[10] "Mirrors of princes" is a term commonly used for medieval ethical treatises used to instruct
rulers in the "wisdom" of their duties.

of the divine plan for redemption. Through the efforts of a godly and just lord it should be possible to restore, at least in part, the primordial state of perfection lost in the fall in Eden. As Nancy Regalado Freeman has demonstrated, marginal comments in manuscripts of the Old French prose Grail romances certainly imply that many lay readers largely understood these works in terms basically secular rather than religious.[11] The same would probably have been true in the case of the *Zifar* although such would not preclude a different perception by those highly trained in the ecclesiastical and liturgical tradition.

In *Kinship and Marriage in Medieval Hispanic Chivalric Romance*, Michael Harney has studied the structures which govern the functions of kinship and marriage in the *Zifar*, the *Amadís* (which will be discussed further along), and several other peninsular romances.[12] One of his most interesting conclusions runs directly counter to the ideas of a number of medievalists who have considered early literature from the perspective of modern feminism. Harney is convinced that these romances advocate the legal and social empowerment of women and that they in no way can be considered a sexist or patriarchal genre dedicated to the furtherance of male dominance.

There are a number of sermons written in the vernacular which date from the late Middle Ages although these works are not, perhaps, of the greatest literary interest. Still, the influence of homiletic structures is of great importance and is apparent in many of the central texts from the period. It is likely that the approaches utilized in the elaboration of medieval sermons affected the writing of the *Zifar*, as the sermonic theme "redde quod debes" ("return what you owe") is certainly of importance in the book. In addition to the *Zifar*, some of the writings of Juan Manuel and also the compendium composed by the Archpriest of Talavera reflect the modes and models often employed by medieval preachers.

Probably the most interesting use of a sermon format in terms of the presentation of what might be called "medieval literary theory" occurs toward the beginning of the fourteenth-century masterpiece of poetic writing, the *Libro de buen amor*, supposedly by one Juan Ruiz, the Archpriest of Hita. After an introductory section of ten stanzas of poetry, there follows a sermon in prose which is ostensibly placed there to help the reader in understanding how to interpret the book. The problem is whether "buen amor" ("good love") refers to an affection directed toward the

---

[11] Nancy Regalado Freeman, "The Medieval Construction of the Modern Reader: Solomon's Ship and the Birth of Jean de Meun." In "Rereading Allegory: Essays in Memory of Daniel Poiron." Ed. Sarah Amer and Noah D. Guynn. *Yale French Studies* 95 (1999), pp. 81–108.

[12] Michael Harney, *Kinship and Marriage in Medieval Hispanic Chivalric Romance*. Westfield Publications in Medieval and Renaissance Studies 11 (Turnhout: Brepols, 2001).

Virgin and Christ, or whether such love should be understood in terms of pleasurable earthly undertakings.

The theme of the sermon has to do with the proper function of memory, will, and understanding. J. K. Walsh has published a brief tract from the late fourteenth or early fifteenth century which consists of an interchange between these three faculties which Saint Augustine had described as being central to the activities of the soul.[13] Saint Bernard of Clairvaux had later elaborated upon the Augustinian position by explaining that a kind of tension or struggle can take place between and among these operations, particularly if one of them becomes overly affected by the influences of earthly desire. This contention, which the poet obviously sees as central to an understanding of the *Libro de buen amor*, must also be one of importance in regard to prose writings in medieval Spanish if ethical considerations are as important there as John Dagenais has suggested in *The Ethics of Reading in Manuscript Culture*.

The most important of the Hispanic novels or romances of chivalry is doubtless the *Amadís de Gaula* which only comes down to us in a version in four volumes put together around 1492 by Garci Rodríguez de Montalvo and printed in 1508. References to the work and some fragments of it date from at least 150 years earlier. The knight Amadís is the epitome of chivalric prowess as well the paragon of the accomplished courtly lover. The influence of the work has been enormous in that Amadís is the model which Cervantes used to produce his parodic opposite don Quijote. It is also clear that the work is a magnificent demonstration of how ideas and examples might be drawn from the Arthurian materials and utilized to prepare paradigms to guide conduct among the noble classes. The basis for the theme of "hacer bien" ("to do good") which is so important in *Don Quijote* is largely conveyed to the Spanish Golden Age by the *Amadís*.

A number of critics have been concerned with possible differences between the so-called "primitive" versions of the work and the definitive text that is available to us. Fernando Gómez Redondo's explanation in *Historia de la prosa medieval castellana* summarizes theories very well and presents a logical explanation of the development of the story of Amadís. He posits a very early version in which the hero serves as the epitome of all knightly virtue, thus exemplifying the role of Tristán as completely committed lover and Zifar as the devoted earthly servant of God. A second version, drawing imagery and thematic materials from the Troy legends, reflected the chaos, disorder, and pessimism of the period of

---

[13] John K. Walsh, *El Coloquio de la Memoria, la Voluntad, y el Entendimiento (Biblioteca Universitaria de Salamanca MS. 1.763) y otras manifestaciones del tema en la literatura española* (New York: Lorenzo Clemente, 1986).

the usurper Trastámara kings, the first of whom began to reign in 1369. The version of the *Amadís* which comes down to us projects the ideals and politico-theological thinking of the era of the Catholic Monarchs, Fernando and Isabel.

Very clearly, works from the Arthurian tradition such as the *Amadís* served as vehicles for entertainment and recreation in the sense described by Glending Olson in *Literature as Recreation in the Later Middle Ages*.[14] In addition, as has been discussed, these stories provided paradigms for the molding of both the individual and society. One important point, however, is that the premodern concept of the individual must have been very different from that notion which prevails in present-day culture. In our post-Freudian era we conceive human character in terms of a complicated interaction of impulses arising from deep within the self which combine with a vast array of outside influences to create a multi-layered, intricately constituted psychological being. The theories of scholars such as Stephen Greenblatt present the late medieval and Renaissance personality as a kind of mirroring of some variety of external textual experience, one which may or may not literally be found in inscribed form.[15] Either a written or oral rendition of a story such as the *Amadís* would have served extremely well as a model for the constitution of both the individual and societal "countertext."

The legends having to do with the deep and overwhelming devotion of Tristán for his lover Isolde certainly inspired a similar reaction in the knight Amadís. If, however, premodern personality is largely constituted as a reflection of some variety of textual experience, it would be possible that the recipient might accept as a model only the obsessive amorous involvement implied in the Tristán material and ignore positive implications found there as well as in other exemplars of a devotional or instructional nature – the genre of the *de regimine principum* for example. The result would be a destructive passion which could lead to despair. This appears to be what occurred in the case of many of the *cancionero* poets of the fifteenth century and with the authors of the so-called "sentimental" novels.

The fifteenth century ushers in what has come to be called, in regard to most Western European literatures, the "premodern" period. Humanistic influences, especially of Italian origin, began to manifest themselves, although scholars and critics debate how profoundly Spain, and especially Castile, was affected by these currents. Traditional genres continued to be important. The *Libro de los exenplos por A.B.C.* ("The Book of Examples

---

[14] Glending Olson, *Literature as Recreation in the Later Middle Ages* (Ithaca, NY: Cornell University Press, 1982).
[15] Stephen Greenblatt, *Renaissance Self-Fashioning: From More to Shakespeare* (Chicago: University of Chicago Press, 1980).

Arranged in Alphabetical Order," *c.* 1400), a grouping probably designed for use by preachers, demonstrates that the traditional interest in the literature of *exempla* continued to be of importance.

This on-going interest in exemplarity problematizes our understanding of a number of other varieties of writing produced during this period. The Marqués de Santillana (1398–1458), best known for his poetry, sent a selection to Dom Pedro of Portugal in 1449 with a prose introduction which traditionally has been taken as one of the earliest examples of literary criticism in Castilian. The Marqués does give some rudimentary discussion of the strong and weak points of the poets to whom he refers, but the rationale for writing in the first place continues to be one related to ethics, or how to entertain while conveying a message.

A large number of chronicles detailing the doings of rulers and dignitaries were composed. In the early part of the century the Castilian Chancellor Pero López de Ayala (1332–1407), a writer accomplished in many fields, produced two chronicles, the *Crónica del rey don Pedro* ("Chronicle of King Pedro") and the *Crónica de Alfonso XI* ("Chronicle of Alfonso XI"), which detailed the happenings during the reigns of important earlier kings. Although the facts listed in these chronicles are doubtless correct, it is also likely that these works are composed to justify the Trastámara uprising against King Pedro I which resulted in his death on the field at Montiel in 1369, slain by his illegitimate half-brother who would become Enrique II. Much later in the century there appeared the *Crónica de don Álvaro de Luna* ("Chronicle of don Álvaro de Luna") which recounted the life of this most important advisor to King Juan II, a man who dominated the political scene in Castile until his downfall. To modern readers the work has also a strong biographical cast which reminds one of the biographical sketches of the *Generaciones y semblanzas* ("Portraits of Illustrious Castilians") of Fernán Pérez de Guzmán (*c.* 1378–1460), and the miscellany probably modeled upon it, the *Claros varones de Castilla* ("Distinguished Men of Castile") of Hernando del Pulgar (*c.* 1425–1490?). The prologue to the *Generaciones y semblanzas* contains a philosophical reflection on the problems of writing history. The way in which such writers viewed the process, however, differs from the modern outlook as is evidenced in the word *afeiçom* utilized by the great contemporary Portuguese chronicler Fernão Lopes (fl. 1434–1454). This refers to the peculiar manner in which writers of the period shaped and misrepresented events to the benefit of benefactors.

Numerous translations into Castilian were also undertaken during the fifteenth century. Ancient Greek sources were generally taken from Latin adaptations (Homer, Plato, and Plutarch) while classical Latin furnished numerous models (Ovid, Seneca, Virgil). Dante, Petrarch, and Boccaccio, who provided the foundation for the Italian literary Renaissance, were, of course, also made available in the vernacular. Again, the primary purpose behind such work was most likely not esthetic but rather a desire to purvey more material for purposes of ethical exemplarity.

The conflict between an evolving sense of differentiation from medieval concepts of Creation and the premodern preoccupation with the doings of the human being is made singularly manifest in the contrast between the early fifteenth-century *Visión deleitable* ("Delightful Vision") (*c.* 1435) of Alfonso de la Torre, almost totally an encyclopedic compendium of medieval wisdom and knowledge, and works which treat more mundane concerns. Enrique de Villena (1384–1434) on the one hand produced the classicizing *Doze trabajos de Hercules* ("The Twelve Labors of Hercules") which gave allegorical treatment to each of the labors and, on the other, his *Tratado de aojamiento* ("Treatise on the Evil Eye") which explained the dangers associated with the much-feared evil eye. It is again important to remember that the functions described by writers such as Enrique de Villena should not be taken as "magical" in the modern sense of the preposterous supernatural but as real phenomena which had to be understood as dangerous if realized with evil intention. Observation and description of real events seemingly portrayed in terms of reality was beginning to impinge upon consciousness as is evident in a work such as the *Relación de los hechos del condestable Miguel Lucas de Iranzo* ("Story of the Deeds of the Constable Miguel Lucas de Iranzo," composed in the 1470s). While to some degree a sense of *afeiçom* may be at play here, the vivid description of festivals and gala events in the life of the constable surely approximates what really occurred.

At the very end of the century two important works treating language were written, the *Universal vocabulario latín y romance* ("Universal Vocabulary of Latin and Romance") by Alfonso de Palencia in 1490 and the *Gramática de la lengua castellana* ("Grammar of the Castilian Language") by Antonio de Nebrija in 1492. Coming at the close of the medieval period, these investigations have their foundations in the kind of study written by Isidore of Seville, and also in a desire to explain the functions of creation through analysis of language, while simultaneously anticipating modern linguistic research carried out for its own sake.

In 1438 Alfonso Martínez de Toledo produced a diatribe which he seems to have called after his professional status as archpriest of Talavera. The subtitle of the book, *Reprobaçion del amor mundano* ("Condemnation of Earthly Love"), gives a true indication of the basic purpose, a disavowal of the objects of earthly desire – in particular of women – and for that reason it has been referred to as misogynistic. The book has also been called the *Corbacho*, because it was mistakenly believed that it had its origins in Boccaccio's *Corbaccio*. It is a heterogeneous collection of sermonic material and examples combined with a great variety of themes garnered from across the medieval didactic tradition. Medicinal and astrological lore mix with popular anecdotal references. The book is obviously a powerful clerical reaction against both the courtly tradition and the melancholic attitude in regard to love which soon produced the so-called "sentimental novel."

The chief literary value of the work has been what seems to be in it a superb portrayal of popular speech, a variety of highly artistic mimicry which might have influenced the masterful monologues and exchanges which occur in *Celestina*. Catherine Brown, building on recent theories having to do with medieval negative writings on women, has proposed that the *maldezir de mugeres* ("speaking Ill of Women") in the work is not so much a faithful reproduction of female speech patterns as a spectacular performance rendering the voices of viragos, shrews, sodomites, effeminates, and hypocrites.[16] It presents a portrayal of an array of marginalized late-medieval individuals.

Imaginative prose fiction is represented in the fifteenth century not only in the romances of chivalry, where love is a positive, elevating force, but also in the writings which have traditionally been referred to as "sentimental novels or romances." These are not, of course, novels in anything like the modern sense; a more appropriate description of them would be tales of woeful or unsuccessful love or amorous passion. These stories, which first appear in the middle of the century and which continued to be written for another one hundred years, represent the mirror image to the idea represented in the courtly tradition that the experience of erotic love can be an ennobling, positive one. Amorous passion represents here an overwhelming and uncontrollable force, desire totally overwhelms the will, and the suffering lover usually comes to an unhappy end.

There has been considerable debate among scholars concerning whether some variety of generic unity exists among these works. It is clear that certain writings in Catalan and Portuguese must certainly be associated with them. Kindred themes can be discerned in other late medieval traditions as well. A wide variety of sources, both direct and intertextual in nature, served as a matrix (for example, classical musings on love popularized by Ovid). In the medieval tradition from which these writings sprang, the chivalresque and courtly had blended with the elegaic, the confessional-penitential, the mirrors of princes, and the didactic as presented in the university treatise. The paratheatre as it must have existed in popular, festive manifestation surely also found voice among the characters of sentimental writings.

---

[16] Catherine Brown, "Queer Representation in the *Arçipreste de Talavera*, or The *Maldezir de mugeres* Is a Drag." In *Queer Iberia: Sexualities, Cultures, and Crossings From the Middle Ages to the Renaissance*. Ed. Josiah Blackmore and Gregory S. Hutcheson (Durham: Duke University Press, 1999), pp. 73–103.

The modern reader not particularly interested in the development of the Hispanic literary prose tradition may find the works in this genre not to be of great interest. There is in sentimental fiction often very little action or plot. These stories recount the emotional process which the chief character undergoes as he suffers the results of misfortune in love. In the premodern period erotic passion was understood to arise in the animal nature of the human being which was viewed in a very different way from modern perceptions. The self was understood as a fragile construct composed of body and mind which was scarcely able to contain the pressures brought upon it by inordinate desire. In regard to the body, control was maintained by regimes of discipline and evacuation and some scholars believe that a medieval man or woman would have conceptualized the body in a very different way from that which prevails in the modern world.

By the fifteenth century there had been considerable change in comparison to earlier medieval modes and manners of expression. Marina Brownlee's study of the manner in which the writers of this period dealt with the tradition of Ovid's amatory letters shows how the ways of treating such materials had varied. In her 1990 book she argues that the Alfonsine exemplary presentation of the *Heroides* was radically altered by Juan Rodríguez in his fifteenth-century rendering, the *Bursario*, which relied heavily upon the Alfonsine translation and adaptations. The author has dismantled the extratextual framework which the earlier writers had utilized to convey a particular authoritative interpretation of the Ovidian opus and has moved toward what will become the modern way of portraying the problem of subjective discourse.

One very important recent critical topic in regard to sentimental writings is the role of women. Scholars suspect that these works reflect a crisis in accepted aristocratic, masculine roles and that writers hoped that traditional ideas concerning women's virtues could be utilized as the basis for the construction of a new variety of male identity and status. If this is true, it is difficult to know what authenticity, if any, one can accord to the female voice in these works. Certainly we know that noble women, Queen Isabel for example, were often among the most influential readers of the sentimental romances.

An important factor which must have contributed to the development of the sentimental writings in the mid fifteenth century is that sense of angst and crisis described by Gómez Redondo. Surely another terribly important fact was the situation of the Spanish Jews and *conversos* (those who had converted or who had pretended to convert to Christianity).[17] Both Diego de San Pedro and Fernando de Rojas were certainly of *converso* stock.

---

[17] See Stephen Gilman, *The Spain of Fernando de Rojas* (Princeton: Princeton University Press, 1972).

The expulsion of the Jews in 1492 and the on-going investigation of the *conversos* by the Inquisition would have created a sense of anxiety and apprehension readily translatable into literary terms.

The earliest of these works is the *Siervo libre de amor* ("slave or Servant Free of Love") composed by a minor Galician noble Juan Rodríguez del Padrón around the middle of the century. The frame is an autobiographical allegory of the author's unhappy love affair which contains within it another short story of difficult love, the *Estoria de dos amadores* ("The Story of Two Lovers"). The frame tale is probably a new type of Augustinian confession describing a psychological journey (of the late medieval type) to the New Jerusalem in which the "slave of love" at the beginning evolves into a "servant of the most high Jesus Christ" at the end. Other mid to late fifteenth-century examples are the *Triste deleytaçion* ("Sad Delight"), written by a Catalan in Castilian, and the *Sátira de la felice e infelice vida* ("Essay Concerning Happy and Unhappy Life") by Dom Pedro, constable of Portugal. The word *sátira* is used here in the old sense of collection or miscellany.

By far the most important writings of this type are those of Diego de San Pedro and Juan de Flores toward the end of the century. The earlier of San Pedro's works is the *Tratado de amores de Arnalte e Lucenda* ("Treatise Concerning the Loves of Arnalte and Lucenda") which demonstrates the hopeless frustrations experienced by the hapless lover. San Pedro's masterpiece is *Cárcel de amor* ("Prison of Love," 1492) which begins when the author finds a captive of love, Leriano, in an allegorical prison of desire in the Spanish Sierra Morena. The action mysteriously moves to Macedonia where the author attempts to help Leriano win the hand of the Princess Laureola. Description of both thought and action is presented in a series of letters exchanged between the characters. At the end, a rejected Leriano commits suicide in a scene which bears eucharistic allusion.

Juan de Flores' two works *Grisel y Mirabella* and *Grimalte y Gradissa*, both printed around 1495, were most certainly composed much earlier. Both of these romances allude strongly to the Italianate tradition and both thematize the problematics of the act of reading. The physical act of love is consummated here but the outcome of the amorous experience is as disastrous as in other examples in sentimental fiction.

In 1499 there appeared the first version of Fernando de Rojas' *Celestina*, undoubtedly the greatest prose masterpiece of the late Spanish Middle Ages and the precursor of the enormous flowering which soon took place in the genre. Although the work is laid out in the form of an extended drama with only the speaking parts of the characters bearing the movement of the action, the relationship to prose writing in both the chivalresque and sentimental traditions is clear. This printing with the title *Comedia de Calisto y Melibea* ("Comedy of Calisto and

Melibea") – the two characters are the two ill-fated lovers in the work – had only sixteen acts. In 1500 there appeared another version with five additional acts and a new title *Tragicomedia de Calisto y Melibea*, which also contained information concerning the author and the work in general. Eventually the work came to be known by the name of the fascinating intermediary who, as go-between, facilitates a relationship between the young lovers: Celestina.

The principal concerns of scholars until recently have largely had to do with authorship and sources. Fernando de Rojas claimed that he found and then built upon what is now the first act, eventually adding what amounts to another twenty, plus introductory and concluding statements. Other material was supplied by editors. Critics have largely attempted in the past to explain *Celestina* in the terms of modern concepts of assigned responsible authorship instead of viewing the work as within the medieval tradition which understood a text as the result of an on-going process of emendation and commentary. Some scholars believe that, while assigning principal credit to Rojas for the masterpiece, it is more logical to speak in terms of the author(s) of the book since often the added material is of considerable value. In regard to sources, the Latin humanistic comedy, Terence for example, as evolved in Italy, along with themes taken from Heraclitus and Seneca, provided inspiration. The influence of Petrarch is considerable as is the whole tradition relating to love and the passions.

Celestina provides an excellent ending for a discussion of the prose tradition of the Spanish Middle Ages. It is a very medieval work in many ways yet bears within it indications of radically new ways of conceiving lengthy discourses in prose. Prose of a traditional kind continued to be produced, of course, but new directions were imminent. Within a very few years the writing of pastoral and picaresque novels prepared the way for one of the greatest moments in all of Western fiction, Cervantes' *Don Quijote* and, with its appearance, modern fiction.

6

The medieval theatre: between *scriptura* and *theatrica*

Charlotte D. Stern

Conventional histories of literature examine the literary qualities of dramatic texts, yet the interrelationship between writing and theatre, between two fundamentally different forms of human creativity, is also a valid concern. Theatre implies a live performance, an essentially evanescent and fluid communal activity; writing embodies a far more stable and enduring personal enterprise. The relationship between writing and performance, between *scriptura* and *theatrica* was particularly complex in the Middle Ages when *theatrum* was broadly defined as a place for sights and sounds, and *theatrica* embraced a wide range of theatrical activities often lacking a verbal script. Yet almost everything we know about the medieval theatre we owe to medieval writing. Some texts are authentic playscripts incorporated into miscellanies. Few such texts survive, however, because directors normally copied the actors' roles on scraps of parchment that eventually went astray. Other texts were intentionally reworked in the process of being transcribed, while still other writings contain not the dialogue but a description of the stage props and costumes, financial costs of mounting the show, audience response, or merely the time and place of the performance. The elite nature of *scriptura* also means that many popular forms of *theatrica* have often gone unrecorded or appear in negative appraisals.

Colorful church rituals including liturgical dramas have endured better than most medieval performances because they were recorded in medieval service books, although the dramatic scripts did not always survive unscathed. In Catalonia strong ties to Italy and France and the shift already in the eighth century from the Visigothic rite to the Roman–French encouraged the assimilation and development of church drama.[1] Especially impressive are several Easter texts recorded in Manuscript 105 erroneously associated with the Benedictine monastery of Ripoll but now identified with the cathedral of Vic. The eleventh-century section of the manuscript contains the earliest known *Quem queritis in sepulcro?* ("Whom do you seek at the sepulcher?") found on Hispanic soil. The

---

[1] For further details on this and what follows, see Richard B. Donovan, *The Liturgical Drama in Medieval Spain* (Toronto: University of Toronto Press, 1958), and Eva Castro, ed., *Teatro medieval I: el drama litúrgico* (Barcelona: Crítica, 1997).

ceremony formed part of the introit of the Resurrection Mass and was preceded by an original processional chant *Ubi est Cristus, meus dominus / et filius excelsi?* ("Where is Christ my Lord and Son of the Most High?"). The chant resurfaces later in various liturgical contexts in other areas of Catalonia and in southern France.

In the twelfth century the *Quem queritis in sepulcro?* was skillfully integrated into a highly original *Visitatio Sepulcri* known as the *Verses pascales de .iii. M<ariis>*, which became part of Easter Matins. In the drama the spice merchant (*unguentarius*), who is missing from the biblical accounts, makes his theatrical debut trumpeting his spices and defending their inflated cost. Original too, but also enigmatic, are the laments of the Marys as they approach the sepulcher. Their final lines lead naturally into the *Ubi est Cristus?* and *Quem queritis?*, although a lone angel responds to the Marys in contrast to the plural *celicole* ("heavenly dwellers") in the *Quem queritis* text. Lexical and metrical recurrences lend coherence to the play. Unfortunately the extant version is flawed. The amanuensis, pressed for space, erased part of the poetic text and recopied it in cramped fashion without regard for the poetry and without the musical notation. Also in the same manuscript is the text of the only Latin *Peregrinus* play from Spain, most likely composed for performance on Easter Monday. Despite its fragmentary and confusing appearance, the play excels for its opening scene in which a distraught Mary Magdalene, searching for Jesus, utters lines redolent with imagery borrowed from the Song of Songs.

The cathedral of Mallorca was renowned for its elaborate performance on Good Friday of a *Planctus passionis* ("Lament of the Passion"), which was later merged with the Descent from the Cross. On Easter Monday, the cathedral staged the *Victimae pascali laudes* ("Praises to the Easter Victim"), composed by the celebrated German poet Wipo (d. 1048–1050). At Christmas the *Quem queritis in presepe?* ("Whom Do You Seek at the Manger?") modeled on the Easter trope was chanted during the third Christmas Mass in the cathedrals of Urgel, Gerona, Palma de Mallorca, Huesca, Vic and the monasteries of Santa Maria de Estany and San Juan de las Abadesas. The antiphon response *Quem uidistis pastores, dicite?* ("Tell, Shepherds, Whom You Have Seen?") of Christmas Lauds of praise is recorded at the monastery of Montserrat and the cathedral of Palma de Mallorca. The *Cantus sibyllae* ("Song of the Sibyl"), doomsday prophecy of the Erythrean sibyl, which is included in the sermon *Contra judaeos, paganos et arianos* ("Against Jews, Pagans and Arians") was sung together with Old Testament prophecies at Christmas Matins. In Palma de Mallorca a lector, cast as Saint Augustine, to whom the sermon was erroneously attributed, summoned the prophets in a full-blown *Ordo prophetarum*.

Unlike Catalonia, Navarre/Aragon did not convert to the Roman–French rite until the 1070s, with little evidence of liturgical drama, although the earliest Aragonese codex containing the new rite includes the *Quem queritis in sepulcro?* The manuscript, however, is a French import, and it is uncertain whether the services at the cathedral of Huesca followed this codex.

The Roman–French rite was imposed on Castile by Alfonso VI at the council of Burgos in 1080. The Cluniac monks who implemented the shift introduced their reform version of the rite which was stripped of those ceremonies lacking a biblical basis. Thus Castilian hostility to the new rite and Cluniac opposition to nonscriptural accretions hindered the assimilation of the liturgical drama. An eleventh-century breviary and an antiphonary from the monastery of Santo Domingo de Silos near Burgos reflect the uncertain fate of the *Visitatio Sepulcri* in Castile. The two manuscripts contain the Roman–French rite, but the handwriting and musical notation are Visigothic. In both codexes the *Visitatio Sepulcri* appears in the margins in Carolingian script and Aquitanian notation. The breviary does not indicate the location of the ceremony in the service, but the antiphonary specifies with an asterisk that the ceremony is to follow the third responsory of Christmas Matins. More explicitly theatrical, it designates the characters as angels and, surprisingly, disciples (*discipuli*) in lieu of the standard *Cristicole* (followers of Christ).

Unlike the Easter drama, Christmas celebrations took hold in central Spain, the *Cantus sibyllae* at Matins at the cathedrals of Leon, Toledo, and Palencia, the *Pastores dicite, quidnam uidistis?* at Lauds in Toledo and Palencia. Missing, however, is the *Quem queritis in presepe?* In western Iberia the eleventh- and twelfth-century examples of the *Quem queritis in sepulcro?* and *Visitatio Sepulcri* from the cathedral of Santiago de Compostela in Galicia exhibit the features of French–Catalan tradition and were designed to please European pilgrims already familiar with the ceremony.

While central Spain evinced limited interest in Latin liturgical drama, the region probably enjoyed a religious theatre in the vernacular from earliest times. The twelfth-century *Auto de los reyes magos* ("The Play of the Magi") was most likely designed for performance not before Benedictine monks but before the Mozarabic laity of Toledo. The play resembles the Latin *Ordo stellae* only superficially. Indeed, original, often ironic, touches have earned it a prominent place in the history of the medieval theatre. The polymetry, symmetrical structure of the opening scenes, vacillating Magi, a befuddled Herod, and rabbis who cannot locate the prophetic passages all suggest the work of a gifted dramatist. Unfortunately, the 144 lines were carelessly transcribed on the last two folios of a manuscript containing Latin exegetical writings. In a different hand from that used elsewhere, the writing appears cramped, the height of the letters uneven, the poetic and dramatic structure virtually ignored, and the spellings so inconsistent as to suggest that the scribe was attempting to reproduce in writing a vernacular tongue that was rarely written down. The play ends abruptly with the rabbis reluctantly admitting the truth. It is not known whether the remaining scenes were equally original or whether the play merged with the liturgy and culminated in the traditional adoration scene.[2]

Gonzalo de Berceo's *Duelo de la Virgen* and *Eya velar*, poems tied to the liturgy, reinforce the claim that Castile possessed an early religious theatre in the vernacular. The *Duelo*, composed in *cuaderna vía*, is a highly dramatic presentation of Holy Week events, in which a solo performer impersonates Mary, Jesus, and Pontius Pilate and recites their exact words. The *Eya velar* is more theatrical. Three choristers, each endowed with a unique personality and cast as *veladores* ("guards"), take up the watch at the sepulcher. The stanzas are distributed among them, but all three join in chanting the refrain. These works could have been performed in a liturgical setting for pilgrims spending the night at the monastery of San Millán de la Cogolla. Consequently they should be examined within the context of medieval Passion drama. That they may have been staged in no way denies their probable use as devotional texts to be read and pondered during moments of private meditation.[3]

The twelfth-century secular theatre included Provençal minstrels who performed in Spain both at court and in the streets. By the thirteenth century they were largely replaced by Iberian entertainers, who created veritable Galician-Portuguese song dramas preserved in *cancioneiros* ("songbooks"). Some songs were dramatic monologues, others dialogues requiring two singers; still others used a soloist and a second *juglar* as mime, while a few called for an entire acting troupe. The satirical pieces may well be the verbal texts for *juegos de escarnio* (satirical plays) that ridiculed homosexuals, abbesses who served as go-betweens, cowardly knights, and other social misfits. Carnivalesque in spirit they inverted the official order to expose the seamy side of medieval Castilian life.[4]

Despite the dearth of historical records it is now clear that a thriving medieval Muslim theatre touched Islamic and Christian Iberia. In his *Risāla fi Fadl al-Andalus* ("Praise of Andalusian Islam"), al-Shaqundi

---

[2] See Charlotte Stern, *The Medieval Theater in Castile* (Binghamton: Medieval and Renaissance Texts and Studies, 1996), pp. 44–48, and Miguel Ángel Pérez Priego, ed., *Teatro medieval II: Castilla* (Barcelona: Crítica, 1997), pp. 39–50.

[3] On the issue of reading and devotional texts, see Germán Orduna, "La estructura del *Duelo de la Virgen* y la cántica *Eya velar*." *Humanitas* 10 (1958), pp. 75–104; Daniel Devoto, "Sentido y forma de la cántica 'Eya velar.'" *Bulletin Hispanique* 65 (1963), pp. 206–237; and Stern, *Medieval*, pp. 153–156.

[4] Francisco Nodar Manso, *Teatro menor galaico-portugués (siglo XIII): Reconstrucción textual y teoría del discurso* (Kassel: Reichenberger, 1990).

(d. 1129) enumerates the performing arts practiced in Úbeda. They include the *khiyāl* (=shadow drama), sword dances, juggling, dancing girls, and a play called the "Villager."[5] The renowned poet Ibn Quzmān (d. 1160) describes these and other vaudeville acts in *zaǧal* 12, an intricate poem that treats theatre as metaphor. The poet explains how the director prepares his Muslim acting company for a variety show that features dances, the "Villager," cross-dressing, a sword dance, musical interludes, a magic show, and two dogs that understand human speech. Yet the theatrical impresario is a metaphor for the poet Ibn Quzmān "in the act of creating a poem."[6]

It is appropriate to mention also the Egyptian ophthamologist Ibn Dāniyāl (d. 1310) who authored at least three genuine comedies to be staged as shadow theatre. These satires of contemporary Egyptian life employ scatological themes and language which have delayed their acceptance as literary works. Since shadow puppets were known in medieval Iberia, it is conceivable that Ibn Dāniyāl plays or others like them were mounted on the peninsula. The comedy *Tayf al-Ḥayal*, for instance, features an impoverished self-pitying old bawd Umm Rašīd, who anticipates Fernando de Rojas' Celestina by 200 years.[7]

The *Libro del arcipreste* (*Libro de buen amor*) ("The Book of Good Love") has been intensely scrutinized as a literary work, yet its arsenal of information on medieval performances remains virtually ignored. Although it was copied, recopied, expanded, and revised, it nevertheless provides important clues to the dynamic process whereby live performances were reworked as a written text (*libro*), which was then recreated as live theatre by minstrels and preachers. It is possible that Juan Ruiz composed the original fragments which were inspired by the minstrel's repertoire and then rewrote and combined these segments over the years to produce the multilayered *Libro*.[8]

Time and again the narrator recounts with unusual verve his amatory failures. He is easily hoodwinked by his go-between, chastized by a *dama cuerda* (wise lady), ridiculed as impotent by an old woman, and repeatedly assaulted by Amazons of the *sierra* (mountains). Interpolated episodes

[5] Shmuel Moreh, *Live Theatre and Dramatic Literature in the Medieval Arabic World* (New York: New York University Press, 1992), p. 35.
[6] See James Monroe, "Prolegomena to the Study of Ibn Quzmān: the Poet as Jongleur." In *El romancero hoy: historia, comparatismo, bibliografía crítica*. Ed. Samuel G. Armistead, Antonio Sánchez Romeralo, and Diego Catalán (Madrid: Cátedra, 1979), pp. 77–129.
[7] Charlotte Stern , "Recovering the Medieval Theater of Spain (and Europe): The Islamic Evidence." *La Corónica* 27 (1999), pp. 142–144. James T. Monroe is preparing a bilingual edition of Ibn Dāniyāl's plays.
[8] John K. Walsh, "The Genesis of the *Libro de buen amor* (from Performance Text to *Libro* or *Cancionero*)." Paper presented at the Modern Language Association Convention, 29 December, 1979.

like the tale of Pitas Payas and the "Enxiemplo del asno y del blanchete" ("Cautionary Tale of the Ass and the Lap Dog") broach such taboo themes as adultery and bestiality. The erotic implications, religious travesty, and obscene humor are difficult to recover because of the verbal pyrotechnics, intentional ambiguities, and omission of bawdy *cantares cazurros* (vulgar songs).[9] Equally complex is the interrelationship between the written text and live performance. Aesop's fables were standard fare of minstrels and preachers. Yet the archpriest so alters the fable of the ass and the lapdog that the minstrel actually performs an obscene parody of the familiar tale. The story of Pitas Payas belongs to traditional farce. Though a narrative in the *Libro*, it abounds in dialogue, while the pseudo-French dialect serves as a useful aid for the performing minstrel.

The Latin comedy *Pamphilus de amore* is reworked in the *Libro* as an exemplary tale that lends itself to dramatization. The narrator/archpriest insinuates himself into the skin of the comic protagonist don Melón. The recently widowed doña Endrina, her mother, and the shrewd old hag Trotaconventos round out the cast of this parody of courtly love. In the *Libro* the narrator describes doña Endrina for the implied reader. In a live performance, however, the narrator as don Melón stands before his audience. If he performs alone, the spectators must imagine the other actors in their stage roles, but if the narrator belongs to an itinerant acting troupe, he could well be summoning them forth to speak their lines and act out their roles. As the action moves toward the denouement, descriptive passages, even phrases like "dixo él" ("he said"), "dixo ella" ("she said"), gradually disappear, and the seduction of doña Endrina, her anguished lament, and the go-between's cynical reaction become pure drama. The *Libro* provides the basic script which is susceptible to diverse theatrical interpretations.

The equally lengthy section on carnival includes the mock battle between don Carnal (Lord Carnival) and doña Cuaresma (Lady Lent). Though rooted in folk tradition the confrontation unfolds in the archpriest's fictional universe where live animals renowned for their sexual drive and procreative excess, as well as cooked meat and fish, replace the disguised human combatants of folk ritual. On Shrove Tuesday a minstrel could easily entertain the spectators with this zany literary parody of the traditional carnival rite.[10]

The burlesque processions celebrating the return of don Carnal and don Amor on Easter Saturday and Sunday turn upside down the triumphal entry of Jesus into Jerusalem on Palm Sunday. The liturgical *exultemus et laetemur* ("let us rejoice and be happy"), *benedictus qui venit* ("blessed

[9] Louise O. Vasvari, "The Tale of 'Tailing' in the *Libro de buen amor.*" *Journal of Interdisciplinary Library Studies* 2 (1990), pp. 13–41.

[10] Louise O. Vasvari, "The Battle of Flesh and Lent in the *Libro del Arcipreste*: Gastro-Genital Rites of Reversal." *La Corónica* 20 (1991), pp. 1–15.

is he who comes"), and *mane nobiscum* ("remain with us") are now directed at the "emperors of food and sex" (James F. Burke's phrase in *Desire Against the Law*).[11] Yet the presence of representatives of the various social classes that make up a Mozarabic community implies that the poet has created a literary parody out of genuine processional drama honoring reigning monarchs.

The Castilian *Danza general de la Muerte* ("The General Dance of Death") exemplifies better perhaps than any other text the permutation of the arts, in this instance the metamorphosis of a dance performance into a mimed sermon which was later reworked as a narrative poem. Long before the outbreak of the plague in 1348 the gravediggers' guild attired in skeleton costumes danced in the cemeteries. With the increase in sudden and violent death preachers intensified their perorations against worldly pleasures and urged repentance. What better way to enliven their sermons than to incorporate the *danse macabre* featuring Death, swathed in all the trappings of popular tradition, luring its reluctant victims from the various estates? The preacher's moral and didactic message conveyed through multiple channels, gestural, rhythmic, terpsichorean, musical, iconographic, and verbal, was delivered against the richly symbolic background of the church interior. Then in the 1380s a gifted poet converted this colorful performance into the literary work, *Danza general de la Muerte*. Composed in *coplas de arte mayor*, this highly polished composition incorporates the preacher into the narrative, replicates the animated exchange between Death and her reluctant partners, and preserves some choreographic details of the live performance. The unique copy of *Danza general*, transcribed in the 1390s and housed in the library of the Escorial, boasts ornamental capitals and flourishes which imply that this visually pleasing text was designed for reading, yet the prologue and the use of the term *trasladación* suggest that the poet has converted (*trasladado*) a mimed sermon into a narrative poem.[12]

A partially translated procession of sibyls (*Ordo sibyllarum*) and a Latin *Planctus passionis* are recorded in an early fifteenth-century manuscript belonging to the cathedral of Cordoba. The document is apparently a Salamancan student's notebook containing carelessly executed exercises. The sibylline procession imitates the *Ordo prophetarum*, but in lieu of prophets the sibyls from classical antiquity predict both the first and second coming of Christ, effectively telescoping the nativity and final

[11] James F. Burke, *Desire Against the Law: The Juxtaposition of Contraries in Early Medieval Spanish Literature* (Stanford: Stanford University Press, 1998), pp. 197–210.
[12] On the "danse macabre" theme, see Florence Whyte, *The Dance of Death in Spain and Catalonia* (Baltimore: Waverly Press, 1931), and Víctor Infantes, *Las danzas de la muerte. Génesis y desarrollo de un género medieval (siglos XIII–XVII)* (Salamanca: Universidad de Salamanca, 1997).

judgment.[13] These sibyls were frequent figures in late medieval iconography where they carried scrolls containing their prophecies. While there is no evidence that the Hispanic *Ordo sibyllarum* was performed, a theatrical version appears at the end of the mammoth French *Mystère du vieil testament* and is inserted into a *Rappresentazione ciclica* from Bologna. The *Planctus passionis* opens with Jesus speaking from the cross and reminding the mourners of Adam's sin. The scene is pieced together from biblical and liturgical texts, some of which have now been identified.[14]

The religious theatre blossomed in the fifteenth century both in the churches and in the streets. Featured at the cathedrals of Leon and Toledo during Christmas Midnight Mass was the Erythrean sibyl, who by now had attracted a supporting cast of angels and torch bearers. The sibyl chanted her doomsday prophecy in Castilian. She intoned the unsettling refrain "Juicio fuerte será dado / cruel y de muerte" ("Harsh judgment will be meted out, cruel and fatal") as eerie music reverberated through the cavernous cathedral. A description and text of the Toledan performance are preserved in Juan Chaves de Arcayos' sixteenth-century account. At Christmas Matins choristers disguised as shepherds processed to the main altar of the cathedral where they remained singing and dancing. At Lauds the Latin antiphon *Quem uidistis pastores?* was followed by a Castilian rendition "Bien vengades, pastores" ("Welcome, Shepherds") in which the shepherds described the manger scene, then sang and danced a *villancico* (carol), chosen from several included in the service book. Thus the *Quem vidistis, pastores?* developed into a lyrical and descriptive dialogue whereas the *Quem queritis in presepe?* recorded elsewhere in Europe evolved into the more theatrical adoration scene.

Several extant manuscripts and printed editions of Fr. Íñigo de Mendoza's *Vita Christi* ("The Life of Christ"), a mistitled infancy narrative, preserve what appear to be multiple versions of a vernacular Christmas drama. In a recently discovered manuscript from Salamanca, the nativity scene consists of brief repartee between two shepherds which is followed by the angel's announcement.[15] In the 1482 printed edition, however, the shepherds expand their initial dialogue, are then joined by

---

[13] José López Yepes, "Una Representación de las Sibilas y un Planctus Passionis en el MS. 80 de la Catedral de Córdoba." *Revista de Archivos, Bibliotecas y Museos* 80 (1977), pp. 545–567; Feliciano Delgado, "Las profecías de sibilas en el MS. 80 de la Catedral de Córdoba y los orígenes del teatro nacional." *Revista de Filología Española* 67 (1987), pp. 77–87.

[14] Castro, *Teatro*, pp. 235–237.

[15] Ana María Álvarez Pellitero, "Indicios de un auto de pastores en el siglo XV." In *Actas del III Congreso de la Asociación Hispánica de la Literatura Medieval (Salamanca, del 3 al 6 de octubre de 1989)* 2 vols. (Salamanca: Universidad de Salamanca, 1994), vol. I, pp. 91–116.

others, and all rejoice at the adoration of the angels. The traditional gift giving, which in a live performance was accompanied by singing and dancing, is narrated in the poem. It leads into a lengthy monologue inspired by the liturgical *Quem uidistis pastores?* These additions, including a special rustic jargon for the shepherds, hispanicize the biblical narrative. They were likely inspired by contemporary Spanish nativity celebrations mounted not in the cathedrals but in rural communities and comparable to the noisy festivities that, two centuries earlier, King Alfonso el Sabio had tried to suppress. The poet of the *Vita Christi* converted the Hispanic shepherds' ritual of thanksgiving and celebration into a comic interlude in order to enliven the terse biblical narrative and heighten the ludic and emotional appeal of his meditative poem.

Gómez Manrique (1412–1491?) inserted *Lamentaciones para semana santa* ("Lamentations for Holy Week") into his lyrical *cancionero*. It is a *Planctus passionis* that stages the final moments of Christ's Passion. Set at the foot of the cross it dramatizes the laments of Mary and John and the silent suffering of Mary Magdalene.[16]

Bookkeeping ledgers from the cathedral of Toledo (1493–1510) confirm that thirty-three Corpus Christi biblical and hagiographic *autos* (plays), whose themes stretched from Creation to Doomsday, were mounted on pageant wagons and performed in Toledo. The ledger abounds in staging details but provides only the opening stanza of an *Auto de los santos padres* ("Harrowing of Hell Play") and the outline of an *Auto del emperador o de san Silvestre* ("The Play about the Emperor, or about Saint Silvester").[17]

The same ledger, however, preserves an *Auto de la Pasión* ascribed to Alonso del Campo. It appears with numerous deletions, insertions, and revisions on several blank pages scattered throughout the ledger. The play, which resembles a work-in-progress, offers valuable clues concerning the compositional techniques used in late medieval biblical and hagiographic plays. The author relies heavily on traditional sources and on two lyric poems, Diego de San Pedro's *Passión trobada* and *Siete angustias*, which he adapts to the theatre. It is not known whether Alonso del Campo polished the play later, or indeed whether it was ever performed. Josep Lluis Sirera believes, however, that its structure is well suited for performance on pageant wagons.[18] The action of the play stretches from Jesus' meditation in the Garden of Gethsemane to Mary's lament at the foot of the

[16] Stanislaw Zimic, "El teatro religioso de Gómez Manrique (1412–1491)." *Boletín de la Real Academia Española* 57 (1977), pp. 381–400.
[17] Carmen Torroja Menéndez, and María Rivas Palá, *Teatro en Toledo en el siglo XV. "Auto de la Pasión" de Alonso del Campo* (Madrid: Anejos de la Real Academia Española, 1977).
[18] Josep Lluis Sirera, "La construcción del *Auto de la Pasión* y el teatro medieval castellano." In *Actas del III Congreso*, vol. II, pp. 1011–1019.

cross. Two additional laments by Peter and John contribute to the play's predominantly lyrical and meditative tone, while the presence of archaic meters and vocabulary argues persuasively for a long tradition of Passion drama in Toledo. The ledger containing the *auto* was found among theatrical paraphernalia belonging to Alonso del Campo. Thus the *capellán* ("chaplain") emerges as both dramatic poet and theatrical impresario, hence a precursor of Golden Age *autores de comedias* ("producers, directors, playwrights").

Yet the Castilian *autos* hardly rival the elaborate church theatre of eastern Spain, particularly the Assumption plays of Tarragona, Valencia, and Elx. Performed on 15 August they commemorated the Virgin's death and assumption. *L'Assumpció de Madona Sancta Maria* ("The Assumption of Our Lady Holy Mary"), staged as early as 1388 in the Plaza del Corral of Tarragona, differs from the others in its close affiliation to the liturgy, the preponderance of song over recitation, and the use of horizontal staging. Prominent in the play are the Jews who are determined that the Virgin's soul should go to Hell and who later are blinded as they attempt to intercept the funeral cortège. The Valencian Assumption play (1420) survives only in the script belonging to the actor impersonating the Virgin. The play performed in the cathedral required both a horizontal and vertical stage that included a canopy heaven equipped with a mechanical lift (*araceli*) designed to lower the angels and Jesus and raise the Virgin. The malevolent Jews do not appear. The 1634 manuscript of the *Misteri d'Elx* is the oldest surviving version of the Elx Assumption play. The presence, however, of liturgical and troubadour melodies attests to the play's fifteenth-century origin. These Assumption plays glorified the Virgin as Mother of God and intercessor for humankind.[19]

In the secular realm, the coronations in Zaragoza of the Aragonese monarchs, Sibila in 1381, Martin I in 1399, and Fernando de Antequera in 1414 generated a flamboyant civic theatre that featured elaborate allegorical pageants called *entremeses*. The pageants were often accompanied by ideological and propagandistic texts, now mostly lost, that apotheosized the monarch. Political satire also flourished during times of social unrest. In the *Farsa de Avila* (1465) the unpopular Enrique IV of Castile is deposed in effigy and his brother enthroned in his place. The extant dialogue poem *Coplas de Mingo Revulgo* ("Verses of Mingo Revulgo," 1465?), which was inspired by Virgil's eclogues and Petrarch's bucolics,

---

[19] For more on this issue, see Ronald Surtz, "Los misterios asuncionistas en el este peninsular y la mediación mariana." In *Teatro y espectáculo en la Edad Media. Actas Festival d'Elx, 1990* (Elx: Instituto de Cultura "Juan Gil Albert" Diputación de Alicante, Ajuntament d'Elx, 1992), pp. 81–97; and Eduardo Juliá Martínez, "La Asunción de la Virgen y el teatro primitivo español." *Boletín de la Real Academia Española* 41 (1961), pp. 179–334.

employs pastoral allegory and a corresponding rustic dialect to urge not that the monarch be deposed but that the people reform. Angus MacKay believes the *Coplas* were staged before a rural audience on Corpus Christi Day, 13 June 1465, in Avila, Salamanca, or Zamora.[20]

The fifteenth-century Castilian court theatre is minutely recorded in the chronicle *Hechos del Condestable Don Miguel Lucas de Iranzo* ("Deeds of the Constable D. Miguel Lucas de Iranzo"). While the chronicler is lavish in his descriptions of the count's ostentatious spectacles mounted in the 1460s, he provides no dramatic scripts. The Magi play, conversion of the king of Morocco, jousts, tourneys, processions, *momos y personajes* (masked entertainers), banquets, and dances celebrated the values and superiority of the medieval knight. Yet the constable's phantasmagorical world concealed only temporarily the harsh political realities of Castile. Miguel Lucas de Iranzo was brutally murdered on 21 March 1473.

The courtly love poems of the *cancioneros* became theatrical scripts for court performances that absorbed both actors and spectators into a play world of make-believe, mimicry, and impersonation. Some poems like Rodrigo Cota's *Diálogo entre el Amor y un viejo* ("Debate Between Love and an Old Man"), the anonymous *Diálogo entre el Amor, el viejo y la Hermosa* ("The Debate Between Love, the Old Man, and the Beautiful Woman," both early sixteenth century), inspired by Cota's work, and Joan Ram Escrivá y Romaní's *Quexa ante el dios de Amor* ("The Complaint Before the God of Love," 1514) were veritable *autos de amores* ("plays of love") that justifiably qualify as theatre. In Francesc Moner's *Momería consertada de seis* ("Mumming Arranged for Six") the poetic script consists of verses (*motes*) and accompanying image that are embroidered on the knights' garments. By the turn of the century the nobility, lured to the pastoral life, masqueraded as shepherds and the courtly love lyrics were reworked as pastoral songs, often in dialogue, that anticipate *églogas* VII and VIII by Juan del Encina (1469 – after 1529).

The fifteenth century also records a religious and secular theatre created specifically for women. Although Spanish nuns were barred from saying Mass or administering the sacraments, a chosen few experienced mystical ecstasies, while others less privileged immersed themselves in the holy by acting in or attending religious plays. Between 1458 and 1468 Gómez Manrique composed *Representación del nacimiento de Nuestro Señor* ("The Play of the Birth of Our Lord") at the urging of his sister María Manrique, abbess of the convent of Poor Clares in Calabazanos

---

[20] Angus MacKay, "Ritual and Propaganda in Fifteenth-Century Castile." *Past and Present* 107 (1985), pp. 1–43.

(Palencia). This remarkable piece, whose structure replicates the liturgy[21] and whose content resembles a veritable *historia humanae salvationis* ("history of human salvation"), was designed to please an audience of female religious. A dream sequence in which an angel dispels Joseph's doubts about Mary and a *momería a lo divino* ("pantomime in a divine style"), in which the Virgin is presented with the instruments of Christ's Passion, are particularly noteworthy. Joseph is portrayed not as the cuck- olded old husband ridiculed in popular farce but as a distraught spouse concerned for his conjugal honor. Mary too retains her dignity as devoted wife and instrument of God's plan for humankind. When she learns of her son's future suffering, she expresses the deep anguish of the *mater dolorosa*. The nuns who participate in singing the *Canción para callar al Niño* ("Lullaby to Quiet the Child") are absorbed into the biblical world and vicariously share Mary's maternal bliss and sorrow.

The anonymous *Auto de la huida a Egipto* ("The Play of the Flight into Egypt") is recorded in a volume of devotional readings for the nuns of the convent of Santa María de la Bretonera in Burgos province. The *auto*, which was likely staged by the women in or near the convent, conflates the flight into Egypt, John the Baptist's sojourn in the wilderness, and the conversion of three thieves and a pilgrim. Poetry prevails over dramatic realism for the *auto* exhibits a variety of meters that shape the dialogue. The five *villancicos* distributed throughout the work further enhance its lyricism.[22]

The celebrated nun Sor Juana de la Cruz (1481–1534) of the Franciscan convent of Nuestra Señora de la Cruz in Cubas, near Toledo, com- missioned a *remembranza de todos los martires* ("The Play of All the Martyrs") for the feast of Saint Lawrence and another *remembranza* for the feast of the Assumption. Nothing is known of the first *remem- branza* but a devotional manuscript belonging to the convent contains two Assumption *autos*, the second one closely resembling the play requested by Sor Juana. The two works, though thematically and structurally different, are designed to appeal to a female community. The first one, composed entirely in *redondillas*, reduces the Assumption narrative to its essential core. Mary is informed by an angel of her imminent death, which is later witnessed by the disciples. Absent are God, Jesus, the malevolent Jews,

---

[21] See Harry Sieber, "Dramatic Symmetry in Gómez Manrique's *La representación del nacimiento de Nuestro Señor*." *Hispanic Review* 33 (1965), pp. 118–135; Alan Deyermond, "Historia sagrada y técnica dramática en la Representación del nacimiento de Nuestro Señor de Gómez Manrique." In *Historia y ficciones: Coloquio sobre la literatura del siglo XV* (Valencia: Universitat de València, 1992), pp. 281–305; Zimic, "Teatro," pp. 353–380.

[22] Ronald E. Surtz, *Teatro Castellano de la Edad Media* (Madrid: Taurus, 1992), pp. 37–42; Pérez Priego, *Teatro*, pp. 101–105.

and the insidious demons. Missing too are scenes depicting Mary's resurrection, assumption, and coronation. The poet emphasizes instead her motherhood and her humanity with the lyrical and devotional aspects all but eclipsing the theatrical. The second Assumption play, which juxtaposes the fall of Lucifer and the Assumption, exploits available stage machinery to maximum effect. In the confrontation between God and Lucifer, God remains hidden in order to make a spectacular appearance after the devil is expelled from heaven. Theatrical suspense is also generated by darkening the stage during the cosmic battle between the good and bad angels. Young men wearing painted wings play the angels, while the role of Mary is entrusted to the handsomest young man. The playwright's poetic sensibility is captured in his lyrical description of Mary that recalls the beloved in the Song of Songs. Enthroned as queen of the angels, she holds the nuns in thrall in her dual role as Mother of God and intercessor for humankind.[23]

Even in the secular world, noble women commissioned plays and often acted in them. Among secular performances Francisco Imperial's *dezir* ("recitation") celebrating the birth of the future Juan II of Castile is the earliest known mumming featuring an all-female cast. The poet/narrator awakens in an idyllic setting, listens to two groups of singers, watches a procession of *dueñas* ("ladies") representing the planets, and looks on as eight angelic women encircle the child and beckon to the poet to step forward and kiss the prince.

Gómez Manrique produced a mumming for his nephew in which he dispenses with the narrator/expositor. Seven noble women embodying the three theological and four cardinal virtues pay homage to the boy in an allegorical piece that paves the way for the Golden Age *auto sacramental* (eucharistic play). He composed another mumming (1467) at the behest of Isabel of Castile to celebrate Prince Alfonso's fourteenth birthday. The women who impersonate the classical muses are disguised as colorful birds. They endow the young prince with the virtues befitting a Christian monarch.

Isabel's fondness for the theatre is further confirmed by her presence at processions and plays, many of them mounted in her honor, like the Seville procession of 1477 and the Barcelona festivities of 1481. At the latter she witnessed the *Representació de Sancta Eulalia* ("The Play of Saint Eulalia"). During the performance the saint stepped briefly out of the dramatic frame, approached the queen, and recited a poem in Catalan which is preserved in the *Llibre des solemnitats de Barcelona* ("Book of Ceremonies of Barcelona"). The ledger also records Isabel's pleasure "en mirar e hoyr la dita representacio" ("in watching and hearing this play").[24] In 1482 the monarch carried a lighted taper in the Corpus Christi procession in Madrid, and in December of that year a platform was erected in the church of San Salvador in Zaragoza from which Fernando and Isabel watched a nativity play. Among the expenses recorded in a bookkeeping ledger is the payment of "medio florín de oro" ("half a gold *florín*") to Maese Piphan for songs that were sung by Mary, Joseph, and the prophets. The scribe's observation that Joseph, Mary, and Jesus were impersonated by a real family implies that the role of Mary was performed by a woman.[25] Ysásaga's glowing account in 1500 of Christmas celebrations at the Portuguese court that included the liturgical *Dicite, pastores* as well as elaborate mummings further confirms Isabel's abiding interest in the theatre.

Consequently, the enigmatic reference in 1677 to a fifteenth-century playbook, no longer extant, *Relación de las comedias que se hizieron el año 1474 a la Reina Isabel y a la Princesa doña Juana, representadas por sus damas* ("Account of the Plays that Were Performed in the Year 1474 Before Queen Isabel and Princess Juana and Staged by Their Ladies in Waiting") becomes less problematic. Despite the anachronistic and misleading use of the term *comedia*, Spain's earliest known drama anthology most likely consisted of poetic *momerías* honoring Isabel at her coronation. Composed by court poets and performed by ladies in her entourage, they were in all likelihood closet dramas similar to Imperial's *dezir* and Manrique's mummings.

In the Middle Ages professional female entertainers from the lower social classes, including *soldaderas* (paid performers), *juglaresas* (minstrels), and *danzaderas* (dancers) were denounced as immoral by church and state. Yet in the fifteenth century noble women apparently did not demean their social station by actively participating in both the religious and secular theatre.

The closing years of the fifteenth century and opening decades of the sixteenth witnessed the burgeoning of theatrical activity and the full emergence of drama as literature. Printed editions of the plays further confirm their literary ascendency. They were perceived to be not only *theatrica* but *scriptura* and, with the advent of printing, became available to a reading public. Since Juan del Encina appended his eight dramatic *églogas* to his vast 1496 *Cancionero* ("Songbook"), the 1514 edition of *Farsas y églogas* by Lucas Fernández (1474–1542), which contains only plays, is the oldest extant Spanish playbook. Well-defined theatrical genres took shape including religious *autos*, mythological and allegorical drama, pastoral

---

[24] Stern, *Medieval*, p. 114.
[25] Charlotte Stern, "A Nativity Play for the Catholic Monarchs." *Bulletin of the Comediantes* 43 (1991), pp. 71–100.

plays, political eulogy and satire, romantic comedy, and rollicking farce. These genres reached impressive heights with the bilingual Gil Vicente (1465–1535/1540) whose *Copilação* ("Collected Works") of forty-four plays was published by his son Luis in 1562.

Encina, enshrined for centuries as the father of the Spanish theatre, shunned the stage reenactment of events from the Bible and the apocrypha. Instead, he composed five narrative poems in traditional meters that are virtually devoid of dialogue. Although the sibyls speak their customary lines, the Magi remain silent; Herod does not rant and rave, and no traditional lament graces the poem *Al crucifijo* ("To the Crucifix"). In his dramatic *églogas* Encina, descendant of *conversos* (converted Jews), appears as a lowly shepherd and explores his ambivalent relationship to the house of Alba, including his feelings of inferiority and his yearning for social equality. The optimism apparent in the early *églogas* yields to increasing disillusionment until finally in the *Égloga de las grandes lluvias* ("The Play of the Torrential Rains," 1498) he openly criticizes his patrons as his position with them worsens. The autobiographical thrust of the plays and Encina's performance in them tie them to secular court mummings onto which Encina has now grafted an oblique treatment of the biblical events. The personal dimension, though still present in the *Égloga de las grandes lluvias*, is dwarfed by the shepherds' complaints about the inclement weather, the angel's announcement, and the shepherds' plans to visit the manger. The heavy rains also sharply differentiate the stage world from the spectators' space. So uncontrollable and devastating is the rain that it forces the shepherds to huddle together for shelter. Yet this harmony turns to discord, only to be restored when the shepherds are transformed by the angel's announcement of Jesus' birth.[26] Encina's Passion and Resurrection plays (*églogas* III and IV), which draw on the Gospels and the apocryphal *Acta Pilati* ("The Acts of Pilate"), emphasize the imperfection of humankind, the Christian doctrine of redemption, and the need for communal solidarity. These themes align Encina with *conversos* like Juan de Lucena and Alonso de Cartagena who earlier pleaded for the reconciliation of Old and New Christians. Henry Sullivan regards these plays, with their medieval themes, absence of action, question-and-answer technique, literalness, and formal style, as the least successful of Encina's dramatic works.[27]

Lucas Fernández's *Égloga o farsa del nascimiento de Jesu Christo* (1500) and *Auto o farsa del nascimiento de Jesu Christo* (1500–1502) ("The Play

---

[26] For more on Encina and Lucas Fernández, see Yvonne Yarbro Bejarano, "Juan del Encina's *Egloga de las grandes lluvias*: The Historical Appropriation of Dramatic Ritual." In *Creation and Re-Creation: Experiments in Literary Form in Early Modern Spain.* Ed. Ronald Surtz and Nora Weinerth (Newark: Juan de la Cuesta, 1983), pp. 7–27; and "Juan del Encina and Lucas Fernández: Conflicting Attitudes towards the Passion." *Bulletin of the Comediantes* 36 (1984), pp. 5–21.

[27] Henry Sullivan, *Juan del Encina* (Boston: Twayne, 1976), p. 54.

of the Birth of Jesus Christ") develop features of Íñigo de Mendoza's nativity scene. The announcement and theological meaning of the divine birth, however, are entrusted to the hermit Macario in the *égloga* and to the shepherd Juan in the *auto*. The rustic gifts and the *villancico* (dance song) figure prominently, but the actual adoration is not staged. Classical allusions in the *égloga* and the polyphonic *villancicos* in both plays bespeak a popular medieval tradition that has been appropriated and transformed by a Renaissance playwright.[28] Fernández's *Auto de la Pasión* ("Passion Play") recalls Christ's Passion in vivid narration. Historical perspective yields to spiritual timelessness as the Christian convert Dionysius of Athens bewails the death of Christ and the Jewish prophet Jeremiah laments the passion and afflictions of the "gran Tetragramaton" at the hands of the Jews. In keeping with the play's anti-Semitic tone, Jeremiah then forecasts the imminent destruction of the Jewish temple. He also brandishes an enormous black banner embroidered in red with the five wounds of Christ. In the early sixteenth century the *Adoratio crucis* ("Veneration of the Cross") or *Ceremonia del pendón* ("Ceremony of the Banner"), which was celebrated at the cathedrals of Oviedo, Leon, Zamora, Palencia, Zaragoza, Granada, and Guadix, featured such a banner, symbol of the cross. It was carried in procession by twelve canons as they chanted the hymn *Vexilla regis* ("Banner of the King"). Although evidence is lacking for this spectacular ceremony at the cathedral of Salamanca, it was so traditional that Fernández must have felt comfortable featuring the banner in his Passion play.

Gil Vicente's *Auto de la sibila Casandra* ("The Play of the Sibyl Casandra," 1513 or 1514) and *Auto de los cuatro tiempos* ("The Play of the Four Seasons," 1516), composed in Castilian, create still more impressive versions of the nativity story, while their multiple levels of meaning challenge a royal Portuguese audience. In the biblical, pastoral, allegorical, and lyrical *Auto de la sibila Casandra*, the Old Testament prophets and ancient sibyls no longer march stiffly in procession but are reinvented as shepherds and shepherdesses and integrated into the dramatic action. The presumptuous Casandra, antithesis of the Virgin and of the beloved in the Song of Songs, believes she is to be the Mother of God. She spurns her suitor Solomon and turns a deaf ear to his uncles Abraham, Moses, and Isaiah. She also ignores the prophecies of Erutrea, Cimeria, and Peresica, only to be persuaded of the truth with the unveiling of a manger scene. The *Auto de los cuatro tiempos* gives cosmic significance to the miraculous birth as personifications of the four seasons join Jupiter and David in paying homage to Mother and Child.

---

[28] John Lihani, *Lucas Fernández* (New York: Twayne, 1973), pp. 118–130.

The *danse macabre* resurfaces as professional drama but in Renaissance trappings in Vicente's *barca* trilogy as the classical images of boat and ferryman replace the gaunt figure of Death engaged in its fatal dance. Only in the *Auto de la barca de la gloria* ("The Play of the Ship of Heaven," 1519), composed in Castilian, does Death appear and hand over to the ferryman of Hell victims of high social and ecclesiastical rank. They are rescued at the last minute through Jesus' direct intervention. Víctor Infantes, in *Las danzas de la muerte*, suggests that Vicente was catering here to his wealthy and powerful patrons,[29] yet Jesus' intercession seems contrived and occurs only after the victims' sins are subjected to harsh criticism. Vicente, too, produced the earliest known Spanish saint's play *Auto de San Martín* ("The Play of Saint Martin," 1504), in which the saint shares his cloak with a beggar. The play dramatizes neither miracles nor martyrdom, the common themes of saints' plays, but a simple act of human kindness. Although it was staged at the convent of Las Caldas in Lisbon before the Portuguese Queen Leonor, its brevity makes it representative of Spanish Corpus Christi *autos*.

In the transition from Middle Ages to Renaissance, the shepherd occupied center stage in early secular drama. An extremely protean figure, he might be the embodiment of the earthy Hispanic rustic, a comic character parodying aristocratic pretentiousness, or a reincarnation of the idealized lovesick shepherd of Virgil's eclogues. In Encina's Carnival play (*égloga* VI, 1494) the shepherd barely recounts the battle between Carnival and Lent before joining his companions for the traditional Shrove Tuesday eating orgy that marks the end of carnival. The peasants' Saturnalian overindulgence is presented as a communal rite, yet the scene is also eminently burlesque. In the topsy turvy carnival world, the actors disguised as shepherds ridicule the peasants' gluttony, while the shepherds in their brief moment as courtiers deride the polished etiquette of the nobility. Lucas Fernández's secular plays deflate the lofty but sterile notion of courtly love by describing lovesickness in scatological language as acute digestive and intestinal malaise. Performed at aristocratic weddings they promote "the unabashed acceptance of the body's preeminent role" in courtship and marriage.[30] The earthy and comic rustic is relegated to the sidelines by his idealized counterpart in Encina's *Égloga de Cristino y Febea* and *Égloga de Plácida y Vitoriano*, both indisputably Renaissance creations.

Francisco de Madrid's politically motivated *égloga* (1495), inspired by the *Coplas de Mingo Revulgo* and composed in *coplas de arte mayor*, employs a thinly veiled pastoral disguise to expatiate on Fernando V's

[29] Infantes, *Las danzas*, pp. 332–333.
[30] Barbara F. Weissberger, "The Scatological View of Love in the Theater of Lucas Fernandez." *Bulletin of the Comediantes* 38 (1986), pp. 193–207.

anticipated defense of Naples and attack on Charles VIII of France. The work opens in a festive vein but ends on an apprehensive note with hostilities about to break out. Alberto Blecua believes the *égloga* was designed to galvanize the audience of Italian ambassadors not to a political response but to a religious one, to pray for the end of war and the coming of a new golden age.[31] The alternation of monologue/dialogue reminiscent of medieval debates, the pastoral allegory, the rustic dialect reflecting the medieval theory of the three styles, and the pre-aesthetic perspective demonstrate the resiliency of a medieval theatrical genre at the height of the Italian Renaissance.

Gil Vicente, too, composed numerous festival plays for the Portuguese monarchy, from the *Exhortação da guerra* ("The Exhortation to War," 1516) to the *Auto da Lusitânia* ("The Play of Lusitania," 1532). A full-blown dramatic script that combines poetic dialogue and traditional songs is grafted onto the medieval pageant with its spectacular stage effects. The plays are court theatre, occasion pieces whose purpose is to praise the monarch and celebrate his achievements. Like the earlier court theatre, the festival plays often breach the barrier separating the theatrical world from the audience's space. The monarch particularly is both silent participant and spectator. The *Auto da Lusitânia* uses the play-within-a-play to depict a contemporary Jewish family and also to dramatize the mythological origin of Portugal. It celebrates the birth of Prince Manuel as it also urges greater tolerance toward New Christians who had come under attack after the earthquake of 1531 in Santarem.[32] Vicente's poetic and musical talents are on full display in the festival plays. Indeed Thomas R. Hart takes pains to emphasize that Vicente's remarkable imagination endows the plays with elements of fantasy and lyricism that sharply distinguish them from the lackluster accounts of the same events recorded in contemporary chronicles.[33]

Yet Vicente was above all the master of popular farce. His characters and plots reflect contemporary Iberian society as they also sink deep roots in the ancient world. His audience, however, was Portuguese royalty and aristocracy. Replete with carnivalesque inversions and slapstick humor, the farces ridicule lecherous old men and women, cuckolded husbands, hypocritical young wives, pompous but destitute squires, venal judges, and avaricious go-betweens. They also attack pressing social ills including

[31] Alberto Blecua, "La *Égloga* de Francisco de Madrid en un nuevo manuscrito del siglo XVI." *Serta Philologica F. Lázaro Carreter natalem diem sexagesimum celebranti dicata* (Madrid: Cátedra, 1983), p. 45.

[32] Stanislaw Zimic, "Nuevas consideraciones sobre el *Auto da Lusitânia* de Gil Vicente." In *Homenaje a A. Zamora Vicente* (Madrid: Castalia, 1991), Vol. III, pp. 356–369.

[33] Thomas R. Hart, ed. *Gil Vicente, Farsas and Festival Plays* (Eugene, OR: University of Oregon, 1972), pp. 44–45.

economic depression, an incompetent judiciary, Christian hypocrisy, state marriages of convenience, domestic squabbles, and male–female relationships that mock courtly love ideals. Portuguese- and Spanish-speaking characters converse easily with one another, which implies that an aristocratic Spanish public would have also understood the Portuguese dialogue. Some plays like the *Tragicomédia do triunfo de inverno* ("The Tragicomedy of the Triumph of Winter," 1528?) blend the farcical with the lyrical, while others contain such detailed stage directions embedded in the dialogue that the attentive reader can easily envision the performance. These passages also suggest that the stage realization of the plays was paramount in Vicente's mind as he composed the dramatic script. In his complex role of scriptwriter, producer, stage manager, set and costume designer, Vicente like Alonso del Campo before him foreshadows the Golden Age *autores de comedias*. His bilingual *Auto da Índia* ("The Play of India"), in which the vivacious Constança entertains a string of male suitors during her husband's sojourn in India, revisits Juan Ruiz's tale of Pitas Payas as it also anticipates Miguel de Cervantes' *Entremés del viejo celoso* ("The Interlude of the Jealous Old Man"), while the *Farsa do Juiz de Beira* ("The Farce of the Judge of Beira"), in which a motley crew of plaintiffs seek justice before an incompetent judge, offers a preview of Cervantes' *Entremés del juez de los divorcios* ("The Interlude of the Divorce Court Judge").

Fernando de Rojas' *Tragicomedia de Calisto y Melibea* ("The Tragicomedy of Calisto and Melibea"), commonly called *Celestina*, was conceived in the spirit of late medieval humanistic comedy, an inordinately popular genre cultivated by accomplished writers. Retitling the work and suppressing its generic affiliation have encouraged its characterization as a novel. Repeated printings of the *Tragicomedia* in the early sixteenth century attest to its readerly appeal. Indeed nothing prevented a private reading, but the author and proofreader had in mind an oral reading, which was a widely practiced form of entertainment even in ancient Rome. A lector or lectors read the dialogue aloud, exploiting fully the marvelous versatility of the human voice in order to convey the characters' identities and moods. The listeners were expected to envision a fictional universe but, because the *tragicomedia* was drama, that universe was perceived as a stage representation with all the necessary theatrical props and effects. D. G. Pattison characterizes this type of drama as "theatre of the mind."[34]

As evidence mounts of theatrical activity in medieval Iberia, the bleak landscape evoked repeatedly in the past must yield to the image of a

---

[34] D. G. Pattison, "The Theatricality of *Celestina*." In *The Medieval Mind: Hispanic Studies in Honour of Alan Deyermond*. Ed. I. MacPherson and R. Penny (London: Támesis, 1997), p. 324.

diverse theatre that defies conventional categorization. Performances in Latin, Castilian, Catalan, Galician-Portuguese, Arabic, Valencian, and Portuguese attest to the cultural pluralism of the region. No particular genre hovers above the others; indeed one must perforce speak of impure or hybrid genres. In this fluid and shifting environment, modern notions of theatre are not adequate; nor does a bright line separate theatre from nontheatre. Since writing absorbs and transforms performances, medieval collections like the *cancioneros* should be revisited as potential sources of performance texts which often present the antiofficial, carnivalesque world view. Only in the transition from Middle Ages to Renaissance is the integrity of the theatrical script respected as plays are increasingly esteemed as literary artifacts. Yet the three major Spanish Golden Age genres, *comedia* (three-act play), *auto sacramental* (eucharistic play), and *entremés* (comic interlude) have not yet taken shape. Throughout this period, the theatre remains close to its ritual origins. The absence of aesthetic distance, the ceremonial and communal nature of the plays, and their performance at religious feasts, civic festivals, or private rites of passage should encourage an anthropological as well as a literary approach to the medieval theatre.

Part IV

Early Modern Spain: Renaissance and Baroque

Jeremy Robbins, Alison P. Weber,
Julian Weiss, E. Michael Gerli,
Anthony J. Close, Mary Malcolm
Gaylord, Margaret R. Greer, Victor
F. Dixon, Evangelina Rodríguez
Cuadros, Jorge Checa

7

Renaissance and Baroque: continuity and transformation in early modern Spain

JEREMY ROBBINS

Each term used to describe the period in which Spain saw a burgeoning of new ideas and new literary forms that helped create a brilliant flowering of prose, poetry, and drama brings with it a distinct view of how that period is to be conceptualized and evaluated. The "Golden Age" refers now by common consent to the literature of both the sixteenth and seventeenth centuries, but critics in previous centuries, excluding on aesthetic grounds seventeenth-century literature from the canon of truly "great" national literature, applied the term only to the sixteenth. Applied now to both centuries it suggests a unified period, not uncoincidentally conterminous with Habsburg rule in Spain (1516–1700), in which differences are outweighed by similarities, the latter often amounting simply to an uncritical notion of literary "greatness" thought applicable to both centuries. In contrast, the terms "Renaissance" and "Baroque" suggest a view of Golden Age literature in which, due to changing intellectual, cultural, and political factors, each century has its own characteristic literary and intellectual ethos. This is what will be argued here, but such a view is especially contentious to those who see the Baroque as a problematic label precisely because, as an anachronistic term developed initially to describe the visual arts, there is little consensus as to its meaning. Its value outweighs the problems inherent in its usage, however, for it not only serves to distinguish seventeenth-century culture from that of the preceding century, but links Spain very broadly to international trends, thereby countering what has long been a forceful element in Spanish historiography, namely the view of Golden Age Spain as intellectually and culturally isolated.

The term "early modern" has gained currency as a descriptive term for the transition from a medieval world view to a more recognizably modern, secular, scientific, and bourgeois one. The Renaissance and Baroque are two key phases in this transitional period which stretched from the late fifteenth to the eighteenth century. The designation "early modern" implies a view of Spain during the Golden Age not always accepted, especially by non-Hispanists, namely that it *was* undergoing a decisive move toward modernity in the sixteenth and seventeenth centuries. It is undeniable, however, that the culture of Golden Age Spain was produced during a protracted period of intense transformation which saw intellectual, social, and religious certainties gradually challenged and eventually changed by the Protestant Reformation of the sixteenth century and the scientific and philosophic revolutions of the seventeenth. This process may have been slower in Spain than in some countries, but it occurred nevertheless. The trends of thought with which Spanish literature was most intimately involved included Erasmianism, Neoplatonism, humanism, Stoicism, and skepticism. Of these the first two had the greatest impact in the sixteenth century and affected both religious and secular works, while the last two more profoundly helped redefine thought and literature in the seventeenth century. The transformations provoked by the intellectual challenges confronting Spain were intensified by the Spanish and Portuguese encounters with the cultures of America and Asia and by the political decline of Spain itself over the seventeenth century. The vibrancy and diversity of Golden Age literature is due in large part to Spaniards attempting to accommodate, advance, or reject the massive intellectual and political changes encountered by the country throughout the early modern period. There is thus a complex causal relationship between literature and intellectual and political developments, a relationship not so much of external influences shaping literary creation as of literature being an integral part of a process of cultural negotiation and national self-definition.

Although external factors exercised decisive influences on literature throughout the Golden Age, a major distinction should be made between the way its two phases related to these. The Spanish Renaissance is the period when the literary models of the Italian Renaissance were adopted. Spanish literature is thus consciously imitative as Spain sought to assimilate a preexisting cultural model whose literary style was largely alien to its native traditions and practices. In sharp contrast, although the Spanish Baroque drew upon European trends in thought, and was a direct response to the major epistemological developments that led elsewhere to the new philosophy and science, there were no preexisting literary models to emulate in assimilating and responding to these. Literature therefore developed its own response, centered on the development of a distinctive nexus of appearance and reality, to express the crisis in European thought. Once the process of direct and conscious emulation of Italian culture was completed by the Renaissance, therefore, Spanish literature gained a far greater degree of cultural autonomy. The Spanish Baroque thus constitutes a unique contribution to European culture, and designates the period when Spanish literature began to come into its own, developing new styles (the aesthetic of wit with its dual aspects of *culteranismo* and *conceptismo*), new genres (the novel and the *comedia*), and a distinctively pessimistic ethos which, despite parallels, was unlike anything else in Europe. It could achieve this, of course, because Spanish literature by the end of the sixteenth century had successfully integrated the existing literary models of the Italian Renaissance. Significantly, in the eighteenth century the seventeenth century came to be seen as an aberration, its style in particular a betrayal of the Renaissance ideals of clarity, harmony, and decorum. Only with the German Romantics at the end of the eighteenth and beginning of the nineteenth centuries (Friedrich and Wilhelm von Schlegel predominantly) and their obsession with Calderón,[1] and the recuperation of Góngora by the Spanish poets of the Generation of 1927 did the writers of the Baroque join the canon. What is significant in this very late recuperation of the Baroque is precisely that it acknowledges the way in which it is sharply divergent from the Renaissance. Such divergence is real, but it should not occlude the ways in which the Baroque transforms Renaissance models to meet the political and intellectual challenges of seventeenth-century Europe. If the Renaissance is thus a conscious break with late medieval literature, the Baroque is the intensification and transformation of aspects of Renaissance culture, rather than a radical departure from them, in ways that took Spain decisively toward a more recognizably modern world view.

Vernacular humanism and Italian literary models had made their presence felt in fifteenth-century Spain and this fact complicates the question of whether the Renaissance was a purely sixteenth-century phenomenon. This said, full exposure to Italian literature and to certain aspects of Italian and northern European humanism and the subsequent decisive transformation of vernacular literature only truly took place in the sixteenth century, largely as a result of political developments. The conquest of Naples in 1503–1504, for example, deepened Spain's direct contact with Italy while the succession of Charles V (Carlos I of Spain) in 1516 exposed Spaniards fully to northern humanism. Humanism and the interest it fostered in literary philology and especially classical antiquity played a dominant role throughout the Golden Age, shaping the conception of the individual, society, and literature. It offered not an integrated or systematic philosophic system but rather a set of values and ideals drawn largely from antiquity from which writers constructed their own eclectic moral system. Given the importance of rhetoric, history, and poetry to the *studia humanitatis* it is hardly surprising that literature became a prime vehicle for the moral philosophy which lay at the heart of humanism as it developed in Spain. Works of entertainment consequently raised the same issues over agency, perception, knowledge, and authority as moral, political, ascetic, and devotional works, a fact which tends to blur the boundaries of what constitutes "literature" in the Golden Age. Humanism's attraction had

---

[1] For a study of the reception of Calderón in northern Europe, see Henry W. Sullivan, *Calderón in the German Lands and the Low Countries. His Reception and Influence, 1654–1980* (Cambridge: Cambridge University Press, 1983).

much to do with the fact that it effectively separated moral thought from philosophy *per se*, creating a literary space thereby in which writers could consider society and the moral responsibilities of the individual without trespassing on the philosophical technicalities of metaphysics and theology, of obvious appeal to a culture darkened by the Inquisition. To a degree, therefore, it fostered a kind of secularization of moral values in so far as religion could be left to one side while purely human affairs were treated. In the sixteenth century the humanist view that the individual could be shaped to fulfill a civic role rested on the fundamentally idealistic notion of the *dignitas hominis*. While there was a strong element of Augustinian pessimism regarding the human condition, this fundamental optimism resulted in a far more confident vision of our capacity for moral improvement: Fernán Pérez de Oliva's *Diálogo de la dignidad del hombre* ("Dialogue on the Dignity of Man," 1546), for example, while offering a pessimistic interpretation of mankind, proposes a stronger argument in favor of human dignity. Such optimism was characteristic of the Spanish Renaissance.

Northern humanism in the shape of the Erasmian movement dominated the first half of the sixteenth century until Erasmus' works were proscribed in the mid century. Erasmus' influence was as much spiritual as literary and many individuals were influenced by his reformism and pietism. Aside from Erasmianism, the Renaissance fostered other reformist and spiritual elements that would shape European culture. Ignatius of Loyola, for example, founded in 1540 the Jesuits, an order which would become synonymous with the Catholic Reformation and the Baroque and whose educational reforms further propagated knowledge of the classics, while the Spanish mystics San Juan de la Cruz and Santa Teresa de Jesús helped shape Counter Reformation spirituality. Spanish mysticism in general, and Jesuit meditation in particular, has also been seen as a source of a heightened awareness of external reality in all its graphic specificity and thus of the literary realism that is a feature of such Spanish genres as the picaresque. Spanish ascetic and religious writing certainly affected Spaniards' perception of reality and led to the complex fusion of the spiritual and the material and the dual focus of seeing matters from both a human and an eternal perspective which are so characteristic of Golden Age literature. This raises the complex question of the relationship between Catholicism and Spanish literature. The latter has frequently been read as profoundly orthodox in its ideas and mentality, an extension of the religious zeal and unquestioning religious commitment taken to be a national characteristic of the period. It would be more accurate to stress less the uniquely Catholic nature of Spanish literature *per se* than the centrality of religion to any early modern mentality. In this way, the influence of religion is not automatically mistaken for authorial piety, nor is Spanish literature seen as more religious than any other national literature. Equally, this allows Spain the capacity for doubt, questioning, and dissent which more accurately reflects aspects of its culture during the early modern period, and recognizes the influence of more "heterodox" thought such as the Cabala or Hermeticism on its literature.

As Spaniards were increasingly exposed to Italian literature, so they began to view the vernacular as a source of patriotism and a worthy vehicle for literature alongside Latin. Juan de Valdés' *Diálogo de la lengua* ("Dialogue on Language," *c.* 1535) was an early expression of interest in perfecting Spanish as a literary language, a process which culminated in the commentaries written on Garcilaso de la Vega's poetry by El Brocense (1574) and Fernando de Herrera (1580). Garcilaso had been one of the first Spaniards successfully to introduce Italian meters and verse forms into Spanish, with his poetry drawing also on the Petrarchan models which rapidly transformed amatory discourse in poetry and prose. The significance of the commentaries on his poetry lay less in their rhetorical analysis of the poetry itself than in the elevation of a Spanish poet to a position of equality with classical writers on whom commentaries were normally written. These commentaries thus mark the beginnings of Spanish literary self-confidence and autonomy.

Garcilaso's verse also popularized the Virgilian bucolic as mediated by Sannazaro, which in turn gave rise to the pastoral novel which offered an idealized portrayal of nature and sought to analyze love in a predominantly Neoplatonic way. This Neoplatonic strain was to dominate Spanish Renaissance literature and was instrumental in imbuing it with its stylistic and thematic emphasis on proportion, balance, and harmony. These aesthetic ideals were posited as underlying creation itself in poems by Francisco de Aldana and Luis de León. Neoplatonism had been formulated in the Italian Renaissance by Ficino and was given influential expression in Spain by Castiglione's *Il cortegiano* ("The Courtier," 1528) and Leone Ebreo's *Dialoghi d'amore* ("Dialogues on Love," 1535). Its vision of the harmony of the universe and the ascent of the soul from material to spiritual reality and its notion of the love of physical beauty leading to the contemplation of the source of beauty itself in God offered an integrated vision of creation, one that exalted the individual's place in the scheme of things and the beauty of creation itself while also simultaneously urging the individual to transcend the material. It offered a means of conceptualizing love and beauty in both the physical and spiritual realms and, by linking the former to the latter, acted as a counterpoint to the Augustinian divide between the body and soul, the world of the flesh and the perfection of heaven. The largely Neoplatonic vision of the harmony between the macrocosm and the microcosm is expressed in magnificent prose works of the period like Luis de Granada's *Introducción del símbolo de la fe* ("Introduction to the Creed," 1583) and Luis de León's *De los nombres de Cristo* ("On the Names of Christ," 1583), and the fact that it also greatly influenced Renaissance amatory and spiritual poetry makes Neoplatonism a defining influence on the Spanish Renaissance.

Once Italian models in prose and poetry and the discourses of Petrarchanism and civic humanism had been assimilated by the Renaissance, Spanish literature began to develop from European literature in more distinct and original ways. This is reflected in the fact that the process of influence began to be reversed, with Spanish literature – Alemán, Cervantes, Lope, Tirso, Gracián, Saavedra Fajardo – being rapidly translated and influencing, for example, the development of French prose, theatre, and moral literature. The relationship between the Renaissance and Baroque as two stages of the early modern period is itself characterized by a process of continuity, intensification, and transformation. Baroque writers take existing elements of Renaissance culture and, due to the changed intellectual and political climate, forge these into a distinct conception of the human condition. There is, of course, a profound intellectual continuity between the Renaissance and Baroque provided above all by the dominance of moral philosophy aimed at practical solutions to emerging moral and political problems rather than a rigid, systematic analysis. Alongside the scholasticism which dominated the university curricula, it is philosophically the very longevity of humanism in Spain which makes Spanish intellectual activity now appear backward. Spain's adherence to Aristotelian and Thomist metaphysics meant that it failed to respond to the seventeenth-century revival of skepticism and Epicurean atomism which, in other parts of Europe, led to the development of mechanistic philosophy. This conception of moral philosophy as a practical discipline characterized by its eclecticism meant that Spaniards eschewed innovative abstract thought and system building and therefore produced no individual figure of major philosophical importance.

The tendency to view the seventeenth century in particular as intellectually bankrupt comes from a failure to see that, faced with the same moral and epistemological issues as elsewhere in Europe, Spain attempted to explore the human aspect of such issues in the humanist tradition rather than via systematic philosophy. Here the lack of a concept equivalent to that of *moraliste* is a major hurdle to the proper evaluation of the way that Spaniards conceived and practiced moral philosophy, for it tends to prevent the type of utilitarian and pragmatic thought which was prevalent in seventeenth-century Spain, and typified by the likes of Baltasar Gracián, Antonio López de Vega, and Francisco Gutiérrez de los Ríos, from being seen as a coherent and intelligent response to a changing political and moral climate. The major contribution to Spain's progress toward intellectual modernity of these writers who effected a reversal of existing paradigms, emphasizing the importance of the contingent over the universal, *parecer* ("to seem to be") over *ser* ("to be"), moral pragmatism over rigid ethical rules, is thereby occluded. For, as Baroque writers of the mid seventeenth century began to reverse such binaries, so they redefined the value system inherited from the Renaissance and laid the intellectual foundations of an empiricist epistemology that made Spain one of the countries most receptive to John Locke (1632–1704), whose *Essay on Human Understanding* (1690) had a major impact on the Spanish eighteenth century.

The dual process of continuity and transformation that characterizes the relationship between Renaissance and Baroque is nowhere more evident than in Golden Age aesthetics. The conception of beauty as the result predominantly of proportion and harmony remains constant. What changes are the effects sought, the desire for novelty and surprise leading poets like Góngora and Quevedo to draw even more heavily than their Renaissance predecessors on Latin syntax (with hyperbaton, or complicated word order, becoming a defining characteristic of Góngora's style in particular), neologisms, and complex conceits to create a dense textual surface. Difficulty rather than clarity was the desired aim, an aim consciously grounded in a pronounced social and literary elitism. Gracián's *Agudeza y arte de ingenio* ("Wit and the Art of Ingenuity," 1642/1648) well illustrates this shift in aesthetic emphasis: many of its examples are drawn from sixteenth-century poets, but the qualities praised are incisive wit and the epigrammatic presentation of striking conceits. In other words, the seventeenth century prized certain qualities of fifteenth- and sixteenth-century verse above others and in foregrounding these theorized them into a new aesthetic. What the new aesthetic of wit with its central concepts of difficulty, surprise, novelty, and wonder encapsulates is the aim of Baroque literature to engage the senses and minds of the reader/spectator, a desire also evident in its far greater dynamism and metatextuality. As a result Spanish literature becomes more sensual in its imagery, more visceral in its descriptions, and more theatrical in its conception of the self.

In general terms the Baroque is the period when the optimism and idealism of the Renaissance gave way to intellectual and existential pessimism. Such pessimism had both political/social and intellectual roots. On the political front, a series of wars, not least the Thirty Years' War (1618–1648) and the war with the French (1635–1659), saw the balance of power shift from Spain to France, the Dutch Republic, and England. While, with the benefit of hindsight, we see this as an inexorable political decline, it is worth stressing that although Spaniards were indeed acutely aware of political and economic crisis – as seen, for example, by the *arbitristas* of the 1590s and early 1600s and later political works such as Quevedo's *Política de Dios* ("Politics of God," 1626/1655) and Diego de Saavedra Fajardo's *Idea de un príncipe político-cristiano* ("Idea of the Political-Christian Prince," 1640/1642) – the decline was a slow one whose outcome was not settled until the mid-century.

Intellectually, Spanish Baroque literature owes most to its engagement with Stoicism and skepticism, two classical philosophies whose rediscovery was one of the most tangible effects of late humanism. The presence of these two philosophies across the entire seventeenth century is both a cause and a consequence of humanism's continued hold on Spain. The seemingly endemic presence of war led to Neostoicism's popularity in Europe. Nowhere did Neostoicism take root as it did in Spain where the ruling elite helped make it an integral component of political thought. Neostoicism taught the individual to separate those things within one's control from those without. In Spain this led to a century of moralists urging individuals to separate appearances from reality and so disabuse themselves of the false values of this world, a state of correct moral and epistemological perception referred to as *desengaño*. The urge to become *desengañado* obviously presupposes that we all live in a state of *engaño*, and thus the notion of deceit infuses all Baroque literature and creates the disjunction between appearances (*parecer*) and reality (*ser*). The interconnected notions of *ser/parecer* and *desengaño/engaño* define more than any other the contours of the sharply antithetical Baroque world view, a mentality of antinomy in which body and soul, heaven and earth, salvation and damnation are violently contrasted, and in which realism and idealism are held in juxtaposition rather than integrated as, for example, in Renaissance Platonism. It is the dominant presence of these concepts and of the world view they seek to express which serves to differentiate Renaissance from Baroque literature, and equally it is the abandonment of them in the final decades of the seventeenth century which signals the Baroque's end and the start of the early Enlightenment in Spain.

The sense of crisis was exacerbated by the rekindling of interest in Academic skepticism and Pyrrhonism which took place in Spain in the opening decades of the seventeenth century. Skepticism further fostered the perception of universal deceit by emphasizing the unreliability of the senses. Raising both epistemological and moral issues, skepticism called into question the possibility of secure and certain knowledge. The existing intellectual disciplines underpinned by Aristotelian scholasticism were thus threatened, and Spaniards were particularly concerned that philosophy would decenter theology, a view that intensified over the Baroque and into the eighteenth century precisely as the *novatores* ("new thinkers") made inroads into the separation of intellectual enquiry from religious dogma. From the start of the seventeenth century Spaniards systematically deployed skeptical arguments and rhetoric that had been part of the humanist rhetorical tradition stemming from Cicero, a tradition that had been present in the previous century in the writings of the Spanish humanist Juan Luis Vives. Now, though, the rhetoric of doubt expressed a widespread intellectual hesitancy and an unfulfilled desire for certainty that was articulated by writers like Cervantes and dramatists like Calderón and Tirso.

Skepticism's influence was most pronounced in the 1640s and 1650s when Saavedra's *Idea de un príncipe político-cristiano*, López de Vega's *Heráclito y Demócrito de nuestro siglo* ("Our Century's Heraclitus and Democritus," 1641), and Gracián's *El Criticón* (three parts 1651, 1653, 1657) addressed the fraught matter of perception and, by fusing skepticism with Neostoicism in ways not found elsewhere in Europe, developed new means of undertaking intellectual enquiry and thus new criteria for what constitutes knowledge. Their concern with the practical rather than the purely theoretical or philosophical impact of skepticism is what sets Spain's engagement with skepticism apart from the rest of Europe's. It is only with the *novatores* that the philosophical issues raised are tackled head-on. What both skepticism and Neostoicism reflect is the waning of the confidence embodied in the humanist tradition whose pessimistic features came to dominate the Baroque. Not surprisingly, the ubiquity of doubt created a counter literature of aggressive assertion as to the absolute truth of Catholicism, extrapolating from such fideism a moral code that was so rigid in its separation of right from wrong that no room was left for skeptical cavillations. In this way, Baroque literature maintains a fraught tension between absolute certainty and radical insecurity.

While appearance and reality, deceit and disillusion, are the hallmarks of Baroque literature, they are found too in many Renaissance texts. The humor and social criticism of *Lazarillo de Tormes* (1554), for example, stems in part from the obvious disparity between outer appearance and inner reality. The difference between the expression of such notions in the Renaissance and in the Baroque has much to do with the impact of Neostoicism and skepticism. While Stoicism had been a feature of fifteenth- and sixteenth-century literature, its overt fusion with Christianity, and its presentation as a philosophy ideally suited to the religious and military upheavals of the early seventeenth century by Justus Lipsius, delivered it to readers as a coherent moral and political stance which taught the individual how to weather the unavoidable vicissitudes of a period of great ideological conflict. Together with skepticism's concurrent questioning of the reliability of our senses, this created a much more cynical and pessimistic mentality which drew on the Christian notion of *contemptus mundi* and led directly to the ubiquity of the terms *ser/parecer* and *desengaño/engaño* to encapsulate the tensions in the prevailing vision of reality. Consequently, texts like Mateo Alemán's *Guzmán de Alfarache* (1599 and 1604) or Gracián's *El Criticón* transform the incidental elements of deception found piecemeal in Renaissance texts and make them central to a vision of society in which deceit is present on every level imaginable: not simply personal and institutional, but sensory, intellectual, and existential.

It has frequently been suggested that the Golden Age in general was marked by the imposition of a monolithic political, religious, and social ideology from which no dissent was possible and that the Baroque in particular was a *dirigiste* culture in which literature, and especially theatre, was deployed to propagate the state's ideology, with the New Historicist twist that subversion was permitted simply so that it could be contained and thus controlled. This model of Golden Age society feeds into the vision of Spain held by most non-Hispanists: an intellectually backward society, isolated from Europe and adhering with increasing rigidity as the period progresses to a political and intellectual world view that was losing ground elsewhere in Europe. This follows many of the contours of the *leyenda negra* ("black legend"), with such things as the Inquisition, censorship, Spain's religious orthodoxy and active extirpation of heterodox thought, and Felipe II's 1559 decree forbidding Castilians from studying abroad all seeming to confirm the picture of an anti-intellectual and reactionary society resisting any transition to the modern world. Such a vision is propagated by the absence of Spain from most non-Spanish accounts of early modern political thought and philosophy. The truth, of course, is more complex. Like most of early modern Europe, Spain resisted change and was conservative. It was, like most European states, particularly inflexible in matters of religious dogma. However, in both the sixteenth and the seventeenth centuries Spain engaged with European thought: the Renaissance was a movement grounded in European intellectual trends while the Spanish Baroque was as responsive in its own way to major shifts in contemporary epistemology as the cultures of any European nation. On this basis alone, it is impossible to speak of Spain's intellectual isolation. Further, the fact that Spain shared with the whole of Europe a common cultural humanist heritage rooted in the classics meant that many of its terms of reference, its models, and its ideals were identical to those being used elsewhere, and such a heritage was a major bridge across the confessional divides. The difference, of course, lies in what Spain did with these models, and that difference becomes most apparent in the seventeenth century when the new philosophy began to redefine philosophy itself by radically breaking with Aristotelian and scholastic thought. Here, in fact, is perhaps the crux of the problem and of Spain's difference vis-à-vis Europe: Spain's inability to move beyond the classical paradigms and develop new modes of thought and enquiry not envisaged by ancient authors. Even at their most radical, Spanish thinkers tend simply to switch from one classical model (e.g. Aristotelianism) to another (e.g. Academic skepticism), and whether this is due to the deep-rootedness of humanism, to the enforcement of orthodoxy and the Aristotelian-scholastic model, or to the lack of institutional support for the new science and philosophy, the result is that Golden Age Spain took decisive steps toward the secularism and empiricism characteristic of modernity but could not break definitively with the prevailing terms of the old metaphysical and epistemological models.

As far as literature is concerned, the notion of a *dirigiste* culture posits writers as propagators of official ideology. Naturally this happened, and the nature of early modern patronage meant that those involved in a client–patron relationship necessarily had critical parameters clearly established. To a large extent, however, those who propound the idea of a *dirigiste* culture put too much emphasis on the anachronistic notions of creative freedom and of literature as personal expression. Informed by humanist ideals and by the classical idea of instruction through entertainment, Golden Age writers rather engaged in a critique of society for the improvement of both the individual and society. In this model, it is not a question of conformity or indeed of subversion, but of engaged and committed criticism and critique which were voiced throughout the Golden Age in both print and, especially, manuscript. Spain permitted a remarkable degree of debate over political and moral matters. Its preferred political model was, in theory and practice, contractual. Literature was thus constantly engaged with social issues. From *Lazarillo de Tormes* and the picaresque, through the stage's constant examination of authority and control and the social concept of honor, to María de Zayas' and Sor Juana Inés de la Cruz's overt feminist polemics and analyses of the political construction of gender roles, literature critiqued social practices and found them wanting. Only recently with studies on the ways colonialism, ethnicity, and sexuality affected literature has the diversity of early modern culture and thus the complexity of Spanish literature's engagement with society begun to be fully acknowledged.

The picture suggested here of Golden Age Spain posits the Renaissance and Baroque as two central yet distinct phases in the country's transition to modernity. The crisis that would lead to a secular and scientific world view began in the Renaissance with the split in Western Christianity. The Renaissance itself introduced Spain to the civic and secular values of Italian humanism which centered on the intense revival of interest in antiquity. It thus made Spain receptive to Neoplatonism and, more importantly, to Stoicism and skepticism, paving the way for the Baroque's gradual reversal of existing paradigms. Although always contested, the process of the secularization of intellectual enquiry nevertheless began to gather momentum across the seventeenth century. It is precisely the negotiation of this paradigm shift which gave rise in Spain to a literature of immense imaginative range, intense human and social engagement, and exquisite force and beauty that truly justifies the term "Golden Age".

8

Religious literature in early modern Spain

ALISON P. WEBER

Much of what was written, published, and read in early modern Spain could be described as "religious literature" – over 3,000 books, by one estimate.[1] The figures for subcategories of religious works are similarly impressive. Melquíades Andrés Martín's recent history of mysticism in Golden Age Spain includes a bibliography of 1,200 "books of spirituality" written in Latin, Catalan, and Spanish; 444 individual hagiobiographies were published between 1480 and 1700, a figure that does not include re-editions, popular collections of saints' lives, or the 507 works on the Virgin Mary. The total figure for "religious literature" would be even greater if we included popular religious printing (inexpensive broadsheets, pamphlet-sized catechisms, and primers, almost all of which have been lost); *farsas* (short mystery plays) and *autos sacramentales* (one-act plays celebrating the Eucharist); ecclesiastical publications (Holy Scripture and works of the church fathers, works on canon law, sermons, and guides for the clergy); devotional poetry; and imaginative literature such as Mateo Alemán's *Guzmán de Alfarache* and Cervantes' *Los trabajos de Persiles y Sigismunda* (both narratives of Christian redemption), or the many chivalric and pastoral novels allegorized "a lo divino" ("in the divine style").[2] Suffice it to say that religious literature, even when the most narrow definition of this term is applied, enjoyed wide diffusion. Inventories of sixteenth-century printer–booksellers reveal stocks of tens of thousands of religious works available for the cost of a few *maravedís* – a fraction of an unskilled laborer's daily wage. Although few of these works, even the "best-sellers" of their day, form part of our contemporary

---

[1] Angelo J. DiSalvo, "The Ascetical Meditative Literature of Renaissance Spain: An Alternative to Amadís, Elisa and Diana." *Hispania* 69 (1986), p. 466.

[2] See José Simón Díaz, *Impresos del XVI: Religión* (Madrid: CSIC, 1964), and Isabelle Poutrin, *Le Voile et la plume. Autobiographie et sainteté féminine dans l'Espagne moderne* (Madrid: Casa de Velázquez, 1995), for further detail. Also, Sarah T. Nalle, "Printing and Reading Popular Religious Texts in Sixteenth-Century Castile." In *Culture and the State in Spain, 1550–1580*. Ed. Tom Lewis and Francisco J. Sánchez (New York: Garland, 1999), pp. 123–153, provides further information on the circulation of popular religious texts and literacy rates during this period.

academic canon, literary historians such as Keith Whinnom[3] and Elizabeth Rhodes[4] have begun to recognize the need to understand their cultural significance and the reasons for their appeal for the men and women of early modern Spain.

Literary histories have traditionally divided religious texts into the moral, the ascetic, and the mystical; however, such distinctions are seldom observed in the works themselves. Moral conduct books often include spiritual as well as ethical advice, and mystical treatises invariably begin with the ascetic preparation for a life of contemplation. It would be similarly mistaken to assume that devotional writers were unconcerned with the aesthetic or entertainment value of their productions. With varying degrees of success, religious writers sought to delight and surprise their audiences, as well as to inspire and instruct them.

With the notable exception of Ramón Llull (*c.* 1232–1316), Christian mysticism did not thrive on the Iberian peninsula during the Middle Ages. At the turn of the sixteenth century, however, a variety of factors – the introduction of the printing press; the end of the Reconquest; the rise of literacy; the spread of spiritual movements such as the *devotio moderna* (a religious movement, with origins in fourteenth-century Holland, that emphasized reading and meditation on Scripture), Franciscan spirituality (which emphasized a desire to imitate the compassion, poverty, and humility of Christ), and Erasmianism; the ecclesiastical reforms of Cardinal Francisco Jiménez de Cisneros (1436–1517; cardinal 1507–1517), and his sponsorship of biblical translation at the University of Alcalá – contributed to a spirit of religious renewal that extended beyond the elite clergy and embraced an increasingly literate laity. Male and female religious, married men and women, aristocrats, artisans, and even farmers and shepherds were avid readers of books of hours, catechisms, saints' lives, guides to Christian conduct, instruction in prayer, and biographies of venerable "servants of God" who had recently lived among them.

Some of the most influential books of the early sixteenth century were translations sponsored by Cisneros during his tenure as cardinal. Most notable are *Contemptus mundi* (known in English as "Imitation of Christ") by Thomas à Kempis, first translated in 1493 and re-edited often afterwards, *Vita Christi* ("The Life of Christ," 1502) by Ludolph of Saxony, and *Vida y milagros de Catalina de Sena* ("Life and Miracles of Catherine of Siena") by Raymond de Capua, translated by Antonio

---

[3] Keith Whinnom, "The Problem of the 'Best Seller' in Spanish Golden Age Literature." In his *Medieval and Renaissance Spanish Literature. Selected Essays.* Ed. Alan Deyermond *et al.* (Exeter: University of Exeter Press, 1994), pp. 159–175.

[4] Elizabeth Rhodes, "Spain's Misfired Canon: The Case of Luis de Granada's *Libro de la oración y meditación.*" *Journal of Hispanic Philology* 15 (1990), pp. 43–66.

de la Peña in 1511. These translations did much to encourage religious enthusiasm in all sectors of society, especially among women. One of the earliest mystical works in Castilian was written by a *beata* (lay holy woman), María de Santo Domingo (*c.* 1486 – *c.* 1524), who enjoyed the patronage of Cardinal Cisneros. An illiterate peasant, María's ecstatic utterances were dictated to an unnamed scribe and published as *Libro de la oración* ("The Book of Prayer," *c.* 1518). Although she was tried for usurping the male clerical privileges of preaching and hearing confession, she was eventually exonerated.[5]

The interior piety, apostolic simplicity, and scripturalism fomented during Cisneros' time as cardinal provided fertile ground for Erasmian humanism, introduced into Spain in the 1520s by Charles V's Flemish courtiers. Erasmus' (1466?–1536) *Enchiridion*, translated into Spanish by Alonso Fernández de Madrid and published in 1526 as *Manual del caballero cristiano* ("Manual of the Christian Soldier"), was so popular that ten more printings followed within two years. Erasmus' most distinguished Spanish disciple, Alfonso de Valdés (*c.* 1500–1533), was the Latin secretary to Charles V. His *Diálogo de las cosas ocurridas en Roma* ("Dialogue Concerning the Events in Rome"), an apology for imperial policy following the Sack of Rome in 1527, and *Diálogo de Mercurio y Carón* (composed *c.* 1528), an acerbic attack on clerical corruption, are primarily examples of religious satire, but they also speak to the Erasmian desire for ethical renewal and interior Christianity. The religious affiliation of Alfonso's younger brother Juan de Valdés (*c.* 1505–1541) remains a matter of debate; he has been described as an Erasmian, a Protestant *sui generis*, and as an *alumbrado*.[6] His only work to be published in his lifetime, *Diálogo de doctrina Cristiana* ("Dialogue of Christian Doctrine," 1529) imagines a cordial discussion between Erasmian reformers and an ignorant but receptive priest. By the 1530s, however, the Erasmists had earned the hostility of the more conservative factions in the Church, who increasingly suspected Erasmists of harboring *alumbrado* and/or Protestant sympathies. Around 1531 Juan de Valdés fled to Italy to avoid an Inquisitorial trial; he attracted a circle of aristocratic disciples in the kingdom of Naples, where he continued to write devotional works and commentaries on the Bible in Italian and Spanish. Other less fortunate Erasmists, notably Juan de Vergara (1492–1557), one of the translators of the Complutensian Polyglot Bible, and Bartolomé de Carranza (1503–1576), author of *Comentarios del Catechismo Christiano* ("Commentaries on the Christian Catechism," 1558), endured long Inquisitorial

---

[5] See Ronald Surtz, *Writing Women in Late Medieval and Early Modern Spain* (Philadelphia: University of Pennsylvania Press, 1995), pp. 86–103.

[6] The *alumbrados* were members of a spiritual movement that emphasized passive union with God and disdained exterior works and ceremonies.

trials. In 1559 the Index of Prohibited Books, promulgated by Inquisitor General Fernando de Valdéz, included almost all of Erasmus' works as well as many by his followers.

The early decades of the sixteenth century witness a remarkable increase in the number of adherents to mental prayer, a form of religious devotion that was to have a profound impact on Spanish religiosity. As opposed to vocal prayer, mental prayer was silent, solitary, and unscripted. Yet it was not without method. Thanksgiving and repentance followed by silent reading and directed meditation on Christ's life were designed to prepare practitioners for the "infused" or divinely granted experience of "recollection," in which the faculties of sense and thought are quieted and become centered on God. Through recollection, individuals hoped not only for assurance of God's love and mercy, but also knowledge of his will. Thus, mental prayer was not considered to be incompatible with secular life; on the contrary, through recollection many laymen and women sought guidance for the bewildering choices they confronted each day. Even Christians of modest status, inspired by the relatively tolerant spirit of the Cisneros period (a tolerance not extended to the recently conquered Moors of Andalusia), were drawn to this practice, which previously was deemed appropriate only for learned, celibate clergy.

Mental prayer was not without stumbling blocks and, after the rise of Protestantism, dangers. Some practitioners were troubled by spiritual "dryness" (the inability to meditate) and by feelings of worthlessness or profound sadness. The experience of prayer was at times intensely physical, giving rise to a flood of tears, uncontrollable vocalization, paralysis, physical pain, or sexual arousal. The devil, it was feared, continually sought to turn souls away from prayer with sensual temptations, or, worse, by counterfeiting God's favors. Consequently, there was an enormous demand not only for instruction in the methods of mental prayer but also in how to discern true from imagined or demonically inspired prayer experiences. In fact, after books of hours and hagiographies, guidebooks to prayer constituted one of the most popular genres of religious literature during the sixteenth century. Between 1500 and 1559, more than twenty-two different guidebooks to prayer were published in Castilian, many of these in multiple editions. (These figures do not include the many translations of works by northern European authors.) In 1559, however, the Valdéz Index of Prohibited Books banned guidebooks to mental prayer such as Francisco de Osuna's *Spiritual Alphabets*, and the works of future canonized saints: Saint Francisco de Borja's *Obras muy devotas y provechosas para cualquier fiel cristiano* ("Very Devout and Beneficial Works for Any Faithful Christian," 1556) and Saint Juan de Avila's *Audi Filia* ("Hearken Daughter," 1556). In the years immediately preceding and during the Council of Trent, when a schism in the Church seemed inevitable,

Inquisitor Valdéz and his allies were determined to curb a practice that side-stepped clerical authority and appeared to discredit the ritual prayer of the church. Opposition eased after 1566, and guidebooks to prayer, with additional chapters extolling vocal prayer and the need for clerical supervision, managed to win Inquisitorial approval.

Francisco de Osuna (*c.* 1492 – *c.* 1540) was one of the most influential early authors of guides to prayer; between 1527 and 1556 twenty-six editions of his *Abecedarios espirituales* ("Spiritual Alphabets") were published in Spain. Although Osuna took pains to affirm the orthodoxy of *recogimiento* ("recollection"), the methodical mental prayer practiced by Reformed Franciscans, as opposed to *dejamiento* ("abandonment"), the passive prayer of the *alumbrados*, all his guides were banned by the Valdéz Index. His style, with its alphabetized lists, fanciful etymologies, and allegorical biblical commentaries is often tedious, but his language is also capable of communicating the enthusiasm of a life transformed by a profound religious experience. His style and method made a durable impression on his most famous reader and admirer, Saint Teresa of Avila.

By far the most widely published work of the genre, and indeed the most popular book in early modern Spain, was *Libro de la oración y meditación* ("The Book of Prayer and Meditation") by Luis de Granada (1504–1588). First published in Salamanca in 1554, it was placed on the Index of Prohibited Books in 1559. However, an expanded and emended version was published in 1566; by 1578 there were sixty-four European editions, and by 1679 there were over one hundred Spanish editions alone. (For the sake of comparison, Cervantes' *Don Quijote de la Mancha* ran to twenty-four editions before the eighteenth century.) The second most popular religious book of the Golden Age is also by Granada; *Guía de pecadores en el cual se enseña todo lo que el cristiano debe hacer desde el principio de su conversión hasta el fin de la perfección* ("The Guide for the Sinner in which the Christian is Taught Everything He Should do from His Conversion to the End of Perfection," 1555) appeared in eighty-one Spanish printings, as well as numerous French and Italian editions. In these works, the Dominican friar offers his reader topics for meditation, advice on resisting temptation and overcoming discouragement, and (in the post-Tridentine versions) recommends that mental prayer be supplemented with exterior works such as vocal prayer, fasting, and alms-giving. A famous orator, Fray Luis skillfully adapts the rhetorical style of the *sermo humilis* for a solitary, silent reader. He appeals to his reader frequently in the singular familiar and varies his instructions with parables, proverbs, and homey comparisons, almost always in a tone that is intimate and consoling rather than reproachful. Although his style, replete with rhetorical questions, exhortations, and exclamations, may strike modern readers as sentimental, his phenomenal publishing record attests to his success in touching the well-springs of early modern sensibilities.

Despite growing suspicions of heterodoxy, Erasmus left a lasting imprint on another important religious genre. In 1534 he published *De praeparatio ad mortem* ("On Preparation for Death"), a humanist's adaptation of a medieval *ars moriendi* ("the art of dying") that emphasized the doctrine of grace and forgiveness over fear of punishment and damnation. Erasmus' handbook was translated into two separate Spanish editions in 1535 and inspired what Marcel Bataillon considered the masterpiece of ascetic literature written during the reign of Charles V: Alejo Venegas' (*c.* 1498–1562) *Agonía del tránsito de la muerte* ("Agony of Crossing Over at Death," 1537). Notwithstanding its grim title this work reflects an Erasmian faith in redemption, while adding an orthodox insistence on the importance of the sacraments of the Church in achieving a "good death." Venegas' *Agonía*, with ten editions, was the most popular *ars moriendi* of the sixteenth century; the Jesuits dominated the genre with a more somber vision in the seventeenth century.[7]

The Discalced Carmelite Juan de la Cruz (1542–1591), though widely acknowledged as one of the most sublime poets of the Spanish Golden Age, has received little critical attention, outside of theological circles, as the author of mystical treatises in prose. His four major works are glosses on his own poems, written but unpublished during the last fourteen years of his life, at the behest of the nuns and friars of his order who were perplexed over the meaning of the mystical eroticism that pervaded his poetry. Contrary to expectations, *Subida al Monte Carmelo* ("The Ascent of Mount Carmel," composed 1579–1585) and its continuation *Noche oscura* ("On a Dark Night," composed 1582–1585) elide the eroticism of the verses they ostensibly gloss (the first three stanzas of the poem *Noche oscura*) and offer instead an extensive treatise on the ascetic preparation necessary for the prayer of union. The commentary on *Cántico espiritual* ("Spiritual Canticle," version A 1584, version B 1586–1591), however, is closer to the ancient tradition of allegorical exegesis of the *Song of Songs*. The gloss on *Llama de amor viva* ("Living Flame of Love," version A 1585, version B 1591), the most aesthetically realized of the commentaries, resembles in many respects a prose poem inspired by the original verse, rather than an allegorical gloss. There is a marked tendency in all the commentaries to multiply rather than restrict poetic-allegorical meanings, which the Hispano-Arabic scholar Luce López-Baralt, in *San Juan de la*

---

[7] On the concept of *ars moriendi*, see Marcel Bataillon, *Erasmo y España: estudios sobre la historia espiritual del siglo XVI*. Trans. Antonio Alatorre (Mexico: Fondo de Cultura Económica, 1966), pp. 558–572, and Carlos M. Eire, *From Madrid to Purgatory: The Art and Craft of Dying in Sixteenth-Century Spain* (Cambridge University Press, 1995), pp. 24–34.

Cruz y el Islam ("Saint John of the Cross and Islam") has attributed to the Sufi mystical tradition. Accusations of *alumbradismo* prevented the publication of his complete works until nearly forty years after his death.

Like Juan de la Cruz, the Augustinian friar Luis de León (1527–1591) is recognized today more for his poetry than for his prose. His audacity in producing a vernacular translation and commentary on the *Song of Songs, Exposición del Cantar de los Cantares* (composed 1561–1562), figured prominently among the charges brought against him in an Inquisitorial trial. His other major Castilian works include a translation and exegesis of *The Book of Job* (composed 1570–1591); a conduct book for married women, *La perfecta casada* ("The Perfect Wife," 1583, revised 1585); and *Los nombres de Cristo* ("The Names of Christ," 1583, revised 1585). In this last work, three fictional characters discuss the meaning of the various biblical names attributed to Christ, such as "spouse," "lamb," "king," and "beloved." The language of the interlocutors, imbued with the cadences of Hebrew and the classics, though hardly colloquial, creates the illusion of uncontrived, cultivated conversation; it is the language not of the courtier or preacher but of a late-Renaissance humanist. Acording to Marcel Bataillon, *Los nombres de Cristo* is an exemplar of veiled Erasmism.[8] Embedded within the Renaissance dialogue, Fray Luis' readers could find not only a biblical anthology in the vernacular (vernacular translations of the Bible had been banned by the Valdéz Index), but also a compendium of Pauline interior Christianity.

Fray Luis dedicated the last years of his life to editing the works of the monastic reformer and founder, Teresa de Jesús (1515–1582; canonized 1622; known in English as Teresa of Avila). This Carmelite nun's first extensive prose work, *El libro de la vida* ("The Book of Her Life," composed 1562–1565), was written at the behest of her confessors, who were concerned that her supernatural visions might be demonic illusions. *Camino de perfección* ("The Way of Perfection," composed 1566–1567), ostensibly a gloss on the Lord's Prayer, is in fact a disguised treatise on mental prayer dedicated to the twelve nuns in the first reformed Carmelite convent in Avila, who had been forbidden to read Teresa's *Life*. *El castillo interior* ("The Interior Castle," composed 1577) is an allegory of the soul's mystical progress to the innermost rooms of a spherical castle. Teresa's style has captivated modern readers no less than her first editor, who praised it for its "elegancia desafeitada" ("unadorned elegance"). Although Teresa was an avid reader of ascetic-mystical literature, she often adopted an exaggeratedly low-register, colloquial style, in part out of sincere distaste for pretentiousness, and in part from the necessity to avoid the appearance of teaching religious doctrine. Accordingly, she

[8] Bataillon, *Erasmo*, pp. 760–770.

sometimes protectively employs a rhetoric of "feminine" ignorance and uncertainty. Ramón Menéndez Pidal famously described Teresa as someone who "speaks through writing."[9] Although she was capable, when she had the time and inclination, to produce more formal prose, many passages are characterized by ellipsis, lapses in agreement, parenthetical digression, lexical archaisms, diminutives (affectionate and ironic), and other features associated with orality. Eschewing learned rhetoric, she developed her own strategies of persuasion to avoid censure and, at the same time, move and inspire men and women who aspired to a more profound religious experience through prayer. Her writings circulated among her followers in manuscript until 1575, when *The Life* was sequestered for Inquisitorial examination. Under the patronage of the Empress Margarita (the sister of Felipe II), her works were edited by Fray Luis de León and published posthumously in 1588.

Although Saint Teresa is by far the most famous woman writer of the period, she was not an anomaly. Despite opposition in important sectors of the Church to women's participation in any form of religious discourse, women's religious writing flourished both before and after the Council of Trent to an extent that has only recently been fully recognized.[10] The reforms initiated by Cardinal Cisneros in the first two decades of the sixteenth century provided women with access to devotional literature – including the lives of famous female mystics – in the vernacular. Post-Tridentine monastic reforms also stimulated (though unintentionally) a renaissance of female writing. Nuns wrote the histories of their convents, biographies of exemplary sisters, devotional poetry, and "vidas por mandato" ("mandated *Lives*") – autobiographical accounts of their supernatural experiences, produced for examination by their confessors. The Discalced Carmelites in particular carried on their founder's literary legacy. María de San José (Salazar) (1548–1603) is the author of the first known dialogue written by a woman in Spanish, *Libro de recreaciones* ("For the Hour of Recreation," composed *c.* 1585). In this humorous and erudite work, two fictional nuns discuss topics ranging from the life of Saint Teresa and the history of their order to women's right to comment on Scripture. Another Discalced Carmelite, Ana de San Bartolomé (1549–1626), is said to have learned to write miraculously by copying Saint Teresa's letters. Despite her late acquisition of literacy, she wrote

[9] Ramón Menéndez Pidal, "El estilo de Santa Teresa." In *La lengua de Cristóbal Colón y otros estudios sobre el siglo XVI* (4th edn. Madrid: Espasa Calpe, 1958), p. 125.

[10] Important work in this regard has been done by Manuel Serrano y Sanz, *Apuntes para una biblioteca de escritoras españolas* (Madrid: Rivadeneyra, 1905; facsimile edn. Madrid: Atlas, 1975); and Electa Arenal and Stacey Schlau, *Untold Sisters: Hispanic Nuns in their Own Works*. Trans. Amanda Powell (Albuquerque: University of New Mexico Press, 1989).

prodigiously, in an unpretentious and markedly colloquial style. By the time she died at the age of seventy-seven, she had penned two spiritual autobiographies, histories of her order, religious guidebooks, over 600 letters, and a small corpus of religious poetry.[11]

Marcela de San Félix (1605–1688), the illegitimate daughter of Lope de Vega, wrote allegorical convent drama, mystical poetry, and biographies of her Trinitarian sisters. Her work is worthy of attention not only because she is the daughter of a famous playwright, but also because of her keen wit, dramatic skill, and lyrical gifts.[12]

Most of convent writing was not intended for publication, although it was copied and circulated among other nuns and patrons. However, the example of Teresa, whose works were published in 1588, just six years after her death, inspired other women religious to record their spiritual lives and visionary experiences and facilitated the transition from manuscript to print. Although such *vidas*, as mentioned above, were nominally written in obedience to the confessor's command, in many cases there is evidence of a close collaboration between the nun and her spiritual director. Many hagiographic biographies of nuns incorporate or paraphrase extensive passages written by the nun herself.

Unlike the many women whose works were never published under their own name, María de Jesús Ágreda (1602–1665) became, albeit posthumously, a publishing phenomenon. A Conceptionist,[13] María de Ágreda was a spiritual confidante to Felipe IV. Her *Mística ciudad de Dios* ("Mystical City of God"), a life of the Virgin Mary supposedly communicated to her through divine revelation, was begun in 1637, examined repeatedly by the Inquisition, and finally published in 1670. There followed 168 Spanish editions and translations. Conceded the title of "Venerable" by Clement X in 1673, Ágreda nevertheless remains a controversial figure today, as Clark Colahan acknowledges.[14]

Convent writing, though far from homogeneous, incorporates a number of recurrent features: an "anxiety of authorship" (that is, the nun's expressed need to legitimate her authority as a writer), frequent expressions of humility and insufficiency (sometimes used ironically), syntax closer to oral than written norms, and a rustic, colloquial, or domestic lexicon. The impression of orality is further enhanced by apostrophic

---

[11] On Ana de San Bartolomé, see Alison P. Weber, "The Partial Feminism of Ana de San Bartolomé." In *Recovering Spain's Feminist Tradition*. Ed. Lisa Vollendorf (New York: Modern Language Association, 2001), pp. 69–87.

[12] For further information on Marcela de San Félix, see Electa Arenal and Georgina Sabat de Rivers, *Literatura conventual femenina: Sor Marcela de San Félix, hija de Lope de Vega* (Barcelona: PPU, 1988).

[13] Member of the Order of Saint Clare, which was founded in the early sixteenth century.

[14] Clark Colahan, *The Visions of Sor María de Ágreda: Writing, Knowledge and Power* (Tucson: University of Arizona Press, 1994).

appeals to an immediate audience of intimate "listeners." We also find, to some extent, indications of the development of a feminist consciousness. That is, some women writers express an awareness of their unjust exclusion from service to the Church and assert their religious, if not civil, equality with men.

Men also wrote spiritual autobiographies (though not "by mandate") and were the subjects of religious biographies. Like the female versions, the latter incorporate hagiographic topoi, folkloric motifs, and more or less plausible testimony from contemporary witnesses. The entertainment value of these works should not be discounted. For example, *La vida y virtudes del venerable Hermano Fray Francisco del Niño Jesus* ("The Life and Virtues of the Venerable Brother Friar Francisco del Niño Jesus," 1624) by José de Jesús María offers moments of humor, wonder, suspense, and pathos as it traces Fray Francisco's (1547–1604) journey from simpleton shepherd to charismatic healer. The Jesuit Pedro de Ribadeneyra (1526–1611; alternate spelling: Rivandeneira) wrote religious biographies of men and women, as well as an autobiography closely modeled on Augustine's *Confessions*. His life of Ignatius of Loyola, first published in Latin in 1572 and in five Spanish editions between 1583 and Loyola's canonization in 1622, combines history, memoir, and first-person accounts of thaumaturgic healings performed by the soldier-saint.[15]

Just as the generic boundaries of the religious tend to overlap with those of imaginative and didactic literature, the reasons why these works held such a strong appeal for early modern Spaniards cannot be described as exclusively "religious." Although it is unlikely that literary merit, however defined, was the major reason for their popularity, it is probable that many readers derived delight as well as edification from these books, whether in narrative invention, rhetorical fireworks, innovative comparisons, rhythmic phrasing, or colloquial style. Ultimately, however, Spaniards were probably willing to spend precious resources on these books because they addressed their spiritual anxieties and longings: the fear of damnation, the hope for salvation, and desire for assurance of God's love.

---

[15] On Ribadeneyra, see Jodi Bilinkoff, "The Many 'Lives' of Pedro de Ribadeneyra." *Renaissance Quarterly* 52 (1999), pp. 180–196.

9

Renaissance poetry

JULIAN WEISS

In his *Proemio e carta al condestable de Portugal* ("Prologue and Letter to
the Constable of Portugal"), written at the threshold of the Renaissance,
Íñigo López de Mendoza, the marqués de Santillana (1398–1458), placed
poetry at the epicenter of human affairs: "Las plazas, las lonjas, las fiestas,
los conbites opulentos sin ella así como sordos e en silencio se fallan. ¿E
qué son o quáles aquellas cosas adonde – oso dezir – esa arte así como nece-
saria no intervenga e no sirva?" ("Public squares, marketplaces, festivals,
opulent feasts are as if deaf and silent without it. What are those affairs
in which – dare I say it – this art does not intervene as if by necessity?").[1]
Poetry literally gives voice to culture, understood in its broad sense as a
whole way of life. Like other early modern European writers, however,
Santillana also elevated vernacular verse, rendering selected aspects of it
into Culture (Culture, with a capital "C," meaning high or learned culture), and investing them with the symbolic capital previously reserved
for the classics. These twin perspectives are fundamental to understanding Spanish verse during a period of expansion and exploration.

If poetry enabled individuals to make sense of themselves and their
society, it was also instrumental in creating those very categories. This
is evident not only in the diversity of Renaissance poetic forms, genres,
and subjects, but also in other material factors. Sixteenth-century verse
circulated orally and in writing, in many forms and contexts, whose social
significance is sometimes obscured by the limited institutionalized forms
and settings in which it is read and reproduced today. When written down,
most poetry circulated in manuscript anthologies whose varied formats
and contents reflect heterogeneous tastes, goals, and audiences. When
printed, the medium of the press transformed verse into commodities
of varied commercial and cultural status: from the popular, ephemeral
pliegos sueltos (chapbooks) to the collected works of an individual nobleman, whose manuscripts might be gathered for posthumous publication
by friends and family anxious to secure his literary posterity and, by
extension, to celebrate his lineage. Early modern verse circulated in other

---

[1] Íñigo López de Mendoza, marqués de Santillana, *Obras completas*. Ed. Ángel Gómez
Moreno and M. P. A. M. Kerkhof (Barcelona: Planeta, 1988), p. 442.

ways too: set to music, incorporated into prose fiction, or as the discourse of the burgeoning national theatre. Poetry therefore was composed, heard, and read in a myriad of settings, as the subject of private, silent reading, or of public or semi-public performance, whether recited in the home, or in literary academies and poetic competitions, in urban or in court circles. Despite its increasingly literate frame of reference, its orality should not be underestimated.

Spanish poetry's geographic horizons also expanded, following soldiers, courtiers, diplomats, and exiled Sephardic Jews into northern Europe, Italy, the Americas, North Africa, and the eastern Mediterranean. As it turned outwards, poetry also turned back in upon itself, redefining its temporal frontiers, pushing back its traditions to antiquity, and acquiring a sense of its own history and historicity. The Renaissance rediscovery of the classics did more than enrich the inherited storehouse of poetic forms and themes, and inspire the composition of a significant body of Latin verse.[2] In a process that mirrored the discovery of perspective, understanding a modern poem meant viewing it in relational terms, reading through the present text to perceive the authorizing models and traditions that stretched out beyond it. *Imitatio* was the key to its poetics.[3]

As agents of "high culture" it was in the sixteenth century that "Spanish poets" acquired awareness of themselves as such, in ways that highlight the intersection of culture and power. The expanding spatial, social, and temporal frontiers demanded, at an ideological level, a stabilizing center. Two obvious examples will suffice. Linguistically, although ballads and other traditional forms continued to be composed in Catalan, this vibrant literary language was overpowered by the cultural hegemony of Castilian, which also drew into its orbit Portuguese poets, like Sá de Miranda (1481–1558) and Luís de Camões (1542–1579). In terms of gender, there were limits and conditions to the spread of lay literacy that determined the changes in poetic culture. Women were patrons, audience, poetic symbols, and the subject of written verse; women's song lay at the heart of the oral lyric tradition; there were also women printers, and, thanks to the perseverance of widows like Ana Girón and Juana de Zúñiga, the works of Garcilaso, Boscán, and Acuña were published when they were. The concept "woman poet," however, continued to be an oxymoron. Although religious women were beginning to carve out a space for their literacy within convents, secular written verse continued to be a

---

[2] Juan Francisco Alcina, *Repertorio de la poesía latina del Renacimiento en España* (Salamanca: Universidad de Salamanca, 1995).

[3] See Antonio García Galiano, *La imitación en el Renacimiento* (Kassel: Reichenberger, 1996).

masculine domain. There were minor exceptions, like Isabel Vega (some of whose love lyrics survive from the late sixteenth century), but no Spanish woman poet either wrote – or managed to have preserved – a body of secular verse to compare with the works of the Frenchwoman Louise Labé or the Italians Gaspara Stampa and Vittoria Colonna. The reasons for this entail a complex intertwining of external and internal pressures, such as the Counter Reformation's emphasis on women's silence, the misogynist underpinnings of natural philosophy (women were associated with the body, not the mind), and the dominant poetic discourses of courtly love, Petrarchism, and Neoplatonism, which elided female experience into a masculinist world view. Women poets would confront these barriers in the seventeenth century.

Renaissance verse poses a serious challenge to periodization. Fifteenth-century poets continued to be read and admired: the *Cancionero general* ("General Songbook," 1511) went into nine editions until 1573, with new material – eventually sonnets – being added, and then provided models of wit for the Baroque. Jorge Manrique's *Coplas por la muerte de su padre* ("Poems on the Death of his Father") and Juan de Mena's *Laberinto de Fortuna* ("Labyrinth of Fortune") acquired the status of national classics. Although the twelve-syllable *arte mayor* became obsolete, the octosyllabic *arte menor* flourished. These poems and metrical forms were not static, but part of a dynamic process of reinterpretation. Numerous poetic glosses fitted new meanings to Manrique's *Coplas* (it being in the nature of the "classic" to straddle past and present), and the octosyllabic line was also adapted to new themes and new stanzaic forms. These older meters did not run parallel to the innovations that came from Italy, but were interwoven with them, for most Renaissance poets made use of both.[4]

Yet a sense of rupture was created. Like the professional humanists who invented the "Dark Ages," the principal innovators, the Catalan Juan Boscán (1487?–1542) and Garcilaso de la Vega (1501?–1536) scorned earlier courtly verse and imagined a new poetic age. This trajectory underpins the structure of Boscán's collected works (1543, posthumously published): the volume moves from Boscán's octosyllabic meters, to his experiments with the new Italian forms, and ends with the works of his late friend, Garcilaso, who successfully adapted Castilian to the rhythms of the hendecasyllable (eleven-syllable line). Boscán's prologue, the *Carta a la duquesa*

---

[4] For more information and analysis of this issue, see José Manuel Blecua, "Corrientes poéticas del siglo XVI." In *Sobre poesía de la Edad de Oro* (Madrid: Gredos, 1970), pp. 11–24; Rafael Lapesa, "Poesía de cancionero y poesía italianizante." In *De la Edad Media a nuestros días: estudios de historia literaria* (Madrid: Gredos, 1967), pp. 145–171; and Antonio Rodríguez-Moñino, *Construcción crítica y realidad histórica en la poesía española de los siglos XVI y XVII* (Madrid: Castalia, 1965).

de Soma ("Letter to the Duchess of Soma"), is a manifesto for the new movement, and it may be read against a mock-serious poem by Cristóbal de Castillejo (*c.* 1490–1550), the "Reprensión contra los poetas españoles que escriben en verso italiano" ("Reproof of Spanish Poets Who Employ Italian Meters"). Both texts betray four concerns: gender (Italian was tainted with effeminacy: the idea recurs in Fernando de Herrera's commentary on Garcilaso); national tradition (the acceptance of the superior authority of Petrarch was seen as a betrayal of national identity); metrical expressivity (the prominence of rhyme in the octosyllabic meter sounded vulgar, particularly when the stress fell on the last syllable); and class (the poems of the *Cancionero general* were too "generally" available: indeed the volume was printed for the bourgeois readership of Valencia). Castillejo used to be regarded as a medieval throwback, whereas in fact he was an archetypal Renaissance courtier-diplomat. This poem, which closes with an ironic demonstration of his mastery of the sonnet form, is an extended example of the wit (*facetia*) and nonchalance (*sprezzatura*) so admired by that arbiter of courtly manners, Baldassare Castiglione.[5]

The sheer abundance and variety of Renaissance verse can be only adumbrated here, under the following overlapping categories: love lyrics and pastoral; satiric and burlesque; popular lyric and ballads; moral and religious verse; heroic, chivalric, and epic.

The Renaissance changed the course of the Spanish love lyric on several levels: it consolidated the eclogue and the sonnet (improving Santillana's earlier experiments in sonnet form); introduced the hendecasyllable (often coupled with seven-syllable lines: a combination known as "lira" after the style adopted by Garcilaso in his fifth Ode); established Petrarchism and Neoplatonism as the dominant erotic discourses; and deployed Ovidian myth in more substantive ways. Although Boscán wrote notable poetry, these changes coalesce in the poetry of Garcilaso, who became, soon after his death in 1536, the benchmark for Castilian lyrics.[6] Garcilaso cultivated the image of the soldier-poet who embodied the union of arms and letters set as an ideal in the previous century. His contacts with Neapolitan intellectuals illustrate how aristocratic poets could form an international network of relationships; indeed, the innovations he championed were set in motion after Boscán's Granadine encounter with the Venetian ambassador Andrea Navagero.

---

[5] See Rogelio Reyes Cano, *Estudios sobre Cristóbal de Castillejo* (Salamanca: Universidad de Salamanca, 2000).

[6] See Rafael Lapesa, *La trayectoria poética de Garcilaso* (Madrid: Istmo, 1985); Ignacio Navarrete, *Orphans of Petrarch: Poetry and Theory in the Spanish Renaissance* (Berkeley: University of California Press, 1994); and Bienvenido Morros, *Las polémicas literarias en la España del siglo XVI: a propósito de Fernando de Herrera y Garcilaso de la Vega* (Barcelona: Quaderns Crema, 1998).

Garcilaso's principal theme was love, which he explored in most of his forty sonnets, five *canciones* (based on the Italian *canzone* not the Castilian form of the same name), and three eclogues. Most scholars no longer accept biographical readings of his love poetry, according to which he was inspired by an impossible love for a Portuguese noblewoman, Isabel Freire. He also wrote on other topics, though, as in his two elegies or his Horatian epistle to Boscán. His handling of the Petrarchan sonnet produced new kinds of poetic subjectivity. Like the Castilian *canción*, the sonnet is an epigrammatic form, but syntactically far more fluid: it de-emphasizes rhyme (which draws attention to the end of lines), and allows for enjambment (the running on of one line to the next). The dynamic relationship between the quatrains and the tercets, coupled with the lapidary final line, produces the sense of an idea – and a mind – in movement. This inner dynamism is produced in part by the turbulent meditation upon an unattainable but alluring beloved, which pulls the lyric subject in opposing directions (a tension underscored by the frequent use of antithesis). There are parallels with courtly love, but the fundamental difference is that whereas the courtly ratiocination of the Castilian *canción* occurs in an eternal present, Petrarchan introspection is played out within a tightly woven framework of past, present, and future, as in the first sonnet, "Cuando me paro a contemplar mi 'stado" ("When I pause to reflect upon my condition"). On another temporal plane, Petrarchism is predicated upon the poet's ambivalent relationship across time with a literary model that is both a legitimizing authority and a rival to be outdone.

These tensions are dramatized in different ways in sonnets of classical inspiration. "En tanto que de rosa y azucena" (no. 23, "While your complexion is the color of rose and lily") and "A Dafne ya los brazos le crecían" (no. 13, "Daphne's arms begin to grow") adapt Horace (the popular "Carpe diem" motif) and Ovid respectively to produce a striking sensuality, a sense of physical presence, of bodies and desires in a state of metamorphosis. A similarly motile conjunction of physical, affective, and psychic states shapes sonnet 5, "Escrito 'stá en mi alma vuestro gesto" ("Your countenance is written upon my soul"). While this poem bears traces of the Neoplatonism that would become so influential in the Renaissance (promoted by León Hebreo's *Dialoghi d'amore* ["Dialogues of Love"] and Boscán's translation of Castiglione's *Il cortegiano* ["The Courtier"]), its echoes of the great Valencian poet Ausiàs March (1379–1459) also illustrate Garcilaso's debt to earlier courtly traditions. As these sonnets suggest, Garcilaso forged his literary modernity through a creative appropriation of a variety of poetic models, and by demanding added depth and breadth from the literate nobleman's cultural literacy.

Garcilaso's sonnets are mainly about love, but they cannot be narrowly restricted to this. As Roland Greene has argued, the discourse of love "was a widely acknowledged staging area for a variety of problems of the time, such as the drives of the subject to find expression in action, the contradictions and incommensurabilities of desire in its many forms, and the distribution of power in unequal situations."[7] This point applies with particular force to Garcilaso's pastoral verse, represented by three eclogues. Since Virgil, the pastoral mode had offered a vehicle for treating a range of human experiences and dilemmas: the pastoral realm of love-lorn shepherds and nymphs is not hermetically sealed, but one that evokes comparisons. Garcilaso's eclogues not only explore the nuances of love against a sparse but exquisitely stylized portrayal of Nature. At the same time, they pose questions of perspective: for example, they view man in relation to Nature, the political to the personal, life to art. The first and third eclogues are considered to be the most successful artistically (the experimental second, nearly 2,000 lines long, was designed for semi-dramatic performance), and of these, the third is the most complex. It represents love in two complementary forms: unrequited (nymphs weave tapestries depicting love lost through separation, metamorphosis, and death) and hopeful (the urgent desires of two shepherds at dusk). This juxtaposition of impossible and possible desires is played out on another level, for the poem is also about the power of representation, or rather the vain desire to halt time and to capture in language shifting emotional and mental states in their full immediacy.[8]

There were many variations upon the lyric conventions crystallized by Garcilaso: indeed, subscribing to a stylistic convention, yet adapting it, meant signaling one's membership of a group and carving out an individual place within it. For example, the sonnets of the powerful grandee Diego Hurtado de Mendoza (1503–1575) have a wider range of rhyme combinations than was usual, and although he has been criticized for echoing the rhythms of *arte mayor* and for persevering with *verso agudo* (verses ending with an accented syllable), this may well be an attempt to continue models established by his prestigious ancestor, the marqués de Santillana. Style becomes a marker of lineage. Style could indicate other affiliations and conditions too. Hurtado de Mendoza wrote about one hundred poems, Italianate and Castilian meters in roughly equal measure. They are hard to date, but the Castilian meters possibly correspond to early and late periods, when he was closely associated with the Spanish court. Hernando de Acuña (1518 – *c.* 1580) chose to combine Italianate and Castilian styles within poems, mixing Petrarchan influences with wordplay and conceptual paradoxes reminiscent of *cancionero* poets. He

[7] Roland Greene, *Unrequited Conquests: Love and Empire in the Colonial Americas* (Chicago: University of Chicago Press, 1999), p. 11.

[8] See Paul Julian Smith, "The Rhetoric of Presence in Lyric Poetry." In *Writing in the Margin: Spanish Literature of the Golden Age* (Oxford: Clarendon, 1988), pp. 43–77.

too may have reverted to simpler "native" Castilian meters at the end of his life. Style marks a return to one's origins.

There were many other distinctive voices, like Gutierre de Cetina (before 1520–1557?), Francisco de Figueroa (1536–1617?), or the mysterious Francisco de la Torre (fl. 1550–1575), who, like Fray Luis de León, was edited by Quevedo and admired for "el corriente de los versos, la blandura, la facilidad" and "lo severo de la sentencia" ("the easy, mellow fluidity of his verse" and the "austerity of his thought").[9] The best mid-century poet was Francisco de Aldana (1537–1578), called "el Divino" ("the Divine") by Cervantes. Born in Italy, he also wrote in Italian, and his best verse possesses a lithe sensuality, as in the famous sonnet which begins "¿Cuál es la causa, mi Damón . . .?" ("What is the reason, Damón?"). This poem shows how the perfect union of male and female (illustrated by the remarkable image of the water-soaked sponge) leads to the Neoplatonic ascent of the soul. However, it also invokes, if only to unsettle, conventional gender identities based on the common scholastic binarism that female is to male as the imperfect is to perfection, and matter is to form. In the quatrains, the female's (feigned?) ignorance of the nature of bodily desire is suffused with a joy that is answered, in the tercets, by the male's theoretical yet profoundly melancholic knowledge.

The Renaissance closes with the major figure of Fernando de Herrera (1534–1597), also called "el Divino." He belonged to the important literary gathering of the Conde de Gelves, and was a prolific writer of prose and verse. He left a powerful and individual stamp upon the Petrarchan tradition, but he also wrote in Castilian meters, and, in an intriguing triangulation of desire, he dedicated his love lyric to doña Leonor, the wife of his patron. Leonor was given names such as Luz, Lumbre, and Eliodora, which are significant for two reasons. Their associations with light and fire symbolize Herrera's yearning for an unattainable aesthetic purity (even at the orthographic level); in the process, Luz, like Petrarch's Laura, becomes a fragmented abstraction. In spite of their common associations, Luz, Eliodora, etc., are after all different names, which in turn echoes not only the multiple voices of Herrera himself, but also the play of coherence and discontinuity within the *rime sparse* ("scattered rhymes") of the originary Petrarchan moment.

Brief mention must also be made of Herrera as literary critic and editor. Three years after El Brocense, he published his famous commentary on Garcilaso's poetry (1580), part of a pugnacious debate over Garcilaso's legacy. Two years later, and exceptionally for the age, he prepared a meticulous edition of his own verse. Both commentary and edition signal

---

[9] Francisco de la Torre, *Poesía completa*. Ed. María Luisa Cerrón Puga (Madrid: Cátedra, 1984), pp. 68–69.

the gradual institutionalization of vernacular "literature" and Herrera's attempt to inscribe himself within an emerging native canon.

The idealizing trends of Renaissance Petrarchism and Neoplatonism find their counterpoint in the rich medieval inheritance of satire, burlesque, and invective. The commercial potential of this legacy, especially among the new urban readership, was soon realized with such publications as the *Cancionero de obras de burlas provocantes a risa* ("Songbook of Poems that Provoke Laughter"; originally part of the *Cancionero general*, but then published independently by a printer with an eye for the market), the obscene *Carajicomedia* ("The Prick's Progress," first printed 1519), and the chapbooks of verse by Rodrigo de Reinosa (*c.* 1500). The range of comic types and topics was already broad, but the expanding literary and social horizons of the early modern period broadened them even further. Reinosa, for example, was the first Castilian to depict the West African slaves of Seville (they had already been the subject of Portuguese burlesque), and also to represent underworld slang (called *germanía*) poetically.

Female sexuality, however, was an obsessive concern, as poets exploited the "low" registers of satire and burlesque to portray models of eroticism, gender, and the female body that transgressed Petrarchan and Neoplatonic traditions. Active, and often dominant and voracious, female sexuality was usually portrayed in an aggressively lewd and ugly mode, but not inevitably so: compare the *Carajicomedia*'s self-mocking depiction of the impotent phallus, sunk in the whore's unfathomable vagina (masculinity's eternal *horror vacui*), with the wider range of comic tones to be found in the playfully erotic *villancicos*, romances, and glosses from the late sixteenth and seventeenth centuries. Fondness for the obscene and the grotesque was by no means alien to Petrarchan poets, as the works of Gutierre de Cetina or Diego Hurtado de Mendoza demonstrate. The latter's *Fábula del cangrejo* ("Fable of the Crab") offers a strikingly lurid example, though he also demythified classical gods, and wrote in praise of mundane objects, like the carrot or the flea. Such verse shows how Petrarchism produced its own mirror image that inverted the idealization of Love and female beauty (youth, golden hair, ivory neck, pearl-white teeth) often taking the form of sonnets excoriating old hags, with white hair, withered skin, and toothless maws. This mode is labeled "antipetrarchism," and although the term usefully draws attention to contemporary awareness of the constraints imposed by the dominant conventions, it also has its limitations. Constructing Petrarchism and anti-Petrarchism as binary opposites obscures their shared ideological underpinnings: they are two ends of a continuous spectrum of misogynist anxieties about the stability of the binarism "masculine/feminine," and about the threat posed by the mutable feminine to the "firmness" of masculinity. Mark Breitenberg has coined the phrase "anxious masculinity" to describe this phenomenon in English Renaissance literature, and we would also do well to recall that the same Spanish courtiers who spread throughout Europe the fashion for somber black also wore suspiciously pronounced codpieces.

One especially noteworthy burlesque and satiric poet was the Sevillian Baltasar del Alcázar (1530–1606). A member, like Herrera, of the Conde de Gelves *tertulia*, he wrote amatory verse in the Petrarchan tradition, characterized by a sensual masochism (e.g. "Tiéneme a una coluna Amor ligado" ["Love has bound me to a column"]), religious sonnets and *villancicos*, and epistles in a variety of meters. He is best known, though, for his satires and parodies, which, like those of his contemporaries Jerónimo Lomas de Cantoral (*c.* 1538–1600) and Juan de Mal Lara (1527–1571), were indebted to the rediscovery of Martial. Alcázar's acerbic wit, as in his coruscating satires of licentious friars, anticipates Quevedo. His parodies of sonnets and epic ballads also display a more genial poetic temperament, as well as his interest in the nature of the literary and creative process. This is also a feature of his *Cena jocosa* ("Jocose Banquet") which links food and sex (commonly associated in his verse) to produce an amusing burlesque not only of Renaissance symposia, but also of narrative itself: foreshadowing Laurence Sterne's *Tristram Shandy*, Alcázar begins a story whose telling is constantly postponed by the lure of the table and of women. Here, and in his numerous octosyllabic epigrams depicting grotesque images of "lost women," the feminine becomes a symbol of desire and confusion. His paradoxical fascination and loathing for the deformed or unrestrained female body is symptomatic of the deeper social conditions of early modern cities like Seville, where, according to Mary Elizabeth Perry, "prostitution was not only acceptable . . . it even acted as a pillar of the moral system that buttressed the existing social order."[10]

Gaping mouths are frequent features of Alcázar's female caricatures, and the association between excess, orality, and the feminine recurs in the poetry of another, more obscure, Sevillian, Cristóbal de Tamariz (fl. 1570–1585). His seventeen comic verse narratives, based on Italian *novelle*, are often directly addressed to women, whose behavior he treats in satiric (though sometimes sympathetic) fashion. These stories were intended for reading aloud in mixed private gatherings, not for print. So of particular interest is Tamariz's admiration for women's natural abilities as storytellers, whose valuable oral tales he turns into writing. His remarks anticipate María de Zayas who, in the middle of the next century, would ironically appropriate the misogynist stereotype of garrulous females – *noveleras* – in her defense of women's literacy.

---

[10] Mary Elizabeth Perry, *Crime and Society in Early Modern Seville* (Hanover: University Press of New England, 1980), p. 213.

The distinction between male literacy and female orality is far from watertight, but it did correspond to real divisions of cultural labor and capital; on a deeper ideological level, these divisions were also played out on the terrain of poetic genre because of the close association between the female voice and the "traditional" or "popular" lyric.[11] These anonymous lyrics – called *villancicos, estribillos, seguidillas,* and so forth – were predominantly female-voiced, but this does not mean that they were necessarily by women, or, even less, that they offer some "pure" unmediated access to female experience. They provide what Mary Gaylord has called "a grammar of femininity" – imagined models of female desire and utterance.[12]

From the early sixteenth century, noblemen like Pedro Manuel Jiménez de Urrea (1486–1535?) continued the earlier interest in these forms, either by imitating them or by using preexisting refrains (*estribillos*) as the basis of their *villancicos*. This assimilation was given added impetus by *vihuelistas* ("vihuela players"; the vihuela is an early form of the guitar) such as Luis Milán, Luis de Narváez, and Alonso Mudarra whose music books were printed in 1535, 1538, and 1546. These compilations culminated in the collective *Cancionero de Upsala* ("Songbook of Upsala"), which was published in 1556, when non-musical anthologies began to appear specifically dedicated to *villancicos* and other popular forms that had previously circulated in *pliegos sueltos* or as part of heterogeneous collections like the *Cancionero general*. As the title of one of these compilations, *Flor de enamorados* ("The Garland of Lovers," 1562), suggests, the overwhelming theme of these lyrics is love, and the subject is explored from a variety of angles (from despair to exultation, from innocence to a knowing eroticism), and it is expressed with an apparent artlessness that belies the poems' evocative power. This capacity to suggest, rather than define, meanings and moods derives from various factors: their dynamic rhythms, assonant rhyme, an incantatory repetition (occasionally based upon structural parallelism), or their reliance on a common stock of symbols, such as hair, skin color, fountains, trees, stags, or bathing. Not only were these symbols polyvalent, but they also had folkloric as well as highly literary connotations. Thus, the two cultural registers "popular" and "learned" could acquire a complementary, rather than conflictive, relationship.

This point extends to the *romancero viejo*, or traditional oral balladry, whose passage from the later Middle Ages to the early modern period follows a similar trajectory to that of the traditional lyric. The first serious interest in their poetic potential was shown by the Isabeline poets, whose verse was sent on its passage through the Renaissance by the *Cancionero general*. These poets grafted their courtly love traditions onto the lyrical

[11] See Margit Frenk, *Lírica española de tipo popular* (Madrid: Castalia, 1978).
[12] Mary Gaylord, "The Grammar of Femininity in the Traditional Spanish Lyric." *Revista / Review Interamericana* 12 (1982), pp. 115–124.

romances, in their glosses of such ballads as "Fontefrida" ("Cool Fountain") or "El prisionero" ("The Prisoner"). *Romances viejos* continued to be transmitted orally and in *pliegos sueltos*, and both oral and written modes of diffusion intermingled to produce the dynamic evolution of particular poems that is so characteristic of this form. Their cultural influence is attested by the fact that as early as the 1520s lines from ballads were being registered as popular phrases. In 1547, drawing on *pliegos sueltos* and oral sources, the famous printer Martín Nucio brought out the first of several editions of his *Cancionero de romances* ("Book of Ballads") whose popularity spawned the abundant *romanceros* that followed. Meanwhile, poets began to imitate traditional ballads to produce *romances artificiosos*, or the *romancero nuevo*, and this process culminated in the publication of the *Flor de varios romances nuevos y canciones* ("Garland of Miscellaneous New Ballads and Songs," 1589), compiled by Pedro de Moncayo. The 1580s, then, marks the emergence of the "new" balladry which would play such a fundamental role in the history of Baroque verse.

Various reasons explain the elevation in cultural status of the ballad and popular lyric. They expanded the available repertoire of expressive effects, and as the century progressed both styles were exploited for assorted poetic ends. Like the sonnet, the ballad became a most capacious vernacular form, capable, as Lope de Vega would put it "no sólo de exprimir y declarar cualquier concepto con fácil dulzura, pero de proseguir toda grave acción de numeroso poema" ("not only to express any conceit with an easy sweetness, but also to narrate any weighty action in a long poem").[13] More broadly, they appealed to a society that in spite of the spread of lay literacy still had a massive oral residue, and in spite of urban development was still predominantly rural. They are also an aspect of the early modern fascination for traditional customs, manners, and speech (in painting one thinks of the *bodegón* ["still life"], and in moral philosophy, the collections of popular wisdom, or *refraneros*). Further, they helped lay the basis for an (unevenly) emerging concept of a "national" culture: to quote Lope again, speaking of the ballads, "y soy tan de veras español, que por ser en nuestro idioma natural este género, no me puedo persuadir que no sea digno de toda estimación" ("I am so truly a Spaniard, that because this genre is natural to our language, no one can persuade me that it is not worthy of the highest estimation").[14] Writers imagined the relative autonomy and richness of that culture precisely because it was understood to be articulated through different, though interdependent, registers. Similarly, broadening the available discourses buttressed

[13] Prologue to his *Rimas*, cited by José Manuel Blecua, *Poesía de la Edad de Oro* (Madrid: Castalia, 1982), p. 14.
[14] Cited in José Manuel Blecua, *Poesía*, p. 14.

Renaissance notions of selfhood: the "dignity of Man" was predicated on the assumption that an "individual" could move freely among all levels of collective experience.

Lastly, traditions are never static, nor simply "there," but constructed and dynamic. The "traditional" lyrics and ballads may be transhistorical, but their function and meanings will evolve along with their changing historical conditions. Menéndez Pidal famously wrote that the "romance vive en sus variantes" ("the romance lives in its variants"), and his observation is also valid for the role played by these forms as cultural memory (which is especially important for the *Ladino* ballads of Sephardic exiles, or for those who took ballads to the New World). They enable readers and listeners to recall and reinterpret the past in the light of the present. The morisco ballad "Abenámar," for example, which treats the process of acculturation between Christian and Muslim, means one thing in the mid fifteenth century, quite another when sung amidst the horrors of the Alpujarra pogroms.

The field of moral verse is dominated by the Augustinian Fray Luis de León (1527–1591), who occupied an ambivalent position within the intellectual establishment. A central figure in the humanist circles of Salamanca, he was also imprisoned by the Inquisition for his views on the Bible. His copious verse falls under three headings: translations, imitations, and original compositions. Within this corpus his twenty-three original poems (not counting his five Petrarchan sonnets, often classed as "imitations") constitute only a minority. He produced powerful yet elegant versions of classical poems (ranging from his principal interests, Horace's *Odes* and Virgil's *Eclogues*, to fragments of the Greeks Pindar and Euripides); biblical verse (the Book of Job and about two dozen Psalms); and a few samples of Italian humanist love lyric (Petrarch and Pietro Bembo). These translations and imitations, particularly of Horace, connect thematically with his original verse and are complementary aspects of the same continuous project. Fray Luis has been described as a Neo-Latin poet writing in the vernacular, and these three creative modes combine to trace a humanist poetic tradition, linking contemporary Castilian verse with the Italian Renaissance, classical antiquity, and its biblical origins. His creative practice, therefore, makes Fray Luis, alongside Garcilaso and Herrera, a key figure in Renaissance constructions of authoritative literary traditions. This process also operates on a formal level, since nearly all his original compositions adopt (and extend the expressive range of) Garcilaso's *lira* form, thus fusing native metrical innovations with classicizing thematic traditions.

Fray Luis' original verse mostly concerns secular ethics, sometimes with a metaphysical dimension. Horace's odes are a major influence, filtered through the Christianized Stoicism, Epicureanism, and Neoplatonism characteristic of Fray Luis' age. Adapting the Horatian "Beatus ille" topos, some poems extol the virtues of solitude and the Golden Mean (e.g. "De la vida retirada," "Al apartamiento," "A la salida de la cárcel" ["On Life in Retirement," "On Solitude," "On Release from Imprisonment"]), while others explore Nature or music to capture the elusive harmony between the inner self and Divine creation (e.g. "Noche serena," "De la vida del cielo," "Oda a Salinas" ["Serene Night," "On the Life of the Heavens," "Ode to Salinas"]). Fray Luis' contemplative side, however, also has a sharp moral edge: he stresses the superiority of individual to inherited nobility, of spiritual to physical beauty, and censures materialism, envy, and avarice, as well as the brutality of war. These ideas were central strands in the broader moral and philosophical currents of the time.[15] Horace, for example, had already influenced the verse epistles of Diego Hurtado de Mendoza, and, in the early Baroque, he would also inspire Francisco de Medrano (1570–1607). The originality and complexity of Fray Luis' verse stem from the way otherwise commonplace ideas are configured and expressed, both within individual poems, and across the corpus as a whole.

Tight organization, clarity, and directness of diction lend his verse simplicity. Yet his vocabulary and metaphors also possess an allusive quality that resonates (often literally, as Senabre has shown) with a plurality of meanings and affective tones. Poems like "De la vida retirada" and the "Oda a Salinas" may invite us to share the serene joy in the simple life or the ecstatic contemplation of the links between man-made music and the divine harmony of the spheres. They also compel us to measure the distance between real and imagined worlds, to explore the inner self, to question man's place in Creation, and to ponder the scope and power of human language.

This "variedad interpretativa" ("interpretive variety"), to use Prieto's phrase, derives from other factors too.[16] His poems circulated in numerous manuscripts, which poses problems for textual critics striving to identify "definitive" texts for work that often underwent a continuous process of refinement. However, around 1580 Fray Luis prepared a collection, perhaps for the press (opinions differ), and although it does not survive, critics often try to identify its authorial structure, believing that the poems are mutually illuminating fragments with an overarching unity. Its prologue begins with a conventional exordial gambit that presents "estas obrecillas" ("these little works") as juvenilia rather than the result of judicious maturity. This modesty distances Fray Luis from his work, and the distance is increased by the fiction that he was a layman whose verse had been stolen by an Augustinian friar. In the context of a corpus that invites

---

[15] See Ricardo Senabre, *Tres estudios sobre fray Luis de León* (Salamanca: Universidad de Salamanca, 1978).

[16] Antonio Prieto, *La poesía española del siglo XVI*. 2 vols. (Madrid: Cátedra, 1998), vol. I, p. 307.

yet also resists biographical readings, this is significant. Like the humanist self of which it is both product and symbol, this body of poetry holds out the prospect of a coherent, controlling subjectivity from the perspective of absence and alienation.

The fluid boundary between moral and religious verse is illustrated by Francisco de Aldana's masterpiece, the *Carta para Arias Montano sobre la contemplación de Dios* ("Letter to Arias Montano on the Contemplation of God," 1577), a poem that bridges the achievements of Fray Luis and San Juan de la Cruz, in a profound and moving meditation on friendship as a pathway to Divine contemplation. Mysticism proper achieves its greatest poetic heights with San Juan de la Cruz (Juan de Yepes, 1542–1591). He wrote various religious poems, including ten ballads on the Gospels and a Psalm, and a few secular lyrics *a lo divino*. These were written in traditional octosyllabic meters, but for his three major poems (*Noche oscura*, *Llama de amor viva*, and *Cántico espiritual* ["Dark night," "Living Flame of Love," "Spiritual Canticle"]), he chose the Italianate *lira* form, inherited from Fray Luis and Garcilaso. These poems treat the soul's mystical union with God, a quest that is represented in the allegorical terms derived from the Song of Songs and the centuries of exegesis upon it. The eight stanzas of *Noche oscura* follow the steps of the female lover (the soul) as she escapes the confines of her "sosegada casa" (the body, with the passions at rest) and journeys anxiously toward ecstatic union with her beloved (Christ):

> ¡Oh noche que juntaste
> amado con amada,
> amada en el amado transformada!
>
> (stanza 5)[17]

(O night that joined / lover and beloved, / the lover transformed into the beloved!)

Following this blissful encounter, the lover dissolves into sensual yet tranquil oblivion:

> Quedéme y olbidéme,
> el rostro recliné sobre el amado;
> cessó todo, y dexéme
> dexando mi cuydado
> entre las açucenas olbidado.
>
> (stanza 8)

(I remained and forgot myself, / my face resting on my beloved; / everything ceased, and I left myself / leaving my cares / forgotten among the lilies.)

---

[17] Juan de la Cruz, *Poesía*. Ed. Domingo Yndurain (Madrid: Cátedra, 2000).

These lines illustrate some of the exquisite qualities of San Juan's finest verse: the syntactic grace, the sparse use of adjectives, the repetition of words, phrases, and rhythms combine to evoke the ineffable while preserving a mood of delicate erotic intimacy.

Some of the underlying ideas of *Noche oscura* are repeated, with variations and from different perspectives, in the intense *Llama de amor viva* (only four stanzas), and in San Juan's longest and most elaborate poem, *Cántico espiritual* (forty stanzas in its second redaction). Here, the lover's journey toward self-negation follows a tripartite structure: stanzas 1–12 describe the "vía purgativa," 13–21 the "iluminativa," and 22–40 the "unitiva" (the paths of "purgation, illumination, and union"). This is no strictly linear narrative, however: the ascent is rendered more complex by abrupt transitions, paradoxes, and a rich web of lexical associations, symbols, and metaphors. Though mostly based on the Song of Songs, the verbal texture of the *Cántico* is infused with an array of linguistic registers and allusions to chivalric romance, *cancionero* verse, Garcilaso's pastoral, and Neoplatonism.

San Juan elaborated the doctrinal and theological underpinnings of these three poems in a long prose commentary (1584), which he wrote at the behest of the Discalced Carmelite nun Ana de Jesús and doña Ana de Peñalosa. While it does explain some of the more esoteric features of the *Cántico*, this commentary was never intended to provide the "key" to these mystical poems, which by definition, according to the author, "no se podrán declarar al justo, [ni] mi intento será tal, sino sólo dar alguna luz general" ("cannot be explained with precision, and my intention will be only to shed some general light on them").[18] Moreover, since we all possess distinct spiritual needs and temperaments, "No hay para qué atarse a la declaración" ("There is no need to be tied to the interpretation"). The idea that meaning could be adjusted to suit the "paladar" ("palate") of individual readers connects these poems with the religious renewal of the sixteenth century, when trends such as the *devotio moderna* ("modern piety") promoted a solitary, "interior" Christianity (see Alison Weber's chapter in the present volume). The female patronage of the commentary also illustrates the role of women, inside and outside the convent, in shaping spiritual developments, as well as the popularity of San Juan's verse in female religious circles of the seventeenth century.

Ana de Jesús also encouraged Fray Luis de León to edit the works of the other great Spanish mystic, Santa Teresa de Jesús (1515–1582). Deploying the octosyllabic forms of popular and courtly traditions, Santa Teresa wrote verse both to strengthen her sisters' faith and to give voice to her

---

[18] San Juan de la Cruz, *Poesía completa y comentarios en prosa.* Ed. Raquel Asún (Barcelona: Planeta, 1997), p. 155.

ascetic or mystic experience.[19] Like San Juan, she portrayed mysticism's anxious yearning in an *a lo divino* gloss of the courtly refrain: "Vivo sin vivir en mí / y de tal manera espero / que muero porque no muero" ("I live without living within myself / and I hope so intensely / that I die because I do not die"). Much of her verse is only attributed, because it was transmitted from convent to convent either orally or in ad hoc copies. This in turn, however, is evidence of the nuns' attempts to construct a religious community around strong female figures.

Of course, the scope of Renaissance religious verse extends far beyond the work of these two poets – especially given the fluidity between the moral and the religious – and its full range can merely be acknowledged here. Among other religious poets of distinction are Gregorio Silvestre (1520–1569; posthumously published, 1582) and Jorge de Montemayor (1520–1561), though the fact that they wrote in both secular and spiritual vein is symptomatic of the age. Whether motivated by the Counter Reformation or to explore the affective and psychic connection between human and divine love, *a lo divino* renderings of secular love lyrics became intensely popular, and even the works of Garcilaso and Boscán were recast in this way, by Sebastián de Córdoba in 1575.[20] Indeed, the 1570s saw an increase in the printing of religious verse, such as López de Úbeda's *Cancionero general de la doctrina cristiana* ("General Songbook of Christian Doctrine") or Cosme de Aldana's *Octavas y canciones espirituales* ("Spiritual Octaves and Songs," both 1579).

Religious discourse also pervades the broad category of epic, chivalric, and heroic poetry. In 1553, Hernando de Acuña dedicated to Charles V his verse rendering of *Le chevalier délibéré* ("The Ardent Knight," by the fifteenth-century Frenchman Olivier de la Marche), arguing that its "doctrina cristiana y militar" ("Christian and military doctrine") constituted the mutually supporting foundations of this monarch's empire. The divine basis of Habsburg power was consecrated in numerous short poems, such as Acuña's sonnet to Charles V, "Al rey nuestro señor" ("To Our Lord King"), or Herrera's patriotic odes "Canción a la batalla de Lepanto" ("Ode to the Battle of Lepanto," 1571) and "Canción por la pérdida del rey don Sebastián" ("Ode to the Loss of King Sebastian," 1578), in which he represents imperial victory and defeat in biblical terms, with Spain as God's chosen people, the new Israelites.

The twin enemies of Protestantism and Islam (both the Ottoman threat and the moriscos, seen as a fifth column) gave impetus to the newly revived epic genre. Taking their place alongside heroic figures from the

---

[19] See Víctor García de la Concha, *El arte literario de Santa Teresa* (Barcelona: Ariel, 1978), pp. 317–376.
[20] See Bruce Wardropper, *Historia de la poesía lírica a lo divino en la cristiandad occidental* (Madrid: Revista de Occidente, 1954).

past (national heroes like Bernardo del Carpio), were Charles V and don Juan of Austria, who were celebrated in such epics as *Carlos famoso* ("Charles the Famous") by Luis Zapata (1566; in fifty cantos, and thirteen years in the making before Cervantes consigned it to the bonfire of unreadable books in *Don Quijote*), and *La Austriada* ("The Austriad," 1584) by Juan Rufo. Not only did the epic christianize the hero as a *miles Dei* ("soldier of God"), it also offered a heroic rendering of Christianity, inspired by hagiographic and literary models, most notably Sannazzaro's *El parto de la virgen* ("The Virgin Birth," Castilian translation 1554). The most interesting Renaissance Christian epic is Cristóbal de Virués' *El Montserrate* (1587, revised 1602), a tale of rape and redemption colored by ideologies of nationhood, race, and gender.[21] The discovery of the New World also provided epic material: Luis Zapata devoted sections of his *Carlos famoso* to this subject, but before him it was treated in Latin verse. However, the encounter between Old and New Worlds is most powerfully treated in *La Araucana*.

Judging by the number of original texts and translations, heroic verse enjoyed a popularity that is not recognized by its place in the modern literary canon,[22] and many works have yet to receive critical attention. Throughout Europe, these poems found particular favor among aristocratic readers,[23] in part because of the latters' investment in their chivalric ethos. The poems' sublime style and literary frame of reference, however, also flattered aristocratic cultural literacy. The poetics of *imitatio* were as central to the epic as to other literary modes, and tested readers' knowledge of Homer (*Ulisea* translated 1550); Virgil (*Eneida* translated 1555, revised 1574); Lucan (*Pharsalia* translated *c.* 1530); the Spanish "classic" Juan de Mena; Luís de Camões (*Os Lusíadas*, 1572, with three Castilian translations between 1580 and 1591); Ariosto (whose *Orlando furioso* was a major influence); and, by the end of the century, Tasso (*Gerusalemme liberata*).

This corpus echoes Antonio de Nebrija's dictum (lifted from Lorenzo Valla) that language was the companion to Empire. In spite of its pervasive triumphalist tone, however, heroic verse is not free of contradiction or self doubt, as in Aldana's profoundly ambivalent sonnet "Otro aquí no se ve . . ." ("No other is seen here"). This poem represents the brutality of slaughter and how it is experienced in and through the body, seen in

---

[21] Elizabeth B. Davis, *Myth and Identity in the Epic of Imperial Spain* (Columbia: University of Missouri Press, 2000), pp. 98–127; and James Nicolopulos, *The Poetics of Empire in the Indies: Prophecy and Imitation in "La Araucana" and "Os Lusíadas"* (University Park, PA: Pennsylvania State University Press, 2000).

[22] See Frank Pierce, *La poesía épica del Siglo de Oro* (Madrid: Gredos, 1961).

[23] Maxime Chevalier, *Lectura y lectores en la España de los siglos XVI y XVII* (Madrid: Turner, 1976), pp. 104–137.

its turn as a fractured body politic. The final line, "¡Oh sólo de hombres digno y noble estado!" ("Oh noble condition worthy only of men!") offers an ironic comment on Horace's "Dulce et decorum est pro patria mori" ("How sweet and fitting it is to die for one's fatherland"). The existence of ideological complexity over a wider range of texts is increasingly being realized, and it has its roots in prevailing political and economic structures. Facile recourse to the terms "imperio" and "España" obscures the nature of a territorial expansion that lacked the resources and infrastructure to support it; was based on annexation, succession, or individual enterprise rather than official state conquest; and was backed by armies of uncertain military capability, made up of men who were increasingly not "Spanish."

All these issues converge in the greatest Spanish epic, *La Araucana*, by Alonso de Ercilla y Zúñiga (1533–1594). This poem (thirty-five cantos in three books, 1569, 1578, 1589) became an early modern best-seller, with continuations, and imitations, as well as partial English and Dutch translations. It narrates the campaigns against the Araucans of Chile, in which the author participated in 1557–1559, as well as the battles of Lepanto and San Quentin, finishing with a defense of Felipe II's claim to Portugal. Ercilla's sources include Virgil, Mena, Ariosto, Garcilaso, Camões, and particularly the "Spaniard" Lucan, who all leave their imprint on the poem's style: his *octavas* (the conventional meter for literary epic) weave together extended epic similes, set speeches, descriptions of the land, battle scenes, erotic interludes, and elements of the fantastic. Ercilla created a model that others, like Juan Rufo, consciously strove to emulate and outdo, just as Ercilla himself was engaged in competitive emulation of his sources.

The exotic portrayal of the Araucans makes the Spaniards appear anodine in comparison, and there is no single Spanish hero, unlike their highly individualized enemies, who embody a contradictory range of qualities: though savage and barbaric, some, like the leader Caupolicán, display a noble valor, dignity, and love of liberty and *patria*. This warrior's horrific execution – impaled and disemboweled – illustrates Ercilla's criticism of Spanish violence and greed, and echoes the bitterness of Camões toward Portuguese brutality. The poem therefore shares in the debate over the rights of the conquered "barbarians," which is infused with a larger preoccupation with the relationship between "nature" and "culture." Politically, the poem is also shot through with doubt. In spite of his eulogy of absolutism, Ercilla poses questions about the reach of the absolutist state, and the security it offers members of his class. Thus, the poem anticipates the *desengaño* that would become so ingrained in the literary and social consciousness of the Baroque.

By way of conclusion, it is significant that one of the most repeated words in the poem is "término" ("boundary, limit"). Whether referring to the "términos" of humanity (Canto XXIII, 40), of an emotion (XXI, 56), of a place (XXII, 6), or of language itself (XVII, 2), the word evokes the Renaissance obsession with mapping boundaries, and the role of poetry in that process.[24]

---

[24] Alonso de Ercilla, *La Araucana*. Ed. Isaías Lerner (Madrid: Cátedra, 1993).

10

The antecedents of the novel in sixteenth-century Spain

E. MICHAEL GERLI

The rise of narrative prose fiction in sixteenth-century Spain is an intricate process that is difficult to synthesize. In a vast universe of texts, it cannot be reduced to a clean outline or progression. Many types of fiction appeared, infiltrated and mutually influenced each other, and extended their individual and collective vitality well beyond the moment of their origins to affect later, newly emerging kinds of narrative. Any history of prose fiction of the period must therefore be constructed by force of generalization and at the expense of detail and objectivity. Two things remain clear, however: the sheer profusion of styles that appeared and the absence of any single controlling tendency, or commanding genre, that eclipsed all others. Five kinds of prose narrative stand out and serve as necessary antecedents for understanding Cervantes and the development of the novel in the early seventeenth century. These are the chivalric, pastoral, Moorish, Byzantine, and picaresque romances, which constituted the core genres, if that is what they may be called, that developed out of a broad and varied process of narrative invention and reciprocal influence in early modern Spain. Put simply, the Iberian peninsula during the sixteenth century can be seen as a vast laboratory for literary experimentation and innovation where the writing of imaginative prose remained a serious and persistent cultural activity. Literary historians have in large part, however, dismissed much of what was produced during this period, banishing it to the footnotes of cultural history, while, with perhaps the exception of *Lazarillo de Tormes*, privileging lyric genres and characterizing the developments in sixteenth-century narrative prose as the necessary but flawed precursors of a later group of mature, transcendent works and forms.

The printing press rescued for the commercial book market many medieval texts that had circulated in manuscript and that now reached a broad readership side by side with more recently composed works intended for the new medium. The emergence of an extended, heterogeneous reading public with new-found wealth and time on its hands produced a demand for both information and diversion that kept printers and authors busy at their craft. The bulk of prose published in sixteenth-century Spain was pious, didactic, or exemplary, especially after the

Council of Trent, but a sizeable portion of it was also aimed purely at entertainment, intended to satisfy the desires of a literate public avid for amusement and eager to appease the cravings of a heightened imagination that resulted from the opening of new geographical, social, and scientific frontiers. One of the most notable outcomes of the advent of printing was the flourishing of these fictional works, many of which possess an intrinsic merit all their own but would also be instrumental in laying the groundwork for Cervantes' later composition of *Don Quijote*, perhaps the single most influential book in the history of the novel.

From script to print: sentimental romances and late humanistic comedy

Although composed and circulated in the late fifteenth century, initially in manuscript, works like Diego de San Pedro's (fl. second half of fifteenth century) *Cárcel de amor* ("Prison of Love," Seville 1492), Juan de Flores' (fl. second half of fifteenth century) *Grisel y Mirabella* (Lérida 1495) – both sentimental romances – and the humanistic comedy *Celestina* (Burgos 1499?) enjoyed vast commercial success in their printed forms, went on to become best-sellers, and would exert a broad influence both inside and outside the Iberian peninsula during the sixteenth century, especially as they were translated into many of the major languages of Europe. San Pedro's work is particularly noteworthy in that it constitutes a bold narrative experiment that uses allegory, dialogue, and epistles to tell its tragic tale of love and minutely dissect the passion of Leriano for Laureola, daughter of the king of Macedonia. As it does this, it reveals a primary interest in the emotional and psychological lives of the characters rather than in the chronicling of events, so that the focus of the work becomes the unfolding of the characters' subjective reactions to what occurs around them, thus establishing an important antecedent in narrative technique for the epistolary and pastoral romances, which materialized around mid century with the publication of Juan de Segura's (fl. mid sixteenth century) *Proceso de cartas de amores* ("The Exchange of Love Letters," Toledo? 1548) and *Los siete libros de la Diana* ("The Seven Books of Diana," Valencia 1559?) by Jorge de Montemayor (*c.* 1520–1561).

    Celestina, a work entirely in dialogue composed during the 1490s, would engender a series of later imitations with a realistic, earthy bent and a tragic or comic tenor. These depicted stories of love and seduction in which the main characters' servants, with the assistance of a go-between, advance the love affairs of their masters or ladies. The most accomplished of the Celestinesque works are the anonymous *Comedia Thebaida*, *Comedia Serafina*, and the *Comedia Hipólita* published together at Valencia in 1521. Others include the *Segunda comedia de Celestina* ("Second Comedy of Celestina"), Medina del Campo 1534 written by Feliciano de Silva (*c.* 1490 – after 1551); the *Tercera parte de la tragicomedia de Celestina* ("Third Part of the Tragicomedy of Celestina"), Medina del Campo 1536 by Gaspar Gómez (dates unknown); the *Tragicomedia de Lisandro y Roselia* ("Tragicomedy of Lisandro and Roselia"), Salamanca 1542 published anonymously but composed by Sancho de Muñón (dates unknown); the anonymous *Tragedia Policiana* (Toledo 1547); Juan Rodríguez Florián's (dates unknown) *Comedia Florinea* (Medina del Campo 1554); and *Comedia Selvagia* (Toledo 1554) by Alonso de Villegas (1522? – before 1565). All of these broadly imitate the original *Celestina* by Fernando de Rojas (*c.* 1475–1541) and constitute important precedents for Lope de Vega's (1562–1635) *La Dorotea* (Madrid 1632), the last example and culminating accomplishment of the tradition.

Although some of the works patterned after *Celestina* have tragic dénouements, the great majority of them are primarily comical in nature as they contrast the lives of masters and servants and revel in the furtive encounters and risk-taking of the lovers. Regardless of the disposition of their plots, all of them share several common characteristics: a material vision of the world with a strong emphasis on the effects of a monied economy on the human passions, an interest in revealing the private lives of people (both high and low status) and in catering to a reading public's desire for risqué narratives that tested the limits of propriety under the guise of moral exemplarity. By far the most interesting of them is the *Comedia Serafina*, which burlesques elements taken from different literary traditions and questions social authority and accepted gender roles in its portrayal of passion.

Francisco Delicado (fl. first half of sixteenth century), a cleric and Spanish expatriate residing in Rome, published his *Retrato de la Lozana andaluza* ("Portrait of the Exuberant Andalusian Woman") anonymously in Venice in 1528. The book is most closely related to the Celestina tradition, although it has often also been seen as a precursor of the picaresque because of the protagonist's brief autobiographical ramble at the beginning and the plot's peripatetic structure. The book's anticlerical satire, use of clever euphemistic language and lowlife jargon, and its portrayal of delinquency and underworld characters also link it thematically to later picaresque narratives. Like the works that imitate *Celestina*, however, *La Lozana* is composed in dialogue and displays an interest in sex, questionable liaisons, and characters who inhabit the margins of society as they make these their business. Nonetheless, the Roman demi-monde of prostitutes and pimps in which it unfolds, and the characters who tell about their experiences in it, more closely resemble the personalities and situations depicted in the racy dialogues of the Italian humanist Pietro Aretino.

Aldonza, the protagonist and humorously lively Andalusian lady referred to in Delicado's title, is a prostitute and procuress in Rome who relates her busy life and adventures, principally among the clergy, in numerous conversations (*mamotretos*) with colleagues and friends. The action takes place just prior to the sack of Rome in 1527 – alluded to at several points in the work in a prophetic way – and provides vivid descriptions of the city at the height of the Renaissance.

Chivalric romances

Amadís de Gaula, an indigenous Iberian chivalric romance, was modeled after French Arthurian romances like the prose *Lancelot*, which continued to circulate in Castilian translation up to the beginning of the sixteenth century. Published in 1508 at Zaragoza by Garci Rodríguez de Montalvo (fl. 1495–1515), a *regidor* (alderman) of Medina del Campo of whom little is known, Montalvo corrected the first three books, rewrote the fourth, and added a fifth of his own to the original *Amadís*, which may be traced back as far as the first part of the fourteenth century. (There are several recorded mentions of the work, the oldest from before 1325.) The original books of *Amadís*, along with Montalvo's additional fifth book entitled *Las sergas de Esplandián* ("The Deeds of Esplandián," Seville 1510), proved an immediate success and were reprinted some thirty times during the rest of the century. Indeed, the work struck such a profound chord in the sixteenth-century imagination that it generated a series of imitations and sequels that exerted a broad influence on European literature, mores, and social ideals. Their popularity provides a standard for measuring the scope and extent of lay reading habits in early modern Spain and prepared the ground for the development of the novel. The chivalric romances were the declared targets of Cervantes' satire at the beginning of the seventeenth century, whose hero Don Quijote is driven mad by reading books like *Amadís* and sallies forth to imitate them and look for adventure, just to crash headlong into an indifferent world.

At first glance, *Amadís* appears to be a work of derring-do adventure with a dizzying multitude of characters and events. Amadís is the prototypical invincible hero, courteous, of noble birth and spirit, whose deeds and heart are moved solely by thoughts of his lady. In this way, his fighting prowess is tempered by courtly values and idealized love to produce a sentimental, heroic vision that came to embody a sixteenth-century aristocratic ideal. (The work was translated into French, was admired by Castiglione, and served as a courtesy book as well as a stimulus to the social imagination.) Essentially a quest romance, the story is conveyed in a plain but elegant, archaizing style. The well-constructed plot is filled with a plethora of characters, increasingly marvelous magical and super-natural elements, and revolves around the revelation of the young hero's hidden noble origins after being raised by a knight. Amadís' loyal love for Oriana, daughter of Lisuarte, king of Britain (facilitated and complicated by Urganda la Desconocida, the sorceress who watches over Amadís), and his combats and adventures in the pursuit of his romantic ideal constitute the thematic core of the narrative.

The action is set in a time shortly after "la Pasión de nuestro Redentor y Salvador Jesu Cristo" ("the Passion of our Redeemer and Savior Jesus Christ") and unfolds in places that, despite some real geographical names, are anything but historical. Born secretly of the clandestine marriage of King Perión of Gaul, a land near Brittany, and Elisena, the youngest and most beautiful daughter of Garínter, king of Brittany, the infant Amadís is set adrift on the waters in a small boat by his mother. He is found on the rugged coast of Scotland by Gandales, a knight who discovers a ring and a sword, along with Elisena's letter, identifying the mysterious castaway as the son of a great king. Known in his youth as "El Doncel del Mar," Amadís is introduced at the court of Languines, king of Scotland, proves his virtue and patrician origins at an early age, and goes on to distinguish himself as the most noble and faithful paladin of his time.

Throughout, the central interest of the story revolves around the hero's unwavering love for the lady Oriana; the obstacles to it placed especially by her father King Lisuarte, who is moved by palace intrigues and jeal-ous rivals; and other adversities the lovers must conquer before their constancy is rewarded by marriage. The main plot of love's loyalty is advanced through a series of intricate subplots that rely principally on description, action, and suspense to maintain narrative interest, at the cost of character development and psychological complexity. (Characters tend to be unidimensional and are either good or evil.) In his quest to prove his love for Oriana, Amadís, aided by his devoted squire Gandalín, battles against giants and other knights (including at one point against his brother Galaor), and is pursued by the evil wizard Arcalaus. After a great deal of bloodshed and personal suffering (a test in the Arco de los Leales Amadores, his transformation into the suffering lover Beltenebros, and his anguished withdrawal from the world to la Peña Pobre to do penance in the name of love while under the impression that Oriana has forsaken him), Amadís emerges victorious from his trials to win his lady's hand. Book three ends with a plethora of activity: the hero's defeat of the supernatural monster *endriago* on the Isla del Diablo, his triumph over the Emperador de Occidente, the liberation and final conquest of Oriana's love, the couple's establishment on the Insula Firme, and the birth of their son, Esplandián, who is the protagonist of the sequel fifth book written by Montalvo.

If the adventures of Amadís embody the tale of the perfect Christian knight, the story of his son, Esplandián, propels his father's personal values into the realm of early sixteenth-century religious sensibilities and Mediterranean politics. In Montalvo's sequel we see the paladin as the embodiment of crusading zeal, a righteous hero whose purpose reflects the affairs of current history and coincides with the policies of the Habsburg state. In *Esplandián*, chivalric ardor is but vanity and serves no purpose unless it is enlisted for the higher aspiration of doing God's work on earth. Esplandián thus consecrates himself to Christ and the defense of Christian civilization in a world threatened by the infidel. The book, filled with a surfeit of devout characters and fervent champions, thus establishes a concrete geography and familiar ideology as the hero's actions are turned against a well-known enemy and the plot's action moves to the eastern Mediterranean to reach its climax in a crusade against the Turks.

Amadís and *Las sergas de Esplandián* were followed by seven continuations plus a vast series of imitations that spawned their own sequels. *Florisando*, Book 6 of the *Amadís* family, appeared in 1510 simultaneously at Salamanca and Toledo and was composed by Páez de Ribera (fl. 1510–1515); *Lisuarte de Grecia*, Book 7 (Seville 1514), was written by Feliciano de Silva, who is known also to have composed Books 8 (another *Lisuarte de Grecia*, Seville 1526), 9 (*Amadís de Grecia*, Cuenca 1530), 10 (entitled *Florisel de Niquea*, Valladolid 1532) and 11 (*Rogel de Grecia*, Medina del Campo 1535, which contains parts III and IV of *Florisel de Niquea*) of the *Amadís* sequence, which ended in 1546 at Seville with the printing of a final and twelfth book, Pedro de Luján's (fl. mid sixteenth century) *Don Silves de la Selva* ("Don Silves of the Forest"). Perhaps the most vigorous of the many series that followed imitating *Amadís* was comprised of the *Palmerín* cycle (*Palmerín de Oliva*, Salamanca 1511 and *Primaleón*, Salamanca 1512, both of uncertain authorship) and the best and most well-known of these was *Palmerín de Inglaterra*, published first in a Castilian translation of 1547, although originally written in Portuguese by Francisco de Moraes (*c.* 1500–1572; the earliest extant Portuguese version is from Evora, 1567). These and many others too numerous to mention comprised the best-read books in Spanish both in and outside the Iberian peninsula. Between 1508 and 1550 romances of chivalry appeared at an average rate of almost one per year, and at least sixty are known to have been published. To be sure, if there was any single genre that could be said to dominate both literary production and tastes during the first half of the sixteenth century, it was the romances of chivalry. The height of their popularity coincided almost exactly with the reign of the emperor Charles V (1516–1555), whose taste for them became legendary. Charles was especially fond of *Belianís de Grecia* (Seville 1545), by Jerónimo Fernández (fl. first half of sixteenth century), and he petitioned a continuation from the author. Although many romances continued to appear well into and beyond the second half of the sixteenth century, it was during the first part of it that they truly flourished, doubtless spurred on by imperial favor and the fashion and acclamation of all chivalric things at court. The last known chivalric romance, *Policisne de Boecia*, appeared in Toledo and Madrid in 1602.

The heroic sense of exalted quest, piety, and heightened imagination at the center of the romances of chivalry were very appealing to a large reading public, including many of the great Spanish mystics like Teresa of Avila, who confessed to reading them with her brother in her youth and being swept away to their mythical landscapes by a sense of awe and adventure. Similarly, Ignatius de Loyola, founder of the Jesuits, was an avid reader of chivalric romances before his spiritual conversion and ultimately adapted their martial ethos, combining action and reflection at the service of a higher good, as a model of piety for his order. Even conquistadors like Bernal Díaz del Castillo read them and used them as a point of comparison. He described the dazzling sights he encountered entering Tenochtitlan, the capital of the Aztec Empire, in 1519 at the side of Cortés.

The enormous popularity of these works can, in fact, be directly traced to their consonance with a certain spirit of the age that combined political militancy with crusading zeal. A reading public anxious to validate a mood of righteous entitlement found in invincible, pious heros like Amadís and Esplandián a reflection of their higher social aspirations and institutional values. In the romances of chivalry we see at work the discourses that are the stuff of empire: a territorialized, expansionist ideology; the cult of the military hero; and the propagation of these ideas through the glorification and institutionalization of chivalry, idealized love, and Christian piety. The romances embody a reaffirmation of many of the forces that shaped civic existence in sixteenth-century Spain: as they tell tales of God-fearing, invincible, romantic paladins and are set in exotic, far-off lands, they fashion a cultural politics forged from an alliance between a literate intelligentsia and the state, where writing is placed at the service of constructing the mythologies of power for a monarchy with imperial aspirations that now embraced the globe. At the same time that they provided both entertainment and escape, these books underscored the fertile union of arms and spirituality, of political authority and religious devotion, that permeated every dimension of Spanish life in the sixteenth century.

The great popularity of the romances of chivalry was tempered, however, by their condemnation by many moralists, theologians, and humanists, who saw in their free fantasies useless, mendacious works of dubious ethical makeup that could provoke readers to mistake lies for truth and plunge the world into moral disorder. Such eminences as Melchor Cano, Fray Luis de Granada, Arias Montano, and Pedro Mexía called for their total suppression in Spain, while abroad as distinguished a scholar as Justus Lipsius characterized *Amadís de Gaula* as the most harmful book ever written, whose sentimental hero was conceived to pervert and ruin the youth of the world. The romances were banned from the Indies in 1531 and again in 1553 (a sure sign that the first prohibition had little effect), while the *Cortes* of Valladolid in 1555 sought their complete abolition. Like all puritanical prohibitions of pleasant things, however, these bans and denunciations fell mostly on deaf ears and did little to diminish the romances' continued popularity and their commercial and artistic success. To be sure, some humanists like Juan de Valdés, although he censured the romances chiefly on aesthetic grounds, had nothing but praise for *Amadís*. Artists, writers, and laypeople everywhere continued to find both diversion and inspiration in them; many were profoundly influenced by their idealized vision of love, loyalty, and virtue, not to mention the artistic freedom and the willingness to experiment they embodied in their composition.

Contrary to narrative forms of classical provenance like epic that were cultivated in Spain during the sixteenth century, chivalric romances did not look to strictly defined, highly theorized literary forebears to emulate. Raised to a theoretical plane, the lack of a consecrated form and convention for chivalric romance offered complete rhetorical liberty and free rein to the imagination. In the romances, writers and readers could range over the complete gamut of human experience, emotion, and fantasy, unconcerned about such things as verisimilitude and the unities of time, character, and place. The romances combined the high with the low, the marvelous with the realistic, and the sentimental with the heroic. At the same time all of them laid claim to being actual histories and were often presented as manuscripts that were serendipitously discovered, or as translations of chronicles of real events originally composed by one or more chroniclers in some exotic language like Greek or Chaldean. The result was the narrative distancing of the events and, at the same time, the internal reduplication of the voices used to relate the story, all of which served as perhaps the chivalric romance's greatest contribution to the truth-making devices employed in many later novels. From the outset of *Amadís*, Montalvo, for example, characterizes himself merely as an editor and corrector of the work, even though he was in fact the author of a substantial portion of Book 4 and all of Book 5. The artifice of the found chronicle would, of course, later be taken up by Cervantes and was artfully exploited, complicated, and refined by him in the composition of *Don Quijote*. It was the crucial narrative strategy that allowed Cervantes to claim that his story was true, based on facts and real events, thus codifying one of the most fruitful narrative devices in the development of the novel.

Like history itself, the stories recorded in the romances of chivalry were always open to further development and to the flow of time and new events. Authors could return to situations in earlier plots, like the birth of Amadís' son Esplandián in Book 3, to mark the beginnings of a continuation that would give the illusion of a series of unfolding occurrences through history and time. This tendency to interlace new plots with old ones always left room for more and reflects the sixteenth-century Spanish chivalric romance's origins in the medieval French romances, just as it marks a crucial structural distinction from the later novel, which sought synthesis, narrative closure, and the sense of a definite ending.

Perhaps it is not idle to note that Montalvo's prologue to *Amadís* focuses on the tension between poetry and history in the work and seeks to make a distinction between them. Although articulated some forty years before the rediscovery of Aristotle's *Poetics* and not developed in any significant way, Montalvo's discussion of poetry and history touches upon the two opposing poles and terms that would act as the intellectual crux of the later debates on Aristotelian literary theory and ultimately lead Cervantes to create *Don Quijote*. As a result of their free fantasies, the Spanish romances of chivalry were cited often as paragons of prevarication and implausibility in the Italian literary polemics centering on the *Poetics* of Aristotle. They circulated widely in Italy, were greatly enjoyed by many readers there, and were responsible for nurturing Spain's literary reputation for fiction in the rest of Europe. In this way, they formed an important part of the sixteenth-century theoretical debates on verisimilitude and the marvelous and, indeed, the nature of literature itself. As such, they served both as background and as a point of contradiction for the appearance of the modern novel with the publication of *Don Quijote* in 1605.

Pastoral romances

At about mid century another significant form of prose narrative appeared that enjoyed great popularity, especially among the aristocracy, and would leave a lasting effect on the development of novelistic discourse in Iberia. This is the pastoral romance, whose immediate antecedents may be traced to Italy with Sannazzaro's *Arcadia* (1502, with Spanish translation in 1547), and the Castilian *Qüestión de amor* ("The Question of Love") by Alonso de Cardona (fl. 1500–1515) (Valencia 1513), an amply circulated, little-studied, thinly veiled *roman à clef* set at the Aragonese court in Naples that encompasses a colloquy in a pastoral setting among several characters disguised as shepherds. By 1530 the bucolic mode of these works had established itself firmly in Spanish narrative with the publication of Feliciano de Silva's *Amadís de Grecia* at Cuenca. This work (Book 9 of the Amadís cycle) incorporates the pastoral interlude of the shepherd Darinel, in love with Silvia, a shepherdess who is in fact the kidnapped daughter of Lisuarte de Grecia. Her uncle, Don Florisel de Niquea, protagonist of Feliciano de Silva's eponymous, multi-part sequel to *Amadís de Grecia* where the pastoral also comes into play (Salamanca 1532, Medina del Campo 1535, Salamanca 1551), falls in love with Silvia and transforms himself into a shepherd to pursue the beautiful shepherdess. Feliciano de Silva's fondness for pastoral characters led him to include one even in his *Segunda Celestina* (Medina del Campo 1534), which incorporates the story of Filínides, a chaste shepherd who provides a droll contrast to the libidinous characters that populate the work. The *Historia de los amores de Clareo y Florisea y los trabajos de Isea* ("History of the Love of Clareo and Florisea and the Trials of Isea," Venice 1552) by Alonso Núñez de Reinoso (fl. first half of sixteenth century) and *Selva de aventuras* ("Forest of Adventures," Barcelona 1565, but with prior lost editions) by Jerónimo de Contreras (fl. mid sixteenth century) are two books that also interject pastoral elements into larger narratives of journeys and adventure.

Jorge de Montemayor's *Los siete libros de la Diana* (Valencia, 1559?) holds the distinction of being the first fully developed Iberian pastoral romance. Indeed, it could be called the prototypical pastoral romance of the sixteenth century since it was translated into all the major languages, circulated widely, and, even more than its Italian precursors, served as a model for such works as Philip Sidney's *Arcadia* and Honorée d'Urfé's *Astrée*. Comprised of several complicated overlapping plots, the main story centers on the shepherd Sireno's search for a cure to love's misery, occasioned by the beautiful shepherdess Diana who has forsaken him to marry another shepherd, Delio. Structured as a journey to the fabled palace of Felicia the Enchantress, who holds the power to dispel all heartache, on the way Sireno is joined by several unhappy lovers who relate their own tales of love's suffering. The action is thus complicated by the appearance of new characters like Félix and Felismena, Belisa, Arsileo, and Filemón, as well as by the advent of nymphs, lustful wildmen, giants, and an assembly of shepherds of lesser importance. At mid journey, the pastoral landscape gives way to a fabulous edifice of shining beauty inhabited by the sorceress, who does in fact liberate the suffering lovers from their plight by means of a magical elixir. Sireno and Silvano, another shepherd rejected by Diana, are freed of their love for her and find happiness. All the characters save Diana, who married and hence cannot easily transform her cares, achieve contentment and are restored to harmony. Although Montemayor promised a continuation to the work, presumably in which Diana's predicament would be examined, he never completed it.

Montemayor (*c.* 1520–1561) writes in the introduction to *Diana* that all the characters in the work are real people disguised as shepherds whose stories have been told in pastoral style. The highly stylized world he creates, filled with convoluted aristocratic sensibilities concealed under pastoral dress, fabulous occurrences, marvelous landscapes, and intense emotions in characters who at first meeting are apt to reveal their most intimate thoughts in a concentrated, poetic idiom (when not actually lamenting their suffering through poetry), makes it difficult, however, to confirm any historical basis for the work. The work is artful, intensely imaginative, and deeply sentimental. Verisimilitude gives way to nostalgic fantasy in *Diana* and to the exacting dissection of the passions of each character in search of love's true meaning. It is this insistence on melancholy introspection and on examining closely the nature of love that lends significance to the work in tracing the history of narrative forms in sixteenth-century Spain. Montemayor's characters, like the ones in the earlier sentimental romances that hark back to Boccaccio's *Fiammeta*, all prove noteworthy experiments in testing ways of telling about and describing the perception of close experience and intimate sensibility.

The pastoral romances, like the earlier sentimental ones, focused their attention on the awareness, display, and analysis of the emotions. Indeed, it could be said that, like the sentimental romances, the pastoral romances made portraying, conveying, and examining feeling and emotion their main task. However, while the sentimental romances unfold in the urbane and decorous setting of the court, the pastoral ones take place in a rarified, primeval, Arcadian landscape presided over by a beneficent Nature that permits lovers to make their cares their sole concern.

The pastoral romance's highly stylized universe and its preoccupation with the nature of love and suffering, contrary to the courtly love of the sentimental romance, finds its intellectual and philosophical roots in Renaissance Neoplatonism as developed from Marsilio Ficino onward. Much of what is said about love in Book IV of *Diana* is taken almost verbatim from Leone Ebreo's *Dialoghi d'amore* ("Dialogues of Love"), a widely read early sixteenth-century dialogue on platonic love. Love is the center around which everything in *Diana* revolves. If it is true, love is chaste and pure, selfless and moved by virtue. False love, on the other hand, springs from the appetites and pursues physical satisfaction. True love is an adornment of every noble soul (lowly spirits are incapable of experiencing it), it is free and born freely of reason and the intellect. Once released by its progenitors, however, it can no longer be governed or restrained by them and can only be effaced by time and fortune. True love inevitably brings suffering to all lovers who pursue beauty, truth, and spiritual union with the beloved, in which constancy must always prevail. All the characters' speeches in this erotic reverie are accompanied by a pervasive sense of melancholy, a sense of the unattainable, and a yearning for peace and flight from the world, that articulates an almost Utopian longing for lost innocence and bygone happiness. If Montemayor's *Diana* alludes at all to contemporary history, it is by means of the urgent expression of this visionary dream and desire.

Like *Amadís*, Montemayor's *Diana* initiated a literary vogue and was followed by a number of continuations and imitations. By 1633 a total of eighteen pastoral romances had been published in Spain. Of these, three in particular stand out: *Diana enamorada* ("Diana in Love," Valencia 1564) by Gaspar Gil Polo (1528?–1591?), which examines the human complexities of love in a refined pastoral setting but seeks a resolution of conflict at the level of the individual without recourse to sorcery, magic elixirs, and other devices; Cervantes' *La Galatea* (Alcalá de Henares 1585), his first published prose work whose promised second part he never completed, populated with interesting, even idiosyncratic, characters who embody every imaginable variety of love's experience; and Lope de Vega's *Arcadia* (Madrid 1598), which includes dazzling descriptions of an idealized Nature and records the love interest of the shepherd Anfriso, a thinly disguised likeness of his early patron the Duke of Alba, while it provides a self-portrait of Lope in the character of Belardo, one of Lope's favorite pseudonyms.

Like the chivalric romances, the pastoral ones were also the object of censure by moralists and theologians, who, despite the books' essentially chaste vision of love, saw in them an unwelcome paganism, a propensity for fantasy and self-pity, and a disregard for Christian values. The classic denunciation can be found in the prologue to *La conversión de la Magdalena* ("The Conversion of the Magdalen," 1585) by Pedro Malón de Chaide (1530–1589), where the Augustinian friar labels the pastoral romances worldly and lascivious. To counter these criticisms, several pastoral romances of a mystical bent were published. One of these was *Clara Diana a lo divino* ("Illustrious Diana in the Sacred Style," Zaragoza 1581) by Bartolomé Ponce de León (fl. last third of sixteenth century), which exploited the figure of the shepherd as an allegory of Christ and Christian love and was written in direct response to Montemayor's *Diana*. The most notable of the Christianized pastoral romances was Lope de Vega's late *Los pastores de Belén* ("The Shepherds of Bethlehem," Lérida 1612), which deals with the events of the nativity (the adoration of the shepherds and the Magi and the Flight to Egypt), and was inspired by Lope's profound sense of piety after a stormy spiritual crisis.

Moorish romances

An elegant, intensely moving narrative of love and chivalry entitled *Historia del Abencerraje y la hermosa Jarifa* ("History of Abencerraje and the Lovely Jarifa"), whose chief protagonists are a pair of noble Moorish lovers and a Christian knight, was probably written around the year 1551, when Antonio de Villegas (1522–1558) applied for a privilege to print his *Inventario*, a collection of assorted prose and poetry. The *Inventario* where the work appears, however, was not actually published until 1565 at Medina del Campo. It is uncertain whether the planned 1551 publication actually contained the *Historia del Abencerraje* or if it was subsequently added to the *Inventario*. In the interim, slightly different versions of the *Historia del Abencerraje* had circulated, notably one as an interpolation in the 1561 Cuenca edition of Montemayor's *Diana*. Set on the Christian and Muslim frontier before the fall of Granada, in it the noble Moor Abindarráez is taken prisoner by Rodrigo de Narváez, a Christian captain, while on his way to marry his beloved, the beautiful Jarifa. Deeply affected by Abindarráez's situation, Narváez agrees to free his captive so that he can keep his appointment. Out of gratitude, the lovers return voluntarily and hand themselves over to the Christian, who again displays his magnanimity and sets the lovers free.

Everything in this brief, moving narrative happens on a human plane and in a known geography. There are no giants, sorcerers, wildmen, or contemplative shepherds. Abindarráez and Narváez are moved by force of conviction and personal feeling and neither is viewed as superior to the other. Although their gallant actions and sentiments are fictional and greatly idealized, and they reflect still the feudo-aristocratic ethos of chivalric romance, they unfold in a conflicted historical setting in which chivalry is no longer a mere pretext for love. In an important advance toward establishing the conventions of the novel, in the *Historia del Abencerraje* fiction moves significantly closer toward imitating historical reality and situating itself in it.

Three other notable works were written in the Moorish vein, one of which could easily be termed a historical novel. This is *Historia de los bandos de los Zegríes y Abencerrajes* ("History of the Factions of the Zegríes and Abencerrajes," Part I, Zaragoza 1595; Part II, Cuenca 1619) by Ginés Pérez de Hita (*c.* 1544 – after 1619), generally referred to as the *Guerras civiles de Granada* ("Civil Wars of Granada"). Fashioned in part from chronicles and ballads dealing with the late fifteenth-century wars for Granada, it romanticizes the rivalries of the major Arab clans of the city up until Boabdil's final capitulation. Filled with brilliant descriptions of battle scenes, Arab customs, and intense love affairs, as the events and characters depicted are fictionally embellished and idealized they are presented as a

Castilian translation of an Arabic source by an Arab named Aben Hamín, an immediate precursor of Cide Hamete Benengeli, the fictional Muslim chronicler who is the chief narrator of Cervantes' *Don Quijote*. The second work, composed in 1589, the year Cervantes was writing the Captive's tale in *Don Quijote*, was Miguel de Luna's *Verdadera historia del rey don Rodrigo* ("The True History of King Rodrigo"). Luna's history, which claims to tell the real truth about his subject, is an entirely fictional one and constitutes a morisco's polemical, contradictory, and highly imaginative rewriting of the legend of the last Gothic king. Moriscos were Spanish Christians of Muslim culture who sought to preserve their use of the Arabic language and many traditional practices. Luna's work was provoked by the appearance two years earlier of Ambrosio de Morales' *Crónica general de España* ("General Chronicle of Spain"), a historical tract among many that marked the revival of an aggressive nationalism and a general resurgence of the myths of the Reconquest, especially the story of King Rodrigo and his violation of the woman known as La Cava Rumía. Finally, the third work, *Ozmín y Daraja*, an interpolated tale that forms part of Mateo Alemán's (1547 – after 1614) picaresque romance *Guzmán de Alfarache* (Madrid 1599), tells the story of a pair of Muslim lovers who find happiness only after their conversion to Christianity. It is important because, in consonance with its picaresque context, hypocrisy, deceit, and disguise supplant the earlier idealizations of the *Historia del Abencerraje* and the *Guerras civiles de Granada* to become integral parts of the narrative as they evoke directly the racial, cultural, and religious tensions articulated in Luna's *Verdadera historia*, and as they adumbrate the so-called "*novela de cautivos*" (a narrative dealing with Christians held captive by Muslims), that would find its optimum expression in the depiction of the trials of Captain Ruy Pérez de Viedma and the Moorish maid Zoraida in *Don Quijote*, Part I.

Quite aside from its esthetic complexity, its greater proximity to novelistic plots, and its claim to historicity, the Moorish romance doubtless resonated profoundly in the contemporary imagination as it pointed toward one of the wrenching internal political conflicts of the age. Readers could not help but see Moorish romances, radically at odds with social and historical reality, as reminders of the intense public debate concerning the Moriscos, touched off by the Alpujarras revolt of 1568–1570, the Turkish menace in the Mediterranean, and the Moriscos' role in Spanish society in the fifty years prior to their expulsion in 1609. The Moorish romance's implicit nearness to this question accorded it a direct social significance that only the picaresque could displace. Works like Luna's *Verdadera historia del rey don Rodrigo*, Pérez de Hita's *Guerras civiles de Granada*, and the *Historia del Abencerraje* constituted both statements of resistance to, and strategies for resolution of, the problem; eloquent rewritings and disavowals of the myth of a fallen Spain brought to its knees by a barbarous oriental race. At the center of these works lies a wish to discredit a belief in a racially pure, Catholic Spanish Empire as defined by its conflict with the Other, and a deep nostalgia for a multicultural world governed by a humane ethos of tolerance, peaceful coexistence, and assimilation. The tales exemplify no small capacity for literary and historical contradiction. In each, mythical and factual materials, past events and contemporary values merge to provoke thought and confront, dismantle, and deny the legitimacy of a triumphant Christian Spain as well as offer up an ideal vision which celebrates its spiritual and ethnic diversity.

Byzantine romances

Humanistic deference to the cultural authority of antiquity led not only to a rediscovery of the great authors of the classical canon, but to the lesser ones of a later age like Heliodorus of Emesa, whose romance of love and adventure, the *Aethiopica Historia* ("Ethiopian History"), was first rendered into Castilian in 1554 as the *Historia etiópica de los amores de Teógenes y Cariclea* ("The Ethiopian History of Theogenes and Cariclea," Antwerp) via Jacques Amyot's earlier French translation of the Greek original. This, along with an Italian adaptation of Achilles Tatius Alexandrinus' *Leucippe and Clitophon*, incorporated by Ludovico Dolce into his *Amorosi ragionamenti* ("Amorous Dialogues," 1546), would come to have a profound influence on the history of narrative in sixteenth-century Spain. Both are stories that relate the trials and wanderings of a pair of separated lovers who, after many amazing adventures and strange turns of events that are accompanied by mythological and descriptive digressions, are reunited in marriage at the end. Each in its own way contributed to the appearance of what are called in Castilian the *novelas bizantinas* ("Byzantine romances") in honor of their late Greek models. In the intellectual contest between ancients and moderns, Heliodorus and the Greek romances were looked to by humanists, especially the Erasmians, as literary paragons that stood in stark opposition to the alarming, mendacious chivalric romances. Many humanists felt that they could perhaps hold the key for perfecting a Neo-Aristotelian poetics of the epic in prose. Two works patterned after Heliodorus and Achilles Tatius are noteworthy for their contribution to this idea and to the origins of the novel in Spain. These are Alonso Núñez de Reinoso's *Historia de los amores de Clareo y Florisea y los trabajos de Isea* (Venice 1552) and Jerónimo de Contreras' *Selva de aventuras* (Barcelona 1565, but with prior lost editions).

Núñez de Reinoso, a Spanish *converso* (a Christian of Jewish ancestry) living in Italy, adapted with some significant modifications lengthy passages and the basic plot from Dolce's translation of Achilles Tatius' *Leucippe and Clitophon* to form the first nineteen chapters of his *Historia de los amores de Clareo y Florisea* (there are thirty-two chapters in all). Dolce apparently approved of the appropriation of the material since he provided a laudatory sonnet for Reinoso's book. Clareo and Florisea are lovers who flee from home to be married but, before this can happen, they must live together for a year as brother and sister to allow Clareo to complete a vow he has made. (Cervantes uses this same device for the main characters in his *Los trabajos de Persiles y Sigismunda* ["The Trials of Persiles and Sigismunda," Madrid 1617].) Traveling disguised as siblings, on their way to Alexandria, Florisea is abducted by pirates, the first in a series of separations, followed by mistaken identities, chance encounters, and amorous entanglements that unfold in a geography dotted with familiar ancient names and conclude at the bucolic, wholly imaginary Insula Pastoril. Chapter XIX marks their wedding and the end of Clareo and Florisea's adventures. After it, we learn that the unfortunate Isea, who in Florisea's absence had become Clareo's intended (Florisea had been given up for dead but later materialized as a slave girl), is in fact the narrator of the work. We realize that Isea, emotionally embroiled with Clareo after she received the false news of her own husband's shipwreck, and who doubtless felt jilted by fortune with her husband's and Florisea's unexpected reappearance, has made herself the subject of the narrative under the guise of telling the story of the runaway lovers. In the last chapters Isea relates her wanderings in search of happiness in the company of Felisendos de Trapisonda, a knight out of the pages of a chivalric romance, and how she comes to the Insula Pastoril seeking peace in the contemplation of Nature, and how finally she attempts to enter a convent but is rejected on the pretext that she lacks a proper dowry, an excuse probably pointing to unacceptable *converso* origins. In addition to challenging socio-ethnic orthodoxies and producing unity of action within a diversity of styles, generating a sense of astonishment and surprise in the reader, and exploring the limits of verisimilitude and the credible by means of these wondrous occurrences, Núñez de Reinoso's *Historia* introduces a feminine narrative voice and experiments with limited point of view. By means of the narrator's direct involvement in the action, the work presents a perspective that can be anything but objective. In this way, the book merits a significant place in the evolution of the styles and methods for telling stories in sixteenth-century Spain. Núñez de Reinoso's work has unfortunately not received the recognition it deserves.

Contreras' *Selva de aventuras* is, as its title indicates, a veritable forest of adventures that centers on Luzmán's love for Arbolea, whom the youth has known since childhood, and to whom he finally proposes marriage. Luzmán, however, is refused by Arbolea, who wishes to enter a convent in their native Seville and dedicate her life to God. Disconsolate, Luzmán dons pilgrim's garb and leaves Seville on a journey to Italy. The strange and marvelous adventures of Luzmán's trek fill out the seven chapters that comprise the romance, as Luzmán and the characters he encounters on his way exchange tales and seek advice from one another to ease their cares. Among many other things, we learn of lovers who retire to die in the desert, of a youth driven mad by love, of the shepherds Ardenio and Floreo, one in love and the other incapable of loving, and how Luzmán visits the cave of the Cumean Sybil, and meets Alfonso V, the Magnanimous, of Aragon in Naples prior to departing for Spain. On his way home, Luzmán again meets adventure. He is taken prisoner by pirates, who transport him to Algiers, from where he is finally rescued to return to Seville, meet with Arbolea, and hear her tell how she has taken the veil. In heartfelt response, Luzmán proclaims his faith, renounces the world, and becomes a hermit.

Though less read and recognized today than even the chivalric and pastoral romances, Núñez de Reinoso's and Contreras' works both gave rise to important narrative patterns, devices, and ideas that greatly influenced Cervantes and provided the bases for the development of the novel. Luzmán's journey in the *Selva de aventuras*, more than an adventure-filled passage through Italy and the landscape of the Mediterranean, comprises in its sojourn and dialogues a symbolic pilgrimage and edifying adventure, a geography of the progress of the human soul. It traces the exemplary development of a lover's care into Christian spiritual perfection and thus points to Lope de Vega's *El peregrino en su patria* ("The Pilgrim at Home," Seville 1604) and Cervantes' *Persiles y Sigismunda*, which Cervantes judged to be the culmination of his work. Similarly, the exotic adventures and strange events that befall Clareo, Florisea, Isea, and the multitude of other characters in Núñez de Reinoso's *Historia*, as they traverse both historically accurate and totally imaginary landscapes, constitute a giant step in the search for a narrative formula that could provide decorum with a sense of unity in diversity. In addition, they produce astonishment and admiration in the reader through the portrayal of places and events that appear to efface the distinctions between truth and fiction, facts and lies. Without either of these now mostly forgotten works, the appearance of the novel would have been long in coming.

Picaresque romances

The year 1554 marks the publication in Alcalá de Henares, Antwerp, Burgos, and Medina del Campo of a little book called *La vida de Lazarillo de Tormes y de sus fortunas y adversidades* ("The Life, Fortunes, and

Adversities of Lazarillo de Tormes"). By 1559 it would be listed on the Index of Prohibited Works. The book, though anonymous, purports to be the autobiography of one Lázaro de Tormes, written in response to a formal query concerning Lázaro's current circumstances from a social superior, addressed in the text only as *vuestra merced*. Since it could have been composed as early as 1525–1526, prior editions may have existed. One thing is sure, however: with it a new type of narrative appeared that would leave a lasting impression on novelistic styles and forms in Europe. This was the picaresque romance. Although *Lazarillo* would have no immediate influence (despite a spurious continuation published at Antwerp in 1555), by the end of the sixteenth century it would be redis-covered by a later generation of prose writers and energize the creation of works like Mateo Alemán's *La vida de Guzmán de Alfarache, atalaya de la vida humana* ("The Life of Guzmán de Alfarache, Watchtower of Human Life," Madrid 1599), Quevedo's *Historia de la vida del buscón llamado don Pablos*, known as *El Buscón* ("The Life of the Petty Thief called Don Pablos," probably written as early as 1605 but not published until 1626 at Zaragoza), and a host of novellas and stories by Cervantes and other authors. The *Lazarillo*'s wicked satire and creativity initiated a type of literature that would in the course of the coming century not only animate a tradition but ultimately come to deny, contradict, and exhaust itself.

Lazarillo is divided into seven *tratados*, or chapters, of varying length, preceded by a prologue. The prologue supports the illusion of the work's autobiographical nature since it occupies a space traditionally reserved for the authorial voice and was purportedly written by Lázaro himself. On the surface, the incidents related in the work are simple enough. Many even find their origins in well-known folk tales dating to the Middle Ages. Told entirely in the first person in response to *vuestra merced*'s unrecorded written request about Lázaro's current circumstances, Lázaro begins at the distant beginning, preferring to tell euphemistically of his ignominious mother and father, his conception and birth on an island in the river Tormes across from Salamanca, and how, when he was a young boy, his widowed mother, occupied with a blackamoor lover and a misbegotten baby half-brother, delivered him over to a crafty blind beggar to be his guide. The beggar's abuse turned into disabuse as the young Lazarillo's hunger for food and retribution taught him to provide for himself and reciprocate, avenging his blind master's brutalities. After the beggar, Lázaro served several other masters: a hypocritical, miserly priest, who fleeced parishioners and starved Lázaro and beat him sense-less; a pretentious, penniless squire, whom Lázaro in the end had to feed and support; a Mercedarian friar who robbed him of his innocence; and a pardoner who crafted bogus miracles and whose histrionics and grasp of life as theatre both enthralled and appalled him. Implicitly having learned life's bitter lessons and the value of keeping silent, Lázaro's fortunes turned when he connected with the ecclesiastical bureaucracy of Toledo and began to serve an entrepreneurial chaplain of the cathedral as a water boy in the chaplain's municipal distribution monopoly. After four years in the chaplain's employ, Lázaro earned enough money to buy a second-hand sword and cape and leave the chaplain to become briefly a bailiff in the Toledo constabulary, before finally landing the job of town crier, a civil service position protected by the Crown under the patronage of his inquisitor, *vuestra merced*. Noting Lázaro's diligence, the archpriest of the church of San Salvador, a subordinate and friend of *vuestra merced*, provided Lázaro with additional employment and even a wife, who now sees to the archpriest's every domestic need. After all of Lázaro's hard work and determination to achieve prosperity and move among the right people, ever sure of his wife's virtue, he tells *vuestra merced*, he must now endure town gossip about this and that and other things as well as his wife's association with the archpriest.

The book's autobiographical narrative is cast as a testimonial given in response to *vuestra merced*'s written interrogation. Crafted as a documentary disclosure, it is in fact a simulacrum that seeks to conceal pervasive corruption and the compromising truth about both Lázaro's and *vuestra merced*'s voluntary moral blindness at the expense of civic trust and to the benefit of their material prosperity. As *vuestra merced*'s missing request for information and Lázaro's published answer to it establish a real-seeming written record – a paper trail – they pay lip service to public pressure for an inquiry into Lázaro's understanding with the archpriest, *vuestra merced*'s friend and subordinate, and constitute a pro forma travesty of process, truth, and justice. In Lázaro's response to *vuestra merced*'s petition for clarification of Lázaro's current circumstances, the judicious reader intrudes upon the text and, like a witness interested but not directly involved in the exchange, begins to detect from a secure distance the crafty verbal strategies for evading issues and glossing the truth; for vouchsafing the moral compromises and accommodations that from top to bottom sustain civic power in Toledo. As he initiates his narrative, the mature Lázaro deflects attention from the present to the very distant past – to the time when he was the callow Lazarillo – and elicits sympathy while manipulating words with the purpose of deceiving, calling things what they are not, so as to turn all truth, shame, and accountability at a distance. Many events portrayed in *Lazarillo*'s biting satire are purposefully fragmented, episodic, and anecdotal and make what is left unsaid as important, or more so, than what is actually related. This is clearly the case, for example, with Tratado IV, that deals with Lázaro's sexual initiation and prostitution at the hands of the Mercedarian friar, artfully glossed over and reduced to a mere paragraph of euphemisms that cannot be lost on any competent reader. The temporal configuration of the narrative is such that, although it is the older Lázaro who tells the tale, interest is always displaced away from controversy and from the present toward the past, to the far-off struggles of an inauspicious youth. The events of most obvious immediate public concern, notably the *ménage à trois* circumlocutiously elided at the very end, are thus minimally developed so as to defuse them and gain sympathy for the narrator through the representation of a life filled with poverty, hunger, and early hardship.

If the narrative dwells on the poverty and hunger of Lázaro's early years, it does so for two reasons: because poverty and hunger were very real historical parts of daily life in sixteenth-century Spain that readers could easily grasp, and because the self-serving narrator exploits them to heighten pity and sympathy as he portrays himself as a self-made man who deserves admiration and respect for conquering adversity. In this way, *Lazarillo de Tormes* marks the emergence of one of the greatest artistic achievements in Iberian narrative: the self-conscious unreliable narrator, a character who perceives a profound personal stake in the act of telling and who is acutely alert to the need to bend the truth and aware of himself as both the subject and the object of his narrative. The artful deployment of this device in *Lazarillo de Tormes* marks a milestone in turning the subtle complexities of character into the focus of narrative attention in fiction.

Several authors have been proposed for this tour de force of irony and social satire. Diego Hurtado de Mendoza (1503–1575), Fray Juan de Ortega (fl. mid sixteenth century), Sebastián Horozco (1510–1580), and both the Valdés brothers, Juan (*c.* 1499–1541) and Alfonso, or someone close to them, are all candidates. The first two were mentioned as possible authors as early as the beginning of the seventeenth century. Regardless of the author's name, *Lazarillo* is a work from the pen of a highly learned individual, probably a scholar trained in the Bible, the classics, and the best of vernacular literature. The author's identity and probable Erasmian social and religious sympathies are of little consequence in measuring the book's artistic achievements or social significance. To be sure, the work is probably intentionally anonymous not so much to hide the author's identity as to heighten the contrast between Lázaro – eager to project personal fame and newly won privilege plus maintain an appearance of respectability through his narrative – and the historical writer who, through the purposeful silencing of his name, implicitly rejects Lázaro and all he represents. If Lázaro in his prologue cites Cicero to assure *vuestra merced* and the reader over his shoulder that honor (confused by Lázaro here with personal reputation) nurtures art, and that authors write only to increase and protect their public standing, the historical author withholds his own identity so as to discredit this belief and his amoral pseudo-autobiographical character who holds it to be true.

With the publication of *Guzmán de Alfarache* in 1599 after a hiatus of nearly fifty years, *Lazarillo* gave rise to a series of some twenty narrative fictions of varying length and complexity commonly referred to as *novelas picarescas* that continued to appear until the mid 1640s. The earliest of these works were composed as fictional autobiographies, although many later ones were told in the third person. All their protagonists were anti-heroes who often struggled in poverty. Some were men and others were women; some lifted themselves up to make good while others became grifters and delinquents, and still others were little more than transparent authorial masks for social satire and ridicule. In many instances, the narrative typology introduced by *Lazarillo* was transformed to such a degree that it is difficult to recognize this work as a clear antecedent of the later narratives. Although the picaresque and its evolution are thus extremely difficult to delineate, one thing remains clear: in contrast to the other types of romance that developed in sixteenth-century Spain, the picaresque's unique contribution to story telling lies in its direct engagement with the brutal, unprincipled side of human existence and its use of irony to open windows on the precarious illusions of life. As it makes the more unseemly parts of life and society the object of its interest, the picaresque assembles a notable cast of sinners, sufferers, and opportunists, and provides them with real-seeming settings for their knavery but, unlike the novel, offers them little or no opportunity or self-perception for the purpose of their own redemption. Lázaro de Tormes and his picaresque progeny are rogues conceived in response to the highly idealized types of narratives like the chivalric romances that circulated during the sixteenth century in Spain. They arose also, however, out of the difficult historical human circumstances of poverty, hunger, unbridled ambition, and moral degradation born of despair in a society in conflict about itself. Their protagonists are not complex, subtly realistic characters *per se*, but they do reflect real social concerns stemming from Spain's economic and social transformation at the beginning of the early modern age. The picaresque's biting portrayal of poverty, delinquency, prostitution, and other civic ills opened the door for the representation of different kinds of realities and for the crafting of deeply ironic ways of telling about them in narrative form while calling attention to the failures of society.

Traditional tales and facetiae (*cuentecillos*)

Finally, traditional tales (*cuentecillos*), or brief stories of folkloric origin with strong traces of their oral roots, contributed to the great fund of narrative that circulated in sixteenth-century Spain and served as a foundation for the development of the novel. These concise, homespun anecdotes, not unlike a variety of jokes, yarns, and tall tales in contemporary Anglo-American folklore, often took the form of a short dialogue or a jest whose sole purpose was the production of wit and laughter. In addition to circulating orally, they were disseminated principally in three printed forms: in several notable compilations (e.g. the two assembled by Juan de Timoneda [1520–1583], *El sobremesa y alivio de caminantes* ["Table Conversation or Balm of Travelers," Valencia 1563], and the *Buen aviso y Portacuentos* ["Good Advice and Portable Tales," Valencia 1564], plus *Floresta española de apotegmas y sentencias* ["Spanish Grove of Maxims and Sayings," Toledo 1574] by Melchor de Santa Cruz de Dueñas [1515? – after 1576]); as stories that were recorded or told by characters in other works (e.g., *El cortesano* ["The Courtier," 1561] by Luis Milán [fl. second half of sixteenth century], and in the many continuations of *Celestina*); and as plot sketches for brief narratives or dramatic interludes (e.g. Timoneda's *El patrañuelo* ["The Hoaxster," Valencia 1567] and *El deleitoso* ["The Delightful One," Valencia 1567] by Lope de Rueda [1510?–1565]). Many *cuentecillos* found their way into works by imaginative prose writers like Mateo Alemán, Quevedo, and especially Cervantes, whose *Don Quijote* incorporates a great deal of folk material with oral origins. With their roots in the oral tradition and their plain colloquial style, the *cuentecillos* served as points of reference for modeling the earthy sensibilities, rustic imaginations, and ordinary speech of characters like Sancho Panza.

Blurred genres and the problems of taxonomy

As early as *Amadís de Gaula* in 1508 it is possible to find a premonition of the pastoral in a chivalric romance. As a result, it is clear that the newly emergent narrative typologies of sixteenth-century Spain from the point of their first appearance began to incorporate elements that blurred and undermined the dominant modes of their representation and relation. With the very first hint of a pastoral episode in chivalric romance it is possible to detect the infiltration of other narrative styles and motifs into an identifiable type of literature, which gives the lie to the notion of the stability of genres and their characterization as taxonomies composed of enduring forms and conventions. Narrative prose fiction, like all types of literature, is continuously subject to modulation, refinement, and change by the interplay of genius, imagination, taste, and even the market. Like all discursive constructions, literary forms and styles evolve and transform themselves as they come into contact with the other forms and styles that populate the vast universe of texts and language. Any historical characterization of a genre or genres therefore, like the written grammar of a language, remains reductive and factitious. It constitutes an artificial synthesis of a dynamic, ever-evolving process into a convenient fabrication that permits access, understanding, and discussion.

Only critics and historians search for process, form, and structure to impose order on the past. Writers and artists simply give expression to their ideas and to the symbolic forms that inhabit their imaginations. There is nothing inherently neat or fixed therefore in the world of sixteenth-century Spanish prose fiction we have described, nor did it possess a teleology. Although each of the kinds of narrative that have been outlined allows for the grouping of certain works, these did not constitute independent, monolithic models, but manifestations of an endless sequence of transactions in continuous flux that took place not only between texts and other texts, but between authors, readers, and patrons, and, even as in the present day, between publishers, booksellers, and the buying public. It is not possible to speak of stable narrative forms and models in sixteenth-century Spain that may serve as the categorical precursors of something we call "the novel" – for which there is also no single narrative paradigm – yet all the books examined here did in one way or another help mold narrative styles and tastes that would lead to the novel's appearance from the hand of Miguel de Cervantes.

Miguel de Cervantes

ANTHONY J. CLOSE

Cervantes' *Don Quijote* was published in 1605. Its immense popularity in Spain, which quickly spread to other European countries – for example, via Thomas Shelton's (1612) and César Oudin's (1614) translations of Part 1 into English and French respectively – stimulated Cervantes into adding a second part in 1615. In the seventeenth century, both in Spain and outside, it was generally perceived as a robust, hilarious work of comedy. The coarse continuation of Cervantes' story by the pseudonymous Alonso Fernández de Avellaneda (dates unknown) (*Don Quijote de la Mancha*, 1614) typifies the tone.[1] This is not the only way in which, from the viewpoint of posterity, the reactions of Spaniards in this period to this work seem somewhat odd and superficial. Despite scores of imitations of particular incidents in it, or allusions to it, in subsequent literature,[2] the only Spanish writers who systematically treat it as a model of fictional prose-narrative are Avellaneda and Alonso Jerónimo de Salas Barbadillo (1581–1635). In this respect, it would not become a canonical paradigm until the eighteenth century. Moreover, despite the high esteem in which it was held by Spanish men of letters, amongst them great writers like Tirso de Molina and Calderón, it was never quite elevated to classic status, as were the works of Garcilaso, Alemán, Fernando de Rojas, Góngora, Lope de Vega, Quevedo, and Calderón.[3] In a way, Cervantes himself contributes to this result. In the prologue of *Don Quijote* Part 1, he makes a virtue of playing up his novel's risibility and popular appeal, and mocks the didactic gravity of contemporary works of literary entertainment – features which, in the eyes of Spanish *litterati*, redeemed two other masterpieces of comic prose, *Celestina* and *Guzmán de Alfarache*. Also, in the course of his story, he takes care to ensure that his novel's rhetorical elegance and

---

[1] With regard to Avellaneda's continuation, see Anthony J. Close, *Cervantes and the Comic Mind of his Age* (Oxford: Oxford University Press, 2000), pp. 71–72; and James Iffland, *De fiestas y aguafiestas. Risa, locura e ideología en Cervantes y Avellaneda* (Madrid: Iberoamericana, 1999).

[2] See M. Herrero García, *Estimaciones literarias del siglo XVIII* (Madrid: Voluntad, 1930); and Ignacio Arrellano Ayuso, "Cervantes en Calderón." *Anales Cervantinos* 35 (1999), pp. 9–35.

[3] Anthony J. Close, "Las interpretaciones del Quijote." In *Don Quijote de la Mancha*. 2 vols. Ed. Francisco Rico (Barcelona: Crítica, 1998), pp. i, cxlii–clxv.

edifying content wear a light and unpretentious air. The transparency of its parody of chivalry books for contemporary readers, and the superb imaginativeness and boisterousness of its many moments of farce – destined to inspire icons, engravings, paintings, music, and opera for centuries to come[4] – encouraged a reaction of hilarity all the more. Consequently, even judicious readers exhibit a curious ambivalence toward the novel, typified by Baltasar Gracián, who, while treating Quijote and Sancho as primary models for the two heroes of his prose allegory of man's pilgrimage of life, *El Criticón* (1651–7), condemns *Don Quijote*, no doubt with some tongue-in-cheek exaggeration, as frivolously unworthy of a man of mature judgment.

The inclusion of *Don Quijote* in the literary canon begins in late seventeenth-century France, an age of literary academicism and "bon goût,"[5] and gathers pace in the eighteenth century, led by England and Spain. A significant milestone is the lengthy prologue contributed by the Spanish Royal Librarian, Gregorio Mayans y Siscar, to the choice edition of *Don Quijote*, in Spanish, published in London in 1738. In this prologue, Mayans defines the broad lines of the approach to *Don Quijote* that would be followed by Spanish criticism of a Neoclassical tendency, culminating in the prologue of Diego Clemencín to his great edition of *Don Quijote* (1833–1839). He assumes that Cervantes had coherent novelistic principles of a Neoclassical nature – for example, those expounded in the canon of Toledo's censure of chivalry books (*Don Quijote* I, 47) – which accord with his practice and make sense of it; that *Don Quijote* is a comic epic in prose comparable in form and merit with the heroic *Iliad*; that Cervantes' attack on chivalry books accords with the reformist motives of Spain's sixteenth-century humanists; and that the serenity and magnanimity of Cervantes the man are complementary to the greatness of his book.

Around 1800, the Neoclassical interpretation of *Don Quijote* was overturned by the German Romantic movement, which took it as a model of the "Romantic" genre par excellence, the novel. The Romantics found in *Don Quijote* poetic grandeur on a level with Shakespeare's, and, more specifically, a bitter-sweet attitude to medieval chivalry, philosophic profundity, a rich polyphony of tones and styles, the ironic sense of the gap between Ideal and Real, and the artist's playful detachment from his own creation. They utterly rejected the treatment of it as a work of coarse comicality suitable for "the digestion hour after dinner," in Friedrich Schlegel's apt phrase. To trace the history of the criticism of *Don Quijote* from this

---

[4] E. C. Riley, "*Don Quixote*: From Text to Icon." *Cervantes* (special issue, winter 1998), pp. 103–115.

[5] Maurice Bardon, "*Don Quichotte*" en France au XVIIe et au XVIIIe siècle, 1605–1815. 2 vols. (Paris: Champion, 1931), chs. 3 and 4.

point on would go beyond the remit of this chapter. Nonetheless, the foregoing brief sketch of how *Don Quijote* has been interpreted is an essential introduction to the history of its relation to its precursors and cultural environment. A tradition three centuries old has accustomed us to assuming without question that *Don Quijote* is a monumental classic. In Cervantes' lifetime, nobody saw it that way; and that includes Cervantes himself, who, though immensely proud of having given such pleasure to so many, and keenly aware of its merits, probably rated *Persiles y Sigismunda* just as, or even more, highly.

So, how does one explain the incongruity between posterity's perception of *Don Quijote* and the seventeenth century's? The answer lies in a combination of distance of perspective and paradigm shifts: features of *Don Quijote* which clamored for attention then are much less noticed now, while others which failed to strike a chord with that century's aesthetics would later appear prophetically to fulfill posterity's. It is a commonplace about literary masterpieces that they have an inexhaustible capacity for self-renewal. In *Don Quijote*'s case, this cliché is strikingly confirmed by historical fact; it has somehow managed to tilt a different facet to each successive age, in which the age can recognize the reflection of its own features. For example, the eighteenth century loved it for Enlightenment reasons. The German Romantics recreated it in their own image. So the process of recreation has continued until Post Modernism which, as we shall see, looks at it through a Bakhtinian lens. In my discussion of *Don Quijote*, I propose to highlight features destined to attract the interest of later centuries, and explain what motivated Cervantes to put them there. In other words, I aim to bridge the apparent abyss between posterity's perception of *Don Quijote* and that of Cervantes' Spain.

First, we must place *Don Quijote* in the context of Cervantes' life and other works,[6] and the social and cultural climate in which he lived. Miguel de Cervantes Saavedra was born in Alcalá de Henares, near Madrid, in 1547. His father was a poor surgeon with a large family. Little is known for certain about his education, save that he completed it at the humanist academy of Juan López de Hoyos in Madrid. In 1569, he suddenly left Spain for Italy, possibly in order to escape the legal consequences of a duel. By 1571, he had enlisted in the allied expedition that was being assembled for a major attack on the Turkish fleet by the powers of Venice, Spain, and the Papacy. In that year, he fought in the historic sea-battle of Lepanto, which he describes in the prologue to *Don Quijote* Part II as "la más alta ocasión que vieron los siglos pasados, los presentes, ni esperan ver los venideros" ("the most exalted occasion seen by ages past, present or to

---

[6] Jean Canavaggio, *Cervantès* (Paris: Mazarine, 1986); Spanish translation, *Cervantes. En busca del perfil perdido* (Madrid: Espasa-Calpe, 1992).

come"), and sustained wounds which left him permanently maimed in the left hand. After further military action in the Mediterranean, he was captured by Berber pirates while returning from Naples to Spain by sea. He spent the next five years in captivity in Algiers; contemporary records testify to his fortitude and kindness to fellow captives during that ordeal, and, also, to his defiant courage, displayed by four unsuccessful escape attempts. This "heroic" decade of Cervantes' life, from 1570 to 1580, is recalled in the Captive's story in *Don Quijote* I, 39–42.

Ransomed in 1580, he returned to Spain, settled in Madrid, and began a moderately successful literary career: he wrote poetry, published a pastoral romance, *La Galatea* (1585), and had some twenty to thirty plays performed without, as he puts it in the prologue to the *Ocho comedias y ocho entremeses* ("Eight Comedies and Eight Farces," 1615), "ofrenda de pepinos, ni de otra cosa arrojadiza" ("offerings of cucumbers or other throwable matter"). After marrying Catalina de Salazar in 1584 and settling with her in her home town, Esquivias, he left the conjugal home and the region of Toledo for Andalucía in 1587, and would spend at least the next ten years there, engaged in humdrum and aggravating occupations: first, as requisitioner of food supplies for the Armada expedition against England (1588), then, as tax-collector. The latter job led to his imprisonment in 1597 as a result of a shortfall in the revenues due to the Spanish Treasury. This misfortune was due to the bankruptcy of the Sevillian banker with whom Cervantes had deposited a sizeable sum of tax money. He confesses in the prologue to *Don Quijote* Part I to having "engendered" Don Quijote in a prison; and tradition has it that he refers to this period of internment.

Let us return to his literary commitments in the 1580s, which have considerable significance for his later career. The genre of pastoral romance, launched by Jorge de Montemayor's influential *La Diana* (1559?), was fashionable in Spain in the second half of the sixteenth century; and Cervantes would always remain attached to it, promising in the preliminaries of his late works to bring out a second part of *La Galatea* – a promise thwarted by his death in 1616. The genre is an extension of pastoral poetry, and, specifically, of the mixture of prose and verse in *Arcadia* (1501), by the Neapolitan Jacopo Sannazaro (1455–1530); it offers a conventionalized, idyllic picture of the lives, and particularly the unrequited loves, of shepherds and shepherdesses in a setting resembling the mythological Golden Age. Montemayor's contribution lay in supplementing the prose-tableaux of Sannazaro with flashback stories, which give a narrative background to the sentiments so exquisitely expressed by the shepherds and shepherdesses in their verse. Beneath the rustic masquerade, the sentiments, concepts, and gallantry of these personages, who stand implicitly for the author's friends, are courtly and literary in nature. Read between the lines, their discussions about love, which in Book IV of *La Galatea* take the form of a full-blown debate between the "loveless" Lenio and the enamoured Tirsi, pose the basic ethical problem of sixteenth-century Spanish love literature: the question of the legitimacy of pre-marital or extra-marital wooing between the courtier and his lady. The solution offered by Tirsi in that debate is a simplified, Catholic Neoplatonism, which defends the goodness of love provided that sensual desire is subordinated to reason and fulfilled only in marriage. Wishy-washy as this conception may seem to us, it provides the criteria for good love, and its converse bad love, basic to Cervantes' subsequent romantic fiction.

Cervantes' enthusiasm for the pastoral genre may strike us as puzzling in view of his ironic mockery of literary implausibility in *Don Quijote*, including that of pastoral. The paradox can be explained in terms of his ambivalence toward the genre, which also extends to other "purple" and idealized literary modes and is reflected in his strategy of parody in *Don Quijote*. On the one hand, he is strongly drawn to pastoral as a poetically heightened medium for the expression of the sentiments of love and the discussion of its psychology, ethics, and metaphysics; on the other hand, his suspicions, as a writer of prose narrative, about literary inverisimilitude, precious excess, and disregard for functional relevance cause him to mock the genre in both *Don Quijote* and *El coloquio de los perros* ("The Dogs' Colloquy"), precisely because these works are primarily concerned to censure such failings. That does not mean that Cervantes' handling of the pastoral theme in the continuation of *La Galatea* would have differed radically from the way in which he treated it in the book published in 1585. The genre, which he designates as "libros de poesía" ("books of verse") in the scrutiny of Don Quijote's library (I, 6), carries implicitly a poetic license denied to other fiction, more strictly governed by the demands of verisimilitude; this, together with its appeal for a sophisticated readership, exempts it from the charge of fabulous nonsense that he makes against chivalry books. While the ridicule that he pours on these is radical, his ironic satire of pastoral preciosity in *Don Quijote*, especially Part I, chs. 12–14, 50–51, is much less damaging.

Of the Cervantine plays performed in the 1580s – the titles of many are given in the "Adjunta" or appendix to Cervantes' *Viaje del Parnaso* ("Voyage to Parnassus") – only two survive, *El cerco de Numancia* ("The Siege of Numancia"), known as *La Numancia*, and *El trato de Argel* ("Life in Algiers"). The latter play creates a poignant picture of the sufferings of Spanish captives in Algiers – a theme also treated in the later play *Los baños de Argel* ("The Prisons of Algiers") and in the already mentioned *novela* of the ex-captive – and is based on Cervantes' own experience. *La Numancia*, a stirring tribute to a Spanish town's heroic refusal to surrender when besieged by Scipio's army in Roman times, is Cervantes' most famous play. One of its modern revivals took place in Madrid during the siege of the city by Nationalist forces in the Spanish Civil War. These two early plays are not to be confused with the eight comedies and eight farces which he published in 1615 and which were probably all written after the interruption of his literary career.

When, around 1600, Cervantes took up writing once again, he must already have been made painfully aware of the huge success of the school of drama led by Lope de Vega – the cause, by his own admission in the revealing prologue of the *Ocho comedias*, written in 1615, of the reluctance of the *autores* ("actor-managers") to buy his plays. In *Don Quijote* (I, 48), the priest of Don Quijote's village, speaking on Cervantes' behalf, delivers a stinging, though reasoned and measured, attack on the New Comedy's violations of the rules of art. Since he attributes them chiefly to the commercially motivated philistinism of the *autores*, one infers that Cervantes, in writing this passage sometime before 1605, had already suffered the rebuff to which he alludes in the prologue of 1615. Not only must it have been mortifying to his pride to be rejected after having enjoyed success as a playwright in the 1580s, but the setback would also have been aggravated by financial loss, the sense of a cheapening of artistic standards and of opportunities lost to luckier rivals, all added to the aggravations suffered in his bureaucratic interlude in Andalucía. The resentment is reflected in the prologue to *Don Quijote* Part I, which wittily and maliciously satirizes the snobbish and pedantic pretensions of contemporary writers, amongst whom Lope de Vega – author of the pastoral romance *Arcadia* (1599) and the Byzantine romance *El peregrino en su patria* ("Pilgrim in His Own Land," 1604) – stands out as the obvious target.

Now, the censure of the *comedia* in *Don Quijote* (I, 48) immediately follows the canon of Toledo's critique of chivalry books in the previous chapter; and the canon treats the errors of one genre as exactly equivalent to those of the other. There is no coincidence in this symmetry; and it helps to explain the polemical motivation of *Don Quijote* and the nature of its parody. In modern times, critics have often questioned that motivation. Why, they ask, should Cervantes have bothered to attack the chivalric genre, which, by around 1600, was virtually defunct in terms of composition if not consumption? The answer is that he saw in its combination of artistic lawlessness and massive popularity the threatening shadow of another genre – the *comedia* – which was very much alive and kicking, and he considered its influence on public taste as spoiling the pitch for the kind of fiction – specifically, heroic romance and, more generally, the romantic *novela* – that he wanted to write. One should remember that the canon of Toledo speaks not of outright demolition of the chivalric genre, but of overhaul and reconstruction, and ends his critique by sketching the outlines of an ideal prose epic which might replace it. Cervantes' Byzantine romance *Persiles y Sigismunda*, published posthumously in 1617, is virtually a fulfillment of that blueprint. The romantic and heroic *novelas* that Cervantes interpolates in *Don Quijote* Part 1 are homogeneous with *Persiles*, since similar *novelas* constitute its episodes. In other words, Cervantes felt that public taste needed to be educated through parodic satire of the chivalric genre, so that the fate which had already befallen his well-crafted plays should not also overtake his well-crafted stories. Generally speaking, in his writings – plays, *novelas, Don Quijote, Persiles* – he aspires to entertain a wide readership while respecting the rules of poetic art: verisimilitude, the reconciliation of pleasure and profit, decorum or fittingness in its many aspects, including plausibility of character-portrayal and the matching of style to theme. His sense of the validity of the traditional poetics is due to something more deeply felt than respect for academic authority: a passionate conviction, repeatedly expressed, of the inventiveness and artistry of his own work. A revealing expression of this pride, which implicitly reflects his high opinion of *Don Quijote*, occurs in the moving prologue to *Persiles*, written when Cervantes was on his deathbed; it contains his farewell to life, and, specifically, to laughter and friends. His priorities are revealing. The prologue also contains the salute to Cervantes by a student, an avid aficionado of his works, whom he met by chance on the road from Esquivias to Madrid just a few days previously: "Sí, sí, éste es el manco sano, el famoso todo, el escritor alegre, y, finalmente, el regocijo de las Musas" ("Yes, yes, it's the whole one-hander, the great celebrity, the merry writer, and, lastly, the Muses' joy"). No doubt Cervantes intended it as his literary epitaph.

Cervantes' theoretical stance toward chivalry books, together with his conception of them as threateningly akin to his own fiction, helps to explain the peculiarly internal nature of his parody of them. He conceives Don Quijote, who aspires to be a hero such as the books describe, as being in some ways a plausible simulacrum of the real thing, intimately familiar with their style and ethos, madly serious, elegantly well-read despite his lurches into effusive excess or banal vulgarity. Yet his re-enactment of them is rendered ridiculous by its merely imitative motives, the archaic and fabulous nature of the model, and his own unsuitability, together with that of the stage and props, for the performance. Consequently, Cervantes perceives Don Quijote as an abortive, frustrated hero of epic romance, who quite often nearly gets it right, but, for the reasons just given, only succeeds in getting it ridiculously wrong. Cervantes also systematically contrasts his personage's ineffectual attempts to live on a plane of heroic achievement or lofty sentiment with interpolated stories where such experience is not confined within literary make-believe.

The success of *Don Quijote* Part I was instantaneous; in the very year of its publication (1605), Don Quijote and Sancho appeared as carnival figures in public festivities held in Valladolid, and, from henceforth, would pass into Spanish, then universal, folklore. The book's enthusiastic reception mellowed Cervantes, appeased his injured vanity, and spurred him to unchecked literary activity until his death – a gloriously creative old age in which he completed *Don Quijote* Part II; his collection of twelve exemplary novels, *Novelas ejemplares* (1613); the collection of eight comedies and eight farces already mentioned (1615); and a long, burlesque fantasy in verse, the *Viaje del Parnaso* (1614) – a satire of contemporary poets, especially poetasters – not to mention works unfinished or unpublished. After his death in 1616 his widow arranged the publication of his Byzantine romance *Persiles y Sigismunda* (1617). In the period 1606–1616, Cervantes lived in Madrid, famous, widely admired, and prominent in literary academies. Toward the end, the patronage of the count of Lemos and the archbishop of Toledo, Bernardo de Sandoval, did something to alleviate his chronic poverty. The preliminaries of *Don Quijote* Part II include an *aprobación* (warrant of inoffensiveness to morals and the faith) by Francisco Márquez Torres, a chaplain of the archbishop; compared with the usual certificate of this kind, it is unusually long and personal, and is one of the most illuminating commentaries on Cervantes written by a seventeenth-century Spaniard. Praising him for his continuation of the edifying project of demolishing chivalry books, the unaffected clarity of his style, the genial urbanity of his satire of customs, and, generally, for his *decoro, decencia, suavidad, blandura* ("decorum, decency, smoothness, mildness"), Márquez Torres goes on to relate a return visit by the retinue of his master, the archbishop, to the French ambassador, then in Madrid to negotiate a royal wedding. When the conversation turned to literature, and Cervantes' name was mentioned, the well-read French courtiers expressed the most lively enthusiasm. The anecdote is a revealing indicator of the qualities of Cervantes that were then particularly esteemed; these include his romantic fiction, *La Galatea* – nowadays an acquired taste.

The preliminaries of the second part of *Don Quijote* also contain Cervantes' riposte to the bitchy personal comments that Avellaneda had made about him in the prologue to his own continuation of *Don Quijote* Part I, published in the previous year. Though the enigma of Avellaneda's identity has not convincingly been unravelled, he gives plainly to understand in his prologue that he considers himself a friend of Lope de Vega, and also a target, with Lope, of Cervantes' satiric attack on the New Comedy in *Don Quijote* Part I. Cervantes, in the prologue to his own Part II, dispatches the reader as emissary to Avellaneda with a couple of jokes about madmen and dogs, which carry disparaging implications about his rival's leaden wit. Considering the provocation that Cervantes had received, his tone is relatively mild; and the humor carries over into the chapters of Part II which allude to Avellaneda's novel (notably, chapters 59, 70, 72). These allusions presumably date from the moment of composition when Cervantes became aware of the publication of his rival's book.

Of the works that he published in the last few years of his life, only the collection of *Novelas* comes anywhere near to rivaling *Don Quijote*'s enduring popularity. In these, Cervantes exploits the thematic diversity and elastic size of the Italian novella derived from Boccaccio's *Decameron*, and uses it as a form in which to synthesize plots and themes popular with Spanish readers. In so doing, he revolutionizes the genre, gives it unprecedented depth, and blends ingredients with startling audacity. For example, the *Coloquio de los perros*, generally acknowledged as the masterpiece of the collection, takes from Apuleius' *The Golden Ass* (second century AD) the theme of man transformed by witchcraft into animal, who then experiences human nastiness at the hands of a succession of cruel, immoral masters. In this case the alleged subjects of metamorphosis are the dogs Berganza and his twin brother Cipión. The narrative of Berganza, who tells the story of his life, obviously also imitates the picaresque, and is especially indebted to Alemán's hugely popular *Guzmán de Alfarache* (1599, 1604) for its satiric denunciation of vices and abuses, its moralistic meditations, and realistic attention to the social here-and-now. The *Coloquio* also echoes the form of the Renaissance didactic dialogue, the allegorical fables of Aesop, and the disenchanted, otherworldly, or infrahuman vision of the human condition of the satires of Lucian of Samosata (second century AD). Since the fictitious author of the dogs' dialogue is the ensign Campuzano, protagonist of the *novela* of *El casamiento engañoso* ("The Deceitful Marriage") by which the dialogue is framed, all this is presented as the invention, or possibly the delirious dream, of the chastened husband of that marriage, which was motivated by greed and duplicity on both sides. The diversity of the *Coloquio*'s literary affiliations is matched by the complexity of its structure, since its somber satire on Spanish society and the human condition, and the narratives of Berganza and Campuzano, together with their fantastic premises, are all subjected to the reactions of skeptical listeners, which constitute a critical meditation on the nature of satire and of story telling, and a rational debunking of the supernatural. To contemporary readers, this thought-provoking manner of handling the *novela*, a genre hitherto solely concerned with telling a pleasing story, and, also, notorious in Spain for its licentiousness – hence on both counts deemed somewhat frivolous – must have seemed extraordinary.

The principal reason for this unfavorable image was that the favorite themes of the Italian *novellieri*, starting with Boccaccio, were jolly, ribald stories about the sexual misdemeanors of randy friars, sexually frustrated wives of old or stupid husbands, hot-blooded youths and maidens, and so on. In such stories, morals go on holiday, and the reader's amused sympathy is invited for the clever circumvention of social or religious taboos. In Spain, from the mid sixteenth century onwards, when the climate of state and religious censorship became severe, this kind of licentiousness was unacceptable; and Spanish translators of Italian *novelle* toward the end of the century become strident in their claims of having repudiated it. Cervantes' protestations of exemplariness in the prologue to his *Novelas* must be understood in that context. They are not mere lip-service to the censor. The avoidance of the amorality associated with the Italian genre can plainly be seen in the tragic dénouements, ironic reversals, and final confessions of error by the husbands of both *El curioso impertinente* ("The Impertinently Curious Husband," interpolated in *Don Quijote* Part I, chs. 33–35) and *El celoso extremeño* ("The Jealous Extremaduran"), these being *novelas* which derive from Italian precursors on the theme of adultery. Both treat the theme as an occasion for serious meditation on the nature of marriage and of each spouse's responsibility for its success. Moreover, Cervantes' audacious blending of heterogeneous strands can be seen in the latter *novela*'s mix of farce and tragedy: the grotesquely exaggerated security measures of the pathologically jealous old husband, who turns the conjugal home into a combination of prison, convent, harem, and kindergarten, are plainly reminiscent of farce; and so are the wiles of the seducer, the sanctimonious hypocrisy of the lewd *dueña*, and the naïve credulity of the other servants. However, the fact that the outwitting of Carrizales is set in the context of his whole life, and culminates in his death-bed contrition and pardon of his wife, gives the story a tragic pathos quite untypical of this species.

Revolutionary experimentation with form is exemplified by the other well-known *novelas*. In *Rinconete y Cortadillo*, Cervantes reduces the *pícaro*'s autobiography to a brief slice of underworld life, told in the third person not the first; effectively, the *novela* concerns what Rinconete and Cortadillo, the two heroes, saw one day in the patio of the Mafia boss of Seville after being inducted into his gang; or, more particularly, what they heard, since the *novela*, which lacks a plot, is largely composed of dialogue and focused on the barbarous mannerisms, the sanctimonious hypocrisy, and "statutes and ordinances" of Monipodio and his underlings. In its dialogic form, it is indebted to comedies and farces about such personages; so here Cervantes synthesizes picaresque novel with theatre, compressing them into a short story. He does something rather similar in *La ilustre fregona* ("The Illustrious Kitchen Maid") and *La Gitanilla* ("The Little Gipsy Girl"). In the first, the picaresque, which normally paints an amusingly sordid picture of delinquent life, is astonishingly hybridized with romantic comedy and pastoral romance. The story is about two young noblemen who run away from their family homes in Burgos to lead the lives of *pícaros*, a project suspended when one of them falls in love with the beautiful, virtuous heroine, apparently a mere serving wench at an inn in Toledo. Despite its base setting, Avendaño's love for Costanza is reminiscent of the nobly spiritual love of Elicio for Galatea in Cervantes' pastoral romance. In the dénouement, Costanza turns out to have a noble pedigree; so a happy ending is achieved without violation of social decorum. Though this kind of theme has precedents in prose romance, it is treated over and over again in Lope's theatre: a model which Cervantes must have had in mind. *La Gitanilla* is similar in plot and theme to *La ilustre fregona* with the difference that the sordid milieu with which the noble hero associates himself is not picaresque but a band of gypsies.

The less famous and popular *novelas* – such as *La española inglesa* ("The Spanish English Girl") and *Las dos doncellas* ("The Two Damsels") – though not much to the taste of modern readers, are a literary species to which Cervantes was very attached, since he cultivates it throughout his career, either as interpolated episode or independent *novela*. Integral to these stories are crises which imperil love, life and honor: capture by pirates, shipwrecks, escapes; compromising escapades by girls pursuing or pursued; providential reunions, wondrous recognitions. The tone is sentimental and decorous; the status of the principals is genteel; the dialogue courtly and rhetorical; the appeal to pathos reinforced by the focus on women's experience of love. Though these stories have precedents in the Italian novella tradition, they are more immediately modeled on contemporary Spanish theatre, where such plots are standard fare.

Cervantes' Byzantine romance, *Persiles y Sigismunda*, is thematically akin to the romantic *novelas* since its main action is diversified by a plethora of episodes, whose plots are very similar to those just described. The story concerns a pilgrimage by two chaste and faithful lovers of royal lineage from northern lands to Rome in order that the hero can pursue his courtship of the heroine, who, before they set out, had been promised in marriage to the hero's elder brother, Magsimino. The pilgrimage also has, of course, a religious purpose: so that both hero and heroine, in Rome, can perfect their instruction in the Catholic faith. On their journey, which takes them from legendary Tile (supposedly somewhere near Norway), to Portugal, Spain, southern France, then Italy, the protagonists, who travel as brother and sister under the assumed names of Periandro and Auristela, are joined by a succession of fellow travelers, all, like them, exiles or victims of misfortune. Each one of them narrates his or her sad story, and these stories represent the episodes mentioned above.

Persiles is epic in length and design. It is largely grandiose and tragic in tone, and ingeniously complex in structure, with the episodes interlocking with the main action and each other like pieces of a jigsaw puzzle, which tantalizingly fall into place in such a way that links and identities are only gradually revealed. For instance, the origins and purpose of the hero and heroine remain shrouded in mystery until very near the end. The plot exemplifies a number of moral/religious themes, including man's relation to divine providence, the nature of good love, the repudiation of violence committed in honor's name, and, overall, the exaltation of Catholic faith above pagan or heretical error. The novel applies with almost painstaking conscientiousness the rules of Neo-Aristotelian poetics and bases itself on a classical model, the *Aethiopica Historia* by Heliodorus, Bishop of Thrace, written in Greek in the third century AD, and much admired by Renaissance humanism for its verisimilitude, ingenious structure, and exemplariness. *Persiles* is Cervantes' most carefully crafted work; and his esteem for it, and ambitious conception of it, are indicated by his claim in the dedicatory to *Don Quijote* Part II that it promises to be either the worst or the best book of entertainment yet written in Spanish. To that he adds that he regrets having said "the worst."

Of the collection of theatrical pieces, the farces (*entremeses*) are brilliant and justly celebrated; however, the comedies are of more uneven quality, showing an ambivalent relationship to the New Comedy of Lope de Vega and his followers. While they sometimes poke fun at its conventions, they show extensive affinities with its themes, character-types, and situations, handling these, however, in a lighter and more ironic way than Lope does.[7] Amongst the more interesting of the *comedias* are *La entretenida* ("The Entertaining Comedy"), *Pedro de Urdemalas*, and *El rufián dichoso* ("The Fortunate Ruffian"). The first of these, a comedy of middle-class manners with a highly intricate plot, parodies, by its anti-climactic dénouement, the New Comedy's typical ending in multiple marriages, and exhibits in various other ways the tendency of Cervantine theatre to allude to itself and to theatrical conventions. It is notable for its vigorous projection of the servants, whose doings are a sophisticated parody of the amatory entanglements of their foolish masters. The character of Pedro de Urdemalas, based on a legendary trickster and changeling of that name, is fascinating for what it reveals about Cervantes' love of the theatre and conception of the ideal actor: in Cervantes' play, the hero comes to realize that this is the profession for which he is destined; and the qualities that he reveals up to that point – quick-wittedness, eloquence, versatility, refusal of permanent attachments – show that Cervantes has conceived his personality, from the beginning, in terms of that culminating self-discovery. The third of the plays named above is about a young ruffian of Seville, magnetically

---

[7] Close, *Cervantes and the Comic Mind*, ch. 3; and Stanislav Zimic, *El teatro de Cervantes* (Madrid: Castalia, 1992).

drawn to the company of cut-throats and prostitutes like Monipodio's gang, and showing something of Monipodio's misplaced religious devotion, though not his stupidity or dishonesty. At the end of the first act he realizes the impiety of his ways, and vows to embrace the monastic life; in the next two acts we see him fulfilling that vow as a saintly friar of the Order of Preachers in Mexico. The portrayal of Lugo, subsequently Fray Cruz, is interesting as a study of a dissolute character who, nonetheless, is born to greatness; the perversely misdirected qualities that he reveals as a ruffian – recklessness, combativeness, chivalrousness, ambition, religious devotion – are continuous with the heroic virtues that he shows in Mexico. He is one of several Cervantine personages who have affinities with Don Quijote.

Something should be said about the society and culture in which *Don Quijote* was written. The Spain of Felipe III (1598–1621) had to cope with the financial exhaustion which had been caused by the imperialistic policies of Felipe II (1556–1598). So it curbed military adventures abroad. However, the Court extravagantly belied this retrenchment, opening the floodgates of gaiety and festivity, at least in the early years of Felipe III's reign, after the solemn sobriety of the previous one. Cervantes lived in Valladolid during two of the five years when it was seat of the Court (1601–1606); and life in that town was described by one intelligent observer as a perpetual comedy or farce in which dissolution was the norm. It is no accident that a spate of comic fiction and satire –including Mateo Alemán's great picaresque novel *Guzmán de Alfarache*, the brilliant sequel to it by Quevedo, *El Buscón* (c. 1605) ("The Sharper"), and, of course, *Don Quijote* itself – were all written after 1598. Another major stimulus to comic writing was the lifting of the ban on the *comedia*, imposed for one year in 1597–98 after Felipe II's death.

Despite the religious fervor of the Counter Reformation, and a spate of projects and books which aimed at social and moral reform, this was in many ways a corrupt society. Powerful Court favorites ran the country for the pious and colorless Felipe III, enriching themselves in the process; and their spectacular rises and falls gave proof of the precariousness of fortune. People swarmed to the capital – Madrid, except for the period 1601–1606, when the capital moved to Valladolid – from the impoverished provinces in order to seek preferment at Court or service in noble households; and the sharpers, beggars, prostitutes, and diverse poseurs who came with them provided a rich quarry for satirists. Aristocrats, attracted by the prospect of power and enrichment, built expensive mansions there, neglecting their country estates. Convents and churches, built with the help of large donations, sprouted in the capital. The rapid expansion of Madrid, and the concentration of the population in the city, created opportunities for literature, which was favored by a combination of factors: aristocratic and Church patronage; academies; the proximity of writers to each other; and, above all, the emergence of a mass market of readers and theatre-goers. Consequently, it flourished in a variety of forms. Though the Church made strenuous efforts to impose norms of decency upon it, and the Inquisition rigorously monitored it for any signs of unorthodoxy, irreverence, or blasphemy, neither of them checked literary creativity.

By its policy of enforced religious unity, Spain avoided the religious conflicts that shook its European neighbors. However, it experienced a different kind of dissension, originating from the socially stigmatized, hence disaffected, descendants of converted Jews and Moors. This was a society hyper-conscious of honor, caste, and status, in which much of the large, hierarchically tiered class of the nobility – apart from those employed in government or other honorable professions – pursued a life of dignified idleness, leaving commerce, manual labor, and agriculture to the lower orders. The combination of gold and silver from the Indies and the insatiable need for borrowed money stoked inflation and had a harmful impact on Spanish commerce; at the same time, it created a new *parvenu* class, determined to buy status with money. "Desengaño" (disenchantment with worldly vanities) and the precariousness of fortune are dominant themes of the literature of the age.

Faced with the social ills of a nation in decline, Cervantes adopts a reticent attitude. It is very unlikely that he intended the politico-historical message that has been discerned in *Don Quijote*, alleged symbol of the nation's incapacity to measure its ambitions to its means. While he offers a grandiose and sweeping picture of the society around him, the tone of his novel is gay, mellow, and picturesque, rather than caustic. Yet the moral themes which run through it and are centered on Don Quijote's and Sancho's careers – the folly of building castles in the air, of empty posturings of honor, of opportunistic social climbing; the ideals of fair justice and zealous government – obviously have wider implications.

In its original conception, *Don Quijote* is a parody of Spanish romances of chivalry, launched by the immensely popular *Amadís de Gaula* (1508). This genre, an offshoot of the medieval *Lancelot* about King Arthur's Knights of the Round Table, presents an escapist version of the medieval code of chivalry, set in a remote era sometime after the death of Christ: a marvelous world of giants, enchanters, castles, forests, tourneys, battles, princesses, dwarves, and dragons, through which heroic knights-errant roam in search of adventure and fame. Cervantes' attack on the genre, motivated primarily by its implausibility, rounds off a chorus of moralistic denunciations by Spaniards dating from the early sixteenth century. Yet his objections are more aesthetic than moral, being based on a Neoclassical conception of what a prose epic should be. As we have already noted,

understanding Cervantes' aesthetic motives for writing *Don Quijote* –
particularly his commitment to heroic romance – helps us to appreciate
how he transformed parody into something much less limited than what
is normally meant by that term. Another motive which needs to be taken
into account are his strong objections to the heavy didacticism of contemporary literature of entertainment, an offense, in his view, against the
principle of decorum or fittingness. The objections are expressed with
waspish wit in the prologue to *Don Quijote* Part 1, which ends with
the recommendations of Cervantes' friend as to how he should write his
novel. The friend tells him that, since his purpose is simply the demolition of chivalry books, "de quien nunca se acordó Aristóteles, ni dijo
nada San Basilio, ni alcanzó Cicerón" ("about which Aristotle never took
note, St Basil was silent, and no news reached Cicero"), he has no need to
go scrounging philosophical maxims, precepts of Holy Scripture, poetic
fables, rhetorical orations, and miracles of saints; all he need do is write
his story in a pleasing, plain, and merry style, concentrate on its argument, and observe verisimilitude, thus provoking the reader to sustained
laughter.

Now, we might see this as a recipe for unremitting levity without the
least concession to gravity or learning. This impression would be mistaken. Since Cervantes shares his age's taste for the display of eloquence,
erudition, and moral sententiousness, *Don Quijote* contains plenty of
"philosophical maxims," etcetera. However, Cervantes cannot be accused
of committing the faults that he condemns. This is because, in incorporating such material in his novel, he takes good care to ensure that it
is genuinely integrated with the main comic theme, by irony, thematic
mirroring, idiosyncrasy of perspective, and other means.

A good example of this is Don Quijote's speech on the Golden Age,
which is both a "poetic fable" and a "rhetorical oration," and forms a
prelude to the pastoral episode of Grisóstomo and Marcela. This precious
and learned rehearsal of a consecrated Classical topos (part 1, ch. 11) is
presented as an aspect of Don Quijote's bookish, chivalric eccentricity.
He is moved to deliver the oration, oblivious of the incomprehension of
his hosts, the goat-herds, merely because he has a full belly after supper,
feels in expansive mood, and holds a bunch of shriveled acorns in his
hand, which puts him in mind of that vegetarian age. Also, he treats the
decline of the mythic age of gold into that of iron as the "historic" circumstance which brought about the genesis of knight errantry, required
to protect wandering damsels from sexual predators. The speech thus
forms a natural introduction to the story of the chaste and independent
shepherdess Marcela, subjected to the pestering of her many male admirers, chief of whom, until his demise, was the shepherd Grisóstomo. The
story of Grisóstomo's love for Marcela, and the drama of his burial and

her eloquent intervention in it, are essentially treated seriously; yet they are harmonized with Don Quijote's doings, first, by being initially presented from the parochial viewpoint of the goat-herd Pedro, which brings the literariness of the behavior of Grisóstomo and his friends and rivals down to earth with a satiric bump, and second, by the excesses of their amatory lamentations, reminiscent of those of Don Quijote for Dulcinea. In essence, Cervantes proceeds in the same sort of way with all the grave matter that he introduces into his novel – the trials and tribulations of Cardenio and Dorotea in the Sierra Morena (I, chs. 23–24, 27–29, 36), Don Quijote's counsels of government to Sancho (II, 42–43), and so on – and, in consequence, he endows it with a suggestive ambivalence. To what extent are Cardenio and Dorotea tarred with Don Quijote's brush? How seriously are we meant to take those counsels, commonplaces of the statecraft of the age? How do we discriminate good romance from bad, one level of fiction from another, "inside" the fictional world from "outside"?[8] For Cervantes and his contemporaries, steeped in cultural presuppositions which allowed them to make such distinctions instinctively, those problems did not exist. Yet for readers of later ages, unfamiliar with those presuppositions, the ambivalence would become ironically mesmerizing. Cervantes appears to present in his novel all the authoritative discourses and forms of talk of his age, and to hold them ironically at arm's length without indicating preference. That at least is how his novel has been interpreted in the twentieth century, from Américo Castro (*El pensamiento de Cervantes*) to Leo Spitzer to Carlos Fuentes; and the interpretation has acquired a new lease of life in the postmodernist age, thanks to the pervasive influence of the "dialogic" theory of Bakhtin.[9] It draws strength from the notorious "metafictionality" of *Don Quijote*: that is, Cervantes' practice of alluding within his novel to its own fictional status, which includes representing the process of creating, consuming, and criticizing fiction. We have an example of this in the Marcela/Grisóstomo episode. Don Quijote, the madman who believes he can live chivalric literature, hears from the goat-herd Pedro the story about the eccentric Grisóstomo and his party, who, for love of Marcela, live the life of *literary* shepherds. Then, he observes Grisóstomo's burial, a solemn literary masquerade, with the mourners, the funeral bier, and ceremony dressed up like a scene from Sannazaro's *Arcadia*. It is as though Don Quijote were reading a version of his own story.[10]

---

[8] E. C. Riley, *Cervantes's Theory of the Novel* (Oxford: Clarendon, 1962); Spanish translation, *Teoría de la novela en Cervantes* (Madrid: Taurus, 1966), pp. 135–148.
[9] Carroll Johnson, "Cómo se lee hoy el *Quijote*." In *Cervantes* (Madrid: Centro de Estudios Cervantinos, 1995), pp. 335–348.
[10] E. C. Riley, *Don Quixote* (London: Allen and Unwin, 1986), pp. 124–132.

From the viewpoint of posterity, the same kind of ambivalence surrounds Don Quijote's motivation. In the early chapters of Part I, it is ridiculously unproblematic. He goes mad as a result of reading too many chivalry books, loses the distinction between them and true history, and resolves to become a knight-errant in the Spain of around 1600. His behavior from that point on, as Sancho aptly observes (II, 10), involves interpreting black as white – windmills as giants, sheep as armies, basins as helmets – with chaotically farcical results. While this black/white dichotomy is basic to a series of centrally significant contrasts through the novel, it is progressively refined by two factors in particular.

The first is Cervantes' internal and empathetic relation to the object of his parody, which affects the nature of his hero's character, particularly the witty inventiveness to which the novel's title alludes. Though Don Quijote's heroic conception of himself and of a consonantly prodigious world exists only in his fantasy, it stylishly and consistently replicates the original in many ways, while, at the same time, capriciously inflating, elaborating, and vulgarizing it. This continually improvised romance is made to absorb, with madly ingenious exuberance, a host of "purple" styles and learned topics, some more or less akin to the chivalric genre (pastoral, epic, history, ballads, Ariosto), and others quite unrelated to it (the Golden Age, the Bible, poetic theory, statecraft, legal jargon, etc.). Don Quijote does not merely play a chivalric role, but lives it, confusing make-believe with reality; and in so doing, he behaves all the time, though he is not aware of it, as an over-enthusiastic, uncritical reader of stories. When, for example, he imagines in a soliloquy how his future chronicler will describe his early morning ride across the plain of Montiel (I, 2), his view of himself at that moment combines simultaneously the roles of narrator of the first chapter of a chivalric novel, reader of it, and, of course, hero of it. Thus he proceeds thereafter, revealing himself to be not just a compulsive reader of chivalry books, but of almost any and every kind of book. Such total, literal personification of the activity of reading incites the actual reader of *Don Quijote*, as Ortega y Gasset shrewdly pointed out,[11] to identify with him; and in this he or she is assisted by a tendency to overlook a distinction that Cervantes takes for granted: that is, the difference between make-believe and really doing or being. We can observe this tendency in Erich Auerbach's famous commentary on the adventure in which Sancho deceives his master into thinking that three village wenches are Dulcinea and two ladies-in-waiting (*Don Quijote* II, 10).[12]

[11] José Ortega y Gasset, "Meditaciones del Quijote. Meditaciones del 'Quijote.'" In *Obras completas*. 9 vols. (7th. edn. Madrid: Revista de Occidente, 1966), vol. I, pp. 380–381.
[12] Erich Auerbach, "The Enchanted Dulcinea." In *Mimesis. The Representation of Reality in Western Literature*. Trans. Willard Trask (Princeton: Princeton University Press, 1953), pp. 334–358.

Let us remind ourselves how this comes about. Before setting forth on his third sally, Don Quijote rides to El Toboso to seek Dulcinea's blessing (II, 8), and expects Sancho to lead him to her palace, since his squire supposedly went there during the second sally to deliver a message to her. As a result, Sancho is put in a terrible pickle, for his account of his embassy to Dulcinea was all a pack of lies (I, 31). Quite apart from that, though Sancho is by now nitwittedly unclear on this point, the palace and Dulcinea's noble status are pure figments of the knight's imagination. After master and squire blunder about El Toboso in the dead of night on their fruitless search (II, 9), Sancho is left to locate Dulcinea on his own; and he resolves on a ruse to get himself out of his jam. Reasoning that his master is mad, and habitually prone to take black for white, he decides to present to his master the first rustic wench that he meets, claiming that she is Dulcinea.

The encounter between Don Quijote and the three girls is dramatically vivid in its oppositions of register, posture, and attitude, and the extremity of its irony. The knight, with bulging eyes and distraught gaze, confronts the moon-faced, snub-nosed "Dulcinea," mounted on her donkey; and one of her companions delivers a coarsely rustic brush-off to Sancho, intermediary of the meeting, on hearing his ridiculously flowery speech of intercession. At this, Don Quijote delivers a preciously wordy entreaty to "Dulcinea" – "Y tú, ¡oh estremo del valor que puede desearse, término de la humana gentileza, único remedio deste afligido corazón que te adora," etc. ("And thou, O limit of desirable worth, ultimate term of human courtesy, only remedy of this afflicted heart that adores thee!") – begging her to look gently and amorously upon him. Auerbach characterizes the speech as nobly eloquent, overlooking its stilted literariness. He is able to take this view because, although Don Quijote overdoes the language of lovers' adoration, he overdoes it marginally, rather than crudely; for Cervantes, the speech's absurdity consists not so much in the style, as in the grotesque mismatch between style and addressee, a failure of decorum which he would not have considered extrinsic to the dignity of expression. Auerbach's misconception is facilitated by Cervantes' characteristic lack of comment on Don Quijote's motives. Why, for example, does the knight fail to transform black into white in this scene, when, in Part I, confronted by wenches quite as hideous as this one, his imagination invariably converts them into paragons of beauty? On this and other questions regarding his attitude to Dulcinea, Cervantes is silent. So the reader is thrown back on Don Quijote's own explanations, which have a crazy inconsequentiality combined with an outwardly stylish and emotive form. Hence many modern readers, including Auerbach, substitute "sublime" for "crazy," as the following quotation shows: "But Don Quijote's feelings are genuine and profound. Dulcinea is really the mistress of his thoughts; he is truly filled with the spirit of a mission which he regards as man's highest duty."[13] From premises like these, a long succession of twentieth-century critics have read this adventure and the ensuing process of the knight's disillusionment as tragedy, not farce.

My purpose here is not to rebut them, but to explain why, since about 1800, there has been a fundamental shift in readers' conception of Don Quijote's mania, no longer seen as a ridiculous, albeit amiable, aberration, but as a paradigm of the human imagination's struggle to transcend the pull of base reality, and thus to achieve some form of salvation, religious, artistic, or other. This, for Ortega y Gasset in his "Meditaciones del 'Quijote'" ("Meditations on Don Quijote"), first published in 1914, is the purpose of all human culture; and Don Quijote's transformation of the windmills on the plain of Montiel symbolizes it. Since, amongst works of fiction, Don Quijote has been the single most important influence upon the development of the European novel after 1800, especially in Spain, Quixotic figures abound in the genre; and while their Quixotry is not always depicted in Ortega's grandiose terms, it tends to be seen as heroic, tragic, or at least pathetic, rather than funny.

The second factor which refines the black/white dichotomy in Don Quijote is Cervantes' conception of the kind of reality that he opposes to his hero's literary fantasies. Grey is often a more adequate symbol for it than black. One of the few chivalry books to be saved from the bonfire in the scrutiny of Don Quijote's library is Tirant lo Blanc ("Tirant the White"), about which the priest says enthusiastically (I, 6): "Aquí comen los caballeros, y duermen y mueren en sus camas, y hacen testamento antes de su muerte, con estas cosas de que todos los demás libros deste género carecen" ("Here knights eat and sleep and die in their beds, and make their wills before dying, with other such things lacking in all the rest of the genre"). Here, the priest pinpoints the stuff of humdrum, everyday life. In focusing upon it, Cervantes opened up a whole new zone of the real world as an object of fictional representation, distinctively different from the kind of exaggerated squalor in which picaresque novelists specialized, and, in dramatizing the interplay between prosaic reality and idealizing fantasy, he discovered a major theme of the European novel from, shall we say, 1800 to 1930.[14] A good example of this focus on the everyday is the last chapter of Don Quijote, in which the priest's words about knights dying in bed and making wills before dying are explicitly recalled and literally come true.

In this, one of the great death-bed scenes in literature, Don Quijote takes up an option which he has hitherto consistently rejected: fulfilling the

---

[13] Auerbach, "Dulcinea," p. 343.
[14] See Harry Levin, "The Example of Cervantes." In Contexts of Criticism (Cambridge, MA: Harvard University Press, 1957), pp. 79–96.

social, personal, and religious obligations incumbent on him as the person he really is, Alonso Quijano el Bueno. He recants his chivalric delusions, which all fly out of his head as though they had never existed, save one: the promise of the island made to Sancho. Why does he remember this particular promise? The answer has to do with the purpose of wills in the Spain of Cervantes' age: to enable the author to depart this world with conscience clear and all debts settled. It was normal for testators to make bequests to faithful retainers in a form of words somewhat similar to the following:

Ítem, es mi voluntad que de ciertos dineros que Sancho Panza, a quien en mi locura hice mi escudero, tiene, que porque ha habido entre él y mí ciertas cuentas, y dares y tomares, quiero que no se le haga cargo dellos, ni se le pida cuenta alguna, sino que si sobrare alguno después de haberse pagado de lo que le debo, el restante sea suyo, que será bien poco, y buen provecho le haga; y si como estando yo loco fui parte para darle el gobierno de la ínsula, pudiera agora, estando cuerdo, darle el de un reino, se le diera, porque la sencillez de su condición y fidelidad de su trato lo merece.

(Item, it is my will that with regard to certain moneys held by Sancho Panza, treated by me in my madness as my squire, these moneys having been the subject of certain reckonings and argy-bargy between us, I do not want him to be held liable for them, nor asked to return any of them, but rather that if there should be any money left over after he has paid himself from what I owe him, and it can't be much, good luck to him; and, remembering how in my madness I was the means of giving him an island, if I could now, in my sanity, give him a whole kingdom, I would do it, because the innocence of his character and loyalty of his service deserve it.)

The words nobly sum up the bond of affection between Don Quijote and Sancho; and they also mimic by their tortuous syntax the wording of real, historic wills. They match the substance too, with obvious differences, which reflect the partly burlesque nature of this testament. We could scarcely imagine a real scribe including in a legal document the idiosyncratic reference to madness and the concession of an island, still less using such colloquial, bread-and-butter expressions as "dares y tomares" or "buen provecho le haga." The whole passage typifies the constant tug in the novel between burlesque fantasy and fidelity to mundane particulars.

In the late twentieth century, the genre of the novel has exhibited a subversive attitude toward cultural and ideological traditions of a monolithic tendency, which harmonizes with its own experimental and self-questioning nature. The novelist – García Márquez, for example – irreverently rewrites history in a mode which blends irony, burlesque, and fantasy; he or she celebrates cultural hybridization and opposes it to exclusive purity (Salman Rushdie, Umberto Eco, Juan Goytisolo), and subjects the authoritarian discourses of the modern age to debunking parody (Rushdie, Milan Kundera). Milan Kundera sums up the Postmodernist potential of *Don Quijote* in the epilogue to his *The Book of Laughter and Forgetting*: "When Don Quixote went out into the world, that world turned into a mystery before his eyes. That is the legacy of the first European novel to the entire subsequent history of the novel. The novelist teaches its reader to comprehend the world as a question." Indeed, though Kundera does not say so explicitly, one infers him to mean that laughter is for Cervantes, as it is for Kundera himself, the means by which ideological certitudes are made to seem problematic. Now, Cervantes and his contemporaries would have found the final sentence of the above-quoted judgment quite mystifying. Considered historically, it makes no sense, though that does not stop modern literary critics interpreting *Don Quijote* from that angle. This is because novels are not inert objects; they are read in a particular ideological climate, which throws into sharp relief those features that appear particularly adapted to it. However, the "postmodernizing" inclinations of the critics have to some extent been checked by a contrary tendency, insistently attentive to the text's historical sense. Caught in this conflict, *Quijote* criticism has stood at the crossroads for a decade or so, uncertain how to proceed. Since it has traditionally taken its cue from novelists, philosophers, artists, and aestheticians, it is doubtless awaiting a new trend-setting "-ism" to give it a fresh impulse forward. As we have seen, *Don Quijote* and its readers have never failed to respond to that kind of prompting.

12

The making of Baroque poetry

MARY MALCOLM GAYLORD

Disapproval of Baroque flourishes was inscribed into modern Spanish literary historiography by Marcelino Menéndez y Pelayo at the end of the nineteenth century, so indelibly that vigorous campaigns from later readers were required to elevate major Baroque poets to the canonical status they enjoy in our time. Meeting on the tercentenary of his death, a brilliant roster of young Spanish writers adopted Luis de Góngora y Argote (1561–1627) as patron saint of their attempts to renovate poetic discourse. Because many of these twentieth-century poets – Federico García Lorca, Pedro Salinas, Jorge Guillén, Dámaso Alonso, Gerardo Diego – contributed significantly to criticism, historiography, and text diffusion, their admiration not only canonized Góngora, but also defined the standards by which seventeenth-century poets would be judged. It is one of the ironies of literary history that the very poets who revered the Baroque master's devotion to language freed from the strictures of conventional logic should also have contributed, over the longer term, to limiting appreciation of his work. In subsequent assessments, Góngora's verse is frequently cited as proof of the definitive exhaustion of classical and Petrarchan imitation. In this view, his brilliant images and dazzling verbal pyrotechnics not only say nothing new: tied to the sensory and the superficial, they seem to spin over an abyss of nothingness. If Baroque verse was "saved" by the creed of linguistic freedom, it was by the same means doomed to irrelevance. The present chapter explores the phenomenon of Baroque poetry, considering the work of major poets in the multiple contexts of literary history, poetics, and the cultural setting of poetic practice, from the last decades of the sixteenth century through the seventeenth. Although seventeenth-century poetry did not always set for itself the goal of imitating real-life characters and customs, it nonetheless left a telling reflection of the imaginative and psychic horizons that were the context of its creation. The stark contrasts, dramatic confrontations, and insoluble paradoxes that abound in Baroque verse are not exclusively literary phenomena, but rather hallmarks of cultural experience in a glorious yet troubled age.

The culture of Baroque poetry

In the early Renaissance, European poets needed not only to defend the writing of poetry as a legitimate enterprise, but to argue for the capacity of vernacular languages to treat serious subjects in an elevated style. By the end of the sixteenth century, with no small help from the rediscovered text of Aristotle's *Poetics*, which set universal poetic truth on a higher plane than historical veracity, poets had won both points. Verse composition, most of it written in the Castilian vernacular, had worked its way into virtually every sphere of Spanish life. Fernando de Herrera's *Anotaciones* (1580) to the poems of Garcilaso de la Vega, and Baltasar Gracián's treatise, *Agudeza y arte de ingenio* ("Art of Wit," 1642, 1648), bring together the leading voices of a culture which prized eloquence, to the point of claiming verbal prowess as native to Spanish genius. The energy of verse plays an important role in a host of new literary enterprises, including the developing genre we know as the novel. When shepherds of pastoral romances explore their intimate feelings in verse, their speech serves as a virtual laboratory for modern novelistic subjectivity. In the national polymetric theatre, forms and diction borrowed from many poetic codes are summoned to construct characters and their sense of themselves in social and political context. To verse composition, moreover, are entrusted subjects of great moment: saints' lives, Christian military triumphs, mystic experience, philosophical meditation, aesthetic treatises, social satire, and political invective. Not surprisingly, poetry's territorial expansion prompted concern in a number of quarters. In his 1611 *Tesoro de la Lengua Castellana o Española* ("Treasury of the Castilian or Spanish Language"), Sebastián de Covarrubias y Horozco (1539–1616) protested that vulgar versifying would besmirch the honor not only of poetry, but of the Castilian tongue, and that verse histories might cast doubt on the authenticity of Spanish New World exploits. The lexicographer's worries would pale beside outcries over Góngora's most difficult poems, circulated in manuscript around 1613–1614. That scandal, however, questioned the legitimacy of a particular kind of poetry; it did not indict an entire genre and can even be seen as evidence of widespread cultural engagement with the poet's art.

Baroque's precursor generation illustrates both the increasingly diverse demographic and the expanding thematic purview of poetic activity. Fernando de Herrera (1534–1597), the Augustinian friar Luis de León (1527–1591), and the Carmelite mystic Juan de Yepes, known as Saint John of the Cross (1542–1591), were born into middle-class families, the latter two of Jewish ancestry. Still to be found were courtier-soldier-poets of Garcilaso's stripe such as the conquistador chronicler Alonso de Ercilla y Zúñiga

(1533–1594), author of a three-volume verse saga of the conquest of Chile entitled *La Araucana* ("The Araucaniad," 1569–1589). Many aristocratic writers like the scholarly Aragonese historiographers, brothers Lupercio Leonardo (1559–1613) and Bartolomé Leonardo (1562–1631) de Argensola, engaged in royal service or ecclesiastical careers. There were self-taught poets, too, however, like Miguel de Cervantes Saavedra (1547–1616), son of an impoverished barber-surgeon, who picked up his humanist credentials on the move as a soldier in late Renaissance Italy.

Publication history offers a telling perspective on the practice of seventeenth-century poetry, both for what it records and for what it does not. It was somewhat unusual for early modern poets to publish their own lyric verse, Lope de Vega being a famous exception. Far more numerous were writers who left the gathering and printing of their poems to a surviving spouse, sibling, or disciple, as did the Argensola brothers and Góngora. The lyrics of Quevedo, who had overseen the publication in 1631 of the verses of Luis de León and Francisco de la Torre (?–1570), appeared posthumously in 1648. During their writing lives, most poets circulated their verses in manuscript among friends and patrons. Pieces penned by Góngora, Lope, and Quevedo found their way into anthologies like the *Romancero general* ("Ballad Collection"), whose first volume appeared in 1600, and the Andalusian Pedro Espinosa's influential *Flores de poetas ilustres* ("Flowers of Famous Poets," 1605). It is not unusual for poems copied into songbooks or *cancioneros* to have circulated in manuscript until the twentieth century. In seventeenth-century Spain, poetry was a shared cultural enterprise. Courts and urban centers promoted exchange and competition among poets; organized "academies" encouraged spontaneous verse improvisation, much now lost; but poetic competitions also fostered multiple treatments of selected topics. In occasional poetry, we can discern Baroque verse's ecphrastic links with such other forms of representation as painting, sculpture, architecture, and the emblem.[1]

Thus interwoven with social experience, poetry had the power to fashion public personas and, in the process, to articulate aesthetic, political, or religious creeds. The previous generation's masters of the schools of Salamanca (Luis de León) and Seville (Fernando de Herrera) were claimed as standard-bearers in contests over the cultural value of poetry. Bitterly fought language wars pitted *conceptistas*, self-appointed heirs to the word-play of fifteenth-century court poets, against Góngora and his *culterano* importers of ancient and Italian ornaments. At the head of the conservative *conceptista* band, Quevedo invoked Luis de León's Castilian purity as antidote to Góngora's strange diction. Both sides sought support from Herrera's vision of poetry as a heroic adventure for which

---

[1] See Aurora Egido, *Fronteras de la poesía en el barroco* (Barcelona: Crítica, 1990).

Spaniards were uniquely equipped. Xenophobia and Counter Reformation orthodoxy came together in the labeling of Góngora's style as *culterano*, a neologism that deforms the word *culto* ("cultivated") to make it resonate with the Castilian *luterano* ("Lutheran"), thereby branding the aesthetic offender as a foreigner, heretic, atheist.[2] For all that scandal seemed to leave little room for neutrality, the truth is that virtually all of Góngora's contemporaries show traces of his influence. While early twentieth-century critics maintained that no two poetic schools could be more distinct from one another, recent scholars have concluded that *conceptismo* and *culteranismo* differ more in theory, and in rhetorical posturing, than in practice. It would be a mistake to conclude that the dust stirred up by Baroque's *enfant terrible* worked only against the prestige of poetry. Although traditionalists and innovators might differ on the relative value of native and imported goods, all coincided in prizing poetic language as cultural treasure. In a society whose glory days of crusading in two hemispheres were receding into memory, poetry offered a substitute field for action and an alternative route to distinction. The Baroque poet no longer needed to see himself as the hero's servant: he could combine the roles of author and actor in the drama of his discourse. Whether hailed as Prince of Light or decried as Prince of Darkness, Góngora seemed to act out Herrera's vision of the Poet as Hero, hurling himself fearlessly into unknown seas and bringing back rich spoils of cultural conquest.

Puzzles of form, riddles of language

While it altered the landscape of Spanish literature dramatically, Baroque poetry, like all revolutions, turned forward in part by turning back. Like its sister arts, Baroque poetry carried on the Renaissance project of dignifying modern national cultures through a return to the ancients. By the end of the sixteenth century, poetic imitation had been raised to the level of a precept. Salamanca grammarian Francisco Sánchez de las Brozas (1523–1600) declared famously that no writer who failed to imitate the best ancients and moderns could be considered an excellent poet.[3] The serious scholars in the Baroque's precursor generation, who produced learned commentaries and literary translations as well as poetry, shared a passion for the archaeology of language: they probed the origins of words, the history of tropes, the rules and rituals of the Castilian language, and its openness

---

[2] Andrée Collard, *Nueva poesía: conceptismo, culteranismo en la crítica española* (Madrid: Castalia, 1967).

[3] Antonio Gallego Morell, ed., *Garcilaso de la Vega y sus comentaristas. Obras completas del poeta acompañadas de los textos íntegros de los comentarios de El Brocense, Fernando de Herrera, Tamayo de Vargas y Azara* (2nd. edn. Madrid: Gredos, 1972), p. 23.

to other tongues. The cult of imitation made poetry self-conscious and metapoetic by definition. Renaissance commentaries invited poets and their audiences to read like paleographers, alert to the writing beneath the writing of palimpsests. Dámaso Alonso, remarking that Góngora's retinas were as old as humanity itself, concluded mistakenly that many-layered imitation prevented the great Cordoban poet from seeing and saying anything new.[4] That new ways of seeing create their own objects and subjects is the lesson of seventeenth-century poetic practice.

Baroque poets could contemplate an array of formal options more diverse than that of any previous generation. Most continued to cultivate seven- and eleven-syllable Italian meters and the stanzaic forms naturalized into Spanish decades earlier. Of all of these, the sonnet proved the enduring favorite, taking over the classical epigram's challenge of memorable brevity. Although autobiographical collections modeled on Petrarch's *Canzoniere* were the exception, virtually every poet cultivated the form which Herrera dubbed not only the most beautiful but also the most welcoming to any subject matter. A favorite in the *comedia*, the sonnet's malleability also made it ripe for *contrafacta*, for parodic treatment, and for deformation. Among longer Italian forms favored by Renaissance poets, the Petrarchan *canción* composed of regular stanzas gradually yielded to the *silva*, whose loose structure was Góngora's choice for his *Soledades* and Lope's for a feline epic, *La Gatomaquia*. Sixteenth-century forms like the eclogue, the madrigal, and the sextina receded, while Garcilaso's *lira* virtually disappeared. Among heroic meters, Dante's *terza rima* (*tercetos*) and Ariosto's eight-line *octavas reales* (octaves) rode the crest of epic's rising popularity. The *octavas'* stately architecture with final rhymed couplet favored the sententious expressions of epic, yet the form continued to be used in lyric and bucolic poems[5] and in mythological sagas like Góngora's *Fábula de Polifemo y Galatea*. Octaves were often called upon to straddle epic and lyric genres, producing one of the period's favorite syncretisms.

With most poets moving back and forth between Italian and Castilian meters, native Spanish octosyllabic forms were cultivated by poets who might half a century before have kept to the presumed aesthetic high ground of imported types. The *romance* ("ballad") was by far the most popular of Castilian forms. In the hands of seventeenth-century poets, free-form octosyllables with assonant rhyme on even verses inherited from the anonymous medieval *Romancero viejo* ("Old Balladry") gave way to more structured four-line stanzas in the authored ballads of

---

[4] *Estudios y ensayos gongorinos* (2nd edn., Madrid: Gredos, 1960), p. 66.
[5] Tomás Navarro Tomás, *Métrica española* (6th edn., Madrid: Editorial Labor, 1983), pp. 252–263.

the *Romancero nuevo* ("New Balladry"). Epic ancestry may explain the form's availability for story telling of all kinds, but the *romance*, like its cousins the ubiquitous *redondilla* ("little round," a metric combination of four octosyllables in which the first normally rhymes with the fourth, the second with the third) and the increasingly popular ten-line *décima*, had long provided a space for lyric expression as well. This formidable threesome of forms, still the bedrock of poetic expression in Spanish, was more than a match for the sonnet's celebrated capaciousness. The *romance* in particular showed itself hospitable to every possible subject and so adaptable to every rhetorical register and purpose that it proved irresistible to the period's greatest poetic geniuses. Octosyllabic verse served as the polymetric *comedia*'s default position for representing the speech of characters drawn from a broad social spectrum. Peppered with *sung* snatches of traditional song, verse *comedias*, *autos sacramentales* (one-act plays based on the Eucharist), and *entremeses* ("interludes") evince poetry's close ties to a shared orality, to music, and to social dance. A variety of forms prospered in various settings: the ancient *cosante*, the *zéjel*, the ubiquitous *villancico*, the *letrilla*, and the *seguidilla*. Góngora and Lope show particular interest in the feminine poetic persona associated with traditional lyric forms. The latter's ballad "Piraguamonte, piragua," worked into the *comedia El Arauco domado* ("Arauco Tamed"), shows traditional oral forms open to new thematic assignments like American experience. Seventeenth-century practice and aesthetic theory embraced hybridity over purity. Most poets worked with equal ease in their culture's two major literary idioms, because they had been raised, as it were, speaking both languages. Most themes easily hurdled relaxed fences of form. At the same time, acute sensitivity to changes in code and register fostered a detachment favorable to parody and other kinds of subversion. Mismatching of form and subject fueled burlesque and satire, as in recruiting of the *romance*, traditional vehicle of Reconquest and chivalric lore, for grotesque retellings of Greek myths and for the low-life sagas of Quevedo's *jácaras*. This rhetorical and prosodic versatility has important implications for the changing nature and reach of poetic voices in the period.

For enthusiasts and detractors alike, the signal features of Baroque poetry are sensory imagery and the ingenious comparison known as the *concepto* or conceit. Baroque images rely on vivid description called *enargeia* in classical rhetoric, meant to produce effects of astonishment and awe conveyed by the Latin term *admiratio*. Among the rhetorical instruments of this project are metaphor, metonymy, synecdoche (the part is used for the whole), prosopopeia (personification), paranomasia (pun), antithesis, and paradox. These very figures, heaped up to excess, one on top of the other, rankled critics like Juan de Jáuregui, who wrote an *Antídoto contra la pestilente poesía de las "Soledades"* ("Antidote to the Pestilential Poetry of the *Soledades*"), and humanist Francisco Cascales, author of the 1634 *Cartas filológicas* ("Philological Epistles"). Beyond the tropes themselves, these critics deplored the experimenter's penchant for altering words (archaisms, foreign borrowings, neologisms, obscure learned references), for rearranging natural Spanish word order to give the effect of Latin syntax, and for failing to provide a clear structure for his poetic fables. In their eyes, Góngora's satanic verses threatened to return language to a primordial chaos where all meaning would be lost.

The controversial poet himself, however, viewed poetic difficulty in very different terms. Góngora saw in competition with the "intricate style" of ancients like Ovid the promise of honor for Spain, mental exercise, and an epistemological odyssey toward the mysterious heart of his tropes. According to Baltasar Gracián, it was the period's queen of figures, the *concepto*, that held out poetry's greatest challenge and its highest gratifications. The poet who crafts a bold conceit performs an aesthetic and intellectual feat, by expressing subtle correspondences between objects. Gracián classifies conceits produced by Roman authors (particularly the epigrammaticist Martial), Church fathers, and Castilian poets according to the kinds of relations they propose (resemblance, difference, proportion, disproportion, equivocation, dissonance, etc.) and according to whether conceits come singly or in the higher form of a complex system of tropes. For the connoisseur of wit, poetry's source lies in the educated writer's storehouse of memory, whose stock has been culled from history, sayings of famous persons, maxims, proverbs, jokes, emblems, allegories, and parables. Memory at its best is only instrumental to ingenuity: superior poetry requires the animating force of an agile intellect to arrange its treasure in arresting designs that appeal to the understanding as well as to the senses. Gracián's *Agudeza y arte de ingenio* not only proposes a logic for the entanglement in practice of *culteranismo*'s gathering of figures and learned allusions, and *conceptismo*'s signifying puzzles, but also suggests why Góngora's conceits were the codifier's favorites.

The subjects of Baroque poetry

In contemporary critical discourses, "subject" has taken on a range of meanings which encompass the subject as protagonist of consciousness, cognition, feeling, verbal expression, syntax, and subject as theme and therefore as object of thought, speech, and writing. Spanish Baroque poetry is perhaps best known for an insistent set of thematic preferences. In the seventeenth century, timeless poetic material – love, desire, Nature,

beauty, power, death – is inflected by a taste for exaggeration, disproportion, violent contrasts, and paradox. Everywhere in Baroque verse
contradictory impulses pull simultaneously in opposite directions: obsession with mortality and decay coexists with yearning for transcendence
and immortality; fascination with ugliness, deformity, monstrosity com-
petes with the lure of hyperbolic beauty; carnal embrace of the world
alternates with scornful withdrawal. It is out of this array of themes and
strategies that the other Baroque subject – the "I" of thought, of feeling,
and of discourse – emerges. If the themes of Baroque poetry are easily
listed, however, its voices prove much more elusive. Owing in part to the
profusion of available codes and to the self-consciousness built into
the poetics of imitation, what prevails in late Renaissance verse is not
the seamless identity of a chosen poetic persona, but instead a degree of
detachment from any and all conventional voices. The Baroque's poetic
speakers embrace a range of postures, from high-toned sententiousness
to satiric perversity, from liturgical reverence to ludic hedonism, from
histrionic exaltation to parodic deformation. In some cases, the joy of
playful impersonation prevails; in others, an alienated speaker who takes
little delight in play can be caught in self-castigation or mourning for lost
coherence. Perhaps most arresting in the period's distinctive voices are
the ways poets negotiate tensions between aesthetic and didactic aims.
Although modern readers may find it difficult to reconcile sensual means
with sober ends, many Baroque poems hang on this very contradiction.
Often trivialized because of its seemingly idle delight in ornamentation,
Baroque poetry in fact uses that surface veneer strategically, cultivating
the very desires it aims to subvert, luring readers into carefully laid pleasure traps where, once ensnared, they will be read bitter lessons of sin
and death. Art thus simulates the human drama of illusion (*engaño*) and
disillusion (*desengaño*). It hoodwinks the reader, but not merely to make
the medicine go down in a swallow of honey: it deceives in order to unde-
ceive; it makes life's truths taste more bitter by contrast, so as to urge
discretion and prudence.

The themes and voices chosen by poetic giants Luis de Góngora
y Argote, Lope Félix de Vega Carpio (1562–1635), and Francisco de
Quevedo y Villegas (1580–1645) suggest the richness and complexity of
poetic practice in the Baroque era. The irresistible pull of urban and court
life brought these writers together in Madrid, where theatres, open-air
corrales, academies, and booksellers provided many venues for artistic
expression and made literary rivalry a feature of everyday life. Although
none of the three would have accepted his likeness to any other, four centuries of hindsight allow us to appreciate the cultural ground and poetic
practices they shared. As readers and writers, they were as adventurous
as they were prolific, each drawn to a range of literary genres extending

well beyond lyric verse. Humanist heirs to ancient, Italian, and Spanish Renaissance classics, they were equally attuned to native Castilian *conceptismo*. In reworking themes from a shared multi-cultural storehouse – pastoral, epic, satire, mythography, Platonism, Stoicism, historical legend, Moorish lore – all became masters of a vast imaginative repertory. Like their contemporary Miguel de Cervantes Saavedra (1547–1616) – best known for his parodic refurbishing of novelistic discourse, but a reinventor of poetic languages as well, notably in the 1614 burlesque epic *Viaje del Parnaso* ("Voyage to Parnassus") – all proved to be master deconstructors of inherited codes. As with *Don Quixote*'s author, self-conscious detachment dictated that their imitations would swing between jest (*burlas*) and earnest (*veras*). Yet, large-scale resemblances notwithstanding, each crafted poetic personas virtually impossible to confuse with any other.

While some would hesitate to anoint Luis de Góngora y Argote as the finest poet of his age, few would deny that he was the most influential. The particular stamp of learned ornament and linguistic difficulty which he impressed on inherited material inspired a host of imitators inside Spain, elsewhere in Europe, and in Spanish America. Published piecemeal or circulated in manuscript during his lifetime, Góngora's works were gathered after his death in 1627 by Juan López de Vicuña under the honorific title *Obras en verso del Homero español* ("Verses of the Spanish Homer") and again in 1633 by Gonzalo de Hozes y Córdoba. In addition, the major poems inspired learned commentaries of the kind that had canonized the poetry of Garcilaso. As is suggested by a title like José Pellicer de Salas y Tovar's 1630 *Lecciones solemnes a las Obras de don Luis de Góngora, Píndaro Andaluz, Príncipe de los Poetas Líricos de España* ("Solemn Lessons on the Works of Góngora, the Andalusian Pindar and Prince of the Lyric Poets of Spain"), most of these were celebratory; but lively controversy about his poetics flourished long after Góngora's death.

Most read in our time is the early Góngora, the one hailed in his own day as Prince of Light. This is the poet of the 1580s, 1590s, and the first years of the new century, who turned out polished sonnets on the one hand, and ingenious Castilian *romances* and *letrillas* on the other. In the period's favorite Italianate form, Don Luis took up standard Petrarchan and classical motifs, dressing them in artifice of unprecedented brilliance. So it is with the famous pair of poems which rework Garcilaso's sonnet 23 ("En tanto que de rosa y d'azucena"), itself glossed on a celebrated epigram ("Collige, virgo, rosas") by the Roman Ausonius. Following Garcilaso, who sandwiched his injunction to the lady to make the most of youth between celebration of her beauty and wry warnings about mutability, Góngora bends the well-worn topos to bold new uses. In "Ilustre y hermosísima María" ("Illustrious and Most Beautiful Maria"), he heightens effects of light and color emanating from the lady's presence, rearranging Garcilaso's argument so that the poem culminates in a joyous double imperative to pleasure. "Mientras por competir con tu cabello" ("While to Compete with Your Hair") exaggerates Garcilaso's flattery by imagining the lady enjoying disdainful triumph over lesser beauties (gold, lilies, carnations, crystal), only to reframe it with hints about transitory loveliness as a dark passage into decay and nothingness. A playful Renaissance *carpe diem* is thus converted to a menacing Baroque *memento mori*. Taken together, these sonnets offer an early indication of one of the starkest contrasts of Góngora's verse, which offers cornucopias of poetic tribute to beauty with one hand and snatches them away – or turns them to dust – with the other. Foreshadowing the dark intensity of mature sonnets like "En este occidental, en este, oh Licio, / climatérico lustro de tu vida" ("In this western, in this, oh Licio, declining stage of life") and "Menos solicitó veloz saeta" ("Less did a swift arrow seek"), "La dulce boca que a gustar convida" ("The sweet mouth that invites to taste") works the Petrarchan topos of the beloved's mouth into a scene of mythical danger and biblical temptation, as the poet cautions lovers that Cupid lurks in the garden of a face, like a serpent ready to unleash deadly venom. The double agenda and rhetorical syncretism of this youthful sonnet reveal the contradictory lines of force – sententiousness and sensuality, scriptural and classical allusion, popular phrase and learned subject – that generate many later works.

This disconcerting mixture of ingredients has prompted many questions about Gongora's poetic persona. To some, the conventional lyric subject, understood as subject of feeling, seems to shine by its absence in his work. The sonnets, in no sense a Petrarchist *canzoniere*, do not recount a sentimental history, even by implication. Many of the finest are heroic, like the 1585 "¡Oh excelso muro, de torres coronadas . . . !" ("Oh lofty wall, by towers crowned") addressed to the poet's native Córdoba, or funereal, like "Esta en forma elegante, oh peregrino" ("This in elegant form, oh pilgrim") for the painter El Greco. Over the full range of their conventional subject matter, moreover, Góngora's sonnets focus little attention on the poetic speaker. When Góngora's "I" makes itself heard as such, it often does so belatedly, as in the 1594 "Descaminado, enfermo, peregrino" ("Wayward, sick, a pilgrim"), where the speaker emerges from a dense thicket of tropes to announce his own death. It would be a mistake to read in this coy first person a general absence of affect. What the sonnets show is a tendency, which flowers in later poems, to allegorize sentimental experience in fables of Desire, Time, and Art.

Perhaps even more popular in his own time than the sonneteer was the Góngora whose *romances* and *letrillas* appeared in collections from the 1590s onward. While their tone is generally light, poems like

"Que pida a un galán Minguilla" ("That Minguilla should ask a gallant gentleman"), "Ándeme yo caliente / y ríase la gente" ("Let me stay warm, and let people laugh"), and "Da bienes Fortuna que no están escritos" ("Fortune bestows unexpected gifts") reveal a mordant muse aimed at social pretensions, courtship behavior, avarice, even New World greed, as in "Escuchadme un rato atentos" ("Listen to me carefully for a while"). From his earliest ballads, Góngora uses mythological figures to burlesque love themes: Cupid in "Ciego que apuntas y atinas" ("You, blind man who aim and hit"); Hero and Leander in "Arrojóse el mancebito / al mar de los atunes" ("The little lad hurled himself into a sea of tuna") and "Aunque entiendo poco griego" ("Though I understand but little Greek"); and Pyramus and Thisbe in "De Tisbe y Píramo quiero" ("Of Thisbe and Pyramus I will") and in "La ciudad de Babilonia" ("The city of Babylon"), a 1618 tour de force considered by its author and many readers to be his parodic masterpiece. While chivalric legends sometimes receive parodic treatment, they also provide the motive for love ballads of vivid sensuality like the 1602 ballad of Angelica and Medoro entitled "En un pastoral albergue" ("In a pastoral inn"), whose ingenious antitheses were much admired by Gracián. Among poems that treat Moorish–Christian relations in a fashion imitated from Ariosto's *Orlando Furioso* and the anonymous novella, *Historia del Abencerraje y la hermosa Jarifa* ("History of Abencerraje and the Lovely Jarifa"), were a Gongorine invention, the ballad of captives, as in "Amarrado al duro banco" ("Lashed to the hard seat"), and poems about Spaniards in North Africa, including "Entre los sueltos cabellos / de los vencidos cenetes" ("Among the loose tresses of the vanquished Zenetes") and "Servía en Orán al rey" ("In Oran served his King"). The earliest ballads introduce a literary self-consciousness that deepens in the mature Góngora. *Romancillos* like "La más bella niña" ("The most beautiful girl") and "Lloraba la niña / (y tenía razón)" ("The girl was crying, and for good reason") explore the aesthetic possibilities offered by the feminine voice of Spanish folk lyric. By lacing traditional forms with learned allusions and conceptual play, Góngora's ballads play host to highly self-conscious exercises in poetic imitation. From so light a form as the *letrilla*, the arch-poet manages to generate metapoetic musings – "Manda Amor en su fatiga / que se sienta y no se diga" ("Love commands in his exhaustion that one feel and not speak") – and teasingly raises the possibility that voice and feeling may not coincide.

The two poems which earned Don Luis the dubious title of Prince of Darkness are long narrative compositions which set stories of love and lovers against the backdrop of a grandly conceived Nature. Both are densely figured, syntactically difficult, and relentlessly intertextual, yet each presents a very different formal aspect: the 504 lines of the *Fábula de Polifemo y Galatea* fall neatly into 63 *octavas reales*, while the irregular *silva* stanzas of the *Soledades* wind through some 2,000 lines before the second *Soledad* breaks off, failing to complete what may have been a four-part plan. *Polifemo*'s structure rests on its Ovidian pretext, the familiar fable of the youth Acis who succeeds in wooing the elusive nymph Galatea, only to lose his life to the jealousy of the singing Cyclops. By contrast, the *Soledades* appear quite amorphous; their openness embraces a number of shorter forms like the ode, the folk dance-song, and the epithalamium. Although the longer poem suffers from no want of literary precedents, it has no one privileged source and no clear structural design.

The two great poems place their narratives and their difficulty at the service of serious meditations on the aims of poetry and the powers of language, as Góngora himself insisted apropos of the *Soledades* in his famous "Carta . . . en respuesta" ("Letter . . . in response"). In both poems, frustrated lovers take on poetic importance as frustrated speakers or singers. Shipwrecked and washed up on a nameless shore, the nameless youth of the *Soledades* wanders through a world of mountain folk, goat-herds, and villagers, toward a rustic wedding. Throughout, as witness to Nature, rituals, and a discourse on the greed-driven New World conquest, he says nothing, either unceremoniously interrupted or silenced by admiration. As a would-be speaker, the estranged wanderer stands in for the poet: like his wordless pilgrim, Góngora the narrator seems to hang back, letting the world and its images speak for him. In *Polifemo*, the contrast between sound and silence becomes starker, thanks to bold jux-tapositions of beauty and ugliness, natural eroticism and tortured passion, cornucopian Nature and cataclysmic violence. The poet sets the sizzling landscape of a Sicilian seaside harvest, where Galatea fends off hordes of suitors before she succumbs to wordless wooing from Acis, against the nocturnal darkness of Polifemo's cave, the shaggy mountainscape of his form, and the destructive force of his passion. A set of ingenious tropes – the barbarous noise Polifemo produces with the bellows of his mouth, the thunderclap of his voice – make the giant's monstrous music into a figure for a new conception of poetic language that privileges cacophony, opacity, disproportion, and shocking contrasts.

If Cervantes was recognized as his age's master of narrative prose, Lope de Vega Carpio was its native genius of verse. While Góngora stood unri-valed in artistic difficulty, Lope was hailed as the incarnation of natural fluency across the full range of poetic idioms available to him. As a poet, he has seemed to many a kind of anti-Góngora: in contrast to the latter's studied impersonality, Lope offers the comforts of colloquial diction and folk musicality. If the Baroque's Prince of Darkness evoked the threaten-ing specters of elitism, foreignness, even atheism, its Monster of Nature (Lope) emerged as arch-champion of Spanish, Old Christian, and popular values. The myth that Lope generated his verses effortlessly does a great disservice to his range and seriousness. Although largely self-taught, the people's poet read as widely in the classics as his most learned contemporaries and shared their acute self-consciousness. On the matter of Lope's proverbial facility, it is impossible to argue with the stereotypes. The 1,500 plays the "Fénix" claimed to have written, averaging 3,000 lines each, add up to some four and a half *million* lines, making the dramatist already an immensely prolific author of verse. Lope contributed in equal abundance to many other poetic fields. He published three volumes of *Rimas*: a 1602 collection of Petrarchan love sonnets seasoned with a dollop of characteristic playfulness; the 1614 *Rimas sacras*, which turn the same secular idiom to religious ends; and the 1634 *Rimas humanas y divinas del Licenciado Tomé de Burguillos* ("Human and Divine Verses of Master Tomé de Burguillos") which ventriloquize parody of Petrarchism and satire of court life through a poetic *alter ego*. From early pastoral and Moorish examples, the *romance* remains a favorite form which the poet intersperses through his plays and uses in his 1624 *Romancero espiritual* to sing the Passion of Jesus in ballads thick with images of Jesus' crown of thorns, prisoner's lashes, and wounds.

Lope stands out among his contemporaries for his devotion to the pastoral mode. Bucolic verses alternate with prose in two pastoral romances – *La Arcadia* (1598) and *Los pastores de Belén* ("Shepherds at Bethlehem," 1612), Spain's only pastoral novel *a lo divino* – and stand alone in three late works: *Amarilis* (1633), *Filis* (1635), and the posthumous *La vega del Parnaso* ("The Meadow of Parnassus"). Stronger yet was Lope's commitment to epic, visible in five major poems – *La Dragontea*, a 1598 saga of Sir Francis Drake's outrages against Spanish New World fleets; *El Isidro*, a 1599 hagiographic celebration of San Isidro Labrador; a 1602 Ariosto spin-off, *La hermosura de Angélica* ("The Beauty of Angelica"); a 1609 Tasso imitation, *Jerusalén conquistada* ("Jerusalem Conquered"); and a 1634 burlesque epic with feline protagonists, *La Gatomaquia*. These poems put on display Lope's versatility, the dizzying spectrum of his subject choices, and his fascination with larger-than-life figures of heroism, piety, and sensuality. Nowhere is the taste for hyperbole more visible than in the *Jerusalén conquistada*, where Lope attempts to out-do Tasso by writing the Castilian king Alfonso VIII anachronistically into the history of the third Crusade. The poem's twenty books, running to more than 22,000 verses, multiply episodic detours, appropriating material from other genres, as happens with the pastoral "chain of love" that binds its major figures together in frustrated desire, and with the Spanish pilgrim's ballad-like recapitulation of the legendary King Rodrigo's fateful passion, in the epic *mise en abîme* of Book VI. Lope's cast of thousands includes supernatural figures like the Virgin and the Devil, the seven deadly sins, and the cross-dressing warrior princess, Ismenia. No shorter on gore than on romance, the poem has Saladin stage a gladiator-style contest between "Asian barbarians" and Christian captives. In *Jerusalén conquistada*, Lope vigorously champions Spanish heroism, not only letting it triumph over Muslim strength, but allowing it to surpass foreign incarnations of Christian purpose like Richard the Lion-Heart.

The mixed forms of epic and pastoral play to one of Lope's greatest strengths by affording him occasions to speak through a staggering variety of personas – including heroes, sinners, monsters, and women. Ludic delight in endless impersonation gives the monumental poetic corpus a Protean quality. In this relentless mask-switching, the poet's intrusiveness is just as striking as his elusiveness: in the guise of the Moor Zaide or the farmer Belardo, Lope uses poetic dress-up to advertise scandalous episodes in his notoriously eventful love-life and to broadcast his mid-life sinner's conversion to Catholic piety. On his lovers, he bestows literary names – Marfisa, Filis, Camila Lucinda, Amarilis – while himself resorting to parodic pseudonyms like Tomé de Burguillos or cultivating the resonances of his various names. Yet behind the screens of versatility and exhibitionism, Lope plays for high stakes in a game which positions him to take personal possession of the poetic idioms he speaks with such fluency. Punning on his evocative surname Vega ("meadow"), in one of the famous "Manso" sonnets, the poet begs his beloved, imagined as a sheep led astray by another shepherd, to come back to her rightful owner and his *vega*. In a ceremony of possession that is both erotic and literary, the poet nominates himself as poet-laureate of Nature. Like his identification with Old Christian Spanish values, Lope's naturalness is at once a fact and a pose. The strategic posture has inadvertently caused a genius to be trivialized by his own fictions of poetic power.

A full generation younger than Góngora and Lope, Francisco de Quevedo y Villegas emerged as a poet of singular talent when seventeen of his poems were published in the 1605 *Flores de poetas ilustres de España*. The son of aristocrats, he enjoyed the social and educational advantages of high rank (study at the Jesuits' Imperial College in Madrid and at the universities of Alcalá de Henares and Valladolid; diplomatic service in Italy), along with a great degree of freedom to devote himself to literature. Access to the inner circles of power proved to be a privilege with heavy costs in later years, when the enmity of Felipe IV's powerful favorite, the Count-Duke of Olivares, earned the writer four years in an underground cell at the Convent of San Marcos in León. Quevedo's work, which Jorge Luis Borges famously called not merely an *obra* ("oeuvre") but a whole literature in itself, encompasses prose genres as diverse as picaresque, Lucianesque satire, biblical exegesis, historiography, political theory, and moral tract. The range of his verse production, little of which saw its way into print during the poet's lifetime, is no less vast. Posthumous collections of poems brought out in 1648 and 1670 distribute very diverse compositions among nine deities of *El Parnaso español*, Spanish poetry's mythic summit.

While Quevedo shares many forms and subjects with his contemporaries – Petrarchan love-language, satiric ballads, ancient myth, chivalric fable, Spanish legend – his poems span the greatest emotional and rhetorical distance of any Baroque poet. With the extraordinary sonnet "Cerrar podrá mis ojos" ("Will close my eyes"), he rises to heights of the Neoplatonic sublime not reached by any of his fellows. In "¡Ay, Floralba!" he approaches the unspeakable dream of consummated desire with the exquisite instrument of the conceit. At his misogynist worst, however, this same poet reviles beauties and hags with equal venom, or else – slumming in his signature picaresque *jácaras* – revels in the tawdry amours of social outcasts. In heroic and moral sonnets such as "Buscas en Roma a Roma, oh peregrino" ("You look for Rome in Rome, oh pilgrim"), "¡Ah de la vida!" ("Is anyone in this life?"), and "Fue sueño Ayer" ("Yesterday was a dream"), Quevedo plumbs yawning depths of despair over the course of history and the transience of all things human. Yet the same poet descends to biting satire and a filthy obscenity that keeps its expressions out of most anthologies. These arresting images and violent swings have fed a controversy that lies, unresolved, at the heart of Quevedo studies: are his extreme expressions fueled by emotion or by intellect?

Much ink has been spilled to argue the intensity of this poet's erotic passion or his experience of *desengaño* since Dámaso Alonso first coined the phrase "el desgarrón afectivo" ("the emotional tear or ripping") to describe the dramatic effects worked by Quevedo's language.[6] In recent years more critics have taken Paul Julian Smith's view that Quevedo has earned his reputation as a love poet "not because of the authenticity or originality of his sentiment, but because of the consummate skill of his expression. Others may have loved more sincerely, few have loved so eloquently."[7] Calculated deployment of tropes ingeniously refurbished and intricately interwoven marks the poet's competitive relation to the shared code of his famous love sonnets. Pointing to twenty-two years of constant passion in the sequence entitled *Canta sola a Lisi*, Quevedo seems to covet Petrarch's place as lord of the love lyric. Ignacio Navarrete, however, argues that this Baroque poet denaturalizes the Petrarchan myth in a subtle parody of the lover caught in the contradictions of Neoplatonic sensuality.[8] As Quevedo twists the beloved's eyes, hair, and mouth

---

[6] *Poesía española: ensayo de métodos y límites estilísticos* (Madrid: Gredos, 1950), pp. 531–618.

[7] *Quevedo on Parnassus: Allusive Context and Literary Theory in the Love Lyric* (London: Modern Humanities Research Association, 1987), p. 175.

[8] *Orphans of Petrarch: Poetry and Theory in the Spanish Renaissance* (Berkeley: University of California Press, 1994), pp. 205–233.

or the lover's soul into conceptual knots, the poet's favorite tropes for erotic "error" not only reveal his signature aversion to all things commercial, foreign, and novel, but sketch the outlines of a new erotic and poetic myth. Sea tempests, shipwreck, drowning, lust for gold – in the famous sonnet "En crespa tempestad del oro undoso" ("In a kinky tempest of wavy gold") – bring together the guilty excesses of sexual desire, greed, and artistic presumption in the familiar figures of Leander, Icarus, the Phoenix, Midas, and Tantalus. The suggestion that these mythic seafarers mask gold-crazed conquistadors and merchant navigators emerges full-blown in "En breve cárcel traigo aprisionado" ("In a brief prison I hold captive"), where the poet recruits the venerable topos of the love prison to style himself as an *indiano*, a returning American traveler or colonist, a proverbial *nouveau riche* social misfit widely satirized for unreliable boasts and absurd pretensions. In this contrived self-immolation, Quevedo makes his Petrarchan persona into an emblem of futile desires, erotic, political, and poetic.

With the satiric, moral, and metaphysical verse, critics have less frequently seen contests between intellect and emotion. Quevedo's extraordinary satiric way with metaphor has been shrewdly dissected by Maurice Molho and Lía Schwartz.[9] Wit forges powerful alliances with class snobbery and racism in celebrated pieces like the *letrilla satírica* "Poderoso caballero es don Dinero" ("A powerful lord is Mr. Money") – which uses the mother–daughter dialogue of traditional lyric to script a perverse confession of love for money, the foundation of the new aristocracy – or the sonnet "Érase un hombre a una nariz pegado" ("There once was a man attached to a nose") in its grotesquely anti-Semitic caricature. In a more elevated mode, wit underwrites lessons from the Stoic *ars bene moriendi* ("art of dying well") laced with synesthesias and antitheses in "Retirado en la paz de estos desiertos" ("Withdrawn to the peace of this deserted place"), anguish over Time's flight in "¡Ah de la vida!" with its stark poetry of grammar, or disenchanted national pride in the psalm "Miré los muros de la patria mía" ("I looked at the walls of my fatherland"). The contemplative intensity of these poems points toward major Baroque figures who lie beyond the scope of this chapter. Pedro Calderón de la Barca (1600–1681) and Mexican "Tenth Muse" Sor Juana Inés de la Cruz (1651–1695) continue to mine the linguistic riches of *culteranismo* and *conceptismo*, using them to stretch the capacity of the Spanish language, to power metaphysical inquiry, and to dismantle poetry's most tenacious myths.

---

[9] Maurice Molho, *Semántica y poética: Góngora, Quevedo* (Barcelona: Crítica, 1977); Lía Schwartz Lerner, *Metáfora y sátira en la obra de Quevedo* (Madrid: Taurus, 1984).

13

The development of national theatre

MARGARET R. GREER

A national, or nationalizing, theatrical tradition developed in early modern Spain through the confluence of several forces: sixteenth-century economic growth and urbanization, local performance traditions, and pan-European interest in renewing classical dramatic forms. The *comedia nueva* that emerged became *the* popular entertainment form for more than a century.

The paradigmatic *comedia* is a three-act, polymetric drama, freely combining comic and tragic elements, noble and baseborn personae in fast-paced plots, in which character is developed more through action than through introspective monologues. *Comedia* serves as the generic term, applied to comic, tragicomic, and tragic works alike. Their thematic range is considerable, including romantic intrigues, "cape and sword" plays, saints' lives, historical, mythological, and biblical themes. Short satirical and burlesque pieces – *entremeses*, *mojigangas*, and *bailes* – entertained the audience between acts and concluded the performance.

History and development

One of the earliest statements of dramatic theory in Renaissance Europe was published by Bartolomé de Torres Naharro (*c.* 1485 – *c.* 1520). Naharro did most of his writing in Rome, where he served in a cardinal's household and wrote the comedias *Soldadesca*, *Trophea*, *Jacinta*, *Tinellaria*, and *Himenea* between 1509 and 1516. Moving to Naples and the service of Fabrizio Colonna, he published his collected dramatic and poetic works as the *Propalladia* (1517). In its *Prohemio* (preface), he briefly summarizes certain classical precepts – the distinction between comedy and tragedy; Cicero's definition of comedy as an imitation of life, a mirror of customs, an image of truth; the six types of comedy, the Horatian recommendation of five-act works, and the importance of decorum – concluding "Todo lo cual me parece más largo de contar que necesario de oir" ("All of which seems to me longer in telling than necessary to hear").[1] His own prescription for the *comedia*, elaborated before the rediscovery of Aristotle's *Poetics*, drew on his experience of performance in private palaces and on observation of the classical models of Plautus and Terence and their contemporary Italian translations. Approving the five-act division, he labels them "jornadas," the length of a day's travel or work, or an audience's attention. Naharro divides comedy into two types: (1) "comedia a noticia," inspired by observed reality, like his *Soldadesca* ("Soldiery") about recruiting troops, or the *Tinellaria*, bawdy, irreverent, polyglot dialogues between the larcenous beneficiaries in the servants' dining quarters (*tinelo*) of a cardinal's palace; and (2) "comedias a fantasía," fictional inventions "with the color of truth," such as *Seraphina* and *Himenea*. For the latter, his most famous work, he drew inspiration for Himeneo and Febea's passion and the servants' roles from *Celestina*, complicated the plot with her brother's obsession with honor, but brought it all to a happy ending. Naharro apparently returned to Spain thereafter, perhaps to Seville, where a second edition of the *Propalladia* was published in 1520. His popularity in Spain is attested in multiple editions before 1559, when it was included in the first Index of Prohibited Books.

Seville and Valencia

Seville and Valencia were important centers for the early development of popular theatre within Spain. As merchant cities that prospered from trade with the Americas and the Mediterranean, respectively, they were open to new social and cultural developments. There and elsewhere in the peninsula, popular religious theatre was the *comedia*'s most important forerunner. A talented contributor was Diego Sánchez de Badajoz (*c.* 1500 – *c.* 1552), who wrote a series of religious "farces" that joined theology, social critique, and bawdy humor into fluid, didactic entertainment, and also penned a number of brief secular pieces. As secular elements of religious theatre multiplied and Counter Reformation pressure to reform clerical discipline increased, these performances were moved from churches to streets and plazas in cities across Spain throughout the sixteenth century.

Corpus Christi performances

One branch of the religious theatre tradition, the Corpus Christi theatrical performances, was particularly important to the growth of the theatrical

[1] Cited in Federico Sánchez Escribano and Alberto Porqueras Mayo, eds., *Preceptiva dramática española del Renacimiento y el Barroco* (2nd. edn. Madrid: Gredos, 1971), p. 63.

institution. The celebration of Corpus Christi – belief in the true presence of the body and blood of Christ in the bread and wine of Communion – was instituted in the thirteenth century. As the culminating point of the liturgical year and a commemoration of the triumph of truth over heresy, this annual celebration of the Eucharist was marked with great popular enthusiasm in Spain, almost as a national rather than a universal obser-vance.[2] The Corpus performances provided a constitutive ritual for the Catholic faith and also for the socio-political community. The symbolism of Corpus Christi is that of society viewed as one body, whose various members are all joined in that of Christ. After the Mass celebrating the sacred presence in the Communion host, it was born in a resplendent mon-strance in procession through the city streets, accompanied by high local or national officials, members of the religious orders, artisans' guilds, and other local groups, and, to make of it a joyful as well as solemn celebra-tion, by variously costumed dancers, a *tarasca* or giant serpent animated by human figures, and by *rocas* or platforms bearing holy statues. The procession ritualistically marked out the consecrated heart of the commu-nity, as well as subtly defining the hierarchical organization of its society, through the order of its participating groups and the route it took. Admin-istration of the festivities eventually passed from the Church to the munic-ipal government in all Spanish cities, and the brilliance of its celebration became a point of local pride. Once the holy statues were replaced by live figures, the dramatic component of the celebration gradually evolved from simple representations of biblical events, saints' lives, and morality plays into elaborate and sophisticated allegorical presentations of Chris-tian history and Catholic doctrine, poetic "sermons in verse" with lavish scenic effects, costuming, music, and dance. By the time of Calderón, these *autos sacramentales* ("sacred dramas") were the highlight of the annual theatrical calendar in Madrid. They were performed on movable carts in city plazas, first for the king, then for councils and public at various points around the city, and, on succeeding days, in the *corrales* (public theatres) and in nearby towns as well. Contracts for performing the *autos* in Madrid and its environs were also central to the financial viability of theatrical companies that secured them.

Emergence of theatre companies

The Corpus Christi performances were equally crucial much earlier in the history of early modern Spanish theatre. Competition between cities to present the most impressive celebration with the most lavish costuming

[2] Bruce Wardropper, *Historia de la poesía lírica a lo divino en la cristiandad occidental* (Madrid: Revista de Occidente, 1954), p. 35.

and best actors is documented as early as 1532 for Seville. Initially, the *autos* were organized, financed, and performed by the local guilds, who also competed to outdo each other. To accomplish this required regular practice and more opportunities for performance by the actors, guild members who, performing as a side-line to their trade, had demonstrated particular histrionic gifts. Scattered references to actors indicate that small local companies organized and performed at least sporadically by the decade of the 1530s, as early as those in Italy that would later travel to Spain.

One company was that of Lope de Rueda (d. 1565–1566), whose career linked the early semi-professional performance tradition to the professional theatre that followed. A native of Seville, Rueda was probably acting in the 1530s, and documents he signed for the Corpus performances there show that he had his own company by 1542–1543. Rueda and his fellow actors were artisans turned actors; he was a goldbeater by trade and others were listed as a silk-spinner, a "dancer and drummer," a stocking-maker, and a carpenter. Cervantes, who said Rueda brought the *comedia* out of swaddling clothes, described his limited resources, the ingenuity of his performances, and his genius at portraying a catalogue of character types. Rueda's skill and career illuminates why, in Spain, theatre-company owners were called *autores de comedias*; first, as actor–director, he was a theatrical entrepreneur, the "author" of each performance; and secondly, he was an author of playscripts in the traditional sense, writing comedies (e.g. *Medora*, *Eufemia*, *Armelina*, schematic versions of Italian comedies drawn from novella plots), pastoral colloquies, and a series of *pasos*, comic interludes that accompanied the *pasos*, brief sketches of rustic farce and folkloric tricks on an array of simpletons. They are the forerunners to the burlesque *entremeses* that in the years to come would be standard accompaniments to comedies and tragedies, public and court plays and Corpus *autos*. His plays were scripts for performance, for entertaining spectacle, without literary ambitions and not intended for publication, but, after Rueda's death, the Valencian bookseller–editor Juan de Timoneda polished and published his works and those of another Sevillian *autor de comedias*, Alonso de la Vega. Rueda's company played in palaces and toured cities around Spain; he signed a long-term contract to write and perform Corpus *autos* in Valladolid, and was planning to equip a theatre there when he died. His career thus illustrates the symbiotic relationship between religious performances and popular secular theatre; to ensure the presence of the best itinerant company to perform Corpus *autos*, municipalities allowed more frequent performances, beyond those on holidays, for a paying public whose growing taste for theatre they fed. A similar symbiosis would facilitate the establishment of public theatres in Lima and Mexico at the end of the sixteenth century.

Diverse contributors shaped the theatrical mix in the second half of that century. Juan de Timoneda's own texts – particularly *Las tres comedias* ("The Three Comedies," 1559), adaptations of Italian erudite prose comedies to Spanish taste – suited his Valencian bourgeois class and the needs of the new itinerant companies that toured cities across Spain, seeking – and forging – their public. Several writers from literary circles in Valencia and Seville wrote works that experiment with modified forms of classical, Senecan, and Renaissance drama. In Valencia, Francisco Agustín Tárrega wrote ten plays, introducing a number of the dramatic formulas that would persist in the *comedia* in plays such as *El prado de Valencia* ("Valencian Promenade"). *Los amantes* ("The Lovers"), the only surviving tragedy of Andrés Rey de Artieda (1544–1613), is the story of lovers fatally separated by a father's avarice. Gaspar de Aguilar makes a merchant the protagonist of *El mercader amante* ("The Merchant Lover") and hints at the direction Spanish theatre might have taken had it continued independent development in the more mercantile atmosphere of Valencia. Another Valencian, Cristobal Virués (1550–1609), left a series of bloody tragedies, *Elisa Dido*, *La gran Semíramis* ("The Great Semiramis"), *Atila furioso* ("Furious Attila"), and *La cruel Casandra* ("Cruel Casandra"), including one, *La infelice Marcela* ("Unhappy Marcela"), that introduces popular types.

Juan de la Cueva (1543–1612), from a distinguished Seville family, wrote comedies and tragedies based on Greek and Roman stories. He also employed Spanish history and legend, as would many future playwrights, to shape a national memory through popular theatre. The plays of both Virués and Cueva may be related to political divisions and intrigues in the reign of Felipe II.

The reach of theatre was also extended by Jesuit school drama and by Italian theatre companies. Jesuit schools, established from 1548 on in many cities, regularly used drama in Latin, and sometimes in the vernacular. This cultivated a wider familiarity with drama and integrated it into community life. The arrival of Alberto Naseli (called "Ganassa") and other Italian actors/directors who traveled to Spain and beyond in the 1560s and 1570s with their mix of Italian comedies, *commedia dell'arte* performances, puppets, and acrobats increased the available repertoire and professionalization of the theatre. Ganassa also advanced the establishment of permanent commercial playhouses and secured permission for regular mid-week performances.

Madrid

Two other factors of crucial importance in the second half of the sixteenth century were: (1) Felipe II's establishment of Madrid as the capital of the monarchy in 1561, and its consequent growth from 9,000 to 80,000 inhabitants in the following forty years, overtaking all cities but Seville, so that this new court city became the principal hub of theatrical activity; and (2) the initiative of charitable brotherhoods (*Cofradías*) in linking theatrical performance to the financing of hospitals, orphanages, and other charities they supported in Madrid and other Spanish cities. Charitable brotherhoods began to sponsor theatrical performances in their courtyards or other rented yards in Madrid in the 1560s. After some initial squabbling, the two principal *Cofradías* agreed to the joint sponsorship of two *corrales*, eventually the Corral de la Cruz established in 1579 and the Corral del Príncipe shortly thereafter. In exchange for official permission for more frequent performances, the *Cofradías* agreed to share part of the proceeds with other charities, including the Hospital General. Over the years, to guarantee a stable income for the hospitals despite fluctuating *corral* receipts, their administration was entrusted to lessee-managers responsible to the Protector of the hospitals, a member of the Council of Castile. The *censor* and *fiscal* charged with reading and authorizing playtexts for performance also answered to the Protector. Payment for the lease of the *corrales* went directly to the city treasury, which guaranteed a fixed subsidy to the hospitals, and municipal dignitaries had a well-positioned box in each theatre from which to view the plays. This association of the public theatres with the hospitals and their incorporation as revenue producers under city and royal administration were important counters to continued moralist objections to the theatre. Theatres were, however, closed during Lent, and during periods of mourning for royal deaths, closures sometimes extended by moralist opposition. Such opposition caused brief attempts to ban actresses, but the compromise reached required that only married women be allowed on stage.

Corrales

In Madrid and other Spanish cities, the *corrales de comedias* were the principle venue for *comedia* performance from about 1580 onward. The designation derives from the fact that earlier, temporary theatres were erected in the patio or courtyard (*corral*) of multi-family houses, inns, or hospitals, and the arrangement they afforded was carried over to buildings specifically adapted for theatrical performances. The rectangular open-air patio was surrounded on three sides by viewing windows or boxes opened or constructed in the neighboring houses and the building's façade; the stage and multi-story acting and tiring room structure stood on the fourth side, opposite the façade. Paying the relatively low entry cost (about one-fifth of a laborer's daily wage) entitled men to stand in the patio, which could be covered by an awning to protect them from the sun; if they paid an extra fee, they could sit on benches in the raked seating that lined the lateral walls. Women paid about one-fifth more, entered by a different doorway and were seated in the *cazuela* ("stewpot"), a gallery that occupied the second level of the façade. There was an upper-level *tertulia* ("gallery") for clerics. Nobility (men and women) and other wealthy viewers or dignitaries occupied the windows and boxes, at much higher prices. Seating arrangements for viewing thus reflected the hierarchical structure of the society, and the wide range of prices allowed at least occasional attendance by most sectors of the community, from laborers, soldiers, and servants up to the wealthiest nobility. Spectators were seated on three sides of the stage, which was several feet above the level of the patio; they could also be seated on the sides of the stage itself if the lateral spaces were not occupied by an imitation mountain or other scenery.

The tiring room structure had two or three levels visible to the public, with doorways for exits and entrances, and an inner space at stage level that could be opened to reveal special effects; otherwise it served as the dressing room for actresses. The men's dressing room was on the level below. Trap doors in the stage floor and stage machinery manipulated from the hidden upper level allowed Don Juan to be pulled down to Hell and saints or mythical gods to "fly" toward the heavens.

The basic *comedia* was performed with iconic stage props and minimal scenery, each scene being "painted" by the text itself, although curtained spaces in the tiring house could be opened to reveal painted scenery. Performance was continuous within the three acts, with the exit of all characters indicating a scene change. Performances of the *loa* ("prologue"), the three acts, the burlesque pieces between acts and the finale lasted about $2\frac{1}{2}$ to 3 hours, and took place in the afternoon, without artificial lighting.

The *autor* (owner-manager) of a theatre company paid playwrights for new plays, which became his property, jealously guarded for about a decade because new works drew larger audiences; they were thereafter published in twelve-play volumes or individual *sueltas*, generally without intervention by the dramatist, and publications were frequently misattributed or based on corrupt texts. Since the playbill was changed every few days, demand for plays was great and production by favored playwrights correspondingly large. Even the most prolific author could not live solely by the pen, however; several were priests, others supported themselves as lawyers, military officers, or served a noble patron.

Ideology

Leaving aside volume of production, similarities between the *comedia* and Elizabethan drama and the theatres in which they were performed are striking, although they developed independently and with little cross-fertilization before the Restoration, when Charles II and his entourage brought familiarity with Spanish drama to England from their Continental exile. Both Spanish and English public theatre emerged from a blend of native popular and Neoclassic learned culture, made possible, according to Walter Cohen, by the nature of the transition from feudalism to capitalism and by the incomplete imposition of absolute monarchy in those two nations. Cohen contrasts this to the case of France, where the rapid passage from fragmented feudal sovereignty to full absolutism and centralized power limited the development of public theatres and the blend of popular and elite traditions.[3]

Juan Oleza Simó suggests that in the latter sixteenth century the aristocracy, previously absorbed in its own private theatre and courtly celebrations, became aware of the growth and potential import of popular theatre and, on the one hand, developed a taste for aspects of its repertoire, while, on the other, they sought to control and reorient it ideologically as a powerful instrument for forging social hegemony.[4] José Antonio Maravall views the Baroque *comedia* as an early form of mass culture, a propaganda tool with which a resilient aristocracy secured broad acceptance of its conservative value system.[5] Certainly the *comedia* formula that prevailed with Lope de Vega and his contemporaries revolved around aristocratic love intrigues and concern for honor, loyalty, courage, (masculine) friendship, and court political intrigue, masking raw economic interests and largely ignoring the existence of merchants and artisans. Plots were played out on two tiers, however, with servants functioning as foil to the dilemmas of their masters and as comic relief, a structure that also provides space for critique of aristocratic codes.

Playwrights

Miguel de Cervantes (1547–1616) wrote a number of plays that, according to his report, were successful in those Madrid *corrales* in the 1580s. Most have not survived, but one, *El cerco de la Numancia* ("The Siege of Numancia"), on the fall of that besieged Celtiberian city to Romans in 133 BC and the collective suicide of its inhabitants, is the best tragedy written in sixteenth-century Spain. He also used his Algerian experience

---

3 *Drama of a Nation. Public Theatre in Renaissance England and Spain* (Ithaca: Cornell University Press, 1985).
4 "Hipótesis sobre la génesis de la comedia barroca y la historia teatral del XVI." In *Teatros y prácticas escénicas.* 2 vols. (Valencia: Institución Alfons el Magnànim, 1984), vol. II, pp. 9–42.
5 *La cultura del barroco: análisis de una estructura histórica* (Barcelona: Ariel, 1975).

in several plays, written in that decade or after the advent of Lopean comedy, but their dramatic construction is imperfect, as is his intriguing semi-picaresque play *Pedro de Urdemalas*. His superb series of *entremeses* – *El retablo de las maravillas* ("The Miracle Show"), *El viejo celoso* ("The Jealous Old Man"), *La cueva de Salamanca* ("The Cave of Salamanca"), *El juez de los divorcios* ("The Divorce Judge"), and others – are comic masterpieces that take on jealousy, ignorance, obsession with purity of blood, and a wide range of human failings. No company owner bought them in his day – perhaps because their open-ended complexity fitted uneasily between acts of a *comedia* – but they merit their wide readership and frequent modern performances. The champion in the genre in his day was Luis Quiñones de Benavente (*c.* 1589–1651), who never wrote *comedias* but dedicated his satirical talents to penning nearly 900 *entremeses*.

The career of Guillén de Castro (1569–1631), a Valencian aristocrat and soldier who moved to Madrid in 1619, is symptomatic of the shift to the court center and its ideology. His most famous play, *Las mocedades del Cid* ("The Young Cid"), invents an honor–love impasse for the historical national hero of the Reconquest of Valencia and his beloved Jimena, incorporating many popular ballads. He also dramatized classical stories, works centering on tyrannical rulers and powerful and jealous women, as in *El conde Alarcos* ("Count Alarcos"), a portrait of the ideal nobleman – now less a warrior than a courtier absolutely loyal to the monarch – in *El perfecto caballero* ("The Perfect Knight"), and a delightful comedy *La fuerza de la costumbre* ("The Force of Custom") about a sister and brother separated at birth, raised by the parent of the opposite sex, and their troubles in adopting the dress and deportment assigned their gender.

Luis Vélez de Guevara (1579–1644), although of humble Andalusian origins and acknowledged *converso* (Jewish) ancestry, enjoyed the patronage of Felipe IV's favorite, the Count-Duke of Olivares. His plays ranged widely, from action-packed or machine-filled dramas to works of delicate Gongorine lyricism. He had a talent for creating characters of impossibly heroic dimensions with sufficient psychological development to render them almost believable. The heroine of *La serrana de la Vera* ("The Mountain-Maid of La Vera") is a manly female outlaw who, seduced and abandoned by a captain, kills a thousand men before being captured and executed. His finest play, *Reinar después de morir* ("Queen After Death"), is a moving dramatization of the execution for political reasons of Inés de Castro, Castilian beloved of a fourteenth-century Portuguese crown prince.

Tirso de Molina – the pseudonym of Gabriel Téllez (1579–1648) – is the third member of early modern Spain's triumvirate of great dramatists, between Lope and Calderón. A Mercedarian friar, he spent two years teaching theology in Santo Domingo (1616–1618) but did not record that experience dramatically, although he did write a trilogy of works on the Pizarro family and their history in Peru. His sharp satirical wit probably contributed to his exile from Madrid in 1625, ostensibly because a government reform council found it scandalous that a friar should write profane comedies but more probably for political reasons or literary rivalries. "Profane" comedies he did indeed write, such as *Marta la piadosa* ("Pious Martha") in which a not-so-pious Martha feigns a religious vocation to gain freedom of action and marry the man of her choice, and *Don Gil de las calzas verdes* ("Don Gil of the Green Britches"), whose heroine cross-dresses and follows her faithless lover to foil his plans to marry a richer woman, creating a dizzying spiral of confused identities. He included ribald sexual humor and satire of religious hypocrisy in other works as well. Tirso was not, as has been conjectured, the illegitimate son of the Duke of Osuna, but he was critical of the aristocracy, and elevates some humbly born characters on the basis of personal qualities: e.g. the beautiful and valiant Galician peasant Mari-Hernández in *La gallega Mari-Hernández* ("The Galician Woman Mari-Hernández"), or the future Pope Sixtus V and his sister in *La elección por la virtud* ("Election by Virtue"). He created the fictional libertine don Juan in *El burlador de Sevilla* ("The Trickster of Seville") who seduces a series of women and laughs at all social and moral codes despite his lackey's repeated warning that he will face divine justice, until he is pulled down into Hell by the stone statue of a would-be victim's father, whom he has slain. That vibrant anti-hero, adapted by Molière, Mozart, José Zorrilla, and a host of other writers, is alone enough to belie the generalization that Spanish comedies feature only types, not complex characters. Similarly complex Tirsian characterizations are the narcissistic Serafina in *El vergonzoso en palacio* ("The Shy Man at Court") and the tormented family of the biblical King David in *La venganza de Tamar* ("Tamar's Revenge"). *El condenado por desconfiado* ("Damned for Despair") dramatizes the theological question of grace and free will through the contrasting fates of a punctilious hermit who despairs of salvation and is condemned, while a bandit is finally redeemed by his love for his father.

Juan Ruiz de Alarcón (1580/1581–1639) was born in Mexico but he finished his legal studies in Spain, and spent much of his life there, writing around thirty plays until he secured a position with the Council of the Indies and stopped writing. The distinctively pragmatic, moralistic tone of his work may have less to do with his place of birth than the cruel treatment he suffered for his physical appearance as a red-headed hunchback. In *La verdad sospechosa* ("The Suspect Truth"), imitated by Corneille and a string of other playwrights, he creates a magnetically self-crafting liar, but punishes him with marriage to the wrong woman. In contrast, the poor and ugly but scrupulously honest hero of *Las paredes oyen* ("The Walls Have Ears") prevails over his handsome but duplicitous rival. The hero of another comedy, *Don Domingo de Don Blas*, places his comfort over social conventions. Although Alarcón contributed – with eight other dramatists – to a play about Hurtado de Mendoza's campaign against the Araucanian indians, there is no overt American presence in his playwriting.

Indeed, of the thousands of sixteenth- and seventeenth-century *comedias* written, only a tiny fraction treat the conquest and colonization of the New World, the more noteworthy being Lope's *El nuevo mundo descubierto por Cristobal Colón* ("The New World Discovered by Cristobal Colón") and Calderón's *La aurora en Copacabana* ("Dawn in Copacabana").

Among the so-called "Calderón cycle" of playwrights, the major figures are Francisco de Rojas Zorrilla (1607–1648) and Agustín Moreto y Cabana (1618–1669). Rojas wrote a series of sensational revenge tragedies, some on classical themes, such as *Progne y Filomena*, but avoided a tragic conclusion in *Del rey abajo, ninguno* ("None Below the King"), a play in which a wealthy commoner is caught between loyalty to the king, whom he thinks is the nobleman trying to seduce or rape his wife, and defense of his conjugal honor. Rojas was a talented developer of the *comedia de figurón* about an exaggerated social type, such as the avaricious old suitor in *Entre bobos anda el juego* ("It's a Fool's Game"), whose fiancée chooses instead his poor but gallant cousin. Moreto's plays tend to urbane comedy of manners, as in *El lindo don Diego* ("The Dandy don Diego"), a delightful *comedia de figurón* about a vain and narcissistic type who spends half his day getting dressed; *El desdén con el desdén* ("Disdain Against Disdain"), in which an aloof woman is defeated by her own tactics; and *No puede ser* ("It Can't Be"), whose intelligent heroine teaches her fiancé, who over-zealously sequesters his sister, that a woman is the only effective guardian of her own honor.

These names and works are but a few highlights of the scores, if not hundreds, of writers of greater or lesser talent and productivity who, between the last decades of the sixteenth century and the end of the seventeenth, wrote thousands of *comedias* to meet the insatiable appetite of the *corral* audiences. Even the best writers also teamed up to write plays by committee, an act apiece by three writers, or even a scene apiece by as many as nine authors.

A few women also wrote plays, but only Ana Caro Mallén de Soto was accorded any professional returns, payment for her contribution in the 1640s to Corpus Christi celebrations in her native Seville. In *Valor, agravio y mujer* ("Valor, Outrage, and Woman"), her heroine cross-dresses to pursue the offender of her honor, outdoing men at swordplay and courting women along the way, and in *El conde Partinuplés* ("Count Part-inuplés"), a young empress tests suitors to decide which to marry. The popular novella author María de Zayas y Sotomayor (1590 – *c.* 1650) wrote one play, *La traición en la amistad* ("Friendship Betrayed"), in which a group of women punish a friend who steals their suitors. Many nuns, including Lope's daughter Sor Marcela de San Félix (1605–1687), wrote varieties of drama for convent performance. Reading these women's works together demonstrates how talented women subtly reshaped *comedia* conventions to communicate their personal views of gender and power relationships.

Court theatre

Court festivities included paratheatrical entertainments (masques, mum-meries, and *entremeses*) as early as the fourteenth century, and early dramatists Encina and Gil Vicente wrote for performance in noble and royal palaces. Carlos I spent little time in Spain, however, and Felipe II was not interested in theatre. Elaborate Court theatre began to develop during the reign of Felipe III, in amateur productions such as *La fábula de Perseo* ("The Myth of Perseus") by Lope and *El caballero del sol* ("Knight of the Sun") by Luis Vélez de Guevara, performed primarily by members of the Court, with impressive stage machinery and music. Its full flower-ing, however, awaited the arrival of the theatre-loving Felipe IV; his prime minister Olivares, eager to use theatre to promote the Spanish Habsburg monarchy; a superb Court dramatist, Calderón; and the 1640 inaugura-tion of a specially equipped Court theatre, the Coliseo, in the new Palace of the Buen Retiro. That conjunction brought to its greatest perfection the Court spectacle drama that had spread from the Courts of northern Italy across Europe beginning in the late fifteenth century, encouraged by humanists' interests in reviving ancient Greek drama and by the rise of absolute monarchs eager to employ spectacle to enhance their prestige and power.

Three splendid 1622 productions in Aranjuez inaugurated Felipe IV's reign: *La gloria de Niquea* ("Niquea's Glory") by the Conde de Villa-mediana; *Querer por sólo querer* ("Love for Love's Sake") by Antonio Hurtado de Mendoza; and *El vellocino de oro* ("The Golden Fleece") by Lope. The scenery and stage machinery for *Niquea* were designed by an Italian engineer, Giulio Cesare Fontana, the first of several Italian experts brought to Spain for that purpose, the most important being Cosme Lotti, between 1626 and 1643, and Baccio del Bianco from 1651 to 1657. In these works, visual effect and music were more important than the poetic texts, based on chivalric, pastoral, or mythological motifs.

The strength of the *comedia* tradition encouraged the use of full-length dramatic texts performed by professional actors, often combining the talents of more than one company, in later Court spectacles for occasions of state. In the Coliseo, they were performed before multiple sets of perspective scenery painted on changeable flats, and with machinery that could make mountains and palaces appear or implode, move the waves on a painted sea, or let characters fly solo or mounted on swans, horses, or clouds. They included dance and traditional strophic music as well as a Spanish version of recitative in which the gods sang, while mortal characters spoke. There were also attempts to introduce Italian Court opera, with *La selva sin amor* ("The Loveless Forest"), a "pastoral eclogue" by Lope, and Calderón's *La púrpura de la rosa* ("The Purple of the Rose") and *Celos aun del aire matan* ("Jealousy Even of the Air Kills"). The Spanish Court, however, preferred a semi-operatic mixed style. Other dramatists wrote Court spectacle plays using the same ingredients, but, with the exception of Francisco Bances Candamo, rarely achieved the dramatic coherence of Calderón's plays.

Court spectacle plays not only served to entertain royalty, court officials, and foreign dignitaries, they also constituted a tool and an expression of absolute monarchy in their lavish production and audience seating arrangement. They sometimes incorporated, along with the exaltation of the monarch, a discreet political lesson for the king, because, as Bances Candamo expressed, performing before the monarch offered an opportunity to instruct him diplomatically by means of the glory and weaknesses of the play's gods and heroes, with whom he was linked. After the opening performance for the royal family, the Coliseo could be opened to a paying public.

Private performances were also given on certain days of the week in simpler theatres in the Alcázar and Buen Retiro palaces, beginning as early as the 1560s for Isabel de Valois, Felipe II's third wife, who did enjoy theatre. The professional companies there performed either plays written for the *corrales*, or dramas written for palace performance which might later be staged in the *corrales* as well.

14

Lope Félix de Vega Carpio

VICTOR F. DIXON

Lope de Vega's life, throughout most of its seventy-two years, was noto-riously turbulent and riddled with contradictions. Baptized in Madrid on 6 December 1562, he was the son of an embroiderer from La Montaña, undoubtedly one of the many craftsmen who were flocking to Spain's new capital. Lope's much-mocked pretensions to noble lineage were certainly unfounded, but twentieth-century suggestions of *converso* antecedents remain unproven too. Having studied, after its foundation in 1572, at the local Jesuit college, between 1577 and 1581 he attended the University of Alcalá (and *may* have studied later at Salamanca). In 1583 he saw active service in an expedition to the Azores.

The next few years were marked by a passion that would haunt him forever after, for Elena Osorio (often *Filis* in his verse), the daughter of an actor–manager for whom he wrote some of his earliest plays. Eventually supplanted by a rich and noble rival, he spread savage poetic libels, for which, early in 1588, he was exiled, for eight years from Madrid and two from Castile. Later that year he abducted and married Isabel de Urbina (*Belisa*), and enlisted to join the Armada, though he may not have left the peninsula. His banishment took the pair to Valencia, to Toledo, and for some years after 1591 to the cultivated court of the fifth Duke of Alba, near Salamanca.

Isabel died there and in 1595 Lope was allowed to return to Madrid, where he was indicted the following year for concubinage with doña Antonia de Trillo (probably his *Celia*). In 1598 he contracted a second marriage, to Juana de Guardo, but by now or shortly after he was more passionately committed to a liaison with Micaela de Luján (*Lucinda*), and the following decade saw him shuttling between two households, in both Madrid and Toledo, with visits to Valencia, Seville, and other cities. In 1610 he settled definitively in Madrid with Juana, but a period of relatively peaceful domesticity was short-lived; 1612 and 1613 saw the deaths both of their dearly loved six-year-old son Carlos Félix and of Juana herself, and in 1614 a spiritual crisis that he had been experiencing for some years culminated in his ordination as a priest. He was nevertheless soon inflamed by new passions: first for an actress, Lucía de Salcedo, and then in

1616 for Marta de Nevares (*Marcia Leonarda* and *Amarilis*), to whom he would remain devoted, despite her later blindness and eventual insanity, for the following sixteen years.

By now he was at the height of popular acclaim, but more deeply embroiled than ever in bitter, personal disputes with literary rivals and critics, though he also had able defenders. Having always hoped, moreover, to transcend his artisan origins, he had served from his teens, mostly briefly, a series of nobly born masters, and from Felipe III's accession in 1598 had repeatedly sought, with limited success, the favor of aristocrats and the court.

Under Felipe IV, he turned his attentions to Olivares and his family, but despite occasional commissions (and a doctorate from the Pope) was never accorded due recognition by the Spanish Crown, and the decade before his death, on 27 August 1635, was soured by poverty, personal sorrows, and disillusion.

His nature, at first sight no less contradictory, was the product of conflicting drives. Intensely emotional, he fell prey to a host of full-blooded passions, of brief or long duration: to love, especially, for many women, some of his offspring, and several friends, though also for his nation and a very personal God, but to less endearing feelings too, like jealousy, envy, and spite. He was driven also, however, more than by poverty, by a yearning for artistic and intellectual eminence and greater social status. Above all, though, he was a writer, with a compulsion to self-projection.

His most obsessive passion was for his pen, through which he sought, with seemingly effortless ease, to satisfy his other passions, or to sublimate his anguish at their frustration. He depicted in his writing every aspect of his life; no author was ever, in the broadest sense, more autobiographical. Many of the characters he created – in essence, all – are re-creations of himself. But in real life, too, he wore a number of masks.

The shamelessness and self-abasement in many of his letters to the sixth Duke of Sessa (whom between 1605 and his life's end he served as a "secret secretary," ghosting adulterous *billets-doux*), though reflecting some complicity and gratitude for small favors, were evidently expected by that vain, egoistic patron. In a similar way, having risen to fame by virtue in part of his fluency, he cultivated the image of the spontaneous, natural genius, and proclaimed the superiority of a plain, pellucid style, but constantly strove to present himself too as a serious, learned author, and so the equal at least of all rivals in every genre of his day. In fact his knowledge was encyclopedic, in more than one sense; some displays of erudition were demonstrably culled directly from compendia, but his ready, retentive memory was remarkably well stocked from experience, popular culture, and wide-ranging first-hand reading, so that his lexis and range of reference were unsurpassed.

Lope's preeminence as a poet and playwright has diverted critical attention from most of his works in prose; yet these were sufficiently diverse,
original, and popular to rival those of any coeval.

Arcadia, published in 1598 (with twenty-one further editions in seventy-
seven years), was an innovatory pastoral romance. Though indebted to
many predecessors, it included more poetry than most (one half of its
lines), and an almost unprecedented weight of didactic discourses. Rather
than interweaving and contrasting many lovers' stories, it centers primarily on two, Anfriso and Belisarda, portraying them more dramatically and
with unusual human depth. Anfriso undoubtedy represents the duke Lope
served in Alba, but the tale does not fit what is known of his life, and many
details came from Lope's. He recognizes in a prologue that "a vueltas de
los ajenos [pensamientos] he lamentado los míos" ("behind others' emotions I have bewailed my own"). In the last of five books, Anfriso cures
his ill-fated love by pursuing learning and virtue. Such ejemplaridad was
another innovation; its introduction seems abrupt, but is announced from
the beginning, and reflects both contemporary concepts of art and Lope's
mid-life mood. These were admirable attempts to update a moribund
genre, but Arcadia gives the impression of excessive improvisation.

In El peregrino en su patria ("The Pilgrim in his Homeland," 1604), he
sought with more success to modernize and personalize a different Renaissance genre, the Byzantine romance of adventure. Characteristically, its
central action, begun in medias res and interwoven with many other tales,
is the travails of a pair of virtuous lovers, repeatedly parted but eventually reunited. Each of its first four books, however, includes a description
in performance of one of Lope's autos; their texts fill over two-fifths of
the book, and point, alongside its polysemic title, frequent devout digressions, and visits to Marian centers, to a different orientation. Pánfilo, the
protagonist, is not only an idealized lover but a pious pilgrim through life
in his native land, an allegorical archetype of the post-Tridentine Christian – the antithesis of the picaresque sinner depicted by Mateo Alemán
(1547–1620?). Erudition, as in Arcadia, is pervasively paraded, but far
better integrated and more evidently germane to the work's doctrinal
aim.

In Los pastores de Belén ("Shepherds at Bethlehem," 1612), dedicated
to Carlos Félix in 1612, he returned to the pastoral mode, but explicitly,
remorsefully, with divine – not human – love as his theme. It retells the
Christmas story from its foreshadowings until the flight into Egypt, but
the contents again are diverse. Lope's shepherds delight in riddles and
contests in verse, reciting a host of poems. He incorporates too some
Old Testament stories of lust, but their narration is restrained, as are his
displays of learning. The overall tone of the work, which proved almost
as popular as Arcadia, is one of ingenuous devotion.

The over-optimistically entitled *Triunfo de la fe en los reinos del Japón* ("The Triumph of the Faith in the Realms of Japan," 1618) is an account of the martyring of Christians there three years before, requested as propaganda by the Dominican order. Lope, who angled in vain over twenty years for a post as royal chronicler, conceived this as a chance to show he could write historical prose. In the main, however, he paraphrased, often verbosely, a missionary's dispatches, though characteristically giving some Christians largely invented speeches.

Far more delightfully idiosyncratic are four *Novelas* dedicated to "Marcia Leonarda": one published with *La Filomena* in 1621 and three with *La Circe* in 1624. These supposedly true but improbable stories, parodies of other novelesque kinds that he might well have written as plays, have traditionally been found wanting in depth and narrative skill. More recent critics, rightly highlighting his many comments to Marta, have seen these solemnly as responses to theories of narrative art (including those of Cervantes), of which he is simply dismissive. Assured of his power to please both his mistress and every other reader, whether ignorant or learned, he throws in, as he says in *La desdicha por la honra* ("Misfortune Caused by Honor"), "cuanto se viniere a la pluma sin disgusto de los oídos, aunque lo sea de los preceptos" ("whatever may come to the pen, without upsetting the ears, even if it may the rules"): brief disquisitions, reflections, anecdotes, seventeen long poems, thirteen verse translations of fragments from classical writers, and innumerable allusions. These unpredictable asides are the essence of his performance. He constantly anticipates his audience's reactions, but (rather than "dialogues" or "epistles") these *Novelas* are one-man shows by an engaging raconteur.

Even more original is his prose play *La Dorotea* (1632), described that year, in lines 403–404 of his *Égloga a Claudio* ("Eclogue for Claudio"), as "póstuma de mis musas . . . y por dicha de mí la más querida" ("the latest product of my muses . . . and perhaps the one I love most"), and often considered his most mature and complex work. Several aspects of its form recall the tragedies of Seneca, but debts to *Celestina* (frequently found elsewhere in Lope) and to the *Eufrosina* (by Jorge Ferreira, 1515?–1585?) are specifically acknowledged, and features reminiscent of Lope's own *comedias* abound. Here, however, the action is often non-linear, the overall tempo is slow, and relatively few plot-incidents serve primarily to reveal its characters' psychology and nature. Lope wrote it in prose, we are told in a prologue, because it was "tan cierta imitación de la verdad" ("so close an imitation of truth"); in fact it is a fictional version of the Elena Osorio affair, many more or less obvious echoes of which had appeared in his novels, poems, and plays. This, however, though it will surface again in *La Gatomaquia*, is its definitive re-creation. Traces remain of a probable early version, but Lope has been transformed by well over half a lifetime's experience, some of it recent; several poems, for instance, inserted late, reflect his disillusionment and loneliness in old age. He portrays all its persons (including his *Doppelgänger* Fernando) with sympathy but ludic, ironic detachment; self-mockingly, perhaps, he has them all indulge in displays of knowledge, but shows them as unaware of deeper truths: the transience of romantic love and earthly life.

Despite their diversity, these prose works have many features in common. All are experimental, all in some degree dramatic, all varied in content and style. In all he seeks to edify, and parades his learning, both spontaneous and secondhand; in almost all he includes a plethora of poems. In all, sometimes autobiographical and frequently first-person, Lope himself is present, self-consciously performing.

Many of the poems in these works were clearly written *ad hoc*, but Lope used them also as additional outlets in print for the flood of verse that poured incessantly from his pen, and in which he displayed, often ostentatiously, a technical proficiency, in every form then conceivable, that seems almost innate.

His earliest surviving poems relate to Elena Osorio. Many are artistic ballads, in which the lover's raw feelings are thinly disguised by attributing them to Moors (Zaide, Gazul) or to shepherds, especially Belardo (forever thereafter his favorite among many pseudonyms). He denied that their traditional, assonantal form was inherently jejune, and its popularity among his generation is attested by a series of ever-larger collections. The poems therein are anonymous, but several are identifiable as his. Both vigorous and sensitive in their expression of emotion, they surpass all but those of Luis de Góngora (1561–1627). He would continue to use the *romance* form, moreover, throughout his life, for instance in four "piscatory idylls" and *A mis soledades voy* ("To My Solitude I Go"), perhaps his most moving poem, inserted in *La Dorotea*. Similarly, he would always employ the octosyllabic line in *redondillas*, *quintillas*, and *décimas*.

His *comedias* and *autos*, moreover, contain a host of traditional-type songs in different meters and styles; indeed many of his plays were inspired by such lyrics, as others were by ancient ballads. Some are authentic folk songs, but the poet was so attuned to the popular muse that these can barely be distinguished from his inventions and re-creations. He knew equally well, however, Spain's pre-Renaissance poets, whose simple works he often glossed; though describing their language as primitive, he admired above all their dense, aphoristic wit.

Nevertheless he admired even more the elegance, musicality, and metaphorical richness of the eleven- and seven-syllable forms inherited by Spaniards like his special idol Garcilaso de la Vega (1503–1536) from Italian Renaissance verse, seeing this in turn as deriving from the poetry of Ancient Rome. He constantly exploited therefore every known combination (*liras, tercetos, silvas, canciones* . . .), and some of his own invention.

Arcadia provided a showcase for a selection of his early poems in these different metrical styles; but his first publications entirely in verse began a series of attempts to demonstrate his capacity as a writer of extended epics, for which *octavas reales* were the established form.

La Dragontea, a ten-canto account of Drake's ill-fated exploits and death in the West Indies two years before, was printed at Valencia (publication in Madrid having been forbidden) early in 1598. Jingoistically bombastic, it demonizes "the dragon" and also criticizes Elizabeth I, though much less savagely than would his *Corona trágica* ("Tragic Crown," 1627), about what he portrayed as the martyrdom of Mary Queen of Scots; it has moments, nevertheless, of vivid description, drama, pathos, and even humor.

El Isidro (1599) was, by contrast, hagiographic; a portrayal, again in ten cantos, of the life and several miracles of his hometown's saintly ploughman, requested by a friar who was promoting Isidro's canonization and provided documentation. Here, wisely eschewing *octavas*, he used traditional *quintillas*, and told Isidro's tale with homely simplicity, but added, less wisely, a series of allegorical characters, sermons delivered by angels, autobiographies by beggars, and a local pious legend dramatized also in his *El alcaide de Madrid* ("The Warden of Madrid").

Fiestas de Denia ("The Festivities at Denia") was a brief though colorful account of some of the celebrations in Valencia of the royal wedding in 1599 (for which he had also written an *auto*, as well as clowning and reciting); but the twenty-canto *La hermosura de Angélica* ("The Beauty of Angelica," 1602) was a much more elaborate work. He claimed to have composed it originally in 1588, but had certainly revised it. Nominally a continuation of the *Orlando furioso* by Ariosto (1474–1533), it is more love-story than epic, a rambling, light-hearted Byzantine romance in verse, replete with both historical and autobiographical digressions, but enlivened by detailed descriptions of martial and amorous encounters.

By then he was probably planning by far his longest and most ambitious epic, *Jerusalén conquistada* ("Jerusalem Conquered," 1609). Though confidently conceived as a sequel and patriotic riposte to the *Gerusalemme liberata* by Torquato Tasso (1544–1595), it is clumsily constructed and far too diffuse. Apocryphally, it supposes that Alfonso VIII participated in the Third Crusade, and its ending is inconclusive, perhaps because Lope added four books to sixteen originally penned.

Though all these attempts to establish himself as Spain's foremost epic poet are partially redeemed by fluently brilliant sections, all are marred by excess, a plethora of digressions insufficiently excused by the conventions of the genre. All, except possibly *Isidro*, must be accounted failures. Lope could not compete, as he hoped, with Ariosto or Tasso.

On the other hand, with his *Angélica* he published for the first time his *Rimas* ("Verses"), a retrospective selection of 200 sonnets of the Petrarchan type, and in the composition of these he was unquestionably a master. Progressively preferring the more exacting four-rhyme forms, he endorsed the central precepts of contemporary theorists: epigrammatically compact, sonnets should develop a single thought to a sonorous, clinching conclusion. Since (including those deployed in his plays) over 1,600 survive, he must be accounted the world's most prolific and proficient sonneteer, and he was surely one of its best.

The themes of these 200 are diverse – some 40, for instance, are dedicated to royalty, nobles, or friends – but by far the most frequent is love. Only a few relate to Elena Osorio, although these include some of Lope's most affecting poems, in which he is moved to meditation by ruins, or casts himself as a shepherd bereft of his favorite sheep; about 30, by contrast, directly name his more recent lover "Lucinda." At least 80, however, refer to no particular woman, distilling into confident, self-conscious art the varied emotions and thoughts of every passionate lover.

Among nearly 50 poems added to a separate edition of *Rimas* (1604), the most engaging is a letter in tercets to Gaspar de Barrionuevo, the first of many such apparently chatty and chaotic but skilfully wrought and allusively witty *epístolas*. The most revealingly autobiographical are one to Francisco de Herrera Maldonado (1623), one to Matías de Porras (1623) – in which he writes movingly (as in an elegy of 1613) of the loss of Carlos Félix – and the mis-named *Égloga a Claudio* (1632).

His spiritual crisis inspired a wealth of devotional verse. In 1612 he published 4 *Soliloquios* ("Soliloquies"), that he would augment to 7, with commentaries, in 1626; in 1613, *Contemplativos discursos* ("Contemplative Discourses"); in 1614, *Rimas sacras* ("Sacred Verses"), in which 49 other poems were preceded by another 100 sonnets. Some 30 of these, dedicated to saints, seem pallid alongside twice that number in which Lope laments his sins or apostrophizes his God, especially the crucified Christ. All are carefully crafted, and some conceits seem contrived, but his sincerity is beyond doubt. Nor would he ever cease thereafter to produce religious verse; later, longer works would include *La Virgen de la Almudena* ("The Virgin of La Almudena," 1623), *Triunfos divinos* ("Divine Triumphs," 1625), and *Corona trágica* (1627).

From late in his fifties, however, he undertook also the composition of extended "pagan" poems. No writer of his age was more directly familiar with Latin authors and classical mythology, but this new enterprise must largely be seen as an attempt to outshine Góngora as a cultured poet. Over forty years their rivalries, tempered by mutual admiration, produced savage personal attacks, though Lope's were mostly directed at his adversary's disciples. His consistent response to Góngora's dazzlingly innovative but "un-Castilian" language was that poetry, though disciplined by art, must be natural in both inspiration and expression; only a poem's content should defy immediate comprehension. To exemplify this, in 1613 he had paraphrased, in a sonnet inserted and explained in his comedy *La dama boba* ("The Dumb Belle"), a section of Pico della Mirandola's Neoplatonic *Heptaplus*. He reprinted this sonnet in *La Filomena* (1621) and (with an exhaustive exegesis) in *La Circe* (1624), and endeavored to encapsulate in 10 others there (plus one in *La Dorotea*) the Neoplatonic philosophy of love. The poems that head those volumes were attempts to challenge the author of *Polifemo* ("Polyphemus") on his own mythological ground (though ironically competition produced some degree of "contamination").

In Part I of *La Filomena* he recreates Ovid's version of that tragic tale with lyrical eloquence and remarkable human feeling. Part II, though inferior, is an amusing invention; in a contest like that of Apollo and Marsias the poet himself, as a nightingale proud of its songs, demolishes – as a pedantic starling – Pedro de Torres Rámila, who had attacked him in 1617. *La Circe*, his longest, most ambitious mythological poem, and in its combination of epic, lyric, and dramatic modes his most impressive, centers in fact on Ulysses, many of whose adventures he relates, adding a descent to Hades and inserting in the Polyphemus episode his own reworking (one of several) of the Galatea story.

With *La Filomena* (alongside nearly thirty other works) he published *La Andrómeda*, a rapid but dramatic retelling of the Perseus myth; with *La Circe* (adding about sixty more), *La rosa blanca* ("The White Rose"). For this he invented a fable in honor of Olivares' daughter María, though it is mainly a compendium of others related to Venus. In *El laurel de Apolo* ("Apollo's Laurel," 1630) he similarly imagined a mythological setting for an enormous list of poets worthy of praise, but also rehearsed the stories of Calixto and Narcissus. Overall, his mythological poems, though unequal in execution, bear comparison with Spain's finest, including his principal rival's.

Far more enjoyable today, however, are his *Rimas humanas y divinas del Licenciado Tomé de Burguillos* ("Human and Divine Verses of Master Tomé de Burguillos," 1634). He attributes them to Tomé de Burguillos, a pseudonym invented in 1620, but barely maintains the pretense. The religious poems, for instance, though popular in style, are simply his own, and only in some 40 of 161 sonnets does Burguillos refer to Lope, himself, or Juana, the plebeian washerwoman he supposedly adores. Over 80 are parodic or satirical, aimed especially at Gongoresque poetasters. At least 30, moreover, are serious; many express the same intense feelings of loss and disillusionment, tempered by stoical resignation, as other admirable poems of this time: several in *La Dorotea* (already mentioned), *Huerto deshecho* ("The Devastated Garden," 1633), and *El siglo de oro* ("The

Golden Age"), in a posthumous compendium *La vega del Parnaso* ("The Meadow of Parnassus," 1637).

The gem among these *Rimas* is *La Gatomaquia*, a hilarious three-canto parody, with cats as its characters, of the classical and Renaissance epic. Even here there are somber moments; Lope's *alter ego* Mamarraquiz is pointedly destroyed by a rifle-toting prince who is out hunting birds. One cannot but be moved, however, to both admiration and laughter by his resiliently free-wheeling sense of fun.

Lope would have preferred to be remembered as Spain's most important writer of prose or verse, but he has better claims as a poetic playwright. No serious scholar accepts a statement by Juan Pérez de Montalbán (in 1636) that Lope wrote (as well as 400 *autos*) 1,800 *comedias*. Only 315 indisputably his are extant (alongside 42 probably authentic, and 73 of dubious attribution), and a likelier though still phenomenal total is from 600 to 700. This means on average, over fifty years, at least one *comedia* a month, but there is evidence for his claim that some were written in twenty-four hours.

Happily, thirty-seven autographs have survived complete, and we have portions of seven more, and some trustworthy transcripts; other texts vary greatly in reliability, including many he published himself. To combat mis-attributions, he printed in his *Peregrino* the titles of 219 *comedias* (adding 219 more in the 1618 edition), and said he would publish 8, but initially his plays were printed by others, principally in three *Partes* (collections of 12). In 1614, however, he collaborated on a fourth, and (having failed to prevent publication of the seventh and the eighth) brought out between 1617 and 1625 (when the printing of *comedias* was banned in Castile) *Partes* 9 to 20. In 1635 (when the ban was lifted) he sought copyrights for three more, and prepared two posthumous volumes for publication. His motives were mixed. Primarily he wanted the profits his predecessors had made, and published with little or no revision whatever texts, good or bad, he could recover; but all the 96 plays in *Partes* 13 to 20 carry separate dedications, mostly to noblemen and crammed with classical quotations. Part of his purpose must have been to stress his seriousness and dominance as a dramatist.

When he started, writing plays for money, for the *corrales*, was a lowly esteemed occupation, scorned by nobles and intellectuals; at his trial in 1588 he declared he had composed them "por su entretenimiento . . . como otros muchos caballeros" ("for his own amusement . . . like many other gentlemen"). In fact they would always be his main and only reliable source of income; he was driven, he often acknowledged, by necessity. In several letters to Sessa he affected to spurn his craft as unworthy, uncon-genial, even whorish (though many of his references elsewhere to mer-cantile verses written for the mob, plays that Italy and France would call barbaric, were partly tongue-in-cheek), and in his old age, when younger rivals won favor, he declared himself loath to continue; indeed only some sixteen plays were unquestionably written after 1625. Nevertheless, he became increasingly proud of his achievements. In his epistle to Antonio Hurtado de Mendoza and his *Égloga a Claudio* he gloried in having brought art to Spanish drama, engendering innumerable disciples. Unfortunately his scanty and rarely specific allusions to previous Spanish dramatists, together with our limited knowledge of his own earliest plays, make it difficult to determine how much he owed to such predecessors, especially the Valencians, but undoubtedly his rapid rise to dominance, attributable to his fecundity, closeness to his public, and genius as both dramatist and poet, had made his works the model, and so had both given the *comedia* its definitive form and proved it could accommodate any content.

Regrettably, he wrote (and performed) much earlier the often jocular but fundamentally serious monologue that provides the only extended exposition of his ideas, his *Arte nuevo de hacer comedias en este tiempo* ("Updated Rules for Writing Plays at This Time," 1609). His apologies to his Neoclassically minded hearers for having pleased his public are patently ironical, but so is his pretended disregard for ancient authors; these, as ever (though scorning their sixteenth-century exegetes), he knows, venerates, and echoes. As a practical playwright, however, he insists that their precepts must be modified in accord with modern taste. Thus he rejects, as contrary to nature and experience, any necessary division between the tragic and comic modes. He accepts, paraphrasing Aristotle, the unity of action (without excluding multiple plots). The unities of time and place, however, may (with caution) be subverted; it depends on the story one is telling. Spanish spectators expect a complete one, not merely a crisis (and Lope takes for granted that none is unsuitable for drama).

He proceeds to give more detailed instruction on his methods. You should write a prose synopsis (some of his have been preserved), devising three acts of continuous, suspenseful, but verisimilar action. Your language should exploit every rhetorical resource, especially ambiguity, but vary to suit both characters and contexts, as also should your verse-forms. His brief remarks on the latter, often mis-interpreted as prescriptive, merely reflect his practice then, and he never ceased to experiment; more significantly, they echo Horace, whose principle of decorum underlies much of this advice. Finally, defiantly, he asserts (line 372): "Sustento . . . lo que escribí" ("I stand by . . . what I have written"); he knows from experience what gives delight, and is therefore right, and works of art embody their own rules. Thus his aesthetic, though partly conservative, was revolutionary in practice.

Many of Lope's *comedias* can be precisely dated, and analysis of his verse-forms has given approximate dates for the rest, but attempts to trace his development by separating them into periods have been only partially successful, largely because demand was such that their sources of inspiration, despite clear shifts of emphasis, remained extremely diverse. Their quality too was always unequal, though the weakest have moments of startling originality, and most reveal more calculation than is commonly acknowledged. Above all, he knew what worked on stage, and wrote "performance texts"; significantly, as his autographs show, his explicit directions, though relatively scant, were in the imperative mood.

A dozen surviving works, some written for the nobility or court but others for the *corrales*, were indebted to classical mythology; the most interesting, perhaps, is his 670-line libretto for the first Spanish opera, *La selva sin amor* ("The Loveless Forest"), spectacularly staged by Cosimo Lotti in 1627. Though justifiably wary of the threat to poetic drama represented by the increasing intrusion of mechanical effects, Lope had to bow to demand. Over thirty works dramatize stories from the Bible, like those of Jacob, Esther, and Tobit; pious legends, as in *La buena guarda* ("The Good Guardian," 1610); and the lives of saints, as in three about Isidro. In an astonishingly metatheatrical masterpiece, *Lo fingido verdadero* ("What's Feigned is True," 1608), he clearly identified with the actors' patron, the Roman martyr Genesius, and half the remainder were written during his religious crisis. All indeed embody deep personal devotion, though many were undoubtedly commissioned. So of course do his many as yet insufficiently studied *autos*; one of the cleverest, though characteristically lyrical, is *La siega* ("The Harvest"), based on the parable of the weeds in Matthew 13: 24–43.

A few, mostly early, *comedias* are in pastoral or chivalresque vein, but more (some thirty) were based on Italian *novelle* – at least eight for instance, early in the new century, on those of Boccaccio (1313–1375) (as "bowdlerized" by Lionardo Salviati [1539–1589]). A far larger proportion, however – at a time of increasing awareness of history, Spain's place within it, and the *exempla* it could afford – were dramatizations of episodes past or present, authentic or supposedly so. Their settings range widely in time and place (and some are essentially fanciful), but the overwhelming majority center on Spain. Based on legends, folk songs, ballads, chronicles, histories, and broadsheets, they cover its every epoch from the distant past to the present, especially the Middle Ages and (in a dozen plays) the time of Fernando and Isabel.

Some thirty are genealogical; they celebrate exploits by noblemen or their forebears, perhaps disinterestedly or merely in hope of favor, but often because they were commissioned as propaganda. *Arauco domado* ("Arauco Tamed"), on the victories in Chile of García Hurtado de

Mendoza (whom Lope had digressed to exalt in *La Dragontea*) was surely one of the first. This, a play about Columbus (*El nuevo mundo* ["The New World"]), and (probably) another about Cortés date from about 1599; but "American" plays were never popular and he wrote only one thereafter, *El Brasil restituido* ("Brazil Restored"), commissioned by Olivares in 1625, which publicized (as did several others) a recent triumph of Spanish arms.

By contrast, many feature peasants, depicted variously as comic, picturesque, or admirable, as in *El villano en su rincón* ("The Peasant in His Corner," 1611) or a pair of plays (1620–1628 and 1625–1630) on *Los Tellos de Meneses* ("The Tello Family of Meneses"), and even as more worthy of honor than noblemen who oppress them, as in *Peribáñez* (1605?), *El mejor alcalde el rey* ("The King the Best Judge," 1620–1623), and *Fuente Ovejuna* (1612–1614). The last, Lope's most-performed (though often perversely adapted) play, dramatizes the murder by peasants in 1476 of their tyrannical overlord, and the solidarity under torture that won them a royal pardon. He insists on their veneration for the Catholic Monarchs, but such clear approval of a peasants' revolt would never have been tolerated then anywhere else in Europe.

These "histories," mostly dramas, highlight (as his *Arte nuevo*, lines 327–330, advised) "casos de honra" ("cases of honor") and "acciones virtuosas" ("acts of heroic virtue"), but always also contain both humor and love, which in its broadest sense was Lope's constant theme. He called few of his plays *tragedias* or even *tragicomedias*, but some of his finest works, like *El duque de Viseo* ("The Duke of Viseu," 1608–1609) or *Porfiar hasta morir* ("Persistence unto Death," 1624–1628) are profoundly and poignantly tragic. The most characteristically lyrical is *El caballero de Olmedo* ("The Knight of Olmedo," probably of 1620), based partly on *Celestina*, but mainly on a well-known semi-historical tale; until well into Act III, life seems to smile on two young lovers, but their idyll is undermined by premonitions of the fate we know awaits.

Lope's tragic masterpiece, however, is *El castigo sin venganza* ("Punishment without Revenge," 1631), a dramatization, via Bandello, of historical events at Ferrara in 1425. It almost complies with the Neoclassical Rules, and echoes of Seneca's *Phaedra* suggest a conscious reworking, though Lope's "Hippolytus" succumbs (as in real life) to his stepmother's advances, and they consummate a guilty but genuine passion. Apprised of this, Lope's "Theseus" secretly (though unhistorically) punishes both with death, but solely, he claims, as Heaven's instrument. His true motivation is problematic, but Lope provokes both condemnation and compassion for all three. As a prologue printed three years later seems to confirm, he probably intended to prove that he could write a tragedy "al estilo español" ("in the Spanish manner"), similar but superior to those of Antiquity.

A month before *El castigo*, perhaps with analogous motives, he had written for a royal garden-party organized by Olivares *La noche de San Juan* ("Midsummer's Eve"), an urban comedy in which (although in this case with highly innovative metatheatricality) he kept ostentatiously close to the Rules, as indeed he had in others, like *La noche toledana* ("Making a Night of It in Toledo") or *Lo que pasa en una tarde* ("What Can Happen in One Afternoon"). He composed throughout his life, alongside numerous *comedias palatinas* (court dramas; located, like most of Shakespeare's comedies, in the faraway realms of romance), such intricately plotted "cloak-and-sword" plays of pre-marital love, confined (like their Roman and Renaissance predecessors) to a specific city, and usually replete with local color and customs. Some early attempts were poorly constructed, with extraneous characters and episodes and overly coarse sexuality, but by mid-career he had perfected what was to be Spain's most distinctive comic genre.

From a host of fine examples, like *La discreta enamorada* ("The Clever Girl in Love," 1606), *El acero de Madrid* ("The Iron Maidens of Madrid," 1607–1609), or *Las bizarrías de Belisa* ("Belisa's Extravagances," 1634), one might single out *La dama boba*. Its stupid heroine, once educated by love, outsmarts her blue-stocking sister and everyone else, though iron-ically the gallant who transforms her seems motivated throughout by desire for her larger dowry. Lope's subtlest comedy, however, is *El perro del hortelano* ("The Dog in the Manger," 1613–1615). Its action springs entirely from a countess's vacillations between jealousy-fueled love for her secretary and veneration for her rank. The issue of love and marriage across rigid social divides is central to several such "secretary-plays" and many others; though treated tragically in Lope's version of the *Duchess of Malfi* tale, *El mayordomo de la duquesa de Amalfi* ("The Duchess of Amalfi's Steward," 1604–1606?), it is usually side-stepped by a last-minute revelation. Here, however, when one is engineered by Lope's cleverest clown, the secretary confesses to the countess that it is false; he has only (line 3294) "nobleza natural" ("natural nobility"). She nevertheless insists that society is happy to accept such shams, and the audience, subversively, is asked to join the conspiracy.

Lope is universally recognized as one of his nation's greatest, most char-acteristic writers, but his reputation has been unduly clouded, both by his popularity (thanks partly to his apparent confessions to having dumbed-down to achieve it) and by his sheer fecundity (on the assumption, despite his contrary claims, that it precluded reflection and polish). In truth much of his writing was excessively spontaneous, but what might seem like improvisation is often underpinned by calculation, intuitive or conscious, and *La Dorotea*, a dozen diverse sonnets, *El castigo sin venganza*, and

El perro del hortelano bear comparison with anything written in Europe during his time.

For far too long, moreover, most of his compatriots have seen him, quite mistakenly, as a "genius of conformity." Some, often quoting over-selectively, from too few plays, pronouncements which are after all those of characters, present him as a lackey of the Establishment, prepared to prostitute his pen to reinforce its dominant ideology. True, he not infrequently wrote to curry favor or to order, and had to serve many patrons, but they never satisfied either his needs or his ambitions; he remained a marginalized and disaffected "wannabe," like many of his public. Like them, he was an orthodox believer and profoundly patriotic, and never thought to question the monarchical system of rule, but was well aware of the abuses and injustices that system could produce. The urban *corrales* he mostly wrote for were the principal public forum and focus for both debate and dissent, and his plays undoubtedly fueled them, for though never a deep philosopher he used many of his plots and characters (censorship nothwithstanding) to insinuate unconventional and often progressive views.

In *Arauco domado*, he duly idealizes his patron, but makes Caupolicán a tragic hero, and while condemning the barbarity of other Chilean natives lets them eloquently proclaim their desire for freedom and denounce the selfish motives of most *conquistadores*, which are clearly exposed again in *El nuevo mundo*. His *El asalto de Mastrique* ("The Assault on Maastricht") suggests doubts about the human costs of Spain's wars in Flanders, and even in his virulently anti-Semitic *El niño inocente de La Guardia* ("The Innocent Boy of La Guardia") he permits his villainous *conversos* to protest at their persecution.

The majority of the monarchs of Spain's (and other countries') past in his histories and pseudo-histories (and even his mythological play about Perseus, *El Perseo)* are depicted, it has been shown, as seriously flawed, and when he idolizes (for instance) Fernando and Isabel he may be covertly rebuking those of his day for showing less direct concern for the common good. In many plays he champions the rights, ideology, and lifestyle of "cristiano viejo" ("Old Christian") peasants vis-à-vis the formerly feudal nobility. He repeatedly raises the issue of upward social mobility, and presents the widest possible range of views on matters of honor. As evidently a feminist as anyone of his day, if he insists that for women (or men) reluctance to love and marry is a perversion, he holds up mostly for admiration many kinds of female protagonists, and validates their rights to education and self-determination. He deserves therefore even more veneration than he is generally accorded, especially by progressively minded Spaniards.

15

Pedro Calderón de la Barca

EVANGELINA RODRÍGUEZ CUADROS

Calderón: witness and mirror to a contradictory century

The year 2000 marked the fourth centenary of Pedro Calderón de la Barca's birth. In addition to the official celebrations – exhibitions, books, conferences – there were brilliant performances of his plays, especially Calixto Bieito's surprising and groundbreaking version of *La vida es sueño* ("Life is a Dream"). Some thought that, at last, Calderón was descending from the erudite library bookshelves onto the boards of present-day stages. However, on 3 December, a harsh article in the Catalan edition of *El País* read:

Si consideramos que un clásico es un autor importante, influyente, imprescindible para entender la historia de la literatura . . . no hay duda de que Calderón es un clásico. Pero si un clásico es aquel que es perpetuamente contemporáneo, aquel que siempre puede ser leído al margen de su contexto histórico, aquel que nos interpreta, que nos habla de nosotros porque habla de cosas que nunca caducan, entonces es perfectamente posible que Calderón no sea un clásico.

(If we consider that a classic is an important and influential author, indispensable to the understanding of the history of literature . . . there is no doubt that Calderón is a classic. But if a classic is an author who is perpetually contemporary, who can always be read outside of his/her historical context, who interprets us, who speaks to us about ourselves because he/she speaks of things that are permanent, then it is perfectly possible that Calderón may not be a classic.)[1]

The author of that article maintained that Calderón was an indubitable genius and the creator of "grandes artefactos teatrales" ("great theatrical artifacts"), but one whose ideology, world view and themes were totally alien to third-millennium man. Rather than being a minority opinion (which is perfectly legitimate), these words convey the heavy burden of prejudices on which Calderón's critical history has been built. The

---

This chapter has been translated from the Spanish by Celeste Delgado-Libero.

[1] Vicenç Villatoro, "¿Y si Calderón no fuese un clásico?" *El País* (3 December 2000; Catalonia edition), p. 3.

centenary made the playwright a part of our national heritage, but it also made him a library classic, without any interest outside the time that created him. Having less vitality than Lope (1562–1635), being less ironic than Cervantes (1547–1616), and less mordant in his nihilism than Francisco de Quevedo (1580–1645), we have come to venerate Calderón, but not because we feel that he is one of us.

Nevertheless, in a work as extensive as it is complex, Calderón demonstrates that to be a classic is to give testimony of the time in which one had to live, not so much in order to judge it, but rather to describe it and, by staging it from different perspectives or dramatic genres, to project its profound contradictions into our present so that we may recognize ourselves (or not) in his mirror. Calderón de la Barca was a heterogeneous and multi-faceted author, much more ambiguous than the critical prejudice makes us believe. For that reason, at times he even managed to be heterodox. Because of his long life trajectory, because of the strategic historic situation in which he lived, and because of the variety of registers of his dramatic writings, he represents, for better and for worse, the Spanish Baroque. His biography, however, reveals attitudes that are sometimes not at all kind toward his milieu. It also reveals the late humanist and the pre-Enlightenment encyclopedic man who got to know Cervantes' mastery, who knew Velázquez (1599–1660) and rendered his paintings in theatrical form, and who was a contemporary of Kepler, Monteverdi, Pascal, Descartes, Espinoza, Hobbes, and Locke, among others.

Calderón was born in Madrid on 17 January 1600. The early years of his education (until 1620) coincided with the last part of the reign of Felipe III (1598–1621) and the influence of the Duke of Lerma (1553–1625) as a *privado* (favorite). Calderón's mother died prematurely in 1610. His father, a member of the bureaucratic *hidalgo* middle class that served the king, had an authoritarian character that controlled his sons' destiny with an iron fist until his death in 1615. These circumstances caused Calderón to grow up strongly influenced by his brothers Diego and José and, above all, by his stay at the Colegio Imperial of the Jesuits (1608–1613) and, later, at the universities of Alcalá and Salamanca. The intellectual baggage provided by such an education structured his culture and his ideology: logic, the theatre as a rhetorical system of persuasion, Jesuit casuistry (a formidable philosophical stance used to judge reality), patristic thought (scholastic Thomism, pre-existentialist Augustinism), Neostoicism (which led him to turn the stage into a field mined by questions and disillusionments), profane and Catholic history, and natural, political, and administrative law. Such complexity has at times been reduced to a contemptuous orthodox Catholicism by modern scholars. Calderón is indeed Catholic, but only if we accept the term in its etymological sense of universal vision which, sometimes, wishes to impose itself with intolerance, transforming theology into science. Other times, with a poignant tragic skepticism, his vision presents the drama of the intellectual (for example, Basilio from *La vida es sueño* or Cipriano from *El mágico prodigioso* ["The Prodigious Magician"]) in search of the elusive truth of that very science. Finally, on other occasions, Calderón is capable of drinking from classical sources (religious or profane) in order to question, from the viewpoint of a radical, solitary humanity, the tragic coexistence of desire and the law.

After several attempts at poetic contests, his first known play, *Amor, honor y poder* ("Love, Honor, and Power") was staged in 1623. The ascension of Felipe IV (1605–1665) to the throne of Spain and the promotion of the Count-Duke of Olivares (1587–1645) brought about a new age which, in contrast with the preceding pacifism, pursued reformist and aggressive politics in order to reaffirm Spain as a European power. Between 1630 and 1640, a decade in which he wrote his best plays, Calderón became a classic of his time, and not only in the *corrales de comedias* (courtyard playhouses): helped by Olivares, Calderón entered the palace and was institutionalized as an official court author. As reward for such services, in 1636 he received the habit of Knight of the Order of Saint James.

This period of creative plenitude was followed by one of crisis: the reformist project fell apart, the Spanish monarchy was incapable of maintaining the country's cohesion, and, after 1640, the rebellions in favor of the *fueros* (local customary statutes) in Catalonia, Portugal, Aragon, or Andalusia became unstoppable. In 1643 Olivares fell from power. The Peace of Westphalia and the Treaty of Münster (1648) marked the independence of Flanders and the beginning of a new European order from which Spain would be progressively marginalized. Calderón was a soldier in the war with Catalonia. His brothers died and (perhaps around 1646) his natural son, Pedro José, was born. This crisis point, which is both external and internal, is also reflected as a break in his dramatic career. The deaths of Queen Isabel of Bourbon (1644) and the heir apparent, Baltasar Carlos (1646), along with the intolerance of moralists, brought about the closing down of public theatres, lasting several years. Calderón underwent a spiritual (and also professional) re-accommodation: his employment as secretary to the Duke of Alba for a few years and his decision to become a priest (1651) cannot be detached from his personal dejection and from the need to maintain an income. His plays became more and more allegorical and abstract, and almost all of them took place in the two theatrical and political spaces that the current circumstances allowed, the Coliseum of the Palace of El Buen Retiro and the stages for the feast of Corpus Christi. He thus entered his last and longest period of dramatic production. When Felipe IV died, the regent, Mariana of Austria, again ordered the theatres closed until 1670. The monarchy, saddened and perplexed by the succession problem, attempted a new reformism and interior cleansing, at the cost of definitively renouncing Europe. Calderón, the last great intellectual of seventeenth-century Spain, had by then seen published almost all the volumes of his compiled works: he had been assembling these since 1636. Nevertheless, just because his plays tended toward allegory or emphasized the concerns of the court or the Church, this did not mean that they lost touch with reality; in his old age, Calderón closely watched the reforms undertaken by Carlos II (1661–1700) and the queen regent. During the carnival of the year 1680, his last play was staged at court: *Hado y divisa de Leonido y Marfisa* ("The Fate, Emblem and Motto of Leonido and Marfisa"). Calderón died on 25 May 1681, before concluding his *auto La divina Filotea* ("Divine Philotea").

Some critics consider such a long career as a prolonged imitation of others, as a synthesis of exhausted inheritances. Rather, Calderón's work can be defined as a "second vanguard" of Spanish classical theatre (after the first vanguard, Lope's *comedia nueva*, which, reasonably, broke away from the Aristotelian norm). Calderón's vanguard perfects the masterful rhythm of the plot and the complication of comedy and subjects them to a reflective maturity. It fills the empty space of the *corrales* with the dream of stage sets and changes of scenery. Moreover, as part of the show, it incorporates the prodigy of the poetic word, of a rhetoric that digs out subjectivity and a passionate debate between the "I" of the character and the world that surrounds him or her. Calderón transforms into theatre all the inventions of the new language created by Luis de Góngora (1561–1627). Of course, there is also the creation of characters that are sometimes stylized in a reiterative manner and sometimes endowed with a powerful personality that brings them close to archetype. These are heroes who doubt and who witness how the initial order of their adventures is different from the order that presides over the end of their trajectories, heroes who get lost in a plot complicated by parallel actions (which complement or contradict one another), from whose labyrinth emerge the disillusionment and the instability that surround all things human.

Four centuries with Calderón: from *casticismo* to the difficult co-existence with post-modernity

In order to grasp the difficulties of received critical opinion concerning Calderón, it is important to review the history of his critical reception. He was a classic for his own contemporaries. In his *Aprobación* to the tome of Calderón's works published in 1682, Manuel Guerra y Ribera (1638–?) stated that what he most admired "en este raro ingenio, fue que a ninguno imitó; nació para maestro, y no discípulo. Rompió senda nueva al Parnaso, sin guía escaló su cumbre; ésta es para mí la más justa admiración, porque bien saben los eruditos que han sido rarísimos en los siglos los inventores" ("in this rare talent, was that he did not imitate anyone; he was born to be a teacher, not a student. He opened a new path toward mount Parnassus, without a guide he climbed to its summit; for me this is the fairest admiration, because the erudite know well that inventors have been extremely rare through the centuries").[2] Together with Molière, Calderón was the most frequently staged playwright in seventeenth-century Europe. Nevertheless, this consensus soon ended. Neoclassicists of the eighteenth century judged Calderón less for his aesthetics than for his perceived ideological motivations. It could be said, as Trías adduces, that "en la diatriba contra Calderón se han puesto de acuerdo las dos Españas, desde los ilustrados afrancesados a lo Moratín hasta el ultra-racionalista . . . Menéndez Pelayo" ("in the diatribe against Calderón the two Spains have come to an agreement, from the enlightened *afrancesados* à la Moratín, to the ultra-rationalist . . . Menéndez Pelayo").[3] The enlightened minority had undertaken a cultural program in which the theatre would conform morally and ideologically to the needs of a civilized, Christian nation. Therefore, they attacked a theatrical canon that propounded a systematic break with verisimilitude and the Aristotelian rules, a complicated *cultista* style, a capricious use of history, and an irrational view of the sacred. When in 1799 Leandro Fernández de Moratín (1760–1828), at the head of the Committee for the Direction and Reform of the Theatres, offered a list of plays "not recommended" for public theatres, he unhesitatingly included *La vida es sueño*.

In the eighteenth century the word *castizo* ("pure") was already associated with the vindication of Golden Age drama, especially Calderón, but it would not be until the following century that such identification became firmly established. Indeed, for August Wilhelm (1767–1846) and Friedrich Schlegel (1772–1829) Calderón became the dramatic bedrock of a cultural nationalism based upon the notion of a spirit of race, and upon chivalric and religious values. However, this grandiose view of Calderón as a Christian poet at the level of Dante exposed the playwright to the manipulation of a pro-Restoration, anti-bourgeois, and counter-revolutionary type of Romanticism, like the one defended in 1814 by Nicolás Böhl de Faber (1770–1836), which identified Calderón with the traditional values of God, monarchy, and honor, setting them against the alleged pro-French or anti-patriotic attitudes of critics like Alcalá Galiano (1789–1865) or Joaquín José de Mora (1783–1864). For Böhl, Spain escaped the evil irruption of modern philosophy thanks to the inoculation of the Calderonian antidote.

---

[2] María José Rodríguez Sánchez de León, *La crítica ante el teatro barroco español (siglos XVII–XIX)* (Salamanca: Ediciones Almar, 2000), p. 66.
[3] Eugenio Trías, *Calderón de la Barca* (Barcelona: Omega, 2000), p. 25.

The identification of Calderón's theatre and the Romantic theatre as manifestations of the Spanish national spirit would play a decisive role years later, in the debate over the so-called "stage realism" and the defense of a type of drama that exalted a poeticized vision of customs as a guarantee of public morals. Calderón would then once again be the great alibi for a conservative and ultramontane ideology like the one defended by Adelardo López de Ayala (1828–1879) in 1870 (upon entering the Royal Academy, in his speech entitled *Sobre el teatro de Calderón* ["On the Theatre of Calderón"]), which supported the return of the monarchy, overthrown two years earlier during the revolution of 1868. Thus, when the overenthusiasm of Catholic orthodoxy led a young Marcelino Menéndez y Pelayo (1856–1912), during the 1881 bicentennial of Calderón's death, to vindicate Calderón as the guarantor of the national spirit – that is, to be opposed to liberal reforms – naturalists and liberals reacted strongly. Most notably, Leopoldo Alas ("Clarín," 1852–1901) depicts the pathetic don Víctor Quintana wielding his sword while reading *El médico de su honra* ("The Surgeon of His Honor") in chapter 23 of *La Regenta*. Menéndez y Pelayo emphasized the conservative nature of Calderón's theatre, while deploring his style and his characters (whose lack of psychological verisimilitude he abhorred). His criticism turned out to be disastrous: it locked Calderón into the anti-modernity of the nineteenth century, where he remained even for lucid thinkers such as Miguel de Unamuno (1875–1939, who considered him to be the champion of his Castilian *casticismo*), Antonio Machado (1875–1939, who detested his poetry), and Ramón María del Valle-Inclán (1869–1936, who, in *Los cuernos de don Friolera* ["The Horns of Don Friolera"], reduced Calderón's concept of honor to a "Judaic popular form" and to biblical dogmatism).

The attempts to recover the classics made by the Generation of 1927 (we cannot forget the moving production of the *auto La vida es sueño* by the La Barraca theatre company, in which Federico García Lorca [1898–1936] himself played Death) were interrupted by the Civil War and Franco's regime, which wretchedly used the imperialist and ultra-Catholic vision of Calderón in lavish performances at Eucharistic conferences or in official theatres. Having been eruditely rescued by Anglo-Saxon criticism (especially by Alexander A. Parker),[4] Calderón has been revised and recovered by contemporary Hispanism only after the centennial of 1981. His difficulty, the excess of all aspects of his theatre, the contrast created by a tragic vision of life that is at the same time carnivalesque, the idea of the theatre as a metaphor for life, and his constant bordering on the world

---

[4] See in particular, *The Allegorical Drama of Calderón: An Introduction to the Autos Sacramentales* (Oxford: Dolphin Books, 1943); and *The Mind and Art of Calderón* (Cambridge: Cambridge University Press, 1988).

of the unreal by looking at man as the matter of his own dreams (something typical of Shakespeare as well), have led post-modernity to approach him in a more interrogative manner, especially when the Calderón of the last twenty years has been revealed to the public in his natural habitat: the stage. Still, most biographical and critical summaries of the author reduce him to a kind of weird peculiarity. Nationalist Germans or Catholic Anglo-Saxons prescribed that, because of his race, faith, temperament, and historical context, Calderón was Spain's best *national* poet, but one incapable of achieving universal transcendence. Even Harold Bloom, who includes Calderón among the indispensable authors in the Hispanic literary canon,[5] describes him, suspiciously, as the only playwright of religious stock who has ever existed in the world, affirming that next to him Paul Claudel (1869–1955) is insignificant. It must be said that what has been interpreted in Calderón as a negative transcendental pessimism is an evident sign of the crisis of modernity, which consists, as Marshall Berman has said, of being "both revolutionary and conservative: alive to new possibilities for experience and adventure, frightened by the nihilistic depths to which so many modern adventures lead, longing to . . . hold on to something real even as everything melts."[6]

History and power: The heterodoxies of a conservative

Indeed, Calderón is not always a fundamentalist, resigned to Christian pessimism or submissive to power. Only recently has the difference between the author's discourse and his characters' discourse been accepted. This opening has permitted us to see the Calderón of the earlier plays, in which his individual passion opposes the iron law of destiny (or of injustice). From his discreet biography, some dissonant facts have been made to stand out. In 1621, for example, Calderón and his brothers were accused of murder. In 1629 he took part in a skirmish involving swords, after one of his brothers was injured by an actor, whom they chased to the Convent of the Trinitarians, where they broke into the nuns' cloister. For that reason, it must not surprise us to find plays by Calderón that can easily qualify as "pre-Romantic," such as *La devoción de la cruz* ("Devotion to the Cross," *c.* 1623–1625) or *Luis Pérez el gallego* ("The Galician Luis Pérez," *c.* 1628), whose protagonists have, as Ángel Valbuena Prat puts it, an "anarchic" profile comparable to the great passions presented

[5] *The Western Canon: The Books and School of the Ages* (New York: Harcourt Brace, 1994), p. 234.
[6] *All That Is Solid Melts Into Air: The Experience of Modernity* (New York: Simon and Schuster, 1982), pp. 13–14.

in Sophocles' or Shakespeare's plays.[7] Eusebio and Julia in *La devoción de la cruz* rebel against the ill-fated authority represented by their father Curcio:

> que mal te puedo negar
> la vida que tú me diste.
> La libertad que me dio
> el cielo es la que te niego.

(because I can hardly deny you the life that you gave me. The freedom that the heavens gave me is what I deny you.)   (Act III)

Luis Pérez unmasks the officials of the judicial system as corrupt and incompetent:

> No quiero amigos letrados;
> que no obligan a los jueces
> las palabras; que ellos hacen
> a propósito las leyes.

(I do not want lawyer friends, because words do not oblige judges, since they make the laws on purpose.)   (II)

Even in later plays such as *Las tres justicias en una* ("Threefold Justice in One Sentence," *c.* 1635), the oedipal rebellion of young Lope de Urrea against his father (who denied him love and an education) bursts on stage as a violent slap in his progenitor's face, a daring breach of decorum for which Calderón was criticized by his own admirers. In *La cisma de Inglaterra* ("The Schism of England," 1627), young Henry VIII (a victim rather than an executioner of the Catholic cause) tries to put an end to the abuse and maliciousness of the court:

> Si a los Grandes hoy les quito
> las rentas y a los que viven
> libres les vuelvo a poner
> leyes, hará que apelliden
> libertad.

(If today I take away the Grandees' income and impose laws again on those who live free, it will cause them to invoke the name of freedom.)   (III)

   Calderón was witness to the spectacular punishment and reprisals with which Olivares began his reform program. Such traumatic violence, the instability of fortune, and the criticism of intolerance left a powerful trace in these plays, which reveal a fascination with the violent energy of

---

[7] *Calderón. Su personalidad, su arte dramático, su estilo y sus obras* (Barcelona: Juventud, 1941), p. 66.

the search for, exercise of, and loss of power. Naturally, Calderón is not explicit in his disagreement: political criticism could only exist at the time couched in ironic ambiguity. As Ruiz Ramón has noted, Calderón offers a clairvoyant example of this attitude in *Darlo todo y no dar nada* ("Giving Everything and Nothing," 1653),[8] which alludes to the legend of Alexander the Great, who asks three painters (Timanthes, Zeuxis, and Apelles) to paint his portrait. Apparently, Alexander had an ugly flaw on his face, which Timanthes attempted to suppress. Zeuxis, in contrast, insisted on highlighting it on his canvas, even exaggerating it. Apelles, finally, opted for a side portrait of the king, which led Alexander to admit, satisfied, that

> Buen camino habéis hallado
> de hablar y callar discreto;
> pues sin que el defecto vea,
> estoy mirando el defecto.

(You have found the right way / to speak discreetly and be silent, / since, without seeing the defect, / I am looking at it.)

That is how Calderón looks at power and history: from the side, discreetly. In this way he can uphold the patriotic exaltation of the Spanish triumph in *El sitio de Breda* ("The Siege of Breda *c.* 1625), presenting the powerful Espínola in a pious attitude toward the victims of the siege and generous toward his opponents, while the protagonist, Flora, wonders about the absurdity of war ("que no hay libertad perdida / que importe más que la vida" ["since there is no lost freedom that matters more than life"]). Calderón can also condemn the despotic intolerance of Emperor Aurelian in *La gran Cenobia* ("The Great Zenobia," 1628) or defend the *moriscos* who rebel against the Christians in the beautiful play *Amar después de la muerte* ("Love After Death," 1633), where, in an unusual anti-xenophobic and tolerant attitude, he pays homage to a people's resistance and struggle (1568–1571) against the dogmatic harshness of Felipe II (1527–1598) and his governors.

The balance of what is known today as "the politically correct" also surfaces in plays that appear to be proselytizing and Catholic, such as the mythicized story about the American evangelization told in *La Aurora en Copacabana* ("Dawn in Copacabana," *c.* 1661). In this play, the conquistadors Pizarro and Almagro confront natives portrayed with an emotive complicity, admiring their courage and nobility, especially those of the protagonist, Yupanqui, whose words evoke a sort of cultural

---

[8] Francisco Ruiz Ramón, "Calderón dramaturgo: el mito del dios de las dos caras." In *Calderón desde el 2000. Simposio Internacional Complutense*. Ed. José María Díez Borque (Madrid: Ollero & Ramos, 2001), p. 281.

crossbreeding: "debe de haber desotra parte / del mar, otra república, otro mundo, / otra lengua, otro traje y otra gente" ("there must be, on the other side / of the sea, another republic, another world, / another language, another dress and another people"). His most important play, *El alcalde de Zalamea* ("The Mayor of Zalamea," *c.* 1636) constitutes perhaps the final confirmation of this reflective look at history interwoven with the human and private levels, where he achieves an exemplary pact between opposing forces. On the one hand the peasantry is exalted in the vibrant figure of farmer Pedro Crespo, whose actions as the mayor (executing the villainous don Álvaro, a nobleman) mythicize the meaning of a horizontal Aristotelian honor (the dignity of the *honra*, patrimony of the soul, above all social classes) and satisfy the municipal powers of Castile, essential to the absolutist design of the Spanish monarchy. On the other hand, the military nobility (loyal to the king), is embodied in the solemn figure of old Lope de Figueroa. King Felipe II himself appears at the end of the scene, forgiving the momentary transgression of Crespo. The king knows that the farmer is willing to go on paying his taxes, send his unruly son to the army, and act, with regard to his daughter Isabel's dishonor, with the rigor that befits the honor of the aristocracy.

Calderón shows the same equivocal attitude regarding women. Of course, no modern feminist trend would tolerate his rigid code of honor (whose tragic victims are always women) or his banal portraits of the stereotypes of the time, whether in allusions to women's fragile will (in *La gran Cenobia*, he writes "Que en la fortuna fuera acción contraria, / siendo mujer, no ser mudable y varia" ["It would be contrary to fortune for a woman not to be mutable and changing"]), or in the pedantry of educated women who resort to a language plagued with outlandish learned words (such as Beatriz in *No hay burlas con el amor* ["There's No Kidding With Love," *c.* 1637]). However, Calderón's female characters can also be possessed by the passion for power, like Semiramis in *La hija del aire* ("Daughter of the Air," 1653). They are also capable of being learned and of governing, as when the protagonist of *El castillo de Lindabridis* ("The Castle at Lindabridis," *c.* 1661) claims the throne of Tartary:

> sin que ley tan sola olvide
> las hembras, pues no lo es
> que el ser mujeres nos quite
> la acción de reinar

(the law should not forget females, for being women does not take away from us the action of reigning.)   (1)

They rebel against social impositions when it comes to their tastes: the wonderful play *Las armas de la hermosura* ("Beauty's Weapons," *c.* 1652) shows young Veturia denouncing before Emperor Coriolanus the misogynist policies of the Senate, which prohibit women from joining the army or the body politic and from wearing the revealing fashions of the time – in seventeenth-century Madrid! Above all, they rebel when it comes to their education and their freedom. For that reason, *La dama duende* ("The Phantom Woman," 1629) is much more than a comedy of intrigue. Rather, it is the self-vindication of a woman (doña Ángela) who, pressured by a claustrophobic moral milieu (she is a widow and has to take care of her brother), decides to find her "own room" by means of the meta-theatrical invention of a stage artifact (a hidden cupboard that leads to her lover's room) and by passing for a ghost ("un enigma a ser me ofrezco" ["I offer to be an enigma"]) in order to seduce her pusillanimous beau.

Light and dark in the comedies

Baroque culture is an urban culture. The city becomes the perfect frame for a theatre whose protagonists (a nobility that can be assimilated into a pre-bourgeois middle class) find happy accommodation in the intrigue of cloak-and-dagger comedies, perfectly located on the simple yet efficacious stage of the *corral de comedias*. In these plays, Calderón shows himself to be at ease, ironic, devoted to entertainment and frantic action that sometimes come close to vaudeville. He prefigures the complexities of Hollywood comedies in *La dama duende* (where he also foreshadows the enlightened reformism of the eighteenth century, in opposition to the doubts about the fiction or the reality of the characters), or in *Casa con dos puertas mala es de guardar* ("A House With Two Doors is Difficult to Guard," 1629), in which a self-assured Marcela stupefies her beau of the moment, when she gives him "favores tales, que me obliga la vergüenza / por mí mismo a que los calle" ("such favors that shame makes me keep silent"). He makes fun of the cloyed Petrarchan and Platonic rhetoric in *No hay burlas con el amor*, where the relationships between men and women are resolved with daring pragmatism (since "temor o atrevimiento / no consiste en otra cosa / que haber o no haber dinero" ["fear or daring are nothing but having or not having money"]). It is true that in plays such as *No hay cosa como callar* ("Silence is Golden," 1638) he slides toward the chiaroscuro of the affairs of honor and the law. He does so, however, in order to unmask the decadence of a certain aristocratic class represented by don Juan de Mendoza, whose personality is divided between his obligation to serve the king in the siege of Fuenterrabía and the rape of Leonor, who has fainted in one of his own father's rooms. The official Spain and the real Spain fold together at the end in a marriage of convenience imposed by paternal authority, as in almost all plays, after the social order has been put to the test.

Comedy, however, is not limited to this register of intrigue and the heroism of the folly of love. In other plays, it offers the elegant view of seventeenth-century palace halls, with more restraint in the use of comic elements (so demanded by the musketeers in the *corrales*) and a greater delicacy in the evolution of characters. Plays such as *Las manos blancas no ofenden* ("White Hands Don't Offend," *c.* 1640), *El galán fantasma* ("The Phantom Gentleman," *c.* 1635), or *El encanto sin encanto* ("Charm without Charm," *c.* 1650–1652) occasionally transform the stage into a ballroom dance and a palace masquerade. This refined Court atmosphere, however, can become a grotesque absurdity in a comedy such as *Céfalo y Pocris*, a burlesque inversion of mythology, which was perhaps staged during the carnival of 1660. Calderón takes a humorous look at his own theatrical possibilities and reduces them to the most vulgar aspects of reality.

From the philosophical dramas to the tragedies

The existence of a Spanish Golden Age tragedy has been denied by some critics on the grounds that in seventeenth-century Spain the orthodox and Christian ideology only allowed the creation of Manichaean conflicts in which there could not be a debate between the individual and a higher power, much less a rebellion against a destiny that, according to Catholic providentialism, responded not to blind forces alien to individual responsibility, but rather to the very moral contribution of human beings to their own existence. Such ideas are naive or partial. Calderón demonstrates the extent to which tragedy, a genre that is not at all univocal, is an open option, resting a good deal of its dramatic structure on the passionate tension between its characters. Starting from a more discerning reading of Aristotle's *Poetics*, the same concept of tragicomedy inaugurated by Lope allowed a more complex and fragmented view of reality and the application of a Neo-Aristotelian model. In the case of Calderón, who never lost his attachment to the Senecan moral tradition (typical of his Neostoic education), this model implied a tragic concept of existence, bound to the vital conditions of man in Baroque society, deeply pressured by rigid taboos, such as the honor code. This leads to an interesting principle, which has been explained by Parker:[9] the responsibility for the tragic destiny of the hero (or heroine) is diffused or shared by all of society, and it is impossible to discern the just from the unjust,

---

[9] Alexander A. Parker, "Towards a Definition of the Calderonian Tragedy." *Bulletin of Hispanic Studies* 39 (1962), pp. 222–237.

the private interest from the public interest, the culpability of the victim from that of the executioner. This is indeed tragedy in a Hegelian fashion, where the bitter principle that understands necessity as the obligatory limit of freedom forces man to renounce his passions. It also forces him to a desire to edify his own reason, or to a vehement insistence on principles, or to a mental shipwreck within the labyrinth of a hostile society that is dominated by the intransigence of absolute principles (honor, reason of state) as opposed to private experience. Hence the diversity of settings that Calderón's tragedy can offer. It can show an exemplary fidelity to the pious values of the eternal gods (in this case, of Christianity) as opposed to political convenience. Fernando, the protagonist of *El príncipe constante* ("The Steadfast Prince," 1629), is in this sense a model character, like Sophocles' Antigone who sacrifices her personal integrity in the interest of fulfilling a destiny in which man's physical annihilation expiates his collective guilt.

In his masterpiece *La vida es sueño* (1635, a tragedy rather than a philosophical comedy, as it has been deemed by many), Calderón offers us an exemplary parable of the acquisition of prudence and the correct use of knowledge (political, ethical) by Segismundo. Through his personal vicissitudes (having to renounce his passionate instincts), this character denounces the abyss that exists between the true law and the cruelty of his father (Basilio) disguised as reason of state. The image of life as a dream, far from being read as a bitter lesson in Baroque disillusionment, represents the birth of a new era in which – as in Descartes around the same time – the priority of experience is proclaimed, together with mistrust of reality's ambiguous signs when it (reality) is interpreted through one's own ambitions or weaknesses. This is what happens in *Los cabellos de Absalón* ("The Hair of Absalom," *c.* 1633–1634), a drama of biblical inspiration in which we witness the tragic conflict between King David's moving filial pity and his children's political treason.

Above all, Calderón is the playwright of freedom ("free will") and of how one must face destiny with it (or, sometimes, with the tragic lack thereof). This gives his characters an admirable depth. Freedom can manifest itself as a blind wish for power or as a passionate desire as the only *raison d'être* (that is what happens in the two admirable parts of *La hija del aire* and *La cisma de Inglaterra*). The terrible absence of freedom, the traumatic lack of power to affirm one's feelings and privacy against imposed codes, is what explains the creation of the space for horror (and the subsequent emotional catharsis) that is achieved in honor plays. In them (from *El médico de su honra* to *A secreto agravio, secreta venganza* ["Secret Vengeance for a Secret Dishonor," both *c.* 1635) the useless heroism of women confronts the monstrous heroism of their husbands, men trapped by the rigor of a society that tries to save itself by means of immovable laws, whose cruelty the playwright makes evident (but does not defend). Honor and its public sense of *honra* thus function as the *fatum* of Greek tragedy. The characters, far from having an open and progressive concept of honor as an individual virtue (which characterized, for example, Pedro Crespo's demands in *El alcalde de Zalamea*), become victims that are sacrificed, literally, in the name of public opinion.

Calderón at Court: mythological comedy and operatic theatre

Understanding the complex symbiosis that exists between art and power is fundamental for the critical appreciation of the plays that Calderón wrote for the court between 1635 and 1680. These plays were the culmination of the great fashion for impressive Court spectacles that were common in sixteenth- and seventeenth-century Europe. The desire to mythicize the Spanish monarchy – the basis of Olivares' politics – promotes constant festive manifestations and, above all, performances in appropriate surroundings, such as palace gardens or the great Coliseum of El Buen Retiro, which housed all the technical mechanisms, machinery, and stage sets that led toward a Wagnerian type of theatre – a synthesis of all the arts – under the direction of great Italian masters such as Cosme Lotti and Baccio del Bianco. Menéndez y Pelayo scorned such manifestations, in which he saw the "prestigio de los ojos" ("prestige of the eyes"), rather than "la lucha de los afectos y los caracteres o la verdad de la expresión" ("the fight of feelings and characters or the truth of expression").[10] In Maraniss' superficial approach, they were a simple exercise in style.[11] In Cascardi's opinion, the playwright, subjected to political power, creates an outlandish entertainment that completely lacks any critical sense.[12] Against these opinions should be juxtaposed the enormous potential of plays whose printed text hardly allows us a glimpse at the polyphony of their dramatic language. Calderón was responsible for introducing opera into Spain through the *stile rappresentativo* imported from Italy, which gave the theatre a new, more distanced, more imaginative, and more spectacular dimension. It also introduced a more transcendental dimension, since it attempted to put on stage the great humanist tradition of the mythological allegory, rendered in a manner that is not only profane, but also intellectual and even moral. In Christianized classical mythographies such as Boccaccio's *De genealogia deorum gentilium* (1375) and in Spanish compendia like Pérez de Moya's *Philosophia secreta* ("Secret Philosophy,"

[10] Marcelino Menéndez y Pelayo, *Calderón y su teatro* (Madrid: A. Pérez Dubrull, 1884), pp. 365–366.

[11] James E. Maraniss, *On Calderón* (Columbia: University of Missouri Press, 1978), p. 87.

[12] Anthony J. Cascardi, *The Limits of Illusion: A Critical Study of Calderón* (Cambridge: Cambridge University Press, 1984), p. 130.

1585) or Baltasar de Vitoria's *Teatro de los dioses de la gentilidad* ("Theatre of the Gentile Gods," 1620), Calderón finds plots in which he always connects the fable with a discreet but evident reference to his own time. In this he may be prompted by a specific event (a wedding, a birth, the birthday of a member of the royal family) or by his maturity, which leads him to advocate political prudence. Such will be plays like *El mayor encanto amor* ("The Greatest Enchantment is Love," 1635), *La fiera, el rayo y la piedra* ("The Beast, the Shaft of Light, and the Stone," 1652), *Fortunas de Andrómeda y Perseo* ("Fortunes of Andromeda and Perseus," 1653), *El laurel de Apolo* ("The Laurel of Apollo," 1657–1658), *Eco y Narciso* (1661), or *La púrpura de la rosa* ("The Crimson of the Rose," 1660, his first attempt at a play that was sung in its entirety). Of course, mythology was not the only source for such royal shows. There is also the fantastic chivalric topic of works such as *El jardín de Falerina* ("The Garden of Falerina," 1648–1649) or *Hado y divisa de Leonido y Marfisa*.

In all of them, the treatment of fables from Antiquity in a free, anachronistic, essential manner that pays no attention to details is much closer to André Gide (1869–1951) or Jean Cocteau (1892–1963) than to the tragedies of Racine (1639–1699), which are subjected to the rigid classical model. In this we can also see the modernity of Calderón's dramas, in an expressive monumentality through which the yearned-for presence of the gods sneaks into the profane world. Thus, he sometimes does not hesitate to speak in favor of an advanced (for its time) utopian ideology. In this sense, we must emphasize *La estatua de Prometeo* ("The Statue of Prometheus," c. 1674), a play that brings Prometheus face to face with his antagonist, the haughty and belligerent Epimetheus. In it, Calderón argues that "más que la fuerza del brazo / vale la de la razón" ("the force of reason is worthier than that of the arm"), subordinates authoritarianism to the right to question, and defends "el anhelo de saber / que es el que al hombre le ilustra / más que otro alguno" ("the wish to know, which is the one that enlightens man more than any other"). The happy ending of this play, in which we are warned that "quien da ciencia, / da voz al barro y luz al alma" ("he who gives science gives a voice to dirt and light to the soul"), is a utopian invitation to the victory of a humanized science and of the teachings that are derived from it. Alcalá Zamora has seen in this a lucid premonition of the enlightenment of the *novatores*.[13]

God on the stage: religious dramas and *autos sacramentales*

The allegorical complexity of the mythological plays could be captured by means of intellectual acuity and also, of course, by means of the fabulous

[13] José Alcalá Zamora, *Estudios calderonianos* (Madrid: Academia de la Historia, 1999), pp. 85–91.

(and sometimes crazy) spectacle of stage sets and machinery. This double reception also occurs in the religious plays, where Calderón proves to be a consummate playwright, producing works that could excite both the uncultured masses (through a didactic and evangelical theatre, whose advantages he had learned in his formative years with the Jesuits) and intellectuals and theologians. For a rationalist and Neoclassical mentality these plays would be a new attack on good taste (Nicholas Boileau [1636–1711] would condemn the lack of verisimilitude of *le merveilleux chrétien*). However, with an approach that is free from rules and from the obligation to produce a realistic effect, Calderón is capable of creating a theatre that, by means of suggestive stage tricks (sudden apparitions of saints or devils, celestial ascensions), instructs in a convincing manner about Christian myths. In *La exaltación de la cruz* ("The Exaltation of the Cross," *c*. 1648) and in *Origen, pérdida y restauración de la Virgen del Sagrario* ("Origin, Loss, and Restoration of the Side Chapel Virgin," *c*. 1637) he does it by mixing historical and supernatural elements. In *El purgatorio de San Patricio* ("The Purgatory of Saint Patrick") and in *La devoción de la cruz*, it is done through the exhortation to conversion in the adventures in the comedies about saints and bandits. Calderón, though, can also transform the stage into a place of intense debate in order to reveal, through arguments typical of scholastic *disputatio*, questions of dogma and Christian theology. In this case, he seeks the complicity of the clergy and other learned men, who would see a vertiginous plot whose main purpose is to underscore the drama of the intense search for the truth, the search for the hidden God (Saint Augustine's *deus ignotus*). That is how plays such as *El mágico prodigioso* (1637) came into being. In this play, Cipriano makes a pact with the devil in exchange for the knowledge of all sciences. Its influence on Johann Wolfgang Goethe's (1749–1832) *Faustus* has been questioned, but when the poet saw the play on the Weimar stage, he understood something that later German Romantics had to learn: that God was to be found not only in patriotic conservatism or monarchic absolutism but also on the stage.

All the plays mentioned speak of the mysteries of Christianity, but they are treated within a frame or context that is absolutely temporal and even profane. This temporal dimension is what distinguishes them from the *autos sacramentales*, a genre to which Calderón applies all his exceptional poetic and intellectual talent, along with the splendor of the performances, atop huge open-air stages and on the *carros* (floats) carrying the impressive stage designs sponsored by the civil power (which thus allies itself with the ideological power of the triumphant Church and the Eucharistic dogma that celebrates the feast of Corpus Christi). The *autos* insistently develop (by means of a variety of plots taken from the Bible, history, the lives of saints, or pagan mythology) the theme of the salvation of man according to the Christian myth of Christ's sacrifice on the cross. This supernatural subject matter determines a theatrical formula that is exempted from any subjection to rules or unity of space or time (Neoclassical critics campaigned against the *autos*, culminating in their prohibition by Carlos III [1716–1788] in 1765). This theatrical space allows the coexistence of abstract characters (Soul, Humanity, the Virtues, Appetite), prophets, deified mythological characters such as Orpheus in *El divino Orfeo* ("Divine Orpheus," 1663, in which the sacred and operatic aspects of music, as a substantial part of the performance, reach their zenith), seducing devils that take the form of "comuneros del empíreo" ("revolutionaries of the heavens") or pirates (*La nave del mercader* ["The Merchant's Ship"], 1673), apostles and Argonauts, Christ and Jason, kings and Court favorites. Calderón even makes the Count-Duke of Olivares into the character of Man, who builds *El nuevo palacio del Retiro* ("The New Palace of the Retiro," 1634), an allegory of the strength of the Church defended by a Felipe IV who is confused with the character of Christ in a not at all disinterested manner. This is a Calderón who catechizes his public (who attend not only a show but also a ritual) in his "sermons put to verse," as he himself defined his plays. This is a Calderón who reflects upon the fugacity of life in *El gran teatro del mundo* ("The Great Theatre of the World," *c.* 1644) and who raises the fires of the Inquisition on the stage itself (*El cordero de Isaías* ["The Lamb of Isaac," 1681). This is also a Calderón who, because of *Las órdenes militares* ("Military Orders") found himself involved in an inquisitorial process when he used the stage as a bitter example of the cruel reality around him by showing Christ himself going through the tests of purity of blood.

A carnival on stage: Calderón's comic short plays

Certainly, Calderón perfects the theatre as a fascinating mechanism of institutional propaganda, but he is also like the gigantic mirror of a gesticulating Spain that, in the absence of a rational and enlightened discourse, generates constant vacillations and counter-myths. Only thus is it possible to understand that the same priest who warns us about the impositions of honor and who, from the *carros* of the feast of Corpus Christi, calls upon us to pursue "A Dios por razón de estado" ("God for reasons of state") allows himself, within the carnivalesque parenthesis that is also the theatre, to write short plays that are grotesque and irreverent, meant to be performed in the course of the *comedias de corral* or even side by side with performances at court and during the sacramental feast of Corpus Christi. Calderón is the author of a number of *jácaras* (plays that are partly sung and which show the underworld of ruffians or "jaques"), *entremeses*, and *mojigangas* in which carnival customs are recreated in an uninhibited manner (*Las Carnestolendas* ["Carnival"]) or honor-driven duels are parodied (*El desafío de Juan Rana* ["Juan Rana's Challenge"]). In *Los guisados* ("Stews"), for example, in the middle of an outlandish parade of Spanish dishes presided by Bacchus, Mrs. Olla Podrida ("Mrs. Well-Seasoned Stew") defends her traditional and "pure" roots against the sophisticated French innovations of Mr. Carnero Verde ("Green Ram"). In *La casa de los linajes* ("The House of Noble Descent") amidst a parade of moors, blacks, barbers, and prostitutes (groups that could not obtain letters patent of nobility in Spain), a tripe seller brags that she comes from the lineage with the most blood, since she sells animal entrails. In *Las visiones de la muerte* ("Visions of Death") a traveler, waking from a nap and seeing a group of actors dressed as Soul, Body, Death, and Angel, theologizes his drunkenness by admitting that indeed "life is a dream." It must be remembered that this play was probably performed during the feast of Corpus Christi in 1673, together with, precisely, the *auto* version of *La vida es sueño*. These are allowances granted to a discreet man, a scholastic erudite, and a master of rhetoric who also knew the therapeutic properties of laughter.

All the masks – whether tragic, cheerful, or grotesque – cover the same face. Calderón always conceived life *sub specie theatrali*. For him the world was a theatre or, rather, a permanent "will of representation." Each one of the genres in which Calderón managed to reflect that will represents for him a hypothesis of reality, a possibility of judgment, a laboratory of ideas. Calderón knew what could be said in each one of them, and what required ambiguity, allegory, or just a grotesque farce. Calderón is not a machine that produces universal values: he is a playwright who produces vulnerable texts. Reading him, studying him, or teaching him with the prejudices with which history has judged him makes him smaller and denies him the universality that his vast culture and his capacity for ironic skepticism demand.

16

Didactic prose, history, politics, life writing, convent writing, *Crónicas de Indias*

JORGE CHECA

Court, language, and empire in the age of Charles V

During the rule of Charles V, Spanish literature achieves an international dimension through the work of Archbishop Fray Antonio de Guevara (1474–1546). His attempt to connect with a new reading public outside restricted humanistic groups accounts for Guevara's immense popularity in Spain and Europe, and makes him into a writer who paved the way for the modern essay and the novel. Guevara's chosen topics are usually entrenched in Renaissance culture, but their didacticism becomes subverted by a lighthearted demeanor, the use of apocryphal sources, or the overwhelming presence of rhetorical devices. *Menosprecio de corte y alabanza de aldea* ("Contempt for Life at Court and a Praise for Life in the Country," 1539) exemplifies his ability to play with a constellation of motives mainly stemming from the medieval controversies about courtly life. Here the author's argumentation annuls the traditional dichotomy announced in the title; his apparent diatribe against the court in favor of country life finally contains a somewhat resigned admission that, with all its evils, only the court grants a certain degree of individual autonomy.[1]

Other authors depart from Guevara's rhetorical self-consciousness. Juan de Valdés (1510–1541) wrote in Italy the *Diálogo de la lengua* ("Dialogue About Language"), which confirms the rise of the vernacular Castilian language as a vehicle of culture. By defending the autonomy of his native language, Valdés aligns himself with Pietro Bembo (1470–1547) or Baldassare Castiglione (1474–1529), who in different ways reveal a similar concern for the Italian language. In Spain, the *Gramática de la lengua castellana* ("Grammar of Castilian Language," 1492), written by Antonio de Nebrija (1444?–1522) constitutes a key reference, but, unlike Nebrija, Valdés follows a non-prescriptive approach. Rather than reducing Spanish to a static system of rules, Valdés considers the evolving nature of linguistic phenomena, and establishes the priority of *use* with the goal

---

[1] Francisco Márquez Villanueva, *"Menosprecio de corte y alabanza de aldea" (Valladolid, 1539) y el tema aúlico en la obra de Fray Antonio de Guevara* (Santander: Universidad de Cantabria, 1999), p. 150.

of approximating written language to the oral speech of the Court (the *Diálogo* itself pretends to transcribe a real conversation). In the *Diálogo* Valdés attributes to the vernacular a power to express his inner concepts ("el concepto de mi ánimo") without unnecessary mediations; as a result, he transfers to language the longing for authenticity he also sought in religious experience.

Reformist trends spreading through Europe in the early sixteenth century share this topic. As far as Spain is concerned, Bataillon emphasized, in a landmark study, the enormous relevance of Desiderius Erasmus of Rotterdam (1466–1536) in Charles V's time, and even beyond.[2] At the center of Erasmian thought there is a sharp criticism of the corruption nurturing the Papacy's secular ambitions and its prominence in the European political scene. According to Erasmus, ecclesiastic power has favored exterior and superstitious forms of popular devotion, which pervert Christ's foundational message. The effort to restore this message in all its purity links Erasmus' impressive work as a philologist to his militant enterprise against the ignorance promoted by jargon-ridden Scholastic commentators. These and other groups who belong to the Church apparatus claim to be closer to perfection than common believers, but Erasmus maintains that virtue can also be achieved in secular life on the condition that it peacefully contributes to the overall harmony of society.

Erasmus' influence in the Iberian peninsula reached the emperor's inner circles, and is evident in Alfonso de Valdés (1490–1532), his Secretary of Latin Letters. The elder brother of Juan de Valdés, Alfonso contributed to the formulation of imperial ideology in the wars for European hegemony. His position may seem to contradict Erasmus' quest for universal peace, but Valdés believed this goal only to be attainable under the religious unity provided by the Empire. As a result of the fragmentation fostered by the rise of Protestantism and the growing power of national states, he notes how the Pope has become an obstacle to the reform of Christianity. Consequently, in the *Diálogo de Lactancio y un arcediano* ("Dialogue of Lactancio and an Archdeacon," 1528), Valdés does not hesitate to see in the infamous Sack of Rome (1527) a manifestation of God's designs. Providential ideology likewise articulates the lucianesque *Diálogo de Mercurio y Carón* ("Dialogue of Mercury and Charon," 1529), in which a detailed account of the conflicts between Charles V and the French king Francis I is interspersed with the judgment of types representing contemporary society. The souls condemned in the other world invert the Erasmian principles that Charles V seeks to restore, and they contrast with the utopian vision conveyed by positive examples. In either case, the *Diálogo* stresses the

---

[2] Marcel Bataillon, *Erasmo y España: estudios sobre La historia espiritual del siglo XVI*. Trans. Antonio Alatorre (México: Fondo de Cultura Económica, 1966).

importance of self-knowledge and individual choice, as seen in the sinful nun sent to the convent against her will or in the blessedness achieved by a married man after he experiences an Augustinian process of conversion. A similar path toward moral awareness follows Polidoro, who personifies the perfect monarch; but his ideals of harmony and concord are already being rendered obsolete by Machiavelli's prince, for whom the end famously justified the means.

Order, human differences, and female representations in the era of Felipe II

The era of Felipe II signals the triumph of the Counter-Reformist mentality inspired by the Council of Trent (1545–1563) and the official rejection of Erasmus. Still, several authors offer some resistance to the dogmatic atmosphere of a country increasingly hostile to foreign influences. Among them is the medical doctor Juan Huarte de San Juan (1529–1588), who in 1575 published the first version of *Examen de ingenios* ("The Examination of Men's Wits"), a widely read treatise based on the "empiricist" assumptions of Hippocratic medicine. Huarte seeks to establish an inclusive theory accounting for the different types of psychological profiles (*ingenios*) found in human beings so that he can determine which profession best suits each *ingenio*. This word also points out our innate ability to "engender" provisional drafts or "representations" of diverse learning fields. At this point Huarte's emphasis on creativity connects him with Juan Luis Vives (1492–1540) and, more generally, revives the Renaissance interest in the practical applications of human differences (according, for example, to Alfonso de Valdés, moral awareness is hardly possible without knowing one's "complexion" or organic predisposition). As Huarte underscores the relevance of his theory for effective social organization, however, he does not ignore the bureaucratic complexity demanded by modern states.

One of the prominent writers of this time is the Augustinian Fray Luis de León (1527–1591), a professor from Salamanca whose biblical and theological work attracted the wrath of the Inquisition (he spent five years in jail). In the dialogue *De los nombres de Cristo* ("The Names of Christ," 1583) – a detailed exegesis of nine denominations attributed to Christ in the Gospels – Fray Luis develops the assumption that names are substantial ciphers of the concepts they represent. The power of sacred language to condense a rich semantic potential is again exemplified in *La perfecta casada* ("The Perfect Wife," 1583), where Fray Luis subjects chapter 31 of Solomon's Proverbs to a moral commentary. Fray Luis focuses on woman's duties within marriage, a debated issue following post-reformist trends and emergent conceptions about the family as a social institution. Admittedly, *La perfecta casada* is partially indebted to misogynist doctrines formulated by early Church authorities; but Fray Luis also sketches a rationalized picture of domestic economy, arguing for a strict distribution of duties among all household members. In the ensuing organization – fashioned like an ideal political community – the wife must preserve the wealth and position achieved by the husband and such a goal demands her exemplary behavior toward children and servants. Virtue and productivity appear to be closely united in Fray Luis' text.

The limitations imposed upon women in the early modern period make of the convent an exceptional locus for female writing. Although studied in a previous chapter, Saint Teresa of Avila (1515–1582) should be mentioned again insofar as she poses an alternative to woman's integration within the domestic hierarchy. Contrary, for instance, to Fray Luis in *La perfecta casada* – with its preestablished role for Christian wives – Saint Teresa creates, in works like *El libro de la vida* ("The Book of Her Life," 1565), an assertive textual space where she struggles to persuade her often suspicious audiences about the truth of her ecstatic experiences. The scene of mystical enunciation is therefore linked in Saint Teresa to the authorial first person as well as to the hidden Reality hinted also in the manner of a secret;[3] all of these elements are private realms, placed at the margins of common norms or institutions.

The *Crónicas de Indias*

The *Crónicas de Indias* comprise a huge textual corpus revolving around the discovery, conquest, and colonization of the New World in the sixteenth and seventeenth centuries. Although often interdependent, these texts touch upon heterogeneous subject matters and disciplines – history, geography, ethnology, theology, etc. While even a summary of such a vast corpus of material is impossible, a few ideas can be presented about the *Crónicas*' cultural significance.

One important question relates to the weight assigned to inherited beliefs and models of thought. Starting with Christopher Columbus (1451–1506), *cronistas* often tend to see in the New World a confirmation of myths or lands which had figured in ancient and medieval sources. The prestige of authorities such as the Bible and Aristotle would prevail over the years; and if experience certainly gains an increasing value, Elliott has remarked how the writers' presuppositions turn out to

---

[3] Michel de Certeau, *The Mystic Fable.* Vol. 1: *The Sixteenth and Seventeenth Centuries* (Chicago: University of Chicago Press, 1992), pp. 99, 145.

be as revealing as the things observed. Discussions about the conquest, its legitimacy, or the merits of recently discovered religions and ways of life are never free of ideological prejudice, hence the polemic character frequently present in the *Crónicas*.[4] A providential view of history, for example, could serve very different interests in the hands of Columbus, Gonzalo Fernández de Oviedo (1478–1557), Hernán Cortés (1485–1547), or the Inca Garcilaso de la Vega (1539–1616). By the same token, the classical distinction between barbarity and civilization remained open to antagonistic uses and interpretations, as did the concept of Nature versus culture. Thus in his *Brevísima relación de la destrucción de las Indias* ("A Brief Account of the Destruction of the Indies," 1552), Bartolomé de las Casas (1474–1566) condemns the violence committed by conquerors and *encomenderos* (colonials who had been granted lands and Indians to work them), while praising the utopian simplicity of their victims. There is a much larger scope in Las Casas' *Apologética historia sumaria* ("Apologetic History," 1559), where he compares American cultures favorably to those developed by ancient and contemporary nations. Partially inspired by Las Casas, Garcilaso de la Vega's *Comentarios reales* ("Royal Commentaries," 1609) will carry out a rehabilitation of Incaic civilization; in humanistic fashion, Garcilaso bases his authority on a deep familiarity with the language and culture of his native ancestors. Methodological rigor and thoroughness had previously informed Bernardino de Sahagún's anthropological work about Mexico.

The latter examples demonstrate that, for some chronicle writers, the notion of authority reaches beyond canonical sources by introducing more immediate perceptions of reality – an attitude permeating earlier accounts of the conquest of Mexico. In the letters of Hernán Cortés to Charles V, both lived history and autobiography are combined in the voice of a military leader who seeks legal sanction for his rebellious enterprise. Bernal Díaz del Castillo – one of Cortés' soldiers – wrote *Historia verdadera de la conquista de la Nueva España* ("The True Story of the Conquest of Mexico," 1568); its proclaimed *truth* enhances the writer's role as witness to events narrated from a non-official, demythologizing perspective.

Problematic identities: history, autobiography, satire, political thought, and secular ethics in the Baroque period

The transition into the seventeenth century is characterized by a widespread feeling of crisis, not only founded on socio-economic causes but

---

4 Mercedes Serna, ed., *Crónicas de Indias* (Madrid: Cátedra, 2000), pp. 50–54.

also on the realization that Spain is irrevocably losing its hegemony. The need to define the identity of a beleaguered monarchy by affirming its Visigothic roots brings forth a renewed interest in national history, mainly promoted by Juan de Mariana (1536–1624) in his *Historia general de España* ("A General History of Spain," first published in 1598). Mariana's monumental project extends from the origins of Spain to King Fernando el Católico, with an addendum which reaches up to 1621. It is imbued with a sense of moral exemplarity, at one point summarized in the call to restore the former strength of values allegedly intrinsic to the nation – frugality, religious piety, mistrust of foreign influences. In a certain sense, other works about institutions and events partake of Mariana's defensive ideology. Pedro de Ribadeneyra (1526–1611) – a distinguished member of the Company of Jesus, like Mariana – published in 1583 his *Vida del Padre Ignacio de Loyola* ("The Life of Father Ignatius of Loyola"), the first biography of the Jesuit founder and a key document to understanding the Company's militant spirit. Ribadeneyra's position as propagandist of Counter Reform ideals is further shown in his influential history of the schismatic movement in sixteenth-century England.

Later on, Luisa de Carvajal (1566–1614) would describe the precarious situation experienced by English Catholics in a collection of letters written between 1605 and 1613. A woman of aristocratic extraction, Carvajal lived poorly in London, where she sought martyrdom in the service of the persecuted cause of Catholicism. Poignant and informative as they are, Carvajal's letters formulate above all a peculiar model of heroic self-fashioning established upon the willingness to sacrifice one's life. It is true that her disposition fits within Baroque religious paradigms; but male autobiographies produced during the same period attribute to the self a protean, even dazzling versatility when relating the protagonist's ordeals in hostile environments. Along with their dubious veracity, this is perhaps the most distinctive trait of the genre known as "soldiers' lives," of which the *Vidas* ("Lives") of Alonso de Contreras (b. 1582) and Diego Duque de Estrada (1589–1647) are the best examples.

An unsurpassed gift for verbal creation constitutes the most evident feature in Francisco de Quevedo's (1580–1645) multifaceted personality as a writer, to the extent that, according to Borges, more than a single author, he is himself a complex literature. In different registers, the voices of the lyric poet, the satirist, the Neostoic philosopher, or the political thinker often complement one another within Quevedo, although it is not unusual that they establish among themselves paradoxical or even contradictory relations. Also, the *Sueños* ("Dreams") – Quevedo's prose satires written between 1605 and 1621 – manifest a radical ambiguity announced in the collection's title. As its narrator suggests, "sueños" refer there to oneiric visions containing revealed truths, but the word may also designate the caprices of his uncontrolled imagination during sleep. Echoing both meanings, the texts generally fluctuate between their proclaimed didactic purpose and their irrepressible drive to dissolve it by means of grotesque associations and ingenious wordplay. In four *Sueños* (there are five in total), this semantic indeterminacy is applied to otherworldly settings or situations; here Menippean conventions such as the mixture of the serious and the comic – mostly borrowed from Lucian – contribute to unmask "the world as it really is" (to paraphrase the title of one piece). It is clear that, for Quevedo, hypocrisy presides over most of the remaining sins, for it disguises them under seemingly positive or harmless "figures" or "figuras."[5] However, his texts are not free of dissimulation as long as many satirical targets appear to be excuses for an exhibition of wit. With its attention to the productivity of language, Quevedo's *conceptismo* ultimately becomes a double-edged instrument – either capable of uncovering hidden realities or perpetuating them through mechanisms of displacement.

Both Quevedo's involvement in power intrigues during the reigns of Felipe III and Felipe IV, and his own work, attest to the centrality of politics in Baroque thought. The urgency to confront the impact of Machiavellism carries with it numerous debates about the "reason of State" – a concept earlier documented in Francesco Guicciardini (1483–1540) and Giovani della Casa (1503–1556), but reformulated by Botero and Ribadeneyra, who try to make it compatible with Catholic principles. Writers more pragmatically and secularly oriented would in turn proclaim themselves disciples of the Roman historian Cornelius Tacitus (55?–120?). Popularized in Spain thanks to the Belgian humanist Justus Lipsius (1547–1606), the movement found in Tacitus a model to interpret present realities, thus stressing the applicability of ancient history. If Tacitism considers history a privileged source of political prudence, it also emphasizes that many outcomes and situations cannot be easily predicted owing to their contingent nature. Prudence then requires an empirical understanding of the circumstances concurring in cases for which no general rules are available, as repeatedly indicated by the diplomat Diego Saavedra Fajardo (1584–1648) in his *Empresas políticas* ("The Royal Politician Represented in One Hundred Emblems," 1640). Saavedra follows here the generic vogue inaugurated by Alciatus' *Emblemata* and combines written texts and visual images with the aim of fashioning the idea of a perfect statesman. In the prologue to his work, Saavedra indicates that the term "idea" means for him a model or epitome as well as an architectonic design, and

---

5 Domingo Ynduráin, "Contradicciones en la obra de Quevedo." In *Homenaje a Quevedo. Academia literaria renacentista*. Vol. II. Ed. V. García de la Concha (Salamanca: Universidad de Salamanca, 1982), p. 478.

hence the *Empresas* seem to point toward an overall discursive coherence. As he does not fail to observe later on, however, slightly different cases may lead statesmen to defend contrary points of view whose uncertainty cancels out the possibility of building a system. That is why, rather than a self-sufficient doctrine, the *Empresas* postulate "a method of creating ideological precautions."[6]

In fact, political paradigms of conduct become so pervasive that the Jesuit Baltasar Gracián (1601–1658) extends them to the sphere of everyday interaction. In *El héroe* ("The Hero," 1637), he already offers the reader "una razón de estado de ti mismo" ("your own reason of state"), and the political image suggests how Gracián sees individual behaviors in the competitive terms usually applied to statecraft. This outlook is emphasized in *Oráculo manual y arte de prudencia* ("The Art of Worldly Wisdom. A Pocket Oracle," 1647), whose 300 aphorisms provide the blueprint for a worldly ethics based on opportunism, dissimulation, and deciphering of others' intentions. With its fragmentary, open-ended form, aphoristic writing shows in the *Oráculo* that the enormous variety of cases and dilemmas confronting us cannot be contained within the limits of any book – even Gracián's. His text therefore puts readers on guard against ready-made formulas, while, from a literary standpoint, it tends to erase generic definitions – something again perceptible in *Agudeza y arte de ingenio* ("Art and Figures of Wit," final version completed in 1648). A treatise exemplifying the poetic figures produced by the faculty of *ingenio* ("wit"), the *Agudeza* explores the epistemological dimension of *conceptismo* as a concrete, temporal way to discover hidden correspondences in reality. Under such light, *ingenio* turns out to be much more than a gift for inventing daring metaphors; according to Hidalgo-Serna it constitutes a method of knowledge in its own right, opposed to abstract and rationalistic thinking.[7] The legacy left by other early modern apologists of human creativity – such as Vives and Huarte de San Juan – is still alive in Gracián's book.

---

[6] Mercedes Blanco, *Les Rhétoriques de la pointe. Baltasar Gracián et le conceptisme en Europe* (Paris: Honoré Champion, 1992), p. 512.

[7] Emilio Hidalgo-Serna, *El pensamiento ingenioso de Baltasar Gracián*. Barcelona: Anthropos, 1993.

Part V

The Enlightenment and Neoclassicism

PHILIP DEACON, JOAQUÍN ÁLVAREZ
BARRIENTOS

17

Spain and Enlightenment

PHILIP DEACON

New light appeared on Spain's intellectual horizons in the 1680s, and for more than a century afterwards the impulse for renewal through skeptical questioning of past truths and methods brought significant changes in cultural attitudes and practices. Yet the context of Spain's intellectual and social life was distinctive, and just as the French experience of Enlightenment was different from Britain's, so Enlightenment in Spain must be examined on its own terms, though from a reasoned comparative perspective.[1] For the intellectual historian, Enlightenment primarily concerns knowledge and the move from authoritative, privileged forms of truth to a skeptical, reasoning, empirically based conception. John Locke's assertion in 1690 of the sense-data basis of knowledge and the role of the human understanding in processing experience gave new significance to the individual and the action of the mind in subscribing to and appropriating truths. An assumption by the individual of responsibility for challenging error or unquestioned authority effected a process of personal emancipation and self-confidence. Locke's theory de-emphasized the reliance on authority, especially religious, and, in combination with Francis Bacon's empirical paradigm of scientific research, this led to the secularized concept of knowledge familiar today.[2] The assault on authoritative knowledge challenged the power of those asserting it, and in Spain the existence of an Inquisition, whose vigilance over theological orthodoxy embraced the sciences and philosophy, implied a lack of freedom and consequent danger when arguing for change. Daring to know, in Immanuel Kant's opportune allusion to Horace (*Sapere aude*), entailed risk in Spain. The Catholic Church asserted a monopoly on knowledge and truth, punishing the written and oral expression of intellectual dissidence.[3]

The objectifying imagery sometimes used to describe intellectual change, as in references to "the Enlightenment entering Spain," can

---

[1] Francisco Sánchez-Blanco, *Europa y el pensamiento español del siglo XVIII* (Madrid: Alianza, 1992).

[2] Roy Porter, *Enlightenment: Britain and the Creation of the Modern World* (London: Allen Lane – The Penguin Press, 2000).

[3] Marcelin Defourneaux, *Inquisición y censura de libros en la España del siglo XVIII* (Madrid: Taurus, 1973).

misrepresent the way in which individuals have actively to assume ideas which involve changes of mentality. Only those already close to adopting new methods and practices can welcome such transformations. If ideas operated in the inexorably physical way that the concept of "influence" suggests, then Spanish Inquisitors who had privileged access to radical foreign texts would have been the most enlightened people in Spain. Human minds rather engage with and appropriate concepts, making them the basis for further thought and action. An inquiry into Enlightenment in Spain would point to the process of intellectual change experienced by growing numbers of educated Spaniards from the 1680s onwards, but admit that too few members of privileged groups with power to alter political and social structures were sufficiently determined to effect radical reforms. Enlightened attitudes can be observed in various Spaniards, apparent in diverse aspects of cultural and social life, and held with varying degrees of conviction. Whereas King Carlos III reduced Inquisitorial powers in the 1760s, he allowed the same Inquisition to put on trial, humiliate, and condemn to imprisonment the politician and intellectual Pablo de Olavide (1725–1803) a decade later, to the dismay of progressive thinkers in Spain and elsewhere.[4]

Enlightenment in Spain is customarily compared with the French experience, often framed in terms of the attack on established religion. Spain undoubtedly witnessed a growing secularization in intellectual and social matters, but beginning from a different starting point and circumscribed by different conditions. A similar, preconceived paradigm of Enlightenment prompts the question as to who was Spain's Voltaire or Diderot, Locke or Hume, unmindful of the limits on expression in Spain which prevented the emergence of comparable individuals. Similarly there was no "little flock" to parallel the authors of the *Encyclopédie*. The clearest evidence of Spain's intellectual vitality is found in the journals of Carlos III's reign (1759–1788) in which most of the articles are unsigned, and significant contributors like Manuel de Aguirre (1748–1800) have only recently been identified; many authors, though, may never emerge from anonymity.

It is the espousal of pluralism and an undogmatic tone which Roy Porter sees as characteristic of the Enlightenment sensibility. Figures at the vanguard of the enlightening process may share broad convictions and sympathies but differ radically on key issues. The multiplication of intellectual fields which the pursuit of knowledge produced led to this fragmentation and the impossibility of over-arching truths. The picture for Spain, like Britain, reveals no systematic set of proposals for

---

[4] Richard Herr, *The Eighteenth-Century Revolution in Spain* (Princeton: Princeton University Press, 1958), pp. 27–29, 78.

implementation, but rather a host of small-scale objectives which would make society more open and pluralistic, less dogmatic and intolerant. Some scholars have focused on economic progress as characteristic of eighteenth-century Spanish reformism, yet the end results would benefit the rich and privileged more than the mass of the population. Even the suggestion that Enlightenment can be equated with the desire to educate is problematic since it depends on whether education is viewed as learning accepted notions from the past or as a skeptical quest in which truth is tentative, always subject to testing and modification.

Turning specifically to Enlightenment in Spain, the objective of "desengaño de errores comunes" ("correcting common errors"), featured in the full title of Benito Feijoo's *Teatro crítico universal* ("Universal Theatre of Criticism"), coincides with the epistemological thrust of Enlightenment across Europe, even though it emphasizes demolishing rather than constructing. The goal of economic reform advocated under Carlos III was pursued in the name of general happiness, a change from previous justifications for action. The secular idea that happiness might belong in this world seems basic to Enlightenment thought and social reform, and the concept of sociability which emphasizes a pragmatic accommodation between individual and society suffuses Spanish Enlightenment texts. Similarly the openness to the outside world, with publications, especially journals, transmitting information, news, and arguments to an eager reading public indicates a desire to learn, to experiment, to benefit from the contemplation of alternatives, and to embrace regeneration. If French influence in eighteenth-century Spain has been emphasized in previous historical accounts, it is principally because French society was a contemporary focus for modernization, and familiarity with the French language made information about it accessible for Spaniards. Even so, intellectual dialogue with Italy continued to flourish, particularly in the arts, legal theory, and historiography. However, it is the interaction with British culture, notably in the spheres of physics, medicine, and epistemology, which, from a methodological and hence more radical perspective, now appears increasingly significant, above all during the early phase of intellectual renewal.[5]

Viewed chronologically, an enlightened mentality is detectable first in small groups of Spanish intellectuals in the 1680s, shared by many more toward the middle of the new century, and fully evident in the wide discussion, questioning, and debate of Carlos III's reign, being an inescapable feature of public discourse in the 1780s. Nevertheless, though significant numbers of articulate Spaniards displayed an enlightened mentality by the 1790s, they were not influential enough to suffuse major centers of

5 Francisco Sánchez-Blanco, *La Ilustración en España* (Madrid: Akal, 1997).

power and prevent the backlash of the French Revolution frustrating the possibility of widespread change. Though the constitutional debates at Cadiz (1810–1812) reveal the prevalence and sophistication of enlightened attitudes, forces of reaction centered on the monarchy, Church, and socially privileged groups impeded the transformation and modernization of society which might have occurred and which Spanish liberalism would later attempt to resume.

The period of the *novatores* (loosely speaking 1675–1725), characterized by small groups of intellectuals dubbed "innovators,"[6] reveals attitudes centered on a rejection of the inherited beliefs, methods, and practices found in medicine and related fields such as physics and biology, subjects then close to philosophy. Research on such figures as the doctors Juan de Cabriada (dates unknown) and Diego Mateo Zapata (1664–1745) makes clear their sense of combating the errors of traditional beliefs in the name of empirical models of truth.[7] Such an attitude was not without risk, and Zapata and Juan Muñoz y Peralta (b. *c.* 1665) had important brushes with the Inquisition. The epistemological basis of past practice was rejected by figures who took their cue from Francis Bacon's empirical methodology and Robert Boyle's practical advocacy of skeptical experimentalism at the Royal Society in London. Methods and errors contained in texts deriving from previously unquestioned authorities were rejected in favor of verifiable truths and proofs which were observable. Locke's epistemology, known early in Spain via Latin or French translations, underlined the focus on the individual mind as the source of knowledge.

Part of the novelty lay in the rejection of universities and an initial focus on the *tertulia*, the private, often informal, gathering of committed seekers after truth. In Seville this led to the creation of the Regia Sociedad Sevillana de Medicina, given royal approval in 1700 before the Bourbon Felipe V ascended the throne.[8] Similar groupings could be found in Barcelona, Madrid, Zaragoza, and Valencia.[9] Their activities found support from government collaborators such as Pedro Portocarrero and Melchor de Macanaz whose reformism, based on accurate appreciation of economic and social realities, adopted an internationalist comparative perspective,

---

[6] Jesús Pérez Magallón, *Construyendo la modernidad: la cultura española en el tiempo de los novatores (1675–1725)* (Madrid: CSIC, 2002).

[7] José María López Piñero, *La introducción de la ciencia moderna en España* (Barcelona: Ariel, 1969).

[8] Antonio Hermosilla Molina, *Cien años de medicina sevillana (La Regia Sociedad de Medicina y demás Ciencias, de Sevilla, en el siglo XVIII)* (Seville: Diputación Provincial, 1970).

[9] Pedro Álvarez de Miranda, "Las academias de los novatores." In *De las academias a la Enciclopedia: el discurso del saber en la modernidad*. Ed. Evangelina Rodríguez Cuadros (Valencia: Edicions Alfons el Magnànim, 1993), pp. 265–300.

while an immediate predecessor like the diplomat Conde de Fernán Núñez revealed a similarly empirical position.

A second phase of Enlightenment is detectable in the 1720s when Martín Martínez (1684–1734) published his *Medicina escéptica* ("Skeptical Medicine," 1722) and *Filosofía escéptica* ("Skeptical Philosophy," 1730), provoking both university and medical establishments. His parallel attack on astrology, *Juicio final de la astrología* ("Last Judgment on Astrology," 1727), attempted to dethrone the reputation of this pseudo-science in universities. Martínez was supported by the Benedictine Friar Feijoo (1676–1764), who began publication of his supremely influential *Teatro crítico universal* in 1726. Each of Feijoo's eight volumes contained sometimes lengthy essays on such topics as national pride, the intellectual equality of women, false miracles, erroneous popular beliefs and superstitions, and more broadly encompassed medicine, physics, and the natural world. The aim of "correcting common errors" was at the forefront of Feijoo's mind, and he taught several generations of Spaniards how to reason and think over the next hundred years, as his writings were constantly reprinted and even sold as individual essays. In 1746 Feijoo switched genre to compile five volumes of *Cartas eruditas y curiosas* ("Letters on Curious and Learned Subjects"). His method was skeptical but positive, taking great care to avoid conflict with the Church establishment, especially the Inquisition, but his writings brought a flood of replies in both book and pamphlet form, some in support, but many in opposition. However, the backing of King Fernando VI (reigned 1746–1759) ensured his continuity. Feijoo's method was firmly empirical. When the traditional belief in the danger of eating after consuming drinking chocolate needed testing, he ate peaches after a good helping of chocolate to prove its falsity.

Feijoo operated from his convent cell in Oviedo, shunning the limelight while ensuring that his words reached a growing readership. A parallel figure, Gregorio Mayans (1699–1781), after a period as Royal Librarian in Madrid, retired to Oliva in Valencia to continue editing and publishing, while influencing scholarly friends via private letters. Mayans' idea of intellectual reform derived from classical humanism, and his main areas of activity were history, literature, and education, in particular through the editing of texts and compiling of manuals on such subjects as rhetoric. Mayans' reformism is based on the recovery of past intellectual virtues, being in that sense backward-looking and less concerned to explore the new or embrace progress.

Both Feijoo and Mayans survived into the 1760s, coinciding with the reign of Carlos III (reigned 1759–1788), when economic upturn favored bolder action. The revolutionary innovation of the period was the intellectual periodical, several being modeled on the English *Spectator* (1711–1714) and *Tatler* (1709–1711) of Joseph Addison and Richard Steele.

An earlier, short-lived, intellectual journal, the *Diario de los literatos de España* ("The Spanish Review of Books," 1737–1742), had provoked the wrath of various authors, including Mayans, who saw their publications submitted to rigorous critiques. *El Pensador* ("The Thinker," 1762–1767), edited by José Clavijo y Fajardo (1728–1808), was by contrast witty and amusing, while also being intellectually provocative. It borrowed and naturalized without acknowledgment texts by Rousseau, Steele, and Swift, making them applicable to Spain, but mainly comprised new materials in the same spirit, reaching eighty-six issues in all, many confessedly not written by the editor. Subject matter ranged over literature, social behavior, relations between the sexes, philosophy, religion, upbringing and education, and differences between nations, mostly conveyed in a light, conversational, ironic style. Formal preferences included argument and response, dialogue, dreams, essays, invective, and letters, all designed to question and provoke. Multiple points of view were common and the desire to stimulate discussion seemed paramount. Responses to *El Pensador* ranged from slim pamphlets to whole new periodicals, ostensibly the product of thinkers, male and female, from Cadiz, Salamanca, and even, supposedly, Heaven.[10] Other rival periodicals featured commerce, foreign news, literary criticism, religion, and textual miscellanies, but most were short-lived, with few surviving the political and economic instability of the mid 1760s.[11]

Not until the 1780s was there a revival, but some of the new titles were intellectually weighty. Publications with a miscellaneous content, appearing once or more a week, with articles usually unsigned, contributed to an intellectual effervescence whose quality and range is extraordinary. Recognized at the time by some as the boldest was the essay-periodical *El Censor* ("The Censor"), edited by the lawyers Luis García del Cañuelo (1744–1801/2) and Luis Pereira (1754–1811), yet incorporating anonymously texts by Gaspar Melchor Jovellanos, Juan Meléndez Valdés, Félix Samaniego, and others hitherto unidentified. Over a six-year period (1781–1787) *El Censor* published 167 numbers, being suspended twice before final closure. Though it appeared to enjoy royal favor, evident in a loosening of censorship in 1785, the motives behind its demise were never clarified, but its articles tackled sensitive areas such as legislation, government policy, ecclesiastical matters, the economy, and moral and philosophical issues usually the preserve of the Church. Subjects were treated from a variety of perspectives, always designed to provoke, and sometimes resorting to stylistic subtlety and obliquity in order to evade

[10] Francisco Aguilar Piñal, *La prensa española en el siglo XVIII. Diarios, revistas y pronósticos* (Madrid: CSIC, 1978).

[11] Paul-J. Guinard, *La Presse espagnole de 1737 à 1791. Formation et signification d'un genre* (Paris: Institut d'Etudes Hispaniques, 1973).

persecution. A government inquiry into authorship ensued in 1789, following Inquisitorial condemnation of many numbers.

The *Correo de los ciegos de Madrid* ("The Madrid Post," 1786–
1791) was a miscellany, with articles frequently stretching over many
numbers. José de Cadalso's extensive meditation on Spain, *Cartas marruecas* ("Moroccan Letters"), first appeared anonymously in its pages in
1789, as did radical texts by Manuel de Aguirre. The tone was often
very serious, with many articles political in outlook, but it ranged widely
over history, philosophy, and social behavior. Current literary activities received coverage, and overall it appealed to serious intellectuals,
as subscription lists testify. The *Espíritu de los mejores diarios literarios que se publican en Europa* ("Epitome of the Best European Cultural
Journals," 1787–1791) contained largely translated material, although
articles by Spanish authors were included. Coverage embraced political, economic, and social matters, and enabled Spanish readers ignorant of foreign languages to keep abreast of intellectual life elsewhere
in Europe. The monthly *Memorial literario* ("Literary Record," 1784–
1808) was a cultural miscellany, including reviews of plays performed in
Madrid, accounts of new books, among them translations, and reports of
academies and public lectures; it covered the Madrid Economic Society's
debate on women's entry (they were denied full membership), but was
generally uncontroversial, except on drama.

Periodicals stimulated cultural life and provoked responses in pamphlets or rival journals, creating intellectual dialogue. The regularity of
publication created a sense of cultural exuberance as one issue gave way
to the next, with censors obliged to turn around copy fast. Since most
articles rarely had names attached to them, translated work might appear
undifferentiated alongside texts by Spanish authors, and more radical
materials could often be inserted unobtrusively. Print runs were not high
but each issue might be consumed by various readers in urban coffee-
houses and inns. Topical debates, like the defense of Spain's reputation
against a French critic in the 1780s, provoked a diversity of responses
and a sense of intellectual dynamism never before experienced. The premature demise of *El Censor* was indicative of the risks involved and of
the threatening ideological climate. However, few could have imagined
that governmental reaction to events in France would bring about the
overnight closure of this enlightening medium on 24 February 1791, on
the orders of the Prime Minister Floridablanca. Fear had taken hold of
the government and the periodical press would never recover such preeminence.

Spain's universities, by contrast, stagnated in the eighteenth century,
attracting a lower proportion of suitably aged students than previously.
Whereas noble offspring might acquire sociability, the aspiring "middle

classes" studied law and theology which led to jobs in the administration, Church, or legal professions. Reforms initiated under Carlos III closed down some institutions and introduced new subjects like natural law, but ideological (usually clerical) control reinforced conformism. Intellectual innovation tended to center on private intellectual gatherings (*tertulias*), which, in principle, were more sheltered from Inquisitorial prying than open meetings, and could challenge the status quo and pursue novelty more readily. Informal groups flourished throughout the century, though details are sometimes hard to come by, information often deriving from unpublished correspondence or Inquisitorial documentation resulting from investigation of their activities. One important literary *tertulia* met in a hotel, the Fonda de San Sebastián, in Madrid; its members variously combined the professions of writer, translator, soldier, professor, historian, and entrepreneur. Discussion centered on poetry, the theatre, bull-fighting, and love affairs, but the informality gave protection against intrusion into sensitive matters, though several members were subject to Inquisitorial investigation.

A major, new, Madrid-based institution began as a private gathering led by a prominent individual. The Real Academia Española, constituted in 1714, had its origins in the Marqués de Villena's *tertulia*. The original idea had been for an academy of all the sciences, not just language and literature, and similar plans for linked institutions were put forward throughout the century although no academy of sciences was established. The Academia began energetically by producing a six-volume dictionary of Spanish (1726–1739), with usage quoted from authoritative sources, and the presiding spirit was reformist in accordance with the academy's motto to "cleanse, establish, and give splendor" to the language. A grammar of Spanish subsequently appeared (1771), but plans for a manual of poetics did not bear fruit. The Real Academia de la Historia (Royal Academy of History) was created in 1738, but though intending to distinguish between truth and myth in Spain's past its influence on historiography was not decisive and its activities rarely reached the public. Meetings were frequently battle grounds between empiricists and those unable to escape from a mythological approach to history, though the Academy attracted intellectuals of the caliber of Jovellanos.[12]

Arguably the most innovative new institutions were the Sociedades Económicas de Amigos del País ("Economic Societies of Friends of the Nation"), of which some hundred were established. The forerunner, at Vergara in the Basque Country (1765), was followed by Madrid (1774), and, once the government attorney Pedro Rodríguez de Campomanes

---

[12] Javier Varela, *Jovellanos* (Madrid: Alianza, 1988), pp. 62–75.

promoted the concept in print, societies sprang up all over Spain.[13] The underlying motivation was to increase prosperity by spreading knowledge and providing mutual support for economic progress, which in turn would promote the well-being and happiness of the population. Those who stood most to gain were the nobles, church hierarchy, land owners, merchant classes, and businessmen, as Campomanes indicated, and, once given official backing, societies recruited significant numbers, including intellectuals. The main meetings involved discussion sessions, usually broken down into the areas most relevant for each location. Madrid focused on agriculture, trades, and manufacturing, and members experimented with seeds and plows; other societies included such subjects as chemistry, fishing, and metallurgy. Being centers of education and information as well as discussion, the societies published accounts of their activities, emphasizing the dissemination of knowledge. In parallel, their libraries accumulated relevant publications and technical data, often from abroad, being allowed to possess the *Encyclopédie* for its scientific and technological entries, although the work was banned by the Inquisition for its philosophical articles. Only the well-to-do with spare time could attend formal meetings but the parallel educational function led to classes in agriculture, arithmetic, botany, chemistry, mechanics, physics, spinning, and weaving, entrusted to hired teachers. While the long-term fruits of the activities are difficult to assess, the desire to question past practices and pool talents for the common good cannot be denied in institutions which had an air of equality about them. Regrettably the atmosphere of suspicion and fear resulting from the French Revolution led to a marked decline in enthusiasm at the end of the century, from which the societies never recovered.

Enlightened questioning of received ideas and practices was countered at all stages by individuals and groups opposed to change. Given the social structures of early modern Spain those most likely to oppose Enlightenment were the universities, clergy, and nobility, whose ideological and socio-economic privileges might seem threatened.[14] Of these the clergy were most prominent in their opposition to Enlightenment. Since the late fifteenth century the Church had entrenched its monopoly over thought, extending from theological beliefs to all forms of spoken, written, and pictorial expression, as well as actions claimed to belong to the realm of orthodoxy. Authors casting doubt on established beliefs would be countered by publications from the pens of ecclesiastical guardians against

[13] Luis Miguel Enciso Recio, "Las Sociedades Económicas de Amigos del País." In *Historia de España*. Vol. xxxi: *La época de la Ilustración*. Part i: *El Estado y la cultura (1759–1808)*. Ed. J. M. Jover Zamora (Madrid: Espasa-Calpe, 1985), pp. 13–56.

[14] François Lopez, "La resistencia a la Ilustración: bases sociales y medios de acción" and "El pensamiento tradicionalista." In Jover Zamora, ed., *El estado y la cultura*, pp. 767–851.

alleged heresy. The writings of Feijoo were answered principally by fellow clerics, and the tally of counter-Enlightenment publications reveals the weight of ecclesiastical opposition, which grew as the century advanced. When an anti-torture debate took off in the 1770s in response to the ideas of Beccaria, Alfonso de Acevedo (an opponent of torture), was promptly countered by a clerical defender, Pedro de Castro, a subsequent adversary of *El Censor*. The teaching of economics at the Aragonese Economic Society was similarly denounced by the Capuchin Friar Diego de Cádiz. One of the harshest anti-Enlightenment satires, *El siglo ilustrado: vida de don Guindo Cerezo* ("The Enlightened Century: Life of don Guindo Cerezo," 1776), a manuscript parody biography of Pablo de Olavide, attributed to a cleric, served to denigrate the former government administrator on the eve of his Inquisitorial trial.

Until the reign of Carlos III, civil censorship was virtually monopolized by clerical figures,[15] but the Holy Office acted as secondary watchdog over culture. Ports and land frontiers were controlled by Inquisition personnel who confiscated anything deemed heterodox. Those caught in possession of prohibited materials, often unaware who might be spying on their cultural choices, were denounced for possession, reading, or lending of prohibited texts. Works criticizing ecclesiastical practices or proposing philosophical alternatives to Catholic orthodoxy were constantly being banned. Voltaire's works suffered a blanket prohibition, as did materialistic or deistic texts, and in the second half of the century the confiscations and condemnations increased. Locke and Montesquieu circulated for decades in French until a final ban, and the pace of prohibitions accelerated between the massive, cumulative Inquisitorial *Index* of 1790 and its 1805 *Supplement*. Illegally imported erotic texts, often searingly anticlerical, were promptly condemned, once identified; a few Spanish poets boldly circulated erotic manuscripts among friends, but all major compositions were eventually banned. Spanish authors and readers of condemned works were admonished and underwent spiritual re-education in convents. Individuals heard airing "propositions" like the denial of Hell, the virgin birth, or the sinfulness of fornication, were similarly punished and humiliated. In spite of Church condemnations, heterodox materials were increasingly circulated and discussed; a readership evidently existed and the punishments failed to deter.

Nevertheless, in clear testimony to the preeminence of the political, the key moments of intellectual repression resulted from political crisis. The widespread riots of 1766 provoked a ban on satirical writings which affected many types of dissent. The crisis of the 1780s, in which the defense

---

[15] Lucienne Domergue, *Censure et lumières dans le règne de Charles III* (Paris: CNRS, 1982).

of Spain's historical reputation was central (a position basically justifying non-Enlightenment), heralded the more comprehensive repression of 1791. The violent turn taken by the Revolution in France led to measures by Carlos IV's government to suffocate enlightened discussion by banning all but government periodicals. In parallel the Inquisition was summoned to defend the status quo, identifying social and cultural reform with the supposed undermining of Church and state. For the next three decades, with brief intervals of respite, the publication and expression of Enlightenment ideas was difficult. Civil censorship reverted largely to clerical hands; novels, frequently deemed useless, were refused examination in 1799. Even the mild criticism of convent education and chiding of superstition in Moratín's *El sí de las niñas* ("A Girl's Consent," 1805) brought a ban on the work in 1819.

If Enlightenment involves effecting a change in mentality, the achievements in eighteenth-century Spain are undeniable, though limited. The empiricism of the *novatores* was increasingly incorporated into scientific thinking as the century advanced, though some institutions were unwilling to accept the decline of authoritative truth. The parallel habit of critical thought, incorporating epistemological skepticism, established the centrality of reason and logical argument in public discourse. State initiatives to reform agriculture provide an example. Government administrators gathered information nationwide and the resulting dossier was passed to the Madrid Economic Society for consultation before Jovellanos' final *Informe* ("Report," 1795) was published. The fact that changed political circumstances impeded its implementation glaringly revealed the strength and nature of anti-Enlightenment forces at that moment.[16]

In the area of religion growing secularization was evident. In the period of the *novatores* the acceptance of "probabilism" as a way of allowing the discussion of heretical beliefs as hypotheses, while notionally admitting their falsity, was a sign of intellectual tolerance.[17] The constant appeal to reform indicated the abandonment of the fatalistic notion that the status quo was enshrined by God. Whereas the survival of the Inquisition bore witness to the hegemony of anti-Enlightenment forces, the fact that its usefulness was questioned, its powers reduced, and its existence finally abolished (1834) was an overdue victory for Enlightenment. Though the Church defended the Holy Office, its practical effects undeniably lessened. Severe punishments, which could include execution, reached minimal levels by the reign of Carlos IV (reigned 1788–1808), though milder ones

---

[16] Antonio Elorza, *La ideología liberal en la Ilustración española* (Madrid: Tecnos, 1970).
[17] Olga M. Quiroz-Martínez, *La introducción de la filosofía moderna en España. El eclecticismo de los siglos XVII y XVIII* (Mexico: El Colegio de México, 1949).

remained. Government use of the Holy Office after 1791 to protect against politically subversive writings resembled a desperate attempt to salvage the political structures of the old regime. Francisco de Goya's evocation of Inquisitorial ceremonies and abuses mostly alluded to the past, notwithstanding the fact that his apparent criticism of ecclesiastical practices led to the withdrawal from sale of his *Caprichos* ("Caprices") in 1799. Writers were harassed into the nineteenth century, while some powerful figures accused the Inquisition of operating against the common good. Though still large, the Church's overall presence in civil society diminished. The Jesuit order was expelled with minimal commotion in 1767; poor relief became increasingly secularized; Church possessions and economic prerogatives declined as the state closed unviable institutions. Confiscation of Church property, begun in 1798, initiated the disentailment process finally completed in the 1860s.

In the area of political and socio-economic privileges advance was less perceptible. Reform signified the increased efficiency of institutions rather than a questioning of their existence. Reports of debates in the London parliament contained in the *Gaceta de Madrid* ("Madrid Gazette") informed Spaniards of representational party politics, but this brought about no lessening of royal prerogatives. The attack on noble privilege, echoing Renaissance concerns, was loud, but change minimal, and, paradoxically, some Spanish nobles were at the vanguard of enlightened discussion, many being active in the Economic Societies.

The debate on women is symptomatic of the age. When Feijoo published his defense of women in 1726 many opponents continued to deny women's intellectual equality. The same arguments for and against were rehearsed as the century advanced. Periodicals of Carlos III's reign indirectly reveal the presence of women as unpublicized participants in the debate, and their effective input to discussion can be gauged from a variety of texts. The debate on entry into the Madrid Economic Society in the 1780s revealed at worst a tolerance of women and at best an eloquent advocacy of their rights. The fact that the Aragonese Society admitted Josefa Amar y Borbón (1749–1833) without controversy demonstrates the insignificance of the issue for some. The *Memorial literario* ("Literary Record") gave publicity to Amar's persuasive advocacy. The intellectual argument seemed incontrovertible, yet tradition weighed heavily against change. The decision, finally taken by the monarch, resulted in women's admission as a separate grouping, devoted to issues thought appropriate for their sex. At the same time the Inquisition was no longer having women burned for witchcraft, suggesting that reason and humanity were prevailing. Goya depicted witches as part of the world of nightmare, as fictions which no enlightened person could endorse. Light was illuminating the obscurity to permit new ways of seeing.

The Enlightenment desire to communicate and reason had a multiple impact on culture. Feijoo's writings revealed a wish to engage a large readership. In the *Teatro crítico universal*, the traditional learned essay was stripped of the formality and pomposity of seventeenth-century style and used to present information and argument in an accessible way, while not omitting the footnotes which empiricism required. Subsequently Feijoo used the more immediate letter format, employing a conversational tone in the hope of widening his audience. The multi-purpose letter became a natural generic preference for the essay-periodical. It facilitated the real or fictitious dialogue between editor and contributors by allowing alternative perspectives, underlining the variety of possible points of view, as well as linking innovative ideas with everyday discourse.

The periodical displayed its varied contents in a diversity of genres. The dialogue or conversation with various participants enabled multiple perspectives to be adopted on a single issue, often disguising authorial point of view. The techniques of periodicals reinforced the Enlightenment sensibility, sometimes undermining traditional ideas via humor and satire. The dialogue in Pensamiento LIII of *El Pensador* has a husband criticizing his wife for extravagance, whereas she questions why he married her if he was unaware that high social status implied high levels of expenditure. The *Conversaciones de Perico y Marica* ("Conversations between Peter and Mary," 1788) employed irony to argue that the government was unlikely to use censorship to restrict debate if it aimed to promote knowledge and discussion. Another conversation suggested that apologists for Spain supported the status quo, instead of questioning untenable practices.

Eighteenth-century Spanish drama, especially in the high culture variants of tragedy, serious comedy, and sentimental comedy, presented contrasting attitudes on topical issues. Jovellanos probed the legal system in *El delincuente honrado* ("The Honorable Criminal," 1773), questioning rigid positions on punishment, the link between goodness and emotion, and attitudes to dueling. Tomás de Iriarte (1750–1791) challenged traditional notions concerning the upbringing of young people in his comedies. Leandro Fernández de Moratín (1760–1828) explored issues surrounding marriage and marital choice in his plays, also taking in religious hypocrisy, social snobbery, convent education, and other polemical topics. Plays exploited emotion and sentiment, as well as reason, in their strategies of persuasion, presenting confrontations between characters espousing opposing viewpoints in order to arrive at pragmatic solutions in accord with reason and the requirements of polite society.

A major strand of eighteenth-century poetry was "philosophical," ranging from praise of individuals for socially desirable virtues to single-focus texts on moral concepts such as egoism, as in a poem by Tomás de Iriarte.

Iriarte presents a secularized view of egoism, arguing for its social benefits in a way at odds with Catholic doctrine, yet in tune with government thinking. In the novel, a genre newly popularized, though encountering difficulties with censors, the lives of the protagonists facilitated the exploration of methods of upbringing and ethical principles as well as questioning the societies in which they moved. Montengón's eponymous protagonist Eusebio, encountering Quakers in the United States, reacted to alternative cultural and ethical choices, provoking questions in his readers. More exceptionally, Luis Gutiérrez's Cornelia Bororquia fell foul of a lecherous archbishop in a novel promptly banned and pursued by the Inquisition in the French editions smuggled into Spain.

The effect of Enlightenment was to extend the range of topics thought worthy of literary treatment. Spanish plays, including popular works, bore witness to the diversity of current issues which drama could present, even though some authors might oppose radical or progressive options. The treatment of topics central to public debate revealed how new subject matter could re-energize literature. In consequence the writer assumed a role in provoking the public conscience, stimulating audiences or readers to observe the playing out of conflict and to rethink matters of personal and public concern. Ideas and their discussion mattered, and the techniques for presenting ideas and their debate took on a new significance. The fact that discussion of reform and change occupied center stage meant that writers assumed a new importance. Authors were increasingly at the heart of public life and, as part of the legacy of Enlightenment, took on a decisive role in public discourse as essential participants in the debate on the modernization of Spanish culture.

18

Eighteenth-century Neoclassicism

PHILIP DEACON

The appeal to classicizing aesthetic principles which characterized the reformist tendency of high culture in eighteenth-century Spain is best understood as a reaction to the dominant literary mode inherited from the previous century.[1] In drama, poetry, and prose writing the renewed emphasis on clarity of communication, respect for generic conventions, and the moral role of literature was thought best exemplified in the tradition deriving from Aristotle and Horace, and elaborated by European, including Spanish, theorists from the sixteenth century onwards.

In poetry the sixteenth-century classicism of Garcilaso, Boscán, Luis de León, and Herrera, and their successors the Argensolas, Esquilache, and Rebolledo, was widely admired, providing models to be imitated by eighteenth-century classicizers.[2] Although printed texts of these predecessors were uncommon until their recuperation in new editions in the second half of the century, the works furnished models of a tradition identified with the revered poets of Augustan Rome (Horace, Ovid, Virgil). Authors such as Quevedo and Góngora, who sometimes abandoned classical clarity in works exploiting the intellectually complex metaphorical play of *conceptismo* and the erudite allusions of the *culterano* style, were nevertheless praised for compositions which coincided with classicism. The rhetoric of *conceptismo* still formed the mainstay of popular versifying, whose reliance on arguably unsubtle wordplay provoked condemnation by classicizers.

In drama it was the dominance of the supposedly hybrid form of tragicomedy, endorsed by the practice of Calderón, Lope, Tirso, and others, which focused debate from the 1730s onwards. An era which increasingly classified scientific and artistic phenomena according to perceived inherent characteristics rejected the flouting of classical conventions as an offense against taste. A parallel respect for the truths of history, geography, and science led to a rejection of literature which disregarded

---

[1] René Andioc, *Teatro y sociedad en el Madrid del siglo XVIII* (Madrid: Castalia, 1987).
[2] Russell P. Sebold, *Descubrimiento y fronteras del neoclasicismo español* (Madrid: Fundación Juan March-Cátedra, 1985), pp. 41–89.

recognized concepts of what constituted knowledge.[3] Thus subgenres of drama such as the spectacular magic comedies, though entrenched in popular entertainment, drew the wrath of classicizers who recalled antecedents in Calderón while raising objections on scientific principles. The eighteenth-century respect for verisimilitude which informed the rejection of unrealistic action also applied to language; Calderón's taste for a style deemed inappropriately artificial for the character speaking was constantly attacked by Neoclassical critics.

The work which heralded the return to classicism was Ignacio de Luzán's *La Poética* ("Poetics"), published in the author's home city of Zaragoza in 1737. Being acquainted with prevailing Italian aesthetic debates as a consequence of his education in Italy, Luzán (1702–1754) produced a sizeable compendium of classical theory, rooted in Aristotle and Horace and enriched not only by Neo-Aristotelian theorizing[4] but also by a knowledge of literary practice. The popular tradition pursued by Spanish dramatists was present, but mostly as a contrasting aesthetic path, rejected or criticized from the perspectives of classicism.

The first two of the four books of *La Poética* dealt with generalities. Literature was asserted to have the same role as moral philosophy, expressed at one point as making virtue attractive and vice abhorrent. However, in addition to being socially useful, literature must provide pleasure. For Luzán, quoting Horace in support, the pleasure derives from the combination of beauty and sweetness (*dulzura*), sweetness being essential in order to influence the reader or spectator. Truth is the basis of beauty, but can be what is real as well as what is thought believable. Literature may thus imitate nature in both a concrete and a general sense, though in the latter case the author should never exceed what is believable. A successful author requires not only imagination and natural talent but also skill and learning.

Following the classical tradition Luzán distinguished three levels of style. The highest was characteristic of epic and tragedy; domestic subjects, by contrast, required a plain, simple style; the middle style combined the simplicity of the latter with the decorativeness of the former, not being associated with any particular subject matter. Luzán recommended that language be clear and appropriate, and the vocabulary pure. On rhetoric, he asserted a major tenet of Spanish Neoclassicism: that metaphors need to be clearly understood in order to be effective, and, mindful of Góngora, he explicitly condemned adding metaphor upon metaphor. He singled out

---

[3] Philip Deacon, "Precisión histórica y estética teatral en el siglo XVIII español." In *Ideas en sus paisajes. Homenaje al Profesor Russell P. Sebold*. Ed. Guillermo Carnero *et al.* (Alicante: Universidad de Alicante, 1999), pp. 141–150.

[4] Russell P. Sebold, *El rapto de la mente. Poética y poesía dieciochescas* (Barcelona: Anthropos, 1989), pp. 98–128.

features of the *conceptista* and *culterano* styles as he condemned wordplay (*agudezas*), extravagant metaphors, and neologistic, erudite terminology. Luzán's main stylistic models were classical Roman ones and he commended for imitation the sound effects of Latin verse.

Drama occupied Book 3 of *La Poética*, augmented by two extra chapters in the posthumous 1789 edition. Luzán set out the classical model of the division of styles: tragedy for serious matters of national concern involving great individuals, and comedy the domain of the domestic, with the unities prescribed for both. Unity of action was deemed indispensable; unity of time might require great ingenuity, but Luzán expected the action to parallel stage time, though in practice the real events might take a little over four hours; unity of place might, if necessary, be stretched to portraying different levels of one basic area. Following Aristotle, plots should have a beginning, middle, and end, and be characterized by changes of fortune and reversals. Tragic events from history were thought particularly effective for dramatization since audiences might know them, however slightly. Countering the dominant mode of the Spanish *comedia*, Luzán echoed Horace in proscribing the low style for tragic action, and recommended a small cast. In the 1789 additions Luzán extended his reservations about Spanish popular drama. His main criticism was that instead of improving conduct it had been detrimental, condoning by its portrayal behavior contrary to public standards. Another major objection concerned the frequent disregard for verisimilitude, as when two characters echoed what each other said. Luzán's most vehement attacks, however, concerned overblown language, repeating his earlier condemnation of the *conceptista* and *culterano* styles.

Although *La Poética* became a benchmark in subsequent decades, the most significant objections on publication came from Juan de Iriarte (1702–1771), in Spain's pioneering *Diario de los literatos de España* ("The Spanish Review of Books"). An extensive summary of Luzán's text, supplemented by praise and approval, was rounded off by reservations in which Iriarte defended the classical origins of tragicomedy, argued in defense of some of Góngora's metaphors, and expressed disagreement as to the alleged intentions of Lope de Vega's *Arte nuevo de hacer comedias* ("New Art of Writing Comedies"). Nevertheless the précis of *La Poética* acquainted a wider readership with Luzán's ideas, in spite of the journal's limited circulation. The objections prompted him to publish a pseudonymous defense (*Discurso apologético* ["Apology"]), reiterating his preference for a simple poetic style, free of extravagant metaphors, affectation, and pomposity. He rejected Góngora's extreme obscurity, subtlety, and ingenuity, and restated his earlier criticism of tragicomedy.

A member of Luzán's literary coterie, Agustín de Montiano y Luyando (1697–1764), advanced the case for Neoclassical tragedy in 1750 in his

Discurso sobre las tragedias españolas ("Discourse on Spanish Tragedy")
accompanied by an example, *Virginia*; the volume was supplemented
in 1753 by further historical argument and another tragedy observing
the classical conventions, *Ataúlfo*, set in medieval Spain. A protégé of
Montiano, Luis J. Velázquez (1722–1772), promoted Neoclassical aesthetic criteria in his *Orígenes de la poesía castellana* ("Origins of Spanish
Poetry," 1754), providing an overview of Spanish verse including the then
still manuscript *Libro de buen amor* as well as living authors. Velázquez
put into circulation the term "Golden Age" for the classicizing era of
Garcilaso, Luis de León, and the Argensolas, condemning *conceptismo*
and *culteranismo* as elitist deviations from true purity of style.

In the 1760s, the leading essay-periodical, *El Pensador* ("The Thinker"),
devoted eighteen of its eighty-six numbers, wholly or in part, to dramatic matters. Pensamiento III contained an ironic conversation between
Spaniards and foreigners in which the latter claimed *comedias* should
observe the unities as contributing to theatrical illusion and promoting
reason and good taste. The Spaniards replied that the unities suggested
a lack of imagination and creativeness, and that the limited number
of characters in foreign plays was similarly a sign of impoverishment.
Later articles were more expository and less ambiguous. Pensamiento IX
set out the Aristotelian norms, principally on the moral character of
tragedy and comedy, while Pensamiento XX criticized Spanish plays for
mixing the comic with the sublime, and for encouraging vice. Pensamientos XXVI–XXVII underlined the ethical function of drama, the need
for verisimilitude in the action, the indispensability of the unities, and
the elevation of tragedy. More controversially Pensamientos XLII–XLIII
questioned whether *autos sacramentales* were drama, advocating their
banning. The final essays on literary theory were equally classicizing:
Pensamientos LVIII–LIX humorously attacked the poetic obsession with
puns and double meanings, while Pensamientos LXIX–LXXI criticized the
treatment of love in Moreto's *No puede ser* ("It Can't Be").

Concurrently with *El Pensador*, two plays by Nicolás Fernández
de Moratín (1737–1780), the comedy *La petimetra* ("The Fashionable
Lady," 1762) and tragedy *Lucrecia* (1763), contained prologues advocating Neoclassical principles. The "Disertación" preceding *La Petimetra*
claimed that poetics is based on reason, and that the purpose of poetry
was the Horatian one of teaching while giving pleasure. The moral function of drama was to make people reject vice and to show virtue triumphant, although few Spanish comedies did so. Moratín asserted what
he saw as the logical justification of the three unities: that actions unfolding over a long historical period cannot reasonably be presented in three
hours and cannot involve major changes of setting, claiming that many
Spanish comedies resembled dramatized history. Moratín emphatically

asserted the centrality of verisimilitude, suggesting that the better it is observed the better the play, noting that Spanish plays frequently offended against it. Appropriate language was equally essential, and Moratín, like Luzán, condemned the elevated style common in Spanish comedies, singling out the mannered, subtle wordplay of many humble characters. In the preface to *Lucrecia*, Moratín echoed Ovid in asserting the dignity of tragedy, following Aristotle in claiming that tragedy purged violent passions while recommending virtue and encouraging heroism. Turning to *Lucrecia*, Moratín stressed his own respect for the unities and history, adding that his principal concern was not to offend against verisimilitude.

Moratín's *Desengaños al teatro español* ("Corrections to Spanish Drama," 1762–1763) restated Neoclassical principles accompanied by practical illustrations, launching into an extended critique of *autos sacramentales* in *Desengaños II* and *III*. The first *Desengaño* repeated the criticism of Spanish comedies for their immorality and bad example, citing Moreto's *No puede ser* as morally pernicious from its very title. Moratín reiterated the idea of theatrical illusion as the objective to which all technical features must contribute. Language has the same purpose, he argued, suggesting that an inappropriate style – and he singled out exaggerated metaphors – destroys theatrical illusion. By way of example he adduced Rosaura's opening words in Calderón's *La vida es sueño* ("Life is a Dream"), arguing that someone having just fallen from a horse is unlikely to use high-flown expressions involving "violent hippogriffs." Calderón was also taken to task for historical and geographical errors. Having argued that drama observes norms, Moratín rhetorically inquired how these might be applied to an *auto sacramental*. If the supreme theatrical convention is verisimilitude, a genre like the *auto* appears nonsensical. If an actor has to represent Spring, how could the role be characterized? Moratín's conclusions about the representability of *autos* came down to questions of taste; for him, sacred matters had no place in a theatre because they needed to be treated reverentially and not mixed with the profane.

An official institution whose activities promoted Neoclassical aesthetics was the Fine Arts Academy, the Academia de San Fernando (founded 1752). The parallel between literature and painting had been a commonplace ever since Horace (*ut pictura poesis*), and the speeches delivered at the Academy's prize ceremonies expounded Neoclassical principles. Competition subjects emphasized classical ideals in a mixture of topics from ancient Greece and Rome, the Old Testament, and Spain's heroic past. Surprisingly perhaps, the Real Academia Española kept distant from the public debate on Neoclassicism in drama, although its poetry competitions, from the late 1770s, were explicitly judged according to classical norms. Though plays in the Neoclassical style were uncommon until the 1780s, evidence shows that classical theory had entered secondary education, where Aristotle and Horace were supplemented by Luzán. Just when Neoclassical works began to have an impact, the emphasis of the important journal, the *Memorial literario* ("Literary Record"), was vehemently classical. Comedies by Tomás de Iriarte (1741–1789) and Leandro Fernández de Moratín (1760–1828) were praised and analyzed in parallel with detailed criticism of works which failed to respect classical norms.

A major summative text expounding both principles and techniques of Neoclassical comedy as viewed by a practicing playwright is the prologue by Leandro Fernández de Moratín to his collected works of 1825 (*Obras*). Moratín's definition of comedy adopted a formula close to Aristotle's for tragedy, coupled with the Horatian aim of teaching and giving pleasure. Moratín claimed to imitate rather than copy nature, because originality consisted in selecting, organizing, and embellishing the materials. Nevertheless, while art may not hold a mirror up to nature, it should nonetheless be realistic. Drama influences by being believable, exploiting the whole apparatus of theatre in the process: costume, staging, movement, gesture, voice. The subjects of comedy should be familiar to the spectator and true to nature, depicting people as they are, drawing on national characteristics, common vices, and the minutiae of domestic life. Comedy is the domain of the middle classes and should deal with behavior disruptive of social harmony or prejudicial to public and private interests; it should portray what is true and impress it on the spectator, correcting prejudice and stupidity. Moratín advocated plots comprising a single action with no subplots, suggesting that unity of action encouraged subtlety in characterization. Whereas unity of action was judged indispensable, those of time and place were essential only for perfection. Moratín concluded that following the "rules" only brought success with audiences when an author had talent, echoing Luzán's similar statement published nearly a century before.

Though Neoclassical aesthetic principles and practices continued to be advocated for over a century after Luzán's trailblazing text, they did little to diminish the appeal of popular drama, which flourished in spite of the absence of explicit theoretical underpinning.[5] What the aesthetic debates made evident was the diversity of tastes in contemporary audiences. It might be argued that published poetry generally adopted increasingly classical styles, yet the emphasis on wordplay and metaphorical inventiveness in popular verse still recalled seventeenth-century models. The debate on drama arguably bore witness to the preference of more educated spectators and readers for classical norms and the desire to create a space for

[5] Emilio Palacios Fernández, *El teatro popular español del siglo XVIII* (Lleida: Milenio, 1998).

classicizing works to be performed. However, as the eighteenth century ended, a variety of new, often hybrid, forms were experimented with to the approval of spectators, revealing that the Spanish theatre thrived on innovation in both subject matter and aesthetics. If the debate in press, pamphlets, and prologues continued to rage, it testified to a widespread enthusiasm for culture rather than a victory for any one stylistic creed.

19

Eighteenth-century prose writing

JOAQUÍN ÁLVAREZ BARRIENTOS

One of the outstanding achievements of eighteenth-century Spanish culture was the rehabilitation of prose as a valid, expressive medium for literary composition. For many years mainstream literary criticism, which tended to privilege the poetry and drama of the Golden Age, interpreted the widespread use of prose in the eighteenth century as a failing. Present-day literary scholarship has reversed that judgment, considering the use of prose in essays, novels, memoirs, polemical writings, satires, and works of scholarship as a major accomplishment.

It can also be argued that some of the more important and successful genres of earlier centuries began to lose their importance in the eighteenth century as culture advanced toward modernity. Among forms which ceased to meet the needs of writers, or for that matter their audiences, were the epic and certain categories of poetry and drama, which were replaced by new prose genres, more up-to-date and in tune with the demands of society. Thus the essay, the novel, and bourgeois drama responded to new social circumstances and the ever-increasing need of the public to see itself and its social world reflected in culture. This required authors to convert contemporary reality into literature, taking models from the world around them rather than looking to writings and literary conventions from the past, and abandoning the traditional imitation of the universal to concentrate on the particular. Being challenged to produce an effect upon the reader or spectator, authors felt obliged to write in prose, setting aside the artifice of poetic meter. Modern Spanish theatre gradually abandoned the use of verse, and one of the achievements of Leandro Fernández de Moratín (1760–1828) was to create a prose that was genuinely poetic, which other writers would only gradually adopt. Yet the persistent jibe was to label as prosaic the writings of authors who used prose for genres previously the preserve of verse.

This chapter has been translated from the Spanish by Philip Deacon and Alvin Sherman, Jr.

Autobiography and memoirs

Contrary to what was thought until quite recently, there exists an abundance of autobiographical writings in eighteenth-century Spain, with their number increasing in the second half of the century. These works, some still unpublished, can be divided into three categories, as recently proposed by Fernando Durán López: lives of saints, comprising autobiographical writings by members of the Church; intellectual memoirs, written by men of letters, politicians, and those belonging to the educated elite; and picaresque memoirs, such as the lives of Diego de Torres Villarroel (1694–1770), Santiago González Mateo, and other lesser-known writers. González Mateo's text, *Vida trágica del Job del siglo XVIII y XIX* ("The Tragic Life of Job in the Eighteenth and Nineteenth Centuries"), is scatological in nature and involves a settling of accounts with the author's father, the Church, and the whole established order.

The quantity of autobiographies, which vary greatly in length, reveals that the exploration of the self held a curious fascination for eighteenth-century readers. The self in question was frequently or constantly problematic, confronting the breakdown of models of behavior inherited from Spain's imperial past and the sense of crisis resulting from the challenges presented by the need for change and renewal.

The most famous of the surviving autobiographies is the *Vida* ("Life," 1743) by Diego de Torres Villarroel. Torres tried his hand at almost every literary genre, especially the more lucrative, popular ones such as almanacs. His autobiography is that of an ordinary man, and the work's success led others to think that they could emulate him, even though their lives might not have been so exceptional or their personalities of historical significance.[1] Thus, from the mid century we find biographical accounts of individuals, such as Joaquín de la Ripa, an artilleryman, and Gómez Arias, that recount often-picaresque adventures. These works invariably focus on the central character's rise to fortune, a topic which can be seen as characteristic of the century. Other memoirs followed: from José de Cadalso (1741–1782), José María Blanco White (1775–1841), Juan Antonio de Armona (1726–1792), José Mor de Fuentes (1762–1848), Juan Sempere y Guarinos (1754–1830), Joaquín Lorenzo Villanueva (1757–1837), and many more, some of whom used the genre to justify their behavior during the Peninsular War.[2]

---

[1] Guy Mercadier, *Diego de Torres Villarroel. Masques et miroirs* (Paris: Editions Hispaniques, 1981).

[2] Known in Spain as the War of Independence (1808–1814), this civil war pitted defenders of the absolutist monarchy against the imperial troops of the "foreign invader" Napoleon. Napoleon placed his brother Joseph on the throne in 1808, but by 1814 the French troops were defeated and Fernando VII returned to Spain.

The novel

The finest examples of prose writing are to be found in the novel, a genre which had been relatively abandoned by the end of the seventeenth century, due primarily to pressure from the Church and factions opposed to the consumption of so-called "works of entertainment." These same powers favored reading matter to which the public could turn repeatedly for inspiration, works of devotion, such as prayer books, saints' lives, and missals, which might halt the alleged harmful effect of the secularization of culture being witnessed throughout Europe, including Spain. In eighteenth-century Spanish society, reading was a group activity which served to consolidate Catholicism when religious works were read, since the faith was not put in doubt. However, if group readings were devoted to novels or literature of entertainment, they turned into discussions about the behavior, ideas, and practices which the texts presented.[3]

Throughout the eighteenth century many earlier novels were re-edited, including *Lazarillo de Tormes* and other picaresque tales, works by Cervantes, and amorous adventure stories (*novelas cortesanas*). However, few new novels appeared during the first half of the century. More common during this period were texts that contained isolated narrative elements, not novels in the strict sense.

It is not until 1758, when Father José Francisco de Isla (1703–1781) published the first part of *Fray Gerundio de Campazas* ("Friar Gerund from Campazas"), that we find a text that can be defined as a true novel, despite its technical defects and excessive didacticism. Isla modeled his work on Cervantes' *Don Quijote*, taking as his subject matter the education of young people. Though the criticism of education was Isla's primary concern, a second focus of the novel is the satire on ecclesiastical oratory. Isla's novel was banned by the Inquisition soon after publication, and the second part initially remained unpublished, although it soon circulated in manuscript form and clandestinely printed copies. Isla organized his narrative material around small segments of plot, distributed over several chapters. In the first chapter of a group he would reflect on a topic and in the following ones provide examples to illustrate his point or dramatize the concept on which he had commented. From a structural point of view, the novel frequently resembles medieval *exempla* and thus underlines the author's educational purpose.

Isla's pioneering example is marred by its excessive didacticism. However, on the plus side, it offers a satirical, dialogical, and intellectual vision frequently found in European narratives of the first half of the eighteenth

3 Joaquín Álvarez Barrientos, *La novela del siglo XVIII* (Madrid: Júcar, 1991).

century, for example, in Henry Fielding's *Tom Jones*, with which Isla's work shares several important features. The model established by *Fray Gerundio* was followed by other writers during the 1770s. However, the most characteristic narrative format in the second half of the century was the sentimental tale, a genre which exalted the expression of emotion, but emotion curbed by reason.

Reason and the emotions are the twin thematic concerns around which the most popular fictional genres revolved. Critics tend to refer to gothic, adventure, epistolary, and sentimental novels, but almost all the texts could fit into more than one category. It might be argued that there are two main types: the gothic novel and the sentimental novel. Originating in England, the gothic novel did not reach Spain until the early nineteenth century. The genre combines mystery and terror, allowing the author to explore the irrational in human behavior, to which are added confrontations over love. Gothic novels are usually set in the countryside, among ruined buildings, as if mirroring the moral breakdown of the characters, and much of the action occurs at night. The stories frequently take place in the past, and the mysterious or fantasy element, which motivates the plot in conjunction with the love interest, achieves resolution by the close. Reason triumphs to provide an explanation for otherwise inexplicable events. Outstanding examples of the genre are Horace Walpole's *The Castle of Otranto* (1764) and Ann Radcliffe's *The Mysteries of Udolpho* (1794) and *The Italian* (1797).

The gothic tale can be located within modern narrative modes in that it develops John Locke's ideas regarding the senses. It is a type of narrative that probes deeply into the mind of the individual, linking irrational and sentimental aspects in order to emphasize a character's subjectivity, a subjectivity which also brings out the negative and malevolent side of personality. In parallel, nature is represented as out of control and at odds with humanity. Sometimes this violent, oppositional view of nature has been taken to represent a rejection of progress and nostalgia for an idealized, unchanging world, increasingly lost in the advance of civilization.

Sentiment is present in all eighteenth-century narrative. The discovery of the self, a basic feature of eighteenth-century memoirs, is equally to be found in the novel. Sentimental novels present the problems associated with love not only in private life but also in the public world of characters, revealing its profound social implications, since love is used as a tool to analyze society. Clashes over love are often used to reaffirm the idea that mutual attraction between two people is a natural feeling, therefore of value and worthy of being respected by social institutions; at the same time the relations between parents and children and associated political structures are questioned in as far as they force obedience by the young in their choice of marriage partner.

In this way sentimental novels assumed ideological significance, since they evoked a utilitarian bourgeois moral code and a vindication of liberty that worried the authorities, to the extent that novels were banned from publication in 1799. However, this prohibition was not strictly enforced and following Spain's War of Independence there was a resurgence in narrative writing, with works incorporating themes of war and patriotism in which love continued to carry out the previous ideological function.

Sentimental novels frequently employed the letter format.[4] The considerable success of the epistolary formula was due to the fact that it deeply involved the reader in central issues and produced an immediate sense of reality. Like the essay, the epistolary novel gave the writer the possibility of tackling everyday events in a language familiar to the reader, thereby giving the author the freedom to switch registers, internalize feelings, analyze situations, and describe scenes. The letter also made it possible to break the plot material into smaller segments. The sentimental novel which best characterizes the epistolary format was *La Serafina* ("Seraphina," 1797) by José Mor de Fuentes. Even though many epistolary novels were written, Mor's was the most successful, being reprinted three times. The novel narrates the difficulties experienced by two lovers living in the bourgeois society of Zaragoza during the latter part of the century. Mor skillfully used the freedoms inherent in the epistolary format to recreate the social life of *tertulias* and strolls in the countryside, recount a dream and insert a Utopian tale, as well as express amorous sentiments and accompanying doubts. The letter became a flexible tool which evoked in readers a sense of reality since what they demanded of literature was a reproduction of the reality with which they were acquainted.

Another important sentimental novel is *La Leandra* by Antonio Valladares de Sotomayor (1740–1820?). Comprising nine volumes in epistolary format, its protagonist is an actress. The novel, "which contains many novels," is an amalgam of all the styles and types of narrative in vogue at the time of its publication, which extended from 1797 to 1807. One finds within its pages sentimental, adventure, gothic, and exotic narratives. Of particular interest is the protagonist's attempt to defend the newly developing role of women in society. Valladares, also well known as a dramatist and journalist, employed a simple, natural style in tune with the conversational tone of the letter format, and established the concept of a novel within a novel as an important structuring feature.

Two other works stand out: *El Valdemaro* (1792) by Vicente Martínez Colomer (1762–1820) and Jerónimo Martín de Bernardo's *El*

---

4 Ana Rueda, *Cartas sin lacrar. La novela epistolar y la España ilustrada, 1789–1840* (Madrid: Iberoamericana, 2001).

emprendedor, o aventuras de un español en el Asia ("The Resourceful Man, or Adventures of a Spaniard in Asia," 1805). Both are adventure stories imitating the style of Cervantes in *Persiles y Sigismunda*, the first being strongly influenced by the fantastic and the latter focusing on the geography of the Orient. They are certainly two of the finest novels produced at the end of the eighteenth century in Spain.

One of the period's most prolific novelists was Pedro Montengón (1745–1824). His five novels are entitled *Eusebio* (1786), *Antenor* (1788), *Eudoxia, hija de Belisario* ("Eudoxia, Daughter of Belisarius," 1793), *Rodrigo* (1793), and *El Mirtilo, o los pastores transhumantes* ("Mirtilus, or the Nomadic Shepherds," 1795). In *Eusebio*, the author's best-known work, Montengón combines both the travel and the rite-of-passage novel, borrowing freely from Jean Jacques Rousseau's 1762 novel *Emile*. Given the work's concern with issues of tolerance and education, it is not surprising that it was promptly censored and expurgated by the Inquisition. *El Mirtilo* is an unusual pastoral story in which the author criticizes urban society and its abandonment of poetic values. The protagonist is a poet who, nostalgic for the past, prefers country life to the rigors of the city. In his other novels, Montengón used the romance variant of the novel, recounting the lives of historical figures and situating the narration in a more distant past.

Alongside original novels there was a significant output of translated works, and the ones chosen were not necessarily those which today would be considered most important or most in need of translation. Rather it was brief, sentimental, epistolary works which attracted the attention of readers and publishers alike, and it was frequently the latter who commissioned authors to provide the Spanish versions. Whatever the case, translations of narrative works served to introduce new ways of writing and thinking into Spain. Their large number evidences an increasing demand for this type of text, which soon appeared in the periodical press where one finds a wealth of short stories and anecdotes, preparing the ground for the serialized novels of the nineteenth century.

If eighteenth-century literature was required to be useful and moral – moral also in the sense of reflecting a country's customs (mores) – the novel found itself in a double bind, criticized first for not conforming to prescribed literary rules and, second, for being considered literature of "entertainment." The debate over the usefulness of literature became more heated as a result of the success and perceived ideological dangers of the novel format. In order to justify fiction writing, authors appealed to its didactic nature, emphasizing the novel's ability to teach the need to love good and reject evil. Authors would frequently portray vices and social defects in detail, justifying their portrayal by saying it was necessary to recognize evil in order to protect oneself against it, an argument which left censors and moralists unmoved. The latter group viewed with alarm readers' adoption of dubious behavior and their embracing of the new values brought by sociability and polite manners. In the novels and debates which the reception of these works provoked one can perceive the crisis of the Old Régime and its accompanying theocratic and medieval value system. In general, the texts published in the eighteenth century reveal the coming into existence of a new model of humanity whose values were based on attitudes which would subsequently be labeled "bourgeois."

Viewed in this light, the eighteenth-century novel is unquestionably moralistic. To the concepts of sensibility and reason which underpin the works must therefore be added a third element, that of morality, which, not infrequently, appeared in the subtitle of the work. By "moral novel," one must understand a type of story that depicts the century's new secularized ethical system based on ideals of usefulness, friendship, and professionalism. It is a novel that pays detailed attention to social context and considers reality, and therefore social behavior, as a suitable subject matter for literature.

Spain's War of Independence and the disruption at the beginning of Fernando VII's reign interrupted the output of novels. However, the genre did not disappear, since the beginning of the new century saw the rise of the historical novel and of narratives dealing with everyday life. It would be impossible to understand the nineteenth-century novel without studying these earlier novels that contributed to the renewal of prose fiction in Spain, preparing the way for future novelists.

Literature of manners (*costumbrismo*)

Within the broad spectrum of eighteenth-century prose works, there are a number of texts that refer to changes in behavior, the majority of which take the form of critical and satirical writings which denounce the appearance of new customs in Spanish society. They tend to see new forms of behavior as attacks on the Spanish nation and on its supposedly inherent traditions. Here, too, prose writing reflected the divisions that Spanish society of the time was suffering. Some texts dealt with changes occurring in the literary world, focusing on the way works came into existence, and theatrical life was not excluded from literary treatment, as can be seen in the until recently unpublished work by Cándido María Trigueros (1736–1798), *Teatro español burlesco, o Quijote de los teatros* ("Spanish Burlesque Theatre, or the Quijote of the Theatres," written *c.* 1784).

From a broader perspective, Alejandro Moya's *El café* ("The Coffee House," 1792–1794) and several works by José de Cadalso stand out. Among Cadalso's works the *Cartas marruecas* ("Moroccan Letters,"

1789) take pride of place, but other texts are most revealing, including *Los eruditos a la violeta* ("The Pseudo-Intellectuals," 1772) and its follow-up *El buen militar a la violeta* ("The Spurious Good Soldier"), which was banned and remained unpublished until 1790.

In *El café*, the author, the possibly pseudonymous Alejandro Moya, describes the atmosphere found in these new venues which provided places of social interaction where people could talk freely. He alludes to the crisis of conscience that many Spaniards were experiencing as they perceived that the outdated ideas that had governed social attitudes for centuries did not address the actual conditions under which they were living. Moya's text is useful because it allows us to reconstruct the spaces, ways of socializing, and topics that were debated in these public places, as well as the sources (whether they came from newspapers or not) that influenced writing and the various currents of thought of the time.

Cadalso's work proves more difficult to pin down. If, for the sake of simplification, we define *El café* as a dialogue, then the generic nature of the *Cartas marruecas* still provokes debate. Some scholars see it as a novel while others consider it to be an essay that presents the changing political and social situation of Spain at the time Cadalso was writing. Other epistolary essays began to appear around the same time, most of them adopting a loose narrative structure. For example, Jerónimo Martín de Bernardo composed *Ocios en mi arresto* ("Idle Thoughts on My Arrest," 1803), an epistolary work on mythology written for young ladies.

Whatever its generic status, Cadalso's *Cartas marruecas* is a landmark in eighteenth-century prose writing. The author comments on physical and social spaces, the masses and the aristocratic classes, problems associated with education, varied forms of entertainment, and Spaniards' relations with their European neighbors. A close reading of Cadalso's epistolary text makes clear his use of Montesquieu's analysis of French customs in *Lettres persanes* ("Persian Letters," 1721) as a structural model. However, Cadalso's approach to his subject matter bears little resemblance to that of his French counterpart. He challenges Montesquieu's image of Spaniards and is more interested in offering his countrymen a critical and constructive image of Spain and at the same time one that appears positive to outsiders. His technique makes use of several voices or points of view, from both an external and internal perspective, the former represented by a Moroccan visitor. In marked contrast with Montesquieu, Cadalso's work lacks plot development. Cadalso makes clear in his prologue that his purpose is to discuss Spanish social behavior, each letter comprising a brief essay resembling a fragmented conversation. The advantage of the epistolary form was that it afforded him the necessary latitude to address a variety of themes, to employ frequent digressions, and to exercise freedom over point of view. As Cadalso stated in the

Introduction, "El mayor suceso de esta especie de críticas debe atribuirse al método epistolar, que hace su lectura más cómoda, su distribución más fácil, y su estilo más ameno" ("The greatest achievement associated with this type of criticism may be attributed to the epistolary method, which makes reading it more straightforward, its dissemination easier, and its style more pleasing"). The same words might equally have been attributed to Benito Jerónimo Feijoo, the father of the Spanish essay. Another work that illustrates and comments upon Spain's social crisis is Gaspar Melchor Jovellanos' treatise entitled *Memoria sobre los espectáculos y diversiones públicas* ("Report on Spectacles and Public Entertainments") published in 1792.

Prose was a most powerful medium of cultural and ideological progress in eighteenth-century Spain, with its resources exploited and displayed in all the major debates of the period. When the need arose to respond to an insulting attack on Spain's national culture by the French intellectual, Masson de Morvilliers, prose was the vehicle for apologies and defenses such as the *Oración apologética por la España y su mérito literario* ("In Defense of Spain and Her Literary Merit," 1786) by Juan Pablo Forner (1756–1797). Forner preferred prose for satires and major writings such as his *Exequias de la lengua castellana* ("Exequies of the Castilian Language," 1792). Jovellanos, too, stands out for his prose, perfecting its differing stylistic varieties in texts ranging from intimate, conversational letters and diaries to more elevated works such as his *Elogio de Carlos III* ("In Praise of Carlos III," 1788) and the justification and defense of his political activities in *Memoria en defensa de la Junta Central* ("Report in Defense of the Central Committee," 1810).

Historians like Luis José Velázquez (1722–1772), Francisco Xavier Lampillas (1731–1810), Juan Andrés (1740–1817), Juan Francisco Masdeu (1744–1817), Francisco Martínez Marina (1754–1833), and others re-affirmed the use of prose for historical writings, while women authors such as Josefa Amar y Borbón (1753–1833) and Inés Joyes y Blake also revealed their literary skills in prose works. Amar y Borbón translated Lampillas' writings from Italian and, in 1790, composed a *Discurso sobre la educación física y moral de las mujeres* ("Discourse on the Physical and Moral Education of Women"). Joyes published a translation from the English, *El príncipe de Abisinia* ("The Prince of Abyssinia," 1798), of the novel by Samuel Johnson also known as *Rasselas*.

20

Eighteenth-century poetry

Joaquín Álvarez Barrientos

Renewal in the field of poetry in eighteenth-century Spain had as twin reference points the debate over the validity of models inherited from the Baroque period, increasingly seen as no longer viable, and the cultivation of a new poetic style to which subsequent criticism would attach the label "Neoclassical." The battles over poetry, of political as well as aesthetic significance and regularly waged in satirical writings, reached their highpoint in the final years of the century.

Verse had long been considered the unquestioned and most valued form of literary expression. For centuries literary norms, accepted as such by writers, dictated that verse was the only valid medium for what was then called "bellas letras" (*belles lettres*), which we now refer to simply as literature; prose, by default, was relegated to the realm of rhetorical writings. If "literatura" was everything written, "poesía" was what was written in verse, whether lyric, epic, or dramatic poetry. Even at the end of the century it was still generally considered unacceptable for theatrical works to be written in prose. Those who did so were accused of not being able to write in verse, since verse demanded subtlety, which, in the opinion of some critics, prose lacked.

In general, eighteenth-century Spanish poetry opted for clarity, even at the risk of being considered prosaic and cold. Eighteenth-century verse embraced a wide variety of styles, from popular forms such as street ballads and prayers, which did not die out until the twentieth century, to the innovative compositions of enlightened or philosophical poetry which reflected new currents of thought appearing at the end of the century. Between the two extremes poets flourished; some were inspired by Neoclassical didacticism, others devoted themselves to satire, to continued use of Baroque modes of expression, or to combining the Baroque national tradition with the new aesthetic and thematic preferences of the Enlightenment.

For convinced Neoclassicists, the most important poetic genres were epic and drama, since by combining instruction with entertainment they fulfilled the primary mission of poetry. By way of contrast, lyric poetry

This chapter has been translated from the Spanish by Philip Deacon and Alvin Sherman, Jr.

occupied a less exalted position, with the writing of amorous verse often being seen as frivolous. Jovellanos advised the poets of the Salamanca group (Cadalso, Meléndez Valdés, and others) to choose more serious subjects for their literary creations, and like several others his wish was to have his verses destroyed on his death so that the poetic activities of his "idle moments" might be forgotten.

Nevertheless, this concept of poetry began to fade by the 1780s, and the author of a major work on poetics, Santos Díez González, expressed the view in 1793 that lyric poetry was then considered the supreme form.[1] Epic poetry and other genres and subgenres which had flourished in earlier times disappeared almost completely from view as energies were directed toward new types of poetry in tune with the spirit of renewal of the age.

Popular poetry

Popular poetry, however, suffered no crisis or decline. Though often marginalized from high cultural debate, popular poetry was constantly criticized and denigrated, despite flourishing throughout the century in its chapbook format. "Literatura de cordel," literally "literature on a string," was so called because it was exhibited at street vendors' stands hanging from a cord. The texts were brief, usually in verse, sometimes containing plays or prose writings, but always cheap. The most common form was the ballad, frequently sold by the blind, who would sing the verses to the accompaniment of a guitar or other musical instrument.

Ballads could be of various kinds.[2] Those belonging to the oral tradition continued to be reprinted in response to public demand. Such compositions featured personalities from the Carolingian cycle, chivalrous themes, or tales of captives. Their protagonists were Charlemagne, the Twelve Peers of France, Count Alarcos, the Cid, and other heroes from the medieval and Renaissance worlds. Though these works have little aesthetic value, they bear witness to a popular worldview that would outlive the eighteenth century.

A second strand comprises historical ballads that narrate deeds, real and invented, of personalities who may or may not have existed. The already existing stock of themes was augmented by recent characters and events, Felipe V and the War of the Spanish Succession, and notorious bandits considered heroes by much of the population. Religious topics frequently appear, sometimes lives of saints or biblical characters, who also figure in

---

[1] José Checa Beltrán, *Razones del buen gusto* (Madrid: CSIC, 1999).
[2] María José Rodríguez Sánchez de León, "Literatura popular." In *Historia literaria de España en el siglo XVIII*. Ed. Francisco Aguilar Piñal (Madrid: Trotta/CSIC, 1996), pp. 327–367.

carols, pastoral songs, and prayers. Ballads incorporate satirical, festive, and amorous elements, as well as horror, violence, and bloodshed.

Although such ballads were frequently banned at the end of the century, they continued to be sold and distributed. Enlightened government agencies, aware that children learned to read via such texts and suspicious of their moral content, attempted to use ballads to disseminate salutary moral lessons by recounting the deeds of worthy heroes and memorable events from Spanish history. However, the plan failed and street literature continued to flourish until finally dying a natural death in the early twentieth century.

Learned poetry in the Baroque style

Roughly speaking, the eighteenth century can be divided stylistically into two halves. The first half was dominated by Baroque style, the second half by Neoclassicism. Literary historians like Luis José Velázquez (1722–1772) held that the poetry of the mid century was decadent and, therefore, bad. Poets who modeled themselves on Góngora were incapable of approaching his quality and their poetry became repetitious in its reliance on commonplaces and formulaic expressions, and mythological and heroic themes.

However, the Baroque manner soon encountered opposition from reformist authors whose experimentation led to the adoption of new literary models deriving from Spanish Renaissance poets and the classical authors of Greece and Rome. It is at this time that the expressions "Edad de Oro" and "Siglo de Oro" ("Golden Age") – the latter first used in Velázquez's *Orígenes de la poesía castellana* ("Origins of Spanish Poetry," 1754) – were applied to the literature of sixteenth-century Spain.

Among the first to promote new poetic standards and models was Gregorio Mayans y Siscar (1699–1781). Mayans criticized the artificiality of style and hollow verbal gymnastics of poetry which privileged meaning over form. It was the beginning of the concept of "buen gusto" ("good taste"), an idea formulated previously by Ludovico Muratori in Italy, which connoted clarity, natural forms of expression, purity of language, concision, and expressive elegance. The efforts to reform versification and the criticism of second-rate contemporary poets led to a reinterpretation of earlier poetry and the first attempts to write histories of Spanish literature. Judgment was passed on poets from the medieval, Renaissance, and Baroque periods, and it is the Renaissance authors – particularly Garcilaso de la Vega, Fray Luis de León, the Argensola brothers, and Esteban Manuel de Villegas – who were subsequently adopted as models.

When Ignacio de Luzán (1702–1754) published *La Poética* ("Poetics") in 1737, he became the champion of the new poetry, rejecting the authority of Baroque models. Supporters and opponents quickly took up positions. Defenders of the Baroque tradition privileged freedom of imagination, while Neoclassicists defended the idea of rules, norms, and conventions as fundamental prerequisites of poetic composition. Debate focused on the dichotomy of Nature versus art, a pairing found in Mayans and Luzán in their advocacy of classicism and Tomás de Erauso y Zavaleta (pseudonym of Ignacio de Loyola Oyanguren, ?–1764) on the side of tradition. Erauso published a text in 1750 in defense of Baroque poetry and drama, viewing Pedro Calderón de la Barca as the supreme exemplar of Baroque style.

The existence of resolute defenders of Neoclassical and Baroque aesthetic creeds did not preclude attempts to reconcile tradition with innovation. Poets such as Alfonso Verdugo y Castilla, Count of Torrepalma (1706–1767), José Antonio Porcel y Salablanca (1715–1794), José de Villarroel (nephew of Diego de Torres Villarroel), Velázquez, Agustín Montiano y Luyando (1697–1764), and others sought a third way which would reconcile opinions and tastes. The *tertulias* where they came together were the Academia del Trípode, situated in Granada (1738–1748), and its successor, the Madrid-based Academia de Buen Gusto (1749–1751). In these academies poetic compositions were read and debated, and discussion led to the production of theoretical and satirical texts, fruits of an environment where friendship did not exclude the possibility of holding differing opinions. In this respect they upheld a major tenet of Enlightenment ideology, the value of friendship.[3]

Although literary history often presents a view of eighteenth-century poets in the Baroque style as vulgar poetasters, there are some whose quality cannot be ignored. Such is the case of Gabriel Álvarez de Toledo (1662–1714), one of the founders of the Real Academia Española. He began as a poet, knew several ancient languages as well as French, Italian, and German, and later in his career wrote important historical texts. Critics have recognized him as one of the most important poets of the early eighteenth century.[4] Álvarez de Toledo was a spirited writer with a fairly difficult style who produced satirical and festive works as well as ones on religious and mythological subjects. Preeminent among his writings is *La burromaquia* ("The Battle of the Donkeys," 1744), a poem in *octavas reales* which embodies all the virtues and defects of the Baroque style, and though at times it recalls Virgil or Lope de Vega, at others it is

---

[3] David T. Gies, *"Ars amicitiae,* poesía y vida: el ejemplo de Cadalso." In *Coloquio Internacional sobre José Cadalso* (Abano Terme: Piovan, 1985), pp. 155–172.

[4] Russell P. Sebold, *El rapto de la mente. Poética y poesía dieciochescas* (Barcelona: Anthropos, 1989).

excessively rhetorical and affected. As was the case with many authors, Álvarez de Toledo's collected works appeared posthumously, published by Diego de Torres Villarroel in 1744.

Another writer in the same vein was Eugenio Gerardo Lobo (1679–1750), a soldier who took up poetry early in life, as exemplified by his poem in praise of the Virgin entitled "El triunfo de las mujeres" ("The Triumph of Women"). Here, the virtues and merits of the most famous women of antiquity are as nothing compared to the Virgin Mary. Being a soldier, Lobo was not interested in pursuing a literary career, nor did he concern himself with publishing his poetry, which appeared without his permission in 1718 under the characteristically Baroque title *Selva de las musas* ("Forest of the Muses"). Lobo wrote lyric, epic, satirical, and religious poetry, as well as festive works (at which he excelled) and drama. Among his better-known compositions are "A una sirvienta arrimona" ("To a Co-Habiting Servant Girl") and "Irónicas instrucciones para ser buen soldado" ("Ironic Instructions for Becoming a Good Soldier"). Even though he imitates Góngora's style in most of his works, his sonnets also reveal traces of Garcilaso de la Vega and the Petrarchan poets.

Diego de Torres Villarroel (1691–1770) achieved fame as an author during his lifetime, modeling himself on the poet and satirist Francisco de Quevedo. Torres was one of the few authors in eighteenth-century Spain who managed to make a living as a writer, and what is more he realized that literature could be a profession like any other. He wrote large quantities of poetry, especially burlesque and satirical verse, though he also experimented with other styles. As a professional author Torres offers his readers a broad range of compositions on contemporary themes, demonstrating an impressively rich vocabulary and wide variety of metrical forms: *silvas, octavas, liras,* sonnets. Perhaps because of his association with Quevedo, a writer of extraordinary poetic range, Torres' verse conveys a depth and immediacy capable of engaging present-day readers. He possessed the capacity to write in various styles and to compose works in serious and popular vein, from learned compositions in the Baroque manner to the popular style of street ballads.

As for Lobo, Torres, and other poets situated in the Baroque camp, they were also acquainted with and sometimes imitated the classical models of Spain's Golden Age. In their attempts to domesticate for a Spanish audience what they believed originated in France they were not alone. Another such author was José Antonio Porcel (1715–1794), a canon from Granada who was a member of both the Real Academia Española and the Real Academia de la Historia and who patterned his work on both Góngora and Garcilaso. His much admired compositions circulated in manuscript until their eventual publication at the end of the nineteenth century. *El Adonis* (published in 1999), his most famous work, recounts in four eclogues the love of Venus and Adonis, following Ovid's *Meta-morphoses*. Despite the limited interest of his work for scholars today, in its time Porcel's poetry exercised considerable influence on contemporary authors, as Velázquez was to claim in his *Orígenes de la poesía castel-lana*. Besides poetry, Porcel was author of an important critique of works read at the Academia del Buen Gusto in his "Juicio lunático" ("Lunatic Judgment").

The Conde de Torrepalma (1706–1767) was a dilettante who opened his home to contemporary poets as well as writing himself. He belonged to the Real Academia Española, the Real Academia de la Historia, and the Real Academia de Bellas Artes, and served as his country's ambassador in Vienna and Turin. Torrepalma wrote on poetic theory, hoping that the debate on literary tastes would bring a qualitative improvement to Spanish poetry. He aimed to domesticate Neoclassicism and update Spanish tradition by restoring a Baroque style that was corrected and purified.[5] As a disciple of Góngora, Torrepalma wrote "Deucalión" (1741), a poem in *octavas reales* after Ovid, which recounts the disappearance of human-ity after the biblical Flood. The sole survivors are Deucalión and Pirra who are destined to repopulate the earth. His "Las ruinas. Pensamien-tos tristes" ("Ruins. Sad Thoughts," 1751) exemplifies his individualistic Baroque style.

Neoclassical poetry

As stated earlier, the stylistic ideal of Neoclassical poetry was "good taste," an unquestioned objective once Neoclassicism became the pre-vailing ideal throughout Europe; and literary good taste went hand in hand with social good taste. The models for the new style of poetry are to be found in ancient Greece and Rome, France in the classical era, and Renaissance Spain. Neoclassical aesthetics, as a definitive body of ide-als, upheld a single, exclusive view of literary practice, with a tendency to eliminate the specific characteristic features of any individual nation. Such a trend was opposed throughout the century by hard-line tradition-alists. Nevertheless, the ideal of good taste lasted beyond 1800 and was still firmly entrenched in the mid nineteenth century.

The strictness of Neoclassical norms underwent a gradual loosening over time, from which new literary models and forms of poetry more open to thematic innovation would emerge. Spanish authors like Herrera and Rioja were complemented by Alexander Pope, James Thomson, Jean François de Saint-Lambert, Edward Young, Solomon Gessner, and

---

[5] Nicolás Marín, *Poesía y poetas del Setecientos* (Granada: Universidad de Granada, 1971).

Voltaire; in Spain, Juan Meléndez Valdés would be considered the embodiment of this new taste in poetry. In the final decades of the century a pure form of Neoclassical poetry co-existed alongside a new style of Neoclassicism containing a philosophical component thought to be more responsive to the contemporary world.

One of the outstanding pure neoclassical poets is Nicolás Fernández de Moratín (1737–1780). Though many of his poetic compositions come under the label "Neoclassical," he also had recourse to Baroque models. He wrote an epic poem, *Las naves de Cortés destruidas* ("The Destruction of Cortés' Ships"); a didactic poem, *La caza* ("The Hunt"); and "Fiesta de toros en Madrid" ("Bullfight in Madrid") and "Oda a Pedro Romero" ("Ode to Pedro Romero"), both relating to bull-fighting, about which he was an enthusiast. The *Arte de las putas* ("The Whores' Art"), a banned work which remained in manuscript until the late nineteenth century, reveals Moratín's profound knowledge of Madrid, especially of its low life. Not only does he feature the haunts and special services of prostitutes, but Moratín also transforms his work into a didactic treatise on physiology and eroticism, entering into details of sexual technique. The poem has frequently been linked to Goya's portrayal of *majas*, go-betweens, and prostitutes.

Erotic poetry was a genre employed by many outstanding authors of the time, not only Nicolás Fernández de Moratín but also such notable figures as Tomás de Iriarte (1750–1791), Felix María Samaniego (1745–1801), Juan Meléndez Valdés (1754–1817), José Iglesias de la Casa (1748–1791), and Nicolás' son, Leandro (1760–1828). Clandestine compositions circulated widely in manuscript form among members of the republic of letters. In these verses, which often employed scatological images, the ideals of good taste were set aside in favor of humor, double meanings, and literary registers more usually encountered in popular poetry. The poems commonly make satirical use of cultured allusions, criticize social groups such as members of the Church, and present an objectified view of the body. In the Neoclassical eighteenth century, erotic poetry becomes a literary space in which transgression of all kinds finds its place. Its subject matter takes in prostitution and homoeroticism, as well as sexual postures and forms of relationship and behavior censured by orthodox thought. With the exception of compositions by Iglesias and Meléndez Valdés, the tone of most of these erotic compositions is intentionally indecent and provocative.

In a literary context it is possible to view erotic works like Samaniego's *El jardín de Venus* ("The Garden of Venus," *c.* 1790) or Moratín's *Arte de las putas* as yet another aspect of Neoclassicism, since allusions to Ovid, Martial, Juvenal, and Catullus abound. Equally present are contemporary philosophical and scientific trends like the theories of sensation which link to forms of clandestine, intellectual libertinism. It is not uncommon for writers to exploit this literary current, proclaiming their opposition to chastity and celibacy, and advocating divorce, regulated prostitution, and educational reforms which would end double standards of morality. Eighteenth-century Spanish erotic poetry awaits detailed study and accessible reliable editions.

Two of Nicolás Moratín's younger contemporaries, Tomás de Iriarte and Félix María de Samaniego, similarly used poetry for satirical and didactic purposes, composing important collections of fables that followed the models established by Aesop, Phaedrus, and La Fontaine. Iriarte's originality in his immensely popular *Fábulas literarias* ("Literary Fables," 1781) stems from his use of literature (as opposed to mores) as the main subject of his fables.

It was not until the second half of the century that the finest Neoclassical poets made their mark. Literary history has recognized José de Cadalso (1741–1782), author of *Ocios de mi juventud* ("Pastimes of My Youth," 1773), as a guiding force behind poetic renewal in Spain.[6] For some critics, his prose poem *Noches lúgubres* (1771) signals the beginning of Romanticism in Spain. In 1773 Cadalso became the mentor of a poetic *tertulia* in Salamanca (often referred to as the Salamanca School) that would follow his lead. The group included Fray Diego Tadeo González (1732–1794), Juan Meléndez Valdés, José Iglesias de la Casa, Fray Juan Fernández, Fray Andrés del Corral, and Juan Pablo Forner (1756–1797). The initial defining characteristic of the group was their adoption of the same concept of imitation (models, meters, and subject matter) espoused by the classical authors of Greece, Rome, and Renaissance Spain. Additional characterizing features were their use of archaic lexical forms, the search for balance, the preference for amorous and sensual themes, the exaltation of friendship, and a marked taste for pastoral topics.

These characteristics associated with the Salamanca School, which some scholars have labeled "rococo," faded once Cadalso left Salamanca and Gaspar Melchor Jovellanos (1744–1811) appeared on the scene. In 1776 Jovellanos composed a "Carta de Jovino a sus amigos salmantinos" ("Letter from Jovino to His Friends at Salamanca") in which he advocated a significant change in subject matter. He proposed more weighty topics, the abandonment of amorous subjects and frivolous, light-hearted issues with little social relevance, and a commitment to moral, philosophical themes. That is, he espoused the ideals of the Enlightenment as apt subject matter for poetry. His underlying wish was that poetry should be useful, serving to promote the concept of the new man of virtue (*hombre de bien*). The result of Jovellanos' letter was that the call for renewal it

[6] Joaquín Arce, *La poesía del siglo ilustrado* (Madrid: Alhambra, 1981).

contained spread through the Spanish republic of letters. Poetry acquired an ethical dimension in tune with the historical moment, allowing for new subject matter which embraced science, and seeking clearer, more accessible means of expression. Its opponents, not surprisingly, dismissed it as prosaic and philosophical.

Like other contemporary poets, Jovellanos had two main sources of inspiration: tradition (evident in the ballads he wrote against Vicente García de la Huerta and Forner) and modern classicism, which gave rise to his philosophical poems. Probably his best poems are the "Sátiras a Arnesto" ("Satires to Arnesto," 1786–1787), two extensive compositions in which he satirized the behavior and deficient education of the nobility.

The greatest poets of eighteenth-century Spain are Juan Meléndez Valdés and Manuel José Quintana (1772–1857). Meléndez, a professor and judge, ended his days as an exile in France for having collaborated with the government of Napoleon's brother, Joseph. He published his first collection of *Poesías* ("Poems") in 1785, achieving immediate success. His compositions embraced themes of philosophy, morality, and love. He wrote eclogues ("Batilo," 1780) and an abundance of odes. In all his work there is a strong feel for classical authors, from Ovid to Propertius, and for Spanish Renaissance poets, as well as the influence of contemporary European authors, poets of the seasons such as James Thomson (1700–1748) and Jean François de Saint-Lambert (1717–1803), who open up new ways of viewing Nature. Meléndez also wrote highly charged erotic poems, like the odes in *La paloma de Filis* ("Filis' Dove") and the Anacreontic texts of *Los besos de amor* ("Love's Kisses"), that remained unpublished until 1894. His social conscience permeates his philosophical and moral poetry. In these latter works his contribution to the renewal of poetic language is much in evidence as is his broadening of the range of topics capable of poetic treatment. Among these, "La despedida del anciano" ("The Old Man's Farewell"), which denounces the effects of war, and "El filósofo en el campo" ("The Philosopher in the Countryside"), an attack on social injustice, stand out. Meléndez also wrote poems about science, progress, happiness, and humanitarian behavior.

Meléndez's disciple, Quintana, enjoyed a long poetic career combined with political activity, his poetry being a combination of philosophical and patriotic themes. As a man of the Enlightenment, his poems bear witness to his faith in progress, science, knowledge, liberty, and a citizen's duty to his country. Among his best-known works are the odes "A la invención de la imprenta" ("To the Invention of Printing," 1800) and "A la expedición española para propagar la vacuna en América" ("To the Spanish Expedition to Promote Vaccination in America," 1806). As a liberal he attacked monarchical tyranny, slavery, and the French, fervently supporting the struggle for liberty during the long war against Napoleon.

This brief view of eighteenth-century poetry cannot ignore authors like Nicasio Álvarez de Cienfuegos (1764–1809), who exploits sentiment in socially and politically committed poems. His inner world is portrayed in intimate compositions such as "El otoño" ("Autumn"). Cienfuegos was an innovator in both language and form, which sets him apart from his contemporaries. Other outstanding poets are Leandro Fernández de Moratín, whose poetry has only recently been re-evaluated by critics; Cándido María Trigueros (1736–1798), forerunner in the exploration of philosophical poetry; Margarita Hickey, author of *Poesías varias sagradas, morales y profanas o amorosas* ("Sacred, Moral and Profane, or Amorous Poems," 1789);[7] and María Gertrudis Hore (1742–1801), a native of Cadiz nicknamed "Hija del Sol" ("Daughter of the Sun"), who published her output of satires, sonnets, sentimental anacreontics, and sensual and pastoral poems in periodicals.[8] Finally, the poets of the so-called "Seville School" should not be forgotten; in addition to the models of Greece and Rome already mentioned, their works reveal a firm political commitment. Members included Manuel María de Arjona (1771–1820), Alberto Lista (1775–1848), Félix José Reinoso (1772–1841), José María Blanco White (1775–1841), and José Marchena (1768–1821), all of whom were better known for their political and journalistic activities than for their poetry.

---

[7] Philip Deacon, "Vicente García de la Huerta y el círculo de Montiano: la amistad entre Huerta y Margarita Hickey." *Revista de Estudios Extremeños* 44 (1988), pp. 395–421.

[8] Russell P. Sebold, "La pena de la *Hija del Sol*. Realidad, leyenda y romanticismo." In *Estudios en honor a Ricardo Gullón*. Ed. Luis T. González del Valle and Darío Villanueva (Lincoln: Society of Spanish and Spanish-American Studies, 1984), pp. 295–308; Constance A. Sullivan, "*Dinos, dinos quien eres*: The Poetic Identity of María Gertrudis Hore." *Michigan Romance Studies* 12 (1992), pp. 153–183.

21

Neoclassical versus popular theatre

JOAQUÍN ÁLVAREZ BARRIENTOS

At the beginning of the eighteenth century Spanish theatre had a well-established tradition of generic models, performing styles, theatrical conventions, and audience preferences.[1] The imaginative power of Spain's Golden Age theatre had resulted in some of the most seminal works in the history of drama, giving birth to mythical characters like don Juan or Celestina. The seventeenth-century stage was supremely responsive to the demands of audiences and developed in close conformity with the dominant mentality of Baroque Spain. Lope de Vega and Pedro Calderón de la Barca created a successful national dramatic tradition whose generic models and principles were followed by most other playwrights.

However, in 1701 a new dynasty ascended the Spanish throne, and the new king, Felipe V, introduced reform at all levels of national life. The idea of change became a constant of the new age and had innumerable repercussions for the theatre. Changes took place in the nation's mental outlook, stimulated by new ideas, written texts, artistic modes, and scientific advances; the new dynasty stimulated changes in Spanish attitudes. The resulting turmoil is reflected most intensely in the theatre because it was the public forum with the deepest ideological significance, enjoying the widest popular favor. Initial confrontations arose out of the questioning of the national theatrical tradition, which promptly took on ideological connotations, but it was from the 1760s onwards that the change in atmosphere became most evident, with the existence of fierce public debate. Defenders of tradition (generally conservative in their thinking) locked horns with Neoclassically minded progressives over the inheritance of the past, each side wishing to claim it as its own. The latter wished to modify and recast works (*refundiciones*) from the existing repertoire, while the former rallied to the defense of authors attacked by the reformists. With hindsight it is clear that the enlightened reformers lost the battle, since conservatism appropriated the discourse of the national tradition; however,

---

This chapter has been translated from the Spanish by Philip Deacon and Alvin Sherman, Jr.
[1] Joaquín Álvarez Barrientos, "Siglo XVIII." In *Historia de los espectáculos en España*. Ed. Andrés Amorós and José María Díez Borque (Madrid: Castalia, 1999), pp. 69–86.

the reformers contributed most to making that legacy known and subjecting it to critical analysis.[2]

The accepted critical view of eighteenth-century Spanish theatre and its significance has undergone radical change over the past few years. Initially only the theatrical practices inspired by Neoclassicism were thought to have value and artistic merit whereas now a more inclusive vision has prevailed which incorporates the broader idea of theatre as spectacle. The result has been an enrichment of historical perspectives embracing dramatic modes which enjoyed enormous success in their time but which for decades were ignored by critics. The new field of study is most often referred to simply as "popular theatre."[3]

Popular theatre

The term "popular theatre," already used by Ignacio de Luzán in *La Poética* ("Poetics," 1737), encompasses a wide variety of forms sharing the same or similar aesthetic principles based on spectacle and an updating of earlier dramatic models. Popular theatre underwent a significant change by the second half of the eighteenth century, abandoning Baroque features linked to social behavior and ethical values, and adopting themes, forms of behavior, and stylistic traits associated with the modernizing tendency of Neoclassicism. This led to a still unresolved debate concerning the degree of classicism espoused by some of the authors traditionally seen as popular and of low aesthetic value. Critics are now reassessing the work of dramatists such as Antonio Valladares de Sotomayor (1740–1820), Gaspar Zavala y Zamora (1760–1812), and Luciano Francisco Comella (1751–1812), focusing on thematic concerns, techniques, and characters until recently thought to be the preserve of enlightened drama and which, taken together, constitute a distinct mental outlook.

Popular theatre comprises a variety of genres whose popularity and characteristics vary through the century. On the one hand there is spectacle-based drama, consisting of comedies about magic, religious, and military subjects; on the other, a type of drama featuring everyday matters, sentimental in nature, and to some extent concerned with social behavior, in which the protagonists are bandits, smugglers, and peasants. Another

---

[2] Joaquín Álvarez Barrientos, "Pedro Calderón de la Barca en los siglos XVIII y XIX. Fragmentos para la historia de una apropiación." In *Estado actual de los estudios calderonianos.* Ed. Luciano García Lorenzo (Kassel: Reichenberger, 2000), pp. 279–324; María José Rodríguez Sánchez de León, *La crítica ante el teatro barroco español (siglos XVII–XIX)* (Salamanca: Ediciones Almar, 2000).

[3] Emilio Palacios Fernández, *El teatro popular español del siglo XVIII* (Lleida: Milenio, 1998).

strand of popular theatre comprises burlesque comedies known as *come-dias de figurón* ("character comedies"), in which character types seen as belonging to the past are caricatured. These are urban plays which ridicule rural behavior and feature members of the lower gentry and other stock types, serving to underline the growing division between city and country. The final strand of popular theatre is the wealth of small-scale dramatic forms: *sainetes* ("comic interlude pieces"), *fines de fiesta* ("end-pieces"), and *tonadillas* ("sung sketches"), which provide illuminating insights into the ideological struggles in town and country deriving from issues such as the civilizing process, progress, and Enlightenment. A *sainete* of 1764 by Ramón de la Cruz, entitled *La civilización* ("Civilization"), centers on this debate, suggesting that the civilizing process constitutes an attack by the city on rural values and behavior.

Magic comedies enjoyed sustained popularity throughout the eighteenth century and even into the twentieth; saints' plays began to die out in the 1760s, a fate which also befell bandit plays, while character comedies evolved into comedies on social behavior. *Tonadillas*, which reached a high point in the final decade of the century, ceased to exist by the time of the War of Independence (1808–1814), giving way to spoken pieces accompanied by music (*melólogos*), monologues, and mime plays. *Fines de fiesta* and *sainetes* would eventually be transformed into popular musical theatre, which enjoyed enormous vitality in the nineteenth century. Small-scale popular theatre, lapped up by audiences, showed great potential to adjust to the times, fashions, and demands of the stage, virtually guaranteeing success as a result of its adaptability. This flexibility was harder to achieve in other genres more constrained by literary conventions, making them less capable of topicality.

Baroque drama, with Calderón to the fore, was staged less and less in the eighteenth century, with the values and forms of behavior it contained ceasing to be relevant to a new Spain in constant evolution, in spite of the on-going debate over the adoption of new value systems or the maintenance of traditional ones. René Andioc and Mireille Coulon have demonstrated the abandonment of classical Spanish drama using the evidence of playbills.[4] Nevertheless, what is significant is that various critical studies have shown how Baroque drama came to be performed in rewritten versions, adapted to reflect the ethical and aesthetic values of the moment, and the same occurred with small-scale pieces. The situation in the early decades of the century was that Baroque drama continued to be staged, although its presence declined notably in the face of authors who attempted to reform and update the style from within the presuppositions of that same tradition.

---

[4] René Andioc and Mireille Coulon, *Cartelera teatral madrileña del siglo XVIII (1708–1808)*. 2 vols. (Toulouse: Presses Universitaires du Mirail, 1996).

One genre which no one attempted to update was the *auto sacramental*. These dramatic compositions linked to the celebration of religious festivals were performed in public processions during the feast of Corpus Christi. The plays were presented on carts or floats that processed on a fixed route lined by the viewing public. The language of such plays was Baroque, rich in comparisons, images, and allegorical references which made them virtually incomprehensible for many in the audience. The high cost of staging *autos*, which the city councils promoting the festivals had to pay for, as well as the fact that from a moral point of view the events were tainted by the presence of actors considered reprobates performing divine mysteries and representing biblical characters, led to a climate which culminated in them being banned. Enlightened reformers as well as politicians and members of the Church, though not all of the latter, agreed on the need to put an end to this vestige of Baroque culture, and prohibition was finally decreed in 1765.

Musical theatre was keenly debated throughout the eighteenth century since Neoclassical theory considered it unrealistic and therefore wrong that music should be present at all and that characters should sing. Yet music was an essential component of almost all forms of contemporary dramatic representation, although the degree of importance varied according to genre. *Zarzuelas* ("operettas") and operas, like *tonadillas* and sung *sainetes*, were all subjected to criticism from a Neoclassical standpoint.

One basic difference between popular and Neoclassical authors was that the latter were incapable of ignoring the rules when it came to writing, whereas the former were flexible enough to compose different types of work according to the moment in the theatrical year: religious works for the Christmas period, magic plays for carnival, and a similar pattern for *sainetes* and *zarzuelas*. This versatility was partly due to the playwrights' need to earn a living from the theatre, a factor which needs to be borne in mind when judging popular works and attempting to comprehend their nature and the requirements of audiences. Ramón de la Cruz (1731–1794) is a case in point. Though he began his career writing in the classical style, he slowly shifted his talents to the most widely appreciated genres, notably the *sainete*, in which he achieved mastery. However, he didn't abandon magic comedies, *zarzuelas*, and other styles popular with audiences. In the field of the *sainete*, Cruz shared the honors with Juan Ignacio González del Castillo (1763–1800) who proved himself to be equally versatile, writing tragedies and classicizing poetry as well as *sainetes*.[5]

---

[5] Mireille Coulon, *Le sainete à Madrid à l'époque de don Ramón de la Cruz* (Pau: Université de Pau, 1993); Josep Maria Sala Valldaura, *El sainete en la segunda mitad del siglo XVIII. La mueca de Talía* (Lleida: Universidad de Lleida, 1993); Josep Maria Sala Valldaura, *Los sainetes de González del Castillo en el Cádiz de finales del siglo XVIII* (Cádiz: Ayuntamiento de Cádiz, 1996).

A single author in the early eighteenth century might compose magic, heroic, and saints' plays, and, in the second half of the century, when these forms died out, a successor might compose works on magic, military, and sentimental subjects, embracing as far as possible the full range of styles preferred by spectators. Among the more prominent dramatists of the first half of the century were Antonio de Zamora (1660?–1728) and José de Cañizares (1676–1750). Zamora produced some magic comedies that differed significantly from Calderón's established format, and, notably, an eighteenth-century version of the don Juan myth: *No hay plazo que no se cumpla ni deuda que no se pague y convidado de piedra* ("Every Deadline Shall be Met and No Debt Remain Unpaid, and the Stone Guest"). On publishing his *Comedias nuevas* ("New Comedies," 1726), Zamora was one of the first traditionalist dramatists to express his intention to reform the theatre, a desire shared by many like-minded authors. Among Zamora's other works worthy of mention are the group on the patron saint of Madrid, Saint Isidore, which to some extent rework plays by Lope de Vega on the same subject.

A younger contemporary, José de Cañizares, contributed more substantially to the renewal of the theatre, not only as dramatist but also as official censor of plays. Among his more important works are the magic comedies *Don Juan de Espina*, *El anillo de Giges* ("Giges' Ring"), *Marta la Romarantina*, and *Juana la rabicortona*, though he also composed mythological, heroic, and saints' plays. Another curious dramatist was Juan Salvo y Vela, though perhaps not as distinctive as some critics have suggested, given the extraordinary figures who inhabited the theatrical world of the time. A tailor by profession, Salvo composed many saints' plays, but his most famous works were the series of five magic plays entitled *El mágico de Salerno* ("The Magician from Salerno"), produced between 1715 and 1720, in three of which the magician protagonist is female. The fact that many of these comedies gave rise to sequels is proof of their success and of the need to offer follow-up story lines based on characters and plots already well received by audiences. In magic plays the magicians manipulate the world in order to make it conform to the desires of characters suffering from some abuse of power or social injustice. This interference with reality often leads to a more harmonious state of affairs and new roles for the protagonists, sometimes including the magician. As the century advances magicians become transformed into more secularized and middle-class characters with power over the world around them, resulting from an informed knowledge of Nature (i.e., knowledge acquired – in the best Enlightenment tradition – through study and experience), not a gift acquired through a pact with the devil or by divine grace, as was the case before.

This theatrical subgenre, which often pokes fun at belief in magic, reflects changes in a society becoming increasingly secular and valuing technological and scientific progress. A similarly evolving pattern can be seen in heroic plays on military themes which become more bourgeois, giving rise to dialogue which suggests a more enlightened mentality. Comella (1751–1812) and Zavala y Zamora (1762–?) are the authors who best reflect this change at the end of the century, composing plays which feature personalities from contemporary European history such as Comella's *Federico II, rey de Prusia* ("Frederick II, King of Prussia," 1788) and *Pedro el Grande, zar de Moscovia* ("Peter the Great, Czar of Muscovy," 1796), or Zavala's plays on Charles II of Sweden, which become a series based on the same historical character.

In a similar way the attention given to women in this type of theatre, making them rulers of the destinies of others, is symptomatic of the new position that women slowly and with difficulty were gaining in society. Women are protagonists in magic comedies of the second half of the century, especially in the plays of Valladares and in works on military and sentimental themes of the same period, notably Comella's *María Teresa de Austria en Landau* ("Maria Theresa of Austria at Landau," 1793).

During the second half of the century the secularizing process accelerates and plots become more related to issues close to the spectator and less associated with subjects deriving from mythology or antiquity. This explains why we also find sentimental comedies as part of popular theatre, differentiated from the Neoclassical model. The fact that authors like Valladares in *El trapero de Madrid* ("The Junkman of Madrid," 1782) and *El fabricante de paños* ("The Cloth-maker," 1784), or Vicente Rodríguez de Arellano in *La reconciliación o los dos hermanos* ("The Reconciliation, or the Two Brothers," 1800), or Comella in the renowned series on *Cecilia*, or Zavala in *El amor constante o la holandesa* ("Constant Love, or The Dutch Girl," 1787), experimented with this type of story with its strong Enlightenment connotations is evidence of an interest in adopting new forms of behavior. The themes formed part of the dominant aesthetic trend and show how different playwrights sought ways to reduce the distance between the contrasting dramatic traditions in vogue at the end of the century. This style of theatre, deriving from existing narrative texts (not for nothing are many plots lifted wholesale from novels), opened the way to new bourgeois attitudes.

Neoclassical theatre

Although drama in the classical style was often presented as something foreign – imported from France – the fact is that in sixteenth-century Spain there had been a demand for plays in the classical style, with Cervantes foremost among the campaigners, and the demand had been met.

The Neoclassical conventions were set out authoritatively in Luzán's 1737 treatise, but in the first half of the century there were few authors who adopted the Neoclassical style. Initial activity centered on literary history in an attempt to resurrect Spanish classical models which might serve to win people over to the new style and domesticate it. Agustín de Montiano y Luyando (1697–1764) wrote a history of Spanish tragedy and composed two original tragedies, *Virginia* (1750) and *Ataúlfo* (1753). Blas Antonio de Nasarre (1689–1751) made a parallel effort on behalf of comedy, publishing Cervantes' plays which Nasarre saw as a reaction against Baroque theatre and Lope's style. In a similar attempt to domesticate Neoclassicism Tomás Sebastián y Latre and Bernardo de Iriarte (1735–1814) adapted comedies and *sainetes* from classical Spanish theatre.

Not until the second half of the century did the best and most significant Neoclassical achievements take place. In the field of tragedy, Nicolás Fernández de Moratín wrote *Lucrecia* (1763), which was never staged, while Cándido María Trigueros managed to get *La Necepsis* (1763) performed, a play on an Egyptian topic which allowed for the extensive exploitation of emotion. Moratín composed two more tragedies, *Hormesinda* (1770) and *Guzmán el Bueno* ("Guzmán the Good," 1777), with their subject matter taken from medieval Spanish history.[6] Trigueros followed up his earlier work with more tragedies: *Las bacanales* ("The Bacchanalian Women," 1767), *Guzmán el Bueno* (1768), *Egilona* (1768), *Los Theseides* (1775), *La Electra* (1781), and others.[7]

José de Cadalso, Gaspar Melchor Jovellanos, and Cristóbal María Cortés (1740–1804) also tried their hands at tragedy, but the biggest success in the genre was Vicente García de la Huerta's *Raquel* (1778). The work was written in 1765 and earned the author exile and prison, making use of Spanish medieval history to criticize the absolutist political system and defend the rights of the nobility in the face of royal authority. By the end of the century tragedy was adapted to the new sensibilities of the gothic manner in the case of Nicasio Álvarez de Cienfuegos (1764–1809). Alternatively, Manuel José Quintana (1772–1857) adapted the tragic model to promote liberal and patriotic ideas, as in his *El duque de Viseo* ("The Duke of Viseo," 1801). Another important tragedy was *Alí-Bek* (1801) by María Rosa de Gálvez (1768–1806). With few exceptions, Spanish tragedy was not favorably received by theatre audiences, although it provided a useful vehicle for aesthetic and ideological innovation which would feed into Romanticism.

Neoclassical comedy takes the form either of comedy of manners or of realistic, character-based comedy, conforming to certain prescribed

---

[6] David T. Gies, *Nicolás Fernández de Moratín* (Boston: Twayne, 1979).
[7] Francisco Aguilar Piñal, *Cándido María Trigueros* (Madrid: CSIC, 1987).

conventions: subject matter taken from everyday life, verisimilitude, and conformity to the unities of time, place, and action. Comedy must teach the spectator and hence uses mockery, although sometimes it also displays an explicit moral content. Many Spanish authors published theoretical writings on Neoclassical comedy, but the person who best summarized the nature of the genre as well as producing the greatest achievements in the medium was Leandro Fernández de Moratín in the 1825 prologue to his plays. Moratín points out that the author should focus on the middle classes in society, as source of characters, situations, and story. Comedy should thus be an imitation in dialogue, in prose or verse, of an event occurring in one place, over a few hours, and between private individuals. The result of this interaction should be that the vices and errors of society are ridiculed and truth and virtue commended. In this way, the didactic dimension of theatre and the realistic modern objective of comedy are made clear, centering discussion on what is specific to society.

In 1762 Leandro's father, Nicolás Fernández de Moratín, published *La petimetra* ("The Fashionable Lady"), based on the life of a modern young lady. Although the work complied with the author's son's requirement to be up to date, it did not achieve the required literary quality. On the other hand Tomás de Iriarte (1750–1791) made significant strides toward establishing a Neoclassical model for comedy in a pair of plays with didactic and moral elements in which ways of bringing up the young were debated: *El señorito mimado* ("The Spoiled Young Man," 1787) and *La señorita malcriada* ("The Ill-Educated Young Lady," 1789), both written in verse and realistic in story line.

However, the Neoclassical playwright who best matched the public's tastes, resulting in the finest comedies of the period, was Leandro Fernández de Moratín. Apart from translating two comedies by Molière and Shakespeare's *Hamlet*, Moratín wrote five original plays including *El barón* ("The Baron"), that appeared first as a *zarzuela* and later, in 1803, as a play, and *El viejo y la niña* ("The Old Man and the Young Girl"), written in 1786 and published in 1789, in which the author criticizes the hypocrisy of marriage based on money and the upbringing given to the young. The issue of upbringing is central to Moratín's plays and figures to a greater or lesser extent in all of them. *La mojigata* ("The Sanctimonious Girl"), completed in 1791 but not staged until 1804, offered the audience two models of upbringing, the traditional one, based on strictness, which encourages lying and distrust; the other, which the play advocates, based on understanding and dialogue.

However, it was in *El sí de las niñas* ("A Girl's Consent"), written in 1801 but not premièred until 1806, that Moratín provided the best formulation of the issues which concerned him most deeply: the upbringing of the young, relations between parents and children, and free choice in marriage. It was the author's greatest achievement. Written in prose, the work presented audiences with up-to-the-moment issues mixed with a dose of sentiment which was more to the fore than in his other plays. As in the earlier comedies there is a love triangle involving a young girl, a young man, and an older man who is the intended husband of the girl, as well as a difference in fortune between the girl and her potential suitors. This basic structure, with only a few additional characters, allows the author to set out a critique of the forms of behavior and evils mentioned above. Moratín's comedies establish the foundations for the analysis of bourgeois modes of conduct.

As a man of the theatre, Moratín was acutely conscious of the state of drama in his time and wrote attacks on the popular genres normally preferred by audiences. He presented his ideas in dramatic form in *La comedia nueva o el café* ("The New Comedy, or the Coffee House," 1792) in which he engineers a confrontation between the two ways of conceiving drama. The comedy enjoyed moderate success, setting in motion a running debate, since the playwright Comella believed himself the model for the character of don Hermógenes. Again in this play Moratín refers to the issue of young people's upbringing or lack of a good one, but he also highlights women's roles, a constant theme in his works, making clear his traditional view of women, whom he did not see as cut out for a career in literature.

A woman who not only wrote a number of dramatic works but also saw them into print was María Rosa de Gálvez (1768–1806), a friend of Moratín who, like him, received patronage from the Prime Minister Manuel Godoy. Gálvez published most of her theatrical works in a collected edition of 1804. One of her comedies, *Los figurones literarios* ("The Literary Charlatans"), is critical of popular theatre and some scholars have seen it as a response to Moratín. Another of her works, *La familia a la moda* ("The Fashionable Family," 1805), features contemporary social behavior in a bourgeois setting, and the unpublished *Las esclavas amazonas* ("The Amazon Slave Women") was performed in Madrid in 1805.

There are certain genres which cannot easily be accommodated within Neoclassical categories. They share classical ideals to a considerable extent but do not belong within Neoclassicism since they use elements which purists proscribed. Sentimental comedies belong to Neoclassicism in their attention to social issues, the middle classes, and their problems, but they also feature sentiment and new currents of contemporary thought. The strong presence of sentiment and emotion combined with the urban setting alters the Neoclassical nature of theatre at the same time as poetry changed under similar psychological and social influences. The importance of the senses for empirical philosophy and the focus on the middle classes as a new subject matter for literature reinforced this dramatic style, which nevertheless had a precedent in Jovellanos' *El delincuente honrado* ("The Honorable Criminal," 1773), not forgetting Luzán's translation *La razón contra la moda* ("Reason versus Fashion," 1751). Sentimental drama advocates a new kind of human being whose ethical values include goodness, utilitarianism, sensibility, and a moral conscience. Jovellanos' work confronts the legal world, the judiciary, and injustice. Trigueros took a similar stand in *El precipitado* ("The Imprudent Man," 1773).

Both Jovellanos' and Trigueros' plays are ideological works that make use of emotion to achieve an impact on the audience. Just as novels used love to criticize the social system, sentimental drama used sentiment to produce a lesson about social failings. This style of drama did not have great success with audiences, who preferred popular sentimental comedies which dealt with similar issues but with notable differences in their treatment.

From the point of view of strict Neoclassicism sentimental drama was initially rejected but grew to be accepted, occupying a place in theoretical writings at the end of the century. In 1789 the theoretical text by the Italian critic Francesco Milizia was translated into Spanish as *El teatro* ("The Theatre"). The author included coverage of "pathetic comedy," pointing out its didactic potential, achievable through sentiment and emotion as well as by the satirical alternation between serious and comic elements. In 1793, Santos Díez González made similar claims in his *Instituciones poéticas* ("Poetic Institutions") in which he singled out what he called "urban tragedy," and, in 1798, Juan Francisco López del Plano (1758–1808) made reference to the "drama of passions."

Sentimental theatre mixed elements of comedy and tragedy, but in the hands of its best practitioners it became an effective way to promote the education of the audience and reform of the stage, paving the way for the drama of the Romantic era.

Part VI

The Forging of a Nation: The Nineteenth Century

DEREK W. FLITTER, DAVID T. GIES,
GREGORIO C. MARTÍN, SUSAN
KIRKPATRICK, MICHAEL IAROCCI, HARRIET
S. TURNER, STEPHEN MILLER, MARÍA
ÁNGELES NAVAL

22

Romanticism in Spain

DEREK W. FLITTER

Definition of "Romantic" appeared less complicated in the early nineteenth century than subsequent critical disputation might suggest. Within the parameters adumbrated by the German critic and poet Johann Gottfried Herder (1744–1803) – for René Wellek "the fountainhead of universal literary history"[1] – application of the term as systematized by the brothers August Wilhelm and Friedrich Schlegel and by Madame de Staël came to be understood and acknowledged all over Europe.[2] It was in 1814 under the heading "Reflexiones de Schlegel sobre el teatro, traducidas del alemán" ("Schlegel's Reflections upon the Theatre, Translated from the German") that Johann Nikolaus Böhl von Faber (1770–1836), an expatriate German merchant and bibliophile resident in the southwest port city of Cadiz, first sought to acclimatize within Spain those new aesthetic doctrines originating in his native land. Using principally the twelfth and fourteenth lectures of A. W. Schlegel's *Vorlesungen über dramatische Kunst und Literatur* ("Lectures on Dramatic Art and Literature") of 1809–1811, Böhl exhorted a return to national traditions, to a literature reflecting popular ideals that was heroic, monarchical, and Christian, the expression of a discernibly Spanish worldview embodied in Golden Age drama; he signed himself an "apasionado de la nación española" ("passionate admirer of the Spanish nation").

There was a significant ideological dimension.[3] Böhl, a Catholic convert with *servil* – i.e. conservative and Absolutist – connections, was combating what he saw as the deleterious consequences of Enlightenment rationalism; he resented the imposition upon Spain of a foreign Neoclassical preference, dismissing detractors of Calderón and of Spain's literary heritage as unpatriotic subversives. His campaign to restore native taste in the face of the bastardized criticism of the philosophical age, as his

---

[1] René Wellek, *A History of Modern Criticism, 1750–1950*. 2 vols. (New Haven: Yale University Press, 1955), vol. 1, p. 183.

[2] René Wellek, "The Concept of Romanticism in Literary History." In *Concepts of Criticism* (New Haven, CT: Yale University Press, 1963), pp. 151–152.

[3] Derek Flitter, "Ideological Uses of Romantic Theory in Spain." In *Romantik and Romance: Cultural Interanimation in European Romanticism*. Ed. Carol Tully (Glasgow: University of Strathclyde, 2000), pp. 79–81.

free translation put it – *Vindicaciones de Calderón y del Teatro Antiguo Español contra los Afrancesados en Literatura* ("Vindication of Calderón and of Ancient Spanish Theatre Against Frenchified Taste in Literature," 1820) – involved, in addition to a Romanticism centered on nationalism and religion, a broad-based attack upon eighteenth-century French literature and philosophical culture. José Joaquín de Mora (1783–1864), Böhl's sparring partner in the expanding literary dispute argued out in Cadiz and Madrid between 1814 and 1820 and generally known as the "querella calderoniana" ("Calderonian debate"), sought to dismantle the Schlegelian perspective by restating the validity of a universal art with eternal rules of taste – this despite his earlier documented liking for Shakespeare and Spanish balladry[4] – viewing the Enlightenment as the pinnacle of human achievement and denigrating Romantic idealization of the Middle Ages; Calderón he regarded crushingly, as did the Swiss literary historian Jean-Charles-Léonard Simonde de Sismondi, as an example of the endemic corruption of his age.

As the polemic developed, Böhl drew upon increasingly varied sources, revealing extensive acquaintance with the intellectual background of his age.[5] His commendation of the German Romantic theorists for their Catholic defense of a traditional social order – Wellek detects in Friedrich Schlegel's lectures a philosophy of history confident in the ultimate victory of Roman Catholicism over the Enlightenment and other forms of secularism[6] – contributed to the widespread association, within Spain, of Schlegelian Romantic theory with political conservatism. Neither Mora nor his friend and supporter Antonio Alcalá Galiano (1789–1865), on the other hand, were *afrancesados* (reformist Spaniards subscribing to the intellectual culture of contemporary France and welcoming its progressive institution within Spain, even under Joseph Bonaparte, hence the label "Frenchified") but liberals living under the authoritarian régime of Fernando VII, and ill-disposed to accept lessons in patriotism from their German adversary. The former would announce in 1820 that his political creed – part and parcel of his opposition to Böhl – was a corollary of Neoclassical taste,[7] a stance representative of the period[8]: we immediately think, in this connection, of the young Francisco Martínez de la

[4] Camille Pitollet, *La Querelle calderonienne de Johan Nikolas Böhl von Faber et José Joaquín de Mora, reconstituée d'après les documents originaux* (Paris: Alcan, 1909), pp. 79–80.

[5] Hans Juretschke, "La presencia del ideario romántico alemán en la estructura y evolución teórica del romanticismo español." *Romanticismo* 1 (1982), p. 13.

[6] Wellek, *History*, vol. II, p. 24.

[7] M. T. Cattaneo, "Gli esordi del romanticismo in Ispagna e *El Europeo*." In *Tre studi sulla cultura spagnola* (Milan: Instituto Cisalpino, 1967), p. 87.

[8] José Luis Varela, "La autointerpretación del romanticismo español." In *Los orígenes del romanticismo en Europa* (Madrid: Instituto Germano-Español de la Sociedad Görres, 1982), p. 129.

Rosa or duque de Rivas. All of which might seem contradictory; however, to describe men like Mora and Alcalá Galiano, as certain modern critics have done, as "existentially" Romantic despite clinging to Neoclassicism in their aesthetic preferences, makes for an even graver distortion.

There has been some reluctance to acknowledge the extent of Böhl's influence. Guillermo Carnero, nonetheless, locating Böhl within the contextual framework of reactionary thought, describes the polemic as a crucial episode in the development of Romantic ideas in Spain, without which it is impossible fully to comprehend the principal ideological thrust of Spanish Romanticism.[9] The defining nature of Böhl's perspective is confirmed by the discussion of Romantic ideas in the Barcelona journal *El Europeo* ("The European") in 1823–1824, principally in articles by Luigi Monteggia and Ramón López Soler deriving from Schlegelian historicism; that of López Soler was clearly mediated by Böhl.[10] As Ermanno Caldera elucidates, Romantic theory and its associated perspectives took on a conservative and nationalistic colouring even in the hands of a political moderate like López Soler.[11] Trenchant Neoclassicist opposition to Schlegelian Romantic theory continued, meanwhile, in the form of Gómez Hermosilla's *Arte de hablar en prosa y verso* ("The Art of Speech in Prose and Verse") of 1826 and Martínez de la Rosa's slightly less intransigent *Poética* ("Poetics") of the following year.[12]

Probably the most influential contribution to the debate was the work of Agustín Durán (1789–1862) in his *Discurso sobre el influjo que ha tenido la crítica moderna en la decadencia del teatro antiguo español y sobre el modo con que debe ser considerado para juzgar convenientemente de su mérito peculiar* ("Discourse on the influence exerted by modern criticism on the decadence of traditional Spanish drama and on the manner in which such theatre ought to be judged if we are duly to assess its unique merits"), published in 1828. Durán followed the Schlegelian periodization of Classical and Romantic, ancient and modern, placing similar stress on chivalry and religion: Romantic drama, he argued, originated in the chivalric way of life, in medieval history and legend, and in Christian spirituality; the apogee of the Spanish stage he linked with military domination and empire. The *Discurso* contained elements of francophobia but was not fanatically anti-classicist. Durán objected most pointedly to the assessment of Golden Age theatre by Neoclassical criteria.

[9] Guillermo Carnero, *Los orígenes del romanticismo reaccionario español: el matrimonio Böhl de Faber* (Valencia: Universidad de Valencia, 1978), p. 19.

[10] Brian J. Dendle, "Two Sources of López Soler's Articles in *El Europeo.*" *Studies in Romanticism* 5 (1965–1966), p. 50.

[11] Ermanno Caldera, *Primi manifesti del romanticismo spagnolo* (Pisa: Università di Pisa, 1962), pp. 27–35, 43–44.

[12] Derek W. Flitter, *Spanish Romantic Literary Theory and Criticism* (Cambridge: Cambridge University Press, 1992), pp. 32–34.

Modern critical reaction to Durán has been mixed. In his edition of the text, Shaw judges the *Discurso* a timid early example of Romantic ideas, its traditionalist vision revealing no dangerous tincture of radicalism, and inadequate in the sense that it contained no intimation of a new and anguished sensibility.[13] David T. Gies is more sympathetic, stressing that Durán deliberately excluded what he regarded as subversive features alien to "genuine" Romanticism.[14] José Escobar likewise underscores the revulsion felt by both Durán and Alberto Lista at the threat of revolution; he identifies in several of Durán's works a counter-revolutionary ideology connecting Romanticism with reactionary cultural nationalism, an idealised *Volksgeist*-dominated vision centered on Golden Age drama that represented the means of *casticista* ("pure") salvation from contemporary radical Romanticism, which Durán was later to label "romanticismo malo" or evil Romanticism.[15] Durán would consistently employ the tenets of Romantic historicism with a Schlegelian content in prefacing the ballad collections or *Romanceros* he edited and published between 1828 and 1832.

There are numerous indications of the growing influence of this set of ideas. The change in Lista's own perspective, from virtually unadulterated Neoclassical preferences toward an acceptance of Schlegelian historicism, is documented, while another important theoretical statement came from Juan Donoso Cortés (1809–1853) in his *Discurso de apertura en Cáceres* ("Inaugural Speech in Cáceres") of 1829. Donoso here declared his preference for the Scottish bard Ossian (whose poems were reproduced in the eighteenth century by James Macpherson) rather than for Greek verse, with pointers to both the Greek rhetorician Longinus and the Irish writer Edmund Burke; he professed the superiority of feeling over rational analysis; he contrasted the "outer man" of classical literature with the "inner man" of the Middle Ages; and, like François René vicomte de Chateaubriand (1768–1848), he accounted for the melancholy tones of contemporary verse by reference to the Christian disposition toward spiritual contemplation. Repudiating literature as the imitation of eternal, unchanging Nature, Donoso included a eulogy of Durán and praised Madame de Staël. Crucial also, in this context, is the contrast between his commendation of Shakespeare, Lope, and Calderón and the degree of superficiality he perceived in eighteenth-century French philosophy. An 1832 issue of the Madrid journal *Cartas Españolas* ("Spanish

---

[13] Donald L. Shaw, "Introducción." In *Agustín Durán. Discurso* (Exeter: University of Exeter, 1973), p. xxvii.

[14] David T. Gies, *Agustín Durán: A Biography and Literary Appreciation* (London: Támesis Books Ltd., 1975), p. 81.

[15] José Escobar, "Romanticismo y revolución." In *El romanticismo*. Ed. David T. Gies (Madrid: Taurus, 1989) pp. 324–328.

Letters"), meanwhile, contained a further defense of Romantic ideas; once more we find the characteristic underscoring of the Schlegelian formula, representative praise for Durán, and repetition of the basic definition of Romanticism as a literature founded upon the ways of being, thinking, and believing of the chivalric Middle Ages.

Romantic theory as professed in Spain in the period prior to 1834 was both coherent and consistent; it was also, as we immediately detect, limited and incomplete, lacking any serious apprehension of literary Romanticism as a contemporary phenomenon: for this reason Shaw elects Alcalá Galiano's prologue to Rivas' *El moro expósito* ("The Foundling Moor") of 1834 as the first genuine Romantic manifesto.[16] Schlegelian theory, however, provided a secure basis for judging, one which later Romantic critics were reluctant to discard. Thus when more radical Romantic works appeared, chiefly in the theatre, their content and vision seemed contrary to established assumptions – *Don Alvaro o la fuerza del sino* ("Don Alvaro or the Force of Destiny," 1835) at first bewildered, and only later outraged, Spanish critics – this helps to explain their speedy rejection. Lista, Durán, and Donoso continued to contribute to the debate, all remaining attached to the earlier Schlegelian formula, restated also, as a working definition, by Antonio Gil y Zárate in his *Manual de literatura* ("Handbook of Literature") of 1842. Enrique Gil y Carrasco (1815–1846), Salvador Bermúdez de Castro (1817–1888), and Ramón de Mesonero Romanos (1803–1882), plus a younger generation of critics like Gabino Tejado and Manuel Cañete, share this approach, which was to define the creative literature of Zorrilla.[17] Even the extensive introduction to Amador de los Ríos' *Historia crítica de la literatura española* ("A Critical History of Spanish Literature") of 1861 is saturated with Schlegelian features, and Amador, typical of his generation, fulsomely praises Durán. Rightly or wrongly, this was the version of Romanticism that prospered.

---

[16] Donald L. Shaw, "Spain. Romántico-Romanticismo-Romancesco-Romanesco-Romancista-Románico." In *"Romantic" and its Cognates: The European History of a Word*. Ed. Hans Eichner (Toronto: University of Toronto Press, 1972), pp. 343–352.

[17] Derek Flitter, *Theory*, pp. 76–112; and "Zorrilla, the Critics and the Direction of Spanish Romanticism." In *José Zorrilla, 1893–1993: Centennial Readings*. Ed. Richard A. Cardwell and Ricardo Landeira (Nottingham: University of Nottingham Press, 1993), pp. 1–15.

23

The theatre in Romantic Spain

DAVID T. GIES

In the 1820s, on the eve of the only sustained Spanish incursion into what was, even at the time, called "romántico," the Spanish theatre was in a muddle. Plagued for years by administrative incompetence, financial instability, ecclesiastical and political censorship, and – in part due to the foregoing reasons – a paucity of new dramatists and quality works, the theatre subsisted on a diet of translations, melodramas, magical comedies, operas, and *refundiciones* ("rewritings") of Golden Age plays. Serious plays – tragedies and comedies – were noticeably absent from the boards. Some attempts were made, of course, to take note of literary trends outside the country, but it was not until the end of the decade, and then, more rapidly following the death of King Fernando VII in 1833, that the Spanish theatre managed to stage imported or home-grown plays that reflected the collective energy and European angst called Romanticism.

Still, Romanticism in Spain was hardly an imported affair, nor would it be restricted to a narrow time period in the first half of the nineteenth century. As I. L. McClelland and Russell P. Sebold have amply demonstrated,[1] the cosmic preoccupation with the self, the obsession with death, and man's sense of being abandoned by greater powers revealed themselves with great clarity during the final years of the eighteenth century in Spain, particularly in the writing of Meléndez Valdés, Jovellanos, and Cadalso, whose sensitivity to the metaphors, symbols, and cosmic worries that would come to dominate Spanish literature fifty years later is now understood. If the Enlightenment, however, can be conceptualized as a time of comedy – that is, as a time of hope, optimism, possible fulfillment, social harmony, balance, renovation, and reform – then the Romantic period inverted that paradigm as a time of failed dreams, tragedy, melodrama, the absence of happy endings, and a confirmation of Francisco de Goya's dictum that the sleep of reason did indeed produce monsters.

The first real revolution in theatre ownership, repertory, and accomplishment took place after 1823 when Juan de Grimaldi (1789–1872),

---

[1] I. L. McClelland, *The Origins of the Romantic Movement in Spain* (Liverpool: Liverpool University Press, 1937; 2nd edn., 1975); Russell P. Sebold, *Trayectoria del romanticismo español* (Barcelona: Crítica, 1983).

a transplanted French soldier, became director of the two main stages in Madrid, the Cruz Theatre and the Príncipe Theatre. Grimaldi had no experience in the theatre, but he had taste, friends, and the conviction that Spain was ripe for a renovation; in quick order he stabilized the finances, hired new actors, commissioned new plays, and made the theatre in Madrid a fundamental, if not obligatory, activity of the middle and upper classes. Then, in 1829, he produced his adaptation of a French magical comedy called *La pata de cabra* ("The Goat's Foot") which was to become the most popular play performed in Spain during the first half of the century. Between 1823 and 1836 Grimaldi hired Mariano José de Larra (1809–1837), Manuel Bretón de los Herreros (1796–1873), and Ventura de la Vega (1807–1865) to write new plays; he staged the works of the duque de Rivas (1791–1865), Francisco Martínez de la Rosa (1787–1862), Antonio García Gutiérrez (1813–1884), and other Romantic playwrights; he improved the material quality of the theatres (seating, set and lighting design, props); and he brought into the companies the actors who would become the stars of the Romantic stage (including his wife, Concepción Rodríguez).

Most of the playwrights who would triumph on the Spanish stage during the 1830s had already written or published works in the previous decade or two. In particular, Rivas – then known simply as Ángel de Saavedra – had written *Ataúlfo* (1814) *Aliatar* (1816), *El duque de Aquitania* (1816), and *Malek-Adhel* (1818), and Martínez de la Rosa had seen some success with his tragedies *La viuda de Padilla* ("Padilla's Widow," 1812), *Morayma* (1818), and *Aben-Humeya o la rebelión de los moriscos* ("Aben-Humeya, or the Revolt of the Moriscos," 1830). It was Grimaldi's staging of Martínez de la Rosa's *La conjuración de Venecia* ("The Venice Conspiracy") on 23 April 1834, however, that shocked the Spanish theatre out of its previous lethargy and complacency. This daring play, which drew on the spectacular tropes of opera and magical comedy (which Madrid audiences loved), presented scenic effects designed to heighten the emotion being expressed on stage by the characters. Its "desenlace . . . en extremo dramático y terrible" ("extremely dramatic and terrifying dénouement"), the words used by Eugenio de Ochoa to characterize it in the pages of the newspaper *El Artista*, captured the new Romantic aesthetic perfectly. The story line tracks the fate of Rugiero, whose dual aspirations include marrying his girlfriend Laura and toppling the tyrannical rule of the Tribunal de los Diez in Venice in 1310 (the work is based on historical fact). These goals fuse into one as it is revealed that Laura's uncle, Pedro Morosini, the president of the Tribunal, is also Rugiero's long-lost father. The "terrifying" finale crushes all hope for any sort of happy ending. As Javier Herrero has noted, Martínez captures perfectly the fusion of political and cosmic terror which fascinated Romantic authors, and which would play

itself out time and again on the Spanish stage.[2] When Mariano José de
Larra saw the play, he was overcome with emotion and clearly aware
that an epochal moment had transpired: "No hemos visto nada mejor
en Madrid" ("We have seen nothing better in Madrid"). The impact
of *La conjuración* on the charged world of post-Fernandine Spain was
decisive.

Larra's own incursion into the field of Romantic drama came just
months after the première of *La conjuración*. *Macías*, a historical drama,
debuted on 24 September 1834 and took the Spanish Romantic theatre
one step further toward authenticity. The play is an accomplished blend of
love, fate, and adverse political circumstances similar to *La conjuración*,
but Larra goes beyond Martínez's model by mixing personal misunderstanding and political conflict with suicide and murder. Elvira, in love with
the troubadour Macías but convinced by her fiancé don Tello that Macías
has married someone else, plunges a dagger into herself, swearing that her
tomb will serve as her impossible nuptial bed. Unlike Martínez's Laura,
who merely faints, Elvira actively participates in her fate and in her rejection of a model of existence that prohibits happiness. Not only the linking
of love and death, but also the recognition that death will become both
the mechanism through which and the place where the unhappy lovers
will finally be united, is central to the Spanish conception of Romanticism.
Larra exploits it skillfully when the tomb and the marriage bed become
one and the same, and both Macías and Elvira recognize that life without
love is not worth living: "¿Qué es la vida? / Un tormento insufrible, si
a tu lado / no he de pasarla ya. ¡Muerte! ¡Venganza!" ("What is life? /
An insuffrable torture if I cannot live it by your side. Death! Revenge!").
Larra, searching for a new way to express aesthetically and symbolically
the tensions he was sensing in his own life and circumstances, captures
in his ill-fated lovers the impassioned and turbulent times in which he
lived.

Romanticism in Europe had rediscovered, and reconfigured, historical
drama. The best-known and most troubling play in the genre was clearly
Rivas' *Don Álvaro o la fuerza del sino* ("Don Alvaro, or the Force of
Destiny"), which premièred on 22 March 1835. Drawing on more recent
history (the eighteenth century rather than the more distant Middle Ages),
Rivas, who had been a proponent of the use of history for theatrical ends
since early in his career, captured in *Don Álvaro* all of the impassioned
angst and symbolic fatefulness of Spanish Romanticism. "The force of
destiny," in its guise of absurd and chaotic fate and pure bad luck, marks

---

[2] Javier Herrero, "Terror y literatura: Ilustración, revolución y los orígenes del movimiento
romántico." In *La literatura española de la Ilustración.* Ed. José Luis Varela (Madrid:
Universidad Complutense, 1988), pp. 131–153.

every step taken by the play's eponymous hero. Álvaro has come to symbolize tragic, Romantic Man, but his tragedy does not flow from a classical tragic flaw, but rather from the mere fact of his existence in a world controlled by whim and chaos. He is neither at fault nor in control of his fate. This is best exemplified in two stunning moments in the play. The first comes early, when don Álvaro, realizing that Leonor's father, the powerful Marqués de Calatrava, opposes their marriage, suppresses the rage he feels when the Marqués insults his supposedly low-class background, and kneels before him in an act of resignation. As he tosses aside the gun he is carrying, it accidentally goes off and mortally wounds Leonor's father, setting in motion a chain of events which will lead to his final, and devastating, act of cosmic defiance. The second comes in the final scenes of the play, when don Álvaro, after years of turmoil in which he thinks that Leonor is dead, discovers that she has in fact been living as a recluse in the craggy mountains near his own monastery (he took religious orders five years previously in an attempt to turn his grief and rage into good works). There, as he rediscovers her, he realizes that her brother Alfonso has just plunged a dagger into her. "¡Te hallé" – he screams – "por fin . . . sí, te hallé . . . muerta!" ("Finally I found you . . . yes, I found you . . . dead!"). His spiritual death occurs at this very moment, but Rivas pushes him yet further, pushes him over a cliff in a dazed, diabolical act of suicide. As he leaps to his death he shouts, "Húndase el cielo, perezca la raza humana; exterminio, destrucción" ("Let the Heavens be buried, let humanity perish; extermination, destruction"), in an act of Romantic defiance that left Madrid audiences confused, angered, and in shock. Viewed as a symbolic drama rather than a realistic one, *Don Álvaro* becomes the first Spanish play to capture fully the step into the modern world's conception of life as something chaotic, lacking reason, and unfair. It revealed to its audiences that there was not necessarily a connection between cause and effect, between misdeed and punishment, good behavior and just rewards. In fact, just the reverse seemed to be true: it demonstrated that good behavior could, for no apparent rational reason, be punished. Eugenio de Ochoa detected in this frightening new moment a "tipo exacto del drama moderno" ("an exact model of modern drama"). Such unnerving views expressed by Rivas and lived by don Álvaro apparently unsettled the author, too, since his post-*Don Álvaro* work draws on more stable, more traditional touchstones. He quickly retreated from the extremist position he staked out in *Don Álvaro* and published work that more closely expressed conservative establishment values. Still, it remains, in Ermanno Caldera's words, as "la obra de ruptura, el primer drama romántico plenamente logrado . . . la obra maestra que llevaba a cabo el arraigo firme y definitivo del romanticismo en el teatro dramático español" ("the work which breaks the mold, the first fully successful Romantic drama . . . the masterwork that carried off the complete and definitive rooting of Romanticism in Spanish dramatic theatre").[3]

Rivas' play surprised the public with its revolutionary and disquieting message, but when Joaquín Francisco Pacheco (1808–1865) staged his vibrant if overwritten *Alfredo* two months after *Don Álvaro* (23 May 1835), the reaction veered between hostility and indifference. Like don Álvaro, Alfredo feels pursued by fate, demonic powers, and a "fantasma" ("ghost") that threatens to take over his life. "¿Será por ventura la fatalidad la única ley del mundo?" he asks ("Can it be that destiny is the world's only law?"). He, too, suffers from a frenetic, "infernal" love, but his passion is not for an innocent young thing but rather for Berta, the "widow" of his absent father, and the suggestion of incest sets this play apart from its predecessors. If the play ultimately fails, crushed by the weight of too many lugubrious images, energetic screams, and precipitous emotional changes, it nevertheless still captures the Romantic mindset. Álvaro sums this up: "Y ¿es acaso culpa mía, si el mundo está dominado por un principio maléfico?" ("And is it my fault that the world is governed by a malevolent principle?"). Alfredo's terrible end echoes don Álvaro's as he takes out a dagger and, with a furious scream of "¡Maldición sobre mí!" ("Damnation upon me!"), plunges it into his breast. This is the new man, the anguished Romantic hero pushed to the limits of his existence.

Similar angst informed the play destined to become one of the most famous phenomena in Spanish theatrical history. The shock produced by Antonio García Gutiérrez on 1 March 1836 with *El trovador* ("The Troubador") is stuff of theatre lore. The play's attention to detail, beautifully conceptualized characters, and Romantic message generated a clamorous ovation and, for the first time in recorded theatre history in Spain, demands that the author come out on stage for public recognition. García Gutiérrez's rebellious hero Manrique pushed the limits of Romanticism into areas that even Larra and Rivas had not gone when he declared that not even God would stand between him and his true love Elvira. *El trovador* is both deeply disturbing and deeply satisfying. It is disturbing because his lovers are crushed by the force of destiny (as happened in *Don Álvaro*), made to abandon even the slightest glimmer of hope or redemption. Evil reigns supreme in Manrique's world, created and sustained by powers – political, social, ecclesiastical, biological, existential – bent on insuring mankind's unhappiness. The tender yet frightening gypsy

---

[3] Ermanno Caldera and Antonietta Calderone, "El teatro en el siglo XIX (1808–1844)." In *Historia del teatro en España. Vol. II: Siglos XVIII y XIX.* Ed. José María Díez Borque (Madrid: Taurus, 1988), p. 458.

Azucena fuses (and confuses) love with vengeance, and her final scream –
"¡Ya estás vengada!" ("Finally you are avenged!") – is spoken as much to
the spirit of her mother as it is to herself, for she has allowed her obsessive
bitterness to bring tragedy and death to everyone in her life, including her
own son (whom she mistakenly threw into a fire in a rage years before).
The play's pessimism goes even deeper, if this is imaginable, than that of
Don Álvaro, whose final act of suicide can at least be interpreted as a
final confirmation of his existential freedom. García Gutiérrez offers us
no such possible redemption. Yet the play is oddly satisfying, too, since
the depth of the characters (Azucena in particular), the care taken in the
writing, and its uncanny capture of the tenor of the times earned it a place
in the minds and hearts of theatre audiences. The newspaper *El Artista*
("The Artist") underscored how it addressed "épocas de revueltas intesti-
nas como la presente, en que las pasiones son todo" ("periods of domestic
upheavals like the present one, in which passions become everything").
Inhabitants of Madrid became obsessed with *El trovador*, lined up at the
box office to buy tickets, suffered scalpers' high prices, bought out the
first printed edition within two weeks, and wandered around repeating
selected verses and scenes from it.

García Gutiérrez had two more Romantic hits with *El paje* ("The
Page") and *El rey monje* ("The Monk King") in 1837. Both plays return
to the role of fate in the lives of men, and both present heroes dominated by passion, daring, and emotion. The opening scenes of *El paje*
present a dizzying amount of information, mystery, secrets to be revealed,
and tension, which culminate later in the play with the breaking of yet
another social taboo: the restriction against incest. Symbolically, both
plays address man's failed struggle for love, happiness, and existence, ideas
consistent with the Romantic cosmology witnessed in the Page's predecessors, Rugiero, Macías, don Álvaro, and the Troubador. Concepts and
images which would by now be standard on the Romantic stage dominate
these plays: the dichotomies life/death, light/dark, good/evil, Heaven/Hell;
the use of hidden identities and disguises; the fusion of the political and
social with the personal; the angst of injustice; and the triumph of pessimism, frustrated love, and despair. Later in his career, García Gutiérrez
returned to the world of Romanticism with *Venganza catalana* ("Catalan
Vengeance," 1864) and *Juan Lorenzo* (1865).

The year 1837 also saw the debut of *Los amantes de Teruel* ("The
Lovers of Teruel") by Juan Eugenio Hartzenbusch (1806–1880). Hartzenbusch drew on a long tradition of European and Spanish work to forge
a drama which gave definitive shape to a well-known legend. While it is
not a drama of rebellion or cosmic angst, it is nevertheless profoundly
Romantic because it deals with a love story played out against the forces
of secular and divine intervention. It shares with other Romantic plays the

belief that true love is transcendent and fundamental to man's happiness, yet impossible to achieve in a world ruled by injustice, evil, bad luck, and fate. Marsilla and Isabel, lovers separated by the twists of fate, are reunited at the end of the play, but only in death. Hartzenbusch infuses the play with high tension and plot twists, including multiple surprises, intense emotion, and a clever blending of the sacred and the profane. While it was not at the time Hartzenbusch's most popular play (his magical comedy *La redoma encantada* ["The Enchanted Flask," 1839] garnered that status), it is the play for which he is best remembered today. Following in the wake of these Romantic dramas, Antonio Gil y Zárate (1793–1862) penned one of the most hyper-Romantic plays in the Spanish repertory, a shocking work that left the public aghast at its daring. Gil, one of the most prolific, interesting, and nearly forgotten dramatists of his generation, was highly respected during his lifetime as a leader in Spanish literary circles. In *Carlos II el hechizado* ("Carlos II the Bewitched," 1838), Gil drew upon all of the now-established Romantic tropes and, in don Froilán, the main character, he created one of the most deliciously and over-the-top evil characters in all of Spanish drama. Froilán's satanic lust for the virtuous Inés, who is later revealed to be the illegitimate daughter of King Carlos II, makes him the very essence of blind obsession. Gil skillfully draws Froilán as a psychologically complex character, motivated by illicit passion yet conscious of both the impossibility of his love and the pleasure of its torments. He struggles against his passion, but fails to dominate it, and the interior battle he undergoes lends depth and subtlety to his character. Froilán expresses his torment in typical Romantic fashion – swearing vengeance, lamenting his "unjust fate," "blind destiny," and "unlucky star" – but he is nonetheless incapable of escaping their power. In the end, crazed and delirious, agonized and confused (in a mental state that reminds us of don Álvaro), he careens out of control. One reviewer, writing in *No me olvides* in 1838 and horrified by the play's excesses, labeled it an "abortion" that pertained to "la escuela satánica, que debía ser enteramente abandonada en este siglo, en el que sabemos muy bien cómo destruir y muy poco cómo edificar" ("the satanic [read 'Romantic'] school, which should be abandoned completely during this century, which knows too much about how to destroy but too little about how to build up").

Needless to say playwrights and audiences did not abandon this "satanic school," although after 1838 the heat began to cool down. Indeed, in spite of appearances, Romantic plays did not completely dominate theatre offerings during the 1830s and 1840s. The repertory was still full of non-Romantic plays, the same amalgam of elements drawn from a rich variety of sources such as eighteenth-century sensualist and sentimental literature, Golden Age comedy, images drawn from the burgeoning

European gothic, French melodrama, historical dramas, and magical comedies.

The play remembered today as the most popular play in the Spanish repertory – not just of the nineteenth century but perhaps of all time – is the astonishingly long-lived *Don Juan Tenorio* by José Zorrilla (1817–1893). Zorrilla was already a well-known poet and playwright when he wrote, in a very short time, his now world-famous *Don Juan Tenorio*. Previously he had enjoyed critical and popular success with such plays as *El zapatero y el rey* ("The Shoemaker and the King," two parts, 1840 and 1842) and *El puñal del godo* ("The Goth's Dagger," 1843). Zorrilla's brilliance in *Don Juan Tenorio* was to draw on the established theatre tradition (historical drama, magical comedy, Romantic tragedy) in order to create not a failed Romantic hero, but rather a successful one, a hero who triumphs over all adversity and overcomes the forces of evil destiny. Clearly, there are those who would argue that, by the very virtue of saving his hero from the world of cosmic angst, Zorrilla by definition removes him from the Romantic cosmos; nonetheless, the play contains enough Romantic language and attitude (particularly in the first part) for it still to be considered an icon of Spanish Romantic theatre. In Part 1 don Juan displays many of the characteristics of his Romantic predecessors – he is arrogant, boisterous, and rebellious. Yet we realize that he is not motivated by generosity or nobility (which mark many of the Romantic heroes of previous plays), but rather by evil and disruption. It is not forces beyond his control which impel him to acts of rebellion but rather his own need for attention and power. The famous words that close Part 1

> Llamé al cielo y no me oyó
> y pues sus puertas me cierra,
> de mis pasos en la tierra
> responda el cielo, y no yo.

(I called out to Heaven but was not heard, and since it closed its doors to me, let Heaven answer for my time on earth, not I)

– echo the rebellious stance of former Romantic heroes, but Zorrilla does not, cannot, leave his main character in that position. Zorrilla uses this moment as a turning point in order to allow don Juan to move away from his life of crime to one of profound repentance for his sins. Inés, transformed from the object of desire and seduction into God's messenger (representing Grace), encourages don Juan to see the evil of his ways, and repent. Such behavior would be inconceivable in other Romantic plays, but Zorrilla's desire to create a character which both attracts and repels his audience succeeded beyond his wildest hope. With one eye on the public taste and the other on the political circumstances in which he was living, he created a hero who could address the need for shock and spectacle and his own (and his audience's) longing for tranquility and stability. His message neatly parallels his society's return to the conservative policies of Ramón de Narváez. Don Juan, in spite of his past misdeeds, is saved through repentance and God's grace. Where other Romantic heroes were rebellious up to (and beyond) their own deaths – Rugiero accepted death proudly, don Álvaro jumped into the abyss, Marsilla dropped dead from "love," etc. – Zorrilla's new hero rejects criminality, begs for forgiveness, repents his past, and floats Heavenward on a bed of flowers to the sound of soothing celestial music. Romanticism in Spanish theatre, for all intents and purposes, is over.

Still, Zorrilla returned to mine Romantic imagery and language once more in 1849, and very successfully, too. *Traidor, inconfeso y mártir* ("Traitor, Unconfessed, and Martyr"), a historical drama, became Zorrilla's favorite play and one of his most dynamic creations. It can be considered both an original work and a kind of *refundición*, since he captured the idea from Jerónimo de Cuéllar's well-known Golden Age comedy called *El pastelero de Madrigal* ("The Pastry Chef from Madrigal"), which had been in the repertories for years, but turned it into a highly original, highly dramatic creation. Like the reformed don Juan, the hero of this play, Gabriel Espinosa, is kind, noble, full of vitality, mysterious, generous, and profoundly Catholic. At key moments in the play Gabriel seems to reveal the "truth," but Zorrilla eschews clarity in order to highlight the hero's character rather than his pedigree. Is he really the aristocratic don Sebastián de Portugal or just the humble cook he claims to be? With its deft versification, dramatic tension, passionate yet tender language, and a dramatic revelation scene at the end, Zorrilla's *Traidor* fits squarely into the Spanish Romantic literary cosmos, but staged as it was in 1849, it came too late to have any impact on the development of theatrical taste in the nineteenth century.

One new and important voice that began to emerge in the 1820s was that of Manuel Bretón de los Herreros (1796–1873), whose first public production was *A la vejez, viruelas* ("A Pox on Old Age"), written in 1818 but not staged until 1824, after Grimaldi had taken over the theatres. Bretón adhered to the classical model of Moratín (whose influence would remain profound throughout the first half of the century), and began to develop a comedy of manners which drew from Moratín's established structures but which addressed more contemporary thematic concerns. *Marcela o ¿a cuál de los tres?* ("Marcela, or Which of the Three Suitors to Choose?" 1831) presented one of the Spanish nineteenth-century theatre's truly independent women. Breton penned and staged dozens of comedies during his long career; he also wrote his own version of the Romantic conflict in *Don Fernando el emplazado* ("Don Fernando the Summoned,"

1837), but had much more success when he wrote in the comic vein, as he had done in his Romantic satires, *Elena* and *Muérete, ¡y verás!* ("Die, and Then You'll See!") that same year. Perhaps his two best-known comedies are *El pelo de la dehesa* ("The Country Bumpkin at Court," 1840) and its sequel, *Don Frutos en Belchite* ("Don Frutos at Belchite," 1845), in which he comically dramatizes the conflict between life in the country and life in the city.

Other dramatists who enjoyed success and public notice during the Romantic years, although they are not known for having written Romantic dramas *per se*, are Ventura de la Vega (1807–1865), Eusebio Asquerino (1822–1892), and Tomás Rodríguez Rubí (1817–1890).

Vega entered Grimaldi's company at the same time as Bretón, writing translations, *refundiciones*, original comedies, and tragedies for several decades. His greatest achievement is undoubtedly what has become known as his anti-don Juan play, *El hombre de mundo* ("Man of the World"), first performed in Madrid on 2 October 1845. *El hombre de mundo* became an instant hit and consolidated Vega as one of the leading lights of the Spanish literary scene of the 1840s and 1850s. The main character, played by the famous actor Julián Romea, is a reformed don Juan type, removed from the Romantic world of passion and angst and ethereal love, and placed squarely into a modern, urban bourgeois existence. What is more, he is married and has a job (two characteristics unassociated with the Romantic heroes that preceded Vega). Vega rejected the excesses of Romanticism, and clearly posited in this drama a restabilization of contemporary society. The Romantic sets of previous plays (cave, cemetery, convent, jail) give way to an elegant sitting room in an upper-middle-class household; the stage becomes a safe cultural space which now reflected the aspirations of the Spanish middle class. As Zorrilla suggested, Spain was ready to return to harmony and comfort, abandoning the traumatic world view put forth by Romantic dramatists.

One month after the debut of *Don Juan Tenorio*, Eusebio Asquerino staged *Españoles sobre todo* ("Spaniards Above All"), a play that became one of the most polemical plays of the decade. An unabashed potboiler which ostensibly dealt with the machinations surrounding the Spanish War of Succession in the early years of the eighteenth century, in reality it addressed issues of contemporary politics. While containing many Romantic elements, it strays from the Romantic cosmos because Asquerino refuses to privilege the love story and opts for a happy ending. The play struck a nerve in a country uncomfortable with the political stagnation it sensed in its body politic (particularly in comparison with what was transpiring in other European nations) and, while Asquerino offered no coherent solutions to the disquiet, his bombastic call for Spaniards to resist foreign domination ("Spaniards above all"), the public received the play with clamorous applause. The debate over its politics remained alive for years.

Tomás Rodríguez Rubí is a key figure positioned between Romanticism and the rise of what came to be called the *alta comedia* ("high comedy"). In his time he was considered to be an equal of Bretón (whose fecundity he rivaled), Gil y Zárate, Hartzenbusch, Rivas, García Gutiérrez, Vega, and Zorrilla, although today he is relatively forgotten. His bourgeois comedies and regional historical dramas garnered the attention of critics and the public. *La rueda de la fortuna* ("The Wheel of Fortune," 1843; second part, 1845) and *Bandera negra* ("Black Flag," 1844) addressed contemporary political issues in the guise of history. Both contain rousing political messages combined with simple love stories and a more modified Romantic language.

Before mid century, few women playwrights had access to the commercial theatre. María Rosa Gálvez had some success, as we have seen, in the first few years of the century, and as early as 1818 we see the publication of *Las minas de Polonia* ("Mines of Poland") by the unknown María de Gasca y Medrano. By the late 1830s and 1840s, several women had managed to publish (if not always have performed) a few dozen comedies and dramas. Among those of whom we have some information are Manuela Cambronero, who staged *Safira* with some success in Valladolid in 1842; Ángela Grassi (1823–1883), who at the age of fifteen published *Lealtad a un juramento* ("Loyalty to an Oath"); Carolina Coronado (1821–1911), whose two plays, *Alfonso el León* (1844) and *El cuadro de la esperanza* ("Portrait of Hope"), signaled the arrival of a fresh, new voice (particularly in poetry); the marquesa de Aguiar; Josefa Rovirosa de Torrentes; Enriqueta Lozano de Vilches (1830–1895); and Joaquina Vera, who penned nine plays in the 1840s alone. Best known among the women dramatists was, of course, Gertrudis Gómez de Avellaneda (1814–1873).

Gómez de Avellaneda's work spanned several decades in the middle of the century. Her first drama, *Leoncia*, was staged in Seville in 1840. After she moved to the capital she published *Alfonso Munio* (1844), followed quickly by *El príncipe de Viana* ("The Prince of Viana," 1844) and *Egilona* (1845). Smart, contentious, and frequently in conflict with the men who controlled Spain's literary universe, Gómez de Avellaneda wrote sixteen full-length plays between 1840 and 1858. Many of her plays are tinged with the Romantic language so dominant in theatre circles at the time, although their themes tend more toward religious and domestic matters. That is, while historical tragedies attracted her attention, historical biblical subjects stimulated her best work. *Saúl*, written in 1844 but not produced or published until 1849, is a tragedy that mixes dramatized history, a Bible story, feminism (Micol, a strong woman figure, stands up for her own love interest), elements from the popular magical comedies, musical interludes, and Romantic language. The deluxe staging it received in Madrid provoked much commentary at the time, controversy repeated by the production of her most successful play, *Baltasar*, which appeared in Madrid in 1858. *Baltasar*, which is neither pure historical drama nor pure biblical playwriting (only three of the characters come from history), echoes Zorrilla's *Don Juan Tenorio* in the creation of a central character who discovers faith and love in his final moments and who earns divine clemency only at his death.

Yet as powerful as the Romantic aesthetic proved to be in Spain for a period of twenty years or so, the second half of the century nonetheless belonged not to Zorrilla and his Romantic brethren but rather to the men and women who looked forward to a more modern Spain, not backward to an older, lamented, lost nation.

24

Mariano José de Larra

GREGORIO C. MARTÍN

Larra (1809–1837), the best journalist in nineteenth-century Spain and one of the century's greatest prose stylists, was the son of an *afrancesado* physician who emigrated to France in 1813. Upon his return to Spain four years later, he enrolled in various courses of study without ever completing a degree. He founded two newspapers – *El Duende Satírico del Día* ("The Satiric Sprite of the Day," 1828) and *El Pobrecito Hablador* ("The Poor Little Chatterer," 1832) – and published numerous articles in other newspapers: *La Revista Española* ("The Spanish Journal," December 1832 – January/February 1835), *El Correo de las Damas* ("The Ladies' Journal," June 1833 – May 1834), *El Observador* ("The Observer," October–December 1834), *El Español* ("The Spaniard," November 1835 – February 1837), *El Mundo* ("The World," December 1836 – January 1837), and *El Redactor General* ("The General Editor," December 1836). The wit and mordacity of his satire drew wide attention and high public praise (he was also well compensated for his work). Larra wrote one historical novel, *El doncel de don Enrique el doliente* ("Don Enrique the Sorrowful's Young Nobleman," 1834), one play, *Macías* (1834), and many adaptations and translations of European plays, but it is his newspaper work which is most remembered today. His writing, marked by both historical and personal events, can be divided into two stages: one of hope and optimism, the other of doubt and despair. Nevertheless, due largely to his ongoing battles with the crushing censorship that severely cramped his style, his despair is evident in both stages, and when that censorship came first to threaten his professional autonomy, and later his personal safety, Larra fled discouraged, first from Spain and then from life itself.

Larra's first article, "El duende y el librero" ("The Sprite and the Bookseller"), published in *El Duende Satírico del Día*, already revealed two facets of his authorial persona – the observer and the cynic. While he recognized the need to criticize society, he was always aware of the risk involved in doing so. At this early point in his career the censors had not yet recognized the skill of the young writer and they often failed to decipher his allusions to King Fernando VII's absolutist government. While

This chapter has been translated from the Spanish by Arantxa Ascunce.

this article addresses the "abusos" ("abuses") and "ridiculeces" ("follies") of society, he puts aside the "ridiculeces" and subtly plays with the word "abusos." In Larra's view the only abuses which needed to be addressed were those perpetrated by the government, whose preferred word when referring to anything related to the press was precisely that – "abuses" of the printing press. The attentive reader of the day would have perceived clearly Larra's oblique references. In this article, Larra, for whom satire and risk are deeply interconnected, introduced two nouns – "gobierno" ("government") and "sociedad" ("society") – and three verbs: "vigilar" ("watch over"), "conspirar" ("conspire"), and "desbaratar" ("thwart"). "El Gobierno vigila sobre la seguridad de los individuos" ("The Government watches over the personal safety of individuals"), says the bookseller to his customer. To this the author replies: "El Gobierno vigila sobre la sociedad" ("The Government watches over society"), which is not the same, because "la sociedad no cesa de conspirar" ("society never stops conspiring"). One conspires in order to "desbaratar los buenos fines del Gobierno" ("thwart the good intentions of the Government"), a phrase taken directly from government propaganda. In this manner, Larra exposes absolutist repression, which the government attempts to justify to the people as "los buenos fines" ("good intentions"), while also capitalizing on the multiple meanings of words in order to justify competing views. It is clear that the government watches over the people not because their vices or abuses might conspire against the state but because the people themselves can conspire. Fooled by this initial tease, the censors did not perceive the aim of Larra's wit, yet once they finally became aware themselves of his cleverness, Larra was forced to develop new rhetorical strategies in order to attain the same ends. The conflict between state power and literary cunning had begun: the mission of the state became to prevent Larra from publishing articles critical of the government and Larra's goal was to avoid censorship so as to continue his critical task.

If in his first article Larra already used the printed word to criticize, his next article, "El café" ("The Cafe") describes a backward world in which attorneys at the café need eyeglasses in order to speak, and the physician shows off his walking stick to those in need of a cure. Larra thus uses the image of the eyeglasses and cane as a disguise for the false wise man. Indeed, he complains that, as time passes, Spaniards fail to re-evaluate their priorities. The symbolic cane of "El café" continues to dominate medical science even five years later, as he states in "El mundo todo es máscaras" ("The Whole World Wears Masks," 1833). Nothing would upset Larra more than the realization that he was preaching in vain and that no one was interested in *being*, only in *appearing*. As he states in "Empeños y desempeños" ("Pawn and Reclaim," 1832), everyone wants to appear like someone they are not. Although this trend depresses Larra, he is hopeful that, having now discovered the vice, a remedy might be found.

When the last articles of *El Duende* fell victim to the censors, his initial suspicions were only confirmed. Whenever he published a new newspaper, Larra aimed to entertain his readers. He claimed in "Dos palabras" ("Two Words," 1832): "Reírnos de las ridiculeces: ésta es nuestra divisa; ser leídos: éste es nuestro objeto; decir la verdad: éste nuestro medio" ("To laugh at our follies: this is our motto; to be read: this is our objective; to tell the truth: this is our means"). His intentions, however, are very serious indeed. Previously he had observed people in a coffee shop. Now, five years later, he watches them in the whole city. He looks for values, but only finds insolence, imprudence, intolerance, whims, and "discordia de pareceres" ("discord of opinions"). For the first time, hope wavers, and he states, "renuncio a mis esperanzas" ("I renounce my hopes") and gives way to doubt. Even though the country has not changed in five years, Larra has, having moved in his personal life from the juvenile idealism of his early marriage to the bitter disappointment of a failed one (reflected in his article, "El casarse pronto y mal" ["Getting Married Quickly and Poorly," 1832]). In 1828, Larra thought that society's failures were the result of ignorance, but by 1832 his personal experience had taught him that the actual source of these abuses in fact lies in the innate wickedness of human beings, regardless of one's enlightenment: "Los hombres que no supieron, y los que saben, todos son hombres, y lo peor es, todos son hombres malos" ("The men who did not know, and the men who do, are all men, and worse of all, they are all wicked men") ("Carta a Andrés," 1832).

State censors showed no mercy with *El Pobrecito Hablador*. On the front page of the early issues, Larra classifies the articles: the first is "robado" ("stolen"), he writes; the second, "nuestro" ("ours"); the third, "enteramente nuestro" ("entirely ours"). When he publishes the fourth, however, it is not "robado" nor "nuestro" but "parecido a otro" ("similar to another one"), which serves to indicate the apparent source that inspires him; it seems (and only seems) like another article that, had it been written, would not have been publishable. In this manner, Larra kept the game alive, and such covert allusions entertained his more enlightened readers. By 1832, however, the censors were not as easy to fool as they were in 1828. Now they "correct" because they understand the allusions, and if they do not entirely understand them, they deny publication because they suspect that something lurks beneath the surface of his prose. Larra pushes the limits of his own obstinate mordacity and those of the law. He would like to know where power stops censoring and justice begins to punish. Although in his "Sátira contra los vicios de la Corte" ("Satire Against the Vices of the Court," 1832) he does not name specific people who restrict artistic freedom and the freedom of speech, he does mention specific jobs, principally those associated with the theatre. Larra seems to know what he is doing and what the risks involved are. Near the end of the article, he writes these lines in which he reveals that not only is risk involved, but so too is "miedo" ("fear"):

> Mas yo, que soy un mísero poeta,
> Antes que por decir verdades claras
> En un encierro un alguacil me meta,
>   Y me cuesten mis sátiras más caras,
> O en el hospicio muera miserable,
> Quiero del riesgo huir doscientas varas:
>   Que ni es lícito hablar donde intratable
> Pone a la lengua la mordaza el miedo,
>   Y ¡ay del primero que rompiéndola hable!

(Even I, a miserable poet, before a cop puts me in prison for the clear truths I speak, and I pay the price of my satires, or I die in a miserable hospice for beggars, I want to flee two hundred yards from risk: for one cannot even speak, where fear places her impossible gag over the tongue. Pity the first person who dares to speak!)

He mentions the fear that Fernando inspires, and fear will be a word he uses frequently in his articles until his trip to Paris in 1835. In order to avoid danger, he writes about the theatre (rather than government, or society, directly), although it is possible that entire articles from the fourth and seventh notebooks were suppressed in addition to one-third of his "Sátira contra los malos versos de circunstancias" ("Satire Against the Bad Poems of Circumstance"). Nevertheless, when he writes "Filología" ("Philology," 1832) he confesses that he understands the power of the word, that "la lengua es para el hablador lo que el fusil para el soldado: con ella se defiende y con ella mata" ("language is for the speaker what the gun is for the soldier: with each he defends himself and with each he can kill"). He knows that the game is no longer a game, but a battle of sorts, and when he takes stock of this period of his life in "Un reo de muerte" ("A Condemned Prisoner," 1835), he will describe his profession with martial imagery – every article is a battle, the pen a weapon: "Esgrimí la pluma contra las balas" ("I brandished my pen against the bullets") he will say, making continued use of this warlike terminology. "Di la cara a dos enemigos" ("I faced two enemies") he writes, in memory of his articles against the rebels fighting against Queen Regent María Cristina's moderate government in the Carlist Wars,[1] and against the "justo medio" ("happy medium") of Martínez de la Rosa, in order to be "desalojado

---

[1] The Carlist Wars, named after Fernando VII's brother Carlos, were civil wars which broke out following the death of Fernando in 1833. Carlos and his followers challenged

de mi última posición" ("kicked out of my last position"), an allusion to the censorship that forced him to cease writing because of "temor de ser rechazado en posiciones más avanzadas" ("fear of being rejected from more advanced posts") and being obligated to "parapetarme en las costumbres" ("take cover in local customs").

Thinking of literature as a battle, Larra was not interested in *costumbrismo* as a mere painting of traditions, as he describes them in "Carta última de Andrés Niporesas al bachiller don Juan Pérez de Munguía" ("The Last Letter from Andrés Niporesas to the Young Don Juan Pérez of Munguía," 1833): "Sencilla relación de las cosas que natural y diariamente en las Batuecas acontecen" ("A simple retelling of the natural and daily things that happen in Batuecas [Podunk]"). The author is a soldier with a clear mission in life: to forge a better life with the (s)word. Writing is an uneven battle in which the author does not intend to annihilate, but rather illuminate; however, as in every battle, the winner is not necessarily the most reasoned individual, but the one who kills the most. For this Larra, "enlightenment" means not prescribing social behavior but uncovering abuses; until things are seen as abuses, he believed, they will never be changed and a new society will never be created. As he states in "Vuelva usted mañana" ("Come Back Tomorrow," 1833), "es muy difícil convencer al que está persuadido de que no se debe convencer" ("it is very difficult to convince the man who is already persuaded that one should not be convinced"). It is for this reason that the disadvantage of the writer originates from ideas and persistence, because, somewhat paradoxically, his worst enemies are those who should make up his army: mankind. However, "cada hombre tiene su cara" ("every man has his own side"), he affirms in "Empeños y desempeños," and "cada hombre [es] un tirano" ("every man [is] a tyrant"), he writes in "Un reo de muerte." Furthermore, since "el hombre es sólo lo que de él hacen la educación y el gobierno" ("man is only what his education and his government make of him") ("Conclusión," 1833), in the particular case of Spain the government has educated the people with fear, so that men "se mueren del miedo de morirse" ("die for fear of dying"), he says in his second letter to Andrés (*El Pobrecito Hablador*, 1832). The instability of various governments, caused by the negative reaction of the populace to new ideas, led liberal politicians to "tener miedo hasta del gas que los ha de levantar" ("fear even the gas that will lift them up") ("El hombre globo" ["The Balloon Man," 1835]). In this manner, fear can be used to justify political inertia and communal indifference, according to the criticism he makes

the legitimacy of Fernando's daughter Isabel to inherit the throne, and fought against Fernando's widow, the Queen Regent María Cristina until 1839. María Cristina and Isabel managed to hold on to power, but the Carlists came back in the 1870s to challenge the Bourbon monarchy once again.

of the opera *Norma*, in which he uses the word "fear" seven times: "El miedo es achaque y pretexto para gobernantes y gobernados" ("fear is the weakness and pretext of the government and the governed," 1834). The power of literature is founded in the relationship of the writer to the reader – so that the word the author writes can germinate in the consciousness of the reader. The need for an enlightened society that would be simultaneously a receptor of such words and their judge springs from this concept; from here also springs Larra's belief that abuse exists where ignorance abounds. Since censorship is born from fear of the power of the word, the state finds a need to censor. This necessity is greater in a "caviloso y débil" ("apprehensive and weak") government because it seeks the power it lacks in the consciousnesses of others, and "teme la palabra" ("it fears the word").

Larra suffered self-doubt for two years, not because of his incapacity to transmit his message, but because of the limits of others to assimilate it. For him, writing was a kind of exordium. Already in "El casarse pronto y mal" he explained that one should always write "de parte de lo que nos parezca verdad y razón . . . según la influencia del momento en que escribamos; y basta de exordio" ("in favor of what we see to be true and reasonable . . . according to the influences of the moment in which we write; and enough with introduction"). He would repeat this message in many other articles. Larra does not claim the use of the word as a means of earning a living, but rather as a natural right that was conceded by God in order to make man superior to the rest of creation. When man does not reclaim this right (to speak freely), he rejects a divine gift and works against Nature. Larra used the simile of a confinement between walls: "Pongámosle . . . cada uno un ladrillito más con nuestras propias manos; vivamos entre nuestras cuatro paredes, sin disputar vanamente si nos ha de sorprender la muerte . . . asados o cocidos" ("Let's lay . . . each one of us, another small brick with our own hands; let's live between our four walls, without vainly arguing about whether or not death will surprise us . . . baked or boiled" ["Conclusión"]). This confinement preoccupied Larra, and he called it "censuras amargas" ("bitter censorships"), referring to it again when he says at the end of the *Pobrecito* that he shudders from head to toe each time he puts pen to paper. It is not a physical fear, but rather a professional suspicion of knowing, a desire that will be met with impotence. "¡Voto a tal!, que nunca le vi la cara al miedo" ("Blast! I've never seen the face of fear"), he would say. He later confesses "que tengo miedo, y que de miedo muero"("I am afraid, and from fear I am dying"). Indeed, he dies for fear of others, for the fear that power has of the power of the word; this is what he calls "pared insuperable" ("an insuperable wall"); a confinement that prohibits him from exorcizing the truth.

On 13 October 1833, a judicial sentence banned Larra from naming actors in his reviews, and on this same date he wrote in "Varios caracteres" ("Several Characters"): "estos días en que el fastidio se apodera de mi alma y en que no hay cosa que tenga color . . . llevo cara de filósofo, es decir, de mal humor . . . cuando el tedio me abruma con su peso, no puedo tener más que tedio" ("during these days in which frustration takes hold of my soul, and in which there is nothing that even has color . . . I wear a philosopher's face, that is, I look unhappy . . . when tedium wears me down with its weight, I cannot bear anything but the tedium"). Larra uses the image of water as a whirlpool in a deep river that Spain must cross. From this point on his bad moods dominate him, and a year later he finds himself forced to fight a duel – something he repudiates but which society, he believes, demands of him – with an actor named Agustín Azcona. Not only did society fail to change but it also caused him – a reformer of traditions – to participate in her worst customs, a reality that must have humiliated him. An acutely sensitive person, Larra thought everything was falling apart for him in late 1834. When he wrote "La calamidad europea" ("The European Calamity"), a truly desolate article published in the collection *Fígaro* in 1835, his failure to maintain hope was palpable: "todo es error y desgracia, todo crimen y confusión en el mundo; todo es, en fin, calamidades" ("everything is error and disgrace, everything is crime and confusion in the world; everything is, in the end, calamity"). Convinced of the impossibility of change, instead of the joy of writing he found a loss of hope for improvement. From this point on his articles became more despairing, and, due to the conflict with Azcona, he wrote in July of 1834 that he could not live without fear. Six months later, he claimed in "La policía" ("The Police," 1835) that everyone is either afraid, or afraid of being afraid. Although he may have been referring to Spain's fear of anarchy, he also possibly feared for his own personal safety: limited by a censorship that blocked more and more of his articles from being published, and troubled by personal problems, he left Spain in despair in 1835.

Larra's trip abroad was therapeutic, at least momentarily, and when he returned from France he was a more optimistic man of ideas. His articles – he calls them "meditations and reflections on forlorn philosophers" – longer in length and now in the form of essays, reveal a seeker of truth who is attempting to exorcize the anguish of a tragic life. Without time to regenerate, he calls for a revolution to "desenredarnos de esta tela vieja en que yacemos miserablemente envueltos" ("disentangle ourselves from this old web in which we miserably rot"). He rejects compromise, and believes that the new Spain must rise from the ashes of the old: "si todo es Viejo aquí, abajo todo" ("if everything here is old, then down

with everything" ["Anthony," 1836]). If he previously viewed Spain as
crossing a turbulent river, now the energy of the new Spain he perceives
is the flooded river that will dismantle the feeble ship of the old Spain.
Once again, he begins hopefully, encouraged by his search for a new
path. In order to anchor himself with hope, he will make professions
of faith without compromising his ideas of freedom and truth, because
"nuestra conciencia puede equivocarse, nunca torcerse" ("our conscience
can be wrong, but it must never deviate") he says in "Ateneo científico y
literario" (1836). He continues the old battle against power, and with the
same weapons: "la palabra es el arma; la tribuna, la prensa; la cátedra
son los campos de batalla" ("the word is the weapon; the tribunal, the
press; and the college the battlefield"). The threat is the same as before,
but for Larra, danger is a spur that stimulates him to polish his style in
such a way as to force the censors and government hacks to permit him to
say what cannot be said but what, in his opinion, must be said. Without
fear, there would be no wit, and without wit, there would be no satire.
Once again, the power of the word combats the power of the state, so
that "sólo el sable es peligroso; la palabra, nunca" ("only the saber is
dangerous; the word, never"), because the word is the "expresión de la
inteligencia, la verdadera arma digna de la humanidad" ("expression of
human intelligence, the true weapon worthy of humanity").

Nevertheless, the same circumstances that beleaguered him before his
trip soon reappeared, because his battle was predisposed by the fear of
others; the fear that power wields over the ideas of new generations. This
affected him as a writer because it resulted in censorship; and censorship
led to prohibition, which led to inertia, then to impotence, and finally
to despair. His fears were made real and events were repeated when he
was threatened with imprisonment in the Canary Islands for the things
he published ("El día de difuntos de 1836" ["The Day of the Dead 1836,"
1836). As a challenge to the censorship that continued to haunt him, the
sensitive, but inflexible, Larra repeated the name of the islands in later
articles as a challenge to authority and an admission of his potential end.
Ultimately, however, he concluded that the battle was too great and the
hoped-for goal too ephemeral. As he wrote in "El día de difuntos de
1836," each article represents a lost battle that buried his hope, and the
word ("hope") means nothing, since the revolution never comes, and all
of his words become nothing more than mere words. When, in 1836,
his personal failures fused with other hardships, Larra's internal crisis
began again. In spite of not accepting compromise by continuing to be
a "periodista por mí y ante mí" ("writer for myself and before myself,"
1835) and "estar casados con nuestra opinión" ("being married to my
own opinions," 1836), he found himself trapped by the fear that others

felt, and by the fear that he felt about himself. The retreat to France was no longer an option. His only way out was to escape from the world. A pioneer of the word, Larra knew how to criticize society's ills in a way that was not only understood by those of his time, but by modern readers as well.

25

Romantic poetry

SUSAN KIRKPATRICK

Significant changes in poetic language, form, and function in Spain reflected a double-faceted response to the seismic shifts occurring in European society at the beginning of the nineteenth century. The reaction against Enlightenment rationalism, materialism, and universalism came first, introduced into Spain by Johann Nikolaus Böhl von Faber (1770–1836). In the course of the 1820s and 1830s, Spanish intellectuals adopted many of the aesthetic ideas derived by Böhl from the German Romantics: the organicist view of culture as the expression of a national spirit (called *Volksgeist*), the primacy of creative imagination, spontaneity, and emotion in artistic production, and the idealization of the Middle Ages as more evocative of those qualities than the decadent and materialistic contemporary world.

The diffusion of these attitudes meant first of all a widespread re-evaluation of the oral poetic tradition, especially Spain's historical ballads, or *romances*. Agustín Durán (1789–1862) spurred interest by publishing his carefully compiled ballad collections in a series of well-received volumes beginning in 1828. There was broad agreement among writers and critics that the *romancero* constituted, in the words of Antonio Alcalá Galiano (1789–1865), "una poesía nacional y natural de consiguiente" ("a national and therefore a natural poetry").[1] This sense that the traditional ballads expressed a unique, unmediated national essence rapidly enhanced their aesthetic value in lettered culture; by the 1830s Spanish poets were creating their own *romances*, adopting the sharp contrasts, dramatic situations, and evocative imagery of the traditional ballads.

Despite historicist Romanticism's nostalgia for medieval organicism, its emphasis on the subjective, on imagination and emotion as the essence of the "poetic," resonated with evolving economic and political formations based on the individual. When Durán in his influential *Discurso* defined the mission of Romantic poetry as the representation of "la historia del hombre interior considerado como individuo" ("the history of the inner

---

[1] Antonio Alcalá Galiano, "Prólogo" to *El moro expósito*, by Ángel Saavedra, duque de Rivas (1834). In *El romanticismo español. Documentos.* Ed. Ricardo Navas Ruiz (Salamanca: Editorial Anaya, 1971), p. 113.

man considered as an individual"),[2] he indicated that the interiority of the individual subject had become the basis of the new aesthetic. This orientation toward expanded poetic exploration of the inner self linked up with the more liberal version of Romanticism that emerged in the mid 1830s, a period of militant liberal reform that abolished the legal basis of aristocratic and ecclesiastical privilege and established a constitutional monarchy. The liberatory desire associated with the struggle to dismantle the *ancien régime* reached its fullest lyrical expression in the poetry of José de Espronceda, which focused on the angst resulting from the failure of the individual's effort to realize self-generated visions of human possibility. Less extreme versions of this theme of disillusionment with an oppressive reality became a staple of Spanish Romantic poetry, as did the exploration of the inner realms of feeling and fantasy. The emphasis on the inner self had another effect related to modernization: as poetry came to be seen as the spontaneous expression of the heart and the imagination, it provided women a path to authorship that was compatible with both their lack of formal education and their socially assigned link to emotionality. Thus, with Romanticism, Spanish women made their appearance in literary history as regular participants in the production first of poetry, and then of other genres.[3]

In his own time and after, José de Espronceda (1808–1842) was seen as the preeminent Romantic poet of Spain. As a youth Espronceda was trained in Neoclassical poetics by Alberto Lista (1775–1848). However, the teenaged poet embroiled himself in liberal conspiracies against the absolutist régime of Fernando VII and in 1827 was sent out of Spain by his family to avoid trouble. Upon his return after Fernando's death, he initiated a new poetics with the publication of "La canción del pirata" ("The Pirate's Song," 1835). Using varied metric forms to suggest the dynamism of an outlaw subject only to his own will, Espronceda's pirate sings joyously of unfettered individual liberty. The poet experimented further with this technique of using the perspective of marginalized figures to criticize social hypocrisy and injustice in four additional *canciones*: "El mendigo" ("The Beggar"), "El reo de muerte" ("The Condemned Prisoner"), "El verdugo" ("The Executioner"), and "El canto del cosaco" ("The Song of the Cossack").

In the years between 1835 and 1840, when a collection of his poetry was published, Espronceda also elaborated a Romantic metaphysics of the self in a series of love elegies. The basic pattern was set in "A una estrella" ("To a Star"), in which the lyrical speaker reads into the faint

[2] Agustín Durán, *Discurso sobre el influjo que ha tenido la crítica moderna en la decadencia del teatro antiguo español* . . . In Navas Ruiz, ed., *El romanticismo español*, p. 85.
[3] Susan Kirkpatrick, *Las románticas. Women Writers and Subjectivity in Spain, 1835–1850* (Berkeley: University of California Press, 1989).

light of a small star the cosmic parallel to the eclipse of his own bright hopes and illusions, dashed in the encounter with a beloved woman. The pain of what is presented as the inevitable abyss between the projections of the desirous imagination and the real world leads the speaker to despairing indifference: "no me importa salvarme o zozobrar" ("I don't care whether I survive or founder"). In "A Jarifa en una orgía" ("To Jarifa in an Orgy"), another lyrical monologue in which the speaker addresses a prostitute, the whore becomes a privileged metaphor for the object world in which the subject attempts and inevitably fails to realize his infinite desires. The pain of frustration drives the speaker to the brothel, but because desire can be neither stilled nor satisfied, the poem itself re-enacts an ever-repeated sequence of emotions – desire, illusion, disappointment, and disgust. Espronceda's conception of the fundamental paradigm of human experience, an element that links his work with other important manifestations of European Romanticism, is epitomized in the canto to Teresa, which despite its inclusion in his epic poem, *El diablo mundo* ("The Devil World"), stands on its own as an elegy to Teresa Mancha, the poet's former lover and mother of his daughter.

In *El estudiante de Salamanca* ("The Salamancan Student"), a long narrative poem first published in its entirety in the 1840 collection, Espronceda splits his central paradigm of human subjectivity between two characters: the fatal will to transcend the limits of reality is represented by the protagonist, don Félix de Montemar, a "second don Juan Tenorio" who brooks no obstacle to the satisfaction of his desires, while the mortal anguish of lost illusion is exemplified in doña Elvira, an innocent young woman he has seduced and abandoned. Narrating the heroine's Ophelia-like descent into madness and death, the poem emphasizes the pathos of her surrender to love: she refuses to relinquish its intensity even when the hopes love inspires have been transformed into the pain of loss and despair. The remaining three sections foreground the masculine *brío*, arrogance, and willfulness of don Félix, yet his also turns out to be a story of descent into death.

The narrative moves from don Félix's duel with Elvira's brother in the shadowy precincts of the Calle del Ataúd ("Coffin Street") on to the fantastic journey of the protagonist's soul as he pursues a veiled feminine figure who mysteriously appears to him. He cannot comprehend the sob with which the veiled phantasm responds to his questions, a sob communicating "su inmenso dolor" ("its immense sorrow"), because he accepts no limits to his will. Indeed, don Félix represents that aspect of the Romantic psyche that strives to transcend the limits of the human condition. As his pursuit leads him into fantastic, otherworldly galleries, his defiance of fear and death becomes grandiose, revealing him as a "segundo Lucifer" ("second Lucifer"):

alma rebelde que el temor no espanta,
hollada sí, pero jamás vencida:
el hombre, en fin, que en su ansiedad quebranta
su límite a la cárcel de la vida.

(rebellious soul undaunted by fear, / battered, yes, but never conquered: / man, in sum, who in his yearning breaks / the limits of life's prison.)

His defiance cannot bend the ineluctable law of life, however; when he reaches the figure he has been pursuing, she is standing at the foot of what is at once a marriage bed and a tomb. The two sides of the human experience have been brought together, but their union reflects Espronceda's pessimism: don Félix's struggle to evade Death's embrace ultimately expires in a "leve, / breve / son" ("light, brief sound"). Espronceda's virtuosity as a poet, manifested in the color and dynamism of the imagery and the expressiveness of the varied meters and rhythms, fuses with powerful thematic material to make *El estudiante de Salamanca* an artistic achievement that no poet of his time was able to match.

Espronceda's most ambitious work was his epic poem, *El diablo mundo*, which remained unfinished at the time of his early death from diphtheria in 1842. Moved, like many other European Romantics, to find a poetic form capable of comprehending the vast and contradictory range of human experience, he sought to combine the philosophical poem modeled by Goethe in *Faust* with the ironic self-consciousness of the Byronic mock-epic. Like the over-reacher evoked as the figure of the human spirit, the poem fails to achieve its impossible ambition and thus in its very incompleteness conveys the poet's vision of the world as an unresolved tension between imagination and corruption, aspiration and frustration.

The introductory canto presents the human condition in terms of a fantastic allegory in which the Luciferian figure of man defiantly challenges the secrets of God from an abyss of desolation and impotence where he is besieged by demon voices expressing contradictory desires and realities. Canto I concretizes the human spirit in the form of an old man seated at a pine table by the light of an oil lamp, a setting that includes everyday contemporary life within the scope of aesthetic representation, in contrast to the medievalizing exoticism of the more conservative brand of Spanish Romanticism. Visited by supernatural spirits, the old man chooses the ceaseless, desire-driven movement of life over the peaceful stasis of death, thus launching the main narrative of his rebirth as natural man in the social world. This canto also introduces Byronic digressions that add irony by representing the relationship between author and readers. By referring to such things as the author's aesthetic intentions, the commercialization of poetry, and contemporary politics, these comments signal his aim of creating a "fiel traslado, . . . cierto trasunto / de la vida del hombre y la quimera / tras de que va la Humanidad entera" ("faithful copy, . . . exact transcription of man's life and the chimera pursued by all Humanity"). The dedication of the entirety of Canto II to the elegy to Teresa further demonstrates this commitment to representing the multiple levels on which the dialectic of desire and disillusion plays out in human life.

Cantos III, IV, V, and VI trace the trajectory of Adam, the reborn old man, from innocence to experience, exploring the social and metaphysical limits of freedom. Adam encounters Spanish society with undiminished *joie de vivre* and expectation of happiness; he is immediately clapped into prison by authorities who believe his lack of inhibition to be a sign of anarchist tendencies. The metaphor equating socialization with imprisonment is explicity developed in Canto IV, where Adam learns language and strategies of social interaction in prison under the tutelage of an experienced criminal. Society is thus associated with injustice, repression, and violence. Edenic possibilities remain in the form of erotic union, represented by Adam's first experience of love with la Salada, a free-living lower-class woman who liberates him from jail. The relentless itch of desire soon impels Adam to seek a greater world of experience. Canto VI, the last completed, begins with his discovery of the world of luxury and sophistication in the palace of a beautiful marquise, but ends with his efforts to comprehend the meaning of mortality and the cruel disparities of human life as he for the first time confronts the underlying reality of human life – death and mourning, represented by an old hag grieving over the body of her dead daughter in the back room of a tavern. Unfinished and uneven as it is, *El diablo mundo* broke new ground in the Spanish poetic tradition, defining an ambitious poetics that included Romantic irony, colloquial language, and scenes of urban lowlife along with the sublime and the lyrical, and introducing modern themes of individual alienation and religious doubt.

Espronceda had few followers in a cultural arena dominated by the conservative doctrines of historical Romanticism. In a certain sense, however, the heirs of his liberal inspiration were the women poets who appeared after 1840, encouraged to write by the Romantic emphasis on emotion and the liberals' assertion of the right to self-expression in conjunction with an expanding press industry. The two most important of these poets, the Cuban-born Gertrudis Gómez de Avellaneda (1814–1873) and Carolina Coronado (1821–1911), while eschewing Espronceda's Luciferian representations of the self as inappropriate to their gender, subtly incorporated emancipatory desire in their lyrical self-representations.

The two principal collections of Gómez de Avellaneda's poetry (1841 and 1850) treat Romantic disillusionment and the compulsions of desire as profound threats to the integrity of the feminine lyrical subject; the dry leaf blown before the wind is a recurring metaphor for the self overtaken by emotion. Carolina Coronado elaborated an even more complex feminine version of Romantic subjectivity that established a long-lived tradition of nineteenth-century women's poetry. The poems in her first volume (1843) focus on the lyricist's response to Nature, particularly flowers, on which she delicately projects the conflict between conventional feminine modesty and fragility and a less socially acceptable desire for recognition and glory. In the poetry written after 1843 and collected in her 1852 volume, her more explicit treatment of the theme of women's suffering reveals the impact of emancipatory Romanticism. In "Cantad, hermosas" ("Sing, lovely women") images of suffocation convey the situation of women, whose "viva inteligencia" ("lively intelligence") and "ardiente genio" ("ardent genius") are smothered in silent domestic tedium. In "Último canto" ("Last Song"), the poet compares herself to a captured insect. The pull of women's social destiny against their artistic aspiration is expressed in recurring imagery suggesting the feminine subject's struggle to escape from enclosure. For example, "El amor de los amores" ("The Love of Loves"), perhaps Coronado's most frequently anthologized poem, characterizes the speaker's quest for the beloved as an expansive movement, from mountain to valley to seashore. In the ceaseless drive to satisfy spiritual longing in the natural world, this poem offers a feminine equivalent to Espronceda's questing spirit of man.

The historicist tendency of Spanish Romanticism found its most representative poet in José Zorrilla (1817–1893). Ironically, he made his appearance on the literary scene at the age of nineteen by reading verses at Larra's funeral, a cultural event that served almost as a manifesto of exalted liberal Romanticism. Having defied his authoritarian father, a Carlist ex-police chief, by abandoning the study of law to try to earn a living in Madrid as a writer, he was initially influenced by Espronceda. After the publication of his first volume of poetry in 1837, however, despair, doubt, and alienation vanished from his verses, and he turned to Spanish national history and tradition for inspiration. A master of versification, expressive rhythms, and colorful imagery, Zorrilla elaborated the varied, improvisitory verse forms that characterized Spanish Romantic poetry. His most significant contribution was in narrative poetry, for which he drew on the oral tradition being recuperated as an expression of the national *Volksgeist* by Durán. Angel de Saavedra, duque de Rivas (1791–1865), had already found in the ballads originating in medieval Spain the material for his long narrative poem, *El moro expósito* ("The Foundling Moor," 1834). Following in this vein, in *Cantos del trovador* ("Songs of the Troubador," 1839–1841) Zorrilla initiated a form he called the *leyenda* ("legend"), which retold stories or anecdotes taken from popular traditions, religious as well as historical. One of the most famous, "Margarita la tornera" ("Margarita the Door-Turner"), for example, tells the story of an innocent nun abducted from her convent and then abandoned, who is miraculously saved by the Virgin Mary. Cases of divine intervention in the cause of justice or salvation are frequent in Zorrilla's *leyendas*, as are stories from medieval history that exemplify Spanish virtues. He declares his aim in the introductory poem of *Cantos*:

> Mi voz, mi razón, mi fantasía
> la gloria cantan de la patria mía
>
> . . .
>
> Y fiel ministro de la gaya ciencia,
> levantaré mi voz consoladora
> sobre las ruinas en que España llora.

(My voice, my reason, my fantasy / sing the glory of my fatherland / . . . / And faithful minister of the troubador's art, / I will raise my consoling voice / above the ruins in which Spain mourns.)

In performing this consolatory, escapist function, Zorrilla's poetry appealed to a society traumatized by invasions, civil war, and a chronically unstable state.

Like Zorrilla, who lived until 1893 and continued to publish poetry in the same vein throughout his life, Spanish poetry became repetitive and formulaic in the middle decades of the century. In the 1860s, however, the Romantic tradition received a fresh impulse. Translations and imitations of Heinrich Heine's *Lieder* ("love poems") between 1857 and 1861, along with the increasing use of the *cantar*, the popular lyric, as a model for cultured poetry, inspired a new aesthetic best exemplified by Gustavo Adolfo Bécquer (1836–1870). The orphaned son of a Sevillian painter, Bécquer went to Madrid in his early twenties to attempt to make a living as a writer. There he became a friend of Augusto Ferrán (1835–1880), whose book of poetry, *La soledad* ("Solitude," 1861), incorporated the new trends. In a review of his friend's book, Bécquer articulated their shared poetics. To the sonorous, declamatory style characterizing earlier Romantic poetry, Bécquer prefers a type of poetry that is "natural, breve, seca, que brota del alma como una chispa eléctrica, que hiere el sentimiento con una palabra y huye, y desnuda de artificio . . . despierta . . . las mil ideas que duermen en el océano sin fondo de la fantasía" ("natural, brief, dry, that springs from the soul like an electric spark, pricks the feelings with a word and flees, and naked of artifice . . . awakes . . . the thousands of ideas that sleep in the bottomless ocean of fantasy").[4] This reconfiguration preserves Romanticism's fundamental equation of poetry

4 Gustavo Adolfo Bécquer, *"La soledad." Rimas, leyendas y otras páginas*. Ed. Jorge Albistur (Montevideo: Ediciones de la Banda Oriental, 1969), p. 152.

with feeling and imagination, but redefines the relationship of language to expression.

Bécquer's *Rimas* ("Rhymes," 1871), the short lyrical poems in which he developed the new Romantic modality, were composed throughout the 1860s, difficult years in which the chronically ill poet struggled to keep his young family afloat by writing for periodicals and serving as the government censor for novels. Although some of the poems saw print in magazines, the whole collection was not published until the poet's friends put together a posthumous version in the year following his death. The sequence in which the poems are ordered and numbered seems to trace the progress of an amorous relationship that follows the familiar Romantic trajectory from illusion to disappointment and frustration. Bécquer made a new contribution to the Spanish Romantic tradition, however, in his vision of the relationship of language, subjectivity, and poetry. In contrast to the earlier Romantic poets, who treated language as if it conveyed their inner experience without mediation, Bécquer dwells explicitly on the inadequacy of words – "el rebelde, mezquino idioma" ("rebellious, miserable language") – to symbolize the sensations, ideas, and emotional colors that constitute the stuff of poetry. Since, as he states in his introduction to the *Rimas*, only language can bridge the abyss between the idea (by which he means the creatures of his inner life) and the form in which they can be externalized, that form is of necessity partial – a suggestion rather than a representation. Thus, in Rima I, he announces that his book offers only fading cadences of the "himno gigante y extraño / que anuncia en la noche del alma una aurora" ("gigantic and strange hymn that announces dawn in the night of the soul") that he would like to sing.

In his effort to evoke the ineffable, Bécquer avoided the declamatory, verbally profuse style of his predecessors and stripped his verse down to the brief four-line stanza and subtly echoing assonant rhyme of the traditional *cantar*. The structuring tension of the *Rimas* is thematized in Rima III, which evokes the poetic process as the eternal struggle between the formless energies of inspiration and the constraining structures of reason. In Bécquer's poetry the spare metric framework and the logic of symmetrically organized analogies play the role of reason, establishing a form whose rigor contrasts with and highlights the imagery of the undefined – the airy shadows, waves, atoms, shimmers, mists, arpeggios, and palpitations that characterize his poetic vocabulary. In many cases the evocative effect is obtained by a rupture of symmetry that gives rise to a light irony, as in Rima XXIII:

> Por una mirada un mundo;
> por una sonrisa, un cielo;
> por un beso . . . ¡yo no sé
> qué te diera por un beso!

(For a glance, a world; / for a smile, a heaven; / for a kiss . . . I don't know / what I'd give you for a kiss!)

Bécquer's incorporation of the dialogic structure implicit in the *cantar*, an enunciation addressed by an "I" to a "thou," gives the *Rimas* the additionally evocative quality of intimacy. Instead of shouting and declaiming, they whisper and insinuate, giving new emotional tone to the Romantic themes of lost illusions and alienation. Ideologically, Bécquer was aligned with the conservative, nostalgic strand of Romanticism, an alignment which is explicit in his prose writing, yet in his perception of the radical alienation of the individual subject in a modernizing world, he points forward to the Modernists of the following century.

The other significant figure in the revitalization of the Romantic lyrical tradition after mid century is Rosalía de Castro (1837–1885). Born out of wedlock in Galicia and separated from her mother until midway through childhood, Castro moved with her family in the mid 1850s to Madrid, where she met Bécquer and other members of his circle. Castro's early poetry followed the Esproncedan vein of emotional self-expression as adapted by Carolina Coronado and other women writers, but in the small volume published after her mother's death, *A mi madre* ("To my Mother," 1864) she expanded the possibilities of this modality by creating symbolic landscapes that reflected a restless, anguished agitation new to the representation of feminine subjectivity. For example, in "Ya pasó la estación de los calores" ("The warm season now is over") her inner state is represented by clouds that fly before the moon, "llenas de amargura y desconsuelo" ("disconsolate and full of bitterness") and "suelto el ropaje y la melena al viento" ("their clothes loosened and their hair in the wind"). By this time, Castro, who had married the Galician nationalist intellectual Manuel Murguía in 1858, was, like Bécquer, turning to popular poetry for inspiration – in her case the rich, deeply rooted oral lyrical tradition in the Galician language. *Cantares gallegos* ("Galician Songs," 1863), a collection of glosses and imitations of traditional songs, was received with enthusiasm in her native region as a first step in the recuperation of Galician as a literary language.

In the *Cantares* Castro's expression, in popular language and imagery, of longing for the familiar landscape and culture of her native land had captured not only her own emotion, but also the experience of Galicians forced by poverty to emigrate to Castile or America. Her next collection of poetry in Galician, *Follas novas* ("New Leaves," 1880), was even more direct in expressing the pain of separation and absence resulting from conditions that made orphans of Galicia's children and widows of its women. In the prologue to *Follas novas*, Castro declared her conviction that poetry must express the feelings shared by the poet's contemporaries: "neste meu novo libro preferín, ás composicións que puderan decirse personales, aquelas outras que . . . espresan al tribulaciós dos que . . . vin durante largo tempo sofrir ó meu arredore" ("in this new book I preferred to the compositions that might be called personal, those that . . . express the tribulations of those whom . . . I saw for a long time suffering around me").[5] Her implicit protest against poverty and exploitation makes Castro an heir to the socially oriented strand of Romanticism present in Espronceda and Coronado.

At the same time, in *Follas novas* Castro gives voice to her own deepening melancholy and existential *angst*, the feelings of abandonment and solitude that resonate with the suffering she sees around her. Her last book of poems, *A las orillas del Sar* ("Beside the River Sar," 1884), written in Castilian, shows her developing this pessimistic vision of human life in poems expressing her intimate responses to Nature, isolation, marital conflict, the birth and death of children, and her own terminal illness (she died of cancer at the age of forty-nine). Resigned suffering as the fundamental reality of woman's lot was the major theme of the feminine poetic tradition based on Romanticism, but Castro transforms it into searching exploration of the human condition that extends even to metaphysical doubt. She confronts her condition head-on, for example, in the poem that begins "¡Ea! ¡aprisa subamos de la vida / la cada vez más empinada cuesta!" ("Come on! Let's hurry up the ever steeper slope of life!"), accepting unflinchingly the solitude of her confrontation with death: "No, ni amante ni amigo / allí podrá seguirme; / ¡avancemos! . . . ¡Yo ansío de la muerte / la soledad terrible!" ("No, neither lover nor friend can follow me there; let's go on! I long for the terrible solitude of death!"). Doubts similar to those of Bécquer about the expressive capacity of language are entertained in this collection, which registers in its experimentation with innovative meters and rhythms – lines of sixteen or even eighteen syllables – Castro's struggle to find formal means of representing the unconventional subjectivity she explored so profoundly.

Romantic poetry was given new life by the innovations of both Bécquer and Castro, as each found poetic language, often inspired by popular forms, for new modalities of individual subjectivity. Thus, these two poets also pointed the way toward the next significant innovations in the Spanish poetic tradition, those that occurred with the Modernist movement at the turn of the century.

---

[5] Rosalía de Castro, "Duas palabras da autora." In *Follas novas*. Ed. Juan Barja (Madrid: Akal, 1985), p. 23.

26

Romantic prose, journalism, and *costumbrismo*

MICHAEL IAROCCI

Even the briefest of engagements with modern Spanish history makes clear
that the cultural production of much of Spain's nineteenth century takes
place against the backdrop of relentless social, political, and economic
upheaval. Indeed, when one contemplates some of the more salient features of that history – a bankrupted monarchy, Napoleonic occupation,
the birth of liberalism in the Cortes of Cadiz (1812), the despotic reign
of Fernando VII's repressive Ominous Decade (1823–1833), the collapse
of empire in South America, repeated constitutional crises, a series of
Carlist civil wars (so-named after Fernando's brother Carlos, pretender
to the Spanish throne), habitual military coups by *pronunciamiento*, etc. –
it is easy to lose sight of the fact that such disparate events are themselves
symptomatic of the more fundamental transformation throughout Europe
that, beginning with the French Revolution, had begun to supplant the
social structures of an aging *ancien régime* with those of a modern bourgeois order.

The literary prose of the Romantic period in Spain is, in the broadest
sense, a register of the cultural turmoil that accompanied this grand transformation. It is the vehicle of public expression for writers whose society
was fitfully working its way toward bourgeois hegemony and a liberal
political order. Romantic responses to this process of social change were
varied, multifaceted, and often contradictory. This was so in part because
their very tools – their modes of knowing and the language they used
to represent it – were themselves immersed in the tumultuous changes
they tried to address. As such, the principal categories into which literary
historians have traditionally subdivided Romantic prose – the historical novel, the *cuadro de costumbres*, and the poetic legend – tend to sit
uneasily, even antithetically, beside one another. Just as the daunting array
of Spain's political crises can be apprehended within a grander narrative
of economic, social, and political transformation, so the various genres of
Romantic prose can usefully be understood as part of the progressive
secularization of literary language that this transformation entailed. The
historicism of the novel, the distinctive mimetic register of *costumbrismo*,
and the lyrical imagination of the legends can thus come into view within

the broader framework of a secularizing cultural process that was at work throughout much of nineteenth-century Europe.

The historical novel's most immediate philosophical forebears were the Germans Johann Gottfried Herder and the Schlegel brothers, Friedrich and August Wilhelm. Their basic tenets – disseminated in Spain by such figures as Johann Nikolaus Böhl de Faber, Luigi Monteggia, and Agustín Durán – had aimed at replacing the classical conception of a universal humanity governed by immutable laws with the notion of a historically contingent and geographically conditioned, malleable human culture. Independent of its most immediate political valences, which were often decidedly conservative,[1] the historicism that began to inform the novel thus represented a significant shift toward a more secular understanding of cultural history inasmuch as the acknowledgment of the historicity of human social structures began to replace longstanding conceptions of a divinely sanctioned, natural social order. This nineteenth-century shift built on the secular historical sensibility that had already taken root among Spanish Enlightenment thinkers during the latter half of the eighteenth century. The historical novel of the early nineteenth century may thus be understood as drawing on both national and pan-European intellectual traditions. If Pedro Montengón's *El Rodrigo* (1793) might be cited as an early representative of the Rousseau-inspired historical novel in Spain, the popularity of the genre would only reach its peak with the introduction of a more decidedly nationalist, post-Napoleonic Romantic historicism in the 1820s, 1830s, and 1840s.[2]

These decades, during which Romantic writers as celebrated as Mariano José de Larra (1809–1837) and José de Espronceda (1808–1842) were drawn to the genre, witnessed the publication of some of the best-known Spanish Romantic historical novels: *Ramiro, conde de Lucena* ("Ramiro, Count of Lucena," 1823) by Rafael de Húmara (dates unknown), *Los bandos de Castilla* ("The Factions of Castile," 1830) by Ramón López Soler (1806–1835), *El conde de Candespina* ("The Count of Candespina," 1832) by Patricio de la Escosura (1807–1878), Espronceda's *Sancho Saldaña* (1834), Larra's *El doncel de don Enrique el doliente* ("Henry the Sorrowful's Squire," 1834), *Cristianos y moriscos* ("Christians and Moriscos," 1838) by Serafín Estébanez Calderón (1799–1867), *El señor de Bembibre* ("The Lord of Bembibre," 1844) by Enrique Gil y Carrasco (1815–1846), and *Doña Blanca de Navarra* ("Lady Blanca of Navarre," 1846) by Francisco Navarro Villoslada (1818–1895). Like its analogues in England, France, and Italy (i.e. novels by Scott, Hugo, Dumas, Chateaubriand, Manzoni), the Spanish historical novel initially appears

---

[1] Derek Flitter, *Spanish Romantic Literary Theory and Criticism* (Cambridge: Cambridge University Press, 1992), pp. 1–22.

[2] Georg Lukács, *The Historical Novel* (Lincoln: University of Nebraska Press, 1983), pp. 19–30.

to flee from its present, frequently taking refuge in medieval settings and in the Manichean plots of romance. Such flight, however, is not an entirely escapist gesture. Along with its temporally exotic settings, its fascination with the gothic macabre, and its sustained interest in the supernatural, the historical novel frequently encoded a series of very contemporary nineteenth-century concerns that allowed it to be read as an allegory of the disquieting present in which it developed.

Enrique Gil's *El señor de Bembibre*, arguably the most successful of Spain's historical novels, is a paradigmatic example of such allegoresis. Set in fourteenth-century León, in the author's native province of El Bierzo, the work intertwines a narrative of impossible love with the history of the dissolution of the Order of the Knights Templar. The representation of medieval León, however, is in large measure a stand-in for the Spain of the 1830s and 1840s. The appropriation of the Templar Knights' properties in the novel resonates eerily with the disentailment of Church properties that the state had begun under Juan Álvarez Mendizábal in 1836.[3] Similarly, the Romantic representation of the heroine Beatriz as an angelic, quasi-disembodied soul finds its correlate in the ideologically charged image of the *ángel del hogar* ("angel of the home") that would increasingly circulate as the prescribed ideal for women in the emergent bourgeois social order.[4] More broadly, the novel's thematic focus on the historical dissolution of all things – the Templars, the protagonists' love, the Middle Ages – speaks to the contemporary anxiety of a society that was itself in the midst of tumultuous historical change.

An equally contemporary facet of the historical novel was the nationalism that accompanied the genre's focus on geographical and cultural specificity. In accordance with Spain's longstanding Castile-centered geopolitics, such nationalism frequently found expression in novels whose basic tropes equated Castilian and Spanish history. Yet Romantic nationalism also authorized and reinvigorated the sense of cultural difference that had historically shaped the regional identities of Iberia. It thus informed many of the foundational writings of the modern regionalist movements, especially in Euskadi (Pablo Pedro de Astarloa, Juan Bautista de Erro y Aspiroa) and in the Catalan *Renaixença* (Ramón López de Soler, Pablo Piferrer, Manuel Milá i Fontanals). Indeed, the legacy of Romantic nationalism would extend well into the twentieth century as the so-called "Generation of 1898" continued to engage Romantic historicism's quest for the imagined origins of the nation.[5]

3 Jean-Louis Picoche, *Un romántico español: Enrique Gil y Carrasco (1815–1845)* (Madrid: Gredos, 1978), pp. 113–115.
4 Bridget Aldaraca, *El ángel del hogar: Galdós and the Ideology of Domesticity in Spain* (Chapel Hill: University of North Carolina Press, 1991), pp. 33–54.
5 E. Inman Fox, "Spain as Castile: Nationalism and National Identity." In *Modern Spanish Culture*. Ed. David T. Gies (Cambridge University Press, 1999), pp. 21–36.

The literary discourse of the historical novel has often been described as a paradoxical hybrid. While its lyrical dimensions resonate with Romanticism's expressive poetics, its reliance on painstaking archival research, its archeological verisimilitude, and its highly detailed natural descriptions reflect more empirical concerns. In this regard it is not difficult to see in the Romantic historical novel the foundations both of modern poetic prose and of a Realist mimesis that would later inform the representation of contemporary society in the novels of Restoration authors such as Galdós, Alas, or Pardo Bazán. By the 1840s, the novel had already become an important vehicle for direct political and social commentary as interest shifted from the remote past to contemporary history in works such as *El poeta y el banquero; escenas contemporáneas de la revolución española* ("The Poet and the Banker; Contemporary Scenes from the Spanish Revolution," 1841–1842) by Pedro Mata (dates unknown), *Madrid y nuestro siglo* ("Madrid and Our Century," 1845–1846) by Ramón de Navarrete (1822–1889), *Doce españoles de brocha gorda. Novela de costumbres contemporáneas* ("Twelve Spaniards Painted with a Broad Brush. A Novel of Contemporary Customs," 1846) by Antonio Flores (1818–1865), and *La república roja o los obreros de París. Novela político-social contemporánea* ("The Red Republic or The Workers of Paris. A Contemporary Socio-Political Novel," 1849) by José Pastor de Rocas (1824–1875).

Among the novels aimed at explicit social commentary, *Sab* (1841), written by the Cuban-born Gertrudis Gómez de Avellaneda (1814–1873), would become a paradigmatic example of the Romantic critique of social injustice. Published ten years before Harriet Beecher Stowe's *Uncle Tom's Cabin* and set on the author's native island, the work fuses the Romantic topos of impossible love with an unflinching abolitionist condemnation of slavery. *Sab* portrays the struggles of its eponymous mulatto hero against the Spanish social structures – state, Church, and aristocracy – that bolster the slave economy. While the novel mounts a searing moral indictment of slavery, its representation of Sab as an exoticized noble savage also reveals the ideological limits within which racial alterity was habitually conceived, even among abolitionists.

One of the most representative figures of both the Romantic novel's social turn and its increasingly commercial status was the politician, publisher, and novelist Wenceslao Ayguals de Izco (1801–1873), whose multiple journals and newspapers were instrumental in establishing the serialized novel, known as the *novela por entregas* or the *novela de folletín*, as one of the most popular narrative forms by the mid century.[6] In addition to writing over forty novels, Ayguals was the principal publisher of the translated works of the popular French novelist Eugène Sue (1804–

---

[6] Ignacio Ferreras, *La novela por entregas, 1840–1900. Concentración obrera y economía editorial* (Madrid: Taurus, 1972), pp. 23–31.

1857) in Spain, and the Spanish writer's republican politics were not far from Sue's utopian socialism. Injustice, poverty, urban squalor, and the social pathologies they engender are among the most persistent of Ayguals' themes, and his highly popular *María, la hija de un jornalero* ("Maria, Daughter of a Day-Laborer," 1845–1846) is a fine example of the way such social concerns were fused with the sentimentally charged rhetoric that would come to define the *folletín*.

Conditioned formally by its intermittent distribution, the *novela por entregas* tended to be highly melodramatic, suspenseful, and tendentious in its plot-construction, often closing its chapters with cliffhangers calculated to prompt interest in subsequent installments. The serialized novel thus foregrounded those elements of Romantic rhetoric that were most effective in maintaining readerly interest across its periodic publication. Enormously successful in commercial terms, the sentimental rhetoric of the *novela de folletín* was destined to become one of the principal targets of Realist/Naturalist authors who eschewed its unabashedly popular registers.[7] Within this rapidly widening panorama of novelistic production, literary historians have traditionally pointed to *La gaviota* ("The Seagull," 1849), by Cecilia Böhl de Faber (1796–1877, who wrote under the pen-name of Fernán Caballero,) as an important benchmark in the development of nineteenth-century Realism. Written in large measure against the sensationalizing *folletinesque* narratives of the day, it portrays the amorous travails of a fisherman's daughter in rural Andalusia. It is not the novel's plot, however, but rather its treatment of setting and character that for many critics announces a new, more Realistic narrative paradigm. Based on years of scrupulous observation and documentation of the social manners of rural Seville, the novel assembled characters and situations that struck readers as authentic, even if presented in a sentimentalized, picturesque form.[8]

The increasing commercialization of literature evident in the *novela de folletín* was itself part of a much broader historical shift in which, over the course of the late eighteenth and early nineteenth centuries, royal, ecclesiastic, and aristocratic control over publication had slowly ceded to the control of market forces. Already by the late eighteenth century, a growing public sphere had developed in Spain as a consequence of the proliferation of the periodic press during the Enlightenment,[9] and this tendency would intensify during the Romantic era, after the death

---

[7] Stephanie Sieburth, *Inventing High and Low. Literature, Mass Culture, and Uneven Modernity in Spain* (Durham: Duke University Press, 1994), pp. 1–26.

[8] Javier Herrero, *Fernán Caballero: un nuevo planteamiento* (Madrid: Gredos, 1963), pp. 283–303.

[9] Joaquín Álvarez Barrientos, François Lopez, and Inmaculada Urzainqui, *La república de las letras en la España del siglo XVIII* (Madrid: Consejo Superior de Investigaciones Científicas, 1995), pp. 7–18.

of Fernando VII, as journals, newspapers, and magazines became the primary medium of public exchange for a growing bourgeoisie.[10] The nature of this shift was profound and far-reaching, for it transformed literary activity to its core: it created the conditions for the emergence of the modern professional writer, it materially transformed the idea of what a text was, and it inaugurated entirely new forms of readerly reception.[11]

The most important periodicals of the Romantic period were *El Artista* (1835–1836) and the *Semanario Pintoresco Español* (1836–1857). Directed by Eugenio de Ochoa, *El Artista* was modeled on the French *L'Artiste*, and it served as an important vehicle for Romantic polemics against a Neoclassical literary establishment perceived to be excessively formulaic and historically out of step. The journal's collaborators included, among others, José de Espronceda, Patricio de la Escosura, Jacinto Salas y Quiroga, and José Zorrilla. The journal also became known for the high-quality graphic art, directed by Pedro Madrazo, that accompanied its essays, stories, and poems, and the interplay between verbal and visual representations in *El Artista* announced a tendency destined to grow stronger over the course of the century as technological advances in the graphic arts – and later, photography – facilitated the juxtaposition of words and images. Indeed, the long-lived *Semanario Pintoresco Español*, directed by Ramón de Mesonero Romanos, owed much of its success to the numerous illustrations that accompanied its articles, and the journal's status as one of the premier vehicles of publication for the brief sketch of social manners that came to be known as the *cuadro de costumbres* depended in large measure on such combinations.

The modern genealogy of the *cuadro de costumbres* can be traced to the Enlightenment shift toward a decidedly empirical epistemology, and the genre's antecedents in eighteenth-century Spain all reveal an increasing focus on the representation of contemporary social life. Early examples of *costumbrista* representation can be found across a wide range of eighteenth-century cultural forms that include, among others, the short essays of José Clavijo y Fajardo's journal *El Pensador* (1762–1767), the social satire of Leandro Fernández Moratín's theatre (in *El café*, for example), the comedic *sainetes* of Ramón de la Cruz, the painter Francisco Goya's satirical *caprichos*, and the folkloric turn of music collectors such as Juan Antonio de Iza Zamácola.[12] Most literary historians have noted, however, that the *cuadro de costumbres* does not become fully established

[10] Leonardo Romero Tobar, *Panorama crítico del romanticismo español* (Madrid: Castalia, 1994), pp. 49–50.
[11] Lee Fontanella, "The Fashion and Styles of Spain's *Costumbrismo*." *Revista Canadiense de Estudios Hispánicos* 6.2 (1982), pp. 175–189.
[12] Rinaldo Froldi, "Anticipaciones dieciochescas del costumbrismo romántico." *Romanticismo* 6 (1996), pp. 163–170.

as a distinctive literary genre until the 1830s, when it crystallizes in the form of a brief newspaper article aimed at a middle-class reading public.

For one of the genre's leading scholars, *costumbrismo* inaugurates nothing less than a fundamentally new form of literary mimesis inasmuch as its object of representation is no longer an abstract, universal human nature, but rather a human subject deeply enmeshed in a specific time and place.[13] In displacing the older universalist premises, *costumbrismo* can thus be understood as performing a secularizing function similar to Romantic historicism, and, like the Realist dimensions of the historical novel, *costumbrismo*'s dominant mode of representation again seems to fly in the face of the lyricism traditionally associated with Romantic rhetoric. The ostensibly objective focus of the *cuadro de costumbres* and the internal world of Romantic poetic expression, however, are in many ways two sides of the same coin. For with few exceptions, and despite Romantic myths to the contrary, the Romantic gaze – whether turned inward to the subject or outward to the objects that surround it – registered a fundamentally bourgeois world view. While poetic representations of Romantic subjectivity provided complex models of the self for an emergent liberalism that had posited the individual as its basic unit of reference, the seemingly more objective qualities of *costumbrista* mimesis worked to connect the external world to the predominantly middle-class perspective that increasingly structured the Spanish polity.[14]

Indeed, taken collectively, the pages of *costumbrista* periodicals display a veritable taxonomy of personages (beggars, laborers, doormen, shopkeepers, bankers, functionaries), public spaces (cafes, restaurants, boulevards, plazas), and shared customs (the siesta, the evening walk, the bullfight, the invitation to a meal, the New Year's Eve celebration). While such an inventory points to the burgeoning classificatory rhetoric of the sciences, the common denominator to this wide array of representations is the figure of the observer himself, the literate narrator who becomes the measure of the reality he attempts to document. Akin to the French *flâneur*, the *costumbrista* is a man about town, an observer who, with notebook in hand, takes in his surroundings in order to represent them as "slices of life" for his readers. Typically male and middle-class, the identity of the *costumbrista* narrator in many ways replicated the ideal citizen – the man of property – predicated by liberal ideology.

The *cuadro de costumbres* additionally reflected and shaped readerly perceptions by performing a series of interrelated social functions: it

---

[13] José Escobar, "*Costumbrismo*. Estado de la cuestión." *Romanticismo* 6 (1996), pp. 117–126.

[14] Susan Kirkpatrick, "The Ideology of *Costumbrismo*." *Ideologies and Literature* 2:7 (1978), pp. 28–44.

became a venue in which the growing bourgeoisie contemplated and analyzed its social world, it established a typology that worked to render
an increasingly heterogeneous society comprehensible and familiar, and,
like the illustrations that increasingly accompanied the genre, it froze for
a moment the fleeting characters, traditions, and institutions of a culture keenly aware of the vertiginous political, economic, and social flux
it was undergoing. Within these broad parameters, however, individual
authors gave the genre highly distinctive inflections. Indeed, one of the
conventions of the *cuadro de costumbres* was to cultivate a unique, personal narrative voice in order to bring to life a quasi-fictional narrator
whose name the *costumbrista* typically used to sign his work. At the height
of their popularity, Ramón de Mesonero Romanos (1803–1882), Serafín
Estébanez Calderón, and Mariano José de Larra, traditionally regarded as
the three foundational figures of nineteenth-century *costumbrismo*, were
thus known primarily by the names of their respective literary alter egos:
"El curioso parlante" "El solitario," and "Fígaro."

The most prolific of the three, Mesonero Romanos became the premier
chronicler of the social customs of Madrid during the 1820s, 1830s, and
1840s. Over the years, he collected and re-edited his *cuadros* several times,
and his best-known volumes include: *Mis ratos perdidos o ligero bosquejo
de Madrid de 1820 a 1821* ("My Leisure Moments or A Light Sketch
of Madrid from 1820 to 1821," 1822), *Manual de Madrid* ("A Manual
of Madrid," 1831), *Panorama matritense* ("Madrid Panorama," 1842),
and *Escenas matritenses* ("Scenes from Madrid," 1842). As he aged,
his work became increasingly retrospective, and his *El antiguo Madrid*
("Old Madrid," 1861) and *Memorias de un setentón* ("Memoirs of a
Seventy-Year-Old," 1880) offer rich insights into the cultural history of
the first half of the century. The narrative voice of Mesonero Romanos'
"El curioso parlante" evokes the image of the middle-class *bon vivant*.
His irony is light and he is rarely mean-spirited. His tone is commonsen-
sical, his outlook is practical. While he carefully avoids explicit political
commentary, his even-tempered judgments model the satisfied comfort of
the class he represents.[15] Even when he ridicules the excesses of Romantic
angst and idealism – as in his well-known parody, "El romanticismo y los
románticos" ("Romanticism and the Romantics") – it is in the name of a
series of tacit bourgeois moral values: work, the family, good citizenship.

Next to Mesonero's "Curioso parlante", Estébanez Calderon's "El solitario" comes into view primarily as a bibliophile, a classically trained
humanist eager to demonstrate his bookish erudition and wit. The minute
observations that characterize the author's *cuadros* often lead, for example, to recondite classical literary allusions, and his ornate prose style

---

[15] Ricardo Navas Ruiz, *El romanticismo español* (Madrid: Cátedra, 1990), p. 204.

carries with it traces of Neo-Baroque complexity. Beyond his style, however, Estébanez Calderón is known today primarily for his *Escenas andaluzas* ("Andalusian Scenes," 1846), one of the first literary treatments by a Spaniard of the longstanding topos of a marginal, picturesque Andalusia. A decidedly localist national pride characterizes many of the articles that constitute the volume, and "El solitario" often incorporates regional dialects and popular jargon into his otherwise bookish registers. He is in this regard representative of the regionalist dimensions that often characterized the *costumbrista* genre. Among the most idiosyncratic of the *costumbristas*, his style has been read as a compensatory gesture for the socially modest milieu in which he was raised.[16]

The most compelling of the nineteenth-century *costumbristas* by far, however, is Mariano José de Larra. His sustained, caustic social criticism, his acerbic political commentary, and the very public anguish he expressed in a series of articles that preceded his suicide in 1837 quickly accorded him iconic status as an emblem of liberal martyrdom. His articles appeared as independent publications – *El Duende Satírico del Día* ("The Satiric Sprite of the Day." 1828), *El Pobrecito Hablador* ("The Poor Little Chatterer," 1832), *Ni por ésas* (1836), *Colección de artículos dramáticos, literarios, políticos y de costumbres* ("Collection of Articles on Drama, Literature, Politics, and Customs," 1835–1837) – and in many of Madrid's newspapers and magazines: *La Revista Española* ("The Spanish Journal"), *El Correo de Damas* ("The Ladies' Journal"), *El Observador* ("The Observer"), *El Español* ("The Spaniard"), etc. In Larra's hands, the *cuadro de costumbres* became a vehicle of social critique and protest. Initially propelled by a belief in the social value of enlightened critique, he cultivated the genre with the hope of effecting change by exposing Spain's social ills. Over the course of his writing, however, such ideals increasingly ceded to his disenchantment over seemingly intractable political problems on one hand and the inertia of his middle-class readers on the other. The faith in the liberal project evident in Larra's early articles thus gives way to concern and uncertainty about the means and ends of liberalism, and this skepticism in turn cedes to a highly subjective, quasi-solipsistic pessimism in his winter essays of 1836.[17] More than six decades after his death, Larra would become a figure of inspiration for the young writers of the so-called "Generation of 1898," who saw in him a modern intellectual deeply concerned with the Spanish nation's problems. Their celebration of the anniversary of his death would in fact become one of

---

[16] Luisa Pavesio, "Sobre el lenguaje de las *Escenas andaluzas*." *Romanticismo* 3.4 (1988), pp. 175–178.
[17] Susan Kirkpatrick, *Larra: el inextricable laberinto de un romántico liberal* (Madrid: Gredos, 1977), pp. 285–288.

the foundational acts of the group of writers who would later become known by that name.

Even as the *cuadro de costumbres* created forms of representation that would work their way into the Realist novel,[18] the idealizing, fantastic, and subjective facets of Romantic poetic discourse were also finding expression in the short prose legend. As a genre, the legend had initially circulated primarily in verse form – e.g. José de Espronceda's *El Estudiante de Salamanca* (1836), Ángel de Saavedra's *Romances históricos* ("Historical Ballads," 1841), José Zorrilla's *Leyendas* ("Legends," 1837–1884) – and it drew on the Romantic privileging of the irrational, the fantastic, and the supernatural. By the 1850s and 1860s, however, shorter, prose narration, already present as early as *El Artista*, began to supplant longer narrative poems. As was the case with much Romantic writing, the designation of such prose pieces – *balada, cuento fantástico, leyenda, tradición* – varied widely, and each of its representative practitioners – Miguel de los Santos Álvarez (1818–1892), Antonio Ros de Olano (1808–1886), Juan Eugenio Hartzenbusch (1806–1880), José Joaquín Soler de la Fuente (dates unknown) – accentuated different facets of what was still a relatively novel, somewhat indeterminate, protean genre.[19]

For most literary historians, however, it is Gustavo Adolfo Bécquer (1836–1870) and his *Leyendas* that represent the definitive, culminating example of the Romantic prose legend. Written between 1858 and 1864, Bécquer's sixteen legends appeared initially in the pages of newspapers such as *El Contemporáneo*, and *La América*. With the exception of the orientalist *El caudillo de las manos rojas* ("The Leader with the Red Hands"), the *Leyendas* drew primarily on longstanding European folk traditions, and they have been celebrated for their highly crafted, poetic style, which led the poet Luis Cernuda to see in Bécquer the origins of the modern Spanish prose poem.[20] In addition, critics have often lauded the psychological sophistication with which Bécquer represents the fantastic. In many of his best-known legends – e.g. *La ajorca de oro* ("The Gold Bracelet"), *El monte de las ánimas* ("The Mountain of Souls"), *Los ojos verdes* ("The Green Eyes"), *El rayo de luna* ("Moonbeam") – a detailed, Realist mode of representation sets the stage for the sudden irruption of the supernatural.[21] Bécquer's interest in the supernatural, however, is not merely a belated instance of Romantic idealism; it also registers the degree

---

[18] José F. Montesinos, *Costumbrismo y novela: ensayo sobre el redescubrimiento de la realidad española* (Madrid: Castalia, 1980), pp. 135–138.

[19] Mariano Baquero Goyanes, *El cuento español: del romanticismo al realismo* (Madrid: Consejo Superior de Investigaciones Científicas, 1992), pp. 35–57.

[20] Luis Cernuda, "Bécquer y el poema en prosa español." In *Prosa completa* (Barcelona: Seix Barral, 1975), pp. 984–993.

[21] Russell P. Sebold, *Bécquer en sus narraciones fantásticas* (Madrid: Taurus, 1989), pp. 17–41.

to which conceptions of the transcendent had themselves been secularized over the course of the Romantic movement.

In this regard, Bécquer's collection of *Leyendas*, like Spanish Romantic prose generally, offers a powerful reminder that the forces of nineteenth-century secularization did not simply demystify the sacred in the name of more worldly values; those forces also sacralized the worldly with increasingly religious or idealist conceptions of the aesthetic.[22] In the end, it is precisely this dialectical interplay of the ideal and the real, of the subjective and the objective, of the poetic and the mimetic, that persistently characterizes the prose of the Romantic era, both in individual works such as the *Leyendas* and across the various genres. For in the hybrid and at times irreconcilable stylistic registers of Spanish Romantic prose are the traces of a more fundamental rift that was opening between the languages of "science" and "art," a rift that is the very hallmark of modern rationality. The paradox with which contemporary reassessments of Spanish Romantic prose continue to grapple is, in this sense, the paradox of the dual character of language in modernity.[23] Along with Spain's political, economic, and social institutions, the country's literary language was itself being transformed by a secularizing cultural machinery, and Spanish Romantic prose became both the record of this change and the first, ambiguous response to it.

[22] Rafael Gutiérrez Giradot, *Modernismo: supuestos históricos y culturales* (Barcelona: Montesinos, 1983; repr. Mexico: Fondo de Cultura Económica, 1988), p. 50.
[23] Max Horkheimer and Theodor Adorno, *Dialectic of Enlightenment* (New York: Continuum, 1997), pp. 17–18.

27

Benito Pérez Galdós

Harriet S. Turner

The term "Realism," whether applied to painting, philosophy, literature, or even to what today is called "the *real* reality TV," always implies a fundamental duality. There is, on the one hand, the perception of a world of things that simply exists – "inanimate, spatially extended, and subject to quantifiable forces" – and, on the other, there is the mind – "the seat of thought, understanding, sensation, and imagination."[1] The mind–body dualism of Descartes (1596–1650) and the inventions and discoveries of Galileo (1564–1642) had shaped for Western civilization the scientific worldview. This view delineated three basic intellectual positions *vis-à-vis* the relationship between mind and world: skepticism, or the idea that what the mind pictures or imagines cannot be a reliable guide to knowledge; idealism, or the conviction that a sensorial and subjective understanding, including certain belief systems, is the only one there is; and Realism, or the perspective that "heroically bridges the gap."[2]

During the nineteenth century, in Spain as in the rest of Europe, the task of bridging this gap, ever widening under the impact of political and social changes as well as scientific discoveries, technological inventions, and industrial advances, became the heroic project of Benito Pérez Galdós (1843–1920), Spain's preeminent Realist novelist. He sought to depict the impact of current political, social, and economic factors that jaggedly shaped everyday life: the resurgence of national consciousness and the imperatives of democracy in forming a nation; the rising presence and power of the bourgeoisie, of industrial growth, and the emergence of an exploited laboring class; the rise of banking, the stock market, the invention of institutional systems of credit and debit, and the introduction of paper money; the opening of railway lines, the spread of gas lighting, the construction of roads and waterways; improved sanitation, a developing interest in public and private health, together with the advances of medicine – anesthesia (1840s), germ theory (1847), antisepsis (1867), vaccination (1876), asepsis (1883), and radiology (1895).[3]

---

[1] Simon Blackburn, "Logical Humanism." *New Republic* (17 and 24 April 2001), p. 96.
[2] Blackburn, "Logical Humanism," p. 96.
[3] Lilian R. Furst, "Introduction." In *Realism* (New York: Longman, 1992), p. 2.

These inventions and discoveries came later to Spain than to the rest of Europe; thus the process of modernization occurred only in a rapid, uneven way.[4] Galdós saw this lately arrived modernity as a tumult generated by the influx of foreign ideas and fashion imposed on native folkways. At the same time, of a liberalizing cast of mind, he proposed to unmask the ways that traditional religious morality opposed new, positivistic views. His aim, as expressed in his great novel, *Fortunata y Jacinta*, was also to expose that "capa con tantos remiendos" ("patched old cloak"[5]) of political maneuvers, since successive reforms had only strengthened ingrained habits of favors and bribes. In Galdós' time, the tensions between such diverse phenomena as coins and credit, free trade and protectionist tariffs, factory work and domestic economy, masculine and feminine, and private and public exacerbated friction among peoples – those of "pueblo" and rural origins, whose voices rasped and whose bright colors raked the eye, and a nascent, insecure bourgeosie who, fearful of the masses, strove to imitate the aristocracy.

Old and new converged also with the question of suffrage and citizenship to aggravate social malaise and political upheavals – Carlist wars, palace intrigues, the Revolution of 1868 and overthrow of Queen Isabel, the brief reign of Amadeo of Savoy, the aborted First Republic and the Bourbon Restoration (1875–1885), which reached Spain from England in the imported person of Alfonso XII. These turbulent events undergird the cultural, historical, and political events of the novels by Galdós to be discussed in this chapter.

Galdós is the author of seventy-seven novels, twenty-six original plays, and numerous occasional pieces, written between 1867 and 1920. These divide into two main categories: the historical and the contemporary social novels, now more appropriately described as "novels of modernity."[6] The forty-six historical novels, called "Episodios nacionales," make up five series, each consisting of ten interconnected novels, except the fifth series, left unfinished. The thirty-one "novels of modernity", published between 1870 and 1915, also divide into two groups: "Novelas de la primera época" ("Novels of the Early Period," 1870–1879) and "Las novelas de la serie contemporánea" ("The Contemporary Social Novels," 1881–1915). The novels of the early period comprise Galdós' first attempts at novel writing, as well as four so-called "thesis novels": *Doña Perfecta* (1876),

---

4 Stephanie Sieburth, *Inventing High and Low. Literature, Mass Culture, and Uneven Modernity in Spain* (Durham: Duke University Press, 1994), pp. 27–30; Jo Labanyi, *Gender and Modernization in the Spanish Realist Novel* (Oxford: Oxford University Press, 2000), p. viii.

5 Benito Pérez Galdós, *Obras completas*. Ed. Federico Carlos Robles (Madrid: Aguilar, 1966), vol. v, p. 295. All subsequent references will be to this edition and will appear in the text.

6 Labanyi, *Gender and Modernization*, p. 91.

the sequel *Gloria* (1876–1877), *Marianela* (1878), and *La familia de León Roch* ("The Family of León Roch," 1878–1879). The next group of novels represents what Galdós called his "segunda manera" – his "second style," a "different kind of writing . . . a more sophisticated and varied mode of narrative presentation."[7]

Born in 1843 in Las Palmas, Canary Islands, the last of ten children, Galdós left home and a domineering mother at the age of nineteen to study law at the University of Madrid, bringing the experience of early years of island life to Spain's capital city. In 1867, having abandoned university classes for cafés, the theatre, and for the heady world of journalism and politics, Galdós made his first trip to Paris, discovered Balzac, and, as he says, "me desayuné" ("I breakfasted" ["Memorias de un desmemoriado," *Obras*, Vol. VI, 1656]) on the novels of *La Comédie humaine* ("Human Comedy"). From Balzac he borrowed the idea of writing a series of interrelated historical and social novels, adapting the technique of using recurring characters. He saw himself as a writer, not a lawyer, and started *La Fontana de Oro* ("The Golden Fountain Café," 1867), his first, full-length novel.

In two essays, written nearly thirty years apart (1870, 1897), Galdós states the premises that shaped his Realist novels: the central role played by the rising middle class; the religious problem, which either divided or dissolved families; adultery and prostitution, which posed the contested question of personal and civil rights; and the rising mix of rural and urban masses, occurring as peasants flocked to the cities after the disentailment of Church lands (1837), the tariff reforms of 1849 and 1868, and as the ensuing boom in real estate development and industrialization began to produce an upper bourgeoisie. We find the mercantile and banking families like the Santa Cruces and Moreno Islas (*Fortunata y Jacinta*) mixing with "indianos," people from impoverished, rural areas who emigrated to the West Indies (Cuba, Puerto Rico), made fortunes as slavers or entrepreneurs, and returned to Madrid to flood the markets with money, as does José María Manso (*El amigo Manso*). Soon "indianos" and the newly rich of Old Madrid's trading neighborhoods evolved into ruthless financiers and speculators like Sánchez Botín in *La desheredada* and the usurer Torquemada, who starts as a ragpicker at the Gate of Toledo (the southern entrance to Madrid) and ends as a mogul, virtually owning the city.

In between rich and poor we find a chafed petty bourgeoisie of moneylenders, laborers, artisans, salesmen, disgruntled office-seekers, civil servants, and, a step up, professional people – pharmacists, lawyers, doctors, and engineers. Galdós celebrates this motley, nascent middle class as the

---

[7] Linda Willem, *Galdós's Segunda Manera* (Chapel Hill: University of North Carolina Press, 1998), p. 12.

"inexhaustible source" of creativity and entrepreneurial energy.[8] One example, which occurs in the first part of *Fortunata y Jacinta*, is the column of an old-fashioned storefront in Old Madrid. Shopkeepers have dressed the column in corsets – red, black, and white – transforming it into an erotically charged, novelistic personage – female, wily, slightly sexual, who beckons provocatively to passers-by. The narrator sees this transformation as a shopkeeper's "sentimiento pintoresco" ("flair for the picturesque" [*Obras*, v, 99]) but now the old notion of "picturesque" has become a culturally transparent sign for the changing status of women. In the novel of modernity women have taken to the streets as consumers, like the matriarch Barbarita Santa Cruz, but also as sexual objects, like Rosalía de Bringas, who squeezes her body into a corset and becomes, literally, a streetwalker who sells that plumped, perfumed body for money to buy luxury items. This surging middle class holds the key to the novel of modernity. Even in the early essay (1870), sure of his mission, Galdós registers doubt and unease about modernity's trends and conflicts – "graves cuestiones" ("serious matters") for which he, as a Realist writer, cannot supply solutions.

At the outset of his career (1870) Galdós saw the retarded development of the new novel as owed to slackers – a reading public that preferred either the nostalgia of archaic folkways (*costumbrismo*) or facile, serialized romance and salon fiction modeled on French writers like Dumas and Soulié. The nation, seduced by popularized serial fiction – in his eyes, a "peste nacida en Francia" ("plague born in France" ["Observaciones," 125]) – seemed to have forgotten the masterpieces of those two great illusionists, Cervantes and Velázquez. In making a plea for a new, national novel, Galdós inveighed against the stereotypes of the French *folletín* and its Spanish imitations – "traidores pálidos y de mirada siniestra" ("pale traitors with a sinister look"), "modistas angelicales" ("angelic seamstresses"), "meretrices con aureola" ("whores with hearts of gold"), "duquesas averiadas" ("wayward duchesses"), "jorobados románticos" ("romantic hunchbacks"), "adulterios, extremos de amor y odio" ("adultery, extremes of love and hate" ["Observaciones," 125]).[9]

Once again, gaps open and contradictions abound. Galdós himself saw foreign writers – Balzac in France and Dickens in England – as masters of the art of the new novel. Through a complex range of narrative

[8] Benito Pérez Galdós, "Observaciones sobre la novela contemporánea." In *Ensayos de crítica literaria*. Ed. Laureano Bonet (Barcelona: Ediciones Peninsula, 1999), p. 130. Subsequent references will be to this edition and will appear in the text.

[9] At the same time – as demonstrated by Alicia Andreu, in her pioneering study *Galdós y la literatura popular* (Madrid: Sociedad General Española de Librería, 1982), and, most recently, by Elisa Martí López in her essay, "The *folletín*: Spain Looks to Europe" (*The Cambridge Companion to the Spanish Novel* [Cambridge: Cambridge University Press, 2003], pp. 65–80) – Galdós relied on the melodrama and the plots of the *folletín* to create the new Realist novel.

perspectives he exploited in his own fiction those self-same, clichéd character types. Further, as feminist critics have shown, Galdós' scorn for the popularized serial novel is another culturally transparent marker for gender bias. Gender stereotyping, which construed the notions of artistic genius and creativity only with male writers, presented women as passive consumers of both fiction and fashion.[10] They become those columns dressed up in corsets, supporting the new economy at the cost of their own degradation. Male critics saw women as congenitally unfit to be creators of the Realist novel, which, when all was said and done, was preeminently masculine – a rational, even scientific, and a nationalistic enterprise. The imprint of gender stereotypes tainted critical opinion about fiction as much as it became manifest in those fictions, for running beneath gender stereotyping was the deeper, branching root of Spain's uneven modernization and what that process implied for women.

Modernization transformed, almost overnight, the "villages" of Madrid and Barcelona into powerful administrative and urban centers but left rural areas virtually untouched. Even after the "Glorious" (i.e. bloodless) Revolution of 1868, which dethroned Queen Isabel and ushered in the First Republic (1868–1871), Spain was more a national territory than a politically and culturally unified nation. For example, in *Doña Perfecta*, obdurate regional strongholds like the town of Orbajosa were rife with factionalism, fanatic Catholicism, and a belief in the Carlist cause, an insurgency led by Fernando VII's exiled younger brother, don Carlos.[11] Orbajosa is a town stinking of garlic ("ajos"), as well as the corruptions of local bossism ("caciquismo"), and as a world all its own ("orb"), Orbajosa opposes deviously and violently the liberalizing mandates of the central government of Madrid. Sporadic civil war was the order of the day in northern Spain.

Thus Galdos' novels not only highlight anew that time-honored gap between mind and world. They also register collective anxieties and interpersonal conflicts arising from a host of new, disconcerting gaps in the social fabric. Such gaps generated a series of troubling interconnections and reversals. As Jo Labanyi notes, one salient example is the "woman question." It soon elided with the "social question," redefining without precedent the meaning both of "woman," which now referred to suffrage, property and civic rights, access to education, and of "social" – a term targeting the disconcerting question of the inclusion of the expropriated masses in civic life.[12] Galdós, like other Realist writers, focused on

---

[10] Alda Blanco, "Gender and National Identity: The Novel in Nineteenth-Century Spanish Literary History." In *Culture and Gender in Nineteenth-Century Spain*. Ed. Lou Charnon-Deutsch and Jo Labanyi (Oxford: Oxford University Press, 1995), p. 128; Labanyi, *Gender and Modernization*, p. 9.

[11] See Rodolfo Cardona's edition of *Doña Perfecta* (Madrid: Cátedra, 1984).

[12] Labanyi, *Gender and Modernization*, p. viii.

married women "because it was not clear where they stood, particularly if they were members of the property-owning class, which by definition constituted society."[13] At the same time, throughout Europe, the old order (patriarchy, religious dogma, and a domestic economy) braced itself against new ideas and actions. Settings large and small registered the gaps, as shown in the heated debate at the table in *Doña Perfecta*, or in a husband's patronizing lecture to his wife in the privacy of their bedroom in *Fortunata y Jacinta* (1886–1887).

In *Fortunata y Jacinta*, Galdós' four-volume masterpiece, triangular relationships, combining with the "woman question" and the "social question," structure the plot. Juanito Santa Cruz, the dauphin or bourgeois prince (as he is called), seduces Fortunata, half-gypsy and a working-class woman. He then marries his first cousin Jacinta but keeps visiting his former mistress. Couples cross as Fortunata marries little Maxi, while Jacinta, the legitimate but spurned wife, imagines a love relationship with the banker Moreno-Isla. Aurora, former lover of Moreno-Isla and new lover of Juanito, betrays Fortunata, while Fortunata, having purposefully conceived a child, before dying delivers that child to Jacinta, bringing about a reconciliation between the two women.

Adultery, identified by Galdós in his early essay (1870) as problematic, blurs boundaries between private and public spaces. As Jo Labanyi observes, "if it is possible to be simultaneously inside and outside, the boundary between the two positions disappears."[14] *Fortunata y Jacinta* illustrates this insight. One instance is the moment when Fortunata, mistress to Juanito Santa Cruz, seizes upon the blurred, reversible status of her own marriage to Maxi and of Juan's to Jacinta. In the intimacy of their affair Fortunata proposes to trade "el nene grande" ("the big boy") – Juan – for "el nene chico," the infant son and heir that Jacinta, supposedly sterile, cannot produce. Fortunata's "gran idea" ("great idea," [*Obras*, v, 280]) of a trade across marriages, from the outside to the inside, turns into a "pícara idea" ("madcap idea" [*Obras*, v, 238]), fleshed out in a real event when she delivers her newborn son by Santa Cruz to her childless rival.

Fortunata's image of both husband and child as a "nene" ("baby boy") also captures the deeper reality of other traded relations within the paired marriages of the Santa Cruces. Responding to Fortunata's "madcap idea," Juan immediately expresses his fear that *any* newborn son would, in the end, supplant *him* and his privileges as the only man-child in the family. Thus he inadvertently discloses the Oedipal nature of the paired Santa Cruz marriages of father, mother, son, and wife. Juan's formidable mother, doña Bárbara, had arranged his marriage to his first cousin Jacinta. Doña

[13] Labanyi, *Gender and Modernization*, p. 40.
[14] Labanyi, *Gender and Modernization*, p. 40.

Bárbara, grooming the "sisterly" Jacinta as a daughter-in-law, transforms her into a kind of "calza" ("leash") that ties son (and husband) to her – doña Bárbara's – maternal rule. Thus the barren Jacinta finds herself brought into the family expressly to mother the son, ironically and to her great grief reinforcing – but also obliterating – any truly maternal ties. For in this marriage, mothering has meant that Jacinta herself will never be a mother.

As literary Realism evolved as part of the twin processes of modernization and nation formation, Galdós adhered to the aesthetic of mimesis, which he understood both as the observance of facts and as a mirror of minds in action; his aim was to reproduce in fiction what in life was "la novela de verdad" ("truly real" ["Observaciones," 124]). Once the moral category of truthfulness became a fundamental premise, the representation – "reproducción" ("reproduction") is his word – of people and places, events and society acquires moral as well as spatial dimensions. The novel, like the human mind, is a huge, hospitable realm where everything has a place although not everything coheres. The "true" and the "real" arise within intermediate spaces between pieces and parts, parts and wholes, and, correspondingly, between the two poles of "exactitud" ("factual accuracy") and what Galdós calls in his later essay (1897) "belleza" ("beauty" or aesthetic design). When things fit together, when the "perfecto fiel de la balanza" ("perfect point of balance") of form and content is achieved, the novel enacts the truth of fiction, since truthfulness perforce encompasses the whole of a thing in its relation to everything else.[15]

Every fact, every response and point of view counts. Thus something as small as a mouse let loose in a convent (*Fortunata y Jacinta*) is as much a catalyst for action as something as large as "la mole aquella" ("that hulking mass" [*Obras*, v, 557]) in *Miau* (1888), in which massive presences trace out the imprint of power in both public and private domains. The heavy tread of Cucúrbitas' wife – a massively overweight woman – reflects in miniature (!) the huge stone façade of the Treasury Building that broods over the Villaamil household, located across from the Women's Prison. Just as Cucúrbitas' wife lurches about the hall, imprisoned in her fat, the meaning of the epithet *Miau* – a catcall referring to the unemployed Villaamil and his luckless family – turns the novel's title into another "mole," a veritable punning, prison house of language.

Similarly, something as illusory as the misguided musings of a professor of philosophy in *El amigo Manso* turns upon linguistic paradoxes. Manso's speculative reasoning has a practical impact: he brings about a

---

[15] Benito Pérez Galdós, "La sociedad presente como materia novelable." In *Ensayos de crítica literaria*. Ed. Laureano Bonet (Barcelona: Ediciones Península, 1999), p. 220.

marriage and a political career; but his "reasoning" points to the fictive-ness of the novel and of its narrated lives. Manso, who declares from the outset that he does not exist, that he arises from an inkwell, having traded his story for a novel, becomes simultaneously author and narrator, character and reader. Manso's declaration of nonexistence, at beginning and end, frames the story of his unrequited love for Irene, of her betrayal, and of the rising power and prestige of the "mental gymnastics" (*Obras*, IV, 1290) of his pupil Manuel in that illusory game of politics. The novel's metafictive frame transcodes spatially and morally an incisive critique of those self-same political and social "fictions" which were only too real in Restoration Spain.

While *El amigo Manso* represents Galdós' most self–conscious metafic-tive experiment, framing devices occur throughout the series of "nov-elas contemporáneas"[16] and, to a lesser degree, in the "Episodios nacionales."[17] One example is the hair-picture in *La de Bringas*, which depicts in miniature the compulsions of both individual and nation – miserly thrift, the hoarding of capital, fetishism.[18] In *Fortunata y Jacinta* bits and pieces of theory about novel writing evolve *within* the novel, one partially reflecting the other. In *Misericordia*, Benina dreams up a fic-tional character who, like Galdós' own fictional characters, turns out to be simultaneously real and imagined.

The complexity of the fictiveness of truthful representation relates also to the central role that Galdos' novels played in "writing the nation" as these texts became, in a development parallel to the writing of legal codes that created citizenship, a "forum for critical debate."[19] Thus the provin-cial, mulish town of Orbajosa evolves as an allegory of rural, Carlist Spain. An impassioned love of luxury, of stylish appearances, which character-izes Isidora Rufete, protagonist of *La desheredada*, becomes a metaphor for the nation.[20] In *La de Bringas*, Manuel Pez, the consummate bureau-crat, is a symbol of the corruptions of the Spanish Civil Service and of the sloe-eyed, sleepy nation, and Rosalía, the "pretty, plumpish" protagonist driven by a desirous, even erotic, passion for fashion, is manifestly an image of Queen Isabel.[21]

[16] Hazel Gold, *Reframing Realism* (Durham: Duke University Press, 1993), p. 2.
[17] Diane Urey, "Galdós and the Fabrication of Historical Reality." In *Toward a Poetics of Realism / Hacia una poética del realismo*. Special issue of *Letras Peninsulares*. Ed. Harriet Turner. Vol. 13, No. 1 (Spring 2000), p. 97.
[18] Hazel Gold, "Francisco's Folly: Picturing Reality in Galdós's *La de Bringas*." *Hispanic Review* 54 (1986), p. 53.
[19] Labanyi, *Gender and Modernization*, pp. 3, 5.
[20] Stephen Gilman, *Galdós and the Art of the European Novel: 1867–1887* (Princeton: Princeton University Press, 1981), p. 121.
[21] Peter A. Bly, *Pérez Galdós, "La de Bringas"* (London: Grant and Cutler, 1981), p. 70.

In *Fortunata y Jacinta*, the narrator takes special care to link births, marriages, and deaths of ordinary people to historically resonant dates, blending fact and fiction to reflect the depth and range of economic, legal, political, and social change. This change was a fitful, uneven process, not at all uniform but rather like "a fugue in which old voices do not cease to sound when new voices enter."[22] Old and new voices mix as history goes on parade in the reminiscences of Estupiñá, old family retainer of the opulently mercantile Santa Cruz family. Jacinta's mother, Isabel Cordero, is as adept at manipulating birth dates as she is at peeling potatoes. The vicissitudes of Juanito Santa Cruz mirror those of his times, and the alternations of marriage and mistress follow the political interchanges between monarchy and republic.

The intersection of public and private discourses oriented the instructional potential of Galdós' novels toward a new objective: the creation of a public-spirited reader. At the same time, a renewed interest in mind–body dualism, which, in the 1880s, took a decisively inward turn toward psychic formation, converged with the need to capture deeper cultural anxieties, arising as high, middle, and lower classes blurred into each other. Thus the notion of "lo cursi" – a derisive epithet applied to those who, like Rosalía Bringas, strive to imitate in fashion and gesture the glossy ways of the aristocracy – becomes a culturally transparent mode.[23] "Lo cursi" manifests obliquely the anxieties accruing to a jumble of class alliances and aspirations taking place in the wake of the new economy and while, in the main, the term applies to women, impoverished dandies like don Frasquito Ponte, in *Misericordia*, are also "cursi." As Labanyi notes, "In emphasizing 'lo cursi' in his *novelas contemporáneas*, Galdós is identifying Spain's insertion into capitalistic modernity, indeed, into a global network of economic relations."[24]

Galdós' novels present an ambivalent critique of the process of standardization and imitation in late nineteenth-century Spain. The novels expose, on the one hand, the human suffering, loss, and waste incurred as "pueblo" – people of rural and working class-origins – either strive or are forcibly molded into "personas decentes" ("decent people," model bourgeois citizens), or as the state invades private life, as in *Miau* (1888), which recounts the story of Villaamil, an elderly civil servant, who is dismissed from the employ of the Minister of Finance. In the case of Isidora (*La desheredada*), her illusions of noble birth transmute into counterfeit – but charismatic – images of artistic, aristocratic bearing, "high" postures that inevitably turn upon the "lows" of prostitution.

---

[22] Raymond Carr, *Spain, 1808–1975* (Oxford: Oxford University Press, 1982), p. 2.
[23] Noël M. Valis, *The Culture of Cursilería* (Durham, NC: Duke University Press, 2002), pp. 149–171.
[24] Labanyi, *Gender and Modernization*, p. 114.

On the other hand, the history of Fortunata shows how a step up the stair to bourgeois respectability can be a good thing. Unlike Papitos, the little gypsy girl found barefoot in the mud holes of Cuatro Caminos – orphaned, illiterate, truly poor, and truly "pueblo" – in the novel, Fortunata emerges midway on the great stone stair, shod in stylish shoes – a manufactured, middle-class article of which she is very proud. Through her liaison with Feijoo, a retired, elderly military man who gives her a Singer sewing machine and who provides in his will for stock options, this working-class woman of the people, who at times had been a prostitute, gains a measure of legitimate financial independence. At the beginning of the novel, wealth, privilege, and political power had placed her seducer, Juanito Santa Cruz, and his powerful family at the top of the social pyramid. At the end, Fortunata, rising from below to form a new family, heroically challenges tradition and entrenched social codes to bridge the gap.

There is the view that Fortunata's incorporation into bourgeois society only illustrates the confounding, tragic result of any attempt to bridge the gap between social classes: as a savage, as "pueblo," she pays the price of death for her striving to become part of the nation's stable, propertied, middle class. Fortunata's death, however, comes not as she gives birth to the Santa Cruz heir and assembles, atop the stair, the kind of new, integrated family of intersecting social relationships to which the nation aspired. A passion for revenge precipitates her death. Gripping a house key like a brass knuckle, Fortunata, once again a savage, lacerates Aurora's face on the floor of Madrid's most fashionable foreign shop. She avenges Aurora's treachery – those aspersions on the legitimacy of the newborn heir and the supreme insult levied against both Jacinta and herself through Aurora's liaison with Juan and the vicious rumor that Aurora has propagated about a liaison between Jacinta and Moreno-Isla. Fortunata's savage behavior, which Jacinta recognizes as a "justiciada" ("righteous action" [Obras, v, 528]), arises from her passionate nature but also from a clear sense of right and wrong, of legitimacy, of civic and natural rights, and from the conviction of being a proper and "propertied" individual: the child is hers and hers to keep or give away.

Not only savages experience passion and a protest against bourgeois norms. Fortunata's ideas and feelings, which evolve as a mix of "pueblo" and bourgeois values, also characterize don Manuel Moreno-Isla, an expatriate, an island ("isla") to himself, a banker of wealth and social prominence allied to the Santa Cruz family. As the novel develops Fortunata's story, it develops also the story of Moreno's obsessive love for Jacinta and his unspoken kinship to Fortunata. The manner of his death prefigures Fortunata's, and it is no coincidence that he owns the building in La Cava where she dies as she contemplates her infant son. Moreno and Fortunata, from opposite poles of the social spectrum, die in a gush of blood, refusing to moderate their passions; the prescriptions of modern medicine (Moreno-Rubio) and mentors (Feijoo) are as nothing before the wave. Each is an island, an orphan; each imagines a child, and each gives birth: Fortunata, a "paloma-madre" ("dove-like mother" [*Obras*, v, 60]), conceives a dove-child. Jacinta imagines that child as belonging to Moreno, and Moreno, thinking of Jacinta, retrieves in himself a lost child, imagines "ideas . . . palomas" ("dove-ideas" [*Obras*, v, 461]) and persists in his passion, which he prizes more than any bourgeois notion of virtue. The plebeian Fortunata, rising on the social stair, and the aristocratic Moreno-Isla, who descends that stair, remain true to those perspectives and passions at the core of life. Each changes, rising and dipping, but each resists the imposition of a common standard in language, thought, morality, and politics. Each functions in his or her own way as a kind of rebel, as do Jacinta, Maxi, and Mauricia *la Dura*, articulating a personally felt resistance to the collective norms of their social world. Those norms, invoked by such fatuous guardians of morality as the priest Nicolás Rubín, are hardly sufficient. Nicolás excoriates his sister-in-law Fortunata for her ruinous behavior, envisaging her degradation as "habas contadas" (something as "countable" as a plate of beans [*Obras*, v, 292]). Fortunata, however, like the others who try "heroically" to bridge the gap between mind and body, masculine and feminine, prescribed roles and individual aspiration, overrides those norms, answering to higher imperatives.

In consequence, given Galdós' two-fold objective of representation and critique, as well as the aesthetic imperative to create, in fiction, the illusion of an autonomous, real, and truthful world, his novels offer deftly mediated narrative points of view. This technique creates a fictional, intermediate space, open to the reader, which, like other gap-like features, allows his novels to become forums of public debate. At the same time Galdós continuously retains control of his story, guiding the reader through the perceptions of both character and narrator via monologue, dialogue, and that effervescent, polyphonic mixture known as the free indirect style. The narrator is styled *as* a character:[25] he evolves as a person; he may or may not be reliable, and he inevitably becomes compromised by what he sees and tells. Yet this sly, winking narrative persona leads the reader to perceive the complexities of his fictional world. As a creator of shifting, intermediate spaces and as one who occupies the vantage point of the reader, who identifies with that reader, and who is, at times, manifestly a reader *himself* of the faces and texts he has invented, the narrator, through various disguises, becomes perhaps the most subtle culturally transparent mode of Galdós' fiction. Now and again, like the blinded Francisco Bringas

---

[25] Ricardo Gullón, *Técnicas de Galdós* (Madrid: Taurus, 1970), p. 18.

who surreptitiously lifts the edge of the band covering his eyes, peeping through a little "ventanita" ("window" [*Obras*, IV, 1614]), the narrator occasionally drops his mask to reveal the unexpected or unseen. He also frames scenes, focalizing through various "ventanitas" – "claraboya" ("transom"), curtains, keyholes, doors set ajar, balconies, even openings in a hedge – to transmute the import of narrative point of view into an image of what is being seen.

The case of *Doña Perfecta* (1876) is instructive. A so-called "thesis novel," it poses oppositions. There is modernity, represented by Pepe Rey, a civil engineer from Madrid, and there is a traditional, entrenched religious intolerance, wielded in the person of doña Perfecta. Perfecta, as her name implies, stands as a stiff-necked icon of the Church. Wishing to repay services rendered by her brother, Juan Rey, Perfecta conceives the plan of offering the hand of her daughter, Rosario, to Juan's son, Pepe Rey. She is eager to welcome him into the family. However, no sooner does Pepe arrive in Orbajosa than troubles begin. With every word, Pepe offends; with every apology, dissension grows; with every courteous gesture, strife ensues. While Rosario and Pepe recognize themselves as betrothed, obstacles proliferate: civil suits over Pepe's land holdings, town gossip, shunning in public places, each of these actions fueled by the persecutory animosity of don Inocencio, Perfecta's spiritual advisor. Soon lines of battle are drawn. Skirmishes over coffee and cigars escalate into civil war. Doña Perfecta locks up her daughter. Pepe moves out of the house to plot an elopement. As he steals into the garden, Perfecta gives to one of her minions the order to fire. Murder, insanity, never-ending penance come to the ironically named don Inocencio, *el penitenciario*, to doña Perfecta, and to the hapless Rosario, consigned to an asylum.

Styled as allegory, *Doña Perfecta* tells the story of made-up words and names, of surfaces and beliefs, of appearances that contradict what is real. The narrator participates in these linguistic shifts. He introduces the novel as artifice. It is manifestly a fiction, a cautionary tale, for the sign "Villahorrenda," name of the train station serving Orbajosa, is conspicuously a piece of allegory, a piece of "propiedad" ("property") owned by him, the narrator–author, in his guise as story teller. Yet it is also Rey's exclamation "¡Villahorrenda! ¡Cinco minutos!" ("Villahorrenda! Five Minutes!" [*Obras*, IV, 407]) that makes up the chapter title. Events appear to have happened. The narrator has seen them and so appends a moral with which he addresses the reader. Now the story of *Doña Perfecta* is akin to fact; it belongs to the history of the nation. The novel is fact and fiction at the same time.

From the beginning the narrator's point of view overlaps with Pepe's. As chronicler, he knows all, just as Pepe knows all, representing as he does modern-day enlightenment. "Intelligence" and "Strength" are Pepe's watchwords, which the narrator sees as engraved upon his character as upon a statue. Pepe, like his adversary doña Perfecta, is an icon. At the same time this narrator appears limited in knowledge. As he tells, he adopts Pepe's point of view in time, taking care to pace chapters according to Pepe's bewilderment or his ignorance. Titles turn into exclamations or questions. Events are structured elusively as phantom chapters, and descriptions of landscape, the town, and its dwellers often coincide so closely with Pepe's thinking as to constitute a kind of free indirect style. Finally, knowledge is deliberately withheld, even dissembled as ignorance, as the narrator feigns astonishment or hazards a guess or tells as if he knows nothing.

Only by chapter 26, near the end, does this bemused narrator refer back to real causes: the plans of María Remedios for her son, an inauspicious rival for Rosario's hand. Through marriage to the landholding family of doña Perfecta, María Remedios, niece to the cleric don Inocencio, aspires to rise above her station. At one time doña Perfecta had employed María Remedios as a laundress, a humiliation still smarting in the consciousness of this working-class woman. So it transpires that the prime mover of the murder of Pepe Rey is not so much religious intolerance or the political system of local bossism that enables Perfecta to give the order to fire. The primal cause is the invidiousness of class distinction, thrust forward by the process of modernization. María Remedios seeks a remedy, a way to step up; thus she manipulates her uncle, who in turn manipulates dona Perfecta to reject, even murder, Pepe, whom she had invited as a suitor for Rosario, only daughter and heir to the Polantinos estate.

Coincidences in narrative point of view not only blur the borders between narrator and character. They call into question the matter of cause and of interpretation. As Galdós' narrator advises, the story told in *Doña Perfecta* is about things that are not as they seem. Pepe appears to be all of a piece and up front; yet he quickly becomes off-guard, speaks out of turn, and unwittingly plays into the verbal deceptions of Orbajosa, becoming, as he himself recognizes, as brutal in counter attack as doña Perfecta. In turn, Perfecta focuses her energies and verbal resources on what she believes to be a just cause – saving Rosario from modernity's monster, Pepe Rey. As in the later novels of adultery, unexpected exchanges and reversals occur. Rather than villain, Perfecta is a victim of unseen ambitions (María Remedios) and of a veiled, active corruption (don Inocencio). The narrator's intermediate, compromised stance communicates these reversals and representations as a moral injunction but also as a lively and tragic process of manipulation and cultural misunderstanding. By showing the intersections of story-telling styles Galdós anticipates the aesthetic and ethical complexities of later novels of modernity.

If *Doña Perfecta* ends with insanity and penance, *La desheredada* begins in Madrid's municipal asylum of Leganés. The narrator now adopts the guise of a doctor, a diagnostician, who sees inmates as objects of study but also as exemplars of humankind. Their aberrant behavior, taken to extremes, simply mirrors what ordinary people think and feel. Leganés is a "masked," mediated world ("Limbo enmascarado del mundo" [*Obras*, IV, 969]) that registers the events, trends, and collusions of the real world of modernity. The mind of Tomás Rufete, Isidora's father, exhibits such a telling mixture of sick and sane. He is a "loco razonable" ("rationally crazy man" [*Obras*, IV, 967]) whose predicament exhibits a novelistic imagination run amuck, the contested question of property rights, the incitations of high capitalism, and the tensions produced by new regulatory systems of medical, social, and national reform.

These tensions arise from a natural affinity between writers of Realist fiction and doctors, emphasized during the latter half of the nineteenth century and characterized by the gradual infiltration of new scientific findings into both medical and artistic thought. The process accelerated rapidly in the 1880s and 1890s. On the one hand, the products of laboratory investigations in physiology and bacteriology were finally shown to be of practical use at the bedside.[26] On the other, observation, hypothesis, experiment, and verification shaped the more or less scientific determinist philosophy that broadly underlay the aesthetic theories of nineteenth-century Realist fiction.[27] *La desheredada* reflects that determinism in the description of inherited traits – stunted growth in street urchins, manias and mental aberrations in adults, delinquency in vagrants and ragpickers, and the brutalizing consequences of industrialization. Juan Bou's rope factory is a case in point.

Galdós articulates these fluid interactions of science and the Realist novel in three major ways: through the propositions of his essays and prologues about Realist fiction (e.g. 1870, 1889, 1897), the recurring presence of doctors and disease in his novels, and the literary figurations that represent the inner workings of the mind of both narrator and character. *La desheredada* opens with an elaborate description of Leganés, which, as a municipal institution, mirrors the operations of state surveillance and control; these operations are "as deranged as Rufete's fantasies of national life."[28] Each sector of Madrid, which Rufete sees as the "Envidiópolis" ("City of Envy" [*Obras*, IV, 967]) finds a correlative in Leganés: correctional officers ("loqueros"), whom the narrator compares to civil servants,

---

[26] Sherwin B. Nuland, "The Uncertain Art." *American Scholar* (Spring 1998), p. 139.
[27] Cecil Jenkins, "Realism and the Novel Form." In *The Monster in the Mirror.* Ed. D. A. Williams (Oxford: Oxford University Press, 1978), p. 2.
[28] Labanyi, *Gender and Modernization*, p. 104.

patrol the grounds; access to living quarters follows social differentiation and gender bias, for the "low life" of the patio for women is more
deprived, more desperate, than that of men; privileged quarters are only
for people who pay. Rufete's head rattles with the business of the state;
he believes he *is* the state, consumed by defaulting payments to the point
of death. Public and private have become fused through his madness in a
manner not dissimilar to the fusions in society at large. Rocking from one
extreme to the other, like the ball of mercury sliding around in Rufete's
brain, all classes, it would appear, are either uprooted, disinherited, or
confined to the dustbin by modernity's capitalistic economy.

Chapter 1 of *La desheredada* frames in a literary way the reversals
of these intersections between madness and sanity, public and private,
old privileges and new civic rights. The title "Fin de otra novela" ("The
End of Another Novel") alludes to the origins of Rufete's own "novel" of
modernity, ending as Isidora's "novel" begins. Rufete and his family come
from La Mancha. Incited by the fictions of a relative, the canon Santiago
Quijano, Rufete believes his daughter Isidora to be the illegitimate grand-
daughter of the Marchioness of Aransis, and so inculcates that image in
her mind – a familiar story line in serialized fiction. Thus the cause and
effect of Isidora's own novel of disinheritance – her illusory claim to an
aristocratic title and her descent into prostitution – evolve in reverse as
a nested structure of fictions, running counter-clockwise to turn "ends"
into retrospective and retroactive beginnings.

While the narrator, in his guise as diagnostician, lays claim to the writing of this novel, Isidora's imagination is far more powerful. She has, he
says, a gift for imagining, for anticipating events, for representing these in
exalted images and "de una manera muy viva" ("in a lively way" [*Obras*,
IV, 977]). It is she who really writes the novel of her disinheritance. Her
conviction of noble lineage is so strong, so deeply rooted, that the narrator himself keeps slipping into that imagined reality. In Chapter 2 she
has already won him over. He can hardly refer to her as Rufete's daughter, thinking of her beauty as somehow consistent with her claim to the
aristocratic title of the Aransis family. The reversed literary format of this
novel, which combines a classic (*Don Quijote*) with popular, serialized
fiction, mirrors the narrator's own reversals about art and life. His slips
from critique to belief in Isidora's image of herself reflect his vulnerability to Isidora and his own fear of modernity, of losing his identity in a
mixed upside-down world. Isidora's claim to the house of Aransis, her
innate sense of style, her artistic temperament, love of art, and her great
beauty are not far from his own ideals. Now the so-called balance between
"exactitud" ("factual accuracy") and "belleza" ("beauty"), which Galdós
proposes in 1897 as the secret of the Realist novel, tilts toward the pole of
aesthetics.

Isidora strives to become the person she imagines herself to be, to exert her rights as a citizen of the nation, to be first among equals, to rise from plebeian origins to occupy her rightful place in society. As Jo Labanyi argues, the lesson Isidora learns when her claim to the Aransis family is rejected is that "wealth is acquired through private initiative in the public sphere of the market."[29] If she cannot be noble, if she is socially disinherited, she will inherit her true self by entering the marketplace; her only property is her person, which she then determines to sell to the highest bidder. That property is alluring. Even the prudish narrator, like Augusto Miquis, senses something dangerously alive in Isidora's ruinous passion for luxury. Both he and Miquis, when confronted with Isidora as she turns before the mirror in the studio of a French dressmaker, waver in their convictions: her beauty seduces them again and again. Isidora's passion responds to something deeper than the mere love of ostentation, as is the case of Milagros in *La de Bringas*. For Isidora, as for her aging, alcoholic godfather, the addiction is existential: "Ser algo por diez minutos" ("to *be* something for ten minutes" [*Obras*, IV, 1150]). The much-maligned doña Pura, housewife in *Miau*, is another case in point. While Pura, like Isidora, is a spendthrift, her behavior owes much to the human need for self-expression, sounded in the second sentence of the novel as a "himno a la libertad" ("hymn to freedom" [*Obras*, IV, 551]); such an attitude is surely justifiable in a person who lives as a shut-in, facing the Woman's Prison House.

Augusto Miquis, rising in society, counsels prudence, thrift, obscurity – the Krausist family ideal achieved by Isidora's cousin who marries an honest man, sews for a living, and cares for Riquín, the illegitimate son whom Isidora has abandoned as she takes to the streets. The narrowness of this regulated ideal, however, cannot hold. The mix, in Isidora, of a gift for high art and the imperative – the social punishment – of a low life exceed the prescriptions of doctor and narrator. A gift for high art, in a woman like Isidora, has nowhere to go but down. We last catch a glimpse of her in *Torquemada en la hoguera* where, fittingly, she reappears as the lover of an impoverished painter. Art trails her skirts, even to the end.

Another example, in *La de Bringas*, of the imagistic power of narrative point of view is the ceremony ("Lavatorio") on Maundy Thursday in which the queen and her courtiers wash the feet of the poor. Perched high on a stair, near the ceiling of the vast interior of the Royal Chapel, children espy through a round, half-window ("claraboya") the particulars of the event. The ceremony appears in bits and pieces, mediated, as it were, by the amazed eyes of the children and giving a staggering, close-up view of paintings on the ceiling: huge, monstrous figures of nymphs and

[29] Labanyi, *Gender and Modernization*, p. 105.

angels tumble in grotesque postures. Down below, where the ceremony is taking place, everything appears in miniature – tiny figures crowding and scurrying to take part in the "pomposo acto de humildad regia" ("pompous act of royal humility"). In this upside-down world, children peering through a half-window register the decadence and deformity of this "comedia palaciega" ("palace farce" [*Obras*, IV, 1585]).

In this way, point of view imprints upon the reader's eye an image of fragments and exaggerations typical of Queen Isabel's reign. Later the child Isabelita Bringas, named for the queen, vomits in reaction to the confusions of the entire event. Like family, like nation, high is low, large is small, Christian is pagan, art is caricature, charity is greed, indeed, governance no more than a parasitical exchange system of favors, bribes, and defaulting payments. The representatives of the poor, humiliated, not honored, by the ceremony, sell their parcels of royal largesse to rapacious agents waiting outside the chapel. Indeed, the narrator himself begins the novel by straying into the labyrinthine inner world of the "palace-city" where the Bringas family lives. He parlays the system of favors and bribes to his own advantage, and while he dismisses the hair-picture as a "mamarracho" ("travesty"), he also "lives" inside that "social picture"[30] and its deceptions, dozing on the terrace, half-hearing, half-seeing, finally to enjoy sexual relations with the protagonist, Rosalía. The hypocrisy and corruption of the narrator illustrates to perfection a cynical comment a character makes in *Miau*: Spain is "el país de las vice-versas" ("the country of vice-versas" [*Obras*, V, 600]).

The decisive factor in Galdós' Realist novels is story telling itself. The notion of "narraciones interiores" ("inside stories")[31] of characters who, in telling, become the makers of their lives, transmutes story telling into the illusion of immediate experience. Family ties, business interests, political affiliations, religious practices, money, fashion, adultery, prostitution – even the luck of the national lottery – fabricate the networks that engender the stories that give rise to the novel that beckons to the reader. In *Fortunata y Jacinta*, the first bits of news about Juanito Santa Cruz blow into the ear of the narrator from friends and acquaintances; thus the genesis of a story about birth and betrayal arises from itself – from its own living speech. The origins of the "Torquemada" series reach back to other novels. It is as if Torquemada, an insistently recurring character, had staked a claim not only to unpaid loans but also to the indignation of the narrator, who now feels compelled to write the four-part series.

---

[30] Bly, "*La de Bringas*", p. 51.
[31] John W. Kronik, "Narraciones interiores en *Fortunata y Jacinta*." In *Homenaje a Juan López-Morillas*. Ed. José Amor y Vázquez and A. David Kossoff (Madrid: Castalia, 1982), pp. 275–291.

Another narrator–character, whining and waving his arms, had claimed Máximo Manso's story, trading pen and ink for a novel.

These examples show how, in Galdós' Realist novels, the meaning of the term "novel" keeps changing as it becomes an image for those various forms of thinking, feeling, and imagining, of dreaming and dissembling, in which people engage as they tell their stories. Some "novelas" are copies or parodies of the social text. Others, evolving through the freedom to think and the power to imagine, redefine social norms and alter perceptions about morality. Still others deliberately deceive and some become letters that either deny or discover or both, while certain "novelas," whole or in part, turn into dialogue, adapted as plays. In all Galdós' novels, however, what is real is alive on the page. For even things as stupidly plain as a plate of beans, which the puffed-up priest Nicolás Rubín compares to the probable outcome of Fortunata's adultery, have an unexpected story to tell.

28

The Realist novel

STEPHEN MILLER

No one alive today has significant personal memories of Juan Valera (1824–1905), Pedro Antonio de Alarcón (1833–1891), José María de Pereda (1833–1906), or Leopoldo Alas "Clarín" (1852–1901). No active scholar or critic can recall Benito Pérez Galdós (1843–1920), Narcís Oller (1845–1930), Emilia Pardo Bazán (1851–1921), Jacinto Octavio Picón (1852–1923), Armando Palacio Valdés (1853–1938), or José Ortega Munilla (1856–1922). By contrast there are still great numbers of persons, in Spain and abroad, whose literary consciousness was formed by generations of novelists, critics, and teachers hostile or, at best, indifferent to much of Spanish culture between the late seventeenth century and the Restoration period. Especially unattractive to these Modernists, Vanguardists, and Postmodernists was and continues to be the Realist imperative to create socio-mimetic fictions centered on the typical or representative people, manners, conflicts, and particular times, places, and settings of regional and national life.

Hence, against the historically and societally homologous fictions of Scott, Balzac, Dickens, Thackeray, Tolstoy, Twain, and the Spanish Realists, there arose early in the twentieth century an opposed way of thinking about all genres of art. Since then this mindset has remained potent. A reminder of its prestige and force was the October 2001 death of the last surviving Spanish Surrealist, Eugenio F. Granell (b. 1914). In a necrological piece in the Madrilenian newspaper *La Razón*, César Antonio Molina cited from Granell's essay, "Apuntes sobre el realismo artístico" ("Notes on Artistic Realism," 26 October): "La realidad mayor en el arte es una independencia absoluta de la vida cotidiana y sus acciones. El arte está fuera de lo diario al hacerse eterno – al hacerse arte y al margen de lo accidental" ("The greatest reality in art is an absolute independence from daily life and its actions. Art is beyond the daily upon making itself eternal – upon making itself art and beyond what is accidental"). Granell simply proclaims that the material of everyday life is not artistic. For all such anti-Realist thought – formulated famously by Ortega in *La deshumanización del arte* ("The Dehumanization of Art," 1925) and later repeated, without acknowledgment, by Juan Benet in *La inspiración y el estilo* ("Inspiration and Style," 1966) – Granell's opinion is canonical truth.

The present chapter discusses the traditions and versions of the Realist art rejected by the Modernists and their heirs. Spanish Realism at its best finds what is universal and eternal in humankind through personages confronting the accidents and issues of human life at given places and moments in time. Against the cosmopolitanism that Valera identified in 1888 as characteristic of the narratives and poems of Darío's *Azul* ("Blue"), the foundational work of Hispanic Modernism, Spanish Realism was essentially regional. For, as the emblematic Realist Galdós came to explain in a series of reviews, articles, prologues, and speeches written between 1870 and 1897, the defining mission of the movement was to observe and recreate what is and has been representative and typical in the lives and memories of contemporary Spaniards in the cities, towns, and countryside of all the nation.[1]

The panoramic view of recent history and current national life which Galdós wrote about was in fact both popular and well-known to the Realists and their audience. Today readers and critics normally have little or no experience with the particularly nineteenth-century format of the most widely circulated magazines. In these magazines, poems, fictions, and articles on history, geography, exotic lands and peoples, biography, and contemporary events were illustrated, first with woodcuts, and then later with photo-engravings intercalated into the text. The wide use of this format was made feasible by technical innovations of the early 1830s in England. These made possible the relatively cheap, simultaneous printing of graphico-lexical pages for periodicals, books, and occasional materials such as *aleluyas* (broadside sheets of illustrations, with captions, often written in rhymed couplets). In 1836 Ramón de Mesonero Romanos (1803–1882), the generational father of Spanish Realism, began publication of the *Semanario Pintoresco Español* ("Picturesque Spanish Weekly," 1836–1857), the first of scores of nineteenth-century Spanish illustrated periodicals. Very important among these was *El Museo Universal* ("The Universal Museum," 1857–1869). Its publishers, Gaspar and Roig, extended the Mesonero model by setting the pattern in Spain for continued success in publishing. They combined publication of a flagship illustrated periodical with that of an illustrated *biblioteca* ("library") of new editions of already popular works (e.g. *Los españoles pintados por sí mismos* ["Spaniards Painted by Themselves"] and Mesonero's *Escenas matritenses* ["Madrilenian Scenes"]), and first and successive editions by new writers (e.g. Alarcón's 50,000-copy best-seller *Diario de un testigo de la Guerra de Africa* ["Diary of an Eyewitness to the War of Africa," 1860] and *De Madrid a Nápoles* ["From Madrid to Naples," 1861]).

---

[1] Stephen Miller, *El mundo de Galdós: teoría, tradición y evolución creativa del pensamiento socio-literario galdosiano* (Santander: Sociedad Menéndez Pelayo, 1983), pp. 13–35.

The Gaspar-and-Roig formula afforded publishers, writers, and graphic artists a steady and increasing market for their collaborative efforts. A vital part of this process was, of course, to be responsive to the public at the same time that it was creating the public's taste for specific writers and illustrators.

Another important dimension of this nineteenth-century graphico-lexical reality also had Mesonero as pioneer. Part of his genius was to make articles on literary history and theory part of the *Semanario*, a precedent followed by the periodical after his editorship ended in 1842, and continued by the *Museo* and, among many other illustrated magazines, its successor *La Ilustración Española y Americana* ("Illustrated Spanish and American Weekly," 1869–1921). In just the 1839 volume of the *Semanario*, the following articles of literary criticism, theory, and history are found: Alberto Lista's discussion of what is then meant by "Romanticism"; the published version of an Ateneo talk on Spanish prose from its origins through the eighteenth century by José de la Revilla, father of Manuel (1846–1881), one of the fundamental critics of Realism and predecessor to Alas;[2] Enrique Gil y Carrasco's discussion of canonical Romantic dramas by comparisons and contrasts with Golden Age practice; and, most significantly for our purposes, Mesonero's essay "La novela" ("The Novel"). Anticipating all the fundamental points of the 1870 manifesto of Spanish Realism, Galdós' "Observaciones sobre la novela contemporánea en España" ("Observations on the Contemporary Spanish Novel"), Mesonero considered what kind of novel the times demanded of any author with literary pretensions. Heavily influenced by all that he judged positive in the Scottish and medieval works constituting Sir Walter Scott's "Waverley" novels (1814–1831), Mesonero proposed a novel that synthesized the best features of the then contemporary novel of manners and the historical novel:

> La novela ... para ser lo que la literatura quiere hoy que sea, ha de describir costumbres, ha de desenvolver pasiones, ha de *pintar* caracteres; si a estas condiciones generales añade la circunstancia de que las costumbres, los caracteres, las pasiones que describa, se enlacen naturalmente con los nombres históricos, vengan a formar el *cuadro* general de una época marcada de la historia de cada país, la novela entonces adquiere un valor sumo y reúne las más ventajosas condiciones del teatro, de la cátedra y de la historia.

> (emphasis added)

> (The novel ... to be what literature wants it to be today, must describe manners, reveal passions, *paint* characters; if it adds to these conditions the circumstance

---

[2] Stephen Miller, *Del realismo/naturalismo al modernismo: Galdós, Zola, Revilla y Clarín (1870–1901)* (Las Palmas: Ediciones del Cabildo Insular de Gran Canaria, 1993), pp. 57–69.

that the manners, the characters, the passions which it describes, naturally connect with historical names, forming thus the general *picture* of a specific time in the history of each country, then the novel acquires a great value and brings together the most advantageous qualities of the theatre, the university, and history.)

Noteworthy here, given the well-known Galdosian cultivation of historical and contemporary fictions in the 1870s (and, not so well known, in the 1860s), is Mesonero's plan for a Realist novel which effectively blurs the distinction between fictional and historical narrative.

This blurring is particularly interesting in light of Scott's and Galdós' practice of equating the contemporary period with that comprehended by the experience and memories of all those living at any given time. In Scott's first novel, *Waverley, or 'Tis Sixty Years Since*, sixty years pass between the 1745 initiation of the story and the 1805 present of the narrator; but 1745 is separated from the 1814 date of publication by sixty-nine years. Galdós makes both the contemporaneity of the first and second series of his famous historical novels, the "Episodios nacionales" ("National Episodes," 1873–1879), and the historical significance of their starting date, clearer than does Scott by giving the first of the series' twenty *episodios* the title *Trafalgar*. Just as 1745 is a watershed date in the history of Scotland, marking the breakdown of the governing patriarchal clan structure and the country's final submission to England, the 1805 Battle of Trafalgar also became a turning point in Spanish history, albeit in a more positive way for having planted the seeds of Spanish independence after a century of French dominance. Galdós' first-person narrator/memorialist, Gabriel Araceli, looks back as an old man in 1873 and sees the 1805 battle, some sixty-eight years earlier, as the place to begin – exactly as Mesonero indicated in 1839 – the intertwining history of Spain and himself. Yet, whereas Scott sets only five of his long fictions in his sixty-eight years of contemporaneity and ranges freely through time back to the eleventh century, Mesonero, Galdós, and Spanish Realism characteristically limit themselves to the contemporaneity of each writer. The stories they tell are witnessed events or events with which eyewitnesses and participants have acquainted them. In the course of narrating, the historical and the fictive fade one into the other.

Hence even though Scott, Mesonero, and Galdós are not commonly counted among important theorists of narrative, they probably would not be much surprised by the theories of Hayden White[3] and Paul Ricoeur[4]

[3] Hayden White, *Metahistory: The Historical Imagination in Nineteenth-Century Europe* (Baltimore: The Johns Hopkins University Press, 1973).
[4] Paul Ricoeur, *The Reality of the Historical Past* (Milwaukee: Marquette University Press, 1984).

on the relations between historical and fictional narration. For the theoretic point being made by Mesonero, as in White and Ricoeur, is that the act of narration is a *sui generis* artistic activity not defined by the elements it synthesizes. Moreover, since Mesonero was living in what the anonymous prologuist to the 1842 Edinburgh edition of the "Waverley" novels called "the age of graphically illustrated Books" ("Notice" 3), he naturally referred to the process of narrating as *pintar* ("painting") and its product as a *cuadro* ("picture"). In so doing he, as a man of his time and editor of the *Semanario*, established also that narration – historical, fictional, historico-fictive – could be lexical, graphical, or, best of all, graphico-lexical.

In light of this discussion, Alarcón's *Diario* takes on a much greater significance than has ever, I think, been accorded it. Even if Alarcón seems to be the most misunderstood and consequently overlooked of the Realists, he was a much-considered, full participant in the historical, political, and literary Spain of his time. When the Spanish–Moroccan war of 1859–1860 was in the offing, the *Museo* publishers Gaspar and Roig backed Alarcón in his desire to cover the war. They did so by forming, from among the regular contributors to the *Museo*, a graphico-lexical team consisting of Alarcón himself, one photographer, and two well-known magazine illustrators: the Spaniard José Vallejo, and the Frenchman Charles Iriarte. Together they produced during several months of battlefield collaboration the *Diario*: 127 woodcuts, based on photos or drawings, intercalated into 320 pages.[5]

For today's readers, very conscious of metaliterary techniques, it is striking how many pages Alarcón devotes to the narration of how the book was being created. While the photographer seems to have simply followed Alarcón's instructions, Alarcón, Vallejo, and Iriarte conferred on events, their meaning, and how best to cover persons, places, and actions. For example, there are pages where the reader both sees Iriarte's illustration and observes through Alarcón's words Iriarte at work on the scene Alarcón himself is at pains to describe and interpret. Hence readers participate in the authors' own eyewitness educations about the war, its people, and its issues, as well as in their struggles to render truthfully and artistically the different dimensions of what they were seeing and, in moments of battlefield peril, acting. Part of this process was explaining the Spanish aims and strategy, and recording the deeds, sacrifices, and valor of the soldiers and officers in many actions. Another part, as the original military goals were met and questions arose of political manipulation of the war from Madrid, was the authors' growing ethnographical understanding

[5] Valeriano Bozal Fernández, *La ilustración gráfica del siglo XIX en España* (Madrid: Alberto Corazón, 1978), pp. 33–34.

and sympathy for Moroccan troops and civilians as they had an ever fuller, more observant experience of them. Even though Alarcón was not writing a novel, he was narrating, in a magnificent graphico-lexical collaboration, historical events and the peoples and customs of the warring land. Precisely because he and Iriarte became especially caught up in the immediacy of all that was happening, the graphico-lexical narrative of the *Diario*, adapting Mesonero's words in "La novela," acquired its particular great value by bringing together the most advantageous qualities of theatre, classroom, and history. The *Diario* was the classroom where the experiences and lessons of literature and history became one.

On the occasion of Alarcón's death in 1891, Galdós published a necrology in *La Prensa* of Buenos Aires. In this, his only considered discussion of Alarcón, Galdós demonstrated a long acquaintance with the author and his work. After mentioning and contextualizing many Alarconian titles, Galdós ranked the works that he most admired: *El escándalo* ("The Scandal," 1875); the *Diario*; *De Madrid a Nápoles*; and *El sombrero de tres picos* ("The Three-Cornered Hat," 1874). In the present context the first two titles are most relevant. For *El escándalo*, the first of the polemical Spanish novels of religious thesis of the 1870s, was followed a year later by Galdós' *Doña Perfecta*. It is noteworthy that, sixteen and fifteen years respectively after Alarcón's novel and his own first of three novels of relogous thesis, Galdós celebrated in 1891 *El escándalo* as "una obra maestra" ("a masterpiece") important to him personally for its effect: "pocas veces he experimentado emoción más viva leyendo una novela" ("rarely have I been so moved reading a novel"). As regarded the *Diario*, Galdós' most substantive 1891 comment is to rank it only after *El escándalo*.

This Alarcón–Galdós connection takes on much greater significance for those specialist readers possessing two types of knowledge: that constituted by familiarity with the contents and textual reality of the four thesis novels and the Galdosian "Episodios"; and, that constituted by theories and critical studies of Stephen Gilman[6] and Thomas Franz[7] concerning the intertextual inspiration and inter-authorial dialogue which they, from different perspectives, show to have characterized Realism. Such readers understand that, independently of any necessarily conscious thought about *El escándalo* and the *Diario*, their themes and techniques, once known to Galdós – and not forgotten by him as late as 1891 – were always available as encouragement to his creations: as forms which he could use and adapt in the rapid elaboration of his own works; as contents with which he could dialogue. Cognizant, then, of the Gilman and

---

[6] Stephen Gilman, *Galdós and the Art of the European Novel: 1867–1887* (Princeton: Princeton University Press, 1981).

[7] Thomas Franz, *Valera in Dialogue / In Dialogue with Valera: A Novelist's Work in Conversation with That of His Contemporaries and Successors* (New York: Peter Lang, 2000).

Franz studies and of Galdós' acknowledgments of Alarcón, very particular meaning accrues to the first words of Galdós' March 1881 prologue to the twenty illustrated *episodios* in the ten-volume deluxe edition of 1881–1885: "Antes de ser realidad estas veinte novelas; cuando no estaba escrita, ni aún bien pensada, la primera de ellas [i.e., *Trafalgar*] . . . consideré y resolví que los *Episodios Nacionales* debían ser, tarde o temprano, una obra ilustrada" ("Before these twenty novels were reality; when the first one of them . . . was not even written, nor even well planned out . . . I thought and decided that the *Episodios Nacionales* should be, sooner or later, an illustrated work"). I would suggest, then, that the Scott–Mesonero–Alarcón line includes Galdós for one more reason: Galdós, also a product of "the age of graphically illustrated Books"[8] and periodicals, began, within a year of the resoundingly successful publication of Alarcón's *Diario*, to create graphico-lexical works. In the clearly historical mode Galdós drew and wrote the conquest of Gran Canaria by forces of the Catholic Monarchs (1861); and his three graphico-lexical satiric narratives, *Gran teatro de la pescadería* ("The Great Fishmarket Theatre," 1862), *Las Canarias* ("The Canaries," c. 1863–1864), *Atlas zoológico* ("Zoological Atlas," c. 1867), recreated contemporary persons and conflicts among Canary Islanders in the Islands and Madrid.[9] Clearly, then, there is every reason to take seriously Galdós' declaration that as early as 1873, he knew the "Episodios" would be complete only when illustrated. Galdós and his graphic collaborators would create for the period from Trafalgar to the Battle of Victoria what Alarcón and his graphic team did for the 1859–1860 war: the narrativized synthesis of history, manners, characters, nation, and graphic illustration.

The reading public, because of the illustrated press, knew the historical narrative into which Galdós entwined the actions of his protagonists. The historical narrative was important in its own terms as a matter of national identity and pride, and the characters' situations and conflicts became significant as demonstrations of the national character revealed, reasserted, and developed during the resistance to and war with the French. Hence Mesonero Romanos, sometimes consulted by Galdós for his eyewitness experience of the period, gave his greatest praise to the Galdós of the "Episodios" in a letter dated 6 December 1877. He stated: "Sobre todo es sorprendente, y más para mí que para ningún otro la intuición con que se apodera de épocas, escenas, y personajes que no ha conocido, y que sin embargo *fotografía* con una verdad pasmosa [emphasis added]" ("Above all, it is surprising, and even more so for me than for anyone else,

---

[8] "Notice." In *Waverley Novels*. Vol. 1: *Waverley* and *Guy Mannering* (Edinburgh and London: Robert Cadell and Houston & Stoneman, 1842), p. 3.

[9] Stephen Miller, *Galdós gráfico (1861–1907): orígenes, técnicas y límites del sociomimetismo* (Las Palmas: Ediciones del Cabildo de Gran Canaria, 2001.)

the intuition with which you appropriate epochs, scenes, and personages that you have not known, and which nevertheless you *photograph* with marvellous truth"). He then implied that this *verdad* ("truth") caused Galdós' productions to manifest "más vida y enseñanza ejemplar que muchas historias" ("more life and exemplary teaching than many histories"). Without recalling specifically his 1839 "La novela," it is clear that the "Episodios," in Mesonero's own opinion, were the realization of his essay's description of the kind of novel that should be written; and, furthermore, that he was in a position to invoke, and judge positively, the "Episodios" by what I call the "touchstone test of realist art."

The touchstone test is at least as old as the 1786 prologue by Ramón de la Cruz (1731–1794) to ten volumes of his theatre, and is customarily stated as a question. An author or critic asks the viewer (of a theatrical work, drawing, or painting) or the reader (of narratives) a question: are not the actions and characters in this work the true copy of what you yourselves have seen, be it in the streets, plazas, and parks of the city, and/or in the countryside, ports, and towns of the provinces? Mesonero evidently asked himself the question and simply affirmed its positive answer to Galdós in 1877. Cruz, however, in discussing his *sainetes*, and Galdós more than eighty years later discussing Cruz's *sainetes* and Ventura Ruiz Aguilera's story collections *Proverbios ejemplares* ("Exemplary Proverbs," 1864) and *Proverbios cómicos* ("Comical Proverbs," 1870), had public audiences and preferred the interrogative rhetorical strategy. Since Cruz and Galdós knew the *sainetes* did not possess the breadth of three- or five-act dramas, and Galdós that the *Proverbios* were not the extended novels of Balzac and Dickens, they had a challenge: convince their readers that truth to observed socio-human reality was the fundamental virtue of a literary work. If Cruz's and Aguilera's productions lacked scale and grandeur, they, like the "Episodios" in Mesonero's authoritative eyewitness opinion, had the fundamental value of transmitting their respective "épocas, escenas, y personajes" ("eras, scenes, and characters"). In so doing Cruz and Aguilera achieved the universal socio-aesthetic aims of Realism: set the life of individuals in the society of a particular place and time before the reader or viewer in a way that lets him or her learn emotively and conceptually about people in history.

The 1880s formed the most intensive decade of long and short Realist narrative in Spain. While, in the 1870s, Alarcón, Valera, Pereda, and Galdós, accompanied especially by the criticism of Revilla, were creating novels which began to define Spanish Realism, in the 1880s Alas, Oller, Palacio Valdés, Pardo Bazán, Picón, and Ortega Munilla continued the older Realists' work in both long and shorter narratives. Upon Revilla's death in 1881 first Alas and then Pardo Bazán also became critical guides to the Realist movement; and Galdós, Palacio Valdés, and Valera contributed prologues, discourses, and newspaper pieces which analyzed important social changes and their consequences for Realist narrative. Ortega Munilla also held various editorial posts, with the most important being that of editor from 1879 to 1906 of *Los Lunes de "El Imparcial"* ("The Mondays of *The Impartial"*). With *La Ilustración Española y Americana*, Ortega's cultural supplement to the Madrid newspaper *El Imparcial* was probably the most consistently important periodical outlet for Realist short fiction, chapters of forthcoming novels, and criticism of and by the Realists. Another figure, not normally considered among the Realists, is a cousin of Oller, the important Catalan theatre critic and editor Josep Yxart (1852–1895). As director in the 1880s of two Barcelona-based illustrated novel collections, first for the library of *Arte y Letras* ("Art and Letters") magazine and later for Henrich and Company, Yxart published novels, often graced with theoretically sophisticated prologues, by all the major Realists, including the Alas of *La Regenta* (1884–1885), but excepting Galdós who was essentially his own graphico-lexical publisher from 1880 until 1907. By having Oller represented in translation in the collections and by securing the collaboration of such important illustrators as the Catalonians José Luis Pellicer (1842–1901) and Apeles Mestres (1854–1936) and the Madrilenians Enrique (1838–1892) and Arturo (1849–1902) Mélida – all of whom worked on the illustrated "Episodios" – Yxart multiplied contacts among the writers who shared illustrators in the creation of first-edition Realist narratives in uniform, luxurious formats. This in turn fomented a greater sense of supra-regional, group identity among the Realists. A remark to Galdós by Pereda at the end of a letter dated 15 February 1887 is relevant here. Aware of the productivity of his companions and his own recent silence, Pereda refers to himself as "el único de la clase que pierde curso este año" ("the only one in the class [of Realist novelists] who skips a course [i.e., does not publish a novel] this year").

Not surprisingly, given the revolution of 1868, the Third Carlist War (1872–1876), and the Restoration of the Bourbon Monarchy in 1875, a basic Realist focus was the comparison and contrast of life in liberal, cosmopolitan Madrid and the more conservative, traditional provinces. Mindful perhaps of Alarcón's *Diario* and *De Madrid a Nápoles*, as well as *Cartas desde mi celda* ("Letters from My Cell," 1864) by Gustavo Adolfo Bécquer (1836–1870), a product of his historico-nationalist Romanticism, Galdós in *Doña Perfecta*, Pardo Bazán in *Los pazos de Ulloa* ("The Ulloa Manor House," 1886), and Pereda in *Peñas arriba* ("To the High Country," 1895) explicitly studied the differences between the center and the provinces of Spain. By recording their city-centered protagonists' travels among the – for them – different, almost foreign peoples and realities of the provinces and their outlying districts, these novelists created an obvious structuring device for observation of and comment on what their protagonists were seeing, and for the responses of the locals as they in turn regarded these visiting strangers. Even though other novelists and these novelists themselves did not normally structure their narratives so obviously through the journey motif, it is clear that much of Realism was a kind of anthropological narrative. Galdós made this explicit in *Nazarín* ("Nazarín," 1895), albeit the journey was only from the solid middle-class parts of upper Madrid, from the Plaza Mayor northward, to the southern, lower-class reaches spreading across the terrain sloping down to the Manzanares River. The narrator of the first of the five parts of the novel cannot tell at first if Nazarín is a priest or an Arab. Then, upon observing the "diversidad de castas humanas que . . . se reunían" ("diversity of human castes which . . . gathered themselves") where Nazarín lives, he decides his visit to this part of Madrid unknown to him "iba resultando de grande utilidad para un estudio etnográfico" ("was becoming very useful for an ethnographic study" [*Nazarín*, Part I, chapter 2; cf. I, 5]). Ethnography was, from the first issues of Mesonero's *Semanario*, as integral a part of the graphico-lexical texts of illustrated magazines as it became in Alarcón's *Diario* and *De Madrid a Nápoles*, and – changing countries, but not literary "-ism," – in Owen Wister's proto-novel of the American west, *The Virginian* (1902), with its travel by train from the civilized east to the increasingly wild and technologically backward west, and intercalated graphic text by Charles Russell.

Another significant ethnographic dimension to the Realist project is revealed in the exchanges of letters among Pereda, Galdós, and Oller. As their Yxart-promoted relations became more frequent and frank, Pereda and Galdós who spoke and wrote in Castilian, came to urge the Catalan Narcís Oller to write his narrative work in the same fine Castilian in which he corresponded with them. At a time when translations from Catalan to Castilian – or from Galician – were not at all so common as they are today, they reasoned that Oller would gain what his work richly merited: many more readers. What they failed to understand, or chose to subordinate to more practical concerns, was Oller's explanation that the complete sociomimetic recreation of his characters must include the linguistic dimension in which he and they thought and acted.

From our perspective today both sides in this debate were right and wrong. In those centrist times even Castilian-speaking provincials could find themselves at a notable socio-political disadvantage when dealing with linguistically centrist speakers (as can be seen in the linguistic deprecation and control of Sevillians by Sanjurjo's "high" Castilian in Palacio Valdés' *La hermana San Sulpicio* ["Sister Saint Sulpice," 1888]). Indeed, the fact is that, because of the linguistic barrier, Oller's narratives never found their way into the canon of the Spanish Realist novel and remain poorly known today. Nevertheless, recalling the "touchstone" formula of Realism, it was necessary to render late nineteenth-century Catalans confronting the challenges of their daily lives in their proper linguistic medium. In this context a new virtue of Alarcón's *Diario*, emulated *mutatis mutandis* by Galdós in the avoidance of anti-French chauvinism in the "Episodios," was its growth toward inter-cultural understanding. That the Realists were not always successful in that enterprise, as happened with Alarcón himself in reporting on Paris in *De Madrid a Nápoles*, and with Galdós and Pereda, only reflects our human imperfections.

Another vexing question of Realism's exploration of Spain is its representation of women. In a society which had rigidly imposed norms for the roles and acceptable conduct of its female half, and in which these roles mostly limited women to the private sphere, it fell mainly to the overwhelmingly male literary establishment to portray women. Hence, for example, while the two consensus masterpieces of Realism, Alas' *La Regenta* and Galdós' *Fortunata y Jacinta* ("Fortunata and Jacinta," 1886–1887), as well as Picón's *Dulce y sabrosa* ("Sweet and Delectable," 1891), received praise for their portrayals of women, Emilia Pardo Bazán was the only major female Realist. Her dilemma was to avoid being pigeonholed in book series and periodicals reserved for women writers and audiences, and to gain access to the same venues as the males of Realism. Her successful solution to the problem entailed, on one hand, using generally male narrators and perspectives to recreate the "touchstone" reality of Spanish society, and, on the other, undermining that reality by means of a subtle twist of viewpoint at the end of the narrative which suddenly placed the narrated action in a woman-sensitive light.[10]

In 1885 Pardo Bazán's best short novel, *La dama joven* ("The Young Lady"), appeared in an eponymously titled volume published by Yxart in his graphico-lexical *Arte y Letras* library. While the prologue contains important reflections relevant to the shorter narrations of the volume and to discussions among Pereda, Galdós, and Oller on the linguistic rendering of characters' thoughts and speech, *La dama joven* itself focuses on the socio-economic situation of women. The protagonist Concha and her elder sister Dolores are long-term orphans who earn their modest living as seamstresses – an archetypical theme of popular literature which Realists such as Ruiz Aguilera, Galdós, and Pardo Bazán revisited and adapted. Because of having been seduced and abandoned when much younger, Dolores mistrusts all men and finds comfort in religion. When chance reveals Concha's talent as an actress, Dolores, guided by her confessor, prefers the married life for Concha – to the ex-actor Ramón – over one

---

[10] Joyce Tolliver, *Cigar Smoke and Violet Water: Gendered Discourse in Emilia Pardo Bazán* (Lewisburg, PA: Bucknell University Press, 1998), pp. 19–42.

in the theatre. For his part, Ramón, blind to Concha's ability, concerns himself only with her being ogled by other men while on stage. The climax occurs when Concha chooses marriage to Ramón over an independent future as a leading lady. Pardo Bazán's particular genius at this point is to close the story with a conversation between the director Gormaz and the eminent actor Estrella. When Gormaz tries to ease his disappointment by suggesting that Ramón might well make Concha happy, Estrella disagrees, and Pardo Bazán subtly changes narrative perspective. For Estrella, in the last words of the story, says: "Lo que le dará ese bárbaro será un chiquillo por año . . . y si se descuida, un pie de paliza" ("What that jerk will give her is a baby a year . . . and, if she's not careful, a kick in the rear" [La dama joven, p. 90]). The attentive reader understands that Concha is going to be controlled by a man of much less ability than her and that the only reason for this is social custom and gender prejudice. Moreover, Pardo Bazán figured in Concha's dilemma some of her own life. Following the success of her La cuestión palpitante ("The Burning Question," 1883), scandalous because it was a woman who wrote on the "unlady-like subjects" treated by French Naturalist writers, Pardo Bazán had to choose between her marriage and her writing. When she decided for her career, the outcome was legal separation from a husband who could not brook having a "public woman" as spouse.

In this context the autobiographical prologue Pardo Bazán wrote for the first edition of Los pazos de Ulloa and letters of the late 1880s to her lover Galdós are extremely important. In the first document she assumed that it was corrrect and important for women to have control over their lives, and argued that that control was not possible until women regularly received the kind of education which would allow them to earn a living. In her letters to Galdós she reasoned that her life was truly hers only when she could pay her and her children's bills and not have to depend upon her family for financial support. These ideas acquired greater literary and "ethnographical" significance when Pardo Bazán's temporary unfaithfulness to Galdós during their liaison ended that relation and provoked a series of novels. Galdós' La incógnita ("The Unknown") and Realidad ("Reality") and Pardo Bazán's Insolación ("Sunstroke"), all published in 1889, glossed the affair from their respective male and female perspectives. The main point to be made here is that Galdós portrayed a wronged, slighted male, and she, artfully playing with the rhetoric of narrative presentation, let the reader see the contradictions between the sexual liberty of males and their – hypocritical – refusal to allow the same freedoms to women. In 1895 Galdós published Tristana, which Pardo Bazán reviewed. Where Galdós demonstrated sensitivity to the social and educational limits confronted by naturally talented women, and showed his protagonist obliged to fall back into the socially accepted role of spouse, Pardo Bazán chafed at the limits being revealed, limits, however, that she did not depict being surpassed in her own work.

During the 1890s and early twentieth century Pardo Bazán, despite being a principal Realist novelist and critic, faced unabated opposition by the male literary establishment to her entry into the Real Academia Español and to a post as university professor. No matter that her accomplishments dwarfed those of most of her male antagonists, she could not overcome the barriers to general recognition of her right to fill positions and hold posts to which no woman for many years afterwards acceded. However, unlike Oller, she wrote in Castilian – instead of the Galician of her home region – which provided her a larger audience than his, one that never allowed her to become as obscured as he, and accords her today a higher level of recognition than ever before.

Because of the forty-seven years separating the first and last death dates of the major Realists (Alarcón in 1891 and Palacio Valdés in 1938), and because of different socio-aesthetic trajectories in each writer, it is hard to say when the nineteenth-century Realist novel ends. Pardo Bazán's 1905 *La quimera* ("The Chimera") may be its last masterpiece. Written as a fictionalized rebuttal to Valle Inclán's *Sonatas* (1902–1905) – themselves a Modernist's memoirs using as foil the Realist autobiography of Gabriel Araceli in the first series of "Episodios" – *La quimera* tells the story of the painter Silvio Lago who masters Realist portraiture and landscape, yet feels impelled to quest for an alternative art form. In this pursuit he becomes entangled with Espina Porcel, a glamorous, decadent Modernist, who is Pardo Bazán's female equivalent to the Marquis of Bradomín, the memorialist of the *Sonatas*. Setting these characters, their art, and life-style against the normal reality of Galicia, Madrid, and Paris, Pardo Bazán's narrator compares and contrasts their alternative lives, works, and theories with that normal reality and the art based upon it. In the end *La quimera* concludes that art inspired in national peoples and customs is superior to life and art pretending to create its own alternative reality. Nonetheless, the dominance of the Realist novel in Spain ended because a majority of strong writers and their public lost their "ethnographical" interest in the peoples, places, and times of the Spain they and their grandparents lived and were witnessing. Today we can see that even when *La quimera* was published, Valle Inclán's Modernist *Sonatas* were marking a future in which the theories and works of Ortega, Granell, and Benet would flourish.

29

The Naturalist novel

STEPHEN MILLER

It is customary to associate Naturalism most frequently with Thomas Hardy (1840–1928) and the experimental novel of Emile Zola (1840–1902). From the beginning of their stories, it is patent that the protagonists are placed in circumstances that will inexorably crush them into hopelessness and death. These circumstances, which affect disproportionately the low-born protagonists usually favored by Naturalism, are those of heredity, birth, gender, and socio-economic class. In Spain this kind of novel, that of "radical Naturalism" or "barricade Naturalism," was cultivated intensely by few writers, with Eduardo López Bago (1853–1931) and Alejandro Sawa Martínez (1862–1909) being most prominent.[1] In the former's tetralogy composed of *La prostituta* ("The Prostitute," 1884), *La pálida* ("The Pallid Woman," 1884), *La buscona* ("The Picara," 1885), and *La querida* ("The Mistress," 1885), and the latter's *El cura* ("The Priest," 1885) and *La mujer de todo el mundo* ("The Woman of All Men," 1885), the little-remembered, never-popular López Bago and Sawa practice the Zola–Hardy deterministic Naturalism explicitly rejected by most Spanish novelists of the period.

This is not to say that these novelists denied the importance and influence of biology, environment, economics, and gender on real people and hence on their fictive counterparts. In *La desheredada* ("The Disinherited Lady," 1881), Benito Pérez Galdós (1843–1920) explored the effect of heredity and socio-economic class on Isidora Rufete and her brother Pecado. In *Los pazos de Ulloa* ("The Ulloa Manor House," 1886) and in *La madre naturaleza* ("Mother Nature," 1887), Emilia Pardo Bazán (1851–1921) observed how the often barbarous conditions of rural life shape persons of all classes; and, in *Los pazos de Ulloa*, *Morriña* ("Homesickness," 1889), and *Insolación* ("Sunstroke," 1889), she treated the gender and economic limitations under which women live. For his part Narcís Oller (1845–1930), the premier Catalan novelist of the period, essayed one deterministic novel in his 1884 *L'Escanyapobres*

---

[1] Pura Fernández, "El naturalismo radical." In *Historia de la literatura española*. Vol. IX: *Siglo XIX (II)*. Ed. Leonardo Romero Tobar (Madrid: Espasa Calpe, 1998), p. 753.

("The Miser"), but never again repeated the Zolaesque "experiment." Also, to abbreviate, Vicente Blasco Ibáñez (1867–1928), an eclectic novelist whose work escapes easy placement in the movements and periodizations of literary history, recreated the lives of Valencian farmers and fishermen living on the edge of disaster. Nevertheless, importantly and typically for the group of writers being considered here, in his best novel, *Cañas y barro* ("Reeds and Mud," 1902), Blasco portrayed how the three generations of one family reacted differently to their similar situations and led different lives as a result. Unlike, then, the international and national novelists of radical Naturalism, the most read and remembered nineteenth-century Spanish novelists rejected that determinism which denied to personages real and fictional the ultimate power to control their lives.

In light of the slight status of Spanish novels of deterministic Naturalism, the goal of this chapter is to explore the criteria for distinguishing between Naturalism and Realism in Spain. The difficulties of this project are several. To begin with, as Pattison documented,[2] the terms "Naturalism" and "Realism" were used interchangeably in nineteenth-century Spain. More than attaining terminological consistency, however, the point of contention among leading novelists in the earlier 1880s was the direction the Spanish novel was taking when Zola's Naturalism was so prominent in Europe.

Pardo Bazán's *La cuestión palpitante* ("The Burning Question"), a collection of twenty newspaper articles first published between November 1882 and April 1883, is the single best source of information concerning the issues at stake, especially in its book form with the June 1883 prologue by critic and novelist Leopoldo Alas (1852–1901). There he limited himself to "decir algo de lo que el naturalismo no es" ("saying something about what Naturalism is not").[3] He identified six stereotypical characteristics of the radical Naturalism which traditionalist and religious Spanish critics found offensive and dangerous, and which he and all other non-radical Spanish novelists also rejected: Naturalism is "la imitación de lo que repugna a los sentidos" ("the imitation of what is repugnant to the senses");[4] Naturalism is "la constante repetición de descripciones . . . de cosas feas, viles y miserables" ("the constant repetition of descriptions . . . of ugly, vile, and miserable things");[5] Naturalism is merely the literary equivalent of Claude Bernard's positivist method of observation and experimentation; Naturalism is pessimism; Naturalism excludes any

---

[2] Walter T. Pattison, *El naturalismo español. Historia externa de un movimiento literario* (Madrid: Gredos, 1969).

[3] Leopoldo Alas, *Los prólogos de Leopoldo Alas.* Ed. David Torres (Madrid: Editorial Playor, 1984), p. 133.

[4] Alas, *Los prólogos*, p. 134.   [5] Alas, *Los prólogos*, p. 134.

other -ism; and, Naturalism is simply a recipe book for making novels. Pardo Bazán's approach is, over twenty weeks/chapters, naturally much more analytic and comprehensive. She studies the history of the French novel leading to Zola and critiques what, in it and him, is and is not of use for the Spanish novel.

The bulk of *La cuestión palpitante* consists of a kind of annotated rewriting of *Les Romanciers naturalistes* ("The Naturalist Novelists," 1881), Zola's author-by-author study of the nineteenth-century French novel. For the purposes of this chapter, more relevant is Pardo Bazán's philosophical and theological reasonings about the issues which stand between the French and the Spanish novel. These issues are, broadly speaking, two: Zola's determinism, and different manifestations of Romantic idealism in philosophy and literature.

Pardo Bazán begins her discussion of idealism by citing Georg Wilhelm Friedrich Hegel (1770–1831). In his *Lectures on Aesthetics* he writes, as quoted by Pardo Bazán, that "la esfera del arte" ("the sphere of art") is "una región superior, más pura y verdadera que lo real, donde todas las oposiciones de lo finito y de lo infinito desaparecen, donde la libertad, desplegándose sin límites ni obstáculos, alcanza su objeto supremo" ("a superior region, purer and truer than the real, where all oppositions between the finite and the infinite disappear, where liberty, unfolding itself without limits or obstacles, reaches its supreme object).["]6 Along with Galdós, Alas, and other prominent Realist/Naturalist novelists and critics, Pardo Bazán had little sympathy for a contemporary literature based on belief in and cultivation of "a superior region" which is "purer and truer" than the real, natural world of everyday experience. Yet the conflicting ideologies in the Spain of the 1870s made such issues religiously and politically polemical.

Between the September revolution of 1868 and the 1875 Restoration of the Bourbon monarchy, six years of liberal experiments with democratic government in Spain were a dismal failure. Traditionalist Catholicism, which was a large part of the Restoration's power base, judged its transcendent, hierarchical conceptions of reality and life more than vindicated before the failures of the immanent, democratic positions of those who supported the revolution. In literature this battling was manifested in what is called the Spanish novel of thesis of the 1870s. Alarcón's novel *El escándalo* ("The Scandal," 1875) and his 1877 talk "Discurso sobre la moral en el arte" ("Discourse on Morals in Art," 1877) represented the transcendent viewpoint, whereas the immanent, secularized view of society was represented by three Galdosian novels: *Doña Perfecta* (1875),

---

6 Emilia Pardo Bazán, *Obras completas*. Vol. III: *La cuestión palpitante*. Ed. Harry L. Kirby, Jr. (Madrid: Aguilar, 1973), p. 583.

Gloria (1877), and *La familia de León Roch* ("The Family of León Roch," 1878).

As was often the case in the Hispanic world, the debate symbolized by the interchanges between Alarcón and Galdós mixed the issues of anticlericalism and politics with those of philosophy and theology. Even though Pardo Bazán was a student of Saint Francis of Assisi, an avowed Catholic, and student of Francisco Giner de los Ríos (1839–1915), an exponent of the idealist Krausist philosophy, she simply could not brook Alarcón's way of Platonizing and Catholicizing Hegel's theory of art. A sample of Alarcón's practice was his claim that the greatest literary works of all times and cultures elevate the reader "a la contemplación del Eterno Ser en quien juntamente residen la Suma Verdad, la Suma Bondad y la Suma Belleza" ("to the contemplation of the Eternal Being in whom reside jointly the Ultimate Truth, the Ultimate Good, and the Ultimate Beauty").[7] In the ideological atmosphere of the times, these words, especially in light of Alarcón's *El escándalo*, signified sponsorship of the militant politico-religious orthodoxy of all the religious, anti-progressive tendencies that, from a secular perspective, had mired Spain in its past. Such hegemonic, didactic idealism was as unacceptable to her as deterministic Naturalism.

Pardo Bazán followed her critique of idealism by differentiating between two kinds of novels inspired in reality: those by such writers as Zola who made their characters products of the materialistic and deterministic world described by Darwin, Comte, and Taine; and other novels that portrayed characters who were responsible for their decisions. Pardo Bazán wrote:

Tocante al naturalismo en general, ya queda establecido que, descartada la perniciosa herejía de negar la libertad humana, no puede imputársele otro género de delito; verdad que éste es grave, como que anula toda responsabilidad y, por consiguiente, toda moral; pero semejante error no será inherente al realismo mientras la ciencia positiva no establezca que los que nos tenemos por racionales somos bestias horribles e inmundas . . . y vivimos esclavos del ciego instinto y regidos por las sugestiones de la materia. Antes al contrario, de todos los territorios que puede explorar el novelista realista y reflexivo, el más rico, el más variado e interesante es sin duda el psicológico, y la influencia innegable del cuerpo en el alma, y viceversa, le brinda magnífico tesoro de observaciones y experimentos.

(Regarding Naturalism generally, it is established by now that, excepting the pernicious heresy of negating human freedom, no other fault can be ascribed to it; truly this is a grave fault, given that it annuls all responsibility and,

---

[7] Pedro Antonio de Alarcón, "Discurso sobre la moral en el arte." In *Novelas completas* (Madrid: Aguilar, 1976), p. 1222.

consequently, all morals; but such an error will not be inherent to Realism until positivist science establishes that we who consider ourselves rational are but unclean, horrible beasts . . . and that we live in slavery to blind instinct and are ruled by the powers of matter. On the contrary, among all the territories that the novelist who is Realist and reflexive can explore, the richest, the most varied and interesting is doubtlessly the psychological; in conjunction with the undeniable influence of the body on the soul, and vice versa, this subject offers to the novelist a magnificent treasury of observations and experiments.)[8]

This paragraph is an expression of the challenge nineteenth-century positivism and Zola's Naturalism presented to Spanish society and its novelists, readers, and critics. Before the claims of materialism and determinism, the vast majority of Spaniards, regardless of how each coordinated their thought and action with respect to Catholic doctrine on other matters, simply maintained orthodox positions on human responsibility and free will. Moreover, as the overall context of the above citation in *La cuestión palpitante* makes clear, Pardo Bazán was suggesting that the best answer to Zola's Naturalism was a reaffirmation and development of Spanish Realism, a theory argued ex post facto by Galdós in his 1901 prologue to a new edition of Alas' *La Regenta* (1884–1885).

The exact direction this Spanish reply should take, in the person of the Spanish "novelist who is Realist and reflexive," is toward the rich "territory" of psychological exploration of characters as beings whose body and soul are inextricably linked and mutually influential. Not only does Pardo Bazán thereby counter radical determinism, but she also suggests that the Spanish Realist novel move its center of gravity from its novelization of typical persons, places, times, and conflicts to a novelization of the inner individual. To understand better what she is proposing and its novelty, it may be useful to review one of the early classics of nineteenth-century Spanish Realism.

The work in question is formed by the ten volumes of the first series of historical novels entitled "Episodios nacionales" ("National Episodes"), published between 1871 and 1875 by the anticlerical, anti-idealist Galdós. Gabriel Araceli is the first-person narrator/protagonist of the series. In the initial novel, *Trafalgar*, Gabriel stresses his very unpromising, impoverished origins: "Doy principio, pues, a mi historia como Pablos, el buscón de Segovia; afortunadamente . . . en esto sólo nos parezcamos" ("I begin, then, my history in the same way as Pablos, the Segovian swindler; fortunately . . . only in this do we resemble each other.")[9] The Pablos to whom he refers is another classic first-person narrator/protagonist,

---

[8] Pardo Bazán, *La cuestión palpitante*, p. 645.
[9] Benito Pérez Galdós, *Trafalgar*. In *Episodios nacionales*. Vol. 1 (Madrid: La Guirnalda, 1882), p. 6.

that of Quevedo's picaresque novel *Historia de la vida del buscón* ("The Swindler," 1626). Not only is this novel often cited by Galdós and historians of the Spanish novel as one of its fundamental texts, but in the last words of Quevedo's novel is found a philosophico-theological point which defines Spanish culture from at least the Counter Reformation through to and beyond Realism/Naturalism. Pablos, whose legal situation in Spain makes flight from the country advisable, decides for America to see "si mudando mundo y tierra mejoraría mi suerte" ("if changing places and climes I would better my luck").[10] He reports, however, that "fuéme peor . . . [porque] nunca mejora su estado quien muda solamente de lugar, y no de vida y costumbres" ("it went worse . . . [because] he who changes only his residence, not his life and habits, does not better himself").[11] Gabriel, constituted from the first page of *Trafalgar* as the anti-picaro, takes care that his life of perseverance and diligence is honorable. This explicit pairing of Gabriel and Pablos by Galdós draws attention to and confirms free will: two young men from backgrounds configured by Galdós to be exact equivalents have different lives because of the respective choices each makes, not because they are determined by anything. Recalling the experimental dimension of the Naturalist novel according to Zola, it seems that Galdós in 1871, long before Zola established himself, performs an "experiment" that demonstrates free will. In that narrow sense *Cañas y barro* could be read as a replication, thirty years later, of the original Galdosian "experiment," and the final word of Spanish Realism/Naturalism on free will and determinism.

The "Episodios" are much more than novels of thesis in which these important philosophical-theological issues are addressed. Reference to the last of the ten volumes of the first series of "Episodios," *La batalla de los Arapiles* ("The Battle of Arapiles" [of Salamanca], 1875), reveals that as he ends his narration, Araceli offers himself as role model for those readers who may find themselves "postergados por la fortuna" ("left behind by fortune").[12] This is possible because he is an exemplary witness and participant in many of the principal events of the War of Independence. Moreover, by also having overcome all deterministic forces in his life, he has become the emblematic citizen of Spain when it took control of its affairs. Following the formula for interrelating fictive and historical persons and events developed by Walter Scott (1771–1832) in the "Waverley" novels, Galdós makes Gabriel's personal history homologous with that of the nation. His personal trials, choices, and

---

[10] Francisco de Quevedo y Villegas, *Historia de la vida del buscón*. In *La novela picaresca española*. Ed. Angel Valbuena y Prat (Madrid: Aguilar, 1943), p. 1101.

[11] Quevedo y Villegas, *El buscón*, p. 1101.

[12] Pérez Galdós, *La batalla de los Arapiles*. In *Episodios nacionales* (Madrid: La Guirnalda, 1885), vol. v, p. 454.

ultimate success occur inseparably from the key events and persons of the epic conflict which won Spanish freedom after more than a century of French hegemony. Nevertheless Galdós will abandon this formula.

Fourteen years after finishing with Araceli, Galdós converts one of his memorable secondary, type characters from the contemporary period, the usurer Francisco Torquemada, into the protagonist of the eponymous *Torquemada* tetralogy published between 1889 and 1895. The tetralogy is important for two reasons. First, it is ideologically consistent with the historical novels protagonized by Gabriel in that its protagonist is a man who takes control of his life to rise from the lower ranks of society – in his youth Torquemada was an halberdier – albeit even more spectacularly than Gabriel. The old usurer becomes one of the richest men in Spain and a figure in European finance. The second reason, which returns the discussion to the reflexive Realist novel, merits separate treatment.

As Torquemada changed from archetypical Madrilenian money-lender to individual studied in his maturity through four novels, the novelistic focus shifted exactly in the way suggested seven years earlier by Pardo Bazán in *La cuestión palpitante*. The physical and spiritual pain Torquemada suffered in the first volume of his tetralogy when his much-loved young son died is what brought his psychology to the fore. Until 1889 – an *annus mirabilis* of Galdosian experimentation[13] – Galdós limited Torquemada to being the stock character of the usurer who came and went as needed through Galdosian novels of the always-broke Madrilenian middle class. Now, though, as reflexive Realist, Galdós wanted to find out about Torquemada as an individual, to see who inhabited the type whose outer self he had been using since his 1883 novel *El doctor Centeno* ("Doctor Centeno"). Moreover, as the emphasis passed from the surface Torquemada to the inner man, something else occurred: the particularities of Madrilenian society became proportionately less important. This is a striking shift in novelistic center of gravity, but not unprecedented. Half of the famous novel *Pepita Jiménez* (1874) by Juan Valera (1824–1905) was epistolary in form. In his letters the protagonist Luis de Vargas revealed his absorbing psychological development from condescending, rationalizing seminarian to a man for whom Pepita Jiménez was very attractive. For occurring before its time, though, Valera's experiment needed years to pass before being seriously imitated. Nonetheless, as early as 1880 Pardo Bazán, in a little-known essay on Galdós, stated that the novelist has two "terrenos" ("domains") through which to roam: "el mundo exterior con sus varias perspectivas y pintorescos accidentes" ("the

---

[13] Stephen Miller, *Del realismo/naturalismo al modernismo: Galdós, Zola, Revilla y Clarín (1870–1901)* (Las Palmas: Ediciones del Cabildo Insular de Gran Canaria, 1993), pp. 153–161.

exterior world with its diverse perspectives and picturesque details") and "el interior que brinda al análisis su inagotable riqueza de sentimientos, con los diversísimos matices que en cada individualidad adopta" ("the interior [world] which offers to analysis its inexhaustible riches of sentiments, with the most diverse individual inflections").[14] In June 1882, Leopoldo Alas, who had mentioned Valera's psychological dimension in an 1879 book review, developed further the "two terrains" concept. The occasion was a piece on Galdós' *El amigo Manso* ("Our Friend Manso") wherein he expressed his preference for that novel as one "de observación psicológica" ("of psychological observation") over the concentration on "el mundo exterior, el fenómeno social" ("the exterior world, the social phenomenon") in *La desheredada*, the immediately preceding Galdosian fiction.[15] He indicated besides that he, who was an enthusiastic reader of earlier Galdós centered in "the exterior world," thought *El amigo Manso* Galdós' best work. Then he added points about Naturalism that anticipated and complemented Pardo Bazán's related ideas in *La cuestión palpitante*, as well as his own in the prologue to that book.

Together with Galdós' *Fortunata y Jacinta* ("Fortunata and Jacinta"), published in 1886–1887, Alas' novel *La Regenta* legitimately lays claim to being the masterpiece of the nineteenth-century Spanish novel. For Alas, Galdosian novels such as *Fortunata y Jacinta* were considered to be "contemporary National Episodes."[16] In addition to everything else he meant by that, Alas was indicating that in his historical "episodes" of the early nineteenth century and in his "episodes" of then contemporary life, Galdós followed the paradigm established by Scott of intertwining the fictitious actions of his characters with corresponding historical events and figures. Hence, in *Fortunata y Jacinta*, the upper-class Juanito Santa Cruz's series of amorous adventures with the working-class Fortunata and his periodic returns to his middle-class wife Jacinta coincide with historical events between the revolution of 1868 and the Restoration of 1875. This parallel structuring device suggests that there is as much capriciousness and self-indulgence in the public sphere as in the private, and that the defects of private life have repercussions in the public sphere. In addition *Fortunata y Jacinta* incorporates many fictional and historical characters from previous Galdosian novels of Madrid into the varied, complex world of the new families and characters invented for the new novel. Moreover,

[14] Cited by Maurice Hemingway, "La obra novelística de Emilia Pardo Bazán." In *Historia de la literatura española*. Vol. IX: *Siglo XIX (II)*. Ed. Leonardo Romero Tobar (Madrid: Espasa Calpe, 1998), pp. 664–665.
[15] Leopoldo Alas, "*El amigo Manso*. Novela de D. B. Pérez Galdós." Cited in John W. Kronik, "La reseña de Clarín sobre *El amigo Manso*." *Anales galdosianos* 15 (1980), p. 67.
[16] Miller, *Del realismo/naturalismo al modernismo*, pp. 110–113.

that Galdosian Madrid may still be walked and viewed today, allowing peripatetic readers to understand better the influence of public spaces on fictional characters. All this is not to say there is no significant psychological dimension to the novel. It is rather that even such prodigious psychological characterizations as Ido del Sagrario and Fortunata's husband Maximiliano Rubín are, in the vast panorama of Galdosian Madrid, mere functions of society, not aesthetic centers of the novel. That center is in the Fortunata of humble origins and spirit who becomes the plaything and pawn of the middle and upper classes, but whose abnegation in the interests of her child by Jacinta's husband says many things about Spanish society. Fortunata's and Jacinta's husbands are timely representatives of their class and gender as their conflicts and resolutions reflect and implicitly comment on those of the public, historical realm.

Starting with its first page, the world of Alas' *La Regenta* differs greatly from that of *Fortunata y Jacinta*. Instead of the vibrant, sprawling Madrid that is the center of fictive and national life, Alas sets his story in Vetusta. This city is portrayed as sleeping a centuries-long siesta, stirring sometimes in its historical backwater to recall it was the court of an important Christian realm when the Moors ran free a thousand years before on the Iberian peninsula. Allusions to contemporary Spain are passing. The lives of the protagonists – Ana Ozores, the "Regenta" or judge's wife of the title, and Fermín de Pas, a locally important priest – revolve around private concerns that develop in a historical vacuum. Scholars can determine that Vetusta is a fictive version of Alas' home city of Oviedo in northern Spain and give reasons for believing the novel's action begins in the late 1870s. Differently, however, from the exterior-world-oriented Galdosian episodes where historical dates, times, and people are specified because they are integral to structuring lives and events, historical materials matter as little in Vetusta as in the subsequent fictionalization by Armando Palacio Valdés (1853–1938) of Vetusta/Oviedo as Lancia in *El maestrante* ("The Grandee," 1893).

La Regenta tells an age-old tale of an attractive young orphan left to the mercy of strangers. In this case the orphan, Ana, is so beautiful that she is shown to out-of-towners as a local sight-to-be-seen. Ana Ozores, however, is also trapped in a marriage of convenience to the old, retired judge, who hunts and reads Calderonian honor plays rather than attend to her. Not surprisingly Ana is viewed as available and is pursued simultaneously by Fermín, whose priesthood is a vocationless economic necessity, and the local don Juan. Much of the novel explores Ana's evolving thoughts about her solitude and her need for true human contact, while having to negotiate a social code that satisfies none of her needs. Despite real feeling for the manipulative Fermín, she submits to the don Juan. Upon learning of his dishonor, her husband challenges her lover to a duel, but, unexpectedly, he is the one who dies in it. Ana is orphaned a second time as all Vetusta, beginning with her lover and the priest, abandon her to a solitude of dishonor and penury. In this tale, then, interpenetration of the conflicts of body and soul is central as Ana, as well as Fermín, live empty, cruel celibacies. Each needs a human relationship which neither's state allows to them. A bad marriage, a job one hates, a bleak future, feeling alone are all sad, commonplace life situations, but Alas, in part through his extensive use of free indirect style, maximizes access to and exploration of the inner Ana and inner Fermín. The priest at least has the priesthood he despises and a social position, but Ana, always essentially alone, has only herself, her feelings and thoughts.

In the time following *La Regenta* psychological interiorization becomes increasingly important in the Spanish novel, with the years 1889–1897 standing out as the most intense period of psychological Naturalism or reflexive Realism. In 1895 Alas revisited the conceptualizations of his review of *El amigo Manso*. In the prologue of that year to his collection of stories *Cuentos morales* ("Moral Tales"), Alas formally announced his adherence to the aesthetic of interiorization, of psychological exploration, not even hinting that it was already essayed by him in *La Regenta*, *Su único hijo* ("His Only Son," 1890), and *Doña Berta* (1891), as well as in short narratives collected in the 1893 volume *El Señor y lo demás, son cuentos* ("The Lord and the Rest, They Are Stories"), and, of course, in *Cuentos morales*. In that prologue to this last title Alas characterized negatively and positively the center of gravity of his psychologically oriented fictions. He explained that they eschewed the "descripción del mundo exterior . . . la narración interesante de vicisitudes históricas, sociales" ("description of the exterior world . . . the interesting narration of historical, social vicissitudes"); and that they stressed instead "los fenómenos de la conducta libre . . . la psicología de las acciones intencionadas . . . el *hombre interior*, su pensamiento, su sentir, su voluntad" ("the cases of free conduct . . . the psychology of intentional actions . . . the *interior man*, his thought, his feelings, his will").[17]

As an indication of how current these views were becoming, the practice of Rafael Altamira (1866–1951), a young writer and disciple of Alas, can be mentioned. In his first collection of critical articles, incorporating pieces published between 1887 and 1891, Altamira as a matter of course differentiated, for example, among authors and works where "*exteriorismo*" ("exteriorism") or "*profundismo*" ("penetrativeness") were dominant.[18] Palacio Valdés was also establishing himself during this

---

[17] Alas, *Los prólogos*, p. 98. Emphasis in original.
[18] Rafael Altamira, *Mi primera campaña* (Madrid: José Jorro, 1893), p. 55; Altamira's emphasis.

time as Spain's principal novelist of abnormal psychology. Starting with
the man-shunning, masochistic Martha of his *Marta y María* ("Martha
and Maria," 1883), Palacio Valdés continued in 1893 the dark world of
physical and sexual abuses, controls, and perversions in *El maestrante*,
and later the self-destruction of the title character through his own depres-
sive egoism in *Tristán o el pesimismo* ("Tristan, or Pessimism," 1906).

Within two years of completing *Fortunata y Jacinta*, Galdós published
in 1889 not only the first volume of the already-discussed *Torquemada*
tetralogy, but also two formally experimental novels that were noteworthy for their "*profundismo.*" The epistolary novel *La incógnita* ("The
Unknown") and the dialogued novel *Realidad* ("Reality") had no descriptive or narrative sections. Instead the characters presented themselves as
completely in their own words as could the dramatis personae of a play in
their monologues and dialogues. With some years of delay, as happened
with Alas as seen above, Galdós explained the aesthetics of previous years'
works. The occasion was the prologue to his 1897 dialogued novel *El
abuelo* ("The Grandfather"). While *El abuelo* was only Galdós' second
novel in that form, he had had eight plays staged between publishing
Realidad and *El abuelo*. Hence, by the 1897 prologue, Galdós' experience with the dialogue form of presentation was significant, especially
because he honed his scripts during intense rehearsals with the actors.
For Galdós, then, the dialogue form, the characters' presentation of themselves through their own words, allowed those characters to imitate more
easily "a los seres vivos, cuando manifiestan su contextura moral con su
propia palabra" ("living beings, when they reveal their moral make-up
through their own words").[19] This was now important to Galdós because
it resulted in the creation of a more efficacious, direct "impresión de la
verdad espiritual" ("impression of the spiritual truth")[20] of his characters.
By this period Galdós valued the psychological aspect of Spanish Naturalism over Realism's socio-historic "territory," and the legitimacy, not to
say triumph, of the Spanish novel of psychological Naturalism was fixed.

One last issue concerning Naturalism may be best accessed by returning
to *La cuestión palpitante*. At the beginning of her study Pardo Bazán stated
that "los períodos literarios nacen unos de otros" ("literary periods are
born one from the other"),[21] that "no basta el capricho de un escritor, ni de
muchos para innovar formas artísticas" ("neither the caprice of one writer,
nor that of many, is sufficient cause for innovation in artistic forms"),
and, finally, that such periods and forms "han de venir preparadas, han de
deducirse de las anteriores" ("must be prepared for, must be deduced from

[19] Benito Pérez Galdós, *Ensayos de crítica literaria*. Ed. Laureano Bonet (Barcelona:
Ediciones Península, 1972), p. 205.
[20] Pérez Galdós, *Ensayos*, p. 205.
[21] Pardo Bazán, *La cuestión palpitante*, p. 577. Subsequent quotes from same page.

anterior ones"). In the present context, the specific version of the question suggested by Pardo Bazán is: why did the main body of Spanish novelists seek alternatives to the Realist socio-historical novel of manners and, having rejected deterministic Naturalism, cultivate the psychologically oriented novel of the inner person?

The answer may be pursued best by once again referencing Galdós. His 1897 entry speech into the Real Academia Española negated the social, political, and historical premises on which he programed the Spanish socio-historic novel of manners in his 1870 Realist manifesto "Observaciones sobre la novela contemporánea en España" ("Observations on the Contemporary Spanish Novel"). From his 1897 standpoint all that seemed positive in Spanish national life during the promise-filled era of the revolution of 1868 had evaporated. He stated: "Examinando las condiciones del medio social en que vivimos como generador de la obra literaria, lo primero que se advierte en la muchedumbre a que pertenecemos, es la relajación de todo principio de unidad. Las grandes y potentes energías de cohesión no son ya lo que fueron" ("Examining the conditions of the social medium in which we live as generator of the literary work, the first thing noticed in the multitude to which we belong is the relaxation of all principles of unity. The great and potent energies of cohesion are no longer what they were").[22] This description of a desolate social panorama explains from a different angle Galdós' emphasis on the individual in his prologue to El abuelo, and thereby invokes both the 1880–1883 period of El amigo Manso and of Pardo Bazán and Alas' early thoughts about psychological narrative, and his own creative practice from 1889 onwards. The artistic material left to the Realist/Naturalist writer who has lost faith in his society is the individual per se. Galdós explains that "Perdemos los tipos, pero el hombre se nos revela mejor, y el Arte se avalora sólo con dar a los seres imaginarios vida más humana que social" ("We lose the types, but the individual better reveals itself to us, and Art justifies itself merely by giving to imaginary beings a life more human than social").[23]

The history of the nineteenth-century Spanish novel, as it evolves from Realism to Naturalism, is the record of the experiments made by writers to create new forms adequate to material "more human than social." This new material also conveyed growing post-Restoration pessimism regarding Spain among novelists, a development which the inept loss of the last vestiges of the Spanish Empire in 1898 served to substantiate. Spain as "the social medium in which [the psychological Naturalists] live[d]" which was "generator of [their] literary work," dictated the inward turn of the Spanish novel. The novelists of psychological Naturalism – or,

---

[22] Pérez Galdós, Ensayos, pp. 176–177.   [23] Pérez Galdós, Ensayos, p. 180.

of reflective Realism – sought the reality of natural women and men, persons for whom historical and present national society is discredited, false, artificial, and, in sum, marginal to their lives. The title and content of Galdós' *Realidad* are emblematic of disillusioned men and women who need to explore what they really, naturally need and want before again taking any social grouping or their role in it seriously.

30

The theatre in Spain 1850–1900

DAVID T. GIES

Women, while still significantly underrepresented as playwrights on Spanish stages, gained slightly more visibility during the second half of the nineteenth century. The model of Gómez de Avellaneda, whose powerful and well-written plays could not be ignored by the establishment (in spite of their continued refusal to recognize her merits publicly with membership in the Real Academia Española), opened pathways to other women who wanted to express themselves in the theatre. Dozens of now semi-forgotten women (we do not even know the birth and death dates of many of them) labored in the margins of the Spanish theatre scene.[1] The best-known woman writer of the second half of the nineteenth century, Emilia Pardo Bazán, while gaining fame as a polemical prose stylist, also wrote several plays.

Many of the plays penned by women fit into traditional "women's" categories such as religious dramas, children's literature, or sentimental comedies, a characterization that makes them no less interesting. In fact, if one were to trace carefully the language, themes, and structures of these plays, one would be able to track more precisely the "domestic" concerns of late nineteenth-century Spanish bourgeois society (this is being done for the novel; the theatre remains largely unexplored territory). Life, love, honor, the place of women, the need for education, the role of constancy and forbearance, and the importance of religion and spirituality in women's lives become the foci of many of these plays. Examples come from the work of Enriqueta Lozano de Vílchez, Adelaida Muñiz y Más, and Rosario de Acuña.

---

[1] Among these dramatists are: Rosario de Acuña (1851–1923), Dolores Arraez de Lledó (fl. 1850s), Julia de Asensi (1859–?), Camila Calderón (1852–?), Emilia Calé (1837–?), Isabel Cheix Martínez (1836–1899), Pastora Echegaray (1850–?), Rosa de Eguílaz y Renart (1864–?), Joaquina García Balmaseda (1837–1893), María Gertrudis Garecabe (?), Enriqueta Lozano de Vílchez (1830–1895), Elisa de Luxán de García Dana (?–1899), Ángela Martínez de la Fuente (fl. 1864–1874), Isabel María Morón (?), Adelaida Muñiz y Mas (?–1906), Rosa Pic de Aldawala (?), Natividad de Rojas (?), Josefa Rovirosa de Torrentes (?), Victoria Sáenz de Tejada (fl. 1890s), Faustina Sáez de Melgar (1834?–1895), María de Soto y Saez (fl. 1890s), Mercedes Velilla y Rodríguez (1852–1918), and Constanza Verea y Núñez (fl. 1870s).

Enriqueta Lozano de Vílchez's historical drama *María o la abne-gación* ("Maria, or Self-Denial," 1854) followed the Neoclassical struc-tural model in that it adhered to the unities of time, place, and action, but grafted onto that model an interesting psychological component drawn from earlier French and Spanish melodramas. In Act II, the heroine, forced to sacrifice her honor in order to save her cousin Raúl, disintegrates into hysteria, convulsive laughter, and temporary insanity, previewing the rep-resentation of women that became all but standardized in the second half of the century.[2] A more mature play, and ultimately a more satisfying one, is *La ruina del hogar* ("The Ruin of the Hearth," 1873), where Lozano works out two issues which concern not only her but the Spanish mid-dle class in general: the role of women in contemporary society, and the central place occupied by money in the middle-class world. Adela, who seems at first to be an embryonic feminist (she complains about being kept at home, bored and unhappy), is revealed to be a superficial, uneducated person overly concerned with glitz, fashion, and the acquisition of money. Money is the motivating force in the play: Carlos needs money to pay for medicine and for a month's stay in the country to regain his failing health; Adela needs money to buy elegant finery; Miguel needs money to repay the funds he illegally spent on a dress and jewels for Adela; Mr. Lara needs money to maintain his business interests; and the parents of Carlos, Adela, and Miguel need money to care for themselves in their old age. Lara is the perfect symbol of Spain's new money-driven society, as he reveals in an ironic updating of classical Anacreontic odes: "Goza del vivir, y déjame trabajar: / tu edad es de disfrutar, / la mía es de adquirir" ("Enjoy your life and let me work: at your age you should be finding pleasure in things; at mine, I should be acquiring them"). This is where Vega's *El hombre de mundo* ends up, where Romantic love has been supplanted by money.

Adelaida Muñiz y Más wrote at least fourteen one- to four-act plays, published and performed in Madrid in the 1890s. She was as comfort-able writing biblical dramas as she was satirical one-acters. Her three-act *Mancha heredada* ("Inherited Stain," 1892) is instructive. Revealing the influence of Henrik Ibsen, Muñiz centers her play around the character of Margarita, orphaned daughter of a jailed convict who has been taken in by the criminal's lawyer, the middle-class don Julián. As the daughter of a notorious criminal, Margarita thinks that she is not worthy of the love of the noble Rafael. Her name has been "stained." Muñiz couches Margarita's dilemma in the context of women's traditional plight (subject to laws created by men), and happiness is denied her when Julián shoots

---

[2] Bram Dijkstra, *Idols of Perversity: Fantasies of Feminine Evil in Fin-de Siècle Culture* (Oxford: Oxford University Press, 1988); Lou Charnon-Deutsch, *Fictions of the Femi-nine in the Nineteenth-Century Spanish Press* (University Park, PA: Pennsylvania State University Press, 2000).

Rafael in a duel. It becomes clear that the "stain," then, is not merely (or even) Margarita's shamed father, but rather the stain of rules upheld arbitrarily by Julián, Rafael's mother (a countess who fights hard to keep Margarita from staining her family's name), and Father Gabriel, all of whom are trapped within a rigid social structure which creates witting and unwitting victims. Margarita sacrifices her love, her freedom, and her happiness in the end, and becomes a Sister of Charity, and tends to her adoptive father in his old age. When Rafael suddenly returns (he had been wounded, not killed, in the duel), Julián thinks this is a prearranged plot (a moment strikingly similar to the ending of Rivas' *Don Álvaro o la fuerza del sino*) and shoots him. The bullet does not kill Rafael, however, but rather Margarita, who had stepped in front of Rafael to protect him. The metaphor is clear: woman's happiness – and, indeed, very existence – is sacrificed between the foolish whims of false honor and false love.

Rosario de Acuña is considerably more radical than her predecessors. Certainly more successful than the other two, she was considered to be a pioneer in Spain's nascent feminist movement for her willingness to confront then-controversial issues such as civil marriage, women's equality, and workers' rights. Her first play, *Rienzi el tribuno* ("Rienzi the Tribune") was staged in 1876, and "praised" (as was the custom with strong-minded women writers) as "manly" for its commitment to the common man and its suspicion of privileged nobility. Acuña was merely echoing what several others had said before her, but she is the first woman to have brought these concerns to the stage. Even more radical is the anticlerical play, *El padre Juan* ("Father John"), which premièred in 1891 and presents a modern, educated, freethinking engineer (reminiscent of Galdós' Pepe Rey in *Doña Perfecta*) as the hero. Acuña rails against what she sees as the oppressive, obscurantist attitudes which crushed Spain's moral and industrial progress, symbolized in the Church. In her play, she brings forth two young people who not only plan to wed in a civil marriage, but who also transform a local religious shrine into a spa to aid – as the convent situated directly in front of it does not – the poor and infirm. Not surprisingly, the play was banned after just one performance.

These were minor trends, of course. The theatre in the second half of the century was built upon the middle class's anxiety about its political and economic stability. Issues previously discussed in the privacy of the home or in cafés around town were now being debated in the public forum of the theatre. Spanish society analyzed itself through the discourse of theatre, debating issues, confronting problems, and finding ways to avoid conflicts it did not wish to confront directly. Society – mostly upper-middle-class society, of course – popularized what became known as the *alta comedia* ("high comedy"), which was in essence dramatized documentation of upper-middle-class behavior and customs. The grand gestures of the

Romantic stage gave way to more intimate condemnations of the greed, vice, ambition, and infidelity that marked too much of the social behavior of the day. Characters now began to whisper and sit in their drawing rooms, rather than shout, declaim, faint, and kill themselves as they had done in the first half of the century. Drawing rooms and offices supplant the cemeteries, jails, and caves of Romanticism. The broad brush strokes with which many Romantic dramatists painted are transformed, by more careful attention to psychological realities and personal motives, into subtle canvases on which are detailed the lives and loves of the bourgeoisie. With the high comedy we begin to detect what can be considered the modern comedy in Spain.

The leading practitioners of Spanish high comedy are Tomás Rodríguez Rubí (1817–1890), Manuel Tamayo y Baus (1821–1898), and Adelardo López de Ayala (1828–1879). Tamayo voiced a desire to paint "moral portraits" of mankind; he created not Realistic plays but rather symbolic ones, laden with heavy doses of conservative, middle-class, Catholic values. Although he began to première plays in 1847, it was not until 1855 and 1856, with the respective appearance of *Hija y madre* ("Daughter and Mother") and *La bola de nieve* ("The Snowball") that his brand of Realism attracted serious attention. *Hija y madre* revolves around class pretensions and social mobility, and how money, business dealings, and class concerns maintain contemporary social structures. Tamayo here, as in many of his plays, resolutely refuses to cave in to tragedy or disappointment, so all ends well as father recognizes daughter, harmony is re-established, and all live happily ever after. Such endings clearly project Tamayo's own hope for the transformation and ultimate salvation of Spanish society. In *La bola de nieve* his subject is envy, for him one of the great ills of his society. This emotion can "snowball" into poisoned relationships, family chaos, and social disruption. Clara, consumed by jealousy over the behavior of her innocent fiancé Fernando, manages to lose not only him but also her best friend María as well. Her obsession threatens the friendship between Fernando and Luis, Clara's brother, and also spills over into Luis' treatment of the household servants, creating thereby a microcosm for society as a whole. Tamayo was a master at moral posturing, and he knew how to write quick-paced dialogue, how to draw out a scene, and how to capture in short strokes the quirks of his characters. His lessons were welcomed and enthusiastically applauded by the mass theatre-going audiences of the 1850s, 1860s, and 1870s who looked around with increasing despair at the immorality of their governments (and of the royal family, above all), and at the corruption of the burgeoning shopkeepers, businessmen, and nouveau riche landowners who seemed to control Spain. Tamayo's *Lances de honor* ("Disputes of Honor," 1863) and *Los hombres de bien*

("The Upright Men," 1870) confirmed his view of Spain's need for moral regeneration.

Four of Adelardo López de Ayala's most interesting high comedies, *El tejado de vidrio* ("The Glass Roof," 1856), *El tanto por ciento* ("The Percentage," 1861), *El nuevo don Juan* ("The New Don Juan," 1863), and *Consuelo* (1878), deal with similar concerns. Of these, perhaps *El tanto por ciento* and *Consuelo* are the most revealing. The former intensifies the conflict between honorable behavior and money, a constant preoccupation with writers in the second half of the century, as we have seen. It was received with nearly unanimous enthusiasm and remembered by Galdós as one of Spain's modern theatre's most "transcendental" works; it clinched López de Ayala's election to the Real Academia Española. *El tanto por ciento* revolves – as did much of Spanish society – around the issue of who has money, who does not, who gets it, who will do what to whom to acquire more, and the consequences of having too much or too little of it. The action on stage concerns what we now call "white-collar crime": Roberto plots ways to swindle his childhood friend Pablo out of land he owns near Zamora, land through which Congress has approved a canal project; whoever owns the land is set to make substantial profits. Interestingly, the money exchanges are not limited only to the "monied" class, as here the servants also get into the act by buying shares in the proposed transaction from Roberto, with money they have managed to save up over the years. Money's ability to corrupt is, of course, Ayala's point (as he is putting the squeeze on Pablo, Roberto coldly states that friendship is one thing, business quite another) and he uses this plot mechanism as a metaphor for what he takes to be the gross materialism of mid nineteenth-century Spain. Still, he opts for a happy ending: whereas villains of the past might have suffered death, banishment, or humiliation, in these high *comedias* they suffer a fate worse than those – they suffer severe economic loss.

Consuelo weaves similar issues into its plot, which is laid out with Ayala's superb handling of dialogue, lyrical pauses, developed characters, convincing situations, and a clear moral vision of individual and social behavior. Consuelo, the play's eponymous heroine, needs to live the "good life," to compete with her peers for social prestige, and to participate in the money culture of the 1870s. She rejects one suitor, a man who truly loves her, for a rich and flashy businessman capable, presumably, of providing her with the finer things in life she craves. She is acquisitive, ambitious, and materialistic. Naturally, at the end of the play she is left without the man who loves her, without her husband, without her mother, her honor, or her self-respect, all because of her ambition to compete in a superficial, valueless society. Once again, she symbolizes what Ayala found most distasteful in the Spain of his day.

Gaspar Núñez de Arce, more applauded for his poetry than for his dramas, nonetheless contributed to the theatre of his day with plays such as *Deudas de la honra* ("Debts of Honor," 1863), *Quien debe paga* ("He Who Owes, Pays," 1867), and the play for which he is most remembered today, *El haz de leña* ("Kindling," written in 1870, premièred in 1872). *El haz de leña* has more connections to Romantic historical dramas than it does to the high comedy *per se*, but it still draws power from the author's look at contemporary society through the filter of the past.

Dozens of other playwrights competed for space in the country's theatres at mid-century and beyond. Most of them are totally (and perhaps unjustifiably) forgotten today, but they participated in a dynamic enterprise which enriched the literary world of the capital and beyond. Theatrical activity was so rich and so diverse, and it so fully captured the attention of Spanish society, that it might be claimed that it became the major site of mid and late nineteenth-century anxiety about what Spain was and what it was becoming. Many plays were purely escapist, of course, but most confronted serious issues in either serious or comic ways. The writing ranged from good to bad to awful, but the subjects dealt with reflected with amazing accuracy the tensions being felt and debated outside of the theatre, in the halls of government, in the pages of the newspapers, and around family dinner tables. Particularly in the period which ranged between the putative end of Romanticism in the 1840s to the rise of the Realist novel in the 1870s, the theatre took over as the major site of self-examination and self-criticism. The theatre struggled to define the identity of the Spanish middle classes, an identity marked by gender, nation, and economic interests.[3]

Among the lesser-known, but still popular household names of their day, are Narciso Serra (1830–1877), Luis de Eguílaz (1830–1874), and Mariano José de Larra's son, Luis Mariano de Larra (1830–1901). Their works share the accomplishments and characteristics of the high comedy, focusing on economic realities, moral posturing, middle- and upper-middle-class characters, and urban environments (predominantly Madrid). We remember, of course, that established playwrights such as Ventura de la Vega and Bretón de los Herreros were still writing major pieces for the theatre. A society in turmoil seethed beneath the surface of hundreds of plays written between 1850 and 1870 and beyond, but high comedy lost steam by the mid 1870s, when the theatre world welcomed new names that would dominate playwriting until the end of the century.

Barcelona had more theatres than Madrid (although Madrid had more seating capacity), so it is not surprising that much of the country's best pieces originated in the Catalan capital. Plays originally written and produced in Barcelona, often in Catalan, were translated immediately to Madrid's stages. Angel Guimerà (1845–1924), a contributor to the Catalan *Renaixença*, penned dozens of enormously successful dramas in his native language which drew on the metaphors and themes of Romanticism (by the second half of the century, following the impact of the dramas of Echegaray, this was now dubbed "Neo-Romanticism"). The lyrical emotion and Romantic passion of his first play, *Gala Placidia* (1879), captured the public's attention in what was described in the pages of the newspaper *El Heraldo de Madrid* (18 November 1891) as "la primera tragedia que figura en la literatura genuinamente catalana" ("the first tragedy of what can be called authentically Catalan literature"). It was *Mar i cel* ("Sea and Sky"), however, that sealed Guimerà's reputation as a respected, even beloved, dramatist; the play itself was seen not just as a regional – Catalan – play, but rather one of national standing, one of the best plays produced in the country in decades. Enrique Gaspar, another well-known playwright, translated it immediately into Spanish for performance in Madrid. *Mar i cel* embraced Romanticism, and from it poured forth a stream of heightened emotionalism, exalted love, tense conflict, sparkling lyricism, individual sacrifice, rhapsodic and melodic moments, and inevitable (Romantic) tragedy. Guimerà turned to more earthly concerns in *Terra baixa* ("Low Country") in 1898, a play again translated immediately into Spanish by yet another major playwright, José Echegaray (it was subsequently translated into a dozen other languages, including English as early as 1902). Compelling, powerful, and full of realistic detail and symbolic meaning, *Terra baixa* deals with the oppression of laborers by the Catalan oligarchy.

Other dramatists focused on gritty social themes in the second half of the century, most notably Sixto Cámara (1826–1862) in *Jaime el Barbudo* ("James the Bearded," 1853) and Fernando Garrido (1821–1883) in *Un día de revolución* ("A Day of Revolution," 1855). It was Eugenio Sellés (1842–1926) and Joaquín Dicenta (1862–1917) who managed to fuse dramas of revolutionary/social concerns with high comedy. Sellés' hit, *El nudo gordiano* ("The Gordian Knot," 1878), confronts women's issues, the time-worn theme of honor, and divorce. In *Las esculturas de carne* ("Statues of Flesh," 1883) he enters the nascent debate on Naturalism and suggests (as did Ibsen) that the sins of the fathers are indeed visited upon the sons. Dicenta's most enduring work, *Juan José* (1895), reflects, directly and indirectly, an awareness of the injustices perpetrated on the lower classes by those who rule society. This is hardly a new discovery, but Dicenta's flair for the structure and language of drama enabled him to articulate more clearly than many others the anger felt by the oppressed in a society judged by many to be unfair and unbalanced. The hero of the play, Juan José, is a simple man who merely struggles to work and make a living, protect his family, and find a place in society, yet he finds himself in conflict with a society that deprives him of those basic rights. The play immediately captured the public's attention and, similar to the case of *Don Juan Tenorio*, established itself as an annual ritual in Spain's theatres (but performed on International Workers' Day, 1 May, rather than All Soul's Day in November, the traditional date of the staging of the *Tenorio*). It was banned, protested, picketed, and criticized, but the basic truth of its message could not be ignored.

One of the most popular and notorious dramatists in Spain in the second half of the century is José Echegaray (1832–1916), whose powerfully melodramatic, Neo-Romantic plays dominated theatres for several decades. Wildly popular, yet scorned by critics both in his own time and today, Echegaray nonetheless mastered the art of writing interesting characters, compelling plots, and dramatic language. His enemies (Azorín called him "el viejo idiota" ["the old idiot"]) never forgave him for winning the Nobel Prize for Literature in 1904, a prize that many thought rightfully belonged to Galdós. As early as 1874 he produced hits – *El libro talonario* ("The Checkbook") and *La esposa del vengador* ("The Avenger's Wife") – which spoke to his public, Spain's upper middle class now fully in control of the social, economic, and political reins of power but still unsure about where that power would take them. He scorned his critics and aimed his plays at the bourgeois men and women who became his staunch defenders. His dramatic power is unquestionable and if at times his language threatens to overwhelm the spectator with high-pitched emotionalism, it nonetheless manages to reach deep into the emotional center of the audience in order to extract a nugget of truth or reveal a deeply hidden human secret. Tapping into Spain's theatrical history, he wrote plays such as *En el puño de la espada* ("At the Hilt of the Sword," 1875), which reminded audiences of Calderón's honor plays as well as the Romantic historical tragedies of Rivas, García Gutiérrez, or Zorrilla. He pushes the Romantic paradigm even further in *O locura o santidad* ("Insanity or Saintliness," 1877), in which he poses, in highly Romantic language, the question of when rationality becomes irrational, when sanity dissolves into insanity. His recognized masterpiece is *El gran galeoto* ("The Great Galeoto," 1881), a play that deals with society's obsession with gossip, jealousy, and suspected infidelity. Galeoto, the individual who served as intermediary between Lancelot and his lover in European legends, came to signify in Spain a person who sowed suspicion through gossip and innuendo; for Echegaray, Galeoto stood for the whole of Spanish society. Echegaray's breakthrough in this play was not the theme but rather the play's structure. While still full of hyperbolic Romantic language and situations, he nevertheless moves toward a pre-Pirandellian model (author-within-the-text).

He sets up a frame into which the real author of the text injects a fictional author who then presents the play he has "written" (this reminds us of Rivas' *El desengaño en un sueño* ["Disillusioned by a Dream"]); in addition, Echegaray includes a prose prologue (the play itself is written in verse) that presents the case study of the play and his own (that is, Echegaray's) *ars poetica dramatica*. The work we see on stage is putatively the one written by the main character, Ernesto. The play's dénouement is tragic and powerful since the play's real villain – malicious gossip – is formless and consequently the punishment must be visited on "real" characters, which is frustrating and unfair, but perfectly logical within the confines of the play itself.

Spain's major nineteenth-century novelist, Benito Pérez Galdós (1843–1920), began and ended his long career as a playwright. As early as 1861, when he was just eighteen years old, Galdós began penning plays, and produced four of them – *Quien mal hace, bien no espera* ("Whoever Does Wrong Should Expect Nothing Good," 1861), *El hombre fuerte* ("The Strongman," 1863–1865), *La expulsión de los moriscos* ("The Expulsion of the Moors," 1865), and *Un joven de provecho* ("A Useful Kid," 1867) – before publishing his first novel, *La Fontana de Oro* ("The Golden Fountain") in 1870. He was as concerned with the quality of Spanish theatre as he was with the state of the novel, and throughout his career he returned again and again to the theatre as a form of artistic expression. He wrote theatre criticism for the newspapers. In his memoirs he remembered: "Mi vocación literaria se iniciaba con el prurito dramático . . . Invertía parte de las noches en emborronar dramas y comedias . . . Respirando la densa atmósfera revolucionaria de aquellos turbados tiempos, creía yo que mis ensayos dramáticos traerían otra revolución más honda en la esfera literaria" ("My literary vocation began with a strong dramatic itching . . . I spent part of my evenings scribbling dramas and comedies . . . Breathing in the dense revolutionary atmosphere of those turbulent times, I thought that my dramatic pieces would bring on another, deeper revolution in literary circles".)[4] His plays were frequently original, often polemical, and in general they were received with alternate doses of praise and scorn, and his reputation as a dramatist declined as his well-deserved fame as a novelist increased.

Galdós wrote two dozen plays, scores of articles of theatre criticism, and his novels are infused with an interest in the theatre. He rejected what he thought of as the facile emotionalism of Echegaray's new Romanticism, and turned instead to the new wave of European dramatists such as Ibsen, Chekov, Hauptmann, and Maeterlinck, whose main characters tended to

4 Benito Pérez Galdós, *Obras completas*. 8 vols. Ed. Federico Carlos Robles (Madrid: Aguilar, 1966), vol. VII, pp. 1430–1431.

think, react, and contemplate rather than scream and shout, gesture, and faint. His dramas contained equal doses of content and form, ideas and technique, and thematically he pursued large social issues rather than individual or intimate matters (the nature of Reality, the search for Truth, the evil of corruption, the need for the regeneration of Spain, the failure of religious education, the evils of hypocrisy, the power of the clergy). The plays are dense, intellectual, and thoughtful, and offer a stark contrast to the hyper-emotionalism of Echegaray. In *Realidad* ("Reality," 1892), Galdós approached the theme of truth and honor, but he resolutely refused to resolve the conflict by recourse to the traditional blood vengeance, which was supposed to "wash" clean a man's stained honor. Rather than give his audience what they expected – blood, passion, and excitement – he dramatized man's marrow and soul rather than his hormones and blood. It is a drama of interiority that marks the subtle shift in Restoration Spain to a more modern sensibility, which the audiences did not entirely understand or appreciate. His critics (who were many) failed to recognize that the conflict Galdós develops in this complex and problematic play is a deep psychological one rather than the superficial blood-and-guts inheritance from the past. It is full of technical innovation, carefully modulated confrontations, stately dialogue, and well-crafted language. Only later was it recognized as a pathbreaking model of "modern" theatre. Other plays followed – *La loca de la casa* ("The Madwoman of the House," 1893), *Gerona* (1893), *La de San Quintín* ("That San Quentin Woman," 1894), *Los condenados* ("The Condemned," 1894), *Voluntad* ("Willpower," 1895), *Doña Perfecta* (1896), *La fiera* ("The Shrew," 1896) – but it was the première of *Electra* in 1901 that made theatre history.

The public and critical reception of *Electra* astonished even those who knew Galdós to be a controversial writer: it ran for 80 consecutive nights in Madrid, another 180 in Paris, 32 in Rome, and provoked an avalanche of commentary in the newspapers. Its first printing sold 30,000 copies in one month. *Electra* was a broadside against intolerance and fanaticism, Spain's mendacious clergy, and the country's refusal to enter the modern scientific world. The young heroine of the play, Electra, became a symbol for Spain in Galdós' mind – undereducated, immature, exposed to dark forces, and in need of liberation – and onto her he projected his hope for a future guided by truth, personal freedom, and scientific objectivity. In the play she is infantilized by fanatical preachers who want to enslave her and reduce her to some sort of angelical object. The battle for Electra's soul (for Spain's soul) between the forces of fanaticism and modern scientific progress (represented in the figure of Máximo) is ultimately won by Máximo, which reveals Galdós' optimism in 1901 that the goal to reform society is not merely a noble one, but also one that can be achieved.

One of the most notable, and not to be forgotten, characteristics of Spanish nineteenth-century drama is its penchant for parody, satire, and slapstick. High Art became, naturally, the subject of literary discourse, theatre criticism, and the educated elite, but lowbrow comedies populated (some would claim overran) the Spanish stage, particularly after mid century. As might be expected, one of the major targets of parodic writers was the hyperbolic and sometimes overblown rhetoric of Romantic dramas, perhaps easy targets for playwrights looking for some laughs. As early as the 1830s, that is, during the height of Romanticism's popularity on the stage, Bretón penned plays which contained spoofs of the exaggerated language and actions of Romantic plays; two examples are *Todo es farsa en este mundo* ("The Whole World's a Farce," 1835) and *Muérete ¡y verás!* ("Die, and Then You'll See!" 1837). Antonio García Gutiérrez even lampooned his own immensely popular *El trovador* in a play called *Los hijos del tío Tronera* ("Uncle Tronera's Children") in 1846, less than ten years after the première of the original. Later, *Venganza catalana* ("Catalan Revenge," 1864) was barely on stage when two spoofs appeared, the first by one of the most prolific parodists of his day, Juan de Alba (fl. 1840–1882), as *La venganza de Catana* ("Catana's Revenge," 1864) and the other by the Catalan writer Frederic Soler as *La venganza de la Tana* ("La Tana's Revenge," 1864). Dozens of examples abound, but without a doubt the most frequently parodied play in the nineteenth-century canon was Zorrilla's *Don Juan Tenorio*. As this work gradually took its place as one of the key plays, if not *the* key play, of the Spanish nineteenth century, imitations, parodies, and "appropriations" of it appeared in such profusion that they became a veritable cottage industry for authors and impresarios for nearly a century following its debut in 1844.[5] While the titles and authors do not necessarily concern us here, it was an important literary phenomenon because it responded to deep impulses stemming as much from Zorrilla's marvellous theatricality as from its religious and social message; it became the property, in a sense, of the society. Every Spaniard came to know Zorrilla's text, or rather, certain moments of it, and that familiarity engendered an intimacy between the spoken or written word and those who heard it or read it. It settled into what we might call the collective consciousness of Spain, and reappeared in a startling number of literary forms throughout the century. Literature began not only to imitate and reflect life, but also to influence it, and *Don Juan Tenorio* entered into a dialogue with playwrights and audiences which on the one hand stretched the parameters of Zorrilla's text while on the other enriched each successive reading of the original.

---

[5] Jeffrey T. Bersett, *El burlado de Sevilla. Nineteenth-Century Theatrical Appropriations of Don Juan Tenorio* (Newark, DE: Juan de la Cuesta Press, 2003).

As the century came to a close, or rather, as the new century dawned, parodies still found a home on Spanish stages (Galdós' controversial play *Electra* became *Electroterapia* at the hands of Gabriel Merino [1860–1903] in 1901), but the thrust and direction of the theatre began to change as new visions and new dramatists took control of the country's stages. Looking back over the century, the theatre tells a tale of dynamic and frequently contentious activity, impressive volume (more than 15,000 plays were written, published, staged, and reviewed over the years), and often memorable quality. Spanish theatre was rich, problematic, and intimately linked to the social and political life of the country. Still, large areas of it remain unexplored and awaiting future study.

31

Poetry in the second half of the nineteenth century

MARÍA ÁNGELES NAVAL

The kind of poetry written during the second half of the nineteenth century – dominated by Gustavo Adolfo Bécquer (1836–1870), Ramón de Campoamor (1817–1901), and Gaspar Núñez de Arce (1832–1903) – tended to be Romantic, and its possible development into modern poetry was affected by the moral, esthetic, and ideological limitations of Spanish Restoration society, a society that was antirevolutionary, at times ultra-Catholic, and almost always idealistic. Poetry was considered to be a mixture of philosophy and science, even though it remained within a didactic realm, as Russell Sebold has indicated in the case of Ramón de Campoamor's "lecciones de realidad" ("lessons in reality").[1] Sebold begins his article on a poet frequently thought of as "Realist" by affirming that Campoamor is not a Realist at all. Still, the term "Realist" has been used by Jorge Urrutia[2] and Marta Palenque[3] to describe the poetry written between 1850 and 1900. Urrutia argues for "materialist" content in poetry of Gustavo Adolfo Bécquer in order to indicate the impact of Realism on his verse. At the other end of the spectrum, Joaquín Marco has commented on the difficulty inherent in considering Campoamor's famous short poem "El tren expreso" ("The Express Train," 1872) as Realist, and proposed viewing the author as a poet more allied with the Spanish Restoration.[4] Bécquer generally appears in Spain's literary history linked to Romanticism, while Campoamor, the author of *Doloras* ("Aches"), has been seen as part of an anti-Romantic reaction.

It is difficult to define Realist poetry in this period, even if it is done in a fashion as provisional and methodological as that proposed by Urrutia: "La poesía realista es la que se escribe entre el final del romanticismo y

This chapter has been translated from the Spanish by Matthieu Raillard.

[1] Russell P. Sebold, "Sobre Campoamor y sus lecciones de realidad." In *La perduración de la modalidad clásica. Poesía y prosa de los siglos XVIII a XIX* (Salamanca: Ediciones Universidad, 2001), p. 268.

[2] Jorge Urrutia, *Poesía española del siglo XIX* (Madrid: Cátedra, 1995).

[3] Marta Palenque, *El poeta y el burgués (poesía y público, 1850–1900)* (Seville: Alfar, 1990).

[4] Joaquín Marco, "El tren expreso y el falso realismo de Campoamor." *Revista de Literatura* 23 (1963), pp. 107–117.

la aparición de la poesía moderna: nuevos planteamientos del 98, modernismo, vanguardia" ("Realist poetry is the poetry written between the end of Romanticism and the arrival of modern poetry: the new problems raised by the generation of 98, Modernism, the vanguard").[5] In reality, Romanticism does not disappear in 1849 with the publication of Fernán Caballero's novel, *La gaviota* ("The Seagull"); on the contrary, it is more reasonable to view what we call Realism as one of the basic components of Romanticism. What is Romanticism if not the perception of contrasts between reality and the ideal and the analysis and artistic interpretation of that reality? Critics have sought, in vain, dates and clues that would clearly mark the end of Romanticism. In 1837 Campoamor published an article that has been given undue importance as heralding the beginnings of an anti-Romantic reaction ("Acerca del estado actual de nuestra poesía" ["Regarding the State of Today's Poetry"] *No me olvides*, 10 December 1837). A close reading of this article, however, shows that, instead of rejecting the new literature, Campoamor joins the ranks of conservative Romanticism, since he invokes Calderón and displays his patriotic and nationalist spirit, all the while favoring a sentimental kind of Romanticism. He rejects truculent Romanticism and its more juvenile aspects, along with the new dress styles and antisocial behavior associated with it. The same attitude was apparent when Mesonero Romanos wrote in that same year in the *Semanario Pintoresco* his article "El romanticismo y los románticos" ("Romanticism and the Romantics"). These supposedly anti-Romantic articles belong in the same ideological context and are noted for their need to define a literature that is both new and national. The same could be said for Martínez de la Rosa's *Poética* ("Poetics," 1831).

At the other end of the political spectrum one finds in Mariano José de Larra's article "Literatura" ("Literature"), written in January of 1836, a veritable manifesto for liberal Romanticism. Campoamor and Larra share, without the latter knowing it, a preoccupation with renovating poetic language. Larra said, in 1836: "Ahora bien, marchar en ideología, en metafísica, en ciencias exactas y naturales, en política . . . y pretender estacionarse en la lengua que ha de ser la expresión de estos mismos progresos, perdónennos los señores puristas, es haber perdido la cabeza" ("Now, going forward in ideology, metaphysics, in exact and natural sciences, in politics . . . and standing still with the very language that is the expression of these same advances, with all due respect to the purists, is to have lost our mind"). Campoamor, in his article from *No me olvides*

[5] Jorge Urrutia, "El camino cerrado de Gaspar Núñez de Arce." *Anales de Literatura Española de la Universidad de Alicante* 2 (1983), p. 492.

presented what would become the crux of his poetics: poetic language should be a faithful reflection of reality, precise in its use of adjectives and loyal to scientific observations of reality.

Another text that has been viewed as marking the end of Romanticism is Juan Valera's essay "Del romanticismo en España y de Espronceda" ("On Romanticism in Spain and On Espronceda," 1854), in which he demonstrates preoccupations of a Romantic nature with respect to the ballad and national literature. These preoccupations are still relevant after the articles of Larra, Campoamor, and Mesonero. In 1867, Ventura Ruiz Aguilera, author of *Los ecos nacionales* ("National Echoes," 1849), published *La Arcadia moderna. Colección de églogas e idilios realistas y de epigramas* ("Modern Arcadia. Collection of Eclogues, Realist Idylls and Epigrams"). In using the label "Realist," Ruiz Aguilera is not moving against Romantic esthetics, but rather that of classicism: "Las dríadas y hamadríadas, las potamides y neliadas, las nereidas y napeas discurren por las cimas del parnaso como sombras de un mundo muerto, a las que el actual, que presume de piadoso, no dejará de conceder sepultura para *in eternum*" ("The Dryads and Hamadryads, the Potamides and Neliads, the Nereids and Napeas dwell amongst the peaks of Parnassus like shadows of a dead world, shadows that the real world, in an effort to appear faithful, cannot abandon and put to rest forever" [vii]). To be in agreement with the Romantic character of these idylls and Realist eclogues, the author of *Ecos nacionales* thus proclaims that the social duty of the poet "ahora como siempre, se inspira además de en los sentimientos personales, en los sentimientos, en las ideas, en las costumbres y en los intereses generosos de su época, y, heraldo del porvenir, marcha delante de la columna de fuego que alumbra el camino de la humanidad" ("now, as always, is inspired by more than personal emotions, emotions, ideas, by the customs and interests of his time, and as herald of the future, walks ahead of the column of fire that sheds light on the path of humanity" [xi]). Even though not as programmatic, this text does not differ much from the end of Larra's article, in which he proclaimed his support for a true and useful literature, capable of encompassing all of human experience as well as the realities of science: "una literatura hija de la experiencia y de la historia y faro por tanto del porvenir, estudiosa, analizadora, filosófica, profunda, pensándolo todo, diciéndolo todo en prosa, en verso" ("a literature born from experience and history, a beacon for the future, studious, analyzing, philosophical, profound, reflecting on and saying all, in prose, in verse"). We find a period of Romantic evolution in which liberal Romanticism faces its conservative counterpart, and in which the manifestations in favor of Realism, the representation of reality, and the incorporation of language and new scientific reality are viewed as being anticlassicist.

Literary polemics of the Restoration period: the end of lyric poetry

The clash between conservatives and liberals is in evidence in the literary polemics of the Restoration.[6] The traditionalist Pedro Antonio de Alarcón defended, in his entrance speech to the Real Academia Española in 1877, didactic art, while at the Ateneo, Manuel de la Revilla, a liberal with Republican tendencies, declared his support for art for art's sake. Barely hidden within these polemics on Realism and Naturalism is an ideological debate. The status of lyric poetry and its possible inferiority to prose inspired Gaspar Núñez de Arce to write on the topic in his speech entitled *Del lugar que corresponde a la poesía lírica en la literatura moderna y juicio acerca de algunos de sus más preclaros cultivadores* ("The Place of Lyric Poetry in Modern Literature and an Evaluation of Some of its Most Eminent Cultivators," 1887). Leopoldo Alas "Clarín" also addressed the topic in *Folletos literarios IV. Mis plagios. Un discurso de Núñez de Arce* ("Literary Pamphlet IV. My Plagiarism. A Speech by Núñez de Arce," 1888). These publications touch upon a theme which concerned not only Spaniards, and posed a fundamental question: faced with the new reality of science and progress, should poetry remain distant from the present and, with time, disappear completely? Melchor de Palau proposes that poetry should ally itself with science and become an expression of a natural and material reality, newly underscored by science. He put this new alliance into practice in his book *Verdades poéticas. La poesía y la ciencia. A la geología. El rayo. El polo ártico* ("Poetic Truths. Poetry and Science. To Geology. The Ray. The Arctic Pole," 1881). Joaquín María Bartrina offers another point of view[7] in his book *Algo* ("Something," 1876). This poet, in accordance with the ideas of Núñez de Arce, and using Bécquer-style rhythms, writes in the poem "De omni re scibili":

> ¡Todo lo sé! Del mundo los arcanos
> ya no son para mí
> lo que llama misterios sobrehumanos
> el vulgo baladí . . .
> Mas ¡ay! que cuando exclamo satisfecho:
> ¡todo, todo lo sé!
> siento aquí en mi interior, dentro mi pecho,
> un algo . . . un no sé qué!

---

[6] M. López, "Los escritores de la Restauración y las polémicas literarias del siglo XIX en España." *Bulletin Hispanique* 81 (1979), pp. 51–74.

[7] José-Carlos Mainer, "Del corazón y la cabeza: sobre la poesía de Joaquín M. Bartrina." In *Pensamiento y literatura en España en el siglo XIX. Idealismo, positivismo, espiritualismo.* Toulouse: Presses Universitaires du Mirail, 1998, pp. 110–122.

(I know it all! Of this world secrets / are no longer to me / what are called supernatural mysteries / by a trivial layman . . . / But, ah, when I exclaim with satisfaction: / All, I know it all! / I feel within me, within my chest, / something . . . something I don't know!)

This contradictory relationship with positivism and science in general arises from a Romantic feeling of loss. Federico Balart, poet and literary and art critic, in his essay *El prosaísmo en el arte* ("Prosiness in Art," 1893) reflected on Romanticism, Naturalism, and the relation between scientific knowledge and creation: "si el arte pudiera morir, el prosaísmo reinante sería su postrera enfermedad" ("if art could die, the prosiness that reigns today would be its last disease").

Authors, works, and poetic genres

If we are to identify different moments in the poetry of the second half of the nineteenth century, the first would come as a result of the conservative backlash against liberal Romanticism that took place toward the middle of the century (1850–1854) and that translates in poetry as a type of sentimental Romanticism, represented by poets who should be regarded as predecessors to Bécquer, although inferior to him (José Selgas, Antonio Arnao and Antonio de Trueba) and also inferior to other Bécquer-inspired contemporaries such as Augusto Ferrán, author of *La soledad* ("Solitude," 1861), or Arístides Pongilioni, author of *Ráfagas poéticas* ("Poetic Gusts," 1865). Another key factor is the political instability of the period between 1868 and 1874. This shift is in evidence in *Gritos del combate* ("War Cries," 1875) by Gaspar Núñez de Arce. In his aforementioned 1887 speech, one finds a reference to "suspirillos germánicos" ("Germanic sighs"), directed not at Bécquer but rather at the overly sentimental authors mentioned above suspected of having been too heavily influenced by German Romanticism. However, Núñez de Arce, a revolutionary in 1854 and 1868, and an enemy of the Republic, found himself in 1874 amongst the supporters of the Bourbon Restoration of Alfonso XII and never again would be counted among the more progressive elements of the political spectrum led by Antonio Cánovas del Castillo (followers, for example, of Ruiz Zorrilla or Castelar). As would be the case with Espronceda and other liberal-progressive writers between 1836 and 1842, Núñez de Arce struggled with the contradictions and the evolution of Spain's liberal bourgeoisie: he shied away from revolutionary ideals. Due to this, Núñez de Arce would, as did Campoamor – albeit in a less politically compromised manner – document and define in his verses the limits of this bourgeoisie, whose moral horizon was becoming saturated with displays of anguish or religious doubt provoked by the *miasmas del siglo* ("miasmas of the century"): science, positivism, and materialism. The moral abyss created by reason and a possible lack of religious beliefs is accompanied in *Gritos del combate* by attacks leveled at Darwinist and scientific philosophies, as well as at bloody revolution, all the while defending family, law, and the importance of voting rights.

Ensconced within this panorama of bourgeois Romanticism are a few poetic styles that begin to acquire a distinctive personality: the sentimental style represented by Bécquer and his followers; the sententious, prosaic and narrative poetry of Campoamor; and the classicist style, one branch of which is seen in the patriotic and Quintana-inspired poetry of Núñez de Arce, and the other, more purist branch, in the poetry of Juan Valera, Gabriel García Tassara, and even Marcelino Menéndez y Pelayo. These tendencies never amounted to specific poetic movements, much less anti-movements; we note, for example, that Núñez de Arce's narrative poems draw in significant ways from the *Pequeños poemas* ("Small Poems") of Campoamor.

Juan María Díez Taboada described the evolution of Romantic poetry around the middle of the nineteenth century: composition of literary fables, a renewed interest in popular poetry and song, and finally the confluence of this popular trend with the influence of imported German texts such as the translations of German authors, in particular those of Heinrich Heine (1797–1856).[8] In the years that separate the publication of Campoamor's *Fábulas orijinales* ("Orijinal [*sic*] Fables") and Augusto Ferrán's *La soledad*, one can begin to note a Romantic poetry of a sentimental vein, with a more symbolic form, one that precedes Bécquer and implies the influence of certain elements of German Romantic poetry. This new slant becomes more concrete with subsequent publications. *La primavera* ("Spring," 1850) by José Selgas, begins to convert the fable into a literary apology ("apólogo"). In *Ecos nacionales* Ventura Ruiz Aguilera unites patriotic poetry with a historical theme and popular lyric expression. The critic Juan María Díez Taboada considers this work a book of ballads, an antecedent to the more popular-styled works of Ruiz Aguilera (*Armonías y cantares* ["Harmonies and Ballads," 1865]).[9] Another definitive text that demonstrates this new tendency is *El libro de los cantares* ("The Book of Songs," 1852) by Antonio de Trueba, which contains glosses and notes on popular songs. Not to be forgotten are Antonio Arnao, Narciso Campillo, and, especially, Eulogio Florentino Sanz, who translated Heine in 1857. In his translations published in the newspaper *El museo universal* ("The Universal Museum"), one finds the rhythmic patterns that inspired some of Bécquer's most famous compositions: double quatrains,

[8] Juan María Díez Taboada, "El germanismo y la renovación de la lírica española en el siglo XIX (1840–1870)." *Filología Moderna* 5 (1961), pp. 21–55.
[9] Díez Taboada, "El germanismo."

combining ten- and seven-syllable lines, with a pronounced rhyme on the –í and –ú. The essays on the renovation of the fable by Campoamor and also by Juan Eugenio Hartzenbusch, as well as the cult of popular song, prepare the literary world for the arrival of the genres that would become characteristic of the poetry of the second half of the nineteenth century: represented by Campoamor's *Doloras* and Bécquer's *Rimas* (1871).

Ramón de Campoamor

Campoamor's first book, *Poesías de D. Ramón de Campoamor*, was published by the Liceo Artístico y Literario in Madrid in 1840, and only in 1847 would it receive the title *Ternezas y flores* ("Endearments and Flowers"), by which it is known. It is the 1846 *Doloras*, however, which is most indicative of his style. *Doloras* represented the arrival of a new lyrical style, brief and concrete not only in its subject matter but also in its philosophical content, a genre first practiced by Campoamor in his *Fábulas orijinales* in 1842. Campoamor owes much of his fame as a skeptical and lightly immoral poet – a facet which critics had already detected in *Ayes del alma* ("Sighs of the Soul") in 1842 – to *Doloras*.

> LAS DOS ESPOSAS
> Sor Luz, viendo a Rosaura cierto día
>   casándose con Blas,
> – ¡Oh, qué esposo tan bello! – se decía.
>   – ¡Pero el mío lo es más!–
> Luego en la esposa del mortal miraba
>   la risa del amor,
> y, sin poderlo remediar, ¡lloraba
>   la esposa del Señor!

(THE TWO WIVES. Sister Luz, upon one day seeing Rosaura / marrying Blas, / "Oh, what a handsome husband!-" she said. / "But mine is even more handsome!" / Later, she saw in the mortal's bride / the laughter of love, / and, unable to prevent it, / the Lord's wife cried!)

In 1872 Campoamor introduced yet another poetic genre in the first installment of the *pequeños poemas*. Like *Doloras*, *Pequeños poemas* generated great public acclaim and strong sales. The most famous of the *Pequeños poemas* is "El tren expreso":

> Habiéndome robado el albedrío
> un amor tan infausto como el mío,
> ya recobrados la razón y el seso,
> volvía de París en tren expreso.

(Having lost my free will / to a love as unfortunate as mine, / having recovered my mind and my reason, / I returned from Paris on the express train.)

The small poems represent an attempt to bring poetic language up to date, cleansing it of Romantic and classicist conventions. This desire for a direct poetic language, a poetry that could reflect reality, is present in Campoamor's oft-reworked *Poética* ("Poetics") from 1883, and has earned him the respect of writers like Luis Cernuda, José Luis Cano, Carlos Murciano, and Leopoldo de Luis. One must remember as well that Rubén Darío, in his magnificent chronicles of *España contemporánea* ("Contemporary Spain"), showed respect toward the decrepitude of Campoamor in his later years, and also expressed admiration for Núñez de Arce.

Campoamor invented his *Humoradas* ("Witticisms") in 1886, a style at once synthetic and sententious. In addition, he cultivated the style of the *Cantares* and wrote long poems, such as *Colón* ("Columbus," 1853) and *El drama universal* ("The Universal Drama," 1869), a poem which echoes the world view first put forth by Espronceda in *El diablo mundo* ("The Devil World," 1840).

Gaspar Núñez de Arce

Núñez de Arce began his literary career as a playwright (*Las cuentas del zapatero* ["The Shoemaker's Bills," 1859]), and by publishing chronicles of the African war in the newspaper *La Iberia* in 1860. His most famous play is *El haz de leña* ("Kindling," 1872). In 1875 he published the book of poems *Gritos del combate*, a title which refers to the political unrest of the time: General Prim's seizing of power, the revolution of 1868, the First Republic, and the upheavals of the Second Carlist War. In "Las arpas mudas" ("The Muted Harps," 1873) Núñez de Arce exhorts his colleagues to abandon lyric poetry until the current political turmoil has passed:

> ¡Poetas! Hasta tanto
> que la borrasca pase,
> colguemos nuestras arpas
> de los llorosos sauces.

(Poets! Until / the squall subsides, / let us hang our harps / from the weeping willows).

Núñez de Arce wrote extensive narrative poems. From these, those that best compare with *Pequeños poemas* are *Maruja* and *La pesca* ("Fishing"). Those dealing with spiritual themes are most characteristic of the author: *La visión de Fray Martín* ("Friar Martin's Vision"), in which he elaborates a monologue spoken by Martin Luther, and *El vértigo* ("Vertigo"), a poem which must be compared with "La duda" ("Doubt"), a poem representative of the moral limits of its author and his contemporaries. In this work he renounces the "musa del análisis" ("the muse of analysis"), and describes the moral and social decadence of the nineteenth century as well as the state in which he finds himself when facing such desolation:

> Noches de soledad, noches de hastío
> En que, lleno de angustia y sobresalto,
> Se agita mi ser en el vacío,
> De fe, de luz y de esperanza falto.

(Nights of solitude, nights of boredom / In which, full of anguish and fright, / My being quivers in the void, / I lack faith, light, and hope).

In *Raimundo Lulio*, *La última lamentación de Lord Byron* ("The Last Lamentation of Lord Byron"), *La selva oscura* ("The Dark Jungle"), and *¡Sursum corda!* he worked on the dramatic monologue. According to Norberto Pérez García, it is possible that his models were Alfred Tennyson and Robert Browning, but this type of exercise did not find followers in nineteenth-century Spain.

Among those who did pattern their work on that of Núñez de Arce we might include José Verlarde, author of the poem "La fe" ("Faith"), which serves as counterpoint to the aforementioned "La duda," and Emilio Ferrari, who in his acceptance speech to the Real Academia in 1905 still maintained the theoretical ideas of the poetry of the Restoration.

The poets of the Restoration – or perhaps it would be more precise to refer to the books of poetry published after Núñez de Arce's "La duda" (1868) and following the posthumous edition of Bécquer's *Rimas* – present an amalgam of special characteristics due to the incorporation and assimilation of three models: Campoamor, Núñez de Arce, and Bécquer. In these verses one finds themes derived from the Romantic taste for both the sublime and the macabre. Contemplation of the abyss opened by death continues to be one of the favorite themes for poets inclined to sentimental expression. Bécquer's *rima* LXXIII ("Cerraron sus ojos" ["They closed their eyes"]) has served, time and time again, as the model for new ways to write about a shop-worn Romantic theme. In Bécquer's poem we detect a specificity, an almost eschatological level of attention to the description of the physical aspects of death, and a simplification of verses. This theme was reprised by, among others, Ventura Ruiz Aguilera in "El dolor de los dolores" ("Pain of Pains"), and by José Selgas in "La sepultura de mi madre" ("My Mother's Tomb/Burial") or "La cuna vacía" ("The Empty Cradle") from *Flores y espinas* ("Flowers and Thorns," 1879). The explicitly Bécquer-styled *Flores de muerto* ("Flowers of the

Dead," 1887) by Luis Ram de Viu offers an extensive range of situations in which he evokes the physical aspects of the body, the cemetery and the tombs, the candles and the catafalque of the wake, even the interment of corpses and their exhumation. Much of the poetry of the Restoration was characterized by empty anguish and a yearning for the sublime.

Finally, we must consider the impact that French Parnassianism and Symbolism[10] may have had on the writers of the last third of the nineteenth century, and also seek to establish a continuity between the poetry of Campoamor and Núñez de Arce and that of the Modernists. Calvo Carilla considers that Campoamor's poetry pointed toward Symbolism, while Núñez de Arce's more toward Parnassian trends, although in both cases the movement is more evident in theory than in practice.[11] Roberto Mansberger stresses the fact that Núñez de Arce and others were aware of French Parnassianism and of the modern literature that we call *fin de siècle*.[12] He points out that within the literary landscape there was a rejection of these trends, not only from conservatives but also from more open individuals such as Clarín. If it is in fact true that the carefully crafted verse of Núñez de Arce confirms a certain degree of classical aspiration, his anguished fervor contradicts the coldness of Leconte de Lisle.

Gabriel García Tassara (1817–1875) was also concerned with the form and sound of verse, so much so that Pere Gimferrer later included him in his *Los raros* ("Oddities"). He wrote almost all of his poems during the Romantic period, but did not publish them until 1872. This diplomat from Seville writes in the prologue to these poems that he has always been "lo que ahora se entiende genéricamente por conservador" ("what is now generically considered to be a conservative"). A little later, he professes his support for the Neo-Catholic party and declares himself a devotee of rational, cosmopolitan poetry, one that intends to emulate "aquel otro movimiento del renacimiento clásico" ("that other Neoclassical movement") as a form of absolute and solemn protest on the part of "Europa tradicional y antepasada contra la Europa moderna y revolucionaria"

---

[10] Parnassianism and Symbolism were poetic continuations of nineteenth-century Romanticism whose subject matter echoed the intimate emotion and aesthetic concerns of earlier poets, but with key differences. Late nineteenth-century poets such as Charles Baudelaire (1821–1867), Paul Verlaine (1844–1896), Arthur Rimbaud (1854–1891), and Stéphane Mallarmé (1842–1898) refrained from excessive sentimentality, rhetoric, prosaic description, or political commentary in an effort to fuse imagination and sentiment in their verses.

[11] José Luis Calvo Carilla, "Reconsideración de la poesía española de la segunda mitad del siglo XIX (a propósito de Núñez de Arce)." *Boletín de la Biblioteca Menéndez Pelayo* 69 (1993), pp. 195–223.

[12] Roberto Mansberger, "Dos discursos restauracionistas en la crisis de fin de siglo: Gaspar Núñez de Arce y Emilio Ferrari." In *Estudios de literatura española de los siglos XIX y XX. Homenaje a Juan María Díez Taboada*. Ed. Francisco Aguilar Piñal *et al.* (Madrid: CSIC, 1998), pp. 282–292.

("traditional and ancestral Europe against modern and revolutionary Europe"). The political, philosophical, and social themes of his *Poesías* ("Poems") allow us to consider him a conservative Spanish Romantic, that is to say, one who harbors an abundance of what Sebold has termed "la modalidad clásica" ("the classical modality").

New authors had begun appearing by the end of the 1870s: Manuel Reina, *Andantes y allegros* ("Andantes and Allegros," 1877), *La vida inquieta* ("The Restless Life," 1894); Ricardo Gil *De los quince a los treinta* ("From Fifteen to Thirty," 1885); and Salvador Rueda *Camafeos* ("Cameos," 1897). These authors have allowed Katharina Niemeyer to suggest the existence of a premodernist stage of poetry in Spain.[13] However, as Richard Cardwell demonstrated in his introduction to *La vida inquieta* in 1978, these works remain grounded in the intellectual context of the Restoration.[14]

One also finds the emergence, during the Restoration, of poetic manifestations that conserve part of the archaeological, historical, and nationalistic spirit of Romanticism and that serve as a starting point for a more regionally inspired poetry: the Jocs Florals (poetry contests) were reinstated in Zaragoza, Barcelona, Sitges, Calatayud, and Salamanca, among other places. José María Gabriel y Galán, who won these Jocs in Salamanca in 1901, was a famous bard from Castille and Extremadura. Vicente Medina, in his *Aires murcianos* ("Murcian Airs") includes, in addition to local themes, linguistic traits of local dialects. This trend would culminate in the so-called "pure" (*castizo*) forms of *modernismo* that already belong to the literary context of the *fin de siècle*.

---

[13] Katharina Niemeyer, *La poesía del premodernismo española* (Madrid: CSIC, 1992).
[14] Richard Cardwell, "Introducción." In *Manuel Reina. La vida inquieta* (Exeter: University of Exeter, 1978), pp. 1–43.

Part VII

The Modern, Modernismo, and the Turn of the Century

Lou Charnon-Deutsch, Joan
Ramon Resina, Nil Santiáñez,
Richard A. Cardwell, C. A. Longhurst,
Nelson R. Orringer

32

Nineteenth-century women writers

LOU CHARNON-DEUTSCH

Nineteenth-century Spanish women writers were hampered by limited access to the means of production coupled with a reigning attitude that a woman's mission was to service and strengthen the family unit by working within the confines of the domestic sphere. Yet despite the fact that they largely embraced the conservative and nationalist ideology of their era, a substantial number of women were sufficiently ambitious to establish their literary reputation even when faced with hostile writing environments. According to Íñigo Sánchez-Llama, early and mid nineteenth-century women writers were not as marginalized as we imagine them to be today; especially those who embraced the reigning Neo-Catholic ideology were able to participate fully in Spanish popular culture ushered in by the expansion of the literary magazine and book trade.[1] This is because Isabeline society, unlike that following the revolution of 1868, held a less "virile" notion of writing that permitted the canonization of a substantial group of writers whose piety, patriotism, and virtue were above reproach. If they are ignored and misunderstood today it is partially because of the rejection of their Neo-Catholic ideology by the generations that followed them. Nevertheless, publishing success both before and after the 1868 revolution implied a delicate balance between professionalism and the celebration, or at least acknowledgment, of the dominant sexual ideologues who looked askance at women's careers in the public sphere. Women seeking validation as writers commonly launched their careers by writing lyric poetry, a mode of expression, according to Susan Kirkpatrick, that afforded greater latitude than prose in which to voice dissatisfactions and desires and which consequently played a significant role in modernizing Spanish society by allowing women to constitute themselves as public figures.[2] Among the women poets, Carolina Coronado (1823–1911), Gertrudis Gómez de Avellaneda (1814–1873), Rosalía de Castro (1837–1885), Josefa Massanés (1811–1887), and Angela Grassi (1823–1883) excelled, largely adapting Romantic

---

[1] Íñigo Sánchez-Llama, *Galería de escritoras isabelinas* (Madrid: Cátedra, 2000).
[2] Susan Kirkpatrick, "Modernizing the Feminine Subject in Mid-Nineteenth-Century Poetry." *Revista de Estudios Hispánicos* 34.2 (May 2000), p. 413.

models to redefine feminine sexuality as complementary to that of men.[3]

With an expanding print industry and growing literacy, especially in the urban centers of Barcelona and Madrid, women prose writers by mid century were also performing significant cultural work, often to the enhancement of the ideological model of femininity dubbed "the angel of the house" by Bridget Aldaraca and Alicia Andreu.[4] As Jo Labanyi has cogently argued, the splitting of the public sphere from the private zone of the home effectively excluded women from participation in civil society,[5] simultaneously putting the domestic sphere under closer scrutiny as its ideal contours became more distinguishable. In its transition to modernity bourgeois society successfully propagated the notion of the family's importance in creating good citizens, and this codification of family life spawned a number of surveillance strategies designed to monitor its health. Women journalists participated fully in this monitoring through the publication of conduct books or advice columns published in installments in the increasingly popular women's magazines such as *Instrucción para la Mujer* ("Woman's Instruction"), *El Ángel del Hogar* ("The Domestic Angel"), *La Mujer* ("Woman"), *El Album del Bello Sexo* ("Album of the Fair Sex"), *Correo de la Moda* ("Fashion News"), *El Pensil del Bello Sexo* ("Garden of the Fair Sex"), *La Educanda* ("The Pupil"), *La Violeta* ("The Violet"), and the very important *Ilustración de la Mujer* ("Women's Illustrated"), a rigorous and influential magazine of the Restoration period in which some of the most prominent women writers of the day collaborated.[6] The success of this feminine press and its influence in shaping the social and moral values of many classes of women cannot be overestimated. In contrast, women writers in general did not gain access to the theatre, and those who did – Gómez de Avellaneda, Enriqueta Lozano de Vilches (1830–1895), Rosario de Acuña (1851–1923), and a handful of others – have been largely "excommunicated" from literary histories.[7]

Well into the 1870s women novelists also took seriously their responsibility as moral beacons for their readers by publishing lives of model

---

[3] Susan Kirkpatrick, *Las románticas. Women Writers and Subjectivity in Spain, 1835–1850* (Berkeley: University of California Press, 1989), p. 289.

[4] Bridget Aldaraca, *El ángel del hogar: Galdós and the Ideology of Domesticity in Spain* (Chapel Hill, University of North Carolina Press, 1991); Alicia Andreu, *Galdós y la literatura popular* (Madrid: Sociedad General Española de Librería, 1982).

[5] Jo Labanyi, *Gender and Modernization in the Spanish Realist Novel* (Oxford: Oxford University Press, 2000), p. 55.

[6] A more complete list can be found in María del Carmen Simón Palmer, *Escritoras españolas del siglo XIX. Manual bio-bibliográfico* (Madrid: Castalia, 1991), pp. 815–824.

[7] David T. Gies, *The Theatre in Nineteenth-Century Spain* (Cambridge: Cambridge University Press, 1994), p. 192.

women, conduct manuals on wifely duties, and treatises on the best ways to mold the family into the emerging bourgeois ideal.[8] When women writers "veered from the enabling Romantic tradition and allowed the constraining angel of the domestic woman to enter into their homes,"[9] they did not suddenly abandon sentimentality and devotion to Romantic ideals, rather they examined those sentiments and ideals within the prism of a domestic sphere which they themselves were newly fashioning as a safe haven from a corrupt society, or, more commonly, as a space under siege from encroaching civilization. While the lyric poetry of Coronado and others explored the frustrations of the feminine writing subject, the novel provided a more substantive platform for examining the trials and tribulations of domestic life, reflecting public debates about the complementary nature of men and women so dear to the Krausists.[10]

In this category, the novels of Cecilia Böhl de Faber (1796–1877), Rosalía de Castro, and Gertrudis Gómez de Avellaneda played a key, though differing, early role during a period that has been characterized by critics as devoid of significant national literature when in fact, as Alda Blanco argues, it was a "cultural moment in which far-reaching discourses (literary and otherwise) were established and elaborated."[11] All three novelists depicted women who were crushed by overwhelming domestic and economic burdens. For example, following the model of Mary Wollstonecraft's *A Vindication of the Rights of Woman* (1792), Avellaneda's *Sab* (1841) negotiated the pressure points and limits of ideal femininity by equating the marriage contract with feminine subjugation.

---

[8] Examples include: María del Pilar Sinués de Marco's *El ángel del hogar* ("The Angel of the House," 1859) and *La misión de la mujer* ("Woman's Mission," 1886); Gimeno de Flaquer's *La mujer española, estudios acerca de la educación* ("Spanish Woman, Studies on Education," 1877), and *Evangelios de la mujer* ("Sermons for Women," 1900); Angela Grassi's primers for mothers and newlyweds such as *El ángel del hogar* ("The Angel of the House," 1874), and *El primer año de matrimonio* ("The First Year of Marriage," 1877); Faustina Sáez de Melgar's *Deberes de la mujer* ("Woman's Duties," 1866), *Un libro para mis hijas* ("A Book for My Daughters," 1877), and *Epistolario manual para señoritas* ("Epistle for Young Ladies," 1877); Joaquina García Balmaseda's *La madre de familia* ("Mother of the Family," 1860), *La mujer laboriosa* ("The Hard-Working Woman," 1876), and *La mujer sensata* ("The Sensible Woman," 1882) – to name but a few.

[9] Alda Blanco, "Domesticity, Education and the Woman Writer: Spain 1850–1880." In *Cultural and Historical Grounding for Hispanic and Luso-Brazilian Feminist Literary Criticism.* Ed. Hernán Vidal (Minneapolis: Institute for the Study of Ideologies and Literature, 1989), p. 372.

[10] Followers of the German philosopher Karl Christian Friedrich Krause (1781–1832) whose ideas exerted immense influence on educational theories in late nineteenth-century Spain. Among these men were Julián Sanz del Río (1814–1869) and Francisco Giner de los Ríos (1839–1915). See Juan López-Morillas, *The Krausist Movement and Ideological Change in Spain, 1854–1874.* Tr. Frances M. López-Morillas (2nd. edn. Cambridge: Cambridge University Press, 1981).

[11] Alda Blanco, "Theorizing the Novel at Mid-Century." *Revista de Estudios Hispánicos* 34.2 (May 2000), p. 423.

Handily appropriating the then popular antislavery rhetoric, she endowed her heroines Carlota and Teresa, like the real slave Sab who served them, with superior sensitivity and capacity for altruism. All three characters wear the "chains" that bind them to the world of a ruthless, white male mercantilism. *Sab*'s antislavery, antimarriage rhetoric has been interpreted as a departure from mid-century fictions in which the "angel of the house" ideology predominated. What it shared with conventional women's fiction, however, was the conviction that civilization was entering into a period of decline and that the reward for suffering could only be secured in the next life. Truly, the domestic fiction of this era is an exploration of delayed rewards and imbalances, unfulfilled desires and making do. What it is not, quite obviously, is an uncritical celebration of domestic bliss. For example, just as for Avellaneda's Carlota, the heroines of Rosalía de Castro's *La hija del mar* ("Daughter of the Sea," 1859), *Flavio* (1861), and *Ruinas* ("Ruins," 1864) discover that the home can be a terrifying place where no amount of feminine virtue guarantees an escape from corrupting civilization that contaminates the relationship between men and women. The connection between civilization, male domination, and sexual exploitation, so often woven into women's fictions of this period, provokes an unusually angry outburst in the narrator of *La hija del mar*, who, echoing the concerns of many women novelists, admonishes future rulers of the world to rethink the meaning of civilization:

Hombres que gastáis vuestra vida al fuego devorador de la política; jóvenes de ardiente imaginación y de fe más ardiente; almas generosas que tantos bienes soñáis para esta triste Humanidad: pobres ángeles que Dios manda a la Tierra para sufrir el martirio, no pronunciéis esas huecas palabras "¡civilización, libertad!": no, no las pronunciéis; mirad a Esperanza y decidme después qué es vuestra civilización, qué es vuestra libertad.

("You men who waste your lives in the devouring fires of politics; youths of ardent imagination and even more ardent faith; generous souls who dream so much good for this sad Humanity: poor angels whom God sends to this earth to suffer martyrdom, do not pronounce those empty words "civilization, liberty!": no, do not pronounce them; look at Esperanza and then tell me, what is your civilization? What is your liberty?")

It has often been remarked that more than any other early novelist, Cecilia Böhl de Faber (known as Fernán Caballero) embodies the contradictions of a woman who has striven for a public voice only to use it to champion traditional feminine virtues that best serve women in the domestic sphere. More conventional in her concept of liberty and civilization than either Castro or Avellaneda, Böhl de Faber established in all her fictions a link between domesticity, sexual normalcy, and women's earthly punishments and rewards. When the pursuit of a career, for example, tempts some heroines to place personal satisfaction above family duty, the results are disastrous for both the woman so bold as to dream of a profession and the family she forsakes. A popular example is the ambitious María of *La gaviota* ("The Seagull", published in 1849 although written decades earlier) who dreams of becoming an opera singer. Her rise to fame and subsequent fall into oblivion when she loses her voice demonstrate Böhl de Faber's rejection of the Romantic stereotype of the passionate Spanish woman unsuited to the duties of family life.[12] Despite Böhl de Faber's conservatism, however, her novels were important for their attention to women's decision-making. While in *La gaviota* and *La familia de Alvareda* ("The Alvareda Family," 1849), the link is established between domesticity, sexuality, and punishment/reward, in *Clemencia* ("Clemencia," 1852) the problems of love, marriage, and wifely duty intersect and are amply explored in relation to a woman's happiness and sense of achievement. By allowing women characters to explore their options in a much more self-determined way, Böhl de Faber, like her contemporaries, acknowledged the relationship between agency and desire. If happiness can be lost through blindness and unrestrained passion as in *La gaviota* or *La familia*, it can also be earned through judicious decision-making during the critical moments of a woman's life. Despite its saccharine morality, *Clemencia* is a tribute not only to patience and prudence, but also to the importance of allowing a woman to reach decisions about her future alone and unadvised, with only reason and the lessons of experience to guide her.

The preoccupation with domesticity did not wane in the decades leading up to and following the 1868 revolution. As more women gained access to the burgeoning publishing industry and especially as the Realist novel began enacting anxieties about the separation between the private and public spheres, the number of novels that championed or challenged the new domestic ideology and women's relation to the social fabric increased. In general these novels are critical of political, economic, and social modernization and insistent on women's maternal attributes that "naturally" relegated them to the private sphere where they nevertheless played an indispensable role as shapers of an ethos of service. Any critique of domestic fiction, consequently, has to recognize that even the most dogmatic and conservative novels are imbued with a deep sense of urgency about what it means to be and to survive as a woman in a society where neglect and poverty are the norm. At a time when men writers, who today count as the scions of the nineteenth-century canon, dominated literary production, hundreds of women writers struggled to define spaces where male

---

[12] José B. Monleón, "Estrategias para entrar y salir del romanticismo (*Carmen* y *La gaviota*)." *Revista Hispánica Moderna* 53 (2000), p. 19.

power may have held sway but where feminine sensibility, refinement, and affiliations were prized instead of denigrated or trivialized. These, now largely ignored, women writers instilled in their readers a sense of self-worth that was sometimes lacking in the works of their male colleagues. Critical rejection of the sentimentality of this writing perpetuates the misunderstanding of the reality in which they participated meaningfully and of the still undetermined effects of this writing on large segments of even the illiterate urban population.

Novelists writing in the decades of the 1860s–1880s, notably Faustina Sáez de Melgar (1833–1895), Concepción Gimeno de Flaquer (1852–1919), Angela Grassi (1823–1883), and María del Pilar de Sinués (1835–1893), most successfully addressed the domestic angel's rewards or consolations, as well as her duties and sacrifices. Not only immensely popular during the period they were written, many of Sinués' novels were re-edited in the last decades of the century and continued to enjoy a wide readership into the twentieth, even as women's domestic roles were being renegotiated. Just as the conservative Sinués de Marco followed in the footsteps of the ultra-traditionalist Böhl de Faber, a more emancipated, but by no means radical, Emilia Pardo Bazán (1851–1921) was influenced by the widely read narratives of Sinués de Marco that explored women's domestic roles in every conceivable context.[13]

It would be a mistake to dismiss this domestic fiction as mere fanfare for conservative domestic ideology. True, these novels do focus very strongly on a problematic concept of the "natural," and therefore desirable, gender roles of a very hierarchical nature: the manifest goal of most domestic fiction, with its glorification of subservience to children and spouse, to the sick and needy, is to teach women always to put the needs and desires of others before their own. It is women who ought, for the sake of brothers, husbands, and fathers, as well as society as a whole, to be self-sacrificing, nurturing, humble, and long-suffering. For the heroines of domestic literature, suffering is a necessary prelude to satisfaction and women must learn to make the best of things even in the face of extreme hardship, so in a way the masochism associated with the domestic novel is a kind of Pragmatism that was more realistic in its approach to women's issues than we

---

[13] For example, Bazán's little studied *Una cristiana* ("A Christian Woman," 1890) and its sequel *La prueba* ("The Test," 1890) are worthy successors to the dozens of Sinués de Marco's domestic novels of earlier decades, among them: *La amiga íntima* ("The Intimate Friend," 1857), *El sol de invierno* ("Winter Sun," 1863), *La senda de la gloria* ("The Path to Glory," 1863), *Una hija del siglo* ("A Daughter of the Times," 1873), *La mujer en nuestros días* ("The Woman of Today," 1878), *La abuela* ("The Grandmother," 1878), and *La expiación* ("Expiation," 1886). These titles represent only a small portion of the approximately seventy-five novels, essay collections, conduct books, and biographies published during her lifetime or posthumously. Today, however, Sinués de Marco's works have been all but forgotten and, like those of Gimeno de Flaquer, Grassi, and Sáez de Melgar, are difficult to access.

commonly concede. Furthermore, in overcoming adversity, women protagonists often develop a keen sense of self-worth and strength, and many, in the process, learn to survive in a world devoid of the Krausist ideal of a supportive, responsible, hardworking spouse that seems strikingly absent from most women's literature. Unlike classic feminine rescue fantasies, as some of these novels admittedly are, many depict a strong feminine presence capable of rescuing men from the evils of modern civilization with its crass materialism (Pardo Bazán's *La prueba*), poverty (Sinués de Marco's *La senda de la gloria*), or atheism (Gimeno de Flaquer's *El doctor alemán* ["The German Doctor," 1880]), through heroic self-sacrifice and ability to withstand adversity. Countless stalwart heroines demonstrated the then widely popular notion that women were the nobler half of humanity whose mission was to elevate men's sentiments. On the other hand, women tempted to flaunt conventional family arrangements by working outside the home, taking a lover, or prostituting themselves were punished with silence, isolation, loss of talent, abandonment, or imprisonment in the strictures of childrearing and housekeeping for which they were, as gender misfits, singularly unsuited.

Though certainly not unique in exploring the darker side of domestic arrangements, the Restoration period fiction of Emilia Pardo Bazán stands out not so much for its challenge to the ideal of the domestic angel, but for its insistence that earth-bound angels can only thrive if men are domesticated alongside them. Pardo Bazán's second novel, *Viaje de novios* ("The Honeymoon," 1881), begins where some (although by no means the majority) of sentimental fictions end, with the marriage of an "angel" who here makes the terrible mistake of marrying a man who is lacking a sense of family solidarity. Going a step further in her most famous novel, *Los Pazos de Ulloa* ("The Ulloa Manor-House," 1886), she paints the heroine Nucha's "home" as a gothic torture chamber where a cruel, uncivilized husband contrasts with the feminized chaplain whose most thrilling moments are spent in the nursery caring for the heroine's daughter. What stands out in Pardo Bazán's fiction is that Civilization is not understood as an unproblematic category to be embraced or rejected wholesale as was the case for many of the preceding generation, rather it holds out the promise of a more just society where men and women can be educated to become better companions.

While all of Nucha's feminine powers are inadequate to the task of "civilizing" her untamed husband, the more educated and resourceful Fe of Pardo Bazán's *Memorias de un solterón* ("Diary of a Bachelor," 1896) marries the bachelor Mauro Pareja after he morphs into the ideal "pareja" ("partner") by becoming her perfect complement. Influenced by John Stuart Mill, whose *The Subjection of Women* (1869) she greatly admired, Pardo Bazán here imagined a marriage contract based on the concept of different but equal partners in the joint enterprise that is the family. Instead of trying to change Fe's unconventional, rebellious character, Mauro allows himself to be molded into her ideal mate, able to recognize and encourage her intelligence, independence, and exceptional talents, but also willing to share her family's economic and emotional burdens. As a man of exceptional powers of observation, Mauro uncovers for female readers the hypocrisy of a male-dominated society, and, more astonishingly, he is willing to suspend all claims to superiority and proclaim that Fe is "su igual en condición y derecho" ("his equal in condition and rights"). Rather than gaining a master, as a husband is imagined in the feudal sexual relations of the period, by marrying him Fe will gain a brother, companion, and lover all rolled into one.

In the latter decades of the nineteenth century and proceeding into the twentieth, women writers began to experiment with characters who, unlike many heroines of the earlier domestic literature, want something more than to be wanted by men or to survive their absence or abuse. It is tempting to assume that, because so much women's literature was concerned with problems relating to the private sphere, women lacked interest in other social issues. In fact, many understood perfectly the contradictions inherent in the cult of domesticity, for example its social isolationism or its clash with patriotic idealism. An important element of feminine education, according to countless conduct manuals like the ones cited above, was the refinement of the notion of women's "natural" capacity for empathy. Responding in part to this century-long ideological project, many women were particularly receptive to the problems of the poor and understood the injustices of the unequal distribution of wealth which they tentatively explored in their essays, novels, plays, and stories. Concepción Arenal, for example, is remembered as one of the most important nineteenth-century reformists, working tirelessly for prison reform and other working-class and women's causes. Freethinker Rosario de Acuña, one of the few successful women playwrights of the late century, explored class conflict in her historical drama *Rienzi el tribuno* ("Rienzi the Tribune") produced in 1876. The anticlerical hero of Acuña's *El padre Juan* ("Father John," 1891) wants to transform a religious shrine into a spa to care for the sick and poor, reflecting "new socialism's desire to reform and transform society through social engineering."[14] Similarly, Adelaida Muñiz y Mas' *El pilluelo de Madrid o Los hijos del pueblo* ("The Little Rogue from Madrid or the Sons of the People," 1893) registers the playwright's dissatisfaction with class stratification. Novelist Dolors Monserdà i Vidal's zeal for working women led her to support the unionization of women textile workers and to incorporate the problems of the

---

[14] Gies, *The Theatre*, p. 210.

working classes in her 1904 novel *La fabricanta* ("The Manufacturer"), echoing the sentiments expressed earlier in Sáez de Melgar's *Rosa la cigarrera* ("Rosa the Tobacco Worker," 1872) and Pardo Bazán's *La Tribuna* ("The Tribune," 1882).

It would be an exaggeration to speak about a revolt against patriarchy by the century's end. Yet turn-of-the-century women writers were clearly more open to questioning the wisdom of subordination to a patriarchal family structure that was increasingly portrayed as alienating and even violent. Some late-century characters gain access to modern notions of individuality and successfully become agents of their own actions rather than mere appendages to husbands and fathers. Those who deviate from conventional roles, like Fe of *Memorias de un solterón*, are less likely to be punished for their rebellion. Some who are crushed by male violence, like La Mila of Albert i Paradis" *Solitut* ("Solitude," 1905), may opt for autonomy and solitude rather than the "chains" of a loveless marriage. A select few, like the sunstruck Asís de Taboada of Pardo Bazán's *Insolación* ("Sunstroke," 1889) even find a mate whose perfection lies in more earthly pleasures that have nothing to do with a comfortable income, an orderly household, and a houseful of offspring.

33

The Catalan *Renaixença*

Joan Ramon Resina

Although possibly inspired in the contemporary term *Risorgimento*, the name *Renaixença* derives from the title of a journal that, from 1871 to 1905, promoted the recuperation of the high-cultural uses of the Catalan language. As a period marker, the term refers to the nineteenth-century retrieval of Catalan culture after the long decline known to Catalan historiography as *La Decadència*. Pierre Vilar has called the *Renaixença* "a *new* datum, in the sense that *the* [Catalan] *language* . . . becomes once more a sign of the social group."[1] This is indeed the primary and, in retrospect, the decisive meaning of the term, which has come to signify the restoration of the cultural uses of the vernacular. Nevertheless, considering the class tensions that played themselves out in this process, the definition demands more precision. The *Renaixença* also represented the growing self-assertion of social groups whose recently achieved economic hegemony required cultural and historical legitimation.

While it would be simplistic to mistake the cultural and, above all, the linguistic reclamation for the political will that enlivened this process, it is true that the *Renaixença* consolidated the values of Catalonia's economic elite. It is not by chance that a latter-day politician like Jordi Pujol, who championed a comparable retrieval of Catalonia's language and political personality in the twentieth century, could assert that "Es difícil que la Renaixença, que anava fent el seu procés lentament, hagués pogut produir el canvi sobtadíssim en quantitat i en qualitat que hi va haver si no hagués tingut el suport d'una classe social i d'una economia creixents" ("Without the support of a growing social class and an expansive economy, it would have been difficult for the *Renaixença*, which advanced slowly, to produce the sudden change in quantity and quality that actually took place").[2] Pujol is undoubtedly right, although his "realism" begs questions about the values involved in the assertion of quality and even of quantity. The *Renaixença* would not have been the same without the support of the

---

[1] Pierre Vilar, "Procés històric i cultura catalana." In *Reflexions crítiques sobre la cultura catalana*. Ed. Pierre Vilar et al. (Barcelona: Departament de Cultura de la Generalitat de Catalunya, 1983), p. 38.

[2] Jordi Pujol, "Les quatre cares de Catalunya (1888–1988)." In *Quatre conferències: analitzar el passat per renovar el projecte* (Barcelona: Edicions 62, 1990), p. 59.

bourgeoisie, or, more to the point, without the ministrations and restraint introduced by that class. Nonetheless, had the bourgeoisie's sponsorship been lacking, and, especially, had the federal republic not been militarily overthrown with the acquiescence of that class, the *Renaixença* would have conveyed more radical values, precisely those favored by the federalist intellectuals who constituted its left wing.

At the origin of this federalist line of thought, and, incidentally, of Spanish *regeneracionismo*, was Antoni Puigblanch (1775–1841), a Romantic exile (he died in London) unaccountably forgotten by Spanish historiography. Puigblanch, author of an uncompromising attack on the Inquisition that brought him imprisonment and exile, was an early advocate of a peninsular confederal structure consisting of three sovereign states and leaving room for the eventual incorporation of Portugal. He was also the first to call for the co-officiality of the Basque and the Catalan languages, anticipating the apologetic affirmation of the vernacular in the speeches and writings of later *Renaixença* figures.

Puigblanch's critique of the Castile-centered monarchy influenced progressive liberals like Pere Mata (1811–1877), author of some poems in Catalan in the 1830s; Antoni Ribot i Fontserè (1813–1871), who in 1838 published poems in Catalan in the Romantic newspaper *El Vapor* (1833–1836); Pere-Felip Monlau (1808–1871), who introduced the pre-Marxian socialism of Fourier and Saint-Simon to Spain; and, especially, Abdó Terrades (1812–1856). A revolutionary leader and a writer of numerous political pamphlets, Terrades was the author of a satiric play against the monarchy, *Lo rey Micomicó* ("King Micomicó," 1838). In 1851, J. B. Guardiola published a critique of centralism in which he anticipated the modern concept of multinationality. Spain, he said, was not a nation but a cluster of nations. This progressive offshoot of the *Renaixença*, which for some time included the young Víctor Balaguer (1824–1901), culminated in Valentí Almirall (1841–1904), one of Spain's keenest political theorists of the left. Almirall was the founder of several publishing ventures: the Republican and anticlerical weekly *La Campana de Gracia*, the Madrid newspaper *El Estado Catalán*, and in 1879 the *Diari Català*, the first newspaper published in Catalan.

After the federal republic was overthrown in 1874, Almirall gave doctrinal expression to the need to reform the state from the periphery and formulated the principles that lie at the core of modern demands for decentralization and self-government. His major work, *Lo catalanisme* ("Catalanism," 1886), is the foundational text for the doctrine of particularism and a historical turning point for the consciousness of Catalanism. Almirall, who used the term *Renaixement* ("Renaissance") to distinguish his political (and positivistic) approach from the apoliticism of the *Renaixença* group, was the most lucid and stringent critic of the Spanish

Restoration. In a series of articles published in Paris in *La Revue du Monde Latin* ("Latin World Review") under the title "L'Espagne telle qu'elle est" ("Spain as it Really Is"), and subsequently issued as a book by Albert Savine in 1887, he remorselessly denounced centralism and the inherent abuses of the political class. Used as writer of the *Memorial de Greuges* ("Memorial of Grievances") delivered by a Catalan commission to King Alfonso XII in 1885, Almirall was later cast off by the compromising bourgeoisie. He remained, however, an important reference for future Catalanists, and a theoretical bridge between nineteenth-century regionalism and the full development of the national theses of the twentieth century.

The culturalist and largely apolitical *Renaixença* is conventionally dated from Bonaventura Carles Aribau's poem "A la pàtria" ("To the Fatherland," 1833). Aribau's well-known verses –

> Plau-me encara parlar la llengua d'aquells savis
> que ompliren l'univers de llurs costums e lleis,
> la llengua d'aquells forts que acataren los reis,
> defengueren llurs drets, venjaren llurs agravis.

(It still pleases me to speak the language of those wise men of yore / who filled the universe with their customs and laws, / the language of those strong men who obeyed their kings, / defended their rights, avenged their grievances.)

– stirred the dormant consciousness of Catalans with respect to their language, which toward the end of the eighteenth century Antoni Capmany (1742–1813) had considered "muerta hoy para la república de las letras" ("dead today for the literary republic"). Less than a nostalgic repository for memories of medieval Catalan grandeur, as is often averred, "A la pàtria" is a summons to mine the modern potential of the language: "It still pleases me . . ." The affirmation of the language's vitality is the key to the poem's success. For Aribau, who wrote the poem while living in Madrid, language merges with the fatherland. To speak or write in Catalan, to live one's culture in Catalan, undoes the physical distance (and assuages the nostalgia) that the poet establishes at the beginning of the poem: "Adéu-siau, turons, per sempre adéu-siau" ("Farewell, ye mountains, forever farewell"). For Aribau, however, and for many poets of the budding *Renaixença*, writing an occasional poem in Catalan was, in Oriol Pi de Cabanyes' words, "la inversió momentània de la pauta, una idealització compensatòria" ("the momentary inversion of the norm, a compensatory idealization [of the actual linguistic practices]").[3]

---

[3] Oriol Pi de Cabanyes, *Apunts d'història de la Renaixença* (Barcelona: Edicions del Mall, 1984), p. 20.

This wavering between the popular idiom and the official language of culture recalls the hesitancy of medieval texts between the lay culture in the vernacular and the written Latin culture of the Church.[4] There is, however, a crucial difference in this latter-day Renaissance. In the nineteenth century the dominant language was no longer the Church's but the state's, and the cultural hierarchy no longer ran along the vertical axis of the holy and the mundane but along the horizontal axis defined by center and periphery, between the culture of an imperial nation (Castile) and that of an erstwhile associate (the Catalan–Aragonese state) that had been subjected militarily in 1640 and 1714. Stripped of its historical franchises after the War of Succession (1705–1714), Catalonia had also been deprived of the educational and religious uses of its language through the "Decreto de Nueva Planta" ("Decree of New Foundation") in 1716. Against this background of political subjugation, the cultural emphasis of the *renaixentistes* takes on a subtler meaning of resistance which did not escape many Castilian authors. The same is true for the Romantic historicism of authors like Pau Piferrer, who in 1839 published two volumes on Catalonia as part of his *Recuerdos y bellezas de España* ("Memories and Beauties of Spain").

Literature and history as a struggle for representation rather than revolutionary zeal characterize this composed strategy of self-repossession. In his presidential address of the Jocs Florals ("Floral Games") of 1864, Joan Cortada (1805–1868), author of historical novels in Spanish and of a series of newspaper articles on the history of Catalonia, "Catalonia y los catalanes" ("Catalonia and the Catalans," 1860), cautiously asserted: "A les lluites polítiques han succeït les lletrades, als crits de guerra lo dolç cant dels trobadors, a les interjeccions d'ira les suavitats de la poesia; mes en lo *fondo* d'unes i altres, sempre s'hi descobreix l'amor a la pàtria, sempre l'entusiasme, sempre l'ardor per mantenir ben altes les glòries catalanes" ("Literary contests have superseded political struggles, war cries have been displaced by the sweet song of the troubadours, the expression of rage by the gentleness of poetry; ultimately, however, at the bottom of each of those alternatives one can always discern the love of the fatherland, the enthusiasm, the zeal to exalt Catalan glories").[5]

The literary *Renaixença* delegated politics to cultural producers in a symbolic gesture that was perfectly understood by the hegemonic power. Valentí Almirall observed that "Es característico que los dirigentes madrileños al no poder impedir estas manifestaciones de la vida

---

[4] Hugo Kuhn, "Esbozo de una teoría de la literatura medieval alemana." In *La actual ciencia literaria alemana*. Trans. Hans Ulrich Gumbrecht and Gustavo Domínguez León (Salamanca: Anaya, 1971), p. 166.

[5] Joan Cortada, "Discurs presidencial dels 'Jocs Florals' de Barcelona de 1864." *Catalunya i els catalans* (Barcelona: Edicions 62, 1965), p. 85.

regional, se han impuesto la consigna de hacer el vacío en torno a ellas, consigna escrupulosamente obedecida por todas las camarillas" ("Typically, Madrid leaders, unable to prevent these manifestations of regional life, have issued the password, which is scrupulously adhered to by all power cells, to cold-shoulder them").[6]

Founded in 1859 with the sponsorship of Barcelona's town council, the Jocs Florals became the *Renaixença*'s emblematic ritual. Ostensibly a revival of the poetry contests held in medieval courts, the Jocs endowed modern Catalan with its first "institution." Deeply implicated in their promotion were Joaquim Rubió i Ors (1818–1899), Víctor Balaguer, Antoni de Bofarull (1821–1892), and Josep Lluís Pons i Gallarza (1823–1894). Rubió, who published numerous poems in Catalan under the pseudonym Lo Gayté del Llobregat ("Llobregat's Bagpiper"), was the first nineteenth-century poet to write assiduously and exclusively in the vernacular. His pseudonym also named the poetry collection he published in 1841, in whose prologue he anticipated Cortada's idea of literature as symbolic compensation for political dependence:

Catalunya pot aspirar encara a la independència; no a la política, puix pesa molt poc en comparació amb les demés nacions, les quals poden posar en lo plat de la balança a més de lo volumen de sa història exèrcits de molts mils hòmens i esquadres de cent navios; però sí la literària, fins a la qual no s'estén ni se pot estendre la política de l'equilibri.

(Catalonia may still aspire to independence; not political independence, because it weighs too little in comparison to the other nations, which can place on the scale not just the volume of their history but also armies of many thousands of men and hundreds of battleships. But it can aspire to literary independence, which is not, nor can it be, comprised of the politics of the balance of power.)

In that very prologue Rubió condemned self-repression, the unmistakable sign of a colonialized consciousness among a dominated people. Remembering the Catalans who fought and fell for their freedom in 1714, he deplored the contrast offered by the generation of his own day, who "ingrats envers sos avis, ingrats envers sa pàtria, s'avergonyeixen de que se los sorprengue parlant en català com un criminal a qui atrapen en lo acte" ("ungrateful to their forefathers, ungrateful to the fatherland, are ashamed to be seen speaking Catalan like a criminal caught in the act").

Rubió's fluvial pseudonym caught on like wildfire, and a plethora of landscape singers appeared on the Catalan scene. Víctor Balaguer, who is better known for his Romantic *Historia de Catalonia y de la Corona de Aragón* ("History of Catalonia and of the Crown of Aragon,"

---

[6] Valentí Almirall, *España tal como es.* Trans. Rosario Fernández-Cancela (Barcelona: Anthropos, 1983), p. 192.

1850–1863), a work from which other poets drew their subject matter, also wrote poetry under the pseudonym "Lo trobador de Montserrat" ("Montserrat's Troubadour"). One of the *Renaixença*'s most emblematic figures was the Mallorcan Marià Aguiló (1825–1897), who launched the Catalan revival in the Balearic islands and promoted its development in Valencia as well. Aguiló was an early champion of the cultural and historical community known today as the "Països Catalans" ("Catalan Lands").

The narrow association of the *Renaixença* with poetry was broken in 1862 with the publication of Antoni de Bofarull's *L'orfeneta de Menàrguens o Catalunya agonitzant* ("The Orphan Girl from Menàrguens or Catalonia in Agony"), a historical novel and the first work of fiction in modern Catalan. Bofarull's work appeared against the background of a copious production of historical novels in Spanish by Catalan authors. It was on the stage, however, that the vernacular reached wide audiences. Víctor Balaguer was the author of *Tragèdies* ("Tragedies," 1876) and *Noves tragèdies* ("New Tragedies," 1879). The unquestioned master of the Barcelona theatre, however, was Frederic Soler (1838–1895), who under the pseudonym "Pitarra" held large audiences captive with low-key comedies in which he parodied the Romantic penchant for medieval themes, satirizing the stilted language of the poets associated with the Jocs Florals. Dreading the theatre's effectiveness in normalizing the use of the vernacular, the government responded with a royal decree in 1866, forbidding the exclusive use of Catalan on stage. Every play staged in Catalonia had to include at least one Spanish-speaking character in the script. Authors responded (to the relish of their audiences) by casting the obligatory Spanish speakers as criminals, authority figures, or military characters, figures that could easily be lampooned. Joan Mañé i Flaquer, editor of the *Diario de Barcelona*, explained in 1893 that this linguistic constraint had been instigated by Spanish writers who feared that the growing popularity of Catalan plays might affect their own incomes.[7]

During the Restoration, literature in Catalan approximated European standards. What had been tentative and incipient matured and reached a degree of formal perfection. Three names represent this achievement: Jacint Verdaguer (1845–1902), Àngel Guimerà (1845–1924), and Narcís Oller (1846–1930).

Verdaguer was Spain's most cultivated poet of the nineteenth century. His epic poem, *L'Atlàntida* ("Atlantis," 1877), is an attempt to render in verse the geotectonic forces involved in the formation of the Iberian peninsula as well as the vanishing of a primal world. *Idil·lis i cants místics*

---

7 Josep Maria Poblet, *Catalunya, 1833–1913: una panoràmica amb el teatre i els Jocs Florals* (Barcelona: Editorial Pòrtic, 1969), p. 69.

("Idylls and Mystical Chants," 1879) is a collection of delicate religious poems inspired by Ramon Llull and Saint John of the Cross. In 1886 he returned to the narrative poem in *Canigó*. Choosing the northern slopes of the Pyrenees as the setting, and invoking medieval legends, Verdaguer conceived his poem as a national epic. The last verses are a dialogue between the bell towers of two romanesque churches that have been on the French side of the border since Catalonia's partition at the Treaty of the Pyrenees in 1659. The final stanza affirms the endurance of creation (and by implication, of the nation) as against the transience of history. Borders come and go, states are made and unmade, but the source of a people's character, says Verdaguer, is beyond both natural disaster and human animosity:

> Lo que un segle bastí, l'altre ho aterra,
> mes resta sempre el monument de Déu;
> i la tempesta, el torb, l'odi i la guerra
> al Canigó no el tiraran a terra,
> no esbrancaran l'altívol Pirineu.

(What one century built up, another century knocks down, / but God's monument remains forever; / and storms, tornados, hatred and war / will not bring down Mount Canigó, / nor lop off the lofty Pyrenees.)

Àngel Guimerà, winner in 1877 of the three awards in the Jocs Florals, a feat that made him "mestre en gai saber" ("master in gay science"), became Catalonia's finest nineteenth-century playwright. A belated Romantic, Guimerà wrote historical tragedies and popular pieces in the tradition of the *tableaux vivants*. He owed his fame, however, to his rural plays: *Maria Rosa* (1894), *La festa del blat* ("The Harvest Festival," 1896), and above all his popular *Terra baixa* ("Low Land," 1897), culminating in *La filla del mar* ("The Daughter of the Sea," 1900). In 1895, he delivered the presidential address at Barcelona's literary and cultural center, the Ateneu, in Catalan. This was the first time anyone did so, and Guimerà's decision caused a commotion but established the practice. From then on, the official use of Catalan in the Ateneu was interrupted only during the twentieth-century dictatorships, when the Catalan language was once again persecuted. Guimerà's work was translated into over a dozen languages, and he was nominated for the Nobel Prize in 1904. His candidacy, however, lacking the support of the Spanish government, could not prosper.

In the area of prose narrative, after the success of historical novels such as Bofarull's *L'orfeneta de Menàrguens*, readers turned to the *tableau* or the article of manners. In his *Aigoforts* ("Etchings," 1892), the Mallorcan Gabriel Maura (1844–1907) distanced himself from the suave vision of other writers of contemporary customs – called *costumistes* – like Emili Vilanova (1840–1905), the chronicler of Barcelona's working-class Ribera district at a time when its traditional life was disappearing under the city's industrial growth. In the Catalunya-Nord (the region the French call Pyrenées Orientales), Carles Bosch de la Trinxeria (1831–1897) published several Realist novels toward the turn of the century, the most memorable of which is *L'hereu Noradell* ("The Noradells' Heir," 1889). Other novelists worthy of note are Martí Genís i Aguilar (1847–1932) and Josep Pin i Soler (1842–1927). Genís tried to overcome stale typicality through the psychological description of characters in novels like *Julita* (1874) and *La Mercè de Bellamata* (1878). More successful is the work of Pin i Soler, especially his distinguished novel *La família dels Garrigues* ("The Garrigues Family," 1887), first part of a trilogy which also includes *Jaume* (1888) and *Níobe* (1889).

The great novelist of the period was Narcís Oller. The French translation of his first novel, *La papallona* ("The Butterfly," 1882), included a flattering prologue by Émile Zola. In *L'escanyapobres* ("The Miser," 1884) Oller studied the process of capitalization, sketching the passion of the money hoarder in the context of industrialization. He next expanded his study of social transformation in *Vilaniu* (1885) and in his master work, *La febre d'or* ("Gold Fever," 1890–1893), a novel about the Stock Exchange and the boom times leading to the crisis of 1886 and the Barcelona World Exposition of 1888. This work was followed by *La bogeria* ("Madness," 1898), a masterful depiction of the mental degradation of a psychopath, whose decline is linked, in Naturalist fashion, to hereditary causes. His last novel, *Pilar Prim* (1906), is a psychological novel about a woman's erotic passion amid social constraints. Its central theme is the clash between desire and bourgeois calculation, a typical *modernista* motif.

The éclat of modern Catalan literature against the grain of great social and political pressures could not have been achieved without a degree of self-reflexivity. Produced at the same time as the literary works outlined above, a stream of articles, speeches, and essays expounded the meaning of the *Renaixença*. Beginning with Félix Torres Amat's inaugural *Memorias para ayudar a formar un diccionario crítico de los escritores catalanes* ("Memoranda for the Compilation of a Critical Dictionary of Catalan Writers," 1836), which laid the foundations of historiographic work on Catalan literature, nineteenth-century Catalan writers could rely on a gradually more refined analytical tradition, culminating in the criticism of Josep Yxart (1852–1895). Yxart, one of the finest nineteenth-century critics in Spain, anticipated reception theory and the idea of interpretive communities: "Per a mi la poesia . . . evoca, desperta, fa vibrar quelcom que porta ja en si qui llegeix . . . En tota obra d'art resideix un valor relatiu, que està més en lo subjecte que en l'objecte" ("In my opinion poetry . . . evokes, arouses, sets aquiver something that is already present in the reader . . . Every work of art contains a relative value, which resides in the subject rather than in the object").[8]

---

[8] Josep Yxart, "Lletra a N'Albert Savine" (1884). In *Entorn de la literatura catalana de la Restauració.* Ed. Jordi Castellanos (Barcelona: Edicions 62, 1980), p. 24.

34
Great masters of Spanish Modernism

NIL SANTIÁÑEZ

Durées and family resemblances of Modernism

As literary terms, *modernismo* and *modernista* entered into the language of writers, artists, and critics at the turn of the nineteenth century. It is commonly believed that Rubén Darío, in 1888, was the first to speak of *modernismo*. It was also at the *fin de siècle* that a significant number of Spanish poets and novelists renewed Spanish letters by producing literary texts deeply influenced by Parnassianism, Symbolism, Pre-Raphaelitism, and decadentism. Some literary critics of that period and many scholars thenceforth have placed this heterogeneous group of innovative writers and their texts under the labels of *modernismo* and *modernista*.

Although many contemporary scholars take for granted that *modernismo* was a syncretic literary movement, at the turn of the century it was still unclear just what *modernismo* was. In an article published as early as 1901, José María Nogués complained that *modernismo* had become an omnibus term, likening it to a prism: all optical illusion with no substance. Writers and critics were so baffled that in 1907, the editors of the journal *El Nuevo Mercurio* ("The New Mercury") decided to conduct a survey aimed at reining in a term as polysemic as *modernismo*. Ramón María del Valle-Inclán, Miguel de Unamuno, Eduardo Chávarri, Ramiro de Maeztu, Ernesto Bark, and Manuel Machado, among many others, defined *modernismo* from very different perspectives and at times in contradictory ways. There has never been complete agreement on the characteristics, origins, or time period of *modernismo*. In describing *modernismo*, the aforementioned critics, and others, observed any number of the following: *modernismo*'s aestheticism and syncretism; its employment of symbolist, decadent, and/or Parnassian techniques and themes; its renewal of and attention to literary form; its search for new modes of expression; *modernismo* as the culture and literature of the modern age; its subversive and oppositional attitude toward the establishment; *modernismo* as the essence of literature itself (an idea developed years later by Paul de Man[1]); and *modernismo* as a synonym of modernity.

---

[1] Paul de Man, "Literary History and Literary Modernity." In *Blindness and Insight* (2nd. edn. Minneapolis: University of Minnesota Press, 1983), pp. 142–165.

These and other traits of *modernismo* would reappear, many years later, in Hispanic and Anglo-American criticism devoted to the study of *modernismo* and Modernism. The turn-of-the-century Spanish debates over *modernismo* therefore anticipated, by several decades, those that took place in literary scholarship in Great Britain and the United States. Given that *modernismo* and Modernism share practically the same semantic field, the English term will be used in what follows.

It is not possible to determine an "essence" of Modernism, or to define it precisely; nor is it adequate to limit the term to the ways it was understood by those who participated in it. Just as we do not reduce "Realism" to what Realist authors of the nineteenth century understood it to mean, we should conceive of Modernism in operative terms that surpass the meanings, at times contradictory and vague, that were given to the term at the turn of the century or after. Wittgenstein's concept of "family resemblances" provides the basis for building a fruitful and pragmatic understanding of Modernism beyond the persistent limitations of Spanish literary historiography dedicated to the analysis of Modernism and of *fin-de-siècle* literature. This chapter will look at some of the most important family resemblances of Modernism in novels and plays: experimental and dislocated language, dissolution of personal identity, spatial form, preponderance of discourse over story (style over plot), tendency toward parody, metaliterature (literature which comments on or refers to literature), emphasis on the multiple meanings of the linguistic sign, religious skepticism, philosophical speculation, distancing from the communicative function of language, employment of multiple or limited narrative voices, perspectivism (the belief that reality is knowable only from the perspective of the individual or group witnessing it at any given moment), relativism (the denial of the existence of an absolute truth and the corresponding view that knowledge is relative to the limitations of the mind and to the perspective of the act of knowing), epistemological uncertainty, unreliable narrators, mixing of genres, and the demand that the reader take an active hermeneutic role.

This morphological description should be complemented by a study of the historical variations of the different families of Modernism. This could be achieved by applying Fernand Braudel's well-known temporal model to literary history.[2] Braudel understood time as plural. History consists, according to him, of a multiplicity of rhythms and of at least three temporal levels (*durées*): a short time span, or a history of events; a conjunctural time span, or a history of social, cultural, and economic conjunctures; and a *longue durée* (long time span). In a *longue durée*, the historical tempo

---

[2] Fernand Braudel, *Ecrits sur l'histoire* (Paris: Flammarion, 1969).

flows slowly. *Longue durée* structures span centuries. Their values, almost immutable throughout an entire historical period, make of *longue durées* the most profound level of history on which the two previous *durées* are built. The historian will therefore convey, from multiple narrative angles, the dialectics between the different temporal strata history is made of. Braudel's model could provide a vision of Modernism, and by extension of any literary problem, that overcomes the chronological limits imposed by literary history, which generally studies periods of short time span and/or conjunctural time span. The linear and discontinuous literary history has proven incapable of seeing continuities between works distanced from each other in time that share a similar poetics. The intertwining of the family resemblances and *durées* of Modernism provides us with the following three-part working hypothesis.

(1) A Modernism of a short time span: in this time period one would look at works commonly associated with the Spanish- and Latin-American modernist movement, published from the end of the nineteenth century through the first decade of the twentieth century. One would have to add to this list a series of novels written by the authors of the so-called "gente vieja" ("old school"), such as *Su único hijo* ("His Only Son," 1890) and *Cuesta abajo* ("Downhill," 1890–1891), both by Leopoldo Alas; *Una cristiana-La prueba* ("A Christian Woman – The Test," 1890), by Emilia Pardo Bazán; and *La incógnita* ("The Unknown," 1889), by Benito Pérez Galdós. The renovation of literary forms was carried out by a group of contemporary writers. The fact that they belong to different chronological generations should not impede their being designated part of the same movement of formal and thematic innovation, that is, among the families of turn-of-the-century Modernism.

(2) A Modernism of a historical conjuncture: in this case, the temporal boundaries would extend from the last twenty years of the nineteenth century until the Civil War of 1936. Within this period, different Modernist families coexist: turn-of-the-century Modernism; the Modernist works of Gabriel Miró, Ramón Pérez de Ayala, and Miguel de Unamuno published in the 1910s and 1920s; and finally, Ramón Gómez de la Serna, José Martínez Ruiz ("Azorín"), Ramón María del Valle-Inclán, Benjamín Jarnés, Enrique Jardiel Poncela, and Rosa Chacel, the most distinctive novelists of the Spanish Avant-Garde.

(3) A Modernism of *longue durée*: as regards the Modernist prose in its time span, it can be said that it is born with *Don Quijote* (1605, 1615). The main traits and techniques of *Don Quijote* are obviously Modernist, for instance its overlapping of narrative voices, its epistemological relativism, metaliterature, the importance of the act of reading in the novel, and the embodiment of literature in Don Quijote and other characters.

The Modernist prose inaugurated by *Don Quijote* continues with *Fray Gerundio de Campazas* (1758, 1768), turn-of-the-century Modernism, the Avant-Garde, and with the experimental prose that, in the post-Civil-War period, was cultivated primarily following the publication of *Tiempo de silencio* ("Time of Silence," 1962).

I shall examine here the literature of some of the great masters of Spanish Modernism in a conjunctural time span: Ramón María del Valle-Inclán (1866–1936), Ángel Ganivet (1865–1898), Pío Baroja (1872–1956), José Martínez Ruiz (1873–1967), and Miguel de Unamuno (1864–1936).

Carnival, language, and politics in Valle-Inclán

Valle-Inclán's work is characterized by a radical search for expressive forms, a resulting revolutionary experimentation with language, and a deliberate heterodoxy with political and epistemological implications. In his writing, Valle acrimoniously criticized the political practices and social decadence of his age, especially dictatorships and militarism. Valle-Inclán's political dissidence went to such extremes that it is impossible to reduce his sympathies to one particular ideological position; in Valle-Inclán converge his early idealization of reactionary Carlism and the antifascism of his last years. The same is the case with his literary theory and practice: he never adopted one single type of literature, as he constantly innovated. Valle-Inclán erased the lines dividing literary genres and ended up creating a language of his own.

In his early years as a writer, Valle cultivated a refined symbolist and decadent prose absolutely opposed to Realism. The most remarkable achievement of that period is his masterful "Memorias del Marqués de Bradomín" ("Memoirs of the Marquis of Bradomín"), a tetralogy of novels made up of *Sonata de otoño* ("Fall Sonata," 1902), *Sonata de primavera* ("Spring Sonata," 1904), *Sonata de estío* ("Summer Sonata," 1903), and *Sonata de invierno* ("Winter Sonata," 1905). The very titles of that quartet establish a musical organization, which is further developed in the narrative form and in the evocative cadence of the sentences and words of the novels themselves. Valle-Inclán rejected the chronological organization of Realist literature, as well as logic, from his first works onwards, and opted instead for a spatial and musical prose favored by symbolists and, years later, by Aldous Huxley in his *Point Counter Point* (1928). In the *Sonatas* three main themes predominate: religion, eroticism, and death, articulated in a series of motifs, spaces, and figures such as cruelty, sadism, *donjuanismo*, satanism, exotic or stylized landscapes and interiors, Pre-Raphaelite characters, and *femmes fatales*. In his next series of novels, a trilogy on the nineteenth-century Carlist wars – *Los cruzados de la causa* ("The Crusaders of the Cause," 1908), *El resplandor de la hoguera* ("The Glow of the Bonfire," 1909), and *Gerifaltes de antaño* ("Notables of Days Gone By," 1909) – Valle-Inclán incorporated into his incessant literary experimentation a social and political criticism that he would never abandon. These three novels are in fact a relentless critique of war, as well as a parodic re-writing of the historical novel. This conjunction of political criticism and linguistic innovation also appears in the "Comedias bárbaras" ("Barbaric Comedies"), a group of three plays thematically related to the trilogy on the Carlist wars published around the same time: *Águila de blasón* ("Heraldic Eagle," 1907), *Romance de lobos* ("Ballad of Wolves," 1908), and *Cara de plata* ("Silver Face," 1922). Due to their linkage of linguistic experimentation with a critical vision of politics and society, the two trilogies constitute a decisive turning point in Valle-Inclán's literary career. The climax of such an interconnection is to be found in the tetralogy "El ruedo ibérico" ("The Iberian Bullring"): *La corte de los milagros* ("The Court of Miracles," 1927), *Viva mi dueño* ("Long Live My Lord," 1928), *Baza de espadas* ("Trick of Spades," 1932), and *Tirano Banderas* ("The Tyrant: A Novel of Warm Lands"), his masterpiece of 1926. In "El ruedo ibérico," the author denounces the ruling classes and the political elite of the reign of Isabel II while re-inventing the historical novel and other literary discourses embedded and re-written. *Tirano Banderas* sharply condemns power structures, dictatorial and militaristic governments, racial discrimination, and the *mauvaise conscience* behind revolutionary politics.

Valle-Inclán undermined rationalism and the traditional concept of linear time through his theory and practice of spatial form. *La lámpara maravillosa. Ejercicios espirituales* ("The Wonderful Lamp. Spiritual Exercises," 1916) constitutes the most extensive exposition of Valle's ideas on the spatial form on which he constructed his works of fiction as well as his plays. In this work, the author overlaps three discourses: aesthetic theory, occultism, and asceticism. *La lámpara*, an aesthetic treatise written in an esoteric *fin-de-siècle* language that by the time of its publication was already somewhat *passé*, is formed by small chapters arranged concentrically. Valle does not proceed through a linear and logical argument, but rather through the repetition of key-motifs organized in thematic blocks. Beyond the visible material world, the "wonderful lamp" illuminates an esoteric, spiritual, and aesthetic reality. The language and structure of the book adequately mimic this irrational, instinctive, unified, and hidden world. According to Valle, both science and reason are insufficient. Reason must be transcended in order to pursue a cosmic as well as epistemological unity eroded by modernity. *La lámpara* blends together several fundamental techniques and themes of Symbolism, among which are the "correspondences," as Charles Baudelaire understood them to be, between empirical reality and a divine universe, the yearning for a transcendent and unified world, the contempt for the rational, the importance of music, and the use of an evocative and polysemic language, by means of which the poet can access levels of reality beyond ordinary language. It is a book whose primary goal is to teach its reader to see "in depth," far beyond empirical phenomena, science, and reason. Its implied world view is mostly aesthetic, and endeavors to lead toward a "liberation" of words from the prison-house of rational language. Besides reason, Valle-Inclán also attempts to transcend chronological time by employing a musical prose. The circular, the eternal, the evocative, and the condensed are opposed to the temporal, the conceptual, and the linear.

Valle-Inclán had already put into practice his theory of spatial form in his acclaimed *Sonatas*. As has been mentioned, the structure of the books, their motivation and their style are built upon musical principles. *El resplandor de la hoguera* is structured in discontinuous sequences; its story is not told linearly, as there are three narrative axes. It presents the Carlist wars in a succession of *tableaux* thus showing characters and situations from multiple and simultaneous points of view without clearly specifying their temporal context. *Tirano Banderas*, on the other hand, can best be described as a cubist novel whose chapters are ordered in concentric sections. "El ruedo ibérico" indicates by its title alone its spatial form, in this case circular. *La corte de los milagros* has a symmetric and circular structure. It is an expressionist and polyphonic novel, in which the Spanish society of Isabel II serves as a protagonist. *La corte de los milagros* uses grotesque language; all sequences are layered in a cubist fashion, creating a fragmentary collection, a type of crucible formed by the overlaying of scenes in a complex temporality that overcomes simple chronological succession. *Viva mi dueño*, like the preceding novel, is a series of interlaced vignettes that correspond to different argumentative lines. This creates a whole that is fragmentary, although united around a symmetrical and circular structure.

Many of the works by Valle-Inclán are inseparable from his theory of *esperpento* ("grotesque"). He put forth his ideas on *esperpento* in the twelfth scene of *Luces de bohemia* ("Lights of Bohemia," 1920), and in the prologue and epilogue of *Los cuernos de don Friolera*, ("The Horns of Don Friolera," 1925), through some authorial characters. According to these characters, *esperpento* consists of a deforming, expressionist technique that transforms all characters into puppets. Life in Spain, these authorial characters remark, can only be portrayed through a systematically deforming language. The author should be a demiurge who sees his creations "from the other bank of the river," that is, from a superior and distant angle. *Esperpento* is thus a poetics of distance, a surpassing of pain and laughter. Valle opposed classical and bourgeois theatre with a carnivalesque, expressionist one. The revolutionary aesthetics of *esperpento* attempts to cause the spectator or reader to reflect on the world that surrounds him. The opposition of *esperpento* to the theatrical tradition is akin to the German playwright Bertold Brecht's alienation effect (requiring critical detachment), the French dramatist Alfred Jarry's absurdist theatre, and Jarry's compatriot Antonin Artaud's theatre of cruelty. The non-mimetic and expressionist language of *esperpento* dramatically alters rational perception and offers new ways of apprehending and understanding reality. *Esperpento* is therefore a radical form of literary and political dissidence, a sort of *engagé* practice of literary expression. *Luces de bohemia* and the three plays grouped in *Martes de carnaval. Esperpentos* ("Mardi Gras. Grotesques," 1930) – *Los cuernos de don Friolera, Las galas del difunto*, published originally as *El terno del difunto* ("The Deceased's Clothing," 1926), and *La hija del capitán* ("The Captain's Daughter," 1927) – which have been considered the most important of Valle's *esperpento*s, are clearly devoted to political and social criticism. It must be added that, although the theory of *esperpento* was developed by Valle during the 1920s, *esperpento* techniques are already manifest in the trilogy of novels on the Carlist wars, published in the first decade of the twentieth century. Moreover, *esperpento* is not limited to Valle's late theatre. Two cases in point are his novel *Tirano Banderas* and the series of "El ruedo ibérico."

The theory and practice of *esperpento* are manifestations of a crucial tendency in Valle-Inclán: the aesthetics of carnival, in the sense proposed by the Russian theorist Mikhail Bakhtin.[3] In fact, Valle's carnivalesque literature has an emblem in the general title of three of his *esperpentos*: *Martes de carnaval*, or *mardi gras*. Some elements of carnival in his literature are: a mixture of genres and styles; the poetry of the prosaic; the parody of genres; the comic and the grotesque; *esperpento* as a constructive and defining principle of puppet-characters; ridicule and debasement of characters; *esperpento* as a poetics opposed to official culture; puppet-characters as the "fools" of carnival; inversion of hierarchies; attraction to the decadent (but also to melodramatic popular culture); erosion of the borders dividing the serious from the comic; the polyglossia (simultaneous presence of several languages interacting with each other) of the marketplace; profanation (memorably personified in the Marqués de Bradomín, but altogether present in many of his works); and the ubiquity of laughter.

In sum, the literature of Valle-Inclán fuses literary experimentation with social and political engagement. Valle's political dissidence cannot be

---

[3] Mikhail Bakhtin, *Rabelais and His World*. Trans. H. Iswolski (Bloomington: Indiana University Press, 1984).

separated from his revolutionary theory and practice of literature. Literary experimentation leads to the subversion of habitual patterns of perception, and confronts the reader and spectator with an unjust society as seen from creative perspectives, the novelty of which invite reflection, and, perhaps, political praxis. Valle-Inclán's works fit in perfectly within Theodor A. Adorno's concept of "modern art."[4] According to Adorno, in a reified world such as the modern age, the meaning of words is contaminated by the capitalist ideology of free exchange. Confronted with this situation, modern art opts to exclude itself from the bourgeois system of representation, centered on mimesis and content. The formal and semantic dislocation of modern artworks is therefore a form of opposition and resistance. The new artistic representation of modern art, while on the one hand treating objectively the irrationality of modernity, on the other presents artistic objects distanced from bourgeois society's modes of perception. Thanks to that, modern art presents itself as the only real alternative that individuals have in a reified, inauthentic world. Valle-Inclán's *esperpento*, his dislocation of expressive forms, and his criticism of certain political and social practices correspond to Adorno's definition of modern art. The literature of Valle-Inclán is predicated upon a simultaneous liberation of both word and world. We cannot assess the social dimension of Valle's works by the same standards we use to study content-oriented literature. The combination of aesthetic experimentation, carnival, and political criticism is neither a dilemma nor a paradox, as some critics have maintained. On the contrary, Valle-Inclán's writing is far more transgressive than content-oriented literature due precisely to its deconstruction of the worn-out expressive forms privileged by the ruling classes.

Ganivet, or the *écritures* of the Self

Ángel Ganivet published a series of essays that were relatively well received at the end of the nineteenth century. In *Granada la bella* ("Granada the Beautiful," 1896), *Idearium español* ("Spanish Idearium," 1897), *Cartas finlandesas* ("Finnish Letters," 1898), and *Hombres del norte* ("Men of the North," posthumous, 1905), he expounds several of his favored themes: urbanism; the rejection of capitalism in favor of a pre-industrial society, an attitude in line with English Pre-Raphaelites; the regeneration of Spain; and finally, art and literature. Nevertheless, of more interest to the historian of Modernist literature are his two novels,

---

[4] Theodor A. Adorno, *Aesthetic Theory*. Trans. R. Hullot-Kentor (Minneapolis: University of Minnesota Press, 1997).

La conquista del reino de Maya por el último conquistador español Pío Cid ("The Conquest of the Kingdom of Maya by the Last Spanish Conquistador Pío Cid," 1897) and *Los trabajos del infatigable creador Pío Cid* ("The Labors of the Tireless Creator Pío Cid," 1898), his symbolist play *El escultor de su alma* ("The Sculptor of His Soul," posthumous, 1904), and his poetics, scattered throughout his essays and his extensive correspondence.

Ganivet's literary theory and aesthetics are derived in part from Arthur Schopenhauer's reflections on art as developed in *The World as Will and Idea* (1819, 1844). For Ganivet, writing and the arts represent the enrichment of the individual, constituting a challenge to the externalism of an alienating capitalist world. Through art and literature, the artist sublimates the harshness of existence. With art, the human being propels himself into self-creation in a process less aimed at the culmination of a work than at the creative act itself. The writer therefore finds himself through the textualization of a creative process that redeems and perpetuates him. Literature and art transfigure man through his experience of pain. In Ganivet's poetics, author and text are practically indistinguishable. In this fusion of writing and writer, the latter recovers the unity that he has lost in his daily interaction with the modern world. Literature acquires an existential dimension. Art, then, should not represent the artist's external reality, but rather the textualization of his creative process. This concept of arts and letters leads Ganivet to reject Realism and Naturalism, which he understands as literary modes solely interested in observing the exterior reality of the human being. Consistent with his poetics, he shows in his essays a preference for spatial form, for polysemic language, and for split characters. Ganivet's literary theory subverts established literary codes such as the communicative function of language. Instead, he develops a theory of literature consolidated years later by other great masters of European Modernism: a writing that plays with its own textuality, discontinuous, polysemic, and always irreducible. All this becomes the basis for a new understanding of literary fiction that Ganivet himself put into practice.

La conquista del reino de Maya por el último conquistador español Pío Cid is a satiric novel narrated by the autodiegetic voice of Pío Cid, the agent of a commercial firm, posted in Africa, who recounts his adventures in the imaginary kingdom of Maya, where he imposes a modern political, social, and economic organization. At the end of the novel, the narrator-protagonist dreams of a dialogue with the shadow of Hernán Cortés in which it is sustained that literary creation is a form of action and self-creation. Intertwined in *La conquista* are several discourses and genres: anticolonialism, satire, travelogues, exoticism, expressionism, the adventure novel, and, finally, metaliterature. This mixture makes *La conquista* a novel that breaks with the representative function of the linguistic sign. By means of satire, Ganivet articulates an episodic and elusive narrative, in which expressionist techniques predominate. Satire requires more effort from the reader in decoding the work of art, a demand characteristic of Modernism. The narrator, Pío Cid, is an unreliable voice akin to other unreliable narrators of European and American Modernism. The plot of the novel, the elusiveness of the narrator's voice, the discourse of the Other and of the violence confronting civilization and reason, are elements that would later re-appear in another classic novel of European Modernism, Joseph Conrad's *Heart of Darkness* (1902). *La conquista* brings into play a metatextual literature. This metanarrative dimension is in perfect harmony with the other primary components of the novel, that is, satire, exoticism, and the grotesque. All of these work to create the Modernism of *La conquista*, found in the way it systematically deforms reality, transgresses the referential pretensions of literature, reveals the crafted nature of the novel, defends the authenticating role of literary creation, and vindicates the exotic spaces abandoned by Realist and Naturalist literature.

Los trabajos del infatigable creador Pío Cid shares its protagonist with *La conquista*, but finds him in an entirely different environment: turn-of-the-century Madrid. The narrator is Ángel, who relates the life of his friend Pío Cid, portrayed this time as a decadent hero. *Los trabajos* is a polyphonic novel that brings together diverse stories and poems written or told by characters in this "novel" by Ángel. The narrating voice fragments and multiplies into other voices, while the main story bifurcates into other narratives and poems that duplicate or comment upon it. Mimesis gives way to metafiction, to the fragmentation of discourse, and to spatial form. There is fluidity between narrative levels, as characters from one level serve as protagonists of a superior level. The confusion between the real and the imaginary forces the reader into awareness of the work's artistic nature and the literary techniques used to achieve it. The mimesis of Realism is undermined, as the novel focuses on itself. The polymorphism and paradoxical nature of the main character, Pío Cid, reflects that of the novel. He is a mysterious character, surrounded by contradictory stories. As an ironist, Pío Cid plays with his own identities. His humoristic ambivalence allows him to avoid committing to any one idea. Through paradox, Pío Cid escapes determinism. Herein lies the impossibility of categorizing his behavior: the comical co-exists with the serious; existential nihilism with ironic petulance. Finally, it is worth noting that several episodes from the author's own life are woven into the fabric of the text. Ganivet refracts his ideas in the voices of a few characters. He creates himself through the dissemination of his voice and life experiences in an autobiographical novel. Given the polymorphism and polyphony of its plot and principal character, *Los trabajos* rejects any possibility of a passive role for its reader. In *Los trabajos*, facts are not lined up in a chronological sequence that gives them meaning; rather, they are left open to the possibility of an endless process of interpretation by the reader. In the face of these diverse, even conflicting, perspectives, confronting this structural chaos and the polymorphism of the protagonist, the reader is obliged to impose his/her own order. Because of this, it could be said that in Ganivet's second and final novel, two of the most important projects of his poetics culminate: the Modernist renovation of literature, and his existential project of creating himself in literature, of merging the search for himself with his artistic creation. Modernist writing is, in Ganivet's case, the writing of a prismatic and fragmentary being in constant and reflexive self-creation.

Pío Baroja: anything goes

Pío Baroja wrote essays – *El tablado de Arlequín* ("The Harlequin's Stage," 1904), *Nuevo tablado de Arlequín* ("The Harlequin's New Stage," 1917), memoirs *Juventud, egolatría* ("Youth, Egotism," 1917), *Desde la última vuelta del camino* ("From the Last Turn of the Road," 1944–1949) – poetry (collected in *Canciones del suburbio* ["Songs of the Suburb," 1944]) – and theatre – *Adiós a la bohemia* ("A Farewell to Bohemia," 1911). Nonetheless, Baroja was above all a writer of novels, the literary genre to which he devoted most of his energy from 1900, the year his first novel, *La casa de Aizgorri* ("The House of Aizgorri"), was published, until his death. His career as novelist is usually divided into two periods separated by the First World War. The first is given over to philosophical concerns, woven into his novels through the discourse of certain characters. *El árbol de la ciencia* ("The Tree of Knowledge," 1911), considered one of his best novels, marks the culmination of this first stage. In the second, Baroja abandons the philosophical dimension predominant in his previous novels, and shows, in his narratives, a greater philosophical skepticism. This classification, privileged by literary historiographers, hides the recurrence of themes and preoccupations in Baroja's novels. His philosophical and moral concerns, for instance, are also found in works published after 1914. Moreover, a variety of techniques and forms are observable in Baroja's novels, originating from a quite liberal understanding of the novelistic genre.

Baroja's poetics is scattered throughout his essays, although the most exhaustive exposition of his literary theory is to be found in "Prólogo doctrinal sobre la novela" ("Doctrinal Prologue on the Novel"), the first pages of *La nave de los locos* ("The Ship of Fools," 1925), with which Baroja responds to Ortega's arguments laid out in *Ideas sobre la novela*

("Ideas on the Novel," 1925). Baroja defines himself as a liberal and antidogmatic writer who has tried different novelistic modes. His theory of the novel, as it is carried out in practice, is sustained by a literary *laissez-faire* that results in a sense that "anything goes." In the aforementioned prologue, Baroja maintains that there is not just a single valid type of novel, and that the contemporary novel is a multiform and protean genre that covers everything, including philosophy, psychology, adventure, the Utopian, and the epic. The novel is a permeable, antidogmatic genre, open to different tendencies; in the novel, anything goes.

Baroja was consistent with this broadmindedness. He practiced various novelistic modes and subgenres. In contrast to Valle-Inclán, Ganivet, and Azorín, Baroja cultivated both Modernist and Realist literature. It would consequently be imprecise merely to label Baroja a Modernist writer, since he also wrote Realist novels, heirs to Pérez Galdós' Realism. There is no logical progression to be discerned in his novelistic evolution, and one could say that what gives unity and coherence to his novelistic trajectory is, precisely, the lack thereof. In Baroja there are recurring themes and tones: pessimism, anticlericalism, skepticism, the tension between willpower and apathy, maladjusted and indolent characters. His novels, like his essays, are conspicuous for their use of imprecise and defective syntax, for a certain stylistic and lexical carelessness, for short paragraphs, as well as for fragmented and apparently slapdash plots.

Several of his more Modernist works are *Vidas sombrías* ("Shadowy Lives," 1900), a collection of short stories; *La casa de Aizgorri*; *Camino de perfección* ("Path to Perfection," 1902); *Paradox, rey* ("Paradox, King," 1906); and *El árbol de la ciencia*. In general terms, one can speak of several family resemblances recurrent in Baroja's Modernist narratives: ekphrasis; the insertion of metaliterary digressions on art and literature; impressionistic descriptions; abundance of dialogue, which in some cases predominates in an exclusive way, as in the novels *La casa de Aizgorri*, *Paradox, rey*, and *La leyenda de Jaun de Alzate* ("The Legend of Jaun de Alzate," 1922); a grotesque and deforming expressionism; parody; perspectivism; epiphanies; a certain nostalgic and melancholic tone in the evocation of space and the depiction of characters; philosophical meditations; a decadent and perverse sexuality; complex characters who suffer from unsolvable internal contradictions; episodic narratives; and, finally, a certain predilection for bohemian worlds, as in his delightful *Aventuras, inventos y mixtificaciones de Silvestre Paradox* ("Adventures, Inventions, and Mystifications of Sylvester Paradox," 1901). Among Baroja's Realist works, his trilogy "Las ciudades" ("The Cities": *César o nada* ["Caesar or Nothing," 1910]; *El mundo es ansí* ["The World is Like That," 1912]; *La sensualidad pervertida* ["Perverted Sensuality," 1920]), as well as his trilogy "La lucha por la vida" ("The Struggle for Life": *La busca* ["The Search," 1904]; *Mala hierba* ["Weed," 1904]; *Aurora roja* ["Red Dawn," 1905]) merit special attention. The latter trilogy describes a Madrid steeped in misery, a mixture of picaresque life and revolutionary conspiracy, almost always of an anarchist bent. In these novels, Baroja puts forth new paths for literary Realism, different from those of classic nineteenth-century Realist writers. Between 1913 and 1935 the twenty-two volumes of the historical novel *Memorias de un hombre de acción* ("Memoirs of a Man of Action") were published. This series of *Memorias* is supported by, and reveals, an important theory of history concealed in Baroja. This theory of history is akin to Azorín's "little things," to Unamuno's "intrahistory," and to Braudel's *longue durée*. The truth of art, Baroja believes, is superior and more authentic than the truth of history. The novelization of the insignificant and the recounting of common things that happen to common people better capture the essence of a historical moment than traditional histories. The Realistic and historical novel, then, is superior to traditional history books.

Baroja was an extraordinary story teller. Manifest in his essays was his preference for writers who narrated adventures. Two of his most remarkable adventure novels are *Zalacaín el aventurero* ("Zalacaín the Adventurer," 1909) and *Las inquietudes de Shanti Andía* ("The Restlessness of Shanti Andía," 1911). His pessimism, already apparent in his doctoral thesis, entitled, significantly, *El dolor. Estudio de psicofísica* ("Pain: A Study of Psychophysics," 1896), and reinforced by his reading of Schopenhauer, was counterbalanced by his taste for entertaining literature and by his remarkable ability to delight his reader with splendid tales. The ultimate compensation for a difficult life resides, in Baroja's work, in the pleasure experienced by author and reader in the narration and reading of entertaining stories. And to achieve such a goal, anything goes.

Azorín: sweet melancholia and will-to-literature

José Martínez Ruiz ("Azorín") lived by and for literature. He began his literary career at the end of the nineteenth century working as a journalist, and during his long writing life produced more than 5,500 articles, stories, plays, and delectable books of essays, among which stand out *Los pueblos* ("Towns," 1905), *La ruta de don Quijote* ("The Route of Don Quijote," 1905), *Castilla* ("Castile," 1912), *Clásicos y modernos* ("Classics and Moderns," 1913), and *Madrid* (1941). Azorín also published sixteen novels, some of which are true jewels of Spanish Modernism: *Diario de un enfermo* ("Diary of a Distressed Man," 1901), *La voluntad* ("Will," 1902), *Antonio Azorín* (1903), *Las confesiones de un pequeño filósofo* ("Confessions of a Little Philosopher," 1904), *Doña*

Inés (1925), *Félix Vargas* (1928), *Superrealismo* ("Surrealism," 1929), and *Pueblo* ("Village," 1930).

Reading Schopenhauer made a lasting impression on Martínez Ruiz (as it had on Ganivet). According to Schopenhauer in *The World as Will and Idea*, the will is a source of pain, as it causes in the subject a never-fulfilled desire to possess. Becoming conscious of the pain produced by will is the first step to overcome it. Asceticism and art lead to domination over, and eventual liberation of, will. Basically, Azorín conceived of the world in these terms after abandoning, around 1903, his early anarchism. He looked for understanding in literature. Perhaps because of this his writing lacks a sense of mimesis. The universe represented by Azorín is openly a verbal construct. His novels and books of essays are usually formed by a series of delicate *tableaux* described in a concise, elegant style. Azorín was a writer gifted with a refined literary knowledge that affected, in the extreme, his career in both its creative and critical facets, often blended together: many of his novels incorporate digressions on literature, while almost all of his essays are impressionistic, poetic, and evocative sketches. Azorín rewrote Spanish literary history through a personal and critical reading of both Spanish classics and lesser-known texts. Undoubtedly, he attempted to transmit to his readers his imperative need to aestheticize life and cultural tradition as a way to dominate irrational, painful will. This is the most enduring social dimension of Azorín's work: to undertake the artistic regeneration of his readers. *In arte veritas* ("in art there is truth") could be Azorín's motto.

Time suffuses Azorín's writing. For him, the passage of time is painful. Time elapses slowly, inexorably. Events repeat themselves in an anguishing and implacable eternal return. The names of the protagonists change; pain and sadness remain. In *La voluntad, Antonio Azorín,* and *Las confesiones de un pequeño filósofo* the narrative voice describes the daily life of remote Spanish villages; in them, there are too many hours, and life slips away monotonously – always the same faces, always the same landscapes, always the same words. Confronted with the monotony and sadness of life, the human being has to resign himself and contemplate the world *sub specie artis.* Azorín wrote entire books around this concept of life and time. One of these is *Castilla,* a collection of charming articles united by the theme of time, as the author himself remarks in the prologue. In order to intensify the dynamics between the passage of time and the eternal return, Azorín inserts, in some essays of *Castilla,* the image of a gentleman seated on a balcony, absorbed by profound meditations, with a sad look, his face leaning on his hand. Everything changes and disappears, except for the pain of living, condensed in the recurrent description of that gentleman. In *Los pueblos,* the narrator insists that everything slides away, that our beloved ones disappear, leaving in our spirits a trail of love and melancholy. In *La ruta de don Quijote*, the painful passage of time is objectified in the artistic descriptions of villages of La Mancha inhabited by resigned, defeated, anonymous beings. In the vast majority of his works, the author writes with the "sweet melancholia" caused by his contemplation and acceptance of universal pain. The contained and elegant cadence of Azorín's style transmits to the reader his experience of melancholy. In Azorín, as in the work of so many other modern writers, melancholy is, simultaneously, comprehension and acceptance, recognition and mourning, contemplation and overcoming.

Involuntary memory is one of the artistic means used by Azorín to represent time. Odors, colors, objects, sounds, and spaces awaken, in the narrative voice of his books, past moments that time has deposited in the mind, and that cannot be evoked but at random. Sensibility is affected by a chance and trivial occurrence that triggers the remembrance of time past. As it also was with the French novelist Marcel Proust in *À la recherche du temps perdu* ("Remembrance of Things Past," 1913–1927), involuntary memory is, at its root, a cancellation of chronological time. The instant is eternalized in the moments of epiphany in which different times in the life of the remembering subject merge. Azorín has explained in different fragments of his work this technique of remembrance. One of its clearest expositions can be found in chapter 2 of *Pueblo*, "La conciencia" ("Conscience"). Although Leopoldo Alas had already used involuntary memory in his Modernist novel *Cuesta abajo*, Azorín would be the writer to consolidate this literary device in Spain. Among the first manifestations of involuntary memory are his article "Un recuerdo: Clarín" ("Remembering Clarín"), published on 24 August 1904 in *España*, later collected in *Los pueblos*, and Part 1, chapter 15 of *Antonio Azorín*. Azorín's involuntary memory culminates in *Doña Inés*, a novel published in 1925 in which his taste for this literary device is reinforced by his reading of Proust. Don Pablo, one of the main characters of this exquisite novel, is gifted with an involuntary memory. The narrator tells us that don Pablo possesses a prodigious memory of sensations, that the spiritual states of the past cannot be evoked at will, and that, unexpectedly, a voice, an incident, make don Pablo relive the same sensation that he had experienced many years before. Unlike Proust's Narrator, don Pablo suffers pain in his recreation of the past. The memory of sensations is agonizing, as it had been for other narrative voices and characters in Azorín's prior works. The sorrow engendered by involuntary memory is certainly consistent with the eternal return as Azorín conceived it, as well as with his sweet melancholia.

Don Pablo is a character typical of Azorín's narrative. For a significant number of the protagonists of his novels and his collections of essays, the will to live is eroded by existential pain. In his first novel, *Diario de un enfermo*, this kind of character appears for the first time. The title itself is rather eloquent: Diary of a "distressed man." The unnamed protagonist and narrator of this novel can be described as an "unhappy conscience" ripped apart by his inability to reconcile intelligence with life. Antonio Azorín (the character whose last name the author took as his own pseudonym from 1905 onwards) is similarly torn in the two following novels by Martínez Ruiz, *La voluntad* and *Antonio Azorín*. His indolence, conditioned, in part, by the lessons of his teacher Yuste as well as the oppressive environment in which he grows up, is an expression of the metaphysical, social, and existential schisms of an "unhappy conscience." The sensations evoked in these two novels, that is, melancholy, death, sadness, the passage of time, and resignation, along with the languid landscapes described, enhance the sense of defeat felt by Antonio Azorín in those two novels. In *Castilla* and in *Los pueblos*, one can easily single out characters of similar torpor, unhappiness, and melancholy who lack a will to live.

The eroding of the will to live is offset, in Azorín, by his constant will-to-literature. Azorín's disdain for literary Realism makes sense in the context of his thinking. Sweet melancholia is consubstantial, in his works, with the aestheticization of reality, that is, with the creation of an autonomous universe governed by its own rules. The literary word is not a compensatory or representational mechanism, but rather an alternative form to reality. Azorín does not pretend to represent the world; he simply builds one. That notwithstanding, the author relates literature and life, word and world through his meditation on existential pain and on will as conceived by Schopenhauer. Literature carries, in Azorín, a critical discourse on reality. Literary writing is the highest form of life, for through it the artist attempts an understanding of life, and, as a result, achieves victory over existential pain. Modernist narrative is better adjusted than Realism to such an existential and literary project. From the beginning of his career as a novelist onwards, Azorín practiced a Modernist discourse, which he continually refined with new techniques. The Modernism of Azorín's narrative distinguishes itself by the following family resemblances: descriptive impressionism, spatial form, metaliterary digressions, poetic prose, musicality of language, layering of narrative voices, involuntary memory, ekphrasis, interiorism, and the importance of sensory perceptions. In some of his novels published in the 1920s, Azorín, always concerned with literary innovation, incorporated surrealist and cubist techniques into his pervasive Modernist writing. *Pueblo*, a novel of 1930, is composed of a series of sketches in which objects and spaces of an anonymous village are described by using cubist layers. *Superrealismo*, a novel published in 1929, is no more than the notes taken by the narrator before writing a novel. It is, as the narrator points out, a "pre-novel" in which scenery, story, and characters are only sketched. The choppy, almost telegraphic style, imitates the spontaneous, unpremeditated act of taking preparatory notes for a paper. *Superrealismo* argues for a poetics of the vague and undefined. The narrator recreates chromatic, auditory, and olfactory sensations, and inserts quotes from several authors. This "pre-novel" is also, therefore, a text woven of quotes, thus unveiling the intrinsically intertextual nature of all texts. In this novel, "surrealism" refers to a reality superior to the ordinary one, beyond conscience and reason.

Azorín's will-to-literature is evident above all in his abundant literary criticism and in the metaliterary reflections of the narrators and characters in his fiction. Consistent with this is the presence of the figure of the writer and intellectual, and of self-referential fragments in many of his novels. In *Diario de un enfermo* the narrator and protagonist meditates on life and on writing. In its prologue, the most conspicuous characteristics of the novel are described. Some fragments transcribe even the moment of writing itself, and in other parts of the novel the narrator summarizes his manifestly Modernist poetics. One of the best-known metaliterary fragments of Martínez Ruiz is to be found in Part 1, Chapter 14 of *La voluntad*, in which a character, Yuste, elucidates a Modernist narrative theory practiced by Azorín in all of his literary works. Yuste advocates a spatial, fragmented, plotless, and multiform narrative, more appropriate than Realism, he believes, to reflect on reality; it is a thesis quite like that defended by Virginia Woolf almost two decades later in her seminal essay "Modern Fiction" (1919). In *Las confesiones de un pequeño filósofo* the objectives, tone, and techniques of the novel are established in the first chapter; it calls for the evocation of the past by involuntary reminiscence to thus create in the reader an iridescent, flexible, naive sense of life as lived by the autodiegetic narrator. In "Confesión de un autor" ("Confession of an Author") from *Los pueblos*, the narrator speaks of the act of writing, of the secret relationships among things, of life, and of the great aesthetic value of the small and insignificant, that is, the "aesthetics of the trivial" postulated, for the first time, in *Las confesiones de un pequeño filósofo*. The autonomy of literature, a constant in Azorín's works, is explained with great clarity in the prologue to *Superrealismo*, a sort of literary manifesto. In this prologue, the narrator claims that words must be liberated from the prison-house in which they have been held by what he labels as "old rhetoric," and that their profound life must be discovered in their autonomy from the world. We should, to use Viktor Shklovski's terminology, "defamiliarize" language in order to return artistic value to words.[5] Obviously, this observation is an implicit attack on Realism as well as a defense of the kind of literature that reflects upon itself. The liberation of

---

[5] Viktor Sklovski, "Art as Device." In *Theory of Prose*. Trans. B. Sher. (Elmwood Park, IL: Dalkey Archive Press, 1990), pp. 1–14.

the word cannot be separated from the need to overcome, through literature, the pain that erodes the will to live. Finally, in the prologue to *Félix
Vargas*, Azorín defends a Modernist literary theory based on ellipses, on
interior reality, on the inorganic, on the fragmentary, and on unconscious
writing. Once again, the liberation of the word and the aestheticization of
the world are the most authentic ways to eliminate the pain of existence.
The rest does not matter.

Unamuno: writing and existence

Miguel de Unamuno was a thinker with a solid literary, historical, philosophical, and theological background. Some of his essays are indispensable to an understanding of Spanish intellectual history, such as *En torno
al casticismo* ("On Tradition," 1895) and *Del sentimiento trágico de la
vida en los hombres y en los pueblos* ("On the Tragic Sense of Life in Men
and Peoples," 1912). He wrote short stories, plays, poetry, and novels such
as *Paz en la guerra* ("Peace in War," 1897), *Amor y pedagogía* ("Love and
Pedagogy," 1902), *Niebla* ("Mist," 1914), *Abel Sánchez* (1917), *Cómo
se hace una novela* ("How a Novel Is Made," 1927), and *San Manuel
Bueno, mártir* ("Saint Manuel Bueno, Martyr," 1931).

From the beginning of his literary and philosophical career Unamuno
adopted the role of intellectual. A significant portion of his work is aimed
at the spiritual regeneration of his readers and of Spain. Unamuno was
an intellectual exiled in the metaphysical sense as postulated by Edward
Said. This intellectual exile is characterized by his constant reorientation,
by his ceaseless movement, and by his questioning of all ideas – others'
and his own. Unamuno was also an exile in the literal sense of the word.
In 1914, he was dismissed from his position as Rector of the University of
Salamanca, and exiled by General Primo de Rivera in 1924. He became
disillusioned with and confronted the leaders of the Second Republic, supported General Franco's rebels, but ended up opposing the fascist uprising
of 1936. "Contra esto y aquello" ("Against This and That"), the title of
one of his collection of essays, succinctly describes his perpetually non-
conformist and rebellious character.

Unamuno's attitude toward life and literature was deeply influenced
by his spiritual crisis of 1897. Although from that point on, he would
frequently raise the issue of his own embodiment of the conflict between
reason and faith, the clearest expression can be found in *Del sentimiento
trágico de la vida* as well as *La agonía del cristianismo* ("The Agony of
Christianity," 1925). Unamuno argues that while the desire for immortality can be given no rational confirmation, neither can reason explain the
finality of the individual's life. Uncertainty, he sustains, is the foundation

upon which the desperation of the vital sense must base its hope. Reason and feeling co-exist at war, and this war must be made the basis for the individual's spiritual life. The impossibility of arriving at a harmonious synthesis is the tragic sense of life: reason is insufficient, but faith cannot be justified by reason. *San Manuel Bueno, mártir* is the novel that best explains the tragic sense of life. Ángela Carballino, its unreliable narrator, reflects this sense. The tension between the implied reader's suppositions about the story and Ángela's account refracts, at the diegetic level, the tension between faith and reason that torments Father Manuel Bueno.

Unamuno's characters typically embody different facets of the tragic sense of life. They are characters in agony, such as Joaquín Monegro, Augusto Pérez, and Manuel Bueno. Unamuno, as he himself says, scrapes in the "sótanos y escondrijos del corazón" ("cellars and hiding places of the heart"), in the "catacumbas del alma" ("catacombs of the soul"). These split characters that so attracted Unamuno could be better portrayed by means of Modernist novel techniques than by using those of literary Realism. The disjointed structure of the Modernist novel perfectly suited the opposing identities of his characters, a phenomenon to which he devoted a certain amount of attention, as in the "Prologue-Epilogue" of his second edition of *Amor y pedagogía*, and in particular in the preliminary pages of *Tres novelas ejemplares y un prólogo* ("Three Exemplary Novels and a Prologue," 1920). The literary representation of the "catacombs of the soul," of "the cellars and hiding places" of the subject is a recurrent theme in the works of this prolific author, making its full debut in *Amor y pedagogía*. Already in this 1902 novel, Unamuno departs from all Realist elements (description of spaces, biographies, effects of reality, the relation of the character with his environment, etc.), elements which he believes hinder the representation of personality, and concentrates instead on the turbulent conscience of his characters.

The tragic sense of life is inseparable from Unamuno's concept of literature. To Unamuno, the written word precedes the oral. Existence and history are given in writing. To narrate life, writes Unamuno, is the most profound way to live it. Every man is child of a legend, written or oral. Accordingly, Unamuno lives within writing, writing his life, for the most authentic way to exist and to think is to write. The blank page is the space of life, and life is made in the act of writing. This is why he rejected closed, architectonic works in favor of fragmentary, contradictory ones. To use two terms proposed by Roland Barthes in *S/Z*, Unamuno counters the text that is "readerly" (*lisible*), finished, subject to the logico-temporal order, unified by the authority of a consciousness (i.e., a character or an author), or by culture, in which the reader is a consumer of a complete product, with one that is "writerly" (*scriptible*), open, plural, contradictory, in perpetual motion, no longer consumed, but produced, by the reader.[6] The different possibilities life offers, the fluidity of existence, the subject's divisions and conflicts, his agony and his tragic sense of life are transformed in literature, the locus of thought and existence. Unamuno's concept of life and the subject is presented in contradictory and paradoxical terms due to the founding premise of his ideology: all is literature, and what matters is to think and live through literature. The written word that, according to Unamuno, preceded everything, necessitates paradox. Rationalization is an act of violence that limits both subject and existence to what can be conceived in the language of reason and science. The junctions and the logic of Realism are, therefore, insufficient. Living literature should express itself through its contradictions, dialogically, endlessly. Unamuno can be considered, in this sense, an intransitive writer. While it is true that he manifested a predilection for certain themes such as love, envy, hate, the tragic sense of life, alterity, the desire for immortality, the personality, and writing itself, in Unamuno what matters is not so much writing about certain topics. Rather, one writes to achieve complete existence, life, through writing itself, through the writing where immortality can also be achieved. Behind Unamuno's existential, religious, political, and literary doubts one can detect a seminal, basic idea: all is literature. It is no surprise, then, that the discourse Unamuno privileged was the novel, not only because he would shape some of his characters autobiographically, but, rather, because the Modernist novel – fragmentary, inwardly directed, self-referential, metaliterary, dominated by dialogue and by the internal conflicts of characters – was the best-adapted literary form to represent Unamuno's particular concept of life and subjectivity.

Unamuno seeks to affect his reader through his writing. He does not look to persuade that reader with logic, but rather to implicate him/her in the dynamic of a text that is *scriptible*. For Unamuno, the reader is also a writer that, in the act of decoding, appropriates the work of art in which he finds himself. The lives of author and reader are enclosed within a text that, because it is *scriptible*, reaches into the future, integrated into the chain of future reader–authors. The most obvious example of this life in literature is *Cómo se hace una novela*, Unamuno's meta-novel *par excellence*, in which he affirms that all truly living fiction is autobiographical. The real author should die to be reborn as a writer, to live his existence and contradictions through literature, and so to become immortal. The true author should sacrifice himself to become another, the other who writes, just as the reader should die as a real reader to be transformed into the implied reader. The author's posterity is made possible only through this act of ritual sacrifice. We die in the text in order to *be*. Writer and reader

---

[6] Roland Barthes, *S/Z* (Paris: Editions du Seuil, 1970).

are creators, they find themselves in literature; they depend on each other upon establishing contact through literature. The reader creates himself, lives, when he reads, as does the author. Reader and author live in an endless narration, for beyond their mortality, both live on in the chain of all reader–authors, in the discursive tradition made up of the intentional acts of writers and their readers. The story is a construction completed by both author and reader, a path to self-knowledge, a form of existence for both, making of all literary works a communion between author and reader by which both are saved from their radical solitude. Unamuno "writer" is an awakener of consciences who incites the reader to think critically, but also to live, truly to exist. The reader understands himself and exists in the text that he himself creates. The dialogue between writer and reader is projected diegetically. In Unamuno's novels, dialogue has an overwhelming presence. Dialogue expresses multiplicity, the construction of the human being, characters' ambivalence and contradictions, paradox, and the impossibility of systematizing thought. Dialogue is thus the ultimate expression of Unamuno's Modernist poetics, epistemology, and ontology.

35

The poetry of *modernismo* in Spain

Richard A. Cardwell

The term *modernismo* is generally applied to the writings of a generation of artists from Latin America and Spain who initiated a revolution in literature in the 1880s in the Americas and the late 1890s in Spain. The literary histories of Spanish *modernismo* written in the period 1936–1955 by Ángel Valbuena Prat, Guillermo Díaz-Plaja, and others, and subsequent accounts based on them have presented an overview which, in the light of recent research, is seriously flawed.[1] First, they contend that the movement began in the Americas with the work of Rubén Darío (1867–1916) and was taken to Spain on his second visit to the peninsula in 1899. Second, *modernismo* is perceived as an essentially aesthetic movement, drawing its inspiration eclectically from European, largely French, literary models. Third, the movement was a homogeneous one, emerging in the late 1890s and largely abandoned by major writers before 1910. Lastly, it was devoid of serious preoccupations and, by the 1950s, held little relevance.

These accounts, with a concentration on aesthetic issues and literary origins, have failed to treat the movement seriously and recognize its complexity. In part this is because, at a very early stage, the *modernistas* explored aspects of experience which seemed, to the conservative establishment, to be in some way subversive. Their affirmation that art could supply meaning and spiritual beauty which a contemporary mercantile and philistine society lacked, their rejection of an art based on the civic and national ideals of a pragmatic bourgeoisie, and their disgust with a discredited political and social system led to what Manuel Machado (1874–1947), in 1913, called "una guerra literaria" ("a literary war"). This war was waged in the literary press and was to color the way the *modernista* experiment was subsequently judged. Indeed, conservative opinion expressed itself in a way which was to nourish the totally false view of *modernismo*.

---

[1] Ángel Valbuena Prat, *Historia de la literatura española*. 2 vols. (Barcelona: Juventud, 1944); Guillermo Díaz-Plaja, *Historia de la literatura española a través de la crítica y de los textos* (Barcelona: La Espiga, 1942); *Modernismo frente a noventa y ocho* (Madrid: Espasa–Calpe, 1951).

In its earliest phase, when the word *modernismo* first came into usage in the early 1890s, the critical establishment, which largely controlled the major organs of dissemination, was at a loss to offer a definition. Even the Real Academia Dictionary Committee itself prorogued an entry until 1899 at its meeting in 1895. In 1900, Almagro San Martín (1882–1947), author of *Sombras de vida* ("Shadows of Life," 1903), a volume of decadent short stories, recorded in his diary the prevailing confusion:

Ahora se habla a troche y moche del modernismo. Yo no sé a punto fijo en qué consiste. Para unos es decir pestes de los viejos autores consagrados . . . , son los muebles "modern style," las cabezas de mujeres con largos cabellos, . . . o los versos de Rubén Darío . . . , la delicuescencia, los lirios, una especie de nuevo romanticismo . . . . [P]odríamos señalar como meollo serio un afán de renovación precedido de una revisión de valores.

(All over the place people are talking about *modernismo*. I am not sure what it means. For some it is to be rude about long-revered writers . . . , or it is Art Nouveau furniture or busts of women with long tresses . . . or the verses of Rubén Darío . . . , general decline, lilies, a new form of Romanticism . . . But, at its core, one can denote a desire to change things preceded by a revision of values.)[2]

In the same year Gómez Carrillo (1873–1927), a *modernista* émigré from Guatemala and prolific disseminator of all the latest European (especially French) artistic trends, was to pose the question "¿Qué es el modernismo *actual* en literatura y arte?" ("What is *today's* modernism in literature and art?") under the byline of "Modernismo" in the pages of *Madrid Cómico* ("Playful Madrid"), a question which began a series of polls which were to produce a surprising outcome as well as an extraordinary range of possible definitions.[3] If Gómez Carrillo was sympathetic to the new trend, by 1902 José Deleito y Piñuela, in another poll in the conservative journal *Gente Vieja* ("Old Guard"), was essentially hostile, a hostility which persisted through two further attacks, one in *La Lectura* ("Reading") magazine in 1911–1912 and another in a major study of 1922. By 1907, with Gómez Carrillo's second poll in *El Nuevo Mercurio*, clear battle lines had been drawn.

If a starting point for the nature of the debate can be identified, it must be the publication, in 1893, of *Entartung* ("Degeneration") by Max

[2] Amelina Correa Ramón, *Melchor Almagro San Martín. Noticia de una ausencia* (Granada: Ficciones. Revista de Letras, 2001), p. 38.
[3] María Pilar Celma Valero, "El modernismo visto por sus contemporáneos: las encuestas en las revistas de la época." In *¿Qué es el modernismo? Nuevas encuestas. Nuevas lecturas.* Eds. Richard A. Cardwell and Bernard McGuirk (Boulder: Society of Spanish and Spanish American Studies, 1993), pp. 25–38.

Nordau (1849–1923). Following the "scientific" theories of Lombroso, he produced a psychopathological study of major literary figures of his day, including Baudelaire (1821–1867) and Oscar Wilde (1854–1900). Through the use of a binary construct – healthy/sick, sane/mad, evolutionary/degenerate – he was able to judge and expel to the margins those who failed the necessary conditions for inclusion within the positive (arch-conservative) aspect of his own binary construct. Rapidly, and especially after the 1902 Spanish translation of Nordau's *Entartung,* the *modernistas* were, almost without exception, stigmatized as "degenerates" (often moral degenerates), "neurotics," and social misfits. This binary categorization set the tone for what was to follow, especially in the literary histories of Valbuena and Díaz-Plaja written during and after the Civil War, works which are still influential in many schools and universities.

Medical terms are inappropriate to literary criticism. Besides, in such a context they express perverted forms of the, then, legitimate scientific discourses of medicine and evolutionism, discourses widely circulated in their day and which exerted no little influence on the public mind. Their use in literary criticism therefore denotes the presence of discourses of power and control. These hidden discourses were powerful enough to condition opinion so that the new literature almost always bore the negative associations of degeneracy and physical and/or mental weakness, even of moral turpitude. By 1912, some *modernistas,* alarmed by this negative reaction and attempting to justify themselves to a younger generation, re-invented themselves as the "Generation of 1898" to offer a more positive and intellectually acceptable identity and, in an apostasy, also affirmed that *modernismo* was a purely aesthetic movement. This revision was soon established in literary histories and, by the late 1930s, the binary of the early 1900s was re-written in terms of Generation of 1898 = good / *modernismo* = bad. After 1940, the Francoist Academia was to construct a hegemonic version of this discursive pattern where the Generation of 1898 was described as "varonil" ("manly"), "robusta" ("robust"), "concienzuda" ("conscientious"), and "castellana" ("Castilian"), while the *modernistas* were marginalized as "femeninos" ("feminine"), "degenerados" ("degenerates"), "neuróticos" ("neurotics"), and "cosmopolitas" ("cosmopolitans").[4] This altogether false picture has bedeviled any proper assessment of the real identity and role of Spanish *modernismo,* especially since many of the works of the so-called "Generation of 1898"

---

[4] Javier Francisco Blasco Pascual, "De 'Oráculos' y de 'Cenicientas': la crítica ante el fin de siglo español." In Cardwell and McGuirk, eds., *¿Qué es el modernismo?* pp. 59–86; Richard A. Cardwell, "Degeneration, Discourse and Differentiation: *Modernismo frente a noventayocho* Reconsidered." In "Critical Essays on the Literatures of Spain and Spanish America." Supplement to *Anales de la Literatura Española Contemporánea* (Boulder: Society of Spanish and Spanish American Studies, 1991), pp. 29–46.

(the essays and travelogues of Martínez Ruiz ["Azorín," 1873–1967], Unamuno [1864–1936], and the early novels of Baroja [1872–1956] and Pérez de Ayala [1880–1962], for example) are in no little way shaped by the aesthetics of *modernismo*. If we reject this binary construct and study the evidence of *modernista* writing itself, a quite different picture emerges.

First, the question of origins. Darío's *Azul . . .* ("Azure . . . ," 1888) and *Prosas profanas* ("Profane Proses," 1896) were held to have helped liberate young Spanish poets from old inhibitions and to usher in a new style. Other, recent accounts, however, relate that Darío was less important and that Spanish *modernismo* emerged from native roots and sources, further shaped by direct contact with progressive French literary ideas. This version seems more probable. In spite of the attack by Juan Valera (1824–1905) on the gallophilia of *Azul . . .* in 1888, Darío's work was not widely known until the late 1890s. *Azul . . .* and *Prosas profanas* were published abroad (in Valparaiso and Paris, respectively) and only a few poems appeared in the Madrid press. It was Darío's physical presence in 1899 which gave a sense of cohesion to the aspirations of the young poets. Darío created a literary coterie with Villaespesa (1866–1936) and invited Jiménez (1881–1957) to join them in April 1900. The Latin American *modernistas* were known in the literary *tertulias* of Madrid, largely through Villaespesa. Yet, despite the dissemination of the new poetic models through the press (Darío, Silva [1865–1896], Jaimes Freyre [1868–1933], Casal [1863–1893], Gutiérrez Nájera [1859–1895], etc.), their influence was limited and is only present in the first two *modernista* works, Jiménez's *Ninfeas* ("Water Lilies") and Villaespesa's *La copa del rey de Thule* ("The Cup of the King of Thule"), both published in 1900. Their major impact was to stimulate a short-lived experimentation rather than a permanent model to be followed. It is arguable that, even without the impact of Latin America and Rubén Darío, who left for Paris in 1900, Spanish *modernismo* would have coalesced into a viable aesthetic of its own accord. Indeed, the 1900 experiment of Villaespesa and Jiménez might never have occurred.

Historians have remarked on the strongly aesthetic emphasis in *modernista* poetry which some critics have termed a "religion of Art." Until 1967, however, the emphasis on aesthetic effects was not properly understood.[5] Darío's late poem, "Yo soy aquel . . ." ("I'm the one . . .") from *Cantos de vida y esperanza* ("Songs of Life and Hope," 1905), with its overt equation of "pure Art" with Christ's *Ego sum lux et veritas et vita* ("I am the light and the truth and the life"), establishes clearly the presence of a displaced theology underpinning much of *modernista* poetry. Art

[5] Donald L. Shaw, "¿Qué es el modernismo?" In Cardwell and McGuirk, eds., *¿Qué es el modernismo?* pp. 11–24.

and the Absolute of Beauty formed the necessary metaphysical structure for writers faced with a crisis of ideals. The creation of an ideal world of Beauty in Art, however, was not merely the search for artifice for its own sake, although Parnassianism is to be found, especially in the poetry of Darío and, briefly, in the 1900 collections of Jiménez and Villaespesa. The *modernista* experiment was more concerned with the investigation of a world of Ideal to be found in what Darío called "el reino interior" ("the inner realm"). The inward search for an aesthetic ideal, the exploration of the imagination and the realm of dreams which seemed to offer a source of spiritual support, had already been explored by Bécquer in the 1860s and in the late poetry of Zorrilla (1817–1893) in the 1870s. The *modernista* (more properly Symbolist) quest, after 1902, for the adequate word and the creation of a wistful understated poetry of nuance and suggestion continued to explore the imaginative world and style of Bécquer's *Rimas* ("Rhymes"), always shaded, subsequently, by the presence of Verlaine (1844–1896), by the poetic theories of Campoamor (1817–1901), and by current medical theories of the mind.

A direct literary link can be established between the 1860s and the late 1890s through *De los quince a los treinta* ("From Fifteen to Thirty," 1885) and *La caja de música* ("The Music Box," 1898) by Ricardo Gil (1855–1908), together with *Efímeras* ("Efemeridae," 1892) and *Lejanías* ("Distant Horizons," 1899) by the Madrid-based Mexican poet, Jorge Icaza (1863–1925). Both employ a similar style and express the same sense of fallen ideals.[6]

A contrastive style of writing, with an accent on artificial effects and a language rich in color and musical resonances, found in Darío, Villaespesa, Jiménez's *Ninfeas* and a number of minor Andalusian poets – Durbán Orozco (1865–1921), González Anaya (1879–1955), Redel (1872–1909), Paso (1864–1901), Domínguez Ortiz (1875?–1935?), Almendros Camps (1865–1912), Ortiz de Pinedo (1880–1959) – also offered a displaced theology of Art. This strain can be linked directly with the experiments of *Andantes y allegros* (1877) and *Cromos y acuarelas* ("Prints and Watercolors," 1878) by Reina (1856–1905), which, in turn, are indebted to the rich and sonorous effects of Espronceda (1808–1842) and Zorrilla, especially the latter's extended poem *Granada* (1852).

Both from Reina and, more powerfully, from France, there emerged the decadent aspect of *modernismo*: the cult of artifice, *dandysme* (excessive attention to appearance and fashion), self-regard, algolagnia,[7] etc. Perhaps the most precocious examples of early *modernista* decadence

---

[6] Richard Cardwell, "El premodernismo español." In *Historia de la literatura española. Siglo XIX (II)*. Ed. Leonardo Romero Tobar (Madrid: Espasa-Calpe, 1998), pp. 309–343.
[7] Algolagnia is a psychiatric condition in which sexual pleasure is derived from receiving or inflicting pain; common examples are masochism and sadism.

are the prose poems of Valle-Inclán (1866–1936) (*Femeninas* [1895] and
Epitalamio [1887]), and Muñoz (1881–1925) (*Miniaturas* ["Miniatures,"
1898] and *Colores grises* ["Grey Tones," 1898]) where all the signs of
the revolt against Nature combined with Romantic skepticism appear.
In major poets like Manuel Machado and Jiménez it proved a passing
fashion and only continued in Villaespesa, Muñoz, and minor poets.

Modernismo did not emerge as an identifiable movement under the
leadership of Darío. Rather, *modernismo* underwent a series of evolu-
tions beginning with Gil and Icaza in the late 1890s, with a second brief
experimental phase in 1900, whose impact was extremely limited, followed by a third phase in 1902–1903 which was to establish an identifiable voice for the movement in both poetry and prose. By the end of the
decade the poetic group, which had gathered around the literary reviews
Alma Española ("Spanish Soul," 1903–1904) and *Helios* (1903–1904),
had dispersed.[8] New journals like *Renacimiento* (1907) had emerged just
as briefly. Darío, still respected but no longer a model, was ill, his *Cantos
de vida y esperanza* left to the care of Jiménez, and the major poets (the
Machado brothers, Villaespesa, and Jiménez), now separated, had begun
to explore new forms of expression.

Modernismo might properly be related to European, as much as to
native, origins. The *modernistas*, especially Gómez Carrillo, Darío, and
the Machado brothers, had resided in Paris before 1900 and were cognizant of all that the city had to offer. The work of D'Annunzio (1863–
1938) was known to Valle-Inclán and Villaespesa at an early date. English
aestheticism in painting and literature was widely discussed, especially
through the contact with Catalan *modernisme*, principally through the
friendship of Rusiñol (1861–1931), Martínez Sierra (1881–1948), and
Jiménez. Thus, the first published forms of *modernista* poetry, *Ninfeas* and
La copa del rey de Thule, express a wide range of aesthetic styles: Romanticism, Parnassianism, Symbolist decadence, and Naturalism. With the
return of the Machado brothers and Jiménez from France in late 1901
and the absence of Darío, the movement was to gain its definitive voice
by 1902–1903. The publication of Manuel Machado's *Alma* ("Soul,"
1902), and Antonio Machado's *Soledades* ("Solitudes") and Jiménez's
Arias tristes ("Sad Airs") in 1903 gave witness to the supremacy of Symbolist aesthetics over other contending styles. In these collections there is
little evidence of Darío and the Latin Americans, no princesses, swans,
and nymphs. Indeed, the tone of *Arias tristes* and *Soledades* is markedly
Realistic, even prosaic at times. These books are more profoundly Symbolist in their use of framing and mirroring devices, the *paysage d'âme*

---

[8] Patricia McDermott, "Modernismo frente a noventayocho: según las revistas de la época
(1897–1907)." In Cardwell and McGuirk, eds., *¿Qué es el modernismo?* pp. 229–255.

(emotion projected out into the landscape), the search for self, the dream world, etc. The eclectic style of 1900 was to disappear save only in the work of minor writers like Emilio Carrère (1880–1947).

Spanish *modernismo* (or, better, the Spanish Symbolist decadence), like other similar movements in Europe and Latin America, has its origins in Romanticism, specifically the negative and profoundly skeptical form expressed by Byron. *Modernismo* expresses the same negative view of existence, of skepticism and doubt, of existential malaise and loneliness that we find in one of *modernismo*'s precursors, Espronceda. The earliest manifestation of Romantic despair, particularly marked in Andalusian writers like González Anaya, Durbán Orozco, Paso, Muñoz, Sánchez Rodríguez (1875–1940), and the early Jiménez and Villaespesa,[9] continues in a less strident form in the post-1903 work of Jiménez and Villaespesa and the Machado brothers, always contained by the allusive style of Symbolism. At no stage is their work devoid of the sense of lost illusions and existential solitude. Indeed, the exploration of the human condition continues in a more sophisticated form in the probing of identity (especially the nature of the artist in the act of creation and the search for an authentic artistic self), in the relationship with the world, and before the question of death, a theme particularly marked in the poetry, especially the late poetry, of Jiménez. One of the more remarkable aspects of this probing was the emergence, especially in Jiménez's poetry after *Arias tristes*, of a decided phenomenological cast where he is concerned with the experiences of the self. This quest, taken up by Ortega y Gasset (1883–1955), was to underpin much of Spanish intellectual life into the 1920s.

The search for ideal worlds and the exaltation of Art and the Absolute of Beauty, so marked in Reina, Darío, and the 1900 collections of Villaespesa and Jiménez, gives way to a less exalted search for spiritual transcendence, especially in the poetry of Jiménez. In *Elejías* ("Elegies," 1908–1910), *Melancolía* ("Melancholy," 1912), *Laberinto* ("Labyrinth," 1913), and, especially, in two post-*modernista* collections, *Diario de un poeta recién casado* ("Diary of a Newly Wed Poet," 1916) and *Dios deseado y deseante* ("God Desired and Desiring," 1949), the pursuit of a transcendent ideal becomes the goal as the poet seeks to recreate himself in his own poetic world. While, up to 1913, there remain many elements of Romanticism and decadence, after that Jiménez explores the potentials of a purer Symbolism (Pure Poetry) to discover himself and his relationship with reality. That is, his total dedication to poetry as a path to ultimate truth evolves into the belief that, out of the struggle with words (the raw stuff

---

[9] Richard A. Cardwell, *Juan R. Jiménez: The Modernist Apprenticeship (1895–1900)* (Berlin: Biblioteca Ibero-americana, 1977).

of poetry), he would reveal the significance of his life. Never rejecting the material world, since his transcendental visionary experience lends it meaning, he accommodates time and change into a vision of an eternal flux, "la corriente infinita" ("the eternal current") that is also an "estación total" ("a total season"). Thus his "dios" is a creature of divine and eternal depths yet also a time-bound human creature, the poet himself. The pursuit of the Absolute of Beauty as a means to sustain some form of faith in the face of Romantic lost ideals and illusions reveals itself as the quest for salvation. In his evocation of a deep flow contrasted with a still totality and his play on oppositions, especially in the poems on death after 1925, he creates a dialectic which is remarkably similar to the philosophies of Unamuno.

If Jiménez's search for a transcendent meaning seems mystical, no less is that of the poetry of Antonio Machado. His *Soledades*, subsequently revised and augmented in 1906 as *Soledades, galerías y otros poemas* ("Solitudes, Galleries and Other Poems"), are profoundly Romantic in tone yet Symbolist in expression.[10] Indeed, in terms of Symbolist practice he is far less sensual, more meditative than Jiménez. We find the Romantic contrast of past happiness and present despair, the sense of time's inexorable erosion of everything always tempered by the belief that memories, dreams, and moments of illumination might recover what has been lost: "De toda la memoria, sólo vale / el don preclaro de evocar los sueños" (Poem LXXXIX) ("In all our memories the only worthy gift is the remarkable one of evoking dreams"). Typically, many poems involve a dialogue between the poet and an object or a moment. He begins on a real plane (a patio, a fountain, a square) but, with the typically Symbolist overlay of emotion on inanimate objects ("triste tarde" ["sad afternoon"]), the reader is raised to the evoked plane, a moodscape, and, in a few poems, to a Symbolic plane where golden fruit, fountains, empty spaces, fleeting shadows suggest the classical myths of the Muses, the fountains of Parnassus, and the golden apples of Helicon, symbolic sources of impossible inspiration. The poems begin with a sense of loss before time's erosion and, thus, failing illusions. They end with the sense that inspiration itself is inaccessible. His poems are, in essence, about their own creation. For this reason he ends on a note of gathering darkness or symbols of death (reflections which look like skulls, a cypress tree). Through many poems there flits the shadow of a huntress or a female figure evoked by a hint of perfume or the rustle of a dress. This allusive style inspired in Stéphane Mallarmé's (1842–1898) "peindre non la chose mais l'effet qu'elle produit" ("paint not the thing itself, but the effect it produces"), and in a

---

[10] Richard A. Cardwell, "Mirrors and Myths: Antonio Machado and the Search for Self." *Romance Studies* 16 (1990), pp. 31–42; Jose María Aguirre, *Antonio Machado, poeta simbolista* (Madrid: Taurus, 1973).

restricted set of images, by accumulation creates the impression of a mystical goal to be sought. Indeed, there is a marked secular mystical strain in this collection which derives from the same source as Jiménez's early mysticism: the widespread discussion, at the end of the century, of mystical practice in the periodical press in France and Spain, the revived interest in Saint John of the Cross, and the mystical element which derives from Symbolism itself. From this rich source Machado was able to discover a personal neo-mysticism which, temporarily at least, was to assuage his profound existential despair.

Two aspects of *modernista* poetry which have been completely overlooked also have their roots in Romanticism and, specifically, German Romanticism. In the late 1830s, as a reaction against the negative strain of Romantic thought and drawing on the theories of the Schlegel brothers, as interpreted by Böhl von Faber (1770–1863), there emerged two theories which were to have a profound effect on the generation of writers who emerged in the late 1890s. These ideas were given strength by the Krausist educational, intellectual, and philosophical experiment from roughly 1865 onwards, ideas transmitted through the Institución Libre de Enseñanza and through the intellectual debates in the Spanish Ateneo. The Machado brothers were educated in the Institución and Jiménez frequented the salons of the *institucionistas* in the period 1901–1904. Their experiences were to have the most profound effects.

The first theory was that literature was, in some way, divinely inspired and that artistic inspiration would illuminate and re-spiritualize mankind. Literary endeavor could heal social divisions and national ills since the artist possessed some supernatural power to conceive a spiritual path forward for a nation in crisis. This response to the crisis of the late 1830s was to be repeated before yet another crisis of values after 1898. In the work of the progressive generation – Ganivet (1865–1898), Unamuno, Baroja, Azorín, Antonio Machado and, especially, Jiménez – we find the pervasive idea that literature can effect spiritual – and, thus, social and political – change. Widely discussed in Krausist circles and given impetus by the translation of Shelley's *Defence of Poetry* (1903), this pervasive idea appears and reappears in *modernista* writing. In 1905, in a review of Unamuno's *La vida de Don Quijote y Sancho* ("The Life of Don Quijote and Sancho"), Machado expressed the view that the cries of anguish and the inward search for a spiritual goal were just as important in the search for a national regeneration as active campaigns. The impact of Krausism on Antonio Machado, as on Jiménez, is very marked. This basic idea forms the center of Jiménez's relationship with Ortega and his essays in *El trabajo gustoso* ("Pleasant Work," 1969, posthumous).

The second theory is based on the Schlegelian and Herderian notion that each nation has a unique identity and personality (*Geist*) and that, in order to prosper, no nation can afford to ignore it. It is the task of the intellectual elite to identify the *Geist*, work in harmony with it, and offer directions for the future. In a sense, this theory is directly related to the first and derives from the same desire to by-pass concrete proposals and plans of action (political or social) and to rely on the intuitions and the visionary activity of the artist. In the case of Machado a direct link between Agustín Durán (1789–1862), one of the major promoters of this idea in the 1820s and 1830s, Machado's grandfather (who married Durán's niece), and father can be established. All of these men believed that in Spanish literature, especially popular literature and the ballads, evidence for the *Geist* could be found. It could also be discovered through travel. Indeed, travel forms a rich source in the poetry of Jiménez and Machado, and in Azorín (a marked Symbolist theorist). This organicist approach was given weight by the addition of apparently positivistic evidence (Machado's father was a positivist), drawn from the burgeoning sciences of evolutionism and determinism. There emerged a heated debate in both scientific and literary circles, further stimulated by the work of Hippolyte Taine (1829–1893), who uses the same notions of the *Geist* leavened by the sciences of causality.[11]

The impact of this amalgam is to be seen in Unamuno's *En torno al casticismo* ("On Tradition," 1895) and Ganivet's *Idearium español* ("An Ideal Model for Spain," 1898). The impact on *modernista* poetry is less palpable but, nonetheless, evident. The first signs are to be found in the nostalgia for a pre-industrial age expressed in the work of Gil. Indeed, by the early 1900s, a strong reaction to the effects of industrialism is evident.[12] Jiménez's cycle of poems from *Arias tristes* ("Sad Arias") to *Pastorales* ("Pastorals," written in 1905 but published in 1911) evokes, in the popular *romance* measure, a rustic idyll (shepherds with flutes herding home their flocks to cottages with smoking chimneys at eventide, the Angelus, grandmothers with children in haycarts) which expresses the "soul" of a given landscape. In his poetic prose evocations in *La ruta de don Quijote* ("Don Quijote's Journey," 1905), Azorín finds evidence of the "soul" in landscape, buildings, furniture, decorative motifs, and in people. Baroja, too, in the more poetic passages of *Camino de perfección* ("The Way of Perfection"), similarly evokes a specific sense of a national or regional "soul." Ramón Pérez de Ayala also explores, in his verse evocations of humble objects and persons in *La paz del sendero* ("The Peace of the Path," 1904), the same ideal organicist structure of society, overlayed with the pietism of Krausism and Francis Jammes (1868–1938). Azorín's

[11] Herbert Ramsden, *The 1898 Movement in Spain* (Manchester: Manchester University Press / Rowman and Littlefield, 1974).
[12] Lily Litvak, *Transformación industrial y literatura en España (1895–1905)* (Madrid: Taurus, 1983).

magazine, *Alma española,* subscribes to the existence of a national *Geist.*
In Antonio Machado's *Soledades* we find glosses of popular verses and
themes which were to be more powerfully expressed in *Campos de Castilla*
("Fields of Castile," 1912; augmented edition 1917), where the barren,
upland landscapes around Soria are evoked to reveal eternal essences and
national character. While this collection of moving poems also laments the
death of his young wife, Leonor, and analyzes some of Spain's modern ills,
the central part of the book and the long "Poema de Alvargonzález" are
directly indebted to the outlook expressed earlier by Böhl and Durán. One
might mention in this context the fervent interest in the *café flamenco* of
the Machado brothers before their journey to Paris in 1899 from which
stems, in part, the strongly popular element in Manuel Machado's verses.
His *Alma,* like the works of his fellow Andalusian *modernistas,* makes
poetry out of folklore and the *cante jondo* ("deep song"), an interest
which was to reappear in *La fiesta nacional* ("National Festival," 1906)
and his later *Cante hondo* ("Deep Song," 1912), both of which were
popular successes. Indeed, apart from the obvious intellectual genealogy
which links Machado with Durán, the finisecular poets of Andalusia (virtually all of the *modernista* poets are Andalusian) seem to have inherited
a similar attraction to popular culture, especially in their glosses of the
tradition of the *cantar* and other distinctly Andalusian verse forms.[13] The
poetry of José Sánchez Rodríguez is a case in point. His early verses follow
in the tradition of the bourgeois taste of the late Restoration. His *Alma
andaluza* ("Andalusian Soul," 1900) and *Canciones de la tarde* ("Songs
of Evening," 1902), however, show evidence of the pervasive search for a
"soul" and exploit popular elements. His Symbolist evocation, in its turn,
is a mirror to the poet's own sense of anguish and fallen ideals rather than
an expression of the real suffering of a marginalized people. The concern
is to delineate an identity, personal and national.

Manuel Machado is, at once, the most Symbolist and the most Avant-
Garde poet of this generation.[14] *Alma,* in part a Symbolist evocation of the
Romantic theme of lost ideals, is also a profound analysis of the realm of
dream and the human psyche. Yet, in its form and its fragmented mode of
expression, in its ludic tone, and, subsequently, in *Caprichos* ("Caprices,"
1905) with its clowns (drawn from Verlaine, Banville [1823–1891] and
Laforgue [1860–1887]), Machado had already begun to anticipate the
aesthetic preoccupations of the Avant-Garde. His *El mal poema* ("The
Evil Poem," 1909) marks a reversal of the cultivation of Beauty through

---

[13] Amelina Correa Ramón, *Poetas andaluces en la órbita del modernismo* (Seville: Alfar,
2001).
[14] Rafael Alarcón Sierra, *Entre el modernismo y la modernidad: la poesía de Manuel
Machado* (Seville: Diputación de Sevilla, 1999).

myth, reverie, dream, and evocation; he performs a reversal of the former aesthetic (with not a little influence from Baudelaire and Laforgue) and ushers in a truly Avant-Garde aesthetic which, after 1914, he was to abandon.

The poetry of Villaespesa after 1900, like that of Manuel and Antonio Machado, is deeply indebted to French models. While his collections express typically melancholy moodscapes, twilight autumnal gardens with shadowy avenues and weeping fountains, all evocations of his own inner disharmony, he lacks the subtlety and intellectual depth of his contemporaries. His poetry, for this reason, seems repetitive and limited in appeal. His use of decadent motifs, like those of the poems Jiménez was to publish in this period of 1902–1905 and to abandon to oblivion, is typical of early *modernismo*. However, he fails to express its lasting values.

In the early 1900s a polemic began between the supporters of Darío and those of Salvador Rueda (1857–1933) as to who was the first *modernista*. In spite of the acrimony of the claim and counter-claim, any analysis of the evidence would reveal that the polemic was less a literary one than an ideological one. In essence, Rueda shared none of the negative metaphysical outlook of the new *modernista* generation and, thus, for him, Art had no transcendental significance nor did it constitute a displaced theology. In spite of the striking rhythmic effects, the extravagant use of color and artifice, in spite of his highly original views on poetic practice expressed in *El ritmo* ("Rhythm," 1894), Rueda's poetry belongs to the Realist and civic emphasis in poetry at the end of the century.[15] A poetry inspired in Leibniz's theory of monads and the Great Chain of Being[16] was hardly conducive to the expression of the inner life and the examination of the experiences of the self. Similarly, the outlook of Zayas y Beaumont (1871?–1945?), for all the Parnassian artifice and Orientalist exoticism of *Retratos antiguos* ("Ancient Portraits," 1902) and *Joyeles bizantinos* ("Byzantine Jewels," 1902), was, as his *El modernismo* (1907) shows, critical of the prevailing pessimism.

Thus poetic *modernismo* was formed of a tightly knit group of poets who set out to explore the human condition through their art. They shared, in varying degrees, a belief that Art and Beauty had some transcendental meaning and that they could reveal truths. They used their art to explore their inner spiritual lives, to examine the way in which sensation and perception are transformed into verbal values as much as into insights into the poetic process itself. They attempted to create a type of

---

[15] Marta Palenque, *El poeta y el burgués (poesía y público, 1850–1900)* (Seville: Alfar, 1990).

[16] The German philosopher Gottfried Wilhelm von Leibniz (1646–1716) held that the Universe consisted of indivisible and indestructible entities ("monads") linked together in an ascending hierarchy of existence.

national aesthetic through which their example might create the conditions for a spiritual regeneration based on the revelation of a national soul, latent in the countryside and its people. They also later created a less allusive, sparer style which was to lead to the advent of Pure Poetry, which Jiménez cultivates in the period 1918–1930, and to the renewed interest in popular rhythms, styles, and motifs in the poetry of two other Andalusian poets and a musician of the 1920s: Federico García Lorca (1898–1936), Rafael Alberti (1902–1999), and Manuel de Falla (1876–1946). Poetic *modernismo*, thus, is more than literary historians allow. It is neither neurotic, degenerate, nor lacks seriousness. It is closely related to the preoccupations of *modernista* novelists. Azorín and Valle-Inclán are Symbolist writers. The former is closely related in his style and outlook to Jiménez and Machado. *Modernismo* cannot be circumscribed in terms of two opposed groups. Rather, it marks a second great flowering of Spanish poetry after the Golden Age, the Spanish version of European Symbolism and Modernism.[17]

[17] John Butt, "Modernismo y *Modernism*." In Cardwell and McGuirk, eds., ¿*Qué es el modernismo?* pp. 9–58.

36

Modernism in Catalonia

JOAN RAMON RESINA

If modernization can be defined as the differentiation of autonomous life spheres within society, then Modernism can be seen as a late phase of this process characterized by the emergence of an autonomous cultural sphere. The appearance of "culture" presupposed the existence of a market for art and literary products and an advanced division of labor that included the specialization of criticism as a distinct literary function. Modernism, in this sense, hardly applies to turn-of-the-century Catalan literature, or to Spanish literature for that matter.[1] Whereas "high" Modernism was an aspect of the imperialism of the most advanced nations,[2] Catalan *Modernisme* was a modest but highly interesting manifestation of a society in the throes of national birth. *Modernisme* is best understood as a liminal moment between the *Renaixença*, a movement of cultural salvage tied to the emergence of a politically articulate national identity, and *Noucentisme*, an aesthetic–civic movement which, among other things, consecrated the intellectual's public role. Its temporal limits could well be set, following Ràfols,[3] between 1890 – the year of the joint exhibition in the Sala Parés of Barcelona by the painters Ramon Casas (1866–1932) and Santiago Rusiñol (1861–1931) together with the sculptor Enric Clarasó (1857–1941) – and 1911 – the year when the poet Joan Maragall (1860–1911) died. Alternatively, *Modernisme* could be dated from 1888, the year of the first Universal Exhibition in Barcelona. This year also marked the start of the second period of *L'Avenç* ("Forward," 1881–1893). Conceived originally as a sequel to Valentí Almirall's *Diari Català* ("Catalan Daily," 1879–1881), *L'Avenç* became, from 1888 until its closure in 1893, the prototypically *modernista* journal.[4] Its founder, Jaume Massó i Torrents (1863–1943), embraced Almirall's determination to invest Catalan literature with "el segell, per a nosaltres essencial, de l'esperit modern" ("the seal, essential for us, of the modern spirit").[5] *Diari*

---

[1] Joan Ramon Resina, *Un sueño de piedra: ensayos sobre la literatura del modernismo europeo* (Barcelona: Anthropos, 1990), chapter 1.
[2] Edward Said, *Culture and Imperialism* (London: Vintage, 1993).
[3] J. F. Ràfols, *Modernisme i modernistes* (Barcelona: Destino, 1982).
[4] Joan Ramon Resina, "Modernist Journals in the *Països Catalans*." *Revista Hispánica Moderna* 53 (2000), pp. 388–398.
[5] Jaume Massó i Torrents, "Els Jocs Florals." *Diari Català* (5 May 1879).

Català had been "polítich i literari," like the *Renaixença* itself. *L'Avenç* would also be "political and literary," assuming both spheres of action to be co-factors in modernization, but in addition it would strive to create a differentiated aesthetic sphere.

The differentiation of the aesthetic as a sphere of action was implicated in a general transformation of the public sphere. At no other moment in recent Spanish history were temperament and outlook so different in Catalonia and central Spain as around 1900. Next to a Spain paralyzed by corrupt parliamentarism, anti-Europeanism, and the circus of "flamen-quismo" -cum-bullfights – the "marasmo" ("paralysis") deplored by the authors of the Generation of 1898 – Catalonia vibrated with expansive energies, social unrest, and a puissant national spirit hankering after homologation with the advanced Western nations. At its most confident, Catalonia's bourgeoisie thought that it could assume political leadership and regenerate Spain. This momentary cohesion of idealism and self-confidence, of feverish "catching up," is the reason why *Modernisme* embraced synchronically what were really two sequential goals: the demarcation of the cultural sphere and the logically prior objective of transforming community into society. If the former aim presupposed the latter, social modernization in turn called for a degree of self-regulation and the achievement of political agency. That is why *Modernisme* had to continue the task of the *Renaixença*, updating it in decisive ways. Crucially, it shifted the focus of values from the country to the city, and from a historical identity to a future-oriented conception of the nation as a task in progress. This transformation had two significant landmarks: the standardization of the Catalan language on the basis of Barcelona's speech and the urbanization of literature.

The first goal was achieved through the orthographic reform of Pompeu Fabra (1868–1948), which *L'Avenç* promoted between 1890 and 1892. In turn, Maragall modernized the literary language. In his influential book on Maragall, Josep Pijoan speaks of Maragall's "miraculous" transformation of the corrupt Barcelona dialect into a modern literary language.[6] Barcelona had already found its great novelist in Narcís Oller (1846–1930), but two younger writers, Raimon Casellas (1855–1910), and Victor Català (1869–1966), a pseudonym for Caterina Albert, exemplified the *modernista* attack on the *Renaixença*'s rural myth. Casellas published *Els sots feréstecs* ("Feral Hollows") in 1901 and Català *Solitud* ("Solitude") in 1905. Also antirural was *La vida i la mort d'en Jordi Fraginals* ("Life and Death of Jordi Fraginals," 1912) by Josep Pous i Pagès (1873–1952). This novel, however, though usually classified as *modernista*, already reflects *noucentista* concerns.

---

[6] Josep Pijoan, *El meu Don Joan Maragall* (Barcelona: Catalonia, n.d.), p. 59.

Classifying *Modernisme*'s works is not always easy, because, from a strictly literary point of view, this movement is ill defined. Exasperated by its eclecticism, some critics have denied the term any aesthetic validity. It would rather denote an attitude, a general disposition to update Catalonia's cultural references.[7] In a programmatic statement for *L'Avenç*, Jaume Brossa (1875–1919) declared: "Antigament se donava exclusiva importància a l'escola, quedant les personalitats ofegades dintre d'ella. Avui dia, al contrari, per més que es tinguin en compte les tendències de cada autor, es busca més aviat lo que de nou porta en ideals, en sensacions, en temperaments i en maneres de veure cada una de les personalitats de l'art" ("In the old days people valued the school to the exclusion of everything else, submerging the writer's individuality. Today, even if one takes stock of the tendencies manifested by each author, we are interested in whatever is new in terms of ideals, sensations, temperament, and viewpoint in each artistic personality").[8] Novelty is given preeminence over stylistic coherence. More precisely, the new arises from this unprecedented indifference to fixed aesthetic guidelines. Content is everything. Form, although important, remains ancillary.

What were the new ideals, sensations, and personalities that resounded among the *modernistes*? In a letter dated in 1893, Maragall announced to his friend Antoni Roura, then stationed in the Philippines, that he was sending him the latest issue of *L'Avenç*, so that he could read Maeterlinck's *L'Intruse*. In that way, he – Roura – would have an idea about the literary movement that was afoot. Then Maragall mentions some of the stars in the new constellation: "[N]o fos cas que al tornar te creguessis que encara Zola és l'amo de tot. No, fill, no: Ibsen, Tòlstoi, Maeterlinck, Nietzsche. Et c'est toujours du nord qui [*sic*] nous vient la lumière" ("Lest upon returning [to Catalonia] you believe that Zola is still the master. No, dear, no: Ibsen, Tolstoy, Maeterlinck, Nietzsche. Et c'est toujours du nord qui nous vient la lumière"). Other names circulating in Barcelona literary circles in the nineties also hailed from the North: Ruskin, Wagner, Strindberg. Wagnerism was introduced to the peninsula by Anselm Clavé in 1862, when his popular ensemble sang the "Pilgrim Chorus" from Tanhäuser. In 1878 musicologist Joaquim Marsillach published a biography of Richard Wagner, mentioning Nietzsche for the first time in Spain. In Barcelona Wagnerism spread like wildfire. After several trips to Bayreuth, Joaquim Pena

---

[7] Joan Fuster, *Literatura catalana contemporània* (Barcelona: Curial, 1971), pp. 22–27; Eduard Valentí Fiol, *El primer modernismo literario catalán y sus fundamentos ideológicos* (Barcelona: Ariel, 1973), p. 25; Joan-Lluís Marfany, "Modernisme i noucentisme, amb algunes consideracions sobre el concepte de moviment cultural." *Els Marges* 26 (1982), pp. 33–36; Joan-Lluís Marfany, "El Modernisme." In *Història de la Literatura Catalana*. Vol. VIII. Ed. Joaquim Molas (Barcelona: Ariel, 1986), p. 78.

[8] Jaume Brossa, "Revista general. Recollim el guant." *L'Avenç* 5 (15 September 1893).

(1873–1944) founded the Associació Wagneriana in 1901 and, assisted by several poets, translated all of Wagner's operas into Catalan. Maragall himself translated *Tristan and Isolde* (1896), followed by parts of *Parsifal* that same year. He was one of the first in Spain to speak of Nietzsche, and the first to write about him in an informed manner. In May 1893 he wrote an article entitled "Federico Nietzsche" for the *Diario de Barcelona* ("Barcelona Daily"). The article ran up against ecclesiastical censorship and was turned down. Maragall then published it in Catalan in the July issue of *L'Avenç*.[9] Soon thereafter he translated fragments from *Thus Spoke Zarathustra* for the same journal.

In Nietzsche it was the doctrine of vitalism that captivated Maragall. Intuitive power, spontaneity, and an explicitly antirhetorical stand inform Maragall's theory of "la paraula viva" ("the live word"), which he formulated in his essay *Elogi de la paraula* ("In Praise of the Word," 1903). A late Romantic influenced by Wagner, Emerson, and Carlyle, Maragall sought to endow Catalan culture with a universal myth. In his poem "El Comte Arnau" ("Count Arnau," 1900–1906) he refashioned a Pyrenean legend with Nietzsche's philosophy of will. In the second part of the poem, however, the Faustian thirst for experience is modified through Novalis' idea of poetry's redemptive power. Arnau, an aspiring *Übermensch*, seduces Adalaisa, a luscious nun. As a mystic who denies her sensuality, the nun represents the spirit of decadence. Her body, however, and especially her eyes, betray her vitality: "Adalaisa, tu que ets tan vividora / i que els ulls els tens plens de voluntat" ("Adalaisa, you who are so full of life / and whose eyes are brimming with your will").

When Adalaisa's life-thirsty spirit defies the poet – "I si ta poesia no pot tant, / si no em pots tornar al món, calla i acaba" ("If your poetry is impotent for that / if you cannot return me to the world, hush and be done") – the latter can only assert his faith in an era that has just begun, and begun precisely through an act of faith:

> Adalaisa, Adalaisa, per pietat,
> al temps hi ha encara coses no sabudes;
> la poesia tot just ha començat
> i és plena de virtuts inconegudes.

(Adalaisa, Adalaisa, have mercy, / in the folds of time there are things unknown; / poetry is just beginning / and is full of unimagined powers.)

Poetry thus becomes the Modernist agent *par excellence*. It promises the rebirth not of a past that cannot recur in any case, but of a spirit awaiting unsuspected reincarnations.

---

[9] Valentí, *El primer modernismo*, pp. 330–331.

If one accepts the oft-repeated notion that *Modernisme* was aesthetically indeterminate, then its emphasis on change and transculturation would mean that origin and contemporaneity rather than style or school were its relevant criteria of value. Although partly true, this view simplifies the matter. There is no doubt that "Modernism" implies an incessant adaptation to the present and the rule of fashion.[10] Taken to its logical conclusion, however, this feverish change for the sake of change would mean having to choose between *being* modern and striving to create a *modern* literature. As Paul de Man pointed out: "The spontaneity of being modern conflicts with the claim to think and write about modernity; it is not at all certain that literature and modernity are in any way compatible concepts."[11] *Modernisme*'s impulse to appropriate a *modern aesthetic* as an icon of Catalonia's desired *modernity* presupposed a reflexivity which necessarily placed this movement at a distance from its models. Because of its tendential, aspiring temperament, Catalan *Modernisme* oscillated between a doctrinaire and an ironic sense of its modernity. In the popular *L'auca del senyor Esteve* ("Mr. Esteve's Story Board," 1907), Santiago Rusiñol humorously resolved the issue of aesthetic emancipation by disclosing art's economic foundation, while in his play *L'Homenatge* ("The Homage," 1914) he lampooned both the bourgeoisie's compulsion to deck itself out with a cultural aura and the poet's dependence on a glory that always comes late and then in perfunctory fashion.

It seems fair to conclude that *Modernisme*'s search for the new blurs the movement's formal consistency, which was weak in any case. On the other hand, historical perspective reveals an unmistakable period style. Even if, as de Man suggests, "[t]he appeal of Modernity haunts all literature,"[12] not all literature is equally afflicted with a passion for absolute beginnings. *Modernisme* did have, if not a style, then an overall predilection that in practice has done duty as a style. This "style" is more apparent in art, and especially in architecture, than it is in literature. Architecture was, not coincidentally, the leading *modernista* domain: it preceded and outlasted the movement's literary manifestations, and left a deeper, more enduring trace in Catalonia's cultural legacy.

The indefinition and marginality of literary *Modernisme* relates to the contradictions between its engagement with tradition and its desire for immediacy. Such a desire can only be satisfied with "the facticity of entities that are in contact with the present," and is therefore unwilling to invest in objects steeped in temporality, as is always the case with linguistic

---

[10] Joan-Lluís Marfany, "Sobre el significat del terme 'Modernisme.'" In *Aspectes del Modernisme* (Barcelona: Curial, 1975), p. 38.

[11] Paul de Man, "Literary History and Literary Modernity." In *Blindness and Insight* (2nd. edn. Minneapolis: University of Minnesota Press, 1983), p. 142.

[12] "Literary Modernity," p. 152.

objects.[13] Literary *Modernisme* could neither satisfy nor forgo its double investment. Vis-à-vis architecture, which could deploy a medievalist symbology of national memory without ceasing to privilege constructive rationalism and to research new techniques and materials, literature remained at a disadvantage. On the one hand, it had to work with a dialectalized language whose most powerful monuments lay far back in the Renaissance and the Middle Ages. On the other hand, its claim to modernity rested on its rejection of tradition. This ruptural impulse, common to many *modernistes*, appears at its most uncompromising in Jaume Brossa: "A èpoques noves, formes d'art noves. El fonament de la cultura d'una generació ha de reposar sobre lo bo de l'anterior; mes si aquesta porta un patrimoni dolent, és preferible menysprear-lo, no fer-ne cas i començar foc nou" ("New times require new art forms. The culture of a [new] generation must be founded upon the best that the former generation was able to create, but if that patrimony is bad, then it is better to disdain it, not pay heed to it, and start a new fire").[14]

"Foc Nou" ("New Fire") was the name of a left-wing *modernista* group composed of Brossa, Alexandre Cortada (1865–1935), Pere Coromines (1870–1939), and the playwright Ignasi Iglésias (1871–1928). An anarchist sympathizer, Coromines was condemned to death during the infamous Montjuïc trials, then pardoned after numerous intellectuals intervened on his behalf in a climate of international outrage. Brossa too had a brush with the authorities. In 1896 he was court-martialed for his pacifist propaganda against the colonial war in Cuba. He managed to escape to France and died in Barcelona shortly after his return during the First World War. Each one of these intellectuals was Catalanist and internationalist at the same time. There was no contradiction, no either/or dilemma to disentangle. Catalanism was the medium, the condition of actuality of their internationalism. They worked to insert Catalonia into the universal sweep of modern life. Brossa, in "L'esperit universalista," expressed their collective purpose with lapidary clarity: "Tant de bo que aviat puguem dir: la regió catalana ha mort! Visca la Humanitat catalana!" ("Let's hope that soon we will be able to say: the Catalan region has died! Long live Catalan Humanity!").[15]

Like the earlier *modernista* group constituted around *L'Avenç* and *Catalonia* (1898–1900), those of Foc Nou contributed to the ferment of ideas that made Catalonia, and especially Barcelona, a uniquely dynamic space in a torpid Spain. They remained a minority, however, on the edge of the cultural and political establishments. It is doubtful that they, in their

---

[13] De Man, "Literary Modernity," pp. 158–159.
[14] Jaume Brossa, "Viure del passat." *L'Avenç* 4.9 (1892).
[15] *El Poble Català* (11 December 1907).

mythopoetic role, really had the sway and the prestige imagined by Joan Fuster when he asserts, speaking of Maragall, that "Ser poeta, allí, entre parlamentaris i anarquistes, entre senyors Esteves i Estevets, tenia, a desgrat de tot, un abast virtual d'influència i d'acció" ("Being a poet at that time, between congressmen and anarchists, between *senyors Esteves* and *Estevets*, had, in spite of all, a virtual range of influence and of action").[16] Maragall enjoyed unprecedented prestige and the respect of the most influential Catalan politicians. Nevertheless, his case was unique. He owed that prestige less to his poetry, which few read, than to his political moderation and his membership in the bourgeois class. His role as *Modernisme*'s emblematic poet was purchased by the life-long efforts and thrift of an enterprising father, a certain *senyor Esteve*. In *L'auca del senyor Esteve* (1906), Rusiñol told the story of many a *modernista*. Their historical problem was how to wrest aesthetic autonomy from the economic mission laid out for them by their elders. In practical terms, the problem was how to redirect the energies marshaled by the previous generation in industrial or commercial concerns and turn them to the production of symbolic value. At the turn of the century bourgeois youth codified their demand for autonomy within their own class as aesthetic revolt. A storm in a teapot, no doubt, but one that left its mark on progressive Catalanism, while contributing to outline the social figure of the artist and the intellectual, a figure that *Noucentisme* would both sanction and restrain.

[16] Joan Fuster, "Maragall i Unamuno cara a cara." In *Obres Completes.* Vol. IV (Barcelona: Edicions 62, 1975), pp. 210–211.

37

Modernist narrative in the 1920s

C. A. LONGHURST

In Spain as elsewhere the 1920s saw a wave of experimentalism in fictional narrative. Modernist narrative, however, cannot be circumscribed to the historical Avant-Garde of the 1920s. Clear precedents can be traced back to the 1890s. The Pío Cid novels (1897–1898) of Ángel Ganivet, as well as some of Galdós' later work, already evince some of the characteristics that will become the hallmarks of Modernist fiction. The well-known 1902 novels of Unamuno, Baroja, Azorín, and Valle-Inclán confirm an emerging trend, but it is the appearance of Unamuno's *Niebla* ("Mist") in 1914 that sets the seal. Here are visibly present many of the central preoccupations of Modernist narrative. Such concerns as the self-conscious text, the nature of artistic autonomy, the role of language, the identity of the self, and authenticity of the image are all given prominence in this work. Baroja was at his most innovative in his early work but, despite a strong defense of Modernism in 1903, never developed into a leading-edge experimental novelist, preferring in his later years to return to a highly personal brand of documentary Realism. Azorín on the other hand moved from an amorphous *Bildungsroman*-type novel in the first decade of the century to a more radical exploration of Modernist themes such as time, writing, and creative doubt in *Doña Inés* (1925), *El caballero inactual* ("The Unmodern Gentleman," 1928), and *El libro de Levante* ("The Book from the Levant," 1929), each more rarified than the preceding one and demonstrating only too well the danger of artistic introversion. Of the older writers – those associated with the so-called "Generation of 1898" – it was Valle-Inclán who, returning to narrative fiction after a lengthy period writing in other genres, produced in 1926–1927 what is arguably the most brilliant experimental novel of the Avant-Garde decade: *Tirano Banderas* ("The Tyrant: A Novel of Warm Lands"). The range of influences absorbed and techniques used in this work is remarkable: cubism, theosophy, the occult, narcosis, time compression, theatricality and performativeness, and a linguistic inventiveness unparalleled in the Spanish novel. The work not only speaks of the human condition in terms of tyranny and enslavement, but succeeds in doing so through the evocation of an artistically stylized world. If Modernism arose as a conscious rejoinder to the scientific pretensions of Naturalism, *Tirano Banderas* proves that the new aesthetic could deal just as effectively with matters of general human import.

Unamuno, Azorín, and Valle-Inclán all contributed work whose taxonomy demands their inclusion under the Modernist label. Of the slightly younger novelists, Ramón Pérez de Ayala (1880–1962) and Gabriel Miró (1879–1930) produced work that conforms to the Modernist paradigm. Possessed of a wide erudition, Pérez de Ayala was a formidable literary essayist and a leading intellectual of his day, but in his novels he wears his erudition lightly and usually to comic effect. He was at the same time, and as a committed Republican, deeply interested in the exploration of themes relevant to his day. In the relatively short span of twenty years, from 1907 to 1926, he produced some of the most original fiction to come out of twentieth-century Spain. His earlier novels, known collectively as the Alberto tetralogy after the main character, evince much the same existential preoccupations as the early novels of Baroja and Azorín, but conveyed with a good deal of humor and satirical intent. His later novels are more overtly experimental and to a degree partake of the interest in metafiction typical of the 1920s, but the human interest and the predilection for the good yarn never wane. *Belarmino y Apolonio* ("Belarmino and Apolonio") the story of two shoemakers, one a linguistic philosopher, the other a dramatist and versifier, is one of the few comic masterpieces of modern Spain and does not disguise the pervasive influence of *Don Quijote*. The potentially trite story of the priest and the prostitute is given a wholly original treatment by the inclusion of a writer-figure, a modern day Cide Hamete who not only happens upon both of these characters quite separately, immediately establishing their linked past, but also becomes rather more interested in the unusual hobbies and personalities of their respective fathers, the two shoemakers, who displace their progeny as the center of interest in the novel. This allows Pérez de Ayala to introduce topical ideas on art and philosophy but to do so within the confines of a comic plot held together by the picturesque personalities of the two shoemakers and their apparently antagonistic attitudes to life. Central to the novel's driving idea and construction is the concept of perspective or vision in depth, which in the physical world is accomplished through the use of two eyes. It is the challenge of achieving such a stereoscopic vision in writing that Pérez de Ayala playfully sets out to meet in *Belarmino y Apolonio*. This he does by employing perspectivistic techniques which invite the reader to see characters and situations from different angles. Virtually everything in the novel is doubled. There are two story lines: the traditional Romantic one and the modern existential one. There are two main narrators. There are two protagonists. The setting is seen through the eyes of two characters of different sensibilities. There are two extra-diegetic figures, one in the prologue and one in the epilogue, who enjoy opposite viewpoints. In addition, virtually all the characters, major and minor, are appraised from radically different perspectives. Viewpoint is everything. The novel is imbued with a modern relativism in which knowledge is created by our cultural baggage, and personal predisposition defines our parameters. In the case of Belarmino this relativism extends to language. The central preoccupation in linguistic philosophy – the connection between language and knowledge – is raised in a mock-serious manner. If language is in some sense knowledge, then knowledge can be recreated by a process of linguistic redefinition, which is exactly what Belarmino attempts to do in his comically creative explorations of the dictionary. Language, then, is one more, perhaps the ultimate, perspective, especially so when the individual using it is a writer.

Pérez de Ayala's final novel, published in two volumes, *Tigre Juan* and *El curandero de su honra.* ("Tiger Juan," 1926), explores and parodies two themes common in Spanish literature, *donjuanismo* and the conjugal honor code, interconnected here through a plot of considerable formal complexity and intertextual richness. The obsessively jealous Calderonian husband appears in the guise of a nineteenth-century Asturian stall-keeper whose tigerish roar is infinitely worse than his bite, while his antagonist don Juan, whom he admires, takes the form of an effeminate and decadent traveling salesman. The seemingly wayward yet ultimately innocent wife is a diffident young woman, fearful of her husband and all too easily impressed by the itinerant don Juan. All three main characters are made to learn their lessons against tradition. Tigre Juan discovers the painful truth that he is no tiger (at least not a Calderonian one), reconciles himself to uncertainty, and bravely confronts social convention. His wife discovers that her amorous suitor is a cowardly wimp, all brag and no heart, and that life with Tigre Juan is infinitely better than the one she happens to witness in the brothel where she is dropped by her reluctant abductor. Finally, the latter is exposed for what he is: a shallow, castrated lover who proves incapable of putting his seductive words into action. These three characters are supported by another three with complementary roles: Tigre Juan's adoptive son, who exemplifies modernity as against Tigre Juan's tradition; the son's girlfriend, who exemplifies utter fidelity to her man irrespective of convention; and the latter's adoptive mother who, after a sterile marriage to an impotent man, finds vicarious satisfaction in acting as a marriage broker, and in a more subtle way by manipulating the events of the novel as if she were the author's fictional persona. Though evidently symbolic, all these and some other more minor characters offer a rich tapestry of human types not often found in twentieth-century fiction. Yet the quintessence of the novel lies in a cultural dialogue with existing literature (especially theatre) and literary themes in the context of modern ideas on love and sex, especially those propounded by the well-known physician and *homme de lettres* Gregorio Marañón. To this modernity of ideas has to be added a modernity of technique, not as marked as in *Belarmino y Apolonio*, but with a number of aspects which must have appeared radically new at the time of first publication. One is the importance given to language. Ayala constantly changes expression depending on character and situation. Language becomes very much an identifying trait: each character is a mode of expression, each situation a mode of composition or perception. The novel as verbal construct is indeed invoked in allusions to the powerful effect of words and to the capacity of language to create illusions. More immediately obvious is the use of musical terminology to suggest pace and symphonic development. The most visually striking innovation is the split-page arrangement for part of *El curandero de su honra*, in which the story line is divided into two separate but parallel strands, each strand occupying one of two columns on the page. The intention behind this technique has caused considerable critical debate; but what can be said with total conviction is that the forced alternation from one column to another makes the reader see connections which would not be noticed if the two strands had been conventionally printed as consecutive chapters. Although Ayala has been criticized in the past for excessive intellectualization, these two novels are much more than just "discussion-fiction" and rank amongst the finest examples of Modernist narrative in Spain.

No less distinctive is Gabriel Miró's final work of fiction, also in two volumes, *Nuestro Padre San Daniel* ("Our Father San Daniel," 1921) and *El obispo leproso* ("The Leprous Bishop," 1926), known together as "the Oleza novels" after the fictitious name of the city in which it is set, the real-life Orihuela in southeastern Spain. Alongside Clarín's *La Regenta*, this must rank as one of the outstanding novels of provincial life in the whole of Spanish literature. To the strength of characterization evident in its nineteenth-century affinity it adds new techniques closely associated with Modernism. The novel as a whole is a subtle but powerful denunciation of the influence exerted by those associated with Carlist traditionalism and its authoritarian and bleak spiritual philosophy. In this sense it follows in the footsteps of Baroja, Azorín, and Pérez de Ayala. The tormented self-denial of the Carlist don Álvaro, his wife Paulina's virtual imprisonment in a loveless marriage, their son Pablo's conflictive childhood and illicit adolescent love, the agony of an enlightened bishop afflicted by a disfiguring disease, the sadistic nature of the austere Father Bellod, the paradoxical humanity of the heterodox priest don Magín, the innocence of the delightfully enticing doña Purita, the prurient malevolence of the sanctimonious doña Elvira: these are but a few of the ingredients of this rich novel whose essential theme is the very human one of unfulfilled expectations of happiness, and whose language is a tour de force of insinuation. Apart from its implacable critique of the clerical right and the richness of its characterization, the work stands out for the use of techniques more usually associated with the Proustian brand of Modernism. Memory is given a special role in the depiction of the characters, with the phenomenon being explored from a fully modern perspective. What interests Miró is not a process of conscious recall but rather the spontaneous unconscious process through which a sense impression suddenly transports us to an experience that took place at some point in our past. Though he never says so directly, the role of the senses in transcending temporal barriers is repeatedly shown to be crucial. What Miró does is to make subtle, almost imperceptible, connections between the then and the now: a shout, an enclosed garden, a face at a window, a picture hook on a wall, the stain on a handkerchief, these apparently intranscendental phenomena are used as triggers of involuntary recall. The "sensación de presencia" ("feeling of presence"), as Miró terms this intrusion, affects different characters in different ways, but underlying the phenomenon is the modern view that our senses do not obey the conventions of time that govern our normal conscious lives. Time has lost its absolute value; what we have is a perception of time, a particularly Modernist approach. Miró's characters, at moments of stress or emotional tension, are transported onto a temporal plane which is more than a mere recall of the past. It is rather an awareness of a space in which past, present, and future coexist simultaneously. "Sentirse en otro tiempo y ahora" ("To feel oneself in another time and in the present"), thinks the unhappily married Paulina as she tries to reconcile past and present. Similarly her adolescent son, caught in a maze of sensuality and moral reprobation, regresses to scenes of childhood security and relives comforting moments of reassurance in which enjoyment did not mean sin. The perception of time is inseparable from the perception of sounds, fragrances, and the objects that surround the characters. Sounds have associations that take the characters back in time; indeed for Miró it is not even the association but the sound itself that has this effect. When the elderly don Daniel hears the church bells on the eve of Saint Peter's Day, the sound takes him back to his childhood, and Miró describes the phenomenon as if don Daniel had physically regressed in time: "Y la esquila tocaba infantilmente" ("And the bell pealed in a childlike way"). Fragrances are even more prominent, for the novel is suffused with olfactory sensations. For don Magín the sensuous scent of flowers becomes a substitute for other kinds of sense experiences which in his condition of priest he has chosen to forgo. Flowers smell of distant happiness, of the "might have been": "casi siempre huelen las flores a un instante de felicidad que ya no nos pertenece" ("flowers nearly always smell of an instant of happiness that is no longer ours"). Of all the Spanish novels of Modernism, *Nuestro Padre San Daniel* and *El obispo leproso* stand out as the most sensitively crafted meditation on the mystery of time.

Several writers among those associated with the historical Avant-Garde of the 1920s tried their hands at the novel, but only two, Jarnés and Gómez de la Serna, did so assiduously. Benjamín Jarnés (1888–1949) was the most accomplished novelist of the *Revista de Occidente* group that coalesced around Ortega y Gasset, but the influence of the latter's aesthetic theories should be seen in terms of the debate which he initiated on the function and appeal of art rather than as the motivation for the novels written by the literary vanguard of the 1920s. *Locura y muerte de nadie* ("Madness and Death of a Nobody," 1929) is the most critically praised of Jarnés' novels, and it is probably significant that it is the most genre-specific of all, with an identifiable theme and an accessible story line. In addition to the original version there is a posthumously published version which was much modified and enlarged by the author to rather dubious effect. The plot is based around the relationships of a foursome: a husband, a wife, and her two lovers; but the theme is the Unamunian one of self-identity, especially that of Juan Sánchez, a dreary, colorless individual who is a failure at whatever he turns to and feels the oppressive weight of anonymity bringing him to increasingly despairing attempts at notoriety, such as planning, but of course failing, to catch his wife *in flagrante* with her lovers in order to kill them. For him, the curse of life is that no-one recognizes what is distinctive about him. Even his deranged attempt to achieve the recognition of others by perpetrating a massive fraud comes to nothing when his assistant is credited with the masterplot and arrested for the crime while Juan is seen as just another of the obscure victims of the deception.

There is more to the novel than Juan's predicament, however, a good deal of the interest coming via the complications wrought by the amorous deviousness of the female character, and partly through the constant reflections of Arturo, one of her lovers, used by Jarnés as the main center of consciousness. Indeed it is clear that for the female co-protagonist each of her three men represents a different facet of the whole man whom she seeks, so that the whole novel can be seen as revolving around personality and its perception. What contributes to the novel's modernity is a number of the techniques employed by Jarnés which also add in no small measure to the novel's originality. Chief among these is the use of cinematic techniques, evoked not only through the presence of screening (of a news reel and a Russian film), but also in the description of other scenes such as the intermittent vision of a woman observed from a distance as she walks behind a succession of arches, or in the reference to an abrupt interruption in the flow of the imagination as a "tijeretazo al celuloide" ("snipping the celluloid"). Oneiric techniques modeled on

surrealist painting are employed repeatedly in the semi-conscious perceptions of the main characters, whether of scenes of scantily clad dancers at
a cabaret, the alluring legs of a young madam dimly seen during a state
of torpor, or, most strikingly, in the closing scene in which a metamorphic
succession of images serves to capture the trance-like state of the eidetic
Arturo waiting for his turn at the bank – just as he was in the opening
scene. Finally Jarnés includes in his novel, albeit discreetly, moments of
narrative self-consciousness in which the novel reflects its own development and refers ironically to its lack of (melo)dramatic content. Indeed
the whole novel is a subtle study in anticlimax and by implication an
ironic critique of the penchant for exaggerated emotions and sensational
plots of popular fiction. Written with an extreme attention to expression,
Locura y muerte de nadie is a paradigmatic specimen of the 1920s novel
for the aesthetically precocious.

Teoría del zumbel ("Theory of the Spinning Top"), published a year
later, is a good deal less circumspect in its use of fashionable metafictional
devices, yet it is, even for 1930, a strikingly original novel that bears
comparison with Milan Kundera's *Immortality* and other Post-modernist
works. A simple plot (a variant on the story of the rake and the virgin in
which, parodically, the rake remains such but the virgin does not) is given
a radically experimental treatment in which the "author" is as much a
character in the novel as are his characters. Unamuno's *Niebla*, although
an obvious precedent, is left well behind in Jarnés' playful exploration
of the relation between author and personages. The image of the spinning top applies both teleologically and novelistically: the world and its
characters will one day run out of spin when God, or the story teller,
finally lays down the spinning cord ("zumbel"). There is no distinction
between (his)story and reflection, between anecdote and compositional
discussion; the author-figure is an observer, but one who mixes comfort-
ably with his characters (as indeed does God himself at one point) and
converses freely with them. Accused in the epilogue of abandoning his
characters, he confesses that his real characters are a cord, a telegram,
and a watch wrecked in an accident, items whose symbolism is evident.
The novel is rich in intertextualities, with both implicit and explicit allusions to such disparate works as *Don Quijote*, Fray Luis de León's *La
perfecta casada* ("The Perfect Wife"), the Bible, and the biography of
Saint Margaret of Cortona. One striking feature is Jarnés' gift for capturing different states of consciousness: drunkenness, daydream fantasies,
erotic dreams, the delirium of a victim of a car accident – these and other
mental experiences are conveyed in a succession of vivid images whose
apparent arbitrariness belies a clever selection of elements without resort
to the labored and over-ornate lexicon that affected some of the writing of
the period. *Teoría del zumbel* is one of those totalizing novels frequent in

Modernism, but it is never a portentous one. On the contrary: it displays a gentle self-mockery that owes not a little to *Don Quijote*.

Ramón Gómez de la Serna (1888–1963), a larger-than-life character who became doyen of the Spanish literary vanguard of the 1920s and 1930s, famed inventor of the *greguería*, a playful Baroque-style conceit which defies definition, suffered a severe decline in his reputation following his exile in 1936. His fecundity, heterogeneity, and willful eccentricity are problems in themselves, but the fragmented and invertebrate nature of his novels appears to have discouraged scholarly analysis, despite his unrivaled talent as the artificer of linguistic pyrotechnics. Though lacking Jarnés' craftsmanship, there can be no doubt that he personifies vanguardism in Spain so far as narrative is concerned. He described his artistic self as a sponge with a hundred eyes, and indeed his novels do reflect a spongiform porosity. *El incongruente* ("The Incongruous Man," 1922) consists of a string of episodes ranging from the improbable to the impossible under the guise of the fictional biography of Gustavo, "un disolvente de todas las leyes de la vida" ("a disrupter of all the laws of life"), in whose presence man-made and natural laws go into a spin. Gómez de la Serna's idiosyncratic linguistic inventions occupy a prominent place in the episodic plot. Unlike Ganivet's Pío Cid, who makes things happen, Gustavo is merely the passive participator in the serendipitous happenings. Fleeing from the unexpected events that befall him whenever he ventures out on the streets, he goes to the movies only to find himself playing the lead role in the film, while the lead actress turns out to be the amorous young lady next to whom he happens to sit. The novel illustrates Gómez de la Serna's strength and weakness as a novelist: his enormous talent for making extraordinary occurrences out of apparently ordinary situations; and his utter incapacity to create literary characters that acquire human relevance and surrogacy. Even *La Quinta de Palmyra* ("Palmyra's Country House," 1923), one of his few serious novels, suffers from the defect of overdrawn characters and arbitrary incidents. Palmyra Talares, living in palatial surroundings on the Portuguese coast (where the novel was written), is a kind of modern Calypso (rather than the Cleopatra she, or her creator, thinks she is) who wastes no opportunity to seduce casual visitors but who feels betrayed when they eventually tire of her incessant need for attention. It is not so much her nymphomania ("inextirpables pensamientos de voluptuosidad" ["ineradicable voluptuous thoughts"]) as her simple adventurism and lack of judgment that make of her a less than credible figure. To judge from the protagonist's susceptibility to Nature, Gómez de la Serna had probably set out to create a tragically sensitive woman; if so it did not quite work. The author's insight seems to be reduced to the character's desire to "volverse a encontrar como objeto de goce" ("find herself once again the object of sexual possession"), which in a full-length novel makes for a sadly shallow psychological portrait. On the other hand there is no denying the narrative resourcefulness with which Gómez de la Serna spins out his tale. The novel is a succession of five failed love affairs, each one less likely than the preceding one. A false and fatuous Spanish aristocrat, a mining engineer given to gambling, a Jewish physician from America, a second-rate concert pianist, and a dour sea-captain all pass through Palmyra's enchanted *quinta*, engage her affections for a while, but do not share her enthusiasm for her Edenic retreat. Entertaining but inconsequential, the various love episodes are mere distractions from the novel's central idea: Palmyra is only truly in love with her country house, not with the men who serve to satisfy her sexuality. In the end the protagonist is forced to recognize "una idea antigua" ("an old idea"), and the novel ends with Palmyra in a lesbian relationship that acts as a mirror of her own "abismo insaciable" ("insatiable abyss"). One suspects nonetheless that the book was never conceived as a study of a lesbian psyche and that the dénouement is another of Gómez de la Serna's idiosyncratic turns. *La quinta de Palmyra* is, all the same, one of the writer's most harmonious novels in which the cult of the clever utterance made for its own sake is kept in check.

El novelista ("The Novelist," 1924), by contrast, brings us back to the consciously anarchical and fragmented approach that is the hallmark of Gómez de la Serna's creativity. The story is not so much of the human personality of the novelist Andrés Castilla as of his diverse production. This suits Gómez de la Serna's wayward talents perfectly, since what we are offered is an ingenious succession of fragments of the various novels with which Castilla is juggling. Most of the book consists of substantial extracts taken from Castilla's novels in progress. We learn at the end that he authored thirty-seven full-length novels, each one recorded under its title. One could of course argue that these compositions are important because the authentic biography of an artist is in his work, not in the humdrum events of his habitual human existence. Yet in some ways Castilla's life is every bit as fantastic as his compositions, since he appears to live on the same plane as his characters, or the characters on his, to judge by their frequent meetings. Gómez de la Serna's novelist is a fragmented being, torn to shreds by his uncontrollable graphomania. It is probably pointless to look for allegorical interpretations based on the idea of self-reflexive fiction that became fashionable in the 1920s. What we have here is simply a process of composition, a process moreover that could end anywhere or not end at all. Gómez de la Serna's restlessness as a raconteur is perfectly reflected in the headlong rush of episodes, whether Castilla is putting pen to paper or desperately searching for copy from the vantage point of the many abodes he rents for the purpose in different quarters of Madrid, visiting jails, hospitals, cafés, hotels, the orphanage, placing advertisements for particular types in newspapers, or traveling to London and Paris to study the gas street lamps for his most unusual novel of all, "El farol número 185" ("Street Lamp Number 185"). *El novelista*, like so much of Gómez de la Serna's work, thrives on the assumption that life is tedious in its essential unintelligibility and that literature can be nothing but a parody of this radical absurdity. For Ramón, the rational world is a temporary illusion which we experience while we wait for the inevitable end of "el mundo que morirá de un apagón" ("the world that will die in a blackout"), as he reminds us in the closing words of the novel.

If Gómez de la Serna bears some relation to Modernist experiments, the equally talented and commercially much more successful Wenceslao Fernández Flórez (1884–1964) stands in intriguing contrast to the Modernist aesthetic, not because he was one of the many epigones of an earlier tradition but rather because he developed in a significantly different direction. Sometimes mistakenly labeled a Realist in literary manuals because of his initial Naturalist leanings, his best-known novels defy easy classification. Indeed in their own way his fictional experiments are as distinctive as the Modernist ones. Their dominant note is satirico-philosophical and they tend toward allegory. *El secreto de Barba Azul* ("Bluebeard's Secret," 1923), although adopting the loose framework of the *Bildungsroman*, is anything but conventional. The biographical trajectory of Mauricio Dossart, an idealistic and leisured gentleman from the imaginary country of Surlandia who falls prey to political intrigue, serves as the connecting thread of a vast and mocking portrait of modern civilization, especially in its political dimensions. Among the many facets to be satirized are patriotism and nationalism, government and monarchy, militarism and the state machine, conspiracy and revolution, heroism and war, crime and punishment, love and procreation, social laws and moral laws. Dossart finds to his suprise that every aspect of political and social life is a hypocrisy, a sham, a well-rehearsed farce. Fernández Flórez's corrosive irony dismantles every ideal. Everything that surrounds us is interpreted according to our own self-serving prejudices. Man deludes himself in searching for his mission, for he has none. He is pure accident. Bluebeard's secret room is laughingly empty. *El secreto de Barba Azul* does share a totalizing approach with some well-known Modernist novels (e.g. Robert Musil's *The Man without Qualities*). It aspires to show up the emptiness and illusory quality of modern civilization and it coincides with Baroja in the denunciation of the "mentiras vitales" ("life-sustaining lies") that serve to pull the wool over our eyes. The ending, too, is reminiscent of Baroja: compassion is the only valid sentiment. Yet Fernández Flórez does not experiment with styles of narration. Apart from the skeptical outlook and absence of ideological commitment that pervade the entire novel, there is nothing distinctively modern about the actual narrative. The plot

is the excuse for repeated reflections on the range of topics already indicated, and each chapter corresponds to a particular theme which is given
satirical treatment through a technique of anecdotal hyperbole and situational bathos often straying into pure caricature. Several of the characters
engage in philosophizing, but it is of a dilettantish kind. All transcendent
beliefs and ideals, whether religious, moral, political, or emotional, are
ironically reduced to self-delusions. It shares the *fin-de-siècle* attitude of
the futility of human existence that we find in *Camino de perfección* and
La voluntad, but with amused detachment rather than despair. A novel
that would be profoundly nihilistic if taken seriously, it remains an entertaining pasquinade, though one laced with Rabelaisian wit.

Las siete columnas ("The Seven Pillars," 1926) is more clearly allegorical. The seven pillars turn out to be the seven deadly sins, without which
modern civilization cannot sustain itself. The anarchist hermit Acracio
Pérez persuades the Devil to abolish temptation and with it the seven sins.
Five years later the country of Negrimia is on its knees. Far from leading to happiness, liberation from the compulsion to sin leads to loss of
will-power and stagnation. Without avarice, industry, agriculture, banking, and all commercial enterprises collapse. Without lust, men do not
desire women and the birth-rate plummets. Without pride, no politician
wants to govern, no inventor wants to invent, no writer wants to write,
and no philanthropist wants to engage in beneficence. Without envy, no-
one wants to outshine his neighbor, property values collapse, and women
no longer strive to outdo one another in attractiveness. Without wrath,
workers no longer feel the anger of exploitation or the urge to confront
their employers and are consequently reduced to poverty. Without sloth,
no-one wants to exert himself because work had been seen as a means
to gain a paradise of leisure. Without gluttony the previously prosperous gourmet food enterprises lose their clients. With the disappearance
of sin comes the disappearance of forgiveness, and without forgiveness
there is no compassion. The allegory of *Las siete columnas* is conveyed
through an entertaining mixture of diverse characters, anecdotes, and
quasi-philosophical dialogues. For all its popular appeal the novel is a
shrewd meditation on the flaws in human nature in general, and modern
man in particular. It is achieved without resorting either to the extravagance of a Gómez de la Serna or the over-refinement of a Jarnés. Although
he uses the Modernist convention of valuing incident above plot, story-
telling remains very much at the forefront of Fernández Flórez's modern
parables. Hence his considerable appeal to a wide readership.

El malvado Carabel ("The Evil Carabel," 1931) is the last of Fernández
Flórez's allegorical novels. Once again it is a humorously engaging study
of human nature, this time in the shape of Amaro Carabel, the humble bank clerk whose loyalty and industriousness are cruelly rewarded

and who comes to realize that honesty and hard work are a recipe for exploitation by others. His decision to improve his lot by taking to crime is nevertheless foiled not just by his own incompetence but by his innate goodness. This is a moral fable in comic form, the lesson of which is clear (and indeed openly enunciated by one of the main characters at the end): one is born either good or evil and there is nothing one can do about it. Evil will always triumph over good because, whereas evil behavior is proactive, resourceful, and assertive, virtuous behavior, being based on an essentially negative code ("Thou shalt not . . ."), is passive, timorous, and self-denying. The world belongs to evildoers. Once again, such a view of the human situation has much in common with that of Pío Baroja, but Fernández Flórez lacks the latter's coherence of vision and ethical consistency. Baroja's agnostic questioning is replaced here by a pervasive irony that comes dangerously close to cynicism. There is, however, no doubting Fernández Florez's inventiveness as a storyteller or his awareness of modern themes. *El malvado Carabel* ends with a delightfully mischievous parody of vanguard poetry when the orphan whom the maladroit Carabel has tried to initiate into the ways of crime is discovered writing surrealist verse. While such impish frivolity inevitably brings Gómez de la Serna to mind, Fernández Florez's gifted creativity is perhaps closer to that of *Los trabajos del infatigable creador Pío Cid* ("The Labors of the Tireless Creator Pio Cid"), with which Modernist narrative in Spain could reasonably be said to have begun.

38

Noucentisme

JOAN RAMON RESINA

Noucentisme designates the dominant cultural movement in Catalonia from 1906, the year of *Solidaritat Catalana* (the Unified Catalanist Front), to 1923, when the political, cultural, and economic *entente* broke down under the dictatorship of Miguel Primo de Rivera. *Noucentisme* is often understood merely to characterize the ideological support given by a group of artists and intellectuals to the Lliga Regionalista de Catalunya. Under the leadership of Enric Prat de la Riba (1870–1917), this reformist party created the Mancomunitat, an embryonic autonomous government. Through a dexterous use of the meager competencies and resources of this institution, Prat developed an inchoate infrastructure with a view to modernizing Catalonia. This entailed, among other things, consolidating its industrial economy. It would be misleading, however, to identify the Lliga narrowly with class interests. As Joan Fuster remarks, to speak about this party as if it were the political equivalent of the Catalan bourgeoisie would be inaccurate, for the bourgeoisie that threw in its lot with Cambó's (1876–1947) and Prat's regionalism was not the same bourgeoisie that followed Alfonso Sala after Primo de Rivera's coup in September 1923.[1]

Prat tackled the difficult task of building proto-governmental structures in a society that was devoid of political power. Lacking the legal basis and the means for actual governance, he laid the foundations of a modern civic society by intervening in the areas of education, technical expertise, and culture. The *noucentistes* saw themselves as purveyors of the idealism required for an ambitious project steered by the politicians and energized by the country's economic leadership. There is no question that in offering their collaboration many *noucentistes* were responding to the challenge and opportunities opened by political action on the margins of the state. As Norbert Bilbeny points out, it was difficult for an intellectual to reject the call for the political autonomy of his or her group, for beyond the immediate social implications this goal always has an unmistakable ethical content. Implied in the universal moral value of "autonomy" is, first of all, the individual subject as it was understood since the Enlightenment.[2]

---

[1] Joan Fuster, *Contra el noucentisme* (Barcelona: Crítica, 1977), pp. 151–152.
[2] Norbert Bilbeny, *Política Noucentista: De Maragall a d'Ors* (Catarroja: Afers, 1999), p. 69.

The issue of autonomy is crucial to an understanding of the Catalan movements in the final decades of the nineteenth century and the first decades of the twentieth. If the *noucentistes* consciously promoted certain political objectives, then this "correlation" of culture with politics cannot be accounted for by the notion of ideological reflection. *Noucentisme* attempted to define and eventually to produce the social and political conditions necessary for intellectual autonomy, and it did it, first of all, by trying to secure professional status for writers. Eugeni D'Ors (1881–1954), *Noucentisme*'s foremost theoretician, made professionalization a precondition for scientific scholarship.[3] The *noucentistes* collaborated with the politicians out of a conviction that high culture requires the existence of institutional vehicles. At times their sense of the primacy of culture – a primacy grounded in Catalonia's modern history – could strain their relations with the politicians. Such tensions were the clearest indication that this group of writers was not, as one often reads, an organic intelligentsia, but rather cultural producers convinced that institutional values originate in the individual's judgment. They conceived of this faculty not as a mere intellectual balance ("seny" in Catalan) but as the capacity for intervention in the world. Posited by D'Ors as the root of all cultural achievement, "albir," from Latin "arbitrium," was conceptualized as the enlivening of reason by the will. Thus, although the *noucentistes* did not derive their ideas from a political program, they conceived those ideas (and the incumbent aesthetic) in social and civic terms; as dignified, so to speak, by their service to the political philosophy expressed in Prat's cultural policies.

Who were they and what were their ideas? Among the group were the poets Josep Maria López-Picó (1886–1959), Josep Carner (1884–1970), Guerau de Liost (pseudonym of Jaume Bofill i Mates, 1878–1933), and Joaquim Folguera (1893–1919), the journalist Eugeni D'Ors, and the critics Josep Lleonart and Manuel de Montoliu. In 1906 they were all in their late twenties or mid thirties, and united in their disdain of the older *modernistes*. *Noucentisme* became a canopy for the cultural producer's commitment to the task of creating an organized, efficient modern society with an expansive culture. Literature in those years took on "un to, podriem dir, de profetisme laic i modern" ("we might say, modern, lay prophetic overtones"), in the nostalgic words of Manuel de Montoliu.[4]

First and foremost, they believed in the repristination of culture. D'Ors understood *Noucentisme* as a special sensibility for the signs of contemporary life, a capacity to discern "les palpitacions del temps" ("the beat

---

[3] See the section, "La invenció de l'intel·lectual." In *Glosari 1906–1910* (Barcelona: Selecta, 1950).

[4] Cited in Margarida Aritzeta i Abad, *Obra crítica de Manuel de Montoliu* (Tarragona: Publicacions de la Diputació de Tarragona, 1988), p. 24.

of the times"), as he put it in 1906, the year in which he launched the *Glosari* and with it the term that would define an entire period. The beat, or rhythm, of the times indicated the arrival of a new cultural category, the *Noucents.* There was nothing unique in this call for a new *epistème.* The expectation of a radical historical break was widespread at the turn of the century.[5] D'Ors adapted *Modernisme's* ruptural rhetoric, merely changing the origin of the regenerating energies. Whereas the *modernistes* sought the guidance of modern, that is, northern European cultures, *Noucentisme* reactively privileged the Latin South.

D'Ors subordinated *Noucentisme* to an idealized Greco-Roman antiquity, or, more precisely, to a new classicism claiming the heritage of the ancient Mediterranean world by virtue of the seaborn Catalan medieval power. From this ancient world, D'Ors drew civic paradigms to galvanize an imperial disposition underwritten by culture (cf. the gloss "Emporium," 19 January 1906). In the same year he published *La ben plantada* ("The Elegant Woman"), a compendium of normative virtues for Catalan society based on the ancient wisdom of the Latin "race." Classicism for D'Ors was not a style but an attitude. Its social translation was civility, the art of "being" in the city, and its political dimension was imperialism, which he conceived as interventionism on a global scale. *Mutatis mutandis,* D'Ors was an early advocate of globalization. He wrote in 1909:

L'Imperialisme diu: "Vulgui o no vulgui, una solidaritat lliga a cada home amb tots els altres, i amb els morts en la història, i amb les generacions a venir; i així mateix els pobles estan units en solidaritat." Per això del destí de cada individu, de cada poble, en són responsables els altres, tant més responsables com més forts i més conscients són. Interveniu, doncs, contínuament, homes, pobles! ("Imperialisme i Liberalisme," 1909)[6]

(Imperialism says: "Whether he means to be or not, each man is solidarily bound to all other men, and to the dead within history, and to all future generations. In the same way, all peoples are united through solidarity." For that reason the responsibility for each individual's destiny lies always with the others, who are all the more responsible the stronger they are and the more conscious they are. Intervene, then, ceaselessly, men, peoples!)

Classicism was, for him, the overcoming of nature, just as imperialism was the antithesis of nationalism's "natural" mode of political association. "Race," a word with very different connotations a century later, did not have for D'Ors the Naturalist implications it already had for the

---

[5] Joan Ramon Resina, *Un sueño de piedra: ensayos sobre la literatura del modernismo europeo* (Barcelona: Anthropos, 1990), chapter 1.

[6] In Eugeni D'Ors, *Glosari.* Ed. Josep Murgades (Barcelona: Edicions 62, 1982), pp. 90–91.

early theoreticians of political Darwinism. Mercè Rius points out the significant fact that Teresa, the Elegant Woman and archetypical figure of the Catalan "race," does not stand for the reproduction of the species. That which D'Ors acclaims as "classic" is not the reproduction of physical traits but the transmission of a cultural disposition, in other words, a tradition.[7] Tradition, he claims, not the individual, is the fountainhead of creativity: "Tot el que no és tradició, és plagi" ("Whatever is not tradition is plagiarism").

Although D'Ors became the foremost exponent of this "classic" Mediterraneism, he was not its originator. In the wake of France's defeat by Prussia in 1871, Jean Moréas had proposed an École romane as a reaction against the dominance of German culture. In an open letter published in *Le Figaro* on 14 September 1891, he urged the renewal of the "chaîne gallique" ("Gallic chain"), allegedly interrupted by Romanticism.[8] It was left to the monarchist Charles Maurras to spell out the nationalist dimension of this *Kulturkampf*: "Le nom de la poésie romane dit clairement notre intention. Il suppose l'unité de l'art du midi de l'Europe qui a trouvé sa plus haute expression dans la littérature française" ("The very name of 'Romance poetry' reveals our intention. It presupposes the unity of the art of southern Europe, which has found its highest expression in French literature").[9] The call for a unification of the Romance cultures found resonance in Catalonia, where the revival of its language and literature had given rise to great expectations. Before D'Ors formalized his doctrine of Mediterranean classicism, the *modernistes* had heeded the summons to join a Romance cultural front. Joaquim Casas-Carbó, chief editor of *L'Avenç*, supported a federation of European Latin states. Alexandre Cortada, a regular contributor, proposed a conference of Latin countries. Pompeu Gener, also associated with the journal, actually co-founded a Society of the Latin Alliance.

Notwithstanding this and other shared interests, the *noucentistes* indicted the older *modernistes* on the same charges which the École romane had levelled against Germanic culture: lack of structure, undisciplined Romanticism, melancholy subjectivity. *Modernisme* had, to be sure, facilitated this attack by admiring the "Northern lights." Even so, it had also inspired the *noucentistes*. D'Ors himself had started out as a regular contributor to *El Poble Català* ("The Catalan People"), a daily affiliated with Republican Catalanism of *modernista* stripe. By the time his attacks on his previous associates began to appear in the Lliga's daily *La Veu de Catalunya* ("The Voice of Catalonia"), however, Josep Carner

[7] Mercè Rius, *La filosofia d'Eugeni D'Ors* (Barcelona: Curial, 1991), p. 131.
[8] Jaume Vallcorba Plana, *Noucentisme, mediterraneisme i classicisme. Apunts per a la història d'una estètica* (Barcelona: Quaderns Crema, 1994), p. 17.
[9] Cited in Vallcorba, *Noucentisme*, p. 15.

and his colleagues in the journal *Catalunya* were already engaged in the distortion and surreptitious adoption of *modernista* tenets.[10]

In France the École romane merged with the proto-fascist Action Française. In Catalonia, as Vincent Cacho Viu remarks, the Lliga's liberal core proved refractory to D'Ors' incitations in that direction.[11] D'Ors' proto-fascist leanings notwithstanding,[12] Mediterraneism provided Catalan intellectuals with a mythico-historical rationale for nation building and a commensurate aesthetic. Arguably, the more interesting realizations are not literary but architectural and, above all, pictorial. In this visual domain, there were stimulating theorizations on the cultural precedence of the image, not only by D'Ors, who was a significant art critic, but also by the painter Joaquim Torres-García (1875–1949). Torres, who would join the Avant-Garde after 1917, criticized Catalan art's "provincial" dependence on northern, especially Parisian models, and prescribed a reorientation toward the Mediterranean tradition and its "classic" rule of line, form, and rhythm.

Politically, Mediterraneism culminates in the doctrine of national classicism of Jaume Bofill i Mates (1878–1933).[13] Synthesizing d'Ors' *Noucentisme* with a poetic classicism derived from the Majorcan Miquel Costa i Llovera, Bofill made this aesthetic aggregate function as a symbol for a harmonious social order in years of extreme labor unrest. He speaks of "social classicism" *and* "political classicism" as functional variations of literary "classicism." The line between art and society is here very thin, as it is in D'Ors. Poetry, wrote the latter in his prologue to Bofill's *La muntanya d'Ametistes* ("The Amethyst Mountain," 1908), consists of "els més bells experiments dins l'alquímia de la tortura" ("the most beautiful experiments in torture's alchemy" [37]). If poetry involves the subjection of "matter" to form, society – D'Ors implies – is also the product of "unnatural" interventions. These interventions, however, must not be capricious. Only by virtue of the model, asserts D'Ors, is creation conceivable. Only achieved perfection renders new perfection possible.

Bofill's concessions to natural determinism seek to reconcile *Noucentisme*'s voluntarism with the traditionalism of Bishop Josep Torras i Bages (1846–1916). This Christian thinker answered the progressive Catalanism of the *modernistes* with a conservative Catalanist theory of his own. Underscoring the nation's natural foundation, he pleaded for continuity

[10] Jaume Aulet, *Josep Carner i els orígens del Noucentisme* (Barcelona: Curial, 1992), p. 220.

[11] Vicente Cacho Viu, *Revisión de Eugenio D'Ors (1902–1930)* (Barcelona: Quaderns Crema, 1997), p. 32.

[12] Narcís Comadira, "Sobre el mediterranisme: unes notes." *Quaderns d'Arquitectura i Urbanisme* 153 (1982), pp. 46–51.

[13] Jaume Bofill i Mates, "Classicisme nacional." In *L'altra concòrdia i altres textos sobre el catalcerisme.* Ed. Jordi Casassas (Barcelona: Edicions de La Magrana, 1983), pp. 3–32.

as against political experimentation. He also advocated an explicitly antimodernist aesthetic, to which the *noucentistes* showed themselves amenable, probably because they shared Prat's conviction that a national party required the confluence of disparate interests. If under Prat's leadership the Lliga Regionalista tried to function as a political canopy for conservative landowners and the urban bourgeoisie, *noucentista* writers, most of them members of the petty bourgeoisie, could rally to Prat's project, because it continued Catalanism's strategy, apparent since the 1880s, of integrating social subgroups.

The *noucentistes* fulfilled *Modernisme*'s goal of demarcating a cultural sphere through a precarious synthesis of cultural and political goals. Joan-Lluís Marfany describes their achievement: "La cultura catalana" ("Catalan culture"), he says, "és el resultat d'una obstinació, i el Noucentisme representa el moment més lúcid, més decidit i més decisiu d'aquesta obstinació" ("is the result of tenacity, and *Noucentisme* represents the most lucid, most resolute and decisive moment of that tenacity").[14] Given its timing, D'Ors' passage from *Modernisme* to *Noucentisme*, marked by his transfer from *El Poble Català* to the more conservative *La Veu de Catalunya*, may reflect his sense of opportunities as much as a more comfortable ideological fit. Above all it suggests his awareness that, if the creation of a social role for intellectuals hinged on the development of a civil society with modern European standards – *Modernisme*'s chief goal – only a broadly based coalition of Catalan forces could bring that society about.

Leaving aside the question of whether his later conversion to Spanish imperialism was anticipated in his antinationalist standpoint, his early alignment with a liberal but on the whole very circumspect political force was entirely coherent with his belief in the virtues of cultural intervention, which he elevated to a creed in his doctrine of "Santa Eficàcia" ("Holy Efficacy"). Until the first decade of the twentieth century, Catalonia's political and fiscal subjugation had hindered the formation of an autonomous cultural sphere. Aware of those limitations, the *noucentistes* embraced the undertaking of developing modern educational and scientific institutions (museums, libraries, technical schools, the Institut d'Estudis Catalans, etc.) on the margins of the state, a project they viewed from the cultural side and for which they promulgated aesthetic criteria as a correlate of what they liked to call "civility." Historically, the convergence of art and politics was as inevitable as it was socially useful. For decades Catalan culture lived from the legacy of the *noucentistes*.

[14] Joan-Lluís Marfany, "Reflexions sobre Modernisme i Noucentisme (a propòsit de *Literatura Catalana Contemporània* de Joan Fuster)." *Els Marges* 1 (1974), p. 54.

39

Ideas, aesthetics, historical studies

NELSON R.ORRINGER

Few twentieth-century Spanish minds match those of Ramón Menéndez Pidal (1869–1968), José Ortega y Gasset (1883–1955), and Eugeni D'Ors (1881–1954). Spanish critics situate Pidal in the Generation of 1898, and Ortega and D'Ors in the Generation of 1914. Non-Castilian by birth like most authors of the Generation of 1898, born around the same date as they, like them Pidal glorified Castile, its landscape, inhabitants, history, and traditions. Ortega and D'Ors, like other coevals, specialized in rigorous theory and produced their first great works around 1914. However, generation theory is losing ground in criticism of Spanish literature: invented in France and Germany, the theory does not apply well to a nation with high illiteracy at the time and a tiny intelligentsia in intimate contact, engaged in intellectual cross-fertilization, ages and birthplaces notwithstanding. Ortega himself, one of the inventors of the notion of 1898, in early writings classified himself as a member of that very generation. Concerned about Spanish decadence, he wrote on similar themes. Probably more universal and precise is the classification of all three as Modernists: all three appreciate modernity in their *métiers* over tradition, and place tradition at the service of the new; all three evince the impact of the crisis between traditional religion and post-Darwinian science; finally, all three – amidst the crisis of religious ideals – apotheosize creative efforts in their own fields of endeavor.

Pidal revolutionized philology in Spain, as Ortega did philosophy. Researching the origins of the Spanish language, Pidal produced such authoritative critical editions of medieval texts that he revived study of medieval Spanish poetry and chronicles. In 1895 he won a contest organized by the Real Academia Española by writing a grammar and vocabulary of the *Poema de Mío Cid*, which he revised and re-edited through 1913. His interpretation of *La leyenda de los Infantes de Lara* ("The Legend of the Infantes de Lara," 1896), has remained unchallenged by world Hispanism. In 1898, Pidal brought his scientific discipline up-to-date by doing postdoctoral study at Toulouse, and in 1899 won a Chair in Romance Philology at the University of Madrid. In 1901, he was elected to the Real Academia Española. Three years afterwards, he published his *Manual elemental de gramática histórica española* ("Elementary Manual of Spanish Historical Grammar"), still universally consulted by beginning Hispanists. While performing his university duties, Pidal joined the Junta for the Expansion of Studies and Scientific Research, a body founded by Krausist reformers, and, as part of the Junta, directed the Center of Historical Studies from 1910 to 1936. In 1914 he founded the prestigious *Revista de Filología Española*. Distinguished philologists owe their formation to Pidal at the Center.[1] In 1925, Pidal was elected Head of the Real Academia Española, and in 1926 published his masterpiece *Orígenes del español* ("Origins of Spanish"), with its new discoveries on linguistic evolution. In 1929, the year he published *La España del Cid* ("The Spain of the Cid"), a biographical exercise in Castilian patriotism studying the eleventh-century hero, he protested in a public letter against closure of Spain's universities by military dictator Miguel Primo de Rivera (1870–1930). Four months after the outbreak of the Spanish Civil War (1936–1939), Pidal, a partisan of the Second Republic, fled to France, Cuba, and the United States, where he served as Visiting Professor at Columbia University (1937–1938). Returning to Franco Spain in 1939, he found himself barred from officially heading philological research in his homeland. Even so, he continued researching, publishing *Los españoles en su historia* ("The Spaniards in History," 1947), the monumental *Romancero hispánico* ("Hispanic Balladry," 1953), and the highly polemical *Padre Las Casas: su doble personalidad* ("Father Las Casas: His Double Personality," 1963). Re-elected Head of the Real Academia Española in 1947, at last in 1959 he received recognition even from the Franco government.

A synthesis of all Pidal's thinking appears in *Los españoles en la literatura* ("The Spaniards in Their Literature," 1949). He argues the existence of permanent Spanish characteristics, the continuity of general psychic norms determining most similar acts, notwithstanding racial and situational change. Spanish literature reflects peninsular sobriety, art for all classes, and ethical and aesthetic austerity. Authors like Góngora and Quevedo, who write for an elite, strike Pidal as inferior in their achievements to the great Castilian poets belonging to the people. Iberian culture possesses such continuity that Pidal links Hispano-Roman letters with Golden Age writing. As against the "individualistic" school of French philologists like Gaston Paris (1839–1903) and Joseph Bédier (1864–1938), who attributed medieval works to learned, individual authors, Pidal holds that each work stems from several authors collaborating with one another, modifying the work in many variations interacting with one another as an anonymous patrimony of the people. One version of a

---

[1] Among these are Amado Alonso (1896–1952), Dámaso Alonso (1898–1990), Rafael Lapesa (1908–2004), Federico de Onís (1885–1966), Claudio Sánchez Albornoz (1893–1984), Tomás Navarro Tomás (1884–1979), and Américo Castro (1885–1972).

given ballad passes to an author who slightly alters it, and like changes take place with virtually every transmission. In the course of time, different literary genres emerge. The *carmina maiorum* ("powerful songs") of the Visigoths generate the epic poems of Castilian *jongleurs*, which, broken into fragments, give rise to ballads, which, in turn, eventually originate Golden Age plays. Pidal's self-styled "Neo-traditionalism" has seemed to critics like Ciriaco Morón Arroyo (1938–) to be a new revision of German Romantic thinking, conceiving a whole people or *Volksgeist* as the author of a work. Pedro Laín Entralgo (1908–2001) has compared Pidal's traditionalism to the early Unamuno's thinking on inner history, a product of the then most current Krausopositivistic thinking. Hence, as in all Modernist culture, tradition or the old serves the new, or the latest intellectual trend, usually derived from abroad, though serving to exalt local culture and to raise it to the level of the times. Further evidence of Pidal's Modernism shows in the secularism of his philology. British philologists criticize his downplaying of the clergy's role in medieval and Renaissance literature. Yet Pidal was clearly influenced by his Krausist friend Francisco Giner de los Ríos (1839–1915), and affected by his break with the Catholic conservatism of family members and teachers like Menéndez y Pelayo (1856–1912).[2] Pidal's own lifelong austerity and selfless devotion to philological study show that, like a good Modernist, he made a religion of his creative vocation.

The same applies to Ortega. Philosopher, journalist, educator, and politician, he hailed from two prominent Madrid publishing families. Educated in Malaga and the universities of Deusto and Madrid, he resolved for patriotic purposes to go beyond the predictable career in journalism, with success guaranteed by his gifts for metaphor and rhythmic prose. Like Pidal, he undertook postdoctoral studies abroad. Supported by a grant (1905–1907) from the Junta for the Expansion of Studies, he studied philology at Leipzig, attended philosophy lectures at Berlin, and discovered his calling for philosophy at Marburg-an-Lahn under the Neo-Kantian culture-philosopher Hermann Cohen (1842–1918). Though awarded in 1910 the Chair of Metaphysics at Pidal's University of Madrid, where he succeeded the Krausist Nicolás Salmerón (1838–1908), he rounded off his philosophical education by returning to Marburg in 1911.

In March 1914, he founded a short-lived reformist party of intellectuals, the League of Political Education, and in July 1914 he published his first book, *Meditaciones del Quijote* ("Meditations on the *Quijote*"), urging his rival thinker Unamuno to join him in the reform of Spanish culture from the roots up. Ortega coined the phrase which would become the touchstone of his philosophy: "Yo soy yo y mi circunstancia, y si no

[2] Steven Hess, *Ramón Menéndez Pidal* (Boston: Twayne, 1982), pp. 89–90.

la salvo a ella no me salvo yo" ("I am myself and my [immediate] circumstance, and if I do not save it, I do not save myself").[3] Among the various journals he founded, *Revista de Occidente* introduced into Spain the most up-to-date ideas of foreign philosophers, historians, scientists, and aestheticians. Ortega resigned from his university chair in 1929 in protest against Primo de Rivera. The protest, however, revealed Ortega's public power: defiant crowds thronged the Infanta Beatriz Theatre in Madrid on 29 May to hear him lecture on the theme "What Is Philosophy?" Ortega then announced the debut of his mature philosophy of human life. Many of these new, existence-based concepts would resurface in his best-known work, *La rebelión de las masas* ("The Revolt of the Masses," 1930), concealing between its lines criticism of the dictator as a mass-man in revolt against his mental and moral superiors.

With the birth of the Second Spanish Republic in April 1931, Ortega revived old political aspirations. Together with the novelist and essayist Ramón Pérez de Ayala, and the physician-essayist Gregorio Marañón (1887–1960) he founded the Movement at the Service of the Republic, a party of intellectuals like the 1914 League, though devoted as well to regional home-rule and liberal socialist economic reform. As Representative of León to the Spanish Parliament, Ortega deplored the polarization of Right and Left throughout Spain. He abandoned politics in 1933, and left Spain shortly before the outbreak of the Civil War. Like Pidal, Ortega wandered through Europe and the New World before his postwar return to Franco Spain (1945). In 1948 Ortega and Julián Marías (1914–), his former student, founded the Institute of the Humanities, a research center with no links to the fascist state. Still, Ortega did not feel at home. During his final years, he lectured abroad whenever possible. He left behind distinguished students in the history of philosophy, among them Xavier Zubiri (1898–1983), José Gaos (1902–1969), Luis Recaséns Siches (1903–1977), and María Zambrano (1904–1991).

Ortega's greatest contributions to Spanish thought are: (1) the invention of a philosophical vocabulary which has become common currency; (2) the introduction into Hispanic culture of contemporary European culture, notably, philosophy and science from German-speaking countries; (3) his impact on political thinking of the Spanish Right (the Falange), Left (the Second Republic), and Center (the Constitution of 1976 providing for home-rule); and, finally, (4) influence on form and content of the Hispanic essay. The most significant vocabulary words did not spring fully grown from Ortega's fertile mind, as his most conservative students maintained, but from his translations of terms derived from his teachers

---

[3] José Ortega y Gassett, *Obras completas.* 9 vols. (Madrid: Revista de Occidente, 1966), vol. I, p. 322.

at Neo-Kantian Marburg and from philosophers read in connection with the phenomenological movement spearheaded by Edmund Husserl (1859–1938) and first brought to Ortega's attention by his teacher Paul Natorp (1854–1924). This we find in Ortega's two best-known books, *La deshumanización del arte* ("The Dehumanization of Art," 1925) and *La rebelión de las masas.*

Many critics see both works as fruits of Ortega's maturity. His most respected critic, Julián Marías, together with Ortega's other students – Paulino Garagorri (1916–), Antonio Rodríguez Huéscar (1912–1990), Luis Diez del Corral (1911–) – find Ortega all but mature around 1910, while still affected by Marburg Neo-Kantianism, Hermann Cohen's culture-philosophy. His works gleam like cold, clear, closed, self-generated, systematic icebergs, hardly evolving after 1914, and more important for what they conceal than what they reveal on their polished surfaces. Yet other critics (José Ferrater Mora, Ciriaco Morón Arroyo, Nelson Orringer, Pedro Cerezo Galán, Javier San Martín, and Thomas Mermall) disagree, finding Ortega more methodical than systematic, more translucent than transparent, more polemical than self-sufficient. Conversing with subtexts and intertexts in endless debate, Ortega creates works which are dialogues with others.

Marías holds that Ortega devises early, but does not practice until 1942, his philosophical method of "razón vital" ("vital reason"). Yet the non-canonical view finds that he puts his method, not fully matured, into practice in *La deshumanización del arte* and *La rebelión de las masas.* This method consists of problem-posing, the definition of the problematic factor through phenomenological reduction, and the narration of the causes of the phenomenon defined with the aim of discovering an orientation with respect to it. Ortega's teacher Cohen contributed methodical problem-posing as of 1910; phenomenological reduction, a method of pinning down essences to resolve philosophical problems, entered Ortega's thought as of 1913; the historical narrative of Dilthey (1833–1911), or cause-and-effect contextualization of intellectual solutions to corroborate them, becomes part of Ortega's method as of 1933 in works like *Historia como sistema* ("History as System," 1935), Ortega's most concise and mature essay. The problem-posing, Ortega admits, shows the influence of Cohen, who converted into problems facts of culture, including aesthetic, psychological, and sociological ones. *Deshumanización* begins with the problem of why Avant-Garde art arouses unprecedented mass hostility, while *Rebelión* starts with the problem of why the masses crowd public places previously reserved for cultural elites. To resolve those problems of culture, Ortega applies Husserlian reduction to their terms. First, he suspends current prejudices to attain a self-evident truth about the problem. Second, he analyzes the truth, distinguishing everything essential from everything inessential to understanding the problem. Third, he synthesizes the essentials into a definition whose aspects he enumerates and describes.

In *Deshumanización*, he rejects the received opinion that the unpopularity of Avant-Garde art will pass. For the new aesthetics transcends the masses' understanding by seeking the purest aesthetic enjoyment. Next Ortega asserts a truth, drawn from phenomenologists Husserl and Moritz Geiger (1880–1937): that aesthetic enjoyment is disinterested contemplation of the aesthetic object as a fiction. The purer the enjoyment, the more stress lain on the fiction, and the less participation art requires in the "human" element (understood with Cohen as experience common to all humankind). "Dehumanizing" artists include cubist painters and poets, playwright Pirandello (1867–1936), and composers Debussy (1862–1936) and Stravinsky (1882–1971). Ortega defines "dehumanized art" with seven characteristics, the most general, "dehumanization," lending the work its title, and the six others described one by one: avoidance of live forms; reduction of art to strictly artistic elements; treatment of art as play; essential irony; forbearance from all falsification and a careful execution of the artwork; and the view of art as intranscendent in scope and meaning.

A like reasoning process pervades *Rebelión*. Ortega suspends the received belief that unprecedented overcrowding in European cultural events stems from political upheaval. He affirms a non-political, self-evident truth: that human society is a dynamic unity of mental and moral elites and masses. The masses of the past followed the examples of the elites; but the masses of the present, Ortega thinks, form a hybrid species, combining traditional inertia with social powers once attributable only to the elite, those who seek excellence in all endeavors. Most of Ortega's best-known book phenomenologically describes today's mass revolt against the elite: on the positive side, the level of history has risen, the insecurity of living today is an adventure, possibilities for self-realization exceed expectations; on the negative side, here preponderant, the masses are overaggressive, antiliberal, historically under-aware, over-specialized, overdependent on the state, and disoriented. Only a European Union can save them.

No city in Spain can boast of more European influence than fiercely public-spirited Barcelona. The Catalonian capital has contributed to twentieth-century Spain a number of outstanding philosophers – besides Eugeni d'Ors, José Ferrater Mora (1912–1991) and Juan David García Bacca (1901–1992), who are considered to be the most universal and original. D'Ors and Ferrater share esteem for the savvy or *seny*, the moderation, and the irony of Catalan culture. D'Ors expresses this appreciation in his journalism, essays, art criticism, and fiction. Son of a Catalan father and a Cuban mother, D'Ors spent his first four decades mostly in Catalonia. He became the leader of the Catalan patriotic movement of *Noucentisme*, a movement displaying the traits of worldwide Modernism. In 1911 he published a program for renovating the cultural politics of Catalonia by creating an academy, a library, and a school of higher studies. The mancomunitat, under the presidency of E. Prat de la Riba (1870–1917), named D'Ors secretary general of the Institute of Catalan Studies. Following the death of Prat de la Riba (1917), succeeded by J. Puig y Cadafalch (1869–1957), D'Ors lost his public offices, left Catalonia, established himself in Madrid, and wrote exclusively in Castilian. He traveled extensively in Europe and served as Spanish representative to the Institute of Intellectual Cooperation in the League of Nations (1927–1934). Favoring the labor union movement, imperialism, authority, and hierarchy, after the Civil War he declared himself in favor of Francoism. From the end of the Civil War until his death, he occupied positions in artistic and educational institutions.

D'Ors considers himself a son of the Mediterranean, source of new ideas. He engages in a struggle for mental light (*heliomaquia*) against obscurity. For almost half a century (1907 to 1949) his *Glosari*, or brief articles, aspire to illumine concrete problems of daily life. These essays, forming a compendium of philosophy, art, politics, science, and daily living, extract from every minute fact the coefficient of universality within it. D'Ors seeks the philosophical category behind the anecdote, as he loves to say. Like Ortega, he strives to surmount the antithesis between rationalism and vitalism. The result is "harmonic reason," comprised of *seny*, a Catalan word denoting practical know-how, but in D'Ors signifying "thinking with the eyes," a plastic, archetypal seeing, uniting concepts with specific intuitions. Teresa, the well-built (*la ben plantada*) heroine of D'Ors' novel by that name, and daughter of Mediterranean luminosity, personifies Catalan *seny*. D'Ors' *Filosofía del hombre que trabaja y que juega* ("Philosophy of the Human Being that Works and Plays," 1914) proposes a doctrine of culture as *seny* put into practice: given the overabundance of energies requiring an outlet, all material of daily labor must be fashioned into a work of art.

40

The Catalan Avant-Garde

Joan Ramon Resina

The specificity of the Catalan Avant-Garde can be explained in terms of the tensions that defined the situation of Catalan writers in the first decades of the twentieth century. The two main axes of these tensions were the strong class polarization and the polarization Catalonia–Spain. A third axis, less conspicuous but crucial for the artist's self-consciousness, was constituted by the range of aesthetic sensibility. Here we find the division between artists or connoisseurs and philistines (or *pompiers*, to use the prevailing terminology). Never mind that this division was internal to the bourgeoisie; it turned out to be crucial for the appearance of the Avant-Garde. The latter depended on the existence of a well-defined aesthetic milieu whose *nomos* it could transgress in the name of the sensibility that generated the milieu. The reason for this double game of affirmation and destruction is simple. Art cannot be assailed from outside its own space without the attacker becoming a philistine. Thus the paradox obtains that the insensitive philistine, whom the *modernistes* had ridiculed in the shape of Rusiñol's *Senyor Esteve* ("Mr. Esteve"), now came under fire for defending art – socially legitimated art, that is.

The specificity of the Avant-Garde in Catalonia, as in the rest of the Spanish state, emanated from the narrowness of art's autonomy. The precariousness of this social space for art, which the *modernistes* had striven to create, accounts for the "tameness" of an Avant-Garde that could not defect from the commitment to forge a differentiated aesthetic sphere. From this perspective, the Avant-Garde appears as an extension of *Modernisme*. It stands for the attainment of an advanced position in the construction of a modern society, modernity being defined by the ability to produce instances of radically contemporary symbolic goods. In practice this attitude, which implied the interaction between tradition and renewal, qualified the Avant-Garde's radicalism. Respect for tradition explains the apparent paradox that certain representatives of the Catalan Avant-Garde resisted the introduction of the most radical forms of the European Avant-Garde. Sensing the dangers of poetic subversion for Catalan, a language that had just been standardized, Josep Vicenç Foix (1893–1987) in 1925 warned that some of the local derivations of Dada threatened to handicap the language at the very moment of its social rehabilitation.[1]

Modernisme and Futurisme

In Catalonia, at the beginning of the twentieth century, the future was invested with extraordinary cultural and political value. The first years of the new century were a hopeful time in a forward-looking society. In its first issue, the anarchist journal *Avenir* ("Future"), which was founded in Barcelona in 1903, asked for contributions by the young, "pera soterrar dogmes en tots els ordres de la vida i del sapiguer" ("in order to bury the dogmas [prevailing] in all spheres of life and knowledge"). The following year Gabriel Alomar (1873–1941) presented his memorable lecture, "Futurisme," in Barcelona's Ateneu. On this occasion he extolled the values that would soon become central to the Avant-Garde: dynamism, youth, the challenge to the state and to tradition, and the future.[2] The impact of this address on the young can be measured by the subsequent appearance of journals entitled *Futurisme* in several Catalan cities: in Barcelona (1907), Terrassa (1908), and Vilafranca del Penedés (1910). Keen interest in the future's Utopian dimension had animated turn-of-the-century journals like *Jugend* in Munich, *Joventut* in Barcelona, and *Juventud* in Valencia, all of them imbued with the vitalism of the period. *Futurisme* entailed a radicalization of that vitalism in the context of a modernizing society that was, however, anchored in a traditional and economically backward state. The parallelism with the Milan-based Italian movement of the same name is obvious, although the question of Marinetti's debt to Alomar remains unclear.

Alomar contributed to the Catalan Avant-Garde as a social visionary rather than as a poet – his poetry remained bound to classical prosody. He was an important link between the *modernistes* and the small group of Catalan Futurists whose figurehead was Joan Salvat-Papasseit (1894–1924). The *modernista* connection, which still remains insufficiently explored, was decisive. The term "Avant-Garde" was first used in Spain by the *modernista* Jaume Brossa, who in 1892 applied it to the radical wing of Catalan *Modernisme*. Many authors from that group, Brossa among them, contributed to Salvat's first publishing venture, *Un Enemic del Poble* ("An Enemy of the People," 1917–1919). *Un Enemic*

---

[1] J. V. Foix, "Algunes consideracions sobre la literatura d'avantguarda" (1925). Repr. in *La literatura catalana d'avantguarda (1916–1938)*. Ed. Joaquim Molas (Barcelona: Antoni Bosch, 1983), p. 192.
[2] Gabriel Alomar, "El Futurisme." In *Assaig*. Ed. Jaume Brossa and Gabriel Alomar (Barcelona: Edicions 62, 1985), p. 72.

was, as the subtitle explained, a leaflet of "spiritual subversion," which included *mots-en-liberté*[3] and typographical experimentation.

Salvat's leaflet inspired a similar enterprise, a journal called *La Columna de Foc. Fulla de Subversió Espiritual* (Reus, 1918–1920), whose title recalls Alomr's first poetry collection (*La columna de foc* ["Column of Fire"]), while the subtitle refers to Salvat-Papasseit's publication.

Noucentisme and the Avant-Garde

If the links between *Modernisme* and the Avant-Garde are easily traceable, the Avant-Garde's relation to *Noucentisme* has largely escaped critical attention. This is due to the conventional understanding of *Noucentisme* as a conservative movement supposedly incompatible with the Avant-Garde. Challenging this dichotomy, Josep Murgardes has devoted an informative study to the relation of Eugeni d'Ors (1881–1954) to the Avant-Garde. D'Ors' idea of "arbitrarism" (the doctrine of impositional reason) shares its philosophical background with the Avant-Garde's "actionism." According to Murgades, the *noucentista* effort to leave behind the Romantic pathos and Naturalist Realism led the movement to adopt certain features of the early Avant-Garde, such as intellectualism, subjective introspection, and the critique of mimesis.[4]

In Barcelona's small literary circles of the early twentieth century, the various coteries interacted as a matter of course. Poets and artists moved with relative ease from one group to the other. The Uruguayan artist, Joaquim Torres-García (1875–1949), for example, was one of the early theoreticians of *Noucentisme*, but he also contributed to Salvat-Papasseit's *Un Enemic del Poble* from the first issue, in which he published some "Consells als artistes" ("Words of Advice for Artists"), stressing the need for an art of the present and for the artist's freedom from norms. Salvat himself was for some time editorial secretary of *La Revista*, the chief *noucentista* journal. There were those who reverted to *noucentista* tenets after briefly but successfully experimenting with the Avant-Garde. That was the case of poet and art critic Josep Maria Junoy (1887–1955). Junoy, who wrote the first book about Cubism in any language, experimented with visual poetry in a highly formal way that recalls the *noucentista* notion of "the well-crafted work of art." This preoccupation with

---

[3] The term *mots-en-liberté* was launched by Emilio Filippo Tommaso Marinetti (1876–1944), one of the founders of Futurism; it became a well-known technique practiced by every Futurist poet.

[4] Josep Murgades, "Visió noucentista del Cubisme segons Ors." In *Els anys vint en els Països Catalans (Noucentisme/Avantguarda)* (Barcelona: Publicacions de l'Abadia de Montserrat, 1997), p. 40.

form, which surfaces in many instances of the Catalan Avant-Garde, is the reason for the latter's manifest artistic value but is also responsible for its slight iconoclastic force. The calligram (the word means "beautiful writing"), by far the favored form, allowed poets to demonstrate their virtuosity deploying something akin to what we might today call multimedia effects. Junoy regularly produced different typographic versions of his calligrams, authorizing only the one he considered most successful. Having published the "wrong" version of Junoy's calligram "Jongleurs" in the catalogue for her Barcelona exhibition of March 1917, the Russian painter Helene Grunhoff had to apologize to the irritated poet. This anecdote demonstrates that, despite the impression of openness and instability made by the proliferating versions of the same poem, artistic fetishism was still at work.

The endurance of aesthetic attitudes that are reminiscent of Symbolism explains in part the Catalans' ambivalence toward the term "Avant-Garde". Loath to forgo the development of an aesthetic legacy in a country (Catalonia) that was struggling to create basic cultural institutions, the poet Joaquim Folguera (1893–1919) – another member of the Avant-Garde – could indulge in the following cautionary pronouncements: "¡És bona, de tant en tant, l'antiacadèmia; però que no em toquin els museus i les biblioteques!" ("Anti-academicism is good from time to time; but hands off the museums and the libraries!").[5] Modernity, in this context, designated above all the poets' control over the artistic media and languages. This semantic choice helps to explain their predilection for Cubism, which emphasizes structure, and for Apollinaire and his disciples, whom Foix esteemed for being "els menys avanguardistes de tota llur turbulenta generació" ("the least Avant-Garde among their whole unruly generation").[6] Dada, on the other hand, became the paradigm of anti-art, a notion the Catalans spurned. Upon finding his name in the list of Dada presidents published in the *Dada Bulletin* of Zurich, Junoy remonstrated that "Cap època havia passat per una vergonya estèticament [i] fisiològica parella. 'Dada' serà la marca infamant d'un vergonyós període d'art despotencialitzat" ("No other period had ever been so embarrassed, both physiologically and aesthetically. 'Dada' will be the opprobrious badge for a shameful period of enervated art").[7] More amiably, Folguera admitted that it was necessary to be open to the cultural works of the present. "No és pas bo dormir amb la finestra del tot tancada" ("It is not good to sleep with the windows completely shut").[8]

[5] Cited in J. V. Foix, *Catalans de 1918* (Barcelona: Edicions 62, 1986), p. 66.
[6] Foix, "Algunes consideracions, p. 194.
[7] Cited in Jaume Vallcorba Plana, *Noucentisme, mediterraneisme i classicisme. Apunts per a la història d'una estètica.* (Barcelona: Quaderns Crema, 1994), p. lxxv.
[8] Cited in J. V. Foix, *Catalans de 1918*, Barcelona: Edicions 62, 1986, p. 66.

Folguera's moderation perfectly illustrates the Catalan Avant-Garde's orientation: it was liberal though not radical, and it advocated the modernization and refinement of Catalan culture. By and large, it legitimated *Noucentisme*'s reformism, rejecting Dada's radical presentism. Almost all of its representative poets refused the negative work of the dialectic, which Bakunin and his Catalan disciples considered the Avant-Garde task *par excellence*.

Preferring Cubism to Dada may have been an expression of partiality for French culture, a partiality that turned into partisanship during the First World War. The *noucentistes* and some of their Avant-Garde associates blamed Prussian culture for the revolutionary violence that afflicted Europe in the early decades of the twentieth century, and implicitly for the social strife that shook Barcelona in those years. In a lecture delivered at Barcelona's Ateneu in 1919, Junoy called the modern period "l'era del gran malentès" ("the era of the great misunderstanding"). All over this era, which supposedly started with the French Revolution and began to decline in the years surrounding the First World War – in other words, roughly at the time of Junoy's lecture – could be seen, according to Junoy, the imprint of the "bruixot de Koenisberg" (*sic*) ("the wizard from Königsberg"). This anti-Romantic gesture – probably inspired by Charles Maurras' *L'Avenir de l'intelligence*, although it is also visible in many of d'Ors' glosses – was part of an ideological rearmament against a closer-to-home reality whose urgency can be perceived in Junoy's shrill rhetoric: "L'onada romàntica s'estén per les cloaques" ("The Romantic surge spreads through the sewers").[9] For Junoy's audience it was apparent that he was referring to the Anarcho-Syndicalist movement, which, with a large and growing following in Catalonia, had been on the brink of revolution in 1917. Neither the emergence of the Avant-Garde nor its evolution can be fully grasped without referring to this background. These were the years of Cubism and the calligram, of *mots-en-liberté* and typographical experimentation, but they were also years in which the employers' federation and the police itself unleashed terror against the syndicalists. Everything pointed in the direction of a coup-de-force, which finally came in the form of a military coup led by Catalonia's Captain General, Miguel Primo de Rivera.

By 1919 the Avant-Garde fever had cooled considerably. Junoy exchanged the calligram for the synthetic, seventeen-syllable haiku, a classic Japanese form. Foix asserted that Avant-Garde procedures amounted to poetic "genres," thereby endowing them with permanence and weakening their shock value. This tendency to moderate the harshest aspects of the Avant-Garde took hold. In 1927, Sebastià Gasch, one of the editors of

---

[9] Cited in Vallcorba, *Noucentrisme*, p. lxxxvi.

L'Amic de les Arts ("Friends of the Arts"), declared: "Cal destruir el mot avantguardisme. Cal foragitar-lo. I cal aclarir per sempre que no defensem la modernitat, ni la revolució, ni les posicions avençades. Les nostres campanyes són afer de bo o de dolent. Defensem la qualitat, vingui de dreta, vingui d'esquerra" ("The word 'Avant-Garde' must be destroyed. It must be expelled. We must state once and for all that we do not defend modernity, revolution, or advanced positions. Our campaigns are a matter of good or bad. We defend quality, whether it comes from the left or from the right").[10] Gasch's attack on the Avant-Garde is all the more significant in that *L'Amic de les Arts* was the primary vehicle for Surrealism in Catalonia. One year later, however, Gasch signed, along with Salvador Dalí and Lluís Montanyà, the notorious "Manifest Groc" ("Yellow Manifesto"), which was inspired by the Futurist manifestos. Even so, the group's distance-taking from revolution and "advanced ideas" in the name of aesthetic principles remained. This attitude, nevertheless, did not reflect the individual subjectivity only. In 1927 Spain was under military dictatorship. Everyone in Catalonia knew what the ambiguous term "advanced ideas" had meant just a few years before.

Form as action

From 1920 to 1921 200 bombs went off in Barcelona. In 1921 alone there were 30 attempts on the lives of employers, 56 against policemen, and 142 against workers.[11] Direct action disabled the intellectuals' mediating role and undermined the hopes for Catalonia's self-government. Salvat-Papasseit remained virtually alone in his commitment to the Avant-Garde's social implications. Conceiving the Avant-Garde as a rupture with social and aesthetic norms, he rejected the attempts to reduce it to a *jeu d'ésprit*. To understand literature as a form of social commitment also implied turning upside down the logic of literary hierarchy as inscribed not only in academicism but also in the notion of legitimate (or official) and illegitimate (or unofficial) cultures. Cultural marginality, in other words, finds a polemical legitimation in the Avant-Garde, understood, in Peter Bürger's sense,[12] as an assault on the institution of (bourgeois) art. Native culture, in Salvat's case, refers us to the proletarian world of turn-of-the-century Barcelona. It consisted of a mixture of anticlericalism, Republicanism, antitraditionalism, left-wing Catalanism,

[10] Sebastià Gasch, "Guerra a l'avantguardisme." *L'Amic de les Arts* 8 (1927), n.p.
[11] Jean Bécarud and Gilles Lapouge, *Los anarquistas españoles.* Trans. Gerard Jacas (Barcelona: Laia, 1972), p. 101.
[12] Peter Bürger, *Theory of the Avant-Garde.* Trans. Michael Shaw (Minneapolis: University of Minnesota Press, 1984).

and the whole spectrum of revolutionary culture, from socialism to anarchism.

Tradition, for Salvat, was not merely a negative force but also an opportunity. If Marinetti "va véncer la seva tradició" ("defeated his own tradition"),[13] Salvat, for his part, fought formalism, which he disparagingly called "tifisme."[14] In a fictitious letter with metapoetic intent, "Fragments de lletres girades" ("Fragments of Mailed Letters," 1921), he dissected the situation of the Avant-Garde poet in Catalonia. Contrasting *noucentista* classicism with Barcelona's reality, Salvat ratified the social value of Avant-Garde form. It is impossible, he says, to read the classics in the Rambles in these days of social struggle, which is why poor Horace is taking a nap on the shelves while the poet writes the calligrams of Barcelona's social life.

Salvat did not conceive of poetic form as something preexisting the creative moment: "La forma?, cap engúnia" ("Form? No Worry"), he wrote in 1922.[15] Rather, he conceived it as a byproduct of action, that is to say, as a law that can be extrapolated from the work only after the act that creates it. Although close to the Avant-Garde notion of performativity, his indifference to models recalls the anarchist doctrine of spontaneity. This connection is in evidence in his early emphasis on "sincerity," which he pits against the "intellectuals who lack dynamism." Salvat may have been influenced by American Pragmatism, which emphasized practical consequences as constituting the best way of ascertaining meaning or truth, as Josep Gavaldà suggests.[16] From the Pragmatist philosopher and psychologist William James (1842–1910), who was known and read in Spain at that time, Salvat could have drawn the conceptual foundation for his poetics of action. Aside from this possible influence, however, there is no doubt that Salvat owed his poetic Pragmatism to syndicalism, that is to say, to a Pragmatic version of anarchism. In his response to a survey carried out by *La Revista* ("The Journal") in 1919, he declared that "El Sindicalisme, métode essencialmente pràctic, no podrà viure sinó obrant, actuant. L'acció és el seu prestigi, com és la seva esséncia" ("Syndicalism, which is essentially a practical method, cannot exist except by doing, by acting. Action is its prestige, its very essence").[17] Action had, therefore, formal value insofar as it applied itself to changing the world.

---

[13] Joan Salvat-Papasseit, *Mots-propis i altres proses*. Ed. Josep Miquel Sobrer (Barcelona: Edicions 62, 1975), p. 68.

[14] In Catalan, a "tifa" is a pompous, ridiculous person, or one incapable of sustaining an opinion that requires some courage.

[15] Joan Salvat-Papasseit, *Epistolari de Joan Salvat-Papasseit*. Ed. Amadeu-J. Soberanas (Barcelona: Edicions 62, 1984), p. 177.

[16] Josep V. Gavaldà Roca, *La tradició avantguardista catalana: proses de Gorkiano i Salvat-Papasseit* (Barcelona: Publicacions de l'Abadia de Montserrat, 1988), p. 50.

[17] Cited in Gavaldà Roca, *La tradició avantguardista catalana*, p. 127.

Marinetti, says Salvat, reproduces war's disorder through prosodic disorder.[18] In like manner, for Salvat the Avant-Garde was the aesthetic equivalent of his own pledge to change reality. Salvat claims that the present requires a commensurate poetic form. He thought he had discerned this form, which is strictly unpredictable, in the dynamism of the Futurists.

Since form precipitates the future in which the necessity of the form will first become apparent, form cannot be an outgrowth of reflection. Even less can it be a result of the poet's recourse to convention. The new form must be wrestled for in the combat against established forms, a combat that is always part of the ongoing social struggle. Aware of the interlacing of symbolic and material strife, Salvat entitled his 1920 "Primer manifest català futurista" ("First Catalan–Futurist Manifesto") "Contra els poetes amb minúscula" ("Against Poets in small caps"). In this manifesto he not only claimed absolute priority for giving a poetic dimension to the chronotope of Future-Catalanism, but he also distanced himself once more from poets who indulge in the aesthetic game with the confidence that only an inert social experience can instill. In the antipodes of classicism and of art for art's sake, he exhorts poets to anticipate new experiences, that is, to consider poetry a tool with which to inject time into the world, and thus to transform it.

[18] Salvat-Papasseit, *Mots-propis*, p. 68.

Part VIII

Twentieth-Century Spain and the Civil War

ENRIC BOU, NIGEL DENNIS,
DRU DOUGHERTY, ANDREW A. ANDERSON

41

Poetry between 1920 and 1940

ENRIC BOU

Groups and poetics

For years literary historians have reluctantly used concepts such as "Generation of 1927" or "Grupo del 27," and "Generation of 1936" to refer to the poetry of the first half of the twentieth century in Spain. Perhaps it is more exact to refer (following María Zambrano's designation) to a "momento histórico" ("historic moment"), that is an impressive convergence that brought together certain individuals and certain poetic modalities which produced publications and public events which had a strong impact on the formation of a literary canon. The 1920s and 1930s were the peak of a period of intense literary and artistic renovation, a period which has justly been called a "Silver Age" in Spanish culture, abruptly interrupted by the Civil War.[1]

Overall we can distinguish a few characteristics which define the moment. One is the vindication (and mixing together) of figures of the Spanish poetic tradition such as Góngora and Garcilaso, Bécquer and Darío, and of course the major poet of the first decades of the century, Juan Ramón Jiménez. All of these poets were considered to be models of a certain artistic purity and interest in poetical form. This implied that new authors were attracted to the Avant-Garde and experimentation with form, and to the consolidation of a model taken from Stéphane Mallarmé: the "Book" as a way to organize poetry collections. Some of the new authors had a genuine sense of verse and rhythm (Federico García Lorca, Rafael Alberti, Miguel Hernández). Others wrote luminous intellectual constructs where everyday life shines under new light (Pedro Salinas, Jorge Guillén). Some transformed a world of secluded love into astonishing Nature-based imagery (Vicente Aleixandre, Luis Cernuda). There was a vindication of new kinds of images (in Ortega's words, "La poesía es hoy el álgebra superior de las metáforas" ["Today poetry is the superior algebra of metaphors"]), and attraction toward intemporality

---

[1] José-Carlos Mainer, *La edad de plata (1902–1939). Ensayo de interpretación de un proceso cultural* (Madrid: Cátedra, 1981).

and aesthetic transcendence.[2] Many devoted attention to art's universality and cosmopolitanism, and echoed popular and traditional poetry
(Lorca, Alberti, Guillén, Manuel Altolaguirre, Dámaso Alonso, and others). Overall, Ortega y Gasset was a strong influence. Later, in the 1930s,
Surrealism and committed literature (in a social or religious sense) became
alternative ways to express new situations and feelings.

The 1920s constitute a case study of a winning strategy for the diffusion
of a new poetical attitude through anthologies, manifestos, journals, and
publishing houses. The celebration of Luis de Góngora's tricentennial in
1927 signified a moment of strength for a group of young writers, and
this moment defined enduring friendships and some literary affinities. The
poet Gerardo Diego warily said about these friends: "no coinciden más
que en cierto programa mínimo, más que nada de escrúpulos morales
y de exclusiones literarias" ("they don't coincide in anything more than
a certain minimal platform of, more than anything else, moral scruples
and literary exclusions"). As discussed at length by Claudio Guillén,[3] this
is more a group than a generation. It is obviously incorrect to refer to
a mere eight poets as a "generation." In any case, they were the most
visible writers of the time, a mere group of friends, who were at the forefront of a renovation in Spanish poetry. Recent publications have changed
the critical understanding of this group: autobiographical writings (collections of letters, etc.) have had a strong impact on our appreciation of
their short life as a group, have changed our readings of some books,
and have confirmed their swiftly changing aesthetic beliefs. Also, publication of the complete works of many of these authors allows us to have
a more comprehensive picture of their evolution and the significance of
their work.

The "Nómina incompleta de la joven literatura" ("Incomplete List of
the New Literature") included Alberti, Jiménez, Lorca, Alonso, Diego,
Espina, Guillén, Jarnés, Marichalar, Salinas, and Claudio de la Torre.
To these we could add some names included in Diego's *Antología de
la nueva poesía española (1915–1930)* ("Anthology of New Spanish
Poetry [1915–1930]"): Aleixandre, Cernuda, Altolaguirre, Prados, Felipe,
Larrea, and Villalón. Other authors could include J. J. Domenchina
(1898–1959) and José Bergamín (1895–1983), the founder of *Cruz y Raya*
(1933–1936), and author of a remarkable autobiography, *Al volver*
("Upon Returning," 1972). In recent years a few women writers have
attracted attention: among them Ernestina de Champourcín (1905–1999),
author of *En silencio* ("In Silence," 1926) and *Ahora* ("Now," 1928); and

---

[2] José Ortega y Gasset, *La deshumanización del arte* (Madrid: Revista de Occidente en
Alianza Editorial, 1981), p. 35.
[3] Claudio Guillén, "Usos y abusos del 27 (Recuerdos de aquella generación)." *Revista de
Occidente* 191 (April 1997), pp. 126–152.

Concha Méndez (1898–1986), who wrote *Inquietudes* ("Worries," 1926) and *Surtidor* ("Gas Pump," 1928). It is also worth mentioning other artists and actresses who made significant contributions: Maruja Mallo, Norah Borges, and Margarita Xirgu.

Poetry journals and literary magazines, many of them short-lived, had significant influence. Among the most important are *Índice* (1921) founded by Juan Ramón Jiménez; the *Revista de Occidente* (1923–1936) founded by Ortega y Gasset; *Carmen* (1927–1928) and its supplement *Lola*; *Litoral* (Málaga, 1926–1927, 1929) founded and edited by Manuel Altolaguirre and Emilio Prados; *Verso y prosa* ("Verse and Prose," Murcia, 1927); and *Los Cuatro Vientos* ("Four Winds," 1933). Many of these journals created publishing houses to distribute their work. Altolaguirre and Prados also founded Imprenta Sur which published many of the best books of the time. Gerardo Diego's influential *Antología* (1932, 1934) established a canon and became a powerful vehicle to assert the existence of a new group. Its exclusions and resulting polemics defined the success of a new group of writers. Several institutions were also instrumental in the diffusion of new ideas. Founded in Madrid in 1910, the Residencia de Estudiantes attracted young artists and writers, among them Lorca, Dalí, Buñuel, and Pepín Bello. An associated publishing house brought out Machado's *Poesía completa* ("Complete Poetry," 1928); many poetry readings took place at the Residencia along with lectures by renowned foreign artists and scholars such as Albert Einstein, André Breton, Louis Aragon, and many others.

A younger group of writers who came of age around 1936 had an extremely difficult time reaching a reading public. The Civil War created strange circumstances: prison, concentration camps, exile, censorship, and repression were some of the hurdles they had to overcome and that marked their work. If anything, they stressed the "subjectivization process," exposing their own selves in their poems. The leading voices were Miguel Hernández, Luis Rosales, Luis Felipe Vivanco, and Leopoldo Panero. One can also mention Idelfonso-Manuel Gil (1912–), Germán Bleiberg (1915–1990), José Antonio Muñoz Rojas (1909–), José María Luelmo (1907–1991), Dionisio Ridruejo, and Juan Gil-Albert (1904–1994). This group had a renewed interest in the poetry of Garcilaso de la Vega, whose fourth centennial was celebrated in 1936, and in San Juan de la Cruz, who also became a model for them. They emphasized a rejection of experimentalism, and a need for "re-humanization." As a result, everyday life permeates their poetical experience. *Residencia en la tierra* ("Residence on Earth," 1935) by Pablo Neruda (1904–1973) became a model for this younger generation of poets. According to Guillermo Carnero, their poetry is "based on experiential daily life, with an existential emotive meaning and comprised of philosophical and ethical transcendence of the adventure that is all individual life in all of its most human and vulgar episodes; a transcendental and emotional reflection of the human condition."[4] It could be said that these poets write a much more "humane" poetry, stressing personal emotion and subjectivity.

Journals such as *Cruz y Raya* edited by Bergamín, and *Literatura*, *El Gallo Crisis* ("The Rooster Crisis"), became their usual means of publication. *Caballo verde para la poesía* ("Green Horse for Poetry," 1935–1936), edited by Pablo Neruda, was a journal that accentuated the attack on Jiménez's model of Pure Poetry. *Nueva España* ("New Spain," 1930–1931) and *Octubre* (1933–1934) emphasized the change in mood and the importance of engagement. Only after the war in Spain could this division be noted. *Escorial* and *Garcilaso* were journals which stressed form and religion, whereas *Espadaña*, founded by Victoriano Crémer, promoted social poetry about the common man.

Poetical modernity

Modernity (and/or modernization) in early twentieth-century Spain encompasses not only the willingness to connect with the Western (i.e., modern) world, but also the impact of certain aesthetic proposals. Critics such as Ricardo Gullón, Andrew Debicki, and Andrés Soria Olmedo have stressed the many similarities between Spanish poetry of the 1920s and 1930s and that of other parts of Europe.[5] That is why it can be very useful to establish a distinction between "Avant-Gardists" and "Modernists." Spanish poets fall into both categories. Some are prone to radical aesthetic activism, and beyond 1929 choose to write engaged literature. Others are more interested in the debate on "Pure Poetry." The letter which Guillén wrote to Fernando Vela defines this parameter: "As I can most simply call it, I resoundly opt for complex and compound poetry, for the poem with poetry and other human things. In sum, a 'pure poetry' *ma non troppo*."[6] For most of them poetry was a way to configure and preserve experiences, thus attaining the Symbolist purpose of elevation and objectivity.

Spanish poetry entered modernity in a two-step process. The first was following Darío's mastery of French Symbolist poetry. Later on,

---

[4] Guillermo Carnero, "La generación poética de 1936 . . . hasta 1939." In *Las armas abisinias* (Barcelona: Anthropos, 1989), p. 243.

[5] Ricardo Gullón, *Direcciones del modernismo* (Madrid: Gredos, 1964); Andrew Debicki, *Historia de la poesía española del siglo XX. Desde la modernidad hasta el presente* (Madrid: Gredos, 1997); Andrés Soria Olmedo, "Introducción." In Soria Olmedo, ed., *Antología de Gerardo Diego. Poesía española contemporánea* (Madrid: Taurus, 1991), pp. 11–59.

[6] Soria Olmedo, ed., *Antología de Gerardo Diego*, p. 404.

around 1920, with the so-called "Joven literatura" ("Young literature") and Avant-Garde "Ultraístas," there is a radicalization in the process of modernization. Darío, a very influential figure, returned the sense of meter and rhythm to Spanish poetry, and introduced free verse and prose poems. J. R. Jiménez encouraged his colleagues "to give verbal form and expression to the sensation of the beauty of things."[7] With a general eagerness for renovation, the Avant-Garde was for all of them (from Salinas to Hernández), to different degrees, a tempting option. Ramón Gómez de la Serna introduced Futurism into Spain in 1909. Journals such as *Ultra* (1921–1922), *Grecia* (1918–1920), *Cervantes* (1919), and *Cosmópolis* (1919) allowed the introduction of a timid Spanish Avant-Garde. The flimsy consistency of "Ultraísmo" and of all Spanish Avant-Garde movements in general is obvious in the pages of these journals: a vague influence of Futurism, attention to metaphor, and some essays of visual poetry, are combined with traditional forms. In sum, art is conceived as play – to liberate poetry from its relationship to reality and servitude to grammar. Guillermo de Torre's *Hélices* (1923) is the highlight of Ultraísta literature. He is better known for his influential and well-informed essays on the European Avant-Garde, *Literaturas europeas de vanguardia*, published in 1925. "Creacionismo" (whose main proponents were Huidobro and Diego) suggested "multiple images" and indeterminate meanings: "The image must aspire to its definitive liberation, to its utmost plenitude." *La Gaceta Literaria* ("Literary Gazette," 1927–1932), with 123 issues, edited by Giménez Caballero and founded by, among others, Guillermo de Torre, was an influential venue for the discussion of Avant-Garde art and literature, but Surrealism turned out to be a much more effective presence. Whereas only Salvador Dalí participated in the activities of French Surrealism, around 1929 many other authors and works show the effects of Surrealist doctrine.[8] Buñuel and Larrea also lived in Paris, close to the Surrealist group. Surrealism was well known in Spain and corroborated radical ethical and revolutionary attitudes, along with shocking images.

Breton went to Barcelona in 1922, lecturing at the Ateneu, and Aragon visited the Residencia de Estudiantes in 1925. Several exhibitions, debates, and essays were amplified in *Gaceta Literaria* and *Revista de Occidente*. In 1929 the Buñuel–Dalí film *Un chien andalou* shocked Parisian society, and many books were written – among them Alberti's *Sobre los ángeles* ("On Angels") and Lorca's *Poeta en Nueva York* ("Poet in New York") – that rather loosely followed the Surrealist example. Previously texts in

---

[7] Debicki, *Historia de la poesía*, p. 28.
[8] Derek Harris, *Metal Butterflies and Poisonous Lights: The Language of Surrealism in Lorca, Alberti, Cernuda and Aleixandre* (Fife: La Sirena, 1998).

Catalan by Dalí and J. V. Foix in *L'amic de les Arts* ("The Friend of the Arts"), or José M. de Hinojosa's novel *La flor de la California* ("The Flower of California," 1928), and poems by Larrea had opened up new forums, although the latter's *Versión celeste* ("Celestial Version") remained unpublished until after 1970. Later Aleixandre and Cernuda also showed an interest in Surrealism. In general, Spanish Surrealism meant a way to renovate poetic images and to validate political engagement.

León Felipe (1884–1968) was an original writer whose voice resonates with classical and Whitmanesque influences (Felipe translated poems by Walt Whitman into Spanish). In *Versos y prosas del caminante* ("The Traveler's Verse and Prose," 1920 and 1929) we detect the presence of moral and religious undertones. Felipe is always seeking an audience; he writes forceful poetry, almost epic in proportion, as he reveals the heroic nature of daily and domestic life. His early poetry deals with a re-reading of Christianity from a non-religious perspective. Later he developed an interest in social issues, which deeply marked his reflections on the Civil War and exile: *España del éxodo y del llanto* ("Spain of Exodus and Weeping," 1939). With direct and powerful language he stresses a moral responsibility when reflecting on the world's condition and the problems of humanity's wellbeing. The result is a poetry that is almost prosaic, energetic, very powerful, and with limited pomposity. Exiled in Mexico, he became a symbol of opposition to the Franco dictatorship.

The early poetry books (*Seguro azar* ["Certain Fate"] and *Presagios* ["Omens"]) by Pedro Salinas (1891–1951) reveal an attraction to objects from modernity (e.g. his well-known "Underwood Girls"), as if he were looking for hidden meanings under those objects. Salinas found his voice when he wrote *La voz a ti debida* ("The Voice Because of You," 1933). Sparked by his affair with Katherine Whitmore, the book can be read as a single poem. Its seventy stanzas deploy a unique metaphysical approach to a reflection on love. He combines the best findings of his early books – tainted by Ultraísmo (a kind of poetic extremism) – as many insightful images attest. The narration of a love story, the definition of love, is illustrated by undermining or de-realizing language and reality itself.[9] As his letters to Whitmore show, the poems of *Razón de amor* ("Reason of Love," 1936) are of a much more circumstantial nature and it is consequently a much weaker collection. *Largo lamento* ("Long Lament," 1937; published posthumously in 1995) chronicles the end of love. His characteristic "desire for clarity" can be traced in *Todo más claro* ("Everything

[9] Robert Havard, *From Romanticism to Surrealism: Seven Spanish Poets* (Totowa, NJ: Barnes & Noble, 1988).

Clearer," 1949). These are long poems devoted to the encounter between a mental city, one that can be recognized in Nature, and another one, that of modernity. Extremely pessimistic in tone, he devotes an entire section, "Cero" ("Zero"), to the fear of the atomic bomb. A shrewd literary critic in newspapers and in the Centro de Estudios Históricos ("Center for Historical Studies"), he devoted considerable attention to emerging poets of his time (Alberti, Aleixandre, etc.). His essays in *El defensor* ("The Defender," 1947) are sharp inquiries into topics of the time: language, letter writing, readership. He also wrote incisive Avant-Garde short stories and dramas.

Jorge Guillén (1893–1984) wrote *Cántico* ("Song") over a period of thirty years, publishing four different editions (1928, 1936, 1945, 1950). The final edition contained 334 poems. A few topics are emphasized: man and things, existence, love's richness, temporality, death, pain, and disorder. In general his poems consist of a gaze – an attention to circumstance learned from Ortega. *Cántico* narrates the world that the senses perceive in a self-conscious voice. The poetic word concedes the possibility of delving deeper into oneself, and of exploring one's surroundings or other beings. Jaime Gil de Biedma stressed the contrast between "immediacy" and "reflection." Guillén's project is "el ser que canta el estar" ("being that sings existence"). Each version of *Cántico* introduces new insights. He starts with aestheticism, goes on to vitalism, and in the last two editions there is a considerable presence of the real world, foreshadowing the turn taken by his latest books. He organizes the poems into symmetrical groupings. The definitive edition follows the model of the 1928 version: five balanced parts in which the initial poems of each section allude to dawn and the final poems to dusk and nighttime. According to Debicki, an "idealistic aestheticism that springs from a modern vision, based on symbolic principles" can be detected in the groundwork of the book.[10] Guillén experimented with metric forms, creating forms such as the "redondilla y cuarteta asonantada" ("little round and quartet with assonantal rhyme") or the "romance breve" ("short ballad"). After publishing *Cántico* he wrote four more books, uneven in quality, among them *Clamor* (1963), subtitled "tiempo de historia" ("time of history"). This book marks a brisk switch in theme and reveals Guillén's interest in engaged literature (see "Potencia de Pérez" ["Pérez's Might"]). It consists of three individual books: *Maremagnum* (1957); *Que van a dar a la mar* ("They Go to the Sea," 1960), and *A la altura de las circunstancias* ("To Rise to the Occasion," 1963). He published his complete poems under the title "Aire nuestro" ("Our Air," 1968). *Lenguaje y poesía* ("Language and Poetry," 1961) is a lucid theoretical reflection in prose on the problems involved in

---

[10] Debicki, *Historia de la poesía*, p. 43.

defining poetic language. *Obra en prosa* ("Work in Prose," 1999) includes *Hacia "Cántico"* ("Toward Cántico"), luminous critical writings from the 1920s.

Gerardo Diego (1896–1987) had an active role in "Creacionismo," together with Vicente Huidobro and Juan Larrea. Books such as *Imagen* ("Image," 1922), *Limbo* (1919–1921), and *Manual de espumas* ("Manual of Foam," 1922), with its distinctive typographical arrangements and twisted syntax, are good examples of this interest. *Fábula de Equis y Zeda* ("Fable of X and Z," 1932) is a challenging interplay between Baroque and Avant-Garde. Like J. V. Foix in Catalan, he skillfully combined tradition and Avant-Garde. Author of more than forty books of poetry, in fact, he was able to combine two quite definite, distinct voices, that of the "poesía de creación" ("poetry of creation"), in which experimentalist poetry creates suggestions for the reader; and that of "poesía de expresión" ("poetry of expression"), where he follows more traditional models, for example in *Ángeles de Compostela* ("Angels in Compostela," 1940) and *Alondra de verdad* ("Lark of Truth," 1941), or in his many religious poems. As is the case with many poets of his generation, Diego was attracted to the arts and incorporated them (music in his case) into his poetry in many ways. *Nocturnos de Chopin. (Paráfrasis románticas) 1918–1962* ("Chopin's Nocturnes. [Romantic Paraphrases] 1918–1962," 1963) was originally written in 1918, but not published until much later. This is a clear indication of Diego's way of working, re-writing his poetry throughout the years. Conceived as an evocation of Chopin's music (see his "Prólogo"), he recognizes his ability to create suggestion in his verses. The poems comment on the music, or evoke scenes from the musician's life, which intersect with scenes from the poet's life. He tried to imitate the music's rhythms with words, as they are the result of saying what playing the music suggests to the poet.

Dámaso Alonso (1898–1990) is better known for his impressive philological work, especially his edition of Góngora's *Polifemo* (he was the intellectual force behind the group's revival of Góngora). Author of remarkable Avant-Garde prose, he achieved notoriety with *Hijos de la ira* ("Children of Ire," 1944), where he dealt with social injustice through the use of bizarre images, everyday language, and free verse. The poems deal with anguish, cruelty, and pain, with existential and religious undertones.

Vicente Aleixandre (1898–1984), a Nobel Laureate, enjoyed an extremely influential presence among the young writers of the sixties (the so-called "Novísimos"). He was instrumental in establishing a connection between the generations. In *Espadas como labios* ("Swords as Lips," 1932), or *La destrucción o el amor* ("Destruction, or Love," 1935), we read dream sequences which mix reality and imagination. Visionary

Surrealist images combine Nature and psychological elements. Union with the beloved is always expressed through fusion with Nature in a series of rich images organized using a convoluted syntax. Love is attained through a desire of union with the universe. Nevertheless, there is an underlying logical vision, one which allows the reader to interpret the poem's apparent impenetrability. Recent studies have emphasized the originality of his "visiones" (Surrealist images) and the influence of Freud, Fray Luis de León, Bécquer, and Darío in *La destrucción o el amor*. A book of love poetry, this masterpiece focuses on the relationship between man and the forces of Nature. For Aleixandre, love equals death, a view culled not only from medieval poetry but also from his own deep pantheism. *En un vasto dominio* ("In a Vast Domain," 1962) reverberates with the same equation between man and Nature, stressing topics such as youth and time past.

Emilio Prados (1899–1962) is well known as the publisher of the journal *Litoral* (1926). Educated in Germany, he wrote his poetry in three very different modes. Under the influence of Surrealism, he tried to found, with Dalí and others, a Spanish "section" of the movement; moved by his political commitment as member of the Communist Party, he wrote engaged poetry in the 1930s and during the Civil War; and tainted by the religious interest he developed later in his life, we read more quasi-mystical verses in his poetry of exile. He employs a complex metaphorical system (of images and personifications) to express the inter-relation between human life and Nature's cycles. He was active politically in his Mexican exile. In *Tiempo* ("Time," 1925) we see an affinity for the type of image that coincides with the aesthetics of the Surrealists. *Cuerpo perseguido* ("Persecuted Body," 1926–1927) is a significant book dedicated to love. *Jardín cerrado* ("Closed Garden," 1946), undoubtedly his masterpiece, represents a memory of solitude and death. By a process of inner analysis the poet tries to salvage his past from oblivion. He has lost the "jardín soñado" ("dreamed garden") of his early poetry and seeks refuge in an interior garden. Prados' work is ruled by a personal sense of unity and symbolism – the process of death and resurrection, light, etc. – which he applies to explain a personal insight. His *Poesías completas* ("Complete Poems") were published in 1975.

Rafael Alberti (1902–1999) started writing poetry deeply influenced by popular models. *Marinero en tierra* ("Sailor on Land," 1925) shows illusion and nostalgia, a love in crisis. Two books from 1929, however, *Cal y canto* ("Lime and Song"), in which he cannibalizes the voice of Góngora, and, in particular, *Sobre los ángeles* ("About the Angels"), initiate an original and radical singularity through Surrealist images representing interior and urban landscapes, marked by disillusionment and anguish. After 1930 he writes social poetry. Only Lorca has exhibited Alberti's sense of verse: a natural facility that translates into a kaleidoscope of voices, registers, and multiple interests. Alberti moves from Neopopularism to Surrealism, and in the 1930s incorporates a poetry of the trenches, engaged politically and socially. An incomplete "complete works" edited by García Montero (1988–1989) gathers together his collections of poetry. *Sobre los ángeles* is a book marked by two clichés: the Surrealist and "the crisis." From a vague mix of autobiographical elements, amorous crisis, and lost youth, he constructs a powerful text riddled with Surrealist-influenced images. Alberti declared (in Berns' translation): "I had lost a paradise, maybe that of my recent years, my clear and first youth, happy and without a care."[11] According to C. B. Morris, four themes can be seen: love, ire, failure, and discord.[12] As with Lorca, we see absurd images and a profound pessimism, but all against a calculated setting. The structure of the book is important: the inter-relations between the poems and the general "plot." The "angels" are the "irresistible forces of the spirit." Visionary images generate strong impressions of a world in decline. *A la pintura* ("To Painting," 1945) offers yet another voice with references to painters and painting techniques. The first two books of *La arboleda perdida* ("The Lost Grove," 1942), an autobiographical account, cover from 1902 to 1917, and from 1917 to 1931, respectively. The title refers to a certain forest of his childhood but addresses a much more general overview, "that of the lost forest of my age." It is also the name of the villa in Argentina where he finished the first two books. His is a powerful account of literary activities, written in a supple prose.

Perfil del aire ("Profile of the Air," 1927), by Luis Cernuda (1902–1963) – published later as "Primeras poesías" in the definitive version of his poetry, called *La realidad y el deseo* ("Reality and Desire," 1977) – presents a world of love and Nature which cannot be attained. Therefore we encounter the distinctive melancholic atmosphere of his poetry. Love was at the center of his poetry and his world, the sole justification of life. *Los placeres prohibidos* ("Prohibited Pleasures," 1931) contains a strong reaction against the inhibitions and controls imposed by society, and a vindication of homoerotic love ("He venido para ver" ["I have come to see"]). Cernuda stresses the importance of eroticism as a crucial element in his fight for an alternative way of life. Many poems pursue Surrealism as a framework of his original visions, as he had already done in a previous volume, *Un río, un amor* ("A River, a Love," 1929). The conflict between truth and appearance, reality and desire, which poetry may help to dispel, becomes the center of this book devoted to a lost ideal, having lost love and youth. After 1935 he combines existential reflection

[11] Rafael Alberti, *La arboleda perdida (libro primero de memorias) y otras prosas* (Mexico: Editorial Séneca, 1942); English translation by Gabriel Berns: *The Lost Grove* (Berkeley: University of California Press, 1981), p. 299.
[12] C. B. Morris, *Una generación de poetas españoles (1920–1936)* (Madrid: Gredos, 1988).

and an ironic approach to life. In recent years he has become one of the most distinguished and appreciated poets of the 1930s. New readings emphasize his explicitly gay love poems. Stunning frankness and syntactic obfuscation permeate his poems. Cernuda combines description with cryptic images, while subjectivity supports his task of analyzing Nature and humanity. According to Philip Silver he searches for the Romantic sublime, halfway between Symbolism and allegorical representation.[13] A shrewd literary critic, Cernuda wrote a highly praised two-volume work, *Poesía y literatura* ("Poetry and Literature," 1965). His *Obras completas* ("Complete Works") in three volumes were published in 1993.

Manuel Altolaguirre (1905–1959) was both a poet and a publisher. During his years in exile in Mexico he developed an interest in screen-writing. He rewrote his most important book, *Las islas invitadas* ("The Invited Islands," 1926), on several occasions, each time adding new material. In his poetry he combines melancholy and happiness, and attention to the sea. His poetry focuses upon vision, trying to establish connections through symbols between the visible and invisible world. According to Cernuda his is a poetry that succeeds in presenting a "misterio penetrado" ("penetrated mystery"). We can also detect an interest in self-analysis – anxiety of ascension toward a goal that looks for expression through the word in the mystical-ascetic tradition and that situates his creation between the apprehension of the natural world and bringing of the objects of the world to their essence – and finally the willingness to establish a "diálogo creador" ("creative dialogue") with humanity. His memoirs, *El caballo griego* ("The Greek Horse"), came out in the first volume of his *Obras completas* in 1986.

The first book by Miguel Hernández (1910–1942), *Perito en lunas* ("Skilled in Moons," 1933), was related to the "pure poetry" aesthetics of Juan Ramón Jiménez, and written in royal octaves. Right from the beginning, one detects his ability to adapt genuinely popular tones and rhythms. Ramón Sijé's enlightening introduction stresses the process of transformation that Hernández experiences when writing these poems: starting from rural motifs he imposes an artistic vision, which allows him to reach a mysterious reality. Born into a working-class family, he was able to join mainstream literary groups thanks to a self-imposed deliberate re-reading of Spanish literary tradition. He suffered harsh incarceration at the end of the Civil War, which eventually caused his death. His name has long been associated with a poetics of resistance to Fascism, and together with García Lorca he became a martyr of war. If we add to this his humble origins – he was a shepherd – we can understand why his poetry has had

---

[13] Philip Silver, *Et in Arcadia ego. A Study of the Poetry of Luis Cernuda* (London: Támesis Books, Ltd., 1965).

innumerable misreadings. *El silbo vulnerado* ("The Damaged Whistle," 1934) is a powerful series of love sonnets with reverberations of San Juan de la Cruz. *El rayo que no cesa* ("The Interminable Thunderbolt," 1936) attests to his interest in Garcilaso and Quevedo. These are forceful sonnets, which are expressions of a personal crisis, in which he uses the image of the bull symbolically, and of an interest in social issues. After 1936 his poems are filled with images related to fatherland, love, and death. In *Viento del pueblo* ("The People's Wind," 1937) he blends his classical poetical education with his populist instinct resulting in an original version of Neopopularism. In *Cancionero y romancero de ausencias* ("Songs and Ballads of Absences," 1938–1941), not published until 1960, he uses Neopopularism (oral poetry and flamenco) and a very somber tone.

Abril (1935) by Luis Rosales (1910–1992) is a book of love poetry with Avant-Garde undertones. It launches an interest in Garcilaso and religious themes, which were two of the marks of postwar poetry. This book was based on well-known symbolism: in it, for example, April indicates natural rebirth, birth of love, life, and poetry. There is an echo of Arab poetic images, and a presence of sentimentality. Undoubtedly the confluence of love and religiosity become a hallmark of this poet. *Abril* was followed by *Segundo abril* ("Second April," written in 1940, published in 1972). These two collections of poetry can be read as two sections of the same book. The first one was written influenced by a sort of experimentalism, the second one with traditional models in mind. Another remarkable volume is *Retablo Sacro del Nacimiento del Señor* ("Sacred Altarpiece on the Birth of the Lord," 1940). Rosales has always been interested in humanity, religiosity, purity, and love, and has written poems about human interaction and temporality. These poems recall Machado's simplicity, combined with the love of poetic play which marked the previous generation.

Luis Felipe Vivanco (1907–1975) embraces a transcendental vision of Nature according to a religious experience. His complete poetic works were published in *Los caminos* ("The Paths," 1974). His poems fall under two rubrics: the everyday and family life, and reflection on religious experience.

Leopoldo Panero (1909–1962) devoted his attention to his family, religion, and the rural landscape. This allowed Dámaso Alonso to describe his poetry as "rooted." *Escrito a cada instante* ("Written at Each Instant," 1949), his most significant book, encapsulates a homage to poets (for example, to García Lorca with the poem "España hasta los huesos" ["Spain to the core"]), a devotion to family, and a deeply felt religious quest. The presence of God permeates his verse.

Dionisio Ridruejo (1912–1974) wrote *Elegías (1943–1946)* ("Elegies [1943–1946]" 1949), which consisted of elaborate, long poems filled with grief and desperation.

Poetry and propaganda During the Civil War

Orality marks the diffusion and great success of poetry during the war. Radio addresses and political meetings, along with many journals and newspapers provide the materials that were later collected in anthologies. New journals also provide space for the diffusion of engaged literature. *El Mono Azul* ("Blue Overalls," 1936) was a publication of the Alianza de Intelectuales Antifascistas ("Alliance of Antifascist Intellectuals") in which Alberti and León had a significant editorial role. Its main objective was to take action against Fascism. *Hora de España* ("Spain's Hour," 1937), an initiative by Antonio Sánchez Barbudo, with Ramón Gaya, Altolaguirre, Juan Gil-Albert, José Moreno Villa, and María Zambrano, wanted to express a higher degree of reflection and investigate Spanish cultural reality at the historical and philosophical level. Several anthologies from the time are instrumental in the dissemination of this poetry through publications controlled by political groups and institutions. On the Republican side Altolaguirre edited *Romancero de la guerra civil* ("Civil War Ballads," 1936), and Prados and Antonio Rodríguez Moñino edited *Romancero general de la Guerra de España* ("General Collection of Ballads about the Spanish War," 1937). Other anthologies include *Romances de CNT* [Confederación Nacional de Trabajadores] ("Ballads of the CNT [National Confederation of Workers]," 1936), *Poesía en las trincheras* ("Poetry in the Trenches," 1937), *Poetas en la España leal* ("Poets in Loyal Spain," 1937), and *Poemas de Guerra* ("War Poems," 1939). Most of them were organized either according to traditional concepts (heroic poems, lyrical poems, etc.) or geographical ones, according to the locations of battles. There is more attention to countryside, "peasants," than to workers. Poems are filled with brutal depictions of war scenes and harsh irony toward betrayal. Well-known writers publish side by side with anonymous ones. Serge Salaün has stressed the epic as a common ground for most of these poems. In his view, the epic "edifies a nascent society's norms . . . and verbally initiates its ideological system in order to initiate a near hegemony."[14] Similarly, the rebels published anthologies of political poetry with titles like *Antología poética del alzamiento* ("Poetic Anthology of the Revolt," 1939), prepared by Jorge Villén; *Cancionero de guerra* ("Anthology of War Songs," 1939) edited by José Montero Alonso; and *Corona de sonetos en honor a José Antonio* ("Crown of Sonnets in Honor of José Antonio," 1939). Some books appeared which were devoted specifically to the war experience, such as Alberti's *Capital de la Gloria* ("Capital of Glory," 1936), Garfias' *Poesías de la guerra española* ("Poems of the Spanish War"), Gil-Albert's

---

[14] Serge Salaün, *La poesía de la guerra de España* (Madrid: Castalia, 1985), p. 288.

Son nombres ignorados . . . ("Their Names are Unknown," 1938), Miguel Hernández's *Viento del pueblo* (1937) and *El hombre acecha* ("Man Lies in Wait," 1939), Manuel Machado's *Horas de oro. Devocionario poético* ("Golden Hours. Poetic Prayerbook"), and *Devocionario poético* ("Poetic Prayerbook"), Pemán's *Poema de la Bestia y el Ángel* ("Poem of the Beast and the Angel," 1939), or Ridruejo's *Poesía en armas* ("Poetry in Arms," 1944), in which he evokes both the Civil War and his fight with the "Blue Division" (a Spanish volunteer division in the Second World War).

42

Prose: early twentieth century

NIGEL DENNIS

In the critical perspectives on the literature of the 1920s and 1930s that were engineered, often opportunistically, in the postwar period, prose writers received scant attention and were usually left to languish in the shadow of a select group of poets. As those perspectives, together with the generic distinctions they stressed, became more entrenched, reiterated in response to pressures that were as much pedagogical as they were political or aesthetic, so the marginal status of the prose writers of the time was reinforced. It has taken a considerable effort in recent decades to pull back into focus the complex realities of the period in order to acknowledge that the climate of renewal and innovation identified with poetry also determined other forms of writing as well as the creative arts as a whole. It has become increasingly evident that during those years prose writers either pursued objectives that complemented those of contemporary poets or developed alongside them their own independent initiatives that helped to shape the literary sensibilities of the time. No credible review of the literature of the so-called "Silver Age" of Spanish letters can now afford to overlook those practitioners of prose. The difficulty lies, rather, in doing justice to the range of their writing and the different directions in which it moved.

It is important to remember that in the years under review little weight was attached to the generic distinctions referred to above. Prose and poetry were published alongside each other with no sense of conflict or incompatibility. All the poets of the so-called "Generation of 1927" also wrote prose. Pedro Salinas (1891–1951) and Antonio Espina (1894–1972) moved effortlessly from one genre to another, while the early reputation of Jorge Guillén (1893–1984) was based on his prose texts. Similarly, many prose writers of the time published texts that were highly polished, densely lyrical, and displayed many of the features associated with the verse of the time. Some were explicitly defined as "poemas en prosa" ("prose poems"); others appeared under different headings: "Girones de prosa" ("Wisps of prose"), "Palabras interiores" ("Inner words"), "Golondrinas" ("Swallows"), and "Estampas" ("Pictures"), for example.[1] Because of its sheer

---

[1] Nigel Dennis, "En torno a la prosa breve en la joven literatura." *Insula* 646 (October 2000), pp. 15–19.

quantity and the distinction of those who practiced it, this kind of writing invites serious study. Two examples are worth noting: the ekphrastic prose poems included at the end of *Yo inspector de alcantarillas* ("I, Inspector of Sewers," 1928), by Ernesto Giménez Caballero (1899–1988), under the title "fichas textuales" ("textual index cards"),[2] and the short lyrical portaits José Bergamín (1895–1983) collected in *Caracteres* ("Characters," 1927).

This blurring of generic boundaries stresses the importance of the "signo lírico" ("lyrical sign") as one of the key defining features of pre-Spanish-Civil War literature.[3] Aesthetic ideals converged; all serious writers aspired to formal perfection, pursuing the finely crafted or ingenious image. This phenomenon owed a good deal to Juan Ramón Jiménez (1881–1958), who nurtured all the young writers of the twenties and instilled in them his own implacable concern for rigor in any genre. The prose texts of *Platero y yo* ("Platero and I," 1914, 1917) and *Diario de un poeta recién casado* ("Diary of a Newly Wed Poet," 1917) were as important to them as models as any of his verse. The example of Ramón Gómez de la Serna (1888–1963), strident champion of innovation, tireless saboteur of conventional genres, however, was more powerful and widespread and was acknowledged by poets and prose writers alike. From 1908, the year he founded his journal *Prometeo*, Ramón embodied the spirit of modernity and in his own diverse writings promoted a new creative outlook and style to which no writer could remain impervious.

Ramón exercised this influence largely through the *greguería*, a gnomic genre invented by the writer himself to accommodate his tendency to focus on isolated fragments of reality and to interpret or recreate them, often lyrically or comically, by means of highly original images or metaphors. Eschewing the principle of discursive continuity, adopting what he called "el punto de vista de la esponja" ("the sponge's point of view"), he privileged the part rather than the whole, believing that this strategy reflected more accurately the nature of reality: "la constitución del mundo es fragmentaria, su fondo es atómico, su verdad es disolvencia" ("the world is made up of fragments, its basis is atomic, its truth dissolves").[4] In his own novels and stories he neglected structural coherence and strict thematic unity and tended to string together *greguerías* like so much decorative bunting. So profound was the impact of his style that Adriano del Valle (1895–1958) called the *greguería* in 1925 the "esperanto de la retórica"

---

[2] María Pao, "Still(ed) Life: The Ekphrastic Prose Poems of Ernesto Giménez Caballero." *Revista Canadiense de Estudios Hispánicos* 25 (2001), pp. 469–492.
[3] Pedro Salinas, "El signo en la literatura española del siglo XX," In *Ensayos completos*. 3 vols. (Madrid: Taurus, 1983), vol. III, p. 181.
[4] Ramón Gómez de la Serna, *Greguerías* (Madrid: Prometeo, 1917), p. 11.

("the Esperanto of rhetoric"), i.e. a basic building block used in the works of all the major prose writers of the 1920s.[5] In effect, in the context I have outlined, Ramón's example prepared the ground for some of the key trends in prose writing of the pre-Civil-War period: the aphorism and its related forms, and the Avant-Garde novel.

Almost as common in the pre-War period as the prose poem, in its various disguises, was the brief critical or reflective note, corresponding to what Salinas described in 1934 as "la ambición de la brevedad" ("the ambition to be brief"), of which the greguería is only one modality.[6] Again there is generic uncertainty here since, though generally aphoristic in nature, i.e. fragmented and discontinuous, these jottings were presented under different headings; consider the "Anotaciones" ("Annotations," 1926) of Luis Cernuda (1902–1963), the "Bengalas" ("Flares," 1924) of Guillermo de Torre (1900–1971), and the "Epigrafías" ("Epigraphs," 1926) of Antonio Marichalar (1893–1973). The only true aphorist is Bergamín whose two books El cohete y la estrella ("The Rocket and the Star," 1923) and La cabeza a pájaros ("Head in the Clouds," 1934) offer the most striking example of systematically fragmented writing. Oscillating in tone between the playful and the lyrical, the morally sententious and the ingeniously paradoxical, Bergamín fixes in pithily elegant formulae his thoughts on subjects as diverse as music, sport, religion, and poetry. The Ejercicios ("Exercises," 1927) of Benjamín Jarnés (1888–1949) are largely made up of similarly truncated reflections, many of which have the nugatory quality of the aphorism and rival Bergamín's with their subtle precision.

Though the novelists of the twenties unanimously rejected the "old" novel, based on the principles of nineteenth-century Realism, they did not have a clear idea about how to write the "new" novel to which they aspired. Critics have proposed various typologies to accommodate the diverse innovations they undertook.[7] There is general consensus, however, on the important role played by Gómez de la Serna and José Ortega y Gasset (1883–1955) in the attempt to devise new novelistic forms. Ramón's formal experimentation in his narrative works from El doctor inverosímil ("The Unlikely Doctor," 1914) to El incongruente ("The

---

[5] Adriano del Valle, "Ramón Gómez de la Serna o el sentido de la universalidad." Alfar 50 (1925), p. 6.

[6] Pedro Salinas, "José Bergamín en aforismos." In Ensayos completos, vol. I, p. 145.

[7] Domingo Ródenas de Moya, Los espejos del novelista. Modernismo y autorreferencia en la novela vanguardista española (Barcelona: Ediciones Península, 1998); Javier Pérez Bazo, "La novela nueva en la época de la vanguardia histórica: una revisión." Ínsula 646 (October 2000), pp. 7–10; José Manuel del Pino, Montajes y fragmentos: una aproximación a la narrativa española de vanguardia (Amsterdam and Atlanta: Rodopi, 1995); C. A. Longhurst, "Ruptures and Continuities: From Realism to Modernism and the Avant-Garde." In Hacia la nueva novela. Essays on the Spanish Avant-Garde Novel. Ed. Francis Lough (Oxford and New York: Peter Lang, 2000), pp. 19–41.

Incongruent One," 1922) and, above all, *El novelista* ("The Novelist," 1923) was crucial in demolishing conventions and legitimizing highly subjective, structurally fragmented, and sometimes metafictional writing.[8] Moreover, the humorous qualities of his work had a wide-ranging influence and gave particular momentum to a type of prose fiction that has long been overlooked, despite its popularity at the time. In 1929, at Ramón's suggestion, Biblioteca Nueva created the "Grandes Novelas Humorísticas" ("Major Comic Novels") collection to which writers like Edgar Neville (1899–1967), Jardiel Poncela (1901–1952), Antoniorrobles (pseudonym of Antonio Robles Soler, 1897–1983) and Samuel Ros (1904–1945), as well as Ramón himself, contributed.

Ortega's journal *Revista de Occidente*, founded in 1923, championed the spirit of renovation and paid special attention to prose. The ideas the philosopher set out in *La deshumanización del arte e Ideas sobre la novela* ("The Dehumanization of Art and Ideas on the Novel," 1925) were decisive in signaling new possibilities. The "Nova Novorum" collection he created in 1926, though short-lived and limited in scope, provided an outlet for some of the best experimental projects undertaken as a result of his stimulus: *El profesor inútil* ("The Useless Professor," 1926) and *Paula y Paulita* ("Paula and Paulita," 1929) by Jarnés; *Pájaro pinto* ("Colored Bird," 1927) and *Luna de copas* ("Toast to the Moon," 1929) by Espina; and *Víspera del gozo* ("Prelude to Pleasure," 1926) by Salinas. Here, the conventions of plot, theme, and characterization were abandoned. The writing became thickly metaphorical and self-referential. *Víspera del gozo* has aged well and stands as a paradigm of Avant-Garde prose. It stresses more the practice of writing and the importance of form than the young protagonist's anticipated encounters, and subtly draws the reader into the process of composition and completion. In *Pájaro pinto* Espina uses a similar model of disconnected narratives, but the fragmentation is more extreme – reminiscent of cinematic montage – and produces little more than shadowy, schematic characters.

The limitations of this kind of playful, ingenious, cerebral, self-reflexive, elitist writing soon became evident. It failed to provide a solution to the "problem of the novel" and until its kinship with the Post-modern sensibility of several decades later was recognized, its indifference to social realities would discredit it. Pérez Firmat ends his inspired reading of the key works of these years by dismissing them as "vacation pieces."[9] Ortega's dissatisfaction with the outcome of the "Nova Novorum" project led him in 1929 to propose an alternative outlet for the talents of his

---

[8] César Nicolás, "Ramón Gómez de la Serna y la novela española de vanguardia." *Insula* 502 (October 1988), pp. 11–13.

[9] Gustavo Pérez Firmat, *Idle Fictions. The Hispanic Vanguard Novel* (2nd. edn. Durham and London: Duke University Press, 1993), p. 140.

young disciples: the biography. This was an opportune initiative in several respects and met with immediate success. With the anchorage of a historical figure, biographers would be able to re-establish contact with the reading public by "humanizing" their work, precisely at a time when the rarified intellectualism and self-indulgent virtuosity of Avant-Garde prose were being criticized. Ortega was also alert both to the impact of a new kind of biographical writing emerging in England and France – Lytton Strachey and André Maurois are two key points of reference – and to the precedents already set within Spain by Gómez de la Serna. As in other contexts, the latter was a genuine precursor. His short biographical sketches of writers were collected in 1929 under the title *Efigies* ("Effigies") and during the years under review he produced independent biographies of such figures as Goya (1928) and Azorín (1930).

As a genre with little tradition in Spain, biography attracted much critical commentary and theoretical reflection.[10] The prevailing view was that biography should aim not to document a life using exact historical data but to recreate it imaginatively, using the subject as a pretext for what was to all intents and purposes a novel. This meant that writers engaged in biographies could make productive use of the skills already acquired when tackling the challenges of the dehumanized, lyrical, metafictional novels of a few years earlier.

In 1929, at Ortega's suggestion, Espasa-Calpe created a special collection "Vidas españolas del siglo XIX" ("Spanish Lives of the Nineteenth Century"). As Rosa Chacel (1898–1994) later recalled, Ortega himself assigned the "personajes novelables" ("novelizable characters") to his disciples: "señaló con el dedo y dijo: Este, este, este, este . . . Nosotros obedecimos" ("he pointed and said: This one, this one, this one, this one . . . We obeyed").[11] The success of this collection – soon widened in scope and re-titled "Vidas españolas e hispanoamericanas del siglo XIX" ("Spanish and Spanish American Lives of the Nineteenth Century") – is evident in the sixty titles it had published by 1936. Other publishing companies launched similar initiatives, recruiting a whole range of writers from Pío Baroja (1872–1956), José María Salaverría (1873–1940), and Manuel Ciges Aparicio (1873–1936) to Juan Chabás (1901–1954), Eduardo de Ontañón (1904–1949), and Rosa Chacel (1898–1994). Even poets tried their hand at the genre: Manuel Altolaguirre (1905–1959) published his *Garcilaso de la Vega* (1933) in yet another collection – "Vidas extraordinarias" ("Extraordinary Lives") – created by Espasa-Calpe. Biography became a notable fashion, enjoying popular and commercial

---

[10] Enrique Serrano Asenjo, *Vidas oblicuas: aspectos teóricos de la nueva biografía en España* (Zaragoza: Universidad de Zaragoza, 2002).

[11] Rosa Chacel, *Poesía de la circunstancia. Cómo y por qué de la novela* (Bahía Blanca: Universidad Nacional del Sur, 1958), p. 29.

success. Between 1929 and 1936 the newspaper *El Sol* published reviews of more than 300 biographies, almost half of which were originally written in Spanish.[12]

In the light of the above, it is unsurprising, perhaps, that the most successful examples of what has come to be termed "Avant-Garde biography" are by writers closely associated with Ortega. Two of the first to appear in the Espasa-Calpe collection were *Sor Patrocinio, la monja de las llagas* ("Sister Patrocinio, The Wounded Nun," 1929) by Jarnés, and *Luis Candelas, el bandido de Madrid* ("Luis Candelas, The Bandit of Madrid," 1929) by Espina. Both were reprinted within a year of publication, a distinction not accorded to either *El profesor inútil* or *Pájaro pinto*. They were joined by Marichalar's highly praised *Riesgo y ventura del duque de Osuna* ("Risk and Fortune of the Duke of Osuna," 1929) and, in a different collection, published by Ulises, *Vida de Greta Garbo* ("Life of Greta Garbo," 1929) by César Arconada (1898–1964), a brilliant example of the fusion of Avant-Garde stylistic inventiveness and the topical interest in the stars of the silent screen.

The year 1930 marked a crisis in the Avant-Garde. The literary world became more politicized and divided as writers sought more radical and effective responses to changing circumstances. *El nuevo romanticismo* ("The New Romanticism") by José Díaz Fernández (1898–1941), published in that year, defined new priorities. The author advocated a "vuelta a lo humano" ("return to the human"), i.e. exploiting the stylistic achievements of the Avant-Garde in order to re-engage with social and political realities instead of making them an end in themselves. This shift of emphasis characterizes the so-called "literatura de avanzada" ("advanced literature") published in the late twenties and early thirties, of which Díaz Fernández's *El blocao* ("The Outpost," 1928) is the finest example. Using the same fragmented structure and metaphorical language evident in the writing of, say, Espina or Salinas, Díaz Fernández drew on his personal experiences as a soldier in North Africa to evoke the dehumanizing effects of the Moroccan war as conducted by inept officers in an alienating colonial context. Less explicitly combative in content, though equally polished in execution, Arconada's *La turbina* ("The Turbine," 1930) embodies the sense of this transition toward a more overtly politicized novel in later years.

El blocao appeared in a collection of "novelas sociales" ("social novels") published by Historia Nueva which also included works by Joaquín Arderíus (1885–1969), César Falcón (1892–1970), and José

---

[12] Francisco Soguero, "Los narradores de vanguardia como renovadores del género biográfico: aproximación a la biografía vanguardista." In *Hacia la nueva novela. Essays on the Spanish Avant-Garde Novel*. Ed. Francis Lough (Oxford and New York: Peter Lang, 2000), p. 208.

Antonio de Balbontín (1893–1977). On the basis of their example, and drawing upon other related sources and influences, a more militant kind of writing took shape that would largely determine the fate of prose narrative in the thirties. It assigned new functions to the novel: to analyze society, identify the nature and causes of its problems, and to work toward resolving them through radical, revolutionary strategies. Consequently, it developed fresh stylistic priorities: simplification and schematization; the privileging of content over form; speed, clarity, and accessibility of the narrative; a narrator whose own ideological affiliations were unequivocally stated; a clear political agenda.[13] It mixed fiction with autobiography and journalistic reporting, creating new hybrid genres that would recur in the prose texts of the Civil War years. In its most radical form it would be known as "la novela proletaria" ("the proletarian novel") – the title of a number of collections published during the Republic by companies like Cenit and Libertad – whose debts to soviet socialist Realism, known in Spain through the dozens of translations made in those years, were openly acknowledged. The quality of this writing, together with the subject matter it dealt with and its treatment of form, vary considerably.[14] The most successful social novels tended to retain elements of the traditional historical novel, though their objectives were more militant. Among the most readable representative texts are *Los pobres contra los ricos* ("The Poor Against the Rich," 1933) and *Reparto de tierras* ("Land Division," 1934), by Arconada; *Campesinos* ("Peasants," 1931) and *Crimen* ("Crime," 1934), by Arderíus; and *Siete domingos rojos* ("Seven Red Sundays," 1932), by Ramón Sender (1902–1982).

The conventional view of the Civil War years has been that the circumstances did not favor the production of prose narratives. While poets and, to a lesser degree, dramatists were able to adapt to the loss of time and tranquility and even to rise successfully to the challenge this represented, prose writers were seen to be severely handicapped. The significant narratives centered on the war would appear later once the trauma of the experience had become distanced and assimilated. There is some truth in this view but it is, perhaps inevitably, an oversimplification, partly a result of the difficulty of locating and, therefore, assessing the relevant texts, and partly a consequence of the uncertain generic status of much of the prose generated by the war. Recent research has shown that even if relatively few novels – in any conventional sense of the term – were written and published between 1936 and 1939, those years produced a good deal of prose writing that, like the poetry and theatre

---

[13] Fulgencio Castañar, *El compromiso en la novela de la II República* (Madrid: Siglo Veintiuno, 1992).

[14] Víctor Fuentes, "La novela social española, 1927–1936: panorámica de un diverso perfil temático y formal." *Letras Peninsulares* 6 (1993), pp. 9–29.

of the time, and in the same combative and often propagandistic spirit, sought to provide an immediate response to the lived experience of war. This "literatura vivencial" ("literature of experience")[15] took the form of brief narrative texts of one sort or another, usually autobiographical and testimonial in approach and journalistic and impressionistic in style. It was published in newspapers throughout the country and in high-profile journals like *El Mono Azul* ("Blue Overalls"), *Milicia Popular* ("Popular Militia"), and *Hora de España* ("Hour of Spain"); the latter had a regular section devoted to "Testimonios" ("Testimonies"). Since many of those who cultivated this kind of writing were well-known figures in the literary and intellectual world – María Teresa León (1903–1988), Vicente Salas Viu (1911–1967), Arturo Serrano Plaja (1909–1978), Antonio Sánchez Barbudo (1910–1995), Juan Gil-Albert, Max Aub (1903–1972), María Zambrano (1904–1991), José Herrera Petere (1910–1977), and Ramón Sender, for example – it deserves to be taken into account.

Given their active involvement in the war and the powerful nature of the real events they witnessed, writers tended simply to record directly their own experiences, unconstrained by the need to transform them imaginatively into conventional narratives. This explains the proliferation of so-called "crónicas" ("chronicles"), evident, for example, in collections like the *Crónica general de la guerra civil* ("General Chronicle of the Civil War") of 1937, edited by María Teresa León, a volume which ought to be read alongside the much better known *Romancero general de la guerra de España* ("General Collection of Ballads of the Civil War," 1936). It contains primarily narrative reporting by more than thirty different writers. Beyond its intrinsic historical and documentary value, this kind of writing also fed into other narrative texts that appeared during the war in which material first published as "crónicas" was recycled.

The same testimonial impulse is detectable in two important collections of short narrative texts from those years: *Valor y miedo* ("Courage and Fear," 1938) by Arturo Barea (1897–1957) and *Entre dos fuegos* ("Crossfire," 1938) by Sánchez Barbudo. Based on the notes and scripts he used for radio programs broadcast in the autumn of 1936, Barea's stories describe – "reproduce" might be a more appropriate term – in simple but vivid language scenes of everyday life in Madrid, peopled by characters that are unexceptional save for their spontaneous acts of heroism. Sánchez Barbudo's book shared the National Prize for Literature in 1938 with Herrera

---

[15] Gemma Mañá, Rafael García, Luis Monferrer, and Luis A. Esteve, *La voz de los náufragos. La narrativa republicana entre 1936 y 1939* (Madrid: Ediciones de la Torre, 1997), p. 52.

Petere's *Acero de Madrid* ("Madrid Steel"). Its five independent narratives offer complementary perspectives on the experience of war, from the uprising in July to the horrors of nationalist repression in a small village in Galicia.

Of the longer prose narratives published during the war, two are worth drawing attention to. Sender's *Contraataque* ("Counterattack") was first published in Britain, the USA, and France in 1937, a year before the Spanish original appeared. It traces the author's movements between May and December 1936, offering a series of fragmentary descriptions of his experiences, especially during the siege of Madrid, peppered with political digressions. Its autobiographical basis has raised doubts concerning its generic status and it is notable that Sender himself viewed it as a book of "recuerdos" ("recollections"), downplaying its literary value. Like many texts of the time in which the author acts as both observer of and participant in the events described, and in which the events themselves require no imaginative elaboration, it is essentially a narrative of personal testimony.

Herrera Petere's *Acero de Madrid* is similarly rooted in the author's own lived experience of the war. The book centers on the history of the Fifth Regiment and the Brigadas de Acero ("Steel Brigades") through the latter half of 1936. It aspires to be an epic novel of popular resistance in Madrid and with its combination of lyricism and ideological militancy is a worthy successor to the "literatura de avanzada" practiced several years earlier by Díaz Fernández and Arconada. Remarkably, Herrera Petere published two other noteworthy novels in 1938: *Cumbres de Extremadura* ("Peaks of Extremadura"), subtitled "novela de guerrilleros" ("novel of guerrillas"), and *Puentes de sangre* ("Bridges of Blood"). Such attempts to produce narrative works that are practically simultaneous to the events they describe help to explain the enthusiastic revision of the Galdós of the "novelas contemporáneas" ("contemporary novels") undertaken during the war by commentators like María Zambrano and Rosa Chacel.

Despite also being something of a generic oddity, *La velada de Benicarló* ("The Benicarló Soirée," 1939) by Manuel Azaña (1880–1940) deserves mention as an impressive example of the literature of the war years, penned by the Republic's most eminent statesman. Although framed by prose texts that remind us of the writer's consummate skills as a stylist, it is not a narrative work. Nor is it a play, despite being written in dialogue form. It is, rather, a rare example of an updated Platonic dialogue, modeled on Alfonso de Valdés' Renaissance dialogues. In a preliminary note, Azaña himself defines it as a "demostración" ("demonstration"), thereby signaling its didactic/dialectic intention. Set in early 1937, it presents a debate among eleven characters, two of whom – Garcés, the ex-minister, and

Morales – represent facets of the writer's own experience, as politician and as intellectual, respectively. The context provides Azaña with the means to reflect on the moral responsibilities of the groups that supported the Republic and to offer a synthesis of his own political philosophy. Despite its gloomy insistence on the destructiveness and ultimate futility of war, the book has undeniable value as a compendium of perspectives on a complex historical situation.

43

The commercial stage, 1900–1936

DRU DOUGHERTY

The theatre in Spain during the first three decades of the twentieth century presents a variety of faces to the historian. It was first and foremost a thriving industry employing thousands of actors and actresses who traveled a circuit of theatres that covered the peninsula and extended to Spanish cities in Africa and the former American colonies, especially Havana and Buenos Aires. Theatres were the favored sites of public entertainment, and, until film achieved rival status in the mid 1920s, they constituted a principal network for communication between social classes. Theatre also provided a reliable, and respectable, source of pleasure, both on and off the stage. Finally, the stage was a space reserved for the nation's self-representation as a collective body, a forum in which national concerns, myths, and memories were debated, celebrated, and debunked.

Theatre thus served society's needs on many levels. Here I will emphasize the commercial, social, and cultural conditions that influenced how plays were written, staged (or suppressed), and received. Because productions were almost entirely financed by private investors, authors who wrote professionally tended to cultivate one of the five established sectors of the market: (1) the one-act play with or without music (*sainete*) based on popular, melodramatic plots involving lower-class types; (2) the elaborate musical comedy (*opereta, revista*) which became the dominant theatrical mode after the First World War; (3) the sentimental comedy that engaged current social problems for the entertainment and elucidation of the middle classes; (4) the farcical comedy aimed especially at petit-bourgeois audiences (*juguete cómico, astracán*); (5) the sophisticated comedy, drama, and musical play (*zarzuela grande*), whose audiences were drawn from the educated elite. On the margins of these sectors, other elements challenged the commercial organization of the theatrical field: Avant-Garde playwrights and directors whose literary, social, or political discourses deprived them of commercial success but ensured their cultural prestige.

Textual histories concentrate almost entirely on comedies and dramas aimed at elite audiences, giving us a canon that represents an important but minor part of the complete theatrical field. Here each sector will receive attention, an attempt to reflect the systemic nature of the theatrical field whose producers of great dramatic texts – especially Benavente, Valle-Inclán, and Lorca – often obscure the rich theatrical horizon on which, historically speaking, they played relatively minor roles. Textual criteria will not simply be ignored, but it is well to remember that this was a cultural field that saw over 1,000 performances each month and more than 200 premières each season in Madrid alone during the 1920s.[1]

The giant of the pre-Civil-war period was Jacinto Benavente (1866–1954), who established a new mode of bourgeois theatre in the last decade of the nineteenth century and set a high literary standard for the stage which did not preclude commercial success. Even Benavente, however, was dwarfed by the vitality of the one-act industry (*género chico*) that constituted the largest sector of the theatrical field up to the 1920s. This festive form of theatre was performed hourly and drew its charm from witty wordplay, stock comic situations, colorful lower-class characters, and musical scores drawn from national, and, occasionally, foreign sources. In 1901 the Teatro Apolo sold almost 4.5 million tickets for its four daily sessions, and that same year more than half of Madrid's nineteen theatres offered one-act programs.[2] In 1909, of the 411 plays premièred in Madrid, 377 were of the one-act variety,[3] and in the 1928–1929 season one-acts still accounted for almost one-third of the commercial hits, including the jewel of the genre, *La verbena de la Paloma* ("The Festival of La Paloma") by Ricardo de la Vega (1839–1910) with music by Tomás Bretón (1850–1923).[4] The enduring popularity of the one-act industry was an index of the genre's usefulness for the bourgeois classes which financed and consumed theatre. The *género chico* retained its comfortable, anachronistic conventions while it gradually and cautiously absorbed erotic influences from Europe (operetta and cabaret), musical rhythms from America (tango and jazz), and social novelties, like the entry of women into the work force. It was a primary means of preserving tradition within a society exposed to radical modernization in its urban centers. After the First World War, the genre was slowly displaced by musical plays of greater extension and more cosmopolitan spirit (the Parisian-style revue or *revista*) but these dazzling, often ribald, spectacles retained characters,

[1] Dru Dougherty and María Francisca Vilches de Frutos, *La escena madrileña entre 1918 y 1926. Análisis y documentación* (Madrid: Fundamentos, 1990), pp. 141–144.
[2] Serge Salaün, "Modernidad -vs- Modernismo. El teatro español en la encrucijada." In *Literatura modernista y tiempo del 98.* Ed. Javier Serrano Alonso (Santiago: Universidad de Santiago de Compostela, 2000), p. 97.
[3] José Francos Rodríguez, *El teatro en España. 1909* (Madrid: Imprenta de Bernardo de Rodríguez, 1910), p. 375.
[4] María Francisca Vilches de Frutos and Dru Dougherty, *La escena madrileña entre 1926 y 1931. Un lustro de transición* (Madrid: Fundamentos, 1997), pp. 362–363.

scenes, and especially music (*chotis*, *pasodoble*) drawn from the one-act tradition.

Central to any one-act play were the customs and stereotypes of lower-class urban neighborhoods: washerwomen, factory workers, street vendors, etc., all of whom coincided in neighborhood festivals (*verbenas*) or religious celebrations (*romerías*) or were drawn into melodramatic plots involving the virtue of an unprotected girl. The paradigm was masterfully set by Carlos Arniches (1866–1943) in *El santo de la Isidra* ("Isidra's Saint's Day," 1898), with music by Tomás López Torregrosa (1863–1913): young and vulnerable, Isidra is stalked by the neighborhood bully, who threatens to force her into prostitution, but is "saved" by Venancio at the annual festival that celebrates Madrid's patron saint, San Isidro. The imperative to protect a young woman was also central to *Es mi hombre* ("My He-Man," 1921) whose protagonist, a lovable coward employed as a bouncer in a seedy bar, overcomes his extreme pusillanimity to defend his daughter. In his review of *¡Que viene mi marido!* ("It's my Husband!" 1918) – a *sainete* stretched into a three-act "grotesque tragedy" – the learned critic Ramón Pérez de Ayala consecrated Arniches as a "serious" author, lifting him above the ranks of market-driven writers.[5] The prestige thus gained was indicative of Arniches' ability to adapt the one-act formula to evolving tastes, while it demonstrated the role of powerful critics (Enrique Díez-Canedo, Enrique de Mesa, Luis Gabaldón, Alejandro Miquis, Rafael Marquina, Melchor Fernández Almagro) in determining who was, and was not, an author worthy of esteem.

The one-act formula was the route to fame for Pilar Millán Astray (1879–1949), one of the few women authors who was successful in the theatre. Her first commercial hit was *El juramento de la Primorosa* ("Primorosa's Oath," 1924), whose protagonist, a mature woman and mother, fights to maintain her family within strict moral guidelines, an example of the strong female characters who appeared in Millán Astray's plays and embodied a traditional, female ethos. In *La tonta del bote* ("The Ugly Duckling," 1925) she reworked the Cinderella myth, expertly fusing sentimentality, comedy, and a close look at social oppression.

Midway between the musical *sainete* and the later full-blown *revista* was *La corte de Faraón* ("Pharaoh's Court," 1910), an operetta written by Miguel de Palacios (1863–1920) and Guillermo Perrín (1857–1923), with music by Vicent Lleó (1870–1922). Taking its plot from the biblical story of Joseph's temptation by Pharaoh's wife (and from the French operetta *Madame Putiphar*), the authors blended sexual innuendo with comic

5 Ramón Pérez de Ayala, "La tragedia grotesca." In *Las máscaras*. Vol. II (Madrid: Saturnino Calleja, 1919), pp. 233–252.

reversals (Joseph has to protect *his* virtue from the women in Pharaoh's palace) in a score that featured a Viennese waltz, Spanish folk tunes, Italianate evocations, and popular *cuplés* from contemporary revues.

The final phase in the development of comic musical theatre was the lavish revue on a Parisian scale. Four producers, José Juan Cadenas and Eulogio Velasco in Madrid, and Fernando Bayés and Manuel Sugrañes in Barcelona, were instrumental in adapting foreign models to the Spanish stage. The resulting hybrid of Spanish, European, and American musical discourses (Andalusian Moorish pieces, Viennese waltzes, the Charleston, cake-walk, and other modes of jazz) drew enthusiastic crowds. Likewise, the action often featured racy French vaudeville twists played by Spanish one-act characters or American gangster types. Relatively free to experiment with staging techniques, the musical revues initiated advances in lighting, elaborate costume effects, and scenographic experiments, all of which drew upon, and competed with, the visual codes of early cinema.

Representative of the hundreds of commercial hits in this genre was *Todo el año es carnaval o Momo es un carcamal* ("Carnival Lasts All Year or, Momo is a Decrepit Old Crock," 1927) by Joaquín Vela and Ramón M. Moreno, with music by Ernesto Rosillo (1893–1968). The revue was a "lyrical fantasy" whose mythical plot of cuckoldry served as a pretext for discreet nudity, popular song and dance, and spectacular staging effects within a festive context of erotic pleasure. Highlights included a Charleston danced by Miss Madness and Uncle Sam, costumes that suggested bisexuality, and actresses who perfumed the spectators during the performance. The revues' hybrid formula regularly incorporated the voyage motif, as in *El Príncipe Carnaval* ("Prince Carnival," 1920) and *Las aviadoras* ("Lady Aviators," 1927) which took the audience on tours of major world capitals during carnival or visited exotic locales like Argentina's pampas or the winesheds of the god Bacchus. Emblems of modernity, pleasure, and sexual fantasy were fused in the discourse of these revues, explaining their dominance of the theatrical field in the 1920s and 1930s.

Some of the theatre's large-scale producers got their start in the one-act industry, notably the Álvarez Quintero brothers and Pedro Muñoz Seca. As they matured, these authors developed longer comic forms that set the tone for light comedy and grotesque farce respectively, theatrical forms that reflected Spain's contemporary reality through the distorting lenses of domestic sentimentality and the absurd.

Serafín and Joaquín Álvarez Quintero (1871–1938 and 1873–1944) were collaborators and regularly had more plays on stage than any other playwrights, a tribute to their prolific output (more than 200 plays) and to their sensitivity to audience anxieties and expectations. Their light comedy regularly centered on the "war of the sexes," providing a rich chronicle of courtship and marriage as these social institutions were subjected to age-old and very modern pressures. *Tambor y cascabel* ("Drum and Bell," 1927) won applause for the delicate exposure of a marriage torn by incompatibilities of character (he is as grave as a bass drum, she as frivolous as a jingle bell). Their plays featured brilliant wit, elegant writing, and humorous plots, making them safe fare for middle-class women. In *Cancionera* (1924), the Quintero brothers created a mythical, colorful Andalusia, anchored by their native Seville, which Federico García Lorca would later set about deconstructing (*Doña Rosita la soltera* ["Doña Rosita the Spinster," 1936] became Federico's answer to *Las flores* ["The Flowers," 1901] through the common trope of woman as flower).

The field of sentimental comedy was broad and lucrative and thus attracted a multitude of talented authors, each of whom specialized in a facet of modern urban life. For the husband-and-wife team of Gregorio Martínez Sierra (1881–1948) and María de la O Lejárraga (1874–1974) (she wrote while he produced), the emotional life of women caught in the transition from traditional to modern paradigms was a rich vein to be worked in comedies like *Canción de cuna* ("Cradle Song," 1911) and *Lirio entre espinas* ("Iris with Thorns," 1911), whose settings are a convent and a brothel respectively. In plays like *Cada uno y su vida* ("Each to His Own," 1919) and *Amanecer* ("Dawn," 1919) we find the themes of "sensible feminism," which fought to educate women, prepare them for self-support if necessary, and free them of legal discrimination, acknowledging all the while that the home was a woman's natural habitat.[6]

The modern woman was also a favorite theme of Luis de Vargas (1892–1949), whose commercially successful comedies, *Charlestón* (1926) and *¿Quién te quiere a ti?* ("Who Loves You?" 1928), featured women from humble origins who become enmeshed in the vices and attractions of the modern metropolis. Vargas addressed the bourgeoisie's fear of social transformation by making of feminist claims a dangerously disruptive force for the traditional family while delighting audiences with performances that put on display the very emblems of modernity – in dress, slang, and music – that he was criticizing.

Luis Araquistáin held that modern comedy was the corrosive solvent that reduced all historical criteria of existence and conduct to the absurd.[7] For Pedro Muñoz Seca (1881–1936), the principal criterion of

---

[6] Pilar Nieva de la Paz, *Autoras dramáticas españolas entre 1918 y 1936* (Madrid: CSIC, 1993), pp. 69–70.
[7] Luis Araquistáin, *La batalla teatral* (Madrid: Mundo Latino, 1930), p. 45.

modern bourgeois society was the equation of individual worth with work, a concept repellent to the *fresco*, a comic stage type devoted to doing nothing and sponging off his friends and family. With this modern picaresque anti-hero, Muñoz Seca dominated the stage with grotesque farces (*astracán*) that outraged the critics but entertained audiences who shared the playwright's irreverence for established authority. The violent and hilarious distortion of things sacred began with the Spanish language itself and extended to emblems of good taste including theatrical genres like Romantic tragedy and European operettas, as in *La venganza de don Mendo* ("Don Mendo's Revenge," 1918) and *Los extremeños se tocan* ("Where Extremeñans Meet," 1926). Unlike Arniches, Muñoz Seca was never consecrated as a "serious" author and thus languished in wealth and popularity as he fed the rebellious streak of the new urban masses season after season.

Offering its practitioners more cultural than financial capital, sophisticated theatre was an elegant site for the staging of issues central to the bourgeoisie's identity: its social and political responsibilities, the role of money, the function of marriage and family, the question of individual autonomy, the place of national consciousness and regional loyalty, etc. In the final years of the nineteenth century, Jacinto Benavente appeared as the architect of a new, bourgeois dramaturgy that was "Mephistophelean" in nature: the playwright would offer his audiences the pleasures of seeing their fears and fantasies played out on stage but would then exact the price of brutal self-recognition. Writing for and from within his own class, Benavente shifted theatrical discourse in Spain from melodrama to irony, giving his well-fed spectators equal doses of complicity and blame in "dramatic comedies" whose literary qualities made him the field's cultural beacon.

In Benavente one finds the rare playwright who was able to attain commercial success without sacrificing his cultural role as privileged observer with a license to speak the truth. The mask he donned was that of the cultivated, disinterested cynic, a figure who appears in *La comida de las fieras* ("Food for Beasts," 1898) and is fully developed in the picaresque Crispín of *Los intereses creados* ("The Bonds of Interest," 1907). Benavente's cynicism, however, was too violent to be disinterested, and in works like *Señora ama* ("M'Lady," 1908), *Pepa Doncel* (1928), or *La melodía del jazz-band* ("Jazz Band Melody," 1931) one perceives what lies behind the mask, i.e., a faith in beauty born of the playwright's education in Symbolist aesthetics and Hispanic *modernismo*. Beauty, usually inscribed in characters capable of sacrificing all for love, becomes the measure against which fashionable society is shown to be cruel, driven by self-interest, and spiritually barren. Teasingly discreet about homosexuality, Benavente left clues in *Teatro fantástico* (1892) and *Los intereses creados*, but a play like *El rival de su mujer* ("His Wife's Rival" – the rival is not another woman) from 1933 openly calls for a gay reading. The characters speak of divorce, communism, and even Marañón's theory of a feminized don Juan, but what cements the friendship between Jaime and Eduardo is left unsaid.

Like Benavente, Eduardo Marquina (1879–1946) found commercial success with plays that were acclaimed for their literary value. Marquina was a Catalan who chose to write in Castilian, and perhaps his origins on the periphery contributed to his desire to turn the stage into a site for historiographic revisionism. Credited with introducing historical plays in verse to the modern stage, Marquina developed a theory of poetic drama whose roots lay in Symbolist poetics. In 1908 he initiated a series of historical dramas to challenge myths that rooted Spain's national identity in medieval Castile (the "heroic" Reconquest) and in the "epic" story of Empire.

In *Las hijas del Cid* ("The Cid's Daughters," 1908), Marquina questioned the patriarchal image of the Cid by masculinizing one of his daughters, Elvira, and giving her a far more heroic role than that of her weakened father. Critics objected loudly at the anemic depiction of Spain's national patriarch and questioned Marquina's patriotism when he dramatized the Flemish rout of the Spaniards – the beginning of the end of the Empire – in *En Flandes se ha puesto el sol* ("Empire's Elegy," 1910). A versatile playwright whom Lorca took as an early model (Marquina, too, was first a poet who turned to the theatre), the Catalan author demonstrated that the theatre could participate in the "reinvention" of Spain after 1898 by eschewing *costumbrismo* for poetry.

History and poetry were often combined in another sophisticated genre, the *zarzuela grande*, Spain's musical drama that combined operatic arias and duos with historical or fantastic plots calling for large orchestras, diva-class singers, and spectacular staging. Instead of questioning national traditions, the *zarzuela* reinforced them, drawing on classic Spanish stories and providing instances of "true Spanish music" in the face of foreign imports, especially Italian opera. Still a favorite with Spanish audiences is *Doña Francisquita* (1923) by Federico Romero (1886–1976) and Guillermo Fernández Shaw (1893–1965), with music by Amadeo Vives (1871–1932). Transposing Lope de Vega's *La discreta enamorada* ("In Love but Discreet") to the nineteenth century, this *zarzuela* retold the age-old story of a young woman, courted by an aged pretender, who uses jealousy to goad a younger suitor to action. The score included boleras, fandangos, and the well-known song "Soy madrileña" ("I'm a Woman from Madrid"), typical nationalist statements that help to explain why the first National Theatre Company was organized to produce *zarzuelas* in 1926.

The remarkable stability of the theatrical field for almost three decades brought cries for reform from many quarters, but the economic interest in maintaining the system, the rich pleasure it supplied, and the useful forum it provided for the bourgeoisie's self-representation prevailed until the end of Primo de Rivera's dictatorship in 1930. The late 1920s and the 1930s saw significant shifts, and these will be reviewed in chapter 44.

44

Theatrical reform and renewal, 1900–1936

DRU DOUGHERTY

Like the field of political power, Spain's theatre was a site of struggle, during the first decades of the twentieth century, between forces of continuity and renewal. The latter term suggests a critical assessment of the theatre as a stagnant institution, one of the main issues in a long debate over the "crisis of the theatre," perhaps the clearest manifestation of the battle to reshape the theatrical field. Critics and playwrights alike took sides, often depending on whether they profited from the status quo, which was governed by commercial interests. The distinction between theatre as business and theatre as art was basic to the language of reform and to the many experiments launched by individuals or small groups during this period.

The many calls for renewal sought to bring Spain's stage up to date (European ventures, like Jacques Copeau's Vieux Colombier and the Moscow Art Theatre, were evident models) by promoting at least four advances: (1) expansion of the stage's thematic range to include questions of sexuality, social justice, and institutional oppression; (2) changes in the economic structure of the free commercial market in favor of state-funded programs, collectives, or companies supported by community subscription; (3) modernization of stagecraft to take advantage of expressive possibilities offered by mechanical innovations like electric lighting and rotating stages; and (4) the staging of Avant-Garde plays in and beyond the small art-theatres, whether by Spanish or foreign companies. These goals were shared by a small but significant coterie of authors, directors, actors, actresses, and critics who occasionally joined forces to launch experimental programs. In the waning years of the Primo de Rivera dictatorship (1923–1930), the pace of reform intensified and then found in the Second Republic (1931–1936) a strong source of support.

While sex was on view nightly in many commercial theatres, sexuality, understood as a social construct, was rarely broached anywhere on stage. A notable exception was *Un sueño de la razón* ("Reason's Dream," 1928) by Cipriano de Rivas Cherif (1891–1967) whose original subtitle, *Un engendro de Lesbos* ("Lesbos' Monster"), was removed from the final manuscript. Dramatized is the passion shared by two women for their unborn child who, they hope, will escape the "fatalidad imperiosa de un sexo en busca de su contrario" ("imperious fate of one sex to search for its opposite").[1] Choosing a prince to father their "monster," Blanca and Livia participate in a ritual designed to "purgar en palabras todos los pensamientos oscuros, los deseos imprecisos, las perversidades del instinto" ("purge through words all obscure thoughts, imprecise desires, the perversities of instinct").[2] With reason, one critic, Paulino Masip, called the play the bravest theatrical experiment ever staged in Spain.[3]

Sexual ambiguity was also explored by Federico García Lorca (1898–1936) in *Amor de don Perlimplín con Belisa en su jardín* ("The Love of Don Perlimplin and Belisa in the Garden," 1933), an "Erotic Aleluya" temporarily confiscated by the police for being "pornographic." Narcissism, fear of female prowess, and the tyranny of heterosexual norms are combined to push a musically structured farce into the dark realm of tragedy. Gender paradigms also underlay Lorca's most scandalous commercial hit, *Yerma* ("Barren," 1935), a rural tragedy in which women's need to be mothers becomes a modern form of fate. The play offended Catholic critics, and the company saw fit to issue a statement that it was *not* an "inappropriate" spectacle for young women.[4]

Just as the musical revues displayed sex without addressing sexuality, many comedies raised the "social question" without confronting the problems of class, economic injustice, and revolutionary violence. In 1930 José Díaz Fernández argued for a "vuelta a lo humano" ("return to human [art]")[5] – an evident answer to José Ortega y Gasset's *La deshumanización del arte* ("The Dehumanization of Art," 1925) – and asked that playwrights address the actual conditions of those who could never afford a ticket to the theatre: "El teatro moderno es un teatro de masas, un teatro para el pueblo" ("Modern theatre is a theatre of the masses and for the common folk").[6] Two years later Ramón J. Sender stated that "proletarian" theatre was "la única modalidad que responde a las íntimas características de nuestra época" ("the only modality that captures the intimate features of our time").[7]

The commercial stage was understandably resistant to calls for revolutionary theatre, and Sender himself finally admitted that proletarian plays

[1] Cipriano de Rivas Cherif, *Un sueño de la razón*. In *Cuadernos El Público* 42 (1985), p. 97.
[2] Rivas Cherif, *Un sueño*, p. 89.
[3] Juan Aguilera Sastre and Manuel Aznar Soler, *Cipriano de Rivas Cherif y el teatro de su época (1891–1967)* (Madrid: Asociación de Directores de Escena de España, 1999), p. 129.
[4] María Francisca Vilches de Frutos and Dru Dougherty, *La escena madrileña entre 1926 y 1931. Un lustro de transición* (Madrid: Fundamentos, 1997), p. 96.
[5] José Díaz Fernández, *El nuevo romanticismo* (Madrid: Zeus, 1930), p. 47.
[6] Díaz Fernández, *El nuevo romanticismo*, p. 207.
[7] Ramón J. Sender, *Teatro de masas* (Valencia: Orto, 1932), pp. 102–103.

were psychologically and aesthetically too simplistic to make a difference. The solution, he suggested, lay in leftist bourgeois writers who could render "una interpretación dinámica y dialéctica" ("a dynamic and dialectic interpretation") of contemporary reality.[8] One such playwright was Alejandro Casona (1903–1965), whose *Nuestra Natacha* (1936) was an impressive box-office hit. The play's heroine, Natacha, is the first woman in Spain to hold a Ph.D. in Education, an honor that gets her a teaching job in a reformatory for teenagers. Her introduction of new educational ideas – elective studies, cooperation between student and teacher, and, especially, coeducation – brings about her dismissal, prelude to the final establishment of a collective school and farm on the estate of one of the students. "Utopias of communist philosophers" complained the critic from Madrid's *ABC*.

Equally Utopian was the dream of finding a new economic structure that would bypass the capitalist exigencies of the commercial theatre. Three avenues were explored: the small amateur group devoted to staging Avant-Garde texts with experimental *mise en scène*; the collective or subscription theatre, usually with a leftist program; and State-funded companies designed to disseminate culture to remote villages and to find in Spain's theatrical tradition a key to national identity.

One of the first attempts to equate theatre with art was the Teatre Intime (1898) of Adrià Gual (1872–1943) in Barcelona, an independent amateur group organized around a modern concept of space, scenic design, and the director's role in shaping the *mise en scène*. Eschewing the pictorial tradition of scene painting, Gual introduced sets conceived to communicate the overall directorial concept behind the staging of Symbolist plays by Maurice Maeterlinck and classics like Aeschylus' *Prometheus Bound*. Another serious experiment was the Teatro de Arte founded by the critic Alejandro Miquis in 1908 and modeled on Antoine's Théâtre Libre. Unlike Gual, Miquis sought less to define a method of directing than to broaden the repertory and raise the level of theatre above localism and entertainment. Hence the choice of George Bernard Shaw's *Mrs. Warren's Profession*, Oscar Wilde's *A Woman of No Importance*, and Maeterlinck's *The Blind* alongside works by Shakespeare and Calderón de la Barca.

Other small groups of note included El Mirlo Blanco, organized by Carmen Monné de Baroja in 1923, Valle-Inclán's short-lived Cántaro Roto (1926), and Rivas Cherif's Caracol (1928). Cipriano de Rivas Cherif directed all three groups and sought to "dignify" the stage with works of proven literary quality drawn from classic and contemporary authors. Thus works by Ramón del Valle-Inclán and Leonid Andreev (1871–1919)

---

[8] Ramón J. Sender, "El teatro nuevo." *Leviatán* 25 (June 1936), p. 370.

appeared on bills with Ramón de la Cruz (1731–1794) and Leandro
Fernández de Moratín (1760–1828). The same literary criterion was
upheld by Pura Maórtua de Ucelay in her Club Teatral Anfistora (1933–
1936), directed by Lorca, that staged Lope de Vega's *Peribáñez y el Comendador de Ocaña* (1935), *Liliom* (1934) by Ferenc Molnár (1878–1952),
and Lorca's own *La zapatera prodigiosa* ("The Shoemaker's Prodigious
Wife," 1933).

The elitist nature of such art groups was denounced by leftists like
José Díaz Fernández, who stated that "hacer teatro de vanguardia para
minorías es tan estéril como escribir en el agua" ("producing Avant-
Garde theatre for a minority is as sterile as writing on water").[9] Their
answer was to organize collectivist companies like the Nosotros group
(1933), directed by César (1872–1970) and Irene Falcón, which staged
plays by Ernst Toller (1893–1939), Maxim Gorki (1868–1936), and
Friedrich Wolf (1888–1953) as part of a program of "proletarian theatre."
Another company, Nueva Escena, directed by Rafael Alberti (1903–
1999) and María Teresa León (1904–1988), staged the Spanish première
of *Esperpento de los cuernos de don Friolera* ("The Lieutenant's Lost
Honor") by Ramón del Valle-Inclán in February 1936, on the eve of the
elections that brought victory to the Frente Popular ("Popular Front").
In that première were joined most of the efforts reviewed here to open
the stage to taboo topics while raising the literary level of the theatre. A
form of tragic farce, the "esperpento" (invented by Valle-Inclán) deconstructed tragic and melodramatic paradigms to create a contemplative
distance between the audience and the genuine suffering of puppet-like
characters. The only "esperpento" staged during the author's lifetime,
Los cuernos de don Friolera spoofed nineteenth-century melodramas by
José Echegaray (1832–1916) and Eugenio Sellés (1842–1926), Calderón's
honor plays and Shakespeare's *Othello*, preserving all the while the
shreds of tragic anguish. The play also satirized the Spanish army, reason enough to make it a favorite underground text during the Franco
dictatorship.

Whether devoted to art or to political propaganda, the small amateur groups were on the periphery of the theatrical field even when they
acquired institutional status thanks to the Second Republic. In 1932 the
government presided over by Manuel Azaña funded the Teatro Universi-
tario la Barraca, directed by Federico García Lorca and Eduardo Ugarte,
an amateur company that, in an effort to spread culture, took classic
Spanish plays to isolated rural areas. A parallel initiative, the Misiones
Pedagógicas, included a traveling group, Teatro del Pueblo, directed by
Alejandro Casona, and featured classic and contemporary popular farces.

[9] José Díaz Fernández, *El nuevo romanticismo*, pp. 207–208.

Both projects were ostensibly educational, but they were also part of a larger movement, the creation of a National Theatre, that sought to identify the Republican state with Spain's long and glorious theatrical tradition. Indeed, the founding of a Lyric (i.e. musical) National Theatre in 1931 was ripe with nationalist overtones. The official decree stated that the genuine expression of Spain's soul lay in its popular music.

The adoption of modern notions of stagecraft was an arduous process, whose liberating effects on authors and directors became apparent only in the late 1920s. In the early years of the century, the pioneer in modern staging practices was Gregorio Martínez Sierra (1881–1948) whose Teatro de Arte in the Teatro Eslava (1916–1926) emphasized the visual aspect of spectacle and sought to create, by coordinating theatre's many sign systems, a unified aesthetic effect. The break with Realist discourse was advanced by scenic artists like Sigfredo Bürmann, Manuel Fontanals, Salvador Bartolozzi, Rafael Pérez Barradas, Santiago Ontañón, and Fernando Mignoni who, for some productions, eschewed perspective and referential scenery in favor of symbolic, three-dimensional sets, suggestive of the spirit of the drama. Bartolozzi's costumes and sets for *El señor de Pigmalión* ("Mr. Pigmalion," 1928) by Jacinto Grau (1877–1958) gave plastic form to this author's disdain for Spanish stagecraft: the prologue's bourgeois illusionism is deconstructed in the following acts by symbolic sets that include a *commedia dell'arte* stage within a stage and a transverse staircase reminiscent of Leopold Jessner's Expressionist emblems. A year later, *Los medios seres* ("Half of One," 1929), an experiment by Ramón Gómez de la Serna (1888–1963), featured costumes and makeup that split each character into opposing halves, a visual sign of the subject's search for his or her "unfinished self." This commercially unsuccessful play slowed the action to a minimum and turned dialogue toward unreal fantasy.

The visit by George Pitoëff's Paris-based Avant-Garde company in February 1927 introduced the expressive effects of side lighting to Madrid's stage, a technique immediately adopted to present *Brandy, mucho Brandy* ("A Lot of Brandy," 1927), a play by Azorín (1873–1967) that the critics violently rejected as anti-theatrical. This is but one example of the vital role played by foreign companies in setting modern standards for stagecraft during the period. Max Reinhardt's resurrection of Calderón's *El gran teatro del mundo* may have inspired Rafael Alberti to write his modern *auto*, *El hombre deshabitado* ("Vacant Man," 1929), whose staging included monstrous masks for the five senses and a helmet worn by the new Adam, signs that were to be read allegorically.

To compete with the dynamic effects of early film, directors sought mechanical means to imitate the rapid rhythms and changes of locale that delighted cinema audiences and were called for by many modern theatrical scripts. Thus, Vicky Baum's international hit *Grand Hotel* (1932) presented four simultaneous actions on as many stages, and Ladszlo Fedor's *El beso ante el espejo* ("Mirror Kiss," 1933) utilized mobile sets that were rolled into place on rails. When the Teatro Español was remodeled in the late 1920s, Valle-Inclán and others criticized the architect for not installing a revolving stage, which would have facilitated the numerous scene changes called for in classic Spanish plays.

Two measures of the effective renewal of Spain's theatre were the inclusion of peripheral theories and techniques in commercial productions, and the box-office success of plays whose Avant-Garde billing made them unlikely hits. The lavish musical revues incorporated the latest innovations in lighting and costume, eroded the three-act plot structure by means of autonomous and discontinuous *cuadros*, restored fantasy to theatrical discourse, and subordinated spoken dialogue to the theatre's concrete semiosis. Impresarios discovered early on that there was a market for renewal, especially in comic genres that appealed to the growing petit bourgeoisie. With *Piezas de recambio* ("Replacement Parts," 1933) Felipe Ximénez de Sandoval (1903–1978) and Pedro Sánchez de Neyra showed that a droll caricature of old-fashioned French vaudeville could become a box-office hit. Like other up-and-coming writers (Enrique Jardiel Poncela [1901–1952], Manuel Abril [1884–1940], Benjamín Jarnés [1888–1950], Ángel Lázaro [1900–1985], Max Aub [1903–1972], Halma Angélico [1888–1952]), Ximénez and Neyra appealed to the audience's impatience with genres that had become out-dated. Irony and humor, mixed with kitsch, were among the best ingredients in the playwrights' recipe for renewal *and* for commercial success. Valentín Andrés Álvarez (1890–1982) also found favor with the public in his *¡Tararí!* ("TaDa!," 1929), a work that pushed madcap farce toward philosophical speculation and made palatable for middle-class audiences the complete withdrawal of reality.

More difficult was the confluence of commercial and Avant-Garde trajectories in serious plays, yet even there the force of renewal proved irresistible and even profitable. After its successful run in Buenos Aires, Lorca's *Bodas de sangre* ("Blood Wedding," 1933), with Lola Membrives in the role of the Mother, became a hit in spite of breaching audience expectations – according to Díez-Canedo – that the rival gypsy families would speak with an Andalusian accent.[10] A year later, *Yerma* (1934) also reached the magical number of 100 consecutive performances, demonstrating that a daring script could indeed become a commercial success.

---

[10] Enrique Díez-Canedo, *Artículos de crítica teatral*. 4 vols. (Mexico: Joaquín Mortiz, 1968), vol. 1, p. 60.

Where the effects of renewal became most apparent, in a well-organized and long-term program, was in Madrid's municipal Teatro Español during the years (1932–1935) that the Margarita Xirgu – Enrique Borrás company played there with expert direction by Rivas Cherif. The semi-commercial venture brought together classic and contemporary Spanish authors noted for their literary excellence (Lope de Vega, Calderón de la Barca, Jacinto Benavente, Eduardo Marquina, Miguel de Unamuno, Federico García Lorca, Rafael Alberti, etc.) and staged contemporary US and European authors (Elmer Rice, Georg Kaiser, Henri-René Lenormand, Luigi Pirandello, etc.) with genuine critical success. The Teatro Español became a showcase of the best Spanish and international theatre, both contemporary and classic, and gave the lie to those who said that Spain's theatre must remain local and moribund.

Emblematic of this achievement was the première of *Divinas palabras* ("Divine Words," 1933), the rural tragicomedy by Valle-Inclán (1866–1936) that had remained unstaged for over a decade. Barbarism, pagan sexuality, and biblical forgiveness were traditional Mediterranean themes that Valle-Inclán reassembled in an Avant-Garde dramatic discourse owing much to Expressionism and Goya's grotesque. Returning to the biblical injunction "Let he who is without blame cast the first stone," the play enacts the greed and lust of Mari Gaila, the faithless wife of a sacristan, who in one scene mounts the back of Satan himself and is transported through the air to erotic ecstasy. Meanwhile her drunken husband makes incestuous advances to their daughter. Also memorable was the première of *El otro* ("The Other") by Miguel de Unamuno in 1932. Received as a modern mystery play, it too joined classic and biblical traditions (Oedipus, Cain and Abel) in probing the divided condition of the modern subject.

Significant spinoffs from the Teatro Español initiative were two schools founded by Rivas Cherif to modernize the stage from within: the Estudio de Arte Dramático del Teatro Español (1933) and the Teatro Escuela de Arte (1934). In both instances, the emphasis was on training young actors, set and costume designers, choreographers, and directors in new methods and theories of staging. The aim was to educate future practitioners in all theatrical arts and thus replace antiquated practices from the ground up.

When the Civil War broke out in August 1936, renewal of the Spanish stage was well underway. Young, talented authors were writing new kinds of plays that were finding knowledgeable critics in the likes of Rafael Marquina and Juan Chabás. Forward-looking directors like Rivas Cherif and Felipe Lluch were working with actresses (e.g. Margarita Xirgu and Irene López Heredia) who thrived on challenging, experimental scripts.

Perhaps the best indicator of the advances made was the fact that Lorca's *Así que pasen cinco años* ("Once Five Years Pass") was in rehearsal in Spring 1936.[11] Once an "impossible," experimental play, this "Legend of Time" had seen the stage evolve sufficiently to make its première finally possible.

[11] Margarita Ucelay, "El Club Teatral Anfistora." In *El teatro en España entre la tradición y la vanguardia (1918–1939)*. Ed. Dru Dougherty and María Francisca Vilches de Frutos (Madrid: CSIC / Fundación FGL / Tabacalera, 1992), pp. 464–466.

45

Federico García Lorca

ANDREW A. ANDERSON

Federico García Lorca (1898–1936) is Spain's most celebrated twentieth-century author. He achieved success and popularity as both poet and dramatist within Spain before his untimely death, and his international reputation has grown steadily since then, resulting in an extraordinary range of editions, translations, critical commentary, productions, and adaptations.

Lorca is most often categorized as belonging to the "Generation of 1927," a group of ten or so writers – predominantly poets – who rose to prominence in Spain in the later 1920s and the first half of the 1930s. The group originated in a number of friendships, some of which went back to childhood, and while its members admired each other's work, that work was, stylistically, very diverse.

Lorca's family and friends expected him to pursue a career in music rather than literature, but a cultural excursion in which he participated in 1916 seems to have been the catalyst that re-oriented him toward letters. Organized by one of his professors at the University of Granada, it involved regular writing assignments, and prose, surprisingly enough, was the first genre that the young Lorca essayed. Soon, however, he was also experimenting with both poetry and drama.

Lorca went on to write some twelve collections of verse plus other shorter sequences of poems, but only six of those twelve were published during his lifetime. Furthermore, of the remaining six, only two were complete at the time of his death.

There are several clearly distinguishable (though sometimes overlapping) phases in Lorca's poetry. His earliest output has been edited by Christian de Paepe and published in 1994 as *Poesía inédita de juventud* ("Unpublished Poetic Juvenilia").[1] This material, written between 1917 and 1919, represents his apprenticeship in verse composition, and the poems betray the influence of writers such as Rubén Darío, Salvador Rueda, Francisco Villaespesa, Antonio Machado, and Juan

---

[1] Federico García Lorca, *Poesía inédita de juventud.* Ed. Christian de Paepe (Madrid: Cátedra, 1994).

Ramón Jiménez. The aesthetic that he initially espoused, then, was unequivocally that of Spanish *modernismo*.

This poetic juvenilia overlaps with his first published collection of poetry, *Libro de poemas* ("Book of Poems," 1921).[2] The poems are squarely in the Romantic–Symbolist tradition, and although the same models and influences persist, they are now generally less pronounced and better integrated. A nascent Avant-Garde had appeared in Spain during 1919 in the form of *Ultraísmo*, but save for a few outlandish metaphors (which probably owe more to Ramón Gómez de la Serna and his *greguerías*), there is no really ground-breaking writing in *Libro de poemas*. There is, though, a striking inventiveness, coherence, density, and richness to be found within the relatively conventional image-making.

At the end of 1920 Lorca deliberately brought to a close what we may term his first poetic manner, and from 1921 onwards he experimented with a very different style, characterized by brief poems, short line lengths, loose and irregular structures, complex imagery, and evocation or ellipsis rather than explicit statement. The result suggests the melding of the traditional Spanish lyric with the haiku, then in fashion in Spain. This is the world of *Suites*, to which, to varying degrees, *Poema del cante jondo* and *Canciones* also belong. Unfortunately, Lorca never published the collection *Suites* in his lifetime; if a definitive manuscript ever existed (which is debatable) it is now lost. The book has been partially reconstructed by André Belamich as *Suites* (1983), and a more thorough edition of the entire corpus of extant poems and versions is currently in preparation.[3] As the name implies, the collection was to have been composed of a number of "suites," a suite being in turn a sequence of several short poems, each of which achieves greater expressiveness within the thematic, imagistic, or narrative context of the progression of the series as a whole.

Poema del cante jondo ("Poem of the Deep Song") is a set of several suites written around the specific topic of *cante jondo*, the purest form of flamenco. They were composed, mainly in November 1921, in anticipation of the Festival de Cante Jondo that Lorca helped to organize in Granada in June 1922, but the collection was not published until 1931.[4] The poems conform to the stylistic pattern of *Suites* and do not attempt to reproduce the metrics of actual *cante jondo*; rather they seek to evoke the impact that a hearing of *cante jondo* lyrics being performed might have on a listener. That impact is considerable, for Lorca conceived of these songs as pure and profound expressions of the gypsy – and more generally the Andalusian – ethos. As such, their dwelling on raw emotion,

[2] Federico García Lorca, *Libro de poemas*. Ed. Mario Hernández (Madrid: Alianza, 1984).
[3] Federico García Lorca, *Suites*. Ed. André Belamich (Barcelona: Ariel, 1983).
[4] Federico García Lorca, *Poema del cante jondo*. Ed. Christian de Paepe (Madrid: Espasa-Calpe, 1986).

the tension of the moment, enigma, death, and above all "pena" ("pain, grief, sorrow, suffering") marked them as a channel through which the Andalusian essence could find release and form.

Canciones ("Songs") was composed over the years 1921–1925. Manuscript evidence demonstrates considerable interference between the corpus of *Suites* and that of *Canciones*, with individual poems being transferred back and forth between them. The collection eventually emerged as a book in 1927, where the concept of the "suite" had all but disappeared.[5] The poems now generally stand alone, and the link with traditional verse forms is even more apparent. Grouped into eleven larger sections (rather than sequences), the tone is also more festive and playful. Compared to *Libro de poemas*, all overtly lyrical outpourings have been banished; emotions, if detected at all, are merely hinted at; the poetry is ludic, enigmatic, elusive; it incorporates ingenious metaphors; and it seems to serve no transcendent purpose. The collection, however, also has its edgier, darker, almost tragic, side, though this remains for the most part below the surface.

Through the 1920s Lorca's poetry began to acquire a considerable reputation among those in the Madrid artistic and intellectual community, but this was based chiefly on his own recitals and the appearance of individual poems in little magazines. The situation changed radically in 1928 with the publication by the prestigious *Revista de Occidente* of Lorca's *Romancero gitano* ("Gypsy Ballad Book"),[6] which enjoyed enormous critical and popular success and which is still favored by many today as his most accomplished collection. The eighteen substantial poems were composed and then polished over the period 1921 to 1927. Here Lorca mined the rich, centuries-old tradition of the Spanish *romance* ("ballad"); in fact, much of the success of *Romancero gitano* may be attributed to the seamless blending that he achieved of traditional and modern elements. On the one hand, the poems are all in ballad meter, they all contain some kind of narrative, and they display a number of other formal, structural, and stylistic features typical of the *romance*; on the other, these are difficult compositions, whose action, content, and theme can be hard to pin down, and they display a dazzling poetic language marked, above all, by the superabundant use of ultra-modern images. The poems' "plots" are sometimes well defined, sometimes much less so, but in all cases they are intended to function as "modern myths." Their protagonists, ostensibly gypsies, are not presented in a picturesque or anthropological vein, but rather serve as atavistic symbols of that which is enduringly Andalusian.

---

[5] Federico García Lorca, *Canciones*. Ed. Mario Hernández (Madrid: Alianza, 1982).
[6] Federico García Lorca, *Romancero gitano*. Ed. Mario Hernández (Madrid: Alianza, 1981).

Thematically, then, *Romancero* follows but develops on *Poema del cante jondo.*

Another project which dates from these same years is that of *Odas* ("Odes"), which, however, was left uncompleted and unpublished. Sporadically between 1924 and 1929 Lorca took up and refurbished several high-art, long-line meters, associated chiefly with poets from Spain's Golden Age, usually combining these elaborate verse forms with the modern language and image-making of the 1920s. The two most notable compositions are "Oda a Salvador Dalí" ("Ode to Salvador Dalí," 1925; published in the *Revista de Occidente*, 1926) and "Oda al Santísimo Sacramento del Altar" ("Ode to the Most Holy Sacrament of the Altar," 1928–1929; published fragmentarily in the *Revista de Occidente*, 1928). The former is a eulogy of the young painter, a token of their close friendship, and an exposition of Dalí's (then) essentially Cubist aesthetic; the latter is a highly heterodox (and again modernistic) meditation on the mystery of the crucified Christ present in the Eucharist – reflecting a brief turning back to Catholicism on Lorca's part. A further group of posthumously published compositions from this same period falls into two categories, parodies and apocryphal poems: *Antología modelna* [*sic*]*, precedida de los Poemas de Isidoro Capdepón Fernández* ("Modeln [*sic*] Anthology, Preceded by the Poems of Isidoro Capdepón Fernández").[7]

Yet another project not brought to fruition is that of the *Poemas en prosa* ("Prose Poems"), whose texts were composed in 1927–1928.[8] The six extant prose poems represent a complete break with the aesthetic and style of both *Odas* and *Romancero gitano.* Although doubtless flattered by the success of the *Romancero*, Lorca felt that its poems were misunderstood by many of its readers, and at the same time his more radical friends, such as Luis Buñuel and Salvador Dalí, were severely critical, finding the collection bourgeois and unadventurous. In this sense, the *Poemas en prosa* may be viewed both as a deliberate distancing from the world of the *Romancero* and as a response to the poems and prose poems that Dalí himself was writing, in Castilian and Catalan, around this same time.

The *Poemas en prosa* are also crucial to understanding how Lorca came to write his next poetical collection, *Poeta en Nueva York* ("Poet in New York"). When the possibility of a trip to the United States arose, Lorca jumped at the opportunity, and soon after his arrival in New York he was at work on the poems that would become *Poeta en Nueva York*. The book is comprised of texts written during his stay (1929–1930) and then polished over the course of the 1930s; had Civil War not broken out in

[7] Federico García Lorca, *Antología modelna* [*sic*]*, precedida de los Poemas de Isidoro Capdepón Fernández*. Ed. M. García-Posada (Granada: Comares, 1995).
[8] Federico García Lorca, *Poemas en prosa*. Ed. Andrew A. Anderson (Granada: Comares, 2000).

July 1936, it would have been published in the Fall of that year (it appeared in 1940, but a definitive critical edition of the recently recovered manuscript is still awaited). In ten sections it charts the poet-*persona*'s passage through debarcation, exploration of New York, a trip to the countryside, return to the city, and final departure for Cuba. As such, the overall shape is transparently autobiographical, but the actual order of composition of the poems and the many liberties of detail belie any presumption of historical accuracy.

The collection covers a number of themes. Sharp contrasts are drawn between the innocence of childhood and the "knowledge" of adulthood; New York is depicted as a compendium of alienation, superficiality, rootlessness, and (hypocritical) organized religion; mankind struggles unsuccessfully to achieve authenticity or any kind of satisfying human relationship; furthermore, as before, mankind is subject to the twin constants of the inexorable passing of time and the inevitability of mortality. Partial exceptions to this rule are the blacks of Harlem, who, although oppressed and denatured, retain (like the gypsies of Andalusia) an atavistic spirituality, and the exemplary figure of Walt Whitman, who was properly "in touch" with himself, others, and Nature. On the social level, Lorca decries the poverty and exploitation he sees around him, criticizes the materialistic capitalism of Wall Street, rails at the Pope, and even looks forward to the day when some kind of cataclysmic upheaval is envisioned as overtaking the city and the rule of Nature will return. On a more personal note, this collection also marks the first appearance of poems that seriously address the topic of homosexuality and homosexual relationships, notably in "Tu infancia en Menton" ("Your childhood in Menton") and "Oda a Walt Whitman" ("Ode to Walt Whitman"). *Poeta en Nueva York* has often been classified as a prime example of Spanish Surrealism, but it is really better thought of as simply Avant-Garde, for Lorca's imagistic practice is quite varied, running the gamut from conventional metaphors to what he called "hechos poéticos" ("poetic acts"), difficult, atmospheric images that resist easy interpretation.

On his return to Spain, Lorca concentrated his efforts on works for the theatre, but did not neglect poetical composition completely. For instance, during trips to Galicia in 1932, he began to write poems in the Galician language, and thus were born some of the texts eventually gathered together as *Seis poemas galegos* ("Six Galician Poems," 1935).[9]

The poems that would eventually be brought together as *Diván del Tamarit* ("Divan of the Tamarit," 1940) were composed between 1931 and 1934.[10] The collection was intended as a homage to the Arabic poets

---

[9] Federico García Lorca, *Diván del Tamarit. Llanto por Ignacio Sánchez Mejías. Seis poemas galegos. Poemas sueltos*. Ed. Andrew A. Anderson (Madrid: Espasa-Calpe, 1988). Hereafter, *Diván*.

[10] Federico García Lorca, *Diván*.

of Muslim Spain ("diván" is an Arabic term for an anthology or collection; Tamarit an Arabic-derived name of a district just outside Granada). As the book took shape in 1934, with its two sections of "Gacelas" and "Casidas" (two Arab-Andalusian verse forms), the earlier compositions were renamed to include one or other denomination in their titles. *Diván del Tamarit* is a diverse collection in that some poems recall the flavor of *Canciones* and others the more meditative style of *Poeta en Nueva York*, but it is nonetheless homogeneous in that all the pieces are situated between the twin axes of "love" and "death," forming not an opposition but most often a complex and ambiguous interpenetration. Anecdotally, a brief, passionate, and seemingly destructive love affair is fleetingly and rather hazily evoked, almost always in the past. The poems are therefore not concerned with any one particular experience, but more with the repercussions of failed or lost love, with meditations on death and death in life, and on the way in which the one almost inevitably leads to (thoughts on) the other.

During the summer of 1934, the bullfighter Ignacio Sánchez Mejías was gored in the ring at Manzanares; gangrene set in and he was dead within thirty-six hours. Mejías was an old friend of several of the members of the Generation of 1927. Only a few weeks after the event Lorca started work on his *Llanto por Ignacio Sánchez Mejías* ("Lament for Ignacio Sánchez Mejías," 1935),[11] a long elegy articulated in four parts that are stylistically and metrically differentiated, but which coalesce in their insistent focus on the dead man and in the narrative progression. Part 1, "La cogida y la muerte" ("The goring and death"), concerned with the goring and the bullfighter's final hours, recounts the events in a number of discrete images, each intercalated with the famous refrain line, "a las cinco de la tarde" ("at five o'clock in the afternoon"). In part 2, "La sangre derramada" ("Spilled blood"), the poet-*persona* cannot bear to contemplate the blood, emblem of Mejías' life force that has flowed from his body and which is left on the sand of the ring, and this is followed by a eulogy in ballad meter that recalls the famous *Coplas en la muerte de su padre* by Jorge Manrique. In part 3, "Cuerpo presente" ("Lying in state"), the body is lying in a chapel before being transported for burial, and the poet urges the mourners to face up to the inescapable fact of physical death as he himself strives to do. Finally, in part 4, "Alma ausente" ("Absent soul"), in a bleak non-Christian framework, Mejías has been long since buried and it is suggested that he is gone and being rapidly forgotten – save by the poet, who has sung, that is, written, of him, fixing his memory for all posterity.

Lorca's last lyric verses are the "Sonetos del amor oscuro" ("Sonnets of Dark Love"), written mainly in November 1935. The eleven extant texts

---

[11] Included in Federico García Lorca, *Diván*.

are first drafts, and they received their first complete edition (as "Sonetos de amor" ["Love Sonnets"]), prepared by Miguel García-Posada for the Madrid newspaper *ABC*, in 1984. The sonnets are all strict Petrarchan hendecasyllabics, and they all depict a lover and his beloved, their relationship, and particularly the lover's sorrows at the beloved's emotional distance or physical absence. Familiar themes reappear: the inability to attain true communion, the inability to achieve lasting solace from the consciousness of time passing and mortality in love and/or sexual abandon, and the paradoxical sentiment that feeling hurt, unhappy, or anguished is better than feeling nothing at all – that it protects one from an emotional "living death." On an autobiographical level, the sonnets were inspired by Lorca's stormy relationship with Rafael Rodríguez Rapún, a young engineering student who was between 1933 and 1935 secretary of La Barraca, a student theatre group that Lorca directed. Nevertheless, despite one legitimate reading of "amor oscuro" as homosexual love, the sonnets can – and probably should – be read much less restrictively, as a broad exploration of love and its trials and sorrows.

Lorca's total poetic output over his lifetime is roughly equal to his dramatic output. He wrote some twelve plays plus numerous other minor and unfinished pieces. These can be loosely grouped in various categories: juvenilia, verse drama, puppet theatre, farce, experimental/avant-garde theatre, and tragedy.

Lorca's first dramatic compositions cover the period 1917–1922. The extant texts (eleven in prose, three in verse) range from brief fragments to complete, substantial dramas, and they have been collected as *Teatro inédito de juventud* ("Unpublished Theatrical Juvenilia"),[12] and as *Cuatro piezas breves* ("Four Short Plays").[13] Lorca made no attempt to have any of them staged. The titles – for example *Dios, el Mal y el Hombre* ("God, Evil and Man") from 1917, or *Cristo. Tragedia religiosa* ("Christ. Religious Tragedy") from 1919–1920 – speak eloquently of his preoccupations over these years: the existence, nature, and disposition of God; the significance of Christ's life and death; the meaning of life itself; social injustice; the conflicts between the spiritual and the carnal; the yearning and quest for an ideal, transcendent love.

These texts also provide the background for Lorca's first performed work, *El maleficio de la mariposa* ("The Butterfly's Evil Spell"),[14] written in 1919 when a Madrid impresario asked him to recast and expand one of his poems (now lost) into a play. The resulting verse drama, whose

---

[12] Federico García Lorca, *Teatro inédito de juventud*. Ed. Andrés Soria Olmedo (Madrid: Cátedra, 1994).

[13] Federico García Lorca, *Cuatro piezas breves*. Ed. Andrés Soria Olmedo (Granada: Comares, 1996).

[14] Federico García Lorca, *El maleficio de la mariposa*. Ed. Piero Menarini (Madrid: Cátedra, 1999).

characters are exclusively insects, principally cockroaches, is patently Symbolist in nature, and suggests inspiration from the Belgian dramatist and Nobel Laureate Maurice Maeterlinck (1862–1949). Completed hurriedly, it premièred in the spring of 1920 and was a resounding failure, closing after only a few performances.

Lorca's next play to receive a commercial production was also a verse drama. *Mariana Pineda* (1928) premièred in Barcelona in 1927, though a first draft was written as early as 1923.[15] In several ways less adventurous than much of his previous dramatic production, *Mariana Pineda* treats, with poetic license, the life of the eponymous protagonist, a historical character from Granada caught up in the liberal revolutionary activity of early nineteenth-century Spain. Many saw in the play an oblique political reference to the Primo de Rivera dictatorship, but the plot is really about the impossibility of attaining – or maintaining – a true love that is reciprocated.

Running in parallel with these early compositions is Lorca's strong interest in puppets. In particular he was concerned with the *cristobicas*, a kind of Andalusian Punch and Judy show, and based on these traditional characters and plot lines he wrote several versions of his own. The manuscript of *Cristobical (Burla)* ("Big Christopher [Jest]"), from 1921 or 1922, is unfinished.[16] A second, completed text dates from 1922 and is entitled *Tragicomedia de don Cristóbal y la señá Rosita* ("Tragicomedy of Mister Christopher and Missus Rosita"; it is also known as *Los títeres de Cachiporra* ["The Billy-Club Puppets"], 1948).[17] At the beginning of the 1930s Lorca produced another, distinct version, that he now entitled *Retablillo de don Cristóbal* ("The Puppet Theatre of Mister Christopher," 1938), and which was performed in Buenos Aires and Madrid in the mid 1930s.[18]

This interest in puppets is also reflected in a collaboration with the composer Manuel de Falla, then resident in Granada, which resulted in a domestic entertainment staged on the eve of Epiphany 1923. Lorca's main contribution was his puppet-play adaptation of a folk tale, *La niña que riega la albahaca y el príncipe preguntón* ("The Basil-Watering Girl and the Prying Prince"; the only extant version is actually an adaptation of Lorca's text made later by an Argentinian puppeteer).[19] With this modest

[15] Federico García Lorca, *Mariana Pineda*. Ed. Luis Martínez Cuitiño (Madrid: Cátedra, 1991).

[16] Federico García Lorca, *Cristobical*. Ed. Piero Menarini. *Anales de la Literatura Española Contemporánea* (1986).

[17] Federico García Lorca, *Tragicomedia de don Cristóbal y la señá Rosita*. Ed. Annabella Cardinali and Christian de Paepe (Madrid: Cátedra, 1998).

[18] Federico García Lorca, *Retablillo de don Cristóbal y doña Rosita*. Ed. Mario Hernández (Granada: Diputación Provincial de Granada, 1992).

[19] Federico García Lorca, *La niña que riega la albahaca y el príncipe preguntón*. Ed. Luis González-del-Valle. *Anales de la Literatura Española Contemporánea* (1984).

success behind them, they proposed a more substantial collaboration, on a comic opera to be entitled *Lola, la comedianta* ("Lola the Actress").[20] The libretto occupied Lorca, on and off, during 1923 and 1924; unfortunately, the project petered out, but some scenes from his text have survived.

The farce-like nature of traditional puppet plays also found expression in two works clearly written for actors. The first draft of *La zapatera prodigiosa* ("The Shoemaker's Prodigious Wife," 1938) was set down in 1924, but it did not reach the boards until 1930.[21] The play picks up the age-old topos of "el viejo y la niña" ("the old man and the young girl") already found in the characters of Cristóbal and Rosita. Lorca provides a simplified, stylized set, costume, and action, while adding a metatheatrical element with a prologue and a kind of play-within-a-play. The piece is one of Lorca's most humorous, and it ends on a broadly cheerful note tinged with ambiguity. The next "human" farce, *Amor de don Perlimplín con Belisa en su jardín* ("The Love of Don Perlimplín and Belisa in the Garden," 1938), drafted in 1925 but not performed until 1933, strikes a distinctly darker chord.[22] Once more using skewed perspectives, symbolic sets and props, and the stylized atmosphere of the eighteenth century, this grotesque and tragic farce presents the traditional figures of an old man married to a young woman, but after touching on impotence and rampant sensuality, it goes on to explore the relationship between fantasy and reality, the desirability of the unknown and the unattainable, and the possibility of the finding of true love in self-sacrifice.

During the latter half of the 1920s Lorca also worked on a number of further dramatic projects; extant manuscript fragments provide titles such as *Diego Corrientes* ("Diego Corrientes," 1926), *Ampliación fotográfica* ("Photographic Enlargement," 1926), *Drama fotográfico* ("Photographic Drama," 1927), *Posada* ("Inn," 1927–1928), *Rosa mudable* ("Mutable Rose," 1928–1929) and *Dragón* ("Dragon," 1929–1930), all of which have been collected as *Teatro inconcluso* ("Unfinished Theatre").[23] While none of these came to fruition, they do testify to the restless, adventurous, experimental spirit that Lorca brought to his writing for the theatre.

This spirit finally bore spectacular fruit during the months spent in Cuba in the spring of 1930, for it was then that Lorca started work on his most extraordinary and revolutionary drama, *El público* ("The Audience").[24] Later versions have been lost or destroyed, but the extant (though possibly

[20] Federico García Lorca, *Lola la comedianta*. Ed. Piero Menarini (Madrid: Alianza, 1981).
[21] Federico García Lorca, *La zapatera prodigiosa*. Ed. Mario Hernández (Madrid: Alianza, 1982).
[22] Federico García Lorca, *Amor de don Perlimplín con Belisa en su jardín*. Ed. Margarita Ucelay (Madrid: Cátedra, 1990).
[23] Federico García Lorca, *Teatro inconcluso*. Ed. Marie Laffranque (Granada: Universidad de Granada, 1987).
[24] Federico García Lorca, *El público*. Ed. Rafael Martínez Nadal (Oxford: Dolphin, 1976).

incomplete) first draft still affords us a powerful impression of the play. Metatheatrical in conception, its use of allegory and total abandonment of verisimilitude suggest fairly close connections with Expressionism. The central theatrical metaphor is used to explore Sartrean notions of acting (for others) and being (in and of oneself); the proposition is put forward that the only (ultimate) truth is death itself; while the action centers on a variety of more or less "inauthentic" and "authentic" relationships mainly between homosexuals, and embodies a plea for a kind of pansexual liberation that would allow everyone to love as their desires dictated. As might be expected, the play was not performed during Lorca's lifetime.

El público represents Lorca's most explicit and extensive treatment of homosexuality, and as such it inevitably invites connection with his personal life. Although he may have been relatively comfortable with his own sexual orientation among a close circle of friends in Madrid during the later 1920s, it was not really until New York and then in particular Cuba that Lorca began to feel that he could – or should – try to write directly about the topic in his literary work. However, beyond the obvious examples of a couple of poems from *Poeta en Nueva York*, the late "Sonetos," and *El público*, there are relatively few other compositions where the theme of homosexuality is openly and directly addressed, and certainly the theme does not appear to be so central to Lorca's output as in the case, say, of his near-contemporary, friend, and fellow member of the Generation of 1927, Luis Cernuda.

Shortly after finishing this play, Lorca commenced work on another, obviously related to it stylistically, that was completed a year later in 1931. *Así que pasen cinco años* ("Once Five Years Pass," 1938), a meditation on the inexorable passing of time and the (existential) need to jump into the river of life, is still Avant-Garde and experimental in manner and technique, but it takes a step back from the extremes of *El público*.[25]

In the last months of his life Lorca started to compose a third experimental and revolutionary piece, which seems to have spun out of continuing work on drafts of *El público*. Only Act I survives of this drama which Lorca planned to entitle *El sueño de la vida* ("The Dream of Life"; published as *Comedia sin título* ["Play Without a Title"]).[26] The set is again a theatre, the performance space includes both stage and auditorium, while a rehearsal of *A Midsummer Night's Dream* is being held somewhere backstage. The Author harangues the audience and gets into an argument; shots ring out, and the theatre collapses into turmoil, while

[25] Federico García Lorca, *Así que pasen cinco años*. Ed. Margarita Ucelay (Madrid: Cátedra, 1995).
[26] Federico García Lorca, *Comedia sin título*. Ed. Marie Laffranque (Barcelona: Seix Barral, 1978).

a workers' uprising rages outside. Clearly then, the increasing politiciza-
tion of the 1930s had had their effect on Lorca also, most of all since the
brutal repression by government forces of the socialist miners' uprising
in Asturias in Fall 1934, and in this unfinished play he sought to combine
previous concerns – authenticity, facing up to the truth, love, death – with
a more explicitly socio-political message.

After the experimentalism of *El público* and *Así que pasen cinco años* in
the early 1930s, Lorca deliberatedly turned back to a more approachable
form of theatre. Almost certainly he had decided that he needed to establish himself as a successful and influential dramatist, and then dictate, from
a position of strength, the staging of his other more challenging works. In
1932 he wrote the first of the tragedies set in the Andalusian countryside,
Bodas de sangre ("Blood Wedding," 1936), and it premièred in 1933.[27]
Manifestly Symbolist in conception, the work is nevertheless decidedly
mainstream in comparison to those that precede it. The first two acts,
although displaying a strong symbolic charge, are relatively Naturalistic,
but there is a significant shift in Act III, where allegorical figures, fantasy,
and verse come to the fore. The dénouement, where the two young men
die and the women are condemned to a life of widowhood, reflects the
bleak vision of the destiny of both those who give free rein to their erotic
passion and those who (try to) suppress it.

Lorca immediately started work on his second tragedy, *Yerma*
("Barren," 1937), composed during 1933–1934 and premièred at the end
of 1934.[28] Overall a little more austere than *Bodas*, in *Yerma* ("Yerma"
is also the main character's name) Lorca nonetheless strove to develop
further the use of the chorus from Greek tragedy, in scenes where washerwomen work and sing, and in a syncretically ritualistic final scene around
the pilgrimage shrine of a saint reputed to cure infertility. The play is
a classic study of frustration and unfulfillment: Yerma's life is focused
exclusively on motherhood, but this is denied her, and with her yearning
to participate in the natural cycle of life unsatisfied she is goaded at the
end of the play to strangle her husband in a frenzy of pent-up resentment.

Lorca did not continue immediately with the third and final part of the
trilogy (*Bodas/Yerma/Bernarda Alba*), but rather diverted his attention
to *Doña Rosita la soltera* ("Doña Rosita the Spinster," 1938), which he
composed in 1934–1935 and premièred late in 1935.[29] The play evokes the
turn-of-the-century city of Granada, and is set in a deliciously pretentious
middle-class ambience. The minimal action is predicated on the symbol of
a rose whose bloom lasts but one day: the eponymous protagonist Rosita

---

[27] Federico García Lorca, *Bodas de sangre*. Ed. Mario Hernández (Madrid: Alianza, 1984).
[28] Federico García Lorca, *Yerma*. Ed. Mario Hernández (Madrid: Alianza, 1981).
[29] Federico García Lorca, *Doña Rosita la soltera*. Ed. Luis Martínez Cuitiño (Madrid:
Espasa-Calpe, 1992).

is its female incarnation, who constantly has to wait and whose whole life, really, is indefinitely postponed. The dénouement leaves her a pale, fading, middle-aged spinster, falling into a faint as the family is forced to move out of their house. The minor-key, nostalgic tone is distinctly Chekhovian; the location and time-frame recall *Mariana Pineda*; the basic theme is reminiscent of *Así que pasen cinco años*.

After the completion of *Doña Rosita*, Lorca then turned to *La casa de Bernarda Alba* ("The House of Bernarda Alba").[30] Commenced in the latter half of 1935, the play existed in draft form by June 1936. Had the Civil War not broken out, *La casa de Bernarda Alba* would doubtless have been premièred in the Fall of 1936; as it was, the play's first performance took place in Buenos Aires in 1945. Lorca continued to pare down the contribution of song and dance, and likewise to eliminate the more overtly symbolic and fantastic elements, though in its monochrome contrasts of black and white, and its extraordinary *dramatis personae* made up exclusively of women, *La casa de Bernarda Alba* is, in its own way, as anti-Realistic and Symbolist as *Bodas* or *Yerma*. The house functions as the central symbol for enclosure and entrapment: under their tyrannical mother's thumb, the daughters adopt different attitudes to their seemingly inevitable fate of frustration and spinsterhood. However, the youngest, Adela, rebels, and takes a secret lover (the fiancé of the eldest sister), but in the long run that is scarcely more satisfactory: their tryst discovered, Bernarda shoots at but misses the fleeing lover, and Adela, thinking the worst, hangs herself.

La casa de Bernarda Alba has been hailed as the culmination of Lorca's dramaturgy, but in assessing this judgment we should remember that he would surely have written many more plays had he not been killed at the age of thirty-eight, and that he himself staked his future primarily in the sphere of *El público* and *Así que pasen cinco años*. Furthermore, there may not be such a disjunction between the experimental dramas and the rural tragedies as first appears. Like Valle-Inclán and other concerned writers, Lorca was severely critical of the state of the theatre in Spain, which he found stagnant, trivialized, and severely over-commercialized. Consequently, *all* of his plays, when focused in this light – as Fernández Cifuentes has shown – can be seen to challenge the status quo.[31] Those which contemporary audiences found easier to accept are subversive of the norms of dramatic composition in more subtle and veiled ways, but in all of them Lorca sought to reinvigorate the Spanish stage, both looking back to ancient and popular traditions (e.g. Greek tragedy,

---

[30] Federico García Lorca, *La casa de Bernarda Alba*. Ed. Mario Hernández (Madrid: Alianza, 1981).

[31] Luis Fernández Cifuentes, *García Lorca en el teatro: la norma y la diferencia* (Zaragoza: Universidad de Zaragoza, 1986).

puppetry) and looking outward to the most modern innovations (e.g. Expressionism).

Besides his poetry and drama, mention should also be made of the prose writings. The earliest of these have been collected as *Prosa inédita de juventud* ("Unpublished Prose Juvenilia").[32] Lorca conceived of these often intensely lyrical outpourings, written between 1916 and 1918, in terms of different subgenres such as "Místicas," "Estados sentimentales," "Meditaciones" ("Mysticisms," "Emotional States," "Meditations") etc. Thematically, they plot the same terrain as the poetic and dramatic juvenilia and, as with the early verse and plays, they also form the backdrop for Lorca's first prose publication. *Impresiones y paisajes* ("Impressions and Landscapes," 1918) predates the première of *El maleficio de la mariposa* by two years and the publication of *Libro de poemas* by three. It is the fruit of the university excursions mentioned above, and contains much of what Lorca wrote on those trips.

In the mid 1920s Lorca composed his *Diálogos* ("Dialogues"),[33] an unfinished and unpublished collection of pieces which, nevertheless, offers the first true evidence of his exploration of Avant-Garde modes of writing several years before *Poemas en prosa*, *Poeta en Nueva York*, or *El público*. These texts are truly transgeneric: in dialogue form with long and elaborate "stage directions," they are not intended for performance but simply to be read. In them Lorca puts much of the "modern spirit" and hence they are much less "Spanish" or "Andalusian" than most of his previous work.

Later, and contemporaneous with *Poeta en Nueva York* and *El público*, was Lorca's single experiment with a film screenplay, *Viaje a la luna* ("Trip to the Moon").[34] Encouraged by a Mexican cinéaste, Emilio Amero, whom Lorca had met in New York, and stimulated no doubt by second-hand accounts of Dalí and Buñuel's recently premièred *Un Chien andalou*, he composed seventy-two brief sequences for a short silent film that Amero made unsuccessful efforts to realize and which was eventually brought to the screen by Frederic Amat in 1998. In the brief "scenes" or sequences of *Viaje a la luna* (that often dissolve one into the other) *montage* is the principal organizational mode: many emblems and symbols appear that are familiar to us from other of Lorca's works, and the piece as a whole renders Lorca's perennial preoccupation with death and sexuality.

In the sphere of non-fiction writing, there are a number of lectures that Lorca composed and delivered throughout Spain and in the countries

---

[32] Federico García Lorca, *Prosa inédita de juventud*. Ed. Christopher Maurer (Madrid: Cátedra, 1994).

[33] Federico García Lorca, *Diálogos*. Ed. Andrew A. Anderson (Granada: Comares, 1998).

[34] Federico García Lorca, *Viaje a la luna*. Ed. Antonio Monegal (Valencia: Pre-Textos, 1994).

to which he traveled (USA, Cuba, Argentina, Uruguay). These texts have been collected as *Conferencias* ("Lectures").[35] Often illuminating of Lorca's own creative works, they broach a wide range of subjects: *cante jondo*, the Spanish lullaby, popular song in Granada, the image in Góngora's poetry, the poetry of Golden Age author Pedro Soto de Rojas, the nature and mechanics of poetic inspiration and composition, and trends in modern art.

In conclusion, Lorca's poetry and drama can be said to express most often a tragic vision (tragic in twentieth-century terms) that is broadly existentialist in nature. He is concerned with the universal experiences, feelings, and intuitions of mankind, of men and women more often than not involved in some struggle with their human limitations. In the world thus portrayed, love is an ideal aspired to by most and fully achieved by few or none. This situation is most commonly played out against the backdrop of the world of Nature, which can echo or contrast, help or hinder, comfort or punish. If this thematic overview sounds bleak, it is, but simultaneously, and paradoxically, Lorca's work is also one of affirmation and celebration – of imagination, fantasy, creativeness, innocence, playfulness, humor, and the resilience of the human spirit, as well as Nature's intrinsic beauty.

[35] Federico García Lorca, *Conferencias*. Ed. Christopher Maurer. 2 vols. (Madrid: Alianza, 1984).

Part IX

In and Out of Franco Spain

MICHAEL UGARTE, JOSÉ MARÍA NAHARRO
CALDERÓN, JANET PEREZ, GUILLERMO
CARNERO, MARTHA HALSEY,
MARVIN D'LUGO

46

The literature of Franco Spain, 1939–1975

MICHAEL UGARTE

In an essay in *El furgón de cola* ("The Caboose," 1976) on the situation of the Spanish writer in the 1960s, Juan Goytisolo (1931–) wrote, "la literatura española contemporánea es un espejo de la lucha oscura, humilde y cotidiana del pueblo español por su libertad perdida" ("contemporary Spanish literature is a mirror of the dark, humble, daily struggle of the Spanish people for its lost liberty").[1] While Goytisolo's views on the literary culture of the Franco period would change in the waning years of the dictatorship, this statement reflects a widely held sentiment on the part of a variety of Spanish intellectuals during the three and a half decades of the regime. Even those writers who had not sided with the Second Republic – Dionisio Ridruejo (1912–1975), José María Pemán (1898–1981), Camilo José Cela (1916–2002), Ernesto Giménez Caballero (1898–1988) are a few examples – were confronted with the daunting obstacles to freedom of expression that had been written into Spanish law. For Goytisolo these prohibitions amounted to what he called "el toro de la censura" ("the censorship bull"),[2] a bull that had gored many Spanish writers regardless of their literary skills.

It would be reductive, however, to subsume all the literature of that period – prose, poetry, essays, drama – into an all-encompassing category of a committed open resistance to the government's impositions. Resistance to the dominant ideology took many forms, often corresponding to the transformations of Spanish economics and politics. Within this pattern the most important developments for literary culture revolved around the censorship laws.

The history of Francoist censorship can be divided into four periods. The first is from the implementation of the Ley de Prensa ("Press Law") in 1938 to the Allied victory in Europe. This period was known as "los años de hambre" ("the hunger years") – although material scarcity endured well into the fifties – and was also characterized by a ruthlessly successful attempt to consolidate power in the face of the defeat of Franco's German and Italian allies as well as residual pockets of armed resistance (albeit

[1] Juan Goytisolo, *El furgón de cola* (Barcelona: Seix Barral, 1976), p. 69.
[2] Goytisolo, *El furgón*, p. 52.

weak), called the "maquis." At this time censorship was the domain of Gabriel Arias Salgado, whose role as Minister of Information and Tourism was to carry out Franco's autarchic project by establishing an "imperio de la verdad" ("empire of truth") in "la gran obra de reconstrucción nacional que el Nuevo Estado ha emprendido" ("enterprise of national reconstruction of the New State").[3] Controls on cultural expression were first directed toward the obliteration of writers and intellectuals who had not sided with Franco. The poet Miguel Hernández (1910–1942) and the playwright Antonio Buero Vallejo (1916–2000), for example, were given death sentences by the Consejo de Guerra ("War Tribunal") under the 1939 Ley de Responsabilidades ("Law of Responsibilities") according to which those who were deemed to have committed crimes before and during the war would be imprisoned or executed, an indicator of what Paul Preston calls "a full-scale institutionalization of a repression".[4] This law was linked structurally and ideologically to the 1938 Press Law.

During a six-year hiatus (1945–1951) censorship was redirected to the Ministry of Education to offer the international community the appearance of constitutional and civilian jurisdiction of cultural dissemination. Yet the prevailing legal obligation to submit publications or media production to the government – the notorious "consulta previa" ("prior consultation") – in accordance with the principle of prohibition of anything that countered the ideals of the Francoist state, remained intact.

In 1951 the new Ministry of Information and Tourism, once again under Arias Salgado, was established to regulate all things cultural. The legal restrictions on editorial freedom in this stage were more bureaucratic than before, yet equally grandiose and vague. It was still a crime to counter the ideals and precepts of the régime, and perceived enemies of the state could be imprisoned for having contradicted those precepts. Criticisms of the Church and the military were prohibited, just as they had been under the original 1938 law. Equally important, if not more so, was chastity in public expression and in the depiction of love relations, imposed to counter what was seen as the salacious nature of the culture of the Second Republic.

In 1962 censorship became the domain of a then young Francoist "liberal," Manuel Fraga Iribarne. With Fraga and the 1966 Ley de Prensa e Imprenta ("Press and Print Law") there was a relaxation of direct censorship, virtual abolition of the "consulta previa," and a new thrust toward what was projected as the responsibility of the artist and intellectual to measure their criticisms of the State with its great accomplishments, such as the highly publicized notion of the "twenty-five years of peace." Also,

[3] Cited by Manuel Abellán, *Censura y creación literaria de España (1939–1976)* (Barcelona: Península, 1980), p. 15, note 4.
[4] Paul Preston, *Franco: A Biography* (New York: Basic Books, 1994), p. 320.

in the realm of the depiction of sexuality, authors and artists were encouraged to write and perform in accordance with the purity of the family and to abide by the teachings of the Church in all depictions of sexual relations. This new emphasis on free will and responsibility, however, was not free of direct reprisals against publishing houses, journals, and theatrical productions that transgressed. In fact, according to Manuel Abellán, in 1966 there were in actuality more governmental interventions against publication of objectionable material than in preceding years.[5]

From the end of the sixties to the death of Franco in 1975 and the ratification of the Constitution of 1978, censorship gradually disappeared, in great part through the determination of writers, editors of journals, film directors and producers, actors, singers, students, of Catalan, Galician, and Basque nationalists, and of common citizens to express themselves without restrictions and to distribute those expressions regardless of governmental interference.

While the above periodization of Spanish censorship may help understand the vicissitudes of cultural regulation at that time, it remains difficult to explain the reasons why some works were censored while others were not. The factor of arbitrariness must not be discounted. What is perhaps more important is the implicit debate concerning the proper response to the régime's prohibitions that the bullish censors engendered. Indeed, the entire gamut of the cultural production of the Franco years was shaped by these codes of restriction.

In the face of the cultural and political division of Spain between the victors and the vanquished and the subsequent impediments to free expression, some writers left the country while others chose to stay and write in the realm of what was called the "possible," that is, to work through, with, against, and around the political and bureaucratic machinations that called artistic freedom into question. For Juan Goytisolo, and others of the so called "Generación de Medio Siglo" ("Mid Century Generation") who considered themselves "imposibilistas," the very act of writing in Spain constituted a subversion regardless of censorship; thus writing to please the censors was a contradiction in terms.

Still, looking back on the politics and aesthetics of the Franco years in the wake of the creation of a modern constitutional democracy, one cannot help giving the "posibilistas" a nod of recognition. If not as a clearly defined strategy to abolish the régime's prohibitions, the predominant ambiguities and evasions of meaning contributed to a weakening (however gradual) of the régime's system of cultural control. Writers left themselves open to their readers' (or spectators', or listeners') interpretation. It has even been suggested that censorship made for the sharpening of the writer's traditional tools: irony, allusion, ambiguity, association,

---

[5] Abellán, *Censura*, pp. 209–215.

multiple signification, and other devices that enhance the sophistication of the writing and the reader's reception of it.

One of the first important novels published after the war was Camilo José Cela's *La familia de Pascual Duarte* ("The Family of Pascual Duarte," 1942). Although initially it was interpreted as a work that reflected the squalid underpinnings of Spanish postwar society (both materially and psychologically), Cela's so-called "tremendismo" (or post-Civil-War grotesque) is perhaps less salient than are the signifying evasions of the narrative through a renewed use of an old form of Spanish prose – the Baroque picaresque. The protagonist is a criminal who offers the story of his low life in the form of a confession. He addresses a specific person – as did his sixteenth-century antecedent, Lazarillo de Tormes – who must decide whether this life-story should be disseminated as an example of bad conduct.

The novel is framed around a series of notes and letters that function not only as narratological distancing devices but as veiled references to the historical circumstances that brought Pascual's manuscript to the hands of its principal implied reader – the "señor" of the first sentence of Pascual's story: "Yo, señor, no soy malo" ("I, sir, am not a bad man"). As it turns out, the "señor" is a friend of Pascual's last victim, the Count of Torremejía whose murder is the reason for Pascual's incarceration and ultimate execution, even though there is no mention of it in the life-story. That all these circumstances occur between 1935 and 1942 make for little doubt that Pascual participated in the events of the war.

Yet the specifics of his participation are precisely what is omitted and thus open to the reader's interpretation. Cela, an expert in censorship due to his own role as censor in the forties, skillfully weaves the taboo of the war into his text with a Baroque wink at the reader, and this wink, this reference to something forbidden, is a dominant characteristic of myriad post-war Spanish works: the Civil War allegories of Ana María Matute (1926–); the objectivist movement of the fifties exemplified by *El Jarama* ("The Jarama River," 1956) by Rafael Sánchez Ferlosio (1927–); many of Buero Vallejo's dramas; travel literature (such as Cela's famous *Viaje a la Alcarria* ["Trip to Alcarria," 1948]); the poetic *Hijos de la ira* ("Children of Wrath," 1944) by Dámaso Alonso (1898–1990), which begins with the famous line: "Madrid es una ciudad de más de un millón de cadáveres" ("Madrid is a city of a more than a million corpses"); the Realist works Juan Goytisolo published before *Señas de identidad* ("Signs of Identity," 1968). One might even include the evasive nature of the popular culture of the time – the celebrated film, *Bienvenido Mister Marshall* ("Welcome, Mr. Marshall," 1954) by Luis García Berlanga (1912–) is one among many – explored poignantly by Manuel Vázquez Montalbán (1939–2003) in his *Crónica sentimental de España* ("Sentimental Chronicle of Spain," 1998).

Related to the ubiquitousness of censorship throughout the Franco years is a factor that informs much of that period's cultural production: the obsession with collective memory. This interest in history was widespread, yet the concept of "memory" predominates over "history" because the former served as an arm of resistance to the dictatorship's univocal and unquestionable rendering of the events. Also, memory, more than history, has to do with each citizen's individual recreation of a national identity based on his/her assimilation of the past, recollections which are by nature shifty, partial, and selective.

It was the flexible and slippery nature of memory that was explored during the Franco years to counterbalance the indisputable truth. Even so, historical truth and memory overlapped; the attempt to re-write Francoist history was pervasive among the period's prominent intellectuals (Juan Benet [1927–1993], Juan and Luis Goytisolo [1937–], Ana María Matute, Montserrat Roig [1946–1991], Carmen Laforet [1921–], Juan Marsé [1933–]) precisely because of history's intimate relation to memory. Indeed, history was transcribed to narrative precisely through the ambiguities and imprecisions of memory as is manifested in Montserrat Roig's *Els catalans als camps nazis* ("Catalans in the Nazi Camps," 1977).

There are several often-cited memoirs of the Franco period whose significance goes beyond their vivid descriptions of life under the régime. Among the most well known are *Años de penitencia* ("Years of Penitence," 1975) by Carlos Barral (1928–1989) and Dionisio Ridruejo's *Casi unas memorias* ("Virtual Memories," 1976). One of the most elucidating both for its sense of documentary reality and for its ability to capture the consciousness of the times is Manuel Vázquez Montalbán's *Crónica sentimental de España* – "sentimental," because, as Antonio Machado asserts in the epigraph, sentiment is essential to the construction of the "patria" ("fatherland") regardless of the wide and conflicting variation of the sentiments. At the same time the *Crónica*'s sentimentality is deceptive, given Vázquez's constant implications that many Spaniards were resisting unwittingly. Indeed the ideological controls of popular culture, particularly of cinematic production through the Compañía Industrial Film Español ("Industrial Film Company of Spain"), made this kind of resistance a necessity.

It is precisely this variance with the regime that shapes Vázquez Montalbán's memories, much in the vein of the filmic memoir-documentary by Basilio Martín Patino (1930–), *Canciones para después de una guerra* ("Songs For After the War," 1977). Both works deal not with high culture, but with familiar songs, ads, films, soccer teams, bullfighters, popular figures (Celia Gámez, Conchita Piquer, Lola Flores), and other images that provide readers and spectators with inroads to understanding three decades of life in Spain. What emerges most pervasively in these evocations is the need to counter the official realities, sometimes openly, other times subtly, and often unwittingly: contraband in the forties as a survival strategy against postwar deprivation; the melodramatic *bolero* of "La bien pagá" ("Paid Off") in *Canciones* accompanied by images of Spaniards in bread lines; Piquer's neurotic infatuation with the sailor in the popular song "Tatuaje" (which later became the basis for one of Vázquez's first detective novels); the difference between the style of bullfighting exhibited by Manolete in the early Franco years – serious and orthodox – and that of El Cordobés in the sixties, who, with his Beatle's haircut, was the tourist's bullfighter – daring, innovative, sexy, and aiming to please the non-*aficionados*. The latter epitomized the post-Second-World War slogan of the Ministry of Information and Tourism, "Spain is different." It is not as much El Cordobés or Conchita Piquer themselves who represent a preoccupation with counter-memory but the reading and assimilation of these cultural figures on the part of Spanish citizens.

These deceptively nostalgic "Chronicles," songs, and other evocations of the Francoist past also suggest (between the lines) that the high counter-culture of the Franco period as witnessed in the novels of Juan Benet, the modern tragedies by Buero Vallejo or Alfonso Sastre (1926–), or the poetry of Blas de Otero (1916–1979) (culture not intended for popular consumption) had its correlations in these more accessible cultural artifacts. In a chapter on "Poetas para el pueblo" ("Poets for the People"), Vázquez Montalbán implies a thematic/aesthetic relation between the popular lyrics in the music of the forties and fifties and the national themes of more serious and exclusive poetry.[6] Equally telling is that many of the popular cultural artifacts evoked in these memoirs were exploited by serious novelists, not the least of which is Juan Goytisolo whose *Reivindicación del conde don Julián* ("Count Julian," 1969) is a devastating demolition of both the high and low cultures of Franco Spain.

A similarly nostalgic yet critical evocation of the Franco years is *Usos amorosos de la posguerra española* ("Love Habits of Postwar Spain," 1987) by Carmen Martín Gaite (1925–2000). Addressing herself not only to the sexual mores of her adolescence, but also to the ideological construction of femininity, the renowned novelist offers a compelling appraisal, both academic and intimate, of women's lives during the dictatorship. Her account covers the early days of the postwar in which women, according to the ideologues of the woman's section of the Falange (Sección Femenina), such as Carmen de Icaza (1898–1979) and Pilar Primo de Rivera (1907–1991), were linked to the determination of the Spanish nation to return to its "true mission." The reconstruction of identity

---

[6] Manuel Vázquez Montalbán, *Crónica sentimental de España* (Barcelona: Planeta, 1998), pp. 62–72.

depended on the purity of women and on their willingness to follow Francoist projections of the examples of the sacred feminine figures of Spanish history and literature: Isabel I (La Católica) and Saint Teresa of Avila.

Yet Martín Gaite does not stop at the forties; even as the autarchy self-destructed with the emergence of US economic domination, the Cold War, and consumer culture, the nationalist constructions of womanhood persisted. In keeping with the historical and cultural themes of subtle resistance to the régime's controls, Martín Gaite treads beyond an objective description of the Francoist politics of gender. At times as if she were transcribing her own experience into a work of fiction, she offers portraits of women in constant battle with their own images: the mistreated bride who waited patiently for the day of her wedding only to shout a resounding "NO" when asked if she would accept her fiancé as her husband (reminiscent of a short story by Emilia Pardo Bazán, "El encaje roto" ["Torn Lace"]), or the university women of the early sixties who imbibed every word of Simone de Beauvoir's *Second Sex*. The Spanish translation of the work of Sartre's "compañera" (comrade/lover) had arrived late along with the Beatles, she affirms, but that did not deprive it of influence, however contaminating, on Spanish women, the kind who "iba a bailar a los boîtes, llegaba tarde a cenar, fumaba, hacía gala de un lenguaje crudo y desollado, había dejado de usar faja, no estaba dispuesta a tener más de dos hijos y consideraba no sólo una antigualla sino una falta de cordura llegar virgen al matrimonio" ("went to dances, arrived late to dinner, smoked, flaunted crude and brazen language, no longer wore sashes, were not fond of the idea of having more than two children, and who considered virginity before marriage not only outdated but a mark of stupidity").[7]

While a good part of Spanish literary culture of the Franco period was integrally linked to the need to recover the loss of liberty after the Civil War, it is significant that toward the end of the régime there was a growing tendency to do away with the obstacles to free expression by forgetting about them and by reaching beyond the thematic limits of Spain. In the seventies, as the official Francoist ideology became less entrenched due both to open political resistance (students, intellectuals, journalists, ETA) and to the contradictions of the régime itself (that is, the need for more political control when authoritarianism had become anachronistic), writers and artists sought links with the world outside Spain. Tourism had become something that Spaniards themselves could partake in – literally and metaphorically.

[7] Carmen Martín Gaite, *Usos amorosos de la posguerra española* (Barcelona: Anagrama, 1987), p. 217.

From 1969 to the death of Franco in 1975 and beyond, writers in various genres (the novel: Torrente Ballester [1910–1999], Miguel Delibes [1920–], Juan and Luis Goytisolo, Lourdes Ortiz [1943–], Juan Marsé (1933–); theatre: Fernando Arrabal [1932–], Francisco Nieva [1927–]; and poetry: Pere Gimferrer [1945–], Gloria Fuertes [1918–], Guillermo Carnero [1947–]) seem more aware than before of innovations in language and structure that were not relegated to a specifically Spanish cultural *milieu*. Their gaze is less focused on their national identities and more on the links between their own writerly projects and those of Europe and Latin America. These are the years of French Structuralism and Poststructuralism as well as the Latin American "Boom," the former arriving in Spain late and the latter directly linked to Spanish publishing houses. It is not that Spanish writers consciously set out to incorporate the currents of Structuralism (the French new novel, for example) or the fantastic epics of Gabriel García Márquez into their own writing. Rather, most internalized the compelling contributions of these movements regardless of their individual appreciations or assimilations of them.

However, Goytisolo's (censorship) bull did not die with a triumphant first thrust. Virtually all the writers of the seventies listed above were still struggling for political/cultural freedom specific to their own circumstances, regardless of their (new) international inclinations. It was the seminal novel by Luis Martín Santos (1924–1964), *Tiempo de silencio* ("Time of Silence," 1961) that helped push the writers of the seventies toward these new aesthetic horizons even though the themes of that novel could not be more Spanish. Likewise, the grand innovator himself, Juan Goytisolo, began the new direction in his writing with *Reivindicación del conde don Julián* whose stated purpose was to demolish the myths of sacred Spain by recreating symbolically the events of the eighth-century Arab conquest.

An indication of the end of the literary culture of the Franco years and the beginning of a new hegemonic democracy was the publication of *La verdad sobre el caso Savolta* ("The Truth About the Savolta Case," 1975) by Eduardo Mendoza (1943–). The novel indicates not only a sharp turn in the form of narrative to which writers and critics of the seventies had been accustomed, but its concerns signal a new intellectual sensibility as well. While the work's preoccupation with Spanish history is a dominant narrative feature, the ways in which history manifests itself have little to do with the obsessions about Sacred Spain which informed much of the writing of the Franco years. The novel is set in the Barcelona of the first two decades of the twentieth century, a city of revolutionary upheaval – strikes, police repression, anarcho-syndicalism, in the context of a constitutional democracy toppled by the "dictablanda" ("bland dictatorship") of Miguel Primo de Rivera. Politics, however, serve as a backdrop for a complicated plot: there have been a series of crimes whose resolution will come to the fore after the reader tunnels through a labyrinth of love relations, political intrigues, interpolated narratives, deceptions, and abuses of power. Yet this resolution, this "truth about the Savolta case," never emerges with clarity, and in the end it is truth itself which remains the object of interrogation – not a political truth, not an exploration of the vicissitudes of Spanish or Catalan identity in the wake of a dictatorship (of the hard kind), but an exploration of the processes of arriving at answers to concrete questions such as "Who killed Savolta?"

Mendoza's novel has an element of the detective story, a narrative subgenre that has become one of the most important features of literary culture of the post-Franco period. Behind Mendoza's entire narrative project is an implicit declaration that the Spanish Civil War along with the culture of Franco – "El Caudillo" ("The Leader") – is no longer an obsession. To put it bluntly, "it's history," and writers and social critics can now move on. A similar rejection of the Francoist past can be detected in many of the writers who have become prominent in the democracy – Vázquez Montalbán, José María Merino (1941–), Antonio Muñoz Molina (1956–), Javier Marías (1951–), Soledad Puértolas (1947–), Rosa Montero (1951–), and Carme Riera (1948–), among others.

Two vastly different cultural transition figures who incarnate this new sensibility are Vázquez Montalbán – himself ironically a victim of Franco's repression – and Pedro Almodóvar (1949–), whose film career began with the transition of 1975–1978. The former wrote a massive *Autobiografía del general Franco* ("Autobiography of General Franco," 1992), whose expressed purpose was to tear down the myth by not treating it as such, as had virtually all the writers of the dictatorship. Similarly, the internationally acclaimed film-maker has manifested a lack of interest in the Franco régime by opting for the depiction of Spanish postmodernity. Vázquez Montalbán and Almodóvar (like many of their contemporaries) have suggested that social realities have proved greater iconoclasts than any cultural figure – in short, that Francisco Franco is indisputably, absolutely, and definitively dead, as US television comics used to affirm repeatedly.

With the end of the twentieth century, Franco (along with the authoritarian culture surrounding him) has become something of an enigmatic figure – strange, remotely connected to Spanish identity, if at all. He has been relegated to history. The European Union, globalization of culture through the market and the internet – phenomena not unrelated to the rejection of the hermetic forms of writing of the seventies – have made for new realities, perhaps the most telling of which is immigration, and it is these realities that will boldly make their ways into the culture of the new millennium.

47

Twentieth-century literature in exile

JOSÉ MARÍA NAHARRO CALDERÓN

Is there such a thing as a literature in exile? Writers such as Camilo José Cela (1916–2002) or Francisco Umbral (1935–), both of whom remained in Spain during the Franco years, have contested the value of the 1939 Spanish *émigrés'* legacy. Francisco Ayala (1906–), one of the most representative intellectuals to emigrate to the Americas (Argentina, Puerto Rico, United States), upon his return to Spain voiced his doubts about exile literature and separated his intraexile or supraexile contributions in an allegorical mode – *La cabeza del cordero* ("The Lamb's Head," 1949), *Los usurpadores* ("The Usurpers," 1949), and *Historia de Macacos* ("Macacos' Tales," 1955) – from any exilic connections. In post-Franco Spain, to disregard exile followed the stream of consensual oblivion regarding the memory of the Spanish Civil War and its aftermath. Ayala, a sociologist by training, understood that in order to be considered within the hegemonic cultural canon in democratic Spain, exile labels had to be rejected.

Still, his position did not reflect the view of most of the individuals who joined the extensive diaspora following the War in 1939. Most intellectuals did not have the chance to return and live through the post-Franco era, nor to view how their history slowly became politically "correct" in the late nineties, particularly when the cultural apparatus of the state signaled that exile was no longer a source of controversy, due to the cushion furnished by chronological distance and the vanishing of the protagonists. More recently, novelist Antonio Muñoz Molina (1956–) and critic Miguel García Posada (1944–) suggested that neither a formal nor a generational justification identified exile as a segregated area of production or study. I could not agree more: it is important to look at literature in exile within a wider spectrum framed also by discourses within territorial Spain – the cultural spaces of what we call interexiles (where texts from inside and outside Spain confront, reflect, and refract each other).[1] One should never erase the ideological contexts surrounding exile, however.

---

[1] For more extensive discussion of the issues raised by exile, see José María Naharro Calderón, *Entre el exilio y el interior: el "entresiglo" y Juan Ramón Jiménez* (Barcelona: Anthropos, 1994); "Por los campos de Francia: entre el frío de las alambradas y el calor de la memoria." In *Literatura y cultura del exilio español de 1939 en Francia*. Ed. Alicia Alted and Manuel Aznar (Salamanca: Varona, 1998), pp. 307–325; and "Por sendas de

On the contrary, it appears that this sort of denial has eventually come back to haunt Spain in its present contradictions: terrorism, immigration, racism, and xenophobia.

The wide and heterogeneous ocean of exile seems to be sailed by a major theme: the longing for return, not only as the historical and physical desire of *émigrés* to regain the lost homeland but as the grounding for their most distinctive metaphor. To return decades later implies the inability to fill in the cultural, political, and psychological gaps found upon rediscovering the once familiar "homespaces." Therefore exile is a double symbol of the void, a hollow representation of Janus, a decentered and ghostly experience for the subject that never reconciles the lost ego with the lost id, an ever changing "trompe l'oeil," fallacious spaces within an inter-textual maze.[2] *La gallina ciega* ("Blind Man's Bluff," 1972) by Max Aub (1903–1972) *Tiempo de llorar* ("Time to Cry," 1979) by María Luisa Elío (1928–) and her *En el balcón vacío* ("On the Empty Balcony," 1962) – the latter filmed by her spouse Jomí García Ascot (1927–1986) as the only film made in exile by exiles – and *El retorno* ("The Return") by Segundo Serrano Poncela (1912–1976), included in his short-story collection *La venda* ("The Blindfold," 1956) are all complex narrative and lyrical examples of the inescapable black hole awaiting the exile's return.

Exile is a perfect analogy for writing and its paradoxical incapacity for full and pristine representation and meaning: the unavoidable distance between sign and referent. Hence, exile texts are removed at least twice from their "original" referent, framing erratic (hi)stories in an attempt to ground "renewed" writing spaces, where diverse and heterogeneous discourse rules of formation emerge. "Retroexile" texts focus primarily on the causes of the diaspora; "infraexile" examples seem buried by the hardships of displacement. These two categories are focused upon and/or remain paralyzed within the trauma of the Spanish Civil War and expulsion from the country. On the other hand, "supraexile" samples appear framed by a transcendental quest (Symbolism, allegory, time spacing) while "intraexile" literature tries to put the expulsion into perspective in a balanced, formal, and meaningful quest and attempts to overcome – but not forget – the tragedy of exile.[3] None of these are representative of

---

la memoria: los exilios de las Españas de 1939." In *La nueva literatura hispánica.* Coord. José María Naharro Calderón (Valladolid: Universitas Castellae, 1999), pp. 87–103.

[2] Francisco Caudet, *Hipótesis sobre el exilio republicano de 1939* (Madrid: Fundación Universitaria Española, 1997); Michael Ugarte, *Shifting Ground: Spanish Civil War Exile Literature* (Durham: Duke University Press, 1989); José María Naharro Calderón, "El sí-no de volver: la gallina ciega del exilio." In *La Chispa: Selected Proceedings.* Ed. Gilbert Paolini (New Orleans: Tulane University Press, 1993), pp. 174–186.

[3] Claudio Guillén, "The Writer in Exile or the Literature of Exile and Counter-Exile." *Books Abroad* 50 (1976), pp. 271–280.

one genre, theme, or author, since their habitats are mixed and muddled within a diverse and tormented ocean of production and reception.

The extraordinary circumstances that allowed a large contingent of writers to emigrate from French concentration camps to the Americas after the Spanish Civil War, primarily to Mexico, where President Lázaro Cárdenas generously opened the doors to them, was conducive to a fruitful production, comically depicted in *La librería de Arana* ("Arana's Bookstore," 1953) by Simón Otaola (1907–1980). Journals flourished throughout the Spanish diaspora and exiles published in them samples of their writings.[4] Prestigious publishing houses such as Losada (Argentina), the primary editor for Nobel Prize-winner Juan Ramón Jiménez (1881–1957), and Fondo de Cultura Económica (Mexico) published many exiles. Joaquín Díez Canedo (1917–1999), creator of the collection Tezontle at the Fondo de Cultura Económica, sent to the presses titles by Manuel Altolaguirre (1905–1959), Max Aub, Luis Cernuda (1902–1963), Pedro Garfias (1901–1967), Francisco Giner de los Ríos (1917–1995), and Emilio Prados (1899–1962).

Other houses, sponsored by exiles, not only published their works but were venues where promising Latin Americans presented their own creations. In Mexico, Séneca published key titles in 1940 such as Federico García Lorca's *Poeta en Nueva York* ("Poet in New York"), or César Vallejo's *España, aparta de mí este cáliz* ("Spain, Let this Cup Pass from Me"). It was directed by José Bergamín, who had reinvented exile as a new pilgrimage and was assisted by former dramatist and *La Vanguardia* editor Paulino Masip (1899–1963) and philosopher Juan David García Bacca (1901–1996), whose phenomenology gravitates around literary readings (Calderón, Machado). Bertomeu Costa-Amic (1911–2002) founded Quetzal (1941–1945) – where Surrealist painter and novelist Eugenio Granell (1912–2001) published *La novela del indio Tupinamba* ("Indian Tupinamba's Novel"), an intraexile reading of the Civil War – and later Ediciones De Andrea with Frank De Andrea, as well as Libro Mex Editores and Editores Mexicanos Reunidos with Fidel Miró. Meanwhile, Grijalbo was established in 1939 by Joan Grijalbo (1911–2002) who published several titles by Marxist philosopher Adolfo Sánchez Vázquez (1915–). Max Aub's attempt to do a transatlantic reading in *Poesía española contemporánea* ("Spanish Contemporary Poetry," 1969) was published by ERA in 1960 (the name was taken from the names of its

---

[4] Among the most important are: *Boletín de la Unión de Intelectuales Españoles, Iberia, Independencia, Don Quijote, La Novela Española* (France); *España Peregrina, Romance, Litoral, Ultra Mar, Las Españas* (Mexico); *Pensamiento Español, De mar a mar, Cabalgata, Realidad* (Argentina); *España libre* (Chile); *La Verónica, Nuestra España* (Cuba); *Temas* (Uruguay); *España libre, Ibérica* (USA); *La poesía sorprendida* (Dominican Republic).

founders: Neus Espresate, Vicente Rojo, and José Azorín). Carlos Barral and Víctor Seix were able to publish in Mexico several titles censored in Spain such as Jaime Gil de Biedma's *Moralidades* ("Moralities," 1966) and Juan Goytisolo's *Señas de identidad* ("Marks of Identity," 1966). Some of Mortiz's books were distributed in Spain, bridging the cultural separation between the two worlds. A similar project had been envisioned as early as 1946 by Julián Calvo (1912–1991) in Mexico and Juan Guerrero Ruiz (1893–1955) in Madrid, while *El Puente*, a journal and a collection sponsored by Editora y Distribuidora Hispano-Americana SA (EDHASA) in the mid sixties was quickly a failure due to censorship. In Ecuador, Alejandro Finisterre (1919–) and his collection Ecuador 0°, 0', 0" published several titles by León Felipe (1884–1968), while, in Chile, Arturo Soria (1907–1980) created Cruz del Sur where a key anthology, *Poetas en el destierro* ("Poets in Exile," 1943) was published with a foreword by dramatist and art critic José Ricardo Morales (1915–).

Nevertheless, the most important and long-lasting intellectual venture of exile took place with the founding of the Casa de España, thanks to Mexican essayists Alfonso Reyes and Daniel Cossío Villegas. This institution, which eventually became El Colegio de México and published the journal *Cuadernos Americanos*, hosted poets Enrique Díez Canedo (1879–1944), Josep Carner (1884–1970), Juan José Domenchina (1898–1959), León Felipe, José Moreno Villa (1887–1955), and Juan Larrea (1895–1980), philologists such as Ramón Menéndez Pidal (1868–1968), and Ortega y Gasset's disciples José Gaos (1900–1969) – who coined the euphemism "transtierro" to signify that Spanish exiles "ideally" had been physically displaced but were spiritually rooted in Spanish-speaking America – and María Zambrano (1907–1991) whose *Pensamiento y poesía en la vida española* ("Thought and Poetry in Spanish Life") and *Filosofía y poesía* ("Philosophy and Poetry"), both published in 1939, represent two of the most lucid contributions to theoretical poetical discourse with an existential basis.

Universities from Buenos Aires to Harvard also opened their doors to Spanish intellectuals who sustained intense debates on Spanish intrahistory as witnessed by Américo Castro (1885–1972) and Claudio Sánchez Albornoz (1893–1984). Others combined writing and teaching, contributing to the decisive expansion of hispanism: novelists Carlos Blanco Aguinaga (1926–), Juan Chabás (1900–1954), Roberto Ruiz (1925–), and Antonio Sánchez Barbudo (1910–1995); poets Germán Bleiberg (1915–1990), Luis Cernuda, Manuel Durán (1925–), Jorge Guillén (1893–1984), Juan Ramón Jiménez, Juan Larrea, Pedro Salinas (1891–1951), and Arturo Serrano Plaja (1909–1979); critics and philologists Joan Coromines (1905–1997), Francisco García Lorca (1904–1976), Claudio Guillén (1924–), Vicente Lloréns (1906–1979), Juan Marichal

(1922–), Luis Monguió (1908–), José F. Montesinos (1897–1972), Homero Serís (1879–1969), Carmen de Zulueta (1916–), and José Ferrater Mora (1912–1991), who published a monumental *Diccionario de filosofía* ("Dictionary of Philosophy," 1977).

For some, however, the road to intellectual freedom was paved by survival memories that recall the concentration camp experiences in southern France after the Catalan Front collapse of 1939 and/or later in Nazi Germany as the Spanish Republicans were captured in the Second World War battlefields or the resistance. Max Aub's *Campo francés* ("French Camp," 1965), a film script, maps his ordeal from Paris at the Roland Garros camp to Le Vernet d'Ariège barbed wires, a symbol for European leftist resistance. In fact, a large part of his writings visit and revisit this pandemonium – for example *Enero sin nombre* ("January Without Name," 1994) – since Aub, a Jewish expatriate, missed deportation to Nazi Germany after living through an accusation saga of communist ideology and chains that drove him to the Djelfa camp in Algeria. *Diario de Djelfa* ("Diary of Djelfa," 1944), a book of verses written away from the eyes of his captors, kept his sanity in focus. On the other hand, Xavier Benguerel's *Los vencidos* ("The Vanquished," 1972) and Roberto Ruiz's *El último oasis* ("The Last Oasis," 1964) show either that some French nationals were solidary with the Spanish Republicans or that children considered their camp as a sort of parenthesis before facing the decenterment of exile. *Otros hombres* ("Other Men," 1956) by Manuel Lamana (1922–1996) is a critical account of the militant's disillusionment after his own escape to France from the Francoist Valley of the Fallen camp along with Nicolás Sánchez Albornoz (1926–).

Nevertheless, Max Aub did not remain entangled in his pathetic memories. Intraexile is also rooted in his works, as they foreshadow the post-Franco oblivion campaign against exile while displaying Post-modern but *engagé* twists. His play *El rapto de Europa* ("The Rape of Europe," 1945), an intertext for Michael Curtis' *Casablanca*, recalls the extraordinary escape routes set up for European intellectuals by a group of courageous resistors led by the quiet American hero, Varian Fry, and Aub's personal friend Margaret Palmer. *Manuscrito cuervo: historia de Jacobo* ("Raven Manuscript: History of Jacob," 1955), a dizzying and ironic tale full of intertextual references to the work of Alfred Jarry, is his more acidic and lasting look at the human condition trapped among the misery of concentration camps, hypocrisy, and petty interests. His play *San Juan* ("Saint John," 1943) recalls the fate of Jewish refugees on a ship that no government allows to dock while predicting and projecting present emigration horror tales across the Straits of Gibraltar or the Indochina Seas.

Jorge Semprún's (1923–) recollections of his deportation and survival in the Nazi concentration camp of Buchenwald lay hidden for decades in his communist political militancy, revealed in his only Spanish "novel" *Autobiografía de Federico Sánchez* ("The Autobiography of Federico Sánchez," 1977). Semprún, later Minister of Culture under the socialist government (PSOE), chose French to deal with his memories, one of the few examples, along with Elena Castedo (1935–) or Agustín Gómez Arcos (1933–), of linguistic syncretism among the Spanish exiles. Others profited from the "transtierro" to "rediscover" the Americas, unaware of the often mythical and mystifying discourses on Hispanicity.[5]

Retroexile texts search for clues in pre-Civil-War years in order to explain intraexile. José Garcés, the protagonist of *Crónica del alba* ("Chronicle of Dawn", 1942–1946) by Ramón J. Sender (1901–1982) – the name combines Sender's own middle and second surname – recalls his life from adolescence in Spain before the Civil War until his agony in the French camp of Argelès-sur-Mer. Max Aub's pentalogy – *Campo cerrado* ("Closed Camp," 1943), *Campo abierto* ("Open Camp," 1951), *Campo de sangre* ("Blood Camp," 1945), *Campo del moro* ("Moorish Camp," 1963), and *Campo de los almendros* ("Camp of the Almond Trees," 1968) – is the most ambitious attempt to map the Spanish universe from the prologue of the Second Republic to the Alicante surrender in 1939. *La forja de un rebelde* ("The Forging of a Rebel," 1951), by Arturo Barea (1897–1957), an autobiographical novel rewritten in Spanish after the English version, recalls the author's youth and adolescence before and during the Civil War.

Ramón J. Sender's *Réquiem por un campesino español* ("Requiem for a Spanish Peasant," 1960) returns to rural Spain before the Civil War where Paco the miller will be betrayed by the local priest Mosén Millán – whose name was the original title for the novella (1953) – allied to the landowners and the military. *Réquiem* is a narrative tour de force that is revealed in the priest's recollection of Paco's life, where reading and narration time unfold simultaneously crossed by polyphonic voices and symbols that mock the assassins' monologism and hypocrisy. Sender's novella is a clear intertext against Camilo José Cela's authoritarian discourse in *La familia de Pascual Duarte* ("The Family of Pascual Duarte," 1942). *Réquiem* rejects Pascual Duarte's genetic fate as a justification for the Civil War while pointing the finger at the religious, economic, and ideological intolerance rooted in Spanish conservative society. This ethical and chronological point of view is shared by the trilogy *Vísperas* by *Las Españas* editor Manuel Andújar (1913–1994) set

---

[5] Marielena Zelaya Kolker, *Testimonios americanos de los escritores españoles transterrados de 1939* (Madrid: Ediciones Cultura Hispánica, 1985); Sebastiaan Faber, *Exile and Cultural Hegemony: Spanish Intellectuals in Mexico, 1939–1975* (Nashville: Vanderbilt University Press, 2002).

in the rural region of La Mancha and its vicinity. It looks at the plain, *Llanura* ("The Plain," 1947); the mine, *El vencido* ("The Vanquished," 1949); and the sea, *El destino de Lázaro* ("Lazarus' Destiny," 1959).

Paulino Masip's *Cartas a un español emigrado* ("Letters to a Spanish Émigré," 1939), however, written on his way to the Americas, and *El diario de Hamlet García* ("The Diary of Hamlet García," 1944) are heteroglossic and autocritical meditations on the endurance needed, failures, and exile responsibilities in dealing with the Civil War and its memories. Hamlet García, a metaphysics teacher and probable alter ego for José Ortega y Gasset, transforms his quixotic escapism into a late social involvement that ends up in failure and insanity. This point of view is prevalent also in women's writings, often divergent from androcentric (male-dominated) and heroic positions. *Memoria de la melancolía* ("Memory of Melancholy," 1970) by María Teresa León (1903–1988), *La Plaça del Diamant* ("Diamond Square," 1962) by Catalan writer Mercè Rodoreda (1909–1983), or the memoirs of Rosa Chacel (1898–1994) are examples, while Esteban Salazar Chapela (1900–1965) uses humor and satire in *Perico en Londres* ("Perico in London," 1947) and *Desnudo en Picadilly* ("Naked in Picadilly", 1959), or laughs at the nuclear menace in *Después de la bomba* ("After the Bomb," 1966).

Nostalgia and even depression may also overcome exile as well as threaten writing and existence as in Serrano Poncela's *Habitación para hombre solo* ("Room for a Lone Man," 1963). Juan Ramón Jiménez's long poem *Espacio* ("Space," 1954) and *Guerra en España* ("War in Spain," 1985) show his deep inner formal and ideological commitment along with his psychological setbacks, recounted also in the *Diarios 1937–1956* (published 1991–1995) of his wife Zenobia Camprubí (1887–1956). Jiménez contended that poetry could not deal with the epic of war and therefore his "Obra" searches for but never reaches the higher ground of supraexile. Emilio Prados' rupture with the logos and Jorge Guillén's enchantment in *Cántico* (1950) place these poets at odds with Luis Cernuda's elegiac *La realidad y el deseo* ("Reality and Desire," 1962), where ekphrasis attempts to frame the lost homeland of infraexile – "¿España? Un nombre. / España ha muerto" ("Spain? A name. / Spain is dead") – through objective correlatives and dramatic monologues into a vision that also fails to escape the dawning of history and his Spanish contemporaries' disdain.

Consequently elegy, as the memory and mourning of lost origins or unavoidable turmoil, appears to be the dominant tone for most exile poets. Pedro Garfias' *Primavera en Eaton Hastings* ("Spring at Eaton Hastings," 1941), Pedro Salinas' *Cero* ("Zero," 1944), and the works of Rafael Alberti (1902–2000), Ernestina de Champourcín (1905–1999), Juan José Domenchina, Juan Gil-Albert (1906–1984), León Felipe, or Juan Rejano (1903–1976,) all reiterate that poetry attempted to appease tragedy and civil strife, echoed by the Spanish inner exiles Vicente Aleixandre or Dámaso Alonso. Even the poets who left Spain as children, and therefore were relatively sheltered from the trauma of uprooting – Manuel Durán, Nuria Parès (1925), Jomí García Ascot, Tomás Segovia (1927), Luis Rius (1930–1984), César Rodríguez Chicharro (1930–1984), José Pascual Buxó, Enrique de Rivas (1931–), Gerardo Déniz (1934–), or Federico Patán (1937–) – are touched by this longing for origins engrained in the melancholy of Antonio Machado or Miguel de Unamuno.

Therefore, it is not surprising that the Francoist cultural apparatus attempted to recuperate those writers whose supraexile discourse would not disturb the ideological dominance of the victors. As much as they failed with Juan Ramón Jiménez, they succeeded with the return of playwright Alejandro Casona (1903–1965) from Argentina in 1962 and the staging of *La dama del alba* ("The Lady of the Dawn", 1944), *Los árboles mueren de pie* ("Trees Die Standing Still", 1949), *La barca sin pescador* ("The Boat without a Fisherman", 1950), and *Prohibido suicidarse en primavera* ("It is Forbidden to Commit Suicide in Spring," 1951). Despite the exilic Symbolism of death as a pilgrim in *La dama del alba*, an image close to Bergamín's analogy, or the drama of rejection upon return in *Los árboles*, close to Benito Pérez Galdós' *El abuelo* ("The Grandfather," 1904), Casona's supraexilic escapist climate fitted perfectly the official version of tolerance in the late Franco régime.

This climate was radically at odds with the theatre of Fernando Arrabal (1932–) who had left Spain a few years previously. Except in *Guernica*, a play that deals directly with the Civil War (*Ciugrena* [1965] was the censored Spanish version), the Melilla-born author built a supraexile corpus full of Spanish cultural symbols, either upon the absurd – *Los soldados* ("Picnic on the Battlefield", 1952) and *El cementerio de automóviles* ("The Car Cemetery", 1958) – or through what he called the "panic" ceremony – *El arquitecto y el emperador de Asiria* ("The Architect and the Emperor of Assyria," 1967) and *Y pondrán esposas a las flores* ("And They Put Handcuffs on the Flowers," 1969). Here, exile is not solely a historical category but a ceremonial and epistemological perception of unattainable reality. Arrabal's theatre had shifted the meaning of exile into the exile of meaning, as a decisive identity mark for the still unfamiliar Spanish interexile culture of the mid twentieth century.

48

Prose in Franco Spain

JANET PEREZ

Flourishing literary, intellectual, and artistic activity during the vanguard and Republic years reflected felicitous confluences of several talented generations, but allegations that the war ended thriving novelistic production are unsubstantiated by canonical novels from those years. Vanguard experimentation produced primarily novellas – stylized, "dehumanized," and relatively unsuccessful with critics and public alike. Literary production generally suffered from the death, exile, and imprisonment of towering figures of earlier generations, and the Civil War left Spain's emerging industry in ruins, destroyed half the nation's housing, and halted agriculture for three years, causing widespread shortages of food, shelter, and other necessities. Understanding postwar Spanish literature requires acquaintance with grim socio-political realities, physical devastation, ideological tyranny, cultural, political, and sexual repression. Readers outside Spain depended mostly on exiles – not too objective or well-informed about the internal literary situation – for early literary and cultural news, resulting in skewed perspectives. The Falange, Spain's only legal political party (closer to Mussolini's than to Hitler's fascism), abolished political associations, activities, and discussion. Immediately following cessation of hostilities, the dictatorship sealed the borders, sending death squads throughout the country to execute or imprison those associated with the Republic, including postal employees and schoolteachers whose jobs dated from the monarchy. Government documents issued to the "politically correct" were required for everything from ration cards to employment, increasing difficulties for the losing side.

Francoist censorship – officially non-existent – scrutinized everything printed in Spain, from playing cards and matchbooks to newspapers. A censorial triumvirate enforced political, religious, and "moral" orthodoxy, prohibiting criticism of the government, its functionaries, the police, military, or Falangist party. Religious censors required positive, orthodox presentation of Catholic dogma and ecclesiastics; moral censorship policed profanity, obscenity, and eroticism, demanding "buenas costumbres" ("proper behavior") in public and print. Offending writers risked arrest, search of their homes, confiscation of manuscripts, and imprisonment. Sympathetic portrayal of the Republic and its adherents was impossible, as was presenting the marginalized losers' perspective. The régime closed all bookstores and purged their inventories, destroying works tainted with liberalism, banning writings by the Generation of 1898 (who "criticized Spain"), and the Generation of 1927 (condemned for association with leftist artists and intellectuals). Nineteenth-century Realists and Naturalists and most foreign writers were outlawed. Medieval and Golden Age canonical works survived, as did orthodox religious texts, Falangist political writings, and works by German, Italian, and Portuguese fascists. An entire generation, growing up under Franco, lost contact with modern literary history, beginning to write in imposed literary innocence, basically reinventing Realism.

Francoist ideology dominated initial novelistic production comprising euphoric, self-idealizing Falangist epics of wartime heroics that – together with vitriolic, partisan essays – constituted "triunfalismo" ("Triumphalism"), exalting "our glorious National Crusade," glorifying Franco, militarism, and fascist values. Paradigmatic of "Triumphalist" authors, Rafael García Serrano (1914–) produced abstract exaltations of life in the trenches. Too skewed to constitute serious historical documents, Triumphalist works appeared sporadically until the 1960s. Rampant anticommunism labeled all who opposed Franco – regardless of ideology – as *rojos* ("Reds"). Triumphalist texts, imbued with fascist myths and aesthetics, extolled patriotism, honor, duty, youth, virility, courage, discipline, force, *machismo*, violence, and brutality, expressing horror of liberals, homosexuals, Masons, Jews, freedom of the press, and feminist emancipation. Given Spain's immediate past, régime anathema included local autonomy, regional cultures (with vernacular languages – Catalan, Galician, Basque, and others – outlawed). Writings favoring divorce, birth control, "career women," or portraying adultery, premarital eroticism, and prostitution were unthinkable (although prostitution flourished privately). Fanatic religiosity and Victorian morality dominated public life, divorce (briefly legalized under the Republic) was abolished, and married women's rights were nearly eliminated Only those poor enough to fill servants' jobs could legally work outside the home under legislation designed to "protect the family" and repopulate the fatherland. Official prizes were awarded for huge families, while women's education emphasized obedience, submissiveness, chastity, frugality, self-abnegation, and matrimony. Women's access to higher education was limited; legally they became perpetual minors, wards of their husbands or male relatives. Spain's period of Empire was idealized, sixteenth- and seventeenth-century models revived and extolled, while government-controlled media purveyed hourly reminders of Franco's having "saved Spain from Communism" (although the Republican government included no communists at the outbreak of the War). While all associated with the Republic were marginalized as *rojos*, additional oppressive measures applied to women. All young women did obligatory "social service," including indoctrination by the Falange's *Sección Femenina* (women's auxiliary); young men faced obligatory military service.

The régime established literary prizes to promote traditional values; promulgation of sixteenth- and seventeenth-century models spurred imitations of picaresque narratives, Garcilaso's pastoral poetry, and modernized *autos sacramentales* (sacramental plays). Some authors subverted these traditional models, including Camilo José Cela (1916–2002). *La familia de Pascual Duarte* ("The Family of Pascual Duarte," 1942) was banned when reader response alerted censors; clandestine editions spurred official, expurgated versions. *Pascual Duarte* and *La colmena* ("The Hive," 1951) – the only works by Cela cited in the Nobel Prize proclamation – contain numerous picaresque elements. Pascual's autobiographical "confession" implies that his violent crimes result from his dysfunctional family – an alcoholic mother and an abusive, criminal father – poverty and ignorance. Rather than Naturalistic biological models or social determinism, Cela evokes the picaresque, parodying opening episodes of *Lazarillo de Tormes*. Attentive readers realize that Pascual is victimized by social structures that produced him; society (implicitly) shares the guilt, while executing him for what in fact is a form of euthanasia (the mercy killing of don Jesús). Pascual's impassive, detailed recounting of shocking, gory crimes (rape, murder, matricide) prompted the label *tremendismo* – echoing readers' tremendous revulsion – and spawned numerous forgettable imitations. Cela rejected the label, but critics nonetheless deemed *tremendismo* Spain's first postwar literary "movement," lumping together writers with little in common but chronological proximity. For some literary historians, *tremendismo* exudes violence, sordidness, aberrations, misery and gore, protests against wartime atrocities, wordless existential *angst*; others see negative aesthetics: Expressionistic deformation, caricature, exaggeration, and gallows humor.

Reaffirming his rejection of *tremendismo*, Cela's *Pabellón de reposo* ("Rest Home," 1943) reflects his confinement in a tuberculosis sanatorium. An experimental novel, its multiple narrative perspectives, *tempo lento*, and lack of action contrast markedly with *Pascual Duarte*: the only violence is psychological – the sadistic indifference of "caregivers" and despair of patients quickly forgotten by healthy family and friends. *Nuevas andanzas y desventuras de Lazarillo de Tormes* ("New Travels and Misadventures of Lazarillo de Tormes," 1944) resuscitates the prototypical sixteenth-century rogue, utilizing picaresque format and protagonist to critique contemporary society (anticipating subversive travel narratives – by Cela and several "social" writers – exposing poverty and injustice in backward areas, officially marginalized and forgotten). Cela rewrote *La colmena* several times between 1945 and 1950; repeatedly prohibited by Spanish censors, it appeared in Buenos Aires and Mexican editions, prompting Cela's expulsion from Madrid's Press Association. This extensive, plotless, anecdotal narrative set in contemporary Madrid during the harsh winter of 1941–1942 presents some 200 to 365 characters – critical counts vary – mostly apathetic, discouraged, hungry, unemployed, or penniless; the remainder are hypocrites, black marketeers, or callous parasites who prey upon the weak and defenseless. Largely colloquial conversations, fragments of seemingly unconnected stories with the city as protagonist, *La colmena* contrasts with *Pascual Duarte*, lacking gore and violence (an unsolved murder notwithstanding). Classed as *tremendismo* for its depressing view of a society divided into victims and executioners, *La colmena* was also hailed as Spain's first Neo-Realist novel. Most critics consider it Cela's masterpiece.

Carmen Laforet (1921–2004) achieved overnight success with her first novel *Nada* ("Nothing," 1945), reconstructing Andrea's year-long sojourn in postwar Barcelona. Arriving from the Canaries to study, the protagonist lives with her grandmother in gothic quarters filled with mentally and emotionally disturbed relatives, shocked by harsh, postwar realities. When Andrea leaves for a promised job in Madrid, abandoning the nightmarish house, she believes her experience was "nothing" (the title allusion). Stronger gothic notes sound in *La isla y los demonios* ("The Island and the Devils," 1952), deemed *tremendismo* by some, a superior "pre-quel" to *Nada* by others. Laforet's later novels received no comparable acclaim, although her brief fiction treating women and adolescents is widely admired. If *tremendismo* involves negative aesthetics and variants of Neo-Naturalism, the label cannot apply to *Nada* or Laforet.

Whether employing chronological parameters or modifications in the prevailing aesthetics, most literary histories divide postwar literature (1939–1975) into at least three periods: the 1940s (*triunfalismo/tremendismo*), the 1950s to mid-sixties ("social" literature, "critical Realism"), the mid-sixties to Franco's death ("new novel," *apertura*). Such generalizations aid grasping the dominant tone of each period but necessarily muffle other notes. Although official ideology was monolithic, this was never true of the postwar narrative. Postwar literary independence was difficult, but novelists soon began defining and occupying non-partisan ground. Ignacio Agustí (1913–1974), Sebastián Juan Arbó (1902–1984), Pedro de Lorenzo (1917–), Eulalia Galvarriato (1905–1997), José M. Gironella (1917–1983), Manuel Halcón (1903–1989), and José Antonio de Zunzunegui (1901–1982), all relatively conservative, avoided both propagandizing and opposition, scoring significant popular successes. Zunzunegui, self-professed Galdosian Realist and admirer of Baroja, produced voluminous novels of Madrid and northern Basque provinces.

¡Ay! ¡Estos hijos! ("Oh, These Kids!" 1943) traces the strict, Catholic upbringing of Luis Larriñaga, bourgeois gentleman of Bilbao who abandons the family business for life in London and Paris. Returning at the outbreak of the War following his mother's death, he embraces religious traditionalism (somewhat like *Javier Mariño*, below, without comparable intellectual density). This politically tainted *Bildungsroman* exhibits picaresque elements common in Zunzunegui works – e.g. *Esta oscura desbandada* ("This Dark Byway," 1952) and *La vida como es* ("How Life Is," 1950), studies of Madrid's seamy demi-monde.

Ignacio Agustí traced development of the Catalan bourgoisie from nineteenth-century cabin artisans through refined twentieth-century industrial society in his saga, *La ceniza fue árbol* ("The Ashes Were Once Trees"), comprising *Mariona Rebull* (1944); *El viudo Rius* ("Widower Rius," 1945); *Desiderio* (1954); *Diecinueve de julio* ("19 July," 1965 [19 July was the day following the outbreak of the Civil War]); and *Guerra civil* ("Civil War," 1972). *El viudo Rius* presents prematurely widowed Joaquín's privileged managerial and capitalistic perspective of economic crises, labor conflicts, and the 1909 anarchist uprising. Agustí's nostalgic "moral portrait" of several Barcelona generations traces individual and collective changes until war ends the Industrial Revolution. Agustí idealizes a past remembered as prosperous, tranquil, and optimistic. His saga shares common ground with the post-Franco trilogy by Montserrat Roig (1946–1991) and *Mirall trencat* ("Broken Mirror," 1978) by Mercè Rodoreda (1909–1983) – both in Catalan – examining Catalan family dynasties in pre-War decades, although the latter two concentrate on female characters, presenting more liberal perspectives.

Examining war and its origins, José María Gironella focuses on divided domestic loyalties representing pre-war divisions, and conflict between generations of a deeply religious family. The tetralogy comprises *Los cipreses creen en Dios* ("The Cypresses Believe in God," 1953), *Un millón de muertos* ("A Million Dead," 1961), *Ha estallado la paz* ("Peace Has Erupted," 1966), and *Condenados a vivir* ("Sentenced to Live," 1971). Set in the Catalan provincial capital of Gerona, *Los cipreses creen en Dios* enjoyed unprecedented success, helping readers decipher scores of pre-war political parties and corresponding ideologies (the cypress tree, associated with Spanish cemeteries, symbolizes death). The devout family portrayed moves farther right in the initial novel. The eldest son abandons the seminary, but his brother replaces him, suffering martyrdom upon the outbreak of hostilities; the daughter subsequently marries a Gerona Falangist. A second runaway best-seller, *Un millón de muertos* controversially depicted atrocities on both sides – the first postwar work to do so. Rumor had it that Franco – portrayed heroically – personally authorized the publication. Additional volumes trace postwar dissolution of ideals in subsequent generations, symbolizing Falangist corruption by decades of power.

With their most significant work behind them, some pre-war novelists continued writing in the 1940s, including Ramón Gómez de la Serna (1888–1963), Ricardo León (1877–1943), and Concha Espina (1869–1955), who (reacting to wartime captivity) produced melodramas praising her Falangist liberators; wartime publications were re-issued, and Espina wrote saints' lives, plus *Princesas del martirio* ("Martyred Princesses," 1941) – the "martyrdom" of three nurses by leftist forces. Opposition to Franco could be openly expressed only in exile, although covert opposition was never completely absent. Like Cela, Gonzalo Torrente Ballester (1910–1999) began early to undermine régime values, subverting Falangist myths and demythologizing official historiography. His *Javier Mariño* (1943), originally authorized, then prohibited, masquerades as the spiritual odyssey of a spoiled, bourgeois playboy who repents his decadent ways and returns, "purified," to wartime Spain to join Franco. Javier, an unappealingly arrogant, indolent, class-conscious, prejudiced pseudo-intellectual, symbolizes Falangist "converts." Torrente undergoes several aesthetic changes, moving through a masterful trilogy of "Social Realism" in the 1960s (*Los gozos y las sombras* ["Joys and Shadows"]: *El señor llega* ["The Master Arrives," 1960], *Donde da la vuelta el aire* ["Where the Air Turns," 1962], *La Pascua triste* ["Unhappy Easter," 1962]) to emerge as leader of the post-Neo-Realist "new novel" of the 1970s.

Initially deemed Catholic and conservative, Miguel Delibes (1920–) has proven a lifelong advocate of the poor, opposing militarism, war, intolerance, and abuse of power. Wartime conscription in Franco's navy made him a lifelong pacifist, defending the marginalized. *La sombra del ciprés es alargada* ("Long is the Cypress' Shadow," 1949) launched his writing career, but his third novel, *El camino* ("The Path," 1950) initiates his definitive, personal, colloquial style, eschewing plot, favoring juvenile or marginal perspectives, and probing rural environments. Like Cela and Torrente, Delibes evolves considerably; his most significant works come later. Without embracing politically charged Objectivism and "Critical Realism" (social literature), Delibes' scores of novels, essays, and story collections indict governmental marginalization of the poor and aged, the mentally retarded, and handicapped, and neglect of backward areas, agriculture, and the environment. In *La hoja roja* ("The Red Leaf," 1959), a desperately penurious, retired public servant and an ignorant young maid, both alone, have no recourse but each other. *Las ratas* ("The Rats," 1962), based on real characters and events, challenges governmental attempts to forcibly relocate primitive, uneducated cave-dwellers, who subsist by hunting rats. *Cinco horas con Mario* ("Five Hours with Mario," 1966) masterfully employs matrimonial conflict, emblematizing the Civil War's class conflict: the widow's self-serving monologue beside her husband's body ironically reveals the ideological abyss separating the aristocratic Carmen from the idealistic deceased professor.

Significant unaligned writers of this period include Elena Soriano (1917–1996), whose trilogy *Mujer y hombre* ("Woman and Man," 1955) was prohibited by Francoist censors. Not re-issued until 1986, the trilogy treats matrimony from a feminist perspective, as essentially antagonistic and problematic. Elena Quiroga (1921–1995), a demanding stylist and structural experimentalist, dealt preferentially with women's condition and psychology, producing numerous novels and stories of adolescents and women. Among her most significant contributions are *Algo pasa en la calle* ("Something's Happening in the Street," 1954) which courageously depicts results of the abolition of divorce, *Tristura* ("Melancholy," 1960) and *Escribo tu nombre* ("[Liberty] I Write Your Name," 1965), indictments of feminine education under Franco. Alejandro Núñez Alonso (1905–1982) cultivated several narrative styles and techniques: the so-called "introspective" novel, the existential novel, and archaeological fictions reconstructing the Roman world of Tiberius. Ricardo Fernández de la Reguera (1916–) authored several existential novels using objective techniques, before beginning a lengthy series of "Episodios nacionales contemporáneos" ("Contemporary National Episodes," 1963–), continuing Galdós' recreation of recent history from the perspective of working-class Barcelona, spanning the time from the Spanish-American War to the Republic. Another independent Realist, Dolores Medio (1911–1996) achieved considerable popular success with novels of quotidian life of ordinary people, abounding in existential anguish, frustration, and solitude, but also featuring strong, autonomous female heroes. Her *Funcionario público* ("Public Servant," 1956) stands almost alone among social novels in obtaining concrete results: a raise in pay for communications workers.

Francisco García Pavón (1919–1989), author of several important story collections, achieved fame as the creator of Plinio, a small-town police chief, exploiting the detective genre's critical potential with humor and irony to satirize officialdom. Another prolific but unaligned creator, Alvaro Cunqueiro (1911–1981) – a pre-war advocate of the Galician independence movement – wrote much of his creative work in the officially marginalized vernacular language (Galician), elaborating a personal universe based on myth, medieval traditions, fable, and legend, cultured fantasies susceptible of symbolic and allegorical interpretation but distant from *engagement*. Typical of his aesthetic experimentation is *Un hombre que se parecía a Orestes* ("A Man Resembling Orestes," 1968), transposing the classical myth to Celtic domains in the Atlantic, using humor and anachronisms to create an anti-heroic farce (with tragic consequences for the actors).

Although classed with the "Mid-century Generation," Ana María Matute (1926–) began publishing in the 1940s. *Los Abel* ("The Abels," 1948) chronicles the decadence and disappearance of rural aristocrats before and during the War. Initially considered *tremendismo*, Matute's novels represent very different aesthetics, denouncing social injustice and inequities lyrically, grotesquely. *Pequeño teatro* ("Little Theatre," 1954) utilizes Renaissance *commedia dell'arte* to subvert aristocratic hypocrisy, prejudice, and indifference to poverty. Matute's initial works enunciate enduring themes: war's underlying causes, Cain and Abel symbolism (conflict within families), love–hate relationships, solitude and loneliness, social-class injustices, exploitation of the poor. These concerns reappear in *Fiesta al noroeste* ("Celebration in the Northwest," 1953), indicting *caciquismo* (local political bossism) and its abuses (cf. Sender's *Mosén Millán*), explored in *Los hijos muertos* ("The Dead Children," 1958), which also portrays wartime Barcelona (as does Matute's prohibited *Luciérnagas* ["Fireflies," 1953]). Expanding the prominence of adolescents, Matute reworks similar themes in her trilogy *Los mercaderes* ("Merchants"): *Primera memoria* ("First Memory," 1959), *Los soldados lloran de noche* ("Soldiers Cry at Night," 1964), *La trampa* ("The Trap," 1969). Contrasting the idealism of the few with the materialism of the majority, she explores war's origins in social inequities, examining the conflict in microcosm – Mallorca – and later exposes its lack of transcendence. *La torre vigía* ("The Watch-tower," 1971), a tenth-century chivalric *Bildungsroman*, incorporates apocalyptic visions to underscore perennial injustice and inequities connecting the tenth century and the twentieth.

Other writers of the "mid-century generation" represent "Social Realism" ("Critical Realism") or Objectivism, and several (José Manuel Caballero Bonald [1926–], Antonio Ferres [1924–], Alfonso Grosso [1928–1995], Juan [1931–] and Luis Goytisolo [1935–]) reflect Marxist influences. Led by Jorge Semprún (1923–), the clandestine communist party (PCE) – Spain's only organized opposition to Franco – courted younger writers: those just mentioned, plus Jesús Fernández Santos (1926–1988), Jesús López Pacheco (1930–1997), and Rafael Sánchez Ferlosio (1927–) – "social" literature's nucleus. Other less politicized but important contributors include Ignacio Aldecoa (1925–1969), Josefina Rodríguez Aldecoa (1926–), Carmen Martín Gaite (1925–2000), Juan García Hortelano (1928–1992), and Juan [Fonseca] Marsé (1933–). Postwar literature's second period and characteristic core, "social" writing was committed and existentially *engagé*, opposing all that Franco represented. With political debate prohibited, "social" writers targeted régime weaknesses: stagnant economy, lagging postwar reconstruction, unemployment, insufficient housing, widespread shortages, and innumerable inequities (marginalization, oppression, and lack of freedom could not be openly broached). Avoiding censorship via impassive, non-judgmental, "objective" presentation of empirical conditions, social literature sketched Spanish society in black and white: rich and poor, evil and good, usually depicting miseries of the long-suffering poor, but also caricaturing the *dolce vita* of the parasitic rich, too jaded even to enjoy their decadence. Typically, social literature employed collective protagonists (miners, fishermen) or generic representatives of groups (shanty dwellers, underpaid functionaries), implicitly denouncing injustices perpetrated upon them and – like Naturalism – demonstrating the need for reform. Several "social novelists" adopted tenets of French Objectivism, employing what had been experimental "laboratory" techniques as mechanisms to circumvent censorship. Avoiding interpretation, judgments, personal commentary, authorial intromission, and psychological presentation, "Objectivists" concentrated upon "scientific" description, eschewing sermonizing, opinions, and conclusions. Cinematographic techniques (modeled especially on Italian Neo-Realist cinema) emphasized dialogue and actions – the visual and audible, only what sound cameras might record. Movement theorists José María Castellet (1926–) and Juan Goytisolo stressed literature as a weapon to change the world: art for art's sake was immoral, and the artist (author) merely another workman, not "I" but part of "we," serving the collective. This altruistic, self-abnegating aesthetic – unfortunately, pedestrian and monotonous – predominated from the early 1950s to the late 1960s among writers who had experienced the War as children or adolescents. Influential Marxist theorists, especially Georg Lukàcs, Jean-Paul Sartre, and Antonio Gramsci contributed to establishing the "generational consciousness," fomented by growing civil disobedience, student unrest, and stagnant economic conditions. With individual variations – notwithstanding collective ideology – social novelists or practitioners of "Critical Realism" included (besides those cited above) Armando López Salinas (1925–), Angel María de Lera (1912–1984), Ramón Nieto (1934–), and many less-known names. The following overview of representative social novels illustrates the movement's themes and thrust.

Ignacio Aldecoa in *El fulgor y la sangre* ("Glare and Blood," 1954) and its sequel, *Con el viento solano* ("With the Desert Wind," 1956), studies stereotypical antagonists, humanizing crime and law enforcement, as a gypsy involved in the death of a Civil Guard is tracked and captured. Aldecoa produced a masterpiece of "Objectivism" in *Gran Sol* ("Big Sole," 1957), portraying the tedium and danger of fishermen's life aboard a North Atlantic halibut vessel. Aldecoa's tender yet cruel portraits of lower-class lives in short-story collections including *Espera de tercera clase* ("Third-Class Waiting-Room," 1955) and *Vísperas del silencio* ("Prelude to Silence," 1955) are artistic masterpieces. Critics argue whether he is a "social" novelist, but agree that his corpus includes some of the postwar's finest narrative achievements.

Carmen Martín Gaite's "social" concerns differ somewhat in placing gender on a par with socio-economic conditions. *Entre visillos* ("Behind the Curtains," 1959) recreates the stifling encloisterment and limited options for females in provincial, postwar towns, underscoring education's crucial significance. Portraying largely interiors and domestic space, the novelist depicts Spanish women's confinement "behind the blinds" that impede their access to the public sphere. *Retahílas* ("Skeins," 1974) presents the tardy, difficult, solitary quest of a mature woman who abandons an unsatisfactory marriage to seek independence and self-realization in a society prohibiting divorce. The writer's novelettes – *El balneario* ("The Spa," 1954), *Las ataduras* ("Bonds," 1960) – and short stories likewise indict Francoist marginalization of women.

Jesús Fernández Santos' *Los bravos* ("The Angry Ones," 1954), a collection of short stories or novelettes, denounces inequities, injustice, poverty, and apathy using cinematographic techniques and preponderant dialogue, aspects of the story collections *En la hoguera* ("In the Bonfire," 1955) and *Cabeza rapada* ("Shaven Head," 1958), likewise focusing on misery, homelessness, and indigence. *Laberintos* ("Labyrinths," 1964) portrays Holy Week in Segovia, juxtaposing lavish religious celebrations with abject poverty. An undervalued artist, Fernández Santos deals in later (post-"social") novels with controversial subjects including conventual life and homosexuality.

Antonio Ferres, in *La piqueta* ("The Pickaxe," 1959), uses the focalizer of young love to study migrants, threatened with homelessness when the city demolishes the tenement they have occupied, as time and hopelessness create tension. López Pacheco's *Central eléctrica* ("Hydroelectric Station," 1958) presents an epic collective struggle against Nature as workers erect a dam and power station, victimized by the indifference of capital and management. *Dos días de setiembre* ("Two Days in September," 1962) by Caballero Bonald, denounces landowners' speculation with migrant labor, exploited by greedy intermediaries, in a chronicle of the Andalusian wine-harvest that contrasts the hypocritically devout, indolent, alcoholic landlord who betrays his own relatives with day laborers lacking even basic necessities. García Hortelano's *Nuevas amistades* ("New Friendships," 1959) critiques young Madrid socialites, a pseudo-liberated group lacking ideals and goals that becomes involved in an ill-fated quest for clandestine abortion. In *Tormenta de verano* ("Summer Storm," 1962), García Hortelano denounces the parasitic existence of the "leisure class." Alfonso Grosso, in *La zanja* ("The Ditch," 1961), provides a contentious, testimonial glimpse of Andalusian village life from dawn to dusk during some eighteen hours in June. Focus on construction of an irrigation canal foregrounds illnesses, showing that tuberculosis is not the same for rich and poor. *El capirote* ("Capuchin Hood," 1966) satirizes Holy Week religiosity in Seville, using Neo-Baroque style and more complex narrative techniques, moving away from "Social Realism" while continuing its political critique.

In *Juegos de manos* ("The Young Assassins," 1954), Juan Goytisolo indicts the empty existence of an adolescent gang of wealthy young delinquents, whose lives of violence, anarchy, and terrorism result from futile searches for meaning and identity. In *Duelo en el paraíso* ("Children of Chaos," 1955), Goytisolo exposes the instinctive barbarity of refugee children, separated from adults on a country estate, who execute another child considered a traitor (imitating adult "war games"). His *Campos de Níjar* ("Fields of Nijar," 1960), the first of three testimonial travel books, offers chilling visions of misery in the arid fields of backward Almería, punctuated by dialogues externalizing fatalism and despair. *La chanca* ("Wooden Sandal," 1962) examines the subhuman living conditions of fishermen near the Almerian capital, including oppression suffered by the politically suspect. Luis Goytisolo, in *Las afueras* ("The Outskirts," 1958) presents seven thematically related stories or novellas, all set in Barcelona eighteen years after the War, whose characters share the same set of names, underscoring the presence of common circumstances and problems. With clear Marxist substrata, the stories denounce the conditions of the working class and the privileged situation of the wealthy, exposing the class structure as immoral.

El Jarama ("River Jarama," 1956), Rafael Sánchez Ferlosio's Objectivist masterpiece, depicts one summer Sunday from sunrise to midnight at a lower-class "swimming hole" near Madrid, not coincidentally the site of a bloody Civil War battle. The limited time-frame and constricted space, common to many social narratives, facilitate privileging dialogue and cinematographic techniques to provide a close-up "snapshot" of *abulia*, resignation, and existential inauthenticity, externalized by banal conversations as the sun slowly crosses the sky. While critics praised the novelist's masterful capturing of colloquial registers and popular discourse, average readers found the novel boring – an inherent limitation of "social" and Objectivist focus on the quotidian, generic, external, and collective, emphatically "here and now." Despite altruistic motivations and the contributions of many talented writers, "Critical Realism" failed with upper-class readers (uncomfortable with their portrayal as parasites), while the impoverished workers it aimed to help could not afford books. Some writers disliked the dualistic, Manichaean world view equating poverty with virtue, wealth with vice and abuse. Intellectual reaction to this over-simplification prompted the Marxist existential psychiatrist, Luis Martín-Santos (1924–1964) to write *Tiempo de silencio*, ("Time of Silence," 1962), a major postwar landmark rejecting over-simplification of concept and techniques while retaining and intensifying the subversive thrust of Critical Realism. Experimental and Neo-Baroque, this extraordinary novel employs multiple subjective perspectives, interior monologues, and flamboyant wordplay in sarcastic demolition of the dictatorship's retouched image of Spain, foreshadowing the "new novel" of the late 1960s.

Juan Marsé's *Encerrados con un solo juguete* ("Locked Up With Only One Toy," 1960) and *Esta cara de la luna* ("This Side of the Moon," 1962) represent an atypical, intimist "Critical Realism"; *Últimas tardes con Teresa* ("Last Afternoons with Teresa," 1966) moves toward radical formal renovation without renouncing social concerns. More polished, *La oscura historia de la prima Montse* ("Obscure History of Cousin Montse," 1970) follows a social misfit, examining contradictions of the contemporary Barcelona class structure. Continuing the experimentation of *Tiempo de silencio, Si te dicen que caí* ("The Fallen," 1973), a critical favorite and an extremely complex, self-referential text, weaves an elaborate intertextual fabric of subversive references to the Falangist hymn (cited in the title). Prohibited by Spanish censors, it appeared in Mexico, remaining banned in Spain until 1977.

International intellectuals, Republican sympathizers, and non-régime critics frequently overlooked or marginalized "uncommitted" writers, including estimable women of several generations: Rosa Chacel (1898–1994), Elisabeth Mulder (1903–1987), Mercedes Salisachs (1916–), Concha Alós (1928–), Mercedes Ballesteros (1913–1995), Concha Castroviejo (1912–), Mercedes Fórmica (1916–), Paulina Crusat (1900–1981), Carmen Kurtz (1911– ; pseud. Carmen de Rafael Marés), to mention only the most prolific and significant. Most treat socio-economic problems or issues related to women's condition, but represent varied ideologies, employing different (non-social) aesthetics, existential perspectives, or psychological approaches – a lack of *engagement* and identification with the "Social Realist" agenda resulting in marginalization by critics opposed to Franco. Likewise often neglected both in Spain and abroad are exiles and expatriates; most works published abroad by exiles could not be legally distributed in Spain until well into the 1970s. For example *Mosén Millán* ("Requiem for a Spanish Peasant," 1953) by Ramón Sender (1901–1982) establishes implicit parallels between the life and passion of Christ and the death of a Spanish socialist peasant leader, ironically focalized via the perspective of the priest, Mosén Millán, who baptized him, officiated at his marriage, and later betrayed him to Falangist executioners. The anniversary requiem mass, attended by conservative landowners and capitalists, adversaries of the deceased, links these pillars of the Franco régime with the Church and Falange in mutual responsibility for the assassination.

Some restrictions against publishing in Catalan were lifted in the late 1950s, and Mercè Rodoreda (1909–1983) published her first important postwar story collection, *Vint-i-dos contes* ("Twenty-Two Stories," 1957), followed by *La plaça del Diamant* ("Diamond Plaza," 1963; translated in 1967 as "The Pigeon Girl" and again in 1981 as "The Time of the Doves"), deemed by Gabriel García Márquez the most beautiful novel published in Spain since the Civil War. Natalia, a simple, working-class woman, recounts her life from her encounter with Quimet (her future husband) shortly before the War through the initial postwar decades. Quimet, an oppressive authoritarian, strips her of her identity and imprisons her in domesticity, estrangement, and pregnancy. Isolated, reduced to tending his doves, she is freed by his reported death in the war but economic straits drive her to contemplate suicide and killing her children, until marriage to an impotent shopkeeper rescues her. *El carrer de les Camélies* ("Camellia Street," 1966) won numerous awards, and with *La meva Cristina i altres contes* ("My Christina and Other Stories," 1967) led to Rodoreda's recognition as the most important Catalan writer of the twentieth century.

Exile works began entering Spain in significant numbers in the late 1960s along with novels of the Latin American "Boom," offering new alternatives to "social" literature. The burgeoning tourist industry brought increasing foreign influences, and a healthier economy rendered "social" emphasis on poverty still less appealing. Objectivism yielded to extreme Subjectivism, anti-aestheticism to renewed formal and linguistic emphases, "Critical Realism" to fantasy, imagination, and mystery, utilitarian *engagement* to new experimentalism. Responding to changing realities, an increasingly pragmatic dictatorship relaxed restrictions; the 1960s "Press Law" regularizing censorship clarified the limits for writers, making Objectivist circumvention unnecessary. Neo-Baroque and Neo-Vanguardist modes found numerous adherents, and Surrealism reappeared. The exuberant Spanish "new novel," emphatically post-Neo-Realist, employed numerous modes, comprising experimental works by Cela, Torrente Ballester, Juan Goytisolo, Miguel Delibes, and newcomers including Juan Benet (1927–1993), the multi-dimensional hybridization and trans-genre writings of Francisco Umbral (1935–), plus a very different experimentalist, Miguel Espinosa (1926–1982), coinciding mainly in their rejection of "Critical Realism," its anti-aesthetic dogma and monotonous themes. Although the "new novel" extends beyond the dictatorship's end (with Franco's death, November 1975), its principal characteristics emerge much sooner.

Cela's calculated experimentation in *Mrs. Caldwell habla con su hijo* ("Mrs. Caldwell Speaks to her Son," 1953) produces a Surrealist second-person monologue comprising some 200 fragments (poems, letters, fantasies) directed by the deranged protagonist to her deceased son. In *Vísperas, festividad y octava de San Camilo del año 1936 en Madrid* ("San Camilo, 1936: The Eve, Feast, and Octave of Saint Camillus of the Year 1936 in Madrid," 1969), the introspective protagonist perambulates about Madrid, invisibly contemplating events public and private during the week of the Civil War's outbreak. An extended, Surreal, second-person monologue of self-loathing, occasionally broken by quasi-omniscient third-person narration, engulfs the contending factions, suggesting that the country's future was decided in bars and brothels – no exalted principles or heroics: all Spain shares the guilt. *Oficio de tinieblas* ("Office of Darkness," 1973) comprises 1,194 unconnected fragments called "monads," lacking any defined space, time, characters, plot, or sequential action. It stands at the far edge of the narrative galaxy, the novelistic *non plus ultra*. Structure and meaning depend upon juxtaposition, reiteration, and lyric devices. Hauntingly Surrealistic, this hermetic work concerns man's inhumanity to man – a *leitmotif* of Cela's – history as fiction, the duplicity of words, truth as illusion. Cela deemed it not a novel but a purging of his heart, expelling disillusionment and pain. Beyond antinovel, it is anti-literature, pushing the limits of logical thought.

Torrente Ballester's best-known contributions to the "new novel" are *La saga/fuga de J. B.* ("The Saga/Flight of J. B.," 1972) and *Fragmentos de apocalipsis* ("Fragments of Apocalypse," 1977). Playfully Post-modern, parodic, intellectually challenging, absurd, and incredibly funny, satirizing critical theorists, both concern narrative theory, reality versus imagination, the joy of invention. Vanguardist techniques, play with language, and self-awareness as fiction pervade these intensely theoretical novels which defy summary, exploring the nature of literary process.

In *Parábola del náufrago* ("The Hedge," 1969), Delibes abandons his accustomed Realism for a Kafkaesque dystopia evocative of Orwell's *Nineteen Eighty-four*. This futuristic fiction presents an oppressive, nightmarish, totalitarian society where emotions are controlled and thoughts punished, provoking the protagonist's mental disintegration (he metamorphoses into a sheep). Delibes uses innovative punctuation and invents an artificial language as his protagonist struggles for sanity. *El príncipe destronado* ("The Prince Dethroned," 1973) depicts the world of adults from the knees down (the toddler's viewpoint), constituting an impressive exercise in perspectivism. *Las guerras de nuestros antepasados* ("Our Forefathers' Wars," 1975) presents putative psychiatric tapes of interviews with a pacifist patient driven mad by his family's generations of warmongers (emblematic of Spain).

Juan Goytisolo switched to the experimental mode with *Señas de iden-tidad* ("Marks of Identity," 1966), whose protagonist searches his family past for his identity, via reverie, dream, and recall, combining myths with Formalist and Structuralist devices and attacking a culture perceived as petrified. In the sequel, *Reivindicación del Conde don Julián* ("Revindi-cation of Count Julian," 1970), Goytisolo's alter ego imagines himself a modern reincarnation of the eighth-century noble who betrayed Spain to the Arabs, launching hallucinatory attacks upon Spanish culture, the Catholic Church, the military and political establishment, the country's language, and literary icons. *Juan sin tierra* ("Juan the Landless," 1975), an intensely literary and intertextual spatial–temporal travelogue, dis-cusses the novel being created, parodies Spain, glorifies sodomy and defe-cation, and experiments with non-language, foreign languages, associative chains, and multiple-person discourse.

Benet's *Volverás a Región* ("You Will Return to Region," 1967) initi-ates a novelistic cycle featuring that mythical microcosm whose history exhibits significant parallels with the nation's. Combining myth and leg-end, history and fantasy, Benet creates detailed geography, flora and fauna, geology, chronicles, dynasties, genealogies, climate, and traditions for Region, a metaphor for existential entrapment, ruin, and despair. Post-modern, hermetic, ultimately undecipherable, his chronicles privilege the element of mystery – ultimate truths forever beyond the grasp of science and humanity.

Espinosa's *Escuela de mandarines* ("School for Mandarins," 1974) – fruit of numerous revisions – a transcendent, innovative, intellectual allegory, aspires to offer moral guidance while meditating continually. The style, doctrinal, logical, and expository, recalls philosophical essays. Espinosa seeks technical and stylistic renovation while remaining as far as possible from Vanguardism. Employing the conventional "life as a voyage" motif, the novel has been compared with Gracián's *El Criticón*. Densely packed with ideas and grandiloquent language recalling the clas-sics, this critique of social structures, human values, attitudes, and customs is situated in the antipodes of "social Realism."

Bemoaning the dark days of censorship, Spanish and international intel-lectuals imagined unpublished masterpieces languishing in drawers, with-held by their authors in fear of reprisal, while awaiting the dictatorship's demise. Perhaps the greatest tribute to the ingenuity of Spain's postwar narrators is that these imaginary suppressed masterworks never appeared: those who had something to communicate managed to do so at the time, despite the censorship, and to do so more artistically in spite of censorial challenges.

49

Poetry in Franco Spain

GUILLERMO CARNERO

The Generation of 1927 in Franco's Spain

Only three ranking members of the Generation of 1927 remained in Spain at the end of the Civil War: Dámaso Alonso (1898–1990), Vicente Aleixandre (1898–1984), and Gerardo Diego (1896–1987).

In the pre-War period Alonso had gained respect and notoriety as a historian, a philologist, and the scholarly promoter of the tercentennial commemoration of Góngora's death in 1927. Yet, with his 1944 book *Hijos de la ira* ("Children of Wrath"), Alonso positioned himself as the leading figure in the movement to "rehumanize" poetry, a tendency which emerged in the years immediately after the Spanish Civil War. This watershed collection deviates from the norms of Garcilasian Neoclassicism, fusing elements of Surrealist "humanization" with the "impurity" of Neruda and Vallejo, and approximating an incipient mode of social poetry, particularly in its treatment of existential anguish and religious distress. The impact of *Hijos de la ira* is fueled by its disquieting imagery, by its Expressionist language culled from the semantic fields of the degraded, the violent, and the repugnant, and by the fiery rhythm of its longish lines. At its core, the book is rooted in an acknowledgment of the injustice and hostile absurdity of reality. The collection presents man not merely as a victim of this reality, but, moreover, as a subject who has come to identify with – and even to see himself as a part of – Nature's intrinsic wrath. Faced with this human tragedy, Alonso appeals to the figure of an indifferent God as he poses unanswerable, yet inevitable, questions concerning the meaning of life, solitude, and death. His *Oscura noticia* ("Dark Message," 1944), an ensemble of poems whose more formal serenity and mystic influence distinguish it from his previous book, still remains true to its ontological focus. Some eleven years later, Alonso published *Hombre y Dios* ("Man and God"), a collection of sonnets and other poems composed in blank verse. With *Gozos de la vista* ("The Joy of Vision," 1981) and *Duda y amor sobre el Ser Supremo* ("Doubt and Love of the Supreme Being,"

This chapter has been translated from the Spanish by Matthew J. Marr.

1985), the poet broke a silence of many years and returned once more to existential and religious reflection.

The poetry of Vicente Aleixandre evolved in the postwar years with a spirit very much akin to that of Alonso, although these points of contact only reveal how different their respective work is. In fact, the similarities between each poet's artistic development attest to the growing importance of the "rehumanization" and existentialist banners in peninsular literature of the period. Aleixandre, for his part, published *Sombra del paraíso* ("Shadow of Paradise") in 1944. This collection continued to cultivate a brand of Surrealism (though comparatively toned down) that had already brought prominence to the author during the previous decade. Its defining characteristic is, above all else, a certain vitality that exalts the elemental, primordial traits of man, as well as his connection with the forces at work in Nature and all living creatures. Aleixandre's great thematic calling is the oblivion of the self before the spontaneous purity of the natural world. He views love, which partially restores for lovers a primitive, natural state by breaking down the limitations of the self, as an anticipation of death: the ultimate moment of reintegration and fusion with Nature. Thus, *Sombra del paraíso* manifests a Utopist dimension that resonates with the myths of the Golden Age and the Christian concepts of Innocence and Fall. The collection's title clearly alludes to these latter notions, as its poems express a sense that a certain sort of atavistic innocence – like a vestige of the lost paradise – remains deep within the heart of man. In effect, the book's pulse of vitality can be said to lend it a critical and, at the same time, hopeful outlook which elevates 1940s humanization to its maximum transcendence.

If *Sombra del paraíso* considered the projection of the self in amorous relationships and identification with Nature, *Historia del corazón* ("History of the Heart," 1954) strongly embraced solidarity and social communion. This sentiment emerges not in the limbo-like context of a Utopia, but, rather, in the realm of the programmatic. In Aleixandre's own words, "El poeta canta por todos" ("The poet sings on behalf of everyone"), a declaration signaling a belief that the poetic self is at once an integral component of the collective and a voice guided by it. This, of course, does not mean that love is absent from *Historia del corazón*, although it is by no means the book's most essential theme. Love does return as a central preoccupation, however, in the 1962 collection *En un vasto dominio* ("In a Vast Dominion"), a systematic poetic project dedicated to praising the body, its parts, and its functions. *Dominio* also maintains the aspect of solidarity initiated in *Historia*, with the poem entitled "Para quién escribo" ("For Whom I Write") providing a foremost example of this tendency. The former offers a series of poems describing common, everyday characters with whom the poet feels solidarity.

This project continues in *Retratos con nombre* ("Portraits with Names," 1965), a book which also evinces similar descriptive and narrative techniques.

If it can be said that *Hijos de la ira* is allied in its characteristics to social poetry, thus placing it in a category of utmost transcendence, an analogous correspondence is discernible in Aleixandre's work between 1954 and 1965. In fact, the poet sought to align himself with this most dominant tendency in Spanish literature following the end of the Civil War, a movement whose influence was paramount for a full quarter-century. Still, Aleixandre managed to write of social truths with a special deftness that kept him at a comfortable distance from the politics *du jour*, and, in the end, he proved himself capable of avoiding the sort of fleeting aesthetics which even Neruda – with whose rhetoric Aleixandre has many points of similarity – cultivated during the same period. In his prologue to the second edition (1945) of *La destrucción o el amor* ("Destruction or Love") Aleixandre rejected the so-called poetry "of minorities" in favor of what he calls "the permanent, the universal" aspect of man. In a speech upon his induction into the Real Academia Española some four years later, he advocated a vision of poetry that "no consiste tanto en ofrecer belleza cuanto en alcanzar propagación, comunicación profunda" ("doesn't consist so much in offering beauty as it does in reaching others, and in profound communication"). In 1955, during a talk given at the Spanish Institute entitled "Algunos caracteres de la nueva poesía española" ("Some Characteristics of the New Spanish Poetry"), he defined the quintessential poetic theme as that of man situated amidst the coordinates of historical time and the social problems of his day. At the same time, moreover, he acknowledged the apparent bankruptcy of self-sufficient aestheticism and the suitability of narrative, realist, and colloquial poetry. Aleixandre embraced a poetics which had been espoused earlier by Unamuno and Machado, and in addition privileged the existentialism, religious strife, Realism, and social criticism which informed poetry later on. Emerging as a sort of inviolate oracle prone to channeling disparate ideologies and tendencies, he forged a transcendent and encyclopedic brand of humanism that showed no unilateral partiality to any single intellectual or spiritual outlook. This progressive, ecumenical stance – free from the limitations of creed or political party – may have played a key role in his selection as a winner of the Nobel Prize in 1977. In accord with the changes ushered into Spanish literature in the mid 1960s, in the final phase of his career Aleixandre abandoned such inclinations, opting instead to craft poems whose metaphysical existentialism was thematically central. In two seminal books, *Poemas de la consumación* ("Poems of Consummation," 1968) and *Diálogos del conocimiento* ("Dialogues of Knowledge," 1974), as well as in the posthumous collections *Nuevos poemas varios* ("Selected

New Poems," 1987) and *En gran noche* ("In the Great Night," 1991), the poet reflects on themes of aging, lost love, and the imminence of death.

The poetry of Gerardo Diego fuses experimental, Avant-Garde, existential, and traditional components to such an extent that his work did not depend on the trends of "rehumanization" so dominant in the wake of the Spanish Civil War. If his poetry can be said to reflect this latter sensibility at all, it does so with tact and in a minor key altogether his own. Diego's production after 1940 was broad and diverse; he published miscellanies and collections of circumstantial poems which frequently revealed the poet's virtuosity in regard to technique, rhythm, and language. Occasionally, however, he was also prone to a risky breed of affectation, an inclination which can turn a frivolous approach to a tragic theme into what seems a joke in bad taste ("A los vietnameses" ["To the Vietnamese"], from *Odas morales* ["Moral Odes"], for example). "'El Cordobés' dilucidado" ("Elucidating 'The Cordovan,'" 1966), with a similar sort of dubious affection, is ostensibly directed toward the mentally disadvantaged. *Ángeles de Compostela* ("Angels of Compostela," 1940) utilizes the sonnet, the ballad, and song forms, as Diego calls on a medley of strophic forms traditional to Spanish verse. *Alondra de verdad* ("Lark of Truth," 1941) immerses itself in a project of recreating the classical sonnet, a tendency very much in vogue during the first postwar period. In this sense, the collection exhibits a certain strain of Garcilasian Neoclassicism, a school whose impersonal style the poet revisits on more than one occasion. In addition to Spanish landscapes and monuments, in the post-Civil War period Diego explores the central themes of religion, bullfighting festivals, and love. This latter theme enjoys sustained consideration in *La sorpresa* ("The Surprise," 1944), *Amazona* ("The Amazon," 1955), *Amor solo* ("Lonely Love," 1958), *Canciones a Violante* ("Songs for Violante," 1959), *Sonetos a Violante* ("Sonnets for Violante," 1962), and *Glosa a Villamediana* ("Gloss to Villamediana," 1961). Within the pages of *Biografía incompleta* ("Incomplete Biography," 1953) and *Odas morales* ("Moral Odes," 1966), Diego approaches what Jorge Guillén called "integral poetry"; he also moves toward social poetry in such poems as "La guerra" ("War") and "En plena bocamina" ("Here in the Mine Entrance," from his 1953 book).

Several other poets should be included in the chronologically derived group which is the Generation of 1927. Foremost among these, perhaps, is Juan Gil-Albert (1904–1994), noteworthy for the poetry he publishes upon returning from exile in 1947 – *El existir medita su corriente* ("Existence Ponders its Own Current," 1949), *Concertar es amor* ("Harmonizing is Love," 1951) – as well as for his final phase of philosophical and ethical reflection, a period which generated *Poesía* (1961), *A los presocráticos* ("To the Pre-Socratics," 1963), *La meta-física* ("Meta-physics," 1974), and *Variaciones sobre un tema inextinguible* ("Variations on an Inexhaustible Theme," 1981). Other significant poets of this group are Ángela Figuera (1902–1984), Rosa Chacel (1898–1994), Agustín de Foxá (1903–1959), Adriano del Valle (1895–1957), José María Pemán (1897–1981), Rafael Laffón (1900–1978), Pedro Pérez Clotet (1902–1966), Joaquín Romero Murube (1904–1969), Rafael Porlán (1899–1945), and Pedro García Cabrera (1905–1981).

The Luis Rosales Group: the *Escorial* and *Garcilaso* reviews

Critics perceive in the "Luis Rosales Group" a conservative ideology which is evident in its rejection of the Avant-Garde and the Neo-Baroque. Literary activity within this group begins before 1936, and it is motivated by an ideal of simplicity and classicism that conjoins sixteenth-century poetics with the collective legacy of Bécquer, Unamuno, Antonio Machado, Juan Ramón Jiménez, Jorge Guillén, and Pedro Salinas. Philosophically speaking, this aesthetic exists within a "rehumanized" and existential framework closely associated with a liberal strain of Catholic thought, the foundations of which are fixated upon love within order, daily life, and the countryside.

These constitute the cardinal elements apparent in the work of Luis Rosales (1910–1992) from his book *La casa encendida* ("The Well-Lit House," 1949) through *Canciones* ("Songs," 1973). *Diario de una resurrección* ("Diary of a Resurrection," 1979) and the three parts of *La carta entera* ("The Whole Letter," 1980), *La almadraba* ("The Trap-Net," 1980), *Un rostro en cada ola* ("A Face on Each Wave," 1982), *Oigo el silencio universal del miedo* ("I Hear the Universal Silence of Fear," 1984) – explore the wonder and misery of love in old age and the irretrievable passage of time.

At the core of Leopoldo Panero's (1909–1962) poetic world, one encounters the theme of religious concern. *La estancia vacía* ("The Empty Room," 1944) and *Versos al Guadarrama* ("Poems for the Guadarrama," 1945) confront the reader with a theocentric concept of reality and human existence. This sensibility permeates *Escrito a cada instante* ("Written in Each Moment," 1949), a collection in which the poet also celebrates love within marriage and the family. Panero's literary career culminates in *Canto personal* ("Personal Canto," 1953), a work written in *terza rima* as a response to Pablo Neruda's *Canto General* ("General Canto," 1950).

Luis Felipe Vivanco (1907–1975) views Nature as a manifestation of God in *Tiempo de dolor* ("Time of Pain," 1940), a book whose long lines of verse cry out with the tone of psalms and prayer. *El descampado* ("The Open Field," 1957) dwells on the topic of human love and the peace to be found within the institution of the family. *Memoria de la plata* ("Memory of Silver," 1958) reveals the influence of Spanish mysticism in addition to the Romanticism of both Spain and Germany. *Los caminos* ("The Paths," 1974) presents, for its part, yet another dosis of marital love as the ideal of bliss.

Primer libro de amor ("First Book of Love," 1939) and *Fábula de la doncella y el río* ("Fable of the Maiden and the River," 1943) by Dionisio Ridruejo (1912–1975) belong to the Garcilasian school. *En la soledad del tiempo* ("In the Solitude of Time," 1944), *Cuaderno de Rusia* ("Russian Notebook," 1944), and *Elegías* ("Elegies," 1948) manifest a sort of "intimist" change bent on posing time-honored questions concerning the human condition and death.

Germán Bleiberg (1915–1990) was one of the most fervent proponents of the Garcilasian school in his *Sonetos amorosos* ("Love Sonnets," 1936), a most influential collection in post-Civil-War Spanish poetry. His work acquires a more pensive, confidential tone with the publication of *Más allá de las ruinas* ("Beyond the Ruins," 1947) and *La mutua primavera* ("Mutual Springtime," 1948).

José Antonio Muñoz Rojas (1909–), a serene and contemplative poet who makes occasional forays into the Garcilasian tradition, can also be situated with the Rosales group.

The intent of *Escorial* – a journal originally founded under the banner of "liberal" Francoism and Rosales' group – was to revive literary life in Spain and to heal the wounds caused by the Civil War. Thus, it adopted a progressive and eclectic tone, lending special attention to sixteenth- and seventeenth-century literature. It also attempted to conform to the Golden Age tradition continued by *Garcilaso*: a review founded in 1943 by a group called "Creative Youth" with José García Nieto (1914–2000) leading the charge. "Garcilasianism" is a poetic school that finds its inspiration in the work of the sixteenth-century poet, Garcilaso de la Vega. Nonetheless, such imitation rarely reached the heights of its model, as it suffered from a lack of emotional depth in its cliché, rhetorical idealization of women, and reconfigured Petrarchan motifs.

Rehumanization, intimism, Neo-Romanticism: the *Espadaña* review

Antonio Machado and Miguel de Unamuno are customarily seen as the forebears of what has become known as the "rehumanization" movement in Spanish poetry of the post-civil-War era. This literary tendency is more definitively set into motion, however, with Miguel Hernández's *Cancionero y romancero de ausencias* ("Songs and Ballads of Absence"), which was composed between 1938 and 1942, and published in 1952.

The *Espadaña* review, launched by Eugenio de Nora and Victoriano Crémer, is the most renowned manifestation of the rehumanization movement, directly opposed in its orientation to the Neoclassicism championed within the pages of *Garcilaso*. *Espadaña* upheld such collections as *Hijos de la ira* and *Sombra del paraíso* as exemplary, thus defending and backing a poetry whose thematics emphasize not only existential and religious questions, but also matters of social and political importance. This Realist inclination toward social protest would become especially prominent in the magazine's final issues.

Eugenio de Nora (1923–) makes his poetic debut with the publication of *Amor prometido* ("Promised Love"). In *Cantos al destino* ("Songs to Destiny," 1945), existential, civic, and religious anguish appear, while *Pueblo cautivo* ("Captive People," 1946) distinguishes itself as the inaugural book of authentically social poetry in Spain. Its project of explicit political protest is carried out anonymously, and the book was published in secret. *Contemplación del tiempo* ("Contemplation of Time," 1948) follows through with this social thrust in part, although in other moments the collection ponders more existential concerns. The poet's 1953 effort, *Siempre* ("Always"), is devoted to the topic of love, while the following year's *España, pasión de vida* ("Spain, Life Passion") returns once more to the repertoire of social themes. From his earliest work, Victoriano Crémer (1907–) allies himself with the sort of existentialism and social protest characteristic of *tremendismo*, often presenting his voice as engaged in a difficult dialogue with God.

The Adonais press, the most influential in postwar Spanish poetry, prints its first collection in 1943: *Poemas del toro* ("Poems of the Bull" by Rafael Morales [1919–]), a book which inaugurates the rehumanization tendency of the 1940s even before the emergence of *Espadaña*, its contributors, and its promoters. The first collection of poems by Blas de Otero (1916–1979), entitled *Cántico espiritual* ("Spiritual Canticle," 1942), contains existential and religious reflection, but without the sense of conflict that later appears in *Ángel fieramente humano* ("Fiercely Human Angel," 1950) and *Redoble de conciencia* ("Drumroll of Conscience," 1951). In 1951, Blas de Otero unconditionally champions the project of social poetry, a move which is readily discernible in *Pido la paz y la palabra* ("I Call for Peace and the Word," 1955), *En castellano* ("In Castilian," 1959), *Que trata de España* ("Concerning Spain," 1964), and *Mientras* ("Meanwhile," 1970). These books reveal a voice which has embraced a new faith based on human and class solidarity, and an author who insists on eliminating lofty rhetoric in favor of a colloquial tone, shorter poems, and simple messages easily appropriated by a broad reading public.

In his books of the 1940s (*Movimientos elementales* ["Elemental Move-ments," 1947], *Objetos poéticos* ["Poetic Objects," 1948], *Las cosas como son* ["Things as They Are," 1949]), Gabriel Celaya (1911–1991) responds to the various existential outlooks prevalent in the period. Begin-ning with *Las cartas boca abajo* ("Showing One's Cards," 1951), he also produces social poetry. *Paz y concierto* ("Peace and Accord," 1953) stresses the need for the poet to act as a collective, non-egocentric voice, denounces injustice and the absence of freedom, and advocates social awareness among its readers. *Cantos iberos* ("Iberian Songs," 1955) places the masses at the forefront in mapping out the struggle for soci-etal regeneration. The collection privileges simple, colloquial language and contains the most famous poem of the social poetry movement: "La poesía es un arma cargada de futuro" ("Poetry is a Gun Loaded with the Future"). Following *Las resistencias del diamante* ("Resistances of the Diamond," 1957), *Episodios nacionales* ("National Episodes," 1962), and from the early 1970s, Celaya favors new experimental directions in what he called his "orphic" period.

Arcángel de mi noche ("Archangel of My Night," 1944) and *Sobre la tierra* ("On Earth," 1945) by Vicente Gaos (1919–1980) are focused on existential problems, recognizing the human quest for transcendence, and man's problematic relationship with God. Unlike Otero, Gaos – whose career culminates with *Última Thule* ("Ultima Thule," 1980) – evolves not toward social protest, but rather, toward a reflective and culturally allusive sort of poetry.

The first period of the poetic output of Carlos Bousoño (1923–) is comprised of three books: *Subida al amor* ("Rising toward Love," 1945), *Primavera de la muerte* ("Springtime of Death," 1946), and *Noche del sentido* ("Night of the Senses," 1957). The first of these falls into a reli-gious mode rooted in faith. The second collection is a meditation on the temporal nature of being and human life. The third doubts the validity of interpreting existential problems in religious terms. It seems, then, that Bousoño – like Blas de Otero – might have replaced his broken faith in reli-gious values with a program of social regeneration. However, in *Invasión de la realidad* ("Invasion of Reality," 1962) he adopts a highly affirmative brand of existentialism in which the real seizes the central place of God, and the world becomes a secular, material cathedral. *Oda en la ceniza* ("Ode in the Ash," 1967) and *Las monedas contra la losa* ("The Coins Against the Counter," 1973) mark a distinct change in the poet's thought and expressive style, as they explore the discursive play of poetry itself and the intellectual development of emotional intuition. The collapse of beliefs that had catalyzed Bousoño's 1962 book is thus redeemed in a new option for salvation: writing's potential for shedding light on the mysteries of reality and the self (who observes and defines the world). *Metáfora del desafío* ("Metaphor for Outrage," 1989) and *El ojo de la aguja* ("The Eye of the Needle," 1993) are, above all else, dense meditations on morality, collections which ponder death and the salvation possible through love and writing.

The crucial reason for the immediate reception and lasting impact of the work of José Hierro (1922–2002) is its underlying foundations in a moderate form of existential thought never prone to tragic exaggeration, as well as its independence from certain dominant trends in post-Civil-War Spanish poetry (tendencies which were once historically pertinent, but which are now obsolete as literary modes). Only in the most minimal sense and with a wholly unconventional approach did Hierro ever compose social poetry. He has categorized his poetic peers as either aesthetic, religious, political, or testimonial in orientation, including himself under this last banner, seeing himself as a witness to turbulent times. Still, his voice emanates from an emotionally inspired, individual perspective, a space in which the poet is able to sidestep the dangers of poeticizing ideological messages. Moreover, unlike Blas de Otero, Hierro has always fashioned his own poetic language with a distinctive simplicity that avoids a sort of self-imposed, conversational triteness. In his desire to explore the enigmatic and the ineffable with clarity, he also espouses an irrational sensibility whose roots can be traced to Symbolism. He perceives two types of poems in his overall production: "reports" (narrative texts with referents in exterior reality; texts of conscience) and "hallucinations" (inquiries into emotion and the haze of the inexpressible). Consequently, his work can be seen as a precursor to the poetry of the Generation of 1950.

Hierro's first books were *Tierra sin nosotros* ("Land Without Us") and *Alegría* ("Joy"), both published in 1947. The *Quinta del 42* ("Class of '42," 1952) offers perhaps the most frequently quoted articulation of his poetics: the poem entitled "Para un esteta" ("For an Aesthete"), a text which introduces Hierro's aforementioned concept of testimonial poetry. His literary production has not been extensive; after *Cuánto sé de mí* ("What I Know about Myself," 1957) and *Libro de las alucinaciones* ("The Book of Hallucinations," 1964), the poet enters a lengthy period of silence which ends only in 1998 with *Cuaderno de Nueva York* ("New York Notebook"), a meditation on consciousness as a synthesis of experience, memory, imagination, and writing.

Several other poets of this cohort should be, at the very least, mentioned in passing: José María Valverde (1926–1996), Carmen Conde (1907–1996), Salvador Pérez Valiente (1919–), Leopoldo de Luis (1918–), Carlos Rodríguez Spíteri (1911–), Ildefonso-Manuel Gil (1912–), Francisco-Javier Martín Abril (1908–1998), Josefina de la Torre (1907–), Manuel Álvarez Ortega (1923–), Alfonso Canales (1923–), and Rafael Montesinos (1920–) have all written poetry worthy of note.

The post-Avant-Garde and experimentation: the *Cántico* review group

The influence of the Avant-Garde greatly waned in the post-Civil-War era. The Surrealist impulse toward irrationalism so present in the 1930s endures only in the most marginal sense until it is embraced once more as an ideal by certain members of the Generation of 1970. A minimal vein of Surrealism survives in the writing of the Rosales Group and the "rehumanization" movement, and – to an even greater extent – in the work of other poets: José Luis Hidalgo (1919–1947), author of *Raíz* ("Root," 1944) and *Los muertos* ("The Dead," 1947); Miguel Labordeta (1921–1969), whose first books – *Sumido 25* ("Submerged 25," 1948), *Violento idílico* ("Violent Idyllic," 1949), and *Transeúnte central* ("Transient in the Middle," 1950) – engage a sort of Surrealist existentialism related in a sense to social poetry (*Epilírica* ["Epilyrics," 1961], *Los soliloquios* ["Soliloquies," 1969]), even if Labordeta always remains at a distance from a populist bent and conversational discourse. The legacy of Surrealism is quite clear in Camilo José Cela's *Pisando la dudosa luz del día* ("Treading on the Doubtful Light of Day," 1945). Yet, the best poet of an Avant-Garde, Surrealist mold during the Franco years is Juan-Eduardo Cirlot (1916–1973), author of numerous short-run collections which found few readers. Among these is his cycle of sixteen pieces published between 1967 and 1971 under the general title *Bronwyn*. Inspired by Franklin Schaffner's 1965 film *The War Lord*, whose symbolic resonance greatly interested the poet, these poems demonstrate Cirlot's profound knowledge of the literary and musical Avant-Garde, Eastern mysticism, Gnosticism, and early medieval literature, as well as his obsessive belief in the possibility of communicating with a deceased lover.

Postism originates under the guidance of Carlos-Edmundo de Ory (1923–) and Eduardo Chicharro (1905–1964). It is primarily a literary movement, given its diffusion in such journals as *La Cerbatana* ("The Blowpipe"), as well as through a number of manifestos. The first of these (1945) declares the movement's links with Surrealism, albeit without the latter's revolutionary element, a practical impossibility within the climate of censorship and self-censorship prevailing at this historical moment in Spain. Postism's advocates, whose philosophy and texts reveal a certain kinship with Dadaism and literature of the absurd, demonstrate a high degree of linguistic irrationalism, as well as frequent gestures toward humor, wordplay, and the imitation of classical forms and meter. From the vantage point of the present, Postism's historical significance lies, for one, in its revivification of the imagination. It also represents an ironic response to both the Neoclassical serenity of the Garcilasian school and the creative limitations of "rehumanized" and social poetry. In later years, Ory promotes two other movements: the so-called "Introrealism" of the

1950s and the Atelier de Poésie Ouverte of the subsequent decade, a movement which backs collective creations of an experimental nature. Ory's *Los sonetos* ("Sonnets," 1963) is perhaps his most representative Postist text, although his best poetic efforts – for instance, *Melos melancolía* ("Melos Melancholy," 1999)– emerge in more recent years. Three other poets are associated, at least in part, with Postism: Gabino-Alejandro Carriedo (1923–1981), Ángel Crespo (1926–1995), and Gloria Fuertes (1918–1998).

Throughout his career, or at least until *Antisalmos* ("Antipsalms," 1978) was picked up by a commercial press, Francisco Pino (1910–2002) remained as unknown as Cirlot. The period of his writing that commences with *La salida* ("The Way Out," 1974) is marked by an experimentalism prone to fragmentary discourse, neologisms, puns, visual play, lyricism, calligrams, and phonetic, atextual poetry.

The Andalusian group of poets formed by Julio Aumente (1924–), Juan Bernier (1911–1989), Pablo García Baena (1923–), Mario López (1918–2003), and Ricardo Molina (1917–1968) bears little aesthetic resemblance to the aforementioned writers of the post-Avant-Garde period. In 1947 this ensemble of poets founds the review called *Cántico*, thus offering a response to both *Garcilaso* and *Espadaña* with a scope conjoining aspects of Modernism, the Generation of 1927, the Renaissance, and, above all else, Spanish poetry of the Baroque period. The group manifests hallmarks which clearly distinguish it from competing poetic tendencies in the 1940s: culturalist intimism, refinement of form and lexical richness, a vitalistic treatment of love as a theme (very much apart from the impersonal stance of Garcilasianism, religious and existential *angst*, and the idealistic vision of marriage of the Rosales group). Younger than the Andalusian group's original founders, Vicente Núñez (1929–2002) is aligned with their project aesthetically.

Social poetry

Several factors combine to produce the emergence of a type of poetry which assails the social injustice and lack of freedom endured by Spain under the Franco régime: the poetry of exile, "rehumanized" poetry, and the evolution of a poetry dealing with religious anguish (like that of Blas de Otero). Francisco Ribes' 1952 *Antología consultada* ("Consulted Anthology") shows social poetry to be the dominant tendency in the 1950s. Faced with the risk of clinging to contemporary problems, to an obsession with Realism, and to colloquial language that Bousoño points out, Celaya – whose own point of view is in keeping with most – embraces testimonial poetry and its key mission of heightening consciousness and changing reality.

The social poetry movement is active from the mid 1940s through the end of the 1960s. Its concerns can be divided into eight main thematic categories: (1) references to the Spanish Civil War, an event which serves as the logical basis for any consideration of the political situation in Franco's Spain; (2) reports of the repressed voice of a discontent people; (3) a satire of figures who fall into line with Franco's policies, whether out of solidarity, fear, skepticism, or desire for wealth (conservative Catholic families, financiers, businessmen, the Church); (4) solidarity with the working class, a theme usually expressed as a portrait of a member of the proletariat whose mentality, customs, desires, virtues, and frustrations are laid bare (a sort of poem that typically suggests the writer should purge himself of his bourgeois values and adopt those of the proletariat); (5) a push for political struggle, a task which not only the people must undertake, but also the poet – as just another man and an enlightening voice for the masses; (6) direct and active political agitation, a theme seen less frequently because of the need to publish in secret or abroad; (7) Spain itself, a topic cultivated in each and every school of postwar Spanish poetry, and a motif which the social poets assimilate with an ideology and critical lens appropriate to their historical moment; (8) international affairs, a phenomenon which in the last phase of social poetry consists of attacking technocratic capitalism and American imperialism as a show of solidarity with other repressed peoples.

The most conscious social poets make an early and thorough effort to criticize themselves too, a tendency manifest in Leopoldo de Luis' 1965 *Antología de la poesía social* ("Anthology of Social Poetry"). Within its pages, José Hierro recognizes the absolute discredit that has befallen social poetry as a result of so many mediocre poets working in the social vein. He demonstrates that this occurs within a cycle of self-absorption among bourgeois intellectuals, a trend that produces a literature of dubious quality in the name of the supposedly urgent content of its message and an undervaluing of the (no less supposed) reading public. José-Ángel Valente, for one, seconds this assessment.

As the product of an awakening of the Spanish intellectual class during the Franco dictatorship, social poetry is a failed project in its indiscriminate appropriation of flawed dogmas: a problematic inherent to art in any instance that it turns itself over to conveying ideology widely.

The Generation of 1950

A cardinal trait held in common among the various writers of the Generation of 1950 (that is, among those poets born between 1924 and 1938) is a sort of ethical intimism, a particular attribute of their work that often serves to transform the quotidian into something much more metaphysical and existential. Nonetheless, this common characteristic does not preclude a great range of styles within this group of poets. Claudio Rodríguez cultivates his visionary irrationalism at one end of this spectrum, while at the opposite pole a cadre of poets absorbs the Realism and colloquial tone of social poetry. Residing on its own somewhere between these extremes is the "Barcelona School," a group whose members include Carlos Barral, Jaime Gil de Biedma, and José Agustín Goytisolo.

The dean of the Generation of 1950, Ángel González (1925–), makes his debut in 1956 with *Áspero mundo* ("Rough World"), a collection featuring an expressive simplicity and colloquial voice characteristic of its author. Love rises above all other themes as the central focus of the book, and it will reappear once more in *Palabra sobre palabra* ("Word upon Word," 1965) and *Breves acotaciones para una biografía* ("Brief Notes for a Biography," 1971). *Grado elemental* ("Elementary Grade," 1962), much like the later collections *Tratado de urbanismo* ("Urban Treatise," 1967) and *Muestra de algunos procedimientos narrativos* ("A Sample of Some Narrative Processes," 1976), considers certain social themes. In the short, joke-form, epigram-like poems of *Prosemas o menos* ("Prosemes or Even Less," 1983), irony surfaces as a prevailing tendency. González's best book, *Otoños y otras luces* ("Autumns and Other Lights," 2001), dwells on a life dedicated to love and other ideals he sees as being degraded by the circumstances of reality.

Las adivinaciones ("Guesswork," 1952), *Memorias de poco tiempo* ("Fleeting Memories," 1954), and *Las horas muertas* ("Dead Hours," 1959) by José Manuel Caballero Bonald (1926–) are books that inhabit an occasionally dark and somber realm. The first two recall the anguished existentialism of the 1940s with poems about the search for God and love, and the misery of the human condition. Working once again within this same frame of mind, the poet takes on the genre of the Andalusian couplet in *Anteo* (1956). An obvious desire for expressive clarity is evident in the socially concerned *Pliegos de cordel* ("Dime-Store Verses," 1963). In *Descrédito del héroe* ("Discredited Hero," 1977), the author composes poetic prose, a project which will culminate in his *Laberinto de fortuna* ("Labyrinth of Fortune," 1984). *Diario de Argónida* ("Diary from Argónida," 1997) sketches places and episodes in a personal history that can be seen as a voyage of the imagination.

Carlos Barral (1928–1989) is influenced by his readings of Mallarmé, Rilke, Eliot, Spanish Baroque writers, and the Greek and Latin classics. *Metropolitano* ("Metropolitan," 1957) offers a dark, though powerfully symbolic, metaphysical discourse concerned with the inhospitable urban world of modernity, a space estranged from Nature where miscommunication and failure flourish. The lone product of Barral's flirtation with

Social Realism is 1961's *Diecinueve figuras de mi historia civil* ("Nineteen Figures of My Civil History"). This book's social commitment – like that of Gil de Biedma – is atypical in its presentation of an upper-middle-class speaker who voluntarily, but hopelessly, struggles to transcend his own class by adopting a socialist ideology. As he strives to reach out to the working class, Barral is wholly conscious (and not without irony) of the failure of such good intentions. The social project dissipates in *Usuras* ("Usury," 1965), *Informe personal sobre el alba* ("Personal Report on Dawn," 1970), and *Lecciones de cosas* ("Lessons on Things," 1986).

Singular and masterful within the modesty of his own limitations, the voice of José Agustín Goytisolo (1928–1999) is first set to the page in *Salmos al viento* ("Psalms to the Wind," 1958). As a poet committed to Social Realism and the theme of love, Goytisolo forges a narrative style built upon expressive simplicity and references to the everyday, contemporary world in *Algo sucede* ("Something Happens," 1968) and *Del tiempo y del olvido* ("Of Time and Oblivion," 1977). His ideology is critical and anti-establishment, while at the same time all his own, a system of values supporting man's liberation from moral and political dogmas. *El rey mendigo* ("The Beggar King," 1988) takes old age as a springboard for melancholy reflection. *Como los trenes de la noche* ("Like the Night Trains," 1994) revisits moments from his life-story, as does *Cuadernos de El Escorial* ("Notebooks from El Escorial," 1995), through the form of short, epigram-like poems.

Jaime Gil de Biedma (1929–1990) has produced a concise list of works: *Según sentencia del tiempo* ("As Time Decrees," 1953), *Compañeros de viaje* ("Fellow Travelers," 1959), *Moralidades* ("Moralities," 1966), and *Poemas póstumos* ("Posthumous Poems," 1968). One of the most personal bodies of work in twentieth-century Spanish poetry, Gil de Biedma's verse is influenced by French sources (Baudelaire), as well as the verse of English (Auden, Eliot) and classical (Catullus) poets. Above all else, Gil de Biedma is a poet fixated on the exaltation and pursuit of fleeting, frequently mercenary, love: a love somewhat limited to the sexual realm, but one which maintains a nuance of nostalgia for more profound emotion. In order to express passion in a way that seems in keeping with the simple, colloquial style typical of his generation, the poet playfully lifts certain expressions and commonplaces from popular song. As a social poet, his chief concern is articulating his consciousness of being little more than a traveling companion never authentically integrated in the onward march of the proletariat.

The first book of José Ángel Valente (1929–2000), *A modo de esperanza* ("In Hopeful Fashion," 1955), proffers a sober reflection on sadness, melancholy, and disappointment before the limits of human existence and the imminent threat of death. Valente also makes discreet allusions to religious dissatisfaction, thus forming a set of preoccupations that resurface once more in *Poemas a Lázaro* ("Poems to Lazarus," 1960). The novelty of *La memoria y los signos* ("Memory and Its Signs," 1966) rests in the presence of elements common to the social poetry repertoire, a mode which the poet will not revisit systematically, although it does appear in *El inocente* ("The Innocent One," 1970) and *Al dios del lugar* ("To the God of the Place," 1989). The last stage of Valente's work falls into line with what has been called a "poetics of silence" – short, fragmentary, and hermetic poems which are written in both verse and prose. This tendency is apparent in *Breve son* ("Brief Sound," 1968), *Treinta y siete fragmentos* ("Thirty-Seven Fragments," 1972), *Interior con figuras* ("Interior with Figures," 1976), and with even more frequency from *Material memoria* ("Material Memory," 1979) to *No amanece el cantor* ("Dawn Without the Singer," 1992). *Fragmentos de un libro futuro* ("Fragments of a Forthcoming Book," 2000) features prolonged reflections on the justification of existence, particularly in light of the imminence of death.

The Generation of 1950 includes at least one feminine voice of note: that of María Victoria Atencia (1931–). Her early books explore a jubilant, trance-like sensibility experienced upon "discovering" the world (*Tierra mojada* ["Wet Earth," 1953]) – an emotion which is ravaged beyond repair by death: an idea poeticized in *Cañada de los ingleses* ("The English Glen," 1961). Beginning with 1976's *Marta y María* ("Martha and Mary"), any traces of idyllic thought disappear and in their place there emerges a pensive consideration of the passage of time and the fluid course of existence. An ideal form for the author, the short poem is adopted as she communicates the importance and transcendence of common situations in everyday settings. While Atencia opts to veil biographical detail in most of her work, the scenes evoked in *La pared contigua* ("The Adjacent Wall," 1989) and *Las contemplaciones* ("Contemplations," 1997) open the possibility of posing questions regarding women's issues or even self-identity.

Ever since the 1960 publication of *Las brasas* ("The Embers"), the poetry of Francisco Brines (1932–) has sustained the most significant degree of self-analysis and ethical contemplation among any of the members of the Generation of 1950. At the core of Brines' problematic is the fluidity of existence itself, the basis of his persistent inquiry into the meaning of human life. These reflections are expressed through elemental language and with a warm, conversational tone. Within his verse, the examination of memory takes on symbolic transcendence, as Brines fashions a self-conscious poetic vision focused on the redemptive power of sensory experience (a notion inexorably linked to the lamentation of its ultimate impermanence). In *El santo inocente* ("Innocent Saint," 1965), a religious solution to the dilemmas of the human condition is dismissed. *Palabras a la oscuridad* ("Words to the Darkness," 1966) and *Insistencias en Luzbel* ("Insistences on Luzbel," 1977) advocate an acceptance of life and love, even though these may not fulfill the highest aspirations of man. In *El otoño de las rosas* ("The Autumn of the Roses," 1986), Brines reconsiders the essence of life through a more optimistic lens, seeing it as a passage toward sensorial pleasure. *La última costa* ("The Last Coast," 1995) views the course of life as a symbolic journey, while its tone despondently alludes to a sort of farewell.

The poetry of Claudio Rodríguez (1934–1999) is characterized from its beginnings – *Don de la ebriedad* ("Gift of Inebriation," 1953) and *Conjuros* ("Spells," 1958) – by a drive to grasp the world through a brand of love fostering self-knowledge and a return to innocence. His writing reveals the greatest degree of irrationalism within the Generation of 1950, as he shapes a symbolic orb whose rural edge is represented through the use of a lexicon focused on the countryside, as well as through the portrayal of farming activities (planting, reaping, sewing), domestic tasks, and the rhythms of the natural world. From its very title, *Alianza y condena* ("Alliance and Condemnation," 1965) alludes to the insurmountable contradiction between the two sides of human existence and interhuman, amorous relationships. The *El vuelo de la celebración* ("Flight of the Celebration," 1976) revisits a sense of nostalgia for lost innocence from a somewhat hopeless perspective, while *Casi una leyenda* ("Almost a Legend," 1991) reconsiders life-long questions that have never been answered as death draws near.

Many other poets of note might be included in the Generation of 1950. They are: César Simón (1932–1997), Ricardo Defarges (1933–), Carlos Sahagún (1938–), Alfonso Costafreda (1926–1974), Aquilino Duque (1931–), Fernando Quiñones (1931–1998), Antonio Gala (1936–), Agustín García Calvo (1926–), Lorenzo Gomis (1924–), Jose Corredor-Matheos (1929–), Enrique Badosa (1927–), Rafael Soto Vergés (1936–2004), Manuel Alcántara (1928–), Miguel Fernández (1931–1993), Julia Uceda (1926–), Eladio Cabañero (1930–), Jaime Ferrán (1928–2000), Francisca Aguirre (1930–), Mariano Roldán (1932–), Rafael Guillén (1933–), Manuel Mantero (1930–), Joaquín Marco (1935–), Félix Grande (1937–), Luis Feria (1927–1998), Antonio Gamoneda (1931–), Manuel Padorno (1933–), Jesús Hilario Tundidor (1935–), and Rafael Ballesteros (1938–).

50

Theatre in Franco Spain

MARTHA HALSEY

The Spanish stage of the early post-Civil-War period reflected the ideological split that continued after Franco's victory in 1939. When Antonio
Buero Vallejo (1916–2000), a former political prisoner who fought on
the losing side in the Civil War, had his tragedy, *Historia de una escalera*
("Story of a Stairway") premièred in 1949, Spain found a new voice and
a new vehicle for revealing a reality absent from a stage dominated by
rightist plays glorifying National Catholicism and the imperial dream, on
the one hand, and by light comedies, on the other. While the first plays
represented an "official" or Francoist culture and the second, a culture
of "evasion," Buero's play represented a dissident culture that brought to
the stage the harsh reality of the early postwar period.

The "official" theatre – heroic pieces by playwrights such as José
María Pemán (1897–1981) and Juan Ignacio Luca de Tena (1897–1975) –
reflected the Franco régime's vision of itself as heir to what it considered
Spain's past glories and national virtues as they idealized a dubious past
while ignoring real problems of their own present. While such plays, of
little lasting value, continued the Spanish Romantic tradition, the serious
comedies of Miguel Mihura (1905–1977), Edgar Neville (1899–1967),
José López Rubio (1903–1996), and Víctor Ruiz Iriarte (1912–1982) participated in international currents of their time. Mihura's *Tres sombreros
de copa* ("Three Top Hats," 1952) has been recognized as a precursor
of the Theatre of the Absurd. López Rubio's and Ruiz Iriarte's plays
are also characterized by experimentation with the absurd as well as by
metatheatre (theatre about theatre) and various forms of theatricalist staging. While they owe a debt to the absurdist comedies of Enrique Jardiel
Poncela (1901–1952) and the poetic theatre of Alejandro Casona (1903–
1965), more significant is their contact with works of Nicolai Evreinov,
Luigi Pirandello, and Jean Anouilh. The playgoer who sought respite from
painful realities favored such comedies, as well as the mediocre plays of
Alfonso Paso (1926–1978).

López Rubio's *La venda en los ojos* ("The Blindfold," 1954), and *El
landó de los seis caballos* ("The Six-Horse Landau," 1950) by the younger
Ruiz Iriarte, represent prototypes of the Spanish comedy of theatricalized
life. Beatriz of *La venda en los ojos* stops the passage of time, shielding

herself from reality, when her unfaithful husband fails to return from a business trip. Feigning madness, she continues returning to the airport every day to meet him. Her aunt and uncle serve as willing spectators for her calculated playacting and, in turn, themselves assume various roles and disguises. The game is interrupted, however, when Beatriz returns one day from the airport with Germán, a man whom she claims is her husband. The brilliant climax is the unexpected return of Eugenio, the real husband who abandoned her. Returning to reality, Beatriz explains why she deliberately chooses illusion rather than face the pain of his betrayal and sends him away forever. The suggestion is that she will find a new life with Germán.

Like *La venda en los ojos*, *El landó de los seis caballos* deals with the role of illusion in human life – a subject treated in much of Casona's theatre. Four young people receive mysterious letters inviting them to a duke's country estate, promising them the possibility of happiness. Upon arrival they discover several elderly persons who live happily in a make-believe world of playacting, taking rides to Madrid parks and having picnics in the countryside, dressed in the style of forty years earlier. With their splendid six-horse carriage – really a sofa –, balloons, and old love ballads, they replace the present with a fictitious past. The four elderly persons, it turns out, are the dead duke's former servants, to whom he left his mansion. The letters were mailed by his doctor in the hope of finding someone to replace Adelita, the servant who took care of the others and created their make-believe world, as she approaches death. Isabel, one of the young guests, finds the happiness promised by the invitation when she remains to assist the aging residents.

Socially committed critics of the 1960s repudiated such plays of poeticized reality as they did Casona's when the latter returned from exile in 1962. During the so-called "Festival Casona" of 1962–1965, the author's plays, most of them performed in Spain for the first time, won overwhelming public acclaim, as they already had in other European and Spanish-American capitals. However, young critics such as Ricardo Doménech and José Monleón attacked Casona's theatre for its lack of commitment to the collective social problems of his time.[1] The harshness of their attacks was understandable given the problems encountered by a new generation of Realistic playwrights in having their plays staged in the 1950s and 1960s. Monleón suggested that the success of Casona's theatre at such a time sent the wrong message, with its emphasis on individual happiness. Such criticism reflected Jean-Paul Sartre's ideas on *engagement*, the writer's obligation to effect an awareness or *prise de conscience*,

---

[1] Ricardo Doménech, "Para un arreglo de cuentas con el teatro de Alejandro Casona." *Ínsula* 209 (1964), p. 15; José B. Monleón, *Treinta años de teatro de la derecha* (Barcelona: Tusquets, 1971).

introduced to Spain in part through the essays of Alfonso Sastre (1926–). Unlike the final tragedies of Lorca or the exile plays of Max Aub, Casona's theatre seemed out of step with the times – despite the originality and lasting value of his most poetic works.

Breaking with the popular escapist plays dominating the boards, Buero's *Historia de una escalera* portrayed families of a Madrid tenement house, underscoring the social and economic immobility of the early postwar years. The worn stairway remains virtually unchanged as three generations trudge up and down it without getting anywhere. Although never mentioned on stage, the Civil War occurs between the second and third acts, and the spectators of 1949 understood the meaning of the blue-collar worker's dreams expressed in Act I and their subsequent betrayal.

When Buero began his career, he expressed the need for a return to the tragic sense that had characterized the most profound works of Spanish art and literature. Some twenty-five years later, Francisco García Pavón was to declare that, for the first time, Spain had an authentic tragedian and that perhaps the greatest tragedy of all, the Civil War, had to occur before that could happen.[2] Buero considered tragedy an expression of the struggle against the bonds – external and internal, social and individual – that enslave, as a search for freedom. His plays reflect his understanding of the dialectical nature of history and are open in that they offer a degree of hope, at least for the spectators, who must answer for the future. Tragedy does not imply, for him, any radical pessimism but rather a desperate hope. This theory of tragic hope soon became associated with his name.

Buero wrote *En la ardiente oscuridad* ("In the Burning Darkness"), which premièred in 1950, just after leaving prison, using a school for the blind as a microcosm of Franco's Spain. The blind students in their seemingly pleasant refuge avoid confronting the truth of their situation. A new student, Ignacio, combats this illusion of normality instilled by the institution. An intransigent realist and, at the same time, a dreamer who speaks of a world of light that exists could they just see it, Ignacio is murdered by Carlos, the student leader supporting the school's official dogmas. The blindness of the students – who prefer comfortable fictions to harsh truths – is not only physical but spiritual. The play's metaphysical thrust is obvious; Ignacio's yearning to see evinces a passion for the absolute. On the political level, the institution represents any established order that perpetuates the myth that its citizens are free and does not hesitate to resort to violence when its authority is challenged. To many critics, the institution suggested Franco's Spain with its injustices and lies.

---

[2] Francisco García Pavón, "Se estrenó *La Fundación* de Antonio Buero Vallejo." *Blanco y Negro* 26 (January 1974), p. 70.

In 1958, Buero's *Un soñador para un pueblo* ("A Dreamer for a People")
introduced to the Spanish stage a kind of historical theatre that examined
the past critically. Buero turned to the past in search of the roots of problems whose essence and reality continued into the spectator's present. This
new historical theatre reflected Hegelian and Marxist theories according
to which history represents an ongoing process culminating in the viewer's
own present. This new direction indicated by Buero in 1958 would become
the model for other committed playwrights of the Franco period. *Un
soñador para un pueblo* returned to the eighteenth century, when the
reactionary mentality of the nobility clashed with the more enlightened
attitude of the *ilustrados* and their visionary minister Esquilache. Buero
sought to bring the spectators to identify with the proponents of progress
in a conflict that remained unresolved. However, he made it clear, through
the words of Esquilache, that ultimately hope for the future rested with
the *pueblo*, or common people.

In *Las Meninas* (1960), Buero portrayed the period of Felipe IV, an
era of economic and moral decadence, of oppression and misery, of pretense and hypocrisy. The parallel with the Franco era, whose officials saw
their régime as heir to the so-called "glories" of Spain's imperial past,
was clear. The play's première, in Madrid's Teatro Español, gave rise to
violent polemics and nearly twenty-five years were to pass before another
of Buero's plays opened in any government-supported theatre in Spain.
Buero's Velázquez is the conscience of his time, and his painting shows
the truth of his Spain: not pomp or grandeur but rather pain. For Buero,
Velázquez's painting represented a judgment on, or perhaps an idea of,
Spain. Only Pedro, the near-blind beggar, once Velázquez's model and
now a fugitive from the law for rebellions he led against injustice and
oppression, understands the significance of the sketch of the proposed
painting that Velázquez has prepared for the king's approval. Pedro envi-
sions the finished painting, describing it as a picture enfolding "toda la
tristeza de España" ("all the sadness of Spain"). The play ends with a
tableau vivant as the characters assume the positions of their namesakes
in the painting. The sketch now becomes visible as the play's spectators
assume Pedro's place to contemplate a theatrical recreation of the finished
painting.

El concierto de San Ovidio ("The Concert at Saint Ovide," 1962)
brought to the stage a group of blind beggars of pre-Revolutionary France,
with all its social and political servitude not unlike the situation in postwar Spain. The originality of Buero's history plays was that he made
historical distancing and emotive identification complementary functions
of dramatic structure and established a dialectical synthesis between past
and present. Each play ends with hope for the future – a tragic hope
embracing both faith and doubt. In words that surely refer to the Franco

dictatorship, Buero's Velázquez states: "el tiempo todo se lo lleva . . . También se llevará esta edad de dolor" ("time carries away all things with it . . . It will also carry away this age of pain").

With *El tragaluz* ("The Basement Window," 1967), Buero introduced a more subjective emphasis that would characterize his subsequent theatre. He focuses on an obscure family forced to take refuge at the War's end in a dark basement apartment where they have remained for close to thirty years. The younger brother Mario, an idealistic dreamer, achieves nothing, paralyzed by his belief that the only path to success is trampling others. His older brother, Vicente, prospers precisely by making victims. The family's story is ostensibly represented through holograms projected by researchers from a future century. Since the latter project some scenes that may be occurring only in the mind of a character seen lost in thought, they bring the audience to identify with that character's viewpoint. Buero carries the spectators to the researchers' future to see, from there, a story of their own times. From there they must observe and judge people not unlike themselves. At the same time, they must feel *themselves* being judged by a future conscience. The researchers underscore the historical dimension of the play, stating that men of action like Vicente did not know how to dream and dreamers like Mario failed to act. Buero urged Spanish viewers of 1967 to examine their own painful and often repressed memories of the postwar period. At the same time, he imparted a sense of hope by having the researchers explain that, in their own far-off century, they have overcome the errors of the family's – and thus the spectators' – present.

With *El sueño de la razón* ("The Sleep of Reason," 1970), Buero continued his cycle of history plays and at the same time intensified his use of a subjective viewpoint on stage. Of all his tragedies, this play about Francisco de Goya, together with *El concierto de San Ovidio* and the later *La Fundación* ("The Foundation"), have won for Buero the greatest international acclaim. The action occurs in 1823, when the aged artist lives hidden in his villa in constant fear of Fernando VII, who has unleashed a reign of terror, torture, executions, and emigration of liberals that suggests the early Franco years. The play makes extensive use of effects of psychic participation or "immersion" that allow the spectators to perceive reality through the protagonist's perspective, a technique associated with Buero's name.[3] The audience shares the deafness that underscores Goya's sense of isolation since words spoken when he is on stage are inaudible. It also shares his terrifying hallucinations: meows, owl hoots, and voices of figures from the phantasmagoric *Pinturas negras* ("Black Paintings") on

---

3 On this topic, see Ricardo Doménech, *El teatro de Buero*; Luis Iglesias Feijoo, *La trayectoria dramática de Buero Vallejo* (Santiago de Compostela: Universidad de Santiago de Compostela, 1982); and Martha T. Halsey, *From Dictatorship to Democracy: The Recent Plays of Buero Vallejo* (Ottowa: Dovehouse, 1994).

the villa's walls. These paintings, which are projected and interpreted by Goya to his friends, show the irrational horrors and monstrous evil of Fernando's time – and, by analogy, Franco's – when reason slept and Spain was plunged into darkness. Buero, an art student and painter before the War, gives many of these paintings a historical and political interpretation. Like Buero's Velázquez, his stone-deaf and half-mad Goya is the conscience of Spain; he, too, paints the truth – just as Buero tells it in his theatre. The psychological Expressionism seen here and in several later plays had an important influence on other Spanish playwrights.

Some twenty-seven years after Buero's release from incarceration, he used his observations as a political prisoner for the basis of a play. *La Fundación*, premièred in 1974, is a key play in Buero's trajectory, not only for its extended use of the "immersion" effect, which turns the protagonist into the play's narrator, but also for the political ideology expressed. In no work of his are the blindness, self-deception, and alienation of postwar society more clearly seen. As the play starts, the action appears to occur in an elegant research center with a picture window opening onto a magnificent Turner landscape. At the end, the spectators find themselves in a prison cell and discover that the characters are not eminent writers and scientists but political prisoners. The audience, although not realizing it until near the end of the tragedy, sees reality through the eyes of Tomás, a young prisoner who, unable to face reality, creates an illusory world. His gradual acceptance of the truth is represented by changes in stage decor as the pleasant furnishings of the "Foundation" vanish to be replaced by the sordid trappings of a cell. When Tomás' fictitious world vanishes and reality emerges, Spanish viewers were to see their own country for the prison that it was under Franco. Buero's play constituted an attack upon political systems that deceive and enslave, but also an expression of hope for a day in which a dark reality may be transformed into the luminous landscape seen by Tomás. Tomás' cellmate, Asel – an author surrogate – tells Tomás that his landscape is true, that it cannot be destroyed even by prison bars. In the dialectical process depicted by the drama, the reality of the prison vanquishes the imaginary "Foundation." Nevertheless, the ideal represented by the luminous landscape remains. To reach this light, it is necessary to excavate the difficult tunnel planned by some of the prisoners. In a key dialogue, Asel speaks of exiting one prison only to enter another. No doubt thinking of the transition toward democracy, Buero explains, through Asel, the importance of each step, each political gain, each concession won from an authoritarian regime, as Spaniards journey toward freedom through a series of concentric prisons from which tunnels must be opened toward the light.

The play contains an important meditation on the legitimate scope of revolutionary violence. Buero's stance is clear. Given the power of the

"Foundation," historical violence or force employed to liberate individuals may be necessary. However, violence must never be gratuitous. A similar debate on the need to reform the revolution was to appear in Buero's very last play, *Misión al pueblo desierto* ("Mission to the Deserted Town," 1999). However, in this final work, portraying a cultural mission during the Civil War to rescue an El Greco painting, Buero totally rejects *all* violence, *all* war, returning to the pacifism of his early *Aventura en lo gris* ("Adventure in Grey"), written in 1949 but banned until 1963.

In 1976, Spaniards finally could see *La doble historia del doctor Valmy* ("The Double Case History of Dr. Valmy"). Buero had written the play in 1964 but refused to make certain changes mandated by the censors. Dr. Valmy, a psychiatrist, dictates to his secretary the story of a National Security policeman who becomes impotent after carrying out an order to castrate a political prisoner. The play's action is the recreation of his story. Even as he narrates the case history, the doctor is seen also observing or even participating in it. Moreover, his patients narrate their own stories to Valmy. Buero uses frames within frames, a theatrical *mise en abyme*. Two of Valmy's former patients inform the spectators that Valmy's story of police torture is false, or, at least, exaggerated. When the audience finally learns that these same patients – subjects of the first case history – had once interrupted the doctor to call him a liar as he was telling the policeman's story to an audience of fellow patients in his asylum, it becomes clear that these fellow patients are the play's spectators, and the theatre is the asylum. The implication is that if the play's spectators doubted the existence of torture in Spain, they were as insane as the two subjects of the first case history.

No image is so central to Buero's theatre as that of the prison. Buero's affinity for the ideas of enclosure, immurement, or entrapment reflected his own condition and that of others of his generation. The institution for the blind, the dark basement apartment, and Goya's hidden villa are all prisons. This Symbolism would continue in Buero's post-Franco plays – as two titles indicate: *Lázaro en el laberinto* ("Lazarus in the Labyrinth," 1989) and *Las trampas del azar* ("The Snares of Fate," 1994). However, to each closed space, there is usually opposed an open space, even though it may exist only in the protagonist's dreams, like the marvelous landscape seen by Tomás. Walls imply an exit, and Buero's purpose is to show the spectator this exit. There is always the potential for freedom. The dialectical structure of Buero's imagery reveals his tragic vision, which is never devoid of hope.

The opening of *Escuadra hacia la muerte* ("Condemned Squad," 1953), only four years after *Historia de una escalera*, marked the beginning of the theatrical career of Alfonso Sastre (1926–), whose theoretical writings on drama were to have a profound impact upon the new committed dramatists of the 1960s. In his book, *Drama y sociedad* ("Drama and Society," 1956), Sastre stressed the social and political function of theatre, emphasizing that it should lead to a prepolitical state of awareness that would result in action of the spectator's own choosing. Preferring agitation over dogmatism, he aimed at disturbing his audience.

Escuadra hacia la muerte, performed by a university group and shut down by the censors after only three performances, is an existential cry for freedom. Six soldiers from a suicide squadron await the enemy's advance in an isolated mountain cabin. Their brutal murder of the fanatical disciplinarian Corporal Goban results not in liberation but a new enslavement as they await the consequences of this action. Written under the threat of a third world war, the play reflected Sastre's disillusioned view of his own generation condemned to the slaughterhouse by a probable atomic conflict. The drama also represented a protest against the nationalist ideals of militarism and the mysticism of death promoted by the Franco régime.

La mordaza ("The Gag," 1954) constituted Sastre's first professional production. Using as point of departure a sensational murder case in Lurs, France, Sastre created the brutal and egocentric figure of Isiah Krapp who, after shooting in cold blood a man who threatened to expose atrocities he committed during the Second World War, imposes a "gag" of silence on his family. The parallel between the gag of fear and intimidation imposed by Krapp and that imposed by Franco was clear to critics and audience alike. Like *La mordaza*, other early plays depicted what Sastre viewed as the tragedy of an unjust social order.

En la red ("In the Net"), performed in 1961 by the Grupo de Teatro Realista ("Realistic Theatre Group") that Sastre had launched earlier, belongs to his dramas of revolution. *En la red* depicts a group of Frenchmen and Algerians united in the ideal of an independent Algeria as a police net slowly closes around them in the apartment where they hide. However, the characters could just as easily have been one of the cells of leftists still existing in Spain at that time, and the drama played in Moscow under the title *Madrid no duerme de noche* ("Madrid Does Not Sleep at Night"). Unities of time and place are tightly maintained and dramatic tension sustained to the end.

Sastre's continuing interest in Realism resulted four years later in a new book that was to be quite influential: *Anatomía del realismo* ("The Anatomy of Realism," 1965). Sastre recognized that Realism takes many forms but all of these, he stressed, must stand in opposition to the escapism of the bourgeois theatre, making the spectators aware of their own situation. The critical and socialist Realism that Sastre espoused came largely from the Marxist theory of the German playwright Bertolt Brecht (1898–1956), the German philosopher Friedrich Engels (1820–1895), and the Hungarian critic Georg Lukács (1885–1971).

Sastre gradually moved from Aristotelian concepts exemplified by his early plays to an epic theatre represented by *Guillermo Tell tiene los ojos tristes* ("Sad Are the Eyes of William Tell," 1962), and *Historia de una muñeca abandonada* ("Story of an Abandoned Doll," 1964), a children's play based on Brecht's *The Caucasian Chalk Circle* – two of Sastre's works performed most widely outside Spain. He next embraced "complex tragedies" such as *La sangre y la ceniza* ("Blood and Ash," 1977). In *La revolución y la crítica de la cultura* ("Revolution and the Critique of Culture," 1970), Sastre explained that his purpose was the creation of powerful revolutionary works that would produce a "complex" reaction embracing and surpassing both Aristotelian catharsis and Brechtian alienation – an effect he called the aesthetics of the "boomerang." Initial indifference would become shock as the drama's full impact hit the spectators only when the drama moved toward its conclusion.

La sangre y la ceniza, a play of some four hours' duration, deals with Miguel Servet, a Spanish physician and theologian persecuted for his revolutionary theory of blood's circulation and for his unitarian theology and burned at the stake in 1553. Deliberate anachronisms designed to produce a shock effect relate the events depicted to the twentieth century. A Nazi hymn, electric shock torture, loudspeakers, and other disconcerting historical anachronisms prevent the audience from being lulled into inattention.

Sastre's important influence on Spanish theatre derived from his essays, not his original plays, which were little staged in Spain although widely taught in literature courses in the United States.

In the early 1960s Sastre initiated an often bitter polemic with Buero on the correct stance of the committed writer in times of censorship, proclaiming that silence was preferable to the literary conventions and masks often used by Buero. Quoting Sartre, the latter responded that committed writers must live their situation and act upon their circumstances, struggling and taking the risk of being censored, striving to make "possible" a theatre that is seemingly "impossible" and avoiding unnecessary provocations that might make "impossible" a theatre that would otherwise be "possible." Buero thus put results over empty gestures and heroic stances, maintaining that playwrights had a duty to make their voices heard, to write plays that had the possibility of being performed.[4] Like Mariano José de Larra, the protagonist of his future play, *La detonación* ("The Shot," 1977), Buero subtly mocked the censors, speaking the truth without avoiding controversial and seemingly – but only seemingly – "impossible" subjects that did not exclude police torture of political prisoners

---

[4] On this polemic, see *Documentación sobre el teatro español contemporáneo.* Ed. Luciano García Lorenzo (Madrid: SGFL, 1981).

(in *The Foundation*). "Posibilismo" in theatre as in politics was Buero's credo, from his youth to his death in 2000. This polemic, which came to be known as the "posibilismo–imposibilismo" debate, was revived by Arrabal in 1975.

The early 1960s, when censorship was temporarily relaxed, saw the emergence of a new generation of playwrights whose vision of Spain was decidedly critical: Lauro Olmo (1923–1994), José Martín Recuerda (1925–), José María Rodríguez Méndez (1925–), and Carlos Muñiz (1927–1994). Although their approaches to theatre varied considerably, these authors came to be known as the "Realistic Generation." The term "Realism" had evolved into an ethical consideration of a dramatist's attitude toward reality and included any theatre supporting a critical, that is, open or dialectical vision of society. Adapting the popular Realism of the brief farce or *sainete*, with its vivid, natural dialogue, music, dance, and local color, to their social thematics, they emphasized the need for a genuinely popular theatre representative of, and directed to, all of society, rather than the theatre-going middle class.

The success of Lauro Olmo's *La camisa* ("The Shirt," 1962), was phenomenal. Originally scheduled for a single performance, it enjoyed two long runs in Madrid and won important awards. Like Buero's *Hoy es fiesta* ("Today's a Holiday," 1956), it is about Spain's poor and their lost dreams and illusions. However, its social criticism surpassed anything previously seen in Spanish theatre. Olmo's setting was the shanty-towns on Madrid's outskirts with their one-room *chabolas* or hovels. Olmo treats two problems of the 1960s: unemployment and the emigration of Spanish workers to find jobs in the more industrialized nations of northern Europe. Just as Buero's tenement dwellers of *Hoy es fiesta* pin their hopes on the lottery, Olmo's characters dream of winning the football pools or of emigrating. The dilemma of whether it was better to remain in their own country, where they firmly believed they had a right to work, or leave for exile was a problem experienced by shanty-town dwellers like Juan in *La camisa* and intellectuals alike. Juan's conviction that it is in Spain where the real solution must be found reflects the personal stance of Olmo, Buero, and other committed dramatists, who refused to leave Spain. Here as in subsequent plays, Olmo gave popular form to a new, implacably Realistic and radically critical vision of Spanish society of the 1960s.

Olmo's play was performed in Frankfurt, Geneva, Buenos Aires, São Paulo, and other cities, sometimes by professional companies in translation but often in the original by workers who had emigrated from Spain. More than any other author of his time, Olmo attempted to create a theatre not only representative of, but directed to, the Spanish working class. His knowledge of the plight of Spain's poor was firsthand: the old white shirt from the flea market that Juan wears in his vain attempt to find work was Olmo's own. In several subsequent plays Olmo focused on the problems of working-class women.

The brief farces that Olmo began to write in 1965 have been considered his most original works. His collection, *El cuarto poder* ("The Fourth Estate"), which he termed a "tragicomic kaleidoscope," deals with the power of the press and its control of the news. Here the farcical and Expressionistic elements present to a limited degree in his early Naturalist plays come to the forefront. Olmo considered the collection an open-ended repertory in which the composition could be constantly varied, a "living newspaper" that could replace his own pieces with those of other playwrights.

An important facet of Olmo's work in the Franco period was his theatre for children, written with his wife, Pilar Enciso. Inspired by tales from the *Panchatantra*, Aesop, and La Fontaine, all have a clear social message. Through lively action, song and dance, humor and poetry, mime and imaginative visual effects, they show how, through solidarity, the oppressed can win their freedom. *Asamblea general* ("General Meeting", 1968) has become a children's classic and is frequently performed internationally.

Olmo's history play, *Pablo Iglesias*, which would open in 1984, honors the founder of Spain's socialist party, a mythic figure admired for his ethics in politics and his support for educating the populace for political democracy. During a long flashback, Iglesias answers a reporter's questions while awaiting the results of the 1910 elections that were to make him Spain's first proletarian congressman. Scanning some sixty years of Spanish history, Olmo's heartfelt tribute to Iglesias includes passages from the latter's own writings, as well as music and poetry. The socialists in power showed little interest in the production – perhaps, as suggested by some reviewers, because it reminded them of their humble origins. One of the most beloved figures in Spain's theatre world, Olmo would die in 1994. Of all the playwrights of his generation he had been the one most adversely affected by government censorship.

Martín Recuerda's plays are set in the towns and villages of his native Andalusia, where for years he directed the theatre of the University of Granada, winning considerable acclaim. *Las salvajes en Puente San Gil* ("The Savages in Puente San Gil," 1963) is a violent and frenzied play that builds upon a series of physical confrontations. Based on a true story, the play depicts a company of chorus girls who arrive at a provincial town to put on a review only to be denounced to Church leaders, attacked brutally by village youths, and used by civil authorities to satisfy their aggressive and ill-repressed sexuality. However, as the actresses are led off by the police, they refuse to be silenced, raising their voices defiantly in a protest song. Like Lorca, Recuerda excels in the creation of female characters, both individual and collective. The work provoked a scandal at its opening, but a popular movie version of it was made in the 1960s and the play returned to the stage, in 1985, some twenty-five years after its polemical première, touring Spain and then enjoying a highly successful Madrid revival.

The opening of Martín Recuerda's *Las arrecogías del beaterio de Santa María Egipciaca* ("The Inmates of the Convent of Saint Mary Egyptian"), in 1977, represented one of the most significant moments in the social and cultural history of post-Civil-War Spain. Subtitled "A Spanish Fiesta in Two Parts," it presents the last days in the life of Mariana Pineda, the Grenadine martyr for freedom in nineteenth-century Spain. As a chorus of young seamstresses wander throughout the theatre singing and dancing, stage and house merge and the 1830s become the 1970s. Suspecting that the convent where Mariana was imprisoned, founded as a reformatory for "immoral" women, was used to hold those of liberal sympathies, Martín Recuerda invents an ensemble of common, uneducated women, anonymous martyrs whose stories are no less significant than hers. At one key moment, the playwright merges the fate of Mariana and her sister prisoners with the audience's. As prisoners in the convent sing of their hopes for rescue, other actors dance outside in the streets of Granada, and the seamstresses sing and dance in the theatre aisles. Then, when Mariana and the other inmates, still singing, descend from the stage to the house aisles, the entire theatre becomes a prison. The play evinces Recuerda's concept of theatre as festival as well as the innovative use of stage space that reflects his considerable experience as director. The example of Mariana, who chooses death rather than name the other conspirators against the despotic Fernando VII, and of her sister prisoners, was relevant to 1977, when members of the Basque terrorist group, ETA, awaited trial in Spain's prisons. This relevance became explicit when the actress who played Mariana addressed the audience, explaining that, had the amnesty later proclaimed been granted in time, Mariana and many like her would have been spared. With applause clearly solicited from the stage, the play became a cry for amnesty and freedom. The première of the play, banned in 1970, marked the virtual end to almost four decades of government censorship of the theatre. Directed by the innovative Adolfo Marsillach, the work met with notable critical and commercial success and was revived in 1978.

The series of high-profile productions of plays by the Realists in the late 1970s and early 1980s, after years of censorship, included the opening of Martín Recuerda's *El engañao* ("The Dupe"), written in 1972. Premièred in 1982, the play brings to the stage Juan de Dios and the wounded soldiers and deserters he shelters in his hospital – victims of the foreign policy of Charles V. Recuerda demythifies the Empire, portraying the poverty of a people bled dry to finance ruinous religious wars. His protagonist is a well-known saint associated with Granada, but equally important are the common people with whom the character identifies: patients, co-workers, and prostitutes who support his hospital. The recitation of verses from Isaiah proclaiming Yahweh's judgment on the wealthy and powerful, as well as chants from the Psalms by choruses of patients and workers, form an integral part of the celebration, contrasting with popular Andalusian songs. Recuerda brings together Juan and another controversial figure, Juana la Loca, who, although judged insane, is the one best able to understand the saint. Juana's vitality and rebellion are symbolized by the carnations she wears. She suggests that Spain has always been divided into two camps: those who love freedom and those who do not, those who wear crowns and those who prefer flowers. Juan is carried off dying after his hospital is sacked; however, the ideals of the man deceived at times even by his co-workers survive. The abuse of power Recuerda attacks is symbolized by the imperial banners torn down at the end.

Las conversiones ("The Conversions"), written in 1974–1978, and premièred in 1983 with the title *Carnaval de un reino* ("Carnival of a Kingdom"), completes Recuerda's trilogy of history plays. Set in fifteenth-century Castile during the persecutions of Jews that inspired terror throughout the central plains, the work dramatizes the possible youth of Celestina. The action occurs in the tanneries outside Salamanca, and the play is a homage to that city, where Recuerda headed the university's theatre department for many years. The play evinces all of the creativity of its author, including the use of choral characters. A chorus of Jews, seated on the tannery floor, incessantly beats stones and drums in a violent rhythm as the spectacle opens and later sings, dances, and metamorphoses into Portuguese revolutionaries, prostitutes from the battlefields, witches and evil spirits, ecclesiastical and royal personages.

The dramatist who portrays Franco's Spain with the most acerbity is Rodríguez Méndez. *Los inocentes de la Moncloa* ("The Innocents of Moncloa," 1961), a key work of his generation, starts as a conventional picture of Spanish student life, but soon becomes a denunciation of the *oposiciones* or public examinations required to obtain professional positions that grant unique status and privileges for life, and, more importantly, of an entire way of life based on dehumanizing competition. Based upon a true story, the play shows how, under the pressure of preparing for the contest, José Luis and other students let a new arrival in the rooming-house die almost unheeded. José Luis' acceptance of the position he wins signifies the triumph of an unjust system.

Rodríguez Méndez' most important plays are popular chronicles that present history as seen through the eyes of its victims. These popular chronicles present a succession of sketches, each of which is significant in

itself. *Bodas que fueron famosas del Pingajo y la Fandanga* ("The Famous
Day When Pingajo and Fandanga Got Wed" [English title by Michael
Thompson]), chosen to open Madrid's newly established Centro
Dramático Nacional, in 1978, had been written in 1965 but banned for
its scenes ridiculing the army, a sacred institution in Franco's Spain. The
play, set in a Madrid shanty-town of 1898, when impoverished and embit-
tered masses of workers and peasants provided cannon fodder for colonial
wars in Cuba and Morocco, chronicles the exploits of a ragged scarecrow
draftee just back from the war in Cuba, and his innocent child bride.
When Pingajo robs the Casino to pay for a splendid wedding feast – the
only way he can command respect in a hostile world – he is executed.

The *zarzuela* – Spain's light opera – and *sainete* are the source of the
local color of the most picturesque of the eight scenes in *Bodas*: the animated sketch of the Retiro Park on a Sunday afternoon and, especially,
of the wedding feast with tables of paellas and wineskins set up in the
street, members of the wedding party decked out in finery bought with
the stolen money, and popular dances. This colorful fresco soon darkens
as the police arrive, fix the guests in their gunsights, and arrest Pingajo
and his accomplices. The bitter epilogue recalls Valle-Inclán's *esperpentos*
or grotesque caricatures as Pingajo is shot, propped up lopsidedly to keep
him from fainting with fear and with a limp cigarette dangling from his
mouth. His body wrapped in a tattered flag – symbol of a debased Spain –
he represents the illiterate and degraded populace of 1898. In 1988 the
play was co-produced in Lima by Spain's Instituto Nacional de Artes
Escénicas y Música ("National Institute of Scenic Arts and Music") and
a Peruvian company.

Rodríguez Méndez' plays often incorporate elements of Spain's popular culture and language. *Historia de unos cuantos* ("Anybody's History,"
1976), one of the first plays of the Realists staged after Franco's death,
depicts ten moments in Spain's history as seen through the eyes of characters taken from the *zarzuela*.

Flor de Otoño ("Autumn Flower"), written in 1972 and reflecting
Rodríguez Méndez's firsthand knowledge of Barcelona, where he spent
many years, opened in 1982. *Flor de Otoño* had been the first choice
of the Centro Dramático Nacional, which finally chose to stage *Bodas*
since the former had previously been made into a film. Inspired by a
picture from an old chronicle of a transvestite singer from Barcelona's
red-light district who was also an anarchist gunman, the play recreates Barcelona of the 1930s, from the respectable middle-class society
to which the protagonist belongs, to the Barrio Chino where he performs
under his alias, to the workers' cooperatives. After assaulting the Fort
of Ataranzanas to obtain arms and leading an aborted anarchist revolution, the singer and his companions are executed before the walls of the
Military Prison of Montjuich. Rodríguez Méndez's chronicles, with their

succession of popular sketches and narrative structure, represented a new dramatic model in post-Civil-War Spain that owed much to Valle-Inclán and Brecht.

Rodríguez Méndez later authored dramatic homages to several figures from Spain's Golden Age of letters. In 1994, he would win the Premio Nacional de Literatura Dramática for *El pájaro solitario* ("The Solitary Bird"), written in 1975, portraying Juan de la Cruz (John of the Cross) who escapes his jailers and is befriended by prostitutes and ruffians who find him hiding in the plaza and are strangely touched by his poetry. Rodríguez Méndez stresses the popular spirit and independence of the subjects of his homages, "reclaiming" these classic figures from Francoist writers who distorted and manipulated them for their own purposes. He is also the author of several controversial books of theatre criticism reflecting the bitter experiences of his generation.

Carlos Muñiz's best-known play is *El tintero* ("The Inkwell," 1961), an Expressionistic tragicomedy about the dehumanization of modern life. Crock, an office worker, rebels against a bureaucratic order that destroys non-conformists. He is denounced by three fellow penpushers: Pim, Pam, and Pum, who speak and act in unison, absurdly supporting with their clichés the regulations of the boss. When Crock is fired for his failure to conform, his superiors toast his dismissal by drinking from their inkwells. Muñiz's tragicomedy approaches the theatre of the absurd and represents a link between the Realist generation and the Avant-Garde. It has been widely performed outside Spain.

When Antonio Gala's *Los verdes campos del Edén* ("The Green Fields of Eden") opened in 1963, critics associated the author with the Realistic generation because the play portrayed the plight of several disinherited persons who took shelter in a cemetery crypt. There they find the happiness denied them by society. However, Gala's muted criticism – largely overlooked by middle-class audiences – differed from the harsh protest of the Realists.

The 1960s that gave rise to the Realistic generation also marked the beginnings of a Symbolist generation that adopted a different aesthetic as the vehicle for socio-political protest. Known as the "New Authors," many of its members maintained ties with independent theatre groups influenced by Artaud and the European vanguard. The American George Wellwarth introduced some of these playwrights in United States' colleges and universities where they became more widely known and staged than in Spain. In his anthology, *Spanish Underground Drama*, he emphasized the importance of three: José Ruibal, Antonio Martínez Ballesteros, and José María Bellido.[5] These "underground" playwrights communicated

---

5 George Wellwarth, *Spanish Underground Drama* (State College, PA: the Pennsylvania State University Press, 1972).

through parable and allegory, using characters that were prototypical. Abstract and dehumanized, their works spoke in a sort of code that the audience had to decipher.

After the death of Franco, when authors were no longer muzzled, this type of play lost much of its appeal. In effect, critics were divided in their evaluation of the playwrights that Wellwarth dubbed "underground" – ignoring the fact that the Realists, too, were silenced by censorship. In his influential *Historia del teatro español: Siglo XX*, Francisco Ruiz Ramón stressed the importance of the Realists and treated the "underground" group less than favorably.[6] A polemic developed and Rodríguez Méndez wrote a witty essay, "Las paradojas de 'Mister W,'" satirizing an American who thought he had discovered another "Golden Age" of playwrights unrecognized in their own country.[7]

José Ruibal's *El hombre y la mosca* ("The Man and the Fly"), written in 1969 and considered by many the most representative work of the "underground" group, is a political parable about Power. After ruling an unnamed country for years, the Man creates a double, molded to his physical and ideological image, to continue his dictatorship without anyone detecting the change. Isolated from the world, the two inhabit a huge dome of glass panels constructed on skeletons of the Man's enemies. When the latter dies, the double rules, guided by the voices of the institutions established by his predecessor. However, the double proves unable to inspire fear in the lowly Fly that alights one day on the outside of the fragile glass. Trying to kill it, he breaks the dome – vulnerable only from the inside – and the structure collapses. Ruibal's subject was the perpetuation of the Franco régime and how to destroy it. While the play was read widely in published form, its long-delayed Spanish première inspired little interest in 1982.

Las hermanas de Búfalo Bill ("Buffalo Bill's Sisters") by Manuel Martínez Medeiro (1937–) was a box-office success, in part because its 1975 première coincided unexpectedly with Franco's death. An aging, gun-toting cowboy (a surrogate for the dictator) tyrannizes his maiden sisters (the national household), keeping them in protective chains so they cannot be seduced by forbidden pleasures of sex. As in other plays by New Authors, sexual freedom is a metaphor for political freedom. One day he returns from maneuvers to defend his house with his chest fatally pierced by an arrow. Big Brother's ghost, however, returns to haunt his household. Martínez Medeiro's work, like Ruibal's, reflects the often-voiced fear of the immortality of Franco's régime. (Fernando Vizcaino Casas'

---

[6] Francisco Ruiz Ramón, *Historia del teatro español. Siglo xx* (2nd. edn. Madrid: Cátedra, 1975).

[7] José María Rodríguez Méndez, "Las paradojas de 'Mister W.'" In *Comentarios impertinentes sobre el teatro español* (Barcelona: Península, 1972).

novel about Franco, *Y al tercer año resucitó* ["And the Third Year He Came Back to Life"] became a best-seller of 1978.)

The Centro Dramático Nacional, which had produced Rodríguez Méndez's *Bodas*, also selected two of the best plays of the New Authors in 1979–1980, pieces whose interest depended on highly creative set design and visual effects: Luis Riaza's *Retrato de dama con perrito* ("Portrait of Lady with Lapdog") and Luis Matilla's two short pieces included in *Ejercicios para equilibristas* ("Exercises for Tight-rope Walkers"). *El Observador* ("The Observer"), one of the latter pieces, also staged in 1980 in New York as part of the program "Spain: Avant-garde Theatre 1980," deals with the loss of personal freedom experienced by Él ("He") and Ella ("She"), whose bedroom is violated by the silent and mysterious Observer, in a futuristic nightmare they cannot escape. The Expressionistic play suggests the control exercised by the state.

Retrato de dama con perrito is a Genet-style metaplay. Its impact is marvelously visual, spectacular, and ceremonial. The stage features an upper space that is the mezzanine of a faded *belle-époque* hotel – the domain of Power – and a lower space that is the service area – the domain of Power's victims. Riaza (1925–) uses transvestism, doubling, and life-size puppets or rag dolls in an elaborate ritual of the death of the aged Lady (Power) and the assumption of her position by her successor. Benito, the hotel manager, grotesquely dressed as a woman, and the chambermaid he tyrannizes, clothed in a Little Lord Fauntleroy suit, serve as doubles of the aged Lady and the Adolescent Artist she victimizes. Each pair is an inverted image of the other. The climax of the ritual is the multiplication and glorification of the image of Lady, that is, of Power, by the macabre puppets all dressed as she is and identically made up. Reflected in a series of mirrors, they create a cemetery-like assembly of mummified figures. The elaborate ceremony ends as Benito kills Lady then dons her dress and picture hat, assuming her identity as Power perpetuates itself. Despite a memorable production and strong critical acclaim, the play was unsuccessful with a public that preferred plays like *Las arrecogías* and *Bodas*. Even Fernando Arrabal, Spain's best-known Avant-Garde playwright, whose residence in France gave him access to theatres around the world, remained controversial in his own country.

Within Spain the most successful proponent of anti-Realistic, non-representational theatre was unquestionably Francisco Nieva (1929–) who, after years in France, returned in the late 1960s to become a distinguished set designer. He differs from the New Authors in the Surrealistic vein of his plays and his magical use of language. His "Teatro Furioso" ("Furious Theatre") is exemplified by *La carroza de plomo candente* ("The Carriage of White-Hot Lead") and the apocalyptical *Coronada y el toro* ("Coronada and the Bull"). The latter, written in 1973 but unperformed until 1982, attacks "Black Spain," subverting established values, exalting freedom – both sexual and political – and celebrating the erotic. Nieva combats *machismo* by portraying its victims: Coronada, the daughter of the mayor Zebedeo, who keeps her chained to preserve her honor, and Marauña, the unwilling bullfighter forced to fight in the most *macho* of rituals. El Hombre-Monja de la Orden Entreverada, the bearded "Nun-Man of the Mixed-Up Order," who suddenly appears, in female dress, through the bullpen to rescue the oppressed, suggests the possibility of a new era of freedom. Buried by order of Zebedeo, he is resurrected. Carried on the back of a peaceful white bull covered with flowers, he ascends through the sky together with the former's victims. Nieva's originality is unmatched by that of any other post-Civil-War Spanish playwright.

The only Catalan to become well-known in Madrid theatre of the Franco era was Jaime Salom (1925–), who wrote in Castilian. His melodramatic *La casa de las Chivas* ("The House of the 'Chivas,'" 1969), portraying life behind the Republican lines outside Barcelona during the Civil War, proved enormously popular. This decidedly non-political play focused on the human side of Republican adherents lodged in the house of the two daughters of a notorious prostitute.

The Franco years saw the work of important playwrights for whom theatre was a vehicle not only for reflecting reality but also for showing it as changeable. They represented the "other" Spain that suffered the restraints imposed by a triumphalist and exclusionist Francoist culture, an "inner" exile that lasted almost four decades. These years witnessed the emergence of Realists and cultivators of the Vanguard whose theatre stood in dialectical opposition to the régime and for whom writing usually meant speaking "against" much of a potential audience. An important theorist, Alfonso Sastre, wrote books whose influence proved substantial. However, the towering achievement was the theatre of Buero, who would win Spain's most prestigious literary award, the Premio Cervantes, in 1986. His plays gave the lie to the myth that little of value could be produced under a repressive régime, that the only alternative for the committed writer was exile or silence. Doménech best explains the importance of Buero's theatre, when he states, speaking of the latter's time, that without him, "no se explicaría el teatro español ni la sociedad española de este tiempo, porque Buero se ha erigido en conciencia de ésta a través de aquél" ("it is impossible to explain Spanish theatre or Spanish society of this time because Buero rose to become the conscience of the latter by way of the former").[8]

---

[8] Ricardo Doménech, "Buero Vallejo, aquí y ahora." In *Antonio Buero Vallejo: Premio Miguel de Cervantes (1986)* (Madrid: Biblioteca Nacional, 1987), pp. 9–10.

51

Film and censorship under Franco, 1937–1975

MARVIN D'LUGO

Film censorship existed in Spain long before the Nationalist government in Burgos established the first Junta Superior de Censura Cinematográfica ("Supreme Film Censorship Board") in 1937. The earliest controls on film exhibition date back to 1913 when the Civil Governor of Barcelona denied public exhibition rights to films that offended public morality. In 1931, the Second Republic formalized its own approach to film exhibition by decentralizing the censorship activity and giving provincial governors broad authority to determine which films could or could not be shown.[1]

Continuing what was by then a decades-old tradition of censorship and suppression of motion pictures, a ministerial order of 2 November 1938 expanded Francoist censorship bureaucracy by authorizing a companion Comisión Nacional de Cinematografía ("National Commission on Film") to the Junta Superior it had established the year before. Whereas the Junta Superior had jurisdiction to review newsreels and documentaries produced by the government, the new board reviewed commercially produced fiction films prior to their distribution. The advent of this elaborate censorship machinery clearly reflected the propagandistic potential that Franco and his Minister of the Interior, Ramón Serrano Suñer, saw in motion pictures.[2] From the start, the Burgos government recognized the need to counter the propaganda campaign in documentaries and newsreels already deftly managed by their Republican adversaries. Now, however, the arrangement for the twin censorship board – the Junta Superior de Censura and the Comisión Nacional – suggested that motion pictures were assuming a more prominent ideological position in the Francoists' design for postwar Spain.

Clearly, they saw motion pictures as an important form of mass communication, rivaling radio and, in a country with a high degree of illiteracy, obviously surpassing newspapers. Unlike other mass media, however, which could be easily censored or suppressed in a single act, film posed multiple problems. Because motion pictures were attractive commercial

---

[1] Juan Antonio Martínez-Bretón, *Libertad de expresión cinematográfica durante la II República Española (1931–1936)* (Madrid: Editorial Fragua, 2000), pp. 55–56.

[2] Román Gubern, *La censura: función política y ordenamiento jurídico bajo el franquismo (1936–1975)* (Barcelona: Península, 1981), p. 26.

commodities that had great popular appeal, they could not be easily suppressed by administrative fiat. Yet, to censor parts of films posed technical problems, involving editing out of specific scenes or images, and the manipulation of the soundtrack through dubbing, which occurred in both foreign and Spanish films. By 1940, surveillance of domestic films was expanded to include "censura previa"("prior censorship") – review of scripts prior to shooting films, as well as review of completed films before their exhibition.

The 1938 ministerial edict was simple and emphatic: the censorship commission was to examine each film and issue a signed authorization for public exhibition.[3] The objective of such censorship review was to eliminate politically and morally offensive material from Spanish movie screens. By 1940 film surveillance would be expanded to include the suppression of even publicity references to Hollywood actors who had publicly supported the Republic, such as Charlie Chaplin, James Cagney, Joan Crawford, Bing Crosby, and Bette Davis.

In Catholic Spain, it was a commonplace to perceive motion pictures as sinful since the decisive center of the international film industry was Hollywood, "corruptor de almas y compañero de viaje de la revolución marxista" ("corruptor of souls and fellow traveler in the Marxist Revolution").[4] In fact, from its inception, the censorship process provided a privileged voice for Church representatives. The censorship boards decreed by the 1938 edict were comprised of representatives of the Falange Party, the army, and the Church.

Importantly, no guidelines were provided to inform the commissions on the appropriateness of the filmed material. It soon became clear that the absence of formal criteria for censorship review could create havoc for producers. Two incidents from the early postwar years demonstrate the problem: Enrique del Campo's naval epic, *El Crucero Baleares* ("The Cruiser *Baleares*," 1941), after a gala première, was removed from circulation owing to the displeasure of navy officials. The following year, a similar fate awaited Carlos Arévalo's *Rojo y negro* ("The Red and the Black") due to the negative reaction of influential military officers. Such sporadic pressures by some officials outside the established censorship channels, combined with the absence of formal censorship norms and the financial risk inherent in any production, led script writers and directors to improvise their own, usually ultra-conservative, version of Francoist ideology and mythology, decisively moving away from material that might offend the military. This kind of self-censorship by the industry worked to

---

[3] Manuel Abellán, *Censura y creación literaria de España (1939–1976)* (Barcelona: Península, 1980), p. 23.
[4] Rosa Álvarez Berciano and Ramón Sala Noguer, *El cine en la zona nacional 1936–1939* (Bilbao: Ediciones Mensajero, 2000), p. 20.

the government's advantage since it effectively made producers, directors, and other film professionals accomplices to the censorship process.

Following the model of fascist Italy, a 1941 Ministerio de Comercio (Commerce Ministry) order called for the imposition of Castilian as the only language permitted for motion pictures shown in Spain. *Doblaje* ("dubbing"), according to the order, could only be done in Spain and by Spaniards, and thus quickly became a wholesale form of censorship, since it was an efficient way to cleanse any ideologically or morally offensive dialogue from films. In addition to these increasingly more elaborate censorship tactics, a film classification policy was established, awarding subsidies for films deemed of "Interés Nacional" ("National Interest"). This provided a financial incentive for the industry to invent narrative rationales and mythology for the Francoist ideology.

With the Axis defeat in the Second World War, the formal censorship administration was reshaped under the jurisdiction of the Ministerio de Educación Nacional ("Ministry of National Education") and given the innocuous name of Junta Superior de Ordenación Cinematográfica ("Supreme Board for Film Regulation"). The Board was to include eleven members, ten designated by the administration and a special representative of the Spanish Church, the latter being the only member of the board with absolute veto power.[5] Although the Junta would regularly excise political dialogue from foreign films, as was the case with the version of *Casablanca* approved for distribution in 1946, the ecclesiastical presence signaled a shift to the new center of censorial activity: the surveillance of morality and the suppression of any sexually suggestive behavior on screen.[6] Spanish producers adjusted to the implicit moral censorship of this new arrangement with little difficulty. The real problem, however, were the foreign films that were gaining increasing presence in Spain. Censorial questions were raised in films ranging from the Hollywood production, *Gilda* (1947), with Rita Hayworth's legendary striptease, to Vittorio De Sica's Neo-Realist film, *The Bicycle Thief* (1948), for which censors imposed their own optimistic voice-over to accompany the final images in order to soften the film's brutal depiction of proletarian life. This kind of tampering prefigured the censors' more active and creative engagement in film production in the coming decade.

After years of being treated as an international pariah, the régime attained diplomatic "normalization" during the 1950s. Because of his strong anti-communist stance, Franco was now viewed as a useful Cold War partner and the USA signed a bilateral treaty with Spain in 1952. The

---

[5] *Diccionario del cine español*. Ed. José Luis Borau (Madrid: Alianza Editorial, Academia de las Artes y las Ciencias Cinematográficas de España, y Fundación Autor, 1998), p. 206.

[6] Alejandro Ávila, *La censura del doblaje cinematográfico en España* (Barcelona: Editorial Cims, 1997), pp. 29–30.

following year, a Concordat with the Vatican helped legitimize Spain's status as an influential Catholic country. Finally, in 1955 Spain became a member of the United Nations. This diplomatic repositioning coincided with efforts in the domestic sphere to modernize the national economy. These included the strategic transformation during the 1950s from a pre-dominantly rural into a progressively more industrial economy and the expansion of foreign tourism as one of the country's principal industries. To further those economic goals, the Ministerio de Información y Turismo (Ministry of Information and Tourism) was created in 1951. Over the next two decades it would be the administrative entity responsible for film censorship. Ultra-conservative Gabriel Arias Salgado was named the first Ministro de Información ("Minister of Information"). Joining him as head of the Ministry's Dirección General de Cinematografía y Teatro ("Office of Film and Theatre Management") was former Falangist, José María García Escudero, who would be the first of a succession of five men to hold the politically volatile appointment over the next decade. García Escudero's tenure was brief, as he was pressured to resign in a matter of months as a result of criticism of his defense of *Surcos* ("Furrows," 1951), a film by José Antonio Nieves-Conde that took a harsh look at the ordeal of a provincial family trying to make a better life in Madrid. The *Surcos* débâcle pointed up the administration's contradictory poli-cies regarding motion pictures. While García Escudero promoted *Surcos* for the "National Interest" award, the censorship commission was busy ordering cuts in scenes that appeared to criticize the régime's policies and Spanish Catholic morality. They also ordered a revised ending to the film, one depicting the family's optimistic return to the countryside.

Re-editing was not an uncommon form of censorship of the period, nor was retouching the dubbed soundtrack of foreign-language films in order to alter dialogue that might prove offensive to Spanish morality. Perhaps the most notorious example of this process was John Ford's *Mogambo* (1953), in which the dialogue was changed to avoid the depiction of an adulterous affair. Turning a married couple into brother and sister had the absurd effect of substituting adultery with an incestuous relation between the film's star, Grace Kelly, and the supporting actor playing her husband.[7]

As Spain became involved in a number of international co-productions during the 1950s, a way was devised to circumvent the censors' zeal through what was commonly known as "dobles versiones" (double ver-sions),[8] one version for Spanish distribution, and one for international markets. The practice was brought to public attention through the scan-dal that surrounded the Spanish–British co-production of Terence Young's

---

[7] Ávila, *La censura del doblaje*, pp. 77–78.   [8] Gubern, *La censura*, p. 130.

That Lady (translated as "La princesa de Eboli," 1954) in which a highly censored version of the film circulated in Spain while the "original" version was shown in international markets.

During the 1950s an open generational conflict emerged around the issue of film censorship, as young filmmakers, recent graduates of the National Film School, were becoming increasingly frustrated by the arbitrariness of the régime's censorial politics. Promising newcomers, like Juan Antonio Bardem and Luis García Berlanga, had to contend with extensive script prohibitions and post-production cuts in their films throughout the 1950s. At a meeting sponsored by the University of Salamanca Film Club in May of 1955, members of the film community denounced the censorship system and the dire state of the Spanish film industry. Rather than calling for its elimination, however, even the young firebrand, Bardem, pleaded only for the administration to "rationalize" film censorship by publishing the norms against which films would be judged.

The "Conversaciones de Salamanca" (the so-called "Salamanca Conversations") suggested some of the pent-up frustration that censorship had created in the film industry. The full extent of the problem was just beginning to become apparent. It eventually became a public secret in the scandal provoked by Luis Buñuel's *Viridiana* (1961), in which the incompetence of the censors was exposed. Having passed through all the appropriate bureaucratic reviews, *Viridiana* was presented at the Cannes Film Festival as the official Spanish entry. It went on to win the coveted Palme d'Or only to be denounced as blasphemous by the Vatican newspaper, *L'Osservatore Romano*. The Spanish government quickly banned the film, and any mention of *Viridiana* or Buñuel in the Spanish press was prohibited. Through events such as these the theme of censorship became part of a public debate to the point that the film journal *Nuestro Cine* ("Our Cinema") even published a poll of members of the film industry and others expressing their views on the subject.

Owing to increased civil unrest, there was a cabinet reshuffling in 1962, which brought Manuel Fraga Iribarne into the Ministerio de Información y Turismo ("Ministry of Information and Tourism"). Considerably more liberal and pragmatic than Arias Salgado, Fraga was one of the principal strategists of Spain's economic modernization. He returned García Escudero to the directorship of the film section and supported the latter's moves to revive the industry. Among the notable achievements of García Escudero's second tenure was the publication in February of 1963 of the Ministry's "Normas de Censura Cinematográfica" ("Film Censorship Norms"). Fashioned after the US Hays Code (1931), the norms were an effort to legitimize film censorship by rationalizing the censorial activity. Other liberal changes included the replacement of the old film classification scheme's propagandistic "National Interest" category with an

"Interés Especial" ("Special Interest") subsidy for films of artistic merit. This was a way for the administration to support the efforts of promising first-time directors. To create a zone of tolerance for the exhibition of more liberal cinema, a 1967 ministerial order created the category of "salas de arte y ensayo" (art houses or experimental and art film screening rooms), small movie houses of no more than 500-seat capacity in provincial capitals and other cities with populations of more than 50,000. These theatres showed recent films from the incipient "Nuevo Cine Español" ("New Spanish Cinema") now promoted by the administration, and, for the first time since the Civil War, foreign-language films with Spanish subtitles.

Despite the appearance of a radical shift in the film administration's approach to censorship, however, film censors remained resolute in their approach to particular films. Anti-establishment directors, like Bardem and Berlanga, continued to struggle with the censors. So much of Berlanga's *Los jueves, milagro* ("Every Thursday a Miracle," 1957) was ordered revised before a shooting license was approved that the director proposed giving screen credit to one of the censors as script writer. Younger filmmakers were beginning to experience comparable problems. Miguel Picazo, the promising director of *La tía Tula* ("Aunt Tula," 1964), complained that censorial "suggestions" reduced that film's polemical force by more than half.[9] A similar fate awaited debut films by young directors, such as Mario Camus' *Los farsantes* ("The Actors," 1963), Francisco Regueiro's *El buen amor* ("Good Love," 1963), and Vicente Aranda's *Brillante porvenir* ("A Brilliant Future," 1964).

One ray of hope appeared in the mid 1960s in the person of the enterprising producer Elías Querejeta, who sought a productive engagement with the censors. In his first collaboration with Carlos Saura, Querejeta assiduously engaged the censors in debates over script revisions for *La caza* ("The Hunt," 1965). Saura later described for interviewers some of the positive effects of that previously unheard-of confrontation with censorship officials. For instance, all direct reference to the Civil War was prohibited, so that characters could only speak of "the war," thus adding additional symbolic weight to the story. For Querejeta over the next decade, active engagement and dialogue with the censors became a strategy that was to bear positive results, not only in the Saura films he produced, but also in works by Víctor Erice (*El espíritu de la colmena* ["Spirit of the Beehive," 1973]), Manuel Gutiérrez Aragón (*Habla mudita* ["Speak, Little Dumb Girl," 1971]), and Antonio Eceiza (*Las secretas intenciones* ["Secret Intentions," 1969]).

---

[9] Román Gubern and Domènec Font, *Un cine para el cadalso: 40 años de censura cinematográfica en España* (Barcelona: Editorial Euros, 1976), p. 126.

By 1967 the liberalization process had come to a halt. A national economic downturn led to administrative downsizing throughout the government, including the elimination of the film office in 1969. The censorship boards, however, continued to function as they would up to and even beyond Franco's death in 1975. Fraga Iribarne abandoned his post at the Information ministry as Admiral Luis Carrero Blanco, who now headed the government's daily operations, appointed to important ministerial offices men who sympathized with his more conservative politics. Alfredo Sánchez Bella, a supporter of the lay Catholic group, Opus Dei, assumed the portfolio for the Information Ministry in October of 1969. A conservative in the style of Arias Salgado, he went to work bringing the censorial process back to the pre-Fraga days. The first victims of his policy of film oversight were foreign films, now heavily censored, often to the point of incomprehensibility. One of the most extreme treatments of a foreign film occurred with Sergio Leone's *Once Upon a Time in the West*, with cuts reducing the film's running time from 190 to 137 minutes, ostensibly for the purpose of eliminating a single rape scene. Other effects of Sánchez Bella's moral crusade included the complete suppression of Fellini's *Roma* and *Satyricon*, and major cuts from Bernardo Bertolucci's debut film, *Before the Revolution*. The administration even altered what they considered lewd publicity posters, replacing Liza Minelli's long mesh stockings and tight shorts with long black pants in the posters advertising Bob Fosse's *Cabaret*.[10] This aggressive approach to foreign films made it all but impossible for the art houses to function, and by 1971 the last of these ceased to operate.

Sánchez Bella's tenure also saw some of the most egregious instances of coercion against Spanish films of this period. These include, among others, the suppression of Basilio Martín Patino's *Canciones para después de una guerra* ("Songs For After a War," 1971) after the film had been released, and the pre-production script mutilations and eventual suppression of the completed version of Josep Maria Forn's *La respuesta* ("The Answer," 1969) due to the film's treatment of a university student strike. Both films were eventually released commercially after Franco's death.

In December 1973, Carrero Blanco was assassinated by Basque terrorists. This led to a complete change in the government with Carlos Arias Navarro assuming the reins of power and naming Pío Cabanillas to replace Sánchez Bella in the Information Ministry. Though Cabanillas was charged with trying to return the administration to the style of the Fraga reform period, it was simply too late. The belligerence of Sánchez Bella's tenure had already demoralized and destabilized much of the film industry.

[10] Gubern, *La censura*, p. 58.

In the Fall of 1975, José Luis Borau's *Furtivos* ("Poachers") received harsh treatment by the censors. Yet, while demanding specific cuts in the film, they temporarily relented, allowing an uncensored version of the film to be shown at the San Sebastián Film Festival. Even before the festival, Borau had refused to comply with the board's demand. When *Furtivos* won top prize at San Sebastián, Borau simply ignored the censors – the régime by this point was clearly in a state of disintegration – and released *Furtivos* for commercial distribution, making it the first Spanish film since 1939 to be released without censorship approval.

During the period following Franco's death in November 1975, the censorship boards continued operating, but with little impact, since it was clear to all that the régime's days were numbered. In 1976 the requirement of prior censorship of film scripts was abolished and the formal censorship apparatus for all forms of public expression disbanded in November of 1977. Thus ended the history of official film censorship in Spain.

Part x

Post-Franco Spanish Literature and Film

José-Carlos Mainer, Juan Cano Ballesta, Brad Epps, Sharon G. Feldman, Susan Martin-Márquez

52

Spanish literature between the Franco and post-Franco eras

JOSÉ-CARLOS MAINER

The death of Franco on 20 November 1975 was not a milestone in the history of Spanish culture. What came to be called discreetly "the inevitable biological fact" was something that politicians had been expecting for some time. It is also commonly accepted that the "Transition" began in 1973, when Admiral Carrero Blanco died in an attack by ETA. As far as intellectual life was concerned, since the beginning of the 1960s the "culture of Francoism" was little more than a phantom, sustained by second-rate writers, by valetudinarian academics, and by functionaries on the payroll of the Ministerio de Información y Turismo ("Ministry of Information and Tourism"). Not even the celebration of "Twenty-five Years of Peace" in 1964, conceived by Minister Manuel Fraga Iribarne with the intention of presenting a less harsh idea of the Franco victory of 1939, had been very well received among intellectuals. Two years later, a new Press Law served to make visible a climate of general discontent which turned into outrage because of the numerous prohibitions and sanctions that its application generated.

By 1975, opposition to the Franco régime was expressed almost openly. It is true that at that time important books still could not circulate: the confessional series by Juan Goytisolo (1931–) initiated by *Señas de Identidad* ("Marks of Identity," 1966) had been published in Mexico, as was *Si te dicen que caí* ("The Fallen," 1973) by Juan Marsé, and *Recuento* ("Retelling," 1973), the tale with which Luis Goytisolo (1935–) initiated his *Antagonía* tetralogy. *Colección particular* ("Personal Collection"), a compilation of Jaime Gil de Biedma's poetry, was banned in 1969 and did not appear until September 1975 as *Las personas del verbo* ("People of the Word"[1]). The vicissitudes of periodicals were even more dramatic: *Cambio 16* ("Change 16"), a moderate center-left weekly, founded by academics and journalists, was suspended for three weeks in March 1975. *Triunfo* ("Triumph"), a leftist illustrated magazine, underwent a four-month prohibition (and received a fine of 250,000 pesetas) in June of

---

This chapter has been translated from the Spanish by Edward T. Gurski.
[1] This title alludes to the Holy Trinity; the Word (*verbo*) is the second person.

that same year, by which time it had become the intellectual and stylistic referent for a wide sector of young, middle-class Spaniards.

As noted above, however, the merry-go-round of threats and sanctions had a double effect: it intimidated many but also created an anxious, claustrophobic atmosphere and helped promote a subjective, anti-Franco consciousness of a markedly cultural nature. Books that mocked the prohibitions, lectures, concerts by the so-called "singer-songwriters," film premières, and independent theatrical productions all acquired much additional significance both as meeting places and as sources of solidarity. In reality, many of those cultural gatherings were complex metaphorical signs: for example, the 1969 theatrical adaptation of Molière's *Tartuffe* by Adolfo Marsillach and Enrique Llovet required its spectators to see in the play's protagonists a cruel satire of the politicians and financiers of Opus Dei; the audience that applauded the Carlos Saura film, *Ana y los lobos* ("Ana and the Wolves," 1972), began with the supposition that, under the sway of their ancient and omnipresent mother, the three brothers who killed the foreign governess – the mystic, the military man, and the crackpot – were the incarnations of the pillars of Francoist power; the success of Victor Erice's fine movie, *El espíritu de la colmena* ("The Spirit of the Beehive," 1973), is astonishing in view of the complex Symbolism of its images and the allegorical tone of the entire narration. However, interpreting written texts or movie stills, deciphering their meaning, was one more form of revenge against a régime that made its victims look foolish and condemned them to vulgarity. In time, the images became more explicit, but the rather masochistic ideas of submission, privation, and defenselessness linked to Francoism never completely disappeared. They are found in films such as Saura's *La prima Angélica* ("Cousin Angelica," 1973), and José Luis Borau's *Furtivos* ("Poachers," 1975); in the almost political "pop" paintings done by Eduardo Arroyo and the Equipo Crónica; or in the splendid cartoons of "Blasillo," the anti-Franco child character, that José María Fraguas ("Forges") drew in the pages of the daily, *Informaciós*, or in the humor magazine, *Por Favor* ("Please").

Still, many changes had taken place. The reincorporation of writers who went into exile in 1939 was not going to offer any striking innovation for readers after the years 1965–1975, during which their editorial presence had already been felt. By 1965, only María Zambrano (1904– 1991) and Rafael Alberti (1902–1999) remained outside the country, and they too would return before long. A writer who returned very early, Juan Gil-Albert (1904–1994), found in the Spain of those years an attention he had never stirred up before, especially for his admirable, evocative discussions of homosexuality: his novel *Valentín* ("Valentine") and the essay "Heracles: sobre una manera de ser" ("Heracles: A Manner of Being") were published in 1974 and 1975, respectively. Francisco Ayala (1906–), perhaps the exiled writer who most actively integrated himself into intellectual life upon his return, enjoyed much success with a new book, *El jardín de las delicias* ("The Garden of Delights," 1971), which accompanied re-editions of his works which had come out during his exile. Ramón J. Sender also found a notable popularity that would then be prolonged in the 1980s by cinematic adaptations of his novels. The only significant disappointment was that of Max Aub (1903–1972), who in 1971 reported in his journal, *La gallina ciega* ("The Blind Hen"), a bitter chronicle of his trip to Spain, a country, in his opinion, without cultural memory and populated by self-satisfied pedants. Still, many of his works were published in Spain between 1970 and 1975.

In any case, the lack of cultural memory signaled by Aub was not the problem. The first Premio Cervantes ("Cervantes Prize") – created in September 1975 by decree of the final Franco government – was awarded to Jorge Guillén, the exiled, anti-Franco poet. The second one went to the Cuban, Alejo Carpentier, an official writer of the Castro régime. The "reclamations" of 1975–1985 was a slogan that served to reflect the reconstruction of the intellectual continuity of Spanish life, so shattered by pro-Francoist prejudices. Young professors who began teaching around 1968 took the lead as they "reclaimed," successively, the heterodoxies of the modern age, of enlightened liberalism, of Krausism and nineteenth-century Institutionalism, the dual history of the workers' movement (anarchist and socialist), the work of the historical vanguards, the political–intellectual commitment of the 1930s, the work of exile, and, in a general way, the regionalist or nationalist movements of the last two centuries. Doctoral dissertations, disseminated as either erudite or popularizing articles, began to be seen just as dangerously "subversive" to the Franco régime and its legacy, as were novels, songs, or poems. These academic works truly involved an intellectual conquest of the past.

Of course, the key event of that past was the Spanish Civil War and, for that very reason, the necessity of understanding it in a manner other than the official one was becoming a pressing problem. Even the pro-Franco Ministry of Information and Tourism understood this, and consequently the "historical" works of one of its employees, Ricardo de la Cierva (1926–1), *Crónica de la guerra de España* ("Chronicle of the Spanish War," 1966), published anonymously, and *Francisco Franco: un siglo de España* ("Francisco Franco: A Century of Spain," 1972), promoted a vision of the war as a collective catastrophe, if, in the end, a providential event. These two works also presented an understanding of the Franco régime as a personal, rather than a fascist, enterprise, as a régime greatly influenced by the political pragmatism of its creator and, in any event, largely redeemed by its economic and social achievements. The discovery of the real significance of the war, however, lay elsewhere. Readers over forty years old perceived this meaning in Luis Romero's reportage in *Tres días de julio* ("Three Days in July," 1965), and in *No fue posible la paz* ("Peace Was Not Possible," 1966) the memoirs of José María Gil Robles (1898–1980). Audiences for commercial theatre recognized it in the play, *El tragaluz* ("The Basement Window," 1967) by Antonio Buero Vallejo (1916–2000), and readers of novels found it in Miguel Delibes' *Cinco horas con Mario* ("Five Hours with Mario," 1966), published the same year as *Ha estallado la paz* ("Peace Has Erupted"), the third part of a trilogy by José María Gironella (1917–2003), preceded by *Los cipreses creen en Dios* ("The Cypress Trees Believe in God," 1953) and *Un millón de muertos* ("A Million Dead," 1961).

In 1969, the return of Camilo José Cela to the long novel form saw, in turn, his personal return to the world of the War, which he had not visited since the now remote book of poems, *Pisando la dudosa luz del día: San Camilo 1936* ("Trampling on the Doubtful Light of Day: San Camilo 1936"). By then, the evocation of the conflict – frequently through a child's eyes – as a source of collective fear, as well as one of complete frustration, was somewhat generalized: it was present in the poems of Jaime Gil de Biedma, José Ángel Valente (1929–2000), and Ángel González (1925–), among others; in the novels mentioned above, particularly those of Juan Marsé; and in the most innovative cinema. It was also significant that, if for older writers such as Buero or Cela the civil conflict became an invitation to assume part of the guilt that touched everyone, for the younger generation – the generation of the "children of war" – it supposed, in contrast, a proclamation of innocence. This outlook can frequently even seem deliberately cynical as happens, for example, in "Intento formular mi experiencia de la guerra" ("I Attempt to Formulate my Experience of the War"), one of the best compositions of Jaime Gil de Biedma, and in "Poema inacabat" ("Unfinished Poem") by Gabriel Ferrater. In the 1980s, the Civil War would appear under the rubric of the myth of origin: that is what links two otherwise different stories such as *Herrumbrosas lanzas* ("Rusty Lances," 1983–1986) by Juan Benet (1927–1993), and Camilo José Cela's *Mazurca para dos muertos* ("Mazurca for Two Dead Men," 1984).

In any case, in 1975, Spanish literature was in the midst of change. The dominant tendency of recent years had been experimentalism, in poetry – where the hegemony of the *novísimos* ("the newest ones") of 1970 was evident – as much as in the novel, as reflected in the most recent catalogue of Barral, and in theatre, where independent groups reigned. The year 1975 was that of *El azar objetivo* ("Objective Chance") by Guillermo Carnero (1947–) who, after this work, remained silent for a significant period, and of *Sepulcro en Tarquinia* ("Tomb in Tarquinia"), two volumes of difficult poems replete with cultural references, by Antonio Colinas (1946–). It was also the year of *Los trucos de la muerte* ("Death's

Deceits") by Juan Luis Panero (1942–), which anticipated a more ele-giac and confessional poetry which would soon come to the fore. Also in 1975, the best-seller by Eduardo Mendoza (1943–), *La verdad sobre el caso Savolta* ("The Truth about the Savolta Case"), was published. This novel signaled a return to a more direct narrative, one not without humor, which contrasted with the studied difficulty of other narratives of the moment. This was the period of the great influence of Juan Benet, a narrator who publicly expressed his loathing for Galdós (although he admired Pío Baroja), and whose most recent work, *La otra casa de Mazón* ("Mazón's Other House") had been published in 1973.

At the same time, the influence of the Latin-American novel, which arose in the 1960s, was still very strong. Without its influence, either direct or indirect, it is not easy to explain the (somewhat limited) suc-cess of works such as *La saga-fuga de J. B.* ("The Saga-Flight of J. B.," 1972) by Gonzalo Torrente Ballester (1910–1999), and *Ágata ojo de gato* ("Cat's Agate Eye," 1974) by José Manuel Caballero Bonald (1926–). Also, a need to recapture one's personal past soon became evident in light of the frustration and hope that dominated the final years of the dictator-ship, a frustration due to impotence, and a hope which had to do with the imminence of freedom. *La búsqueda de interlocutor* ("The Search for an Interlocutor," 1973), a collection of essays by Carmen Martín Gaite (1925–2000), was more than just an apt title. Also seeming to search for a complicit reader were Rafael Sánchez Ferlosio (1927–) in the dis-cursive essays of *Las semanas del jardín* ("Garden Weeks," 1974) and Agustín García Calvo (1926–) in *Cartas de negocios de José Requejo* ("José Requejo's Business Letters," 1974), and the quests through mem-ory carried out by Jaime Gil de Biedma (1929–1990) in *Diario del artista seriamente enfermo* ("Journal of the Seriously Sick Artist," 1973) and Carlos Barral in *Años de penitencia* ("Years of Penitence," 1975). Like-wise, a 1976 film by Jaime Chávarri, *El desencanto* ("Disenchantment"), searched through monologues by members of a real family in crisis, that of the former "official" poet, Leopoldo Panero: a fragile, dreamy wife and children who oscillated between foppishness and rage, all of them as prone to exhibitionism as disposed to hide behind a condition of victim-hood. Without doubt, that diagnosis applied to many other Spaniards in the early stages of the new post-Franco régime.

The changes that the slow arrival of democracy introduced referred fun-damentally to the institutional framework in which Spanish letters were evolving. Freedom did not mean the discovery of unpublished or marginal-ized works, but rather it revealed the possibility of treating previously ignored themes. The abolition of censorship in 1977 was noted, above all, in the expression of erotic themes: customs changed quickly, nudity was everywhere, and some popular films revealed the crisis of antiquated values. Comedies such as Jaime de Armiñán's *¡Jo, papá!* ("Hey, Dad!"

1976) and José Luis Garci's *Asignatura pendiente* ("Pending Matters," 1977) described with great accuracy the collapse of taboos. In addition, by the middle of the 1980s, the "comedia madrileña" ("Madrid comedy") as it became known, with directors such as Fernando Colomo and Fernando Trueba, depicted an entirely new society, where the persistence of family ties and the cult of friendship, which could be thought of as sociologically archaic, coexisted with a lack of prejudices and a freedom equivalent to or even greater than that of Italian or French society of the same era.

Another great innovation was the advance of "state culture." On 5 July 1977 the Ministry of Culture and Social Well-Being (after February 1978 simply the Ministry of Culture), which had very little to do with the former Ministry of Information and Tourism, was created. Its budget and importance kept growing in succeeding years and many of the activities that it has promoted since then are now indispensable realities. The new Ministry intervened in theatrical life, which had been in open crisis throughout the 1970s, with the creation in 1978 of the Centro Dramático Nacional ("National Drama Center"), which filled the void left by the near-disappearance of privately funded theatre. Auditoriums were built in places where there was already a musical tradition and in others that had not previously had one. A policy promoting large-scale exhibitions of the plastic arts was pursued, and then, in the 1980s, of constructing ambitious art centers. In turn, the new autonomous governments created Culture Councils which organized their own cultural infrastructure, and not always on a reduced scale. A policy of restoration of the artistic patrimony, the creation of museums and galleries, the formation of symphony orchestras, and the foundation of institutes of theatre and film, all contributed to make the word "culture" a complex term and a catchword that was repeated ad nauseam.

After 1980, the results of all this activity began to be visible. Spanish culture lost a certain willful and combative tone and began to be guided by more commercial parameters. One spoke of "disenchantment" in the face of whatever was unsatisfactory in the new political life but the reality is that in a very brief time some important progressive magazines disappeared: for example, *Cuadernos para el Diálogo* ("Notebooks for Dialogue") closed in 1978 and then *Triunfo* in 1982. Their replacements were daily newspapers: most importantly, *El País* ("The Country") began publication on 4 May 1976, followed in the same year by a magazine, *Interviú* ("Interview"), which nimbly alternated political sensationalism and photos of nude women with work by prestigious authors. Many significant book publishers disappeared as well, which produced a commercial concentration from which emerged several powerful "multimedia" groups – for example, Planeta and Santillana y Anaya – although independent entities were consolidated too: the novelistic collections of

Anagrama and Tusquets were born in the early eighties, and, together with Alfaguara (part of Santillana) and Planeta, had the majority of prominent writers; in the same way, two private enterprises, Hiperión and Visor (with Pre-Textos of Valencia), occupied center stage in the world of poetry.

Writers, though, benefited from these changes. It is certain that a majority of well-known poets, as well as almost all of the essayists, continued to belong to the academic establishment, but novelists, who were accustomed to living on their royalties, frequently supplemented their income with newspaper articles or participation in radio discussions (called *tertulias*), a genre that had acquired an unusual importance. This new situation had both advantages and disadvantages. The novelist doubtless produces too many novels and, on not a few occasions, exploits themes which found acceptance in his or her previous novels, or others of predictable popularity. In many ways, the novel became a reliable barometer of the country's life, often because it resembled reporting or the essay, and authors themselves have become celebrities. On the other hand, many writers have been translated into other languages. If the presence of the writers of the 1950s in some European catalogues was the exception, an exception conceded thanks to their anti-Franco significance, now it is an everyday occurrence. Spanish letters of the 1980s undoubtedly reflected a more self-satisfied literary society. What was called "poetry of experience" evoked the insularity of a left-wing which felt disillusioned and triumphant, sentimental and a bit cynical, all at the same time. The abundance of writers' journals and memoirs, which grew so much in the 1990s, reveals on the one hand the public recognition of the writer, and, on the other, the hegemony of the intimate and personal as thematic material.

In regard to the above, one could think – after the upheavals of 1981 and the socialist victory in the elections of 1982 – that another era had opened. However, things are not so simple. The "Transition," another loaded word which itself reflects a process rather than a change, lasted several more years. Perhaps 1986 is the moment of its actual end: by then fifty years had passed since the beginning of the Civil War and now not a single soldier who had participated in the War remained on active duty; Spain officially entered the European Community on 1 January that year and, in March, a referendum supported Spain's continuation in NATO, closing a chapter in the dreams of the left; finally, on 1 December, Fraga Iribarne abandoned the presidency of the Alianza Popular ("Popular Alliance") and a party began to gestate which, with vestiges of the Francoist past, would assume its status as an alternative party of the Right.

53

Post-Franco poetry

JUAN CANO BALLESTA

Filled with social tensions and political turmoil, the last years of Franco's régime mark the demise of engaged and social poetry and see the beginning of the strong leadership of a group of poets called the *novísimos* ("newest"), even while a large number of contemporary poets maintained their own independent voices and particular styles. It was José María Castellet who started using the term *novísimos* in 1970 in his anthology *Nueve novísimos poetas españoles* ("Nine Newest Spanish Poets"), in which he includes some of the most distinguished poets of the time: Manuel Vázquez Montalbán (1939–2003), Antonio Martínez Sarrión (1939–), José María Álvarez (1942–), Félix de Azúa (1944–), Pedro Gimferrer (1945–), Guillermo Carnero (1947–), Leopoldo María Panero (1948–), Vicente Molina Foix (1946–), and Ana María Moix (1947–). From the very beginning this group sought to overcome the primacy of social poetry. The sense of social and political engagement and the hegemony of Realism had brought to poetry a certain platitudinous tone that urgently called for renewal. The new poetic language was sensorial, refined, and acquired a certain aesthetic primacy; as Castellet states, "la forma del mensaje es su verdadero mensaje" ("the form of the message is its true message").[1] Mass culture (movies, detective stories, rock music, popular myths), the camp sensibility (as defined and popularized in Spain by Susan Sontag), and all kinds of literary, historic, and artistic references enrich the poems of the *novísimos*, which reflected the improved economic and cultural standards of the country. These poets believed that art should not serve any practical purpose and they rebelled against the use of poetry as a weapon to achieve social or political change. On the contrary, they tended toward a poetry that is culturalist, elitist, and ludic: "me parece una especie de juego" ("it seems to me like a kind of game"), says J. M. Álvarez.[2] Poets sympathize with Surrealist trends and are prone to formal experimentation. The *novísimos* had a profound

---

[1] José María Castellet, *Nueve novísimos poetas españoles* (Barcelona: Barral Editores, 1970), p. 34.
[2] Pedro Provencio, *Poéticas españolas contemporáneas. La generación del 70* (Madrid: Hiperión, 1988), p. 63.

impact on the lyric production of their time and became a necessary point of reference for the poetry of the years to come.

There were other outstanding poets like Antonio Carvajal (1943–), Antonio Colinas (1946–), Jenaro Talens (1946–), Alejandro Duque Amusco (1949–), Jaime Siles (1951–), Luis Alberto de Cuenca (1950–), and Luis Antonio de Villena (1951–), among others, whose lyricism diverged in some or in many respects from the *novísimos* aesthetics, offering a rich variety of tones, new topics, and resources. *Sepulcro en Tarquinia* ("Tomb in Tarquinia," 1975), by Antonio Colinas and *Hymnica* (1979), by Luis Antonio de Villena, initiate creative techniques that avoid splendor and brilliance by using less luxurious and culturalist elements in order to stress instead lyric emotion[3] and create a new kind of poetry, in which aestheticism informs the personal experiences of the poet. The poetry of Alejandro Duque Amusco, author of important books like *Del agua, del fuego y otras purificaciones* ("On Water, Fire, and Other Purifications," 1983) coincides in a certain Neo-Romantic tone and in classic or Hellenic echoes with Colinas.

Critics have expressed the most divergent opinions in evaluating the poetry of the eighties and nineties. Some consider these poets to be prisoners of culturalism, *preciosismo*, and aestheticism, or accuse them of being unable to overcome social poetry or the poetry of the *novísimos*. Andrew Debicki states that "the new poetry published in Spain in the 1980s seems less obsessed with linguistic creativity, with allusiveness, and with self-reflexivity."[4] Other critics have suggested that the poetry of the 1980s follows prior clichés and artistic trends or that, in sharp contrast with the *novísimos*, "the poets of the 1980s remain satisfied with the essentially conservative vision of this genre."[5] It is difficult to agree with most of these opinions. The poets of the 1980s and 1990s offer a rich, diverse, and sophisticated poetic production that shows significant innovations in almost every subgenre that they cultivate, as can be seen in the abundance of civic or political poetry, or in the poetic production of "dirty Realism," Neosurrealism, new eroticism, erotic expression by women, and the new meaning that these poets give to culturalism and Hellenism. Many critics agree that profound changes were taking place during the late seventies and early eighties and detect a constant poetic renewal brought about by a deeper understanding and revisiting of the

---

3 Miguel D'Ors, *En busca del público perdido. Aproximación a la última poesía española joven (1975–1993)* (Granada: Impredisur, 1994), p. 15.
4 Andrew Debicki, *Spanish Poetry of the Twentieth Century. Modernity and Beyond* (Lexington: The University Press of Kentucky, 1994), p. 179.
5 Jonathan Mayhew, *The Poetics of Self-consciousness. Twentieth Century Spanish Poetry* (Lewisburg: Bucknell University Press, 1994), p. 131.

old masters. Young poets developed a personal voice and lyrical accent re-adapting past styles and experimenting with new techniques.

The last two decades of the twentieth century constitute a very rich period in lyrical production and dissemination of it, due largely to several important anthologies that have reached a wide reading public, to numerous magazines, which are frequently of regional or local character, and to a publishing industry that is deeply engaged in the publication of old and new poetry: Visor (Madrid), Hiperión (Madrid), Renacimiento (Seville), Pre-Textos (Valencia), Tusquets (Barcelona), and Cátedra (Madrid).

Perhaps the best way to understand the nature of recent poetry is to apply to it the aesthetics and critical concepts of Post-modernity. For the Post-modern artist the past is no longer a burden that must be shaken off, but rather a treasure chest containing valuable riches. The literary texts and topics of modernity can now be recycled from a mimetic or parodic perspective, imbued with a new spirit and recast in a different cultural context. Post-modernism, writes Matei Calinescu in referring to Post-modern architecture, "reinterprets the past in a multiplicity of ways, going from the endearingly playful to the ironically nostalgic, and including such attitudes or moods as humorous irreverence, oblique homage, pious recollection, witty quotation, and paradoxical commentary."[6] These are common reactions of recent poets to the texts of the literary tradition. The revisitation of old cultures and their artistic treasures becomes a highly fertile and enriching experience.

From culturalism to life

The beginning of the 1980s brings with it the demise of culturalism and of metapoetic practice, an increasing striving for philosophical meaning, and a certain classical taste together with the fact that "se afianza la poesía del silencio y se regresa a la tradición de la poesía pura" ("the poetry of silence becomes stronger and moves closer to the tradition of pure poetry").[7] Debicki says about this poetry: "It grew out of the striving for concision, for exact form, and for the reduction of expression to pure sign that had already appeared during the second phase of the 1970s and was best illustrated by Siles's verse."[8]

Amparo Amorós (1950–) has studied the development of this *poetry of silence* and how it originates in a search for precision and brevity. This trend looks to the great masters, Octavio Paz, José Angel Valente, Jorge

---

[6] Matei Calinescu, *Five Faces of Modernity* (Durham: Duke University Press, 1995), p. 283.
[7] José-Carlos Mainer, "Introducción." In *El último tercio del siglo (1968–1998). Antología consultada de la poesía española* (Madrid: Visor, 1999), p. 28.
[8] Debicki, *Spanish Poetry*, p. 182.

Guillén, and the Austrian Paul Celan, while searching for a naked, intellectual, and pure poem. Outstanding poets in this line are José Luis Jover (1946–), who speaks of poetry as "the form of silence," writing verses such as: "Es el poema / una metáfora / del silencio" ("The poem is / a metaphor / of silence," *Retrato de autor* ["Portrait of the Author," 1982]), together with Andrés Sánchez Robayna (1952–), María Victoria Atencia (1931–), Justo Navarro (1953–), Amparo Amorós, José María Bermejo (1947–), Carmen Pallarés Molina (1950–), Jenaro Talens, Luis Suñén (1951–), José Carlos Cataño (1954–), Miguel Martinón (1945–), and César Simón (1932–1997), among many others. Jaime Siles stands out with his books *Música del agua* ("Water Music," 1983) and *Columnae* (1984). Many other poets such as José Gutiérrez (1955–), Alvaro Valverde (1958–), Carlos Marzal (1961–), or Justo Navarro cultivate this mode of creation only in certain moments or in specific books. More recently, Ada Salas (1965–) has published with Hiperión *Variaciones en blanco* ("Variations in White," 1994) and *La sed* ("Thirst," 1997). Both collections communicate intense sensations in short sentences and in verses that reach full emotional intensity with minimal verbal resources.

In the aesthetic pluralism of the Post-modern era, critics point to important changes that took place after 1975 and intensified their impact in the following decade. Miguel García Posada sees a general trend "del culturalismo a la vida" ("from culturalism to life").[9] The intimate and autobiographic remembrance, confessionalism – carefully avoided by the *novísimos* – an urban sensibility, a return to emotionalism and to metaphysical meditation became common topics. The poetry of the last two decades, however, is primarily individualistic, personal, light, and mostly hedonistic. Federico Gallego Ripoll reminds us that in our time, "no hay que luchar por las grandes palabras porque han perdido en gran manera su sentido" ("we do not have to fight for the great words, because most of them have lost part of their meaning"), and "vivimos una extraña época de facilidades artísticas, de poca responsabilidad y menor compromiso" ("we live in a strange era of artistic easiness, of little responsibility and less engagement").[10] Therefore, poetry becomes a "private pleasure": daily experience, the trivial love adventure, and an evening out with friends are some of the frequent settings of an unworried and hedonistic lyricism. These poets write diaries about common life events: Eloy Sánchez Rosillo, *Páginas de un diario* ("Pages from a Diary," 1981), Jon Juaristi, *Diario del poeta recién cansado* ("Diary of the Newly Tired Poet," 1985), Luis

---

9   "Del culturalismo a la vida." In *El lugar de la poesía*. Ed. Luis Muñoz (Granada: Diputación Provincial de Granada, 1994), p. 28.
10 Federico Gallego Ripoll, "El laberinto transparente. Renovación en los poetas de los ochenta." In *La Poesia Spagnola Oggi: una generazione dopo l'altra*. Ed. Mario Di Pinto and G. Calabro (Naples: Vittorio Pironti Editore, 1995), p. 89.

García Montero, *Diario cómplice* ("Accomplice Diary," 1987), Vicente Gallego, *La luz de otra manera* ("The Light in Another Way," 1988). They abandon the high pedestal of the *novísimos* in order to pay more attention to private emotions and experiences. Leopoldo María Panero throws his intimate experience of living into his poems, considering them as a sort of psychoanalysis, while for Luis Antonio de Villena art is life and life should be lived as art. During the 1980s and 1990s poetry slides from an intense culturalism to the other extreme that places life (thought, emotions, even daily experiences) at the center of attention.

Poetry of experience

The poetry of experience is perhaps the most visible trend in contemporary poetry. It incorporates and absorbs ideas and currents that are in the cultural ambience of the 1980s and 1990s.

Luis García Montero (1958–), Alvaro Salvador (1950–), and Javier Egea (1952–1999) initiate a poetic renewal with the manifesto and anthology published in 1983 under the title *La otra sentimentalidad* ("The Other Sentimentality"). Overcoming aspects of the *novísimo* aesthetics, they attempt to bring the arts closer to life and to make a connection with the generation of social poets, particularly Jaime Gil de Biedma (1929–), Claudio Rodríguez (1934–), and Francisco Brines (1932–), who tended to merge biography and poetry while keeping a historical perspective. Some ideas of *La otra sentimentalidad* were developed and completed by Luis García Montero in later publications. First, he denounced in traditional poetry "el espejismo de la sinceridad y . . . la pureza tramposa de lo espontáneo" ("the mirage of sincerity and . . . the fallacious purity of spontaneity") and he asserted that the poem is "una puesta en escena, un pequeño teatro para un sólo espectador" ("a staging, a little play for only one spectator").[11] Second, he offers a warm welcome to the feelings and emotions that appear in the new poetry which is a "confesión directa de los agobiados sentimientos, expresión literal de las esencias más ocultas del sujeto" ("direct confession of confused feelings, verbal expression of the most hidden essences of the subject"),[12] while also accepting the most common daily events and experiences of life. Third, García Montero points out that a certain theoretical Marxism and the friendship of Rafael Alberti leads some of these young writers to a recovery of Realism and social engagement that they share with poets of the 1950s: "La poesía no

[11] Luis García Montero, *Confesiones poéticas* (Granada: Excma. Diputación Provincial, 1993), pp. 221 and 187 respectively.
[12] García Montero, *Confesiones*, pp. 185–186.

es un arma cargada de futuro sino de presente" ("Poetry is not a weapon loaded with future, but with present").[13] Thus, in the 1980s and 1990s there appear poets who, distancing themselves from *novísimo* aesthetics, vindicate lyrical engagement and attack – mostly with acid irony – the world in which they live.

The label of this trend comes most likely from William Blake's *Songs of Experience* and from the book *The Poetry of Experience* by Robert Langbaum, which presents an image of the poet as an iconoclast who, after rejecting traditional values, "discovers his own feelings and his own will as a source of value in an otherwise meaningless universe . . .; exhibiting as much emotion and will as possible."[14] The poet comes to believe only in himself and in "his infinite capacity for experience, his capacity for feeling something about everything in the world."[15] Gil de Biedma and Luis Cernuda, avid readers of the poets studied by Langbaum (William Blake, Wordsworth, Browning, Tennyson), offer young poets a view of existence forged in both the Romantic and Modernist rebellions which led to the disappearance of all certainties and values previously provided by religion, philosophy, and ideology. What interests the young poets of today are their own feelings and experiences through which they leave their personal mark on the cultural tradition that they inherited. Personal emotions and experiences now fill the void that in the past was occupied by transcendental truths.

An important technique that the poets since the 1980s have used is the so-called "dramatic monologue," or the use of a lyric voice different from that of the poet. The poet invents a character, frequently a mask of himself, who tells his own story, explains his world view, ideals, desires, and fears. The reader perceives the experience as it is narrated by the poetic voice from its own perspective and personal interests. The poet uses an identity other than his or her own to diminish the immediacy of feelings, while dramatizing the story and the emotions it contains.

These ways of understanding poetry have had a great impact in the last two decades on a large number of poets who wrote, at least partially, in this artistic environment. In spite of his severe criticism of the theory and poetic practice of this trend, even a rather hostile critic like Antonio Ortega names Luis García Montero, Felipe Benítez Reyes (1960–), Carlos Marzal (1961–), Vicente Gallego (1963–), Alvaro García (1965–), and

---

[13] García Montero, *Confesiones*, p. 204.
[14] Robert Langbaum, *The Poetry of Experience. The Dramatic Monologue in Modern Literary Tradition* (New York: W. W. Norton and Co., 1963), p. 16.
[15] Langbaum, *Poetry of Experience*, p. 17.

Benjamín Prado (1961–) "las cabezas jóvenes más visibles y consagradas" ("the most visible and famous young poets") of this poetic trend.[16]

In the steps of Jaime Gil de Biedma and other writers of the 1960s, these poets show their dislike for the Avant-Garde (as does García Montero), use a more colloquial language, and get closer to the common reader. As opposed to the elitism of the Avant-Garde, they prefer daily life, believing that "es importante que los protagonistas del poema no sean héroes . . . sino personas normales" ("it is important that the protagonists of the poem not be heroes . . . but normal people").[17] Even if they grow out of a common theoretical and aesthetic position close to the poetry of experience, they practice a great variety of poetical forms, tones, and lyrical styles. Nevertheless Javier Salvago (1950–), Felipe Benítez Reyes, Jon Juaristi, Alvaro García, Carlos Marzal, Vicente Gallego, and José Luis Piquero (1967–) cultivate a kind of lyricism that is close to the one practiced by Luis García Montero, Javier Egea, Alvaro Salvador, Luis Muñoz (1966–), Benjamín Prado, and Inmaculada Mengíbar (1962–). Some outstanding names from different trends deserve to be stressed.

Carlos Marzal portrays a disenchanted world and a certain bohemian life of night-time urban adventures, as the titles of two of his books suggest: *El último de la fiesta* ("The Last of the Party," 1987) and *Los países nocturnos* ("Night Countries," 1996), but he also makes use of satire and of a fine irony of skeptical moral convictions.

Jon Juaristi (1951–) displays an original voice and a great variety of registers in his books *Diario del poeta recién cansado*, *Suma de varia intención* ("Sum of Diverse Intentions," 1987) and *Mediodía* ("Noon," 1994). In addition to satire and the melancholic remembrance of youth, he also cultivates a certain kind of civic poetry, speaking with passion and irony of the terrible tensions of living in the Basque Country.

Abelardo Linares (1952–) can be considered a promoter of the poetry of experience. His lyrics had at the beginning a certain culturalist accent and fervor (referring back to the Baroque practices of Quevedo, for example) but later on became more personal, sensual, and sophisticated, focusing also on oneiric experiences, his own existence as reality or dream, and on similar metaphysical problems. Important books of his are *Sombras (Poesía 1979–1985)* ("Shadows [Poetry 1979–1985]," 1986) and *Espejos (1986–1991)* ("Mirrors [1986–1991]," 1991).

Juan Manuel Bonet (1953–) uses impressionistic techniques and knows how to capture in few words the atmosphere and feelings of the instant. His books include *La patria oscura* ("Dark Country," 1983), *Café des exilés* ("Exiles' Café," 1990), and *Praga* ("Prague," 1994).

[16] Antonio Ortega, "Entre el hilo y la madeja: apuntes sobre la poesía española actual." *Zurgai* (July 1997), p. 47.
[17] García Montero, *Confesiones*, p. 36.

José Gutiérrez (1955–) shakes off the culturalist legacy of his early poems to write a poetry of intimacy that could be called poetry of experience in a melancholic remembrance of fleeting youth; his love poems take place in an urban setting. *De la renuncia* ("On Renouncement," 1989) and *Poemas 1976–1986* (1997) contain his most important work to date.

The most significant representative of the poetry of experience and its theoretical foundation is Luis García Montero. He considers lyric poetry as the expression of experiences that frequently include elements of fiction. García Montero enjoys feeling the pulse of everyday life, open to individual and collective sentiments, in an urban environment full of the symbols of Post-modern life: telephones, cars, airports, shop windows, lights, etc. José Antonio Mesa Toré (1963–), Vicente Gallego, Alvaro García, and Luis Muñoz are, each in his own way, close to this mode of expression.

This poetry of experience becomes an adventure "en busca del público perdido" ("in search of the lost audience"), as Miguel D'Ors' book by that title suggests. It awakens interest among wide circles of readers, who give it a support never enjoyed before. This trend brings with it significant sociological and cultural consequences, as Antonio Candau has pointed out:

La hegemonía de una corriente poética supone, entre otras cosas, acceso a premios, fondos públicos, facilidades de publicación, recepción crítica, etc. La literatura de cada sociedad tiene, según la denominación de Pierre Bourdieu (1992), sus "reglas del arte" y aunque la poesía no alcanza el poder de influencia de la novela o el cine, ni está en el nivel de importancia económica de, por ejemplo, la arquitectura, es indudable que sí tiene su pieza en el rompecabezas de la sociedad cultural.

(The hegemony of a poetic trend, entails, among other things, access to prizes and public funds, advantages in publishing and critical reception, etc. The literature of each society has, in the words of Pierre Bourdieu (1992), its own "art rules" and even if poetry does not reach the power of influence of the novel or of the cinema, and is not at the level of economic relevance of, let's say, architecture, it is undoubted that it has its importance in the puzzle of a cultivated society).[18]

Other trends

Pedro Provencio establishes a clear opposition between the poetry of experience – that rejects "no sólo el yo romántico sino el vanguardista" ("not

[18] Antonio Candau, "Jorge Riechmann y la metamorfosis de la experiencia." *España Contemporánea* 13 (Spring 2000), p. 13.

only the Romantic but also the Avant-Gardist I"), with García Montero leading the trend – and the poetry of those who proudly follow the spirit of the Avant-Garde, with Jorge Riechmann (1962–) excelling among them.[19] Some critics are pleased to announce the decline of the Avant-Garde (García Montero) or proclaim its death (Mayhew), while others such as Antonio Ortega defend it enthusiastically. The latter, in his anthology *La prueba del nueve*, presents nine poets who, in his words, maintain "una percepción no dogmática de la tradición y de la modernidad" ("a non-dogmatic perception of tradition and modernity"), believe that the Avant-Garde contributed important formal and conceptual innovations to art, and invite us to undertake "una reflexión crítica sobre la realidad" ("a critical reflection on reality").[20] In the words of Antonio Candau, Ortega considers "los hallazgos de las vanguardias históricas un legado irrenunciable" ("the discoveries of the historic Avant-Garde an indelible legacy").[21] These differences among rival groups have provoked passionate and bitter debates.

The admirers of the achievements of the Avant-Garde, also called "poets of high modernity," reject everything that sounds Post-modern. Antonio Ortega in *La prueba del nueve* includes in this trend such names as Miguel Casado (1954–), Juan Carlos Suñén (1956–), Jorge Riechmann, Esperanza López Parada (1962–), Vicente Valero (1963–), Olvido García Valdés (1950–), Miguel Suárez (1951–), Ildefonso Rodríguez (1952–), and Concha García (1956–). Pedro Provencio considers this trend, led by Jorge Riechmann, to be open to poetic exploration and experimentation and opposed to the poetry of experience, naming Luisa Castro, Blanca Andreu (1959–), Juan Carlos Suñén, and José María Parreño (1958–) as its principal practitioners.

Miguel Casado is a poet of pictorial intentions but one who also knows how to meet the outside world with a gaze that reveals its deep mysteries and its metaphysical dimension, as we can see in *Falso movimiento* ("False Movement," 1993) and *La mujer automática* ("The Automatic Woman," 1996).

Juan Carlos Suñén, Roger Wolfe (1962–), and Jorge Riechmann stand out among the few poets who raise their independent voice to resist power, war, and injustice, while developing their own critical understanding of reality. They write a kind of civil poetry concerned with problems of our time and far from any aestheticism or culturalism.

Surrealist modes unfold in the poetry of Blanca Andreu; she had a major impact on her contemporaries with the publication in 1981 of her book

---

[19] Provencio, *Poéticas españolas*, pp. 45–46.
[20] Antonio Ortega, *La prueba del nueve (Antología poética)* (Madrid: Cátedra, 1994), pp. 9–10.
[21] Candau, "Riechmann," p. 8.

De una niña de provincias que se vino a vivir en un Chagall ("About a Girl from the Provinces Who Came to Live in a Chagall"). Her poems are built of long free verses that exhibit brilliant and unexpectedly fascinating irrational images. As Andrew Debicki writes, these poems "unfold a luxuriant view of elemental love and life impulses, blending into morbid apprehensions of death and destruction."[22] The overflowing imagination of Blanca Andreu together with her attention to the tastes and experiences of young people of her time (drugs and their hallucinatory visions) produced a unique language that awakened great enthusiasm and stimulated young women poets – Luisa Castro (1966–), Amalia Iglesias (1962–), Concha García, and Almudena Guzmán (1964–) – but also men who practiced Surrealistic irrationalism such as Luis Miguel Rabanal (1957–), César Antonio Molina (1952–), José Carlón (1954–), Juan Carlos Mestre (1957–), Fernando Bertrán (1956–), and Angel Muñoz Petisme (1961–).

Poetry written by women bloomed during the eighties and nineties. New and original voices were heard and a great number of books were published. Women became conscious of the need to win access to a wide audience and important anthologies of women poets appeared: Ramón Buenaventura published *Las diosas blancas: antología de la joven poesía española escrita por mujeres* ("White Goddesses: Anthology of Young Spanish Poetry Written by Women," 1985) and Noni Benegas and Jesús Munárriz published *Ellas tienen la palabra. Dos décadas de poesía española* ("They Have the Word: Two Decades of Spanish Poetry [by Women]," 1997). Original women's voices achieved vigorous expression and showed an uncommon vitality. Some followed the trends of the moment, others invented a new language and developed the old topics of love and eroticism from a woman's perspective, creating innovative and subversive verses.[23]

Pluralism and diversity are, in the opinion of many critics, the most characteristic trait of recent poetry in Spain. Perhaps the proximity of this process does not allow for a comprehensive, panoramic perspective of this rich and complex literary reality. Yet one thing seems clear: *novísimo* poetics lost its predominance during the 1970s and has been replaced by a

---

[22] Debicki, *Spanish Poetry*, p. 210.
[23] Besides the name of Ana Rossetti – sensual, innovative, and hedonistic, and one of the best poets of female eroticism – we should add those of María Victoria Atencia (1931–), Amparo Amorós (1950–), Rosa Romojaro (1948–), Fanny Rubio (1949–), María del Carmen Pallarés (1950–), Concha García, María Sanz (1956–), Blanca Andreu, Almudena Guzmán, Luisa Castro, Juana Castro (1945–), Amalia Iglesias, and Andrea Luca (1957–). Among the forty women poets included in *Ellas tienen la palabra* some already enjoy a secure prestige (Olvido García Valdés [1950–]) while others are promising figures with an important *oeuvre* (Isla Correyero [1957–], Aurora Luque [1962–], Amalia Bautista [1962–], Ada Salas).

number of new trends and poets that are no longer fascinated by foreign artists and exotic topics. They do not turn their backs on the Spanish literary tradition, as many of the *novísimos* did. On the contrary, they find some of their most admired poets in Cernuda, Gil-Albert, Gil de Biedma, and Ángel González, poets who are closer to today's Spaniards and to their shared life experiences. Many of these authors make use of narrative discourse: they like to narrate, to tell stories in their poems; but if the poets of the 1960s poeticized "collective experiences" and suppressed the "I" as a bourgeois intrusion, today's poets write of personal and individual experiences.

The poetry of the last fifteen years shows as one of its most visible traits the triumph of individualism and hedonism. Social and political poetry, to the extent that it continues to be written, speaks in a totally new voice and becomes limited to a few young writers (Roger Wolfe, Juan Carlos Suñén, Jorge Riechmann, Fernando Beltrán, among others) while most of the poets write of events of daily life in modern cities, where "enseignes lumineuses, architectures urbaines, design automobile, mode vestimentaire, maquillage, deviennent les nouveaux topoi de cette poésie urbaine" ("lighted signs, urban architecture, automobile design, clothing fashions, make-up, become the new *topoi* of this urban poetry") and are raised to the "catégorie d'objets esthétiques" ("category of aesthetic objects").[24] Today's poetry appears open to wide horizons, and does not avoid colloquial or even sordid language. It can also use select, elegant, and elevated discourse and turn willingly to its prestigious Spanish elders.

---

[24] Claude Le Bigot, "Janus polycéphale ou le discours postmodern de la poésie espagnole contemporaine." In *Postmodernité et écriture narrative dans l'Espagne contemporaine* (Grenoble: Cerhius, 1996), p. 304.

54

Spanish prose, 1975–2002

BRAD EPPS

The death, after a protracted agony, of Francisco Franco on 20 November 1975 has left its mark on Spanish historiography. The mark may be indelible, but it remains contentious. Many have attempted to ignore or eschew the death, the dictator, and the date as so many attributes of a conception of history still in thrall to powerful people, famous proper names, and neat chronologies. Many others preserve and even promote Franco's passing as a watershed event, indispensable to any serious reflection on modern Spain. Still others point to the assassination by ETA of Franco's likely successor, Admiral Luis Carrero Blanco, in late 1973 as the event to remember. Regardless, the terms "post-Franco" and "post-Francoist" hold for literary historians and critics in ways that do not obtain for the writers themselves. Nor are the problems of such classificatory moves resolved by invoking Post-modernism, which, despite some critics' claims to the contrary, constitutes yet another classification. As Manuel Vázquez Montalbán notes, post-Francoism and Post-modernism alike are indicative of a "voluntad de síntesis" ("will to synthesis") that is necessarily reductive.[1] That Post-modernism should signify synthesis and reduction is ironic, and partly accounts for its increasingly nugatory status as an epistemic and heuristic category. The decline of Post-modernism does not, however, invalidate its "successes," significantly among them, as Gonzalo Navajas observes, "la legitimación definitiva de discursos prohibidos y minoritarios" ("the definitive legitimization of prohibited and minoritized discourses").[2] Spain in the wake of Franco did indeed seem to refashion itself into a Post-modern playground of raucous desires. The persistence and rise of unemployment, terrorism, drug abuse, AIDS, political corruption, and consumerism, however, gave the lie to Utopian stylizations and radical ideological breaks. Dreams of new beginnings competed with specters of the past, and history, once again, was re-written.

The writing, re-writing, and even erasure of history has its place in literature. *En el día de hoy* ("On the Day of Today," 1976), by Jesús

---

[1] Manuel Vázquez Montalbán, *Crónica sentimental de España* (Barcelona: Planeta, 1998), p. 13.

[2] Gonzalo Navajas, "Una estética para después del posmodernismo: la nostalgia asertiva y la reciente novela española." *Revista de Occidente* 143 (1993), p. 106.

Torbado (1943–), winner of the first Planeta Prize after Franco's death, carries revisionism to an extreme by imagining the victory of Republican forces in 1939. Other re-workings of historical subjects include *El ingenioso hidalgo y poeta Federico García Lorca asciende a los infiernos* ("The Ingenious Gentleman and Poet Federico García Lorca Ascends into Hell," 1980) by Carlos Rojas (1928–), and, later on, *Autobiografía del general Franco* ("Autobiography of General Franco," 1992) by Manuel Vázquez Montalbán (1939–2003). The "what if" of such endeavors at once points to and turns from codified reality; the effects, not surprisingly, can be quite varied. More a cultural curiosity than anything else, Torbado's novel is hardly a "great work" of literature and has received virtually no critical attention. The point is important, inasmuch as Franco's death and the subsequent transition to democracy were accompanied by great expectations. Somewhere, somehow, after so many years of censorship and oppression, a daring work of breathtaking genius must surely lie in waiting. Some assumed that it might spring from the pen of an unknown, while others assumed that it might be the work of a writer already established before 1975. Neither assumption proved accurate. While seasoned writers such as Juan (1931–) and Luis (1935–) Goytisolo, Camilo José Cela, Carmen Martín Gaite (1925–2000), Ana María Matute (1926–), Miguel Delibes (1920–), Gonzalo Torrente Ballester (1910–1999), Juan Garcia Hortelano (1928–1992), Juan Marsé (1933–), Rafael Sánchez Ferlosio (1927–), and Rosa Chacel (1898–1994) continued to publish after Franco's death, and while younger writers such as Javier Marías (1951–), Juan José Millás (1946–), Rosa Montero (1951–), and Eduardo Mendoza (1948–) burst onto the scene, no one work or author – including Cela, 1989 Nobel Prize-winner – enjoyed undisputed praise.

In many respects, the expectations that attended literature after Franco matched the expectations, at least by many on the left, for profound political change and a truly new social order. Juan Goytisolo's riotously self-reflective *Juan sin tierra* ("Juan the Landless," 1975) gestures at breaking not merely with the Francoist past but with the entirety of Spanish history. After a page in which the Spanish language is twisted and transformed, *Juan sin tierra* closes in Arabic, as if saying that Spanish can no longer account for Spain. Goytisolo's move led more than one critic to expect the author to abandon the Spanish language and literary tradition. Others, of course, read the move from Spanish to Arabic as an intricately literate, if overtly politicized, attempt to bring the act of writing, and reading, resoundingly to the fore. Far from the mimetic transparency of Social Realism, which Goytisolo himself had once cultivated, *Juan sin tierra* partakes of the "linguistic turn" that characterizes such opaque works as *Tiempo de silencio* ("Time of Silence," 1962) by Luis Martín Santos

(1924–1964) and *Volverás a Región* ("Return to Region," 1967) by Juan Benet (1927–1993). Unlike its predecessors, however, *Juan sin tierra* is not "grounded" in Spain and engages a variety of places – primarily Cuba and Morocco – that, while implicated in Spain's colonial history, remain sufficiently autonomous to constitute a sort of cultural dissonance. The history of Spanish literature, in Goytisolo's view, is bound up in a history of conquest, expansion, solidification, and retrenchment in which difference is sacrificed to sameness. Goytisolo's insistence on a heterodox literary and critical practice in which other voices, long stigmatized and suppressed, are unearthed and vindicated takes, however, some rather self-reflective, if not self-serving, turns.

The turn to language brings Goytisolo face to face with himself, not as a discrete, verifiable individual but as a conflicted persona. Uncovering and recovering the past, Goytisolo produces an ambivalent theorization of the authorial self in two surprisingly best-selling autobiographical works: *Coto vedado* ("Forbidden Territory," 1985) and *En los reinos de taifa* ("Realms of Strife," 1986). The petty politics of publishing and personal fame vie with the grand politics of social transformation and revolution. Goytisolo's *mise en question* of Spanish society, no less than his attempts to claim a place for himself in a modern Spanish critical tradition that includes Francisco de Goya, Mariano José de Larra, José María Blanco White, and Luis Cernuda, have earned him both accolades and criticism as a moralist. Goytisolo's moralism entails, however, the celebration of "immoral" and "amoral" acts and identities and runs throughout his later novelistic production. *Makbara* (1980), *Paisajes después de la batalla* ("Landscapes After the Battle," 1982), *Las virtudes del pájaro solitario* ("The Virtues of the Solitary Bird," 1988), *La saga de los Marx* ("The Marx Family Saga," 1993), *El sitio de los sitios* ("The Siege of Sieges," 1995), and *Las semanas del jardín* ("The Garden of Secrets," 1997) – the latter published without Goytisolo's name on the cover, only his picture – all remit to the author's life. They do so while confronting racism, genocide, terrorism, war, and AIDS, to be sure. The self-referential text here becomes a text that refers to the author's self. Asserting his marginal status as a modern-day *poète maudit* and purveyor of truth, Juan Goytisolo is nonetheless a canonical author.

Carmen Martín Gaite, whose prose is as different as possible from Goytisolo's, also scatters autobiographical signs throughout her writing, most memorably in *El cuarto de atrás* ("The Back Room," 1978), in which a mysterious man in black queries the narrator – designated only as "C" – about her past, her country, and her writing. Like Goytisolo, Torrente Ballester, Vázquez Montalbán, Sánchez Ferlosio, Antonio Muñoz Molina (1956–), and Carme Riera (1948–), to name but a few, Martín Gaite cultivated the critical and historical essay along with narrative fiction.

Her *Usos amorosos de la postguerra española* ("Love Customs in Post-war Spain," 1987) explores the varieties of amorous experience, many of which do not figure in conventional histories centered on "great men." Martín Gaite attends to the "novela rosa," or "romance novel," and to relatively obscure women writers and cultural producers. She attends, furthermore, to how such a popular sentimental form of representation can coincide with rigid and often aggressive formulations of gender, family, nation, and duty found in the Falange and in the Sección Femenina. The memory of both organizations marks *El cuarto de atrás* and troubles the fuzzy nostalgia that often accompanies the passing of time. Rosa Chacel's *Barrio de maravillas* ("The Maravillas District," 1976), referring to a central area of Madrid and published shortly after the author ended an exile of almost forty years, likewise explores the past in a manner that complicates nostalgia. Whatever the turns of nostalgia in Martín Gaite's and Chacel's works, in post-Francoist Spain nostalgia was most succinctly expressed in two apparently contradictory, but actually quite complementary, phrases: "with Franco we lived better" and "against Franco we lived better." Martín Gaite, along with the Goytisolo brothers, Marsé, Jorge Semprún (1923–), and others, refused to fall prey to nostalgia even as they engaged it in their writing. History and fiction collided, at times even appeared to fuse, while nonetheless remaining relatively autonomous.

Self-referential fiction, self-referential non-fiction: in a series of texts metanarrative slides into autobiography. The idea that autobiography is little practiced in Spain – convincingly contested by a number of critics – intersects with the idea that literary experimentation is little practiced too. Comparisons with other national literary traditions notwithstanding, autobiographically inflected experimental, metafictional writing enjoyed substantial critical success in Spain in the seventies and eighties. For Robert Spires, Juan Goytisolo's *Juan sin tierra* "could well be considered the manifesto for the whole Spanish self-referential novel movement."[3] Whether or not there was a "movement," a number of texts contribute to that impression. *Novela de Andrés Choz* ("Novel of Andrés Choz," 1976) by José María Merino (1941–), centering on a mortally ill man and an extraterrestrial, *La tríbada falsaria* ("The False Lesbian," 1980) by Miguel Espinosa (1926–1982), highlighting erogenous transgression, and Juan García Hortelano's *Gramática parda* ("Tawny Grammar," 1982), all challenge referentiality. Luis Goytisolo's *Los verdes de mayo hasta el mar* ("The Greens of May until the Sea," 1976) is, however, one of the most notable examples of self-referential narrative. Less given to attitudinizing and autobiographical allusions than his brother Juan, Luis Goytisolo pens

---

[3] Robert Spires, *Beyond the Metafictional Mode. Directions in the Modern Spanish Novel* (Lexington, KY: University of Kentucky Press, 1984), p. 76.

novels whose complexity is only partly measured by their intertextuality. *Los verdes de mayo* is one of four titles in the ambitious and innovative *Antagonía*, the others being *Recuento* ("Recount," 1973), *La cólera de Aquiles* ("The Anger of Achilles," 1979), and *Teoría del conocimiento* ("Theory of Knowledge," 1981). Spanning the last years of Francoism and the first years of democracy, *Antagonía* provides a lesson in the process of writing and reading. *Teoría del conocimiento*, with its philosophically portentous title, contains at least three narrators who vie for authority and explicitly cites the passing of Franco. The real historical death of the dictator dovetails in compelling ways with the highly symbolic death of the author.

Martín Gaite's *El cuarto de atrás*, Marsé's *La muchacha de las bragas de oro* ("Golden Girl," 1978), and *L'hora violeta* ("The Violet Hour," 1980) by Montserrat Roig (1946–1991) are among the many novels that cite Franco's passing. They do so within a story about the embattled resiliency of authority, that of the political leader and of the story teller alike. Authority, authoritarianism, and authorship comprise a tense trio in which politics and literature are intricately implicated. It is almost as if the dream of total narrative control were rendered nightmarish under the weight of totalitarian projects, from both the right *and* the left. *Panfleto contra el Todo* ("Pamphlet against Totality," 1978) by Fernando Savater (1947–), provides a philosophical gloss of totality, but one of the most trenchant critiques of totalistic thought is an intensely reticular personal account: Semprún's *Autobiografía de Federico Sánchez* ("The Autobiography of Federico Sánchez," 1977). The real autobiography of a quasi-fictional entity, Semprún's text shuttles between the dizzying days of the Transition and a more somber day in 1964, when Semprún was expelled from the Spanish Communist Party for questioning its oppositional strategies, authoritarianism, and selective historical memory. Federico Sánchez was Semprún's pseudonym during his clandestine days as a communist militant, but the text – drawing on party documents, newspaper articles, police files, poems, and letters – also recounts Semprún's experiences in the Civil War, the French Resistance, and Buchenwald concentration camp. With its less than flattering portrayal of Dolores Ibárruri, "La Pasionaria," and Santiago Carrillo, leader of the Spanish communist party, *Autobiografía de Federico Sánchez* shattered a Manichaean understanding of history in which good and evil, right and wrong, were clearly demarcated.

Democracy, with all its inconsistencies, challenges, and ambiguities, entailed not only more open and nuanced examinations of Francoism, capitalism, and technocracy, but also of communism, socialism, and other anti-Francoist formations. To varying degrees, Semprún, Goytisolo, Savater, Marsé, Roig, and Vázquez Montalbán, among many others, undertook a reassessment of politics that often assumed the guise of a personal critique. The rhetoric of heroic integrity, already troubled in the sixties (e.g. *Tiempo de silencio*), became increasingly fraught with problems and often veered into the absurd. The broken heroes of *Luz de la memoria* ("Light of Memory," 1976) by Lourdes Ortiz (1943–), *La noche en casa* ("The Night at Home," 1977) and *El río de la luna* ("Moon River," 1981) by José María Guelbenzu (1944–), and Marsé's *Un día volveré* ("One Day I Will Return," 1982) – novels in which, respectively, insanity, sexual obsession, mediocrity, and imprisonment predominate – signal the collapse of master narratives that supposedly marks the "Postmodern condition." For José-Carlos Mainer, the general collapse of master narratives entails the "shipwreck" and "bankruptcy" of the "leftist tradition."[4] Mainer's rhetoric betrays a certain fractured grandeur of its own, but it accurately conveys a sense of an ending that surpassed the death of Franco. In other words, the death of the dictator was bound up in the disintegration of grand redemptive projects, whatever their political content, and in the ascendancy of a hybridized global order that resisted and even ridiculed totalization. However totalizing such configurations may themselves prove to be (grand propositions have hardly vanished), a significant strain of narrative does put into practice the ambiguous virtues of fragmentation and partiality.

Rather than clear-cut guilt and innocence, complicity appears to hold sway. Juan Benet's repudiation of *engagé* literature and his refusal to clarify the implications of the Civil War sustained a literary practice that irked some and that bewitched, even influenced, others – notably Millás and Marías. Complicity, not clear commitment, suffuses Benet's texts, including the twelve-part, triple-volume *Herrumbrosas lanzas* ("Rusty Lances," 1983–1986), with maps and battle plans, and the more modest *En la penumbra* ("In the Penumbra," 1989), in which two women reflect on their lives while waiting for a messenger. Benet's penchant for enigma, for him a mainspring of *poesis*, and his fascination with the Civil War make for difficult stories that concede little, if anything, to popular culture. Anti-consumerist, uncompromising, elitist, and yet widely recognized as a contemporary literary master, Benet remains an exceptional literary force. It is not that Benet is the only demanding writer, but that he is one of the few from the Francoist period whose "politics" were not made clear in his writing (though for some critics the very lack of clarity was a sign of support for the status quo). The dissatisfaction with established leftist politics that suffuses many later works by Juan Goytisolo, Semprún, and Marsé,

---

4 José-Carlos Mainer, "1975–1985: los poderes del pasado." In *La cultura española en el posfranquismo: diez años de cine, cultura y literatura (1975–1985)*. Ed. Samuel Amell and Salvador García Castañeda (Madrid: Playor, 1988), pp. 19, 20.

along with the discomfort that attends, in retrospect, the rightist politics of certain early works by Torrente Ballester and Cela, does not quite hold for Benet. Despite their differences, all of these writers challenge – some more resoundingly than others – a mimetic principle of representation even as they refer to historical reality.

For David Herzberger, "double referencing [to other texts and to 'reality itself'] makes the postmodern emphasis on words more than a playful game of literary manipulation. It makes it, in fact, a political act of dissent."[5] Playful games and political dissent vary, of course. Although a multi-focal discourse runs against the grain of the monolithic discourse of Francoist historiography, it tends to circumscribe itself to a relatively small circle of literary initiates. Gonzalo Sobejano has called the self-referential novel of the early 1980s "ensimismada" ("self-absorbed," "introspective," or "narcissistic"–the latter term taken from Linda Hutcheon) and has underscored its unpopularity.[6] Benet's venture into popular culture, the detective story *El aire de un crimen* ("The Air of a Crime," 1980), was written on a dare from friends who maintained that he could *not* "reach the masses." Appearing the same year as Benet's punctilious and poetic *Saúl ante Samuel* ("Saul Before Samuel," 1980), *El aire* was hardly a huge commercial success, though it did garner the rather lowbrow Planeta Prize, as did Marsé's *La muchacha de las bragas de oro*. Marsé's foray into consumerism was different, because *La muchacha*, whose title gives an ironic high-cultural nod to Balzac's *La fille aux yeux d'or* ("The Girl with the Golden Eyes"), toys with writing in a society whose values are monetary. Less incisive in its depiction of class struggle than *Últimas tardes con Teresa* ("Last Afternoons with Teresa," 1966) and less convoluted in its depiction of resistance and its dissolution than *Si te dicen que caí* ("The Fallen," 1973), *La muchacha* focuses on a *Falangista* who dictates his personal history to his niece. The tale examines the ageing of those who lived through the Civil War, enjoyed the spoils of the victors, and attempted to refashion themselves, and their history, in a more socially palatable manner. Rebuked by more than one critic for "selling out," Marsé returned to more demanding, if still relatively accessible, stories in *Ronda del Guinardó* ("Guinardó Circle," 1984), *Teniente Bravo* ("Lieutenant Bravo," 1987), and *El embrujo de Shanghai* ("The Spell of Shanghai," 1993).

The tension between commercial and critical success, significant in the late nineteenth century, endures in the late twentieth century. Torrente Ballester's *Fragmentos de Apocalipsis* ("Fragments of Apocalypse," 1977)

---

[5] David K. Herzberger, *Narrating the Past: Fiction and Historiography in Postwar Spain* (Durham: Duke University Press, 1995), p. 143.

[6] Gonzalo Sobejano, "La novela ensimismada (1980–1985)." *España Contemporánea* 1.1 (1988), p. 11.

and *La isla de los jacintos cortados* ("The Island of Cut Hyacinths," 1980), though not as impressive as *La saga/fuga de J.B.* ("The Saga/Flight of J.B.," 1972), are here germane: all three novels combine a love of story telling, all but essential to popular (commercial) success, with an appreciation of formal innovation, so dear to many critics. Imbued with Galician and Spanish codes, Torrente's later novels bring to mind the fabulative fire of Gabriel García Márquez, the humor of Cabrera Infante, and the intellectual acrobatics of Borges. Despite Torrente's attempts to temper such comparisons by references to Cervantes and fellow Galician Álvaro Cunqueiro, a transatlantic relay appears inevitable. Camilo José Cela's Galician heritage distinguishes many of his works too, including *Mazurca para dos muertos* ("Mazurka for Two Dead Men," 1983), which wavers between the jocular, the erotic, and the sordid. Cela's dalliances with Francoism – he worked briefly as a censor – as well as his unabashed *machismo* led some to dismiss his work as reactionary cant. Many others, however, praised his dazzling command of the Spanish language – evidenced in his *Diccionario secreto* ("Secret Dictionary," 1968–1972) – as well as his familiarity with the varieties of narrative form. Though *La familia de Pascual Duarte* ("The Family of Pascual Duarte," 1942) and *La colmena* ("The Hive," 1951), both temporarily censored, overshadowed his later works, Cela remained a vibrant, if cantankerous, force in Spanish letters until his death in 2002. While the critical and commercial success of novels by Torrente and Cela was far from even, more recent works enjoyed both. Eduardo Mendoza's *La ciudad de los prodigios* ("City of Marvels," 1986), in which a man vies with Barcelona for protagonism, and Javier Marías' *Corazón tan blanco* ("A Heart So White," 1992), in which an enigmatic suicide inaugurates an elegant reflection on truth, were best-sellers in Spain and abroad.

Then again, neither Mendoza nor Marías indulges in perplexing word games, whose extremes are arguably Julián Ríos' *Larva* (1983) and *Poundemonium* (1985), two "anti-novelas"[7] which take on James Joyce and Ezra Pound. Contesting the idea that Spanish is wanting in puns and homonyms, Ríos offers a torrent of literary and linguistic "pranks" that include triple entendres, heteroglossic turns, onomatopoeic japes, rambunctious notes, and the tangled thread of a plot. Marías may have translated *Tristram Shandy*, but Ríos attempts to perform it – as a transmuted *Finnegan's Wake*. Celebrated by Juan Goytisolo, Severo Sarduy, and other mavens of Hispanic culture, Ríos appears deliriously out of sync with the recuperation of narrative that attends the end of the twentieth century, when experimentation is not so much extinct as deprived of its combative aura. The debatable premise that good writing is socially

---

[7] Sobejano, "La novela ensimismada," p. 17.

significant *and* experimental becomes increasingly untenable as Franco fades. Ríos' lack of social engagement seems even more pronounced than Benet's, for whom the Civil War and its legacy remained unremittingly present. More interestingly, Ríos' ludic vein complements even as it contradicts the rule of popular entertainment. Fun and games – including high cultural games of intellectual recognition – come together in a movement that propels Spain into the international spotlight.

However successful the writers may be, the dominant cultural figure in the aftermath of Franco is a maker of movies: Pedro Almodóvar. The ascendancy of the visual that characterizes late capitalism inflects *la movida*, a movement of urban reaffirmation centered in Madrid. As term and concept, *la movida* has its origins in the "drug culture" of rock, punk, and new wave music. Artificial paradises of the late nineteenth century and counter-cultural hallucinations of the 1960s and 1970s give way to consumer indulgence. The anti-censorial effervescence of *el destape*, the unveiling of (usually female) bodies tied to *la movida*, left its mark on literature, particularly in the Sonrisa Vertical ("Vertical Smile") series of erotica as well as in a generalized loosening of expression. Cela's *Mazurca*, peppered with quasi-pornographic scenes, is outstripped by Almudena Grandes' *Las edades de Lulú* ("The Ages of Lulú," 1989) and María Jaén's *Amorrada al piló* (translated as *El escote* ["Cleavage"], 1986). In a country where feminism remains embattled, the realization that young women can write as salaciously as older men provokes diverse reactions. Regardless, both Grandes and Jaén – an Andalusian who cultivates Catalan – have grown in stature with *Malena es un nombre de tango* ("Malena is a Tango Name," 1994) and *La dona discreta* ("The Discreet Woman," 1997), respectively. Cinematic adaptations of their works, especially Bigas Luna's version of *Las edades*, signal the "interest" in translating certain graphic literary scenes into audiovisual images.

Cinematic adaptations are clearly not limited to the lewd, however, and the renewal of Spanish film encompasses Delibes' *Los santos inocentes* ("The Innocent Saints," 1981), Adelaida García Morales' *El sur* ("The South," 1985), Muñoz Molina's *Beltenebros* ("Prince of Shadows," 1989), Marsé's *El amante bilingüe* ("The Bilingual Lover," 1990), and Mendoza's *La ciudad de los prodigios*, as well as *La colmena* and *Tiempo de silencio*. The eighties saw a proliferation of videos and comics, often violent and sexually explicit, and of such irreverent journals as *La Luna de Madrid* ("The Moon of Madrid"), which first appeared in 1983. Many writers, notably among them Terenci Moix (1942–2003), Marsé, and Lourdes Ortiz, incorporated techniques from visual culture into their work. Moix, whose *El día que va morir Marilyn* ("The Day Marilyn Died," 1969) made clear his interest in celluloid, divas, and glamor (Marilyn Monroe), continued to pay homage to film in *El cine de los sábados* ("Saturday Cinema," 1990), the first volume of his memoirs, *El peso de la paja* ("The Weight of Straw," or "The Weight of Masturbation"). Ortiz drew on the movies for *Luz de la memoria* and on classical paintings and televized video clips for *Arcángeles* ("Archangels," 1986) to explore the impact of information technologies, speed, and hyperstimulation on literature and consciousness. A decade later, Luis Goytisolo incorporated a CD-ROM in his book of African adventures, *Mzungo* (1997). The modern exotic note was not confined to Goytisolo, however. Jesús Ferrero (1952–) – whose novels *Bélver Yin* (1981) and *Opium* (1986), along with his collaborations with Almodóvar on *Matador*, catapulted him into pop stardom – made refined exoticism fashionable again. For a few vertiginous years, Ferrero himself became a virtual icon of a highly mobile postmodernity.

Although *la movida* had a vigorous run in Galicia and elsewhere, Madrid capitalized on it most. The Italian philosopher Gianni Vattimo proclaimed Madrid "capital of the twentieth century," just as Walter Benjamin had proclaimed Paris "capital of the nineteenth century." Such hype – with foreign thinkers aiding national cultural pundits, scholars, bureaucrats, and journalists – lent an air of excitement to a city, and a nation, confronted with soaring unemployment and entrenched social problems. Enrique Tierno Galván, humanist intellectual and socialist mayor of Madrid, was a guiding force behind the capital's symbolic transformation and was spoofed in Vázquez Montalbán's *Asesinato en el Comité Central* ("Murder in the Central Committee," 1981) and celebrated in Umbral's *Y Tierno Galván ascendió a los cielos* ("And Tierno Galván Ascended into Heaven," 1990). The invented status of *la movida*, however, hardly compromises its symbolic power. Almodóvar's own incursion into writing, *Patty Diphusa y otros textos* ("Patty Diphusa and Other Writings," 1991), includes references to US hegemony and participates in debates over American military bases and Spain's membership in NATO.

The attentiveness to non-normative modes of desire, glitzy as it can be, veers into social commentary in other works as well. *L'anarquista nu* ("The Naked Anarchist," 1979) by Lluís Fernàndez (1945–), Terenci Moix's *Nuestro virgen de los mártires* ("Our Lady of the Martyrs," 1983), *Plumas de España* ("Plumes of Spain," 1988) by Ana Rossetti, *Siete contra Georgia* ("Seven Against Georgia," 1987) and *Una mala noche la tiene cualquiera* ("Anyone Can Have a Bad Night," 1982) by Eduardo Mendicutti (1948–) all flirt with extravagance. Mendicutti's novels spring from specific historical events: the arrest of two gay men in Georgia that led to the US Supreme Court case of Bowers *v.* Hardwick and, more momentously for Spain, the attempted *coup d'état* by Lieutenant Colonel Antonio Tejero on 23 February 1981. Centered on lusty queens and sharp-tongued transvestites, these stories of rebellious sexual experience are stamped by religious and legal systems that are not amused by the vindication of desire. These texts evoke such real figures as Ocaña, a well-known Barcelona transvestite, and, more popularly, Bibi Andersen, whose transsexual "transition" from man to woman becomes a metaphor for the Transition, sparking the imagination of Vázquez Montalbán, Umbral, and others. The partial "queering" of Spanish culture includes Lluís Pasqual's 1987 production of Federico García Lorca's long-censored *El público* ("The Public," 1929–1930), Salvador Dalí's recollections about his relationship with Lorca, Fernando Savater's meditatively hip *El dialecto de la vida* ("The Dialect of Life," 1985), and the languid, lyrical *Mimoun* (1988) by Rafael Chirbes (1949–). Other works related the "coming out" of democracy in ways that flattered virtually no-one. Vázquez Montalbán's *Los alegres muchachos de Atzavara* ("The Merry Lads of Atzavara," 1987), harking back to 1974, criticizes the Transition by criticizing people who play at being "liberated." *Chicos* ("Boys," 1989) by Luis Antonio de Villena (1951–) is set in Madrid when socialist-dominated conceptions of culture effected a Spanish version of *la gauche divine*, and *El joc del mentider* ("The Liar's Game," 1994) by Lluís Maria Todó (1950–), replete with neo-libertine games, recalls the Transition from a Catalan perspective.

However problematic the figurations, gay men were visible in ways that simply did not hold for lesbians. Shadowed forth in Ana María Moix's *Julia* (1970) and Carme Riera's "Te deix, amor, la mar com a penyora" ("I Leave You, My Love, the Sea as a Token," 1975), it is not until *El mismo mar de todos los veranos* ("The Same Sea as Every Summer," 1978) by Esther Tusquets (1936–) that lesbian desire is fleshed out. All three works present same-sex relations as inter-generational (between teachers and students), though Tusquets' alone tarries with explicit sexual scenarios. *El mismo mar* is noteworthy for how it recalls certain theoretical practices of Western feminism, among them *écriture féminine* ("feminine writing"), a non-holistic, non-linear, and non-teleological textuality. *El mismo mar*, like *El amor es un juego solitario* ("Love is a Solitary Game," 1979) and *Varada tras el último naufragio* ("Stranded," 1980) with which it forms a trilogy, is, however, far from radical in its sobering fixation on bourgeois culture: repeatedly, women are torn apart by domineering men. Yet, as Biruté Ciplijauskaité remarks, *El mismo mar* offers a cutting critique of the myths and rituals of the bourgeoisie.[8] In Moix's "Las virtudes peligrosas" ("Dangerous Virtues," 1985), the silence, invisibility, and separation of women persist, though agency is

---

[8] Biruté Ciplijauskaité, *La novela femenina contemporánea (1970–1985): hacia una tipología de la narración en primera persona*. (Barcelona: Anthropos, 1988), p. 174.

curiously reaffirmed. Later texts, such as *La passió segons Renée Vivien* ("The Passion According to Renée Vivien," 1994) by Maria Mercè Marçal (1952–1998) provide a more culturally nuanced presentation of female same-sex desire. Not for women writers alone, lesbianism is explored by a number of men as well. *Extramuros* (1979) by Jesús Fernández Santos (1926–1988), set in a sixteenth-century convent, gives historical depth to the erotic, ethical, and political implications of women's community. More recently, *El amante lesbiano* ("The Lesbian Lover," 2000) by José Luis Sampedro (1917–) explores the limits of gender and sexuality: the lesbian in question is a man in love with being a woman. The political implications of representation and authorship – who represents whom, what, and how – are such that virtually every work flirts with polemic. The relations between lesbianism and feminism, for example, appear vexed in works by Martín Gaite, Roig, and others. Roig's *El temps de les cireres* ("The Time of the Cherries," 1977) and *L'hora violeta*, one scene of which presents a Neptune-like Franco rising from the sea to censure a lesbian fantasy, wrestle, moreover, with the connections and contradictions between the workers' movement and the women's movement. Challenging the monopoly of political discourse by men, various novels by women intervene, programmatically or not, in the politics of gender.

Novels such as Ortiz's *Urraca* (1982), centered on the relatively obscure life of an early twelfth-century queen of Castile and León, or *El rapto del Santo Grial* ("The Ravishment of the Holy Grail," 1984) by Paloma Díaz-Mas (1954–), constitute, amid considerable irony, feminist deconstructions of masculine discourse. Drawing on Arthurian legends and traditional Spanish *romances*, Díaz-Mas weaves a story of illusion and disillusionment rich with contemporary meaning. Of those who seek the Grail, only the young believe in the quest; the others are actually saddened by the prospect of attaining the desired object. Díaz-Mas' reworking of Arthurian legend allows for a relay with *Amor de Artur* ("Love of Arthur," 1982) by Xosé Luis Méndez Ferrín (1938–), in which a Galician national dimension – further evident in his *Bretaña, Esmeraldina* (1987) – is crucial. The interplay of gender, sexuality, and class involves nationality, a fact variously portrayed in such Catalan texts as *Pedra de tartera* ("The Rolling Stone," 1985) by Maria Barbal (1949–), Riera's *Qüestió d'amor propi* ("A Matter of Self-Esteem," 1987), *Joana E* (1992) by Maria-Antònia Oliver (1946–), and *La salvatge* ("The Savage," 1994) by Isabel Clara Simó (1943–). In Simó's novel, male desires for control lead to brutality, just as in Díaz-Mas' they sustain the machinery of war. No less critical of male privilege is Rosa Montero, whose *Crónica del desamor* ("Absent Love: A Chronicle," 1979) and *La función Delta* ("The Delta Function," 1981) grapple with both the "sexual revolution" and the women's movement. With humor, Montero conveys a nagging sense of discontentment and a far from sanguine view of the future (*La función* is partly set in

2010). *Te trataré como a una reina* ("I Will Treat You Like a Queen," 1983), a quasi-detective novel with feminist undertones, accentuates the somber side of modern life.

Montero's fascination with the banal and sordid indicated that some things were still the same, if not indeed worse, in the days of democratic euphoria. Suspicion rather quickly solidified into disenchantment, *el desencanto*, another term that gained currency during the Transition. The disenchantment is often dated from 1978 to 1982, year of the socialist electoral victory; yet the temporal coordinates of what is effectively a mood or feeling are actually quite diffuse. Umbral's melancholy chronicle *Mortal y rosa* ("Mortal and Pink," 1975) is an account of the death of a beloved child and resonates with the (anticipated) death of the father. Published shortly before Franco's death, Umbral's text mines the Symbolism of broken, and unbroken, timelines. Later, in *La década roja* ("The Red Decade," 1993), Umbral authors a chronicle in which socialism, sex, money, corruption, and disenchantment loom large. Both chronicles grapple with loss, be it of another being, a way of life, or an ideal. Other chronicles, including Vázquez Montalbán's *Crónica sentimental de la transición* ("Sentimental Chronicle of the Transition," 1985), also confront disenchantment, though fiction arguably offers the most compelling takes. Juan José Millás' *Visión del ahogado* ("Vision of the Drowned Man," 1977) is about people who do not become better, just older. Loss marks other novels by Millás, from the turgid *Cerbero son las sombras* ("The Shadows Are Cerberus," 1975) to the self-enclosed *Letra muerta* ("Dead Letter," 1984) to the playfully serious *El desorden de tu nombre* ("The Disorder of Your Name," 1988). Many works published in the late seventies and early eighties are not optimistic about substantive change and recognize that injustice, inequality, and exploitation continue in democracy. One corollary of disenchantment is, to be sure, depoliticization, a phenomenon popularly known, especially among the young, as "pasotismo." Carefree attitudes can belie an excess of cares that issues in a sort of overwhelmed "dropping out." The parallels with the depoliticization or "pacification" of the populace through soccer matches, bullfights, and mass culture under Franco are considerable. Typically, the city is the locus of disenchantment, but the countryside is also implicated. *La lluvia amarilla* ("Yellow Rain," 1988) by Julio Llamazares (1955–), where "yellow rain" evokes a "black sun" of melancholy, and *Camí de sirga* ("Cord Road," 1988) by Jesús Moncada (1941–) center on the abandonment of rural environments. The consolidation of an urbanized nation in which rural locales seem antiquated, quaint, or inconsequential bears on *la movida* and *el desencanto*, marking and exceeding both.

Disenchantment, with its somber turns, finds a prominent place in detective fiction, especially when it engages the less savory aspects of history. Whatever the validity of *el desencanto*, the blend of historical and detective fiction constitutes one of the most significant strains of late twentieth-century literary production. According to Joan Ramon Resina, Eduardo Mendoza's *El misterio de la cripta embrujada* ("The Mystery of the Haunted Crypt," 1979) and *El laberinto de las aceitunas* ("The Labyrinth of Olives," 1982) parody, or "carnivalize," detective fiction.[9] The psychologically probing *Cándida, otra vez* ("Cándida, Again," 1979) by Marina Mayoral (1942–) might also be read as a parodic extension of detective fiction, but it is Mendoza's *La verdad sobre el caso Savolta* ("The Truth About the Savolta Case," 1975) that has garnered the greatest amount of critical attention and praise. Published at a time when experimentalism held sway, Mendoza's work gives a relatively clear, though actually quite complex, account of class conflict in Barcelona. For all the attempts at clarity, the *truth* of history, Mendoza suggests, is not at all easy to ascertain. The story teller as historian and detective: such is the upshot of a significant portion of Vázquez Montalbán's production as well. *Galíndez* (1990), about the assassination of an exiled Basque Republican critical of Franco and Trujillo (of the Dominican Republic), and, in a departure from the detective mode, *El pianista* ("The Pianist," 1985), about a musician whose career is "interrupted" by the Civil War, offer many memorable characters. Vázquez Montalbán's most original creation is Pepe Carvalho, a private investigator of Galician origin, an ex-communist, a former CIA agent, a gourmet, a cynic, and a "passive lover," who first appeared in *Yo maté a Kennedy* ("I Killed Kennedy," 1972). The "Carvalho series" includes *La soledad del manager* ("The Angst-Ridden Executive," 1977), *Los mares del Sur* ("Southern Seas," 1979), *La rosa de Alejandría* ("The Rose of Alexandria," 1984), *El laberinto griego* ("An Olympic Death," 1991), and other fast-paced, slang-strewn, hard-hitting works in which political commentary careens into entertainment. Another master of detective fiction is Muñoz Molina, whose *El invierno en Lisboa* ("Winter in Lisbon," 1987) and *Beltenebros* at times read as if they were *film noir* scripts. Muñoz Molina's election, at a young age, into the Real Academia Española became the most visible sign of his canonization, confirmed in the success of *El jinete polaco* ("The Polish Horseman," 1991) and *Plenilunio* ("Full Moon," 1997). Disenchanted or not, the return to narration seems secure.

Detective fiction was not the only mode of story telling to be reinvigorated in the eighties and nineties. Fantasy, horror, adventure, romance, and farce all had their triumphs. The mischievous *El castillo de la carta cifrada* ("The Castle of the Coded Letter," 1979) and *Amado monstruo* ("Beloved Monster," 1985) by Javier Tomeo (1932–) are cases in point.

[9] Joan Ramon Resina, *El cadáver en la cocina: la novela criminal en la cultura del desencanto* (Barcelona: Anthropos, 1997), pp. 245, 229.

So too are the darkly witty ecological revision of *Robinson Crusoe* in *El año de Gracia* ("The Year of Grace," 1985) by Cristina Fernández Cubas (1945–) and her semiotically sophisticated *El ángulo del horror* ("The Angle of Horror," 1990), in which horror is an effect of doubles, angles, and flickering signs. The venerable Ana María Matute turned to the Middle Ages for inspiration to write the mammoth *Olvidado rey Gudú* ("Forgotten King Gudú," 1996) and *Aranmanoth* (2000), in which the influence of fairy tales is manifest. The meticulously researched and rather conventionally rendered action-adventure romps by Arturo Pérez-Reverte (1951–), including *El maestro de esgrima* ("The Fencing Master," 1988), *La tabla de Flandes* ("The Flanders Panel," 1990), *El club Dumas* ("The Dumas Club," 1993), and *La piel del tambor* ("The Seville Communion," 1995), were commercial blockbusters. Antonio Gala's *La pasión turca* ("The Turkish Passion," 1993), and Terenci Moix's *No digas que fue un sueño* ("Don't Say It Was a Dream," 1986) and *El sueño de Alejandría* ("The Dream of Alexandria," 1988), proved that kitsch, camp, and Orientalism could still be profitable, while *¡Oh es él! Viaje fantástico hacia Julio Iglesias* ("Oh, It's He! Fantastic Voyage to Julio Iglesias," 1986) by Maruja Torres (1943–), proved that kitsch, camp, and *españolismo* (Spanish cultural nationalism) could be too. By the late eighties and early nineties, amid the fanfare surrounding the Olympics in Barcelona and the World's Fair in Seville (both held in 1992, the year of the polemical five hundredth anniversary of Columbus' voyage), Spain seemed far from the poverty, hunger, and authoritarianism that characterized, for many, years of Francoist rule.

Impugned *and* applauded as more show than substance, the "new" Spain of consumerist spectacle ironically conditioned more discreet narrative endeavors. *Relatos sobre la falta de sustancia* ("Tales About the Lack of Substance," 1977) and *El héroe de las mansardas de Mansard* ("The Hero of the Big House," 1983) by Álvaro Pombo (1939–), *Alguien te observa en secreto* ("Someone Secretly Observes You," 1985) by Ignacio Martínez de Pisón (1960–), *Historia de un idiota contada por él mismo* ("The Story of an Idiot as Told by Himself," 1986) by Félix de Azúa (1944–), *Burdeos* ("Bordeaux," 1986) and *Todos mienten* ("Everyone Lies," 1988) by Soledad Puértolas (1947–), and Marías' *El hombre sentimental* ("The Sentimental Man," 1986) and *Todas las almas* ("All Souls," 1989) are neither flashy, opaque, nor confrontational. Navajas notes how Azúa's novel avoids the histrionics of a Juan Goytisolo and charts a more truly tentative, even humble, course.[10] The lack of justice, redemption, or grand meaning does not issue into a sweeping repudiation of history or a gaudy assumption of irrelevance but into a

---

[10] Navajas, "Una estética," p. 115.

fragile negotiation of fictionalized reality. Puértolas grapples with falsity, solitude, and powerlessness, and Pombo wonders if the much-trumpeted lack of substance – the "unbearable lightness of being" – is not made deceptively good by dreams of literary substance. The presence of low-keyed, almost forgettable stories of individuals who attempt to carve out a place for themselves in an uncaring world is insistent. Montero's *Amado amo* ("Beloved Boss," 1988), centered on the petty power plays of the work force, and Millás' *La soledad era esto* ("That Was Loneliness," 1990), focused on a middle-aged woman's attempts to cope with death, isolation, and anonymity, present the age of democratic consolidation and European integration as a neo-liberal rat-race. Spain officially enters the European Union in 1986, but the end of centuries of marginalization does not spell the end of sadness and disillusionment. The brilliant *Juegos de la edad tardía* ("Games of an Elderly Age," 1989) by Luis Landero (1948–) provides a temporally dense meditation on the fate of the artist as hero: through the obsessive encouragement of a friend, a despondent man named Gregorio becomes the dashingly successful, but absurd, Faroni. Competition of a more recognizable sort (in sports, specifically track and field) runs through *La media distancia* ("The Middle Distance," 1984) by Alejandro Gándara (1957–), reminiscent of Alan Sillitoe's *The Loneliness of the Long-Distance Runner* (1975).

Competition has national vectors as well. If in the sixties Social Realism came apart, it is also then, as Mario Santana remarks, "that the national conception of Spanish literature collapsed."[11] The "collapse" occurs by way of "a reemergent pluricultural conception of the Spanish state" articulated primarily in Galicia, Euskadi, and Catalonia, and the success of the Latin American "Boom."[12] The impact of García Márquez, Cortázar, Carpentier, and Vargas Llosa, variously promoted by Carlos Barral (of Editorial Seix Barral) and others, both invigorates and intimidates Spanish authors, many of whom struggle with being in the shadow of Latin America. The divide is not easy, however, and Darío Villanueva, for one, finds the separation of literatures written in basically the same language increasingly untenable.[13] The Peruvian Vargas Llosa, like the Paraguayan Augusto Roa Bastos and the Uruguayans Juan Carlos Onetti and Cristina Peri Rossi, move to Spain and in some cases become Spanish citizens, a fact that troubles their national categorization. The movement to Spain recalls movement from it, an exile conditioned by war, scarcity,

---

[11] Mario Santana, *Foreigners in the Homeland: The Spanish American New Novel in Spain, 1962–1974* (Lewisburg, PA: Bucknell University Press, 2000), p. 17.

[12] Santana, *Foreigners*, p. 18.

[13] Darío Villanueva, "Los marcos de la literatura española (1975–1990): Esbozo de un sistema." In *Historia y crítica de la literatura española. IX: Los nuevos nombres 1975–1990*. Ed. Francisco Rico. (Barcelona: Crítica, 1992), p. 13.

and state-sponsored violence. The "Mexican years" of Luis Buñuel, Max Aub, and Luis Cernuda are not reducible to some intrinsic "Spanishness," however much invoked. *Chromos* by Felipe Alfau (1902–1999), written in English in 1948 but not published until 1990 (after the success of the reissue of *Locos*), raises further questions about nationality, language, location, and time. Is the date of composition more important than the date of publication? Is the place of birth more, or less, important than the place of production? Does language determine national pertinence? Is Spanish literature written in Spain, in Spanish, by native-born Spaniards, or is it something else? The reaffirmation of literary production in Galician, Catalan, and Basque brings these questions "home." The equivalence of Spanish and Castilian is implicitly questioned by the National Literature Prize, awarded to *Xa vai o Griffón no vento* ("The Griffon") by Alfredo Conde (1945–) in 1986, *Obabakoak* by Bernardo Atxaga (pseudonym of Joseba Irazu Garmendia; 1951–) in 1989, Riera's *Dins el darrer blau* ("In the Last Blue") in 1995, and *¿Qué me queres amor?* ("What Do You Want of Me, Love?") by Manuel Rivas (1957–) in 1996.

Atxaga, Conde, and Riera engage the promises and pitfalls of writing in so-called "minor" or minoritized languages and advance pluralistic conceptions of the past and the present. Riera's *Dins el darrer blau* narrates the persecution of a group of Mallorcan Jews during the Inquisition, while her *Cap al cel obert* ("Toward the Open Sky," 2000) confronts racism and anti-Semitism in colonial Cuba. Conde's *Griffon*, moving between an Inquisitorial past and a democratic present, presents Galicia as suffering under intolerant Castilian-speaking forces, while Atxaga's *Obabakoak*, drawing on Maupassant and Chekhov, provides a subtle picture of an imaginary Basque town that is *not* determined by intolerance, extortion, and terrorism. Celebrated as *Obabakoak* is, *Ene Jesus* (*Ay de mí, Jesús*; "Woe is Me, Jesus," 1976) by Ramon Saizarbitoria (1944–) and *Eta emakumeari sugeak esan zion* (*Y la serpiente dijo a la mujer*; "And the Serpent Said to the Woman," 2000) by Lourdes Oñederra (1958–) help fortify a burgeoning literary culture in Euskera. Galician and Catalan, as Romance languages, present fewer problems of intercommunication and translation into Castilian than Basque, and draw more confidently on flourishing medieval and modern traditions (hence Atxaga's half-serious defense of plagiarism in *Obabakoak*). *Ilustrísima* ("His Grace," 1980) by Carlos Casares (1941–2000), *A ceo aberto* ("Open Sky," 1981) by Xosé Fernández Ferreiro (1931–), *Polaroid* (1986) and *Land Rover* (1988) by Suso de Toro (1956–), and Marina Mayoral's novel for young readers, *Tristes armas* ("Unhappy Weapons," 1994), along with *La teranyina* ("The Spider's Web," 1983) by Jaume Cabré (1947–), *Les primaveres i les tardors* ("Springs and Falls," 1986) by Baltasar Porcel (1937–), *El perquè de tot plegat* ("The Reason for It All," 1993) by Quim Monzó

(1952–), and *Gràcies per la propina* ("Thanks for the Tip," 1994) by Ferran Torrent (1951–) are only a few of the diverse novels and stories – some virtual memoirs and others gems of the imagination – that appear in a more pluralistic Spain. Yet, for all the advances, the status of texts written in Basque, Galician, and Catalan – not to mention Bable – remains contested, with the government itself intervening in the construction of canons and reading lists. The unity of Spain is still articulated, it seems, in Spanish (Castilian), and recent moves by the Valencian government have actually attempted to promote said unity by fostering the disunity of Catalan. Marsé's *El amante bilingüe*, set in Barcelona, gives a devastatingly tendentious view of Catalan linguistic policy and makes a case for a hybrid, "bastardized" language conveyed, nonetheless, almost entirely in Castilian.

The complication, if not collapse, of a national conception of Spanish literature is not limited to the Iberian periphery or the Americas. The "grupo leonés," or "León group," is a construction that privileges a place of origin, with three quite diverse writers – José María Merino, Luis Mateo Díez (1942–), and Juan Pedro Aparicio (1941–) – linked as much by geography, common cultural history, and friendship as by style, theme, or ideology. Díez's *Las estaciones provinciales* ("Provincial Times," 1982) and *La fuente de la edad* ("The Fountain of Age," 1986), Aparicio's *El año del francés* ("The Year of the Frenchman," 1986) and *Retratos de ambigú* ("Portraits of Ambigú," 1989), and Merino's *El caldero de oro* ("The Cauldron of Gold," 1981) and *La orilla oscura* ("The Dark Shore," 1985) are disparate works that deploy a variety of narrative techniques, including temporal overlaps, dialogism, and metafictionality. Earlier in his career, Díez, as a poet and a member of the "grupo Claraboya," had criticized the *castellanidad* of much social (Realist) literature and the perceived frivolity of much experimental literature. Indeed, a variety of narratives in Castilian, many of them set in the countryside, do not partake of the facile patriotism often associated with regional constructions (Spain as a nation "rich" in regions as opposed to Spain as a plurinational state). Sampedro's *Octubre, octubre* ("October, October," 1981) and *La sonrisa etrusca* ("The Etruscan Smile," 1985), with their affirmative reflections on aging, death, family, and tenderness, and *El silencio de las sirenas* ("The Silence of the Sirens," 1985) by Adelaida García Morales (1945–), set in a village in Las Alpujarras, are not hegemonic works. Nor are Martín Gaite's *Nubosidad variable* ("Variable Cloudiness," 1992) or Díaz-Mas' *El sueño de Venecia* ("The Dream of Venice," 1992), or *Azul* ("Blue," 1994) by Rosa Regás (1933–), or any number of other titles. Writing in Spanish, the authors of these works may not have to contend with the problems that face those writing in the other languages of the state, but they are not, for that reason, any less inclined to grapple with the pains and pleasures of expression. The extrapersonal dimensions of language; the status of nations and states (the Spanish Constitution distinguishes between the "duty" to know Castilian and the "right" to know Catalan, Basque, and Galician); the conflicting versions of history, and so on, are only some of the factors that mark literary endeavors.

The shape of Spanish narrative at the end of the twentieth century and the beginning of the twenty-first is far from clear. The relatively strong divisions and connections between social engagement and aesthetic experimentation that characterized the sixties and seventies seem to have weakened, fragmented, or proliferated in ways that make any classification not based on genre, date, place, and ostensibly more embodied signs of identity (such as gender, sexuality, nationality, and race), quite tentative. Of course, classification of any sort is increasingly contested, as if the truth were indeed nowhere – or perhaps everywhere – to be found. Crime, disease, addiction, and militarism in *Días contados* ("Numbered Days," 1993) by Juan Madrid (1947–), Vázquez Montalbán's *El estrangulador* ("The Strangler," 1994), and Muñoz Molina's *Ardor guerrero* ("Warlike Ardor," 1995) seem to function as if *they* were the truth. Yet, such topics also become something of a fad with the promotion, under the rubric of "dirty realism," of José Ángel Mañas' *Historias del Kronen* ("Stories of Kronen," 1994) and Ray Loriga's *Lo peor de todo* ("The Worst of All," 1992) and *Caídos del cielo* ("Fallen from Heaven," 1995). Mañas (1971–) and Loriga (1967–) are of the same "generation" – another disputable classificatory term – as Belén Gopegui (1963–), whose *La escala de los mapas* ("The Scale of Maps," 1993) and *Tocarnos la cara* ("To Touch Our Faces," 1995) explore, respectively, the fear of shared intimacy and the self-interest that persists in communal endeavors. If Mañas writes with a directness that seems to empty prose of poetry, Gopegui's prose becomes poetic in its reliance on ellipsis, understatement, and repetition. A masculine/feminine divide might be – indeed has been – adduced, but only to be troubled by the presence of other men and women writing in at least four languages and from a variety of perspectives. Whatever the "crises" of literature, something still holds: be it a war-torn past – as in *Historia de una maestra* ("A Teacher's Story," 1990) by Josefina Aldecoa (1926–), Rivas' *O lapis do carpinteiro* ("The Carpenter's Pencil," 1998), and *Soldados de Salamina* ("Soldiers of Salamina," 2001) – by Javier Cercas (1962–) or a consumer-driven present. Or something else: the future, as always, remains to be seen.

55

Post-Franco theatre

SHARON G. FELDMAN

In the multiple realms and layers that comprise the contemporary Spanish theatrical landscape, "crisis" would seem to be the word that most often lingers in the air, as though it were a common mantra, ready to roll off the tongue of so many theatre professionals with such enormous ease, and even enthusiasm, that one is prompted to wonder whether it might indeed be a miracle that the contemporary technological revolution – coupled with perpetual quandaries concerning public and private funding for the arts – had not by now brought an end to the evolution of the oldest of live arts, or, at the very least, an end to drama as we know it.

In 1996, José Ramón Fernández, a playwright based in Madrid, went so far as to underscore the presence of a curious inclination toward self-destruction in the theatre profession in Spain, where grim prognostications and dismal portrayals of the current theatrical panorama are surpassed only by the horrors of Francisco de Goya's black paintings.[1] In the year 2000, Barcelona playwright/poet Joan Casas (1950–) dared to pose the provocative hypothesis that the often-cited "new Catalan dramaturgy," in effect, might be merely a "mirage." ("Dramaturgy," in Spain, generally refers to the art of writing plays and/or the textual organization and design of the *mise en scène*.) Furthermore, during the past decade, the tempestuous cultural-political *milieu* surrounding the construction and reconstruction of several architecturally striking and ostensibly lavish public theatre venues – which include, in Barcelona, the Teatre Nacional de Catalunya, the new Teatre Lliure, and the Gran Teatre del Liceu, and, in Madrid, the Teatro Real, the Teatro Olimpia, and the Teatro María Guerrero (the historic home of Spain's Centro Dramático Nacional [CDN]) – has spawned a hallucinatory display of melodramatic moments, impassioned accusations, and hysterical outbursts, witnessed both on and off the stage.

Yet, history has shown that in Spain, as well as other Western societies, crisis is perhaps not only a necessary condition, but also a *raison d'être* for

[1] José Ramón Fernández, "Quince años de escritura dramática en España: un camino hacia la normalidad." *ADE Teatro* 50 (April–June 1996), p. 80.

the theatre, for it implies an essential attitude of risk and rupture, a sense of being on edge or on the verge of collapse, that underlies its dynamic drive toward survival. Only complacency – not crisis – could lead to death, or to what Peter Brook calls "deadly theatre." The Polish theatre director Jerzy Grotowski (1933–1999), for whom the stage was always a place of provocation, once declared that the theatre has meaning only "if it allows us to transcend our stereotyped vision, our conventional feelings and customs, our standards of judgment." Imbedded in Grotowski's theory of acting is the implicit paradox that only after having cast aside all masks and relinquished all pretense, can the actor "unveil" and then embrace, "in a state of complete defenselessness," the process of self-discovery and transcendence that is the experience of performance.[2] It is a method that may be painful, shocking, or polemical, and that, when superimposed onto the broader context of the Spanish stage, would seem to be the very same process that underpins the arduous evolution of theatre history subsequent to the death of Francisco Franco. One need only recall the forty-year period of Civil War and dictatorship, in which censorship and multiple manifestations of exile and diaspora meant the disappearance, obstruction, or severe limitation of the work of those theatre professionals who refused to succumb to the aesthetic–political–linguistic norms of the official culture, in order to begin to understand that the Spanish stage has come a long way since 1975.

Since the transition to democracy, the theatre of Spain has evolved into a cacophonous state of aesthetic heterogeneity, cultural diversity, and linguistic plurality that is truly unprecedented in modern times. While cynicism may be a long-established premise, it may also be tempered by existing signs that contemporary theatrical life in Spain, far from languishing upon its deathbed, in fact may be enjoying at this new turn of the century relatively good health. In stark contrast to the years of dictatorship, a situation of synchronicity exists whereby several generations of dramatists, directors, designers, and performers are able to lead parallel lives, writing and working side by side within the Spanish state, offering a broad range of performance practices and theatrical traditions intended to garner the interest of diverse and overlapping groups of spectators. A commercial theatre of bourgeois sensibilities, conventional comedies, and the so-called "aesthetic of the boulevard" (from Juan José Alonso Millán [1936–], Ana Diosdado [1940–], and Santiago Moncada [1928–] to Neil Simon and Stephen Sondheim) continues to thrive, and no doubt always will, but it exists alongside a gamut of Avant-Garde, and multilingual, alternatives.

---

[2] Jerzy Grotowski, "Statement of Principles." In *The Twentieth Century Performance Reader*. Ed. Michael Huxley and Noel Witts (New York: Routledge, 1996), p. 188.

In the realm of experimental theatre, the hierarchical distinction between text-based drama and pure performance is no longer valid, and all possible amalgamations and variations of the theatrical spectacle co-exist: from the multimedia "actions" of companies such as La Fura dels Baus, Sèmola, and Comediants, enormously physical and highly visual in conception; to the plays of Carles Batlle (1963–), Lluïsa Cunillé (1961–), Ignasi Garcia (1964–), Juan Mayorga (1965–), and Borja Ortiz de Gondra (1965–), in which the word is action and action is word; to the hybrid language of Rodrigo García (1964–) and Sara Molina (1958–), at once profoundly rooted in both the aesthetic tendencies of installation art and the exploitation of the text. Catalan dramatist and director Sergi Belbel (1963–) aptly summarized this cross-disciplinary, eclectic sensibility when he declared, "if I like both La Fura dels Baus and Molière, it's not a contradiction."[3]

In keeping with the contemporary obfuscation of distinctions between high and low, the phenomenon of "crossover" – in Madrid and Barcelona, as on Broadway – is no longer a taboo necessarily synonymous with "sell-out." This situation can at times lead to beneficial effects of aesthetic hybridism and intellectual cross-fertilization. Such is the case of the tremendously popular adaptations of canonical works of literature by the Barcelona musical theatre company Dagoll Dagom, under the creative supervision of Joan Lluís Bozzo and Anna Rosa Cisquella. Their *Antaviana* (1978/1985) was based on the short stories of Pere Calders, while *Mar i cel* ("Sea and Sky," 1988) was derived from the eponymous play by Àngel Guimerà. *Cacao* (2000), with cast members from both Spain and the Caribbean, and music by rock icon Santiago Auserón, was inspired by a short story written by Gérard Lauzier. It is a musical that revealed, beneath its uplifting rhythms and comic episodes, a serious political engagement with issues of immigration, identity, uprootedness, and the plight of those living in Spain without legal documentation. Another telling example of this phenomenon of crossover is the Catalan musical *El temps de Planck* ("Planck Time," 2000), written by Belbel and experimental composer Òscar Roig, an unconventional and compelling blend of metaphysics and melodrama, whose unforgettable melodies resonate with an energy comparable to that of any Broadway show.

Curiously, the common tendency among many contemporary playwrights to cross over from drama to television screenwriting – Álvaro del Amo (1942–), Belbel, Josep M. Benet i Jornet (1940–), Fermín Cabal (1948–), Toni Cabré (1957–), Jordi Galceran (1964–), Garcia, Rafael González (1966–), Ignacio del Moral (1957–), Antonio Onetti (1962–),

[3] Sharon G. Feldman, "Si me gustan La Fura dels Baus y Moliére, no es una contradicción: Conversaciones con Sergi Belbel." *España Contemporánea* 13.1 (2001), pp. 71–86.

Josep Pere Peyró (1959–), David Plana (1969–), Sergi Pompermayer (1967–), Jordi Sánchez (1964–), Paco Sanguino (1964–), Mercè Sarrias (1966–), Rodolf Sirera (1948–), – has created intriguing relationships between the stage and the small screen. Beginning in the 1990s, Benet i Jornet transformed the face of Catalan language television, and by extension, Catalan theatre, with his popular serial melodramas. The enormous success of television series such as these has helped fuel the rise in theatre spectatorship in Catalonia, not only because audiences have become more likely than ever before to recognize the name of the author, but also because the crossover has engendered a "star system" composed of some of Spain's finest stage actors, who move regularly from the television screen, to the stage, and back, enticing spectators and "fans" to move with them.

As the foregoing descriptions suggest, the history of theatre in Spain is no longer a tale of just one city; rather, the ontological limits that define the contemporary Spanish stage extend well beyond the geopolitical borders of Madrid. The same issues of self-determination, national identity, and cultural legitimacy – the often-cited forces that stem from both the center and the periphery – that have left a lasting imprint on the history of the modern Spanish state, have likewise informed the cultural-political backdrop of post-Franco theatre. The CDN was established in Madrid in 1978, and subsequently, throughout the 1980s, a vast shift toward decentralization ensued with the emergence of several national "drama centers," funded by local governments in Andalusia, Catalonia, Galicia, Valencia, Extremadura, and the Balearic Islands. These generally well-endowed public institutions (some of which were only short-lived ventures), created according to varying principles of international projection, nationalism, and protectionism, were established, in theory, to promote and showcase autochthonous theatre from distinct historical repertoires, as well as the work of contemporary playwrights.

The employment of a language other than Spanish on the stage has been a crucial marker and affirmation of identity, and even a sign of resistance; of course, this was also the case during the dictatorship. As director Lluís Pasqual (1951–), founding member of Barcelona's Teatre Lliure, has affirmed, "Catalan theatre and the Catalan language were strangled, but they were not able to suffocate or kill us . . . To speak Catalan at that moment meant: communist, separatist, whatever!"[4] Raúl Dans (1964–), a playwright with ties to the Centro Dramático Galego, has remarked that his use of the Galician language in post-Franco times is "a way of reclaiming one's own space . . . when faced with the strong thrust of

---

[4] Interview in Ytak, *Lluís Pasqual: Camí de teatre*. Trans. Albert de la Torre (Barcelona: Alter Pirene / Escena, 1993), p. 36.

more powerful dramaturgies."[5] In plays such as *Lugar* ("Place," 1994), and *Derrota* ("Defeat," 1998), Dans has shown how being "on the edge of the world" is not only a geographic situation, but also an existential condition, which translates into a "geopathological" meditation on the relationship between place and theatrical space.

In effect, a sweeping view of cultural activities in contemporary Spain reveals large and small enclaves of substantial theatrical undertakings in peripheral locations that are often far detached from the bravado of grandiloquent public or commercial infrastructures. Such is the performance garage in Santiago de Compostela known as La NASA (Nave de Servicios Artísticos), established in 1992 as a center for Avant-Garde artistic endeavors and home to the Galician theatre company Chévere. On the island of Menorca, each November since 1970, the Cercle Artístic de Ciutadella has granted the coveted Born Prize, one of Spain's most revered and lucrative theatre awards, to a play written in either Spanish or Catalan. The Basque town of Rentería is home to the awarding-winning Ur Teatro (1988), whose influential director Helena Pimenta has gained international notoriety for her contemporary stagings of Shakespeare. Although the list of playwrights who create Basque-language drama is small (Yolanda Arrieta [1963–], Bernardo Atxaga [1951–], Aitzpea Goenaga [1959–], Xabier Mendiguren [1945–], Xavier de Soto, Patxi Zabaleta [1947–], Ramón Barea [1949–], among others), there was a fleeting attempt, during the late 1990s, to establish a Teatro Público de Guipúzcoa with a stable company performing in both Spanish and Euskera. Ignacio Amestoy (1947–) and Xabi Puerta (1959–) have taken up issues of Basque identity in plays written in Spanish.

Since its founding by Salvador Távora in 1971, La Cuadra de Sevilla has unfailingly displayed – with spectacles such as *Quejío* ("Moan," 1972), *Andalucía amarga* ("Bitter Andalusia," 1979), and more recently, *Don Juan de los ruedos* ("Don Juan of the Bullrings," 2000) – a commitment to deconstructing the mythologized images of Andalusia that were perpetuated by the culture of the dictatorship. Jerez de la Frontera is center of operations for La Zaranda (1978), a theatre company whose dark, brooding visions, depicted in *Perdonen la tristeza* ("Forgive the Sorrow," 1992) and *Cuando la vida eterna se acabe* ("When Eternity Comes to an End," 1996), are evocative of the canvasses of the Andalusian Baroque painters.

A key showcase for contemporary drama in Spain is the Muestra de Autores Contemporáneos, held annually in Alicante since 1993, under the

---

[5] Raúl Dans, "Un dramaturgo en el fin del mundo." In "Les darreres generacions teatrals del segle." Special issue of *Assaig de Teatre: Revista de l'Associació d'Investigació i Experimentació Teatral* 24 (September 2000), p. 140.

direction of Guillermo Heras (1952–). This is one of numerous theatre festivals organized each year throughout the Autonomous Community of Valencia, where theatre in post-Franco times has grown steadily in keeping with the cultural resurgence of its capital city. One of the watershed plays of the democratic Transition, *Plany en la mort d'Enric Ribera* ("Lament for the Death of Enric Ribera," 1972), was written by coveted Valencian playwright Rodolf Sirera. This "biographic symphony" takes the form of a complex impressionistic collage, with visual projections and text interwoven in both Spanish and Valencian Catalan. Sirera's experimental play, which finally premièred in 1977, was an explicit vehicle for expressing his preoccupations with issues of Valencian identity and the future of the Valencian stage. Perhaps, years later, upon contemplating the growth of the theatre in this community, he was able to experience a sense of recompense for his enormous efforts on behalf of its survival and revitalization.

Director Carles Alfaro (1960–) and his Valencian company Moma Teatre (1982) have received national recognition for their stagings of Pinter and Camus. The operatic spectacles of Valencian director, composer, and pianist Carles Santos (1940–) – *L'esplèndida vergonya del fet mal fet* ("The Spendid Shame of the Deed Badly Done," 1996), *Ricardo i Elena* (2000), *Sama Samaruck Suck Suck* (2002) – have presented audiences at international venues including the Edinburgh Festival with an uncanny, Surrealistic blend of the sacred and the profane. Playwrights Pasqual Alapont (1963–), Carles Alberola (1964–), Chema Cardeña (1963–), Roberto García (1968–), Rafael González, Alejandro Jornet (1956–), Manuel Molins (1946–), Carles Pons (1955–), Paco Sanguino, and Paco Zarzoso (1966–), part of a veritable "boom" in theatrical writing in Valencia, are gradually gaining ground and national prizes. Zarzoso, who regularly writes in Spanish, has revealed in the minimalist brushstrokes of *Umbral* ("Threshold," 1997), *Valencia* (1977), and *Mirador* ("Lookout," 1998) a sharp sense of the relationship between liminal exterior spaces of transgression and the interior torment of his characters.

In post-Franco Spain, Barcelona and Madrid have emerged unequivocally as the two major axes of theatrical creation, production, and exhibition, creating what Pimenta has termed a "bipolarización" of the Spanish stage.[6] Along with cultural, political, social, and economic factors, the magnetic draw that these cities have had with regard to the evolution of theatre during the democratic period is also a consequence of their role as pedagogical centers. They are home to the two principal conservatories, the RESAD (Real Escuela Superior de Arte Dramático) in Madrid

---

[6] Helena Pimenta, "El euskara, ¿una ausenca teatral?" In "Les darreres generacions teatrals del segle," p. 117.

and the Institut del Teatre in Barcelona, as well as numerous workshops, seminars, university groups, and publications supervised by a long inventory of established playwrights and theatre "gurus" that includes José Luis Gómez (1940–) and Guillermo Heras in Madrid, and Ricard Salvat (1934–) in Barcelona. In 1995, Gómez founded the award-winning Teatro de la Abadía in Madrid, an experimental theatre laboratory devoted to intellectual reflection, social debate, and the pursuit of "el placer inteligente" ("intelligent pleasure"). José Sanchis Sinisterra (1940–), a Valencian dramatist, director, and theorist, has been a decisive pedagogical force and inspiration to many playwrights in Madrid and Barcelona, as well as Latin America.

Significantly, the dramatists and theatre practitioners who have come of age during the democratic period have had a level of academic training in the theory and mechanics of writing *and* staging plays that has never before been seen in Spain. Many of these playwrights have strong ties to one or more of the nearly thirty *salas alternativas*, or "alternative venues" (similar in conception to the performance spaces located "off-off" Broadway or on the London "fringe"), which are scattered about the Spanish State (e.g. La NASA and the Sala Beckett). A phenomenon that emerged during the mid 1980s, these generally small hives of creativity (approximately nine in Madrid, seven in Barcelona) are today dynamic spaces of Avant-Garde energy, where banality and reckless expenditure are replaced with risk, commitment, experimentation, research, and pedagogy, and where the artists are hardly impervious to international recognition.

Stemming from the *salas alternativas* are pioneering cadres of theatre artists such as the Grupo El Astillero (composed of playwrights José Ramón Fernández [1962–], Juan Mayorga, Luis Miguel González [1965–], and Raúl Hernández [1964–]), with connections to the Sala Cuarta Pared in Madrid. Javier Yagüe, artistic director of the Cuarta Pared and its resident company, created, along with playwrights Yolanda Pallín (1965–) and José Ramón Fernández, the immensely successful *Trilogía de la juventud* ("Trilogy of Youth," 1999–2002), which was seen in more than fifty cities. In Barcelona, the Sala Beckett and the initiatives of Sanchis Sinisterra and director Toni Casares (1965–) have nurtured the careers of Àngels Aymar (1958–), Carles Batlle, Sergi Belbel, Lluïsa Cunillé, Manel Dueso (1954–), Beth Escudé (1963–), Ignasi Garcia, Enric Nolla (1966–), Josep Pere Peyró, David Plana, Sergi Pompermayer, and Mercè Sarrias.

As was suggested earlier, the long road from the democratic Transition to what Fernández and others have termed the "normalization" of the Spanish stage has hardly been devoid of episodes of anguish. For the group of dramatists commonly known as the "new Spanish theatre," which emerged during the *apertura* (gradual "opening" of Spain to foreign influence) of the 1960s, the transition was a time of disenchantment, as they were forced to contend with a persistent denial of historical memory, a rejection of the allegorical evocations of injustice that had been constants in their theatre. Born in the 1920s, 1930s, and 1940s, Luis Riaza (1925–), José Ruibal (1925–), Ramón Gil Novales (1928–), Antonio Martínez Ballesteros (1929–), Miguel Romero Esteo (1930–), Jesús Campos (1938–), Manuel Martínez Mediero (1938–), Luis Matilla (1939–), Jordi Teixidor (1939–), Angel García Pintado (1940–), Alberto Miralles (1940–), María-José Ragué-Arias (1941–), Carmen Resino (1941–), Jaume Melendres (1941–), Jerónimo López Mozo (1942–), Manuel Lourenzo (1943–), and Roger Justafré (1944–) were part of a long list of playwrights who, in general, were known to employ anti-Realist/ anti-classical modes of representation (absurdist allegory, Expressionism, collage, *esperpento*) as a seemingly innocent mask for an intensely critical subtext whose sphere of reference remained, but was not limited to, authoritarian Spain. These *nuevos* were branded with epithets that included "underground," "Symbolist," "prohibited," and even "the most prized and the least staged." This last appellation certainly held true, for, during the political Transition, a so-called "Realist" playwright, such as Antonio Buero Vallejo, whose long career culminated with the historic *mise en scène* of *La Fundación* ("The Foundation," 1974) at the CDN in 1998, was much more likely to see his works staged than any of the *nuevos*.

Amid frequent bouts of historical amnesia on the part of audiences, producers, and national drama centers, the Transition was also a period marked by several uneven attempts to rescue the quintessentially Spanish anti-Realist traditions of the carnivalesque, the grotesque, the Surreal, and the *esperpento*. Several productions of Ramón del Valle-Inclán's theatre (which had already seen the light of day during the *apertura*) were met with success, but, as Enrique Centeno noted, the effort to return to the recent past in order to settle matters that the dictatorship had left unresolved was fruitless in the case of Rafael Alberti (1902–1999) and that of Fernando Arrabal (1933–).[7] (Arrabal did finally receive the National Theatre Prize in 2001 for Juan Carlos Pérez de la Fuente's *mise en scène* of *El cementerio de automóviles* ["The Automobile Cemetery," 1977] at the CDN.) In 1979, Centeno speculated in the pages of *El País* that audiences during the Transition were generally unwilling to decipher a series of codes that were no longer relevant to their immediate reality of democracy and freedom.

The case of Francisco Nieva (1927–), however, was different. Nieva, who had worked extensively during the 1960s as a set designer and

---

[7] Enrique Centeno, "Cambio y comunicación en el teatro posfranquista." *El País* (16 September 1979): VIII ("Arte y Pensamiento").

director in both Spain and abroad (especially France), did not see his plays reach the Madrid stage until 1976, with the première of *Sombra y quimera de Larra* ("Shadow and Chimera of Larra"). From then on, throughout the 1970s and on into the 1990s, he was a regular presence on the Madrid stage. Perhaps Nieva's delirious, Baroque, "gothic," "furious," "calamitous" sense of farce, his derisive critique of the establishment, and the transgressive nature of this theatre, which was largely influenced by the plastic arts, was especially attractive to the culture of the *destape* and, later, that of the *movida* (terms that encapsulate the atmosphere of indulgence, permissiveness, and decadence that characterized the culture of the political Transition). What is undeniable is that plays such as *La carroza de plomo candente* ("The Carriage of White-Hot Lead," 1976), *Coronada y el toro* ("Coronada and the Bull," 1982), *El baile de los ardientes* ("The Dance of the Raging Flames," 1990), and *Los españoles bajo tierra* ("Spaniards Underground," 1993) have established Nieva's place in Spanish theatre history as one of the most original voices to emerge during the post-Franco period.

Among the politically engaged playwrights who struggled against oppression, the case of Agustín Gómez-Arcos (1933–1998) represents an extraordinary paradox. Like Nieva, and in keeping with the tradition of Valle-Inclán's *esperpentos*, the theatre of Gómez-Arcos is a place where defiance and dissent are converted into an aesthetic. Censorship prompted his voluntary exile to France in 1968, making him a kind of phantom figure of the Spanish stage. His subsequent publication of several novels, written in French, earned him international acclaim. His rebellious cries were long forgotten in his native Spain, until the early 1990s, when the revival of three of his plays at the hands of director Carme Portaceli – *Interview de Mrs. Muerta Smith por sus fantasmas* ("Mrs. Dead Smith's Interview with her Phantoms," 1972), *Los gatos* ("The Cats," 1962), and *Queridos míos, es preciso contaros ciertas cosas* ("My Dear Friends, It's Time We Get Certain Things Straight," 1966) – at publicly funded theatre venues in Madrid, re-established overnight his prestige as a Spanish dramatist. Hence, his life had come full circle in that the Spanish Ministerio de Cultura that once denigrated his work, with the advent of democracy was finally promoting it.

It is those artists who, like Nieva and Gómez-Arcos, have displayed a daring and defiant ingenuity that enables them to transcend generational groupings and slick categorization who are also the best expression of a theatrical Avant-Garde. Indeed, the Avant-Garde theatre of the post-Franco period did *not* spring forth from a cultural void; rather, it represents the culmination of a trajectory of experimental theatre in Spain that began in Barcelona in the late 1950s. Concurrent with the emergence of the "new" Spanish theatre, Spain's theatrical landscape witnessed the genesis of a variety of workshops, pedagogical environments, and communitarian performance troupes that were conceived as non-official and non-professional "underground" alternatives to commercial and government-subsidized theatre. Throughout Spain, the so-called "independent" theatre movement explored the implications of collective creation and opened its doors to the most experimental tendencies and repertoire of the twentieth-century international stage. The Agrupació Dramàtica de Barcelona, the Escola d'Art Dramàtic Adrià Gual, Els Joglars, and Comediants in Catalonia, Tábano and Los Goliardos in Madrid, Teatro Geroa in the Basque Country, and La Cuadra in Andalusia are among the most prominent examples. Liberated from the shackles of the official culture of the dictatorship and inspired in large part by the parallel activities of performance troupes such as the Living Theatre, the San Francisco Mime Troupe, and Bread and Puppet, the independent theatre groups embarked upon an interrogation of the conventional hierarchy of artistic invention that had once subordinated the theatrical to the literary, the *mise en scène* to the author, and the theatre to life itself. Their questions seemed to echo Artaud's influential struggle against logocentrism, textual authority, and the notions of repetition and representation that are embodied in that struggle. They approached the value and integrity of linguistic structures from a perspective of ambivalence, giving preference to the construction of visual *tableaux* that would accentuate the pictorial, sculptural, and spatial features of the performance.

It will always be a curious and absurd paradox that, during these post-Civil-War years, the denial of freedom of expression, in a sense, seemed to fuel creativity and change, and that the confining socio-cultural, and linguistic, circumstances surrounding the independent theatre movement became a catalyst for aesthetic innovation. Following Franco's death, the majority of the independent theatre troupes eventually reached an impasse, or suffered a crisis of identity, as they were forced to re-examine their *raison d'être* when their main cause for rebellion had suddenly ceased to exist. The independent theatre, however, can be considered the most decisive turning point in the history of contemporary drama and performance in Spain, and its considerable legacy continues to be felt in the twenty-first century, for it served as a breeding ground for some of the most dynamic members of the post-Franco theatre scene: José Luis Alonso de Santos (1942–), Josep M. Benet i Jornet, Albert Boadella (1943–), Fermín Cabal, Jesús Cracio (1946–), Mario Gas (1947–), José Luis Gómez, Guillermo Heras, Anna Lizaran, Josep Montanyès (1937–2002), Joan Ollé (1955–), Lluís Pasqual, Fabià Puigserver (1938–1991), Ricard Salvat, José Sanchis Sinisterra. Moreover, on an aesthetic level, the experience of the independent theatre engendered in Spain a new, post-Franco theatrical identity (or identities) vis-à-vis its transnational transactions and intercultural associations. In Grotowski's terms, it was a vehicle through which the post-totalitarian face of Spanish theatre was able to transcend stereotyped visions, conventional feelings, customs, and standards of judgment.

A crucial cluster of Catalan groups, collectives, and performers – Els Joglars (1962), Comediants (1971), Dagoll Dagom (1974), Albert Vidal – which originated in the margins of Francoist oppression and censorship, continues to thrive today, having achieved an impressive degree of commercial success and/or professional consolidation in democratic times. These groups essentially paved the way for the appearance of a new generation of Catalan companies established during the post-Franco period: Teatre Lliure (1976), La Fura dels Baus (1979), Sèmola (1978), El Tricicle (1979), La Cubana (1980), Vol Ras (1980). On the whole, these groups have continued to investigate the aesthetic precepts of the independent theatre movement; namely, the Artaudian interrogation of the borders situated between performer and spectator. As they seem to suggest, if we are able to locate a place where representation is completely denied, then we will have uncovered "the real": pure presence in its most untainted state and a place where theatre truly does equal life.

In the tumultuous *curriculum vitae* of the eminently insolent Albert Boadella and his company Els Joglars, the moments in which real life has been confused with spectacle have emerged with extraordinary frequency. Court martial, imprisonment, a dramatic escape from jail, flight into exile, subsequent amnesty, gun shots fired at a theatre, knife wounds inflicted upon an actor, bomb threats, and public remonstration by a group of bishops were just some of the entries in this CV, which landed on the pages of the daily press during the political transition. Over time, Els Joglars have modified their aesthetic values (gradually incorporating the word into their theatre) and adjusted their point of attack in accordance with the most ardent political issues of any given moment. If there is a provocative question that surfaces throughout their entire forty-year trajectory, it is the role that art can, and should, play in the articulation of a cultural identity and the construction (and deconstruction) of a national culture.

Under the direction of founding-member Joan Font (1949–), Comediants may be one of Spain's most international, well-traveled theatre companies, but they have never had to stray very far in order to find their most important source of inspiration: the culture of the Mediterranean and its festive iconography. Faithful to a 1960s Utopian ideal, their hedonistic, Epicurean, carnivalesque spirit, their anarchistic appropriations of pagan celebrations, and their recuperation of street theatre (a performance genre that was expressly prohibited during much of the

Franco period), become elements of rebellion, capable of affirming and stimulating a Catalan historical memory.

La Fura dels Baus emerged as a collective during the period of political paradox, cultural renaissance, and frenzied activity that characterized the democratic transition and the *movida*. This "urban tribe" has recontextualized the Mediterranean rhetoric of its origins within a contemporary technological environment, employing a multimedia aesthetic of collage in presenting its delirious obsessions. According to La Fura's radically extended concept of *mise en scène*, poetic primitive ritual of the past intermingles with urban iconography of the present, audacious pyrotechnics clash with futuristic machinery, and circus-like acrobatics overlap with recycled industrial refuse.

The independent theatre had opened the way to a shift in emphasis to director-centered productions (de-emphasizing the role of the playwright). This, combined with the success of "visual" theatre (de-emphasizing the role of the literary text), created a period of profound difficulties for many dramatists during the late 1970s and early 1980s, some of whom sought refuge in television and film. It did not help matters that many theatres, such as the Lliure, one of the most vital cradles of repertory theatre in Spain, had been inclined to privilege a "universal repertoire" in lieu of the work of autochthonous playwrights. Toward the mid 1980s, the pendulum began to shift, and theatre in Spain, as in Europe and North America, began to witness what has been dubbed "the return of the word." New prizes, such as the Marqués de Bradomín (1985), granted by the Instituto de la Juventud, were established with the intention of encouraging young people to create dramatic literature. Competitions for grants established by national drama centers, were among the other incentives that have since contributed to the process of recuperating and reinvigorating Spain's national "dramaturgies."

The theatre of the word returned with renewed energy, force, and prestige; however, once it "returned," it was not the same. Whereas the points of reference for previous dramatists had been Antonio Buero Vallejo, Bertolt Brecht, Arthur Miller, Eugene O'Neill, or Josep Maria de Sagarra, now they are Samuel Beckett, Thomas Bernhard, Edward Bond, Bernard-Marie Koltès, Tony Kushner, David Mamet, Heiner Müller, Harold Pinter, Sam Shepard, and Botho Strauss. In the experimental strain of text-based drama, there are no thematic limits. In terms of aesthetic construction, quite often, the action not only precedes the word; the action *is* the word. Monologue is often employed as a way of confronting the traumas of remembrance and forgetting. Plot and characterization are frequently established through subjective fragments and shreds, not through objective/naturalistic/psychological approaches. Theatrical space is more apt to portray interior realities than exterior landscapes. Meaning is established elliptically and enigmatically, "relatively," or "in relation to" as Carles Batlle puts it, through silences, pauses, and gaps, or through strategies of repetition, regression, conflation, and simultaneity.[8]

In intricately structured plays that include *¡Ay, Carmela!* (1986), *Crímenes y locuras del traidor, Lope de Aguirre* ("Crimes and Madness of the Traitor, Lope de Aguirre," 1986), *El cerco de Leningrado* ("The Siege of Leningrad," 1989–1993, which premièred in 1994 with Núria Espert), and *El lector por horas* ("The Hired Reader," 1996), José Sanchis Sinisterra demonstrates that it is still possible to create a compellingly valid, politically committed theatre in democratic times. His investigation and inquiry with regard to the "borders" of metatheatricality (he founded a company named El Teatro Fronterizo in 1977) appear to be guided by a relentless desire to call attention to the creative processes at work in the construction of the theatrical text, as well as the theatricalized body, and thereby expose the performance practices that underlie the inscription of historical memory.

Fermín Cabal, like Sanchis, is not apt to shy away from political engagement, and some of his most mature works to date, *Ello dispara* ("It Shoots," 1989), *Travesía* ("Passage," 1991), and *Castillos en el aire* ("Castles in the Air," 1995), express a less than subtle air of disenchantment in reaction to the landscape of fallen idols and shattered Utopian ideals that was left following the decline of the social-democratic government of Felipe González. Here, an implicit commentary on the Post-modern crisis of authority, on the evaporation of monolithic cultural discourses, is invoked in Cabal's portraits of frivolous expenditure, escalating corruption, and government scandals (with references to the morally ambiguous "dirty war" against Basque terrorism). It is a crisis that is also played out in a subtle interrogation of the notion of theatrical representation, the relationship between sign and referent, and the word as the traditional locus of authority in the theatre.

Juan Mayorga, one of the most intellectually sophisticated of Spanish playwrights, appears to be well aware that performance, as Joseph Roach reminds us, hinges in essence upon a tenuous rapport between the living and the dead.[9] In plays that display an innovative sense of temporality, such as *El traductor de Blumemberg* ("Blumemberg's Translator," 1993), *El sueño de Ginebra* ("Geneva Dream," 1996), and *Cartas de amor a Stalin* ("Love Letters to Stalin," 1998), he creates a "theatre of ideas" that engages in hypothetical creations and recreations of history, and of struggles between artists and power, stretching the borders of reality and

---

[8] Carles Batlle, "El drama relatiu." In *Suite* (Barcelona: Proa / Teatre Nacional de Catalunya, 2001), pp. 17–23.

[9] Joseph Roach, *Cities of the Dead: Circum-Atlantic Performance* (New York: Columbia University Press, 1996).

fiction, and inviting us to reflect upon the subjective construction of the past and the violence implicit in our words and actions.

Josep M. Benet i Jornet is a Catalan playwright whose ability to rise above generational gaps has made him one of the most influential and internationally recognized contemporary dramatists. The première of *Desig* ("Desire," 1989) at Barcelona's Teatre Romea in 1991, under the direction of Sergi Belbel, was a defining moment in the evolution of text-based drama in Spain, considered a revelation by playwrights in both Madrid and Barcelona. In this play, as in *Fugaç* ("Fleeting," 1992), *Testament* ("Legacy," 1995), and, most recently, *L'habitació del nen* ("The Thirteenth Hour of the Night," 2001), an atmosphere of mystery encloses a poetic transcription of physical space, revealed as an immanent, interior, immaterial, psychic reality. Benet's theatre reveals a yearning for continuity, transcendence, and immortality, a concern with projecting oneself beyond what is our mundane, quotidian existence. His interest in perspectivism, subjectivity, and perception has evolved in conjunction with his creative complicity with Sergi Belbel.

Belbel, who is presently at the forefront of his theatrical generation, and whose reputation abroad earned him a French Molière prize, has played a leading role as a playwright, director, and translator in revitalizing the tradition of text-based drama in Spain. In plays that include *Elsa Schneider* (1987), *Tàlem* ("Fourplay," 1989), *Caricies* ("Caresses," 1991), *Després de la pluja* ("After the Rain," 1993), *Morir* ("To Die," 1994), *La sang* ("Blood," 1998), and *El temps de Planck*, he has offered original approaches to formal construction and design. For Belbel, the role that verbal communication may play in apprehending reality has always been a matter of investigation and even a point of contention. In essence, Belbel's theatre is about pain, for it is within the realm of anguish and affliction that the fissure between the visible and the invisible, sign and referent, becomes most unmistakably apparent. "Cultural aphasia" would seem to be the governing metaphor here; an inability to express verbally the conditions of a culture that has become morally bereft, ethically corrupt, spiritually dispossessed, and wholly void of compassion. Belbel's pain is capable of assassinating the word, of shaking language to its very foundations, or, in the words of David Le Breton, "it slices up language and liberates anguish."[10]

It is this same type of cathartic awe that in the theatre of Rodrigo García is converted into provocation, into a flood of images. With his own company La Carnicería (1989), García grounds his work in the plastic arts: installations, environments, and collages made with recycled materials,

---

[10] David Le Breton, *Antropología del dolor*. Trans. Daniel Alcorba (Barcelona: Seix Barral, 1999), p. 42.

which disturb and unnerve, as well as incite curiosity. "Autism," a concept that has likewise emerged in the work of Robert Wilson, perhaps would be an apt metaphor for works that include *Notas de cocina* ("Notes on Cooking," 1994) and *Conocer gente, comer mierda* ("Meet People, Eat Shit," 1999): abnormal introversion and egocentricity, an acceptance of fantasy rather than reality. García dares to venture into the most vulgar dimensions of daily life; however, within the most prosaic of realms, he is also capable of revealing a hidden poetry and even a sense of the spectacular. And just when García leads us to believe that image is everything, and that everything is transparency and visibility, he uncovers a textual dimension to his theatre of extraordinarily lyrical and rhythmic beauty.

Finally, in the untamed sea that is the "new Catalan dramaturgy," Lluïsa Cunillé, who writes in both Spanish and Catalan, is undoubtedly the most prolific, and, along with Belbel, the most consolidated of playwrights. Her enigmatic theatrical universe, created with minimalist lines, subtle shadings, and hidden meanings, is what Sanchis Sinisterra has called "a poetics of subtraction." In *La venda* ("The Sale," 1994), *Privado* ("Private," 1996), and *Apocalipsi* ("Apocalypse," 1998), an atmosphere of uncertainty reigns, and Cunillé's tenuous and circumstantial landscapes seem disquietingly devoid of action. Paradoxically they are also so disquietingly real (or hyperreal), so devoid of referentiality, that she seems to have erased the barrier between art and life.

Perhaps Cunillé, as well as the other playwrights described here, have in effect "unveiled" realities that many may not wish to see, for each reveals through varying methods the traumas, the violence, and the wounds that permeate our contemporary existence both within Spain and without. The question that lingers, however, is the extent to which the contemporary unification of Europe and its inherent ambiguities and indeterminacies, coupled with new conceptions of the relationship between the local and the global, will have a significant bearing on how we perceive Spain's contemporary theatrical identity.

56

Spanish literature and the language of new media: from film adaptation to digitized cultural interfaces

SUSAN MARTIN-MÁRQUEZ

M, it would appear, felt violated.

M, for those who are not intimately acquainted with the *succès de scandale* in question, is the much-lauded Spanish novelist Javier Marías, who published a petulant article in *El País* concerning his treatment at the hands of the father–daughter team, Elías and Gracia Querejeta, producer and director, respectively, of the film adaptation of Marías' novel *Todas las almas* ("All Souls," 1989). While it is not in the least unusual for writers to decry publicly the inadequacies of films that have been based on their work, what is notable here is the way in which Marías makes explicit the subtext of sexual deviance that, as Robert Stam suggests,[1] usually only lurks beneath the surface of such discussions of filmic "infidelity." For Marías is uncomfortable, above all, with the film's specific representations of sexuality. Indeed, the author begins his article by recounting (in the third person, and using the initials M, Q, and Q for the three parties concerned) a conversation that he has had with Q senior concerning the homosexuality of one of the characters (Cromer-Blake), and the possibility of a sexual relationship between that character and another male protagonist (Toby Rylands). Marías insists that such a relationship is unthinkable, and then records his astonishment at Q senior's response: "Aun así Q insistió con una pregunta en verdad genialoide: '¿Estás seguro?' M pudo haber sido sarcástico pero no lo fue, se limitó a contestar lo obvio: '¿Cómo no voy a estar seguro, si el libro lo he escrito yo?' M, ingenuo, respiró con alivio creyendo haber atajado a tiempo un grave malentendido de lectura" ("Even so Q insisted with a truly brilliant-ish question: 'Are you sure?' M could have been sarcastic, but he wasn't, he limited himself to responding with the obvious: 'How could I not be sure, if it is I who wrote the book?' M, ingenuous, sighed with relief thinking that he had prevented a grave misreading, just in time"). Marías' sigh of relief, however, is premature, for the resulting film, *El último viaje de Robert Rylands* ("Robert Ryland's Last Journey," 1996), does in fact make reference to

---

[1] Robert Stam, "Beyond Fidelity: The Dialogics of Adaptation." In *Film Adaptation*. Ed. James Naremore (New Brunswick, NJ: Rutgers University Press, 2000), p. 54.

a homosexual relationship between the two men; moreover, according to Marías, the cinematographic work utterly lacks the irony of the original, falling instead into the sort of melodramatic excesses characteristic of the soap opera. Marías' association of the film with all forms of such "feminine" excess is clear when the adaptation is subtly personified as a madly promiscuous woman: "más que libre era loca" ("she [it] was more crazy than loose"). The author ends the article declaring that he will never again permit his novels to be adapted, for fear that cases of on-screen incest or pedophilia might result.

In this article, besides indulging in sexist and homophobic flights of fancy, Marías presents a surprisingly narrow understanding of the processes of intertextuality in general, and of film adaptation in particular. While Marías himself has frequently recycled earlier literary masterpieces in his own writings, sometimes in rather "perverse" ways – what, for example, would William Shakespeare think of Marías' variations on Lady Macbeth in *Corazón tan blanco* ("A Heart So White," 1992)? – he is evidently unwilling to grant filmmakers a similar degree of freedom when they adapt literary works (or at least, when they adapt *his* novels). His article includes the obligatory insistence upon faithfulness to the letter and spirit of the literary text, and concludes, "[t]anto si *El último viaje de Robert Rylands* es una obra maestra como si es espantosa, en todo caso tiene muy poco de la letra y nada del espíritu de *Todas las almas*" ("whether *El último viaje de Robert Rylands* is a masterpiece or a frightful mess, in either case it has very little of the letter and nothing of the spirit of *Todas las almas*"). In her article on the controversy Dona Kercher defends the Querejetas' respect for the spirit of *Todas las almas*,[2] but I would prefer instead to highlight Marías' theoretical inconsistency. Curiously, Marías' essay lacks much of the deliciously self-aware irony and convoluted Post-modern playfulness that tend to characterize his work – including *Todas las almas* and the more recent novel *Negra espalda del tiempo* ("Dark Back of Time," 1998), both of which serve to confound the issue of autobiographical identities, since the narrator of *Todas las almas* is a Spanish writer and visiting professor at the University of Oxford, as was Marías. In the *El País* essay, by contrast, the autobiographical game is reduced to the initial transposition of the narrative into the third person, and the substitution of the full name "Marías" for initials, which are later baldly clarified and rectified: "Y como M no era otro que quien esto firma, paso sin dificultades a la primera persona" ("And since M was none other than he who signs this, I shift without difficulty into the first person"). Marías' *Robert Rylands* article, in short, is uncharacteristically unsophisticated.

---

[2] Dona Kercher, "Children of the European Union, Crossing Gendered Channels: Javier Marías's Novel, *Todas las almas*, and Gracia Querejeta's *El último viaje de Robert Rylands*" *Cine-Lit* 3 (1997), pp. 100–112.

Yet Marías' essay is not unrepresentative of the state of Spanish adaptation studies, which has for the most part failed to stray from the same traditional and problematic questions of letter and spirit. Moreover, in the larger European and American context, adaptation studies has only very recently begun to attain some level of theoretical sophistication. For decades, a handful of increasingly outdated book-length treatments and an overwhelming number of individual case studies, published as discrete articles or anthologized, have served to mark out the parameters of the field. Despite the occasional renunciation of issues of fidelity, the vast majority of essays on adaptation have returned to that most sanctified ground to register with pained regret the multifarious ways in which (sometimes well-meaning) films fail to reflect the artistic greatness of their source texts. Their authors have tended simply to reiterate stock claims concerning the film medium's presumed incapacity to accomplish "uniquely literary" tasks such as the representation of thought and other subjective states, or to narrate in anything other than the present tense. Taking stock of this vast body of material, Robert Ray has written very recently, and refreshingly bluntly, that "most of this criticism was useless, based as it was on the severely curtailed definition of *the movies* that Hollywood had successfully naturalized."[3]

Efforts to eschew subjectivity and impressionism, and to present a presumably more rigorous semiotic and narratological approach to adaptation – which reflects an on-going desire to legitimize film studies in general by presenting a theory now argued to be "scientific" – are hardly more illuminating. These studies rely upon the notion that narrative is a universal phenomenon, and that adaptation is best understood as a special form of translation or transcodification; for that reason, they tend to focus on the minutiae of media-specific differences. Brian McFarlane's *Novel to Film* works in very methodical fashion to "set up procedures for distinguishing between that which can be transferred from one medium to another (essentially, narrative) and that which, being dependent on different signifying systems, cannot be transferred (essentially, enunciation)."[4] According to Imelda Whelehan, approaches such as McFarlane's have the advantage of rejecting traditional notions of fidelity and accepting that alterations are an inevitable, unavoidable part of the adaptation process, which should be mined for what it reveals of the nature of the two artistic media rather than simply condemned.[5] Even so, the sad refrain

---

[3] Robert Ray, "The Field of 'Literature and Film.'" In Naremore, ed., *Film Adaptation*, p. 46.

[4] Brian McFarlane, *Novel to Film: An Introduction to the Theory of Adaptation* (Oxford: Clarendon Press, 1996), p. vii.

[5] Imelda Whelehan, "Adaptations: The Contemporary Dilemmas." In *Adaptations: From Text to Screen, Screen to Text*. Ed. Deborah Cartmell and Imelda Whelehan (London and New York: Routledge, 1999), pp. 10–11.

that "something is always lost in translation" may continue to reverberate in these studies. That loss is more frequently associated with the cinema, the "absent signifier" (in Christian Metz's famous formulation) *par excellence*.[6]

Another – and ultimately more productive – school of adaptation studies has emerged out of reader-response and reception theory, and begins to allow for notions of supplementation, for a conceptualization of adaptation grounded in presence and plenitude instead of absence and lack. Beginning in the 1980s, more progressive theorists such as Joy Gould Boyum had come to consider film adaptations as individualized "readings" of the source text; filmmakers were seen as akin to literary critics, presenting, through properly cinematographic channels, one of a multiplicity of possible interpretations. Yet this approach was still limited by the notion that some readings were inherently more legitimate than others; the consensus of interpretive communities served as the yardstick of an adaptation's success, while the literary text was still deemed the ultimate source of authority. As Boyum writes, "[t]he text may spark countless interpretations, numerous individualized works of art, but it nonetheless places certain constraints on what a reader can sensibly, even commonsensically, do with it."[7] Perhaps given this hegemonic maintenance of traditional, hierarchical notions of high and low cultural forms, and of the proper role of the consumer of texts that are readily assignable to one category or another, James Naremore has argued that adaptation studies has comprised "a system of critical writing that tends to reproduce a bourgeois mode of reception."[8]

An insistence on adaptations that are somehow "true to the spirit" of the original assumes, moreover, not only that divining that essential (and essentially agreed-upon) spirit is indeed possible, but also that all, or most, viewers desire that kind of fidelity, or look with absolute reverence upon literary texts. In fact, a majority of viewers may not have read, and may never read, the works in question. Even those who are intimately familiar with a literary source may be secretly thrilled by an adaptation that compels them to contemplate that particular text in a completely new light. Their engagement with an alternative perspective may lead them to a more nuanced understanding, or to a rigorous interrogation, of the original or of their initial reaction to it – decidedly intellectual pleasures – or to somewhat less purely cerebral and more playfully creative practices of give-and-take with the cultural texts in question. As Whelehan observes:

---

[6] Christian Metz, *The Imaginary Signifier: Psychoanalysis and the Cinema*. Trans. Celia Britton *et al.* (Bloomington: Indiana University Press, 1977).

[7] Joy Gould Boyum, *Double Exposure: Fiction into Film* (New York: Plume, 1985), p. 72.

[8] James Naremore, "Introduction: Film and the Reign of Adaptation." In Naremore, ed., *Film Adaptation*, p. 10.

Clearly the adapter "poaches" from the original in most crucial ways, but perhaps the seasoned consumer of adaptations begins to find the process itself equally participatory, welcoming the opportunity to recapture the experience of a first encounter with the original text in a different formulation. Alternatively, perhaps there are pleasures to be found in first encountering a "version" which appears to iconoclastically demolish the "literary" shaping of its original.[9]

Indeed, more traditional reader-response-inspired theories of adaptation now need to absorb the ideas developed by cultural studies scholars who have focused on the concept of resistant or negotiated readings, and who have explored the phenomenon of fandom. As Stuart Hall has detailed, not all readers choose (consciously or unconsciously) fully to submit to the text's aesthetic and ideological manipulations as they undertake the practice of decodification.[10] By extension, when adapting literary works, filmmakers may also prefer to engage in a radically oppositional reading. Viewers of the resulting film adaptation, in turn, may choose to resist or accept the various parameters of the cinematic text; that choice may also be influenced in complex ways by the nature of their original reception of the literary source, if they have in fact read it. Henry Jenkins' work on fandom, which is grounded in Michel de Certeau's notion of poaching, can provide a model for understanding the dynamics of film adaptation and reception as potentially more interactive, creative, or even subversive processes than had previously been allowed. Readers, filmmakers, and viewers alike can now be seen as willful appropriators of preexisting cultural texts, reshaping their meanings to serve many different, and possibly unforeseeable, purposes.

Within the context of Spanish cinema of the post-Franco era, one of the most intriguing examples of this sort of "resistant" adaptation is Josefina Molina's *Función de noche* ("Night Performance," 1981), which is inspired, somewhat indirectly, by a novel and play by Miguel Delibes. In the novel, *Cinco horas con Mario* ("Five Hours with Mario," 1966), a widow named Carmen rails against her dead husband, over whose body she holds vigil, in a series of monologues; yet ironically her unrelentingly bitter criticisms lead the reader to condemn Carmen while exalting the silent and lifeless figure of her intellectual spouse. The novel, participating in a gesture not uncommon among the Spanish left (and even, it must be admitted, among female leftists in Spain), apparently casts the blame for political backwardness on women. However, when the novel was adapted for the stage in 1979, the mere physical presence of the actress Lola Herrera in the role of Carmen, along with a few textual modifications, tended to inspire audiences to "read" her character as more sympathetic.

9 Whelehan, "Adaptations," p. 16.
10 Stuart Hall, "Encoding/Decoding." In *Culture, Media, Language*. Ed. Stuart Hall *et al.* (London: Hutchinson, 1980), pp. 128–138.

At the same time, the shock of finding herself identifying with a character that she had initially found so repugnant provoked the actress herself to experience a profound personal crisis, which led her to faint onstage on the night of the Barcelona debut. These events are recreated in Molina's film, and snippets of the play are intercut with selections from a lengthy, supposedly impromptu conversation between Lola and her estranged husband, the actor Daniel Dicenta, which was shot on multiple cameras positioned behind two-way mirrors in a recreated stage dressing room. Thus the monologue of the Delibes novel and play becomes a dialogue in the film, but in this case the husband loses much by gaining a voice. Dicenta's words, now juxtaposed with Carmen's monologue, reveal his hypocrisy and selfishness, while the camera records the subtle gestures – for example, he looks at his watch when Lola brings up the subject of their wedding night – that betray his least attractive qualities. *Función de noche* is a film adaptation of the most radical sort, which subjects the Delibes text to an unflinching ideological interrogation, revealing (among many other things) that even men who considered themselves opposed to Francoism may have blithely participated in the Francoist-style oppression of women. The spectator's interface with *Función de noche* will also be extraordinarily complex, depending in part upon the nature of his or her negotiation of and with the multiple layers of textuality.

Other productive new approaches to film adaptation explore the historical relationships between specific audiences and literary and filmic texts. How and why is the past "consumed" through the process of the creation and reception of film adaptations? Why do filmmakers of one era preferentially turn to literary works from another? How do multiple adaptations of a given literary text shift according to the period in which each adaptation is produced? (Of course these questions are further complicated when geographical and cultural, as well as temporal, differences are also introduced.) If adaptations seek to capture an idea of the past – or, I might add, of other, more spatial forms of remoteness – studying the specific fashion in which such ideas are represented cinematographically might be especially illuminating. Furthermore, it might also prove intriguing to analyze how consumption of a particular version of temporal, geographical, or cultural difference in a particular time and place, most especially as it is presented in the adaptation of highly admired canonical literary texts, enables viewers to acquire what Pierre Bourdieu has referred to as "cultural capital." That is to say, viewers of adaptations of literary works marked off as prestigious might benefit from the afterglow of the aura of cultural worth that normally accrues to readers of those works.

Within the Spanish context, there is remarkably little divergence of critical opinion concerning the significance of the historiographical tendencies within dominant film adaptation practice during the socialist years. Appointed by Felipe González as Director General de Cinema in 1982, Pilar Miró promulgated a law which attempted to shore up the national industry through generous governmental subsidies, and which sought as well to boost the status of cinema – in the aftermath of the execrable nudie comedies that dominated the late Franco and early Transition periods – in part by supporting films associated with a more prestigious artistic medium: literature. The so-called "Miró Law" (1983) thus favored "cinema of quality" literary adaptations, while also promoting a particularly self-interested vision of the recent past. In her incisive analysis of film adaptation during the socialist years, which draws upon a broad range of critical opinion, Isolina Ballesteros observes that "reinterpretar el patrimonio histórico y cultural resultó prioritario para deshacer el ocultamiento y la manipulación del pasado franquista, y evidenciar la necesidad y conveniencia del presente socialista" ("reinterpreting the historical and cultural legacy became a priority in order to undo the concealment and manipulation of the Francoist past, and to prove the necessity and advantage of the socialist present").[11] Ballesteros signals two dominant tendencies: the production of filmic homages to and hagiographies of writers who had been marginalized or even eliminated by the Franco régime (most particularly Lorca), and the adaptation of Social Realist novels – or perhaps more accurately, the Social Realist adaptation of novels – produced during the dictatorship. According to Ballesteros even the most experimental of 1960s and 1970s novels were apt to be treated as if they simply carried on the Social Realist tradition, and were characteristically adapted as straightforward, documentary-like depictions of the sordid reality of life under Franco. As a case in point, Ballesteros analyzes Vicente Aranda's 1986 version of Luis Martín Santos' *Tiempo de silencio* ("Time of Silence," 1962), a novel which functioned in part as a scathing criticism of the artistic poverty of Social Realism, but which in the film adaptation is excised of all of its discursive inventiveness, in order to fulfill a more straightforward commercial and/or pedagogical mission. Similar arguments have been made by Ballesteros and others concerning a multiplicity of adaptations of the era.

What is perhaps most surprising is that, a quarter-century after the transition to democracy, this hijacking of literary texts to serve as vehicles for the filmic representation of Francoist hellfire and brimstone and, occasionally, Second Republic prelapsarianism, is still taking place. *La lengua*

---

[11] Isolina Ballesteros, "Convergencias y alianzas culturales: las adaptaciones fílmicas de obras literarias en el periodo socialista." *Cine (ins)urgente* (Madrid: Fundamentos, 2001), p. 158.

de las mariposas ("Butterfly's Tongue," 1999), based on a collection of short stories by Manuel Rivas and directed by José Luis Cuerda, presents "the most exportable perspective that foreign cinema has discovered":[12] the innocent, or perhaps more appropriately, naive view afforded by focalization of history through the eyes of a child. This heavily formulaic film also attests to the remarkable on-going box office success of a particular packaging of events surrounding the Spanish Civil War, in which political allegiances are clearly and predictably drawn (the film was picked up for US distribution by Miramax, and played on screens in New York City for a remarkable several months). In an article published in the *Guardian*, David Archibald describes *Lengua* (together with the Oscar-winning *Belle Epoque*) as:

> sugar coated history. Republican Spain seen through rose-tinted glasses; a harsh and bitter world, magically transformed into an idyllic and pre-modern utopia about to be cruelly crushed by fascism. There is a refusal to engage with a concrete historical past, and what is presented in both films is a nostalgic recreation of a republican Spain that never was. These two films highlight the fact that right-wing myths of the past are slowly being undone but they are being replaced with myths of a different kind.[13]

Soft history, however, particularly when coupled with soft porn, sells. Structured as a coming-of-age story, the narrative features the requisite adorable (and in this case undeniably talented) young actor (Manuel Lozano, in the role of Moncho), and includes a hackneyed scene of Moncho witnessing the glories of heterosexual sex (all two minutes of them), which enthusiastic audiences consumed with delight. Although the film's last image – in which Moncho succumbs to the social pressure to throw rocks at the schoolteacher who has nurtured his intellectual and human growth, as he is carted away by fascists – briefly rescues the work from the realm of the absolutely predictable, it also might be seen as symbolizing the stance of the vast majority of these adaptations: ultimately, they present a surprisingly united resistance to change, a rejection of any but the most traditional forms of Manichaean representation.

Oddly, however, as the Spanish nostalgia industry flourishes, an apparently opposite tendency is emerging: since the mid 1990s or so, publishers have stacked the tables and filled the shelves of local and chain bookstores with wildly popular facsimiles of Franco-era school texts, comic books, and periodicals, as well as with literary memoirs illustrated with various and sundry forms of textual ephemera, such as print ads and propaganda posters. The critical narratives that frame or accompany

---

[12] Sean Axmaker, "'Butterfly' Alights Only Briefly on Politics But Lingers on Nostalgia." *Seattle Post-Intelligencer* (23 June 2000).
[13] David Archibald, "The War that Won't Die." *The Guardian* 28 July 2000.

some – but by no means all – of these new editions tend to adopt a tone of benevolent bemusement. This is literature meant to evoke a memory and provoke a smile. Jessamy Harvey observes that some of these texts initially provided the means for "exorcising the past through laughter,"[14] but she also voices the concern that once the publishing industry began to flood the market with copycat products, many readers abandoned their critical stance simply, in essence, to wallow in nostalgia. Moreover, according to Harvey, women readers in particular may have been left with nothing to laugh at, as the reprinted texts themselves reproduce the sexual oppression that they ostensibly are designed to parody.[15] Now, these texts are being adapted to the stage and screen, to enable mass audiences to share in the more collective pleasures of nostalgic recollection. Since 1996, the Basque group Tanttaka Teatroa's staging of Andrés Sopeña Monsalve's *El florido pensil: memoria de la escuela nacionalcatólica* ("The Flowering Garden: Memoirs of National-Catholic School," 1994) has been seen by over a million theatregoers; the film version, directed by Juan José Porto, was released in March 2003, and sold a quarter of a million tickets in the first month. Though these pieces would appear to differ radically from the Manichaean literary adaptations set in the Civil War and postwar era, both series of works may function to avoid an intellectually and ethically rigorous engagement with the Francoist past.

Furthermore, the preferential adaptation of texts set in the years from 1931 to 1975 also edges out the filming of earlier works. While in the Anglo cultural context, the continual and oftentimes dizzyingly inventive cinematographic mining of Shakespearean plays, as well as the recent popularity of heritage films inspired in nineteenth-century novels, have given rise to renewed critical considerations of the processes of adaptation, nostalgia, and historical representation, such has not been the case in Spain. Occasionally, pseudo-nineteenth-century novel adaptations will make an appearance, such as Pedro Olea's *El maestro de esgrima* ("The Fencing Master," 1992), based on the 1988 novel by Arturo Pérez-Reverte; or the beautifully shot and curiously "literary" *A los que aman* ("To Those Who Love," 1998), directed by Isabel Coixet, which is only a simulated adaptation of a romantic novel (and in this sense might be compared with Jane Campion's *The Piano* [1992]). Yet there are almost no modern film versions – and certainly no artistically or ideologically stimulating adaptations – of texts by the likes of Galdós, Pardo Bazán, or Clarín. Nor have Spanish viewers been treated to *La [mo]vida es sueño*, or *Segismundo:*

---

[14] Jessamy Harvey, "The Value of Nostalgia: Reviving Memories of National-Catholic Childhood." *Journal of Spanish Cultural Studies* 2.1 (2001), p. 115.
[15] Harvey, "The Value of Nostalgia," pp. 116–117.

Civil War Prisoner; all possible permutations of Calderón de la Barca
are utterly absent from the ranks of the current cinematographic field.
Pilar Miró's final film, the highly lauded adaptation of Lope de Vega's
El perro del hortelano ("The Dog in the Manger," 1996), still remains
the exception that proves the rule: in modern-day Spain, the Golden Age
is nowhere to be found on the silver screen (and only rarely appears on
the small screen). Indeed, before her untimely death in 1997 Miró had
embarked upon a one-woman crusade to change that scenario, inspired
by critically acclaimed and commercially successful contemporary Shakespearean films such as Kenneth Branagh's *Henry V* or *Much Ado About
Nothing*. *Perro*, conceived of as the first in a trilogy of Golden Age play
adaptations, banked on the star power, scintillating chemistry, and fault-
less diction of its two stars, Emma Suárez and Carmelo Gómez, as well
as on exquisite cinematography, music, and locations (the Portuguese
palaces at Sintra, Setubal, and Lisbon), and vividly symbolic, over-the-
top "period" costumes; it was a box office hit, and nearly swept the Goya
awards (the Spanish equivalent of the Oscars). In her intelligent discussion of this film, as well as of Miró's theatrical staging of several other
classical plays, Pilar Nieva de la Paz observes that the director – embit-
tered by the (in some cases misogyny-laden) scandals that had plagued her
tenure as Directora General de Cinematografía and Directora General de
la Radio Televisión Española – clearly chose to take on works that enabled
her to lodge a pointed critique of the contemporary socio-political situation, and that also centered around strong, independent female characters. Nieva de la Paz concludes that Miró's problems stemmed from
the unconventionality of her work, which allows for a questioning of
social "law" and for a modern vindication of the individual, as well as
from her own highly publicized life experiences (she encountered resistance when she attempted to maintain her independence within the established political structures).[16] Now, several years after Miró's death, it
still remains to be seen if other Spanish film directors will be similarly
inspired to view the national literature of earlier eras as a form of "usable
past."

If the revered, time-tested classics of the national literary canon are
largely absent from their movie screens, how then do Spanish viewers
manage to accumulate "cultural capital" (assuming, of course, that like
viewers in other parts of the world, they mostly fail to do so the old-
fashioned way: by reading)? According to Marvin D'Lugo, in Spain the
notion of film authorship – and perhaps by extension the cultural val-
orization of cinema – has enjoyed a different, rather less fraught history,

---

[16] Pilar Mieva de la Paz, "Pilar Miró ante el teatro clásico." *Anales de la Literatura Española
Contemporánea* 26.1 (2001), pp. 255–276.

than elsewhere; for D'Lugo, since the 1950s film authors such as Bardem, Berlanga, Buñuel, and Saura have been seen as romantic figures of political resistance, and as defenders of artistic integrity against the impoverishment of Franco-era film production.[17] Although these high-prestige directors have rarely adapted literary texts, nonetheless they have been considered creative geniuses in their own right, on a par with the most revered of Spanish authors, and, for that reason, viewing their films may indeed allow Spanish spectators to acquire highly prized forms of cultural capital; it is a tendency that continues with the newer *auteurs* who have emerged since the transition to democracy, such as Pedro Almodóvar and even younger writer-director figures like Julio Medem. Moreover, D'Lugo has shown how Almodóvar's films themselves engage in a self-reflexive exaltation of a literary creation closely linked to the filmmaking process; though they acknowledge the perils of crass commercialization to which literature is always subject, they also represent literary authorship as a uniquely valuable mode of individual, familial, and national regeneration.

It is interesting, however, that the only literary text that Almodóvar has adapted thus far has been an English-language work, British crime novelist Ruth Rendell's *Live Flesh* (which inspired the 1997 *Carne trémula*). In fact, within the realm of film production in Spain the accumulation of capital – cultural and otherwise – is now often linked to questions of international prestige and reach; film projects are more and more frequently undertaken in English, with non-Spanish casts and, sometimes, settings and crews; and the adaptation of foreign authors, or even more particularly, of Spanish authors who enjoy a certain level of renown abroad – such as Javier Marías, or Antonio Muñoz Molina, whose 1989 novel *Beltenebros* was filmed in English and with British stars by Pilar Miró in 1991 – may be considered a more bankable endeavor. Moreover, within the contemporary Spanish film industry global/local niche marketing is also frequently tied to the practice of film adaptation. For example, the Catalan theatre and film director Ventura Pons has, since the late seventies, made a series of critically and commercially successful films, many of which are based on contemporary Catalan narrative works and plays (for example, *Carícies* ["Caresses," 1997], based on Sergi Belbel's homonymous play; *Amic/Amat* ["Beloved Friend," 1999], based on Josep Benet i Jornet's play *Testament* ["Legacy"]; or *El perquè de tot plegat* ["What It's All About," 1994], inspired in a collection of Quim Monzó stories). Besides appealing in particular to the Catalan filmgoing public (they are shot in Catalan, and are shown elsewhere in Spain with Castilian subtitles), Pons' works often

---

[17] Marvin D'Lugo, "Pedro Almodóvar y la autoría literaria." In *Literatura española y cine*. Ed. Norberto Minguez (Madrid: Complutense, 2002), pp. 75–92.

tap into an international gay market (as well as some of the customary museum, archive, and art house circuits), and have won awards at gay film festivals abroad. Clearly a participant in many of the trends outlined thus far, in January 2003 Pons premièred his fourteenth film, *Food of Love*, which was shot in English, and is an adaptation of the novel *The Page Turner* by the acclaimed gay British writer David Leavitt.

The ways in which the circulation and consumption of films such as Pons' may circumvent the boundaries of the traditional nation-state attest to what Michael Hardt and Antonio Negri have signaled as the perfect correspondence between the Post-modern celebration of difference and the capitalist ideology of the world market.[18] Other forms of niche marketing, intimately tied to the practice of film adaptation, continue to follow the vicissitudes of the Spanish, and global, publishing industry. For example, for several years in the nineties, the so-called "Generation X" novelists enjoyed particular success on Spanish screens when films such as *Historias del Kronen* ("Stories of Kronen," 1995), directed by Montxo Armendáriz, and *Mensaka* ("Motorbike Messenger," 1998), directed by Salvador García, both based on novels by José Angel Mañas, appeared to be targeted at a guaranteed public of disaffected urban youth; films by other young directors, such as Daniel Calparsoro, while not based on literary works, still seemed to tap into Gen-X cultural preferences and patterns of consumption. It is a trend, however, that in Spain, as elsewhere, may now have passed (though a filmmaker as talented as Calparsoro will most certainly continue to produce significant works).

Contemporary literary texts are also routinely brought to the screen for their narrativization of the concerns that dominate Spanish newspapers, particularly the on-going violent conflicts with ETA and immigration issues. The multiple Goya award-winning *Días contados* ("Numbered Days," 1995), directed by Imanol Uribe and based on the Juan Madrid novel, while it shared some ground with Gen-X films (for example, in its treatment of Javier Bardem's drug addict character), was also considered one of the first films to present an ETA member (played by Carmelo Gómez) in a not wholly unsympathetic light. A number of films have also begun to sketch out the complexities of Spain's new role as gatekeeper of "Fortress Europe." The highly polemical *Bwana* (1996), also directed by Uribe, borrowed most of the details of its representation of an ill-fated encounter between a shipwrecked African immigrant, a Spanish taxi driver's family, and a group of young neo-Nazi tourists, from the play by Ignacio del Moral, *La mirada del hombre oscuro* ("The Dark Man's

---

[18] Michael Hardt and Antonio Negri, *Empire* (Cambridge, MA: Harvard University Press, 2000), pp. 150–152.

Gaze," 1992). However, other films such as the recent *Salvajes* ("Savages," 2001), directed by Carlos Molinero, may supplement their literary source material with additional pointed references to current events topics. In fact, the somewhat bittersweet José Luis Alonso de Santos play on which the latter is based – centered around the evolving relationship between a soon-to-retire police detective (Imanol Arias), and the terminally ill Berta (the magnificent Marisa Paredes), a nurse who has struggled and sacrificed to raise her orphaned nephews, who nevertheless have become drug addicts and skinheads – includes only a few brief references to the plight of African and South American immigrants in Spain. The film, by contrast, employs natural lighting and an imperfectly framed and focused, sometimes frantically hand-held digital camera to capture the sordid details of Berta's personal life, and the horrific nature of her nephew's crime: beating a Senegalese immigrant nearly to death. While the detective of the play expresses empathy for immigrant victims of racist violence in Spain, in the film he makes little effort to hide his prejudice as he interviews the family of the victim and works to solve the crime. Perhaps the most fascinating aspect of the film is its ending, which diverges dramatically from the theatrical text's sentimental promise of a trip to the Cape of Good Hope: rather, in the film a tragic dénouement, in which Berta cradles the dying detective in her arms after his fatal encounter with a group of desperate illegal immigrants, is suddenly reframed through a video camera whose time codes are visible; "fiction" is now replaced by "reality," as the actors begin to relax and the crew enters the frame. The final credits then roll over a documentary-like segment featuring brief interviews with several African immigrants, including an Equatorial Guinean, who chides Spaniards for not acknowledging their responsibility toward their former colonial subjects in Africa: "el guineano tiene que estar aquí como el de Las Palmas o Tenerife" ("Guineans should be here just like people from Las Palmas or Tenerife").

It is difficult to underestimate the potential significance of this trend toward documentary-style or documentary-influenced filmmaking – much of which is beginning to be produced, as in the case of *Salvajes*, using digital technology – and some of which engages in self-conscious explorations of the presumed indexical relationship between film and reality, as well as of the presumed Realist tradition within Spanish literature. These films may very well function to shift the status of literary adaptations on the national cultural scene, by subjecting the "truth-factor" of literature, cinema, and literature-inspired cinema to interrogation. It might even be argued that in 1981 *Función de noche*, with its unusual melding of literary adaptation and *cinéma-verité* style documentary, anticipated this more recent development. Although the films in question refuse to reject adaptation altogether, they do appear to share something of the sentiment expressed by the Iranian director Abbas Kiarostami, who once stated: "I always think that directors who look for stories in books are like those Iranians who live next to a stream full of fish, but eat out of tins."[19]

Though digital film technology may enable some Spanish films to offer fresher, less "canned" perspectives, the impact of the so-called "new media" on the relationship between literature and cinema promises to be far-reaching and eminently varied. While it is unlikely that more traditional forms of literary adaptation will disappear any time soon, increasingly such processes may be supplemented by alternative forms of digitized cultural interfaces, that potentially function to expand the horizons of literature, and film, in fascinating new ways.

Luis Goytisolo's novel and CD-ROM of African tourism, *Mzungo* (1996), might be considered a pioneer in the exploration of this new technological terrain as well. The CD-ROM includes a video game, which the back cover of the novel characterizes as a "prolongación lúdica del relato" ("ludic extension of the narrative"). The player identifies with one of the novel's protagonists, and then must try to avoid a series of dangers that include, according to the final page of the novel, drowning at sea, being devoured by crocodiles, or falling into the hands of a cannibalistic tribe (although those with rudimentary gaming abilities may find it difficult to advance beyond the first round of the game, which features poisonous snakes and falling coconuts). It is interesting, however, that while the novel foregrounds the multiple layers of racist discourse through which meditations on Africa still tend to be filtered – and might, as a consequence, stimulate the reader to react critically to those different discourses – the videogame reproduces the most infantile stereotypes of African ways of life, and (through its somewhat crude cartoon imagery) the most racist and sexist depictions of Africans themselves, which players are simply forced to accept as they attempt (perhaps more literally than might first be apparent) to "save their skins." If the novel, for example, highlights (albeit somewhat problematically) the European tendency to reduce Africa to a series of spectacularly violent narrative kernels of contemporary life – such as death by "necklacing" – the videogame also repeats the violent fantasies of an earlier generation: the "savage" dangers of African nature and natives. While it might be argued that intellectually engaged readers and players could be prompted to think through the implications of these representations, it is perhaps more likely that, after finishing the novel (or not), readers who are also aficionados of computer gaming will simply exploit the CD-ROM for its entertainment value (or lack thereof, given the game's relatively low level of technological

---

[19] Farah Nayeri, "Iranian Cinema: What Happened in Between?" *Sight and Sound* (December 1993), p. 27.

sophistication). Indeed, the current trend in video game tie-ins is not particularly promising: "Torrente: El Juego" ("Torrente: The Game"), by Virtual Toys, the first Spanish film-inspired videogame – and a significant commercial success – gleefully exploits the in-your-face "political incorrectness" of Santiago Segura's 1998 box-office hit, *Torrente: el brazo tonto de la ley* ("Torrente: The Stupid Arm of the Law," aka "Torrente: The Dumb Arm of the Law," aka "Torrente: The Wrong Arm of the Law").

Mzungo's CD-ROM features music by Carlos Padrissa, a member of the Barcelona-based experimental theatrical troupe La Fura dels Baus, which has played a leading role in the cultivation of linkages between literature, performance, and new media in Spain. One of the group's latest series of projects, for example, is an exploration of the Faust theme in a variety of different media, including theatre, opera, and film – as well as in a virtual solar eclipse (the Java-based *La Sombra de Fausto / Faust Shadow*), which, right on cue, morphed into the real thing on 11 August 1999 (the latter project was sponsored by SUN Microsystems and the organization Catalonia en Red, which hoped to encourage Catalans to use the internet more extensively). Fura's staged "adaptations" of the Goethe text, as well as other on-going productions inspired in Shakespeare and Cervantes, carry the Avant-Garde elimination of the theatrical "fourth wall" and the opening up of the space between performers and audience into new domains, as their "digital theatre" invites thousands of cybernauts to participate in the artistic process. Thus Fura's ever-changing website (www.lafura.com) includes pages that allow participants to register, for example, their personal obsessions so that they may be incorporated, in real time, into the performance (in the case of their *Macbeth* adaptation), or to forward on original musical compositions to be added to the score (in the case of the opera based on *Don Quijote*); the site has also featured links to near-immediate retransmissions of the works as they are being shown in various cultural venues around the world.

While new media technologies might seem to fulfill the promise of ultimate interactivity anticipated in some of the most modern currents of adaptation theory, however, it is important to recognize that many of the seemingly limitless advantages of the digital realm might, in fact, be illusory. As Lev Manovich observes in *The Language of New Media*, digitized interfaces tend to be menu-based, and as such are much more restrictive than may first be apparent; though we may presume we are creating unique structures, for example, when we explore interactive pathways, we are instead merely adopting predetermined identities.[20] Moreover, according to Manovich:

[20] Lev Manovich, *The Language of New Media* (Cambridge, MA: MIT Press, 2001), p. 129.

there is the danger that we will interpret "interaction" literally, equating it with physical interaction between a user and a media object (pressing a button, choosing a link, moving the body), at the expense of psychological interaction. The psychological processes of filling-in, hypothesis formation, recall, and identification, which are required for us to comprehend any text or image at all, are mistakenly identified with an objectively existing structure of interactive links.[21]

Fura dels Baus' digital theatre manifesto (available through the website) does demonstrate considerably more optimism concerning the liberation of collective and individual subjectivities potentially afforded by digital technology. To its credit, though, the group would also seem to acknowledge that the interactivity which takes place across the audience member's personal "mindscreen" is still as significant as any other ancillary forms of interactivity that might be effected through the computer screen, or through the enormous video screens of their staged multimedia performances.

Moreover, the development of intriguing new forms of interactivity and/or modes of experiencing intertextuality (beyond the more traditional notion of adaptation) is not necessarily dependent upon advances in new media technology. A case in point would be Julio Medem's film *Tierra* ("Earth," 1996), and his publishing tie-in *Tierra / Mari en la tierra* ("Earth / Mari On Earth," 1997). Timed to coincide with the film's release on video, the Planeta book included the filmscript on one side, and on the flip side (printed upside down with respect to its sister text), a diary of the main female character of the film, written by Medem himself. Thus through this very textual configuration, film and literary work are positioned as mutually, and endlessly, supplemental: viewers of *Tierra* will find new depths in *Mari en la tierra* and readers of the diary will discover hidden meaning in the film.

For example, although they both feature interlocking love triangles, each emphasizes one of the triangles at the expense of the other. In *Tierra*, Angel, the other-worldly male protagonist, is torn between two women: Angela, the pale, blonde, earth-mother, and Mari, the dark and earthily sensual seductress. Viewed in isolation from the diary, the film has some difficulty avoiding the repressive virgin–whore dichotomies of patriarchal discourse. Mari's diary, however, provides a window onto her subjectivity, otherwise unavailable in the film, which is allied with Angel's perspective. Her writing serves to highlight the crises in masculinity that produce such a reversion to patriarchal representational dichotomies, as well as the seductive attraction that traditional forms of masculine identity still hold for women who, theoretically, "know better." In this text's dominant

---

[21] Manovich, *New Media*, p. 57.

triangle, Mari vacillates between the violently animalistic Patricio, and the fragmented but incipient "new man" Angel. Initially Mari is seduced by the traditional homosocial triangle; she is fascinated by masculine confrontation, and she thrills at the thought that two men might resort to violence on her account. Yet Mari is also conscious that maintenance of this traditional configuration of gender roles requires her to engage in a very particular form of performance. When she is with Patricio, for example, Mari props up his masculinity by allowing him to win at billiards, all the while positioning her body for maximum display. The lucidity with which she describes these performances, however, would indicate that she is not simply swallowed up by the image; rather she works to produce an image that will be consumed by, and eventually consume, others. Even as she creates this all-knowing, all-consuming spectacle of femininity, Mari begins to take pleasure in observing a new form of male display, as she finds herself drawn to Angel's vulnerability, as he struggles to distance himself from a gendered identity based upon violent conflict. Angel is eventually forced to admit his fear in a confrontation with Patricio, and Mari awaits the private spectacle of Angel's broken masculinity: "Me detengo sin dejar de mirarle esperando que se vuelva para verme. Y lo hace, sólo un instante maravilloso, sólo para mí, roto, desolado" ("I halt but continue to gaze at him, in the hope that he will turn around to look at me. And he does so, only for a marvelous instant, only for me: he is broken, disconsolate"). This, in fact, is the man with whom Mari will drive off into the sunshine at the end of the film and the diary.

I would not wish this particular reading of the two texts, however, to shut down the potentially endless generation of meaning that Medem's unique new mode of intertextual linkage promotes; there are enough gaps and contradictions between the two texts to provide ample resistance to interpretive closure. Moreover, Medem's curious act of narrative "transvestism" in *Mari en la tierra* (as well as in the prologue that accompanies the diary) might function as a metaphor for new ways of fashioning or of re-vamping preexisting cultural forms. While Javier Marías expressed discomfort with all but the most "orthodox" of relationships between literature and cinema, Medem, by contrast, may be said to celebrate rather more "perverse" couplings. It is precisely these new forms of cross-media creative experimentation that leave the Spanish cultural scene greatly enlivened, as well as enriched.

Bibliography

Abellán, José Luis. *Historia crítica del pensamiento español*. Vol. II: *La Edad de Oro (siglo XVI)*. Madrid: Espasa-Calpe, 1979.
Historia crítica del pensamiento español. Vol. III: *Del Barroco a la Ilustración I (siglos XVII y XVIII)*. Madrid: Espasa-Calpe, 1981.
Abellán, José Luis, Coord. *El exilio español de 1939*. Madrid: Taurus, 1976.
Abellán, Manuel. *Censura y creación literaria de España (1939–1976)*. Barcelona: Península, 1980.
Acín, Ramón. *Narrativa o consumo literario*. Zaragoza: Prensas Universitarias de Zaragoza, 1990.
Adorno, Theodor A. *Aesthetic Theory*. Trans. R. Hullot-Kentor. Minneapolis: University of Minnesota Press, 1997.
Aguilar Piñal, Francisco. *Cándido María Trigueros*. Madrid: CSIC, 1987.
"Poesía." In *Historia literaria de España en el siglo XVIII*. Ed. Francisco Aguilar Piñal. Madrid: Trotta/CSIC, 1996. 43–134.
La prensa española en el siglo XVIII. Diarios, revistas y pronósticos. Madrid: CSIC, 1978.
ed. "La novela española del siglo XVIII: el rescate de un género." *Insula* 546 (1992): 9–20.
Aguilera Sastre, Juan, and Manuel Aznar Soler. *Cipriano de Rivas Cherif y el teatro de su época (1891–1967)*. Madrid: Asociación de Directores de Escena de España, 1999.
Aguirre, José-María. *Antonio Machado, poeta simbolista*. Madrid: Taurus, 1973.
Aguirre, Manuel de. *Cartas y Discursos del Militar Ingenuo al Correo de los Ciegos de Madrid*, ed. Antonio Elorza. San Sebastián: CSIC, 1974.
Alarcón, Pedro Antonio de. "Discurso sobre la moral en el arte." In *Novelas completas*. Madrid: Aguilar, 1976. 1201–1223.
Alarcón Sierra, Rafael. *Entre el modernismo y la modernidad: la poesía de Manuel Machado*. Seville: Diputación de Sevilla, 1999.
Alarcos, Emilio. *La poesía de Blas de Otero*. Salamanca: Anaya, 1966.
Alas, Leopoldo. "*El amigo Manso*. Novela de D. B. Pérez Galdós." In John W. Kronik, "La reseña de Clarín sobre *El amigo Manso*." *Anales galdosianos* 15 (1980): 63–71.
Los prólogos de Leopoldo Alas. Ed. David Torres. Madrid: Editorial Playor, 1984. 132–139.
Alberti, Rafael. *La arboleda perdida (libro primero de memorias) y otras prosas*. Mexico: Editorial Séneca, 1942. (English translation by Gabriel Berns: *The Lost Grove*. Berkeley: University of California Press, 1981.)

Alborg, Juan Luis. *Historia de la literatura española*. 2nd. edn. 2 vols. Madrid: Editorial Gredos, 1970.
Hora actual de la novela española. Madrid: Taurus, 1958; repr. 1968.
Alcalá Galiano, Antonio. *Historia de la literatura española, francesa, inglesa é italiana*. Madrid: Imprenta de la Sociedad Literaria y Tipográfica, 1845.
"Prólogo" to *El moro expósito* by Angel Saavedra, duque de Rivas. 1834. In *El Romanticismo español. Documentos*. Ed. Ricardo Navas Ruiz. Salamanca: Ediciones Anaya, 1971. 107–127.
Alcalá Zamora, José. *Estudios calderonianos*. Madrid: Academia de la Historia, 1999.
Alcina, Juan Francisco. *Repertorio de la poesía latina del Renacimiento en España*. Salamanca: Universidad de Salamanca, 1995.
Aldaraca, Bridget. *El ángel del hogar: Galdós and the Ideology of Domesticity in Spain*. Chapel Hill: University of North Carolina Press, 1991.
Aldaraca, Bridget, Edward Baker, and John Beverley, eds. *Texto y sociedad: problemas de historia literaria*. Amsterdam and Atlanta: Rodopi, 1990.
Allegra, Giovanni. *El reino interior*. Madrid: Ediciones Encuentro, 1986.
Allen, John J., and José M. Ruano de la Haza. *Los teatros comerciales del siglo XVII y la escenificación de la comedia*. Madrid: Castalia, 1994.
Allen, Judson Boyce. *The Ethical Poetic of the Later Middle Ages: A Decorum of Convenient Distinction*. Toronto: University of Toronto Press, 1982.
Almirall, Valentí. *España tal como es*. Trans. Rosario Fernández-Cancela. Barcelona: Anthropos, 1983.
Alomar, Gabriel. "El Futurisme." In *Assaig*. Ed. Jaume Brossa and Gabriel Alomar. Barcelona: Edicions 62, 1985. 53–89.
Alonso, Álvaro, ed. *La poesía de cancionero*. Letras Hispánicas, 247. Madrid: Cátedra, 1995.
Alonso, Dámaso. *Estudios y ensayos gongorinos*. 2nd. edn. Madrid: Gredos, 1960.
"Poesía arraigada y poesía desarraigada." In *Poetas españoles contemporáneos*. Madrid: Gredos, 1969.
Poesía española: ensayo de métodos y límites estilísticos. Madrid: Gredos, 1950.
Altamira, Rafael. *Mi primera campaña*. Madrid: José Jorro, 1893.
Alvar, Carlos. "La letteratura castigliana medievale." In Valerian Bertolucci *et al.*, *L'area iberica. Storia delle letterature medievali romanze*. Rome: Laterza, 1999. 97–324.
La poesía trovadoresca en España y Portugal. Barcelona: Planeta, 1977.
Álvarez Barrientos, Joaquín. *La novela del siglo XVIII*. Madrid: Júcar, 1991.
"Pedro Calderón de la Barca en los siglos XVII y XIX. Fragmentos para la historia de una apropiación." In *Estado actual de los estudios calderonianos*. Ed. Luciano García Lorenzo. Kassel: Reichenberger, 2000. 279–324.
"Siglo XVIII." In *Historia de los espectáculos en España*. Ed. Andrés Amorós and José María Díez Borque. Madrid: Castalia, 1999. 69–86.
Álvarez Barrientos, Joaquín, François López, and Inmaculada Urzainqui. *La república de las letras en la España del siglo XVIII*. Madrid: Consejo Superior de Investigaciones Científicas, 1995.
Álvarez Berciano, Rosa, and Ramón Sala Noguer. *El cine en la zona nacional 1936-1939*. Bilbao: Ediciones Mensajero, 2000.

Álvarez de Miranda, Pedro. "Las academias de los novatores." In *De las academias a la Enciclopedia: el discurso del saber en la modernidad.* Ed. Evangelina Rodríguez Cuadros. Valencia: Edicions Alfons el Magnànim, 1993. 265–300.

Palabras e ideas. El léxico de la Ilustración temprana en España (1680–1760). Madrid: Real Academia Española, 1992.

Álvarez Pellitero, Ana María. "Indicios de un auto de pastores en el siglo XV." In *Actas del III Congreso de la Asociación Hispánica de la Literatura Medieval (Salamanca, del 3 al 6 de octubre de 1989).* Vol. I. Salamanca: Universidad de Salamanca, 1994. 91–116.

Alzieu, Pierre, Robert Jammes, and Yvan Lissorgues, eds. *Poesía erótica del siglo de oro.* Barcelona: Crítica, 1984.

Amador de los Ríos, José. *Historia crítica de la literatura española.* 7 vols. Madrid: Imprenta de José Rodríguez, 1861–1865.

Anaya, Angel. *An Essay on Spanish Literature, Containing its History, from the Commencement of the Twelfth Century, to the Present Time . . .* London: Boosey & Sons, 1818.

Anderson, Benedict. *Imagined Communities: Reflections on the Origin and Spread of Nationalism.* Rev. edn. London and New York: Verso, 1991.

Andioc, René. *Teatro y sociedad en el Madrid del siglo XVIII.* Madrid: Castalia, 1987.

Andioc, René, and Mireille Coulon. *Cartelera teatral madrileña del siglo XVIII (1708–1808).* 2 vols. Toulouse: Presses Universitaires du Mirail, 1996.

Andrés Martín, Melquíades. *Historia de la mística de la edad de oro en España.* Madrid: Católica, 1994.

Andreu, Alicia. *Galdós y la literatura popular.* Madrid: Sociedad General Española de Librería, 1982.

Aradra, Rosa María. "El canon en la literatura española (siglos XVIII y XIX)." In *Teoría del canon y literatura española.* Ed. Rosa María Aradra and José María Pozuelo Yvancos. Madrid: Cátedra, 2000. 143–303.

Araquistáin, Luis. *La batalla teatral.* Madrid: Mundo Latino, 1930.

Arce, Joaquín. *La poesía del siglo ilustrado.* Madrid: Alhambra, 1981.

Archibald, David. "The War that Won't Die." *Guardian* 28 July 2000.

Arellano Ayuso, Ignacio. "Cervantes en Calderón." *Anales Cervantinos* 35 (1999): 9–35.

Arenal, Electa, and Georgina Sabat de Rivers. *Literatura conventual femenina: Sor Marcela de San Félix, hija de Lope de Vega.* Barcelona: PPU, 1988.

Arenal, Electa, and Stacey Schlau. *Untold Sisters: Hispanic Nuns in their Own Works.* Trans. Amanda Powell. Albuquerque: University of New Mexico Press, 1989.

Aritzeta i Abad, Margarida. *Obra crítica de Manuel de Montoliu.* Tarragona: Publicacions de la Diputació de Tarragona, 1988.

Armistead, Samuel G., et al. *Judeo-Spanish Ballads from Oral Tradition.* 2 vols. to date. Berkeley: University of California Press, 1986–.

Arpa y López, Salvador. *Historia compendiada de la literatura española.* Madrid: Succesores de Rivadeneyra, 1889.

Arróniz, Othón. *La influencia italiana en el nacimiento de la comedia española.* Madrid: Gredos, 1969.

Asensio, Eugenio. *Itinerario del entremés desde Lope de Rueda a Quiñones de Benavente.* Madrid: Gredos, 1965.

Asís Garrote, María Dolores de. *Última hora de la novela en España.* Madrid: Eudema, 1990.

Auerbach, Erich. "The Enchanted Dulcinea." In *Mimesis. The Representation of Reality in Western Literature.* Trans. Willard Trask. Princeton: Princeton University Press, 1953. 334–358.

Aulet, Jaume. *Josep Carner i els orígens del Noucentisme.* Barcelona: Curial, 1992.

Avalle-Arce, Juan Bautista. *La novela pastoril española.* 2nd. edn. Madrid: Istmo, 1974.

Ávila, Alejandro. *La censura del doblaje cinematográfico en España.* Barcelona: Editorial Cims, 1997.

Axmaker, Sean. "'Butterfly' Alights Only Briefly on Politics But Lingers on Nostalgia." *Seattle Post-Intelligencer* 23 June 2000.

Ayerbe-Chaux, Reinaldo. "El uso de *exemplum* en la *Estoria de España* de Alfonso X." *La Corónica* 7 (1978–1979): 28–33.

Bailey, Michael D. "From Sorcery to Witchcraft: Clerical Conceptions of Magic in the Later Middle Ages." *Speculum* 76 (2001): 960–990.

Bakhtin, Mikhail. *Rabelais and His World.* Trans. H. Iswolski. Bloomington: Indiana University Press, 1984.

Ballesteros, Isolina. "Convergencias y alianzas culturales: las adaptaciones fílmicas de obras literarias en el periodo socialista." In *Cine (ins)urgente.* Madrid: Fundamentos, 2001. 153–174.

Baquero Goyanes, Mariano. *El cuento español: del romanticismo al realismo.* Madrid: Consejo Superior de Investigaciones Científicas, 1992.

Bardon, Maurice. *"Don Quichotte" en France au XVIIe et au XVIIIe siècle, 1605–1815.* 2 vols. Paris: Champion, 1931.

Barrajón, Jesús. *La poesía de José Hierro.* Cuenca: Universidad de Castilla – La Mancha, 1999.

Barrero Pérez, Oscar. *Historia de la literatura española contemporánea (1939–1990).* Madrid: Istmo, 1992.

Barthes, Roland. *S/Z.* Paris: Editions du Seuil, 1970.

Bataillon, Marcel. *Erasmo y España: estudios sobre la historia espiritual del siglo XVI.* Trans. Antonio Alatorre. Mexico: Fondo de Cultura Económica, 1966.

Batlle, Carles. "El drama relatiu." In *Suite.* Barcelona: Proa / Teatre Nacional de Catalunya, 2001. 17–23.

Bécarud, Jean, and Gilles Lapouge. *Los anarquistas españoles.* Trans. Gerard Jacas. Barcelona: Laia, 1972.

Bécquer, Gustavo Adolfo. *"La soledad." Rimas, leyendas y otras páginas.* Ed. Jorge Albistur. Montevideo: Ediciones de la Banda Oriental, 1969. 150–160.

Berceo, Gonzalo de. *Milagros de Nuestra Señora.* Ed. Fernando Baños Vallejo. Biblioteca Clásica, 3. Barcelona: Crítica, 1997.

Obra completa. Ed. Isabel Uría. Madrid: Espasa-Calpe, 1992.

Obras completas. Ed. Brian Dutton. 2nd. edn. 3 vols. London: Támesis, 1984. Vol. 1.

Berman, Marshall. *All That Is Solid Melts Into Air: The Experience of Modernity.* New York: Simon and Schuster, 1982.

Bernikow, Louise. *The World Split Open: Four Centuries of Women Poets in England and America, 1552–1950.* New York: Vintage, 1974.

Bersett, Jeffrey T. *El burlado de Sevilla. Nineteenth-Century Theatrical Appropriations of Don Juan Tenorio.* Newark, DE: Juan de la Cuesta Press, 2003.

Bertolucci, Valerian, *et al. L'area iberica. Storia delle letterature medievali romanze.* Rome: Laterza, 1999.

Bessiére, Bernard. *La culture espagnole. Les mutations de l'aprés-franquisme (1975–1992).* Paris: L'Harmattan, 1992.

Beverly, John. *Aspects of Gongora's Soledades.* Purdue University Monographs in Romance Languages, 1. Amsterdam: John Benjamins, 1980.

Bhabha, Homi. *The Location of Culture.* London: Routledge, 1994.

ed. *Nation and Narration.* London: Routledge, 1990.

Biglieri, Aníbal. *Hacia una poética del relato didáctico: ocho estudios sobrel El Conde Lucanor.* North Carolina Studies in the Romance Languages and Literatures, 233. Chapel Hill: Department of Romance Languages, University of North Carolina, 1989.

Bilbeny, Norbert. *Política Noucentista: De Maragall a d'Ors.* Catarroja: Afers, 1999.

Bilinkoff, Jodi. "The Many 'Lives' of Pedro de Ribadeneyra." *Renaissance Quarterly* 52 (1999): 180–196.

Blackburn, Simon. "Logical Humanism." *New Republic* (17 and 24 April 2001): 95–96.

Blackmore, Josiah. "*Afeiçom* and History-Writing: the Prologue of the *Crónica de D. Joao I.*" *Luso-Brazilian Review* 34 (1997): 15–24.

Blackmore, Josiah, and Gregory S. Hutcheson, eds. *Queer Iberia: Sexualities, Cultures, and Crossings From the Middle Ages to the Renaissance.* Durham: Duke University Press, 1999.

Blanco, Alda. "Domesticity, Education and the Woman Writer: Spain 1850–1880." In *Cultural and Historical Grounding for Hispanic and Luso-Brazilian Feminist Literary Criticism.* Ed. Hernán Vidal. Minneapolis: Institute for the Study of Ideologies and Literature, 1989. 371–394.

"Gender and National Identity: The Novel in Nineteenth-Century Spanish Literary History." In *Culture and Gender in Nineteenth-Century Spain.* Ed. Lou Charnon-Deutsch and Jo Labanyi. Oxford: Oxford University Press, 1995. 120–136.

Narradoras de la domesticidad en la España isabelina. Granada: Universidad de Granada, 2001.

"Theorizing the Novel at Mid-Century." *Revista de Estudios Hispánicos.* 34.2 (May 2000): 423–431.

Blanco, Mercedes. *Les Rhétoriques de la pointe. Baltasar Gracián et le Conceptisme en Europe.* Paris: Honoré Champion, 1992.

Blanco Aguinaga, Carlos. *El Unamuno contemplativo.* Mexico City: El Colegio de México, 1959.

Blanco García, Francisco. *La literatura española en el siglo XIX.* 3 vols. Madrid: Aguado, 1891–1894.

Blasco Pascual, Francisco Javier. "De 'Oráculos' y de 'Cenicientas': la crítica ante el fin de siglo español." In *¿Qué es el modernismo? Nuevas encuestas. Nuevas lecturas.* Ed. Richard A. Cardwell and Bernard McGuirk. Boulder: Society of Spanish and Spanish American Studies, 1993. 59–86.

Blecua, Alberto. "La *Égloga* de Francisco de Madrid en un nuevo manuscrito del siglo XVI." In *Serta Philologica F. Lázaro Carreter natalem diem sexagesimum celebranti dicata.* Madrid: Cátedra, 1983. 39–66.

"Sobre la autoría del 'Auto de la Pasión.'" In *Homenaje a Eugenio Asensio.* Madrid: Gredos, 1988. 79–112.

Blecua, José Manuel. "Corrientes poéticas del siglo XVI." In *Sobre poesía de la Edad de Oro.* Madrid: Gredos, 1970. 11–24.

Poesía de la Edad de Oro. Madrid: Castalia, 1982.

Bloom, Harold. *The Western Canon: The Books and School of the Ages.* New York: Harcourt Brace, 1994.

Bly, Peter A. *Pérez Galdós, "La de Bringas."* London: Grant and Cutler, 1981.

Bofill i Mates, Jaume. "Classicisme nacional." In *L'altra concòrdia i altres textos sobre el catalanisme.* Ed. Jordi Casassas. Barcelona: Edicions de La Magrana, 1983. 3–32.

Bonet, Laureano. *La escuela de Barcelona y la cultura del medio siglo.* Barcelona: Edicions 62, 1994.

Borau, José Luis, ed. *Diccionario del cine español.* Madrid: Alianza Editorial, Academia de las Artes y las Ciencias Cinematográficas de España, y Fundación Autor, 1998.

Borges, Jorge Luis. *Ficciones.* Ed. and trans. Anthony Kerrigan. New York: Grove Press, 1962.

Bourdieu, Pierre. *Distinction: A Social Critique of the Judgement of Taste.* Trans. Richard Nice. Cambridge, MA: Harvard University Press, 1984.

Bouterwek, Friedrich. *Historia de la literatura española.* Trans. Jose Gomez de la Cortina and Nicolas Hugalde y Mollinedo. Madrid: Imp. de E. Aguado, 1829.

History of Spanish and Portuguese Literature. 2 vols. London: Boosey and Sonse, 1823.

Boyum, Joy Gould. *Double Exposure: Fiction into Film.* New York: Plume, 1985.

Bozal Fernández, Valeriano. *La ilustración gráfica del siglo XIX en España.* Madrid: Alberto Corazón, 1978.

Braudel, Fernand. *Ecrits sur l'histoire.* Paris: Flammarion, 1969.

Breitenberg, Mark. *Anxious Masculinity in Early Modern England.* Cambridge: Cambridge University Press, 1996.

Bretz, Mary Lee. *La evolución novelística de Pío Baroja.* Madrid: Porrúa Turanzas, 1979.

Brook, Peter. *The Empty Space.* New York: Atheneum, 1968.

Brossa, Jaume. "L'esperit universalista." *El Poble Català* 11 December 1907.

"Revista general. Recollim el guant." *L'Avenç* 5 (15 September 1893).

"Viure del passat." *L'Avenç* 4.9 (1892).

Brossa, Jaume, and Gabriel Alomar, eds. *Assaig*. Barcelona: Edicions 62, 1985.

Brown, Catherine. "Queer Representation in the *Arçipreste de Talavera*, or The *Maldezir de mugeres* Is a Drag." In *Queer Iberia: Sexualities, Cultures, and Crossings From the Middle Ages to the Renaissance*. Ed. Josiah Blackmore and Gregory S. Hutcheson. Durham: Duke University Press, 1999. 73–103.

Brown, Joan L. *Women Writers of Contemporary Spain: Exiles in the Homeland*. Newark: University of Delaware Press, 1991.

Brown, Marshall. "Rethinking the Scale of Literary History." In *Rethinking Literary History*. Ed. Linda Hutcheon and Mario J. Valdés. Oxford: Oxford University Press, 2002. 116–154.

——. ed. *The Uses of Literary History*. Durham: Duke University Press, 1995.

Brownlee, Marina Scordilis. *The Severed Word: Ovid's "Heroides" and the "Novela Sentimental."* Princeton: Princeton University Press, 1990.

Bürger, Peter. *Theory of the Avant-Garde*. Trans. Michael Shaw. Minneapolis: University of Minnesota Press, 1984.

Burke, James F. *Desire Against the Law: The Juxtaposition of Contraries in Early Medieval Spanish Literature*. Stanford: Stanford University Press, 1998.

——. *History and Vision: The Figural Structure of the Libro del Cavallero Zifar*. London: Támesis, 1972.

——. *Vision, the Gaze and the Function of the Senses in "Celestina."* University Park, PA: Pennsylvania State University Press, 2000.

Butt, John. "Modernismo y *Modernism*." In *¿Qué es el modernismo? Nuevas encuestas. Nuevas lecturas*. Ed. Richard A. Cardwell and Bernard McGuirk. Boulder: Society of Spanish and Spanish American Studies, 1993. 39–58.

Cacho Blecua, Juan Manuel. *Amadís: heroísmo mítico cortesano*. Madrid: Cupsa, 1979.

Cacho Viu, Vicente. "Els modernistes i el nacionalisme cultural (1881–1906)." In *Els modernistes i el nacionalisme cultural. Antologia*. Trans. Jordi Cassassas i Ymbert. Ed. Vicente Cacho Viu. Barcelona: Edicions de la Magrana, 1984. v–xlii.

——. *Revisión de Eugenio D'Ors (1902–1930)*. Barcelona: Quaderns Crema, 1997.

Caldera, Ermanno. *Primi manifesti del romanticismo spagnolo*. Pisa: Università di Pisa, 1962.

——. *El teatro español en la época romántica*. Madrid: Castalia, 2001.

——. ed. *Teatro di magia*. Rome: Bulzoni, 1983.

Caldera, Ermanno, and Antonietta Calderone. "El teatro en el siglo XIX (1808–1844)." In *Historia del teatro en España. II. Siglos XVIII y XIX*. Ed. José María Díez Borque. Madrid: Taurus, 1988. 377–624.

Calinescu, Matei. *Five Faces of Modernity*. Durham: Duke University, 1995.

Callahan, William J., *Church, Politics and Society in Spain, 1750–1874*. Cambridge, MA: Harvard University Press, 1984.

Calvo Carilla, José Luis. "Reconsideración de la poesía española de la segunda mitad del siglo XIX (a propósito de Núñez de Arce)." *Boletín de la Biblioteca Menéndez Pelayo* 69 (1993): 195–223.

Cañas Murillo, Jesús, and Miguel Ángel Lama, eds. *Juan Pablo Forner y su época*. Mérida: Editorial Regional de Extremadura, 1998.

Canavaggio, Jean. *Cervantès*. Paris: Mazarine, 1986. (Spanish translation: *Cervantes. En busca del perfil perdido*. Madrid: Espasa-Calpe, 1992.)

Candau, Antonio. "Jorge Riechmann y la metamorfosis de la experiencia." *España Contemporánea* 13 (Spring 2000): 7–36.

Cano Ballesta, Juan. *La poesía española entre pureza y revolución (1920–1936)*. Mexico, DF: Siglo Veintiuno Editores, 1996.

Cantar de mio Cid. Ed. Alberto Montaner. Biblioteca Clásica, 1. Barcelona: Crítica, 1993.

Cardona, Rodolfo, and Anthony Zahareas. *Visión del esperpento. Teoría y práctica en los esperpentos de Valle-Inclán*. Madrid: Castalia, 1982.

Cardwell, Richard "Degeneration, Discourse and Differentiation: *Modernismo frente a noventayocho* Reconsidered." In *Critical Essays on the Literature of Spain and Spanish America*, supplement to *Anales de la Literatura Española Contemporánea*. Boulder: Society of Spanish and Spanish-American Studies. 29–46.

"Introducción." In *Manuel Reina. La vida inquieta*. Exeter: University of Exeter, 1978. 1–43.

Juan R. Jiménez: The Modernist Apprenticeship (1895–1900). Berlin: Biblioteca Ibero-americana, 1977.

"Juan Ramón, Ortega y los intelectuales." *Hispanic Review* 53 (1985): 329–350.

"Juan Ramón Jiménez and the Decadence." *Revista de Letras* 23–24 (1974): 291–342.

"Mirrors and Myths: Antonio Machado and the Search for Self." *Romance Studies* 16 (1990): 31–42.

"El premodernismo español." In *Historia de la literatura española. Siglo XIX (II)*. Ed. Leonardo Romero Tobar. Madrid: Espasa-Calpe, 1998. 309–343.

Cardwell, Richard, and Bernard McGuirk, eds. *¿Qué es el modernismo? Nuevas encuestas. Nuevas lecturas*. Boulder: Society of Spanish and Spanish-American Studies, 1993.

Carnero, Guillermo. *Estudios sobre el teatro español del siglo XVIII*. Zaragoza: Universidad de Zaragoza, 1997.

"La generación poética de 1936 . . . hasta 1939." In *Las armas abisinias*. Barcelona: Anthropos, 1989. 238–255.

El grupo "Cántico" de Córdoba. Madrid: Editora Nacional, 1976.

"La novela española del siglo XVIII: estado de la cuestión." *Anales de literatura española* 11 (1995): 11–45.

Los orígenes del romanticismo reaccionario español: el matrimonio Böhl de Faber. Valencia: Universidad de Valencia, 1978.

Carr, Raymond. *Spain, 1808–1975*. Oxford: Oxford University Press, 1982.

Carrasco Urgoiti, María Soledad. *The Moorish Novel*. Boston: Twayne, 1975.

Carruthers, Mary. *The Craft of Thought: Meditation, Rhetoric, and the Making of Images, 400–1200*. Cambridge: Cambridge University Press, 1998.

Casas, Joan. "El miratge de la 'nova dramatúrgia catalana.'" *Serra d'Or* 481 (2000): 34–37; repr. in Spanish in *ADE Teatro* 83 (2000): 161–164.

Cascardi, Anthony J. *The Limits of Illusion: A Critical Study of Calderón*. Cambridge: Cambridge University Press, 1984.

Caso González, José Miguel. *La poética de Jovellanos*. Madrid: Prensa Española, 1972.

Castañar, Fulgencio. *El compromiso en la novela de la II República*. Madrid: Siglo Veintiuno, 1992.

Castellet, José María. "La novela española quince años después." *Cuadernos del Congreso por la Libertad de la Cultura* 33 (1958): 48–52.

Nueve novísimos poetas españoles. Barcelona: Barral Editores, 1970.

Castells, Ricardo. "'A la presençia de Calisto se presento la deseada Melibea': la memoria en el argumento general de *Celestina*." *Celestinesca* 24 (2000): 115–122.

Castro, Americo. *El pensamiento de Cervantes*. Madrid: Hermando, 1925.

The Spaniards: An Introduction to their History. Trans. Willard F. King and Selma Margaratten. Berkeley: University of California Press, 1971.

Castro, Americo, and Hugo A. Rennert. *Vida de Lope de Vega (1562–1635)*. With additions by Fernando Lázaro Carreter. Salamanca: Anaya, 1968.

Castro, Eva, ed. *Teatro medieval*. Vol. 1: *El drama litúrgico*. Barcelona: Crítica, 1997.

Castro, María Isabel de. *La poesía de cantares en la segunda mitad del siglo XIX*. Madrid: Universidad Complutense, 1988.

Castro, Rosalía de. "Duas palabras da autora." In *Follas novas*. Ed. Juan Barja. Madrid: Akal, 1985. 16–27.

Cattaneo, M. T. "Gli esordi del romanticismo in Ispagna e *El Europeo*." In *Tre studi sulla cultura spagnola*. Milan: Instituto Cisalpino, 1967. 75–137.

Caudet, Francisco. *Hipótesis sobre el exilio republicano de 1939*. Madrid: Fundación Universitaria Española, 1997.

"El modernismo visto por sus contemporáneos: las encuestas en las revistas de la época." In *¿Qué es el modernismo? Nuevas encuestas. Nuevas lecturas*. Ed. Richard A. Cardwell and Bernard McGuirk. Boulder: Society of Spanish and Spanish American Studies, 1993. 25–38.

Centeno, Enrique. "Cambio y comunicación en el teatro posfranquista." *El País* 16 September 1979: VIII ("Arte y Pensamiento").

Cerezo Galán, Pedro. *Las máscaras de lo trágico. Filosofía y tragedia en Miguel de Unamuno*. Madrid: Trotta, 1995.

Cernuda, Luis. "Bécquer y el poema en prosa español." *Prosa completa*. Barcelona: Seix Barral, 1975. 984–993.

Certeau, Michel de. *The Mystic Fable*. Vol. 1: *The Sixteenth and Seventeenth Centuries*. Chicago: University of Chicago Press, 1992.

Chacel, Rosa. *Poesía de la circunstancia. Cómo y por qué de la novela*. Bahía Blanca: Universidad Nacional del Sur, 1958.

Chandler, Richard E. *A New History of Spanish Literature*. Rev. edn. Baton Rouge: Louisiana State University Press, 1991.

Charnon-Deutsch, Lou. *Fictions of the Feminine in the Nineteenth-Century Spanish Press*. University Park, PA: Pennsylvania State University Press, 2000.

Narratives of Desire: Nineteenth-Century Spanish Fiction by Women. University Park: Pennsylvania State University Press, 1994.

Checa Beltrán, José. *Razones del buen gusto*. Madrid: CSIC, 1999.

Checa Beltrán, José, Juan Antonio Ríos, and Irene Vallejo. *Poesía del siglo XVIII*. Madrid: Júcar, 1992.

Checa Puerta, Julio Enrique. *Los teatros de Gregorio Martínez Sierra*. Madrid: Fundación Universitaria Española, 1998.

Chevalier, Maxime. *Folklore y literatura: el cuento oral en el Siglo de Oro*. Barcelona: Crítica, 1978.

Lectura y lectores en la España del siglo XVI y XVII. Madrid: Turner, 1976.

Ciplijauskaité, Biruté. *La novela femenina contemporánea (1970–1985): hacia una tipología de la narración en primera persona*. Barcelona: Anthropos, 1988.

Clavería, Carlos. *Temas de Unamuno*. Madrid: Gredos, 1970.

Close, Anthony J. *Cervantes and the Comic Mind of His Age*. Oxford: Oxford University Press, 2000.

"La crítica del *Quijote* desde 1925 hasta ahora." In *Cervantes*. Madrid: Centro de Estudios Cervantinos, 1995. 311–333.

Don Quixote. Cambridge: Cambridge University Press, 1990.

"Las interpretaciones del Quijote." In *Don Quijote de la Mancha*. 2 vols. Ed. Francisco Rico. Barcelona: Crítica, 1998. cxlii–clxv.

The Romantic Approach to "Don Quixote." Cambridge: Cambridge University Press, 1978.

Coenen, Lily. "M. Menéndez Pelayo: Literary History in the Context of a Religious Question." *Yearbook of European Studies* 12 (1999): 173–183.

Cohen, Ralph. "Genre Theory, Literary History, and Historical Change." In *Theoretical Issues in Literary History*. Ed. David Perkins. Baltimore: Johns Hopkins University Press, 1991. 85–113.

Cohen, Walter. *Drama of a Nation. Public Theater in Renaissance England and Spain*. Ithaca: Cornell University Press, 1985.

Colahan, Clark. *The Visions of Sor María de Ágreda: Writing, Knowledge and Power*. Tucson: University of Arizona Press, 1994.

Cole, Peter. *Selected Poems of Shmuel Ha-Nagid*. Princeton: Princeton University Press, 1996.

Selected Poems of Solomon Ibn Gabirol. Princeton: Princeton University Press, 2000.

Collard, Andrée. *Nueva poesía: conceptismo, culteranismo en la crítica española*. Madrid: Castalia, 1967.

Colmeiro, José E. *La novela policiaca española: teoría y crítica*. Barcelona: Anthropos, 1995.

Comadira, Narcís. "Sobre el mediterranisme: unes notes." *Quaderns d'Arquitectura i Urbanisme* 153 (1982): 46–51.

Los conceptos de rococó, neoclasicismo y prerromanticismo en la literatura española del siglo XVIII. Oviedo: Cátedra Feijoo, 1970.

Convivencia: Jews, Muslims and Christians in Medieval Spain. Ed. Jerrilyn Dodds, Vivian Mann, and Thomas Glick. New York: George Braziller and the Jewish Museum, 1992.

Coope, Marian G. R. *Reality and Time in the Oleza Novels of Gabriel Miró*. London: Támesis, 1984.

Correa Ramón, Amelina. *Melchor Almagro San Martín. Noticia de una ausencia.* Granada: Ficciones. Revista de Letras, 2001.

Poetas andaluces en la órbita del modernismo. Seville: Alfar, 2001.

Cortada, Joan. "Discurs presidencial dels 'Jocs Florals' de Barcelona de 1864." In *Catalunya i els catalans.* Barcelona: Edicions 62, 1965. 85–93.

Cossío, José María de. *Cincuenta años de poesía española (1850–1900).* Madrid: Espasa-Calpe, 1960.

Coulon, Mireille. *Le Sainete à Madrid à l'époque de don Ramón de la Cruz.* Pau: Université de Pau, 1993.

Criado de Val, Manuel. *Historia de Hita y su Arcipreste. Vida y muerte de una villa mozárabe.* Madrid: Editora Nacional, 1976.

Croce, Benedetto. "Introduction." In Francesco de Sanctis, *History of Italian Literature.* Trans. Joan Redfern. New York: Harcourt, Brace, 1931.

Cruz, Anne J. *Discourses of Poverty: Social Reform and the Picaresque Novel in Early Modern Spain.* Toronto: University of Toronto Press, 1999.

Cruz, Juan de la. *Poesía.* Ed. Domingo Ynduráin. Madrid: Cátedra, 2000.

Poesía completa y comentarios en prosa. Ed. Raquel Asún. Barcelona: Planeta, 1997.

Culture and Gender in Nineteenth-Century Spain. Ed. Lou Charnon-Deutsch and Jo Labanyi. Oxford: Oxford University Press, 1995.

Dagenais, John. *The Ethics of Reading in Manuscript Culture: Glossing the "Libro de buen amor."* Princeton: Princeton University Press, 1994.

Damian-Grint, Peter. *The New Historians of the Twelfth-Century Renaissance: Inventing Vernacular Authority.* Woodbridge, England: Boydell, 1999.

Dangler, Jean. *Mediating Fictions: Literature, Women Healers and the Go-Between in Medieval and Early Modern Iberia.* Lewisburg, PA: Bucknell University Press, 2001.

Dans, Raúl. "Un dramaturgo en el fin del mundo." In "Les darreres generacions teatrals del segle." Special issue of *Assaig de Teatre: Revista de l'Associació d'Investigació i Experimentació Teatral* 24 (September 2000): 131–152.

Davis, Elizabeth B. *Myth and Identity in the Epic of Imperial Spain.* Columbia: University of Missouri Press, 2000.

De Looze, Laurence. "*El Conde Lucanor*, Part V, and the Goals of the Manueline Text." *La Corónica* 28 (2000): 129–154.

"Subversion of Meaning in Part I of *El Conde Lucanor.*" *Revista Canadiense de Estudios Hispánicos* 19 (1995): 341–355.

Deacon, Philip. "Precisión histórica y estética teatral en el siglo XVIII español." In *Ideas en sus paisajes. Homenaje al Profesor Russell P. Sebold.* Ed. Guillermo Carnero *et al.* Alicante: Universidad de Alicante, 1999. 141–150.

"Vicente García de la Huerta y el círculo de Montiano: la amistad entre Huerta y Margarita Hickey." *Revista de Estudios Extremeños* 44 (1988): 395–421.

Debicki, Andrew. *Historia de la poesía española del siglo XX. Desde la modernidad hasta el presente.* Madrid: Gredos, 1997.

Poetry of Discovery: The Spanish Generation of 1956–1971. Lexington: Kentucky University Press, 1982.

Spanish Poetry of the Twentieth Century. Modernity and Beyond. Lexington: Kentucky University Press, 1994.

Defourneaux, Marcelin. *Inquisición y censura de libros en la España del siglo XVIII.* Madrid: Taurus, 1973.

Delgado, Feliciano. "Las profecías de sibilas en el MS. 80 de la Catedral de Córdoba y los orígenes del teatro nacional." *Revista de Filología Española* 67 (1987): 77–87.

Del Pino, José Manuel. *Montajes y fragmentos: una aproximación a la narrativa española de vanguardia.* Amsterdam and Atlanta: Rodopi, 1995.

"Novela y vanguardia artística (1923–1934)." In *La vanguardia en España. Arte y literatura.* Ed. Javier Pérez Bazo. Toulouse: CRIC, 1998. 251–274.

Del Río, Angel. *Historia de la literatura española.* 2 vols. New York: Holt, 1948, 1963.

del Valle, Adriano. "Ramón Gómez de la Serna o el sentido de la universalidad." *Alfar* 50 (1925): 6–7.

Dendle, Brian J. "Two Sources of López Soler's Articles in *El Europeo.*" *Studies in Romanticism* 5 (1965–1966): 44–50.

Dennis, Nigel. "En torno a la prosa breve en la joven literatura." *Insula* 646 (October 2000): 15–19.

ed. *Studies on Ramón Gómez de la Serna.* Ottawa: Dovehouse Editions, 1988.

Devoto, Daniel. "Sentido y forma de la cántica 'Eya velar.'" *Bulletin Hispanique* 65 (1963): 206–237.

Deyermond, A. D. *El "Cantar de mio Cid" y la épica medieval española.* Biblioteca General, 2. Barcelona: Sirmio, 1987.

Historia de la literatura española. Vol. 1: *La Edad Media.* Barcelona: Ariel, 1973.

"Historia sagrada y técnica dramática en la *Representación del nacimiento de Nuestro Señor* de Gómez Manrique." In *Historias y Ficciones: coloquio sobre la literatura del siglo XV.* Valencia: Universitat de València, 1992. 291–305.

A Literary History of Spain: The Middle Ages. London: Ernest Benn, 1971.

Tradiciones y puntos de vista en la ficción sentimental. Mexico City: Universidad Nacional Autónoma de México, 1993.

ed. *Historia y crítica de la literatura española.* Vol. 1: *La Edad Media.* Gen. ed. Francisco Rico. Barcelona: Crítica, 1980.

ed. *Historia y crítica de la literatura española.* Vol. 1: *La Edad Media: primer suplemento.* Gen. ed. Francisco Rico. Barcelona: Editorial Critica, 1991.

Diago, Manuel. "Lope de Rueda y los orígenes del teatro profesional." *Criticón* 50 (1990): 41–65.

"La práctica escénica populista en Valencia." In *Teatros y prácticas escénicas.* 2 vols. Vol. 1: *El Quinientos Valenciana.* Ed. J. Alonso Asensio *et al.* Valencia: Institució Alfons el Magnànim, 1984. 329–353.

Díaz Fernández, José. *El nuevo romanticismo.* Madrid: Zeus, 1930.

Díaz Mas, Paloma, ed. *Romancero.* Biblioteca Clásica, 8. Barcelona: Crítica, 1994.

Díaz-Plaja, Guillermo. *Historia de la literatura española a través de la crítica y de los textos*. Barcelona: La Espiga, 1942.

Historia general de las literaturas hispánicas. Barcelona: Editorial Barna, 1949.

A History of Spanish Literature. Trans. Hugh A. Harter. New York: New York University Press, 1971.

Modernismo frente a noventa y ocho. Madrid: Espasa-Calpe, 1951.

Díaz y Díaz, Manuel C. *Index scriptorum Latinorum Medii Aevi Hispanorum*. 2 vols. [Salamanca]: Universidad de Salamanca, 1958–1959.

Diego, Gerardo. *Carmen y Lola*. Facs. edn. Madrid: Turner, 1977.

Díez Borque, José María. *Sociedad y teatro en la España de Lope de Vega*. Barcelona: A. Bosch, 1978.

ed. *Historia de las literaturas hispánicas no castellanas*. Madrid: Taurus, 1980.

Díez-Canedo, Enrique. *Artículos de crítica teatral*. 4 vols. Mexico: Joaquín Mortiz, 1968.

Díez de Revenga, Francisco Javier. *Panorama crítico de la generación del 27*. Madrid: Editorial Castalia, 1987.

Díez Taboada, Juan María. "El germanismo y la renovación de la lírica española en el siglo XIX (1840–1870)." *Filología Moderna* 5 (1961): 21–55.

Dieze, Johann Andreas. *Geschichte der spanischen Dichtkunst*. Ed. Luis Jose Velázquez de Velasco, Marqués de Valdeflores. Gottingen: V. Bossiegel, 1769.

Dijkstra, Bram. *Idols of Perversity: Fantasies of Feminine Evil in Fin-de–Siècle Culture*. Oxford: Oxford University Press, 1988.

DiSalvo, Angelo J. "The Ascetical Meditative Literature of Renaissance Spain: An Alternative to Amadís, Elisa and Diana." *Hispania* 69 (1986): 466–475.

D'Lugo, Marvin. "Pedro Almodóvar y la autoría literaria." In *Literatura española y cine*. Ed. Norberto Minguez. Madrid: Complutense, 2002. 75–92.

Dodds, Jerrilyn. *Al-Andalus. The Art of Islamic Spain*. New York: The Metropolitan Museum of Art, 1992.

Architecture and Ideology in Early Medieval Spain. State Park: Pennsylvania University Press, 1990.

Doménech, Ricardo. "Buero Vallejo, aquí y ahora." In *Antonio Buero Vallejo: Premio Miguel de Cervantes (1986)*. Madrid: Biblioteca Nacional, 1987. 9–10.

"Para un arreglo de cuentas con el teatro de Alejandro Casona." *Ínsula* 209 (1964), p. 15.

El teatro de Buero Vallejo. Madrid: Gredos, 1973.

Domergue, Lucienne. *Censure et lumières dans le règne de Charles III*. Paris: CNRS, 1982.

Le Livre en Espagne au temps de la révolution française. Lyon: Presses Universitaires de Lyon, 1984.

Domínguez Ortiz, Antonio. "La España del Quijote." In *Don Quijote de la Mancha*. 2 vols. Ed. Francisco Rico. Barcelona: Crítica, 1998. lxxxvii–civ.

Donovan, Richard B. *The Liturgical Drama in Medieval Spain*. Toronto: University of Toronto Press, 1958.

Doron, Aviva. "La poesía de Todros Ha-Levi Abulafia como reflejo del encuentro de las culturas: la hebrea y la española en la Toledo de Alfonso X El Sabio." In *Actas del X Congreso de la Asociación Internacional de Hispanistas.* 4 vols. Ed. Antonio Vilanova *et al.* Barcelona: PPU, 1992. Vol. I. 171–178.

D'Ors, Eugeni. *Glosari 1906–1910.* Barcelona: Selecta, 1950.

    Glosari. Ed. Josep Murgades. Barcelona: Edicions 62, 1982.

    "Prologue" to *La muntanya d'Ametistes.* In Guerau de Liost, *Obra poètica completa.* Ed. Enric Bou. Barcelona: Selecta, 1983. 35–38.

D'Ors, Miguel. *En busca del público perdido. Aproximación a la última poesía española joven (1975–1993).* Granada: Impredisur, 1994.

Dougherty, Dru. *Guía para caminantes en Santa Fe de Tierra Firme. Estudio sistémico de "Tirano Banderas."* Valencia: Pre-Textos, 1999.

    Talía convulsa: la crisis teatral de los años 20. In *2 ensayos sobre teatro español de los 20.* Murcia: Universidad de Murcia, 1984.

Dougherty, Dru, and María Francisca Vilches de Frutos. *La escena madrileña entre 1918 y 1926. Análisis y documentación.* Madrid: Fundamentos, 1990.

Dunn, Peter N. *Spanish Picaresque Fictions. A New Literary History.* Ithaca: Cornell University Press, 1993.

Durán, Agustín. *Discurso sobre el influjo que ha tenido la crítica moderna en la decadencia del teatro antiguo español . . . 1828.* In *El Romanticismo español. Documentos.* Ed. Ricardo Navas Ruiz. Salamanca: Ediciones Anaya, 1971. 54–100.

Durán López, Fernando. "La autobiografía moderna en España: nacimiento y evolución." Ph.D thesis. 2 vols. Universidad de Cádiz, 2001.

Dutton, Brian, with Jineen Krogstad, eds. *El cancionero del siglo XV.* Salamanca: Biblioteca Española del Siglo xv/Universidad de Salamanca, 1990–1991.

Egido, Aurora. *Fronteras de la poesía en el barroco.* Barcelona: Crítica, 1990.

Egido, Teófanes. "Los anti-ilustrados españoles." In *La Ilustración en España y Alemania.* Ed. R. Mate and F. Niewöhner. Barcelona: Anthropos, 1989. 95–119.

Eire, Carlos M. *From Madrid to Purgatory: The Art and Craft of Dying in Sixteenth-Century Spain.* Cambridge: Cambridge University Press, 1995.

Eisenberg, Daniel. *Romances of Chivalry in the Spanish Golden Age.* Newark, DE: Juan De la Cuesta, 1982.

Elliott, John H. *El viejo mundo y el nuevo.* Madrid: Alianza Editorial, 1972.

Elorza, Antonio. *La ideología liberal en la Ilustración española.* Madrid: Tecnos, 1970.

Enciso Recio, Luis Miguel. "Las Sociedades Económicas de Amigos del País." In *Historia de España.* Vol. XXXI: *La época de la Ilustración.* Part I: *El Estado y la cultura (1759–1808).* Ed. J. M. Jover Zamora. Madrid: Espasa-Calpe, 1985. 13–56.

Enríquez de Salamanca, Cristina. "¿Quién era la escritora del siglo XIX?" *Letras Peninsulares* 2 (1989): 81–107.

Ercilla, Alonso de. *La Araucana.* Ed. Isaías Lerner. Madrid: Cátedra, 1993.

Escobar, José. "Costumbrismo. Estado de la cuestión." *Romanticismo* 6 (1996): 117–126.

"Un episodio biográfico de Larra, crítico teatral en la temporada 1834." *Nueva Revista de Filología Hispánica* 24 (1976): 45–72.

Los orígenes de la obra de Larra. Madrid: Prensa Española, 1972.

Escobar, José. "Romanticismo y revolución." *Estudios de Historia Social* 36–37 (1986): 345–351.

Evans, Peter. "CIFESA: Cinema and Authoritarian Practices." In *Spanish Cultural Studies*. Ed. Helen Graham and Jo Labanyi. Oxford: Oxford University Press, 1995. 215–222.

Even-Zohar, Itamar. "Literature as Goods, Literature as Tools." www.tau.ac.il/~itamarez/papers/lit-g-t.html. Also forthcoming in *Neohelicon*, a special issue In Memoriam György Mihaly Vajda.

"The Role of Literature in the Making of the Nations of Europe." www.tau.ac.il/~itamarez/papers/rol_lit.html. Also published in *Applied Semiotics / Sémiotique appliquée* 1 (1996): 20–30. (Latter is a refereed periodical on the WWW: www.chass.utoronto.ca/french/as-sa/index.html.)

Fabbri, Maurizio. *Un aspetto dell'Illuminismo espagnolo: l'opera letteraria di Pedro Montengón*. Pisa: Libreria Goliardica, 1972.

Faber, Sebastiaan. *Exile and Cultural Hegemony. Spanish Intellectuals in Mexico, 1939–1975*. Nashville: Vanderbilt University Press, 2002.

Fabra Barreiro, Gustavo. "El pensamiento vivo de Larra." *Revista de Occidente* 50 (1967): 129–152.

Feldman, Sharon G. "'Si me gustan La Fura dels Baus y Molière, no es una contradicción': Conversaciones con Sergi Belbel." *España Contemporánea* 13.1 (2001): 71–86.

Fernández, José Ramón. "Quince años de escritura dramática en España: un camino hacia la normalidad." *ADE Teatro* 50 (April–June 1996): 80–86.

Fernández, Pura. "El naturalismo radical." In *Historia de la literatura española*. Vol. IX: *Siglo XIX (II)*. Ed. Leonardo Romero Tobar. Madrid: Espasa-Calpe, 1998. 751–761.

Fernández Cifuentes, Luis. "Fenomenologías de la vanguardia: el caso de la novela." *Anales de Literatura Española de la Universidad de Alicante* 9 (1993): 45–60.

García Lorca en el teatro: la norma y la diferencia. Zaragoza: Universidad de Zaragoza, 1986.

Teoría y mercado de la novela en España: del 98 a la República. Madrid: Gredos, 1982.

Fernández Montesinos, José. *Estudios sobre Lope de Vega*. Salamanca: Anaya, 1969.

Fernández Utrera, María Soledad. *Visiones de estereoscópico. Paradigma de hibridación en al ficción y el arte de la vanguardia española*. Chapel Hill: University of North Carolina Press, 2001.

Ferreras, Juan Ignacio. *La novela en el siglo XX (desde 1939)*. Madrid: Taurus, 1988.

La novela por entregas, 1840–1900. Concentración obrera y economía editorial. Madrid: Taurus, 1972.

Fitzmaurice-Kelly, James. *Historia de la literatura española: desde los orígenes hasta el año 1900*. Trans. Adolfo Bonilla y San Martín. Madrid: La España Moderna, 1901. (Translation of English original published in 1898.)

Flitter, Derek W. "Ideological Uses of Romantic Theory in Spain." In *Romantik and Romance: Cultural Interanimation in European Romanticism*. Ed. Carol Tully. Glasgow: University of Strathclyde, 2000. 79–107.

Spanish Romantic Literary Theory and Criticism. Cambridge: Cambridge University Press, 1992.

"Zorrilla, the Critics and the Direction of Spanish Romanticism." In *José Zorrilla, 1893–1993: Centennial Readings*. Ed. Richard A. Caldwell and Ricardo Landeira. Nottingham: University of Nottingham Press, 1993. 1–15.

Fogelquist, James Donald. *El "Amadís" y el género de la historia fingida*. Madrid: José Porrúa Turanzas, 1982.

Foix, J. V. "Algunes consideracions sobre la literatura d'avantguarda." 1925; repr. in *La literatura catalana d'avantguarda (1916–1938)*. Ed. Joaquim Molas. Barcelona: Antoni Bosch, 1983. 193–198.

Catalans de 1918. Barcelona: Edicions 62, 1986.

Folger, Robert. *"Generaciones y semblanzas." Memory and Genealogy in Medieval Iberian Historiography*. Munich: University of Munich, 2002.

Images in Mind: Lovesickness, Sentimental Fiction and Don Quijote. Chapel Hill: University of North Carolina Studies in Romance Languages and Literatures, 2002.

Fontanella, Lee. "The Fashion and Styles of Spain's *Costumbrismo*." *Revista Canadiense de Estudios Hispánicos* 6.2 (1982): 175–189.

Foucault, Michel. *The Archeology of Knowledge*. Trans. A. M. Sheridan-Smith. New York: Harper, 1972.

The History of Sexuality. New York: Vintage, 1990.

The Order of Things: An Archaeology of the Human Sciences. Trans. of *Les Mots et les choses*. New York: Random House, 1970.

Fox, E. Inman. *Azorín: guía de la obra completa*. Madrid: Castalia, 1992.

"Spain as Castile: Nationalism and National Identity." In *The Cambridge Companion to Modern Spanish Culture*. Ed. David T. Gies. Cambridge: Cambridge University Press, 1999. 21–36.

Fraker, Charles F. *Celestina: Genre and Rhetoric*. London: Támesis, 1990.

Franchini, Enzo. *El manuscrito, la lengua y el ser literario de la "Razón de amor."* Madrid: CSIC, 1993.

ed. *Los debates literarios en la Edad Media*. Madrid: Laberinto, 2001.

Franco Carrilero, Francisca. *La expresión poética de Carlos Bousoño*. Murcia: Universidad de Murcia, 1992.

Francos Rodríguez, José. *El teatro en España. 1909*. Madrid: Imprenta de Bernardo de Rodríguez, 1910.

Franz, Thomas R. *Valera in Dialogue / In Dialogue with Valera: A Novelist's Work in Conversation with That of His Contemporaries and Successors.* New York: Peter Lang, 2000.

Freeman, Nancy Regalado. "The Medieval Construction of the Modern Reader: Solomon's Ship and the Birth of Jean de Meun." In "Rereading Allegory: Essays in Memory of Daniel Poiron." Ed. Sarah Amer and Noah D. Guynn. *Yale French Studies* 95 (1999): 81–108.

Frenk, Margit. *Lírica española de tipo popular.* Madrid: Castalia, 1978.

Froldi, Rinaldo. "Anticipaciones dieciochescas del costumbrismo romántico." *Romanticismo* 6 (1996): 163–170.

Fuentes, Carlos. *Cervantes, o la crítica de la lectura.* Mexico: J. Mortiz, 1976.

Fuentes, Víctor. "La narrativa española de vanguardia (1923–1931): un ensayo de interpretación." *Romanic Review* 63 (1972): 211–218.

"La novela social española, 1927–1936: panorámica de un diverso perfil temático y formal." *Letras Peninsulares* 6 (1993): 9–29.

Funes, Leonardo. *El modelo historiográfico alfonsí: una caracterización.* London: Department of Hispanic Studies, Queen Mary and Westfield College, 1997.

Furst, Lilian R. *"All is True": The Claims and Strategies of Realist Fiction.* Durham: Duke University Press, 1995.

"Introduction." In *Realism.* New York: Longman, 1992. 1–23.

Furst, Lilian, ed. *Realism.* London: Longman, 1992.

Fuster, Joan. *Contra el Noucentisme.* Barcelona: Crítica, 1977.

Literatura catalana contemporània. Barcelona: Curial, 1971.

"Maragall i Unamuno cara a cara." In *Obres Completes.* Vol. IV. Barcelona: Edicions 62, 1975. 197–222.

Gabriele, John P., ed. *Summa valleinclaniana.* Barcelona: Anthropos, 1992.

Galerstein, Carolyn L., and Kathleen McNerney, ed. *Women Writers of Spain: An Annotated Bio-Bibliographical Guide.* New York: Greenwood Press, 1986.

Gallego Morell, Antonio, ed. *Garcilaso de la Vega y sus comentaristas. Obras completas del poeta acompañadas de los textos íntegros de los comentarios de El Brocense, Fernando de Herrera, Tamayo de Vargas y Azara.* 2nd. edn. Madrid: Gredos, 1972.

Gallego Ripoll, Federico. "El laberinto transparente. Renovación en los poetas de los ochenta." In *La Poesia Spagnola Oggi: una generazione dopo l'altra.* Ed. Mario Di Pinto and G. Calabro. Naples: Vittorio Pironti Editore, 1995. 87–98.

García de la Concha, Víctor. *El arte literario de Santa Teresa.* Barcelona: Ariel, 1978.

La poesía española de 1935 a 1975. Vol. I: *De la preguerra a los años oscuros 1935–1944.* Madrid: Cátedra, 1992.

García Galiano, Antonio. *La imitación en el Renacimiento.* Kassel: Reichenberger, 1996.

García Lara, F. ed. *Actas del Primer Congreso Internacional sobre novela del siglo XVIII.* Almería: Universidad de Almería, 1998.

García Lorenzo, Luciano, ed. *Documentación sobre el teatro español contemporáneo*. Madrid: SGFL, 1981.

García Montero, Luis. *Confesiones poéticas*. Granada: Diputación Provincial de Granada, 1993.

García Pavón, Francisco. "Se estrenó *La fundación* de Antonio Buero Vallejo." *Blanco y Negro* 26 (January 1974): 70.

García Posada, Miguel. "Del culturalismo a la vida." In *El lugar de la poesía*. Ed. Luis Muñoz. Granada: Diputación Provincial de Granada, 1994. 15–33.

La nueva poesía 1975–1992. Barcelona: Crítica, 1996.

Gasch, Sebastià. "Guerra a l'avantguardisme." *L'Amic de les Arts* 8 (1927).

Gavaldà Roca, Josep V. *La tradició avantguardista catalana: proses de Gorkiano i Salvat-Papasseit*. Barcelona: Publicacions de l'Abadia de Montserrat, 1988.

Gaylord, Mary. "The Grammar of Femininity in the Traditional Spanish Lyric." *Revista/Review Interamericana* 12 (1982): 115–124.

Geary, Patrick J. *The Myth of Nations: The Medieval Origins of Europe*. Princeton: Princeton University Press, 2002.

Gerli, E. Michael. "Leriano and Lacan: The Mythological and Psychoanalytical Underpinnings of Leriano's Last Drink." *La Corónica* 29.1 (2000): 113–128.

ed. *Medieval Iberia: An Encyclopedia*. New York and London: Routledge, 2003.

Gibson, Ian. *Federico García Lorca*. Vol. I: *De Fuente Vaqueros a Nueva York (1898–1929)*; Vol. II: *De Nueva York a Fuente Grande (1929–1936)*. Barcelona: Grijalbo, 1985, 1987.

Gies, David T. *Agustín Durán: A Biography and Literary Appreciation*. London: Támesis Books Ltd., 1975.

"*Ars amicitiae*, poesía y vida: el ejemplo de Cadalso." In *Coloquio Internacional sobre José Cadalso*. Abano Terme: Piovan, 1985. 155–172.

Nicolás Fernández de Moratín. Boston: Twayne, 1979.

"Spanish Theater and the Discourse of Self-Definition." *Revista de Estudios Hispánicos* 34 (2000): 433–442.

The Theatre in Nineteenth-Century Spain. Cambridge: Cambridge University Press, 1994.

Gies, David T., ed. *El romanticismo*. Madrid: Taurus, 1989.

Gil Casado, Pablo. *La novela deshumanizada española (1958–1988)*. Barcelona: Anthropos, 1990.

Gil y Zárate, Antonio. *Manual de literatura: principios generales de poética y retórica y resumen histórico de la literatura española*. 1844 10th. edn. Paris: Garnier, 1889.

Gillet, J. E. *Propalladia and Other Works of Bartolomé de Torres Naharro*. 4 vols. Philadelphia: University of Pennsylvania Press, 1943–1962.

Gilman, Stephen. *Galdós and the Art of the European Novel: 1867–1887*. Princeton: Princeton University Press, 1981.

The Spain of Fernando de Rojas. Princeton: Princeton University Press, 1972.

Giner de los Ríos, Hermenegildo. *Manual de literatura nacional y extranjera antigua y moderna. Primera parte*. Madrid: Victoriano Suárez, 1899. [no second part was published].

Gold, Hazel. "Francisco's Folly: Picturing Reality in Galdós's *La de Bringas.* *Hispanic Review* 54 (1986): 47–66.

Reframing Realism. Durham: Duke University Press, 1993.

Gómez de la Serna, Ramón. *Greguerías.* Madrid: Prometeo, 1917.

Gómez Redondo, Fernando. *Historia de la prosa medieval castellana.* 2 vols. to date. Madrid: Cátedra, 1998.

ed. *Poesía española.* Vol. 1: *Edad Media: juglaría, clerecía y romancero.* Páginas de Biblioteca Clásica, 1. Barcelona: Crítica, 1996.

González-Echevarría, Roberto, Enrique Pupo Walker, and David T. Haberly, eds. *The Cambridge History of Latin American Literature.* 3 vols. Cambridge: Cambridge University Press, 1996.

González Stephan, Beatriz. "The Early Stages of Latin American Historiography." Trans. Gwendolyn Barnes and Néstor E. López. In *1492–1992: Re/Discovering Colonial Writing.* Ed. René Jara and Nicholas Spadaccini. Minneapolis: Prisma Institute, 1989.

La historiografía literaria del liberalismo hispano-americano del siglo XIX. Havana: Casa de las Américas, 1987.

Gossy, Mary S. *The Untold Story: Women and Theory in Golden Age Texts.* Ann Arbor: University of Michigan Press, 1989.

Gould Levine, Linda, Ellen Engelson Marson, and Gloria Feiman Waldman, eds. *Spanish Women Writers: A Bio-Bibliographical Source Book.* Westport, CT: Greenwood Press, 1993.

Goytisolo, Juan. *El furgón de cola.* Barcelona: Seix Barral, 1976.

Gracia García, Jordi. *Hijos de la razón. Contraluces de la libertad en las letras españolas de la democracia.* Barcelona: Edhasa, 2001.

La pasión fría. Lirismo e identidad en la novela de Benjamín Jarnés. Zaragoza: Institución Fernando el Católico, 1988.

Graham, Helen. "Gender and State: Women in the 1940s." In *Spanish Cultural Studies.* Ed. Helen Graham and Jo Labanyi. Oxford: Oxford University Press, 1995. 182–195.

Greenblatt, Stephen. *Renaissance Self-Fashioning: From More to Shakespeare.* Chicago: University of Chicago Press, 1980.

"Rethinking Memory and Literary History." In *Rethinking Literary History.* Ed. Linda Hutcheon and Mario J. Valdés. Oxford: Oxford University Press, 2002. 50–62.

Greene, Roland. *Unrequited Conquests: Love and Empire in the Colonial Americas.* Chicago: University of Chicago Press, 1999.

Greer, Margaret. *The Play of Power: Mythological Court Dramas of Calderon de la Barca.* Princeton: Princeton University Press, 1991.

"A Tale of Three Cities: The Place of the Theatre in Early Modern Madrid, London and Paris." *Bulletin of Hispanic Studies* 77 (2000): 391–419.

Grinstein, Julia Bordiga. *La rosa trágica de Málaga. Vida y obra de María Rosa de Gálvez. DIECIOCHO* Anejo 3 (2003).

Grotowski, Jerzy. "Statement of Principles." In *The Twentieth Century Performance Reader.* Ed. Michael Huxley and Noel Witts. New York: Routledge, 1996: 187–194.

Gubern, Román. *La censura: función política y ordenamiento jurídico bajo el franquismo (1936–1975)*. Barcelona: Ediciones Península, 1981.

Gubern, Román, and Domènec Font. *Un cine para el cadalso: 40 años de censura cinematográfica en España*. Barcelona: Editorial Euros, 1976.

Guillén, Claudio. "Literature as Historical Contradiction: El Abencerraje, The Moorish Novel, and the Eclogue." In *Literature as System*. Princeton: Princeton University Press, 1971. 159–217.

——— *Teorías de la historia literaria: ensayos de teoría*. Madrid: Espasa, 1989.

——— "Usos y abusos del 27 (recuerdos de aquella generación)." *Revista de Occidente* 191 (April 1997): 126–152.

——— "The Writer in Exile or the Literature of Exile and Counter-Exile." *Books Abroad* 50 (1976): 271–280.

Guillén, Jorge. *Language and Poetry. Some Poets of Spain*. Cambridge, MA: Harvard University Press, 1961.

Guinard, Paul-J. *La Presse espagnole de 1737 à 1791. Formation et signification d'un genre*. Paris: Institut d'Etudes Hispaniques, 1973.

Gullón, Germán. *La novela moderna en España (1885–1902)*. Madrid: Taurus, 1992.

Gullón, Ricardo. *Autobiografías de Unamuno*. Madrid: Gredos, 1964.

——— *Direcciones del modernismo*. Madrid: Gredos, 1964.

——— "La generación poética del 1925." In *La invención del 98 y otros ensayos*. Madrid: Gredos, 1969.

——— "Introducción." In Benito Pérez Galdós, *La de Bringas*. Englewood Cliffs: Prentice Hall, 1967. 1–26.

——— *Técnicas de Galdós*. Madrid: Taurus, 1970.

——— ed. *El modernismo visto por los modernistas*. Madrid: Guadarrama, 1980.

Gutiérrez de los Ríos y Córdoba, Francisco, Conde de Fernán Núñez. *El hombre práctico, o discursos varios sobre su conocimiento y enseñanzas*. Ed. Jesús Pérez Magallón and Russell P. Sebold. Córdoba: Cajasur, 2000.

Gutiérrez Giradot, Rafael. *Modernismo: supuestos históricos y culturales*. Barcelona: Montesinos, 1983; repr. Mexico: Fondo de Cultura Económica, 1988.

Gwara, Joseph J., and E. Michael Gerli, eds. *Studies on the Spanish Sentimental Romance*. London: Támesis Books, 1997.

Hall, Stuart. "Encoding/Decoding." In *Culture, Media, Language*. Ed. Stuart Hall *et al.* London: Hutchinson, 1980. 128–138.

Halsey, Martha T. *From Dictatorship to Democracy: The Recent Plays of Buero Vallejo*. Ottowa: Dovehouse, 1994.

Hardt, Michael, and Antonio Negri. *Empire*. Cambridge, MA: Harvard University Press, 2000.

Harney, Michael. *Kinship and Marriage in Medieval Hispanic Chivalric Romance*. Westfield Publications in Medieval and Renaissance Studies, 11. Turnhout: Brepols, 2001.

Harris, Derek. *Metal Butterflies and Poisonous Lights: The Language of Surrealism in Lorca, Alberti, Cernuda and Aleixandre*. Fife: La Sirena, 1998.

Hart, Thomas. "A History of Spanish Literary History, 1800–1850." Diss. Yale University, 1952.

    ed. *Gil Vicente. Farces and Festival Plays.* Eugene: University of Oregon Press, 1972.

Harvey, Jessamy. "The Value of Nostalgia: Reviving Memories of National-Catholic Childhood." *Journal of Spanish Cultural Studies* 2.1 (2001): 109–118.

Havard, Robert. *From Romanticism to Surrealism: Seven Spanish Poets.* Totowa, NJ: Barnes & Noble, 1988.

Hayward, Louise M. "'La Escura Selva': Allegory in Early Sentimental Romance." *Hispanic Review* 68 (2000): 415–428.

Heiple, Daniel L. *Garcilaso de la Vega and the Italian Renaissance.* University Park: Pennsylvania State University Press, 1994.

Hemingway, Maurice. "La obra novelística de Emilia Pardo Bazán." In *Historia de la literatura española.* Vol. IX: *Siglo XIX (II).* Ed. Leonardo Romero Tobar. Madrid: Espasa-Calpe, 1998. 661–681.

Hermosilla Molina, Antonio. *Cien años de medicina sevillana (La Regia Sociedad de Medicina y demás Ciencias, de Sevilla, en el siglo XVIII).* Seville: Diputación Provincial, 1970.

Herr, Richard. *The Eighteenth-Century Revolution in Spain.* Princeton: Princeton University Press, 1958.

Herrero, Javier. *Ángel Ganivet: un iluminado.* Madrid: Gredos, 1966.

    Fernán Caballero: un nuevo planteamiento. Madrid: Gredos, 1963.

    "Terror y literatura: Ilustración, revolución y los orígenes del movimiento romántico." In *La literatura española de la Ilustración.* Ed. José Luis Varela. Madrid: Universidad Complutense, 1988. 131–153.

Herrero García, M. *Estimaciones literarias del siglo XVIII.* Madrid: Voluntad, 1930.

Herzberger, David. *Narrating the Past: Fiction and Historiography in Postwar Spain.* Durham: Duke University Press, 1995.

Hess, Steven. *Ramón Menéndez Pidal.* Boston: Twayne, 1982.

Heugas, Pierre. *La Célestine et sa descendance directe.* Bordeaux: Institut d'Études Ibériques et Ibéro-américaines de l'Université de Bordeaux, 1973.

Hidalgo-Serna, Emilio. *El pensamiento ingenioso de Baltasar Gracián.* Barcelona: Anthropos, 1993.

Hillgarth, J. N. *The Spanish Kingdoms: 1250–1516.* 2 vols. Oxford: Clarendon, 1976–1978.

Hita, Arcipreste de. *Libro de buen amor.* Ed. Eric W. Naylor. 2nd. edn. Clásicos Hispánicos, II.9. Madrid: Consejo Superior de Investigaciones Científicas, 1972.

Hobsbawn, Eric. *Nations and Nationalism since 1780: Programme, Myth, Reality.* Cambridge: Cambridge University Press, 1990.

Holsinger, Bruce W. *Music, Body, and Desire in Medieval Culture: Hildegard of Bingen to Chaucer.* Stanford: Stanford University Press, 2001.

Holt, Marion P. *The Contemporary Spanish Theater (1949–1972).* Boston: G. K. Hall, 1975.

Horkheimer, Max, and Theodor Adorno. *Dialectic of Enlightenment*. New York: Continuum, 1997.

Hurtado y Jiménez de la Serna, Juan, and Angel González Palencia. *Historia de la literatura española*. Madrid: Tipografía de Archivos, 1921.

Hutcheon, Linda. "Preface. Theorizing Literary History in Dialogue." In *Rethinking Literary History*. Ed. Linda Hutcheon and Mario J. Valdés. Oxford: Oxford University Press, 2002. ix–xiii.

"Rethinking the National Model." In *Rethinking Literary History*. Ed. Linda Hutcheon and Mario J. Valdés. Oxford: Oxford University Press, 2002. 3–49.

Iffland, James. *De fiestas y aguafiestas. Risa, locura e ideología en Cervantes y Avellaneda*. Madrid: Iberoamericana, 1999.

Iglesias Feijoo, Luis. *La trayectoria dramática de Buero Vallejo*. Santiago de Compostela: Universidad de Santiago de Compostela, 1982.

Iglesias Santos, Montserrat. *Canonización y público. El teatro de Valle-Inclán*. Santiago: Universidad de Santiago de Compostela, 1998.

Illades Aguiar, Gustavo. *"La Celestina" en el taller salmantino*. Publicaciones de *Medievalia*, 21. Mexico: Universidad Autónoma de México, 1997.

Impey, Olga. "En el crisol de la prosa literaria de Alfonso X: unas huellas de preocupación estilística en las versiones del relato de Dido." *Bulletin Hispanique* 83 (1982): 5–23.

Infantes, Víctor. *Las danzas de la muerte. Génesis y desarrollo de un género medieval (Siglos XIII–XVII)*. Salamanca: Universidad de Salamanca, 1997.

Ingenschay, Dieter, and Hans Neuschaffer, eds. *Abriendo caminos. La literatura española desde 1975*. Barcelona: Lumen, 1995.

Jagoe, Caterine, Alda Blanco, and Cristina Enríquez de Salamanca, eds. *La mujer en los discursos de género*. Barcelona: Icaria, 1998.

Jayyusi, Salma Khaddra, ed. *The Legacy of Muslim Spain*. Leiden: Brill, 1992.

Jenkins, Cecil. "Realism and the Novel Form." In *The Monster in the Mirror*. Ed. D. A. Williams. Oxford: Oxford University Press, 1978. 1–16.

Jenkins, Henry. *Textual Poachers: Television Fans and Participatory Culture*. New York and London: Routledge, 1992.

Jiménez, José Olivio. *Cinco poetas del tiempo*. Madrid: Ínsula, 1964.

La poesía de Francisco Brines. Seville: Renacimiento, 2001.

Johnson, Carroll. "Cómo se lee hoy el *Quijote*." In *Cervantes*. Madrid: Centro de Estudios Cervantinos, 1995. 335–348.

Johnson, Roberta. *Crossfire: Philosophy and the Novel in Spain, 1900–1934*. Lexington: The University Press of Kentucky, 1993.

Jones, Margaret E. W. *The Contemporary Spanish Novel, 1939–1975*. Boston: Twayne Publishers, 1985.

Juliá Martínez, Eduardo. "La Asunción de la Virgen y el teatro primitivo español." *Boletín de la Real Academia Española* 41 (1961): 179–334.

Poetas dramáticos valencianos. 2 vols. Madrid: Tipografía de la Revista de Archivos, 1929.

Juretschke, Hans. "La presencia del ideario romántico alemán en la estructura y evolución teórica del romanticismo español." *Romanticismo* 1 (1982): 11–24.

Kellner, Hans. "Language and Historical Representation." In *The Postmodern History Reader*. Ed. Keith Jenkins. London: Routledge, 1997. 127–138.

Kelly, Douglas. *The Conspiracy of Allusion: Description, Rewriting, and Authorship from Macrobius to Medieval Romance*. Leiden: Brill, 1999.

Kercher, Dona. "Children of the European Union, Crossing Gendered Channels: Javier Marías's Novel, *Todas las almas*, and Gracia Querejeta's *El último viaje de Robert Rylands*." *Cine-Lit* 3 (1997): 100–112.

Kinder, Marsha. *Blood Cinema. The Reconstruction of National Identity in Spain*. Berkeley: University of California Press, 1993.

Kirkpatrick, Susan. "The Ideology of *Costumbrismo*." *Ideologies and Literature* 2.7 (1978): 28–44.

　　Larra: el inextricable laberinto de un romántico liberal. Madrid: Gredos, 1977.

　　"Modernizing the Feminine Subject in Mid-Nineteenth-Century Poetry." *Revista de Estudios Hispánicos* 34.2 (May 2000): 413–422.

　　Las románticas. Women Writers and Subjectivity in Spain, 1835–1850. Berkeley: University of California Press, 1989.

Kraye, Jill, ed. *Introducción al humanismo renacentista*. Cambridge: Cambridge University Press, 1998.

Kronik, John W. "Narraciones interiores en *Fortunata y Jacinta*." In *Homenaje a Juan López-Morillas*. Ed. José Amor y Vázquez and A. David Kossoff. Madrid: Castalia, 1982. 275–291.

Kuhn, Hugo. "Esbozo de una teoría de la literatura medieval alemana." In *La actual ciencia literaria alemana*. Trans. Hans Ulrich Gumbrecht and Gustavo Domínguez León. Salamanca: Anaya, 1971. 163–179.

Labanyi, Jo. "Censorship or the Fear of Mass Culture." In *Spanish Cultural Studies*. Ed. Helen Graham and Jo Labanyi. Oxford: Oxford University Press, 1995. 207–214.

　　Gender and Modernization in the Spanish Realist Novel. Oxford: Oxford University Press, 2000.

LaCapra, Dominick. "Rethinking Intellectual History and Reading Texts." In *Modern European Intellectual History: Reappraisals and New Perspectives*. Ed. Dominick LaCapra and Steven L. Kaplan. Ithaca: Cornell University Press, 1982. 47–86.

Lama, Miguel Ángel. *La poesía de Vicente García de la Huerta*. Badajoz: Universidad de Extremadura, 1993.

Langbaum, Robert. *The Poetry of Experience. The Dramatic Monologue in Modern Literary Tradition*. New York: W. W. Norton and Co., 1963.

Lapesa, Rafael. "Poesía de cancionero y poesía italianizante." In *De la Edad Media a nuestros días: estudios de historia literaria*. Madrid: Gredos, 1967. 145–171.

　　La trayectoria poética de Garcilaso. Madrid: Istmo, 1985.

Lázaro Carreter, Fernando. *"Lazarillo de Tormes" en la picaresca*. Barcelona: Ariel, 1972.

Le Bigot, Claude. "Janus polycéphale ou le discours postmoderne de la poésie espagnole contemporaine." In *Postmodernité et écriture narrative dans l'Espagne contemporaine*. Grenoble: Cerhius, 1996. 289–305.

Le Breton, David. *Antropología del dolor*. Trans. Daniel Alcorba. Barcelona: Seix Barral, 1999.

Letras españolas 1976–1986. Madrid: Castalia – Ministerio de Cultura, 1987.

Levin, Harry. "The Example of Cervantes." In *Contexts of Criticism*. Cambridge, MA: Harvard University Press, 1957. 79–96.

Lida de Malkiel, María Rosa. *La originalidad artística de "La Celestina."* Buenos Aires: EUDEBA, 1962.

Lihani, John. *Lucas Fernández*. New York: Twayne, 1973.

ed. *Poema de Fernán González*. East Lansing, MI: Colleagues Press, 1991.

Lipking, Lawrence. "A Trout in the Milk." *Modern Language Quarterly* 54.1 (1993): 7–13.

Lista, Alberto. "Discurso sobre la importancia de nuestra historia literaria." In *Vida, obra y pensamiento de Alberto Lista*. Ed. Hans Juretschke. Madrid: CSIC, 1951. 466–478.

Literatura de caballerías y origen de la novela. Ed. Rafael Beltrán. Valencia: Universitat de Valencia, 1998.

Litvak, Lily. "The Birth of the Idea of Pan-Latinism in Catalonia." *Catalan Review* 2.1 (1987): 130–136.

España 1900. Modernismo, anarquismo y fin de siglo. Barcelona: Anthropos, 1990.

Transformación industrial y literatura en España (1895–1905). Madrid: Taurus, 1983.

Livingstone, Leon. *Tema y forma en las novelas de Azorín*. Madrid: Gredos, 1970.

Llull, Ramon. *Selected Works of Ramon Llull (1232–1316)*. 2 vols. Ed. and trans. Anthony Bonner. Princeton: Princeton University Press, 1985.

Lombardero, Manuel. *Campoamor y su mundo*. Barcelona: Planeta, 2000.

Longhurst, C. A. "Ruptures and Continuities: From Realism to Modernism and the Avant-Garde." In *Hacia la novela nueva. Essays on the Spanish Avant-Garde Novel*. Ed. Francis Lough. Oxford and New York: Peter Lang, 2000. 19–41.

Lopez, François. "Los novatores en la Europa de los sabios." *Studia Histórica / Historia Moderna* 14 (1996): 95–111.

"El pensamiento tradicionalista." In *Historia de España*. Vol. XXXI: *La época de la Ilustración*. Part 1: *El estado y la cultura (1759–1808)*. Ed. J. M. Jover Zamora. Madrid: Espasa-Calpe, 1988. 813–851.

"La resistencia a la Ilustración: bases sociales y medios de acción." In *Historia de España*. Vol. XXXI: *La época de la Ilustración*. Part 1: *El estado y la cultura (1759–1808)*. Ed. J. M. Jover Zamora. Madrid: Espasa-Calpe, 1988. 769–812.

López, M. "Los escritores de la Restauración y las polémicas literarias del siglo XIX en España." *Bulletin Hispanique* 81 (1979): 51–74.

López-Baralt, Luce. *San Juan de la Cruz y el Islam*. 2nd. edn. Madrid: Hiperión, 1990.

López Estrada, Francisco. *Introducción a la literatura medieval española*. 4th. edn. Madrid: Gredos, 1979.

Los libros de pastores en la literatura española. La órbita previa. Madrid: Gredos, 1974.

López de Mendoza, Íñigo, marqués de Santillana. *Obras completas*. Ed. Ángel Gómez Moreno and M. P. A. M. Kerkhof. Barcelona: Planeta, 1988.

López-Morillas, Juan. *The Krausist Movement and Ideological Change in Spain, 1854–1874*. 2nd. edn. Trans. Frances M. López-Morillas. Cambridge: Cambridge University Press, 1981.

López Piñero, José María. *La introducción de la ciencia moderna en España*. Barcelona: Ariel, 1969.

López Yepes, José. "Una *Representación de las Sibilas* y un *Planctus Passionis* en el MS. 80 de la catedral de Córdoba." *Revista de Archivos, Bibliotecas y Museos* 80 (1977): 545–557.

Lorenzo-Rivero, Luis. *Larra: técnicas y perspectivas*. Madrid: José Porrúa y Turranzas, 1988.

Lough, Francis, ed. *Hacia la nueva novela. Essays on the Spanish Avant-Garde Novel*. Oxford and New York: Peter Lang, 2000.

Lukács, Georg. *The Historical Novel*. Lincoln: University of Nebraska Press, 1983.

MacCormick, Sabine. *Religion in the Andes: Vision and Imagination in Early Colonial Peru*. Princeton: Princeton University Press, 1991.

MacKay, Angus. "Ritual and Propaganda in Fifteenth-Century Castile." *Past and Present* 107 (1985): 1–43.

Macklin, John. *The Window and the Garden: The Modernist Fictions of Ramón Pérez de Ayala*. Boulder: University of Colorado Press, 1988.

Mainer, José-Carlos. *Análisis de una insatisfacción: las novelas de Wenceslao Fernández Flórez*. Madrid: Castalia, 1975.

"Del corazón y la cabeza: sobre la poesía de Joaquín M. Bartrina." In *Pensamiento y literatura en España en el siglo XIX. Idealismo, positivismo, espiritualismo*. Toulouse: Presses Universitaires du Mirail, 1998. 110–122.

"1975–1985: los poderes del pasado." In *La cultura española en el posfranquismo: diez años de cine, cultura y literatura (1975–1985)*. Ed. Samuel Amell and Salvador García Castañeda. Madrid: Playor, 1988. 11–26.

La edad de plata (1902–1939). Ensayo de interpretación de un proceso cultural. Madrid: Cátedra, 1981.

Historia, literatura, sociedad (y una coda española). Madrid: Biblioteca Nueva, 2000.

"Introducción." In *El último tercio del siglo (1968–1998). Antología consultada de la poesía española*. Madrid: Visor, 1999.

"La invención de la literatura española." In *Literaturas regionales en España*. Ed. José-Carlos Mainer and José María Enguita. Zaragoza: Institución Fernando el Católico, 1994. 23–45.

"Poesía lírica, placer privado." In *De Postguerra (1951–1990)*. Barcelona: Grijalbo-Mondadori, 1994. 161–170.

ed. *Modernismo y 98*. Barcelona: Crítica, 1980.

Mainer, José-Carlos, and Santos Juliá. *El aprendizaje de la libertad 1973–1986. La cultura de la transición*. Madrid: Alianza, 2000.

Man, Paul de. "Literary History and Literary Modernity." In *Blindness and Insight*. 2nd. edn. Minneapolis: University of Minnesota Press, 1983. 142–165.

Mañá, Gemma, Rafael García, Luis Monferrer, and Luis A. Esteve. *La voz de los náufragos. La narrativa republicana entre 1936 y 1939*. Madrid: Ediciones de la Torre, 1997.

Mangini, Shirley. *Jaime Gil de Biedma*. Madrid: Júcar, 1977.

Manovich, Lev. *The Language of New Media*. Cambridge, MA: MIT Press, 2001.

Mansberger, Roberto. "Dos discursos restauracionistas en la crisis de fin de siglo: Gaspar Núñez de Arce y Emilio Ferrari." In *Estudios de literatura española de los siglos XIX y XX. Homenaje a Juan María Díez Taboada*. Ed. Francisco Aguilar Piñal *et al*. Madrid: CSIC, 1998. 282–292.

Maraniss, James E. *On Calderón*. Columbia: University of Missouri Press, 1978.

Maravall, José Antonio. *La cultura del barroco: análisis de una estructura histórica*. Barcelona: Ariel, 1975.

Estudios de historia del pensamiento español. Madrid: Ediciones de Cultura Hispánica, 1984.

Teatro y literatura en la sociedad barroca. Madrid: Seminarios y Ediciones, 1972.

Marco, Joaquín. "El tren expreso y el falso realismo de Campoamor." *Revista de Literatura* 23 (1963): 107–117.

Marfany, Joan-Lluís. "El Modernisme." In *Història de la Literatura Catalana*. Vol. VIII. Ed. Joaquim Molas. Barcelona: Ariel, 1986. 75–142.

"Modernisme i noucentisme, amb algunes consideracions sobre el concepte de moviment cultural." *Els Marges* 26 (1982): 31–42.

"Reflexions sobre Modernisme i Noucentisme (a propòsit de *Literatura Catalana Contemporània* de Joan Fuster)." *Els Marges* 1 (1974): 49–71.

"Sobre el significat del terme 'Modernisme.'" In *Aspectes del Modernisme*. Barcelona: Curial, 1975. 35–70.

Marías, Javier. "El novelista va al cine: disensiones de un autor." *El País* 3 November 1996: 35.

"Quién escribe." In *El personaje novelesco*. Coord. Marina Mayoral. Madrid: Cátedra, 1990. 91–99.

Marín, Nicolás. *Poesía y poetas del Setecientos*. Granada: Universidad de Granada, 1971.

Márquez Villanueva, Francisco. "*La Celestina* as Hispano-Semitic Anthropology." *Revue de Littérature Comparée* 61 (1987): 425–453.

Espiritualidad y literatura en el siglo XVI. Madrid: Alfaguara, 1968.

Lope de Vega: vida y valores. San Juan: Editorial de la Universidad de Puerto Rico, 1988.

"Menosprecio de corte y alabanza de aldea" (Valladolid, 1539) y el tema aúlico en la obra de Fray Antonio de Guevara. Santander: Universidad de Cantabria, 1999.

Martí López, Elisa. "The folletín: Spain Looks to Europe." In *The Cambridge Companion to the Spanish Novel*. Ed. Harriet S. Turner and Adelaida López de Martínez. Cambridge: Cambridge University Press, 2003, 65–80.

Martín, Gregorio. *Hacia una revisión crítica de la biografía de Larra (nuevos documentos)*. Porto Alegre: PUC-EMMA, 1975.

"Larra y el teatro: censura crítica e histórica." *Kentucky Romance Quarterly* 33 (1986): 431–437; and 34 (1987): 345–350.

Martín Gaite, Carmen. *Usos amorosos de la posguerra española.* Barcelona: Anagrama, 1987.

Martín Rodríguez, Mariano. *El teatro francés en Madrid (1918–1936).* Boulder: Society of Spanish and Spanish American Studies, 2000.

Martínez-Bretón, Juan Antonio. *Libertad de expresión cinematográfica durante la II República Española (1931–1936).* Madrid: Editorial Fragua, 2000.

Martínez Cachero, José María. *La novela española entre 1936 y el fin de siglo. Historia de una aventura.* Madrid: Castalia, 1997.

Martínez Palacio, Javier, ed. *Pío Baroja.* Madrid: Taurus, 1974.

Massó i Torrents, Jaume. "Els Jocs Florals." *Diari Catalá* (5 May 1879).

Maurizi, Françoise. *Théâtre et tradition populaires: Juan del Encina et Lucas Fernández.* Aix-en-Provence: Université de Provence, 1994.

Mayans y Siscar, Gregorio. "Oración en que se exhorta a seguir la verdadera idea de la elocuencia española." In *Escritos literarios.* Ed. Jesús Pérez Magallón. Madrid: Taurus, 1994.

Mayhew, Jonathan. *The Poetics of Self-consciousness. Twentieth Century Spanish Poetry.* Lewisburg: Bucknell University Press, 1994.

McClelland, I. L. *The Origins of the Romantic Movement in Spain.* Liverpool: Liverpool University Press, 1937; 2nd. edn. 1975.

McDermott, Patricia. "Modernismo frente a noventayocho: según las revistas de la época (1897–1907)." In *¿Qué es el modernismo? Nuevas encuestas. Nuevas lecturas.* Ed. Richard A. Cardwell and Bernard McGuirk. Boulder: Society of Spanish and Spanish American Studies, 1993. 229–255.

McFarlane, Brian. *Novel to Film: An Introduction to the Theory of Adaptation.* Oxford: Clarendon Press, 1996.

McGann, Jerome. "Canonade. The Academic War Over the Literary Canon." *New Literary History* 25.3 (1994): 487–504.

McKendrik, Melveena. *Playing the King: Lope de Vega and the Limits of Conformity.* London: Támesis, 2000.

Theatre in Spain, 1490–1700. Cambridge: Cambridge University Press, 1989.

Women and Society in the Spanish Drama of the Golden Age. A Study of the "mujer varonil." Cambridge: Cambridge University Press, 1974.

Medina, Raquel. *El surrealismo en la poesía española de posguerra.* Madrid: Visor, 1977.

Meléndez Valdés, Juan. *Obras en verso.* Ed. J. H. R. Polt and Jorges Demerson. Oviedo: Cátedra Feijoo, 1981.

Membrez, Nancy. "The 'teatro por horas.'" Doctoral dissertation. Santa Barbara: University of California, 1987.

Menéndez Peláez, Jesús. *Los Jesuitas y el Teatro en el Siglo de Oro.* Oviedo: Universidad de Oviedo, 1995.

Menéndez Pidal, Ramón. "El estilo de Santa Teresa." In *La lengua de Cristóbal Colón y otros estudios sobre el siglo XVI.* 4th. edn. Madrid: Espasa-Calpe, 1958. 119–142.

Menéndez Pidal, Ramón, ed. *Reliquias de la poesía épica española*. Madrid: Espasa-Calpe, 1951.

Menéndez y Pelayo, Marcelino. *Antología de poetas líricos castellanos*. 10 vols. Madrid: CSIC, 1944–1945. (Originally published between 1890 and 1906.)

Calderón y su teatro. Madrid: A. Pérez Dubrull, 1884.

Historia de las ideas estéticas en España. 5 vols. Madrid: CSIC, 1940. (Originally published between 1883 and 1891.)

Obras completas. Vol. XIII: *Orígenes de la novela*. Santander: Edición Nacional, 1943.

Menocal, Maria Rosa. *The Ornament of the World*. New York: Little, Brown, 2000.

Menocal, Maria Rosa, Raymond Scheindlin, and Michael Sells, eds. *The Cambridge History of Arabic Literature: Al-Andalus*. Cambridge: Cambridge University Press, 2000.

Mercadier, Guy. *Diego de Torres Villarroel. Masque et miroirs*. Paris: Editorial Hispanique, 1981.

Meredith-Jones, C., ed. *Historia Karoli Magni et Rotholandi ou Chronique du Pseudo-Turpin* (Geneva: Slatkine Reprints, 1972 [1936].

Metz, Christian. *The Imaginary Signifier: Psychoanalysis and the Cinema*. Trans. Celia Britton *et al*. Bloomington: Indiana University Press, 1977.

Mignolo, Walter D. "Rethinking the Colonial Model." In *Rethinking Literary History*. Ed. Linda Hutcheon and Mario J. Valdés. Oxford: Oxford University Press, 2002. 155–193.

Milá y Fontanals, Manuel. *Principios de literatura general y española*. Barcelona: Imprenta Barcelonesa, 1877. (Volume reads: "Nueva edición.")

Miller, Stephen. *Del realismo/naturalismo al modernismo: Galdós, Zola, Revilla y Clarín (1870–1901)*. Las Palmas: Ediciones del Cabildo de Gran Canaria, 1993.

Galdós gráfico (1861–1907): orígenes, técnicas y límites del socio-mimetismo. Las Palmas: Ediciones del Cabildo de Gran Canaria, 2001.

El mundo de Galdós: teoría, tradición y evolución creativa del pensamiento socio-literario galdosiano. Santander: Sociedad Menéndez Pelayo, 1983.

Molho, Maurice. *Semántica y poética: Góngora, Quevedo*. Barcelona: Crítica, 1977.

Monedero, Carmen, ed. *Libro de Apolonio*. Clásicos Castalia, 157. Madrid: Castalia, 1987.

Monleón, José B. "Estrategias para entrar y salir del romanticismo (*Carmen* y *La gaviota*)." *Revista Hispánica Moderna* 53 (2000): 5–21.

Treinta años de teatro de la derecha. Barcelona: Tusquets, 1971.

Monroe, James T. trans. "Muammad ibn Dāniyāl (d. 1310). ayf al-Hayāl, Ajīb and Garīb, and al-Mutayyam and the Wretched Little al-Yutayyim." Manuscript.

"Prolegomena to the Study of Ibn Quzmān: the Poet as Jongleur." In *El Romancero hoy: historia, comparatismo, bibliografía crítica*. Ed. Samuel G. Armistead, Antonio Sánchez Romeralo, and Diego Catalán. Madrid: Catedra, 1979. 77–129.

Montesinos, José F. *Costumbrismo y novela: ensayo sobre el redescubrimiento de la realidad española*. Madrid: Castalia, 1980.

Moreh, Shmuel. *Live Theatre and Dramatic Literature in the Medieval Arabic World*. New York: New York University Press, 1992.

Morley, S. Griswold, and Courtney Bruerton. *Cronología de las comedias de Lope de Vega*. Madrid: Gredos, 1968.

Morón Arroyo, Ciriaco. "La teoría crítica de Menéndez Pidal." *Hispanic Review* 38 (1970): 22–39.

Morris, C. B. *Son of Andalusia. The Lyrical Landscapes of Federico García Lorca*. Nashville: Vanderbilt University Press, 1997.

Una generación de poetas españoles (1920–1936). Madrid: Gredos, 1988.

Morros, Bienvenido. *Las polémicas literarias en la España del siglo XVI: a propósito de Fernando de Herrera y Garcilaso de la Vega*. Barcelona: Quaderns Crema, 1998.

Murgades, Josep. "Visió noucentiste del Cubisme segons Ors." In *Els anys vint en els Països Catalans (Noucentisme/Avantguarda)*. Barcelona: Publicacions de l'Abadia de Montserrat, 1997. 35–63.

Naharro Calderón, José María. *Entre el exilio y el interior: el "entresiglo" y Juan Ramón Jiménez*. Barcelona: Anthropos, 1994.

"Falacias de exilio." In *Sesenta años después: el exilio literario de 1939*. Ed. María Teresa González de Garay and Juan Aguilera Sastre. Logroño: Universidad de la Rioja, 2001. 351–357.

"Por los campos de Francia: entre el frío de las alambradas y el calor de la memoria." In *Literatura y cultura del exilio español de 1939 en Francia*. Ed. Alicia Alted and Manuel Aznar. Salamanca: Varona, 1998. 307–325.

"Por sendas de la memoria: los exilios de las Españas de 1939." In *La nueva literatura hispánica*. Coord. José María Naharro Calderón. Valladolid: Universitas Castellae, 1999. 87–103.

"El sí-no de volver: la gallina ciega del exilio." In *La Chispa: Selected Proceedings*. Ed. Gilbert Paolini. New Orleans: Tulane University, 1993. 174–186.

"Y para qué la literatura del exilio en tiempo destituido?" In *El exilio literario español de 1939: Actas del Primer Congreso Internacional*. Vol. 1. Ed. Manuel Aznar. San Cugat del Vallès: Gexel-Cop d'Idees, 1998. 63–83.

Naharro Calderón, José María, ed. *El exilio de las Españas de 1939 en las Américas: "Adónde fue la canción?"* Barcelona: Anthropos, 1991.

Nalle, Sarah T. "Literacy and Culture in Early Modern Spain." *Past and Present* 125 (1989): 65–96.

"Printing and Reading Popular Religious Texts in Sixteenth-Century Castile." In *Culture and the State in Spain, 1550–1580*. Ed. Tom Lewis and Francisco J. Sánchez. New York: Garland, 1999. 123–153.

Naremore, James. "Introduction: Film and the Reign of Adaptation." In *Film Adaptation*. Ed. James Naremore. New Brunswick, NJ: Rutgers University Press, 2000. 1–16.

"Los narradores de vanguardia como renovadores del género biográfico: aproximación a la biografía vanguardista". In *Hacia la nueva novela. Essays on the Spanish Avant-Garde Novel*. Ed. Francis Lough. New York: Peter Lang, 2000.

Navajas, Gonzalo. "Una estética para después del posmodernismo: la nostalgia asertiva y la reciente novela española." *Revista de Occidente* 143 (1993): 105–130.

Naval, María Ángeles. *El sentimiento apócrifo (un estudio del cantar literario en Aragón 1880–1900)*. Zaragoza: Institución Fernando el Católico, 1990.

Navarrete, Ignacio. *Orphans of Petrarch: Poetry and Theory in the Spanish Renaissance*. Berkeley: University of California Press, 1994.

Navarro Tomás, Tomás. *Métrica española*. 6th. edn. Madrid: Editorial Labor, 1983.

Navas Ruiz, Ricardo. *El romanticismo español*. Madrid: Cátedra, 1990.

ed. *El romanticismo español. Documentos*. Salamanca: Anaya, 1971.

Nayeri, Farah. "Iranian Cinema: What Happened in Between?" *Sight and Sound* (December 1993): 26–28.

Nicholas, Robert L. *Unamuno, narrador*. Madrid: Castalia, 1987.

Nicolás, César. "Ramón Gómez de la Serna y la novela española de la vanguardia." *Insula* 502 (October 1988): 11–13.

Nicolopulos, James. *The Poetics of Empire in the Indies: Prophecy and Imitation in "La Araucana" and "Os Lusíadas."* University Park, PA: Pennsylvania State University Press, 2000.

Niemeyer, Katharina. *La poesía del premodernismo español*. Madrid: CSIC, 1992.

Nieva de la Paz, Pilar. *Autoras dramáticas españolas entre 1918 y 1936*. Madrid: CSIC, 1993.

"Pilar Miró ante el teatro clásico." *Anales de Literatura Española Contemporánea* 26.1 (2001): 255–276.

Nirenberg, David. *Communities of Violence: Persecution of Minorities in the Middle Ages*. Princeton: Princeton University Press, 1996.

Nodar Manso, Francisco. *Teatro menor galaico-portugués (siglo XIII): reconstrucción textual y Teoría del Discurso*. Kassel: Reichenberger, 1990.

Nora, Eugenio G[arcía] de. *La novela española contemporánea (III)*. Madrid: Gredos, 1962.

"Notice." In *Waverley Novels*. Vol. I: *Waverley* and *Guy Mannering*. Edinburgh and London: Robert Cadell and Houston & Stoneman, 1843. 3–4.

Nuland, Sherwin B. "The Uncertain Art." *American Scholar* (Spring 1998): 137–142.

O'Callaghan, Joseph F. *The Learned King: The Reign of Alfonso X of Castile*. Philadelphia: University of Pennsylvania Press, 1993.

Ojeda Escudero, Pedro. "'Del romanticismo en España y de Espronceda.' Significado y alcance del artículo de Don Juan Valera." In *Actas del primer congreso internacional sobre don Juan Valera*. Ed. Matilde Galera. Cabra: Ayuntamiento, 1997. 375–386.

Oleza Simó Juan *et al.* "Hipótesis sobre la génesis de la comedia barroca y la historia teatral del XVI." In *Teatros y prácticas escénicas*. 2 vols. Valencia: Institució Alfons el Magnànim, 1984. Vol. II, 9–42.

Olson, Glending. *Literature as Recreation in the Later Middle Ages*. Ithaca: Cornell University Press, 1982.

Ordóñez, Elizabeth. *Voices of Their Own (Contemporary Spanish Narrative by Women)*. Lewisburg: Bucknell University Press, 1991.

Orduna, Germán. "La estructura del *Duelo de la Virgen* y la cantica *Eya velar*." *Humanitas* 10 (1958): 75–104.

Orozco Díaz, Emilio. *Manierismo y barroco.* 4th. edn. Madrid: Cátedra, 1988.

Ortega, Antonio. "Entre el hilo y la madeja: apuntes sobre la poesía española actual." *Zurgai* (July 1997): 42–50.

La prueba del nueve (antología poética). Madrid: Cátedra, 1994.

Ortega y Gasset, José. *La deshumanización del arte.* Madrid: Revista de Occidente en Alianza Editorial, 1981.

"Meditaciones del Quijote. Meditaciones del 'Quijote.'" In *Obras completas.* 9 vols. 7th. edn. Madrid: Revista de Occidente, 1966. Vol. I, 309–400.

Palacios Fernández, Emilio. *La mujer y las letras en la España del siglo XVIII.* Madrid: Laberinto, 2002.

"Teatro." In *Historia literaria de España en el siglo XVIII.* Ed. Francisco Aguilar Piñal. Madrid: Trotta/CSIC, 1996. 135–233.

El teatro popular español del siglo XVIII. Lleida: Milenio, 1998.

Palenque, Marta. *El poeta y el burgués (poesía y público, 1850–1900).* Seville: Alfar, 1990.

Pao, Maria. "Still(ed) Life: The Ekphrastic Prose Poems of Ernesto Giménez Caballero." *Revista Canadiense de Estudios Hispánicos* 25 (2001): 469–492.

Pardo Bazán, Emilia. *La cuestión palpitante.* In *Obras completas.* Vol. III. Ed. Harry L. Kirby, Jr. Madrid: Aguilar, 1973. 574–647.

Parker, Alexander A. *The Allegorical Drama of Calderón: An Introduction to the Autos Sacramentales.* Oxford: Dolphin Books, 1943.

The Mind and Art of Calderón. Cambridge: Cambridge University Press, 1988.

"Towards a Definition of the Calderonian Tragedy." *Bulletin of Hispanic Studies* 39 (1962): 222–237.

Patterson, Lee. "Chaucer's Pardoner on the Couch: Psyche and Clio in Medieval Literary Studies." *Speculum* 76 (2001): 638–680.

Pattison, D. G. "The Theatricality of *Celestina*." In *The Medieval Mind: Hispanic Studies in Honour of Alan Deyermond.* Ed. I. MacPherson and R. Penny. London: Támesis, 1997. 317–326.

Pattison, Walter T. *El naturalismo español. Historia externa de un movimiento literario.* Madrid: Gredos, 1969.

Pavesio, Luisa. "Sobre el lenguaje de las *Escenas andaluzas*." *Romanticismo* 3.4 (1988): 175–178.

Pedraza Jiménez, Felipe, and Milagros Rodríguez Cáceres. *Manual de literatura española.* XII. *Posguerra: narradores.* Pamplona: Cenlit Ediciones, 2000.

Pérez, Janet. *Contemporary Women Writers of Spain.* Boston: G. K. Hall, 1988.

Pérez de Ayala, Ramón. "La tragedia grotesca." In *Las máscaras.* Vol. II. Madrid: Saturnino Calleja, 1919.

Pérez Bazo, Javier. "La novela nueva en la época de la vanguardia histórica: una revisión." *Insula* 646 (October 2000): 7–10.

Pérez Firmat, Gustavo. *Idle Fictions. The Hispanic Vanguard Novel.* 2nd. edn. Durham and London: Duke University Press, 1993.

Pérez Galdós, Benito. *La batalla de los Arapiles.* In *Episodios nacionales.* vol. V. Madrid: La Guirnalda, 1885.

Doña Perfecta. Ed. Rodolfo Cardona. Madrid: Cátedra, 1984.

Ensayos de crítica literaria. Ed. Laureano Bonet. Barcelona: Ediciones Península, 1972.

Obras completas. 8 vols. Ed. Federico Carlos Robles. Madrid: Aguilar, 1966.

"Observaciones sobre la novela contemporánea" and "La sociedad presente como materia novelable." Reprinted in *Ensayos de crítica literaria*. Ed. Laureano Bonet. Barcelona: Ediciones Península, 1999. 123–139; 218–226.

Trafalgar. In *Episodios nacionales*. Vol. 1. Madrid: La Guirnalda, 1882. 5–157.

Pérez Magallón, Jesús. *Construyendo la modernidad: la cultura española en el tiempo de los novatores (1675–1725)*. Madrid: CSIC, 2002.

En torno a las ideas literarias de Mayans. Alicante: Instituto de Cultura "Juan Gil-Albert," 1991.

Pérez Priego, Miguel Ángel, ed. *Teatro medieval*. Vol. II: *Castilla*. Barcelona: Crítica, 1997.

Pérez Vidal, Alejandro. "Introducción." In *Fígaro. Colección de artículos dramáticos, literarios, políticos y de costumbres*. Barcelona: Editorial Crítica, 1997.

Perkins, David. *Is Literary History Possible?* Baltimore: Johns Hopkins University Press, 1992.

ed. *Theoretical Issues in Literary History*. Cambridge: Cambridge University Press, 1991.

Perriam, Chris, Michael Thompson, Susan Frenck, and Vanessa Knights, eds. *A New History of Spanish Writing: 1939 to the 1990s*. Oxford: Oxford University Press, 2000.

Perry, Mary Elizabeth. *Crime and Society in Early Modern Seville*. Hanover: University Press of New England, 1980.

Pi de Cabanyes, Oriol. *Apunts d'història de la Renaixença*. Barcelona: Edicions del Mall, 1984.

Picoche, Jean-Louis. *Un romántico español: Enrique Gil y Carrasco (1815–1845)*. Madrid: Gredos, 1978.

Pierce, Frank. *La poesía épica del Siglo de Oro*. Madrid: Gredos, 1961.

Pieters, Jürgens, ed. *Critical Self-Fashioning: Stephen Greenblatt and the New Historicism*. Frankfurt am Main: Peter Lang, 1999.

Pijoan, Josep. *El meu Don Joan Maragall*. Barcelona: Catalonia, n.d.

Pimenta, Helena. "El euskara, una ausenca teatral?" In "Les darreres generacions teatrals del segle." Special issue of *Assaig de Teatre: Revista de l'Associació d'Investigació i Experimentació Teatral* 24 (September 2000): 115–130.

Pitollet, Camille. *La Querelle caldéronienne de Johan Nikolas Böhl von Faber et José Joaquín de Mora, reconstituée d'après les documents originaux*. Paris: Alcan, 1909.

Poblet, Josep Maria. *Catalunya, 1833–1913: una panoràmica amb el teatre i els Jocs Florals*. Barcelona: Editorial Pòrtic, 1969.

Polt, J. H. R. *Batilo: estudios sobre la evolución estilística de Meléndez Valdés*. Oviedo: Centro de Estudios del Siglo XVIII / University of California Press, 1987.

Pont, Jaume. *El Postismo*. Barcelona: Del Mall, 1987.

Pope, Randolph D. *Novela de emergencia. España 1939–1954*. Madrid: Sociedad General Española de Librería, 1984.

Porter, Roy. *Enlightenment: Britain and the Creation of the Modern World*. London: Allen Lane – The Penguin Press, 2000.

Poutrin, Isabelle. *Le Voile et la plume. Autobiographie et sainteté féminine dans l'Espagne moderne*. Madrid: Casa de Velázquez, 1995.

Pozuelo Yvancos, José María, and Rosa María Aradra Sánchez. *Teoría del canon y literatura española*. Madrid: Cátedra, 2000.

Prat, Ignacio. *Estudios sobre poesía contemporánea*. Madrid: Taurus, 1982.

Preston, Paul. *Franco: A Biography*. New York: Basic Books, 1994.

Prieto, Antonio. *La poesía española del siglo XVI*. 2 vols. Madrid: Cátedra, 1998.

Prieto de Paula, Ángel L. *Introducción a la poesía de Claudio Rodríguez*. Salamanca: Universidad de Salamanca, 1993.

Provencio, Pedro. *Poéticas españolas contemporáneas. La generación del 70*: Madrid: Hiperión, 1988.

"Las últimas tendencias de la lírica española." *Cuadernos Hispanoamericanos* 531 (1994): 31–54.

Pujol, Jordi. "Les quatre cares de Catalunya (1888–1988)." In *Quatre conferències: analitzar el passat per renovar el projecte*. Barcelona: Edicions 62, 1990. 53–81.

Quevedo y Villegas, Francisco de. *Historia de la vida del buscón*. In *La novela picaresca española*. Ed. Angel Valbuena Prat. Madrid: Aguilar, 1943. 1036–1101.

Quiroz-Martínez, Olga V. *La introducción de la filosofía moderna en España. El eclecticismo de los siglos XVII y XVIII*. Mexico: El Colegio de México, 1949.

Ràfols, J. F. *Modernisme i modernistes*. Barcelona: Destino, 1982.

Ragué-Arias, María-José. *El teatro de fin de milenio en España (de 1975 hasta hoy)*. Barcelona: Ariel, 1996.

Ramsden, Herbert. *The 1898 Movement in Spain*. Manchester: Manchester University Press / Rowman and Littlefield, 1974.

Ray, Robert. "The Field of 'Literature and Film.'" In *Film Adaptation*. Ed. James Naremore. New Brunswick, NJ: Rutgers University Press, 2000. 38–53.

Redondo, Agustin. "Acercamiento al *Quijote* desde una perspectiva histórico-social." *Cervantes* (Madrid: CEC, 1995): 257–293.

Regalado, Antonio. *Calderón. Los orígenes de la modernidad en la España del Siglo de Oro*. 2 vols. Barcelona: Destino, 1992.

Remie Olivia, Constable, ed. *Medieval Iberia: Readings from Christian, Muslim and Jewish Sources*. Philadelphia: University of Pennsylvania Press, 1997.

Resina, Joan Ramon. *El cadáver en la cocina: la novela criminal en la cultura del desencanto*. Barcelona: Anthropos, 1997.

"Hispanism and its Discontents." *Siglo XX / 20th Century* (1996): 85–129.

"Modernist Journals in the *Països Catalans*." *Revista Hispánica Moderna* 53 (2000): 388–398.

"The Sublimation of Wealth and the Consciousness of Modernism in Narcís Oller's *La febre d'or*." *Journal of Hispanic Research* 3 (1994–1995): 259–276.

Un sueño de piedra: ensayos sobre la literatura del modernismo europeo. Barcelona: Anthropos, 1990.

Revilla, Manuel de, and Pedro de Alcántara García. *Principios generales de literatura é historia de la literatura española.* 2 vols. 2nd. edn. Madrid: Librerías de Francisco Iravedra y Antonio Novo, 1877.

Rey Hazas, Antonio. "Introducción a la novela del Siglo de Oro, I (formas de narrativa idealista)." *Edad de Oro* 1 (1982): 65–105.

Reyes Cano, Rogelio. *Estudios sobre Cristóbal de Castillejo.* Salamanca: Universidad de Salamanca, 2000.

Poesía erótica de la Ilustración española. Seville: El Carro de la Nieve, 1989.

Rhodes, Elizabeth. "Spain's Misfired Canon: The Case of Luis de Granada's *Libro de la oración y meditación*." *Journal of Hispanic Philology* 15 (1990): 43–66.

Richmond, Carolyn. "Introducción." In *La quinta de Palmyra* by Ramón Gómez de la Serna. Madrid: Espasa-Calpe, 1982.

Rico, Francisco. "El destierro del verso agudo (con una nota sobre rimas y razones en la poesía del humanismo)." In *Homenaje a J. M. Blecua.* Madrid: Gredos, 1983. 525–551.

"Historia del texto." In *Don Quijote de la Mancha* by Miguel de Cervantes. 2 vols. Dir. Francisco Rico. Barcelona: Crítica, 1998. 1: cxcii–ccxclii.

The Spanish Picaresque Novel and the Point of View. Trans. Charles Davis. Cambridge: Cambridge University Press, 1984.

El sueño del humanismo: de Petrarca a Erasmo. Madrid: Alianza, 1997.

Ricoeur, Paul. *The Reality of the Historical Past.* Milwaukee: Marquette University Press, 1984.

Riera, Carmen. *Aproximaciones a la poesía de José A. Goytisolo.* Barcelona: Anthropos, 1991.

La Escuela de Barcelona. Barcelona: Anagrama, 1988.

La obra poética de Carlos Barral. Barcelona: Edicions 62, 1990.

Riley, E. C. *Cervantes's Theory of the Novel.* Oxford: Clarendon, 1962. (Spanish translation: *Teoría de la novela en Cervantes.* Madrid: Taurus, 1966.)

Don Quixote. London: Allen and Unwin, 1986. (Spanish translation: *Introducción al "Quijote."* Barcelona: Crítica, 1990.)

"*Don Quixote*: From Text to Icon." *Cervantes* (Special Issue, Winter 1998): 103–115.

"A Premonition of Pastoral in *Amadís de Gaula*." *Bulletin of Hispanic Studies* 59 (1982): 226–229.

Ríos Carratalá, Juan Antonio. *Vicente García de la Huerta (1734–1787).* Badajoz: Diputación Provincial, 1987.

Riquer, Martí de. *Història de la literatura catalana; Part Antiga.* 3 vols. Barcelona: Ariel, 1982.

Risco, Antonio. *Azorín y la ruptura con la novela tradicional.* Madrid: Alhambra, 1980.

Rius, Mercè. *La filosofia d'Eugeni D'Ors*. Barcelona: Curial, 1991.

Rivas Cherif, Cipriano de. *Un sueño de la razón. Cuadernos El Público* 42 (1985): 61–99.

Rivers, Elias. "The Horatian Epistle and its Introduction into Spanish Literature." *Hispanic Review* 22 (1954): 175–194.

"The Pastoral Paradox of Natural Art." *Modern Language Notes* 77 (1962): 130–144.

ed. *La poesía de Garcilaso de la Vega. Ensayos críticos*. Barcelona: Ariel, 1974.

Roach, Joseph. *Cities of the Dead: Circum-Atlantic Performance*. New York: Columbia University Press, 1996.

Robbins, Jeremy. *The Challenges of Uncertainty: An Introduction to Seventeenth-Century Spanish Literature*. London: Duckworth, 1998.

Ródenas, Domingo. "Introducción." In *Prosa del 27. Antología*. Madrid: Espasa-Calpe, 2000. 11–118.

Ródenas de Moya, Domingo. *Los espejos del novelista. Modernismo y autorreferencia en la novela vanguardista española*. Barcelona: Ediciones Península, 1998.

Rodríguez, Isaías. "Autores espirituales españoles (1500–1572)." In *Repertorio de historia de las ciencias eclesiásticas en España*. Vol. III: *Siglos XIII–XVI*. Salamanca: Instituto de Historia de Teología Española, 1971. 407–655.

Rodríguez Cuadros, Evangelina. *Calderón*. Madrid: Editorial Síntesis, 2002.

La técnica del actor español en el barroco. Hipótesis y documentos. Madrid: Castalia, 1998.

Rodríguez Cuadros, Evangelina, and Antonio Tordera. *Calderón y la obra dramática corta del siglo XVII*. London: Támesis Books, 1983.

Rodríguez Méndez, José María. "Las paradojas de 'Mister W.'" In *Comentarios impertinentes sobre el teatro español*. Barcelona: Península, 1972.

Rodríguez Mohedano, Rafael, and Pedro Rodríguez Mohedano. *Apología del tomo V de la Historia literaria de España, con dos cartas sobre el mismo asunto . . .* Madrid, 1779.

Historia literaria de España, desde su primera población hasta nuestros días . . . 10 vols. Madrid: Antonio Pérez de Soto, 1769–1791.

Rodríguez-Moñino, Antonio. *Construcción crítica y realidad histórica en la poesía española de los siglos XVI y XVII*. Madrid: Castalia, 1965.

Rodríguez Puértolas, Julio. *Literatura fascista española*. 2 vols. Madrid: Akal, 1986–1987.

Rodríguez Sánchez de León, María José. *La crítica ante el teatro barroco español (siglos XVII–XIX)*. Salamanca: Ediciones Almar, 2000.

"Literatura popular." In *Historia literaria de España en el siglo XVIII*. Ed. Francisco Aguilar Piñal. Madrid: Trotta/CSIC, 1996. 327–367.

Romero Tobar, Leonardo. "Algunas consideraciones del canon literario durante el siglo XIX." *Insula* 600 (1996): 14–16.

"Entre 1898 y 1998: la historiografía de la literatura española." *Rilce* 15.1 (1999): 27–49.

"Las historias de la literatura y la fabricación del canon." In *Cànon literari: ordre i subversió*. Ed. Jaume Pont and Josep M. Sala-Valldaura. Lleida: Institut d'Estudis Ilerdencs, 1998.

Panorama crítico del romanticismo español. Madrid: Castalia, 1994.

Root, Jerry. *"Space to Speke": The Confessional Subject in Medieval Literature*. New York: Peter Lang, 1997.

Rovira, Pere. *La poesía de Jaime Gil de Biedma*. Barcelona: Del Mall, 1986.

Rozas, Juan Manuel. *Estudios sobre Lope de Vega*. Madrid: Cátedra, 1990.

Significado y doctrina del "Arte nuevo" de Lope de Vega. Madrid: Sociedad General Española de Librería, 1976.

Rubio, Fanny. *Las revistas poéticas españolas, 1939–1975*. Madrid: Turner, 1975.

Rubio Jiménez, Jesús. *El teatro poético en España. Del modernismo a las vanguardias*. Murcia: Universidad de Murcia, 1993.

Rueda, Ana. *Cartas sin lacrar. La novela epistolar y la España ilustrada, 1789–1840*. Madrid: Iberoamericana, 2001.

Ruggles, D. F. *Gardens, Landscape, and Vision in the Palaces of Islamic Spain*. State Park: Pennsylvania State University Press, 2000.

Ruiz Aguilera, Ventura. *La Arcadia moderna. Colección de églogas e idilios, realistas y de epigramas*. Madrid: Imprenta de Rojas y Cia., 1967.

Ruiz Ramón, Francisco. "Calderón dramaturgo: el mito del dios de las dos caras." In *Calderón desde el 2000. Simposio Internacional Complutense*. Ed. José Maria Díez Borque. Madrid: Ollero & Ramos, 2001. 275–289.

Historia del teatro español. Desde sus orígenes hasta 1900. Madrid: Cátedra, 1979.

Historia del teatro español. Siglo XX. 2nd. edn. Madrid: Cátedra, 1975.

Russell, P. E., ed. *Spain: A Companion Guide to Spanish Studies*. London: Methuen, 1973.

Said, Edward. *Culture and Imperialism*. London: Vintage, 1993.

Sala Valldaura, Josep Maria. *El sainete en la segunda mitad del siglo XVIII. La mueca de Talía*. Lleida: Universidad de Lleida, 1993.

Los sainetes de González del Castillo en el Cádiz de finales del siglo XVIII. Cádiz: Ayuntamiento de Cádiz, 1996.

ed. *Teatro español del siglo XVIII*. 2 vols. Lleida: Universidad de Lleida, 1996.

Salaün, Serge. "Modernidad -vs- Modernismo. El teatro español en la encrucijada." In *Literatura modernista y tiempo del 98*. Ed. Javier Serrano Alonso. Santiago: Universidad de Santiago de Compostela, 2000. 95–116.

La poesía de la guerra de España. Madrid: Castalia, 1985.

Salcedo, Angel. *Resumen histórico-crítico de la literatura española, según los estudios y documentos más recientes*. Madrid: Saturnino Calleja, 1910.

Salinas, Pedro. "El signo en la literatura española del siglo XX." In *Ensayos completos*. 3 vols. (Madrid: Taurus, 1983). III (1927): 181–189.

"José Bergamín en aforismos." In *Ensayos completos*. 3 vols. Madrid: Taurus, 1983. Vol. I (1934): 144–148.

Salomon, Noël. *Lo villano en el teatro del Siglo de Oro*. Madrid: Castalia, 1985.

Salvat-Papasseit, Joan. *Epistolari de Joan Salvat-Papasseit*. Ed. Amadeu-J. Soberanas. Barcelona: Edicions 62, 1984.

Mots-propis i altres proses. Ed. Josep Miquel Sobrer. Barcelona: Edicions 62, 1975.

Sánchez, José A. *La escena moderna. Manifiestos y textos sobre teatro de la época de vanguardias.* Madrid: Akal, 1999.

Sánchez, José Rogerio. *Historia de la lengua y literatura española.* Madrid: Renacimiento, 1915.

Sánchez-Blanco, Francisco. *El Absolutismo y las Luces en el Reinado de Carlos III.* Madrid: Marcial Pons, 2002.

Europa y el pensamiento español del siglo XVIII. Madrid: Alianza, 1992.

La Ilustración en España. Madrid: Akal, 1997.

La mentalidad ilustrada. Madrid: Taurus, 1999.

Sánchez Escribano, Federico, and Alberto Porqueras Mayo, eds. *Preceptiva dramática española del Renacimiento y el Barroco.* 2nd. edn. Madrid: Gredos, 1971.

Sánchez-Llama, Íñigo. *Galería de escritoras isabelinas.* Madrid: Cátedra, 2000.

Sánchez Zamarreño, Antonio. *La poesía de Luis Rosales.* Salamanca: Universidad de Salamanca, 1986.

Sanchis Sinisterra, José. "Una poètica de la sostracció." Intro. to *Accident* by Lluïsa Cunillé. Biblioteca Teatral, 92. Barcelona: Institut del Teatre de Barcelona, 1996.

Santana, Mario. *Foreigners in the Homeland: The Spanish American New Novel in Spain, 1962–1974.* Lewisburg, PA: Bucknell University Press, 2000.

Santiáñez, Nil. *Ángel Ganivet, escritor modernista.* Madrid: Gredos, 1994.

Investigaciones literarias. Modernidad, historia de la literatura y modernismos. Barcelona: Crítica, 2002.

Sanz Ayán, Carmen, and Bernardo J. García García. *Teatros y comediantes en el Madrid de Felipe II.* Madrid: Editorial Complutense, 2000.

Sanz Villanueva, Santos, *et al.*, eds. *Historia y crítica de la literatura española.* Vol. VIII: *Época contemporánea: 1939–1975. Primer suplemento.* Barcelona: Crítica, 1999.

Sarrailh, Jean. *La España ilustrada de la segunda mitad del siglo XVIII.* Madrid: Fondo de Cultura Económica, 1977.

Sartre, Jean-Paul. *Qu'est-ce que la littérature?* Paris: Gallimard, 1948.

Scanlon, Larry. *Narrative, Authority, and Power: The Medieval Exemplum and the Chaucerian Tradition.* Cambridge: Cambridge University Press, 1994.

Schack, Adolfo Federico, Conde de. *Historia de la literatura y del arte dramático en España.* Madrid: M. Tello, 1887.

Schwartz Lerner, Lía. *Metáfora y sátira en la obra de Quevedo.* Madrid: Taurus, 1984.

Sebold, Russell P. *Bécquer en sus narraciones fantásticas.* Madrid: Taurus, 1989.

Descubrimiento y fronteras del neoclasicismo español. Madrid: Fundación Juan March – Cátedra, 1985.

Novela y autobiografía en la "Vida" de Torres Villarroel. Barcelona: Ariel, 1975.

"La pena de la *Hija del Sol.* Realidad, leyenda y romanticismo." In *Estudios en honor a Ricardo Gullón.* Ed. Luis T. González del Valle and Darío Villanueva. Lincoln: Society of Spanish-American Studies, 1984. 295–308.

El rapto de la mente. Poética y poesía dieciochescas. Barcelona: Anthropos, 1989.

"Sobre Campoamor y sus lecciones de realidad." In *La perduración de la modalidad clásica. Poesía y prosa de los siglos XVIII a XIX.* Salamanca: Ediciones Universidad, 2001. 265–270.

Trayectoria del romanticismo español. Barcelona: Crítica, 1983.

Sellés, Manuel, *et al.*, eds. *Carlos III y la ciencia de la Ilustración.* Madrid: Alianza, 1988.

Sells, Michael. *Approaching the Qur'an: The Early Revelations.* Ashland, OR: White Cloud Press, 1999.

Stations of Desire: Love Elegies from Ibn 'Arabi and New Poems. Jerusalem: Ibis Edition, 2000.

Senabre, Ricardo. *Tres estudios sobre fray Luis de León.* Salamanca: Universidad de Salamanca, 1978.

Sender, Ramón J. *Teatro de masas.* Valencia: Orto, 1932.

"El teatro nuevo." *Leviatán* 25 (June 1936): 365–375.

Sentaurens, Jean. *Séville et le théâtre: de la fin du Moyen Age à la fin du XVIIe siècle.* Bordeaux: Université de Bordeaux III, 1984.

Serna, Mercedes, ed. *Crónicas de Indias.* Madrid: Cátedra, 2000.

Serrano Ansejo, Enrique. *Vidas oblicuas: aspectos teóricos de la nueva biografía en España.* Zaragoza: Universidad de Zaragoza, 2002.

Serrano y Sanz, Manuel. *Apuntes para una biblioteca de escritoras españolas.* Madrid: Rivadeneyra, 1905; facs. edn. Madrid: Atlas, 1975.

Shafer, Robert J. *The Economic Societies in the Spanish World.* Syracuse: Syracuse University Press, 1958.

Shaw, Donald L. "Introducción." In *Agustín Durán. Discurso.* Exeter: University of Exeter, 1973.

"Qué es el modernismo?" In *¿Qué es el modernismo? Nuevas encuestas. Nuevas lecturas.* Ed. Richard A. Cardwell and Bernard McGuirk. Boulder: Society of Spanish and Spanish American Studies, 1993. 11–24.

"Spain. Romántico-Romanticismo-Romancesco-Romanesco-Romancista-Románico." In *"Romantic" and its Cognates: The European History of a Word.* Ed. Hans Eichner. Toronto: University of Toronto Press, 1972. 341–371.

Shergold, N. D. *A History of the Spanish Stage from Medieval Times Until the End of the Seventeenth Century.* Oxford: Oxford University Press, 1967.

Shklovski, Viktor. "Art as Device." In *Theory of Prose.* Trans. B. Sher. Elmwood Park, IL: Dalkey Archive Press, 1990. 1–14.

Sieber, Harry. "Dramatic Symmetry in Gómez Manrique's *La representación del nacimiento de Nuestro Señor.*" *Hispanic Review* 33 (1965): 118–135.

Sieburth, Stephanie. *Inventing High and Low. Literature, Mass Culture, and Uneven Modernity in Spain.* Durham: Duke University Press, 1994.

Silver, Philip. *La casa de Anteo. Ensayos de poética hispana (de Antonio Machado a Claudio Rodríguez).* Madrid: Taurus, 1985.

Et in Arcadia ego. A Study of the Poetry of Luis Cernuda. London: Támesis Books, Ltd., 1965.

Simón Díaz, José. "Hagiografías individuales publicadas en español de 1480 a 1700." *Hispania Sacra* 30 (1977): 421–480.

Impresos del XVI: religión. Madrid: CSIC, 1964.

Simón Palmer, María del Carmen. *Escritoras españolas del siglo XIX. Manual bio-bibliográfico.* Madrid: Castalia, 1991.

Sirera, Josep Lluis. "La construcción del *Auto de la Pasión* y el teatro medieval castellano." In *Actas del III Congreso de la Asociación Hispánica de Literatura Medieval.* 2 vols. Ed. María Isabel Toro Pascua. Salamanca: Universidad de Salamanca, 1989. II: 1011–1019.

"*Una quexa ante el Dios de amor* del comendador Escrivá como ejemplo posible de los autos de amores." In *Literatura Hispánica: Reyes Católicos y Descubrimiento.* Barcelona: Promociones y Publicaciones Universitarias, 1989. 259–269.

Sismondi, J. C. L. Simonde de. *Historical View of the Literature of the South of Europe.* 4 vols. London: H. Colburn and Co., 1823.

Smith, Colin, ed. *Spanish Ballads.* Oxford: Pergamon, 1964.

Smith, Paul Julian. *Quevedo on Parnassus: Allusive Context and Literary Theory in the Love Lyric.* London: Modern Humanities Research Association, 1987.

"The Rhetoric of Presence in Lyric Poetry." In *Writing in the Margin: Spanish Literature of the Golden Age.* Oxford: Clarendon, 1988. 43–77.

Snow, Joseph T. *Celestina by Fernando de Rojas: An Annotated Bibliography of World Interest, 1930–1985.* Madison: Hispanic Seminar of Medieval Studies, 1985.

Sobejano, Gonzalo. "La novela ensimismada (1980–1985)." *España Contemporánea* 1.1 (1988): 9–26.

Novela española de nuestro tiempo (en busca del pueblo perdido). 2nd. edn. Madrid: Prensa Española, 1975.

Soguero, Francisco. "Los narradores de vanguardia como renovadores del género biográfico: aproximación a la biografía vanguardista." In *Hacia la nueva novela.* Ed. Francis Lough. New York: Peter Lang, 2000. 199–217.

Soldevila Durante, Ignacio. *La novela española desde 1936.* Madrid: Alhambra, 1980.

Solomon, Michael. *The Literature of Misogyny in Medieval Spain: The "Arçipreste de Talavera" and the "Spill."* Cambridge: Cambridge University Press, 1997.

Soria Olmedo, Andrés, ed. *Antología de Gerardo Diego. Poesía española contemporánea.* Madrid: Taurus, 1991. 11–59.

¡Viva don Luis! 1927. Desde Góngora a Sevilla. Madrid: Publicaciones de la Residencia de Estudiantes, 1997.

Soufas, Teresa, ed. *Women's Acts: Plays by Women Dramatists of Spain's Golden Age.* Lexington: University Press of Kentucky, 1997.

Spires, Robert. *Beyond the Metafictional Mode: Directions in the Modern Spanish Novel.* Lexington: University Press of Kentucky, 1984.

Transparent Simulacra. Spanish Fiction, 1902–1926. Columbia: University of Missouri Press, 1988.

Spitzer, Leo. "Perspectivismo lingüístico en el *Quijote*." In *Lingüística e historia literaria.* Madrid: Gredos, 1955. 161–225.

Stam, Robert. "Beyond Fidelity: The Dialogics of Adaptation." In *Film Adaptation*. Ed. James Naremore. New Brunswick, NJ: Rutgers University Press, 2000. 54–76.

Stern, Charlotte. "Juan del Encina's Carnival Eclogues and the Spanish Drama of the Renaissance." *Renaissance Drama* 8 (1965): 181–195.

The Medieval Theater in Castile. Binghamton: Medieval and Renaissance Texts and Studies, 1996.

"A Nativity Play for the Catholic Monarchs." *Bulletin of the Comediantes* 43 (1991): 71–100.

"Recovering the Medieval Theater of Spain (and Europe): The Islamic Evidence." *La Corónica* 27 (1999); pp. 119–153.

Sullivan, Constance A. "*Dinos, dinos quién eres*: The Poetic Identity of María Gertrudis Hore." *Michigan Romance Studies* 12 (1992): 153–182.

Sullivan, Henry W. *Calderón in the German Lands and the Low Countries: His Reception and Influence, 1654–1980*. Cambridge: Cambridge University Press, 1983.

Juan del Encina. Boston: Twayne, 1976.

Tirso de Molina and the Drama of the Counter Reformation. Amsterdam: Rodopi, 1981.

Surtz, Ronald E. *The Birth of a Theater: Dramatic Convention in the Spanish Theater from Juan del Encina to Lope de Vega*. Princeton and Madrid: Castalia, 1979.

El libro del consorte. Barcelona: Puvill Libros, 1982.

"Los misterios asuncionistas en el este peninsular y la mediación mariana." In *Teatro y spectáculo en la Edad Media. Actas Festival d'Elx, 1990*. Elx: Instituto de Cultura "Juan Gil Albert" Diputación de Alicante, Ajuntament d'Elx, 1992. 81–97.

Writing Women in Late Medieval and Early Modern Spain. Philadelphia: University of Pennsylvania Press, 1995.

ed. *Teatro castellano de la Edad Media*. Madrid: Taurus, 1992.

Taine, Hippolyte. *Histoire de la littérature anglaise*. 4 vols. Paris: Hachette, 1863–1864.

Tarr, F. Courtney. "Reconstruction of a Decisive Period in Larra's Life (May–November, 1836)." *Hispanic Review* 5 (1937): 1–24.

Teijeiro Fuentes, Miguel Ángel. *La novela bizantina española. Apuntes para una revisión del género*. Cáceres: Universidad de Cáceres, 1988.

Terés, Elías. "La literatura arábigoespañola." In *Historia general de las literaturas hispánicas*. 6 vols. Ed. Guillermo Díaz-Plaja. Barcelona: Editorial Vergara, 1949–1968. Vol. I: 215–256.

Terry, Arthur. *Catalan Literature*. London: Benn, 1972.

Thomas, Gareth. *The Novel of the Spanish Civil War (1936–1975)*. Cambridge: Cambridge University Press, 1970.

Thompson, Colin P. *The Strife of Tongues: Fray Luis de León and the Golden Age of Spain*. Cambridge: Cambridge University Press, 1988.

Ticknor, George. *History of Spanish Literature*. 3 vols. New York: Harper and Brothers, 1849.

Tolliver, Joyce. *Cigar Smoke and Violet Water: Gendered Discourse in Emilia Pardo Bazán.* Lewisburg, PA: Bucknell University Press, 1998.

Torre, Francisco de la. *Poesía completa.* Ed. María Luisa Cerrón Puga. Madrid: Cátedra, 1984.

Torre, Guillermo de. *Literaturas europeas de vanguardia.* Madrid: Caro Raggio, 1925.

Torres-García, Joaquim. *Escrits sobre art.* Ed. Francesc Fontbona. Barcelona: Edicions 62, 1980.

Torroja Menéndez, Carmen, and María Rivas Palá. *Teatro en Toledo en el siglo XV. "Auto de la Pasión" de Alonso del Campo.* Madrid: Anejos de la Real Academia Española, 1977.

Tortosa Linde, María Dolores. *La Academia del Buen Gusto en Madrid (1749–1751).* Granada: Universidad de Granada, 1988.

Trías, Eugenio. *Calderón de la Barca.* Barcelona: Omega, 2000.

Trigueros, Cándido María. *Discurso sobre el estudio metódico de la Historia literaria.* Madrid: Benito Cano, 1790.

Trueblood, Alan S. *Experience and Artistic Expression in Lope de Vega: The Making of "La Dorotea."* Cambridge, MA: Harvard University Press, 1974.

Turner, Harriet. *Galdós, "Fortunata y Jacinta."* Cambridge: Cambridge University Press, 1992.

Ucelay, Margarita. "El Club Teatral Anfistora." In *El teatro en España entre la tradición y la vanguardia (1918–1939).* Ed. Dru Dougherty and María Francisca Vilches de Frutos. Madrid: CSIC / Fundación FGL / Tabacalera, 1992. 453–467.

Ugarte, Michael. *Shifting Ground: Spanish Civil War Exile Literature.* Durham: Duke University Press, 1989.

Ullman, Pierre L. *Mariano José de Larra and Spanish Political Rhetoric.* Madison: University of Wisconsin Press, 1971.

Umbral, Francisco. *Diccionario de literatura. España 1941–1995: de la posguerra a la posmodernidad.* Barcelona: Planeta, 1995.

Unamuno, Miguel de. *La tía Tula.* Ed. Carlos A. Longhurst. 9th. edn. Madrid: Cátedra, 1999.

Urey, Diane. "Galdós and the Fabrication of Historical Reality." In *Toward a Poetics of Realism / Hacia una poética del realismo.* Special issue of *Letras Peninsulares.* Ed. Harriet Turner. 13.1 (Spring 2000): 97–116.

Uría, Isabel. *Panorama crítico del mester de clerecía.* Literatura y Sociedad, 63. Madrid: Castalia, 2000.

Urrutia, Jorge. "Bécquer, poeta materialista?" *Boletín de la Real Academia Española* 53 (1973): 399–410.

"El camino cerrado de Gaspar Núñez de Arce." *Anales de Literatura Española de la Universidad de Alicante* 2 (1983): 491–508.

Poesía española del siglo XIX. Madrid: Cátedra, 1995.

"Reconstrucción de la poesía realista del siglo XIX." In *Reflexión de la literatura.* Seville: Universidad de Sevilla, 1983. 85–115.

Valbuena Prat, Ángel. *Calderón. Su personalidad, su arte dramático, su estilo y sus obras*. Barcelona: Juventud, 1941.

Historia de la literatura española. 2 vols. Barcelona: Juventud, 1944.

Valdés, Mario J. "Rethinking the History of Literary History." In *Rethinking Literary History*. Ed. Linda Hutcheon and Mario J. Valdés. Oxford: Oxford University Press, 2002. 63–115.

Valentí Fiol, Eduard. *El primer modernismo literario catalán y sus fundamentos ideológicos*. Barcelona: Ariel, 1973.

Valis, Noël M. *The Culture of Cursilería*. Durham, NC: Duke University Press, 2002.

Vallcorba Plana, Jaume. "Introducció." In *Obra poètica* by Josep Maria Junoy. Ed. Jaume Vallcorba Plana. Barcelona: Quaderns Crema, 1984. xi–cxviii.

Noucentisme, mediterraneisme i classicisme. Apunts per a la història d'una estètica. Barcelona: Quaderns Crema, 1994.

Valverde, José María. *Azorín*. Madrid: Planeta, 1971.

Van Doren, Carl, *et al*. *The Cambridge History of American Literature*. 3 vols. Cambridge: Cambridge University Press, 1917.

Varela, Javier. *Jovellanos*. Madrid: Alianza, 1988.

Varela, José Luis. "La autointerpretación del romanticismo español." In *Los orígenes del romanticismo en Europa*. Madrid: Instituto Germano-Español de la Sociedad Görres, 1982. 123–136.

Larra y España. Madrid: Espasa-Calpe, 1983.

Varey, J. E. *Cosmovisión y escenografía: el teatro español en el Siglo de Oro*. Madrid: Castalia, 1987.

Vasvari, Louise O. "The Battle of Flesh and Lent in the *Libro del Arcipreste*: Gastro-Genital Rites of Reversal." *La Corónica* 20 (1991): 1–15.

"A Tale of 'Tailing' in the *Libro de Buen Amor*." *Journal of Interdisciplinary Library Studies* 2 (1990): 13–41.

Vázquez Montalbán, Manuel. *Crónica sentimental de España*. Barcelona: Planeta, 1998.

Vega, Garcilaso de la. *Obra poética y textos en prosa*. Ed. Bienvenido Morros. Barcelona: Crítica, 1995.

La "Vida de San Alifonso por metros" (ca. 1302). Ed. John K. Walsh. Supplement to *Romance Philology* 46.1. Berkeley: University of California Press, 1992.

Vilanova, Antonio. *Novela y sociedad en la España de la postguerra*. Barcelona: Lumen, 1995.

Vilar, Pierre. "Procés històric i cultura catalana." In *Reflexions crítiques sobre la cultura catalana*. Ed. Pierre Vilar *et al*. Barcelona: Departament de Cultura de la Generalitat de Catalunya, 1983. 9–51.

Vilarós, María Teresa. *El mono del desencanto. Una crítica cultural de la transición española*. Madrid: Siglo XXI de España, 1998.

Vilches de Frutos, María Francisca, and Dru Dougherty. *La escena madrileña entre 1926 y 1931. Un lustro de transición*. Madrid: Fundamentos, 1997.

Villanueva, Darío. *Estructura y tiempo reducido en la novela*. Valencia: Bello, 1977.

"Los marcos de la literatura española (1975–1990): esbozo de un sistema." In *Historia y crítica de la literatura española.* Vol. IX: *Los nuevos nombres 1975–1990.* Ed. Francisco Rico. Barcelona: Crítica, 1992. 3–40.

Villatoro, Vicenç. "Y si Calderón no fuese un clásico?" *El País* 3 December 2000, Cataluña edition: 3.

Walsh, John K. *El Coloquio de la Memoria, la Voluntad, y el Entendimiento (Biblioteca Universitaria de Salamanca MS. 1.763) y otras manifestaciones del tema en la literatura española.* New York: Lorenzo Clemente, 1986.

"The Genesis of the *Libro de Buen Amor* (from Performance Text to *Libro* or *Cancionero*)." Paper presented at the Modern Language Association Convention, 29 December 1979, San Francisco, CA.

Wardropper, Bruce. *Historia de la poesía lírica a lo divino en la cristiandad occidental.* Madrid: Revista de Occidente, 1954.

Introducción al teatro religioso del Siglo de Oro. Madrid: Revista de Occidente, 1953.

Weber, Alison P. "The Partial Feminism of Ana de San Bartolomé." In *Recovering Spain's Feminist Tradition.* Ed. Lisa Vollendorf. New York: Modern Language Association, 2001. 69–87.

Teresa of Avila and the Rhetoric of Femininity. Princeton: Princeton University Press, 1990.

Weckmann, Luis. *The Medieval Heritage of Mexico.* Trans. Frances M. López-Morillas. New York: Fordham University Press, 1992.

Weiss, Julian. *The Poet's Art: Literary Theory in Castile c. 1400–60.* Medium Ævum Monographs: New Series, 14. Oxford: The Society for the Study of Mediæval Languages and Literature, 1990.

Weissberger, Barbara F. *Repairing Spain's Broken Body: Gender Ideology in the Age of Isabel the Catholic.* Minneapolis: University of Minnesota Press, 2002.

"The Scatological View of Love in the Theater of Lucas Fernández." *Bulletin of the Comediantes* 38 (1986): 193–207.

Wellek, René. "The Concept of Romanticism in Literary History." In *Concepts of Criticism.* New Haven, CT: Yale University Press, 1963. 128–198.

"The Fall of Literary History." In *The Attack on Literature and Other Essays.* Chapel Hill: University of North Carolina Press, 1982. 64–77.

A History of Modern Criticism, 1750–1950. Vol. I: *The Later Eighteenth Century;* Vol. II: *The Romantic Age.* New Haven: Yale University Press, 1955.

Wellwarth, George. *Spanish Underground Drama.* University Park, PA: Pennsylvania State University Press, 1972.

Whelehan, Imelda. "Adaptations: The Contemporary Dilemmas." In *Adaptations: From Text to Screen, Screen to Text.* Ed. Deborah Cartmell and Imelda Whelehan. London and New York: Routledge, 1999. 3–19.

Whinnom, Keith. "The Form of *Celestina.* Dramatic Antecedents." *Celestinesca* 17 (1993): 129–146.

"El género celestinesco: origen y desarrollo." In *Literatura en la época del Emperador*. Ed. Víctor García de la Concha. Salamanca: Academia Literaria Renacentista de la Universidad de Salamanca, 1988. 119–130.

La poesía amatoria de la época de los Reyes Católicos. Durham Modern Language Series: Hispanic Monographs, 1. Durham: University of Durham Press, 1981.

"The Problem of the 'Best Seller' in Spanish Golden Age Literature." In *Medieval and Renaissance Spanish Literature. Selected Essays*. Ed. Alan Deyermond et al. Exeter: University of Exeter Press, 1994. 159–175.

Spanish Literary Historiography: Three Forms of Distortion. Exeter: University of Exeter, 1967.

White, Hayden. *Metahistory: The Historical Imagination in Nineteenth-Century Europe*. Baltimore: The Johns Hopkins University Press, 1973.

Whyte, Florence. *The Dance of Death in Spain and Catalonia*. Baltimore: Waverly Press, 1931.

Wilcox, John C. *Women Poets of Spain, 1860–1990: Toward a Gynocentric Vision*. Urbana: University of Illinois Press, 1997.

Willem, Linda. *Galdós's Segunda Manera*. Chapel Hill: University of North Carolina Press, 1998.

Wright, Eleanor. *The Poetry of Protest Under Franco*. London: Támesis, 1986.

Wright, Roger. *Late Latin and Early Romance in Spain and Carolingian France*. Liverpool: Francis Cairns, 1982.

A Sociophilological Study of Late Latin. Utrecht: Brepols, 2002.

Yarbro Bejarano, Yvonne. "Juan del Encina and Lucas Fernández: Conflicting Attitudes towards the Passion." *Bulletin of the Comediantes* 36 (1984): 5–21.

"Juan del Encina's *Egloga de las grandes lluvias*: The Historical Appropriation of Dramatic Ritual." In *Creation and Re-Creation: Experiments in Literary Form in Early Modern Spain*. Ed. Ronald Surtz and Nora Weinerth. Newark: Juan de la Cuesta, 1983. 7–27.

Ynduráin, Domingo. "Contradicciones en la obra de Quevedo." In *Homenaje a Quevedo. Academia literaria renacentista*. Vol. II. Ed. V. García de la Concha. Salamanca: Universidad de Salamanca, 1982. 475–481.

Yxart, Josep. "Lletra a N'Albert Savine" (1884). In *Entorn de la literatura catalana de la Restauració*. Ed. Jordi Castellanos. Barcelona: Edicions 62, 1980. 19–26.

Ytak. *Lluís Pasqual: Camí de teatre*. Trans. Albert de la Torre. Barcelona: Alter Pirene / Escena, 1993.

Zahareas, Anthony, and Rodolfo Cardona, eds. *Ramón del Valle-Inclán. An Appraisal of his Life and Works*. New York: Las Américas Publishing Company, 1968.

Zelaya Kolker, Marielena. *Testimonios americanos de los escritores españoles transterrados de 1939*. Madrid: Ediciones Cultura Hispánica, 1985.

Zimic, Stanislav. "Nuevas consideraciones sobre el *Auto da Lusitânia* de Gil Vicente." In *Homenaje a A. Zamora Vicente*. Vol. III. Madrid: Castalia, 1991. 359–369.

El teatro de Cervantes. Madrid: Castalia, 1992.

"El teatro religioso de Gómez Manrique (1412–1491)." *Boletín de la Real Academia Española* 57 (1977): 353–400.

Zink, Michel. *Medieval French Literature: An Introduction*. Trans. Jeff Rider. Binghamton, NY: Medieval and Renaissance Texts and Studies, 1995.

Zulueta, Emilia de. *Arte y vida en la obra de Benjamín Jarnés*. Madrid: Gredos, 1977.

Index

Calderón de la Barca (*cont.*)
268; *El divino Orfeo*, 281; and
Donoso, 348; *Eco y Narciso*,
279; *El encanto sin encanto*,
276; *La estatua de Prometeo*,
279; *La exaltación de la cruz*,
280; *La fiera, el rayo y la piedra*,
279; *Fortunas de Andrómeda y
Perseo*, 279; *El galán fantasma*,
276; *La gran Cenobia*, 273, 274;
El gran teatro del mundo, 281,
591; *Los guisados*, 282; *Hado y
divisa de Leonido y Marfisa*,
268, 279; *La hija del aire*, 274,
277; honor plays, 277, 443,
590; *El jardín de Falerina*, 279;
El laurel de Apolo, 279; *Luis
Pérez el gallego*, 271; and magic
comedies, 308; *El mágico
prodigioso*, 267, 280; *Las
manos blancas no ofenden*, 276;
El mayor encanto amor, 279; *El
médico de su honra*, 277;
mythological plays, 278–9; *La
nave del mercader*, 281; *No hay
burlas con el amor*, 274; *No hay
cosa como callar*, 275; *El nuevo
palacio del Retiro*, 281; and
opera, 278; *Las Órdenes
Militares*, 281; *Origen, pérdida
y restauración de la Virgen del
Sagrario*, 280; and political
criticism, 273–4;
"pre-Romantic" plays, 271; *El
príncipe constante*, 277; *El
purgatorio de San Patricio*, 280;
La púrpura de la rosa, 250, 279;
*A secreto agravio, secreta
venganza*, 277; *El sitio de
Breda*, 273; tragedies, 276–8;
and tragicomedy, 307; *Las tres
justicias en una*, 272; *La vida es
sueño*, 267, 269, 270, 277, 282,
311; *Las visiones de la muerte*,
282
Calila e Digna, 99

Calinescu, Matei, 696
calligram, 548
Calparsoro, Daniel, 750
Calvo Carilla, José Luis, 457
Calvo, Julián, 623
Cámara, Sixto; *Jaime el Barbudo*,
442
Cambio 16, 687
Cambronero, Manuela; *Safira*, 360
Camões, Luís de, 160; *Os Lusíadas*,
175
La Campana de Gracia, 471
Campillo, Narciso, 453
Campo, Alonso del, 133; *Auto de la
Pasión*, 123–4
Campo, Enrique del; *El Crucero
Baleares*, 678
Campoamor, Ramón de, 448, 453,
454–5, 456, 457, 504; *Ayes del
alma*, 454; *Cantares*, 455;
Colón, 455; "Acerca del estado
actual de nuestra poesía," 449;
Doloras, 448, 454; *El drama
universal*, 455; *Fabulas
orijinales*, 453, 454; *Humoradas*,
455; "lecciones de realidad,"
448; *Pequeños poemas*, 453,
454; *Poesías de D. Ramón de
Campoamor* (*Ternezas y flores*),
454; *Poética*, 455; poetics, 449;
"El tren expreso," 448, 454
Campos, Jesús, 731
Camprubí, Zenobia; *Diarios
1937–1956*, 626
Camus, Mario; *Los farsantes*,
682
Canales, Alfonso, 651
Canals, Antoni, 53
Canción para callar al Niño, 126
Cancionero de Estúñiga, 90
*Cancionero de obras de burlas
provocantes a risa*, 166
Cancionero de Palacio, 90
Cancionero de Upsala, 168
Cancionero general, 90, 94, 161,
162, 166, 168

CPSIA information can be obtained
at www.ICGtesting.com
Printed in the USA
LVHW02s2154090118
562401LV00016B/340/P